Microeconomic Theory

This book introduces the main concepts of microeconomics to upper-division undergraduate students or first-year graduate students who have undergone at least one elementary calculus course. The book fully integrates graphical and mathematical concepts and offers over 150 analytical examples demonstrating numerical solutions.

The book has a strong theoretical basis, but shows how microeconomics can be brought to bear on the real world. New features for this edition include:

- an incorporation of the theory of stock externalities associated with greenhouse gases;
- development of the section on insurance, with particular reference to the new US health-care program;
- greater integration of game-theoretic concepts throughout the book.

The book's style is accessible, but also rigorous. Mathematical examples are provided throughout the book, in particular for key concepts, and the result is a balanced approach in terms of prose, graphics, and mathematics.

Michael E. Wetzstein is Professor of Agricultural and Applied Economics at The University of Georgia, USA.

Microeconomic Theory

Concepts and connections

Second edition

Michael E. Wetzstein

Routledge
Taylor & Francis Group
LONDON AND NEW YORK

First edition published 2005
by South-Western

Second edition published 2013
by Routledge
2 Park Square, Milton Park, Abingdon, Oxon OX14 4RN

Simultaneously published in the USA and Canada
by Routledge
711 Third Avenue, New York, NY 10017

Routledge is an imprint of the Taylor & Francis Group, an informa business

British Library Cataloguing in Publication Data
A catalogue record for this book is available from the British Library

Library of Congress Cataloging in Publication Data
Wetzstein, Michael Eugene.
Microeconomic theory / Michael Wetzstein. – 2nd ed.
p. cm.
Rev. ed. of: Microeconomic theory: concepts and connections. c2005.
1. Microeconomics. 2. Economics, Mathematical. I. Title.
HB172.W48 2012
338.5–dc23 2012008345

ISBN: 978-0-415-60369-0 (hbk)
ISBN: 978-0-415-60370-6 (pbk)
ISBN: 978-0-203-09835-6 (ebk)

Typeset in Times New Roman
by Cenveo Publisher Services

MIX
Paper from responsible sources
FSC® C004839

Printed and bound in Great Britain by the MPG Books Group

Contents

1 Introduction

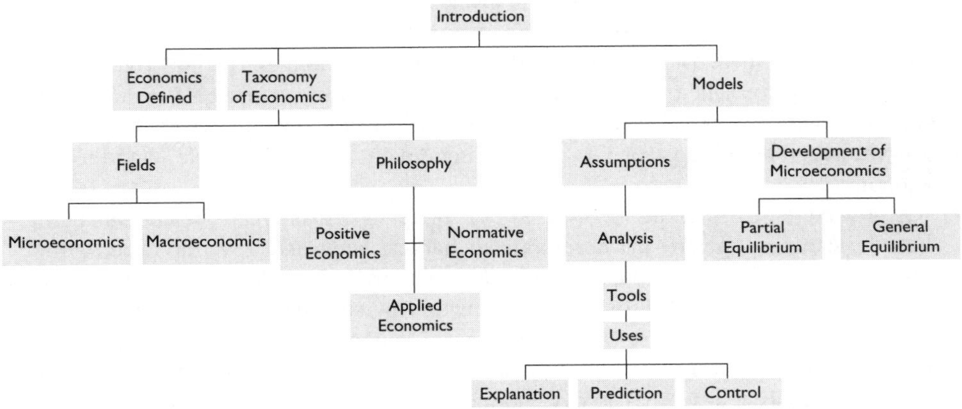

Outline and Conceptual Inquiries

What is economics? Limits and tradeoffs

Would you be sorry if all your wants were satisfied?

Why study economics?

Economics dissected

Microeconomics versus macroeconomics

Why will a team full of outstanding players not necessarily win?

Positive versus normative economics

Why can two people agree on the price of a movie, but possibly not agree on whether to go?

Value of applied economics

Why are economists artists?

Application: Business schools spawning from applied economics

Building models

Making assumptions

How do humans differ from other animals?

Doing analysis

How did the Babylonian and Greek scientists differ?

Using tools

How is Adam Smith's invisible hand made visible?

Application: Economists as engineers

Models provide scientific explanation, prediction, and control

Origins of microeconomics

Application: An alternative to the Marshallian cross?

Partial-equilibrium versus general-equilibrium models

Why are apertures changed on economic lenses?

Summary

Key concepts

Key equation

Questions

Internet case studies

An economist is armed and dangerous. Watch out for the invisible hand (One of the top 10 reasons to study economics).

Ever think about how our very complex economic and social world operates? Do we live in a centrally controlled system like the *Matrix* movies that makes choices for us? No, such a system generally only occurs in movies. Instead, we live in a decentralized market system where each of us self-determines our own choices. But how is it possible for each of us to make our own choices and yet the system as a whole is efficient in satisfying our choices? The simple answer is market prices operate as signals directing our choices. The full answer lies in revealing Adam Smith's invisible hand through economic theory.

Knowledge of economic theory creates a price-signal roadmap for understanding how the economy operates in a decentralized market system and how individuals within this economy interact as groups of consumers and producers. With this roadmap, you can be armed and dangerous by knowing how this invisible hand works. The economic theory roadmap describes how a decentralized system of resource allocation can result in efficiently allocating our limited resources. The ability to understand economic theory and apply it to your everyday choices will provide you with the power to make correct choices and understand the choices made by others. The roadmap can aid us in addressing practical, realistic problems such as environmental degradation, cartels, dishonest used car salespeople, and discrimination.

However, the economic profession is often criticized for its lack of realism in addressing practical problems. As an example, consider the following poem:

Our economic methodology
is full of fine epistemology.
But when we come to problems practical
our theories are too didactical.
If economics is a science,
it needs to foster the alliance
of theorist and statistician,
with manager and prognostician;
To tie the work of mathematicist
to problems of the market strategist.

Herman Southworth

Epistemology is a field of philosophy that critically investigates the nature, grounds, limits, and criteria or validity of human knowledge. It is a theory of cognition, the act or process of knowing. And economic theory does contain a great deal of epistemology. Economists have gone to great lengths in developing a theory for examining how human behavior affects economic decisions. For example, economists have worked effortlessly on specifying the exact minimal number of assumptions required for characterizing an individual consumer's preferences. This type of epistemology lends itseif well to classroom instruction, so it is didactical in the sense it is suited for teaching. Hence, Southworth (and others) contend that economic theory is more an instructional exercise than a science addressing practical realistic problems.

For economics to be a science, it should foster an alliance with fields that address practical problems, applying economic theory to these problems, to yield feasible solutions. As discussed in this chapter, this is exactly what an *applied economist* does: combining economic theory with knowledge of institutions and the environment to address practical problems. In the subsequent chapters, we develop the concepts and connections of microeconomic theory, yielding feasible solutions for practical problems. However, prior to a discussion of the practical applications of economic theory, we should investigate how the focus of economics is on limits and tradeoffs.

What is economics? Limits and tradeoffs

My riches consist not in the extent of my possessions, but in the fewness of my wants.
(J. Brotherton)

Riches in terms of fewness of wants are what economics is all about. Unfortunately, from early childhood, we learn we are unable to satisfy all of our wants; there are limits. For a society, these limits take the form of scarce (limited) resources. For example, a society has a limited amount of land, water, energy, labor, and physical capital for satisfying wants. Economics is the study of how to allocate these limited resources to satisfy our wants. Specifically, **economics** is a social science concerned chiefly with the way society chooses to employ its limited (scarce) resources, which have alternative uses (tradeoffs), to produce goods and services for present and future consumption. Note that economics is a social science, in contrast to a natural science. A *social science* deals with human society or its characteristic elements, such as the individual, family, or state. A **society** is the interaction of individuals within an environment. Unfortunately, there is scarcity in all environments. *Scarcity* means there are not enough resources around to satisfy every possible desire for them. Using resources in one way has an opportunity cost (tradeoff) of not being able to use them in another way. For example, an opportunity cost of allocating time (a resource) for studying is the lost enjoyment of facebooking instead.

Economics. A social science concerned with the allocation of scarce resources for satisfying unlimited wants. *E.g., with your limited income, do you go out to eat or eat at home? Do we pay down the national debt, maintain social programs, or fly to Mars?*

Society. The interaction of individuals within an environment. *E.g., the United States and other countries.*

These scarce resources are continuously changing through time. Nonrenewable resources, such as petroleum, are declining and renewable resources, including fish and timber, may increase or decline over time. Capital, both human and physical, will depreciate through time and must be augmented to maintain or increase present levels. This is assuming individuals' wants are insatiable (they want more and more goods) and the change in resources is a constraint (limitation) that prevents complete satisfaction. Individuals' wants are also continuously changing, depending on age, location, and even time of day. Thus, economics is concerned with the way society chooses to allocate a continuously changing set of limited resources among a continuously changing set of unlimited wants.

Would you be sorry if all your wants were satisfied? Yes, we would often be sorry if all our wants were gratified, for tomorrow these current wants will change. Everybody who has ever rubbed the magic oil lamp realizes the three wishes given to them by Genie Abdul only satisfied their current wants.

> *One of the most venturesome things left us is to go to sleep. For no one can lay a hand on our dreams.*
>
> (E.V. Lucus)
>
> *Translation: When you sleep you are in global bliss; your dreams have no limits.*

As our definition of economics implies, economics is a philosophical inquiry into the process of resource allocation (tradeoffs). Economic theory outlines how a society allocates its scarce resources to achieve prosperity and well-being for its citizens. Thus, the objective of economics is to maximize the happiness for society as a whole (**social welfare**) subject to limited resources. Economic theory provides a framework for obtaining **local bliss**, where for a given resource constraint social welfare is maximized. In contrast, **global bliss** (or simply bliss) is where there are no resource constraints, and thus all wants are satisfied. An example of global bliss is our dreams, in which we are free from the scarce resource constraints in our awaking hours.

Social welfare. Happiness for society as a whole. *E.g., economists have suggested modifications to a country's gross national product as a surrogate measure for social welfare.*

Local bliss. A state where social welfare is maximized for a given resource constraint. *E.g., a time of peace and prosperity.*

Global bliss (or bliss). A state in which there are no resource constraints and all wants are satisfied. *E.g., our dreams.*

For obtaining or at least moving toward local bliss, economics provides a theory for determining what commodities to produce, when to produce them, how to produce them, and for whom. The theory describes the economic environment in which **agents** (households and firms) interact. Having knowledge of this environment provides an understanding of how an **economy** operates. Thus, economic theory offers both an explanation for and predicts how agents within an economy operate. Agents must understand this operation of an economy to make efficient decisions on how to allocate resources. In general, with the understanding of economic theory, the ability to explain, predict, and control our economy is possible. Economic theory could then be used as a basis for the design of policies by governments wishing to influence (control) the outcome of a program or for a critique of the control actions governments might take.

Agent. A household or firm within an economy. *E.g., you.*

Economy. A group of agents interacting to improve their individual and joint satisfaction. *E.g., the interaction of buyers and sellers in a free society.*

For example, economic theory can describe how the price of oil affects auto production, why a large increase in the gasoline price results in little reduction in the demand for gasoline, why a cattle rancher will continue to stay in business even if she is losing money, and why a firm with monopoly power can charge a higher price for its commodity than can a competitive firm. These are just a few of the practical questions that can be answered with economic theory. The following chapters provide the necessary tools to answer many such practical problems.

Economic theory, like poetry, is a very nonlinear use of language; that is implications are more than just the sum of the parts. For example, economic theory may explain how consumers increase satisfaction and firms enhance profits, but, taken together, these two explanations reveal how an efficient allocation of resources is possible—an explanation beyond the sum of the parts. This ability of economic theory to reveal additional implications makes it a very powerful and exciting field of study.

Why study economics? At this level, microeconomic theory is very interesting in terms of offering solutions to practical problems, so take the time to understand and enjoy the theory (poetry).

Economics dissected

Economics may be dissected into a number of divisions both in terms of economic philosophy (positive and normative) and in terms of major fields (microeconomics and macroeconomics). Economists tend to specialize in one of the major fields. Within their field, they will apply economic theories to reach conclusions useful for understanding an economic problem. In their applications, they will generally employ both positive and normative economic philosophies.

Microeconomics versus macroeconomics

Microeconomics is concerned mainly with the economic activities of individual consumers (buyers) and producers (sellers) or groups of consumers and producers in determining prices, known as **markets**. For example, microeconomics is concerned with consumers' demand for food, cost to a firm for a particular volume of production, and the per-unit price a firm charges for a specific volume of its output. Studying microeconomics reveals how consumers and producers interact in a market and how market price signals allocate resources. With this knowledge, consumers, producers, and government policymakers can make informed decisions. **Macroeconomics** is concerned with the behavior of economic aggregates or the economy as a whole. For example, macroeconomics is concerned with the total volume of output for a nation, the general level of prices and employment, and the total level of income and expenditures.

Microeconomics. Investigates the interactions of individual consumers and producers (agents). *E.g., determines the efficient allocation of resources.*

Market. A mechanism for consumers (buyers) and producers (sellers) of a good or service to interact in determining the market price. *E.g., the New York Stock Exchange.*

Macroeconomics. Investigates the economy as a whole. *E.g., determines how to achieve full employment with stable prices.*

These two fields complement each other. Microeconomics deals with efficient allocation of resources within an economy, and macroeconomics deals with maintaining a stable economic environment resulting in full employment with stable prices. If macroeconomists are unable to maintain full employment of resources, then microeconomists need not worry about efficiently allocating these resources, since the unemployed resources are not limited. Thus, microeconomics is of limited use unless resources are fully employed. The reverse is also true: If microeconomists are unable to efficiently allocate resources, then even with fully employed resources social welfare will not be maximized.

We can further investigate the relationship between micro- and macroeconomics by considering the fallacies of composition and division. The **fallacy of composition** states that what is true of the parts is not necessarily true of the whole. For example, consider the statement: "Because players A, B, C, and D are excellent ball players, a team composed of these players is sure to win the season's championship." This statement contains an error in reasoning: a successful team requires not only good players but also the ability to work together. In terms of economics, generalizations made at the microeconomic level may not always be true at the macroeconomic level. For example, rising unemployment may result in workers increasing their savings. Microeconomics would then predict an increase in individual savings. However, the rising unemployed may decrease savings to maintain their living standards. The macroeconomic effect of saving may result in a decrease in savings when considering the saving of both the employed and unemployed (this is called the *Paradox of Thrift*).

Why will a team full of outstanding players not necessarily win? Fallacy of composition: what is true of the parts is not necessarily true of the whole.

Fallacy of composition. What is true of the parts is not necessarily true of the whole. *E.g., one student can get up and walk out of a classroom within one minute, but all the students at one time cannot do this.*

The converse of the fallacy of composition is the **fallacy of division**, which states that what is true of the whole is not necessarily true of the parts. An example is the inference that because a particular college course is excellent, every lecture or discussion within this course is excellent. Likewise, generalizations made at the macroeconomic level may not always be true at the microeconomic level. As an example, in the aggregate (macro), the level of prices may be stable. Specifically, there is no **inflation**, defined as a general rise in prices. However, in a particular market (micro), prices may be rising or declining rapidly.

Fallacy of division. What is true of the whole is not necessarily true of the parts. *E.g., a presidential candidate who wins the national popular vote has not necessarily received a majority vote in every state.*

Inflation. A general rise in prices. *E.g., the United States experiencing a 2 percent annual rise in the Consumer Price Index.*

Micro- and macroeconomics are not distinct areas of study. They both can be used to investigate the same policy action. For example, an increase in government taxes affects consumers and producers. The increase can be analyzed with microeconomic tools to investigate the effect on the markets for specific commodities, such as housing or automobiles. The tax increase can also be investigated with macroeconomic tools to analyze the effect on aggregate employment, inflation, and national income.

Positive versus normative economics

Opposites attract, they make the best marriages.

(Bill Hybels)

In terms of economic philosophy, **positive economics** is concerned with what is, was, or will be; **normative economics** is concerned with what ought to be. Positive economics considers actual conditions that have occurred or will occur in an economy. In contrast, normative economics involves value judgments—statements about what is good and what is bad, what ought to have occurred, or what ought to occur in an economy. If two people disagree over positive statements in economics, they should be able to settle their controversy by logical thinking and appealing to the facts. However, if they disagree over normative statements, they are disagreeing over value judgments, and may not be able to reach an agreement. For example, the statement "a 10 percent increase in the price of gasoline will have no effect on the number of vacationers going skiing" is a positive statement because it can be tested by empirical research. The number of skiers before a price hike can be compared with the number of skiers after. In contrast, the statement "only Bohemia residents should be allowed to vacation in Bohemia" is a normative statement. It is a value judgment that cannot be tested; empirical evidence cannot be used to destroy one's belief about the issue. Such a distinction is revealed by the terms *wants* and *needs*. The positive study of economics deals with people's wants as opposed to their needs. People want or demand a certain amount of ice cream at a given price. Needs imply value judgments. "People ought to have or need a certain amount of ice cream" is a value judgment. As another example, note that the first part of this subsection's opening quote, "opposites attract," is a positive statement that can be tested by bringing together opposites. In contrast, the second half of the statement is a value judgment. What makes the best marriages is a value statement about which people are unlikely to reach total agreement.

Why can two people agree on the price of a movie, but possibly not agree on whether to go? The price of the movie can be determined by just checking the Internet; whether you should go is a value judgment.

Positive economics. The study of what is, was, or will be. *E.g., investigating the statement "firms generally attempt to maximize their profits."*

Normative economics. The study of what ought to be. *E.g., investigating the statement "firms should attempt to maximize our social desires instead of their profits."*

Value of applied economics

Economists who have escaped from the fine epistemology and didactical nature of economic theory are applied economists. Although **applied economics** is closely related to the categories of normative and positive economics, it also encompasses a third category called the *art of economics*. This three-part distinction dates back to the father of John Maynard Keynes, John Neville Keynes,[1] who placed his discussion of the art of economics under the heading "Applied Economics." According to Keynes, positive economics is the study of what is and the way the economy works; it is pure science, not applied economics. Normative economics is the study of what should be; it is also not applied economics. The **art of economics** is applied economics that accepts some set of goals determined in normative economics and discusses how to achieve those goals in reality, given insights of positive economics. It relates the conclusions derived in positive economics to the normative goals determined in normative economics.

Applied economics. The application of economic theory and statistics, combined with a knowledge of institutions, to explain the behavior of real world phenomena. *E.g., why dentists' incomes are higher in California than in West Virginia.*

Art of economics. Relating the conclusions derived from positive economics to the goals determined in normative economics. *E.g., developing the conditions necessary for providing the basic level of nutrition to all our children.*

Positive economics would suffer from the lack of an art of economics. If a separate art is not delineated, positive economic inquiry faces pressures to have practical-problem relevance, which constrains imaginative scientific inquiry. Imagine, for example, that theoretical physics were required to maintain practical-problem relevance. Einstein's thought experiments would have been seen as a waste of time. Likewise, positive economics is abstract thinking about abstract problems. Immediate or even future relevance is of little or no concern to a positive economics researcher. That relevance is the domain of the applied economist.

The methodology for the art of economics is much broader, more inclusive, and far less technical than the methodology for positive economics. Applied economics requires knowledge of institutions and of social, political, and historical phenomena. Mechanisms for using available data in addressing current economic problems are developed as economic art.

With the normative economic objective of maximizing social welfare, applied economics relies on all the other disciplines to support the positive economics required for advancing toward maximizing that objective. For example, the disciplines of engineering, biology, and ecology are improving the technology for producing more desirable commodities from limited resources. The disciplines of mathematics, computer science, and statistics are developing new tools for advancing both applied economics and positive economic theory. In developing conditions for maximizing social welfare, applied economics incorporates theories from political science, sociology, and psychology. Thus, all other disciplines' discoveries are funneled into applied economics and then directed by positive economic theory to the normative goal of maximizing social welfare.

Why are economists artists? As an artist takes a brush and paint to canvas, an applied economist takes economic theory to find solutions to real world problems.

Application: Business schools spawning from applied economics

As discussed by B.E. Kaufman, in its early years (1910–1930) business education was regarded as applied economics. Prior to the mid-1910s, only a handful of universities had established a business school (generally called a school of commerce). There was strong sentiment against specialized business degrees, as many felt that business subjects lacked intellectual content and were vocational. The early business schools were considered by some as little more than glorified typing and secretarial schools. However, a demand for college-graduated business professionals resulted in 65 business schools by 1918, and by 1922 the number had more than doubled to 147. Employers were searching for such things as methods to mitigate high employee turnover rates and labor unrest, and graduates from business schools had the unique education to develop such methods.

Prior to 1930, economics served as the principal intellectual discipline around which business curriculums were established, and most business faculty were trained economists. Courses in finance, accounting, marketing, and management were typically viewed as offerings in applied economics. Economics during this period was generally defined as a science concerned with scarcity of wealth and how society overcomes this scarcity through the process of production and distribution. Markets were considered as just one mechanism for production and distribution, and greater emphasis than today was placed on the role of firm organization and management.

After 1930, substitutes for economics as the foundation of business education emerged. Engineering in terms of scientific management, the development of administrative and organizational sciences, and the influence of behavioral sciences (psychology and sociology) complemented economics as a business foundation. This led to a gradual separation of business education from applied economics. The process of specialization and division of labor in the production and dissemination of knowledge precipitate this separation.

Source: B.E. Kaufman, "Personnel/Human Resource Management: Its Roots as Applied Economics," *History of Political Economy* 32 (Suppl. 2000): 229–256.

Building models

Your paradigm is so intrinsic to your mental process that you are hardly aware of its existence, until you try to communicate with someone with a different paradigm.

(Donella Meadows)

The economic world today is a very complex system, with billions of agents interacting. To individuals who have not studied economics, this economic world may seem confusing and unpredictable. However, economics is based on the belief that most behavior can be explained by assuming agents have stable well-defined preferences and make rational market choices consistent with these preferences. In fact, economics is distinguished from other social sciences by its general acceptance of this belief in its objective to explain how agents allocate their limited resources. Thus, this belief is a **paradigm** in economics. This synthesis, achieved by reaching a consensus on a paradigm, defines the field of economics and creates a mechanism by which scientific progress can be made. Until a possible new paradigm is developed, applied economists then employ this paradigm as an aid in solving practical problems.

> **Paradigm.** A theory that is tested a number of times and its explanatory power accepted. *E.g., a competitive firm's objective is profit maximization.*

This paradigm—that agents have stable, well-defined preferences and make rational market choices—is a foundation for building economic models. **Models**, which are simplified representations of reality, are the basic tool used by scientists to increase our understanding of the real world. Reality is simplified in different ways in a model, depending on the objectives of the model and the particular economic situation. For example, a map is a simplified model of the world, but not all the information about the world can be placed on one map. Thus, if depicting soil types is the major objective, then roads and cities may not be identified on the map (model). Likewise, the particular economic objectives to be depicted will determine how a situation will be simplified in the model.

> **Models.** Simplified representations of reality. *E.g., models that the National Weather Service use for predicting the path of a category five hurricane.*

Making assumptions

In modeling, reality is simplified by employing a set of assumptions to form a model from which conclusions are logically deduced about some system. A **system** is a group of units interacting to form a whole. For example, consumers and producers interact to form a market system. **Assumptions** are assertions about the properties of a system that are observable in the real world, and thus can be evaluated for their degree of realism. **Properties** are the traits and attributes of a system. A model describes the essential features of a system, based on theory, in a way that is simple enough to understand and manipulate yet close enough to reality to yield meaningful results.

As an example, consider a model of consumer behavior with the following assumptions:

1. A consumer is rational and attempts to maximize satisfaction (utility).
2. This consumer has a fixed level of income.
3. Commodities (goods and services) vary continuously, and the utility the consumer derives from them is measurable.
4. The consumer has a given set of preferences for these commodities.
5. Commodity prices are constant.

System. A group of units interacting to form a whole. *E.g., faculty and students form a university.*

Assumptions. Statements about the conditions of some system. *E.g., faculty forming classes for student instruction.*

Properties. The traits and attributes of a system. *E.g., within a university, faculty sharing knowledge.*

Based on this set of assumptions, we can conclude that a consumer will maximize utility by equating the marginal (additional) utility per dollar for all the commodities he purchases.[2] In this model, the **variables**—commodity prices, income, and consumer preferences—are assumed to influence a consumer's purchases of commodities. Such variables are called **exogenous variables**. Based on economic theory, which determines the cause-and-effect relationship among the variables, we can develop a model where these exogenous variables cause a change in other variables called **endogenous variables** (in this case a consumer's purchases).

Variable. A symbol, such as "x," that changes within a model. *E.g., the level of a fraternity's beer consumption.*

Exogenous variables. Variables whose values are predetermined outside a model. *E.g., commodity prices and income for a model describing what commodities consumers purchase.*

Endogenous variables. Variables whose values are determined within a model and depend on the values of the exogenous variables. *E.g., the commodities consumers purchase based on a model with given prices and income.*

Assumptions characterize the type of world for which a model is intended, but the model is not an exact representation of reality. For example, when at the supermarket you do not count the level of utility you receive per unit of the commodities. However, the model does provide a reasonable abstraction from which to consider the likely conclusion. In general, consumers attempt to determine the marginal worth of an item and compare this with the price of the item and related commodities. But the assumption (paradigm) of realism—where agents have the disposition to face a problem and deal with it practically—may not exactly represent reality. For example, emotion may also play a role in dealing with a problem. Even so, such an assumption may yield valuable conclusions about agents' market behavior.

Abstracting from reality is part of the **scientific method** and is employed throughout the sciences. The scientific method prevents smart people from coming up with excellent explanations for mistaken points of view. As a process of abstracting from reality and thus constructing a reliable, consistent, and non-arbitrary representation of reality, the scientific method minimizes the influences of personal and cultural beliefs in explaining reality. Thus, economists employ the scientific method to develop and test models that are accurate representations of reality.

This abstraction capability differentiates humans from other animals, making humans alone capable of widespread generalizations. Examples are the assumption of a frictionless state in physics and the concept of a field in electrical theory. The situations characterized by these models are admittedly hypothetical. However, such hypothetical models are important in any science. Even if these models may be artificial (their assumptions do not conform to reality), such constructs are extremely useful. The real test of such models is whether they lead to conclusions that help to further our scientific objectives of explanation, prediction, and control.

How do humans differ from other animals? Humans alone are capable of abstraction and thus making widespread generalizations.

Scientific method. Reducing the complexity of reality to manageable proportions, formulating a hypothesis that explains reality, and then testing the hypothesis. *E.g., developing a hypothesis to explain the price a monopoly sets and then testing the validity of the hypothesis.*

Doing analysis

In the following chapters, we will discuss models and their uses in terms of analyzing practical economic problems. The value of these models is not in the realism of their assumptions, but how useful are the conclusions derived from them. As illustrated in Figure 1.1, economists employ the scientific method for analyzing these models. Considering reality (the real world) as a starting point, an economist reduces the complexities of reality to manageable proportions by developing a model of a real-world system based on economic theory. This results in a logical model that is suited to explain the system observed. By logical argument (deduction), logical or model conclusions can be derived. These logical conclusions are **hypotheses** of the relationship among the variables. The hypotheses are then transformed, by means of theoretical interpretation, into conclusions about the real world.

Hypothesis. A logical conclusion based on a theoretical model. *E.g., competitive markets will efficiently allocate resources.*

In addition to a theoretical model, economists may employ **econometrics** (the application of statistics to economics) to analyze reality. For developing an econometric model,

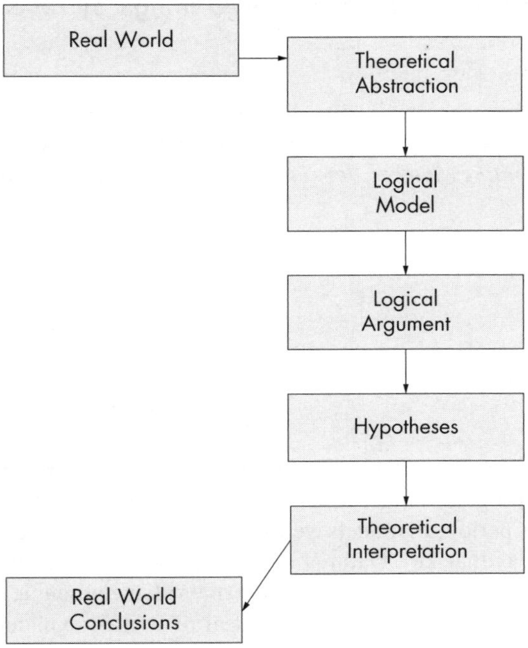

Figure 1.1 **Scientific method.** A model reduces the complexities of reality to manageable proportions.

economists use experimental abstraction based on economic theory, which leads to experimental design. The model is then useful in testing hypotheses derived from economic theory. Thus, the theoretical and econometric models complement each other in developing real world conclusions.

The relative emphasis on theoretical versus statistical models has changed over time depending on the preference for computation. Greek tradition proves things with abstract principles (theoretical models); for example, the proof of the Pythagorean Theorem does not depend on the particular size of a right triangle.[3] In contrast, the Babylonian tradition discovers things by computation, such as the fact that a million different right triangles all have the same relation among the squares of their sides. In modern economics, the Greek tradition prevailed in the works of past Nobel laureates such as Paul A. Samuelson and Kenneth J. Arrow, who applied mathematical reasoning to a minimum of data. Currently, the ever decreasing cost of computation due to advanced technology has increased the cost of Greek science (theoretical modeling) relative to Babylonian science (econometric modeling). In other words, elegant analysis still costs as much time and effort as it ever did, but number crunching becomes ever cheaper. Furthermore, the kinds of practical questions consumers, firms, governmental policymakers, and economists are asking are more amenable to answers with new Babylonian economics. For example, an econometric model can show the magnitude of a reduction in pollution from a change in a pollution standard. In contrast, a theoretical model will generally only provide an indication of the direction of the change and not the magnitude.

How did the Babylonian and Greek scientists differ? The Greeks proved things with abstract principles; the Babylonians proved things by repeated computation.

Econometrics. Based on economic theory, the application of mathematical statistics to economic data. *E.g., estimating market demand and supply functions for labor.*

Using tools

> *If the only tool you have is a hammer, you tend to see every problem as a nail.*
>
> (Abraham Maslow)

Tools employed for developing theoretical models and deriving conclusions are prose, geometry, mathematics, and computer programming. Prose is the ordinary language of people in speaking or writing. In the prehistoric period, all models were developed and communicated in spoken prose. The disadvantage was that key features of a model were lost as it was verbally transmitted or imitated among individuals. The invention of written communication solved this problem, but for relatively detailed models a great deal of written explanation was required.

The advent of geometry alleviated this limitation—"a picture is worth a thousand words." Geometric illustrations that complement the writing allow a model to be communicated and conclusions to be developed with greater efficiency. Geometry is an excellent tool for describing a model with two variables, such as price and quantity. This two-dimensional model can be drawn on a geometrical plane—a piece of paper, a chalkboard, or a computer tablet. Unfortunately, geometry is limited by its dimensions. With some difficulty, geometry can also represent three dimensions (such as two variable inputs and an output) by drawing the illusion on a geometrical plane of one of the axes protruding from the surface. However, geometry is not able to represent the fourth, fifth, or any higher dimension, which is required of a model with more than three variables.

In such cases, a tool that frees us from our three-dimensional world is required. Such a tool is mathematics. With mathematics, we can enter the worlds of higher dimensions and explore their vast areas with mathematical models designed to provide insights into their workings. If a picture is worth a thousand words, mathematics is worth the universe.

How is Adam Smith's invisible hand made visible? As discussed in the Mathematical Review, mathematics makes Adam Smith's invisible hand visible.

A model can always be communicated without mathematics, but the language of mathematics greatly reduces a model's description and expresses it in a very concise manner. As these mathematical models become more complex, **analytical solutions** to the models become difficult or impossible. However, the advancement of computer programming provides **numerical solutions** to these complex models. In fact, computer programs have provided solutions to some models that previously could not be solved.

Thus, economists have many more tools than a hammer and are not limited to models that view every problem as a nail.

Analytical solution. Solving a mathematical model with algebra. *E.g., given linear demand and supply equations, solving for the equilibrium price by equating quantity demanded to quantity supplied.*

Numerical solution. Solving a mathematical model by computation. *E.g., given highly nonlinear demand and supply equations, using a mathematical search algorithm (recipe) to find the equilibrium solution.*

Application: Economists as engineers

In the 1990s, economists, particularly game theorists, started to take a substantial role in the design of markets. Two examples are the design of a labor clearinghouse used by American doctors and the design of auctions in which the US Federal Communications Commission sells the rights to transmit on different parts of the radio spectrum. As addressed by A. Roth, this design of markets is spawning a new discipline in economics, called design economics, which develops and maintains markets. This new discipline will require new tools supplementing existing economic analysis tools. In addition, game theory and experimental and computational tools in economics will require refining and further development.

Just as engineering relies on physics and medicine relies on biology, market design will increasingly rely on computer programmers based on scientific literature of design economics, especially as the marketplace proliferates on the Internet. Such market designs will share a number of common characteristics. First, the designs must be fast. Once a demand exists for a market, only a limited time exists for economic input into its design. Second, the designs must be flexible, to allow for refinement based on initial experiences. Third, the designs must mesh with the political and social realities. Finally, the tools for designs should be based on economic theory, historical observation, experimentation, and computation.

In the design of a market clearinghouse, Roth discovered economic theory does offer an excellent guide to designing markets and approximated the properties of a large complex market fairly well. The theory organized the discussion in developing intuition of how people behave in various circumstances and in identifying the tradeoffs involved when altering these circumstances.

In conclusion, Roth notes that design is important because markets do not always grow like weeds. Some are like hothouse orchids, requiring the establishment of time and place and rules for interaction. The real test of economic theory is not only how well it provides an understanding of how an economy operates, but how well economists can apply the tools developed from it to solve practical questions of microeconomic engineering. A measure of the success of microeconomic theory will be the extent to which it becomes the source of practical advice on designing the institutions through which people interact.

Source: A. Roth, "The Economist as Engineer: Game Theory, Experimentation, and Computation as Tools for Design Economics." *Econometrica* 70 (2002): 1341–1378.

Models provide scientific explanation, prediction, and control

It is possible to store the mind with a million facts and still be entirely uneducated.
(Alec Bourne)

An educated person is someone who is able to explain relationships among facts. Neither a list of facts nor a compilation of summary statistics from a survey are explanations. These are generally called **data**, and an **explanation** is the general relation underlying these data. Data are interpreted or explained by applying theory to account for relationships among the data variables. If a model does well at explaining the relationships, it can be used for prediction. **Prediction** is deriving some conclusion before it is observed. The distinction between explanation and prediction is this: explanation is a conclusion observed first, with a model in support of the conclusion provided afterwards. Prediction is a conclusion deduced from a model before the conclusion is observed. If correct predictions can be made when these conditions are not fulfilled, then this is prediction without explanation.

Data. A collection of values for model variables. *E.g., commodity prices and quantity for a firm over time.*

Explanation. Determining relationships among variables. *E.g., the 10 percent price increase is the cause for the 20 percent decline in sales.*

Prediction. Deriving conclusions before they are observed. *E.g., the 10 percent price increase will result in a 20 percent decline in sales.*

Control is the altering of one or more exogenous variables in a model to predict a particular outcome. Examples are changing the price of a commodity to predict the change in a consumer's purchases or changing the pollution standard in a model to predict the change in pollution. For purposes of control, a model that provides valid explanations as well as accurate predictions is required. Models with the ability to control provide valuable insights into the possible effects that various programs and policies will have on an economy and on the agents within this economy.

Control. Altering a model's exogenous variables to predict a particular outcome. *E.g., increasing prices by 10 percent, and predicting that sales will fall by 20 percent.*

In the following chapters, we develop models of consumer and firm behavior, based on microeconomic theory, and relate the models to actual agent behavior. Based on these models, we investigate changes in (control of) exogenous variables—such as prices, wages, and income—by comparing one equilibrium position with another. Such an investigation is called comparative statics analysis. Table 1.1 lists a collection of optimization models along with comparative statics analysis developed and discussed in the ensuing chapters. All optimization models involve either maximizing or minimizing an objective function. Given a fixed level for the exogenous variables, the endogenous variables are varied for determining the optimal level of the objective function. Generally, the objective function is

Table 1.1 Collection of optimization models developed in this text

Operation	*Objective function*	*Variables*		*Constraint*	*Comparative statics*
		Endogenous	*Exogenous*		
Maximize	Household's utility	Commodities	Prices, income	Income	Prices, income
Maximize	Household's utility	Work, leisure	Time, wages	Income, time	Wages
Minimize	Firm's costs	Inputs	Input prices, output	Output	Input prices
Maximize	Firm's profit	Price	Output	Technology	
Maximize	Firm's profit	Output, inputs	Prices	Technology	Prices
Maximize	Firm's revenue	Output	Prices	Profit	
Maximize	Social welfare	Agents' utilities	Commodities	Technology	
Minimize	Firms' costs	Firms' emissions	Total emissions	Total emissions	
Maximize	Firm's profit	Output, emission	Tax	Technology	Tax

subject to some constraint, such as limited income or a given level of technology. In fact, underlying each agent's objective to maximize their well-being is that all agents are faced with limits (constraints). As indicated in Table 1.1, these limits may be income and time for households and technology for firms. Additional implications from the models are possible with comparative statics analysis by varying the exogenous variables.

Origins of microeconomics

At a fundamental level, the ensuing chapters are just an explanation and elaboration of neoclassical economics stemming from the Marshallian-cross analysis developed by the English economist Alfred Marshall (1842–1924) in *Principles of Economics* 1890.[4] An illustration of this Marshallian cross is provided in Figure 1.2, where the per-unit price of a commodity, p, is measured on the vertical axis and the quantity of the commodity, Q, on the horizontal axis. This Marshallian cross is represented by market demand and supply curves. As the price decreases, quantity demanded for a commodity by consumers is expected to increase, which results in a downward or negatively sloping demand curve. In contrast, firms supplying this commodity are expected to react to this price decline by decreasing the supply of the commodity, which results in an upward or positively sloping supply curve. These demand and supply curves result in the Marshallian cross, where their point of intersection (crossing) represents the market equilibrium level of price and quantity (p_e, Q_e). **Market equilibrium** is where

$$\text{Quantity Supplied} = \text{Quantity Demanded}$$

so there is no incentive for consumers or firms to change their market behavior. Firms will be willing to supply Q_e units of the commodity at p_e and consumers will be willing and able to purchase Q_e units at p_e. As outlined in the following chapters, this market-clearing price p_e is the most efficient mechanism for allocating our scarce resources among unlimited wants. It is the underlying ability of a decentralized decision system to efficiently allocate resources.

Microeconomic theory is also called *price theory*, given this major role of prices in providing an efficient allocation mechanism for buyers and sellers. Such a role for price signals exists in a decentralized system where consumers and firms attempt to maximize their own individual well-being (utility) with their given limited resources. This is in

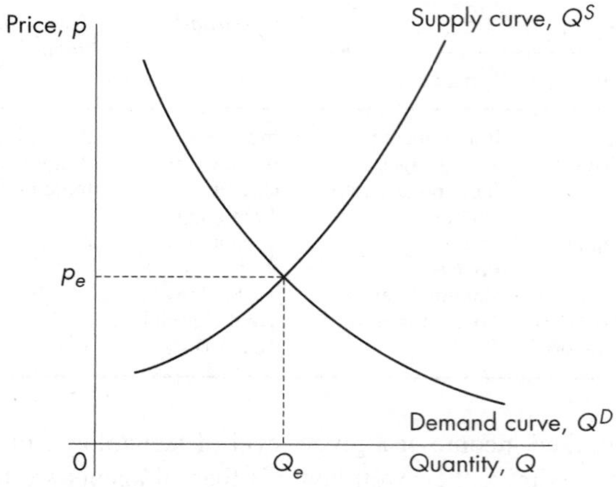

Figure 1.2 **Marshallian cross.** The market demand and supply curves establish a market equilibrium price p_e and quantity Q_e.

contrast to a centralized control system, such as North Korea and the former Soviet Union, determining for each agent what, when, and how their scarce resources, goods, and services should be allocated. As we will see in the ensuing chapters, individual agent decision in a decentralized price system is poetry in that it results in an efficient allocation of resources, goods, and services. The efficiency of price signals results in markets where buyers and sellers interact. These markets include the local supermarket, the hotdog stand at a track meet, the Internet markets, or an international commodities market. Lack of a market for a particular item results in an absence of market price signals, leading to inefficiencies, such as polluted lakes and streams.

Market equilibrium. State of balance in the market. *E.g., a market price where quantity supplied equals quantity demanded.*

Investigations over the past century have led to a greater understanding of the factors underlying these market supply and demand curves, and this Marshallian-cross analysis has been applied to a wide range of social behavior. For example, the Marshallian cross can explain markets not only for the commodities that consumers consume but also for natural resources, commodities delivered in the future, and commodities involving uncertainly (e.g., lottery tickets and common stocks).

Application: An alternative to the Marshallian cross?

As outlined by G.M. Koot, at the start of the twentieth century when Marshall's more theoretical conception of economics was taking hold in the form of neoclassical economics, opposition came from English historical economists. Historical economists maintained that the study of economic history and applied economics was the preferred foundation for developing public policy. These historical economists pioneered the systematic study of business and public administration. They saw an economist as a practical adviser rather than a detached expert, and economic theory as less significant than its application. For example, the historical economist W.A.S. Hewins rejected neoclassical economic theory out of distaste for individualistic theory. He maintained that an individualistic economic theory based on the individual maximizing satisfaction (economic man) and employing a model of perfect competition was erroneous. Instead, Hewins subscribed to an organic view of society that emphasized the ties of family, race, religion, and patriotism as the key elements. In other words, society determines the individual, and economics is a part of a larger social study.

The historical economists did not produce a discipline as Marshall's followers did. English historical economics was too diffuse, too untheoretical, and too committed to economic history, and lacked leadership. However, their important contribution was the central concept that economists solve pressing contemporary problems for which orthodox theory offers little guidance. Applied economics molds this central conception of early historical economists into economic theory for the development of solutions to contemporary problems.

Economists are also continuously extending neoclassical economics (the Marshallian cross) by importing newly discovered theory and conclusions from other sciences, such as psychology and sociology. Termed *recent economics* by J.B. Davis, these departures are challenging the standard neoclassical paradigm. They are not being advanced so much as to supplant the paradigm but instead to support its extension.

Sources: G.M. Koot, "An Alternative to Marshall: Economic History and Applied Economics at the Early LSE," *Atlantic Economic Journal* 10 (1982): 3–17; J.B. Davis, "Akerlof and Kranton on Identity in Economics: Inverting the Analysis," *Cambridge Journal of Economics* 31 (2007): 349–362.

Partial-equilibrium versus general-equilibrium models

Although the Marshallian cross is a useful tool, it is a partial-equilibrium model. **Partial-equilibrium models** only consider one market at a time rather than all the markets in an economy. For some questions, this narrowing of perspective gives valuable insights and analytical simplicity. For other broader questions about the efficiency and welfare implications of economic activities, such a narrow viewpoint may prevent the discovery of important interrelations.

Partial-equilibrium model. Modeling one market with limited effects from other markets. *E.g., only determining the equilibrium market price and output for oranges without also considering other related markets.*

For answering broader questions, a **general-equilibrium model**, which models the whole economy or some major subset, is required to investigate the interrelationship among various markets and agents. The French economist Leon Walras (1831–1910)[5] created the basis for such an investigation by representing the economy with a number of simultaneous equations. Realizing that in some cases, it is inappropriate to analyze a single market in isolation, Walras created a model that permits the effects of a change in one market to be carried through into other markets. Many recent theoretical developments in economics have been in the field of general-equilibrium analysis. In a sense, current macroeconomics is simply an example of applied general-equilibrium analysis. The two fields of economics are converging at this point of general equilibrium.

General-equilibrium model. Modeling the interrelationships among a number of markets or the whole economy. *E.g., determining the equilibrium prices and outputs for all fruit markets.*

To illustrate partial and general equilibrium, let us consider the change in the price of wheat. Marshall (partial equilibrium) would seek to understand implications of this price change by looking at conditions of supply and demand in the wheat market. In contrast, Walras (general equilibrium) would look not only at the wheat market but also at repercussions in other markets. An increase in the price of wheat increases cost for bakers, which affects the supply curve for bread. Also, an increase in the price of wheat may increase land prices for landowners, which affects the demand curves for all products landowners buy. As you see, the effect of any price change may eventually spread throughout the whole economy.

Why are apertures changed on economic lenses? To address (focus on) a particular type of problem, an alternative economic analysis (aperture) is employed.

Summary

1. Economics is the study of how society allocates its scarce resources among its unlimited wants.
2. Microeconomics is the study of individual agent interactions and the efficient allocation of resources. Macroeconomics is the study of the economy as a whole.
3. Positive economics is concerned with what is, was, or will be, and normative economics is concerned with what ought to be.
4. Applied economics is the application of economic theory to the solution of practical problems facing an economy. The art of economics is applied economics that takes goals from normative economics and determines how to achieve them using positive economics.
5. Based on the scientific method, models are simplified representations of reality with a set of underlying assumptions.
6. Methods employed for developing models are prose, geometry, mathematics, and computer programming.
7. Models are constructed for explanation, prediction, and control. Explanation determines the relationship among variables. If the conclusions from a model

are not yet observed, then the model will predict them. Control involves altering one or more of a model's exogenous variables to predict a particular outcome.

8. The Marshallian cross represents the crossing of the supply and demand curves. At the intersection, the equilibrium price and quantity are determined. In equilibrium, there is no tendency for the price and quantity to change.
9. Partial-equilibrium analysis results from considering the equilibrium in only one market with limited effects from other markets. General-equilibrium analysis considers the equilibrium among a number of markets or the whole economy.

Key concepts

agent, 4
art of economics, 8
analytical solution, 14
assumptions, 10
applied economics, 8
control, 16
data, 16
econometrics, 12
economics, 3
economy, 4
endogenous variables, 11
exogenous variables, 11
explanation, 16
fallacy of composition, 6
fallacy of division, 6
general-equilibrium model, 19
global bliss, 4
hypotheses, 12
inflation, 7
local bliss, 4
macroeconomics, 5
market equilibrium, 17
markets, 5
microeconomics, 5
models, 10
normative economics, 7
numerical solution, 14
paradigm, 10
partial-equilibrium model, 19
positive economics, 7
prediction, 16
price theory, 17
properties, 10
scientific method, 12
social science, 3
social welfare, 4
society, 3
system, 10
variables, 11

Key equation

$$\text{Quantity Supplied} = \text{Quantity Demanded}$$

Market equilibrium is where quantity supplied equals quantity demanded. There is no incentive for consumers or firms to change their market behavior.

Questions

A genius is a talented person who does his or her homework.

(Thomas Edison)

1. Critically analyze this statement: *Wants are not insatiable, because I can get all the coffee I want to drink every morning at breakfast.*

2. *Life has value because we are going to die.* Explain.
3. Generally, people may question whether scarcity is a major problem in the United States. They may argue the major problem is insuring full employment of our resources and distributing commodities in a fair and equitable manner. Given these concerns, can economists still maintain that scarcity is the problem? Explain.
4. *If you filled a room with economists, they would all point in different directions.* Evaluate this statement in terms of positive and normative economics.
5. *The study of economic theory is interesting as a mental exercise, but it has little to do with how societies really allocate their resources.* True or false? Explain.
6. *Facts are of limited value until they are arranged, and how they are arranged is theory. Theory is the arrangement and interpretation of facts, which allows generalizations for understanding how things happen.* Analyze and explain these statements.
7. Is there a tradeoff between the realism of the assumptions of a model and its tractability (the logical conclusions)? Explain.
8. *That's just a coincidence; it doesn't prove anything.* How does theory enable us to distinguish relevant evidence from mere coincidence?
9. Why do economists limit their analyses to marginal (additional) rather than total quantities? Do economists believe marginal quantities are more useful than the corresponding total quantities? Explain.
10. Why is it not necessarily evil to make unrealistic assumptions when constructing models?

Internet case studies

1. Develop a list of the frequently occurring errors in reasoning and provide an example of each.
2. Examine a normative economic concept used in economic theory and how it is used.
3. Discuss a number of the new paradigms in economics and how they may lay the foundation for advancement of economic theory.
4. Definitions of the scientific method vary from being very broad to quite narrow. Compare a very broad definition of the scientific method with a narrow definition. Under what conditions may one definition be preferred over the other?

Part I

Consumers' sovereignty

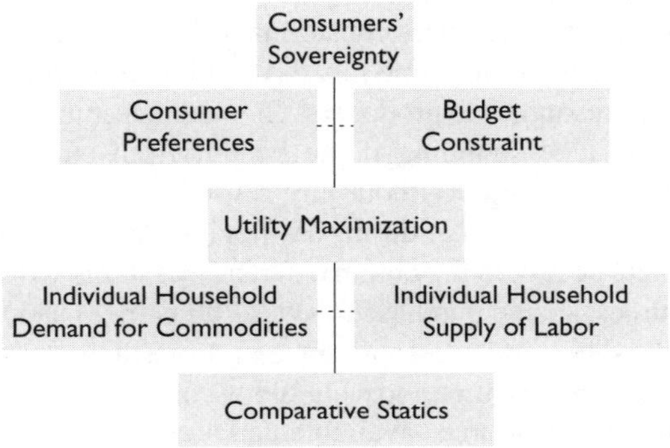

Chapters

2. **Consumer preferences**
3. **Utility maximization**
4. **Comparative statics: analysis of individual demand and labor supply**

Nobody HAS to do ANYTHING.

(Charles McCabe's Law)

Translation: A student never gets penalized for cutting a class, if she does not decide the advantages exceed the drawbacks.

From the quote, the student may have decided instead to go shoe shopping. When shopping, why would she purchase only one particular pair of shoes instead of others and how did the shoe store know to have the shoes she wanted? Was she just lucky or is it magical? Well if it is magical, then magic is happening all the time as individual market transactions, mating demand with supply for a pair of shoes, are repeated constantly between buyers and sellers. In fact, we generally take it for granted that we can go shopping and find the type of shoes we want. How is this possible? Well society is composed of agents (e.g., the student in the above quote), categorized as consumers (buyers) and producers (sellers), attempting to individually and collectively increase their well-being. Through these individual attempts to maximize their well-being, the shoes will be there for her to purchase. It is magic in the sense that price signals (the invisible hand) will mate demand with supply.

Now, why did she purchase this particular pair of shoes and not the other? Well, generally consumers attempt to satisfy their wants by consuming commodities (goods and services), limited by their resource constraint. This resource constraint is generally composed of time (there is limited time in a day) and income derived from supplying labor and other owned resources to producers. Given this resource constraint, a student will cut class and go shoe shopping if the benefit from cutting is more than the satisfaction gained in attending. Without any resource constraints, the student may purchase more shoes. For example, during Philippine President Ferdinand Marcos's reign, he had complete access to the country's treasury, so his wife Imelda R. Marcos had unlimited resources, so she purchased over 2,700 pairs of shoes.

Producers (e.g., the sellers of shoes) attempt to improve their well-being by satisfying consumer wants, limited by resource and technology constraints. It is generally assumed there is a fixed amount of resources available and a given technology for combining these resources into outputs that satisfy consumers' wants.[1] To understand how society can optimally allocate these limited resources among unlimited wants, we need to know how agents make allocation decisions. Without this knowledge, developing a theory for the optimal allocation of society's resources, given consumers' and producers' decisions, is impossible.

It is appropriate to first study how consumers optimally allocate their limited resources; for without consumption there would be no justification for production. In **free markets** (unregulated by any governmental authority), consumer sovereignty exists. Thus, consumers generally have the freedom to choose which set of commodities they wish to consume, given their constraints.

Free markets. Markets not controlled by any governmental constraints. *E.g., the invisible hand.*

Consumer theory is basically a theory of how you and I behave, so it is something we all can relate to. Consumer preferences are the foundation of this theory. Defining consumer preferences provides a method for describing how consumers may prefer one commodity over another. In Chapter 2, we develop a theory of consumer behavior in which consumers are able to order (rank) their preferences for one group of commodities over another. In Chapter 3, based on these preference orderings and consumers' limited income, we develop a theory on how consumers determine the commodities they consume. Then, in Chapter 4, we discuss a theory of individual consumer demand for commodities and supply of labor.

The overall objective of Part 1 is to derive a consumer's demand for a commodity. Then, in Part 2, Chapter 5, we sum the individual consumer demand for a commodity over all consumers to derive the market demand for the commodity. The associated market demand curve is one arm of the Marshallian cross. Thus, Part 1 is an investigation of how consumers' preferences are reflected in the market by aggregate demand.

We also derive the individual supply of labor curve in Part 1, based on labor's work/leisure choice. In Part 7, Chapter 16, we sum this individual worker's supply of labor over all workers to derive the market supply for labor. The associated market supply curve is the other arm of the Marshallian cross for the labor market. With an understanding of the determinants underlying market supply and demand, Adam Smith's invisible hand of how markets efficiently allocate resources is revealed.

2 Consumer preferences

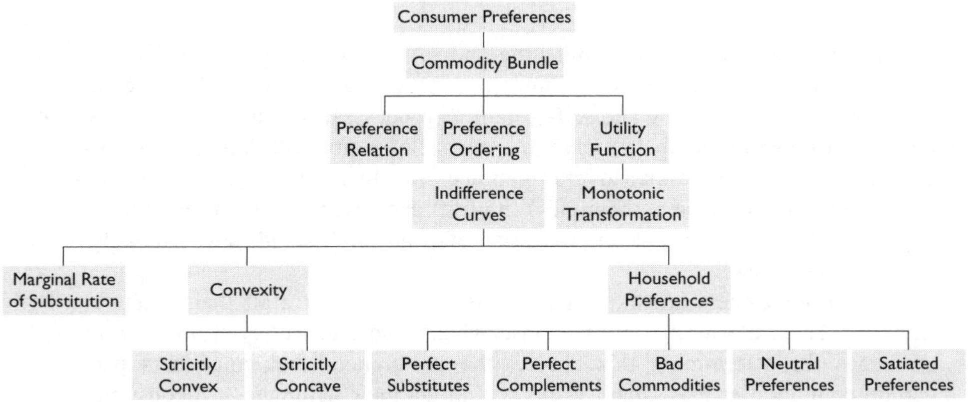

Outline and Conceptual Inquiries

Household preferences and grocery carts

How many grocery carts are there anyway?

The world of only two commodities

How are two commodities really k commodities?

Preference relation: arranging grocery carts

Preference ordering: ranking grocery carts

When waiting in line at a supermarket, can you rank the various grocery carts?

Application: Households' rationality may be bounded

Utility functions dissected

Application: Economic man as a moral individual

Do utility functions have personalities?

Indifference curves: apathy

Can you read a utility-relief map?

How much are you willing to substitute partying for studying?

Are averages preferred to extremes?

Are extremes preferred to averages?

How indifference curves represent household preferences

Imperfect substitutes: apples and oranges

Perfect substitutes: brown and white eggs

When are earrings perfect substitutes?

Application: Only a bad reproduction is a good reproduction

Perfect complements: shoes and shoe laces

When are earrings perfect complements?

Application: Big business versus big government—are they perfect complements?

Bad commodities: cigarettes

Neutral preferences: inert ingredients

Do zombies have neutral preferences?

Satiated preferences: heaven

Are there economists in Shangri-La?

Summary

Key concepts

Key equations

Questions

Exercises

Internet case studies

Appendix to chapter 2

How to measure utility

Is there a hedonimeter?

Application: Is a hedonimeter feasible?

What is a positive monotonic transformation of a utility function?

When does $U = U^{1/2}$?

Question

Exercises

Commodities may not always bring happiness; but there is no happiness without commodities.

(Michael Wetzstein)

Life is an object that performs signaling and self-sustaining processes. To perform, life consumes energy, which for humans (consumers) is supplied by consuming commodities. For signaling and self-sustaining processes, consumers are interested in consuming commodities that satisfy some wants. For example, they obtain food, shelter, and clothing to increase their overall happiness. In fact, without these commodities, there would probably be no happiness (no life). However, not all commodities bring happiness. For example, bad water, leaky roofs, and smelly clothes would likely yield unhappiness instead.

Because consumers are faced with limited resources, not all their wants can be satisfied. Thus, consumers must choose which wants to satisfy from their limited resources. In determining this choice, the preferences that consumers place on certain commodities that satisfy wants will affect their willingness to consume these commodities. For example, if, for the same resource allocation, fish consumption offers a higher level of satisfaction than lamb consumption, a consumer who attempts to maximize satisfaction will choose the fish. *Consumer preferences* are thus central to how consumers behave in allocating their limited resources to satisfy as many wants as possible.

The aim of this chapter is to investigate how consumer preferences are employed by consumers in making their individual commodity choices. Such a decentralized decision process directly allows us to relate individual consumer preferences to society's overall consumer choices. No central authority is required for determining overall consumer choices. As revealed in subsequent chapters, price signals and decentralized consumer choice based on consumer preferences underlies an efficient allocation of resources.

In this chapter, we investigate consumer preferences for commodities in terms of models that describe consumer behavior. These models are based on a consumer preference relation, which allows the development of a number of assumptions called *preference axioms*. Given these preference axioms, *utility functions* defining the power of commodities to satisfy consumers' wants can be specified. Depending on the nature of consumer preferences for commodities, utility functions can take on various forms. We will investigate properties associated with a number of utility functions.

The main objective in investigating these utility functions—and in general developing a model of consumer behavior—is to derive demand functions based on consumer preferences, prices, and income. **Demand** is defined as how much of a commodity consumers are willing and able to purchase at a given price. We intuitively, understand that as the price of a commodity declines, quantity demanded for the commodity will increase. This **Law of Demand**, theoretically developed in the following chapters, is illustrated in Figure 2.1.[1] Note the inverse relationship between price and quantity demanded: increase price, quantity demanded declines; decrease price, quantity demanded increases.

Demand. How much of a commodity consumers are willing and able to purchase at a given price. *E.g., you may be willing and able to purchase 5 pounds of bananas at the supermarket price of 59¢ per pound. You have the income (ability) to purchase more bananas, but you are not interested in purchasing more (unwilling to purchase more).*

Law of Demand. As the price of a commodity declines, quantity demanded for the commodity increases. *E.g., once at the supermarket, you notice the store has a special on bananas for 39¢ per pound. As a result of this price decline, you are now willing to purchase 7 pounds instead of 5 pounds.*

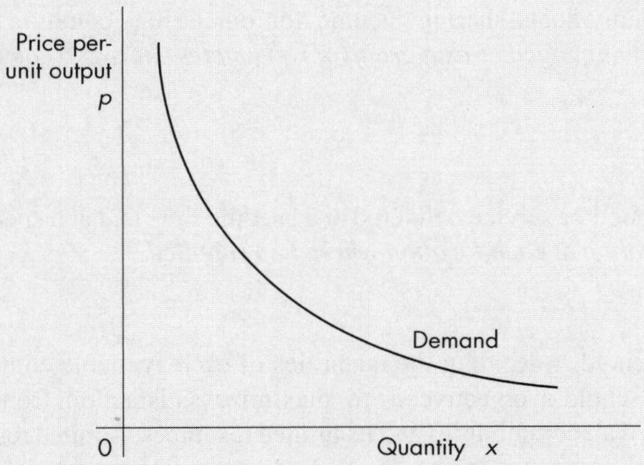

Figure 2.1 **Law of Demand.** The downward-sloping demand curve illustrates the inverse relationship between price and quantity demanded.

Knowledge of consumer demand for commodities is critical for firms in attempting to maximize profits. Without this knowledge, firms would not know which direction to take in product development, sales promotion, or production levels. Thus, to determine consumer demand, large firms will employ applied economists to model the demand for their products. For example, the credit card company American Express employs hundreds of applied economists to model the demand for their credit cards and the characteristics of consumers likely to default, commit fraud, or always pay their minimum balances.

Demand functions are based on the assumption that consumers attempt to maximize their satisfaction by consuming commodities. Out of an infinite combination of commodities, they choose a particular set of commodities that maximize satisfaction. Unfortunately, this maximization is constrained by limited resources. (Only in our dreams can we achieve unconstrained satisfaction.)

Household preferences and grocery carts

Even as the cell is the unit of an organic body, so the household is the unit of society.
(Ruth Nanda Anshen)

The central foundation of consumer theory is the model of consumer or household preferences. A **household** is any group of individuals who share income to purchase and consume commodities. Each household is a unit of society attempting to maximize its happiness based on its preferences for commodities. A **commodity** is a particular good or service delivered at a specific time and at a specific location. Commodities consumed at different times and locations should be viewed as distinct commodities. However, in practice, economic models often involve some aggregation over time and location (space), because data are often aggregated by time and space (e.g., monthly county data). The assumption is that commodities being aggregated are sufficiently similar, so few economic implications are lost.

Household. A group of individuals sharing income for purchasing commodities. *E.g., parents and children living together or a group of roommates sharing a common food budget.*

Commodity. A particular good or service delivered at a specific time and at a specific location. *E.g., Brand X gasoline at each location where it is supplied.*

The problem facing a household is deciding the quantities of each available commodity it should consume. The household's objective is to maximize satisfaction from these commodities, given the prices of all commodities and its limited resources. Limited resources are represented as a monetary constraint in the form of income. **Income** represents the monetary return from resources owned by a household at a given time period. For example, the number of hours a household devotes to working times a wage rate would be a household's income from working.[2]

Income. The monetary return from resources owned by a household at a given time period. *E.g., the sum of your earnings from working and any unearned income (line 22 on IRS form 1040).*

Especially considering the time and space characteristics of a commodity, there are an infinite number of commodities. For developing models of consumer behavior, economists abstract by assuming a finite number of k commodities. Depending on the objectives and nature of a model, k could be restricted to just two commodities or be unrestricted and take on any value. Associated with each of these k commodities is the amount each individual household may consider consuming. Let the variable x_j represent this quantity of the jth commodity a household may consume, $j = 1, 2, \ldots, k$. For example, x_1 could be the amount of meat consumed, x_2 the amount of bread, x_3 the amount of hair spray, and so on.

The level of consumption may be zero for some commodities. For example, consumers generally consume zero levels of antique buses or trips into outer space.

A bundle making up all the k commodities a household may consume is called a **commodity bundle** (or a market basket), and is represented as

$$\vec{x} = (x_1, x_2, \ldots, x_k).$$

Commodity bundles will vary by the quantity of each commodity in the bundle. Assuming these quantities for each commodity are unrestricted, an infinite number of commodity bundles are possible. Each of these commodity bundles can be thought of as a grocery cart filled with goods and services. The next time you are in a grocery store, look at people's grocery carts and observe the different commodities they have in their carts. There are an infinite number of possible bundles within these carts. Also, for investigating small (marginal) changes in consumption, assume each commodity is perfectly divisible so any nonnegative quantity can be purchased. For example, assume it is possible to split open a package of hotdog buns and just purchase one bun.[3]

How many grocery carts are there anyway? An infinite number.

Commodity bundle. A set of commodities that a household may consume. *E.g., given your weekly income, all the commodities you consume during the week.*

The world of only two commodities

For graphical presentation, we often assume a household is faced with a choice of only two commodities (x_1 and x_2), such as sodas and fries or pork and beef. These two commodities could be either the only two commodities a household consumes or the only two commodities it can vary. In this two-commodity assumption, all other commodities are fixed in terms of some given quantity. We then represent the commodity bundle as

$$\vec{x} = (x_1, x_2 | x_3, \ldots, x_k),$$

where all commodities to the right of the bar | are considered fixed and cannot be varied by the household.

This two-commodity assumption can be generalized by assuming one of the commodities is a **composite commodity** (called the **numeraire commodity**) composed of all other commodities. As an example, x_1 could be the amount of bread consumed by a household, with x_2 the composite commodity consisting of all other commodities except bread.

How are two commodities really k commodities? Making one of the two commodities a composite of all other commodities results in two commodities being k commodities.

Composite commodity (numeraire commodity). A group of commodities represented as one combined commodity. *E.g., an amusement park can be a composite commodity of the rides and entertainment inside the park.*

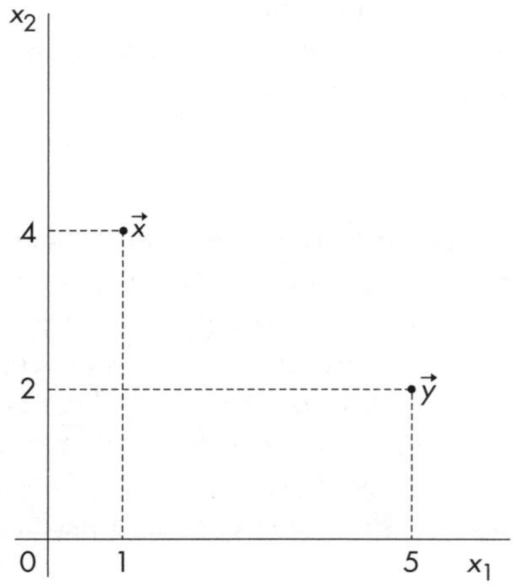

Figure 2.2 **Commodity space.** The commodity space is the nonnegative quadrant in a graph. Bundles $\vec{x} = (1, 4)$ and $\vec{y} = (5, 2)$ represent two possible bundles in this commodity space.

In a graph of two commodities, x_1 and x_2, a commodity bundle is a point in the commodity space (Figure 2.2). A **commodity space** is a set of all possible commodity bundles. As illustrated in Figure 2.2, a household cannot consume a negative amount of a commodity, so the commodity space is represented by the nonnegative quadrant. In this commodity space, commodity bundle $\vec{x}$ contains 1 unit of x_1 and 4 units of x_2, and bundle $\vec{y}$ contains 5 units of x_1 and 2 units of x_2. Any nonnegative combination of x_1 and x_2 makes up a commodity bundle, so the commodity space still exists as x_1 and x_2 approach infinity.

Commodity space. The set of all possible commodity bundles. *E.g., all the grocery carts in the world.*

Preference relation: arranging grocery carts

The objective of a household is to consume the commodity bundle that yields the highest satisfaction it can afford. A household's choice of this preferred commodity bundle depends not only on commodity prices and the household's limited income but also on the tastes and preferences of the household. These tastes and preferences can be summarized by the *preference relation*, "is preferred to or indifferent to," written $\succsim$, where $\succ$ denotes preferred to and $\sim$ denotes indifference to. The term

$$\vec{x} \succsim \vec{y}$$

where $\vec{x}$ and $\vec{y}$ are commodity bundles (alternative grocery carts), means a household either prefers $\vec{x}$ or $\vec{y}$ or is indifferent to $\vec{x}$ and $\vec{y}$. **Indifference** means the household would be just as satisfied, based on the household's preferences, of consuming $\vec{x}$ as it would be consuming $\vec{y}$.

Indifference. A household is just as satisfied consuming one commodity bundle as it is consuming some other commodity bundle. *E.g., faced with a number of grocery carts filled with different quantities of commodities, you are just as satisfied with any of the carts.*

Preference ordering: ranking grocery carts

Happiness is not an absence of problems, but the ability to deal with them.

(H. Jackson Brown)

The preference relation provides a method for modeling how a household orders or ranks a set of bundles from the most to the least desirable. This preference ordering is often done unconsciously, but, especially in the case of large purchases such as buying an automobile, it is also done consciously. Without this preference ordering, a household cannot determine its preferred consumption bundle.

Two assumptions, *preference axioms*, regarding a household's preferences are required to order a set of bundles. These assumptions are basic axioms in consumer theory, where an axiom is an assumption that is generally accepted as true.

Axiom 1. Completeness

If $\vec{x}$ and $\vec{y}$ are any two commodity bundles, a household can always specify exactly one of the following: $\vec{x} \succ \vec{y}$, $\vec{y} \succ \vec{x}$, or $\vec{x} \sim \vec{y}$.

Commodity bundles within an area of household indecision as illustrated in Figure 2.3 cannot be ordered in terms of a household's preferences. Thus, the Completeness Axiom precludes areas of indecision, assuming that members of a household completely understand the contents of each bundle and can always make up their minds.

Households generally can make up their minds within their range of common experience. However, there might exist some extreme cases, possibly involving life or death comparisons,

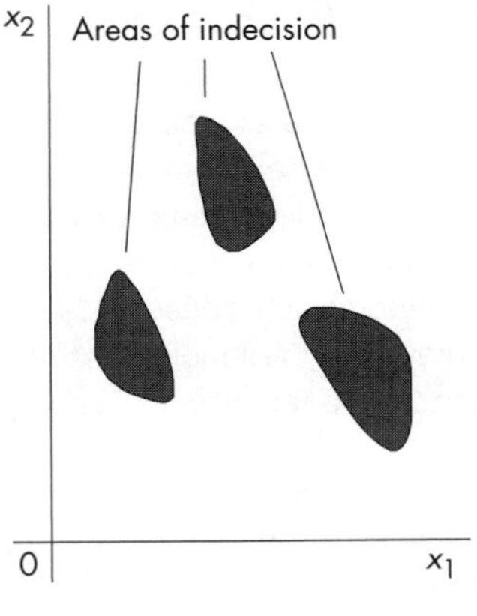

Figure 2.3 **Gaps of indecision in the commodity space.** As a result of household indecision, bundles within the shaded areas cannot be ranked in terms of most to least preferred.

where comparison of alternatives would be difficult. Such extremely difficult situations are rare (and generally only occur in the movies). Thus, the Completeness Axiom assumes that households have taken the time for evaluating alternative commodity bundles and can make decisions on the preference ordering of these bundles.

Axiom 2. Transitivity

If a household states $\vec{x} \succsim \vec{y}$ and $\vec{y} \succsim \vec{z}$, then it must also state $\vec{x} \succsim \vec{z}$.

The Transitivity Axiom states that a household's preferences for alternative commodity bundles cannot be cyclical. An example of cyclical preferences is where partying Friday night is preferred to a Saturday football game and a Saturday football game is preferred to going to church on Sunday, but then going to church is preferred to Friday partying. Ruling out such cyclical preferences is necessary for any discussion of preference maximization. Without this axiom, households cannot order their commodity bundles from most to least desirable. Such an ordering is necessary for maximizing satisfaction, given an income constraint and fixed commodity prices.

Preferences based on these two axioms characterize rational household behavior. **Rationality** means households can ordinally rank (see the Mathematical Review) a set of commodity bundles to maximize their satisfaction of wants given limited resources.

When waiting in line at a supermarket, can you rank the various grocery carts? If you are rational and thus obey the Completeness and Transitivity Axioms, you can rank the grocery carts in terms of most to least preferred.

Rationality. Households can maximize satisfaction by ranking a set of commodity bundles. *E.g., ranking the selection of commodities for your grocery cart to maximize your satisfaction.*

Application: Households' rationality may be bounded

Bounded rationality is a theory that households are limited by available information, their cognitive abilities, and limited time for decision making. It was developed by Herbert Simon (1916–2001) as an alternative to the mathematical modeling of preference ordering. In rational choice, information processing becomes more complex as the number of feasible consumption bundles increases. When the number of bundles becomes large, rational choice may be cognitively demanding, so households may replace maximization with a simpler choice rule. They may apply rationality only after greatly simplifying the available choices. Households are then a "satisficer," seeking a satisfactory solution rather than the optimal one.

Salant provides the following example of bounded rationality where order of alternatives affects decision making. In 1981, American Airlines determined that travel agents booked the first flight that appeared on their computer screen 53 percent of the time and a flight that appeared somewhere on the first screen almost 92 percent of the time. American Airlines then manipulated the order in which flights were listed on the

American "Sabre" computer reservation system that dominated the market for electronic flight bookings. This led to the US federal government regulating screen display in computer reservation systems. Salant determines that households, in an attempt to simplify the complexity of ordering bundles, consider the order in which the bundles appear. This results in additional behavioral regularities, including choice overload and default tendency. These effects emerge as optimal when a rational household attempts to reduce the costs of ordering bundles.

Sources: H. Simon, "A Behavioral Model of Rational Choice," in *Models of Man, Social and Rational: Mathematical Essays on Rational Human Behavior in a Social Setting*, New York: Wiley (1957); Y. Salant, "Procedural Analysis of Choice Rules with Applications to Bounded Rationality," *American Economic Review* 100 (2011): 724–748.

Utility functions dissected

Political theorist Jeremy Bentham introduced a ranking of commodity bundles.[4] This ranking may be represented by a **utility function**

$$U = U(\vec{x}) = U(x_1, x_2, \ldots, x_k).$$

Utility is the ability or power of a commodity or commodity bundle to satisfy wants when a household consumes the commodity or bundle. For example, you receive a certain level of utility (or satisfaction) from reading microeconomic theory. Utility functions indicate how a household ranks commodity bundles by assigning a numerical value to each level of satisfaction associated with each commodity bundle. The higher the preference ranking, the larger is the number assigned. The household then determines which bundle maximizes this utility function given the household's limited income and fixed commodity prices.

Utility function (U). A function that orders commodity bundles based on household preferences. *E.g., a function that tells you which grocery cart to choose from a given set of carts.*

Utility. Ability or power of a commodity to satisfy a want. *E.g., having pizza and Coke during a study break satisfies your hunger.*

Again, for graphical presentation, we assume that only two commodities can vary and hold all other commodities constant. In this case, the utility function is represented as

$$U = U(x_1, x_2 | x_3, \ldots, x_k),$$

or, suppressing the fixed commodities, $x_3, \ldots, x_k$,

$$U = U(x_1, x_2),$$

where x_1 and x_2 are the only commodities allowed to vary.

Application: Economic man as a moral individual

Generally a household's behavior is affected by moral considerations. In an article by Dowell, Goldfarb, and Griffith, a variety of approaches for introducing moral considerations into economic analysis are reviewed. These approaches can be categorized into three areas: introducing moral values as part of preference functions, introducing moral norms as constraints, and introducing such norms as decision rules in strategic interactions (game theory, Chapter 14).

As an application of the first area, the authors maintain the concept of a utility function representing preferences. However, they modify the function so the utility from consuming a given commodity bundle varies in a lumpy way, depending on the current moral content of the household. Thus, a household's moral behavior affects the utility function's position in the commodity space. One example is a retail businessperson choosing not to open a gun shop in a low income area.

Specifically the Dowell, Goldfarb, and Griffith model considers the utility function

$$U = U(\vec{x}, H),$$

where H represents some moral value such as honesty, so $\Delta U/\Delta H > 0$. If H were continuous, it would be just like any other commodity in the commodity space. However, the authors model H as a dichotomous variable, taking on the value of 1 if a household behaves morally, and 0 if it behaves immorally. A change from immoral to moral behavior will then shift the utility function outward. The utility function is then higher for any commodity bundle if the household behaves morally. Immorality generates guilt, which lowers (poisons) a household's consumption of the resulting commodity bundle. Thus, a moral lawyer (oxymoron?) will not represent an immoral client if the additional commodities she could purchase from taking the case are sufficiently poisoned by her feelings of guilt.

Source: R.S. Dowell, R.S. Goldfarb, and W.B. Griffith, "Economic Man as a Moral Individual," *Economic Inquiry* 36 (1998): 645–653.

Do utility functions have personalities?

Who is rich? He that is content. Who is that? Nobody.

(Benjamin Franklin)

Depending on the particular assumptions concerning a household's preferences, utility functions and indifference curves derived from them can take on a number of shapes. For example, as illustrated in Figure 2.4 and discussed in the Appendix to this chapter, the classical shape of a utility function assumes a commodity is desirable. Greater amounts of the commodity increase utility. This desirability assumption is stated in the following axiom.

Axiom 3. Nonsatiation

More of a commodity is preferred to less.

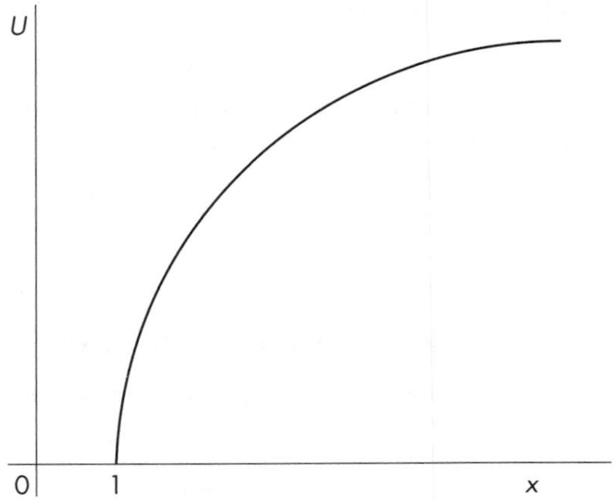

Figure 2.4 **Utility curve for the function $U(x) = \ln x$.** As the commodity x increases, utility U increases at a decreasing rate.

The Nonsatiation Axiom states that a household can always do a little bit better by consuming more of a commodity. Such a commodity is termed a **good** (or **desirable**) **commodity**, as opposed to a **bad** (or **undesirable**) **commodity**. A bad commodity results in a decline in utility as more of the commodity is consumed. More of the commodity is not preferred to less. Garbage, defined as a commodity that yields negative utility, by definition is a bad commodity.

Good (or desirable) commodity. More of the commodity is preferred to less. *E.g. food.*

Bad (or undesirable) commodity. More of the commodity is not preferred to less. *E.g., dirty air.*

Assuming the utility function $U(\vec{x})$ is differentiable, the Nonsatiation Axiom requires all first-order partial derivatives of the utility function—the **marginal utilities (MU)**—be positive. Thus, increasing the consumption of any commodity, holding the consumption of all other commodities constant, increases utility. In other words, nobody is content with their current level of any commodity. For example, assuming a household ranks commodities by the utility function

$$U = U(x_1, x_2, \ldots, x_k).$$

Then

$$\mathrm{MU}_j = \frac{\partial U}{\partial x_j} > 0, \quad j = 1, \ldots, k.$$

MU_j is the extra utility obtained from consuming slightly more of x_j while holding the amounts consumed of all other commodities constant. The value of marginal utility depends on the point at which the partial derivative is to be evaluated; that is, how much $x_1, x_2, \ldots, x_k$

the household is currently consuming. However, only the sign of MU is important; the actual magnitude is meaningless since utility is only an ordinal ranking.

Marginal utility of x_j (MU_j). The extra utility obtained from consuming slightly more of x_j while holding the amounts consumed of all other commodities constant. *E.g., having that additional cup of coffee is very satisfying.*

Example 2.1. How to derive marginal utilities from a utility function

Few things are harder to put up with than the annoyance of a good example (Mark Twain).

Consider the following utility function with two commodities (x_1 and x_2)

$$U = x_1 x_2.$$

The marginal utilities of x_1 and x_2 are then

$$MU_1 = \frac{\partial U}{\partial x_1} = x_2 > 0, \quad MU_2 = \frac{\partial U}{\partial x_2} = x_1 > 0.$$

Thus, this utility function satisfies the Nonsatiation Axiom.

The result of the Nonsatiation Axiom, for two commodities x_1 and x_2, is illustrated in Figure 2.5. Every point or bundle within the positive quadrant represents a commodity bundle. For example, the commodity bundle $\vec{x}$ contains x_1' units of x_1 and x_2' units of x_2. The Nonsatiation Axiom states that given an initial commodity bundle $\vec{x}$, every commodity bundle with more of at least one commodity will be preferred to $\vec{x}$. The shaded area in Figure 2.5 represents the preferred set of bundles; $\vec{u}$, $\vec{y}$, and $\vec{z}$ are all preferred to $\vec{x}$. In contrast, $\vec{v}$, $\vec{r}$, and $\vec{s}$ may not be preferred to $\vec{x}$ because they have less of at least one of the commodities.

Axioms 1 and 2 provide the necessary assumptions for household preference ordering. They determine the **indifference sets** of commodity bundles, where within each set a household receives the same level of satisfaction. A household is indifferent between any two bundles within an indifference set. For example, a household may be willing to give up a six pack of cola for a pound of candy with no change in satisfaction. Axiom 3 provides the direction for increasing utility given a change in a commodity bundle. Thus, in terms of preferences, these three axioms are all that is necessary for determining the utility-maximizing bundle. A list of these preference axioms (along with the last axiom, Axiom 4) and the major implications in terms of assumptions on household preferences for each axiom are provided in Table 2.1.

Indifference set. The set of all commodity bundles where a household receives the same level of satisfaction for each bundle consumed. *E.g., a group of grocery carts with commodities offering the same level of satisfaction.*

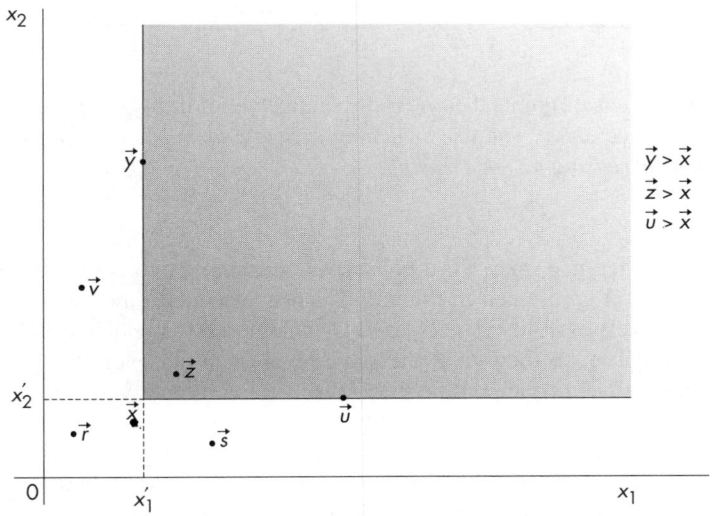

Figure 2.5 **Nonsatiation, more is preferred to less.** The shaded area, including the boundary with bundles $\vec{y}$ and $\vec{u}$, represents commodity bundles with at least more of one commodity than $\vec{x}$. These bundles are all preferred to $\vec{x}$. The bundles outside this shaded area, including bundles $\vec{v}$, $\vec{r}$, and $\vec{s}$, represent bundles with less of at least one commodity than $\vec{x}$. Based on the Nonsatiation Axiom, these bundles may not be preferred to $\vec{x}$.

Table 2.1 Preference Axioms

	Axiom	*Implication*	
1	Completeness	No gaps in the commodity space. Any two bundles can be compared	Rational household (Axioms 1 and 2)
2	Transitivity	Orders bundles in terms of preferences	
3	Nonsatiation	A household can always do a little bit better	Necessary for utility maximization (Rational household and Axiom 3)
4	Diminishing marginal rate of substitution (strict convexity)	Averages are preferred to extremes	

Indifference curves: apathy

Based on these three axioms, the indifference sets are a set of curves, where each **indifference curve** is a locus of points (commodity bundles) that yield the same level of utility. Every point (commodity bundle) along an indifference curve represents a different combination of two commodities and each combination is equally satisfactory to a household. Each combination yields the same level of total utility, so these commodity bundles can be represented by an indifference space. An *indifference space* is analogous to a relief map, where contour lines or curves represent equal levels of satisfaction or utility instead of equal elevation.

Indifference curve. A locus of points that yield the same level of utility. *E.g., as you walk along an indifference curve, you are switching grocery carts but your level of satisfaction is neither increasing nor decreasing.*

Figure 2.6 shows an indifference space for a household consuming two commodities x_1 and x_2 (say sodas and fries). Represented in this indifference space are three indifference curves yielding different levels of utility (U_1, U_2, and U_3). Commodity bundles $\vec{x}$ and $\vec{y}$ are on the same indifference curve, so they yield the same level of utility even though they represent different combinations of the commodities. (More of commodity x_2 and less of commodity x_1 are consumed at $\vec{x}$ than $\vec{y}$.) Commodity bundle $\vec{z}$ is on a higher indifference curve, so, compared with $\vec{x}$ and $\vec{y}$ it yields a higher level of total utility. According to the Nonsatiation Axiom, increasing either or both of the commodities shifts the household to higher indifference curves until the household approaches global bliss. Some households will never reach global bliss. In this case, there are an infinite number of indifference curves. However, between any two indifference curves—say U_1 and U_2 in Figure 2.6—there are a finite number of curves. A household will not be able to distinguish between two

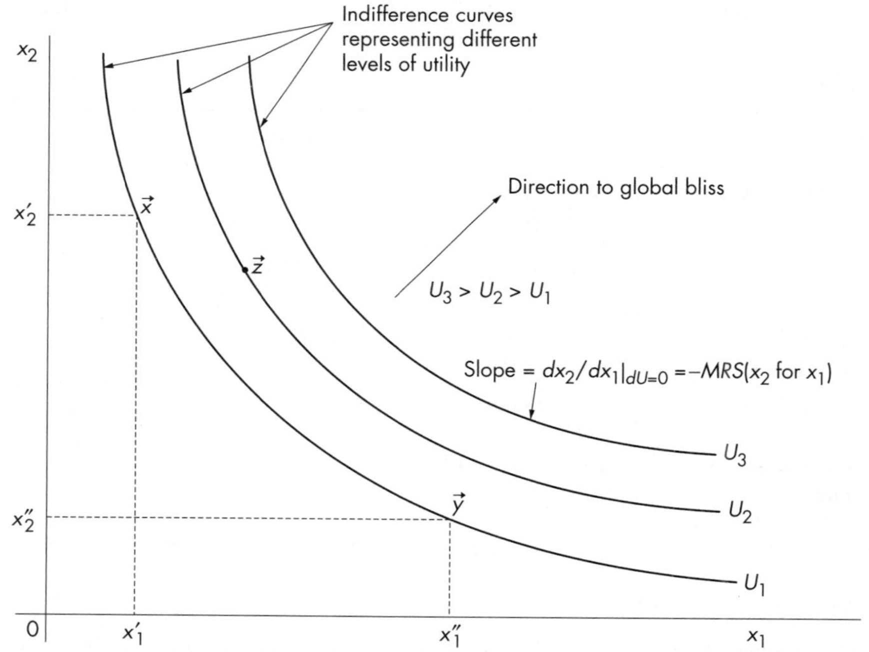

Figure 2.6 **Indifference space, MRS(x_2 for x_1).** Commodity bundles $\vec{x}$ and $\vec{y}$ lie on the same indifference curve U_1, so they yield the same level of utility. Bundle $\vec{z}$ lies on a higher indifference curve, U_2, so it yields a higher level of utility compared with $\vec{x}$ and $\vec{y}$.

indifference sets that are very close to each other, but as the sets diverge the distinction will become apparent.[5]

Can you read a utility-relief map? Yes, different commodity bundles on the same contour line yield the same level of utility and higher contour lines yield a higher level of utility.

Note that as with contour lines on relief maps, indifference curves cannot intersect. As illustrated in Figure 2.7, the Transitivity Axiom is violated if indifference curves intersect. In the figure, $\vec{x} \succ \vec{y}$, $\vec{z} \succ \vec{u}$, and $\vec{y} \sim \vec{z}$. Thus, given the Transitivity Axiom, $\vec{x} \succ \vec{u}$; however, $\vec{x}$ and $\vec{u}$ are on the same indifference curve, so $\vec{x} \sim \vec{u}$. This results in a contradiction when indifference curves intersect.

Example 2.2 How to derive an indifference curve from a utility function

Consider again the utility function in Example 2.1:

$$U = x_1 x_2.$$

A listing of commodity bundles yielding a utility level of 12 is shown in the table and graphed in the figure.

x_1	x_2	U^o
1	12	12
2	6	12
3	4	12
4	3	12
6	2	12
12	1	12

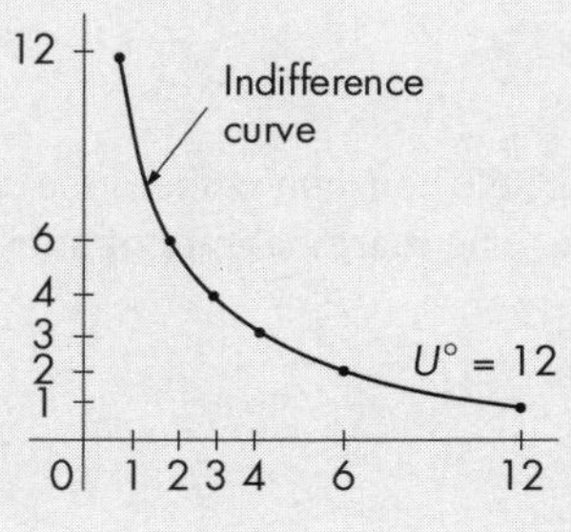

Marginal rate of substitution (MRS)

Additional peace and quiet is worth sacrificing some convenience.

(Michael Wetzstein)

The (generally) negative slope of an indifference curve implies that if a household is forced to give up some x_1, it must be compensated by an additional amount of x_2 to remain indifferent

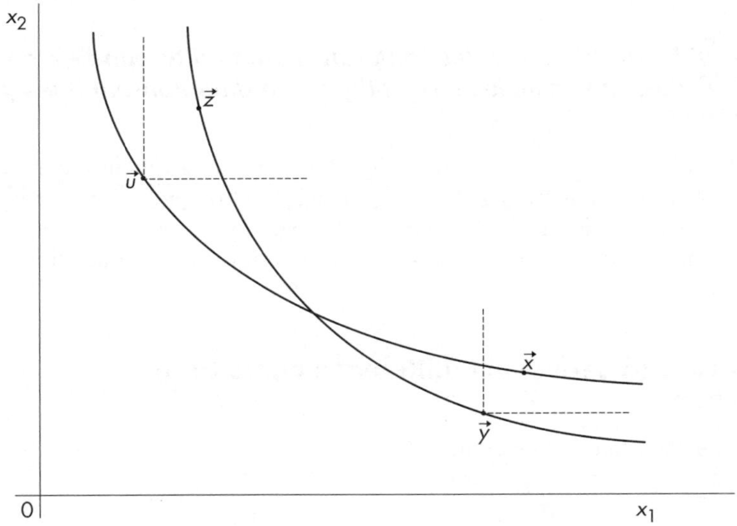

Figure 2.7 **Indifference curves cannot intersect.** Commodity bundle $\vec{x} \succ \vec{y}$, $\vec{z} \succ \vec{u}$, and $\vec{y} \sim \vec{z}$, so, assuming the Transitivity Axiom, $\vec{x} \succ \vec{u}$. However, $\vec{x}$ and $\vec{u}$ are on the same indifference curve, which implies $\vec{x} \sim \vec{u}$. This results in a contradiction, and thus indifference curves cannot intersect.

between the two bundles. For example, the household gives up some convenience of living in town to obtain additional peace and quiet, by living in the suburbs. A measure for this substitution is called the **marginal rate of substitution (MRS)**, defined as the negative of the slope of an indifference curve. It is equal in magnitude to the indifference curve's slope. For the two commodities x_1 and x_2 (illustrated in Figure 2.6), the slope of an indifference curve is

$$\text{Indifference Curve Slope} = \frac{dx_2}{dx_1}\bigg|_{U=\text{constant}},$$

where $U = \text{constant}$ ($dU = 0$) indicates that utility is being held constant as the slope changes. This represents a movement along an indifference curve. The marginal rate of substitution (x_2 for x_1) is then defined as

$$\text{MRS}(x_2 \text{ for } x_1) = -\frac{dx_2}{dx_1}\bigg|_{U=\text{constant}}.$$

For a negatively sloping indifference curve, $(dx_2/dx_1)_{U=\text{constant}} < 0$, so $\text{MRS}(x_2 \text{ for } x_1) > 0$. MRS measures the rate at which a household is just on the margin of being willing to substitute commodity x_2 for x_1. Stated differently, MRS measures how much a household, on the margin, is willing to pay in terms of x_1 in order to consume some more of x_2.

How much are you willing to substitute partying for studying? The value of your MRS, at a given combination of partying and studying, measures how much you are are willing to substitute partying for studying and will give you the answer.

Marginal rate of substitution x_2 for x_1 [MRS(x_2 for x_1)]. The rate at which a household is willing to substitute commodity x_2 for x_1. *E.g., if substituting 2 chips for 1 fry maintains the same level of satisfaction, then the MRS of chips for fries is 2.*

Alternatively, how much a household is willing to pay in terms of x_2 in order to consume more of x_1 is measured by the MRS(x_1 for x_2)

$$\text{MRS}(x_1 \text{ for } x_2) = -\frac{dx_1}{dx_2}\Big|_{U=\text{constant}}.$$

Example 2.3 Calculating the marginal rate of substitution, MRS

The MRS for the utility function

$$U = x_1^{1/2} x_2^{1/2}$$

is obtained as follows

$$\text{MU}_1 = \tfrac{1}{2} x_1^{-1} U = \tfrac{1}{2} x_1^{-1/2} x_2^{1/2},$$

$$\text{MU}_2 = \tfrac{1}{2} x_2^{-1} U = \tfrac{1}{2} x_1^{1/2} x_2^{-1/2},$$

$$\text{MRS}(x_2 \text{ for } x_1) = \frac{MU_1}{MU_2} = \frac{x_2}{x_1},$$

$$\text{MRS}(x_1 \text{ for } x_2) = \frac{MU_2}{MU_1} = \frac{x_1}{x_2}.$$

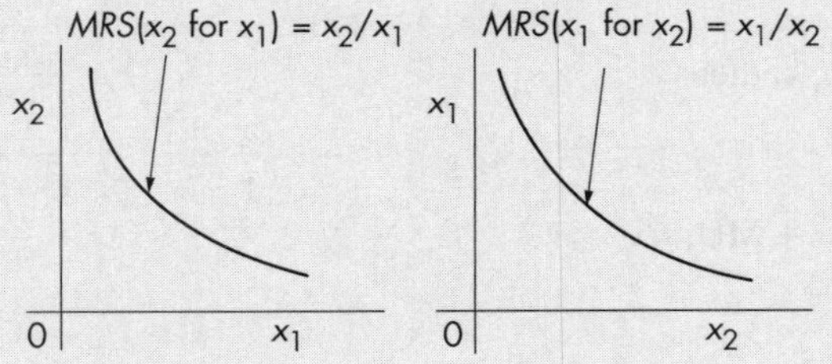

As illustrated in Figure 2.8, this results in flipping the axes: commodity x_1 is measured on the vertical axis and x_2 on the horizontal axis.

MRS, as a measure of a household's marginal willingness to pay, is directly related to a household's marginal utilities for each commodity

$$\text{MRS}(x_2 \text{ for } x_1) = \frac{\text{MU}_1}{\text{MU}_2}.$$

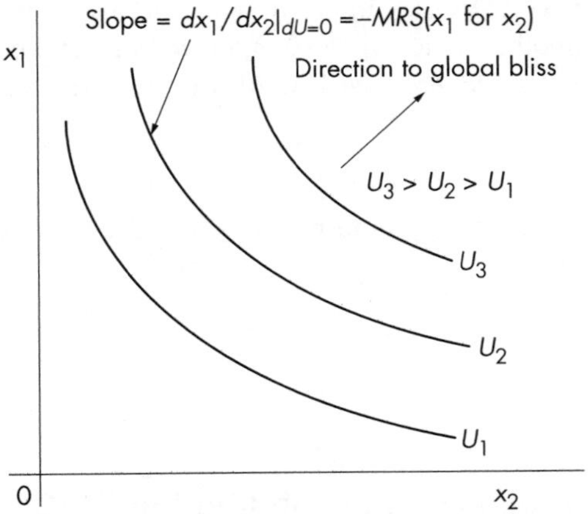

Figure 2.8 **Indifference space, MRS(x_1 for x_2).** Flipping the axes, so x_1 is on the vertical axis and x_2 is on the horizontal axis results in the slope and MRS inverting.

This relationship will be very useful in interpreting the utility maximization conditions discussed in Chapter 3. The relationship is derived by first considering the extra utility obtainable from consuming slightly more $x_1, x_2, \ldots, x_k$ as the sum of the additional utility provided by each of these increments. Specifically, taking the total differential of $U = U(x_1, x_2, \ldots, x_k)$,

$$dU = \frac{\partial U}{\partial x_1}dx_1 + \frac{\partial U}{\partial x_2}dx_2 + \ldots + \frac{\partial U}{\partial x_k}dx_k.$$

Noting $\text{MU}_j = \partial U/\partial x_j$, $j = 1, 2, \ldots, k$, then

$$dU = \text{MU}_1\, dx_1 + \text{MU}_2\, dx_2 + \ldots + \text{MU}_k\, dx_k.$$

In words, the change in utility, dU, is equal to the influence a change in x_1 has on utility, MU_1, times how much x_1 changes, dx_1, plus the influence a change in x_2 has, MU_2, times how much x_2 changes, dx_2, plus this influence for the remaining commodities, $x_3, \ldots, x_k$. The concept of MRS changes only the level of two commodities (say x_1 and x_2) keeping the household indifferent ($dU = 0$). This implies that all dx's are equal to zero except dx_1 and dx_2:

$$dU = 0 = \frac{\partial U}{\partial x_1}dx_1 + \frac{\partial U}{\partial x_2}dx_2 = \text{MU}_1\, dx_1 + \text{MU}_2\, dx_2.$$

All other goods are held constant ($dx_3 = \ldots = dx_k = 0$). This is the same assumption employed in the development of indifference curves. Rearranging terms yields

$$\mathrm{MU}_1\, dx_1 = -\mathrm{MU}_2\, dx_2, \text{ s.t. } dU = 0 \ (\textit{Note}: \text{ s.t.} = \text{ subject to}),$$

$$\left.\frac{dx_2}{dx_1}\right|_{dU=0} = -\frac{\mathrm{MU}_1}{\mathrm{MU}_2} = -\frac{\partial U/\partial x_1}{\partial U/\partial x_2},$$

$$\mathrm{MRS}(x_2 \text{ for } x_1) = -\left.\frac{dx_2}{dx_1}\right|_{dU=0} = \frac{\mathrm{MU}_1}{\mathrm{MU}_2} = \frac{\partial U/\partial x_1}{\partial U/\partial x_2}.$$

This equation is an application of the *Implicit Function Theorem*, and illustrates the relationship of MRS to the ratio of marginal utilities.

Strictly convex indifference curves: preferring averages to extremes

> *Moderation in all things.*
>
> (Terence)

> *Variety is the soul of pleasure.*
>
> (Aphra Behn)

If given a choice, most consumers would prefer a combination of beer and hot wings to all beer and no hot wings or all hot wings and no beer. Not always, but in general, households would prefer consuming a variety of items rather than the extreme of concentrating all their consumption on one commodity. Strictly convex indifference curves (drawn in Figures 2.6 and 2.8) indicate this type of tradeoff a household is willing to make and is based on the following axiom.

Axiom 4. Diminishing marginal rate of substitution (strict convexity)

Diminishing MRS exists when the value of MRS(x_2 for x_1) approaches zero as x_1 increases.

For example, in Figure 2.9, as x_1 increases, the slope of the indifference curve tends to zero, becoming less negative. Because MRS is the negative of the slope, MRS is decreasing toward zero as x_1 increases. For very low values of x_1, a household is willing to give up a larger amount of x_2 to get one more unit of x_1. At $\vec{x} = (x_1', x_2')$,the household is willing to give up a units of x_2 for one more unit of x_1. In contrast, at $\vec{y} = (x_1'', x_2'')$, the household is only willing to give up b units of x_2 for one more unit of x_1. Note that $a > b$. This assumes indifference curves form a convex set of commodity bundles that yield at least the same level of utility represented by an indifference curve. As x_1 increases, the household is willing to give up less of x_2 to obtain one more unit of x_1. Similarly, as x_2 increases, the household is willing to give up less of x_1 to obtain one more unit of x_2. In terms of beer and hot wings, as the amount of beer increases, the household is willing to give up fewer hot wings to obtain one more beer.

A set of points is a ***convex set*** if any two points within the set can be joined by a straight line contained completely within the set. Using this definition of convexity, we can determine an implication of the Diminishing MRS Axiom. As illustrated in Figure 2.9, suppose a

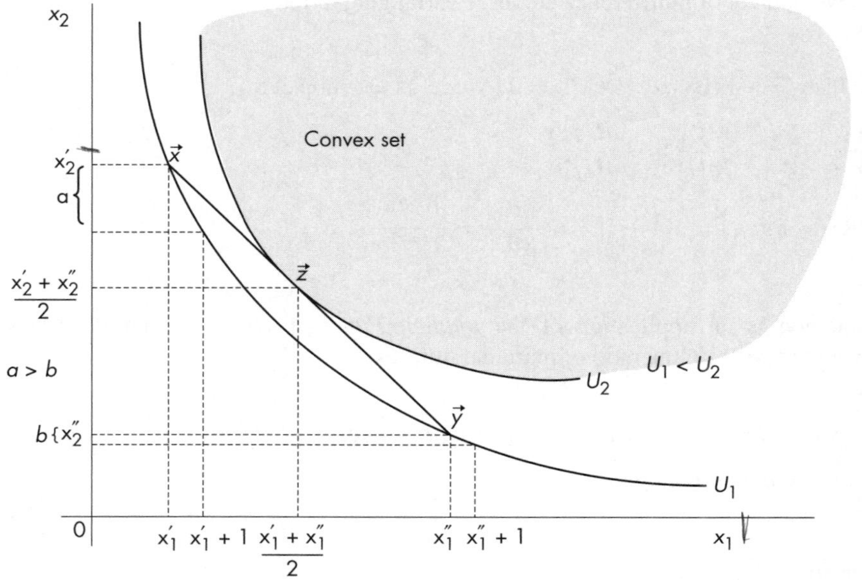

Figure 2.9 **Indifference curves with diminishing marginal rate of substitution.** The household prefers the average bundle $\vec{z}$ to the two extreme bundles $\vec{x}$ and $\vec{y}$.

household is indifferent between bundles $\vec{y} = (x_1'', x_2'')$ and $\vec{x} = (x_1', x_2')$. The Diminishing MRS Axiom states that the combination bundle

$$\vec{z} = \left(\tfrac{1}{2}(x_1' + x_1''),\ \tfrac{1}{2}(x_2' + x_2'')\right)$$

will be preferred. In Figure 2.9, $\vec{z} \succ \vec{x} \sim \vec{y}$. Thus, strict convexity is equivalent to the assumption of diminishing MRS, provided linear combinations of the commodities are possible. Intuitively, the implication of diminishing MRS is that well-balanced, diversified bundles of commodities are preferred to bundles that are heavily weighted toward one commodity. In other words, the household prefers averages to extremes. Given Axiom 4, a household would prefer a combination of beer and hot wings instead of all beer or all hot wings.

Are averages preferred to extremes? If well-balanced commodity bundles are preferred to unbalanced bundles, then averages are preferred to extremes.

Example 2.4 Demonstrating diminishing marginal rate of substitution, MRS

For negatively sloping indifference curves, diminishing MRS(x_2 for x_1) requires

$$\frac{d\text{MRS}}{dx_1} < 0.$$

This implies

$$-\frac{d\text{MRS}}{dx_1} = \frac{d^2x_2}{dx_1^2}\Big|_{dU=0} > 0.$$

Setting the utility function in Example 2.1, $U = x_1x_2$, equal to some constant U^o, so $dU = 0$

$$U^o = x_1x_2.$$

Solving for x_2,

$$x_2 = \frac{U^o}{x_1}.$$

Evaluating the derivatives,

$$-\text{MRS} = \frac{dx_2}{dx_1}\Big|_{dU=0} = -\frac{U^o}{x_1^2} < 0,$$

$$-\frac{d\text{MRS}}{dx_1} = \frac{d^2x_2}{dx_1^2}\Big|_{dU=0} = \frac{2U^o}{x_1^3} > 0.$$

This implies $d\text{MRS}/dx_1 < 0$.

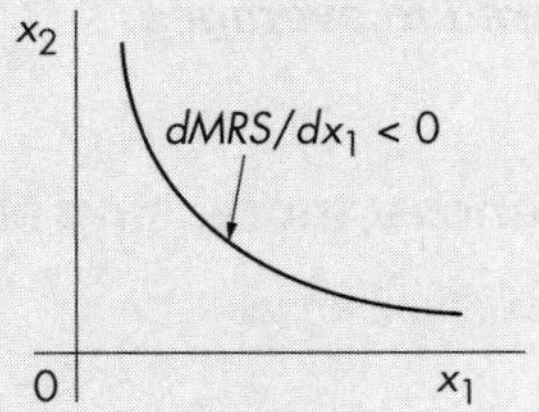

Strictly concave indifference curves: preferring extremes to averages

Music with dinner is an insult both to the cook and the violinist.

(G.K. Chesterton)

If a household's preferences were represented by strictly concave preferences, as illustrated in Figure 2.10, the household would prefer extremes to averages. In Figure 2.10, the household prefers the extreme commodity bundles (x_1'', x_2') and (x_1', x_2'') to the average $\left(\frac{1}{2}(x_1' + x_1''),\ \frac{1}{2}(x_2' + x_2'')\right)$. Generally, households do attempt to diversify, which rules out these concave preferences; however, there are rational choices that imply concave preferences. Examples are a household preferring either alcohol or driving over consuming both together and preferring grades of all As instead of some combination of As and Bs.

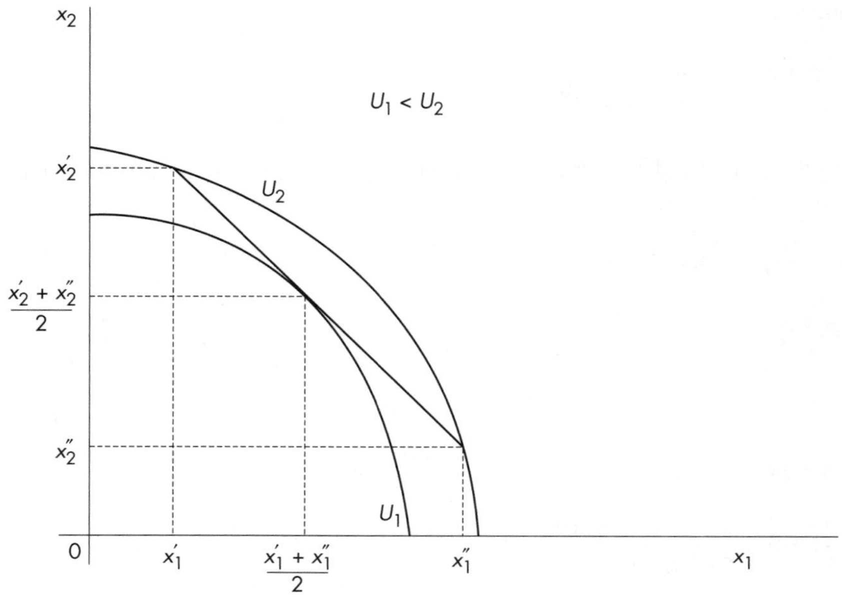

Figure 2.10 **Indifference curves with concave preferences.** The household prefers extremes to averages.

Are extremes preferred to averages? In instances where commodities do not mix well, like oil and water, extremes will be preferred to averages.

Example 2.5 Demonstrating concave preferences, increasing MRS

Consider the following utility function representing concave preferences

$$U = x_1^2 + x_2^2.$$

Holding utility constant at $U = U^{\text{o}}$ and solving for x_2 yields

$$U^{\text{o}} = x_1^2 + x_2^2,$$

$$x_2^2 = U^{\text{o}} - x_1^2,$$

$$x_2 = (U^{\text{o}} - x_1^2)^{1/2}.$$

Evaluating the derivatives using the product rule for the second derivative results in

$$-\text{MRS} = \left.\frac{dx_2}{dx_1}\right|_{dU=0} = -x_1(U^{\text{o}} - x_1^2)^{-1/2} < 0, \text{ given } x_2^2 > 0,$$

$$\text{then } (U^{\text{o}} - x_1^2)^{-1/2} > 0,$$

$$-\frac{d\text{MRS}}{dx_1} = \frac{d^2x_2}{dx_1^2}\Big|_{dU=0} = -(U^o - x_1^2)^{-1/2} - x_1(-1/2)(U^o - x_1^2)^{-3/2}(-2x_1)$$
$$= -(U^o - x_1^2)^{-3/2}[(U^o - x_1^2) + x_1^2]$$
$$= -U^o(U^o - x_1^2)^{-3/2} < 0.$$

This implies $d\text{MRS}/dx_1 > 0$, and increasing MRS.

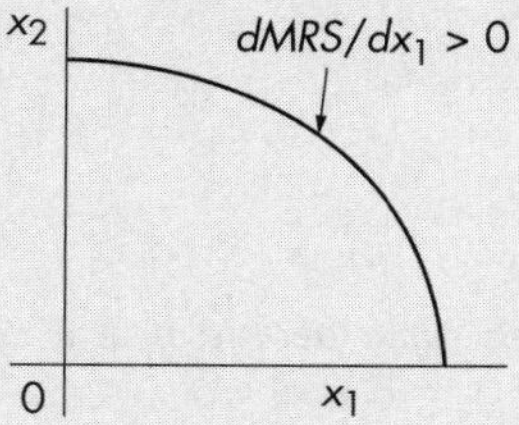

How indifference curves represent household preferences

Imperfect substitutes: apples and oranges

We have seen that indifference curves represent individual households' preferences for commodities. Suppose a household may prefer consuming relatively more of commodity x_2 over commodity x_1. For the household to be willing to give up a small amount of x_2, it would have to be given a relatively large quantity of x_1. As illustrated in Figure 2.11,

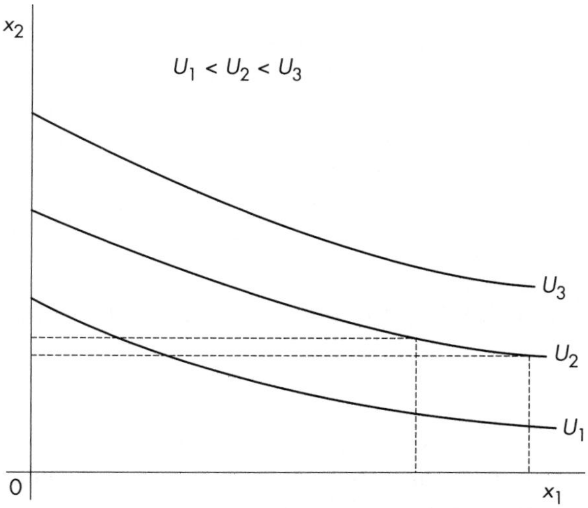

Figure 2.11 **Indifference curves where commodity x_2 is relatively more preferred to x_1.** For a household to be willing to give up x_2, it must be compensated with relatively more of x_1.

this results in relatively flat indifference curves, and is an example of imperfect substitutes. **Imperfect substitutes** are characterized by the four preference axioms and most household preferences for most commodities fall into this category. We discuss more extreme preference relations that violate one or more of the axioms next.

Imperfect substitutes. As the amount of consumption for a commodity decreases, a household would be willing to substitute more of other commodities for an additional unit of the commodity. *E.g., given an initial small quantity of beer, you are willing to give up a lot of hot wings for a little bit more beer.*

Perfect substitutes: brown and white eggs

> *Facebook is so big, so powerful and pointless that for some people it is a complete substitute for life.*
>
> (Michael Wetzstein)

A utility function of the form

$$U = ax_1 + bx_2$$

where a and b are positive parameters (constants) represents preferences associated with **perfect substitutes**. For perfect substitutes, MRS(x_2 for x_1) is

$$\text{MRS}(x_2 \text{ for } x_1) = -\left.\frac{dx_2}{dx_1}\right|_{dU=0} = \frac{\text{MU}_1}{\text{MU}_2} = \frac{\partial U/\partial x_1}{\partial U/\partial x_2} = \frac{a}{b}.$$

The slope of the indifference curve does not change as one commodity is substituted for another. In general, perfect substitutes are associated with MRS = constant, which violates the Diminishing MRS Axiom. The MRS does not change as the relative quantities of the commodities consumed change. As illustrated in Figure 2.12, the indifference curves are parallel straight lines with a constant slope. An example of perfect substitutes may be two different brands of colas. In this cases, $a = b$ in the utility function; the household is indifferent in terms of how much it has of one or the other, but does care about the total amount of cola.

When are earrings perfect substitutes? If you only wear one, then earrings are perfect substitutes.

Perfect substitutes. A household's willingness to exchange one commodity for another is constant and does not depend on the relative quantities of the commodities consumed. *E.g., pink and yellow grapefruit, or slick tires and skid tires, which offer the same exhilarating ride.*

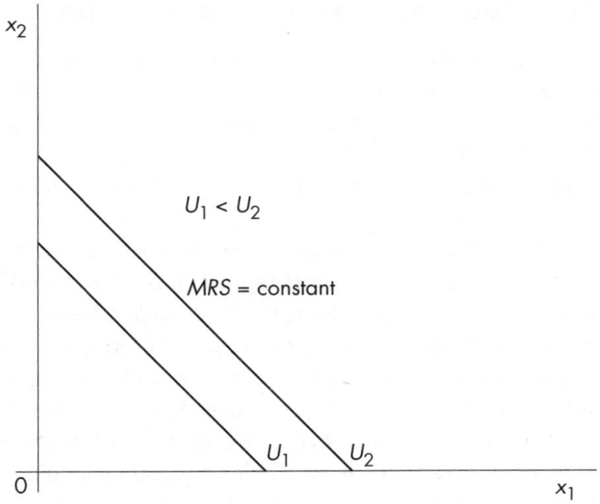

Figure 2.12 **Perfect substitutes.** A household's willingness to substitute one commodity for another is constant all along an indifference curve.

Example 2.6 How to derive indifference curves from perfect-substitute preferences

Consider the following utility function representing perfect substitutes as preferences

$$U = 5x_1 + 2x_2.$$

$$\text{MRS}(x_2 \text{ for } x_1) = \text{MU}_1/\text{MU}_2 = 5/2.$$

At every commodity bundle along an indifference curve, the household is willing to substitute 5/2 units of x_2 for one unit of x_1. This willingness to substitute is constant throughout the entire length of an indifference curve, so for $U = 10$, $x_2 = -(5/2)x_1 + 5$. Note that $d\text{MRS}/dx_1 = 0$, indicating constant, instead of diminishing, MRS.

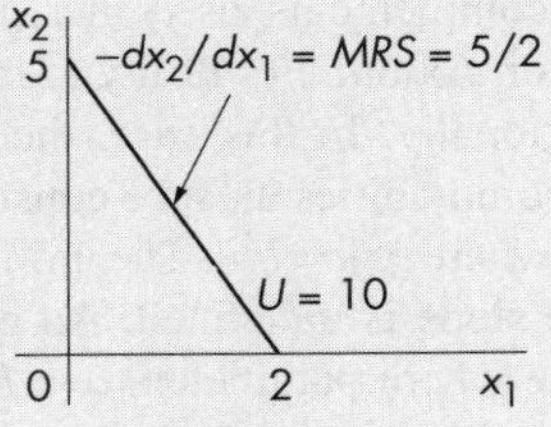

Application: Only a bad reproduction is a good reproduction

Art historians have made a cult out of owning an original work of art despite the fact that perfect reproductions offer the same aesthetic experience. As addressed by Pommerehne and Martin, a perfect reproduction is a copy that is totally true to the original, but is not produced by the artist. Highly skilled craftspeople as well as computer-based methods can create perfect reproductions that are indiscernible from the original simply by observation.

Pommerehne and Martin investigated what individuals (households) seek when acquiring works of art. Their hypothesis is that a perfect reproduction may function as a substitute for an original work of art with respect to aesthetic considerations. As a test of this hypothesis, they measured individuals' willingness to pay for reproductions, specified in relative terms as a percentage share of the willingness to pay for the original. Their underlying theory is that the greater the number of reproductions in existence, the lower is the individual willingness to pay. From this, they developed conclusions on the substitutability between an original and reproductions. Their empirical estimation of willingness to pay did not reject their hypothesis. In terms of aesthetics, a reproduction is a perfect substitute for an original.

Source: W.W. Pommerehne and G.J. Martin, "Perfect Reproductions of Works of Art: Substitutes or Heresy?" *Journal of Cultural Economics* 19 (1995): 237–249.

Perfect complements: shoes and shoe laces

Proverb: A man with one chopstick will go hungry.

Perfect complements can be represented by the nondifferentiable utility function:

$$U = \min(ax_1, bx_2).$$

This function states whichever value (ax_1 or bx_2) is smaller is the level of utility. Figure 2.13 illustrates perfect complements. If $1/a$ units of x_1 and $1/b$ units of x_2 are employed, then $U = 1$. If we add more units of x_1, say $2/a$ units, holding x_2 constant at $1/b$, then the utility remains constant at $U = 1$. Similarly, adding more units of x_2 holding x_1 constant does not increase utility. In the case of perfect complements, as x_2 increases, the marginal utility of x_2 is zero, which violates the Nonsatiation Axiom. For utility to increase, consumption of both commodities must increase proportionally. In this case, there is no possibility of substituting one commodity for another; the commodities must be consumed in the same fixed proportion. The MRS is therefore undefined where $ax_1 = bx_2$. The indifference curves have a kink where $ax_1 = bx_2$, and at this kink the slope is undefined. An example of perfect complement preferences is a right and left shoe where parameters $a = b$. More interesting examples are "tomatoes and oregano make it Italian and wine and tarragon make it French" (Alice May Brock).

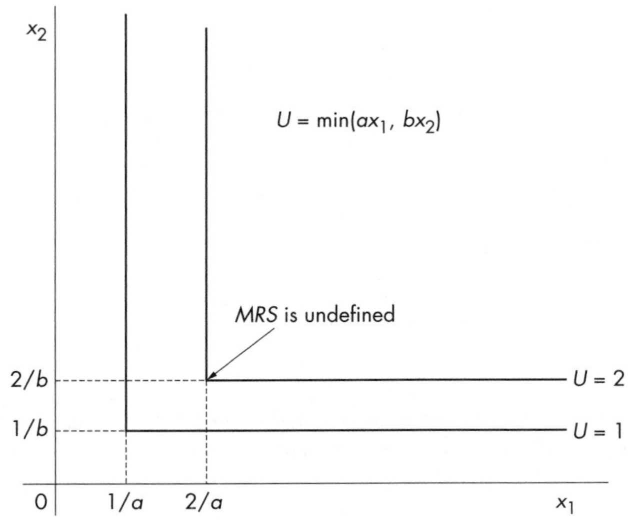

Figure 2.13 **Perfect complements.** A household is unwilling to substitute one commodity for another. The commodities are consumed in a fixed proportion.

When are earrings perfect complements? If you wear a pair of earrings, one in each ear, then earrings are perfect complements.

Example 2.7 How to derive indifference curves from perfect-complement preferences

Consider the following utility function representing perfect complements as preferences:

$$U = \min(x_1/2, x_2/3).$$

This utility function is not differentiable. Although it is continuous, the slope where $x_1/2 = x_2/3$ is undefined, so it is not smooth. Thus, we cannot use calculus to characterize the shape of the indifference curves. Instead, we construct a table listing the utilities associated with alternative commodity bundles.

x_1	x_2	U
2	3	1
2	4	1
2	5	1
3	3	1
4	3	1

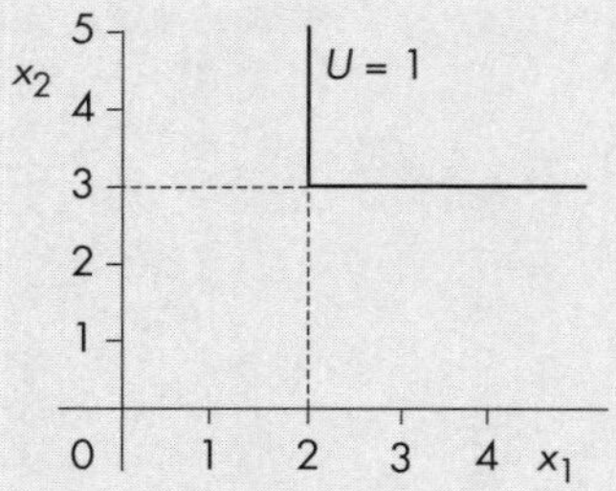

Perfect complements. Commodities consumed in a fixed proportion. *E.g., some individuals may consume peanut butter and jelly or fruitcake and Christmas cake in fixed proportion.*

Application: Big business versus big government—are they perfect complements?

> *I draw the conclusion that, assuming no important wars and no important increase in population, the economic problem may be solved or be at least within sight of solution, within a hundred years. This means that the economic problem is not—if we look into the future—the permanent problem of the human race.*
>
> (John Maynard Keynes, 1930)

As outlined by Lin, neoclassical economics generally treats the economy and politics as distinct subjects and isolates economic analysis from the political process. Markets are self-sustaining and not subject to state forces. The recent Great Recession has questioned this self-sustaining ability. In contrast, heterodox economists see interactions between the political process and markets. This interaction has led public choice advocates such as J.M. Buchanan (1986 Nobel laureate) and G. Tullock to advocate less government involvement and institutionalists such as J.K. Galbraith and W.J. Samuels to criticize big business and favor big governments (major government market intervention).

Lin's hypothesis is that big business and big government have become perfect complements—they are symbiotic. Decreasing big government without also checking big business will not improve social welfare, and vice versa. Instead, Lin argues for a systematic reduction in both if we are to move toward sustainable social welfare improvements. He suggests that it is socially desirable to move toward more decentralized government and business control, with local government and business promoting the local community. Such a joint lowering of the complements (big business and big government), Lin hypothesizes, is consistent with the current trend toward sustainable development (think globally, act locally).

Source: B.C. Lin, "More Government or Less Government? Further Thoughts for Promoting the Government," *Journal of Economic Issues* 42 (2008): 803–821.

Bad commodities: cigarettes

If the headache would only precede the intoxication, alcoholism would be a virtue.
(Samuel Butler)

Recall that a bad commodity is a commodity a household does not like, say cigarettes. Preferences for such a commodity are illustrated in Figure 2.14 with another commodity, say food. For the household to be willing to consume additional cigarettes and maintain the same level of utility, it must be given more food along with this increase in cigarettes. Bad commodities violate the Nonsatiation Axiom: more is not preferred to less, given that more of the bad commodity reduces utility. The concave indifference curves, drawn in Figure 2.14, assume averages are preferred to extremes, Axiom 4.

A utility function representing preferences for x_2 as a bad commodity is

$$U(x_1, x_2) = x_1 x_2^{-2}.$$

$\text{MRS}(x_2 \text{ for } x_1) = -x_2/(2x_1) < 0$, indicating positively sloped indifference curves. We can determine the concavity of these indifference curves by setting utility equal to a constant,

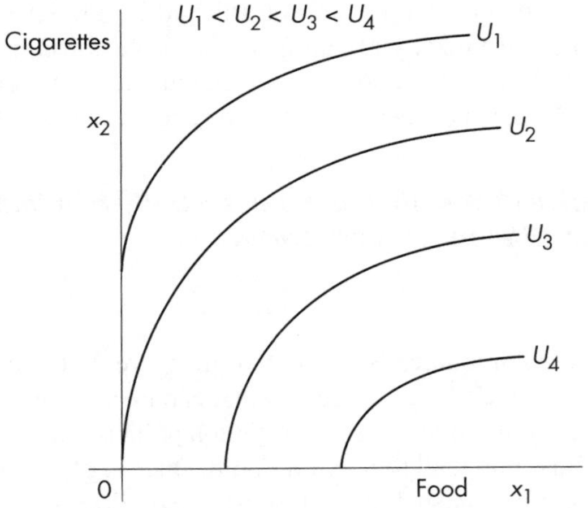

Figure 2.14 **Bad commodities.** For a household to be willing to consume more of the bad commodity (cigarettes), it must be compensated with more of the good commodity (food).

$U = U^{\circ}$, and solving for x_2:

$$U^{\circ} = x_1 x_2^{-2},$$
$$x_2 = (x_1/U^{\circ})^{1/2}.$$

Evaluating the derivatives

$$-\text{MRS}(x_2 \text{ for } x_1) = \frac{dx_2}{dx_1}\bigg|_{dU=0} = \frac{1}{2}(U^{\circ})^{-1/2} x_1^{-1/2} > 0,$$
$$-\frac{d\text{MRS}}{dx_1} = \frac{d^2 x_2}{dx_1^2}\bigg|_{dU=0} = -\frac{1}{4}(U^{\circ})^{-1/2} x_1^{-3/2} < 0.$$

Thus, as x_1 increases, the MRS increases toward zero (becomes less negative); representing diminishing MRS.

Neutral preferences: inert ingredients

A commodity is a *neutral commodity* if a household does not derive any utility from it. The commodity does not enter a household's utility function, so it does not affect the level of utility. A household only cares about the consumption of other commodities. An example is the inert ingredients in many pharmaceutical products. A household would generally only be interested in the active ingredients, so the utility function is

$$U = U \text{ (active ingredients)};$$

the inert ingredient does not enter into the utility function.

As illustrated in Figure 2.15, the indifference curves are not affected by the levels of the neutral commodity (inert ingredient) consumed. Only an increase in the consumption of the active ingredient increases utility. Any increase in the inert ingredient has no effect on satisfaction, so Axiom 3 is violated. Also, averages are not preferred to extremes, which violates Axiom 4.

Do zombies have neutral preferences? Yes, they are a dead body reanimated with no change in preferences for different grocery carts.

Satiated preferences: heaven

The satiation point (bliss point) for two commodities is illustrated in Figure 2.16. At this bliss point, all of the household's wants for the two commodities that can be consumed are satisfied. As illustrated, if more than two commodities exist, the satiation point is only a local satiation point (local bliss). Prior to the bliss point, all four axioms hold. Once in global bliss, who cares which axioms hold? There are no longer limited resources, so allocation is no longer a problem.

Are there economists in Shangri-La? Some may have made it there, but they are unemployed.

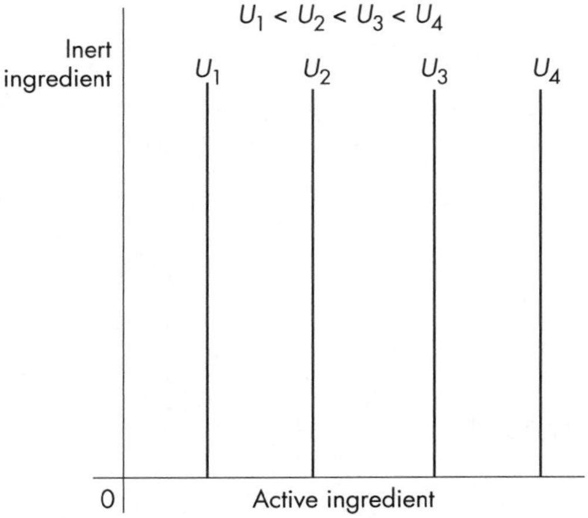

Figure 2.15 **Neutral commodity.** A household's level of satisfaction is unaffected by the neutral commodity (inert ingredient).

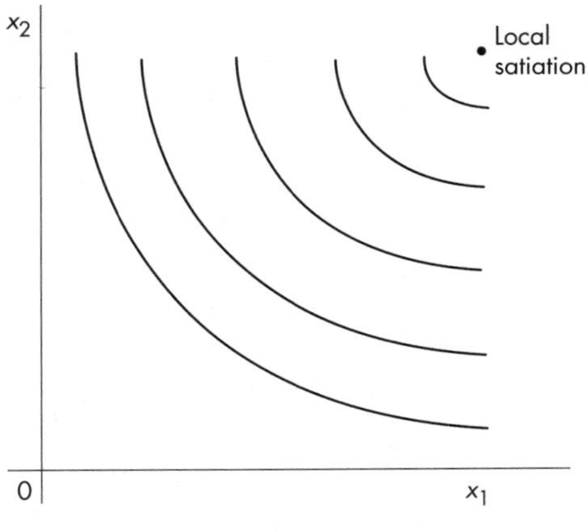

Figure 2.16 **Local satiation or local bliss point.** At the local satiation point, a household is completely satisfied by its consumption of x_1 and x_2.

Example 2.8 Illustrating satiated preferences

Consider the following utility function

$$U = 4x_1 - x_1^2 + 6x_2 - x_2^2.$$

Utility is maximized with the following first-order conditions (FOCs):

$$\frac{\partial U}{\partial x_1} = 4 - 2x_1^* = 0 \Rightarrow x_1^* = 2,$$

$$\frac{\partial U}{\partial x_2} = 6 - 2x_2^* = 0 \Rightarrow x_2^* = 3.$$

Thus, this household is satiated (maximizes utility) at $x_1^* = 2$ and $x_2^* = 3$.

For $x_1 < 2$ and $x_2 < 3$,

$$MU_1 = \frac{\partial U}{\partial x_1} = 4 - 2x_1 > 0,$$

$$MU_2 = \frac{\partial U}{\partial x_2} = 6 - 2x_2 > 0,$$

indicating Axiom 3 (Nonsatiation) is satisfied. Also,

$$MRS(x_2 \text{ for } x_1) = \frac{4 - 2x_1}{6 - 2x_2} = \frac{2(2 - x_1)}{2(3 - x_2)} = \frac{2 - x_1}{3 - x_2} > 0,$$

for $x_1 < 2$ and $x_2 < 3$, indicating negatively sloping indifference curves. Finally, these indifference curves are strictly convex, indicated by diminishing MRS.

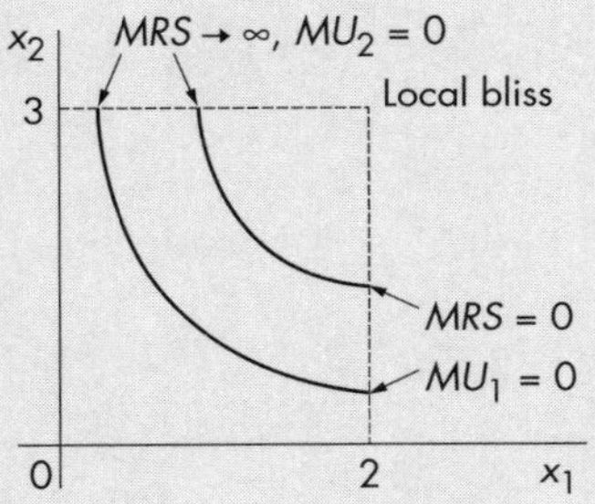

Summary

1. The problem facing a household is deciding how much of each available commodity it should consume to maximize satisfaction.
2. A household must compare tastes and preferences for alternative commodity bundles to determine which bundle yields the highest satisfaction it can afford. Such a comparison is determined by the preference relation, "is preferred to or indifferent to."
3. The preference relation provides a method for ordering the set of consumption bundles from the most to the least preferred. The two axioms, Completeness and Transitivity, allow this ordering of bundles.
4. The preference ordering of bundles may be represented by a utility function, which assigns a numerical value to each commodity bundle. Because utility functions are ordinal, it is not possible to determine the magnitude of a change in satisfaction between two commodity bundles.

5. Assuming nonsatiation (more of a commodity is preferred to less), all marginal utilities are positive. Marginal utility is the additional utility derived from consuming an additional unit of a commodity while holding the consumption of all other commodities constant.
6. Indifference curves are based on three axioms: Completeness, Transitivity, and Nonsatiation. An indifference curve is a locus of points (commodity bundles) yielding the same level of utility.
7. The negative of the slope of an indifference curve is the marginal rate of substitution (MRS). MRS measures the rate at which one commodity can be substituted for another, that is, how much a household is willing to pay to substitute one commodity for another.
8. Strictly convex indifference curves imply the Diminishing Marginal Rate of Substitution Axiom. This axiom states that the willingness to give up some of a commodity decreases as the amount of the commodity declines. Households will then choose a diversified commodity bundle over a bundle concentrated in one particular commodity. In other words, households prefer averages to extremes.
9. Preferences where two commodities are perfect substitutes result in a constant MRS. The willingness to give up one commodity for another does not depend on the amount of the commodities consumed. In contrast, for preferences where commodities must be consumed in the same fixed proportion (perfect complements), a household is unwilling to substitute one commodity for another.
10. A bad commodity is one that decreases satisfaction when it is consumed. For a household to be willing to consume additional amounts of this bad commodity, it would have to be compensated with additional units of some desirable commodity.
11. A commodity is neutral if a household does not derive any utility from it. The commodity does not have any effect on the household's level of satisfaction, so it does not enter into a household's utility function.
12. A household is satiated when further increases in the commodities it is consuming do not result in any enhancement of satisfaction.
13. *(Appendix)* A household's preferences for substituting one commodity, represented by a utility function measured on an ordinal scale, will not change if the utility function is transformed by any positive monotonic transformation.

Key concepts

bad commodity, 37
cardinal utility, 63
commodity, 30
commodity bundle, 31
commodity space, 32
composite commodity, 31
convex set, 45
demand, 28
free markets, 24
good commodity, 37
household, 30
imperfect substitutes, 50
income, 30
indifference, 32
indifference curve, 39
indifference sets, 38
indifference space, 40
Law of Demand, 28
marginal rate of substitution (MRS), 42
marginal utilities (MU), 37
numeraire commodity, 31
ordinal utility, 63
perfect complements, 52
perfect substitutes, 50
rationality, 34
utility, 35
utility function, 35

Key equations

$$\vec{x} \succsim \vec{y}$$

This preference relation indicates commodity bundle $\vec{x}$ is preferred to or indifferent to bundle $\vec{y}$.

$$U = U(\vec{x}) = U(x_1, x_2, \ldots, x_k)$$

The utility function represents the level of satisfaction an agent receives from consuming a commodity bundle $\vec{x}$.

Questions

Knowing is not enough; we must apply. Willing is not enough; we must do.

(Samuel Beckett)

1. Discuss the relationship between the Nonsatiation Axiom and the idea of scarcity that underlies microeconomics.
2. Is the marginal utility of income uniquely defined?
3. Why does the statement "more is preferred to less" imply downward-sloping indifference curves?
4. Explain what information the slope of an indifference curve conveys about household preferences.
5. You probably would not want to eat pickles and ice cream out of the same bowl. Thus, are your indifference curves for these two goods concave rather than convex? Explain.
6. What is the marginal rate of substitution for a neutral commodity substituted for a desirable commodity, MRS (neutral commodity for desirable commodity)? What is MRS (desirable commodity for a neutral commodity)?
7. Boys will generally only wear an earring in one ear, whereas girls will wear earrings in both ears. Which have perfect complement preferences for a pair of earrings? Which have perfect substitute preferences?
8. Does a rational household prefer more of a commodity to less and prefer averages to extremes?
9. The preference relation, "is preferred to or indifferent to," is called the *weak preference relation*. The *strong preference relation* just states "is preferred to." Can the weak preference relation be used to derive the strong preference relation? Explain.

Exercises

Every exercise has a gift for you in its hands.

(Richard Bach)

1. Determine whether the following utility functions have strictly convex indifference curves consistent with the Diminishing MRS Axiom
   a. $U = x_1^{3/5} x_2^{4/5}$.
   b. $U = x_1^{1/2} + x_2^{1/2}$.
   c. $U = x_1^{3/2} + x_2^{3/2}$.
   d. $U = (x_1 + x_2)^3$.
   e. $U = \min(x_1/5,\ x_2/2)$.
2. Demonstrate which preference axioms are satisfied and which are not satisfied by the following statements:
   a. General William T. Sherman stated, "War is Hell."
   b. "Things go better with Coke."
   c. A.E. Housman stated, "For nature, heartless witless nature will neither care nor know."
   d. I like to eat dinner at 7:00 p.m. However, I am willing to eat earlier or later if I am sufficiently compensated.
   e. Margarine is just as good as butter.
3. Determine the shape of the indifference curves from the following utility functions.
   a. $U = Ax_1^{1/2} x_2^{1/3}$.
   b. $U = 6x_1^{1/3} x_2^{2/3} + 10$.
   c. $U = 10x_1^{2/3} x_2^{3/4} + 23.7$.
   d. $U = 59x_1^{5/8} x_2^{1/8}$.
   e. $U = x_1^{3/4} x_2^{1/4}$.
   f. $U = (x_1^{1/3} x_2^{2/3})^{10}$.
   g. $U = 3x_1 + 4x_2$.
4. Valentia loves to throw parties. At her parties, she prefers to have exactly as many males (M) as females (F), represented by the utility function

   $$U(F, M) = \min(2F - M, 2M - F).$$

   Determine the shape of Valentia's indifference curves.
5. In 1891, Irving Fisher argued that a poor community would likely not distinguish quality grades of a commodity like beef, whereas a rich community would. Construct indifference curves for low- and high-quality beef at low and high levels of income. Why should different beef qualities be better substitutes at low incomes than at high incomes?

6. Mr Smell derives utility from hamburgers and from living away from a landfill. His utility function is

$$U = H + 4D,$$

where H denotes the per-unit consumption of hamburgers and D is distance from the landfill. Assume he initially has 40 hamburgers ($H = 40$) and lives right next to the landfill ($D = 0$).

   a. Graph his indifference curve associated with his initial allocation.
   b. What is the greatest number of hamburgers he is willing to pay to move 1 unit of distance away from the landfill?
   c. Assume a farmer owns the land away from the landfill and can either sell land to Mr Smell or use it to produce one hamburger. Will the farmer sell her land to Mr Smell? Where will Mr Smell choose to live?

7. Assume a household gains utility from clean air and hamburgers. If it locates in Denver, it will receive 50 hamburgers (H) and 20 units of air quality (A). If it locates in Los Angeles, it will receive 100 hamburgers and 0 units of air quality. The household's utility function is

$$U = 10H + 5A.$$

Give conditions for when the household will choose to live in Los Angeles, when it chooses to live in Denver, and when it would be indifferent between living in either city.

8. Consider the following utility functions:

   a. $U = x_1^4 x_2^4$;
   b. $U = x_1^{1/4} x_2^{1/4}$;
   c. $U = x_1 x_2^2$;
   d. $U = 5x_1 + 3x_2$;
   e. $U = x_1 x_2/(x_1 + x_2)$;
   f. $U = \min(x_1, x_2)$;
      i. Determine whether each utility function satisfies the axioms of consumer preference.
      ii. Find the function, if it exists, for the marginal rate of substitution for each utility function.
      iii. Graph the indifference curve for $U = 1$ for each utility function.

9. Illustrate how you might formally represent a change in tastes in favor of one commodity.

10. Illustrate how you might formally represent a set of preferences in which one household is altruistic toward another household. Then, illustrate a household envious of another household.

Internet case studies

1. Provide a brief history of the development of cardinal and ordinal utility.
2. Critically discuss two methods for teaching the concept of indifference curves.
3. Find a number of examination questions on the marginal rate of substitution and answer them.
4. Critically discuss the Law of Diminishing Marginal Utility.
5. Discuss the concept of rationality. Is it overrated? Does it vary by culture?
6. Provide some applications of the Weber–Fechner Law.

APPENDIX TO CHAPTER 2

How to measure utility

Classical economists of the eighteenth and nineteenth centuries assumed it was possible to measure the level of satisfaction or utility from consuming a commodity. Just as you measure the size of a commodity, they assumed there was a hedonimeter to measure the intensity of satisfaction. In particular, it was thought consumers responded in proportion to the logarithm of the stimulus x:

$$U(x) = \ln x.$$

This utility function is illustrated in Figure 2.4. The slope of this utility function is

$$\frac{dU}{dx} = \frac{1}{x} > 0,$$

and utility increases at a decreasing rate,

$$\frac{d^2U}{dx^2} = -\frac{1}{x^2} < 0.$$

If utility were measurable (say in utils) on at least a *cardinal scale* (see the Mathematical Review), many economic questions could be directly answered. For example, the optimal distribution of commodities among people and the exact level of maximum social welfare could be determined.

The ability of households to determine the change in magnitude of satisfaction among bundles is called **cardinal utility**. However, it is generally accepted that households can only rank a set of commodity bundles based upon their preferences (called **ordinal utility**) on an *ordinal scale* (see the Mathematical Review). In general, households can measure neither their level of satisfaction from a particular commodity bundle nor the magnitude of a change in satisfaction. Thus, we can only state that $\vec{x} \succsim \vec{y}$ not by how much. In other words, which bundle is first in the relation "is preferred to or indifferent to," can be determined between two bundles, but the magnitude or distance between these two bundles is unobservable.[6]

Is there a hedonimeter? No. Utility is measured on an ordinal scale, so it is not possible to measure the magnitude of utility between commodity bundles.

Application: Is a hedonimeter feasible?

The hope that a hedonimeter to measure cardinal utility may be within reach emerged from a symposium on the issue in the *Economic Journal* (November 1997). Such a meter would reinstate cardinal utility as a foundation of positive economic modeling. And with such a meter a social welfare function could be developed for ranking society's preferences.*

If current knowledge could be applied specifically to its development, a hedonimeter might be feasible. As outlined by Zizzo, there are two sets of arguments supporting the practical feasibility of a hedonimeter: verbal responses, requiring a high correlation between verbal responses and hedonic states, and neurobiological evidence. In terms of the latter, electrical stimulation of the brain appears to produce pleasure, so it may be possible to correlate electrical stimulation with hedonic experience along some interval scale. However, Zizzo demonstrates that current evidence falls short in supporting the practical feasibility of a hedonimeter. While progress is being made, the degree of correspondence between choice and hedonic experiences is still unknown. A problem is that individual verbal responses are imperfect measures of actual hedonic experiences. Also, the electrical stimulation of the brain tends to be saliency rather than pleasure. Thus, at least for the foreseeable future, economics will not have its hedonimeter as tool for improving social welfare. However, E. Fehr and A. Rangel review recent advances in neuroeconomics indicating that experimentally induced variations in brain neural activity can change an individual's willingness to pay, have more impatience, be more selfish, violate social norms, and cheat.

Sources: D.J. Zizzo, "Neurobiological Measurements of Cardinal Utility: Hedonimeters or Learning Algorithms?" *Social Choice and Welfare* 19 (2002): 477–488; E. Fehr and A. Rangel, "Neuroeconomic Foundations of Economic Choice: Recent Advances," *Journal of Economic Perspectives* 25 (2011): 3–30.

*See Chapter 20. An ordinal ranking of individual preference cannot yield a social ranking unless some reasonable assumptions are violated.

What is a positive monotonic transformation of a utility function?

Recall that MRS is a measure of a household's preferences for two alternative bundles. As we have seen, this preference relation is based on an ordinal ranking of bundles. Thus, taking a monotonic transformation of the utility function does not change the preference ordering. As discussed in the Mathematical Review, a *positive monotonic transformation* is defined as a strictly increasing function $U = U(x_1, \dots, x_k)$, and a transformation $V(U)$, V is positive monotonic if $V'(U) > 0$. For example, given a transformation on U of $V(U) = U^2 + 5$, $V'(U) = 2U > 0$, indicating that V is a positive monotonic transformation on U.

When does $U = U^{1/2}$? When utility is measured on an ordinal scale, $U = U^{1/2}$.

Example 2A.1 Monotonic transformation of a utility function and household preferences

Consider the utility function in Example 2.3,

$$U = x_1^{1/2} x_2^{1/2},$$

and let $V(U) = U^2 = x_1 x_2$, so $V'(U) = 2U > 0$. MRS(x_2 for x_1) for $V(U)$ is then

$$\text{MRS}(x_2 \text{ for } x_1) = \frac{\partial V/\partial x_1}{\partial V/\partial x_2} = \frac{x_2}{x_1},$$

and MRS(x_2 for x_1) for U is

$$\text{MRS}(x_2 \text{ for } x_1) = \frac{\partial U/\partial x_1}{\partial U/\partial x_2} = \frac{\frac{1}{2}x_1^{-1}U}{\frac{1}{2}x_2^{-1}U} = \frac{x_2}{x_1}.$$

Both utility functions $V = x_1 x_2$ and $U = x_1^{1/2} x_2^{1/2}$ describe the same preference relation, and thus yield equivalent MRS's.

This is not true for a negative monotonic transformation of a utility function, because such a transformation does not preserve the preference ordering. For example, consider the transformation $V(U) = U^{-2} = x_1^{-1} x_2^{-1}$; then $V'(U) = -2U^{-3} < 0$, a negative monotonic transformation. MRS(x_2 for x_1) for $V(U)$ is the same:

$$\text{MRS}(x_2 \text{ for } x_1) = \frac{\partial V/\partial x_1}{\partial V/\partial x_2} = \frac{x_2}{x_1}.$$

However, the marginal utilities switch from positive to negative:

$$\text{MU}_1 = \tfrac{1}{2}x_1^{-1}U > 0 \text{ and } \text{MU}_2 = \tfrac{1}{2}x_2^{-1}U > 0,$$

$$V'(U)\text{MU}_1 = -x_1^{-1}V < 0 \text{ and } V'(U)\text{MU}_2 = -x_2^{-1}V < 0.$$

The negative monotonic transformation results in a preference reversal. Good commodities become bad commodities.

A positive monotonic transformation, $V[U(x_1, x_2)]$, does not change the MRS or the signs of marginal utilities:

$$\frac{\partial V}{\partial x_1} = V'(U)\mathrm{MU}_1, \text{ and if } \mathrm{MU}_1 > 0, \text{ then } \frac{\partial V}{\partial x_1} > 0,$$

$$\frac{\partial V}{\partial x_2} = V'(U)\mathrm{MU}_2, \text{ and if } \mathrm{MU}_2 > 0, \text{ then } \frac{\partial V}{\partial x_2} > 0,$$

$$\mathrm{MRS}\,(x_2 \text{ for } x_1) = \frac{V'(U)\mathrm{MU}_1}{V'(U)\mathrm{MU}_2} = \frac{\mathrm{MU}_1}{\mathrm{MU}_2}.$$

A household's indifference curves and preference order remain unchanged with a positive monotonic transformation of the utility function. This is true for any monotonic transformation, including multiplying a utility function by a positive constant or raising the function to the power of some positive constant. Thus, any positive monotonic transformation of a utility function can represent the same preference ordering for a household. This result occurs because the signs of the marginal utilities remain unchanged and when calculating the MRS, the units of utility measurement cancel out $[V'(U)/V'(U) = 1]$, resulting in x_2 per unit of x_1 as the measure for MRS(x_2 for x_1).

The monotonic transformation of the utility function must be positive for the Nonsatiation Axiom to hold. Given $V'(U) > 0$, then $V'(U)\mathrm{MU}_1 > 0$ and $V'(U)\mathrm{MU}_2 > 0$, which still satisfies Axiom 3. The preference ordering has not changed. However, if $V'(U) < 0$ (a negative monotonic transformation), then $V'(U)\mathrm{MU}_1 < 0$ and $V'(U)\mathrm{MU}_2 < 0$, which violates the axiom. The preference ordering of bundles has changed.

For example, a household's preference ordering does not change if it is represented by $U = x_1^{1/4}x_2^{3/4}$ or $V = x_1x_2^3$, because $V = U^4$ and $dV/dU = 4U^3 > 0$. Note that in terms of taking derivatives, representing preferences by $V = U^4$ may be relatively easier than $U = x_1^{1/4}x_2^{3/4}$. Thus, for ease of obtaining analytical solutions, it may be useful to first take a monotonic transformation.

Question

1. Does taking a monotonic transformation of a utility function change the marginal rate of substitution? Explain.

Exercises

1. Suppose Tim's utility function for commodities x_1 and x_2 is

$$U(x_1, x_2) = x_1^2 x_2.$$

   a. Demonstrate that his indifference curves are downward sloping. Are they strictly convex? Explain.

b. Now consider the transformation on Tim's utility function

$$V(x_1, x_2) = \ln U(x_1, x_2).$$

Show that the marginal rate of substitution is the same as in (a).

c. Are any of the utility functions in Exercise 8 monotonic transformations of one another? Explain.

3 Utility maximization

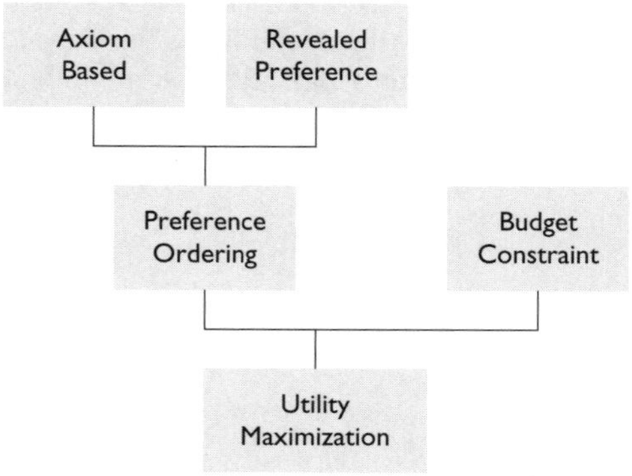

Outline and Conceptual Inquiries

Consider a household's budget constraint: feasible grocery carts

Consuming discrete commodities

Can you consume one-third of an airline ticket?

Assuming continuous choice

Do you bargain with grocery clerks?

Application: India households shift their budget constraints for boys' healthcare relative to girls'

Nonlinear budget constraints

At a grocery store, why does it not matter which commodity you purchase with the small change you found on the floor?

Application: Why not ration commodities instead?

Application: Which is preferable: an excise or an income tax?

Application: Which is preferable: subsidized price or income?

Why is there a black market for food stamps?

How to choose a household utility maximum bundle

What is the tangency condition?

What have you done when you are in a grocery checkout line?

Understanding the marginal utility per dollar condition

Application: Understanding marginal analysis

Should you study or spend time with your significant other?

Problems with nonconvexity

Possible corner solutions

Why will you only purchase apples when you could purchase a combination of apples and oranges?

The invaluable Lagrangian tool

Implications of the FOCs

Summary

Key concepts

Key equations

Questions

Exercises

Internet case studies

Appendix to chapter 3

Revealed preference: observed grocery cart ordering

Principle of rationality: observing rational choices

Is your observed market behavior rational?

Questions

Exercises

Households seek in society comfort, use, and protection.

(Michael Wetzstein)

At a very basic level, wants may be classified as comfort and protection, and households are able to purchase these wants by being useful to society. We provided a convenient way to represent consumer preferences for these wants in Chapter 2. The basic hypothesis is that a rational household will always choose a most preferred bundle from the set of feasible alternatives. This belief in utility maximization belongs to the Austrian School of thought,[1] which holds that the maximization hypothesis is the fundamental axiom of human action that is known to be true a priori. This is a form of hedonism doctrine (the doctrine that pleasure is the chief good in life). The competitive market model, which is another element of the Austrian School, is often used as an argument for profit maximization. Firms that do not maximize profits are driven out of the market by competitive forces.

Households are rewarded for their usefulness to society by receiving compensation in the form of income. They can then take this income and purchase commodities within the market to satisfy some of their wants. Our aim in this chapter is to show how household choices among alternative commodity bundles are determined for satisfying these wants. A household is constrained in its ability to consume commodity bundles by market prices associated with each commodity and a fixed level of income with which to purchase commodities. This constraint is called a *budget constraint*. Given this budget constraint and a utility function representing preferences, we can determine the utility-maximizing commodity. This decentralized determination of the utility-maximizing bundle by each household, based on price signals, is a key element in the efficient allocation of society's limited resources.

Following our development of the utility-maximization hypothesis based on the preference axioms, an alternative utility-maximization hypothesis (called revealed preference) is presented in the appendix to the chapter. Revealed preference is based on observed market choice and does not rely on the preference axioms discussed in Chapter 2.

Economists do not directly estimate the utility-maximizing set of commodities for each household. It is not possible to estimate individual utility functions and then determine the optimal consumption bundle for each consumer. Even if it could be done, this is not the objective of economics. Economists are interested in efficient resource allocation for society as a whole. They are interested in the aggregate (market) response of households to prices and income choices. However, as discussed in the applications, the utility-maximizing hypothesis for individual households does yield some interesting conclusions associated with government rationing of commodities, taxes, and subsidies.

Consider a household's budget constraint: feasible grocery carts

My problem lies in reconciling my gross habits with my income.

(Errol Flynn)

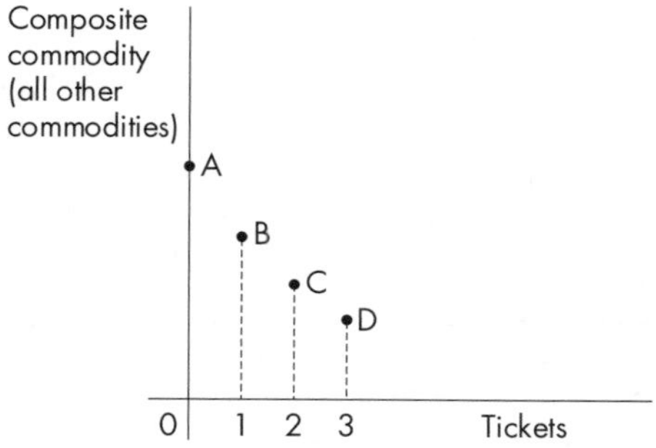

Figure 3.1 **Airline tickets representing a discrete commodity.** Tickets can only be purchased in discrete increments. For example, it is impossible to purchase one-third of a ticket. Bundles A, B, C, and D all yield the same level of utility, but a household cannot purchase a bundle between these discrete commodities.

The major determinant of consumer behavior, or specifically utility maximization, is the utility or satisfaction we receive from commodities. However, commodity prices and a household's income are also of primary consideration. Thus, in choosing a commodity bundle, the household must reconcile its wants with its preference relation (or utility function) and its given budget constraint. Certain physical constraints may also be embodied in the consumption set and further limit the choice of commodity bundles.

Consuming discrete commodities

An example of a *physical constraint* is a commodity that must be consumed in discrete increments. For example, a household can either purchase an airline ticket and fly to a given destination or not. It cannot purchase a fraction or continuous amount of a ticket. Figure 3.1 illustrates the discrete choice for airline tickets along with the continuous choice of a composite commodity. Each point or commodity bundle—labeled A, B, C, and D—yields the same level of utility. As the ability to consume more units of the discrete commodity (airline tickets) within a budget constraint increases, the discrete bundles blend together and form an indifference curve. Generally, in econometrics, five or more discrete choices can be analyzed as a continuous-choice problem. Thus, we will assume that households have a relatively large number of choices in terms of the number of units or the volume of a commodity, so we can investigate household behavior as a continuous-choice problem.

Can you consume one-third of an airline ticket? No, unless you also have a parachute (Did D.B. Cooper do it on November 24, 1971?).

Assuming continuous choice

There ain't no such thing as a free lunch.

(Robert Heinlein)

Translation: The cost of a lunch is the lost opportunity of doing something else at lunchtime.

Consider first the two-commodity case in graphical analysis, where the two commodities could be food and clothing or any other pair of commodities. We denote the parameter I

as income to be allocated between commodities x_1 and x_2 with associated per-unit prices p_1 and p_2. Prices are based on the assumption that commodities are traded in a market and are publicly quoted. This is called the *principle of completeness* or *universality of markets*.[2] Note that a price for a commodity could be negative, which means the household is actually paid to consume the commodity. An example is the bad commodity pollution. However, in this chapter, we will assume all prices are positive. (In Chapter 21, we consider the possibility of negative prices for bad commodities [negative externalities].) Also, it is assumed that all prices are constant, which implies households are **price takers**. That is, they take the market price for a commodity as given. A household is then constrained by a *budget set* (also called a *feasible* or *opportunity set*),

$$p_1x_1 + p_2x_2 \leq I.$$

The left-hand side is a household's total expenditure for the two commodities x_1 and x_2. The first term, p_1x_1, is expenditure for x_1, per-unit price times quantity, and the second term, p_2x_2, is the expenditure for x_2. For example, if x_1 is your level of candy consumption at school, then p_1x_1 is your total expenditure on candy. The level of a household's total expenditure on x_1 and x_2, $p_1x_1 + p_2x_2$, is constrained by its income I. Total expenditures on the purchase of x_1 and x_2 cannot exceed this level of income. The budget set, illustrated by the shaded area in Figure 3.2, contains all the possible consumption bundles that this household can purchase.

Do you bargain with the grocery clerks? No, you take the price offered by the grocery store as fixed. If you try bargaining, the store manager will ask you to leave.

Price taker. An agent who considers the prices associated with the commodities as fixed. *E.g., when you go to the supermarket, you do not dicker with the grocery clerk for a better price on your cornflakes.*

A boundary associated with this budget set is the **budget line** (also called a **budget constraint**);

$$p_1x_1 + p_2x_2 = I.$$

The bundles (set of commodities x_1 and x_2) that cost exactly I are represented by this budget line, and the bundles below this line are those that cost strictly less than I. The budget line represents all the possible combinations of the two commodities a household can purchase at a particular time, given the market prices of the commodities and the household exhausts all its income. Consumption bundles on the budget line represent all the bundles where the household spends all of its income purchasing the two commodities. Bundles within the shaded area, in Figure 3.2 but not on the budget line represent bundles the household can purchase and have some remaining income.

Budget line, or budget constraint. A set of bundles that exhaust a household's income. *E.g., for a given level of his savings, all the various travel destinations a student can go to on spring break.*

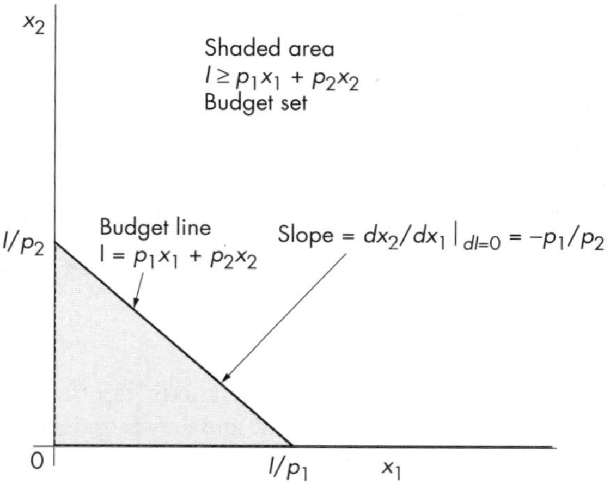

Figure 3.2 **Budget set.** Every commodity within the shaded area can be purchased at or below income I.

Rearranging this budget line by subtracting p_1x_1 from both sides and then dividing by p_2 results in

$$x_2 = \frac{I}{p_2} - \frac{p_1}{p_2}x_1.$$

This is the equation of a line with a vertical intercept of I/p_2 and a slope of $-p_1/p_2$ (Figure 3.2). The equation indicates how much commodity x_2 can be consumed with a given level of income I and x_1 units of commodity 1. If a household only consumes x_2 ($x_1 = 0$), then the amount of x_2 consumed will be the household's income divided by the price per unit of x_2, I/p_2. In Figure 3.2, this corresponds to the budget line's intercept on the vertical axis. Similarly, if only x_1 is purchased ($x_2 = 0$), then the amount of x_1 purchased is I/p_1, corresponding to the horizontal intercept. The slope of the budget line measures the rate at which the market is willing to substitute x_2 for x_1. Specifically, the slope of the budget constraint is

$$\left.\frac{dx_2}{dx_1}\right|_{dI=0} = -\frac{p_1}{p_2}.$$

The subscript $dI = 0$ indicates that income is remaining constant, so the change in income, dI, is zero. If a household consumes more of x_1, it will have to consume less of x_2 to satisfy the budget constraint. This is called the **opportunity cost** of consuming x_1, and the slope of the budget line measures this opportunity cost as the rate a household is able to substitute commodity x_2 for x_1. It is the tradeoff the market imposes on a household to substitute x_2 for x_1.

Opportunity cost. The cost of increasing the consumption of one commodity measured by the resulting decrease in consumption of another commodity. *E.g., the opportunity cost of purchasing a home entertainment center may be the loss of a European vacation.*

A change in price will alter this slope, and thus the opportunity cost. For example, as illustrated in Figure 3.3, an increase in the price of p_1, from p_1° to p_1', will tilt the budget line inward. An increase in the price of p_1 to p_1' does not change the vertical intercept. The price of x_2 has not changed, so if the household does not consume any of x_1, it can still consume the same level of x_2. However, the opportunity cost does change. The rate at which a household can substitute x_2 for x_1 has increased from p_1°/p_2 to p_1'/p_2. Increasing consumption of x_1 from x_1° to x_1' results in a decrease in x_2 of a at price p_1°. In contrast, at price p_1', the decrease is b. As illustrated in the figure, $b > a$, indicating the opportunity cost for increasing x_1 is higher at price p_1' than at p_1°. Alternatively, a change in income does not affect this opportunity cost. Income is only an intercept shifter, so it does not affect the slope of the budget line. As Figure 3.3 shows, an increase in income from I° to I', holding prices constant, results in a parallel shift upward of the budget line.

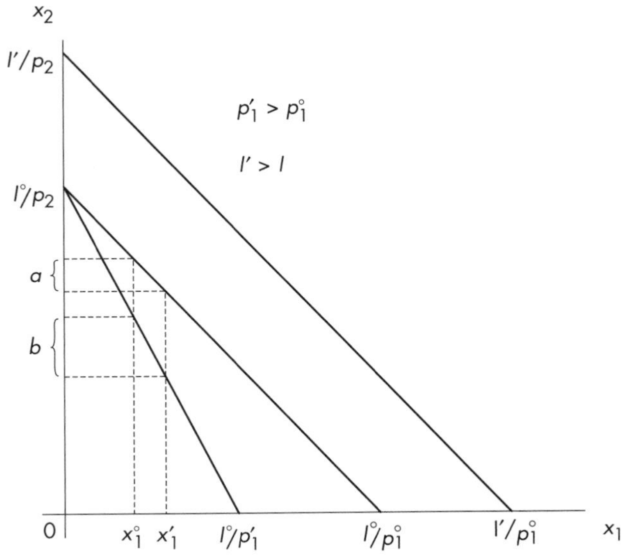

Figure 3.3 **Increased opportunity cost from an increase in p_1 and constant opportunity cost for an increase in *I*.** An increase in p_1 increases the opportunity cost of x_1. In contrast, an increase in I does not change the opportunity cost.

Example 3.1 Shifting versus tilting the budget constraint

Letting $p_1 = \$3$ and $p_2 = \$5$, with $I = \$60$, a household's budget constraint is then

$$3x_1 + 5x_2 = 60.$$

Solving for x_2 gives

$$x_2 = 12 - \frac{3}{5}x_1.$$

If all of the household's income was spent on x_2 ($x_1 = 0$), then 12 units of x_2 could be purchased. Similarly, if all of the income was spent on x_1 ($x_2 = 0$), then 20 units of x_1 could be purchased. For the household to stay within the income limit of \$60, increasing the consumption of x_1 by one unit would require reducing the consumption of x_2 by 3/5 of a unit. The opportunity cost of increasing x_1 by one unit is the 3/5 loss of x_2.

Increasing income from \$60 to \$90 yields a parallel shift upward of the budget line with no change in the slope. The opportunity cost of increasing x_1 remains the same. In contrast, an increase in the price of x_1 from 3 to 4 results in an inward tilt of the budget line with an associated increase in the opportunity cost of consuming more of x_1. The budget constraint with this increase in p_1 is

$$4x_1 + 5x_2 = 60,$$
$$x_2 = 12 - \frac{4}{5}x_1.$$

The opportunity cost of increasing x_1 by one unit is now a 4/5 loss in x_2. This results in a 1/5 increase in the opportunity cost.

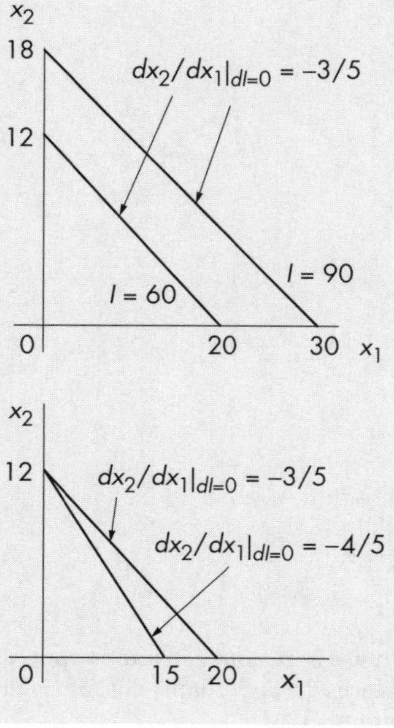

Application: India households shift their budget constraints for boys' healthcare relative to girls'

In 2001, there were 35 million more males than females in India, and this gender gap continues to grow. Female infanticide is a major cause of this "missing women" dilemma, but, as addressed by Asfaw, Lamanna, and Klasen, gender discrimination in the provision of healthcare is also a major factor. They hypothesize that households who face tight budget constraints are more likely to spend their meager resources on hospitalization of boys rather than girls. In terms of providing healthcare commodities for boys, households will make more of an effort to shift the budget constraint outward, so they will receive more healthcare service relative to girls. With empirical estimation of survey data, the authors reveal boys are much more likely to be hospitalized than girls. The budget constraint for boys will be shifted outward by borrowing, sale of assets, or help from friends and relatives to a greater degree than for girls. Consistent with economic theory, their results also indicate the gender gap is inversely related to income—poorer households will attempt to shift their budget constraint for boys more than the rich.

Source: A. Asfaw, F. Lamanna, and S. Klasen, "Gender Gap in Parents' Financing Strategy for Hospitalization of Their Children: Evidence from India," *Health Economics* 19 (2010): 265–279.

Nonlinear budget constraints

A budget constraint is linear only if the per-unit commodity prices are constant over all the possible consumption levels. In some markets, per-unit prices will vary depending on the quantity of the commodity purchased. Firms may offer a lower per-unit price if a household is willing to purchase a larger quantity of the commodity.[3] For example, the per-unit price of many food items—such as breakfast cereals, soaps, and candy—is lower when purchased in bulk. Such quantity discounts result in a nonlinear (convex) budget constraint, where the price ratio varies as the quantity of a commodity changes for a given income level. Figure 3.4 shows a convex budget constraint, given quantity discounts for Internet access with an assumed constant price for food, p_F. The price per minute for limited Internet usage, p_I°, is higher than the price for moderate usage, p_I', and the lowest price per minute, p_I'', is reserved for the Internet addict, so $p_I^\circ > p_I' > p_I''$.

How to choose a household utility maximum bundle

Life consists not in holding good cards but in playing those you hold well.

(Josh Billings, pen name of Henry Wheeler Shaw)

Playing well the cards you hold implies maximizing the happiness given the cards you were dealt. These cards are the household's budget constraint, which contains information on market prices and the household's income. The budget constraint, along with the household's preferences, provides the necessary information required to determine the consumption

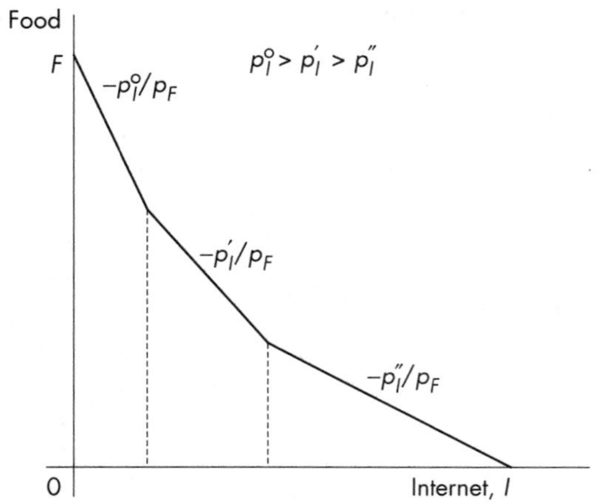

Figure 3.4 **Quantity discount resulting in a convex budget constraint.** The price per unit of time declines in three pricing increments as the amount of time spent on the Internet increases.

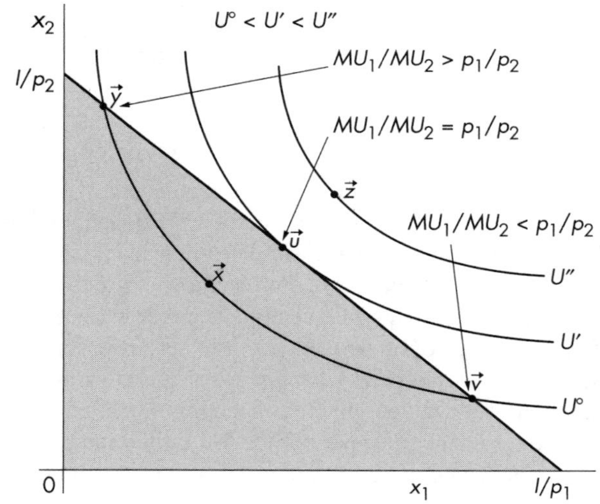

Figure 3.5 **Budget set superimposed on the indifference map.** For a given level of income, $\vec{u}$ represents the utility-maximizing bundle.

bundle that maximizes the household's utility. Recall that the indifference curves contain information on a household's preferences. Superimposing the budget constraint on the household's indifference space (map) results in Figure 3.5. The budget line indicates the possible combinations of x_1 and x_2 that could be purchased at given prices of x_1 and x_2 and income. Moving along the budget line, the possible combinations of x_1 and x_2 change but a household's income and market prices remain constant. The indifference curves U°, U', and U'' indicate the various combinations of x_1 and x_2 on a particular indifference curve that result in the same level of utility. For example, moving along indifference curve U°, total utility does not change but the consumption bundles containing x_1 and x_2 do. In contrast, shifting from indifference curve U° to U' does increase total utility.

According to the Nonsatiation Axiom, a household will consume more of the commodities if possible. However, a household cannot consume a bundle beyond its budget constraint. For example, a household cannot obtain a level of utility corresponding to bundle $\vec{z}$ in Figure 3.5 or achieve global bliss, because its limited income constrains it to a lower level of utility. Within the shaded area of the budget set, say at commodity bundle $\vec{x}$, a household has the income to purchase more of both commodities and increase utility. Thus, for utility maximization subject to a given level of income (represented by the budget line), the household will pick a commodity bundle on the budget line. For example, bundle $\vec{y}$ can be purchased with the household's limited income. The question is whether bundle $\vec{y}$ is the utility-maximizing bundle for the household's given level of income. If it is possible to increase utility by moving along the budget line from bundle $\vec{y}$, then $\vec{y}$ is not the utility-maximizing bundle. For example, moving down the budget line away from $\vec{y}$ toward $\vec{u}$, the combinations of x_1 and x_2 purchased are changing; commodity x_1 is being substituted for x_2. The household is also shifting to higher indifference curves. Total utility is increasing. Thus, the household will move from bundle $\vec{y}$ toward bundle $\vec{u}$ and increase its utility.

From bundle $\vec{u}$, further movements down the budget line do not result in increased utility. From bundle $\vec{u}$ toward $\vec{v}$, total expenditure remains constant, but the household shifts to lower indifference curves. The resulting level of utility declines. Thus, at bundle $\vec{u}$, the household will maximize utility for a given income and fixed commodity prices. At all alternative bundles, the budget constraint cuts through an indifference curve, so utility can be increased. However, at $\vec{u}$ the constraint is tangent to an indifference curve. Thus, the tangency point indicates that there is no possibility of increasing utility by moving in either direction along the budget constraint.

In reality, complications may prevent a consumer from reaching this theoretical maximum level of utility. For instance, consumer tastes change over time due to new products, advertising, and consumers growing tired of some commodities. Also, prices of commodities change through time. Households are constantly adjusting their purchases to reflect these changes.

What is the tangency condition?

> *The truth is that all of us attain the greatest success and happiness possible in this life whenever we use our native capacities to their greatest extent.*
>
> (Smiley Blanton)

Geometrically, the tangency at commodity bundle $\vec{u}$ is where the slope of the budget constraint,

$$\left.\frac{dx_2}{dx_1}\right|_{dI=0} = -\frac{p_1}{p_2},$$

exactly equals the slope of the indifference curve at point $\vec{u}$,

$$\left.\frac{dx_2}{dx_1}\right|_{dU=0} = -\text{MRS}\,(x_2 \text{ for } x_1).$$

The term $dU = 0$ indicates that utility remains constant along the indifference curve. In Figure 3.5, only at this tangency point $\vec{u}$ are the slopes of the budget and indifference curves equal along the budget line. Thus, for utility maximization, the MRS should equal the ratio of the prices:

$$\text{MRS}(x_2 \text{ for } x_1) = p_1/p_2.$$

This is called the **optimal choice** for a household. The price ratio p_1/p_2 is called the **economic rate of substitution** or *marginal rate of transformation*, so at the utility-maximizing point of tangency, the economic rate of substitution equals the marginal rate of substitution (MRS). The per-unit opportunity cost p_1/p_2 that a household is able to substitute one commodity for another is equal to how much the household is willing to substitute, MRS.

What have you done when you are in a grocery checkout line? Once in line, you have selected the optimal grocery cart for your given budget. So your marginal rate of substitution based on your preferences is equal to the economic rate of substitution.

Optimal choice. The point where utility is maximized for a given budget constraint. *E.g., when you have completed your grocery shopping and are waiting in the checkout line.*
Economic rate of substitution or marginal rate of transformation. The market rate at which one commodity can be purchased in place of another holding income constant. *E.g., given a per-unit price for apples of 2 and for bananas 1, the market rate of substitution is two bananas for one apple.*

Understanding the marginal utility per dollar condition

Suppose a teenager reconsiders his purchases of socks and CDs on the way home from a shopping trip. He decides the socks were a good buy but the CDs not. Given a choice, he would have increased his purchases of socks and decreased his purchases of CDs. As we will see, the reason for this reconsideration is that the marginal utilities per dollar for socks and CDs are no longer equal. Recall that $\text{MRS}(x_2 \text{ for } x_1) = \text{MU}_1/\text{MU}_2$, so a relationship between the price ratio, p_1/p_2, and the ratio of marginal utilities at the utility-maximizing bundle is

$$\frac{p_1}{p_2} = \frac{\text{MU}_1}{\text{MU}_2}.$$

Dividing by p_1 and multiplying by MU_2 yields the condition of equating the marginal utility per dollar for maximizing utility with a given income and fixed prices:

$$\frac{\text{MU}_1}{p_1} = \frac{\text{MU}_2}{p_2}.$$

When deciding what commodities to spend its income on, a household attempts to equate the marginal utility per dollar for the commodities it purchases. This equalization of marginal utility per dollar is a basic condition for utility maximization and is called the *equal marginal principle*. For k commodities, the purchase condition is

$$\frac{\mathrm{MU}_1}{p_1} = \frac{\mathrm{MU}_2}{p_2} = \ldots = \frac{\mathrm{MU}_k}{p_k},$$

which expresses a household's equilibrium. In this case, equilibrium is a condition where the household has allocated its income among commodities at market prices in such a way as to maximize total utility.

Also, this equation is equivalent to stating that for a household to be in equilibrium the last dollar spent on commodity 1 must yield the same marginal utility as the last dollar spent on commodity 2 (as well as all the other commodities). If this does not hold, a household would be better off reallocating expenditures. Marginal utility per dollar indicates the bang or addition in total utility from spending an additional dollar on a commodity. If the marginal utility per dollar for one commodity is higher than the marginal utility per dollar for another commodity, a household can increase overall utility by spending one less dollar on the commodity with the lower marginal utility per dollar and one more dollar on the commodity with the higher marginal utility per dollar.

For example, suppose

$$\frac{\mathrm{MU}_1}{p_1} > \frac{\mathrm{MU}_2}{p_2},$$

which is represented by bundle $\vec{y}$ in Figure 3.5. The household is not in equilibrium and thus not maximizing total utility given its limited income. The per-unit opportunity cost of increasing x_1, p_1/p_2, is less than how much the household is willing to pay for increasing x_1, MRS. The household can increase its total utility by increasing its consumption of x_1 and decreasing its consumption of x_2. More additional total utility per dollar is received from x_1 than from x_2. Thus, if one more dollar were used to purchase x_1 and one less dollar for the purchase of x_2, total expenditures would remain constant, but total utility would increase. The household can continue to increase total utility by simply rearranging purchases until

$$\frac{\mathrm{MU}_1}{p_1} = \frac{\mathrm{MU}_2}{p_2},$$

which results in the maximum level of utility for a given level of income. This equality of marginal utility per dollar corresponds to bundle $\vec{u}$ in Figure 3.5.

Application: Understanding marginal analysis

At the bare essentials, economic analysis is just marginal analysis, and some economists even use the word marginalism for referring to economic logic. Economic theory is marginal analysis because it assumes that decisions are always reached by comparing additional benefits with the associated additional costs. For example, assume your significant other calls you at 10:00 p.m. while you are cramming for your midterm economics examination. She wants you to come over for just an hour or so. Unhappily, you tell her no and explain you must study. She responds, "Economics must be more important than me." Demonstrating how well you have been studying, you respond, "Only at the margin."

The issue is not the value of your significant other versus economics. Instead, it is whether the utility per hour of studying is greater than the utility per hour with her. For example, air is more important than candy. However, we generally would be unwilling to pay for one breath of air but willing to pay for a piece of candy (especially if it is chocolate). It is the level of utility of an additional unit of air that influences how much we are willing to pay, not the value of the total amount of air we consume. What we would be willing to pay for one breath versus one piece of candy is not what we would be willing to pay to have air or candy.

Your significant other is viewing the problem in terms of totals. The choice is either economics or me. However, that was not the choice. The real choice is the marginal choice of an additional time studying or being with her. Generally, the choices we face are marginal choices. Rarely is the choice in terms of absolute all or nothing of commodities.

Should you study or spend time with your significant other? If the marginal utility per hour for studying is greater than the marginal utility per hour spending time with your significant other, then study.

Problems with nonconvexity

The optimal choice illustrated in Figure 3.5 involves consuming some of both commodities and is called an **interior optimum**. The tangency condition associated with this interior optimum is only a necessary condition for a maximum. As illustrated in Figure 3.6, tangency point $\vec{y}$ is inferior to a point of nontangency $\vec{z}$. The true maximum is the tangency point $\vec{x}$. If the optimal choice involves consuming some of both commodities, the Diminishing MRS

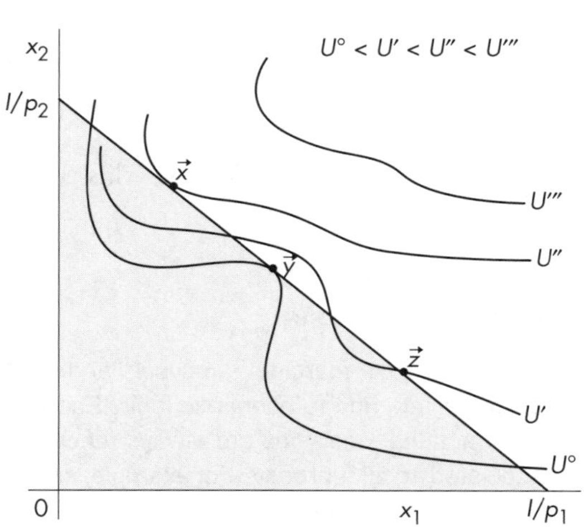

Figure 3.6 **The tangency rule is only a necessary condition for a maximum.** The tangency at $\vec{y}$ is not the utility-maximizing point.

Axiom (Strict Convexity) and the tangency condition are a necessary and sufficient condition for a maximum.

Interior optimum. The utility-maximizing solution results in some of all commodities being consumed. *E.g., considering two commodities, you purchase a combination of apples and bananas.*

Possible corner solutions

When going to the store, a couple may intend to purchase a combination of chicken and beef for this week's dinners. However, at the store, there is a weekly special on chicken, so the couple decides only to purchase chicken. This decision to not purchase a combination of the commodities is called a **corner solution** (boundary optimal).

An example of a corner solution, when the assumption of strict convexity holds, is shown in Figure 3.7. In this case, the utility-maximizing bundle would be to consume only x_2 (chicken) and none of x_1 (beef). At this boundary optimal, the tangency condition does not necessary hold. Specifically, the boundary-optimal condition in Figure 3.7 is

$$\frac{\mathrm{MU}_1}{p_1} \leq \frac{\mathrm{MU}_2}{p_2}.$$

It is possible that the marginal utility per dollar is larger for commodity x_2, so the household would prefer continuing substituting x_2 for x_1. However, further substitution at the boundary, where $x_1 = 0$, is impossible.

Why will you only purchase apples when you could purchase a combination of apples and oranges? The extra satisfaction per dollar from purchasing another apple may be greater than the extra satisfaction per dollar from purchasing oranges.

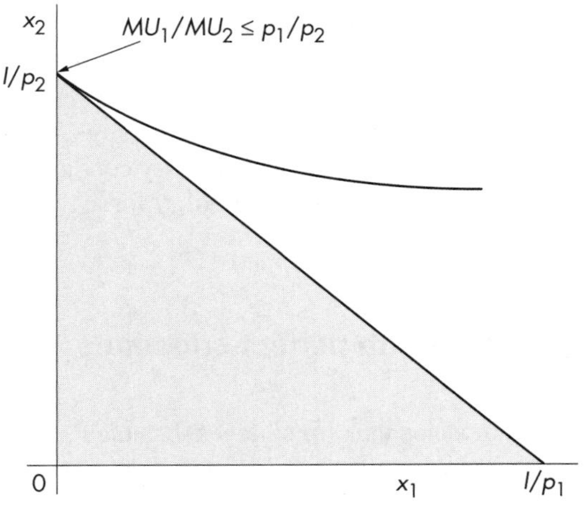

Figure 3.7 **A boundary-optimal solution with only commodity x_2 being consumed.** A household would prefer reallocating expenditures from x_1 to x_2, but there is no expenditure on x_1 to reallocate.

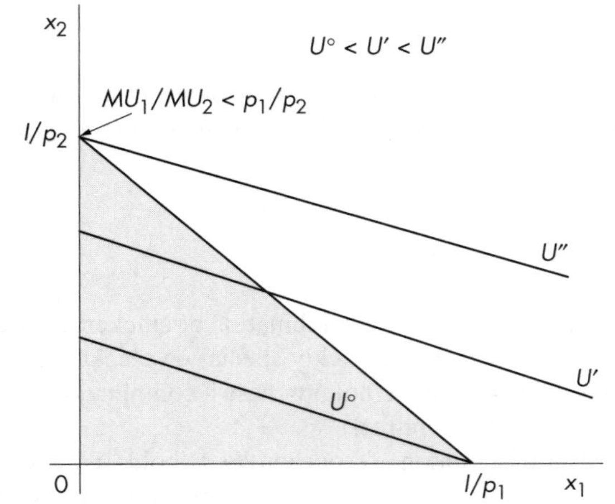

Figure 3.8 **A corner solution for perfect substitutes.** A household's utility is maximized for a given level of income I by only purchasing commodity x_2.

Corner solution. An optimal solution at one of the axes. *E.g., you intend to purchase apples and bananas. But due to the relatively high price of bananas, you purchase only apples.*

A corner solution will always occur when the Diminishing MRS Axiom is violated over the whole range of possible commodity bundles. For example, with perfect substitutes as preferences (say two brands of colas), a household will consume only the commodity with the largest marginal utility per dollar. In Figure 3.8, the household only consumes x_2 and purchases I/p_2 units. Similarly, for a household with strictly concave preferences (increasing MRS), extremes are preferred (say, drinking and driving), so the optimal allocation will be at an extreme boundary. This occurs where the marginal utility per dollar for one of the commodities is maximized. In Figure 3.9, this results in the household again only consuming x_2 and purchasing I/p_2 units. Note that at point A in Figure 3.9, the tangency condition MRS $= \text{MU}_1/\text{MU}_2 = p_1/p_2$ results in minimizing rather than maximizing utility for a given level of income.

Example 3.2 How to maximize utility with perfect-substitute preferences

Consider a household consuming two commodities that are perfect substitutes. Specifically, let the perfect substitute preferences be represented by the following utility function:

$$U(x_1, x_2) = 5x_1 + 3x_2,$$

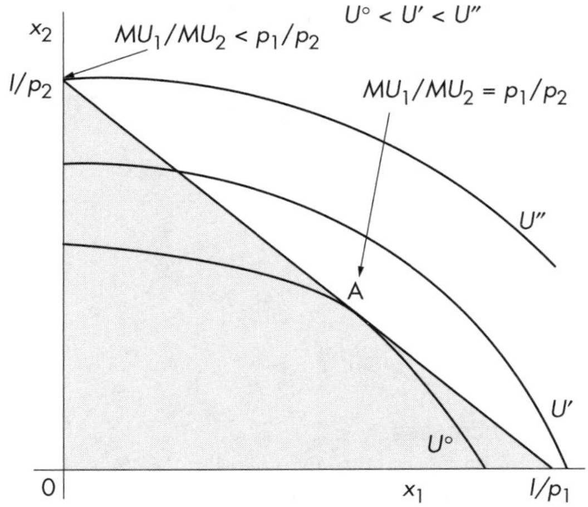

Figure 3.9 **A corner solution with strictly concave preferences.** A household's utility is maximized by consuming the extreme bundle containing only x_2 and none of x_1.

with prices, $p_1 = 4$ and $p_2 = 3$, and income $I = \$96$. Then MRS($x_2$ for x_1) $= MU_1/MU_2 = 5/3 > 4/3 = p_1/p_2$, the economic rate of substitution. As illustrated in the graph, this results in the linear indifference curve being steeper than the budget line. The optimal commodity bundle then comprises $x_1 = 24$ and $x_2 = 0$.

Comparing the marginal utilities per dollar, we have

$$\frac{MU_1}{p_1} = \frac{5}{4} > \frac{3}{3} = \frac{MU_2}{p_2}.$$

The household will allocate all of its income to x_1, where the marginal utility per dollar is the highest.

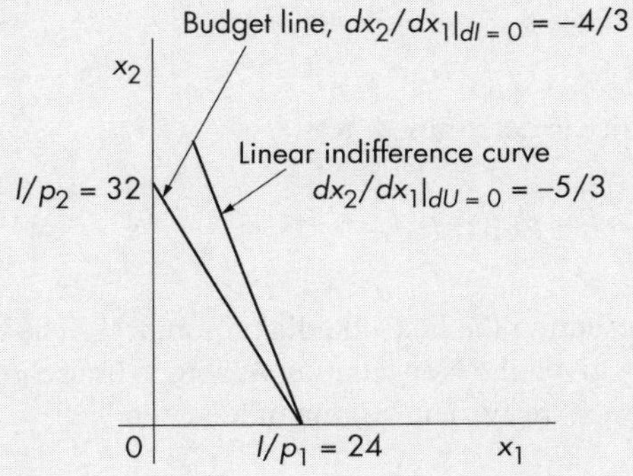

Example 3.3 How to maximize utility with strictly concave preferences

Consider a household with strictly concave preferences. As developed in Example 2.5, these preferences may be represented by the utility function

$$U(x_1, x_2) = x_1^2 + x_2^2,$$

with prices $p_1 = 4$ and $p_2 = 3$, and income, $I = \$96$

$$\text{MRS}(x_2 \text{ for } x_1) = \frac{\text{MU}_1}{\text{MU}_2} = \frac{2x_1}{2x_2} = \frac{x_1}{x_2},$$

which results in the MRS increasing as x_1 increases.

The indifference curves are strictly concave, so the Diminishing MRS Axiom is violated. The household prefers extremes to averages. Thus, its optimal consumption bundle will comprise only x_1 or only x_2, but not any combination of them. If the household allocated all of its income to the consumption of x_1, it could purchase 24 units of x_1. At this level of consumption, the household's marginal utility per dollar for x_1 is $48/4 = 12$. Alternatively, if the household allocates all of its income to x_2, its marginal utility per dollar for x_2 is $64/3 = 21.33$, with $x_2 = 32$. The marginal utility per dollar is higher for consuming only x_2 than for consuming only x_1, so the household's optimal bundle is 32 units of x_2 and 0 units of x_1.

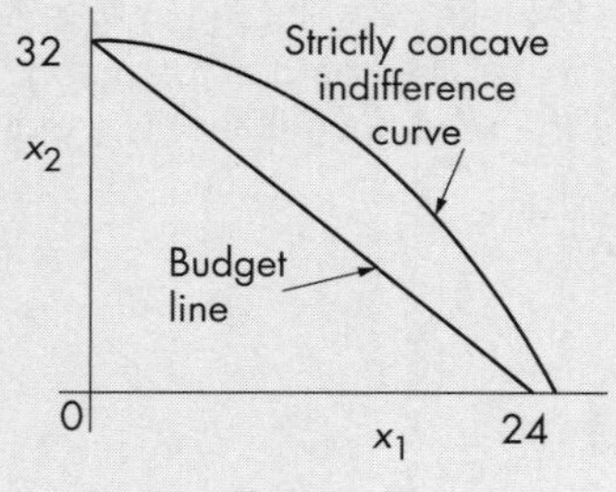

The invaluable Lagrangian tool

Mathematically, the maximum level of utility is determined by

$$\max_{(x_1, x_2)} U = \max U = \max U(x_1, x_2), \quad \text{s.t. } I = p_1x_1 + p_2x_2,$$

where $U(x_1, x_2)$ is the utility function representing the household's preferences. The budget constraint is written as an equality because, given the Nonsatiation Axiom, a household will spend all available income rather than throw it away. The Lagrangian is then

$$\mathcal{L}(x_1, x_2, \lambda) = U(x_1, x_2) + \lambda(I - p_1x_1 - p_2x_2).$$

First-order conditions (FOCs) are

$$\frac{\partial \mathcal{L}}{\partial x_1} = \frac{\partial U}{\partial x_1} - \lambda^* p_1 = 0,$$

$$\frac{\partial \mathcal{L}}{\partial x_2} = \frac{\partial U}{\partial x_2} - \lambda^* p_2 = 0,$$

$$\frac{\partial \mathcal{L}}{\partial \lambda} = I - p_1 x_1^* - p_2 x_2^* = 0.$$

Example 3.4 How to maximize utility subject to an income constraint

Let x_1 be the amount of food consumed by a household and x_2 the amount of clothing. Assume that the household's preferences are represented by the specific utility function

$$U = U(x_1, x_2) = 5 \ln x_1 + 3 \ln x_2, \text{ or } V = x_1^5 x_2^3,$$

where $V = e^U$, $V' = e^U > 0$. Note that both functions represent the same preference ordering, so they will yield the same optimal commodity levels. Also, assume that it faces a per-unit price for food, p_1 = \$10 and clothing, p_2 = \$2 with a given level of income I = \$96. The household's budget constraint is then

$$\begin{aligned} 96 &= p_1 x_1 + p_2 x_2 \\ &= 10x_1 + 2x_2. \end{aligned}$$

In implicit form,

$$96 - 10x_1 - 2x_2 = 0.$$

The Lagrangian is then

$$\mathcal{L}(x_1, x_2, \lambda) = 5 \ln x_1 + 3 \ln x_2 + \lambda(96 - 10x_1 - 2x_2).$$

FOCs are

$$\frac{\partial \mathcal{L}}{\partial x_1} = \frac{5}{x_1^*} - 10\lambda^* = 0,$$

$$\frac{\partial \mathcal{L}}{\partial x_2} = \frac{3}{x_2^*} - 2\lambda^* = 0,$$

$$\frac{\partial \mathcal{L}}{\partial \lambda} = 96 - 10x_1^* - 2x_2^* = 0.$$

This results in three equations and three unknowns (x_1, x_2, and λ). Solving for these unknowns provides the utility-maximizing quantities of x_1^* and x_2^* along with the marginal utility of income λ^*. One method for solving these equations, yielding some economic implications, is adding λ^* times the price to both sides of the first two equations and taking their ratios:

$$\text{MRS}(x_2 \text{ for } x_1) = \frac{5x_2^*}{3x_1^*} = \frac{10}{2} = 5 = \frac{p_1}{p_2}.$$

This is the tangency condition where the MRS equals the economic rate of substitution. Solving for x_2^* yields

$$x_2^* = 3x_1^*.$$

As discussed in Chapter 4, this equation is called the *income expansion path*. The problem now is reduced to finding the two unknowns, commodities x_1 and x_2, given this expansion path and the last FOC, the budget constraint. Substituting the income expansion path into the budget constraint, by replacing x_2^* with $3x_1^*$ in the budget constraint, yields

$$96 - 10x_1^* - 6x_1^* = 0,$$

$$x_1^* = 6.$$

We determine the optimal level of commodity x_2, x_2^*, for maximizing utility by either substituting x_1^* into the income expansion path or the budget constraint. This results in $x_2^* = 18$. Thus, the utility-maximizing bundle for $96 of income is $x_1^* = 6$ and $x_2^* = 18$.

Finally, we determine the marginal utility of income, λ^*, at an income of $96 by substituting the optimal levels of the commodities into either the first or second FOCs. Specifically, taking the first condition,

$$\frac{\partial \mathcal{L}}{\partial x_1} = \frac{5}{x_1^*} - 10\lambda^* = 0,$$

and substituting $x_1^* = 6$ yields

$$\frac{5}{6} - 10\lambda^* = 0.$$

Solving for λ^*, $\lambda^* = 1/12$. An extra dollar of income would yield approximately 1/12 unit of additional utility. For example, if the extra dollar was spent on clothing, this would buy a $^1/_2$ unit of clothing (clothing costs $2.00 per unit). The MU_2 at the optimal commodity bundle is

$$MU_2 = \frac{\partial U}{\partial x_2} = \frac{3}{x_2^*} = \frac{3}{18} = \frac{1}{6}.$$

The additional $^1/_2$ unit of clothing times MU_2 is the addition to total utility from having an additional dollar in income. The result is

$$\frac{1}{2} \cdot \frac{1}{6} = \frac{1}{12},$$

which is the marginal utility of income, λ^*.

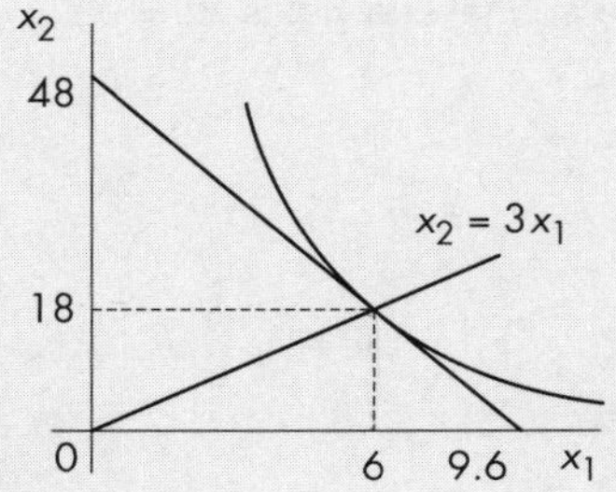

Example 3.5 How to maximize utility with perfect-complement preferences

Consider the following utility function representing a household's preferences for perfect-complement commodities x_1 and x_2:

$$U(x_1, x_2) = \min(4x_1, 3x_2).$$

Assume the household is facing prices $p_1 = 1$ and $p_2 = 3$, with a given level of income $I = \$120$. This yields the budget line

$$x_1 + 3x_2 = 120.$$

The utility function, although continuous, is not smooth. As illustrated in the figure, at the points where $4x_1 = 3x_2$, the function is kinked, so the slope is not unique. Thus, it is not possible to take the derivative of this utility function and determine the tangency of the indifference curve with the budget line. However, as indicated in the figure, the utility-maximizing bundle corresponds to the kinked surface ($4x_1^* = 3x_2^*$) of the indifference curve. Solving for x_2^* yields

$$x_2^* = \frac{4}{3}x_1^*,$$

which is the income expansion path connecting all the utility-maximizing bundles as income is varied. The optimal bundle, for a given level of income, is then obtained by solving the two equations (the income expansion path and budget line) for x_1 and x_2. These two equations may be solved by substituting the income expansion path into the budget line

$$x_1^* + 3\left(\frac{4}{3}x_1^*\right) = 120.$$

Solving for the optimal level of x_1^*,

$$5x_1^* = 120,$$

$$x_1^* = 24.$$

Substituting x_1^* into either the expansion path or the budget line yields $x_2^* = 32$.

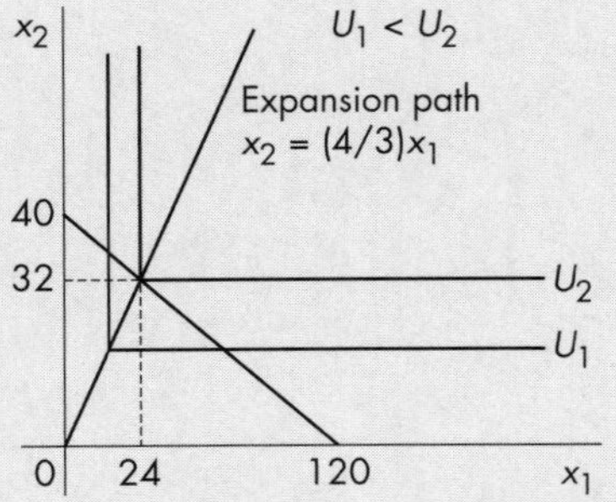

These three FOCs along with the three variables (the two commodities and the Lagrange multiplier λ) can be solved simultaneously for the optimal levels of x_1^*, x_2^*, and λ^*.

In terms of the second-order condition (SOC), the Diminishing MRS Axiom is sufficient to ensure a maximum. The possibility of not maximizing utility when this axiom is violated is illustrated in Figures 3.6 and 3.9.

Implications of the FOCs

Understanding the tangency condition

Rearranging the first two FOCs by adding λ^* times the price to each side yields

$$\frac{\partial U}{\partial x_1} = \lambda^* p_1,$$

$$\frac{\partial U}{\partial x_2} = \lambda^* p_2.$$

Taking the ratio,

$$\frac{\partial U/\partial x_1}{\partial U/\partial x_2} = \frac{\text{MU}_1}{\text{MU}_2} = \text{MRS}(x_2 \text{ for } x_1) = \frac{p_1}{p_2}.$$

For maximizing utility, how much a household is willing to substitute x_2 for x_1, as measured by MRS(x_2 for x_1), is set equal to the economic rate of substitution, p_1/p_2. As illustrated in Figure 3.5, this result is identical to the tangency condition for utility maximization between the budget line and the indifference curve.

Marginal utility per dollar condition

Dig where the gold is, unless you just need some exercise.

(John M. Capozzi)

The gold is the marginal utility per dollar for a commodity, so dig (consume) where the marginal utility per dollar is the highest. This results in equating marginal utility per dollar for all commodities consumed. From the FOCs, this marginal utility per dollar condition is derived by solving for λ^* in the first two equations:

$$\lambda^* = \frac{\partial U/\partial x_1}{p_1} = \frac{\partial U/\partial x_2}{p_2}$$
$$= \frac{\text{MU}_1}{p_1} = \frac{\text{MU}_2}{p_2}.$$

At the utility-maximizing point, each commodity should yield the same marginal utility per dollar. Thus, each commodity has an identical marginal-benefit to marginal-cost ratio. The extra dollar should yield the same additional utility no matter which commodity it is spent on. The common value for this extra utility is given by the Lagrange multiplier of income I. The multiplier λ^* can be regarded as the marginal utility of an extra dollar of consumption expenditure and called the **marginal utility of income (MU_I)**. Specifically, $\lambda^* = \partial U/\partial I = \text{MU}_I$. It is commonly referred to as the *shadow value* and indicates the marginal rate of change in the objective function—in this case utility—as the constraint is relaxed—income.

Marginal utility of income (MU_I). The additional satisfaction received from an additional unit of income. *E.g., the pleasure you receive from spending your birthday money on a concert.*

Solving each of the first two conditions for price yields

$$p_j = \text{MU}_j/\lambda^*, \quad \text{for } j = 1, 2.$$

$\text{MU}_I = \lambda^*$ results in the conversion unit between dollars and utility, so MU_j/λ^* is the dollar equivalent of the change in utility. The equation states that for a commodity, the price of this commodity represents a household's dollar evaluation of the utility associated with the last unit consumed. The price represents how much a household is willing to pay for this last unit of the commodity. If $\text{MU}_j/\lambda^* < p_j$, a household will not purchase any more units of commodity j.

At a grocery store, why does it not matter which commodity you purchase with the small change you found on the floor? The additional satisfaction per dollar for each of the commodities you will purchase are all the same, so it does not matter which commodity you purchase with the change on the floor.

Application: Why not ration commodities instead?

Rationing: The art of satisfying only bureaucrats.

(Michael Wetzstein)

Limited resources and unlimited wants result in insufficient commodities for the satisfaction of wants, so some mechanism for allocating these commodities to households is required. A common and efficient method of allocation is through reliance on the free-market price system. With price signals, the market automatically allocates limited supply in such a way that quantity supplied equals quantity demanded. This ability of the market to freely allocate supply is called the *invisible hand*. Adam Smith, father of economics, coined this term in a book entitled the *Wealth of Nations*, published in the very famous year of 1776.

Without a free market, some other design of mechanism is required for commodity allocation. Generally, this requires a social organization (government) determining a policy for allocation. For example, instead of relying on a decentralized allocation with market price signals, a government may establish a centralized allocation mechanism, based on ideological, humanitarian, or political reasons. Ideological reasons stem from either an underlying disbelief in markets' ability to optimally allocate commodities or possible religious convictions that conflict with a market-based allocation system. Temporary shortage of a commodity resulting from war (e.g., World War II) or other economic disturbances (e.g., an oil embargo) may result in a government deeming a market price for the commodity excessive (inhumane).

One type of governmental mechanism for commodity allocation is allocating a fixed quantity of a commodity for each household. For example, during World War II, ration stamps were issued in the United States for certain commodities, including gasoline and chocolate. For a household to be willing and able to purchase those commodities, it required not only money but also a ration stamp issued by the federal government. A problem with ration stamps is determining how many to issue, how to issue them, and who receives them. This requires a governmental agency to do what the free market does automatically.

The effects of a governmental rationing program are illustrated in Figure 3.10. A household wishes to consume bundle (x_1^*, x_2^*), but rationing limits the quantity of x_1 available to each household to an amount x_R. At the prevailing price, x_1^* is not attainable. The effective budget constraint then becomes OCBx_R and some other constrained utility-maximizing commodity bundle must be chosen (point B). Rationing has decreased the household's utility from U^* to U'. Note that rationing only has an effect on household preferences if $x_R < x_1^*$. However, the likelihood of x_1^* exceeding x_R will increase with x_1^* increasing as income rises.

For this rationing program to work, it must be illegal for households to sell their ration stamps. Otherwise, the effect is the same as just letting the market allocate commodities. If a market for buying and selling ration stamps develops, then the governmental issuance of such stamps just amounts to a redistribution of income; the effect would be the same as if the government just gave out money instead. In fact, the ability to buy and sell stamps makes the stamps just another form of currency.

Without laws and penalties to enforce governmental rationing, there are incentives for the households to find some way of moving from B to A in Figure 3.10. Even with laws, some households will generally be willing to engage in illegal activities and purchase more than their legal allocation. In Chapter 10 (on economic efficiency), we discuss problems associated with black markets (illegal markets) supplying commodities. Thus, the main effect of rationing, besides allocating the limited supply, is the establishment of a governmental rationing agency and additional governmental enforcement of laws against allowing a free market for the ration stamps. Governmental bureaucrats are very pleased with lending a hand in replacing the invisible hand.

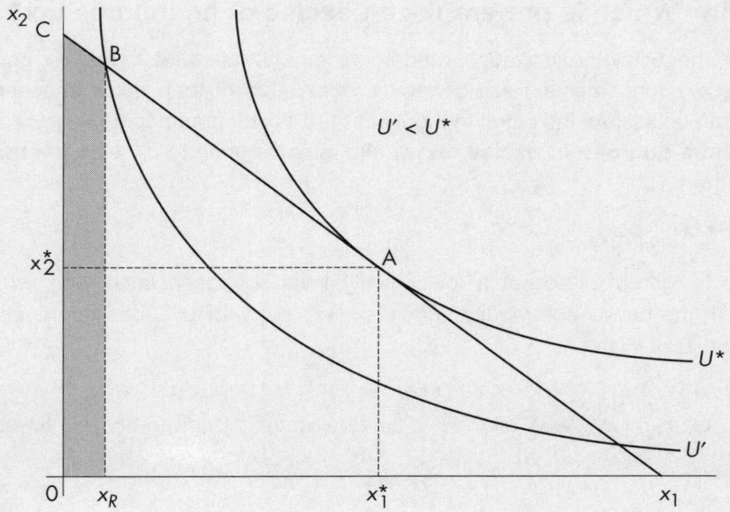

Figure 3.10 **Governmental rationing.** Rationing restricts a household's choice to the shaded area OCBx_R, which lowers its utility from U^* to U'.

Source: Adam Smith, *The Wealth of Nations*, New York: Modern Library (1937).

Example 3.6 Reduced utility from rationing

Consider the utility function and budget constraint in Example 3.4. Without any rationing, the optimal consumption levels are $x_1^* = 6$ and $x_2^* = 18$. This results in $U^* = 5\ln 6 + 3\ln 18 = 17.63$. Suppose commodity x_1 is rationed at $x_R = 3$. In maximizing utility, a household will purchase the entire rationed amount of x_1 and with its remaining income purchase x_2. Total expenditure for x_1 is \$30 = 10(3), so the budget constraint for x_2 is then

$$96 = 30 + 2x_2.$$

Solving for x_2, the household will purchase 33 units of x_2. Utility associated with this ration allocation is then $U' = 5\ln 3 + 3\ln 33 = 15.98 < 17.63 = U^*$.

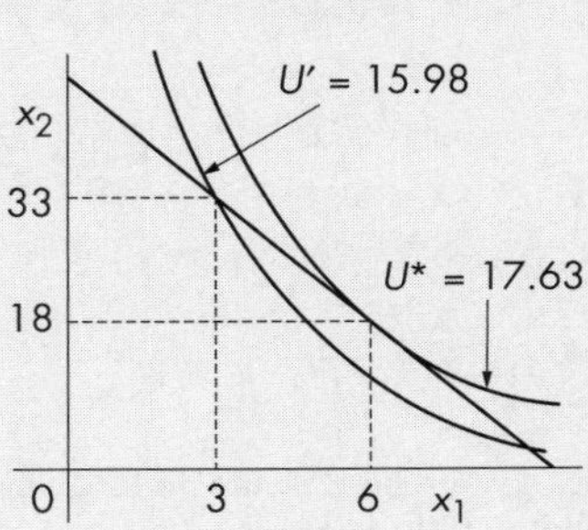

Application: Which is preferable: an excise or an income tax?

We can use the utility-maximization model to demonstrate that taxes on general purchasing power (income tax) are generally more efficient than taxes imposed on individual commodities. As indicated in Figure 3.11, a tax on commodity x_1 of τ dollars per unit (called a **quantity or excise tax**) would raise its price to $p_1 + \tau$. The budget constraint is then

$$I = (p_1 + \tau)x_1 + p_2x_2.$$

A household is forced to accept a lower utility level, U', associated with (x_1', x_2') compared with the pretax commodity bundle of (x_1^*, x_2^*) with U^*. Total tax revenues, TR_T, would be $TR_T = \tau x_1$.

Quantity (excise) tax. A tax on the per-unit amount of a commodity purchased. *E.g., the federal tax on gasoline.*

A general purchasing power tax (called a **lump-sum income tax**), which also collects TR_T dollars in revenue, is determined by

$$\begin{aligned} I &= (p_1 + \tau)x_1 + p_2x_2 \\ &= p_1x_1 + \tau x_1 + p_2x_2 \\ &= p_1x_1 + TR_T + p_2x_2, \\ I - TR_T &= p_1x_1 + p_2x_2. \end{aligned}$$

That is, income minus the tax results in an after-tax income of $I - TR_T$.

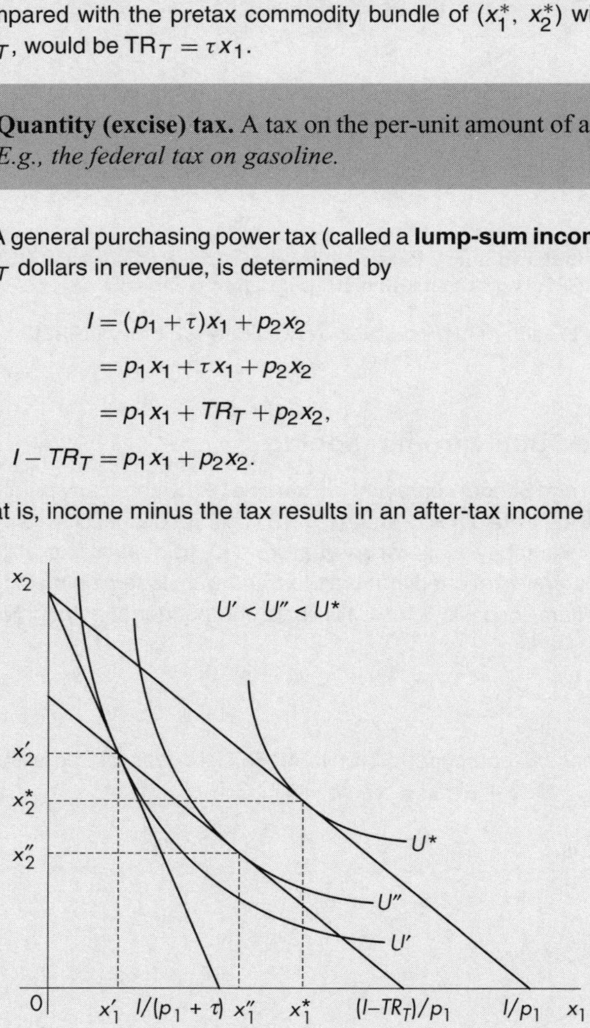

Figure 3.11 **Taxation and the lump-sum principle.** A household would prefer an income tax resulting in U'' over an excise tax with utility U'.

Lump-sum income tax. A tax on income. *E.g., federal and state tax on personal income.*

In contrast to the excise tax, the relative prices remain the same with an income tax. Only the household's purchasing power has declined. As illustrated in Figure 3.11, the consumer will choose to consume (x_1'', x_2'') at utility level U''. Thus, even given that the household pays the same tax bill in both instances, the bundle chosen under the purchasing-power tax yields a higher utility than does the single-commodity tax. The reason for this is that a single-commodity tax affects a household's well-being by decreasing general purchasing power and directing consumption away from the taxed commodity. In contrast, an income tax only decreases general purchasing power. No distortion in the market prices occurs, so the household is still maximizing utility by equating the marginal utility per dollar for the two commodities. Under an excise tax, a distortion in market prices occurs, which prevents the household from achieving the utility-maximizing combination of commodities. With an excise tax, the equilibrium level of commodities x_1' and x_2' is not associated with the equality of the marginal utilities per dollar.

This is the theoretical rationale for the idea that income taxes are superior to equal-revenue excise or sales taxes on individual items. However, income taxes are more efficient in terms of offering a higher level of utility only to the extent they do not incorporate distorting price effects by changing the price ratio p_1/p_2.

Several limitations exist with this result. First, it only applies to one household. The amount of the income tax will generally differ by household. Thus, an income tax for all households is not necessarily better than an excise or sales tax for all households. For example, a household that does not purchase any of the commodity would prefer an excise or sales tax on that commodity. Second, the income tax may have some negative incentives to work, which might result in households substituting leisure activities for work. Third, there may be a supply response to this excise tax, which would require further investigation for a complete analysis. Specifically, firms may adjust downward their quantity supply of the commodity when faced with an excise or sales tax.

Example 3.7 Taxation and the lump-sum principle

Consider the utility function and budget constraint in Example 3.4. Without any taxation, the optimal consumption levels are $x_1^* = 6$ and $x_2^* = 18$. This results in $U^* = 5\ln 6 + 3\ln 18 = 17.63$. A quantity (excise) tax of \$2 per unit on x_1 will increase the price of x_1 from \$10 to \$12. For utility maximization,

$$\text{MRS}(x_2 \text{ for } x_1) = \frac{\text{MU}_1}{\text{MU}_2} = \frac{5x_2'}{3x_1'} = \frac{p_1 + \tau}{p_2} = \frac{12}{2} = 6.$$

Solving for x_2 yields

$$x_2' = \tfrac{18}{5} x_1'.$$

Substituting into the budget constraint results in

$$96 - 12x_1' - \tfrac{36}{5}x_1' = 0,$$

$$x_1' = 5,\ \ x_2' = 18,\ \ \text{TR}_T = \tau x_1' = \$10,\ \ U' = 16.72.$$

Instead of the excise tax, suppose an income tax of $\text{TR}_T = \$10$ is imposed. The budget constraint is then

$$86 - 10x_1 - 2x_2 = 0.$$

For utility maximization,

$$\text{MRS}(x_2 \text{ for } x_1) = \frac{\text{MU}_1}{\text{MU}_2} = \frac{5x_2''}{3x_1''} = \frac{p_1}{p_2} = \frac{10}{2} = 5.$$

Solving for x_2'' yields

$$x_2'' = 3x_1''.$$

Substituting into the budget constraint results in

$$86 - 10x_1'' - 6x_1'' = 0,$$

$$x_1'' = 5.38, x_2'' = 16.13, \text{TR}_T = \$10, U'' = 16.76.$$

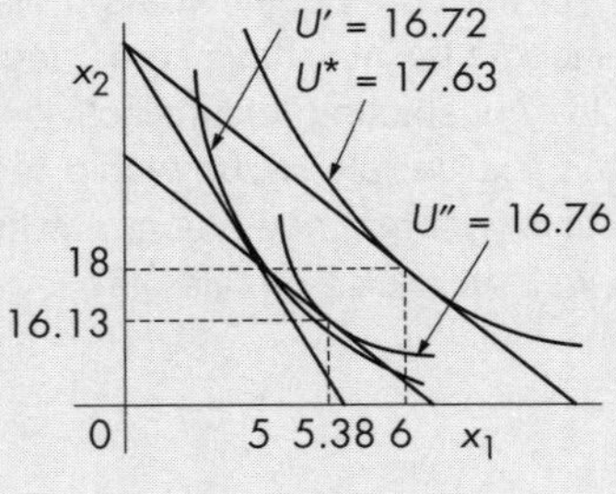

Application: Which is preferable: subsidized price or income?

Cheap bread is no substitute for money.

(Michael Wetzstein)

The argument presented for positive taxes applies to negative taxes (subsidies) as well. As illustrated in Figure 3.12, a general **income subsidy** can be shown to be a more effective way of raising utility than a provision that results in purchasing some commodities at below market prices. A **subsidized price** for commodity x_1, $p_1 - s$, where s is the per-unit level of the subsidy, tilts the budget line outward. This results in the commodity bundle (x_1', x_2') with utility increasing from U^* to U'. However, a direct income subsidy of S dollars, resulting in the household having the same purchasing power, yields a higher level of satisfaction with commodity bundle (x_1'', x_2''), $U'' > U'$.

Why is there a black market for food stamps? By selling food stamps on the black market, households will increase their satisfaction more than using the stamps for food.

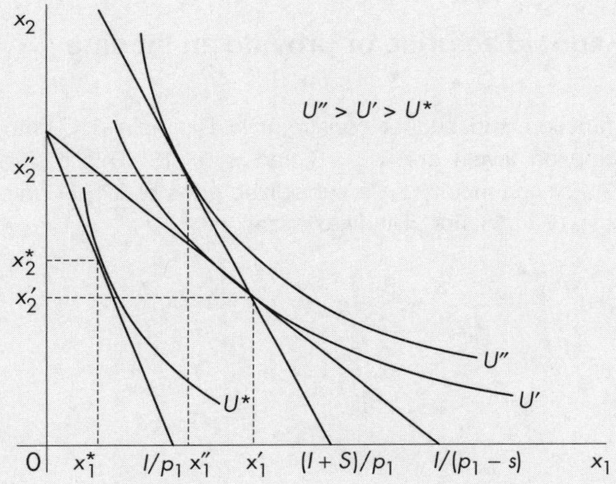

Figure 3.12 **Subsidy.** A household would prefer a general income subsidy yielding utility U'' over a subsidized price for x_1

Income subsidy. Direct cash payment to a household. *E.g., a welfare payment or an agricultural crop deficiency payment.*

Subsidized price. A payment-in-kind reducing the price per unit of a specific commodity. *E.g., food stamps and agricultural export subsidies.*

Similar to a tax, an income subsidy, equivalent to a subsidized price in purchasing power, is determined by

$$I = (p_1 - s)x_1 + p_2x_2$$
$$= p_1x_1 - sx_1 + p_2x_2$$
$$= p_1x_1 - S + p_2x_2,$$
$$I + S = p_1x_1 + p_2x_2.$$

This result—that households generally prefer an income subsidy over a subsidized price—has important policy implications for anti-poverty programs. In recent years, the most rapidly growing programs to aid the poor have been those that provide commodities at subsidized prices (food stamps, subsidized housing, and Medicaid). Our analysis indicates that anti-poverty funds might be more effectively allocated by a greater reliance on direct income grants. However, if an objective of these programs is also to provide incentives for purchasing more of a particular commodity, say food, then a subsidized price for food may possibly be more effective.

Example 3.8 Want to subsidize price or provide an income subsidy?

Consider again the utility function and budget constraint in Example 3.4. With no subsidy, the optimal consumption levels are $x_1^* = 6$ and $x_2^* = 18$. This results in $U^* = 5\ln 6 + 3\ln 18 = 17.63$. For commodity x_1, a subsidized price of \$2 per unit will decrease the price of x_1 from \$10 to \$8. For utility maximization,

$$\text{MRS}(x_2 \text{ for } x_1) = \frac{\text{MU}_1}{\text{MU}_2} = \frac{5x_2'}{3x_1'} = \frac{p_1 - s}{p_2} = \frac{8}{2} = 4.$$

Solving for x_2' yields

$$x_2' = \frac{12}{5}x_1'.$$

Substituting into the budget constraint results in

$$96 - 8x_1' - \frac{24}{5}x_1' = 0,$$

$$x_1' = 7.5,\ x_2' = 18,\ S = sx_1' = \$15,\ U' = 18.75.$$

Instead of the subsidized price, suppose a lump-sum subsidy of $S = \$15$ is imposed. The budget constraint is then

$$111 - 10x_1 - 2x_2 = 0.$$

For utility maximization

$$\text{MRS}(x_2 \text{ for } x_1) = \frac{\text{MU}_1}{\text{MU}_2} = \frac{5x_2''}{3x_1''} = \frac{p_1}{p_2} = \frac{10}{2} = 5.$$

Solving for x_2'' yields

$$x_2'' = 3x_1''.$$

Substituting into the budget constraint results in

$$111 - 10x_1'' - 6x_1'' = 0,$$

$$x_1'' = 6.94, x_2'' = 20.81, U'' = 18.79.$$

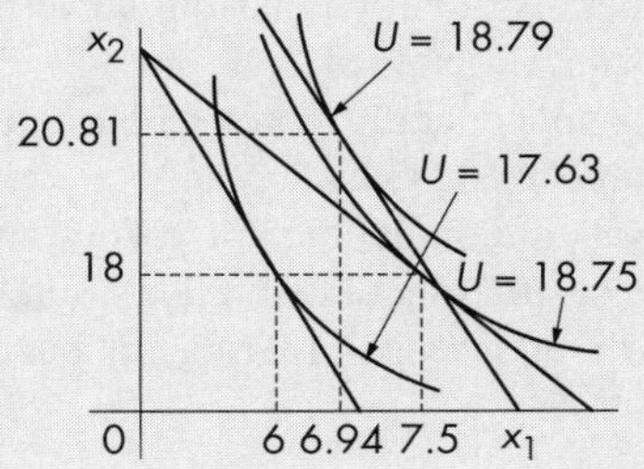

Summary

1. The major determinant of utility maximization is the satisfaction a household receives from a commodity bundle. Unfortunately, the choice of the utility-maximizing bundle is constrained by the budget set.
2. The budget set is the set of all commodity bundles that can be purchased at a given level of income and a fixed set of prices.
3. A boundary of the budget set is the budget line, whose slope measures the opportunity cost of increasing the consumption of one commodity by the resulting decrease in consumption of another commodity.
4. A household will maximize utility for a given budget constraint by shifting to higher indifference curves until the point of tangency is reached between an indifference curve and the budget constraint. At this tangency point, the slope of the indifference curve is equal to the slope of the budget line. The household's utility is then maximized for the given budget constraint. This corresponds to where the marginal rate of substitution is equal to the economic rate of substitution.
5. At the utility-maximizing bundle for a given budget constraint, the marginal utilities per dollar for all commodities that a household purchases are equal. A household is in equilibrium when the last dollar spent on one commodity yields the same additional utility (marginal utility) as the last dollar spent on another commodity.
6. The utility-maximizing conditions can be solved mathematically by using the Lagrangian. This results in the identical tangency condition between the budget line and an indifference curve, with the further result of the marginal utility per dollar of each commodity equaling the Lagrangian multiplier. In this case, the multiplier is the marginal utility of income.
7. An application of utility maximization subject to a budget constraint is government rationing of commodities. Such a mechanism design allocates a fixed quantity

of a commodity to each household. Unfortunately, rationing generally results in decreasing households' satisfaction. This creates incentives for households to enter the black market in order to increase their satisfaction.

8. In terms of increasing households' satisfaction, a purchasing power tax (income tax) is generally more efficient than taxes imposed on individual commodities. No distortions in the market prices occur under a general purchasing power tax, so the utility-maximizing commodity bundle can be obtained.
9. Similar to a tax, a direct income grant (subsidy) will generally increase households' utility more than providing commodities at subsidized prices.
10. *(Appendix)* Revealed preference theory is an alternative to an axiom-based approach for characterizing consumer preference ordering of commodity bundles. Revealed preference determines a household's preference ordering for bundles based on the observed market choices it makes.

Key concepts

Key equations

$$p_1x_1 + p_2x_2 = I$$

Total expenditure is the price per unit of commodity 1 times the amount consumed plus the price per unit of commodity 2 times the amount of commodity 2 consumed. Total expenditure is exhausted if it is equal to the household's income.

$$\text{MRS}(x_2 \text{ for } x_1) = \frac{p_1}{p_2}$$

A condition for maximizing utility subject to a given budget constraint. The marginal rate of substitution is equal to the economic rate of substitution.

$$\frac{MU_1}{p_1} = \frac{MU_2}{p_2} = \ldots = \frac{MU_k}{p_k}$$

When deciding what commodities to spend its income on, a household attempts to equate the marginal utility per dollar for all the commodities it purchases.

Questions

In the beginner's mind there are many possible answers, but in the expert's mind there are few.

(D.T. Suzuki)

1. How does the availability of credit affect a household's budget constraint over a brief period? Over a longer time period?
2. Why is the probability higher that a couple will go to an expensive restaurant if they have to employ a babysitter than if they are childless?
3. What does it cost to sleep through 1 of 50 lectures in a course for which you paid \$3000 in tuition?
4. An advertisement promoting traveling by Greyhound bus stated, "Take a bus and leave the driving to us." Why might it be cheaper to fly instead?
5. After returning home from a supermarket and contemplating the purchases, it is common to consider some purchases as good buys and others as possibly a mistake. What do these thoughts imply about the equilibrium condition of equating marginal utility per dollar for all purchases? Explain.
6. In poor countries, the poor are thin compared with the rich. In contrast, in relatively rich countries the poor tend to be obese and the rich thin. How could this be?
7. In terms of horticulture, even gardeners not formally schooled in the principles of economics know the bottom-line objective is to get as much vegetable output as possible from the seed, fertilizer, water, and labor inputs used in the garden. Is this the correct objective? Explain.
8. It is likely more people would prefer a Lexus over a Camry; however, more people purchase Camrys. True or false? Explain.
9. Assume a household can allocate income among a number of commodities. Is it rational for the household to purchase the quantity of any commodity that will maximize its total utility for that commodity? Explain.
10. Discuss the equilibrium condition of equating the marginal utility per dollar of all commodities. Why will this condition not hold for increasing marginal rate of substitution between two commodities?

Exercises

When I'm working on a problem, I never think about beauty. I think only how to solve the problem. But when I have finished, if the solution is not beautiful, I know it is wrong.

(Buckminster Fuller)

1. Sara is a frequent flyer whose fares are reduced through coupon offerings. She receives a 20% reduction on fares after she flies 20,000 miles a year and a 40%

reduction after she flies 40,000 miles. Illustrate her budget constraint and indicate how her level of utility will change given these frequent-flyer coupons.

2. Assume that the budget line is

$$p_1x_1 + p_2x_2 = I.$$

Suppose the government places an income tax of T and places a quantity tax of τ on commodity x_1 and a subsidy of s on x_2. What does the budget line now look like?

3. Assume $p_1 = \$2$, $p_2 = \$4$, and $I = \$100$. Derive the utility-maximizing consumption bundle for each of the following utility functions:
   a. $U = x_1^4 x_2^4$;
   b. $U = x_1^{1/4} x_2^{1/4}$;
   c. $U = x_1 x_2^2$;
   d. $U = 5x_1 + 3x_2$,
   e. $U = x_1x_2/(x_1 + x_2)$.
   f. $U = \min(x_1, x_2)$.
4. Suppose Sean views butter and margarine as perfect substitutes for each other.
   a. Draw a set of indifference curves that describe Sean's preferences for butter and margarine.
   b. Are these indifference curves strictly convex? Why or why not?
   c. If butter costs \$2 per pound while margarine is only \$1 and Sean has \$10 allocated for their purchases, how much butter and margarine will he purchase? Graphically illustrate the result.
5. Mr Rush has no time for breakfast, so will only have milk, M, and orange juice, O, according to the utility function

$$U(M, O) = M^2 + O^2.$$

Determine Mr Rush's utility-maximizing bundle if $p_M = \$1.00$, $p_O = \$1.50$, with \$6.00 to spend.

6. Assume that an indifference curve for a household consuming x_1 and x_2 can be described by $x_2 = 32/x_1$. Given the budget constraint $x_1 + 2x_2 = 18$, how much of x_1 and x_2 will the household choose to purchase?
7. Demonstrate that an equal percentage tax on all commodities, collecting the same revenue from a household as a lump-sum tax, is identical to the lump-sum tax in terms of household choice.
8. Demonstrate that if food stamps can be resold in a black market, providing food stamps is equivalent to providing a lump-sum grant.
9. Show that if Ms Constrained is forced to spend a fixed amount of income on a particular commodity, her level of utility will be lower than if she could freely allocate her income.
10. A governor wants to subsidize daycare and is considering two proposals. Under Proposal 1, a household would receive a subsidy of s dollars for each day a child

attends a daycare facility. Under Proposal 2, a household with a child in a daycare facility receives a lump-sum subsidy. The state would spend the same amount of money on either proposal. The governor is confronted with conflicting support for each proposal. Daycare providers support Proposal 1, but households with children support Proposal 2. Using indifference curves, show that more daycare would be purchased under Proposal 1, but households' utility would be higher under Proposal 2.

Internet case studies

1. Determine the various methods economists employ for revealing the preferences of agents.
2. Explore the various aids for helping individuals make optimal choices, and relate these aids to the economic theory of utility maximization.
3. Discuss one incidence of rationing in history and the effects it had on a society.
4. Derive a list of all the various governmental subsidies.

APPENDIX TO CHAPTER 3

Revealed preference: observed grocery cart ordering

Tell me what you eat, and I will tell you what you are.

(Anthelme Brillat-Savarin)

Translation: By observing households' purchases, their preference orderings for commodity bundles can be determined.

An alternative approach to the axiom-based utility-maximization hypothesis is the **revealed preference theory**, which is based on market-observable quantities. This observed-market-behavior approach is less epistemological and didactical than the axiom-based approach. Using this choice-based approach, we can uncover households' preferences from observing their market behavior rather than making assumptions on their behavior. For example, the preferences a college student has for alternative bundles of cola and pizza should be revealed by what she actually consumes instead of based on some preference assumptions. Assuming a household's preferences remain unchanged, observing its behavior defines a principle of rationality, which is used to reveal the household's preferences.

In Chapter 3, we figured out how preferences and budget constraints determine choices. In this appendix, the process is reversed. If we know the household's choices, we can figure out its preferences.

Principle of rationality: observing rational choices

The principle of rationality in the revealed preference approach is the relation "is revealed preferred" (denoted $\succ^*$) between pairs of bundles. If a household purchases commodity bundle $\vec{x}^1 = (x_1^1, x_2^1)$ at prices (p_1^1, p_2^1) and given income I^1, when it could have, at these prices and income, purchased another bundle $\vec{x}^2$, then $\vec{x}^1$ is revealed preferred to $\vec{x}^2$. The revealed preference relation is written

$$\vec{x}^1 \succ^* \vec{x}^2,$$

and it indicates that when a household was confronted with two consumption bundles within its budget set, $\vec{x}^1$ was chosen and $\vec{x}^2$ was not, where $\vec{x}^2$ is no more expensive than $\vec{x}^1$. The statement $\vec{x}^2$ is no more expensive than $\vec{x}^1$ at prices (p_1^1, p_2^1) is

$$p_1^1x_1^1 + p_2^1x_2^1 \geq p_1^1x_1^2 + p_2^1x_2^2.$$

Thus, $\vec{x}^1 \succ^* \vec{x}^2$, if $I^1 = p_1^1x_1^1 + p_2^1x_2^1 \geq p_1^1x_1^2 + p_2^1x_2^2$.

The expenditure on $\vec{x}^1$, which was actually purchased at certain prices, is no smaller than the expenditure required at these prices to purchase $\vec{x}^2$. The principle of rationality states that the choices households make are preferred to the choices they could have made. As indicated in Figure 3A.1, the household chose bundle $\vec{x}^1$when it could have purchased bundle $\vec{x}^2$ at prices (p_1^1, p_2^1), $\vec{x}^1 \succ^* \vec{x}^2$. If bundle $\vec{x}^2$ is chosen, at alternative prices (p_1^2, p_2^2) associated with income I^2, $\vec{x}^2 \succ^* \vec{x}^1$, then bundle $\vec{x}^1$ is not affordable. If $\vec{x}^2$ is chosen with income I^3 at prices (p_1^3, p_2^3), then both bundles $\vec{x}^1$ and $\vec{x}^2$ could be purchased, which violates the principle of rationality. Given income I^3, some alternative bundle, say $\vec{x}^3$, will be purchased.

Is your observed market behavior rational? If the choices you make are preferred to the choices you could have made, then your behavior is rational.

Revealed preference then ranks commodity bundles given the household's market choice for various commodity prices and incomes rather than based on some assumed ordering of preferences. In Figure 3A.1, $\vec{x}^3 \succ^* \vec{x}^1$ and $\vec{x}^1 \succ^* \vec{x}^2$, so $\vec{x}^3 \succ^* x^2$. Observing household market choices directly provides information on household preference ordering.

From Figure 3A.1, the violation of the principle of rationality if $\vec{x}^2$ is chosen with I^3 at prices (p_1^3, p_2^3) is stated in the following axiom.

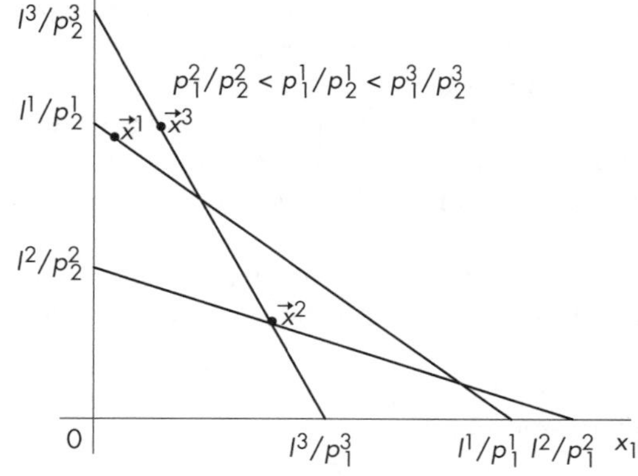

Figure 3A.1 **Revealed preference.** Bundle $\vec{x}^3 \succ^* \vec{x}^1$ and $\vec{x}^1 \succ^* \vec{x}^2$, so $\vec{x}^3 \succ^* \vec{x}^2$.

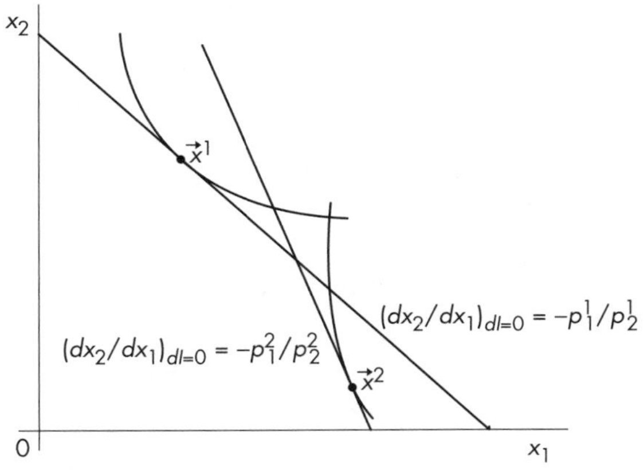

Figure 3A.2 **Weak Axiom of Revealed Preference.** At (p_1^1, p_2^1) a household chose $\vec{x}^1$, so at (p_1^2, p_2^2) it is not possible for the household to choose $\vec{x}^2$.

Weak Axiom of Revealed Preference

If bundle $\vec{x}^1$ is revealed preferred to bundle $\vec{x}^2$, then bundle $\vec{x}^2$ cannot be revealed preferred to bundle $\vec{x}^1$.

Thus, the revealed preferred relation is asymmetric:

$$\vec{x}^1 \succ^* \vec{x}^2 \rightarrow \vec{x}^2 \not\succ^* \vec{x}^1,$$

or

$$p_1^1x_1^1 + p_2^1x_2^1 \geq p_1^1x_1^2 + p_2^1x_2^2 \rightarrow p_1^2x_1^2 + p_2^2x_2^2 < p_1^2x_1^1 + p_2^2x_2^1.$$

This Weak Axiom of Revealed Preference states that if at prices (p_1^1, p_2^1) a household could have purchased $\vec{x}^2$, but instead chose $\vec{x}^1$, then if $\vec{x}^2$ is chosen at prices (p_1^2, p_2^2), it should be impossible at these prices for the household to purchase $\vec{x}^1$. An illustration of how it is impossible for this situation to occur without indifference curves intersecting is depicted in Figure 3A.2. If at prices (p_1^1, p_2^1) a household chose $\vec{x}^1$ and at prices (p_1^2, p_2^2) it instead chose $\vec{x}^2$, then the indifference curves associated with these choices would intersect. Thus, if at prices (p_1^1, p_2^1) a household chose $\vec{x}^1$, it should be impossible at prices (p_1^2, p_2^2), associated with household choice $\vec{x}^2$, to purchase $\vec{x}^1$.

The Weak Axiom of Revealed Preference involves a relationship between two bundles. As illustrated in Figure 3A.1, for preference ordering of bundles, transitivity is required among a set of bundles. Explicitly this transitivity assumption is stated in the following axiom:

Strong Axiom of Revealed Preference

If bundle $\vec{x}^1$ is revealed preferred to bundle $\vec{x}^2$, bundle $\vec{x}^2$ is revealed preferred to $\vec{x}^3$, …, bundle $\vec{x}^{k-1}$ is revealed preferred to bundle $\vec{x}^k$, then bundle $\vec{x}^k$ cannot be revealed preferred to $\vec{x}^1$:

$$\vec{x}^1 \succ^* \vec{x}^2, \vec{x}^2 \succ^* \vec{x}^3, \ldots, x^{k-1} \succ^* \vec{x}^k, \text{ then } \vec{x}^k \not\succ^* x^1.$$

This axiom implies the Weak Axiom of Revealed Preference when $k = 2$. If observed behavior by a household is rational so the household is maximizing utility, it must satisfy the Strong Axiom of Revealed Preference. This axiom provides a foundation for utility-maximization theory based on comparisons of observed market behavior of households. With market behavior as the foundation of revealed preference, behavior as a basis for individual decision making provides an alternative to introspection of a household's rationality.

Example 3A.1 Observed market behavior satisfying the Weak Axiom of Revealed Preference

Consider the following three observed consumption patterns for a household faced with alternative sets of prices:

Observation	*Prices*		*Commodities*		*Expenditures*		
	p_1	p_2	x_1	x_2	$\vec{x}^1$	$\vec{x}^2$	$\vec{x}^3$
1	1	1	3	3	6	4*	5*
2	1	2	3	1	9	5	8
3	2	1	2	3	9	7*	7

We determine expenditures by calculating total expenditures for each commodity bundle at each of the three sets of prices. For example, expenditure for bundle $\vec{x}^1$ at observed prices 1 is $6 = 1(3) + 1(3)$. Alternatively, expenditure for bundle $\vec{x}^1$ at prices 2 is $9 = 1(3) + 2(3)$. The diagonal elements under the expenditure columns ($6, $5, and $7) are the actual expenditures a household incurs at each observed price. The off-diagonal elements under the expenditure columns are the expenditures a household would have incurred if it purchased an alternative bundle.

To determine a household's revealed preference for the three alternative bundles, we compare the expenditures actually incurred (the diagonal elements) with the two off-diagonal elements in the same row. For example, in the first row, at observed prices 1, the expenditure actually incurred is $6 for bundle $\vec{x}^1$. Instead of purchasing bundle $\vec{x}^1$, the household could have purchased bundles $\vec{x}^2$ and $\vec{x}^3$, with an expenditure of $4 for $\vec{x}^2$ and $5 for $\vec{x}^3$. Thus, bundle $\vec{x}^1$ is revealed preferred to both bundles $\vec{x}^2$ and $\vec{x}^3$. An asterisk next to the expenditures for bundles $\vec{x}^2$ and $\vec{x}^3$ at price 1 indicates this revealed preference. Similarly, at observed prices 3, the expenditure for bundle $\vec{x}^2$ is equal to the expenditure for the purchased bundle $\vec{x}^3$, so bundle $\vec{x}^3 \succ^* \vec{x}^2$. Bundle $\vec{x}^1$ with an expenditure of $9 could not be purchased with the actual expenditure of $7 for $\vec{x}^3$ at price 3. Thus, $\vec{x}^3$ is not revealed preferred to $\vec{x}^1$. For observed price 2, both the alternative bundles $\vec{x}^1$ and $\vec{x}^3$ require expenditures in excess of purchased bundle $\vec{x}^2$, so $\vec{x}^2$ is not revealed preferred to either bundle $\vec{x}^1$ or $\vec{x}^3$.

If a household's preferences are asymmetric, the Weak Axiom of Revealed Preference is satisfied. In the example, preferences are asymmetric if the asterisks are asymmetric, where an asterisk in say row *i* column *j* does not result in an asterisk in row *j* column *i* of the expenditure columns. For example, an asterisk is in row 1 column 2 but not in row 2 column 1 of the expenditure columns, so $\vec{x}^1 \succ^* \vec{x}^2$ and $\vec{x}^2 \not\succ^* \vec{x}^1$. Similarly, an asterisk is in row 1 column 3, but not in row 3 column 1, so $\vec{x}^1 \succ^* \vec{x}^3$ and $\vec{x}^3 \not\succ^* \vec{x}^1$. Also, there is an asterisk in row 3 column 2 but not in row 2 column 3, so $\vec{x}^3 \succ^* \vec{x}^2$ and $\vec{x}^2 \not\succ^* \vec{x}^3$.

Thus, the observed market behavior of this household does satisfy the Weak Axiom of Revealed Preference, so, by this axiom, the household is considered rational and attempts to maximize utility by choosing utility-maximizing bundles.

Example 3A.2 A violation of the Weak Axiom of Revealed Preference

Consider a change in the three observed consumption patterns for a household presented in Example 3A.1:

Observation	*Prices*		*Commodities*		*Expenditures*		
	p_1	p_2	x_1	x_2	$\vec{x}^1$	$\vec{x}^2$	$\vec{x}^3$
1	1	1	~~3~~2	3	5	4*	5*
2	1	2	3	1	8	5	8
3	2	1	2	3	7*	7*	7

As a result of this change, the expenditures for the three commodity bundles change along with the household's revealed preference for the bundles. Symmetry now exists with one of the paired off-diagonal elements, so the Weak Axiom of Revealed Preference is violated. Specifically, row 1 column 3 and row 3 column 1 of the expenditure columns both have an asterisk. This implies $\vec{x}^1 \succ^* \vec{x}^3$ and $\vec{x}^3 \succ^* \vec{x}^1$, which violates the axiom. An irrational circular preference pattern exists.

Example 3A.3 Using the Strong Axiom of Revealed Preference to order bundles

From Example 3A.1, the household's preference ordering for the bundles is transitive:

$$\vec{x}^1 \succ^* \vec{x}^3, \vec{x}^3 \succ^* \vec{x}^2, \text{ and } \vec{x}^1 \succ^* \vec{x}^2,$$

which is consistent with the Strong Axiom of Revealed Preference. In contrast, in Example 3A.2, the household's preferences are not transitive, which violates the Strong Axiom of Revealed Preference.

Questions

1. If you observed a household choosing consumption bundle A when B is available, can you conclude that bundle A is revealed preferred to B?
2. Are indifference curves with linear segments consistent with the Weak Axiom of Revealed Preference?
3. Suppose Brian chose to dine at a different restaurant each night. Assuming prices remain constant along with Brian's income, does Brian's choice violate the Strong Axiom of Revealed Preference?

Exercises

1. Hazel is consuming two commodities x_1 and x_2. When $p_1 = 4$ and $p_2 = 8$, she consumes $x_1 = 1$ and $x_2 = 2$ of the commodities. When the prices are $p_1 = 12$ and $p_2 = 6$, she consumes $x_1 = 2$ and $x_2 = 1$ of the commodities. Is Hazel rational and attempting to maximizing utility? Explain.
2. Consider the following partial information concerning Andrea purchasing two commodities:

Commodity	*Year 1*		*Year 2*	
	Quantity	*Price*	*Quantity*	*Price*
1	50	50	60	50
2	50	50	?	40

   Over what range of quantities of commodity 2 consumed in year 2 would you conclude her behavior violates the Weak Axiom of Revealed Preference?
3. Sara is observed to purchase $x_1 = 40$, $x_2 = 20$ at prices $p_1 = 4$ and $p_2 = 12$. She is also observed to purchase $x_1 = 36$, $x_2 = 8$ at prices $p_1 = 6$ and $p_2 = 10$. Are her preferences consistent with the Weak Axiom of Revealed Preference?
4. Mark's entire food budget is spent on cereal and milk. Based on two weeks of consumption, determine if his preferences are consistent with utility maximization.

	Week 1	*Week 2*
Price of milk	2	3
Price of cereal	3	6
Consumption of milk	6	5
Consumption of cereal	9	10

5. Over a three-year period, the Young household reveals the following consumption behavior:

Year	p_1	p_2	x_1	x_2
1	3	3	7	3
2	4	2	5	4
3	5	1	6	5

Is the Youngs' behavior consistent with the Strong Axiom of Revealed Preference?

4 Comparative statics

Analysis of individual demand and labor supply

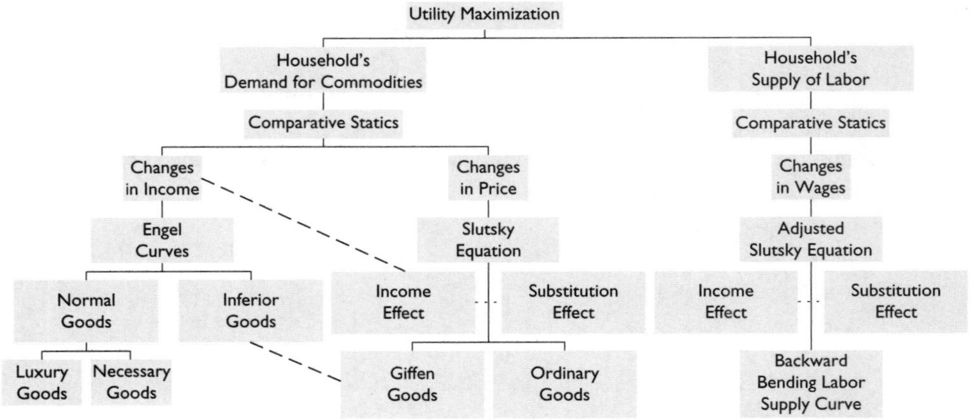

Outline and Conceptual Inquiries

Deriving household demand
Shifting demand versus a change in quantity demanded
How to invert demand curves
Is quantity dependent on price or is price dependent on quantity?
Application: How to bid on eBay
Generalizing to k commodities

Understanding comparative statics
What are homogeneous of degree zero demand functions?
Do you have money illusion?
Application: Do criminals suffer from money illusion?
Changing income
What kind of preferences do deeply religious individuals have?
How do you measure poverty?
Changing price
When the price of a commodity decreases, why do you consume more of it?
Giffen's paradox: homeless alcoholic
Application: Why did Marshall introduce Giffen's paradox?
Why consider compensated price changes?
Should your grandmother receive the full cost of living increase in her monthly Social Security check?
Application: Consider a gas tax with an income tax rebate
How do we decrease our dependence on foreign oil?
Changing the price of another commodity

Summary
Key concepts
Key equations
Questions
Exercises
Internet case studies

Appendix to chapter 4

How the Slutsky equation relates to the household's supply of labor
Considering both time and income constraints
Is time a constraint on happiness?
Doing utility maximization
Understanding substitution and income effects
Using the adjusted Slutsky equation
Deriving household's supply-of-labor curve
Given a wage increase, will you always work more?
Application: Empirical estimates of an income/leisure indifference function
Questions
Exercises
Internet case study

When I hear somebody sigh, "life is hard," I am always tempted to ask, "compared to what?".

(Sydney J. Harris)

In the Looney Tunes cartoon the *Road Runner*, Wile E. Coyote is never quite able to catch Road Runner. Something always happens that prevents his capture. Like Wile E. Coyote, rational households in their effort to find local bliss by maximizing utility for a given level of income and a fixed set of prices are never quite able to make it. Ever-changing prices and income require households to continuously adjust their commodity bundle. We can study these changes by comparing one utility-maximizing equilibrium with another. This comparison, called **comparative statics analysis**, investigates a change in some parameters, holding everything else constant, including preferences (***ceteris paribus***). With preferences constant, individual indifference curves remain fixed, and comparative statics investigates the effects of shifting the budget constraint by changing its parameters (income and prices). Comparative statics is not concerned with *dynamics*—the movement from one equilibrium position to the next. Instead, comparative statics analysis investigates the sensitivity of a solution to changes in the parameters. The question of why a parameter changes—for example, why a price increases—will be addressed in subsequent chapters. In terms of comparative statics, the statement "life is hard" does not provide much information. The relative relationship of life now compared with life at another point in time or place would be more informative.

Comparative statics analysis. Investigating a change in one parameter, holding all other parameters constant. *E.g., a cook developing a new recipe by changing one ingredient and comparing the taste to the original recipe.*

Ceteris paribus. With all other factors remaining the same. *E.g., changing only your lipstick and not the rest of your makeup.*

In this chapter, we use a comparative statics framework to investigate a change in one commodity's price. This enables us to derive a household's demand curve for each commodity and to illustrate such curves for alternative household preferences. We then investigate a change in income, holding all prices constant, and develop *Engel curves* and *Engel's Law* associated with income changes. Based on the shapes (slopes) of demand and Engel curves, commodities are generally classified as normal, luxury, or inferior goods, in terms of an income change, and ordinary or Giffen for a price change. We then discuss how the *Slutsky equation* considers the total effect of a price change as shown to be the sum of a substitution effect and an income effect. Using the Slutsky equation, we illustrate the theoretical possibility of a positively sloping demand curve (called *Giffen's paradox*).

We discuss the use of the Slutsky equation to measure compensated price changes (price changes holding utility or purchasing power constant) and the *Laspeyres index* to measure the Consumer Price Index (CPI). We then extend the Slutsky equation to changes in the price of another commodity. In this discussion, we develop the concepts of gross and net substitutes and gross and net complements.

In the appendix to this chapter, we derive a household's labor supply curve and discuss the adjusted Slutsky equation associated with this labor function. The income and substitution effects given a change in wages determine the slope of a household's labor supply curve.

Our objective in this chapter is to derive a household's demand functions for the commodities it purchases and its labor supply function. Intuitively, quantity demanded should generally decline as the price of a commodity increases and demand should generally increase with a rise in income. We investigate the underlying determinants for this response of quantity demanded for a change in the price and income parameters. In terms of labor supply, the determinants of a household's supply of labor given a rise in wages may result in supply increasing, declining, or remaining unchanged. With an understanding of how household demand for commodities and supply of labor are derived, we can develop the aggregate (market) demand and supply. These market supply and demand functions will provide a foundation for investigating the efficient allocation of society's resources.

Applied economists do estimate consumer demand and labor supply functions for determining how responsive consumers and labor are to changes in prices, wages, incomes, sales promotion, and various governmental programs. Consumer demand is a very large area in economics—some universities even have a separate consumer economics department. Labor economics is also a large area, where the impacts of government welfare programs, working conditions, exploitation, immigration, and unions are extensively studied.

Deriving household demand

To attract students to their bar on a week night, the owners will reduce the prices of drinks. This decline in price results in an increase in the quantity demanded by students. A student's quantity demanded is based on his or her preferences, limited resources (income), and the prices for drinks. With indifference curves representing preferences and budget lines as income constraints, we can derive a theoretical relation between price and a student's quantity demanded. Consider the case of a price change in one of two commodities x_1 and x_2, which could be drinks and entertainment, beef and pork, food and clothing, or any other set of commodities. The budget line is then

$$I = p_1x_1 + p_2x_2,$$

where I, p_1, and p_2 represent income, per unit price of commodity 1 and per unit price of commodity 2, respectively. For example, if $I = 10$, $p_1 = 2$, and $p_2 = 1$, then the budget line is

$$10 = 2x_1 + x_2,$$

with a slope

$$\left.\frac{dx_2}{dx_1}\right|_{dI=0} = -\frac{p_1}{p_2} = -2.$$

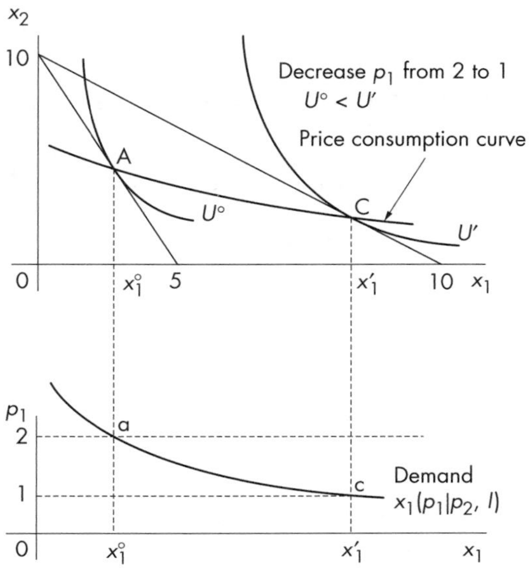

Figure 4.1 **Derived demand for a decrease in p_1.** Decreasing the price of x_1 from $p_1 = 2$ to $p_1 = 1$ results in a new equilibrium point C with an increase in the consumption of x_1.

A graph of this budget line is represented in Figure 4.1 with an x_1 intercept of 5 units and an x_2 intercept of 10 units. A household maximizes its utility for a given level of income, 10, at a point on the budget line tangent with an indifference curve (commodity bundle A). This equilibrium bundle (at a given income level and prices) corresponds to one point on the household's demand curve (point a). Additional points on the household's demand curve for x_1 are obtained by changing the price of commodity x_1 while holding income and price of x_2 constant. For example, decreasing the price of x_1 from 2 to 1 ($p_1 = 1$) results in the budget line tilting outward. The slope of the budget line is now

$$\left.\frac{dx_2}{dx_1}\right|_{dI=0} = -\frac{p_1}{p_2} = -1,$$

with intercepts of 10 units for both the x_1 and x_2 axes. With this new price for p_1, commodity bundle C represents the new equilibrium level of utility maximization, for a given \$10 of income, and a new point on the household's demand curve (point c).

Further changes in p_1 will result in additional tangencies of a budget line with an indifference curve and a corresponding point on the household's demand curve. Connecting all these points results in the **household's demand curve** for commodity x_1. Each point on the demand curve corresponds with a point of tangency between an indifference curve and a budget line. Specifically, at each point on the demand curve, the household is maximizing utility for a given income level and the market price of commodity x_1. Each point on a household's demand curve illustrates how much of the commodity a household is willing and able to purchase at a given price. For example, at a price of $p_1 = 2$ with $p_2 = 1$, the household is willing and able to purchase x_1° units of commodity x_1. When the price p_1

declines to $p_1 = 1$ with the price of p_2 remaining unchanged at 1, the household is willing and able to increase its purchases of x_1 to x_1'.

Example 4.1 How to derive demand functions from a household's utility-maximization problem

Consider again the following problem from Example 3.4:

$$\max_{(x_1,\, x_2)} U(x_1, x_2) = \max(5 \ln x_1 + 3 \ln x_2), \quad \text{s.t. } I = p_1 x_1 + p_2 x_2.$$

Based on this utility function, we derive the household's demand functions by forming the Lagrangian:

$$\mathcal{L}(x_1, x_2, \lambda) = 5 \ln x_1 + 3 \ln x_2 + \lambda(I - p_1 x_1 - p_2 x_2).$$

The first-order conditions (FOCs) are then

$$\frac{\partial \mathcal{L}}{\partial x_1} = \frac{5}{x_1^*} - p_1 \lambda^* = 0,$$

$$\frac{\partial \mathcal{L}}{\partial x_2} = \frac{3}{x_2^*} - p_2 \lambda^* = 0,$$

$$\frac{\partial \mathcal{L}}{\partial \lambda} = I - p_1 x_1^* - p_2 x_2^* = 0.$$

From the first two FOCs, we have

$$\text{MRS}(x_2 \text{ for } x_1) = \frac{5x_2^*}{3x_1^*} = \frac{p_1}{p_2}.$$

Solving for x_2 results in the income expansion path

$$x_2^* = \frac{3}{5} \frac{p_1}{p_2} x_1^*.$$

This reduces the problem down to two equations (the income expansion path and the budget constraint). Substituting the income expansion path into the budget constraint (the third FOC) yields the demand function for x_1:

$$p_1 x_1^* + p_2 \frac{3}{5} \frac{p_1}{p_2} x_1^* = I,$$

$$p_1 x_1^* \left(1 + \frac{3}{5}\right) = I,$$

$$\frac{8}{5} p_1 x_1^* = I,$$

$$x_1^* = \frac{5I}{8p_1}, \text{ the demand function for } x_1.$$

Taking the partial derivative of this demand function with respect to its own price p_1,

$$\frac{\partial x_1}{\partial p_1} = -\frac{5I}{8p_1^2} < 0,$$

which indicates a negatively sloping demand curve. The second derivative,

$$\frac{\partial^2 x_1}{\partial p_1^2} = \frac{5I}{4p_1^3} > 0,$$

indicates that the demand function is convex. If $I = 80$, then at $p_1 = 1$, $x_1^* = 50$, and at $p_1 = 2$, $x_1^* = 25$.

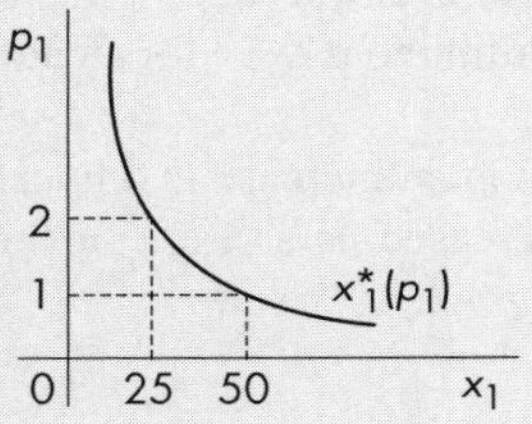

Substituting this demand function for x_1 into either the budget constraint or the income expansion path yields the demand function for x_2:

$$x_2^* = \frac{3I}{8p_2}, \text{ the demand function for } x_2.$$

For these demand functions, there are no cross-price effects. Demand for x_1 is not a function of p_2 and demand for x_2 is not a function of p_1. This implies that commodities in the household's utility function are independent. For example, a price change in x_2 does not affect the quantity demanded of x_1. Such an assumption for household preferences would generally be unrealistic. However, a more realistic assumption for household preferences would involve complicating the solution and possibly making an analytical solution impossible. Also, note that the demand functions are homogeneous of degree zero in prices and income. Doubling of all prices and income will leave the quantities demanded unchanged.

We can derive the Lagrange multiplier λ^* by substituting the demand function for x_1 into the first FOC:

$$\frac{5}{5I/8p_1} - p_1\lambda^* = 0,$$

$$\lambda^* = \frac{8}{I}.$$

As income increases, λ^* decreases. This implies that diminishing marginal utility of income is represented by this utility function. As a household's income increases, the additional satisfaction received from an additional increase in income declines.

Household's demand curve. A curve illustrating how much of a commodity a household is willing and able to purchase at a given price. *E.g., when the price for bananas drops, you move down along your demand curve for bananas and are willing and able to purchase more bananas.*

From Figure 4.1, at $p_1 = 2$ associated with $x_1 = x_1^\circ$, the MRS(x_2 for x_1) = 2, so the household is willing to give up 2 units of x_2 for 1 additional unit of x_1. Specifically, the household is willing to pay 2 units of x_2 for 1 additional unit of x_1. The price per unit of x_2 is \$1, so the cost of 2 units of x_2 is \$2. Thus, the household is willing to pay \$2 for an additional unit of x_1. Note that as the price p_1 declines, the household's MRS(x_2 for x_1) declines, so how much it is willing to pay for an additional unit of x_1 also declines. For example, at $p_1 = 1$ associated with $x_1 = x_1'$, MRS(x_2 for x_1) = 1, so the household is only willing to pay \$1 for an additional unit of x_1.

Also, as illustrated in Figure 4.1, a decline in price results in an increase in a household's level of utility. The household's purchasing power has increased as a result of this price decline, which enhances the household's satisfaction.

Example 4.2 How to derive demand for a household with perfect substitutes as preferences

Returning to Example 3.2, with utility function $U = 5x_1 + 3x_2$, the household will only consume commodity x_1 as long as the marginal utility per dollar for commodity x_1 remains greater than the marginal utility per dollar for commodity x_2. In this case, the household's income expansion path is the x_1 axis represented by the equation $x_2 = 0$. We then derive the household's demand function for x_1 by substituting this income expansion path into the budget constraint:

$$p_1x_1 + p_2 0 = I.$$

Solving for x_1 results in the demand function for x_1, $x_1^* = I/p_1$. Technically, and for completeness, the demand function for x_2 is $x_2^* = 0$.

With $p_2 = 3$ and $I = 96$, $p_1 > 5$ results in $x_1 = 0$ and the household will only consume x_2. At $p_1 = 5$, the household is indifferent between purchasing x_1 or x_2, and at $p_1 < 5$, the household's demand for x_1 is $x_1 = I/p_1$.

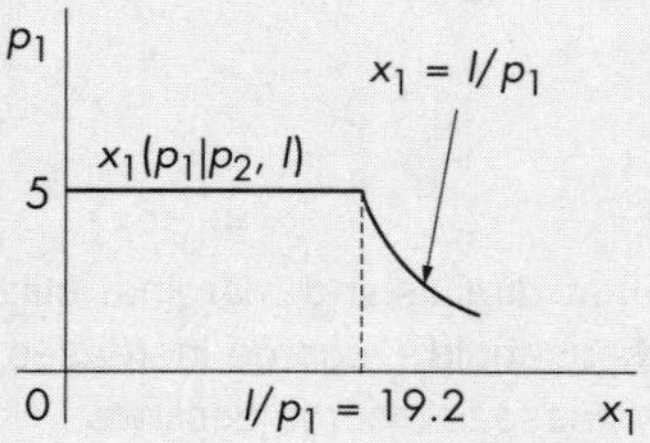

Example 4.3 How to derive demand for a household with perfect complements as preferences

Consider the case of perfect complements in Example 3.5 with $U = \min(4x_1, 3x_2)$. The income expansion path is $x_2 = \frac{4}{3}x_1$. Substituting this expansion path into the budget constraint and solving for x_1 yields the demand function for x_1:

$$p_1 x_1 + p_2\left(\frac{4}{3}x_1\right) = I,$$

$$x_1^* = \frac{I}{p_1 + \frac{4}{3}p_2}.$$

Substituting this demand function into the expansion path or the budget constraint yields the demand function for x_2:

$$x_2^* = \frac{I}{\frac{3}{4}\,p_1 + p_2}.$$

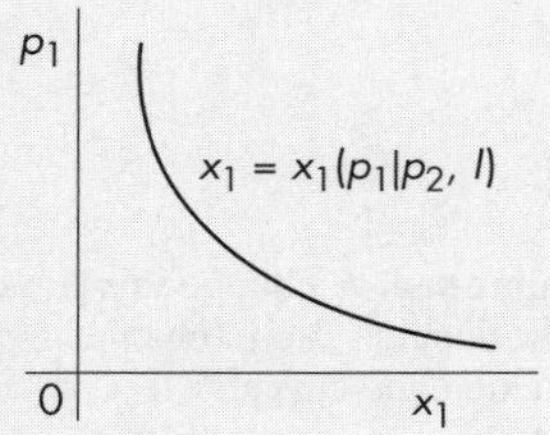

Shifting demand versus a change in quantity demanded

Beware of the man who will not be bothered with details.

(William Feather)

It is convenient to graph x_1 as a function of its own price p_1, with the understanding that income and all other prices are being held constant. As illustrated in Figure 4.1, assuming two commodities and considering a change in p_1, the demand function for x_1 is

$$x_1 = x_1(p_1|p_2, I),$$

where quantities to the right of the bar, p_2 and I in this case, are held constant. By varying p_1, the *price consumption curve* traces out the locus of tangencies between the budget line and the indifference curve. A negatively sloped demand curve can be derived from this price consumption curve, where a decrease in p_1 will result in an increase in quantity demanded (a movement along the demand curve). Alternatively, a change in p_2 or I will shift the demand curve. This difference in a change in quantity demanded versus a shift in demand is illustrated in Figure 4.2. At bundle A, a decrease in p_2 from p_2° to p_2' results in a movement

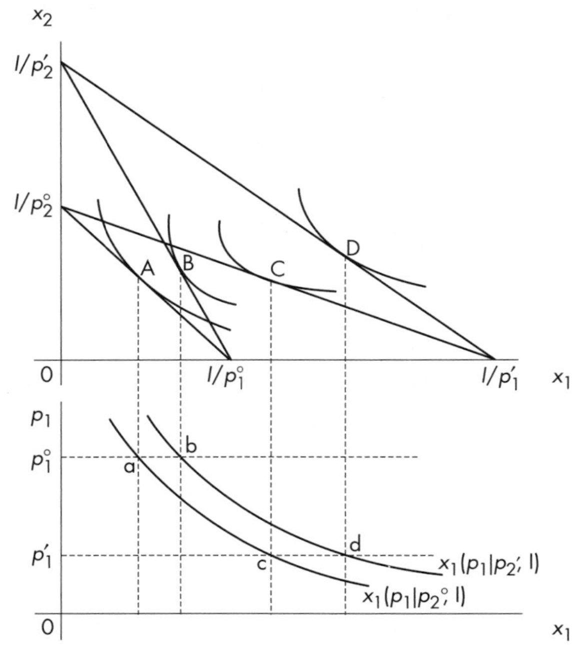

Figure 4.2 **Shift in demand versus change in quantity demanded.** A change in p_1, measured on the vertical axis, results in a movement along the demand curve (change in quantity demanded). A change in p_2 results in a shift in the demand curve.

from bundle A to B, which shifts the demand curve. This shift is depicted as a shift from point a on the demand curve $x_1(p_1 | p_2^\circ, I)$ to point b on $x_1(p_1 | p_2', I)$. In contrast, a decrease in p_1 from p_1° to p_1', at bundle A, results in a movement from bundle A to C. This causes a movement along the demand curve $x_1(p_1 | p_2^\circ, I)$ from point a to c, a change in quantity demanded. Similarly, at bundle C, a decrease in p_2 from p_2° to p_2' shifts the demand curve from point c on $x_1(p_1 | p_2^\circ, I)$ to point d on $x_1(p_1 | p_2', I)$.

In general, the two variables measured on the axes (p_1 and x_1 in Figures 4.1 and 4.2) are allowed to vary, and all other factors (p_2 and I) are held constant (*ceteris paribus*). A change in either of the variables on the axes causes a movement along a curve; whereas, any change in a factor not measured on one of the axes causes a shift in the curve. For example, a change in income or preferences will shift a demand curve.

How to invert demand curves

The demand functions depicted in Figures 4.1 and 4.2 are sometimes called **inverse demand functions** because generally the dependent variable is on the vertical axis and the independent variable is on the horizontal axis. Price as the dependent variable states what the level of quantity demanded for a commodity would have to be for the household to be willing to pay this price per unit. It reflects a household's *marginal willingness to pay*—the maximum price a household would be willing to pay for an extra unit of the commodity. For example, in auctions (see Chapter 13), the price is dependent on the quantity demanded of a commodity. A single item would generally go for a higher per-unit price than a lot containing 100 of the items. Thus, inverse demand functions represent price as a function of quantity demanded as opposed to quantity demanded as a function of price (depicted in **direct demand functions**). Inverse demand functions and direct demand functions provide different perspectives on the same relation of household-maximizing behavior. Thus, it will generally be recognized the axes are just reversed and the meaning of Figures 4.1 and 4.2 is quantity demanded as a function of price.

Is quantity dependent on price or is price dependent on quantity? If the price per unit a consumer receives for a commodity is fixed, then quantity demanded is dependent on this fixed price.

Inverse demand functions. Price per unit is a function of quantity demanded. *E.g., purchasing a larger quantity of laundry detergent results in a lower per-unit price.*

Direct demand functions. Quantity demanded is a function of price. *E.g., the price of apples determines the quantity you will purchase.*

Application: How to bid on eBay

The auction site eBay works by incrementally increasing the price of an item. For example, if the current price is \$5 and you place a bid of \$15, the price will not adjust upward to \$15. Instead, the price will adjust upward by some increment that is determined by eBay. So your \$15 bid will result in the price increasing to \$5 plus the increment. If no one else bids, then you will receive the item for \$5 plus the increment. If another bid is received below \$15, the price will increase to this other bid plus the increment and you will still be the highest bidder, and with no other bids you will receive the item at this other bid price plus the increment. If the other bid exceeds your \$15 bid, then with no other bids the other bidder will receive the item for \$15 plus the increment. The utility-maximizing strategy is to then bid your maximum willingness to pay plus some small amount. You will then be guaranteed to receive the item at or below your willingness to pay. For example, if your willingness to pay is \$15, then bid \$15.15. If the next highest bid plus the increment is \$15, you will win the auction and pay \$15. This is a called a *second-bid auction* (see the Appendix to Chapter 13)

Generalizing to k commodities

In general, from the FOCs for maximizing utility, we can solve for the optimal levels of $x_1^*, x_2^*, \ldots, x_k^*$, and λ^* as functions of all the parameters (prices and income). The quantities of $x_1, x_2, \ldots, x_k$ demanded by the household will depend on the shape of the utility function (consumer preferences) and on $p_1, p_2, \ldots, p_k$ and I. Mathematically, the demand functions are represented as

$$\begin{aligned} x_1 &= x_1(p_1, p_2, \ldots, p_k, I), \\ x_2 &= x_2(p_1, p_2, \ldots, p_k, I), \\ &\vdots \\ x_k &= x_k(p_1, p_2, \ldots, p_k, I). \end{aligned}$$

Demand functions state how much a household is willing and able to consume of a commodity at given prices and income. Given the demand functions for $x_1, x_2, \ldots, x_k$ and values for $p_1, p_2, \ldots, p_k$, and I, the amount of each commodity that a household will purchase can be determined.

Understanding comparative statics

> *Comparative statics could be frightening when comparing your waistline before and after the holidays.*
>
> (Michael Wetzstein)

Comparative statics associated with a household's demand function for x_1 investigates what happens to x_1 when prices and/or income change.

What are homogeneous of degree zero demand functions?

In many developing countries (such as Brazil) the history of high rates of inflation has resulted in price and income indexing. For example, if inflation is running at 10 percent annually, then incomes are automatically adjusted (indexed) upward by 10 percent. This keeps households' purchasing power the same, and, assuming no money illusion (where purchasing power is the same for an increase in income and prices, but the household is under the illusion of increased purchasing power), does not change their demands for commodities. To understand why there is no change in households' demands; consider the effect on the budget constraint when all prices and income change proportionately. As illustrated in Figure 4.3, if all prices and income are doubled (or multiplied by some positive constant), the optimal quantities demanded would remain unchanged. Specifically, considering the budget constraint

$$p_1x_1 + p_2x_2 = I,$$

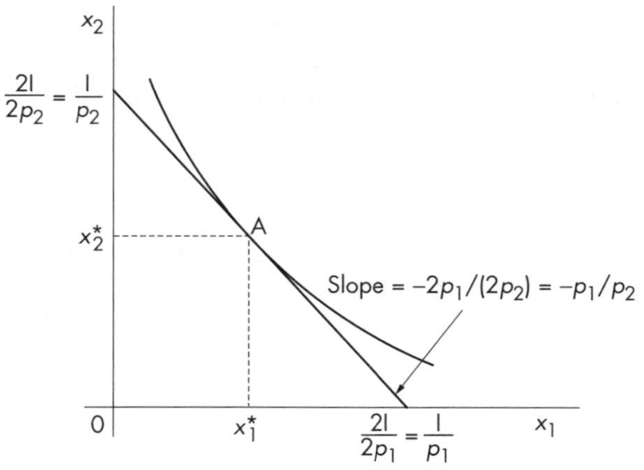

Figure 4.3 **Homogeneity of demand functions.** Multiplying prices and income by some positive constant, for example 2, does not change the budget set or the amount demanded.

if all prices and income are doubled, the new budget constraint is

$$2p_1x_1 + 2p_2x_2 = 2I,$$

which is equivalent to the first constraint. The slope and intercepts of the budget constraint do not change. Generally, if prices and income are multiplied by some positive constant α, the same budget constraint remains:

$$\alpha p_1x_1 + \alpha p_2x_2 = \alpha I \Rightarrow \frac{\alpha p_1x_1}{\alpha} + \frac{\alpha p_2x_2}{\alpha} = \frac{\alpha I}{\alpha} \Rightarrow p_1x_1 + p_2x_2 = I.$$

Given no change in the budget constraint from multiplying prices and income by $\alpha > 0$, the quantity demanded by a household will also not change:

$$x_j = x_j(\alpha p_1, \alpha p_2, \ldots, \alpha p_k, \alpha I) = x_j(p_1, p_2, \ldots, p_k, I) \quad \text{for all } \alpha > 0 \text{ and } j = 1, \ldots, k.$$

This type of function is called *homogeneous of degree zero*. In this case, consumer demand functions are homogeneous of degree zero in all prices and income. Household demands are not affected by pure inflation. For example, a household does not experience the illusion of increased purchasing power when a doubling of income corresponds with a doubling of prices.

Do you have money illusion? Assuming a commodity cost the same in the United States and France, if you purchase more of the commodity in France because the exchange rate results in more of the foreign currency, then you have money illusion.

Application: Do criminals suffer from money illusion?

S. Cameron investigated the hypothesis that one reason for increases in crime is criminals have money illusion. This hypothesis is tested by determining if criminal activity increases with a rise in prices. Criminal activity is assumed to be a form of labor supply generating income. If criminals did not suffer from money illusion, then as prices increase there should be no associated increase in crime. A rise in prices would be reflected in the value of property stolen.

As a test of this hypothesis, Cameron related the supply of crime to an index of prices in a multivariable regression equation. For theft and auto-theft, the results indicate rejecting the null hypothesis of no money illusion at the 5 percent significance level. Thus, one explanation of increased criminal activity may be that criminals do suffer from money illusion.*

Source: S. Cameron, "Do Criminals Suffer from Money Illusion?" *Rivista Internazionale di Scienze Economiche e Commerciali* 39 (1992): 457–466.

* Risk-loving (seeking) has also been advanced as an argument for committing a crime (see Chapter 18).

Numeraire price

A useful result of homogeneous of degree zero demand functions is that we can divide all prices and income by one of the prices. Then the demand for a commodity depends on price ratios (called *relative prices*) and the ratio of money income to a price (called *real income*). Specifically, picking any price, say p_1, and multiplying the demand function by $1/p_1$ results in

$$x_j = x_j(p_1, p_2, \ldots, p_k, I) = x_j(1, p_2/p_1, \ldots, p_k/p_1, I/p_1),$$

where α in this case is $1/p_1$. This has the effect of setting $p_1 = 1$, which is the relative price with which all the other prices and income are compared (called the **numeraire price**).

Numeraire price. The relative price with which all other prices and income are compared. *E.g., the price of a standard computer system, where additions, deletions, and upgrades are all compared with this price.*

Changing income

What is a recent economics graduate's usual question in his first job?
"What would you like to have with your French fries sir?".

(Pasi Kuopamäki)

A college graduate's income will generally substantially increase upon landing that first professional job. This change in income I, holding all prices fixed, results in a change in the graduate's purchasing power. As indicated in Figure 4.4, an increase in income will result in an expected increase in purchases. This is represented by parallel shifts in the budget lines. Only I has changed, so the price ratio remains constant. A curve intersecting all points where the indifference curves are tangent with the budget lines (the locus of utility-maximizing

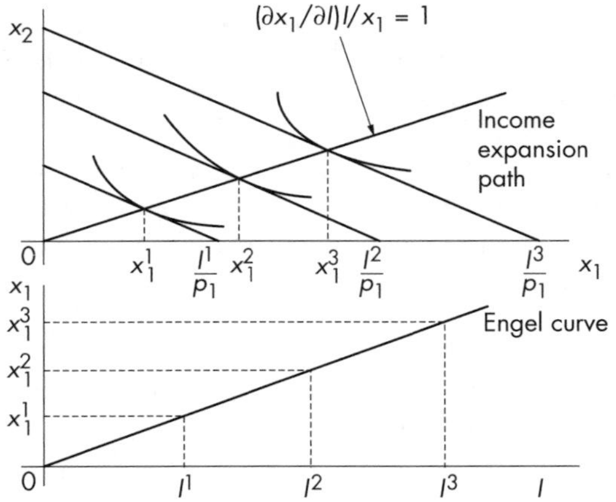

Figure 4.4 **Income expansion path and Engel curve for homothetic preferences.** A household consumes the same proportion of commodities x_1 and x_2 at all levels of income.

bundles) is called the *income consumption path* or income expansion path. Every point on an income expansion path represents the demanded bundle at that level of income.

Example 4.4 Deriving Engel curves from demand functions

Given the demand functions derived in Example 4.1,

$$x_1 = \frac{5I}{8p_1}, \qquad x_2 = \frac{3I}{8p_2},$$

we determine the Engel curves by holding prices constant and allowing the commodities x_1 and x_2 to vary as a result of I changing. For these demand functions, the slopes of the Engel curves are the constants

$$\frac{\partial x_1}{\partial I} = \frac{5}{8p_1}, \qquad \frac{\partial x_2}{\partial I} = \frac{3}{8p_2},$$

with zero intercepts, so the preferences associated with these demand functions are homothetic.

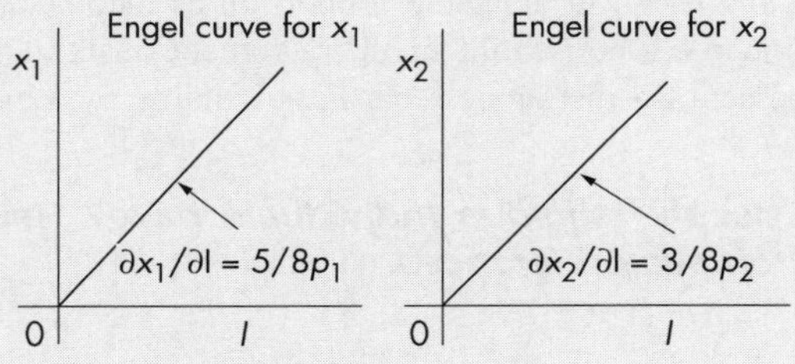

Engel curves

From the income expansion path, we can derive a function that relates income to the demand for each commodity at constant prices. Such functions are represented by Engel curves (after the Prussian economist Ernst Engel, 1821–1896). As illustrated in Figure 4.4, as income rises from I^1 to I^2 and then to I^3, the demand for x_1 increases from x_1^1 to x_1^2 and then to x_1^3. Plotting this increased demand with the rise in income yields an Engel curve. Thus, *Engel curves* illustrate a relationship between the demand for a commodity and income. In Figure 4.4, the Engel curve has a positive slope. In general, Engel curves can have either positive or negative slopes. Positively sloped Engel curves, with $\partial x_1/\partial I > 0$, are called **normal goods**. Given a normal good, an increase in income results in more of the commodity being purchased.

Normal good. An increase in income results in purchasing more of the commodity. *E.g., increasing your consumption of eating out as your income increases.*

Homothetic preferences: tithing

> *When I was a teenager, I spent 80 percent of my allowance on clothing to look older. Now I spend the same percentage of my income to look younger.*
>
> (Michael Wetzstein)

As illustrated in Figure 4.4, if the income expansion paths, and thus each Engel curve, are straight lines (linear) through the origin, a household will consume the same proportion of each commodity at every level of income:

$$\frac{x_1^1}{I^1} = \frac{x_2^2}{I^2} = \frac{x_3^3}{I^3} = \frac{\partial x_1}{\partial I}.$$

This assumes that prices are held fixed. Preferences resulting in consuming the same proportion of commodities as income increases are called **homothetic preferences**. In this case,

$$\frac{\partial x_j}{\partial I}\frac{I}{x_j} = 1, \ j = 1, 2.^{1}$$

The commodities are just scaled up and down in the same proportion as income changes. For example, if at a given level of income a household spent 10 percent of its income on insurance, it would still spend 10 percent on insurance regardless if its income increased or fell.

What kind of preferences do deeply religious individuals have? Religious individuals who tithe have homothetic preferences.

Homothetic preferences. Consumer preferences resulting in the proportion of income spent on a commodity remaining the same at all levels of income. *E.g., a household that tithes to a particular religious organization. The household gives 10 percent of its income to the organization regardless of its income level.*

Luxury and necessary goods: diamonds and food

We can further divide normal goods into luxury and necessary goods, if the income expansion path bends toward one commodity or the other. As illustrated in Figure 4.5, the income expansion path bends toward commodity x_1, making x_1 a **luxury good**. Specifically, x_1 is a luxury good if $(\partial x_1/\partial I)I/x_1 > 1$. As income increases, the household spends proportionally more of its income on x_1. Examples of luxury goods are fine wines and silk suits. If as income increases the household spends proportionally less of its income on a commodity, that commodity is a **necessary good**. In Figure 4.5, x_2 is a necessary good where $(\partial x_2/\partial I)I/x_2 < 1$. Examples of necessary goods are gasoline and textbooks. As the household receives more income, it wishes to consume more of both commodities, but proportionally more of the luxury good than of the necessary good. Observe that for the two-commodity case, if one commodity is a luxury good, then the other must be a necessary good.

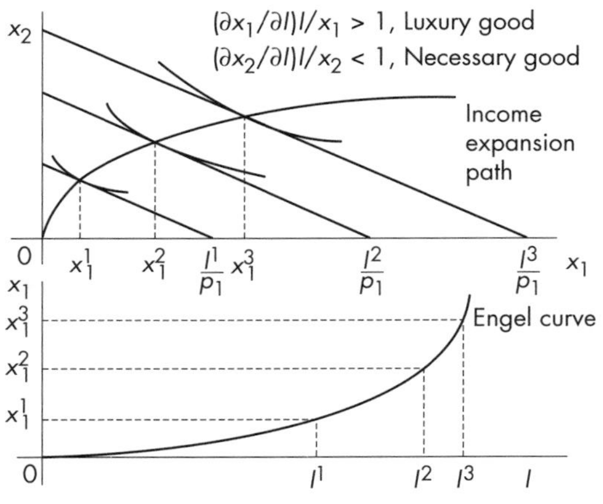

Figure 4.5 **Income expansion path and Engel curve for a luxury good x_1.** As income increases, a household spends proportionally more of its income on x_1.

Luxury good. The proportion of income spent on a commodity increases as income rises. *E.g., the percentage of your income spent on stylish clothing increases as income increases.*

Necessary good. The proportion of income spent on a commodity decreases as income rises. *E.g., the percentage of your income spent on food declines as income increases.*

Inferior goods: used prom dresses

A negatively sloped Engel curve is associated with an income expansion path that bends backwards. In this case, with an increase in income, a household actually wants to consume less of one of the commodities. In Figure 4.6, as income increases, consumption of x_1 declines. Such a commodity is called an **inferior good** and is defined as $\partial x_1/\partial I < 0$. Examples of inferior goods are cheap wine and used books.

Inferior good. The expenditures on a commodity decline as income increases. *E.g., doing your own automobile repairs.*

Engel's law: poverty indicator

The relationship between income and the consumption of specific items has been studied since the eighteenth century. Engel was the first to conduct such studies, and developed the following important generalization about consumer behavior. The proportion of total expenditure devoted to food declines as income rises. Food is a necessity whose consumption rises less rapidly than does income. This is known as **Engel's Law** and has been verified in

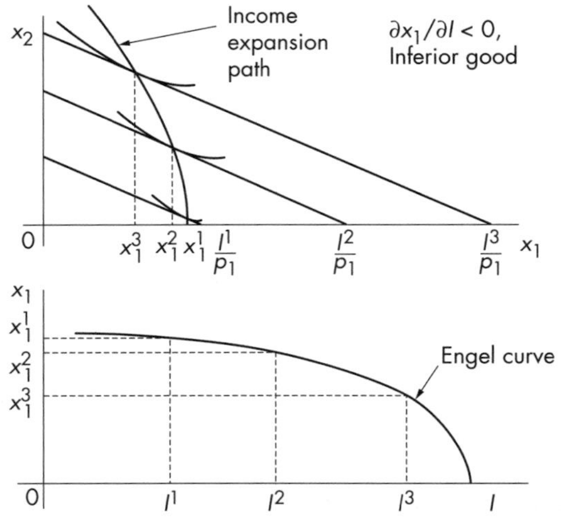

Figure 4.6 **Income expansion path and Engel curve for an inferior good x_1.** As income increases a household purchases less of the inferior commodity x_1.

numerous subsequent studies. Engel's Law appears to be such a consistent empirical finding that some economists have suggested the proportion of income spent on food might be used as an indicator of poverty. Families that spend more than say 40 percent of their income on food might be regarded as poor.

How do you measure poverty? One measure of poverty is the proportion of income spent on food.

Engel's Law. The proportion of total expenditure devoted to food declines as income rises. *E.g., the proportion of expenditures spent on food by a college student's parents is less than the proportion spent by the student.*

Changing price

In searching the Internet for cheap airfares to Europe, a vacationer finds a great fare, but decides to think about it. Returning to the website the next day, he finds that the fare is no longer available and has to settle for a higher one. This is the case, again, of a price change holding income fixed. As illustrated in Figure 4.7, if p_1 is allowed to vary holding p_2 and I fixed, the budget line will tilt. The locus of tangencies will sweep out a price consumption curve. Recall that a price consumption curve, from varying p_1, is a curve connecting all the tangencies between indifference curves and budget lines for alternative price levels.

Ordinary good: food, clothing, shelter

The price consumption curve for an ordinary good is illustrated in Figure 4.7, where

$$\frac{\partial x_j}{\partial p_j} < 0$$

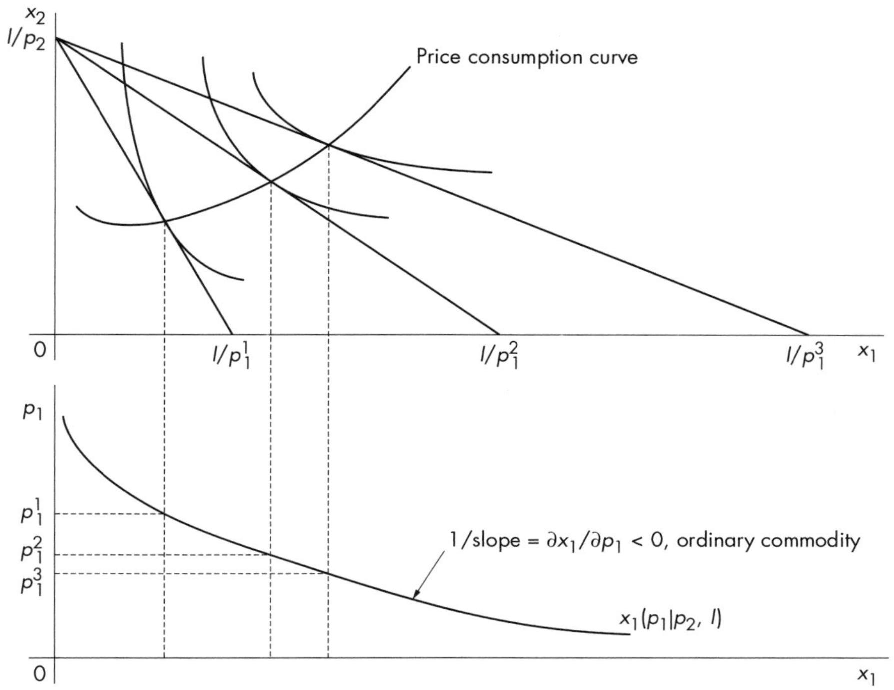

Figure 4.7 **Price consumption curve and a demand curve derived from utility maximization.** The price consumption curve traces out the utility-maximizing commodity bundles for changes in the price of x_1. The demand curve is then derived from this price consumption curve where at every point on the demand curve a household is maximizing utility for the given prices and income.

defines an **ordinary good**. The demand curve derived from the price consumption curve has a negative slope, indicating an inverse relationship between price and quantity of the commodity consumed.

Ordinary good. Price and quantity demanded move in opposite directions. *E.g., as the price of watermelon declines, you purchase more watermelons.*

Giffen good: homeless alcoholic

The slope of a demand curve could be positive:

$$\frac{\partial x_j}{\partial p_j} > 0,$$

which defines a **Giffen good**. For a Giffen good, a decrease in p_1 results in a decrease in demand for x_1 (Figure 4.8). The household's demand curve for this Giffen good has a positive slope.[2]

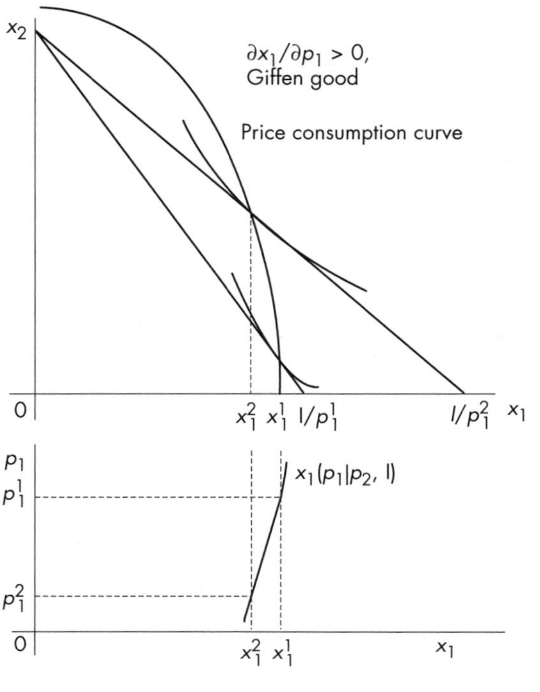

Figure 4.8 **Price consumption curve for a Giffen good.** As the price of x_1 increases, the demand for x_1 also increases.

Giffen good. Price and quantity demanded move in the same direction. *E.g., an alcoholic's purchases of cheap wine.*[3]

Substitution and income effects

In the summer of 2008, the price of gasoline shot up to over $4.00 per gallon and households cutback on their gasoline purchases. Two effects, called the **substitution** and **income effects,** of this gasoline price increase explain their cutback. First, households will substitute other commodities for gasoline in an attempt to mitigate the loss in satisfaction from the price increase. Second, the higher price of gasoline reduced households' real income, and their total purchasing power declined. This negative income effect further reduced their consumption of gasoline. The direction and magnitude of these two effects combine to determine whether a commodity such as gasoline is an ordinary good, a Giffen good, or in general the slope of the demand curve.

The substitution and income effects of a price change for the case where p_1 decreases are illustrated in Figure 4.9. The initial budget constraint is

$$I = p_1^{\circ}x_1 + p_2x_2,$$

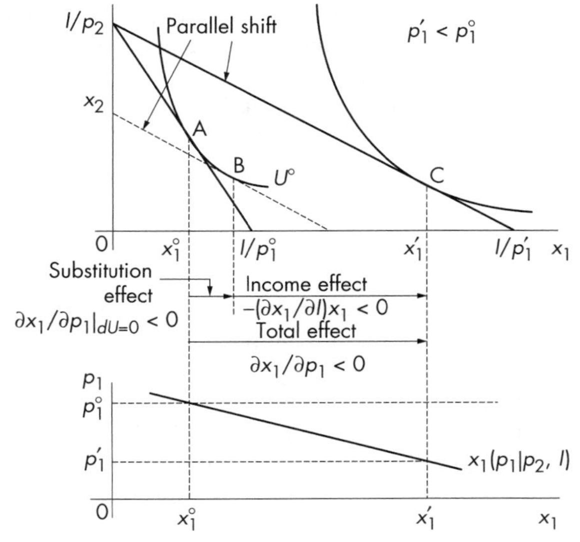

Figure 4.9 **Income and substitution effects for a decrease in p_1 from p_1° to p_1'.** The total effect, A to C, resulting from the price decline may be decomposed into the substitution effect, A to B, and the income effect, B to C.

and the new budget constraint is

$$I = p_1'x_1 + p_2x_2,$$

where $p_1' < p_1^\circ$. In Figure 4.9, a price decrease in p_1 from p_1° to p_1' results in the quantity demanded of x_1 increasing from x_1° to x_1'. This increase in quantity demanded is the total effect of the price decline

$$\text{total effect} = \frac{\partial x_1}{\partial p_1} < 0.$$

This *total effect* can be decomposed into the substitution and income effects:

$$\text{total effect} = \text{substitution effect} + \text{income effect}.$$

Substitution effect

In 2002, Canadian automobiles generally cost from 20 percent to 35 percent less than in the United States. For example, adjusting for the differences in the exchange rate, Ford sold its Windstar LX minivan to Canadian dealers at an invoice price of \$15,373 (\$16,448 suggested retail price) compared with an invoice price of \$20,844 (\$22,340 suggested retail price) to US dealers. With the fall of trade barriers and harmonizing of environmental and safety regulations, the only differences between new cars made for sale in Canada and those made for the United States are the speedometers and odometer, and, in some instances, minor differences in daytime running lamps. Thus, US automobile buyers attempt to substitute

Canadian cars for US ones. This illustrates the **substitution effect** (also called the **Hicksian substitution**)—as an incentive for consumers to purchase more of a lower-priced commodity (Canadian automobiles) and less of a higher-priced commodity (US automobiles), given a change in the price of one commodity relative to another.

To determined the substitution effect, we hold the level of utility constant at the initial utility level U° and consider the price change for x_1:

$$\text{Substitution Effect} = \left.\frac{\partial x_1}{\partial p_1}\right|_{dU=0}.$$

If a household were to stay on the same indifference curve, consumption patterns would be allocated to equate the MRS to the new price ratio. In Figure 4.9, this is represented by a budget line that is parallel to the new budget line but tangent to the initial indifference curve. This tangency, point B, illustrates a household's equilibrium for a level of utility U° with p_1' as the price of x_1. Bundle A represents consumer equilibrium for the same level of utility as bundle B, but at price p_1° instead of p_1'. The decrease in p_1, from p_1° to p_1', results in the consumer purchasing more of x_1 and less of x_2, with the level of utility unchanged. The movement from bundle A to B is the substitution effect.

Substitution effect (Hicksian substitution). The incentive to purchase more of a lower-priced commodity and less of a higher-priced commodity. *E.g., if there is a sale on clothes, you may purchase more clothes and not eat out.*

Compensated law of demand

In Figure 4.9, the Strict Convexity Axiom makes it impossible for a tangency point representing the new price ratio p_1'/p_2 (bundle B) to occur at the left of bundle A. If p_1 decreases, implying p_1/p_2 decreasing, then MRS also decreases. The only way for MRS to decrease is for x_1 to increase and x_2 to decrease. Thus, decreasing x_1's own price p_1, holding utility constant, results in the consumption of x_1 increasing, so the own-substitution effect is always negative, implying $\partial x_1/\partial p_1|_{dU=0} < 0$. This is known as the *Compensated Law of Demand*, where price and quantity always move in opposite directions for a constant level of utility.

Income effect

As the cost of prescription drugs for a senior citizen on a fixed income increases, the senior's purchasing (buying) power can decline to the point of having to choose between eating or taking the medicine. In general, a change in the price of a commodity that a household purchases changes the purchasing power of the household's income. This is called the **income effect**. As in the example, an increase in the price of drugs decreases the ability to purchase both drugs and food. This decreased ability to purchase the same level of commodities represents a decline in purchasing power. The change in price has the same effect as if the household experienced a change in income.

Income effect. The change in purchasing power resulting from a price change. *E.g., an increase in your rent reduces your purchasing power.*

Specifically, a price decline of x_1 has the effect of increasing a household's purchasing power or real income. As illustrated in Figure 4.9, the movement from bundle A to B (the substitution effect) represents a price decline of p_1, with utility remaining constant. The income necessary to purchase bundle B is less than the income required to consume the bundle I/p_2 where $x_1 = 0$. If the household were to purchase bundle B, it would not spend all of its income. The decline in p_1 results in an increase in real income or purchasing power. This increase in real income is represented by a parallel outward shift in the budget line associated with the new price p_1'. The budget line with prices (p_1', p_2) shifts outward until the entire increase in real income is accounted for. This occurs where the intercept of the budget line is I/p_2. At this intercept, the income necessary to purchase I/p_2 of x_2 is restored. The equilibrium tangency then shifts from point B to C, which is the measurement of the income effect.

Mathematically, given the budget constraint

$$I = p_1 x_1 + p_2 x_2,$$

the change in income from a change in p_1, holding consumption of the commodities x_1 and x_2 constant, is

$$\frac{\partial I}{\partial p_1} = x_1.$$

The substitution effect, a movement from A to B in Figure 4.9, will equal the total effect if, given a decline in p_1, income also falls by x_1. If income is not reduced, then this decline in p_1 represents an increase in real income I_R. Specifically, a decline in p_1 results in an increase in I_R of x_1:

$$\frac{\partial I_R}{\partial p_1} = -x_1.$$

The minus sign results from the condition that a change in price and a change in real income move in opposite directions. Thus, this change in real income depends on how much x_1 a household is consuming. If purchases of x_1 are small, the impact of a price change will be minor. For example, a 10 percent price change in salt will have little impact on purchasing power, but a 10 percent change in rent generally has a significant impact.

Multiplying this impact on real income from the change in price, $-x_1$, by the influence of this change in income has on the consumption of x_1, $\partial x_1/\partial I$, results in

$$\text{Income Effect} = -\frac{\partial x_1}{\partial I} x_1.$$

The partial derivative $\partial x_1/\partial I$ may be either positive (normal good) or negative (inferior good), and thus the sign of the income effect is indeterminate.

Example 4.5 Illustrating the Slutsky effect for a household with perfect complements as preferences

Returning to the utility function

$$U(x_1, x_2) = \min(4x_1, 3x_2),$$

first presented in Example 3.5, let the price of p_1 increase from \$1 to \$2 while holding p_2 at \$3 and $I = \$120$. As indicated in the figure, this tilts the budget line inward and results in a reduced commodity bundle C containing 20 units of x_1 and approximately 26.7 units of x_2. The movement from A to C represents the total effect of this price change, which is composed entirely of the income effect. The substitution effect is zero. Shifting up the new budget line representing the increase in price of p_1 results in it touching the original indifference curve at bundle A. Given perfect-complement preferences, there are zero possibilities for substituting one commodity for another.

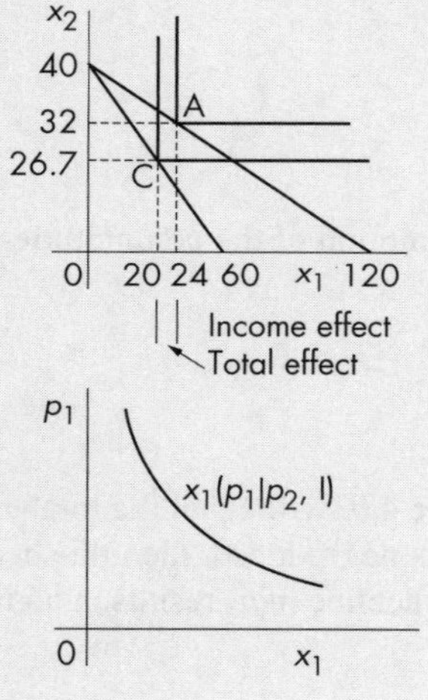

Slutsky equation dissected

Combining the equations for substitution and income effects yields

$$\text{total effect} = \text{substitution effect} + \text{income effect}$$

$$\frac{\partial x_1}{\partial p_1} = \frac{\partial x_1}{\partial p_1}\bigg|_{U=\text{constant}} - \frac{\partial x_1}{\partial I} x_1.$$

This is called the **Slutsky equation**, after the Russian economist Eugene Slutsky (1880–1948). The Slutsky equation mathematically defines the substitution and income effects, where their sum is the total effect of a price change. The total effect is a movement from bundle A to bundle C or a movement along the demand curve for a change in p_1 (Figure 4.9). The substitution effect defines a change in the slope of the budget line, which would motivate a household to choose bundle B if choices had been confined to those on the original indifference curve U°. The income effect defines the further movement from B to C resulting from a change in purchasing power. Price p_1 decreases, which implies an increase in real income. If x_1 is a normal good, a household will demand more of it in response to this increase in purchasing power. As illustrated, again, in Figure 4.9, the own-substitution effect

$$\left.\frac{\partial x_1}{\partial p_1}\right|_{U=\text{constant}} < 0$$

always holds. If $\partial x_1/\partial I > 0$, a normal good, then $-(\partial x_1/\partial I)x_1 < 0$, so the total effect $\partial x_1/\partial p_1 < 0$. This results in a negative income effect, $-(\partial x_1/\partial I)x_1 < 0$, which reinforces the negative substitution effect, $\partial x_1/\partial p_1|_{U=\text{const}} < 0$. Thus, the total effect is the sum of these two negative effects, so it also is negative: $\partial x_1/\partial p_1 < 0$, an ordinary good. This result of an ordinary good given a normal good is known as the *Law of Demand*. The demand for a commodity will always decrease given its price increased, if demand increases with an increase in income.

When the price of a commodity decreases, why do you consume more of it? If demand increases with an increase in income, then the income effect will also be negative and reinforce the negative substitution effort.

Slutsky equation. An equation that decomposes the effects of a price change. *E.g., the total effect of a change in the price of a commodity can be decomposed into the substitution and income effects.*

Example 4.6 Illustrating the Slutsky effect for a household with perfect substitutes as preferences

Recall the utility function representing specific perfect substitutes in Example 3.2:

$$U(x_1, x_2) = 5x_1 + 3x_2.$$

At $p_1 = \$4$ and $p_2 = \$3$, MRS $= 5/3 > 4/3 = p_1/p_2$, indicating that the household would only consume commodity x_1. However, if p_1 increases, say to \$6, the inequality will reverse. At $p_1 = \$6$, MRS $= 5/3 < 6/3 = p_1/p_2$. Now only commodity x_2 will be consumed. As illustrated in the figure, the household has completely substituted x_2 for x_1. The income effect on the consumption of x_1 is zero because the household is no longer purchasing any x_1. The movement from bundle A to B is the substitution effect and the movement from B to C is the income effect. In terms of the impact that the price change has on x_1, the total effect equals the substitution effect.

At $p_2 = 3$, $I = 96$ and $p_1 = 5$, the household is indifferent between consuming x_1 or x_2. At a price above $p_1 = 5$, the demand for x_1 is zero; for $p_1 < 5$, the demand for x_2 is zero. When $x_2 = 0$, the budget constraint is $p_1x_1 = I$, and solving for x_1 yields the demand function for $x_1 = I/p_1$.

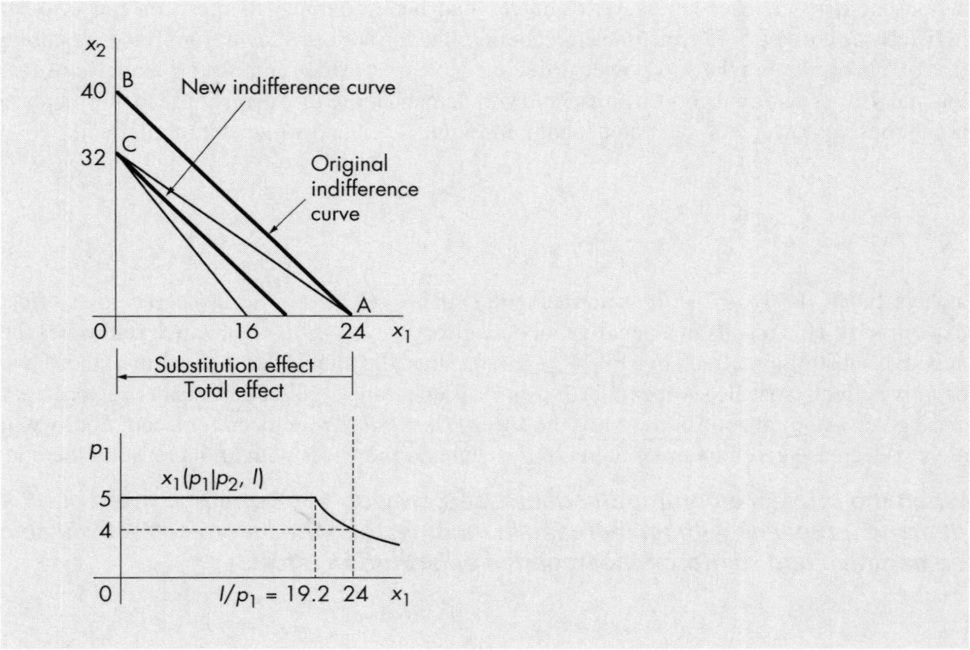

The income and substitution effects can also be illustrated for a price increase in commodity x_1. Figure 4.10 represents such a condition. Assume the price of p_1 increases from p_1° to p_1'. This results in an inward tilt of the budget line, with a new equilibrium point of tangency C instead of the initial tangency point A. The substitution effect represents the price increase holding the level of utility constant. Bundle B is a tangency of a budget line, given the new increase in price, p_1', with the initial indifference curve. The movement from bundle A to B is the substitution effect. The increase in price of p_1 results in a decrease in purchasing power or real income. The income effect measuring this decrease in real income is represented by a parallel leftward shift in the budget line from a point of tangency at B to the new point of tangency C. The total effect is the sum of the income and substitution effect representing a movement from A to C. Again, as in Figure 4.9, the income effect is negative and reinforces the negative substitution effect.

Not all commodities are normal goods resulting in a negative income effect reinforcing the negative own-substitution effect. Some commodities are inferior, where a rise in income will yield a decrease in their consumption, $\partial x_1/\partial I < 0$. For these inferior goods, the income effect is positive, $-(\partial x_1/\partial I)x_1 > 0$. Thus, instead of the income effect reinforcing the negative substitution effect, it will now partially or completely offset the substitution effect. If the income effect does not completely offset the negative substitution effect, the total effect will still be negative, $\partial x_1/\partial p_1 < 0$. Specifically, if

$$-\frac{\partial x_1}{\partial I}x_1 < \left|\frac{\partial x_1}{\partial p_1}\bigg|_{dU=0}\right|,$$

then $\partial x_1/\partial p_1 < 0$, so x_1 is still an ordinary good.

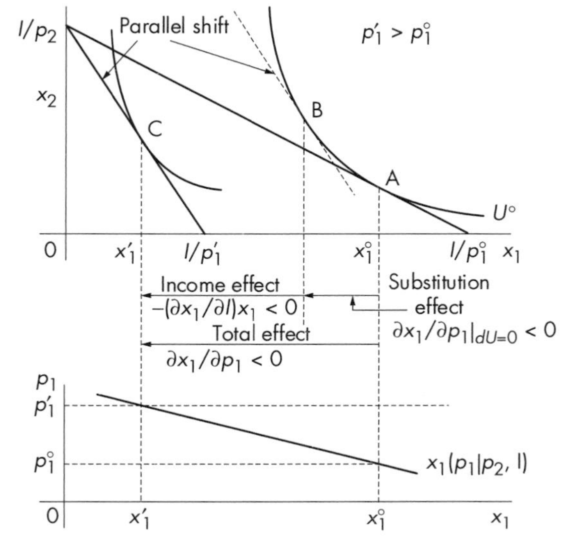

Figure 4.10 **Substitution and income effects for an increase in p_1 from p_1° to p_1'.** The total effect, A to C, resulting from a price increase is decomposed into the substitution effect, A to B, and the income effect, B to C.

Figure 4.11 illustrates these effects for an inferior and ordinary good for a decrease in the price of p_1 from p_1° to p_1'. The movement from A to B resulting from this price change, holding utility constant, is the substitution effect. A decline in price results in an increase in the consumption of x_1 holding utility constant, which illustrates the negative own-substitution effect. The income effect, movement from B to C, partially offsets this negative substitution effect. As illustrated in the figure, if this positive income effect does not completely offset the negative substitution effect, then the total effect is still negative. This results in an ordinary but inferior good. Recall examples are cheap wine and used books.

Giffen's paradox: homeless alcoholic

In general, if x_1 is an inferior good, $\partial x_1/\partial I < 0$, the sign of the total effect, $\partial x_1/\partial p_1$, is indeterminate. That is, it can be either positive or negative. The substitution effect is negative and the income effect is positive. Thus, the positive income effect can be large enough to produce the perverse result

$$\frac{\partial x_1}{\partial p_1} > 0,$$

as illustrated in Figure 4.12. Instead of the demand curve being negatively sloping, it has a positive slope. In this case, an increase in price results in an increase in quantity demanded.

Although such a result is rare, it may be possible. For example, the English economist Robert Giffen claims to have observed the effect in nineteenth-century Ireland. An increase in the price of potatoes resulted in an increase in consumption of potatoes. If x_1 represents potatoes, then $\partial x_1/\partial p_1 > 0$, a Giffen good. Potatoes were a large part of total expenditure

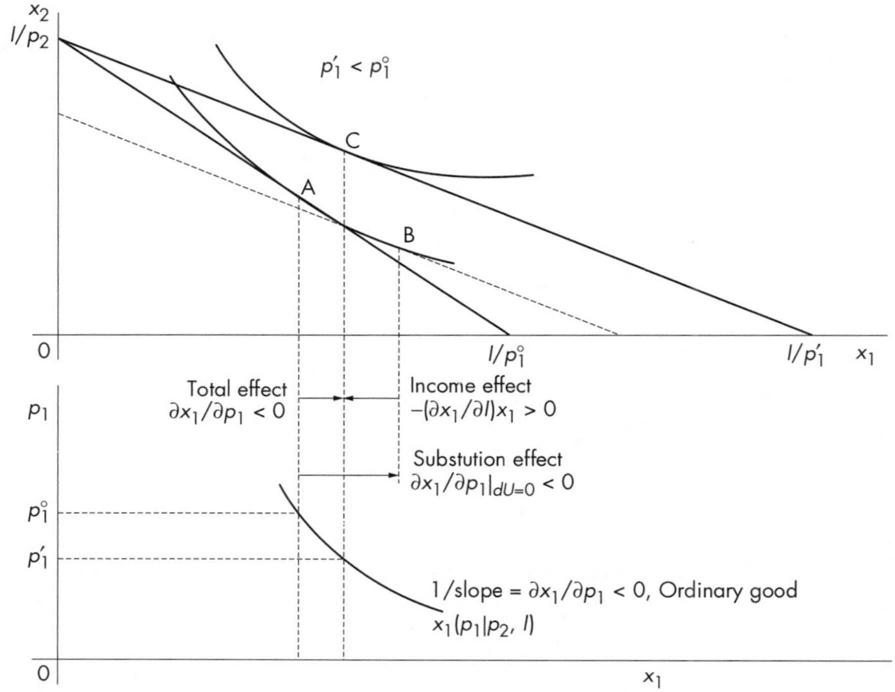

Figure 4.11 **Substitution and income effects for an inferior and ordinary good x_1.** A decline in p_1 from p_1° to p_1' results in the negative substitution effect, a movement from A to B. This substitution effect is partially offset by a positive income effect, a movement from B to C. The total effect is then the sum of these two effects, a movement from A to C.

in nineteenth-century Ireland, and an increase in I would lead to an increase in meat and a decrease in potato consumption. An increase in the price of potatoes, due to the shortage of potatoes, resulted in a decrease in real income, with an associated decrease in meat and an increase in potato consumption (Figure 4.12). The own-substitution effect is still negative, $\partial x_1/\partial p_1|_{U=\text{constant}} < 0$. An increase in p_1 reduces the consumption of x_1, holding utility constant, from A to B. However, the income effect is positive, $-x_1 \partial x_1/\partial I > 0$. Commodity x_1 is an inferior commodity, $\partial x_1/\partial I < 0$, which results in the positive income effect. This positive income effect offsets the negative substitution effect. As illustrated in Figure 4.12, if it completely offsets the substitution effect, the total effect is positive, $\partial x_1/\partial p_1 > 0$, defining a Giffen good.

As illustrated in Figure 4.12, a Giffen good requires a relatively large and positive income effect. The size of this income effect depends on the proportion of income spent on the commodity. The more of a household's income is spent on a commodity, the larger will be the income effect. Generally, commodities, such as food and shelter, associated with a large proportion of a household's income are normal goods rather than inferior goods. Thus, it is very rare to encounter a Giffen good. One example would be an alcoholic who spends a large amount of her income on cheap wine, an inferior good. As the price of cheap wine increases,

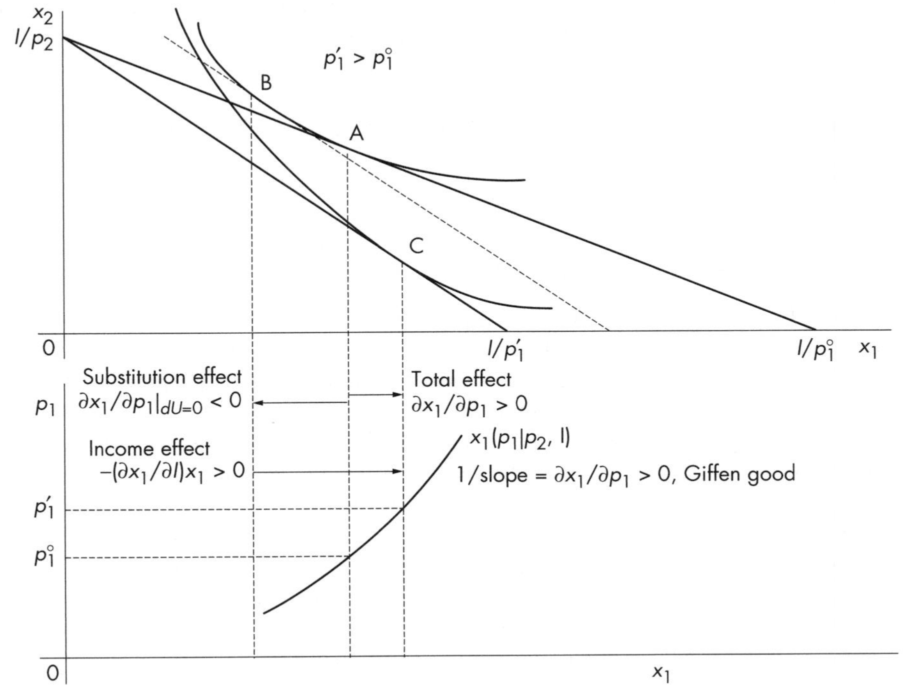

Figure 4.12 **Giffen's paradox.** An increase in the price of x_1 results in an increase in the consumption of x_1. The negative substitution effect, A to B, is completely offset by the positive income effect, B to C.

her real income declines, so she consumes more cheap wine. A more mundane example is a college fraternity with a fixed food budget for a football party. The fraternity is considering having chips and salsa along with a fruit and vegetable tray. However, once at the market, they discovered the price of chips and salsa had increased, so to make sure there would be enough food they had to purchase a smaller fruit and vegetable tray and more chips and salsa.

Application: Why did Marshall introduce Giffen's paradox?

As recounted by P. Dooley, F. Edgeworth objected to the notion of a Giffen good, so A. Marshall wrote him a letter in 1909 containing the following illustration:

> "Suppose a man was in a hurry to make a journey of 150 kilos. He had two florins for it, and no more. The fare by boat was one cent a kilo, by third class train two cents. So he decided to go 100 kilos by boat, and 50 by train: total cost two florins. On arriving at the boat he found the charge had been raised to $1\frac{1}{4}$ cents per kilo. 'Oh: then I will travel $133\frac{1}{3}$ kilos (or as near as may be) by boat, I can't afford more than $16\frac{2}{3}$ by train.' Why not? Where is the paradox?"

This example by Marshall is a subsistence argument for a Giffen good. Marshall considered a Giffen good to be a rare and unimportant exception to his theory of consumer demand and consumer surplus, so he introduced it as a paradox.

Source: P.C. Dooley, "Why Did Marshall Introduce the Giffen Paradox?" *History of Political Economy* 24 (1992): 749–752.

Summary of ordinary, Giffen, inferior, and normal goods

The relationships among an ordinary good ($\partial x_1/\partial p_1 < 0$), a normal good ($\partial x_1/\partial I > 0$), an inferior good ($\partial x_1/\partial I < 0$), and a Giffen good ($\partial x_1/\partial p_1 > 0$) are illustrated in Figure 4.13 for an increase in p_1 from p_1° to p_1'. (Similar relationships could be established for a price decrease in x_1.) Initially a household is consuming x_1° at prices (p_1°, p_2) associated with commodity bundle A. A price increase in p_1 from p_1° to p_1' results in the negative own-substitution effect, a movement from A to B. If $\partial x_1/\partial I > 0$ (normal good), then the income effect will reinforce this negative substitution and further decrease the consumption of x_1. For example, the total effect may result in x_1 decreasing from x_1° to x_1'. In contrast, if x_1 is an inferior good, $\partial x_1/\partial I < 0$, then the income effect will partially or completely offset the negative own-substitution effect. If the income effect completely offsets the negative own-substitution effect, a Giffen good results in which the consumption of x_1 will increase as a result of p_1 increasing. For example, if as a result of p_1 increasing, x_1 increases from x_1° to x_1''', then a Giffen good results. As shown

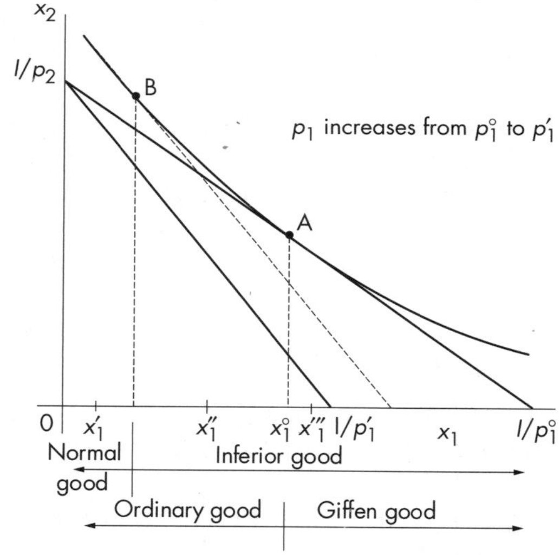

Figure 4.13 **Summary of ordinary, normal, inferior, and Giffen goods.** For a price increase holding utility constant, the substitution effect results in a decline in consumption of x_1, a movement from A to B. A normal good reinforces this negative substitution effect, further decreasing x_1. An inferior good will either partially or completely offset this negative substitution effect. If it completely offsets the negative substitution effect, x_1 is a Giffen good.

in the figure, a necessary condition for a Giffen good is that it is an inferior good. If the income effect does not completely offset the negative own-substitution effect, then an ordinary good results, in which the price increase in x_1 yields a decline in the consumption of x_1. For example, a movement from x_1° to x_1'' represents the total effect, in which x_1 is an ordinary and inferior good. Thus, a Giffen good must be an inferior good, whereas an ordinary good could be either inferior or a normal good. How a household reacts to prices represented by the slope of the indifference curves, along with its initial utility-maximizing bundle, determines the type of good.

The Law of Demand is also illustrated in Figure 4.13. If x_1 is a normal good, then it will be an ordinary good, yielding an inverse relationship between price and quantity.

Why consider compensated price changes?

In very cold winters, the price per therm for natural gas generally rises as a result of increased demand. These increases in price are especially hard on the poor, who spend a larger proportion of their income on heating. In an effort to aid these poor families, government programs provide direct income compensation to offset these higher heating costs.

To determine how much compensation is required, we rewrite the Slutsky equation as

$$\text{substitution effect} = \text{total effect} - \text{income effect}$$

$$\left.\frac{\partial x_1}{\partial p_1}\right|_{U=\text{constant}} = \frac{\partial x_1}{\partial p_1} + \frac{\partial x_1}{\partial I}x_1.$$

The Diminishing MRS Axiom assures that this own substitution effect will always be negative. This substitution effect, also called a *compensated price effect*, is the sum of two components that are observed (revealed) in markets. The compensated price effect indicates the effect from a pure price change, where the level of consumption is adjusted for any beneficial or adverse effects from a change in real income, so utility remains unchanged. The income effect is removed from the total effect, resulting in this pure price effect.

As result of the higher price for natural gas, households' real incomes have declined, which reduces their satisfaction. Compensating households for this loss in satisfaction by increasing their income results in the compensated price effect. Their utility then returns to the same level prior to the price rise. The compensated price effect is calculated from estimates of the observed total effect and income effect.

Example 4.7 How to measure compensated price changes

Given the demand function for x_1 derived in Example 4.1,

$$x_1 = \frac{5I}{8p_1},$$

we determine the compensated price change for a change in p_1 by first calculating the total and income effects:

$$\text{total effect} = \frac{\partial x_1}{\partial p_1} = -\frac{5I}{8p_1^2} = -\frac{x_1}{p_1},$$

$$\text{income effect} = -\frac{\partial x_1}{\partial I} x_1 = -\frac{5x_1}{8p_1}.$$

The compensated price change is then

$$\text{compensated price change} = \left.\frac{\partial x_1}{\partial p_1}\right|_{dU=0} = -\frac{x_1}{p_1} + \frac{5x_1}{8p_1} = -\frac{3x_1}{8p_1}.$$

If $I = \$1280$ and $p_1 = 10$, then $x_1 = 80$, with a total effect of -8, an income effect of -5, and a compensated price change of -3.

Hicks versus Slutsky compensation

I am a Slutsky woman. Between holding my utility constant versus my purchasing power, I would take the latter.

(Michael Wetzstein)

The compensated price effect, which compensates households back to their initial level of satisfaction is called *Hicks compensation*, introduced by J.R. Hicks and based on Pareto's discussion of compensation.[4] An alternative type of compensation is *Slutsky compensation*. Instead of adjusting income to the same level of utility prior to a price change, Slutsky compensation adjusts income so a household can purchase the original consumption bundle. In contrast to Hicks compensation, which holds utility constant, Slutsky compensation keeps a household's purchasing power constant. As illustrated in Figure 4.14, an increase in the price of x_1 (say natural gas) from p_1° to p_1' results in the Hicks compensation bundle B, where the budget line with the new price ratio is tangent to the original indifference curve. In contrast, Slutsky compensation adjusts income to where the budget line, with prices (p_1', p_2), intersects the original commodity bundle (A) prior to the price change. Slutsky compensation

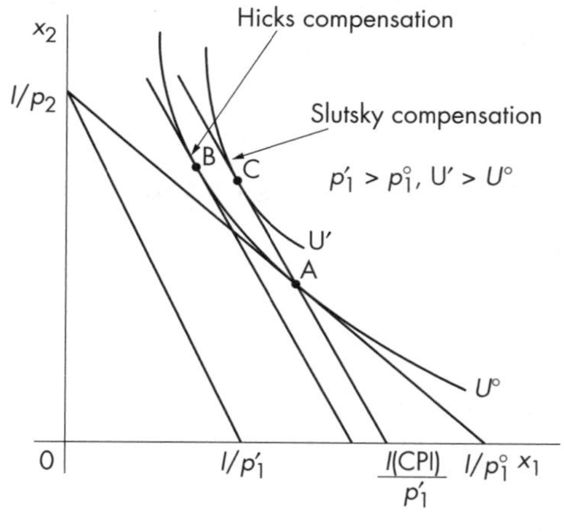

Figure 4.14 **Hicks and Slutsky compensation.** For the increase in price of x_1, Hicks compensation is represented by the movement from A to B holding utility constant. Slutsky compensation is the movement from A to C holding purchasing power constant.

requires the ability to just purchase this original bundle A. Thus, the Slutsky compensated budget line cuts the original indifference curve U°, so by additional substitution a household can obtain bundle C. Commodity bundle C yields a higher level of utility than bundles A and B, $U' > U^\circ$.

Although the degree of compensation and resulting satisfaction level differ, the form of the Slutsky equation does not change when considering these two types of compensation. In the limit as the price change tends to zero, the Hicks and Slutsky compensations are identical. Thus, it will in general not matter which type of compensation is used, provided the price change is small. As discussed later, Hicks compensation has the desirable property for policy analysis of compensating a household to the point where its level of satisfaction is unaffected by a price change; however, such compensation is not directly revealed in the market. Slutsky compensation *is* revealed, and thus can provide an approximation for Hicks compensation.

Example 4.8 Measuring the bias in the CPI, given perfect complements and perfect substitutes as preferences

Let's consider first the case of perfect complements. As indicated in Example 4.5, there is no substitution effect. Thus, the bias in the CPI is zero. From Example 4.5, the original bundle is (24, 32) with prices (1, 3) associated with $I = \$120$. Increasing p_1 from \$1 to \$2 results in a required income level of \$144 [(24)(2) + (32)(3) = 144] to obtain bundle A. Thus, a CPI of 144/120 = 120 percent will exactly compensate a household for the price change.

In contrast, consider the case of perfect substitutes as preferences, Example 4.6. Here a price increase from \$4 to \$6 results in a complete substitution from x_1 to x_2. Hicks compensation would compensate the household back to the original indifference curve bundle B. This would require an income level of (40)(3) = \$120 versus the original income level of (32)(3) = \$96, or a 24/96 = 25 percent increase. In contrast, Slutsky compensation is (24)(6) = \$144, yielding a CPI of 144/96 = 150 percent. This Slutsky compensation results in the household consuming 48 units of x_2 and obtaining a higher level of utility compared with the original bundle A. Thus, due to the ability of the household to substitute, the CPI is overestimated by 25 percent in terms of compensating a household back to the same utility prior to the price increase.

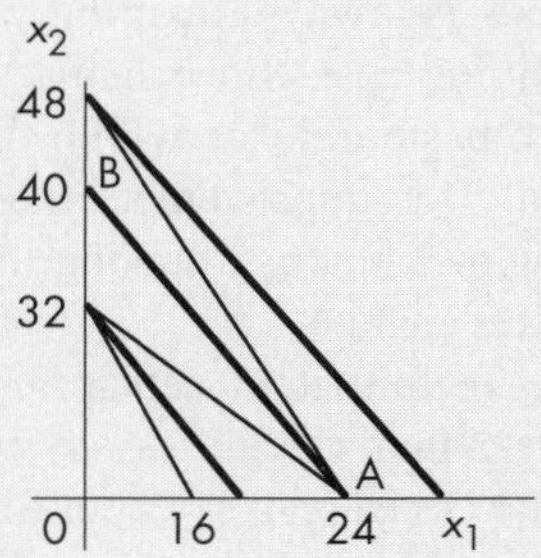

Laspeyres index

The *Laspeyres Index*, used by the United States and other countries to define the **Consumer Price Index (CPI)**, is a Slutsky compensation index. This index computes the change in quantity of commodities consumed using the initial set of prices as weights: for example prices (p_1°, p_2) in Figure 4.14. The CPI states, in percentage, the amount of income required in the current year to purchase the same consumption bundle in some base year. In Figure 4.14, I is the amount of income required to purchase bundle A with the initial set of prices (p_1°, p_2), and I(CPI) is the amount of income required to purchase bundle A at the new set of prices (p_1', p_2). Calculating the CPI with the Laspeyres index does not account for households adjusting to price changes by changing their consumption bundle. For example, instead of consuming bundle A with income I(CPI) and prices (p_1', p_2), a household will adjust its consumption and consume bundle C. Thus, adjusting households' income for any price increases, with the CPI, may result in households increasing their utility. Since the Laspeyres index does not account for the possibility of households substituting other commodities, it biases the CPI upward. Households are over-compensated when adjusting their incomes for price increases. However, for small relative price changes, the bias should not be large, given the good approximation of Slutsky compensation to Hicks compensation.

Should your grandmother receive the full cost of living increase in her monthly Social Security check? No, if the cost of living is designed to maintain her current happiness, then she should receive less than the full cost-of-living increase.

Consumer Price Index (CPI). An index that states the amount of income required in the current year to purchase the same consumption bundle in some base year. *E.g., if the CPI increased by 2 percent this year, then it would take a 2 percent increase in income to purchase the same commodities as last year.*

The US CPI, measured by the Bureau of Labor Statistics, consists of consumer prices for a bundle of 364 categories of commodities. These prices are compared with what was charged for the same items in a base period.[5] The Congressional Budget Office estimates the CPI has grown faster than the cost of living by between 0.2 and 0.8 percentage points annually. This failure to gauge the possibility of households substituting other commodities has cost the Federal Government $300 billion over the past few decades. Social security payments, civil service pensions, and earned-income tax credits are all based on the CPI.

Why not fix the CPI? Well the Bureau of Labor Statistics is always tinkering with the CPI in attempts at moving it closer to a truer measure of living cost. Since January 1999, a *geometric mean formula* has been used to calculate most basic indexes within the CPI. Specifically, the prices within item categories are averaged. This improvement moves the CPI somewhat closer to a Hicks compensation cost-of-living measure by allowing for some consumer substitution as relative prices within item categories change.

But, this mean formula is used only to average prices within item categories, so it doesn't account for consumer substitution taking place between item categories, say between vegetables and meat. In 2002, as a complement to the CPI, the US Bureau of Labor Statistics began producing a new index called the *Chained Consumer Price Index* for All Urban Consumers that better approximates the true cost-of-living. This index utilizes expenditure data in adjacent time periods to reflect effects of substitution that consumers make across item categories in response to changes in relative prices. But without being able to determine households' underlying preferences (utility functions), it is unlikely that the problems of defining living standards and measuring changes in their cost of attainment over time will ever be resolved completely.

Application: Consider a gas tax with an income tax rebate

In January 2009, a federal commission proposed raising the federal excise tax on gasoline. Are there any merits to this proposal? Such a proposal would have two potential beneficial effects. First, the policy would reduce the level of automobile emissions, and thus improve air quality and reduce greenhouse gases. Second, the policy would provide economic incentives for the development of alternative energy sources. However, a large tax increase could dangerously reduce consumer purchasing power and possibly cause a recession.[a] There is also the question of equity (changes in the distribution of income). Such a tax would be harder on low-income groups, who spend a larger proportion of their income on gasoline. One method for offsetting this loss in purchasing power is to take the revenue collected from the excise tax and return it to households as a tax rebate. Payroll and Social Security taxes not only hit the poor harder than the rich, but they account for an increasingly large proportion of total taxation. These taxes artificially increase the cost of hiring people, and thus discourage employment. Imposing taxes on gasoline and lowering taxes on wage earners could make the price of both gasoline and wages more closely reflect their social costs.

This results in a policy to implement a compensated price change as a way of reducing gasoline consumption (Figure 4.15). Implementation of the excise tax alone would tilt the budget constraint inward from consumption bundle A to bundle C. Gasoline purchases would decrease from x_1° to x_1', and utility would decrease from U° to U'. However, the inclusion of the tax rebate as part of the proposal would shift the budget constraint upward, to commodity bundle B. Gasoline consumption would increase slightly from what it would have been under the pure excise tax, but the policy combination would result in a reduction of the original gasoline purchases with no loss in utility.

We can investigate this policy combination with the Slutsky equation. Let τ denote the price impact of the gasoline excise tax. Then

$$\tau \frac{\partial x_1}{\partial p_1}\Big|_{U=\text{constant}} = \tau \frac{\partial x_1}{\partial p_1} + \tau \frac{\partial x_1}{\partial I} x_1,$$

where τ is the price change ($\tau = dp_1$). This equation indicates the net change in gallons of gasoline purchased as a result of the tax policy. As an example, consider a \$1.50 increase in the price of gasoline. Such a tax would account for the major external costs of driving: oil dependency, greenhouse gases, air pollution, accidents, and congestion. We measure how a household will respond to this increase by the percentage decrease in gasoline consumption given the percentage increase in its price. This measure is called *elasticity of demand* and is estimated by economists to be on average −0.26.[b] Given this estimate, a household driving 20,000 miles per year at 20 miles per gallon would decrease gasoline consumption from 1000 to 870 gallons (130 gallons) when faced with a \$1.50 increase in the price of gasoline.[c] Thus,

$$\tau \frac{\partial x_1}{\partial p_1} = -130 \text{ gallons.}$$

Also, given the initial 1000 gallons of gasoline consumption, real income would decline by \$1500 as a result of the \$1.50 excise tax increase:

$$\$1.50(1000) = \$1500 = \tau x_1^\circ.$$

For Slutsky compensation, this would require a rebate of \$1500 to offset this real income decline, and for Hicks compensation, illustrated in Figure 4.15, it would require slightly less compensation, T^C. Assuming annual compensation T^C produces a 14 gallon increase in annual gasoline purchases per household; then the income effect would be 14 gallons.[d] The overall effect of the excise tax and tax-rebate plan would be to reduce annual gasoline sales by 116 (130–14) gallons per household with a household's level of satisfaction remaining unchanged. However, this is not a revenue-neutral policy. The total revenue collected would be $\tau x_1'' = 1.50(1000 - 116) = \$1326$. A Slutsky rebate of \$1500 would require additional revenue, and even a Hicks rebate requires a rebate greater than \$1326. This is because, in order to afford bundle B, (x_1'', x_2''),

$$I^\circ + T^C = (p_1^\circ + \tau)x_1'' + p_2 x_2'',$$

$$I^\circ + (T^C - \tau x_1'') = p_1^\circ x_1'' + p_2 x_2'',$$

$$T^C - \tau x_1'' = (p_1^\circ x_1'' + p_2 x_2'') - I^\circ.$$

However, $p_1^\circ x_1'' + p_2 x_2'' > I^\circ$, bundle B is outside the budget constraint, and so $T^C > \tau x_1'' = \$1326$.

If additional revenue is not allocated to this program, the average household will be worse off as a consequence of the program. That the program is neither revenue-neutral nor "utility-neutral" negatively impacts its appeal. Note that this result of the household being worse off, even after the rebate, without some revenue enhancement is for the average household. Households that consume less than the average amount of gasoline may actually benefit from the program.

How do we decrease our dependence on foreign oil? One method that may result in little if any loss in satisfaction is to impose higher excise taxes on gasoline with an accompanying cut in payroll taxes.

[a] A recession is defined as a two-quarter decline in real gross domestic product accompanied by lower real income and higher unemployment.

[b] See Chapter 5. Elasticity of demand is defined as the percentage change in quantity demanded given a percentage change in price. Table 5.1 lists the estimates of this quantity demanded to a change in price with a short-run measure for gasoline of −0.26.

[c] Assuming an initial price of \$3.00, the \$1.50 increase represents a 50 percent increase in this price. The decrease in gasoline consumption is then 13 percent [(50 percent)(−0.26)]. Thirteen percent of 1000 gallons is 130 gallons.

[d] A household with an annual income of \$50,000 would experience a 3 percent increase in income from a \$1500 rebate. In Table 5.3, a short-run responsiveness (percentage increase) of a household's gasoline consumption to a percentage

increase in income is listed as 0.47. This yields a 1.41 percent increase in gasoline consumption [(3 percent)(0.47)]. With the household consuming 1000 gallons prior to the excise tax and tax rebate, the 1.41 percent increase in gasoline consumption represents approximately a 14 gallon increase.

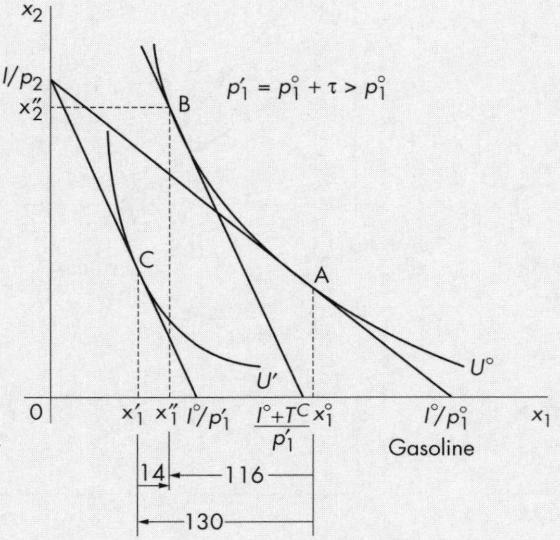

Figure 4.15 **Excise tax on gasoline with an income tax rebate.** An excise tax increasing the price of gasoline results in a movement from A to C. Compensating the household for the tax, in the form of income tax relief, shifts the budget constraint to point B, yielding the same level of utility prior to the excise tax.

Changing the price of another commodity

In many cases, shoppers are faced with determining how much of one commodity to purchase when the price of a related commodity changes. For example, when apples are harvested in the fall, their price declines, which is likely to have an effect on the amount of oranges a shopper purchases. We can use the Slutsky equation to express this change in x_1 (oranges) when p_2 (price of apples) changes:

$$\text{total effect} = \text{substitution effect} + \text{income effect}$$

$$\frac{\partial x_1}{\partial p_2} = \frac{\partial x_1}{\partial p_2}\bigg|_{U=\text{constant}} - \frac{\partial x_1}{\partial I} x_2.$$

Income effect represents $\partial x_1/\partial I$ times the change in income as a result of changing p_2. The sign of $\partial x_1/\partial p_2|_{U=\text{constant}}$ is generally indeterminate for three or more commodities, but in a two-commodity case, this *cross-substitution effect*, $\partial x_1/\partial p_2|_{U=\text{constant}}$, will be positive, assuming diminishing MRS. When utility is held constant, a decrease in the price of x_2 will tend to cause purchases of x_1 to decrease due to diminishing MRS (Figure 4.16). Given the strict convexity of the indifference curves (Axiom 4), it is impossible for this tangency—representing the

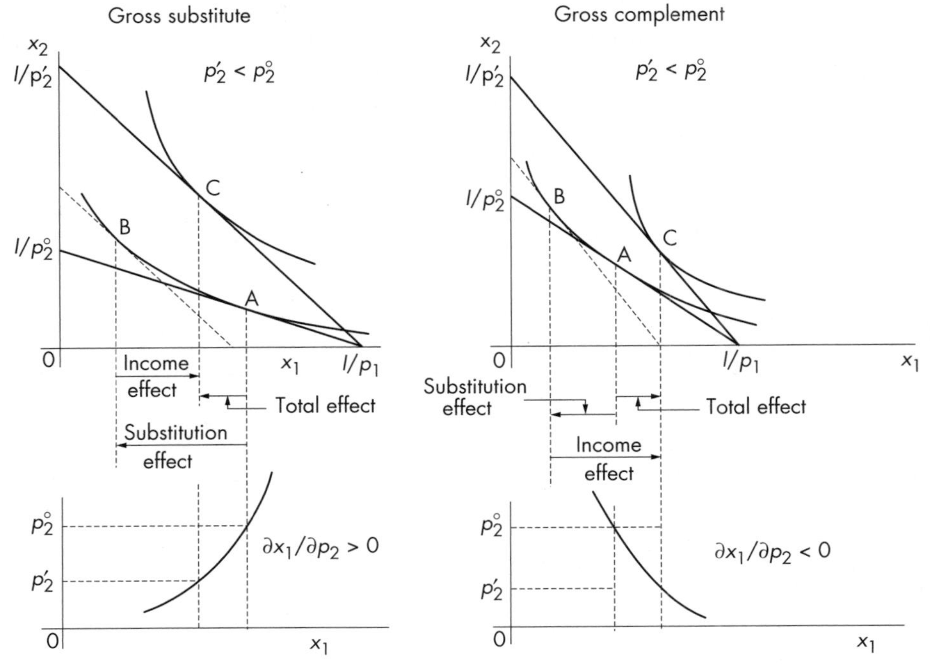

Figure 4.16 **Gross substitutes and complements.** For the two-commodity case, the cross-substitution effect from a price decrease in x_2 on consumption of x_1 is always positive. If the income effect completely offsets this positive substitution effect, then x_1 is a gross complement; otherwise x_1 is a gross substitute for x_2.

new price ratio p_1/p_2' (bundle B)—to occur at the right of bundle A. If p_2 decreases, implying p_1/p_2 increasing, then MRS also increases. The only way for MRS to increase is for x_1 to decrease and x_2 to increase. This implies $\partial x_1/\partial p_2|_{dU=0} > 0$, given two commodities. If x_1 is a normal good, the income effect is negative. Therefore, the total effect, $\partial x_1/\partial p_2$, may be either positive or negative depending on the relative strengths of the cross-substitution and income effects.

Substitutes and complements

The magnitude and signs of the substitution and income effects will determine if the commodities are substitutes or complements. Two commodities are substitutes if one commodity may, as a result of a price change, replace the other. Examples are two brands of cola or gasoline. Two commodities are complements if one commodity is consumed with another good. Examples of complements are pancakes and syrup, gasoline and automobiles, and a baseball bat and ball. Specifically,

$$\frac{\partial x_1}{\partial p_2} > 0, \text{ gross substitute,}$$

$$\frac{\partial x_1}{\partial p_2} < 0, \text{ gross complement.}$$

For a price decrease in x_2, Figure 4.16 illustrates this gross substitute and gross complement relationship. Note that because only two commodities are considered, for both the gross substitute and gross complement cases, the cross-substitution effect is positive. A decrease in the price of x_2 results in the consumption of x_1 decreasing. However, the income effect overwhelms this positive cross-substitution effect for the gross complement case. For completeness, two commodities are *independent goods* if a price change in one commodity does not affect the consumption of another. Specifically, if

$$\frac{\partial x_1}{\partial p_2} = 0,$$

then commodity x_1 is independent of x_2. An example of independent commodities is bottled water and laundry detergent. If the price of bottled water declines, a household might purchase more bottled water, but this price decline for water would generally not influence the demand for detergent.

We can use the price consumption curve to determine whether commodities are gross substitutes or complements. In Figure 4.1, the price consumption curve has a negative slope, which indicates that a fall in the price of x_1 results in a decline in the consumption of x_2. Thus, a negatively sloping price consumption curve illustrates that commodity x_2 is a gross substitute for x_1. In contrast, if the price consumption curve has a positive slope (Figure 4.7), a fall in the price of x_1 results in an increase in the consumption of x_2, and x_2 is a gross complement for x_1. In the case of independent goods, the price consumption curve is horizontal for a change in the price of x_1. This change in p_1 has no effect on the consumption of x_2.

Example 4.9 What are the gross complements for perfect-complement preferences?

In Example 4.3, we derived the following demand functions for a perfect-complement set of preferences:

$$x_1^* = \frac{I}{p_1 + \frac{4}{3}p_2},$$

$$x_2^* = \frac{I}{\frac{3}{4}p_1 + p_2}.$$

Note that these commodities are gross complements of each other:

$$\frac{\partial x_1}{\partial p_2} = -\frac{\frac{4}{3}I}{(p_1 + \frac{4}{3}p_2)^2} < 0,$$

$$\frac{\partial x_2}{\partial p_1} = -\frac{\frac{3}{4}I}{(\frac{3}{4}p_1 + p_2)^2} < 0.$$

Example 4.10 Independent goods

In Example 4.1, we derived the following demand functions:

$$x_1^* = \frac{5I}{8p_1}, \quad x_2^* = \frac{3I}{8p_2}.$$

These commodities are independent goods of each other:

$$\frac{\partial x_1}{\partial p_2} = \frac{\partial x_2}{\partial p_1} = 0.$$

The price consumption curve for a change in the price of x_1 is then horizontal.

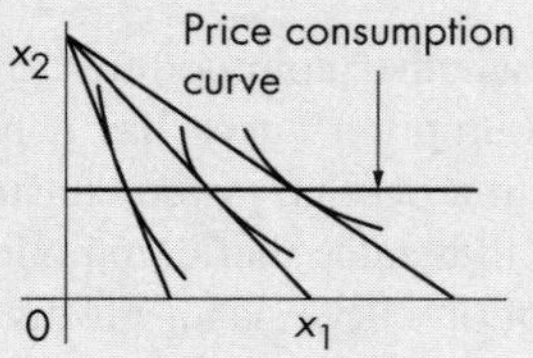

It is possible, given these definitions, for x_j to be a substitute for x_i and at the same time for x_i to be a complement of x_j. The presence of income effects can produce this paradoxical result. For example, consider the consumption of two items (food and books). Decreasing the price of food may lead to ∂(books)/∂(price of food) < 0. Food is an important item in consumption; a decline in its price will increase real income and may increase the demand for books. Thus, a book is a gross complement for food, as illustrated in Figure 4.16 by letting x_1 be books and x_2 food. This increase in real income completely offsets the cross-substitution effect, resulting in a gross complement. In contrast, decreasing the price of books may result in ∂(food)/∂(price of books) > 0. The income effect will be relatively small if the total amount of expenditure on books is small. Thus, as illustrated in Figure 4.16 for a gross substitute, where x_1 is now food and x_2 is books, the income effect does not offset the positive cross-substitution effect. Thus, food is a gross substitute for books.

This asymmetry of effects can be eliminated by removing the income effect, which results in alternative definitions (called *Hicksian substitutes* and *complements* or *net substitutes* and *complements*). Specifically, net substitutes and complements are defined as

$$\left.\frac{\partial x_j}{\partial p_i}\right|_{U=\text{constant}} > 0, \text{ net substitute},$$

$$\left.\frac{\partial x_j}{\partial p_i}\right|_{U=\text{constant}} < 0, \text{ net complement}.$$

With this definition, the cross-substitution effects are completely symmetric:

$$\left.\frac{\partial x_j}{\partial p_i}\right|_{U=\text{constant}} = \left.\frac{\partial x_i}{\partial p_j}\right|_{U=\text{constant}}.$$

The income effect is removed and only the substitution effect is considered.

Summary

1. An individual household's demand function for a commodity is a theoretical relation between price and quantity. This demand function is derived from utility maximization and is based on commodity prices, household preferences, and income.
2. A household's demand curve illustrates how much of a commodity the household is willing and able to purchase at a given price.
3. A shift in demand results when one of the parameters being held constant changes. For example, a change in income will result in the demand curve shifting. In contrast, a change in quantity demanded occurs when the own price of the commodity, which is not being held constant, changes.
4. An inverse demand curve represents price being dependent on quantity, and a direct demand curve represents quantity being dependent on price.
5. Comparative statics associated with a household's demand function investigates the effect on the demand for a commodity when price and/or income change.
6. Homogeneous of degree zero demand functions result when demands are not affected by pure inflation. For example, doubling all prices and income does not affect a household's demand for commodities.
7. Engel curves relate income to the demand for each commodity, holding prices constant. Positively sloped Engel curves are associated with normal goods and negatively sloped curves with inferior goods.
8. The total effect of a price change may be decomposed into the substitution and income effects, with the aid of the Slutsky equation. The own-substitution effect is always negative and if the commodity is a normal good, the income effect will also be negative. In this case, the Law of Demand states that a commodity will always change opposite to any change in its own price. If the income effect is positive, the sign of the total effect is indeterminate.
9. The compensated price effect indicates the effect from a pure price change, where the level of consumption is adjusted for a change in real income. The two major types of compensation are Hicks and Slutsky compensations. Hicks compensation compensates a household to the point where its level of satisfaction is unaffected by a price change. Slutsky compensation keeps a household's purchasing power constant.
10. The Slutsky equation can also be expressed for a change in the consumption of a commodity resulting in a change in the price of a related commodity. Substitutes and complements for a commodity are then determined by the associated substitution and income effects.
11. *(Appendix)* There is a Slutsky-type equation for determining a household's labor supply curve. A labor supply curve is derived by households maximizing utility subject to a limited amount of time as well as an income constraint.
12. *(Appendix)* A household's labor supply curve illustrates how much labor a household is willing and able to supply at a given wage rate.

Key concepts

Key equations

$$x_j = x_j(\alpha p_1, \alpha p_2, \ldots, \alpha p_k, \alpha I) = x_i(p_1, p_2, \ldots, p_k, I)$$

Demand functions are homogeneous of degree zero in prices and income.

$$\frac{\partial x_1}{\partial p_1} = \frac{\partial x_1}{\partial p_1}\bigg|_{U=\text{constant}} - \frac{\partial x_1}{\partial I} x_1$$

Slutsky equation, which states that the total effect can be decomposed into the substitution and income effects.

$$\frac{\partial h}{\partial w} = \frac{\partial h}{\partial w}\bigg|_{U=\text{constant}} + \frac{\partial h}{\partial I}\ell$$

Adjusted Slutsky equation for the effect that wages have on leisure.

Questions

1. What main assumption underlies comparative statics analysis? In general, will this assumption ever hold in reality? Explain.
2. Is the substitution effect or the income effect more important in accounting for downward-sloping demand curves? Explain.
3. Why, without considering an income effect, must a demand curve have a negative slope? For a normal good, must a demand curve continue to be negatively sloping when the income effect is considered?

4. Why can Giffen's Paradox hold only over a limited range of the price consumption curve? Can the price consumption curve ever circle around and rejoin itself at its starting point?
5. The daycare industry opposes a lump-sum subsidy. What does this indicate about the sign of the income effect?
6. Empirical evidence indicates that as a country's per-capita income increases, its birth rate declines. Assuming that household preferences remain constant, does this indicate that children are inferior goods? Explain.
7. If the income of a household increases and one of the prices for a commodity that the household consumes decreases, will the household be at least as well off? Explain.
8. In the analysis of consumer behavior, it may appear logical to define complementarity between two commodities x_1 and x_2 as occurring where MU_1 rises as more of x_2 is consumed. Specifically, $\partial^2 U/\partial x_1 \partial x_2 > 0$. In economic theory, complementarity is not defined this way. Why not? How is it defined?
9. Higher heating costs forced many low-income households to reduce their food consumption during a hard winter. This indicates food is a substitute for heat. True or false? Explain.
10. Sara requires \$20,000 to maintain her present standard of living at existing prices. She currently purchases 50 CD's a year, so an increase in the price of CD's by \$10.00 indicates she would require \$20,500 to maintain her standard of living. True or false? Explain.

Exercises

One is not likely to achieve understanding from the explanation of another. Understanding is achieved by solving problems.

(Michael Wetzstein)

1. Consider the following utility functions:
   - i. $U(x_1, x_2) = x_1^{3/5} x_2^{4/5}$;
   - ii. $U(x_1, x_2) = x_2 + \ln x_1$, *quasilinear utility*;
   - iii. $U(x_1, x_2) = 3(x_1 x_2)^{1/4} + \ln 5$;
   - iv. $U(x_1, x_2) = A x_1^{1/2} x_2^{1/3}$;
   - v. $U(x_1, x_2) = \frac{1}{2}\ln x_1 + \frac{1}{3}\ln x_2$;
   - vi. $U(x_1, x_2) = 156 x_1^{1/2} x_2$;
   - vii. $U(x_1, x_2) = 10 x_1^{2/3} x_2^{3/4} + 23.7$.

   a. Derive the demand functions for x_1 and x_2.
   b. Geometrically illustrate the demand and Engel curves for commodity x_2.

2. Consider the following utility functions:
   - i. $U(x_1, x_2) = x_1^4 x_2^2$;
   - ii. $U(x_1, x_2) = x_1^{1/4} x_2^{1/4}$;
   - iii. $U(x_1, x_2) = x_1 x_2^2$;
   - iv. $U(x_1, x_2) = 5x_1 + 3x_2$;
   - v. $U(x_1, x_2) = x_1 x_2/(x_1 + x_2)$;
   - vi. $U(x_1, x_2) = \min(x_1, x_2)$.

   a. Derive the demand functions for x_1 and x_2 as functions of p_1, p_2, and I.
   b. Determine if the demand functions are downward-sloping.

c. Are the commodities normal or inferior? Explain.
d. What are the cross-price effects of x_1? Is x_1 a substitute for or a complement for x_2? Explain.

3. Consider the following utility function:

$$U = x_1 x_2.$$

a. Assuming a rational household with preferences represented by this utility function, maximize utility, U^*, and derive the demand functions for x_1 and x_2.
b. Suppose that instead of maximizing utility at U^*, the household attempts to minimize expenditures to achieve utility level U^*. Set up the optimization problem and solve it. How does the answer differ from (a)? How is it similar?

4. Assume preferences represented by the utility function $\min(x_1, x_2)$. What is the Slutsky equation that decomposes the change in the demand for x_1 in response to a change in its price? What is the income effect? What is the substitution effect?
5. Geometrically illustrate the Slutsky equation and derive the demand curve for the following:
   a. An ordinary and normal good
   b. An ordinary and inferior good
   c. A Giffen good
6. The income expansion path of a household is derived with prices of commodities x_1 and x_2 held constant. After the price of x_1 falls, a second income expansion path is derived. Use the Slutsky equation to explain why the two expansion paths cannot cross.
7. Assume Katherine receives five football tickets, and she may either attend the games or scalp them. In one season, she may attend some games and sell tickets for the games she does not attend. Assume her decisions are independent of whom the home team is playing. If the price at which she can sell her tickets increases, determine the effect on the number of games she chooses to attend.
8. Consider the utility function

$$U = x_1/x_2, \quad \text{s.t. } x_1, x_2 \geq 0.$$

If $x_2 = 0$, then $U = x_1$. Derive the demand functions for commodities 1 and 2 as they depend on prices and income.

9. Assume a local sales tax on food is removed. Using the Slutsky equation, explain how this tax change will affect a household's food consumption.

Internet case studies

1. Determine what your current cost of going to college would have been for your parents.

2. Find examples of a Giffen good.
3. Find a number of other price indexes besides the Laspeyres index and discuss how they are used.

APPENDIX TO CHAPTER 4

How the Slutsky equation relates to the household's supply of labor

I finished last, but I got to sleep in.

(Michael Wetzstein)

Translation: Work/leisure choice.

Labor is an integral part of production. In all production processes, labor is employed either directly or indirectly through the development of physical capital. Thus, some economists adhere to the philosophy that all returns from production should accrue to labor. As discussed in Chapter 16, the amount of returns accruing to labor is determined by the labor market supply curve, which is based on the individual labor supply curves of households.

We derive a household's labor supply curve similar to the way we derive a household's demand curve for a commodity. This labor supply curve is based on the household maximizing utility when confronted with the problem of time allocation. Because there is only a fixed amount of time in a given day, week, month, or year, households and individuals within a household must decide how many hours to work, consume, and sleep. In terms of an individual, the wage or salary an individual obtains can be expected to influence this time allocation and, in particular, determine the supply of labor.

We can simplify the problem of time allocation by reducing the choice to either work or leisure, where an individual derives satisfaction directly from leisure activities (such as reading, hunting, or attending concerts) and indirectly from working to obtain income to spend. With this choice, we can investigate the effects of a wage change in a two-commodity utility model. The two commodities are leisure h and a composite commodity I that contains all other commodities. Setting the price of the composite commodity as the numeraire price (so it is equal to 1), we represent utility as

$$U = U(h, I).$$

Considering both time and income constraints

I still find each day too short for all the thoughts I want to think, all the walks I want to take, all the books I want to read, and all the friends I want to see.

(John Burroughs)

Households are all endowed with the same time budget, but time allocation between work and leisure (walks, books, and friends) differs owning to heterogeneity in preferences and income constraints. A household's objective is then to maximize utility subject to the following constraints:

$$\ell + h = 24,$$

where ℓ is hours of work per day, and

$$I = w\ell + Y,$$

where w is the hourly wage rate and Y is the daily nonwage income. The nonwage income could be unearned income in the form of interest, dividends, or parent's income, so it is assumed $Y > 0$. (An alternative allocative assumption would be assuming $Y < 0$, where Y could then be a tax.) The first constraint indicates there are only 24 hours in the day to be allocated between work and leisure. This time constraint is assumed fixed. The second constraint is an income constraint, where the wage rate w times the hours worked ℓ, plus nonwage income, determines an individual's income level. Income is used for purchasing the composite commodity with a numeraire price, so the level of consumption is equal to I. This income constraint can vary from a maximum of $24w + Y$, where an individual devotes all 24 hours to work, to a minimum of Y, where an individual does not work ($\ell = 0$).

Combining the two constraints gives

$$I = w(24 - h) + Y,$$
$$I + wh = 24w + Y.$$

Given the Nonsatiation Axiom and an individual's attempt to maximize utility, the total expenditures on consumption and leisure ($I + wh$) will equal an individual's total potential income. The price of leisure, h, is the opportunity cost of not working, w. If $h = 24$, the individual does not work, so $Y = I$ and income I cannot fall below Y with $h \leq 24$. Thus, an additional constraint is $h \leq 24$. The constraints are illustrated in Figure 4A.1. For $Y > 0$, we solve for I to obtain

$$I = 24w + Y - wh,$$

where $24w + Y$ is the maximum level of consumption with no leisure time, and the slope $-w$ measures the opportunity cost of forfeiting income for leisure. At $h = 24$, the constraint $h \leq 24$ truncates the ability for transforming income into leisure.

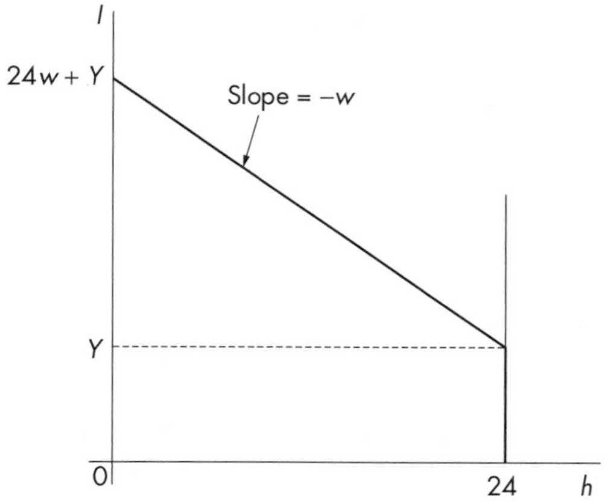

Figure 4A.1 **Time and income constraints for $Y > 0$.** If $h = 0$, income is the sum of earned income, $24w$, and unearned income Y. As h increases, income falls at a rate of w until $h = 24$.

Is time a constraint on happiness? Yes, time is a limited resource that prevents households from achieving global bliss.

Doing utility maximization

Given that a household is interested in maximizing utility subject to this constraint, the Lagrangian is

$$\mathcal{L}(h, I, \lambda) = U(h, I) + \lambda(24w + Y - I - wh).$$

The FOCs are then

$$\frac{\partial \mathcal{L}}{\partial h} = \frac{\partial U}{\partial h} - w\lambda^* = 0,$$

$$\frac{\partial \mathcal{L}}{\partial I} = \frac{\partial U}{\partial I} - \lambda^* = 0,$$

$$\frac{\partial \mathcal{L}}{\partial \lambda} = 24w + Y - I^* - wh^* = 0.$$

These FOCs result in

$$\text{MRS}(I \text{ for } h) = \frac{\partial U/\partial h}{\partial U/\partial I} = w.$$

As illustrated in Figure 4A.2, this FOC is represented by the tangency, at point A, between a household's indifference curve for income and leisure and the constraint. At this tangency the household is maximizing utility in terms of the work/leisure choice by engaging in h^* hours of leisure and working $24 - h^*$ hours. Working $24 - h^*$ yields an optimal level of income I^*. The negative of the slope of this indifference curve is MRS(I for h), and the

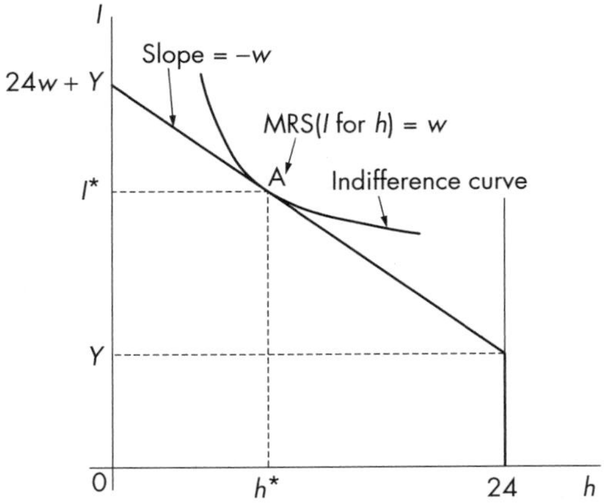

Figure 4A.2 **Work/leisure choice for maximizing utility.** At the tangency point A, MRS(I for h) $= w$, so the household will maximize utility by engaging in h^* hours of leisure and spending I^* on consumption.

slope of the constraint is the negative of the wage rate w. A movement down this constraint transforms income into leisure based on the wage rate. The wage rate is the income foregone by not working. For example, giving up income in the amount of w will allow one more hour of leisure. The slope is $-w/1$.

Understanding substitution and income effects

By investigating the effect a wage rate change has on this income/leisure choice, we can derive the household's labor supply curve. As with a household's demand curve, the total effect of a wage change can be decomposed into income and substitution effects. As illustrated in Figure 4A.3, a rise in the wage rate from w° to w' results in a substitution effect represented as a movement from A to B on the same indifference curve, U°. As a result of this substitution effect, the household engages in less leisure, substituting work for leisure, holding utility constant.

In contrast, assuming leisure is a normal good, $\partial h/\partial I > 0$, an increase in income will result in more leisure. Thus, the income effect from a rise in wages is opposite to that of the substitution effect. As illustrated in Figure 4A.3, the income effect, resulting in a movement from B to C, offsets a portion of the substitution effect. The total effect, a movement from

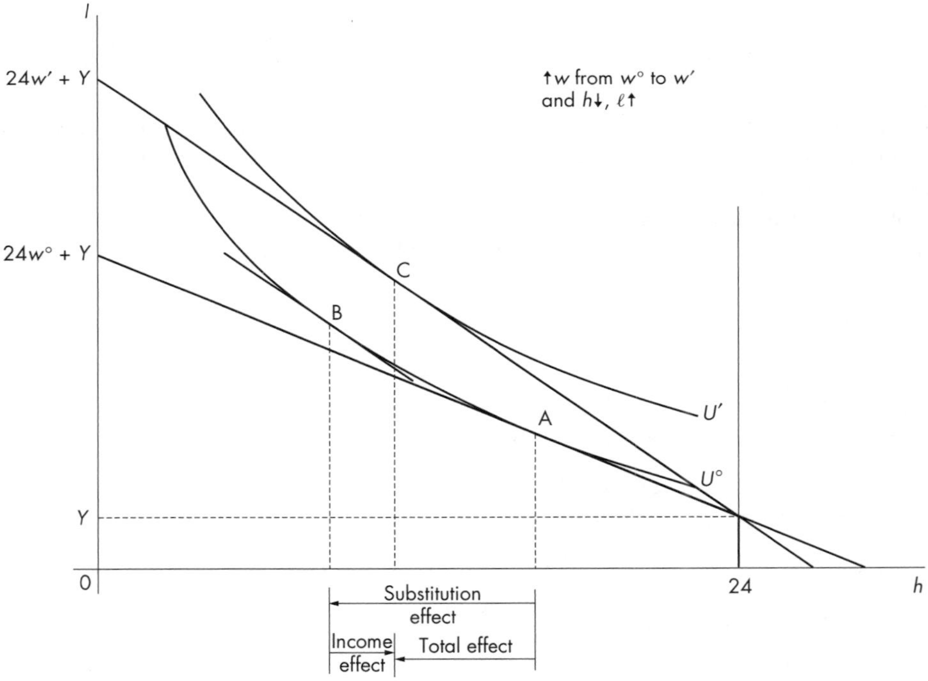

Figure 4A.3 **Substitution and income effects for the work/leisure choice, given an increase in wages resulting in an increase in hours worked.** An increase in wages results in the total effect A to C, with a movement from A to B representing the substitution effect and a movement from B to C the income effect. In this case, the income effect does not completely offset the negative substitution effect, so the total effect of a wage increase decreases leisure.

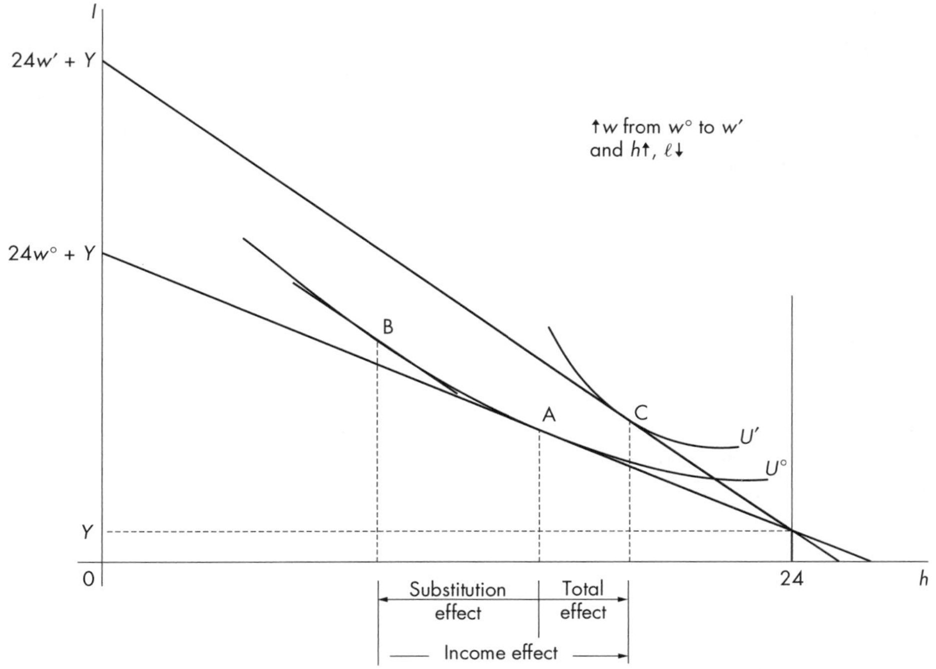

Figure 4A.4 **Substitution and income effects for the work/leisure choice, given an increase in wages, resulting in a decrease in hours worked.** An increase in wages results in the total effect A to C, with a movement from A to B representing the substitution effect and a movement from B to C the income effect. In this case, the income effect completely offsets the negative substitution effect, so the total effect of a wage increase increases leisure.

A to C, is thus less than the substitution effect, but it is still negative, $\partial h/\partial w < 0$. Alternatively, as illustrated in Figure 4A.4, the income effect can completely offset the substitution effect, resulting in a positive total effect, $\partial h/\partial w > 0$. The total effect, the movement from A to C, results in the household's income still increasing, but the household is interested in allocating more time to spend this increased income.

Using the adjusted Slutsky equation

Similar to the Slutsky equation for a price change of a commodity, an equation exists for decomposing the total effect from a change in wages. This adjusted Slutsky equation is

Total effect = Substitution effect + Income effect

$$\frac{\partial h}{\partial w} = \left.\frac{\partial h}{\partial w}\right|_{dU=0} + \frac{\partial h}{\partial I}\ell.$$

Note that the positive sign between the two terms on the right-hand side results from real income increasing with a wage increase, as opposed to real income falling with a commodity price increase.

The *adjusted Slutsky equation* considers an additional income effect when wages are changed. The standard Slutsky equation developed in this chapter assumes that income is held constant given a price change. In the case of a wage rate change, income is not held constant. For example, an increase in wages will increase potential income. An adjustment to the income component of the Slutsky equation is then required to account for this change in potential income. The adjustment is the change in demand for leisure when income changes, $\partial h/\partial I$, times the change in potential income when wages change. This change in potential income when wages change is determined by

$$I = 24w,$$

$$\frac{\partial I}{\partial w} = 24.$$

The partial derivative $\partial I/\partial w$ indicates how potential income changes when wages change. Given 24 hours in a day, if wages increase by \$1, potential income will be enhanced by \$24. Thus, the adjustment to the income effect is $24\partial h/\partial I$. Incorporating this adjustment into the standard Slutsky equation yields the adjusted Slutsky equation:

$$\begin{aligned}\frac{\partial h}{\partial w} &= \frac{\partial h}{\partial w}\Big|_{dU=0} - \frac{\partial h}{\partial I}h + 24\frac{\partial h}{\partial I}\\ &= \frac{\partial h}{\partial w}\Big|_{dU=0} + (24-h)\frac{\partial h}{\partial I}\\ &= \frac{\partial h}{\partial w}\Big|_{dU=0} + \frac{\partial h}{\partial I}\ell.\end{aligned}$$

Deriving household's supply-of-labor curve

Suppose an HMO doctor receives a large salary increase. As a result of this increase in income, she decides to take Wednesdays off to play golf. In this case, the doctor's labor supply curve has a negative slope. An increase in wages results in her working less. In general, a **household's labor supply curve** illustrates how much labor a household is willing and able to supply at a given wage rate. The relative magnitude of the substitution and income effects will determine the sign of the total effect, and thus, the slope of a household's labor supply curve, $\partial \ell/\partial w$. Specifically,

$$h = 24 - \ell,$$

$$\frac{\partial h}{\partial w} = -\frac{\partial \ell}{\partial w}.$$

If the total effect is negative, $\partial h/\partial w < 0$ (Figure 4A.3), then the slope of the labor supply curve will be positive, $\partial \ell/\partial w > 0$ (Figure 4A.5). The larger the substitution effect, the more responsive an individual is to a change in wages, so the less steeply sloped will be the supply curve. For example, a high-school graduate who does not have an option of going to college may be willing to work for almost any wage just to gain some experience. Alternatively, as the number of hours this individual works increases, the income effect may increase, which will tend to offset the substitution effect so that the supply curve might become more

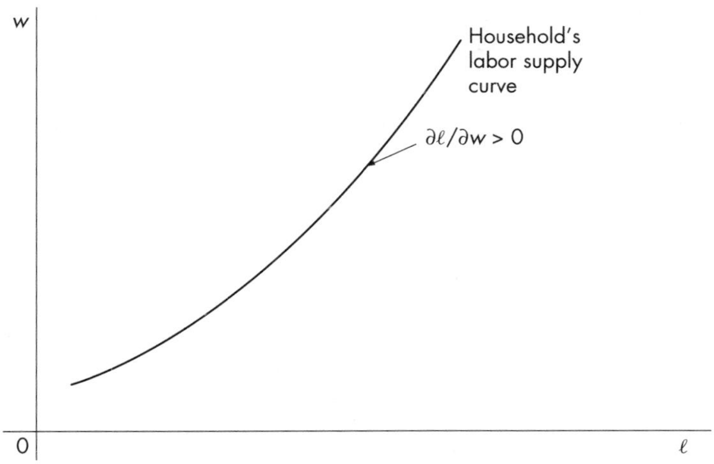

Figure 4A.5 **Positively sloped household's labor supply curve.** As wages increase, the quantity supplied of labor by a household increases.

steeply sloped. As the number of hours working increases, the household may be unresponsive to any further increase in wages.

Eventually, a point may be reached where any increase in wages results in a positive total effect, $\partial h/\partial w > 0$. The household will decrease hours worked given a wage increase, $\partial \ell/\partial w < 0$ (Figure 4A.6). As illustrated in Figure 4A.6, this results in a negative sloping household supply curve for labor (called a **backward-bending labor supply curve**). As wages increase, at first the household may increase hours worked. However, at some point the household may decrease the number of hours worked if wages continue to increase and will allocate more leisure time to consume I.

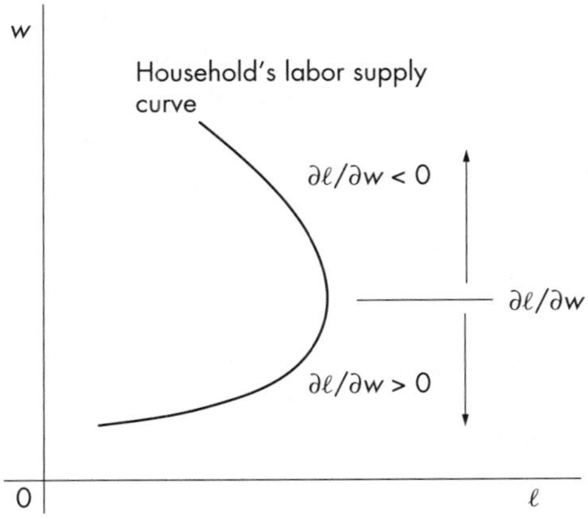

Figure 4A.6 **Backward-bending household's labor supply curve.** As wages increase, the quantity supply of labor at first increases. But at some point, further increases in wages result in a decrease in quantity of labor supplied.

Given a wage increase, will you always work more? No. The income effect from an increase in wages may completely offset the substitution effect of increased hours worked, so you will work less.

If one segment of the household consumes and another segment works, the income effect may not offset the substitution effect. For example, putting children through college may, for particularly low-wage households, result in a large negative substitution effect and a small income effect.

Data on the average work week over the past century supports the theory of a backward-bending household labor supply curve. At the end of the nineteenth century, the average working week was approximately 60 hours. As relative wages rose, the average working week declined to approximately 40 hours by the late 1920s. During this time, leisure was substituted for income as incomes increased. However, in the United States, the average working week has not fallen much below 40 hours. The substitution effect of higher wages has almost exactly balanced the income effect. However, since the mid twentieth century, the number of two-income households has increased significantly, partially as a result of higher wage opportunities developing for women. Thus, the household labor supply curve over the past half-century may not be backward-bending. Currently, the lack of household leisure time has resulted in some households allocating more leisure time as income continues to rise. Time will tell if this trend is significant.

Application: Empirical estimates of an income/leisure indifference function

L.E. Dunn has derived indifference curves for the income/leisure choice and labor supply curves based on a survey of textile workers in a southeastern US cotton-mill town. In an oral interview, each worker was asked how much, if any, money per week he or she would be willing to pay in order to have on his or her job a specified non-pecuniary return (e.g., improved working conditions, pension plan, or lunch break). Workers were also asked how much longer they would be willing to work with no extra pay to have this return.

Specifying an indifference function satisfying the preference axioms resulted in empirically estimated sharply bending curves with labor and income approximately constant to the left and right of the bend, respectively. This indicates close but not perfect complements between income and leisure. A high degree of inflexibility in choice between income and leisure exists, which may be explained by workers being conditioned to a subsistence level of living. Dunn estimated that the associated labor supply curve resulting from the textile workers' preferences has a negative slope throughout the entire range of working hours. This is in contrast to a backward-bending labor supply curve, where the slope is positive at low incomes and becomes negative at high incomes. The subsistence level of income results in workers possessing a target level of income behavior. Workers desire to maintain approximately a given level of subsistence income, so they will work more to maintain their income as wages fall.

Source: L.E. Dunn, "An Empirical Indifference Function for Income and Leisure," *Review of Economics and Statistics* 6 (1978): 533–540.

Example 4A.1 Determining the household's work/leisure choice

Consider the following utility function for leisure h and income I:

$$U(h, I) = h^{1/4} I^{1/2}.$$

A household is interested in maximizing utility subject to time and income constraints

$$\ell + h = 24 \quad \text{and} \quad I = w\ell + Y,$$

where Y is some nonwage income. Solving for ℓ in the income constraint

$$\ell = \frac{I}{w} - \frac{Y}{w}$$

and substituting the result into the time constraint yields

$$\frac{I}{w} - \frac{Y}{w} + h = 24.$$

Multiplying through by w and representing the equation in implicit form yields the combined constraint

$$24w + Y - I - wh = 0.$$

The resulting Lagrangian is then

$$\mathcal{L}(h, I, \lambda) = h^{1/4} I^{1/2} + \lambda(24w + Y - I - wh).$$

The FOCs are

$$\frac{\partial \mathcal{L}}{\partial h} = \frac{1}{4} h^{*-1} U - \lambda^* w = 0,$$

$$\frac{\partial \mathcal{L}}{\partial I} = \frac{1}{2} I^{*-1} U - \lambda^* = 0,$$

$$\frac{\partial \mathcal{L}}{\partial \lambda} = 24w + Y - I^* - wh^* = 0.$$

From these FOCs,

$$\text{MRS}(I \text{ for } h) = \frac{\partial U / \partial h}{\partial U / \partial I} = \frac{\frac{1}{2} I^*}{h^*} = w.$$

Solving for I^* yields the expansion path, $I^* = 2h^* w$. Substituting this expansion path into the constraint yields

$$24w + Y - 2h^* w - wh^* = 0$$

$$3h^* = \frac{Y}{w} + 24,$$

$$h^* = \frac{Y}{3w} + 8, \text{ household's leisure demand function.}$$

This demand function has the properties

$$\frac{\partial h}{\partial w} = -\frac{Y}{3w^2} < 0,$$

$$\frac{\partial^2 h}{\partial w^2} = \frac{2Y}{3w^3} > 0.$$

The supply function for labor is then

$$\ell^* = 24 - h^* = -\frac{Y}{3w} + 16,$$

with

$$\frac{\partial \ell}{\partial w} = \frac{Y}{3w^2} > 0,$$

$$\frac{\partial^2 \ell}{\partial w^2} = -\frac{2Y}{3w^3} < 0.$$

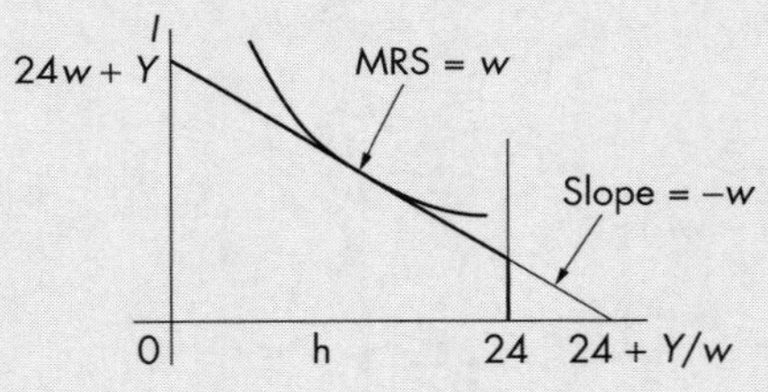

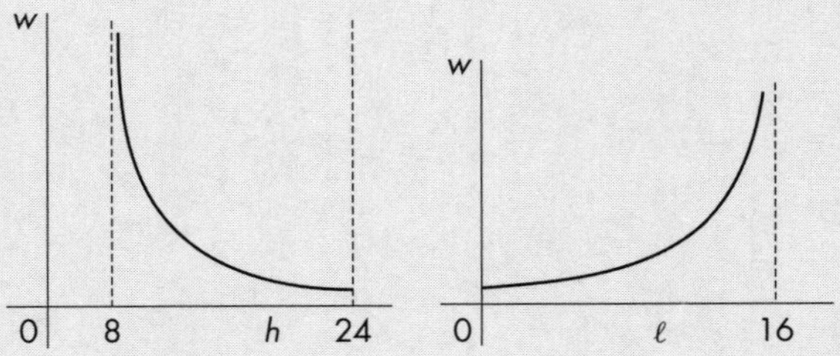

Example 4A.2 Deriving a negatively sloping labor supply curve

The following utility function will yield a negatively sloping labor supply curve:

$$U = \ln(I - b) + 2\ln h, b < I.$$

For U to be positive a threshold, b, of income is required. MRS(I for h) $= 2(I - b)/h$. Equating MRS to the economic rate of substitution, $w/1$, and solving for I yields the expansion path

$$\frac{2(I^* - b)}{h^*} = w,$$

$$I^* = \frac{1}{2}h^* w + b, \quad \text{expansion path.}$$

Substituting the expansion path into the constraint results in

$$24w + Y - I^* - h^* w = 0,$$

and solving for h^* yields the demand function for leisure:

$$24w + Y - \left(\tfrac{1}{2}h^* w + b\right) - h^* w = 0,$$

$$\frac{3}{2}h^* w = 24w + Y - b,$$

$$h^* = 16 + \frac{2(Y - b)}{3w}, \quad \text{demand function for leisure.}$$

This demand function has the properties

$$\frac{\partial h}{\partial w} = -\frac{2(Y - b)}{3w^2} > 0 \quad \text{if } b > Y,$$

$$\frac{\partial^2 h}{\partial w^2} = \frac{4(Y - b)}{3w^3} < 0.$$

The supply function for labor is then

$$\ell^* = 24 - h^* = 24 - \left[16 + \frac{2(Y - b)}{3w}\right] = 8 - \frac{2(Y - b)}{3w},$$

with

$$\frac{\partial \ell}{\partial w} = \frac{2(Y - b)}{3w^2} < 0 \quad \text{if } b > Y,$$

$$\frac{\partial^2 \ell}{\partial w^2} = -\frac{4(Y - b)}{3w^3} > 0.$$

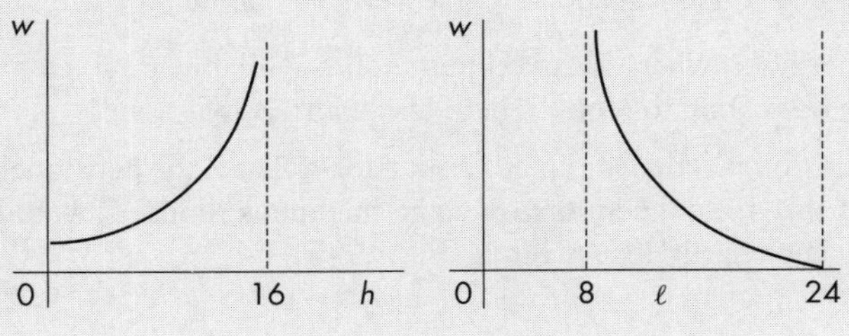

Questions

1. What is the price of your leisure?
2. In the last century, real wealth and real wages have steadily increased in the United States. However, average working hours in market employment have remained relatively constant. What does this condition indicate in terms of the income and substitution effects of labor?
3. In the nineteenth century, managers of African mines had a difficult time getting enough native workers. When they raised the wage rate, they found the workers worked for shorter stints before returning to their native villages. The European managers attributed this behavior to laziness. Do you agree? Explain.
4. If the supply curve for labor is backward-bending, leisure is a luxury good. True or false? Explain.
5. An increase in the income tax rate will induce employees to work more to offset the net decline in income. True or false? Explain.

Exercises

1. Draw the indifference map and budget line for Dr Toil, who prefers working for a living to receiving the same income as unemployment relief.
2. Assume a Negative Income Tax System (NITS) is introduced where each worker is given \$50 a week and then taxed at a rate of 25 percent on all earnings.

   a. Would individuals earning \$200 a week prior to the NITS reduce their supply of labor?
   b. What about individuals earning \$320 a week?

3. Assume Andrea has preferences represented as $U = I + 2h^{1/2}$, where I is the composite commodity and h is leisure.

   a. Derive Andrea's labor supply function.
   b. What is the minimum wage for which she is willing to work?
   c. How will her supply of labor respond to a lowering of an income tax?

4. Donald is paid \$20 per hour, where his maximum hours available are fixed by his employer. Would he be willing to moonlight at less than \$20 per hour?
5. Assume a tax-free pension is reduced (taxed) dollar-for-dollar if the pensioner has any wage income. If this 100 percent tax on wage income is reduced, would the government treasury necessarily lose revenue?

6. Ms Tight is currently paying her workers \$10 an hour for the first 40 hours per week and \$15 per hour for overtime. Overtime averages 10 hours per week. Ms Tight also pays \$20 a week in Social Security contributions per employee, regardless of the number of hours they worked. The workers now lobby for a contract that abolishes overtime and replaces it with a fixed wage of \$11 per hour. Will Ms Tight accept the contract? Explain.

7. Kelly receives utility from leisure consumed during a day, h, and from a daily income I, according to preferences

$$U(h, I) = h^{3/4} I^{1/4}.$$

Kelly attempts to maximize utility subject to the constraints

$$\ell + h = 24, \quad I = w\ell + Y,$$

where ℓ is the number of hours worked and Y is income from nonlabor sources.

a. If $Y = 0$, determine Kelly's labor supply curve. How many hours will he work if $w = \$4$?

b. Assume Kelly has an outside income of \$16 per day. How will this income shift the supply of the labor curve? Now how many hours will be worked if $w = \$4$?

8. Sara receives utility from leisure consumed during a typical day, h, and from income received during the day, I, according to the utility function

$$U(I, h) = h^{2/3} I^{1/3}.$$

Sara attempts to maximize utility subject to two constraints

$$\ell + h = 24,$$

and

$$I = w\ell.$$

Calculate Sara's labor supply curve.

9. Assume Marjean has the income/leisure preferences

$$U(h, I) = h^{1/3}(I + 45)^{2/3}.$$

At a wage rate of \$15 per hour, determine the optimal hours of work per day.

10. Mr Marich has preferences represented by the utility function

$$U = h^{1/2} I,$$

where h is hours of leisure activities and I is consumption. Mr Marich maximizes his utility at $U = 640$ when he works 8 hours a day. If Mrs Gass offered him \$20, would he be willing to give up an hour of his leisure time to drive her to the mall? Explain.

Internet case study

Determine the average salaries in a number of occupations and the likelihood the labor supply curves are backward-bending.

Part II

Markets and consumer interaction

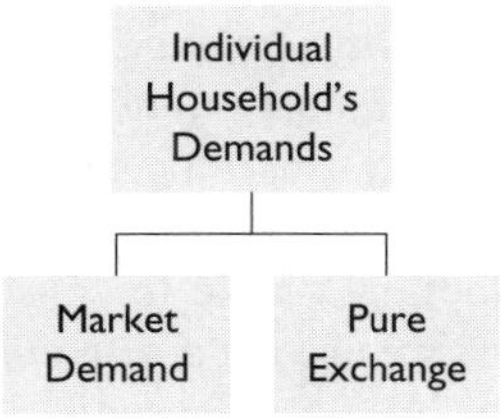

Chapters

Market economy is where even the price for a kidney is known.

(Michael Wetzstein)

For firms to know what and how many commodities consumers would like them to produce, they must receive some type of a signal. Economic theory reveals that the only signal firms require is the price signal, which is based on the market demand and supply of a commodity. Without any centralized organization, the market transforms households' demands for commodities into price signals for firms.

In Part 1 (Chapters 2–4), we derived household demands for commodities when individual households maximize their utility (happiness) constrained by limited resources embodied as an income constraint. Individual demand functions are based on this decentralized decision process. These demand functions state how much of each commodity a household is willing and able to consume at given prices. For enhancing social welfare, household demands for commodities should be closely matched with the production and supply of these commodities, which requires price signals based on the sum of all individual household demands for a commodity. Producers can then base their production decisions on this aggregate household demand.

We develop this concept in Chapter 5. An economy where commodities demanded by households are available for purchase at known prices is called a *market economy*. In contrast, a barter economy is where commodities demanded by households can only be obtained by exchanging other commodities. There are no set commodity prices to serve as market signals. To understand how a market economy functions and equilibrium prices and quantities are determined, economists employ both partial-equilibrium and general-equilibrium analyses.

As the name implies, *partial-equilibrium analysis* considers equilibrium in a subset of an economy. For example, a household's solution to its utility-maximization problem is a partial-equilibrium analysis if we assume that the household's solution is not affected by other households (as we did in Chapter 3). However, a household's determination of which consumption bundle to consume generally is influenced by other households' choices. Thus, we use *general-equilibrium analysis* to consider the influence each household choice has on other households' choices (Chapter 6). This analysis investigates how commodities are optimally allocated among households, so aggregate demand is equal to a given supply of the commodities. An economy where this is true is a *pure-exchange economy*, where the supply of all the commodities is fixed (there is no production).

5 Market demand

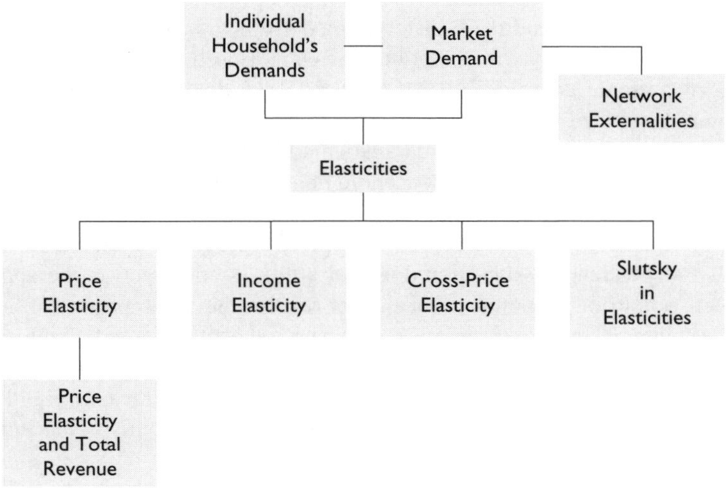

Outline and Conceptual Inquiries

Deriving the market demand

Understanding network externalities

Would you purchase a fax machine if no one else had one?

Application: Network externalities in consumption of international multi-ingredient foods

Did you purchase a pet rock, an Elmo, Power Ranger shoes, or Pokémon cards?

Application: Why technology adoption has a bandwagon effect

Elasticity dissected

Units of measurement

Deriving a unit-free measure of responsiveness

Why a logarithmic representation?

Price elasticity of demand

What is your demand for living?

Application: Measuring the impact of an airport on travelers' expenditures

Relationship between price elasticity and total revenue

Why do farmers always seem to complain about the prices they receive or their yields?

Application: How to adjust prices: US versus French wine producers

Price elasticity and the price consumption curve

Income elasticity of demand

Cross-price elasticity of demand

Slutsky equation in elasticities

Summary

Key concepts

Key equation

Questions

Exercises

Internet case studies

Appendix to chapter 5

Behavioral economics

Will you eat a doughnut or a cup of yogurt?

Do stock and commodity traders suffer from loss aversion?

What will provide you with more satisfaction: a diamond necklace or a family vacation?

Everybody wants excellence in their local schools, but when it comes to paying for this excellence many are unwilling to pay the price.

(Michael Wetzstein)

The demand for a commodity is differentiated from a want in terms of society's willingness and ability to pay for satisfying the want. Based on individual households' demands for a single commodity (in Chapter 4), we determine in this chapter the total amount demanded for a commodity by all households (called *market demand* or *aggregate demand*). As we will see, market demand is the sum of individual household demands, assuming that individual household demands are independent of each other. For example, one individual's demand for going to a volleyball game is independent of another individual going. However, we will explore cases called *network externalities,* where this independence assumption does not hold. As addressed in the appendix to this chapter, a field of economics that further relaxes the assumptions on household behavior is called behavioral economics. A behavioral economist will combine related disciplines, principally psychology, to investigate how considering alternative, possibly less restrictive, assumptions can enrich our ability to understand the household decision process. A behavioral economist's goal and that of other economists is to improve on our understanding of markets and how prices are determined.

Major determinants of market demand for a commodity are its own price, the price of related commodities, and households' incomes. *Elasticity of demand* is a measure of the influence each of these parameters has on market demand. We first investigate own-price elasticity of demand as elastic, unitary, or inelastic, depending on its degree of responsiveness to a price change. Relating own-price elasticity to households' total expenditures for a commodity, we demonstrate how the own-price elasticity of demand determines whether total expenditures for a commodity will increase, remain unchanged, or decline, given a price change. We then define income elasticity of demand and elasticity of demand for the price of related commodities (called *cross-price elasticity*).

Applied economists are very active in estimating elasticities for all of the determinants (parameters) of market demand. Knowledge of the influence these determinants have on market demand provides information for firms' decisions on pricing, sales promotion, production, and product development. Government policymakers can also employ estimates of elasticities to determine the nature and impact of various programs on markets, firms, and household behavior. Armed with reliable estimates of elasticities based on economic models, economists have the ability to explain, predict, and control agents' market behavior.

Deriving the market demand

Enjoy your own life without comparing it with that of another.

(Marquis De Condorcet)

Market demand is one arm of the Marshallian cross. It conveys jointly each individual household's preferences for a commodity given its budget constraint. This **market demand** (or **aggregate demand**) is the sum of all individual households' demands for a single commodity. Let's consider only two households—Robinson (R) and Friday (F)—and two commodities:

$$x_1^R = x_1^R(p_1, p_2, I^R),$$
$$x_1^F = x_1^F(p_1, p_2, I^F),$$

where x_1^R and x_1^F are, respectively, household Robinson's and household Friday's demands for commodity x_1. Both households are facing the same per-unit prices for the two commodities p_1 and p_2, and we will assume each household is a price taker. Also, both households are bound by their budget constraints, with I^R and I^F representing income for Robinson and Friday, respectively.

Market (aggregate) demand. The total amount of demand for a commodity by all households. *E.g., the total demand for watching the Super Bowl on TV.*

The market demand Q_1 is the sum of the amounts demanded by the two households:

$$Q_1 = x_1^R + x_1^F = x_1^R(p_1, p_2, I^R) + x_1^F(p_1, p_2, I^F),$$

or

$$Q_1 = Q^D(p_1, p_2, I^R, I^F).$$

Holding p_2, I^R, and I^F constant, we obtain the market demand curve for x_1 in Figure 5.1. For a private good,[1] the market demand curve is the horizontal summation of the individual household demand curves:

$$Q_1^* = x_1^{R*} + x_1^{F*}.$$

As illustrated in Figure 5.1, at p_1^*, Robinson demands 5 units of Q_1 and Friday's demand is 3 units. Summing these demands at the price p_1^* yields the total market demand of 8 units. Varying the price will result in other associated levels of market demand, which will then trace out the market demand curve for Q_1. Given that x_1 is an ordinary commodity for both households, $\partial x_1^R/\partial p_1 < 0$ and $\partial x_1^F/\partial p_1 < 0$. Then, for changes in p_1, the market demand curve will have a negative slope, $\partial Q_1/\partial p_1 < 0$.

Example 5.1 Deriving market demand from individual households' demands

Assume two households, R and F, with demand functions for commodity x_1, and let the specific representations of these functions be the demand functions derived

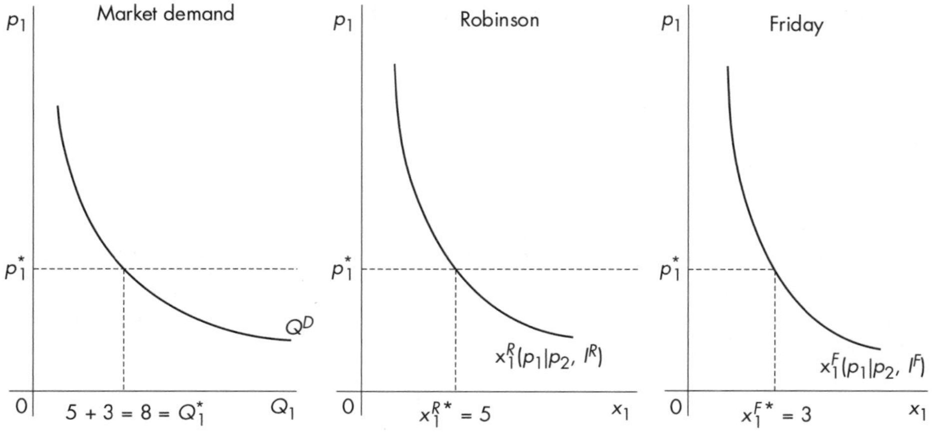

Figure 5.1 **Market demand for commodity Q_1 as the horizontal summation of individual households' demands.** For a given price, the level of quantity demanded in the market is determined by horizontally summing the individual household's quantity demanded.

in Example 4.1:

$$x_1^R = \frac{5I^R}{8p_1} \text{ and } x_1^F = \frac{5I^F}{8p_1}.$$

Also, let the incomes for households R and F be $I^R = \$104$ and $I^F = \$136$. Market demand for Q_1 is then the horizontal summation of these household demands:

$$Q_1 = x_1^R + x_1^F = \frac{5I^R}{8p_1} + \frac{5I^F}{8p_1} = \frac{5}{8p_1}(I^R + I^F).$$

Substituting in the given levels of income gives

$$Q_1 = x_1^R + x_1^F = \frac{5}{8p_1}(240) = \frac{150}{p_1}.$$

As illustrated in the figure, this is a negatively sloped convex market demand curve. Specifically,

$$\frac{dQ_1}{dp_1} = -\frac{150}{p_1^2} < 0,$$

$$\frac{d^2Q_1}{dp_1^2} = \frac{300}{p_1^3} > 0.$$

Note that if aggregate income increases, say by \$80, the market demand curve will shift to the right. For example, at $p_1 = \$50$, market demand at an aggregate income of \$240 is 3 units, but an increase in aggregate income to $320 results in a market demand of 4 units.

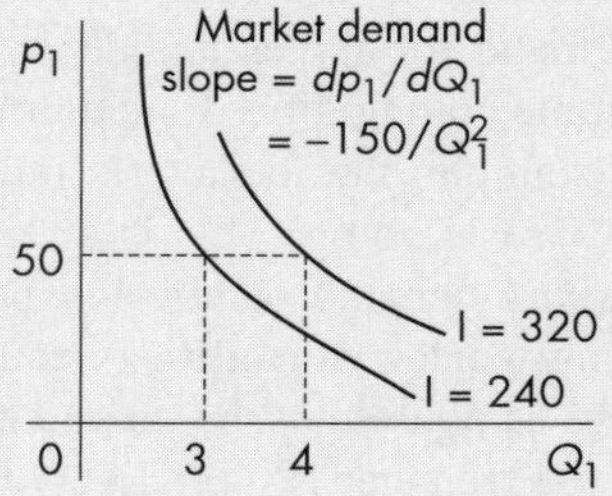

It is possible that $\partial x_1/\partial p_1 > 0$, a Giffen good, for some households. However, for market demand to have a positive slope, $\partial Q_1/\partial p_1 > 0$, a large portion of households would have to consider x_1 a Giffen good, which is unlikely. Thus, we assume that market demand for a commodity is inversely related to its own price. Also, shifts in the market demand will occur if there is a change in household preferences, income, price of another commodity, or population. As illustrated in Figure 5.2, the market demand curve will shift outward from Q^D to $Q^{D'}$ for an increase in income, population, or the price of substitute commodities, or a decrease in prices of complement commodities.

Understanding network externalities

It is in the nature of very few people to admire without envy a friend who has prospered.

(Aeschylus)

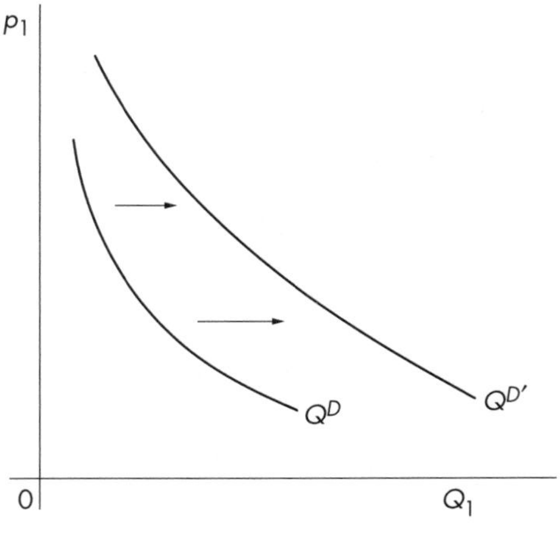

Figure 5.2 **Shift in market demand.** An increase in income, population, or the price of a substitute commodity will result in an outward shift of the market demand curve. A decrease in the price of a complementary commodity will also result in an outward shift.

A teenager talking about an upcoming party was heard saying, "I will go if you go, but I would not be caught dead going if he is there." This statement has a direct impact on the demand for the party. The horizontal summation of households' demand functions assumes individual demands are independent of each other (households do not compare their lives with that of another). For example, one household's demand for apples is independent of another household's demand for apples. However, for some commodities, one household's demand depends on other households' demands. For example, the teenager's interest in (demand for) going to the party is dependent on who else is going. This is an example of *network externalities*, which exist when a household's demand is affected by other households' consumption of the commodity. **Positive network externalities** result when the value one household places on a commodity increases as other households purchase the item. For example, network externalities are positive if the teenager is more likely to go to a party if her friend is also going. In contrast, **negative network externalities** exist if the household's demand decreases as a result of other households' actions. For the teenager, negative network externalities are present if he goes to the party.

Would you purchase a fax machine if no one else had one? No, unless it could be used as a copier.

Positive network externalities. The value one household places on a commodity increases as other households purchase the item. *E.g., demand for fax machines, DVDs, and cell-phone plans.*

Negative network externalities. The value one household places on a commodity declines as other households purchase the item. *E.g., you will not go to an amusement park if increased demand results in congestion.*

Application: Network externalities in consumption of international multi-ingredient foods

The consumption of multi-ingredient foods is increasing around the world. Examples range from packaged mixed salads to frozen pizzas. Ingredients derived from all parts of the world are mixed to form the final product sold to consumers. Producing, processing, and supplying these products presents new and challenging problems. The potential for cross-contamination increases with greater consumption of these multi-ingredient foods. Traceability systems for identifying the sources of all the ingredients used in a product offer improved management of information within and between firms. Such systems allow firms to respond to consumer demands for ingredient sources and reduce the risk of food safety hazards in supply chains. In response to food safety concerns with multi-ingredient foods, the European Parliament and the Council created the European Food Safety Authority, requiring mandatory traceability by 2005.

Souza-Monteiro and Caswell analyzed the economic implications of a voluntary traceability system in a supply chain producing multi-ingredient foods. They modeled inter-firm traceability as a coordination problem, investigating the conditions under which none, a limited number, or all firms provide traceability. Their model incorporated the potential for improved logistics operations and reduced incidence of food safety hazards, along with traceability costs of gathering, storing, and sharing information.

Consideration was also given to the uneven distribution of benefits across the supply chain, which may lead to adoption of suboptimal traceability systems.

Their results identified significant horizontal and vertical positive network externalities. Horizontal externalities occur as the increase in the level of traceability in one ingredient positively affects the demand for similar increases in other ingredients. Vertical network externalities may arise from initial suppliers increasing their traceability, leading to increased demand for intermediate and final suppliers to similarly respond. For an optimal traceability system, an accounting of such network externalities is required.

Source: D. Souza-Monteiro and J. Caswell, "The Economics of Voluntary Traceability in Multi-Ingredient Food Chains," *Agribusiness* 26 (2010): 122–142.

Example 5.2 Deriving market demand from individual households' demands with positive network externalities

Consider a modification of the demand functions for households R and F from Example 5.1:

$$x_1^R(p_1, p_2, I^R, x_1^F) = \frac{5I^R}{8p_1} + \frac{x_1^F}{4},$$

$$x_1^F(p_1, p_2, I^F, x_1^R) = \frac{5I^F}{8p_1} + \frac{x_1^R}{4},$$

where now each household's demand is also a function of the other household's demand. Specifically,

$$\frac{\partial x_1^R}{\partial x_1^F} = \frac{\partial x_1^F}{\partial x_1^R} = \frac{1}{4},$$

indicating that an increase in one household's individual demand (say Friday's) will also generate an increase in Robinson's demand (positive network externality). Households' market demand for Q_1 is determined by solving these two demand functions simultaneously for x_1^R and x_1^F. We do this by first substituting Friday's demand function into Robinson's. The result yields demand functions for households R and F solely as a function of p_1, p_2, and incomes I^R and I^F:

$$x_1^R = \frac{5I^R}{8p_1} + \frac{1}{4}\left(\frac{5I^F}{8p_1} + \frac{x_1^R}{4}\right)$$

$$= \frac{5I^R}{8p_1} + \frac{5I^F}{32p_1} + \frac{x_1^R}{16},$$

$$\frac{15}{16}x_1^R = \frac{5I^R}{8p_1} + \frac{5I^F}{32p_1},$$

$$x_1^R = \frac{2I^R}{3p_1} + \frac{I^F}{6p_1}, \text{ Robinson's demand for } Q_1.$$

Similarly, we derive the demand for F by substituting R's demand function into F's:

$$x_1^F = \frac{2I^F}{3p_1} + \frac{I^R}{6p_1}, \text{ Friday's demand for } Q_1.$$

Market demand is then

$$Q_1 = x_1^R + x_1^F = \frac{2I^R}{3p_1} + \frac{I^F}{6p_1} + \frac{2I^F}{3p_1} + \frac{I^R}{6p_1} = \frac{5}{6p_1}(I^R + I^F).$$

As assumed in Example 5.1, if aggregate income equals \$240, then $Q_1 = 200/p_1$. At $p_1 = 50$, market demand is 4 units, which is larger than the market demand assuming no positive network externalities in Example 5.1. As a result of positive network externalities, the market demand curve shifts to the right.

Bandwagon effect: Wearing the latest fashion

The best way to predict the future is to invent it.

(Alan Kay)

The teenager's demand for going to the party (his behavior) is influenced by a particular set of individuals going or not going—if a friend goes or if he does not go. A field of economics investigating such behavior is called **behavioral economics**, which relaxes assumptions on economic behavior by considering individual behavior based on theories from psychology and other disciplines. In this case of a teenager's demand, a *peer effect* exists that relaxes the assumption of independent teenager behavior. Positive network externalities also exist when individual household demand is affected by the number of other households consuming a commodity (called the **bandwagon effect**). The greater the number of households consuming a commodity, the more desirable the commodity becomes for an individual household. A person develops a demand for a commodity simply because many other people demand it. In fact, the key to marketing most toys and clothing is to create a bandwagon effect. Examples are toys and clothing based on a movie character: the movie creates the bandwagon. A bandwagon effect results in the market demand curve shifting outward as individual household demand increases in response to increased demand by other households. It explains how successful revolutions or strikes grow by leaders motivating others to join, such as the 2011 Arab Spring with revolutions in Bahrain, Egypt, Libya, Syria, Tunisia, and Yemen.

Did you purchase a pet rock, an Elmo, Power Ranger shoes, or Pokémon cards? If you did not, you missed the bandwagon.

Behavioral economics. A field of economics that relaxes assumptions on economic behavior by incorporating findings from related disciplines such as psychology and sociology. *E.g., someone buys a computer tablet on impulse without considering his budget constraint.*

Bandwagon effect. Individual demand is based on the number of other households consuming a commodity. *E.g., a toy based on a TV cartoon character that a child demands because "everyone has one."*

Application: Why technology adoption has a bandwagon effect

Modern economics may be called network economies, as technologies and innovations increasingly require households and firms (agents) to interface with other agents. It is critical for agents to adopt technologies that are capable of interfacing with other internal and external systems, and have complementary additional products available together with a high level of support. A community (network) of users then develops around the technology, providing increasing benefits to adopters. Agents will switch from one technology only if they believe others will also switch (bandwagon effect). Their own preferences may be offset by their expectations concerning what others will do. This desire for compatibility creates a market characterized with network externalities.

As addressed by Lange, McDade, and Oliva, this bandwagon effect creates a discontinuity in market adoption. Adoption occurs once the network externality benefits exceed the benefits from not networking. In markets where technology compatibility is important, agents are better off if they are on the same market standard. Results from Lange et al. indicate that awareness of a technology is a strong measure of benefits. As awareness increases, it provides a sense of security regarding the adoption of a new standard. Whatever an agent's decision is, it wants others to make the same choice. In terms of adoption, Lange et al.'s complementary good variable was a strong indicator of adoption. For example, for a software product's operating system, compatibility is the critical issue. This is why Mac computers initially suffered in the market: the initial lack of compatible software relative to the large number of PC-compatible products. Once software compatibility was not an issue, Macs became very competitive with PCs.

Source: R. Lange, S. McDade, and T. Oliva, "Technological Choice and Network Externalities: A Catastrophe Model Analysis of Firm Software Adoption for Competing Operating Systems," *Structural Change and Economic Dynamics* 12 (2001): 29–57.

Market effect

A simple summation of individual household demands without taking into consideration possible network externalities will not result in the true market demand for a commodity. If positive network externalities exist, the summation of individual household demands does not take into account households' increase in demand when other households increase their demand for the commodity and will underestimate the true market demand. The effect on market demand in the presence of positive network externalities is illustrated in Figure 5.3. The individual household demand curves are positively influenced by other households'

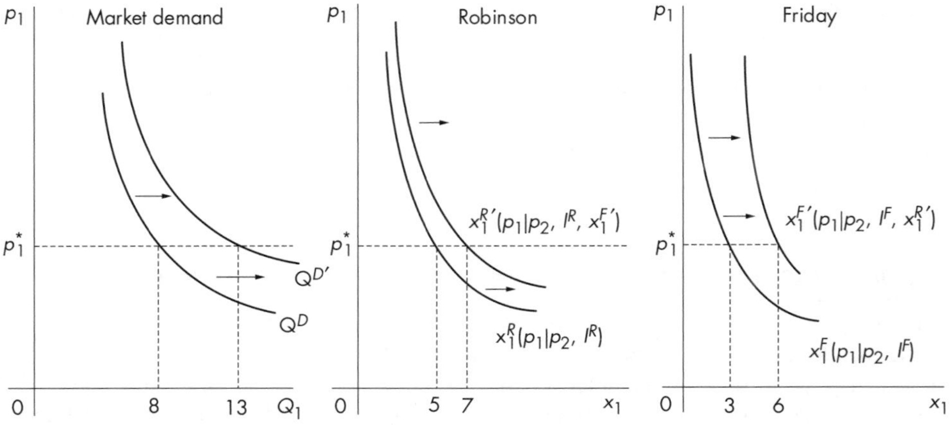

Figure 5.3 **Market demand for commodity Q_1 with positive network externalities.** Individual demand curves are positivity influenced by other households' level of demand for the commodity. This results in market demand beyond the horizontal summation of individual demand.

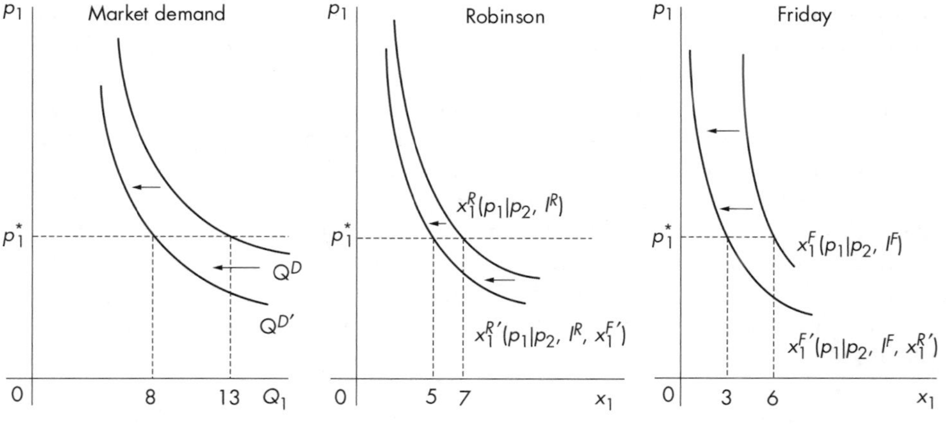

Figure 5.4 **Market demand for commodity Q_1 with negative network externalities.** Individual demand curves are negatively influenced by other households' level of demand for the commodity. This results in market demand below the horizontal summation of individual demands.

level of demand for the commodity. This results in a further outward shift of the individual household demand curves $x_1^{R'}$ and $x_1^{F'}$ and the market demand curve $Q^{D'}$. As illustrated, instead of the market demand being the sum of 5 plus 3 units at price p_1^*, positive network externalities result in a market demand of 7 plus 6 units. Similarly, as illustrated in Figure 5.4, if negative network externalities exist, the summation of individual household demands will overestimate the true market demand. This results in an inward shift of the individual household demand curves $x_1^{R'}$ and $x_1^{F'}$, with a corresponding inward shift in the market demand curve $Q^{D'}$.

Example 5.3 Deriving market demand from individual households' demands with negative network externalities

Consider another modification of the demand functions for households R and F from Example 5.1:

$$x_1^R(p_1, p_2, I^R, x_1^F) = \frac{5I^R}{8p_1} - \frac{x_1^F}{4},$$

$$x_1^F(p_1, p_2, I^F, x_1^R) = \frac{5I^F}{8p_1} - \frac{x_1^R}{4},$$

where now each household's demand is also a function of the other household's demand. Specifically,

$$\frac{\partial x_1^R}{\partial x_1^F} = \frac{\partial x_1^F}{\partial x_1^R} = -\frac{1}{4},$$

indicating that an increase in one household's individual demand (say Friday's) will generate a decrease in Robinson's demand (negative network externality). Households' market demand for Q_1 is determined by solving these two demand functions simultaneously for x_1^R and x_1^F. As in the case of a positive externality (Example 5.2), we do this by first substituting F's demand function into R's. The result yields demand functions for households R and F solely as a function of p_1, p_2 and incomes I^R and I^F:

$$x_1^R = \frac{5I^R}{8p_1} - \frac{1}{4}\left(\frac{5I^F}{8p_1} - \frac{x_1^R}{4}\right)$$

$$= \frac{5I^R}{8p_1} - \frac{5I^F}{32p_1} + \frac{x_1^R}{16},$$

$$\frac{15}{16}x_1^R = \frac{5I^R}{8p_1} - \frac{5I^F}{32p_1},$$

$$x_1^R = \frac{2I^R}{3p_1} - \frac{I^F}{6p_1}, \quad \text{Robinson's demand for } Q_1.$$

Similarly, we derive the demand for F by substituting R's demand function into F's:

$$x_1^F = \frac{2I^F}{3p_1} - \frac{I^R}{6p_1}, \quad \text{Friday's demand for } Q_1.$$

Market demand is then

$$Q_1 = x_1^R + x_1^F = \frac{2I^R}{3p_1} - \frac{I^F}{6p_1} + \frac{2I^F}{3p_1} - \frac{I^R}{6p_1} = \frac{1}{2p_1}(I^R + I^F).$$

As assumed in Example 5.1, if aggregate income equals \$240, then $Q_1 = 120/p_1$. At $p_1 = 50$, market demand is 2.4 units, which is smaller than the market demand assuming no negative network externalities in Example 5.1. As a result of negative network externalities, the market demand curve shifts to the left.

Elasticity dissected

Wooing before marriage is like transforming derivatives into elasticities, it adapts the partners so they can be matched.

(Michael Wetzstein)

A recent slump in the regional economy has left a local department store with a large inventory of unsold garments. The sales manager is interested in moving this merchandise by cutting prices—having an inventory clearance sale. The big question is how much to slash prices. The store's market demand for garments reveals the answer by providing a relationship between price and quantity demanded. Specifically, it shows that quantity demanded is inversely related to price. But of greater interest to the sales manager, and in general to firms and government policymakers, is *how responsive* quantity demanded is to a change in price. The function's downward-sloping demand curve indicates that if a store increases its price, quantity demanded will decline, but it does not show the magnitude of this decline. To measure the magnitude of responsiveness, we use the derivative or slope of the curve. For example, if a change in one variable, x, affects some other variable, y, then $\partial y/\partial x$ measures how responsive y is to a small change in x. The larger the partial derivative, the more responsive is y.

Units of measurement

One problem in using the derivative for measuring these effects or responsiveness is the units of measure. By changing the units of measurement—say from dollars to cents or pounds to kilograms—we cause the magnitude of the change or the value of the derivation to vary. For example, if y is measured in pounds and x in dollars, and $\partial y/\partial x = 2$, then the measurement is 2 pounds per dollar. For each \$1 increase in x, y will increase by 2 pounds. However, if we change the scale used to measure y to ounces, then $\partial y/\partial x = 32$. Now for each \$1 increase in x, y will increase by 32 units. Just changing the scale makes it appear y is more responsive to a given change in x. This is an example of how to lie with statistics. Whenever viewing statistical phenomena presented by a graph or diagram, beware that the message conveyed may, to a certain extent, be influenced by the scale on the two axes (the units of measurement).

Deriving a unit-free measure of responsiveness

On September 23, 1999, prior failure to convert from the English to the metric system of measurement caused the loss of the *Mars Climate Orbiter*, a spacecraft designed to orbit Mars. In economics, to avoid making such errors in comparing responsiveness across different factors with different units of measurement, we use a standardized derivative, **elasticity** that removes the scale effect. The derivative is standardized (converted into an elasticity) by weighting it with levels of the variables under consideration, which results in a percentage change in y, given a percentage change in x. This provides a unit-free measure of the responsiveness that can then be compared across different factors. This degree of responsiveness is analogous to a spaghetti noodle. When it is dry, it is not responsive at all toward efforts to stretch it (inelastic), but once wet it responds to such efforts by stretching (elastic).

Elasticity (ε). A standardized (unit-free) measure of responsiveness. *E.g., if elasticity of demand is −2, a 1 percent increase in price results in a 2 percent decline in quantity demanded.*

For example, consider the function

$$y = f(x).$$

The elasticity of y with respect to x, denoted by ε, is

$$\varepsilon_{y,x} = \lim_{\Delta x \to 0} \frac{\%\Delta y}{\%\Delta x} = \lim_{\Delta x \to 0} \frac{\Delta y/y}{\Delta x/x} = \frac{\partial y}{\partial x}\frac{x}{y},$$

where Δ denotes change. This expression indicates the percentage response of y to a small percentage change in x. For example, if $\varepsilon_{y,x} = 3$, then a 1 percent increase (decrease) in x leads to a 3 percent increase (decrease) in y.

Although the partial derivative, $\partial y/\partial x$, also indicates how y changes when x changes, it is not as useful as the elasticity measurement. For example, if y is measured in pounds and x in dollars, then $\partial y/\partial x$ is in terms of pounds per dollar. When we multiply this partial derivative by x/y, the measurement units cancel out:

$$\frac{\partial y}{\partial x}(\text{pounds per dollar})\frac{x}{y}(\text{dollars per pound}) = \frac{\partial y}{\partial x}\frac{x}{y},$$

yielding the elasticity in terms of only percentage change:

$$\varepsilon_{y,x} = \frac{\partial y}{\partial x}\frac{x}{y}.$$

Changing the units of measurements—for example, from pounds to ounces—does not change the elasticity:

$$\frac{\partial y}{\partial x}(\text{ounces per dollar})\frac{x}{y}(\text{dollars per ounce})$$

still yields

$$\varepsilon_{y,x} = \frac{\partial y}{\partial x}\frac{x}{y}.$$

Why a logarithmic representation?

As noted, this weighting of the slope results in measuring the percentage change of y given a percentage change in x. Thus, as a percentage change measure, elasticity can be expressed in logarithmic form:

$$\varepsilon_{y,x} = \frac{\partial y}{\partial x}\frac{x}{y} = \frac{\partial \ln y}{\partial \ln x}.$$

Specifically,

$$\frac{\partial \ln y}{\partial \ln x} = \frac{\partial \ln y}{\partial y} \frac{\partial y}{\partial x} \frac{\partial x}{\partial \ln x}.$$

The first term on the right-hand side is

$$\frac{\partial \ln y}{\partial y} = \frac{1}{y}$$

and the remaining terms are

$$\frac{\partial y}{\partial x} \frac{\partial x}{\partial \ln x} = \frac{\partial y}{\partial x} x,$$

given $e^{ln\ x} = x$. and

$$\frac{\partial e^{\ln x}}{\partial \ln x} = e^{\ln x} = x.$$

Thus,

$$\frac{\partial \ln y}{\partial \ln x} = \frac{1}{y} \frac{\partial y}{\partial x} x.$$

Price elasticity of demand

Price **elasticity of demand** for a market quantity Q is defined as

$$\varepsilon_{Q,p} = \frac{\partial Q}{\partial p} \frac{p}{Q} = \frac{\partial \ln Q}{\partial \ln p}.$$

Elasticity of demand indicates how Q changes, in percentage terms, in response to a percentage change in p. In the case of an ordinary good, $\partial Q / \partial p < 0$, which implies $\varepsilon_{Q,p} < 0$, given that p and Q are positive. Examples of demand elasticities are provided in Table 5.1. Note that all the elasticities of demand listed in the table are negative, indicating an inverse relation between price and quantity demanded (a negatively sloping demand curve).

Elasticity of demand. The percentage change in quantity demanded given a percentage change in price. *E.g., if the elasticity of demand for gasoline is −0.26, a 1 percent increase in the price of gasoline will result in a 0.26 percent decrease in the quantity demanded of gasoline.*

Table 5.1 Estimates of price elasticities of demand

Commodity	*Price elasticity of demand*
Food[a]	
Bread	−0.354
Poultry	−0.644
Vegetables	−0.724
Fruit	−0.720
Juice	−1.011
Automobiles[b]	−0.87
Gasoline[c]	
Short run	−0.26
Long run	−0.58
Cigarettes[d]	−0.3 to −0.7
Alcohol[e]	−0.70
Illicit drugs[e]	
Marijuana	−0.50
Cocaine	−0.55

[a]K.S. Huang and B.-H. Lin, "Estimation of Food Demand and Nutrient Elasticities from Household Survey Data," Economic Research Service, USDA, Technical Bulletin Number 1887, 2000.
[b]P.S. McCarthy, "Market Price and Income Elasticities of New Vehicles Demand," *Review of Economics and Statistics* 78 (1996): 543–547.
[c]M. Espey, "Gasoline Demand Revisited: An International Meta-Analysis of Elasticities," *Energy Economics* 20 (1998): 273–295.
[d]J.S. Ringel and W.N. Evans, "Cigarette Taxes and Smoking During Pregnancy," *American Journal of Public Health* 91 (2001): 1851–1856.
[e]Abt Associates, Inc., *Illicit Drugs: Price Elasticity of Demand and Supply,* prepared for the National Institute of Justice, February 2000.

Perfectly inelastic demand, $\varepsilon_{Q,p} = 0$: Drug addicts

> *Give me liberty at any price.*
>
> (Michael Wetzstein)
>
> *Translation: The demand for liberty is perfectly inelastic.*

As noted by the Sierra Club, global warming is an experiment to see what will happen to our planet when we make drastic changes in our climate. Some will argue that this experiment should be stopped at any price. This implies the elasticity of demand for stopping global warming has the largest possible value, so $\varepsilon_{Q,p} = 0$. If $\varepsilon_{Q,p}$ is zero, a change in price results in no change in quantity demanded. This is called **perfectly inelastic demand**. The perfectly inelastic demand curve represented in Figure 5.5 is vertical, and at every price level quantity demanded is the same. Examples of $\varepsilon_{Q,p} = 0$ (perfectly inelastic) are difficult to find due to the lack of households with monomania preferences. Generally, there will always be at least some quantity response to a price change. However, any household that spends all its income on one commodity would have a perfectly inelastic demand for this one commodity. For example, alcoholics and drug addicts would have highly inelastic demands over a broad range of quantity, which indicates a perfectly inelastic individual demand curve.

What is your demand for living? Life is priceless; so your demand would be perfectly inelastic.

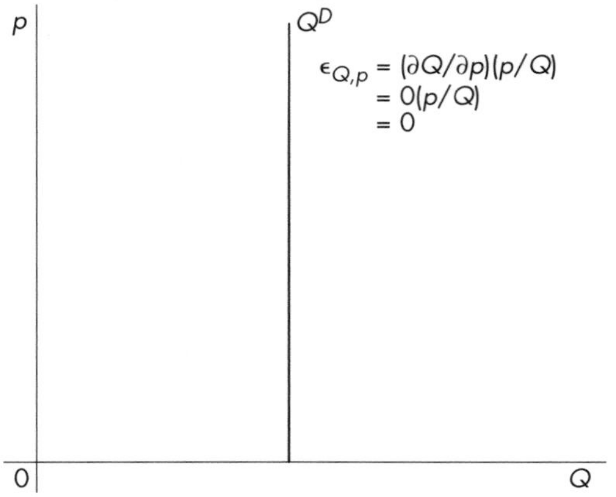

Figure 5.5 **A perfectly inelastic demand curve.** Quantity demanded is unresponsive to any change in price.

Perfectly inelastic demand ($\varepsilon_{Q,p} = 0$). Quantity demanded is not at all responsive to a price change. *E.g., a diabetic, who will die without insulin, would be willing to pay any price for the proper life-saving level of insulin.*

Perfectly elastic demand, $\varepsilon_{Q,p} = -\infty$: An Iowa corn farmer

> *No matter how much I produce the price is always the same: too low.*
>
> (Michael Wetzstein)
>
> *Translation: The producer is facing a perfectly elastic demand curve and feels the price is too low.*

The smallest possible value of $\varepsilon_{Q,p}$ is for it to approach negative infinity. If $\varepsilon_{Q,p} = -\infty$ (negative infinity), demand is called **perfectly elastic**. A very slight change in price corresponds to an infinitely large change in quantity demanded. For any small price increase, quantity demanded is driven to zero, and, in reverse, for any small decrease in price, quantity demanded approaches infinity. A perfectly elastic demand curve is illustrated in Figure 5.6. As discussed in the chapters on market structure (Parts 5–8), there are many examples of perfectly elastic demand curves. Whenever, a firm takes its output price as given, no matter what its level of output, it is facing a perfectly elastic demand curve. For example, in agriculture, individual producers generally have no control over the price they receive for their output, and thus are facing a perfectly elastic demand curve.

Perfectly elastic demand ($\varepsilon_{Q,p} = -\infty$). Quantity demanded is infinity responsive to a percentage change in price. *E.g., if a farmer offers her crop at a price slightly above the market price, she will not be able to sell any of the crop.*

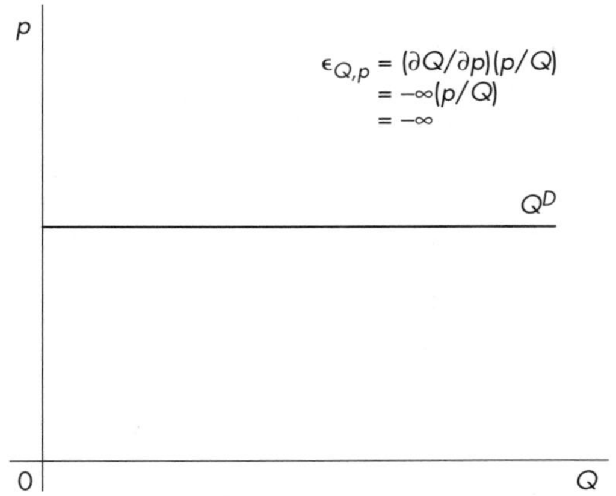

Figure 5.6 **A perfectly elastic demand curve.** Quantity demanded is infinity responsive to even a very small change in price.

Classifying elasticity

Between these elasticity limits, from $-\infty$ to 0, elasticity may be classified in terms of its responsiveness as follows:

- $\varepsilon_{Q,p} < -1$, elastic, $\left|\frac{\Delta Q}{Q}\right| > \left|\frac{\Delta p}{p}\right|$.

  The absolute percentage change in quantity is greater than the absolute percentage change in price. Quantity is relatively responsive to a price change.

- $\varepsilon_{Q,p} = -1$, unitary, $\left|\frac{\Delta Q}{Q}\right| = \left|\frac{\Delta p}{p}\right|$.

  The absolute percentage change in quantity is equal to the absolute percentage change in price.

- $\varepsilon_{Q,p} > -1$, inelastic, $\left|\frac{\Delta Q}{Q}\right| < \left|\frac{\Delta p}{p}\right|$.

  The absolute percentage change in quantity is less than the absolute percentage change in price. Quantity is relatively unresponsive to a price change.

Application: Measuring the impact of an airport on travelers' expenditures

The economic impact of an airport is the change in economic activity in an area directly as a result of the airport. Such an impact can be sizable. For example, not long after World War II, in 1950, the cities of Atlanta, Georgia and Birmingham, Alabama had approximately the same population, with Atlanta at 331,000 and Birmingham with

326,000. However, in 2009, their populations were 5.5 million for Atlanta (metropolitan Atlanta) and only 1.2 million for Birmingham (metropolitan Birmingham). One of the major explanations of this divergence is the development of Atlanta's transportation system with its airport Hartsfield-Jackson Atlanta International Airport as the center.

In estimating the economic impact of an airport, applied economists have generally assumed the number of visitors traveling to the local area would be zero without the airport. This assumes a perfectly elastic demand for air travelers, where any increased travel cost and time associated with not having a local airport results in a complete loss of demand in traveling to the area. However, this assumption is generally too restrictive. Some people would travel to the local area using alternative modes. Thus, the demand for air travelers is probably not perfectly elastic.

Studies estimating an airport's economic impact also fail to consider the increased local-area expenditures by residents who would reduce travel in the absence of the local airport. This implicitly assumes that the demand for travel by residents is perfectly inelastic. Regardless of the cost, residents will not curtail their travel plans.

J. Desalvo develops a methodology for avoiding both of these restrictive assumptions of perfectly elastic and inelastic travel demands. Applying his methodology to the Tampa International Airport for the year 1996, Desalvo illustrated how these restrictive assumptions result in overestimating the direct impacts of the airport by six times.

Source: J.S. DeSalvo, "Direct Impact of an Airport on Travelers' Expenditures: Methodology and Application," *Growth and Change* 33 (2002): 485–496.

Measuring elasticity with linear demand

A linear demand curve will exhibit all three of these elasticity classifications. For example, consider the linear demand function for commodity x_1:

$$x_1 = 120 - 2p_1,$$

which is plotted in Figure 5.7 with the elasticity of demand represented as $\varepsilon_{11} = (\partial x_1/\partial p_1)(p_1/x_1)$. The size of the elasticity coefficient, ε_{11}, increases in absolute value for movements up this linear demand curve because the slope remains constant, $\partial x_1/\partial p_1 = -2$, while the weight, p_1/x_1, increases.[2] For example, at point D in Figure 5.7, the weight is $p_1/x_1 = 15/90 = 1/6$; at point B, the weight is $p_1/x_1 = 45/30 = 3/2$. Because $3/2 > 1/6$, the ε_{11} is greater in absolute value at B than at D. At point B,

$$\varepsilon_{11} = \frac{\partial x_1}{\partial p_1}\frac{p_1}{x_1} = -2 \times \frac{45}{30} = -3, \text{ elastic,}$$

whereas at D,

$$\varepsilon_{11} = \frac{\partial x_1}{\partial p_1}\frac{p_1}{x_1} = -2 \times \frac{15}{90} = -\frac{1}{3}, \text{ inelastic.}$$

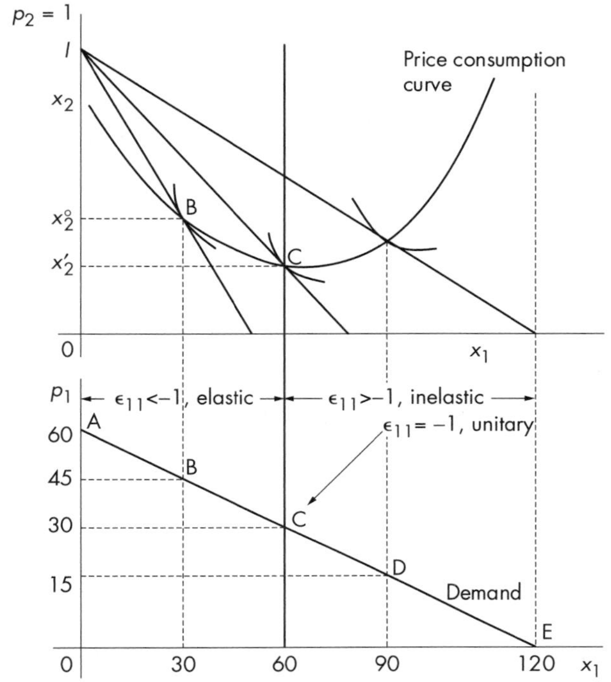

Figure 5.7 **Linear demand curve and its relation to the range of demand elasticities and the price consumption curve.** For movements along a demand curve, the slope of a linear demand curve remains constant while the weight p_1/x_1 is changing.

At the midpoint of the demand curve (point C), the elasticity of demand is unitary, $\varepsilon_{11} = -2(30/60) = -1$, and at the limits (points A and E), demand elasticity is $-\infty$ and 0, respectively. Thus, ε_{11} is elastic to the left of the midpoint C and inelastic to the right.

A general functional form for a linear market demand function is represented by

$$Q_1 = a + bp_1, b < 0,$$

where Q_1 denotes the market demand for commodity 1 and p_1 is the associated price per unit. Note that partial derivative $\partial Q_1/\partial p_1$ is equal to the constant b, so elasticity of demand ε_{11} is not constant along a linear demand curve:

$$\varepsilon_{11} = \frac{\partial Q_1}{\partial p_1}\frac{p_1}{Q_1} = b\frac{p_1}{Q_1}.$$

As p_1/Q_1 increases, the demand curve becomes more elastic. In the limit as Q_1 approaches zero, elasticity of demand approaches negative infinity, perfectly elastic. The other extreme is when $p_1 = 0$, resulting in perfectly inelastic elasticity of demand, $\varepsilon_{11} = 0$.

A straight line (linear) demand curve is certainly the easiest to draw (Figure 5.8). However, such behavior is generally unrealistic, because a linear demand curve assumes $\partial Q_1/\partial p_1$ = constant. This implies that a doubling of prices, say from \$0.25 to \$0.50, will

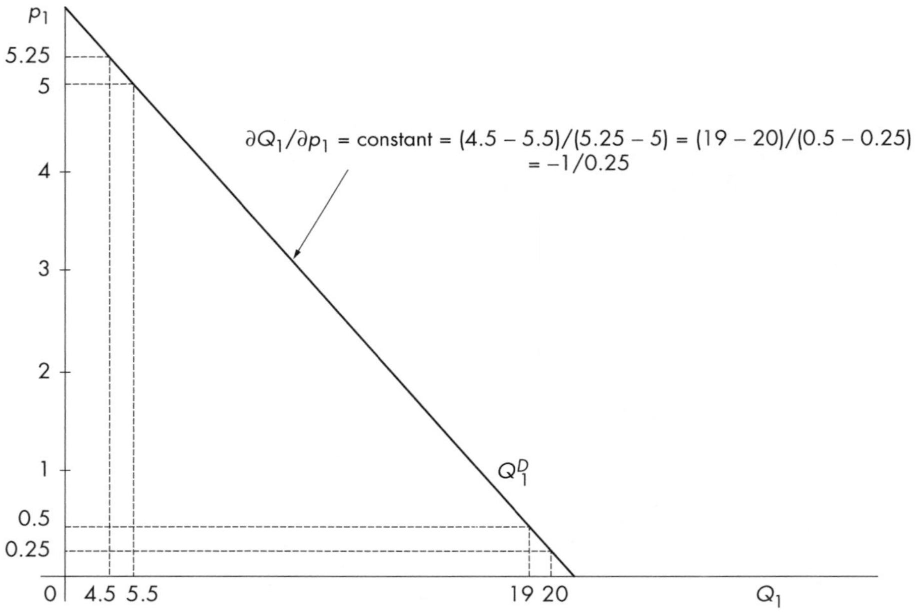

Figure 5.8 **A linear demand curve.** Doubling of prices from \$0.25 to \$0.50 has the same effect on quantity Q_1 as a 5 percent price change from \$5.00 to \$5.25.

have the same effect on Q_1 (a decrease of 1 unit) as a 5 percent increase, say from \$5.00 to \$5.25. However, a 100 percent increase in price generally would have a greater impact on quantity demanded than a 5 percent increase.

Proportionate price changes

Assuming households respond to proportionate rather than to an absolute changes in prices, it may be more realistic to consider the demand function

$$Q_1 = ap_1^b, \quad a > 0, \quad b < 0,$$

or, equivalently,

$$\ln Q_1 = \ln a + b \ln p_1.$$

The elasticity of demand is

$$\varepsilon_{11} = \frac{\partial Q_1}{\partial p_1}\frac{p_1}{Q_1} = bap_1^{b-1}\frac{p_1}{Q_1} = bap_1^b p_1^{-1} p_1 Q_1^{-1} = bQ_1Q_1^{-1} = b,$$

or, equivalently,

$$\varepsilon_{11} = \frac{\partial \ln Q_1}{\partial \ln p_1} = b.$$

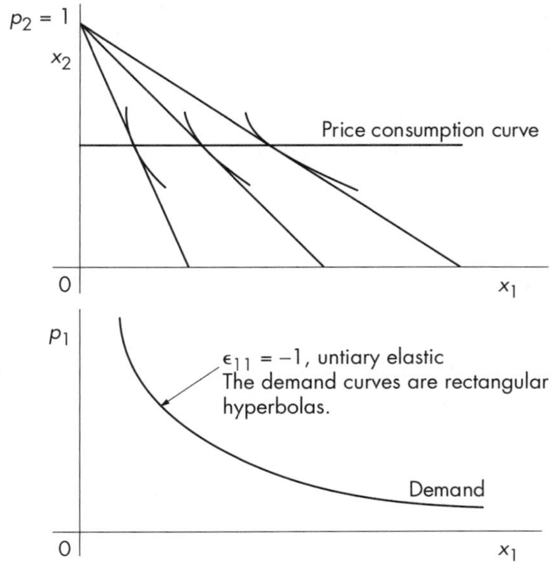

Figure 5.9 **Constant unitary elasticity of demand is represented by a rectangular hyperbola.** The elasticity of demand does not vary along the demand curve. It is -1 at every price and quantity combination.

This case illustrates the condition

$$\varepsilon_{11} = \frac{\partial \ln Q_1}{\partial \ln p_1} = \frac{\partial Q_1}{\partial p_1} \frac{p_1}{Q_1}.$$

The elasticity of this demand curve is constant, equal to b, along its entire length. A constant elasticity-of-demand curve, with $b = -1$, is illustrated in Figure 5.9, for an individual household's demand for x_1.

Relationship between price elasticity and total revenue

Price and quantity demanded are like two children on a seesaw, when one goes up the other comes down. What about total revenue?

To maintain federal and state subsidy support, a regional transit manager must boost revenues from ridership to cover at least 25 percent of total operating cost. The manager decides to consult with an economist for advice. The first thing the economist wants to know is the elasticity of demand for ridership. One of the most valuable uses of elasticity of demand is to predict what will happen to households' total expenditures on a commodity or to producers' total revenue when the price changes. **Total revenue (TR)** and **total expenditures** are defined as price times quantity (p_1Q_1). Considering total revenue accruing to a firm, a change in price has two offsetting effects. A reduction in price has the direct effect of reducing total revenue for the commodity, but it will also result in an increase in quantity sold that increases total revenue.

Why do farmers always seem to complain about the prices they receive or their yields? The inverse relationship between price and quantity demanded results in low prices when yields are high and high prices when yields are low.

Total revenue (TR). Per-unit price of a commodity times the quantity a firm sells. *E.g., the amount of apples purchased from a supermarket times the per-unit price of apples is the total revenue the supermarket receives from its apple sales.*

Total expenditures. Per-unit price of a commodity times the quantity a household purchases. *E.g., the amount of apples you purchase times the per-unit price of apples is your total expenditure for apples.*

Considering these two opposing effects, total revenue from a commodity price change, may go up, go down, or remain the same. This effect on total revenue depends on how responsive quantity is to a change in price, which is measured by the elasticity of demand. The relation between total revenue and elasticity of demand may be established by differentiating total revenue (p_1Q_1) with respect to p_1. Using the product rule of differentiation and noting that Q_1 is a function of p_1, we have

$$\frac{\partial(p_1Q_1)}{\partial p_1} = Q_1 + p_1\frac{\partial Q_1}{\partial p_1}.$$

Dividing both sides by Q_1 gives

$$\frac{1}{Q_1}\frac{\partial(p_1Q_1)}{\partial p_1} = 1 + \frac{\partial Q_1}{\partial p_1}\frac{p_1}{Q_1}$$
$$= 1 + \varepsilon_{11}.$$

Multiplying both sides by $p_1/p_1 = 1$ yields the *total revenue elasticity*, $\varepsilon_{TR,p}$:

$$\frac{\partial(p_1Q_1)}{\partial p_1}\frac{p_1}{p_1Q_1} = \frac{\partial \text{TR}}{\partial p_1}\frac{p_1}{\text{TR}} = \varepsilon_{\text{TR},p} = 1 + \varepsilon_{11}.$$

The total revenue elasticity measures the percentage change in total revenue for a percentage change in price. The sign of $\varepsilon_{TR,p}$ depends on whether ε_{11} is greater than or less than -1. If $\varepsilon_{11} > -1$, demand is inelastic and $\varepsilon_{TR,p} > 0$. Thus, price and total revenue move in the same direction; an increase in p_1 leads to an increase in total revenue. (Agricultural products, in general, exhibit an inelastic demand (Table 5.1). An increase in p_1, due possibly to poor yields from bad weather, leads to an increase in expenditures on food.) In contrast, if $\varepsilon_{11} < -1$, demand is elastic, and $\varepsilon_{TR,p} < 0$, so an increase in p_1 is associated with a decrease in total revenue. If elasticity of demand is unitary, $\varepsilon_{Q,p} = -1$, then $\varepsilon_{TR,p} = 0$. Total revenue remains unchanged for a price change. The percentage change in quantity exactly offsets any percentage change in price, $| \Delta Q_1/Q_1 | = | \Delta p_1/p_1 |$.

If elasticity of demand is elastic, quantity demanded will increase by a larger percentage than price decreases. In this case, total revenue will increase with a price decline, $\varepsilon_{TR,p} < 0$. The opposite occurs when demand is inelastic. A price decline results in total revenue declining because quantity demanded increases by a smaller percentage than price decreases.

For example, in Figure 5.7, total revenue at point B is (45)(30) = \$1350 and at point C it is (30)(60) = \$1800. The decline in price from 45 to 30 results in an increase in quantity demanded of 30, along with an increase in total revenue of \$450. Total revenue increases for this price decrease, because the price change occurred in the elastic portion of the demand curve. In contrast, points in the inelastic portion of the demand curve result in total revenue falling for a price decline. For example, from revenue of \$1800 at point C, a price decline from 30 to 15 results in total revenue falling to (15)(90) = \$1350, at point D.

In summary, in the elastic portion of the demand curve, price and total revenue move in opposite directions; in the inelastic portion, price and TR move in the same direction. This relation between own-price elasticity of demand and total revenue for a price change is summarized in Table 5.2 and illustrated in Figure 5.10. In the elastic portion of the demand curve, a decrease in price results in an increase in TR; in the inelastic portion, a decrease in price yields a corresponding decline in TR. Why did the economist inquire about the elasticity of demand for ridership? So he will know if a price hike or a price cut would be required for enhancing total revenue.

Table 5.2 Response of total revenue to a price change

Demand	*Price*	*Total revenue* $TR = p_1 Q_1$
Elastic, $\varepsilon_{11} < -1$, $\varepsilon_{TR,p} < 0$	Decreases	Increases
	Increases	Declines
Inelastic, $\varepsilon_{11} > -1$, $\varepsilon_{TR,p} > 0$	Decreases	Declines
	Increases	Increases
Unitary, $\varepsilon_{11} = -1$, $\varepsilon_{TR,p} = 0$	Decreases	Unchanged
	Increases	Unchanged

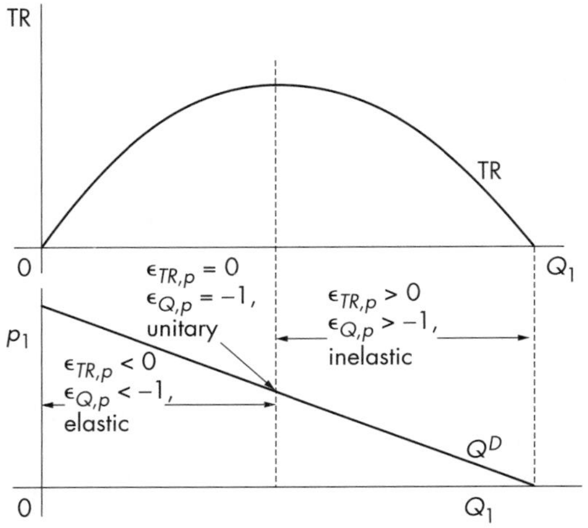

Figure 5.10 **Elasticity of demand and total revenue for a linear demand function.** In the elastic portion of the demand curve, $\varepsilon_{TR,p} < 0$; in the inelastic portion, $\varepsilon_{TR,p} > 0$.

Application: How to adjust prices: US versus French wine producers

Even considering the Great Recession, US wine consumption has steady increased since the mid 1990s. Americans are only behind Italy in the volume of wine consumed and the United States is the fourth largest producer of wine. With wine imports growing by 36 percent from 2004 to 2008 and now representing more than a quarter of the US market, the question is how should the US wine industry respond to maintain revenue and compete with imports.

Seale, Marchant, and Basso's estimates of foreign and domestic wine elasticities provide the answer. They estimate demand elasticities of US red wine imports from five countries accounting for over 90 percent of imports—Italy, France, Spain, Australia, and Chile. These estimates are compared with US domestically produced red wine. Empirical results suggest that US red-wine producers could increase their total revenue by decreasing prices. The estimated demand elasticity for domestically produced wine is −1.63 resulting in a total revenue elasticity of −0.63. With a 1 percent price decline, their total revenue will increase by 0.63 percent. In contrast, the demand elasticity for French wine is estimated to be −0.31, leading to a total revenue elasticity of 0.69. If French wine producers lower their prices by 1 percent, they will lose 0.69 percent of their revenue. This indicates that the US domestic wine industry may want to consider price-competing with French wines.

Source: J. Seale, M. Marchant, and A. Basso, "Imports versus Domestic Production: A Demand System Analysis of the U.S. Red Wine Market," *Review of Agricultural Economics* 25 (2003): 187–202.

Price elasticity and the price consumption curve

This relation between total revenue and elasticity of demand aids in understanding the association of elasticity of demand with the slope of the price consumption curve, illustrated in Figures 5.7 and 5.9. Setting p_2 as the numeraire price, $p_2 = 1$, then

$$p_1x_1 + x_2 = I,$$

and solving for total revenue (expenditures) for x_1 yields

$$p_1x_1 = I - x_2.$$

Thus, on the vertical axis in Figure 5.7, at $p_1 = \$45$, income I is initially allocated between total expenditures for x_2, x_2^o, and total expenditure on x_1, $I - x_2^o$. Decreasing p_1 from \$45 to \$30 results in total expenditure for x_2 declining from x_2^o to x_2' and total expenditure for x_1 increasing by $x_2^o - x_2'$. The movement from B to C in the indifference space results in a negatively sloping price consumption curve. This declining price consumption curve, resulting in a decrease in p_1, is associated with an increase in total expenditures on x_1, indicating $\varepsilon_{11} < -1$ (elastic demand). Thus, the negatively sloping portion of the price consumption curve is associated with the elastic portion of the demand curve. Similarly, a positively sloping price consumption curve is associated with the inelastic portion of the demand curve. Decreasing p_1 from \$30 to \$15 results in total expenditures for x_2 increasing and thus total expenditures for x_1 declining, indicating $\varepsilon_{11} > -1$ (inelastic demand). Finally, as illustrated throughout Figure 5.9 and at point C in Figure 5.7, if the price consumption curve has a zero slope, unitary elasticity exists. A change in the price of x_1 changes the total expenditure for neither x_2 nor x_1, indicating $\varepsilon_{11} = -1$, unitary elasticity.

The slope of the price consumption curve is determined by the magnitude of the income and substitution effects. Recall that the total effect of a price change is the sum of these two effects. The closeness of substitutes for a commodity directly influences the substitution effect. The more closely related the substitutes are to the commodity, the larger will be the substitution effect. A relatively large substitution effect will decrease the slope of the price consumption curve and thus make the demand curve more elastic. If a commodity has a close substitute and if the price of the substitute remains constant, a rise in the price of the commodity will divert households' expenditures away from the product and over to the substitute. For example, a specific make and model of an automobile (say a Ford Taurus) has a number of close substitutes (other makes and models of automobiles), which results in a relatively large substitution for a price change in the Taurus. Thus, the price elasticity of demand for a Taurus is elastic (−2.1) with an associated negatively sloped price consumption curve.[3] In contrast, automobiles in general have relatively few substitutes, resulting in a relatively small substitution effect. This results in a positively sloping price consumption curve and inelastic demand (Table 5.1).

Another important determinant of the slope of the price consumption curve and elasticity of demand is the proportion of income allocated for a commodity and if it is a normal or inferior commodity. The smaller the proportion of income allocated for a commodity, the larger will be the slope of the price consumption curve and the more inelastic the demand. The income effect is relatively small for a commodity requiring a small fraction of income. A relatively small income effect results in a more inelastic demand for the commodity. For example, demand for commodities such as salt, matches, toothpicks, and soft drinks tends to be relatively inelastic. Each of these commodities is a relatively small part of households' total expenditures, so a change in their prices results in a small change in relative income and a corresponding small income effect. An inferior commodity will tend to result in a positively sloping price consumption curve and associated inelastic demand curve. If the inferior nature of a commodity results in a Giffen good, then a backward-bending price consumption curve and a positively sloping demand curve will result.

A final major determinant of demand elasticity is the time allowed for adjusting to a price change. Elasticities of demand tend to become more elastic as the time for adjustment lengthens. The longer the time interval after a price change, the easier it may become for households to substitute other commodities by adjusting their tastes and habits of consumption toward these other commodities. For example, the demand for electricity is highly inelastic right after a price change (−0.184).[4] However, over time, households may adjust toward substitutes for electricity such as gas dryers and stoves and energy-efficient appliances. This results in a more elastic long-run demand for electricity (−0.329).

Income elasticity of demand

A lottery winner states, "Good-bye to synthetic wool hello fur".

(Michael Wetzstein)

The lottery winner's increase in fur and decline in synthetic wool consumption represents a response of quantity demanded to a change in income. This response can also be measured in terms of elasticity. Recall from Chapter 4 that the relationship between the change in quantity demanded and change in income may be represented by the slope of an Engel curve. Weighting this slope with income divided by quantity results in **income elasticity**, denoted as $\eta_Q = (\partial Q/\partial I)(I/Q)$. Income elasticity of demand measures the percentage change in quantity to a percentage change in income, and is classified as follows:

$$\eta_Q = \frac{\partial Q}{\partial I}\frac{I}{Q} = \frac{\partial \ln Q}{\partial \ln I} > 0, \quad \text{normal good;}$$

$$< 0, \quad \text{inferior good, synthetic wool;}$$

$$> 1, \quad \text{luxury good, fur;}$$

$$< 1, \quad \text{but} > 0, \text{ necessary good.}$$

Table 5.3 lists the income elasticities for various foods, new automobiles, and gasoline. From this table, automobiles, fruits, and juices are luxury goods ($\eta_Q > 1$), whereas bread, poultry, vegetables, and gasoline are necessary goods ($\eta_Q < 1$). Considering the income elasticity of a new automobile $\eta_Q = 1.70$, a 1 percent increase in I results in a 1.7 percent increase in new automobile purchases.

Income elasticity (η). The percentage change in quantity given a percentage change in income. *E.g., if the income elasticity of demand for DVD players is 3, a 1 percent increase in income would result in a 3 percent increase in demand for DVD players.*

Table 5.3 Estimated income elasticities

Commodity	*Income elasticities*
Food[a]	
Bread	0.578
Poultry	0.900
Vegetables	0.976
Fruit	1.160
Juice	1.042
Automobiles[b]	1.70
Gasoline[c]	
Short run	0.47
Long run	0.88

[a] K.S. Huang and B.-H. Lin, "Estimation of Food Demand and Nutrient Elasticities from Household Survey Data," Economic Research Service, USDA, Technical Bulletin Number 1887, 2000.
[b] P.S. McCarthy, "Market Price and Income Elasticities of New Vehicles Demand," *Review of Economics and Statistics* 78 (1996): 543–547.
[c] M. Espey, "Gasoline Demand Revisited: An International Meta-Analysis of Elasticities," *Energy Economics* 20 (1998): 273–295.

Table 5.4 Estimated cross-price elasticities of demand for selected food commodities

	Price				
Commodity	*Bread*	*Poultry*	*Vegetables*	*Fruit*	*Juice*
Bread	−0.354	0.013	−0.046	−0.010	−0.006
Poultry	−0.018	−0.644	−0.091	−0.000	−0.012
Vegetables	−0.086	−0.049	−0.724	−0.029	−0.001
Fruit	−0.092	−0.023	−0.087	−0.720	−0.046
Juice	−0.066	−0.025	−0.006	−0.067	−1.011

Source: K.S. Huang and B.-H. Lin, "Estimation of Food Demand and Nutrient Elasticities from Household Survey Data," Economic Research Service, USDA, Technical Bulletin Number 1887, 2000.

Cross-price elasticity of demand

For a graduation gift, a high-school senior's parents were planning on giving their son a Toyota Camry, but a sale on the Honda Accord changed their mind. Generally, quantity demanded for a commodity, such as an automobile, will depend not only on its own price but also on the prices of other related commodities and on income. We measure the responsiveness of demand to a price change in a related commodity by the **cross-price elasticity**. Cross-price elasticity of demand for commodities x_1 and x_2 is defined as

$$\varepsilon_{12} = \frac{\partial Q_1}{\partial p_2}\frac{p_2}{Q_1} = \frac{\partial \ln Q_1}{\partial \ln p_2} > 0$$

when Q_1 is a gross substitute for Q_2 and

$$\varepsilon_{12} = \frac{\partial Q_1}{\partial p_2}\frac{p_2}{Q_1} = \frac{\partial \ln Q_1}{\partial \ln p_2} < 0$$

when Q_1 is a gross complement for Q_2. Cross-price elasticity can then be either positive or negative, depending on whether Q_1 is a gross substitute or complement for Q_2. Table 5.4 presents a matrix of cross-price elasticities for selected food commodities. In all the cases, except the cross-elasticity of demand for bread given a change in the price of poultry, the elasticities are negative (representing gross complements). In the case of bread and poultry, bread is a gross substitute for poultry but poultry is a gross complement for bread.

Example 5.4 Calculating elasticities of demand for demand functions

We can calculate the price and income elasticities for the household demand functions derived in Example 4.1,

$$x_1 = \frac{5I}{8p_1} \quad \text{and} \quad x_2 = \frac{3I}{8p_2},$$

by taking the logarithms of these functions:

$$\ln x_1 = \ln\frac{5}{8} - \ln p_1 + \ln I,$$

$$\ln x_2 = \ln\frac{3}{8} - \ln p_2 + \ln I.$$

The price elasticities of demand are then

$$\varepsilon_{11} = \frac{\partial \ln x_1}{\partial \ln p_1} = -1, \quad \varepsilon_{12} = \frac{\partial \ln x_1}{\partial \ln p_2} = 0,$$

$$\varepsilon_{21} = \frac{\partial \ln x_2}{\partial \ln p_1} = 0, \quad \varepsilon_{22} = \frac{\partial \ln x_2}{\partial \ln p_2} = -1,$$

indicating unitary own-price elasticities and zero cross-elasticities. The demand functions are unresponsive to a change in the price of the other commodity. They are independent goods.* The income elasticities are

$$\eta_1 = \frac{\partial \ln x_1}{\partial \ln I} = \eta_2 = \frac{\partial \ln x_2}{\partial \ln I} = 1,$$

indicating unitary income elasticities.

* See Chapter 4. Two commodities are independent goods if a price change in one commodity does not affect the consumption of the other commodity.

Cross-price elasticity (ε_{ji}). The percentage change in quantity of commodity x_j given a percentage change in the price of commodity x_i. *E.g., if the cross-price elasticity of demand for apples, given a price change for oranges, is 3, a 1 percent increase (decrease) in the price of oranges will then result in a 3 percent increase (decrease) in the consumption of apples.*

Example 5.5 Calculating demand elasticities for the perfect-complement demand functions

The demand functions derived from the perfect-complement utility function in Example 4.3 are

$$x_1^* = \frac{I}{p_1 + \frac{4}{3}p_2},$$

$$x_2^* = \frac{I}{\frac{3}{4}p_1 + p_2}.$$

The price and income elasticities of demand for x_1 and x_2 are then

$$\varepsilon_{11} = \frac{\partial x_1}{\partial p_1}\frac{p_1}{x_1} = \frac{-x_1}{p_1 + \frac{4}{3}p_2}\frac{p_1}{x_1} = \frac{-p_1}{p_1 + \frac{4}{3}p_2} = \frac{-1}{1 + \frac{4}{3}(p_2/p_1)} > -1, \quad \text{inelastic,}$$

$$\varepsilon_{12} = \frac{\partial x_1}{\partial p_2}\frac{p_2}{x_1} = \frac{-\frac{4}{3}x_1}{p_1 + \frac{4}{3}p_2}\frac{p_2}{x_1} = \frac{-\frac{4}{3}p_2}{p_1 + \frac{4}{3}p_2} = \frac{-1}{\frac{3}{4}(p_1/p_2) + 1} > -1, \quad \text{gross complement,}$$

$$\varepsilon_{22} = \frac{\partial x_2}{\partial p_2}\frac{p_2}{x_2} = \frac{-x_2}{\frac{3}{4}p_1 + p_2}\frac{p_2}{x_2} = \frac{-p_2}{\frac{3}{4}p_1 + p_2} = \frac{-1}{\frac{3}{4}(p_1/p_2) + 1} > -1, \quad \text{inelastic,}$$

$$\varepsilon_{21} = \frac{\partial x_2}{\partial p_1}\frac{p_1}{x_2} = \frac{-\frac{3}{4}x_2}{\frac{3}{4}p_1 + p_2}\frac{p_1}{x_2} = \frac{-\frac{3}{4}p_1}{\frac{3}{4}p_1 + p_2} = \frac{-1}{1 + \frac{4}{3}(p_2/p_1)} > -1, \quad \text{gross complement,}$$

$$\eta_1 = \frac{\partial x_1}{\partial I}\frac{I}{x_1} = \frac{1}{p_1 + \frac{4}{3}p_2}\frac{I}{x_1} = 1 > 0, \quad \text{normal good,}$$

$$\eta_2 = \frac{\partial x_2}{\partial I}\frac{I}{x_2} = \frac{1}{\frac{3}{4}p_1 + p_2}\frac{I}{x_2} = 1 > 0, \quad \text{normal good.}$$

Note that the denominator in the own-price elasticities will always be greater than 1 (1 plus a positive number is greater than 1), so the own-price elasticities will always be inelastic, regardless of the prices. This is because of the zero substitution effect associated with perfect complements (see Example 4.5). This zero substitution effect results in the price consumption curve having a positive slope, yielding inelastic demand.

As an example of determining own-price, income, and cross-price elasticities, consider the market demand function

$$Q_1 = ap_1^b p_2^d I^o.$$

This demand curve is linear in logarithms:

$$\ln Q_1 = \ln a + b\ln p_1 + d\ln p_2 + o\ln I.$$

The own-price elasticity of demand is

$$\varepsilon_{11} = \frac{\partial \ln Q_1}{\partial \ln p_1} = b,$$

and the cross price and income elasticities are

$$\varepsilon_{12} = \frac{\partial \ln Q_1}{\partial \ln p_2} = d,$$

$$\eta_1 = \frac{\partial \ln Q_1}{\partial \ln I} = o.$$

These elasticities are constant throughout the ranges of prices and income.

Slutsky equation in elasticities

Recall the Slutsky equation from Chapter 4:

$$\frac{\partial x_1}{\partial p_1} = \frac{\partial x_1}{\partial p_1}\bigg|_{U=\text{constant}} - \frac{\partial x_1}{\partial I} x_1.$$

Multiplying through by p_1/x_1 yields

$$\frac{\partial x_1}{\partial p_1}\frac{p_1}{x_1} = \frac{\partial x_1}{\partial p_1}\frac{p_1}{x_1}\bigg|_{U=\text{constant}} - p_1 x_1 \frac{\partial x_1}{\partial I}\frac{1}{x_1}.$$

Multiplying numerator and denominator of the final term by I gives

$$\frac{\partial x_1}{\partial p_1}\frac{p_1}{x_1} = \frac{\partial x_1}{\partial p_1}\frac{p_1}{x_1}\bigg|_{U=\text{constant}} - \frac{p_1 x_1}{I}\frac{\partial x_1}{\partial I}\frac{I}{x_1}.$$

We denote what is called the *substitution elasticity* as

$$\xi_{11} = \frac{\partial x_1}{\partial p_1}\frac{p_1}{x_1}\bigg|_{U=\text{constant}}.$$

This indicates how the demand for x_1 responds to proportional compensated price changes. The Slutsky equation in elasticity form is then

$$\varepsilon_{11} = \xi_{11} - \alpha_1 \eta_1,$$

where $\alpha_1 = p_1 x_1 / I$ is the proportion of income spent on x_1. This Slutsky relationship in elasticities form indicates how the price elasticity of demand can be disaggregated into substitution and income components. The relative size of the income component depends on the proportion of total expenditures devoted to the commodity in question. Given a normal good, the larger the income elasticity and proportion of income spent on the commodity, the more elastic is demand. This income effect will be reinforced by the substitution effect. The larger the substitution effect, the more elastic is demand.

Summary

1. Assuming individual households' demand curves are independent of each other, the market demand curve for a commodity is determined by horizontally summing these individual household demand curves.
2. Network externalities exist when an individual household's demand for a commodity is dependent on other households' level of consumption. Positive (negative) network externalities exist when one household's value for a commodity increases (decreases) as other households purchase the item.

3. Elasticity is a measure of how responsive one variable is to a change in another variable. As a unit-free measurement, it is a standardized measurement of this responsiveness.
4. Elasticity is determined by weighting the derivative associated with the variables, which results in a measure of the percentage change in one variable to a percentage change in another variable. As a percentage change measurement, elasticity can be expressed in logarithmic form.
5. Elasticity is classified in terms of its responsiveness. This responsiveness is called elastic (inelastic) if the percentage change of the dependent variable is greater (less) than the percentage change in the independent variable. Unitary elasticity results when the percentage changes are equal.
6. The change in total revenue from a price change is dependent on the elasticity of demand. If demand is elastic (inelastic), price and total revenue move in the opposite (same) direction. Unitary elasticity results in total revenue remaining constant for any price change.
7. Income elasticity of demand measures the percentage change in quantity to a percentage change in income. Cross-price elasticity of demand measures the percentage change in quantity to a percentage change in the price of a related commodity.
8. The Slutsky equation in elasticity form indicates how the price elasticity of demand can be disaggregated into the substitution and income effects. The relative size of the income effect depends on the proportion of total expenditure devoted to the commodity.
9. (*Appendix*) Behavior economics is a field of economics that relaxes assumptions on economic behavior by incorporating finding from related disciplines.

Key concepts

aggregate demand, 169
bandwagon effect, 174
behavioral economics, 174
cross-price elasticity, 193
elastic, 183
elasticity, 178
elasticity of demand, 180
income elasticity, 192
market demand, 168
negative network externalities, 172
perfectly elastic demand, 182
perfectly inelastic demand, 181
positive network externalities, 172
total expenditures, 187
total revenue, 187

Key equation

$$\varepsilon_{11} = \xi_{11} - \alpha_1 \eta_1$$

The Slutsky equation in elasticity form indicates how the price elasticity of demand can be disaggregated into the substitution and income components.

Questions

1. If there is a single all-consuming commodity that absorbs all of a household's income, what is its price elasticity and income elasticity of demand?
2. Assume that, as a possible consequence of an oil cartel, the quantity of gasoline suddenly and permanently decreased by 20 percent. The prediction is the price of gasoline will increase immediately, but will then decline over time, although possibly not to the previous level. Do you generally agree or disagree with this statement? Explain.
3. Is the demand for a particular brand of a product, such as Head skis, likely to be more price-elastic or price-inelastic than the demand for the aggregate of all brands, such as downhill skis? Explain.
4. A friend tells you he will drink the same amount of coffee whether its price is 50 cents or $1.50 per cup. Is the market demand for coffee perfectly inelastic in this range of prices? Explain.
5. How does ignorance affect elasticity of demand?
6. If an anti-drug program is effective and causes the price of drugs to increase, it should reduce the quantity of drugs consumed and increase the total amount spent on drugs. Do you agree or disagree with this statement? Explain.
7. Assume that the regents of a major state university system decide to generate an increase in revenue by changing their tuition policy. They vote an 18 percent increase in state resident tuition and a 5 percent reduction in out-of-state tuition. What are the regents assuming about the elasticities of demand for state residents and out-of-state students? Explain.
8. Given an inelastic demand curve for beef, what would be the effects on price, quantity, and total revenue if mad-cow disease occurs in the United States? Explain.
9. Insurance agents receive a commission on the policies they sell. Would higher or lower insurance premiums raise the income of agents? Explain.
10. Hazel is the seller of a commodity that has zero costs to produce and a high income elasticity of demand of 25. She determines she can maximize profits by giving the customers money. She reasons that this increases their incomes and greatly increases the demand for her product. Why is this plan irrational?

Exercises

I know the answer. The answer lies within the heart of all mankind. The answer is five.

(Charles Schultz)

1. Sandra's income elasticity of demand for food is 1, and her price elasticity of demand is $-\frac{1}{2}$. Also, assume she allocates $10,000 per year on food, the price of food is $2 and her income is $25,000.

a. If a \$2 tax on food causes the price of food to double, what would happen to her consumption of food?
b. Assume that, after accounting for the sales tax effect in (a), she is given a tax rebate of \$5000 to ease the effect of this tax. What would be her resulting level of food consumption?
c. Is Sandra better or worse off when given a rebate equal to the tax payments? Discuss.

2. The Young household consumes two commodities, x_1 and x_2. What is the Youngs' demand function for x_1, if x_1 and x_2 are perfect complements? What is the cross-price elasticity of demand?
3. A firm's DVD players have a price elasticity of demand of -1 in the short run, while the price elasticity for its CD players is -2. If the firm decides to raise the price of both products by 10 percent, what will happen to its sales and revenue?
4. A negative relation between the price of a commodity and its market consumption would be observed even if every household chose at random. With the aid of the budget constraint, explain why this is true.
5. See Exercise 2 in Chapter 4. For the utility functions (i) through (iv) and (vi), calculate the own-price elasticities, income elasticities, and cross-price elasticities.
6. Andrea says peanut butter and jelly are perfect complements when used in the fixed proportion of one glob of peanut butter to one glob of jelly. Assume that the price of a glob of peanut butter is the same as a glob of jelly.

   a. Show that the own-price elasticity of demand for peanut butter is $-1/2$.
   b. Show that the cross-price elasticity of a change in the price of jelly on peanut butter consumption is also $-1/2$.
   c. If the price of peanut butter is twice the price of jelly, how does this affect the answers in (a) and (b)?

7. Consider the following household utility function:

   $$U(x_1, x_2) = x_1^{1/5} x_2^{3/5}.$$

   a. Derive the demand functions for x_1 and x_2.
   b. Assuming all 100 households have identical preferences, derive the market demand functions.
   c. Calculate the market price elasticities of demand.

8. Assume Sean's income elasticity of demand for junk food is 1 and he spends 10 percent of his income on junk food. If his price elasticity of demand for junk food is -0.3, what is his substitution price elasticity?
9. Over the last 10 years, 33 convicted murderers have been executed per year on average. Over the same 10 years, the murder rate has averaged 2150 per year. The demand for murder is highly inelastic with respect to capital punishment. Based on data during the last 10 years, this elasticity figure is only -0.008. If one more

murderer had been executed each year, how many fewer murders would there have been over the last 10 years?

10. Assume that the demand function for a firm's output q_1 is estimated to be

$$q_1 = 255 - 465.40p_1 + 979.34p_2 + 82.56A_1 - 89.67A_2 + 3.49I,$$

where p_1 and p_2 denote prices of products q_1 and q_2, respectively; A_1 and A_2 represent advertising expenditures for q_1 and q_2, respectively; and I denotes income. The mean values of the variables are

$$p_1 = 9, p_2 = 4, A_1 = 45, A_2 = 35, \text{ and } I = 456.$$

a. Calculate the own- and cross-price elasticity of demand for q_1.
b. Calculate the own- and cross-advertising elasticity of demand for q_1.

Internet case studies

1. Develop a list of commodities affected by network externalities.
2. Find the elasticity of demand for a number commodities, and show that the own-price elasticity of demand becomes more inelastic as the commodity classification becomes more aggregated.

APPENDIX TO CHAPTER 5

Behavioral economics

We are interested in determining the efficient allocation of resources for improving social welfare. As such, we are concerned with households' attempting to maximize their utility only in terms of using it as a foundation for deriving household demand and then aggregating these household demands into market demands for commodities. These market demands can then be used along with market supply for deriving market prices. In a decentralized market system, these market prices are signals yielding an efficient allocation of resources. With this objective, we are not as concerned with determining the realism of the assumptions underlying utility maximization for all households.

Instead, it is assumed in general that households can order their available commodity bundles, have limited income, and can then maximize satisfaction. This is the classical approach to microeconomic theory. However, these simplifying assumptions are not true for all households. Less restrictive assumptions on human behavior may better explain household demand. As an example, consider how network externalities can shift demand curves.

A field of economics considering alternative assumptions on behavior is behavioral economics. Behavioral economics combines related disciplines, principally psychology, to investigate how considering alternative, possibly less restrictive, assumptions can enrich our ability to understand the household decision process. The goal is to not develop fine epistemology, but instead to improve on our understanding of markets and how prices

Table 5A.1 Behavioral economics

Modification	*Description*	*Example*
Availability	The effect of the availability of an alternative commodity on the demand for a commodity	The availability of chocolate cake decreases the demand for a healthier bowl of fruit
Reference point	The point at which a decision is made	A firm setting a price and then providing a 20 percent discount
Endowment (divestiture aversion)	A commodity is valued higher if a household already has it	Valuing a coffee mug more if you already own it
Anchoring (Focalism)	Choice determined by relying on prior information	Ignoring the cost of checking baggage when purchasing an airline ticket
Paradox of choice ("More is less")	Reducing choice can increase utility	A firm bundling options
Status quo bias	The tendency not to change behavior	Keeping your car rather than replacing it
Relative consumption satisfaction	Households derive utility not just from their own consumption but also from how they compare to other households	Keeping up with the Jones by purchasing a new car
Hedonic adaption (Hedonic treadmill)	Households return to a relatively stable level of utility after a large life change	An increase in income yields no permanent gain in utility
Peer	Network externality	Wearing the latest fashion
Law of small numbers (Hasty generalization)	Reaching a conclusion based on insufficient evidence	Herd behavior in stock market investing after a short stock market rise
Hyperbolic discounting	Discounting outcomes in the short run more than outcomes in the long run	Preferring to receive $50 now rather than $100 a year from now, but preferring $100 in ten years over $50 in nine years
Cooperation	Working together toward a fair common goal	Charitable giving

are determined. For example, firms will in many cases use these household behavioral assumptions as a foundation in their marketing decisions (setting prices and outputs).

Some major modifications emerging from behavioral economics are listed in Table 5A.1. Underlying the *availability effect* is the idea that households' demand for a commodity bundle is not only determined by the classical microeconomic assumptions but also by impulsive or passion behavior. Easy availability of a commodity can lead to impulsiveness trumping the cognitive classical assumption. Eating the available chocolate cake will taste good now, but make you fatter and less healthy. Firms generally will attempt to profit from this availability effect behavior by providing commodities with easy access. At grocery checkouts, impulse commodities, including snack foods, magazines, and DVDs, are available for easy selection; and firms will advertise on signs outside their shops that a commodity is available—"Hot Doughnuts Now."

Will you eat a doughnut or a cup of yogurt? Only if the doughnut is available and your impulsive behavior trumps your cognitive behavior.

Behavioral economics asserts that the valuation a household places on commodities is dependent on the household's point of reference. This *reference point effect* is a determinant in the resulting demand for a commodity. Consumers going to a manufacturers' outlet mall and finding bargains are using retail prices as a reference point for considering that outlet mall prices are low (a bargain). Firms will attempt to set the reference price for their commodities and offer the commodities at a discount from this reference price. Consumers using a firm's reference price are then happy when they purchase the commodities on sale.

The *endowment effect* is a type of reference point where households tend to value a commodity more if they own it. If a household purchases a ticket to some event and could later sell it at a higher price, classical economics assumes the household will sell it and increase its utility. What the household is willing to pay for the ticket should be the same as what it is willing to sell the ticket. The price should be the same. However, behavioral economics indicates the household will keep the ticket and go to the event. This behavioral result is based on *loss aversion*, which states a feeling of loss exists when a household loses something it once owned. A major type of household endowment effect based on loss aversion is the selling of securities (stocks and bonds). Households may tend to be reluctant to sell a security at a loss and invest the proceeds in another asset with the likelihood of higher returns. Behavioral economics explains this reluctance by the endowment effect, where facing the loss in the security when selling it is greater than the satisfaction gained in reinvesting the proceeds in another asset.

Do stock and commodity traders suffer from loss aversion? No—otherwise they would be out of business.

If it ain't broke why fix it?[5] Similar to the endowment effect, *status quo bias* indicates that households tend not to change established behavior unless there is a strong incentive to do so. In contrast, classical economics assumes no inertia on the part of households. They take every opportunity that increases utility. Status quo bias is related to the endowment effect given the status quo is part of a household's endowment. Thus, loss aversion exists resulting from household inertia. Similar to other behavioral effects, the effects may be so subtle that households are not aware of it. Classical economics assumes astute utility maximizing households break out of these behavioral effects.

Some households may also rely too heavily (*anchor*) on a piece of information when making decisions. Decisions can be very complex and costly in terms of spending time and energy in evaluating all the potential benefits and costs. This is particularly true when information asymmetry exists between the buyers and sellers.[6] The seller may have more information about the item than the buyer. This asymmetric information and resulting cost of acquiring information may lead households to use a simple rule of thumb in making a decision. They may decide on a major purchase based on the information that a neighbor, co-worker, or relative purchased it. Such anchoring can save time and effort. For example, some firms will base where they are going to locate their retail outlets on another retail outlet's location decision. The firm can save by anchoring their location decisions on the other firm's decisions. Households may also ignore other information when making purchasing decisions. When booking an airline flight or rental car or buying an item on the Internet, households may only concentrate on the initial price quote and not consider the hidden costs of baggage fees, insurance, or shipping costs.

There is a paradox associated when a household has a large set of choices to choose from. At first, as the number of choices increase, the likelihood of finding a specific item that meets a household's criteria increases, which enhances utility. However, the *paradox of choice* states that it is possible that at some point additional choices can lead to a poor decision or failure to make a decision at all. Classical economics states that more choice is always preferable because a household can just ignore the less desirable choices. A teenage girl would much rather go shopping at a large mall in a big city than a strip mall in a small town. However, behavioral economics indicates that *hyperchoice* can lead to diminishing utility. Making a decision on the right cold medication can be challenging given the wide assortment of brands and symptom reliefs. The research supporting the paradox of choice indicates that firms could reduce product choice and improve their sales. However, evidence on firm behavior does not support this result. Supermarkets are full of cold medications and other differentiated products. In fact, firms attempt to differentiate their products in an attempt to increase return by filling every market niche.[7]

Classical economics assumes no *relative consumption satisfaction effect*, where one household's utility is dependent on other households' income or consumption. Behavioral economics considers this satisfaction effect. An example is where an employee receives a bonus. Classical economics would conclude the employee gains utility from the bonus; behavioral economics would conclude the gains in utility would depend on the bonuses received from her colleagues. If her bonus was lower, her utility might decline rather than increase. Commodities, including autos, houses, electronics, and fashion items, are relative commodities where a household's utility is dependent on the quantity and quality of these commodities consumed by the household's comparison group (keeping up with the Jones). In contrast, absolute commodities such as health, safety, and relationships are commodities that the associated level of utility is not dependent on other households' income or consumption. Thorstein Veblen (1857–1929) coined the term *conspicuous consumption,* where purchasing commodities is mainly for demonstrating wealth and social status. A household's conspicuous consumption is a form of the relative consumption satisfaction effect.

It is generally accepted in psychology that households have a set hedonic level of happiness. This level of happiness can increase with income up a point, but then further income increases will generally not add much to happiness. A large increase in income may at first increase happiness, but with time the increase in happiness will tend to dissipate. At low levels of income, household utility does increase with income up to around $75,000, but then it levels off. Households tend to adapt (*hedonic adaption*) to changes in income, family deaths, or debilitating accidents. Since the mid 1950s, real (inflation-adjusted) per-capita income has generally steadily increased, with the associated average level of household satisfaction remaining constant. Long-run happiness tends to be associated with nonmarket family and friends activities compared with short-run happiness associated with the purchase of commodities such as flat-screen TVs and automobiles.

What will provide you with more satisfaction: a diamond necklace or a family vacation? The relationships developed with family and friends provide long-run happiness.

The *peer effect* was investigated in the section on network externalities, where considering this effect will shift the demand curve. We will investigate the *law of small numbers* after probability has been discussed in Chapter 18 and the *hyperbolic discounting effect* once the idea of discounting future utility has been presented in Chapter 19.[8] Heard behavior is when households act together without planned direction. Finally, the *cooperation effect* states that households generally want to cooperate with others and not increase their utility at the expense of others. Such cooperative behavior as opposed to competition is investigated in Chapter 14 with game theory. Generally, households do not attempt to maximize utility from consumption at all costs. Instead, they are interested in the fairness of their allocation decisions.

6 Pure exchange

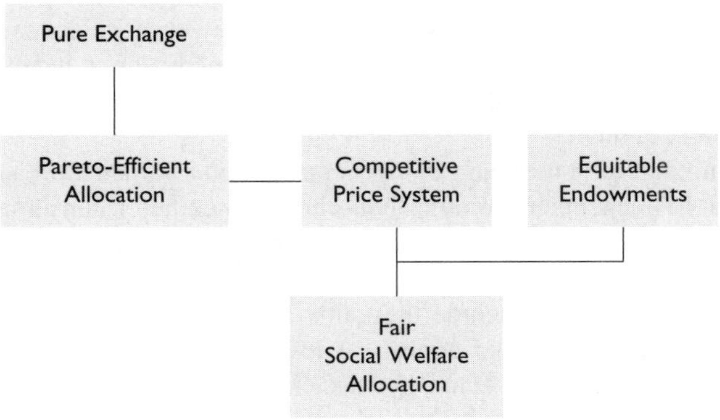

Outline and Conceptual Inquiries

There are gains from trade
Consider a two-commodity and two-household economy
How do you feed the multitudes?
Edgeworth box
Can you put a whole economy in one box?
Application: Why the Edgeworth box is not a Pareto box
Understanding a Pareto-efficient allocation
Contract curve (Pareto-efficient allocations)

Why are price-signals efficient?
Why should you love free markets?
Application: POW camp
Illustration of the first fundamental theorem of welfare economics
How much are you willing to exchange apples for oranges?

Walras' law and the beauty of price signals
Is there excess demand in an economy?
Improving social welfare
Why have equal-opportunity legislation?
Application: Equitable allocations and equal access

Summary
Key concepts
Key equations
Questions
Exercises
Internet case studies

The question is not if there are gains from trade, but who receives them.
(Michael Wetzstein)

The treatment of a cancer patient can take a number of forms depending on the nature of the cancer. If the cancer is predominantly localized, a surgical procedure may be appropriate for the condition. However, if it has spread to a number of organs or throughout the body, surgery would be ineffective and instead chemotherapy may be used to address the condition (problem). Similarly, economists have different treatments for addressing economic problems. If the problem of allocation is generally localized in one market (organ), then a partial-equilibrium analysis would provide the correct solution. Instead, if it is more of a general problem infecting numerous markets (organs) or the whole economy (body), a general-equilibrium analysis would be in order.

In previous chapters, we investigated the utility-maximization conditions for an individual household mostly in isolation from all other households. This type of analysis is called **partial-equilibrium analysis**, where only one segment of an economy is analyzed without consideration of possible interactions with other segments. For example, partial-equilibrium analysis of utility maximization for a household considers only the demand for commodities without considering the supply. Partial-equilibrium analysis may also consider the market (demand and supply) for just one commodity—say pizza—without considering the interactions of other commodities—say burgers and dogs.

However, in general, a market for a commodity will be influenced by the market effects for other commodities. The study of this interaction among agents (households and firms) across markets within an economy is called **general-equilibrium analysis**. A (general) equilibrium model of all markets, where supply and demand for each commodity are equated, will result in necessary conditions for economic efficiency. This equilibrium of supply and demand in all markets is achieved by agents trading commodities in order to increase their utility. Agents will engage in trading commodities until all the gains from trade are exhausted.

Partial-equilibrium analysis. Only one segment of an economy is analyzed without consideration of possible interactions with other segments. *E.g., a firm determining its optimal level of output and price without considering the effects this may have on the prices in other related markets.*

General-equilibrium analysis. Analysis of the interaction among agents across markets within an economy. *E.g., prior to the European conquest, how native North American tribes, on the east coast, interacted.*

The efficiency gains from agents' trading are most apparent when only agents are households, who are initially endowed with some quantities of commodities, and there is no production. This is called a **pure-exchange economy**, where there are no firms producing the commodities. The supply of each commodity is then the sum of each household's endowment of that commodity. The only agents are households and each household is initially endowed with a given quantity of each commodity. Households will then trade commodities based on their initial endowments and preferences for commodities. When all the gains from trade are exhausted, an efficient allocation of commodities exists.

Pure-exchange economy. Households trading, given they are initially endowed with some quantities of commodities and there is no production. *E.g., children in the lunch room trading various items in their lunch boxes.*

In this chapter we first explore gains from trade in a pure-exchange economy. The *Edgeworth* box is a method of illustrating these gains for two agents (traders). After determining the efficient allocation, or *Pareto-efficient allocation*, for agents, we investigate the efficiency of a free-market price system for allocating commodities and relate this to the Pareto-efficient allocation using the First and Second Fundamental Theorems of Welfare Economics. We then develop the *tâtonnement* (trial and error) process of establishing an equilibrium set of prices and relate this to the optimal social-welfare allocation. Given this tâtonnement process, the question of who receives the gains from trade is answered by the market. In a normative (value-judgment) context, this market solution may not maximize social welfare, given that social welfare is also dependent on an equitable distribution of initial commodities (resources) among the agents. At the end of this chapter, we discuss a fair allocation of initial resources, yielding an optimal social-welfare allocation.

The conclusion that free markets – resulting in an efficient allocation of resources through a tâtonnement process and requiring no centralized governmental decision process – are best is central to many applied economic analyses. Applied economists will take this conclusion and apply it to the various resource allocation problems. In cases where externalities, supply of public goods, and asymmetric information result from missing markets, they will recommend and develop mechanisms for establishing those markets. Where free markets fail in terms of some agents having market power (monopoly power), applied economists measure the degree of this monopoly power and associated inefficiency and, if warranted, develop mechanisms for correcting this inefficiency.

There are gains from trade

Gains from trade are neither myth nor invention, but fruit.

(Michael Wetzstein)

In 1626, a Dutch West India Company agent named Peter Minuit swapped wampum beads, metal knives, and wool blankets for Manhattan Island.[1] Such swaps, possibly not as historic, have occurred through the ages. For example, archeologists have discovered seashell necklaces at sites far removed from an ocean beach. Thus, at least since the dawn of modern man there have been gains from trade. In such pure-exchange economies, we assume a certain amount of various commodities exist, and the problem is to allocate these commodities among households in an efficient way. An allocation of the existing commodities is efficient if no one household can be made better off (by reallocating the available commodities) without making some other household worse off. The necessary condition for such an efficient allocation of commodities is

$$\text{MRS}_1 = \text{MRS}_2 = \ldots = \text{MRS}_n,$$

where the subscripts denote households, n represents the number of households, and MRS measures how much a household is willing to trade one commodity for another. When how much each household is willing to trade one commodity for another is the same, gains from trade are exhausted. Any reallocation of the commodities will not increase the utility of one household without decreasing the utility of another.

Consider a two-commodity and two-household economy

As an illustration of this necessary condition for an efficient allocation of commodities, consider an economy with two commodities, bread and fish, and two individuals (households), Robinson (R) and Friday (F). Note that we can develop all of the aspects of general-equilibrium analysis based on such a two-commodity, two-household economy and then generalize to k commodities and n households.

In our hypothetical pure-exchange economy, 50 units of bread and 100 units of fish are to be allocated and can be allocated in various ways. All of the commodities could be allocated to Robinson, all to Friday, or some combination between the two. An egalitarian allocation would divide the commodities equally between Robinson and Friday. However, such an allocation may not be efficient if Robinson and Friday have different preferences for bread and fish. In such a case their MRSs will not be equal at this equal allocation.

Suppose Robinson's MRS_R (bread for fish) $= 2/1$ at an equal allocation where Robinson obtains 25 units of bread and 50 units of fish. Robinson is willing to give up two units of bread to obtain one more fish. For an equal allocation, let Friday's MRS_F (bread for fish) $=$ 1/1. Friday is willing to trade 1 for 1. This equable allocation does not result in an efficient allocation, because

$$\text{MRS}_R = 2 \neq 1 = \text{MRS}_F.$$

As indicated in Table 6.1, if 2 units of bread are taken from Robinson with 1 unit traded to Friday for 1 fish, the level of utility remains the same, with 1 bread left over. By trading, the utilities of Robinson and Friday remain unchanged, with 1 unit of bread left over. This 1 unit of bread represents the gains from trade, which could then be divided between Robinson and Friday, resulting in their utility increasing. This may be how it is possible to feed people in the wilderness.

How do you feed the multitudes? By facilitating exchange of commodities, it is possible to feed the multitudes.

As long as MRSs between Robinson and Friday are unequal, gains from trade are possible. There are many possible trades that will result in gains. As shown in Figure 6.1, we can use Robinson's and Friday's initial endowments and indifference curves (representing their preferences) to determine all possible trades leading to gains. We denote Robinson's consumption bundle as (x_1^R, x_2^R), where x_1^R represents the quantities of fish Robinson consumes and x_2^R the quantities of bread he consumes. Similarly, Friday's consumption bundle is (x_1^F, x_2^F). An initial endowment consists of an initial commodity bundle. For Robinson, this endowment bundle is (e_1^R, e_2^R), where e_1^R and e_2^R are Robinson's initial endowments of fish and bread, respectively. Similarly, Friday's initial endowment bundle is (e_1^F, e_2^F).

Table 6.1 Gains from trade

Household	*Initial allocation*		*Trade*		*MRS*	*Utility*	*Final allocation*	
	Fish	*Bread*	*Fish*	*Bread*			*Fish*	*Bread*
Robinson	50	25	1 demand	2 supply	2/1	Unchanged	51	23
Friday	50	25	1 supply	1 demand	1/1	Unchanged	49	26
Total	100	50					100	49
Gains from trade			0	1				

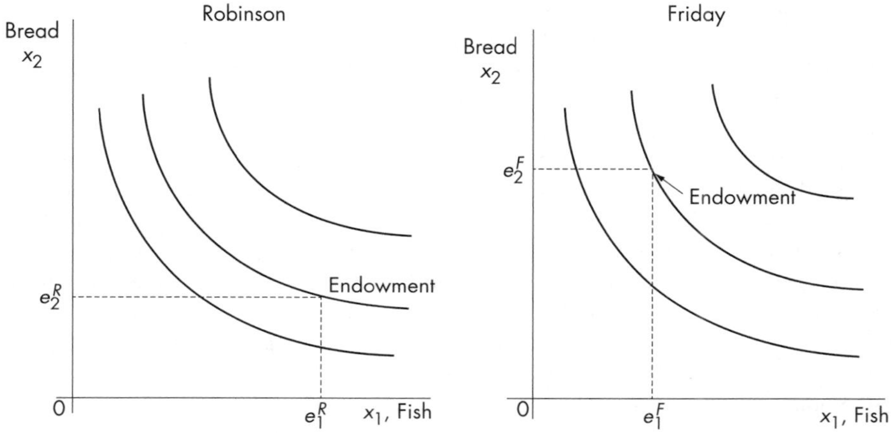

Figure 6.1 **Preferences and endowments for the two-commodity, two-household pure-exchange economy.** Robinson and Friday are each endowed with an initial allocation of fish and bread. Preferences for these two commodities are represented by indifference curves.

Edgeworth box

Put the economy into a box and watch the gains from trade pop out.

(Michael Wetzstein)

An **Edgeworth box** diagram (Figure 6.2) provides a convenient method for representing the two households' preferences and endowments in one diagram. We construct an Edgeworth Box by turning the preference space for Friday (in Figure 6.1) 180° and placing it on top of Robinson's preference space at the point where their endowments are together, point C in Figure 6.2. The horizontal width of the box represents the total quantity of fish available, $e_1^R + e_1^F$, and the vertical height represents the total quantity of bread available, $e_2^R + e_2^F$. Therefore, the size of the box depends on the total amount of fish and bread available in the economy. If the total amount of fish is increased, the width of the box expands. The height expands with an increase in the total endowment of bread. Every point inside the box represents a *feasible allocation* of fish and bread between Robinson and Friday. An allocation

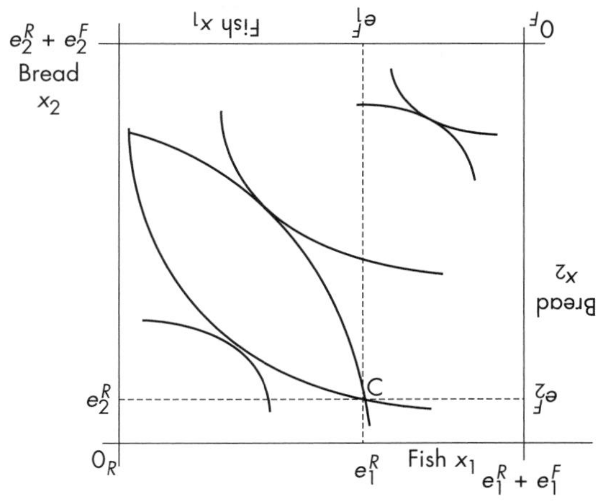

Figure 6.2 **Edgeworth box in a pure-exchange economy.** The sum of household endowments determines the size of the box. Every point inside the box corresponds to a feasible allocation.

is feasible if the total quantity consumed of each commodity is equal to the total available from the endowments (supply). Specifically,

$$x_1^R + x_1^F = e_1^R + e_1^F, \quad \text{commodity 1, fish,}$$

$$x_2^R + x_2^F = e_2^R + e_2^F, \quad \text{commodity 2, bread.}$$

An allocation where Robinson receives nothing, (0, 0), and Friday receives all ($e_1^R + e_1^F$, $e_2^R + e_2^F$), is a feasible allocation represented by the origin O_R in Figure 6.2. At this allocation, Robinson's utility is minimized and Friday's utility is maximized for this level of total endowments. Similarly, at the origin O_F, the allocation is (0, 0) for Friday and ($e_1^R + e_1^F$, $e_2^R + e_2^F$) for Robinson, so Friday's utility is minimized and Robinson's maximized. Feasible allocations between these two extreme points represent combinations of commodities with varying in level of satisfaction for both Robinson and Friday. For a movement toward O_R, Friday receives more of fish, bread or both, which increases her utility, and Robinson receives less, which decreases in his utility. The reverse occurs for a movement toward O_F. Points outside the box are not feasible, because insufficient levels of fish, bread, or both are available.

Can you put a whole economy in one box? Yes, given a fixed level of commodity endowments there are a finite number of feasible allocations, so these feasible allocations will fit into a box.

Edgeworth box. A diagram illustrating the feasible allocations of two commodities between two agents. *E.g., Bonnie and Clyde dividing up the guns and liquor they stole.*

Application: Why the Edgeworth box is not a Pareto box

The Edgeworth box was developed by Vilfredo Pareto (1848–1923) and was only popularized by Francis Y. Edgeworth (1854–1926). As addressed by J. Weatherby, the Edgeworth box got its name because Marshall took a diagram by Edgeworth that contained the box and incorporated it fully into the second edition of his *Principles*. The *Principles* textbook was very popular in Britain and the United States even into the late 1930s. Pareto was unknown in these countries until Hicks introduced his ideas in the late 1930s. As in football, the player who picks up the ball and runs with it gets the fame.

Source: J. Weatherby, Jr, "Why Was It Called an Edgeworth–Bowley Box? A Possible Explanation," *Economic Inquiry* 14 (1976): 294–296.

Understanding a Pareto-efficient allocation

In Buddhism, any act that increases the total of human suffering is immoral and any act that reduces suffering is moral. This viewpoint directly results in a Pareto-efficient allocation. Specifically, a **Pareto-efficient allocation** can be described as an allocation where there is no way to make all the households better off. Stating it differently, there is no way to make some households better off without making someone else worse off, so all of the gains from trade are exhausted. A Pareto-efficient allocation is illustrated in Figure 6.3. In the figure, point C is not Pareto-efficient, because it is possible to reallocate the commodities in such a manner that one household can be made better off without making someone else worse off. For example, moving along Friday's indifference curve toward point A, by giving Robinson more bread and less fish and giving Friday more fish and less bread, Friday's utility remains

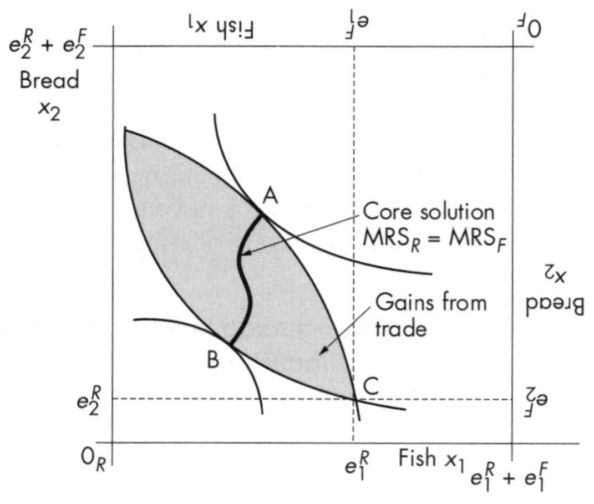

Figure 6.3 **Efficiency in a pure-exchange economy.** Any allocation within the shaded area is a Pareto improvement over allocation C. The Pareto-efficient allocations are represented by the core solution curve between allocations A and B.

unchanged and Robinson's utility increases. This remains true until point A is reached. At point A, it is not possible to increase the utility of one household without decreasing the utility of the other household.

Pareto-efficient allocation. There is no way to make one agent better off without making some other agent worse off. *E.g., two children dividing up a cupcake.*

At point C, the indifference curves for Robinson and Friday cross, so the MRSs at point C are not the same. In fact, $\mathrm{MRS}_R < \mathrm{MRS}_F$. Thus, gains from trade are possible, and any point within the shaded lens represents a gain (called a **Pareto improvement**). Points A, B, and points on the chord connecting the two are where $\mathrm{MRS}_R = \mathrm{MRS}_F$ and are Pareto-efficient allocations. This chord from points A to B is called the core solution. The **core solution** of a pure-exchange economy is where all gains from trade are exhausted. The exact solution point within this core, which results from Robinson and Friday trading, depends on the bargaining strength of the two agents. If Friday is a relatively strong bargainer, then she will receive more of the gains from trade and the solution will be closer to point B. Alternatively, if Robinson has the upper hand, he will receive a larger portion of the gains and the solution will approach point A.

Pareto improvement. A reallocation of commodity bundles among agents resulting in at least one agent being made better off without any loss incurred by another agent. *E.g., two schoolchildren increasing their satisfaction by trading cookies and chips.*

Core solution. Points where all gains from trade are exhausted. *E.g., a point where trading among classmates during lunch has ended and the students eat their lunch.*

Contract curve (Pareto-efficient allocations)

> *The advantage of a classical education is that it enables you to despise the wealth that it prevents you from achieving.*
>
> (Russell Green)

In Mark Twain's classic 1881 book *The Prince and the Pauper*, two agents switch their initial endowments for a number of days. The pauper (Tom Canty) receives the prince's endowment and the prince (Prince of Wales) receives the pauper's. This trading of endowments directly affects their resulting optimal allocations (their experiences). Like the prince and the pauper, the optimal allocation resulting from allocating the commodities between Robinson and Friday will depend on how the initial total endowment of bread and fish is divided between them. If Robinson initially has most of the bread and fish (a prince), then an optimal allocation near point D in Figure 6.4 may result. The value of this initial endowment is the wealth or income of the households. The more fish and bread a household initially has, the higher the level of utility that can be achieved. Thus, the distribution of income determines the resulting Pareto-efficient allocation. By varying the allocation of initial endowments, we can trace out the complete set of Pareto-efficient allocations (called

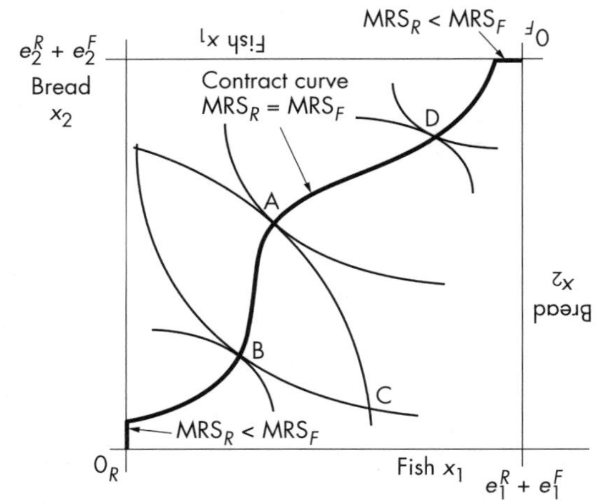

Figure 6.4 **Contract curve in a pure-exchange economy.** The contract curve represents the Pareto efficient allocations.

a **contract curve**) (Figure 6.4). As illustrated in Figure 6.4, the contract curve represents a curve in the interior of the Edgeworth box intersecting the tangencies between the indifference curves for the two agents, where their MRSs are equal. If efficient allocations exist, where an agent will not consume a positive amount of all commodities, the contract curve will correspond with a segment of an axis (corner solution) and MRSs will not equate. Any point not on this contract curve—for example point C—is inefficient. Given the appropriate set of endowments, the agents will adjust their terms of trade until a contract, represented by a point on the contract curve, is made.

Contract curve. The locus of Pareto-efficient allocations. *E.g., the resulting amount of cookies and chips each schoolchild consumes given that one child has all the cookies and chips, or the other child has all the cookies and chips, or any combination between these two extremes.*

The contract curve represents all the Pareto-efficient allocations. Every point on the contract curve results in economic efficiency, but social welfare is not maximized at every point. A movement along a contract curve will increase one agent's utility at the expense of reduced utility for the other agent. Maximum social welfare depends not only on economic efficiency but also on an optimal distribution of income. Thus, only a point on the contract curve that corresponds to an optimal distribution of income will maximize social welfare. Pareto optimality does provide a necessary condition for an allocation to maximize social welfare. At a Pareto-efficient allocation, no inefficiencies in resource allocation exist, which is a necessary condition for maximum social welfare.

The major inadequacy of the Pareto-welfare criterion is it does not lead to a complete social ranking of alternative allocations for an economy and thus is a useless criterion in the context of many policy propositions. However, some analytical results can be obtained with a Pareto-welfare criterion. For example, point rationing is ordinarily better than fixed ration quantities. Point rationing is where households are given a fixed amount of points and must use these points along with money for the purchase of commodities that vary not only in price but also in point value. Fixed ration quantities implies households receive a given amount of each rationed commodity. Point rationing may permit every household to benefit by adjusting its purchases in accord with its own tastes and preferences. An example of point rationing is a grammar school carnival with a number of activities in which the children can participate. Providing each child with tickets and requiring various number of tickets for each activity (point rationing) is generally preferred to allowing each child to participate in each activity a fixed number of times (fixed ration of quantities). Point rationing allows a child to allocate the tickets so he participates more in those activities from which he receives the most happiness (Moon jumps) and not participate in activities that he dislikes (finger painting).

Unfortunately, there are many other policy proposals that cannot be evaluated with the Pareto criterion. Generally, such policies will result in a gain by one agent associated with a loss by another agent. This is not a Pareto-efficient improvement, so the Pareto criterion will not help in determining the social desirability of the policy.[2]

Example 6.1 Determining the Pareto-efficient allocations, contract curve

Consider the following utility functions for Robinson and Friday:

$$U^R = x_1^R (x_2^R)^{1/2} \quad \text{and} \quad U^F = x_1^F x_2^F,$$

with $e_1^R + e_1^F = 100$ and $e_2^R + e_2^F = 50$. The contract curve or Pareto-efficient set is where

$$\text{MRS}_R(x_2^R \text{ for } x_1^R) = \text{MRS}_F(x_2^F \text{ for } x_1^F),$$

$$\frac{2x_2^R}{x_1^R} = \frac{x_2^F}{x_1^F}.$$

This condition is determined by maximizing one household's utility subject to holding the other's utility constant. For example, consider maximizing Robinson's utility holding Friday's utility constant:

$$\max_{(x_1^R, x_2^R)} \left[x_1^R (x_2^R)^{1/2}\right], \quad \text{s.t. } U^F = x_1^F x_2^F.$$

Noting that $x_1^F = 100 - x_1^R$ and $x_2^F = 50 - x_2^R$, the Lagrangian for this problem is

$$\mathcal{L}(x_1^R, x_2^R, \lambda) = x_1^R (x_2^R)^{1/2} + \lambda[U^F - (100 - x_1^R)(50 - x_2^R)].$$

FOCs are then

$$\frac{\partial \mathcal{L}}{\partial x_1^R} = (x_1^R)^{-1}U^R + \lambda(50 - x_2^R) = 0,$$

$$\frac{\partial \mathcal{L}}{\partial x_2^R} = \frac{1}{2}(x_2^R)^{-1}U^R + \lambda(100 - x_1^R) = 0,$$

$$\frac{\partial \mathcal{L}}{\partial \lambda} = U^F - (100 - x_1^R)(50 - x_2^R) = 0.$$

Taking the ratio of the first two conditions gives

$$\text{MRS}_R(x_2^R \text{ for } x_1^R) = \frac{2x_2^R}{x_1^R} = \frac{50 - x_2^R}{100 - x_1^R}$$

$$= \frac{x_2^F}{x_1^F} = \text{MRS}_F(x_2^F \text{ for } x_1^F).$$

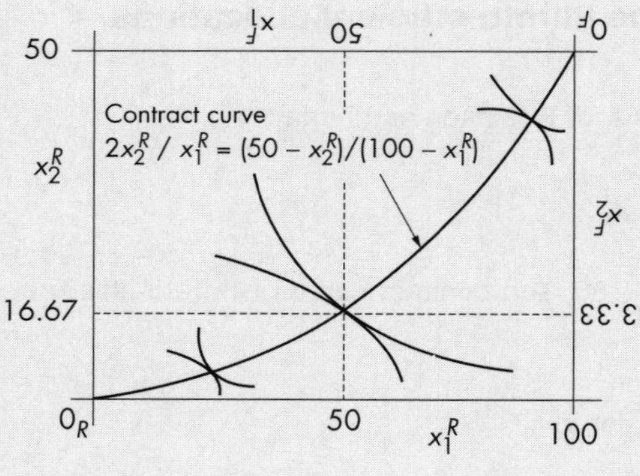

Why are price signals efficient?

After the Russian revolution in 1917, currency issued by Tsar Nicholas II, with his portrait on it, survived for years as the major medium of exchange within communist Russia. As long as agents are willing to accept a particular medium of exchange for commodities, it will be used. Such a medium of exchange is particularly useful as the number of households increases and the process of bartering becomes cumbersome.[3] All commodities are valued by this medium, and the medium is accepted in exchange for commodities. This medium of exchange is money. Money is accepted not for the direct utility it provides but for the indirect utility via the commodities it can purchase. This characteristic of money results in the famous paradox: "The essence of money is in its absolute worthlessness."

Based on money as a medium of exchange, the allocation device that has received by far the greatest attention (by economists) is the **price system,** which assumes all commodities are valued in the market by their money equivalence. Relying on the self-motivation of many decision makers, the price system permits the decentralization of allocation decisions. In contrast, in a central-planning system, allocation decisions are made within one central organization. Relative to central planning, an interconnected market system provides a method for relating household preferences with supply at a reduced cost for society. Prices act as signals to economic agents in guiding their supply-and-demand decisions. Under a **perfectly competitive price system,** households have no control over the market prices and thus take such prices as given. This price-taking characteristic of perfectly competitive markets yields a Pareto-efficient market system.

Price system. All commodities are valued in the market by their money equivalence. *E.g., all the commodities at the supermarket have an associated price.*

Perfectly competitive price system. Agents have no control over the market prices, so they take such prices as given. *E.g., at the checkout counter in a supermarket, you do not haggle over the prices.*

In a perfectly competitive price system, the correspondence between a Pareto-efficient allocation of resources and a perfectly competitive price system is exact. This is called the **First Fundamental Theorem of Welfare Economics**. Every perfectly competitive allocation is Pareto-efficient. For competitive markets, the first fundamental theorem provides a formal and very general confirmation of Adam Smith's invisible hand. The **Second Fundamental Theorem of Welfare Economics** states that every Pareto-efficient allocation has an associated perfectly competitive set of prices. This second theorem is a converse of the first. It states the possibility of achieving any desired Pareto-efficient allocation as a market-based equilibrium using an appropriate distribution of income. However, not every Pareto-efficient allocation is a social-welfare optimum. Thus, although a competitive price system may bring about an efficient allocation of resources, economists must be careful when assessing the social desirability of such an allocation.

First Fundamental Theorem of Welfare Economics. Every perfectly competitive allocation is Pareto-optimal. *E.g., if there are market prices for cookies and chips, the resulting trades by children taking these prices as given would be Pareto-efficient.*

Second Fundamental Theorem of Welfare Economics. Every Pareto-efficient allocation has an associated perfectly competitive set of prices. *E.g., let the price of a cookie be the numeraire, so it is \$1. If the children's trading yields a Pareto-efficient allocation of 5 chips for 1 cookie, then the competitive prices would be \$1 for a cookie and \$0.20 for a chip.*

We can establish this correspondence between Pareto-efficient allocations and perfectly competitive prices by first recalling that Pareto efficiency in exchange requires the condition

$$\text{MRS}_1 = \text{MRS}_2 = \ldots = \text{MRS}_n,$$

for the n households in an economy. For utility maximization subject to a wealth or income constraint, each household equates its MRS with the price ratio:

$$\text{MRS}(x_2 \text{ for } x_1) = p_1/p_2.$$

Every household faces the same price ratio. Thus,

$$\text{MRS}_1 = \text{MRS}_2 = \ldots = \text{MRS}_n = p_1/p_2.$$

The market, in equilibrium (called a *Walrasian equilibrium* after the French economist Leon Walras, 1834–1910), creates a society rate of tradeoff that is a correct reflection of every household's tradeoff rate. Information on this tradeoff rate, if it could be gathered, would require large expenditures by a government. Instead, this tradeoff can, at zero governmental cost, be generated by the perfectly competitive interaction of supply and demand.

Why should you love free markets? A perfectly competitive market system will result in an efficient allocation of resources.

Application: POW camp

A prisoner-of-war (POW) camp provides an actual example of a simple pure exchange economy where every agent (prisoner) receives roughly an equal share of commodities (Red Cross food parcels) and then realizes gains in satisfaction through trading. As recorded in a now famous article by R.A. Radford, during World War II, Allied prisoners in Europe actively traded all consumer goods and some services. However, a minority felt all trading was undesirable because it created an unsavory atmosphere and occasional frauds. Certain forms of trading were condemned more than others. Trade with Germans was generally criticized, and price controls were tried without success.

Most trading was for food against cigarettes, and cigarettes became a form of currency where the market value of all other commodities was expressed in terms of cigarettes (price). At first, after the POWs were captured, simple direct barter occurred, such as a nonsmoker exchanging cigarettes for a chocolate ration. Within a couple of weeks, the volume of trades increased into a well-developed market in which a market value was placed on all commodities. For example, a tin of jam was worth a half pound of margarine plus something else, a cigarette issue was worth several chocolate issues, and a tin of diced carrots was just about worthless.

As mentioned, cigarettes became the common commodity to express the market value of all other commodities. Cigarettes performed all the functions of a paper or metallic currency: a unit of account, a measure of value, and a store of value. They were homogeneous, reasonably durable, of a convenient size, and difficult to counterfeit. There was one disadvantage, as with precious (gold and silver) coins—cigarettes could be clipped or sweated by rolling them between the fingers so some tobacco fell out.

In the permanent camp Stalag VIIA at Moosburg in Bavaria, with 50,000 prisoners of all nationalities, shops were organized as nonprofit public utilities. Prisoners would deposit the commodities they wished to sell at a market price in cigarettes. Only sales in cigarettes were accepted, with no haggling (bargaining) or barter. For example, shirts sold from 60 to 120 cigarettes, depending on the age and quality of the shirt. Without labor or production, a market was created and prices were determined by the supply and demand for commodities.

In April 1945, just before the camp was liberated by the 30th US Infantry Division, chaos replaced the orderly market. Prices were unstable making trades difficult. On liberation day, April 12, 1945, the need for the science of allocating limited resources to unlimited wants (economics) ended. The age of plenty was ushered in (global bliss).

Source: R.A. Radford, "The Economic Organization of a P.O.W. Camp," *Economica* 12 (1945): 189–201.

Illustration of the first fundamental theorem of welfare economics

To illustrate the First Fundamental Theorem of Welfare Economics, we reconsider our two-household, two-commodity pure-exchange economy. Each agent (Robinson, R, and Friday, F) is initially endowed with a certain amount of the two commodities (fish x_1 and bread x_2). The ratio in which these two quantities can be traded is given by the market price ratio of commodities, p_1/p_2, where p_1 and p_2 are the per-unit prices for fish and bread, respectively.

Offer curve

To aid our illustration, we use the concept of an offer curve. An *offer curve* traces out the points where the household maximizes utility for a given level of income across various ratios of prices (Figure 6.5). At each point on the offer curve, a household's indifference curve is tangent to a budget constraint for a given price ratio. The offer curve represents how much a household is willing to offer one commodity in exchange for the other at a given price ratio.

An offer curve is analogous to the price consumption curve, with the focal point at the initial endowment e. At alternative price ratios, the endowment is affordable and every point on the offer curve is at least as good, in terms of utility, as the agent's endowment point e. An offer curve represents a set of demanded bundles (grocery carts), with each demanded bundle associated with a price ratio. For example, in Figure 6.5, p'_1/p'_2 is associated with demanded bundle A. At this price ratio, the agent is willing and able to supply $e_1 - x'_1$ in exchange for $x'_2 - e_2$. As the price of fish, x_1, increases relative to the price of bread, x_2, the slope of the budget line increases in absolute value (the budget line becomes steeper). This will result in a new demanded bundle—for example, point B associated with the price ratio p''_1/p''_2. As the price ratio continues to increase, new demanded bundles unfold. The locus of all these demanded bundles associated with all possible prices is the offer curve.

How much are you willing to exchange apples for oranges? Your willingness to exchanging apples for oranges is how much you offer on the market to make such an exchange.

Each household has an offer curve and initial endowment of the commodities. Relating the offer curves and endowment of the two households in an Edgeworth box, the Walrasian equilibrium is illustrated in Figure 6.6. Where the two offer curves intersect, at point A, the price ratio p^*_1/p^*_2 is the same for both Robinson and Friday. At this price ratio, the demanded

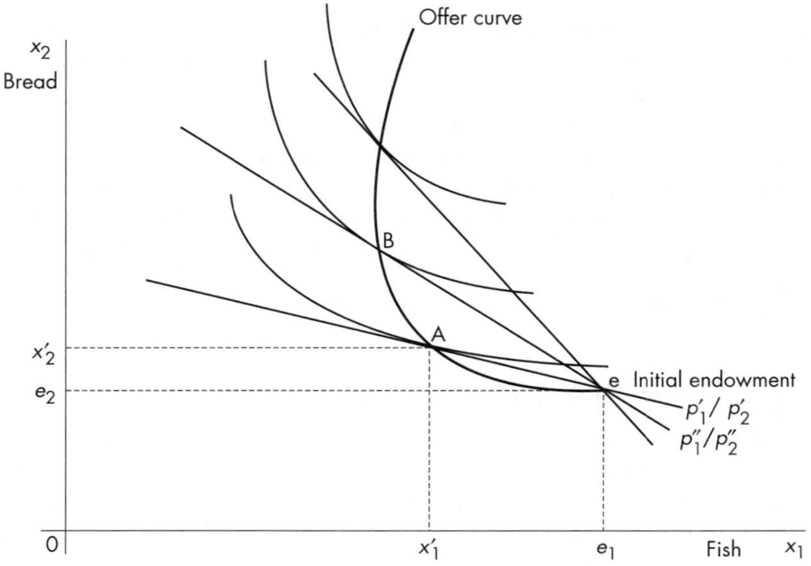

Figure 6.5 **Offer curve.** For alternative price ratios, each point on the offer curve represents how much a household is willing to offer one commodity in exchange for another commodity.

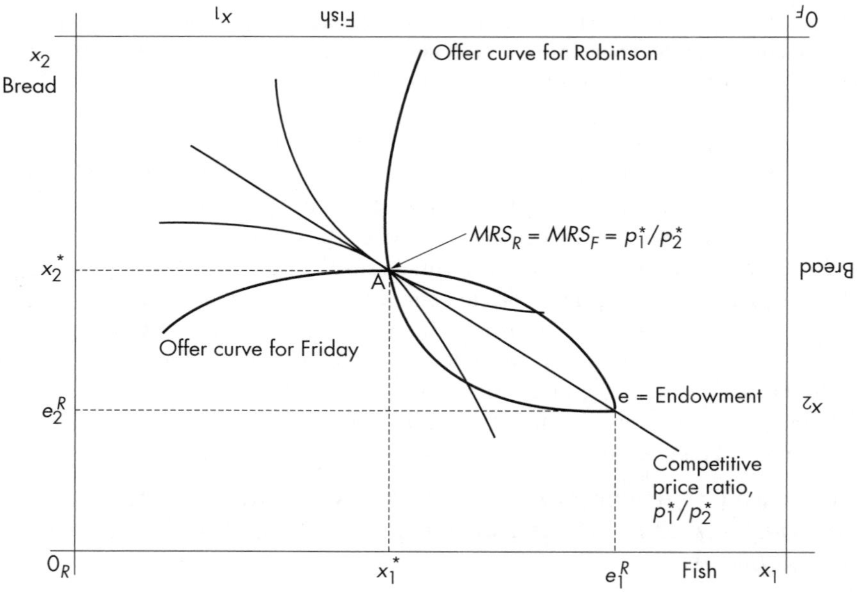

Figure 6.6 **Pareto efficiency and competitive pricing.** A Walrasian equilibrium is established where the two offer curves intersect. At this intersection, MRSs are equal to the competitive price ratio, p_1^*/p_2^*.

bundles exactly match the supply. For example, Robinson is willing to supply $e_1^R - x_1^*$ of fish in exchange for $x_2^* - e_2^R$ of bread, and Friday is willing to supply $x_2^* - e_2^R$ of bread for $e_1^R - x_1^*$ of fish. At this equilibrium, the MRSs for Robinson and Friday are equated, which yields the one-to-one correspondence between Pareto efficiency and perfectly competitive markets (First Fundamental Theorem of Welfare Economics). A Pareto-efficient allocation corresponds to where the two households' offer curves cross. At this point, the households' offers are based on the same price ratio, so their MRSs are both equal to this price ratio, p_1^*/p_2^*. Where the two offer curves cross, aggregate supply equals aggregate demand for each of the commodities and the households are maximizing their utility.

Walras' law and the beauty of price signals

As scarce as truth is, the supply has always been in excess of the demand.

(Josh Billings)

Translation: In equilibrium there is no excess demand for any commodity.

A feature that distinguishes economics from other fields, such as physics, is that the theoretical results are generally static equilibrium conditions. An example is the pure-exchange equilibrium condition of the MRSs equaling the price ratio. In contrast, results in other fields are often dynamic conditions (laws) describing how a system will evolve through time. Unfortunately, an economy does not operate on a set of natural laws that describe its evolution. Thus, the process of how an economy in disequilibrium reaches an equilibrium state (called tâtonnement stability) can be described in only limited detail.

Tâtonnement. French for trial and error. *E.g., attempting to get a computer to perform some task by clicking on various menus.*

Tâtonnement stability was first described by Walras, where **tâtonnement** is French for groping or trial and error. For example, if at the price ratio p_1'/p_2', quantity demanded for fish is greater than quantity supplied and quantity demanded for bread is less than quantity supplied, then the price ratio p_1'/p_2' will rise. As this ratio increases, the quantity demanded for fish will decline and demand for bread will increase. This adjustment of prices in response to demand and supply conditions will continue until prices converge to the competitive equilibrium levels (p_1^*, p_2^*). The adjustment assumes prices will respond to market shortages and surpluses. If prices are rigid, possibly as a result of some governmental price controls, then the tâtonnement process will not work.

Mathematically, let $x_1^{F*} = x_1^F(p_1, p_2, e_1^F, e_2^F)$ and $x_2^{F*} = x_2^F(p_1, p_2, e_1^F, e_2^F)$ be Friday's demand functions for commodities x_1 and x_2, respectively. Similarly, let $x_1^{R*} = x_1^R(p_1, p_2, e_1^R, e_2^R)$ and $x_2^{R*} = x_2^R(p_1, p_2, e_1^R, e_2^R)$ be Robinson's demand functions. The Walrasian equilibrium set of prices (p_1^*, p_2^*) is where, for both commodities, aggregate demand equals aggregate supply:

$$x_1^{F*} + x_1^{R*} = e_1^F + e_1^R,$$
$$x_2^{F*} + x_2^{R*} = e_2^F + e_2^R.$$

Alternatively, this Walrasian equilibrium may be represented in terms of aggregate excess demand functions:

$$z_1^* = x_1^{F*} + x_1^{R*} - (e_1^F + e_1^R) = 0,$$

$$z_2^* = x_2^{F*} + x_2^{R*} - (e_2^F + e_2^R) = 0,$$

where $z_j > 0$ states that commodity j is in excess demand and $z_j < 0$ that commodity j is in excess supply, for $j = 1, 2$. A Walrasian equilibrium then exists when these aggregate excess demand functions are zero.

Is there excess demand in an economy? No, in equilibrium, there is no excess demand.

A result of specifying markets for commodities in terms of excess demand is called **Walras' Law**, which states that the value of the aggregate excess demand is zero:

$$p_1 z_1(p_1, p_2, e_1^F, e_2^F, e_1^R, e_2^R) + p_2 z_2(p_1, p_2, e_1^F, e_2^F, e_1^R, e_2^R) = 0.$$

This states that the aggregate excess demand is zero for not only the equilibrium set of prices (p_1^*, p_2^*) but also for all possible prices. In the two-commodity economy, if $z_1 > 0$ (excess demand), then, given positive prices, $z_2 < 0$ (excess supply) for Walras' Law to hold.

Walras' Law. The value of aggregate excess demand is zero. *E.g., given the two commodities bread and fish, if fish is in excess demand, then the value of this excess demand will equal in absolute value the value of the excess supply of bread.*

The proof of Walras' Law involves adding up the households' budget constraints and then rearranging terms. Consider first Friday's budget constraint:

$$p_1 x_1^F + p_2 x_2^F = p_1 e_1^F + p_2 e_2^F,$$

where the right-hand side is Friday's income, represented as the value of Friday's endowments of x_1 and x_2. Thus, the budget constraint states that total expenditures on x_1 and x_2 will equal this value of endowments. Rearranging terms,

$$p_1(x_1^F - e_1^F) + p_2(x_2^F - e_2^F) = 0.$$

We now define Friday's excess demands for commodities 1 and 2 as

$$z_1^F = x_1^F - e_1^F,$$

$$z_2^F = x_2^F - e_2^F.$$

If $z_1^F > 0$, Friday has excess demand for x_1, and, in contrast, if $z_1^F < 0$, Friday has excess supply. We can then represent Friday's budget constraint as

$$p_1 z_1^F + p_2 z_2^F = 0.$$

The value of Friday's excess demand for the two commodities is zero. For satisfying the budget constraint, the cost of commodities that Friday demands must equal the income from the commodities Friday supplies.

Similarly, Robinson's value of excess demand for the two commodities is also zero:

$$p_1 z_1^R + p_2 z_2^R = 0.$$

Note that the aggregate excess demand for x_1 and x_2 is the sum of individual household excess demands:

$$z_1 = z_1^F + z_1^R,$$
$$z_2 = z_2^F + z_2^R.$$

Adding Friday's and Robinson's values of excess demand together yields Walras' Law:

$$p_1 z_1^F + p_2 z_2^F + p_1 z_1^R + p_2 z_2^R = 0,$$

$$p_1(z_1^F + z_1^R) + p_2(z_2^F + z_2^R) = 0,$$

$$p_1 z_1 + p_2 z_2 = 0.$$

Thus, Walras' Law is derived: the value of aggregate excess demand must be zero, given that the individual households' value of excess demand equals zero.

Relative prices

An important result of Walras' Law is that if aggregate demand equals aggregate supply in one market, then, for a two-market economy, demand must equal supply in the other market. Generalizing to k commodities, if aggregate demand equals aggregate supply in $k-1$ markets, then demand must equal supply in the remaining excluded market. We can establish this result by noting that Walras' Law holds for alternative prices in a market and in particular holds for the equilibrium prices in market 1:

$$z_1^* = z_1(p_1^*, p_2^*, e_1^F, e_2^F, e_1^R, e_2^R) = 0.$$

Then, by Walras' Law,

$$p_1^* z_1^* + p_2^* z_2^* = 0.$$

If $p_2^* > 0$, then $z_2^* = 0$.

Thus, a set of prices where aggregate demand for one market equals aggregate supply will result in the other market clearing (aggregate demand equaling aggregate supply).

Example 6.2 Deriving Pareto efficiency: two-agent and two-commodity pure-exchange economy

Consider the following utility functions for Robinson, R, and Friday, F:

$$U^R = x_1^R x_2^R \quad \text{and} \quad U^F = x_1^F x_2^F,$$

with initial endowments of

$$e_1^R = 15, \quad e_2^R = 150, \quad e_1^F = 85, \quad e_2^F = 50.$$

We can determine the competitive equilibrium allocation and prices by equating total demand to total supply for each commodity. Total supply for a pure-exchange economy is the sum of the endowments for each commodity:

$$e_1^R + e_1^F = 100, \quad \text{total supply of commodity 1, fish,}$$
$$e_2^R + e_2^F = 200, \quad \text{total supply of commodity 2, bread.}$$

Total demand is the sum of individual agents' demands for the commodities. Given that the agents have the same preferences (utility functions), we can derive the demand function for agent j, $j = 1, 2$. Agent j will maximize utility subject to the budget constraint

$$p_1 x_1^j + p_2 x_2^j = p_1 e_1^j + p_2 e_2^j, \quad j = 1, 2,$$

where $p_1 x_1^j + p_2 x_2^j$ is agent j's total expenditures and $p_1 e_1^j + p_2 e_2^j$ represents agent j's value of the endowment (income). The Lagrangian for this problem is

$$\mathcal{L}(x_1^j, x_2^j, \lambda) = x_1^j x_2^j + \lambda(p_1 x_1^j + p_2 x_2^j - p_1 e_1^j - p_2 e_2^j).$$

The first-order conditions (FOCs) are then

$$\frac{\partial \mathcal{L}}{\partial x_1^j} = x_2^j + \lambda p_1 = 0,$$

$$\frac{\partial \mathcal{L}}{\partial x_2^j} = x_1^j + \lambda p_2 = 0,$$

$$\frac{\partial \mathcal{L}}{\partial \lambda} = p_1 x_1^j + p_2 x_2^j - p_1 e_1^j - p_2 e_2^j = 0,$$

From these FOCs, MRS(x_2^j for x_1^j) $= x_2^j / x_1^j = p_1 / p_2$, which yields the income expansion path $x_2^j = (p_1/p_2) x_2^j$. Substituting this expansion path into the budget constraint results in agent j's demand functions:

$$p_1 x_1^j + p_2 x_2^j = p_1 e_1^j + p_2 e_2^j,$$

$$p_1 x_1^j + p_2 (p_1/p_2) x_1^j = p_1 e_1^j + p_2 e_2^j,$$

$$p_1 x_1^j + p_1 x_1^j = p_1 e_1^j + p_2 e_2^j.$$

Solving for x_1^j yields Robinson's and Friday's demand functions for commodity 1:

$$x_1^R = \frac{p_1 e_1^R + p_2 e_2^R}{2p_1} = \frac{15p_1 + 150p_2}{2p_1},$$

$$x_1^F = \frac{p_1 e_1^F + p_2 e_2^F}{2p_1} = \frac{85p_1 + 50p_2}{2p_1}.$$

We obtain Robinson's and Friday's demand functions for commodity 2 by substituting these demand functions into the income expansion path:

$$x_2^R = \frac{p_1 e_1^R + p_2 e_2^R}{2p_2} = \frac{15p_1 + 150p_2}{2p_2},$$

$$x_2^F = \frac{p_1 e_1^F + p_2 e_2^F}{2p_2} = \frac{85p_1 + 50p_2}{2p_2}.$$

Summing these demand functions for x_1 and equating them to total supply of x_1, with p_1 as the numeraire price ($p_1^* = 1$), yields the competitive-equilibrium price for x_2:

$$(15 + 150p_2)/2 + (85 + 50p_2)/2 = 100,$$

$$p_2^* = \tfrac{1}{2}.$$

The equilibrium allocations are then

$$x_1^R = \frac{15p_1 + 150p_2}{2p_1} = 45,$$

$$x_1^F = \frac{85p_1 + 50p_2}{2p_1} = 55,$$

$$x_2^R = \frac{15p_1 + 150p_2}{2p_2} = 90,$$

$$x_2^F = \frac{85p_1 + 50p_2}{2p_2} = 110.$$

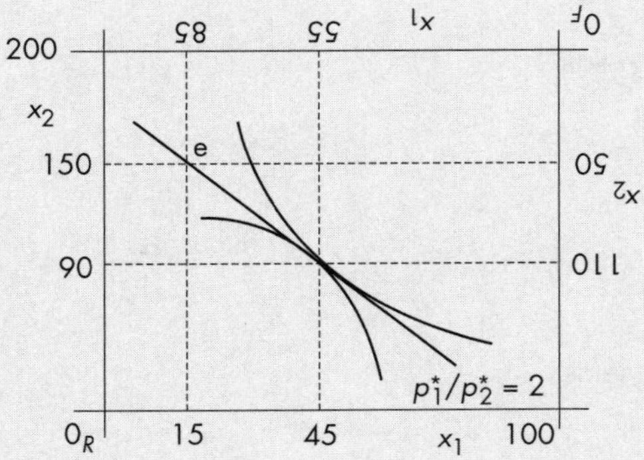

Mathematically, this implies $k-1$ independent equations in a k-commodity model. With one less equation than the k-number of market clearing prices, we cannot solve the system for a set of k independent prices. Instead, we can determine only relative prices. Specifically, in general equilibrium, each household's income is the value of the endowment at given prices. Thus, each household's budget constraint is homogeneous of degree zero in prices. For example, multiplying prices by some positive constant α does not change Friday's budget constraint:

$$\alpha p_1 x_1^F + \alpha p_2 x_2^F = \alpha p_1 e_1^F + \alpha p_2 e_2^F,$$

$$\alpha(p_1 x_1^F + p_2 x_2^F) = \alpha(p_1 e_1^F + p_2 e_2^F),$$

$$p_1 x_1^F + p_2 x_2^F = p_1 e_1^F + p_2 e_2^F.$$

This implies if (p_1^*, p_2^*) is a set of Walrasian equilibrium prices, then $(\alpha p_1^*, \alpha p_2^*)$ is as well. In general equilibrium, only relative prices are determined, given all households' budget constraints are homogeneous of degree zero in prices. Multiplying all prices by some positive constant does not change households' demand and supply for commodities. Thus, as discussed in Chapter 4, setting one price equal to 1 (the numeraire price) we can measure all other prices relative to this numeraire price. For example, letting the price of commodity 1 be the numeraire price, multiplying all prices by $\alpha = 1/p_1$ results in the price of commodity 2 being measured relative to the price of commodity 1, p_2/p_1.

Example 6.3 Deriving offer curves in a pure-exchange economy

The intersection of the offer curves yields a competitive equilibrium allocation and prices. Such an intersection may be demonstrated by deriving offer curves and then solving them for the equilibrium allocations. Let's reconsider Example 6.2.

The equation for agent *j*'s income expansion path is $x_2^j = (p_1/p_2)x_1^j$, $j = 1, 2$. This income expansion equation establishes the tangency point between a budget line and an indifference curve. We determine an offer curve by solving this expansion path for the prices and substituting it into the budget line. Specifically, solving for p_1 gives

$$p_1 = \frac{x_2^j}{x_1^j} p_2.$$

Substituting this into the budget line yields

$$p_1 x_1^j + p_2 x_2^j = p_1 e_1^j + p_2 e_2^j,$$

$$p_2 x_2^j + p_2 x_2^j = \frac{x_2^j}{x_1^j} p_2 e_1^j + p_2 e_2^j.$$

Dividing by p_2 and multiplying by x_1^j yields

$$x_1^j x_2^j + x_1^j x_2^j = x_2^j e_1^j + x_1^j e_2^j,$$

$$2x_1^j x_2^j = x_2^j e_1^j + x_1^j e_2^j,$$

$$x_1^j = \frac{x_2^j e_1^j}{2x_2^j - e_2^j}, \quad \text{offer curve for agent } j, \quad j = 1, 2.$$

Letting $e_1^R = 15$, $e_2^R = 150$, $e_1^F = 85$, and $e_2^F = 50$, Robinson's and Friday's offer curves are then

$$x_1^R = \frac{15x_2^R}{2x_2^R - 150}, \quad \text{Robinson's offer curve, } O^R,$$

$$x_1^F = \frac{85x_2^F}{2x_2^F - 50}, \quad \text{Friday's offer curve, } O^F.$$

We can solve these offer curves for the competitive equilibrium allocation of fish, x_1, and bread, x_2, for both Robinson and Friday by solving the two offer curve equations along with the two equations for equating demand with supply, $x_1^R + x_1^F = 100$ and $x_2^R + x_2^F = 200$. Note that the offer curves are nonlinear, and so it appears that no analytical solution is available. Thus, some type of numerical solution may be required. (Refer to a numerical analysis book for solution methods.) Alternatively, we could use a tâtonnement process (similar to reality). The solution is the same solution as found in Example 6.2, where total demand is determined and equated to total supply.

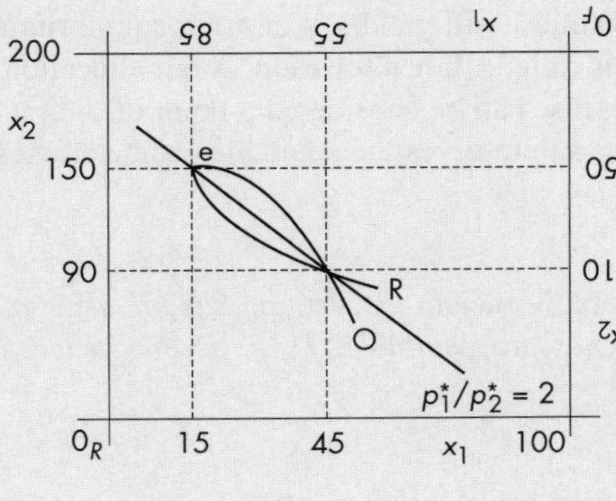

Improving social welfare

Legend has it that Robin Hood was an outlaw who poached the King's deer in the royal hunting forest of Sherwood, and stole riches from the noble travelers through the forest. The saying goes that Robin Hood took from the rich and gave to the poor. Whether Robin Hood is myth or man is not important; what is important is that the Walrasian equilibrium may not be an optimal social-welfare point. A Robin Hood may be required for maximizing social welfare. A Walrasian equilibrium does result in a Pareto-efficient allocation; however, it assumes a given distribution of the initial endowments. If the endowments are distributed in such a way that one agent receives a relatively small share of the initial endowments and the other agent receives a relatively large share, social welfare may not be maximized. For maximizing social welfare, the optimal distribution of initial endowments along with competitive prices is required. Thus, one criticism of perfect competition (capitalist markets in general) involves the restriction that perfectly competitive markets take this distribution of initial endowments as given. With any initial distribution of endowments that society deems as "unfair," perfect competition will not maximize social welfare.

Equitable distribution of endowments and fair allocations

The problem of determining an optimal distribution of initial endowments is normative in nature—it involves value judgments concerning the satisfaction households receive from their endowments. A possible normative solution is an optimal distribution of initial endowments that is equitable. An **equitable** initial allocation may be defined as an allocation of endowments where no household prefers any other household's initial endowment. That is, no household is envious.

Equitable. No household prefers any other household's initial endowment. *E.g., no child prefers the lunch a mother packed for another child.*

For example, one equitable allocation of initial endowments is an equal division of commodities—each household has the same initial commodity bundle. As is demonstrated in Table 6.1, this equal division will probably not be Pareto-efficient. A competitive market, given this initial equal division of commodities, will yield a Walrasian equilibrium that is Pareto-efficient. Such a market allocation is called a **fair allocation**. A fair allocation is both equitable and Pareto-efficient and in this sense can be considered a point of optimal social welfare. Thus, a perfectly competitive market preserves the equitable characteristics of the initial endowment.

Fair allocation. An equitable and Pareto-efficient allocation. *E.g., if all students purchase the cafeteria lunch, the lunches are equitable. Then, as they trade food, a Pareto-efficient allocation will result.*

We can show a fair allocation resulting from a competitive reallocation of equitable initial endowments by contradiction. Assume the allocation is not fair and Robinson is envious. He prefers Friday's allocation to his own:

$$(x_1^{*F}, x_2^{*F}) \succ_R (x_1^{*R}, x_2^{*R}),$$

where $\succ_R$ represents Robinson's preferences. If Robinson prefers Friday's allocation over his own utility-maximum allocation at prices (p_1^*, p_2^*), then Robinson cannot afford Friday's allocation:

$$p_1^* x_1^{*F} + p_2^* x_2^{*F} > p_1^* x_1^{*R} + p_2^* x_2^{*R}.$$

However, the equal distribution of initial endowments implies that the value of the initial endowment must be the same, so

$$p_1^* e_1^F + p_2^* e_2^F = p_1^* e_1^R + p_2^* e_2^R.$$

Thus, Friday also cannot afford her optimal allocation, which results in a contradiction. It is impossible for Robinson to envy Friday at the Pareto-efficient allocation, so a competitive equilibrium from equitable initial endowments is a fair allocation.

Some societies have unfortunately achieved this equal division in value of initial endowments by reducing the size of the Edgeworth box. Through war, pestilence, and famine, current and future generations of households within these societies are or will be at a near-subsistence level. In such cases, social welfare is not maximized by achieving an equitable distribution of endowments.

One problem with achieving an equal distribution of initial endowment values is that incentives to work and invest are reduced. If each generation is to start out with an equal distribution of value of endowments, there is no incentive for a household to will its next generation additional endowments. In a communist society, working for the common good is meant to replace these individual incentives and result in an enlargement of the Edgeworth box for all our comrades. However, this degree of altruism may be too much to ask of individual households.

An alternative to an equal distribution of value of endowments is providing equal opportunities for enriching a household's endowments. Equal opportunity was one of the driving forces for the large migration of households to the United States in the nineteenth century. Providing an initial endowment consisting of equal opportunities is an equitable allocation and provides an underlying justification for equal-opportunity legislation ranging from minority rights to funding for public education.

Why have equal-opportunity legislation? Improvements in equal education and employment opportunities result in a more equitable allocation of endowments and when mated with free markets can increase social welfare.

The history of the United States indicates that mating equal opportunity with free markets can greatly enlarge the Edgeworth box. This results in increasing all households' utilities, and results in fair allocations leading to an optimal social-welfare allocation of commodities. However, a great deal of poverty exists within the United States. The reversal in the 1980s of a more equal distribution of wealth indicates the United States has not reached local bliss (maximum social welfare). Other societies—for example many European countries—that are generally more socialistic than the United States are not willing to have such a large inequality in wealth. Thus, these societies generally strive for a more equal distribution of endowments at the expense of incentives to work. Which system is preferred is a value judgment. In terms of economists' value judgment, in a 2004 poll, 69 percent of those surveyed strongly favored government redistributive policies—including transfer and aid programs and tax progressivity—with only 17 percent opposed and 14 percent having mixed feelings.[4] The US Department of Commerce and the Internal Revenue Service indicate that declines in income inequality in the mid twentieth century were replaced with increases since the 1970s. In 2010, the top 20 percent of Americans earned almost 50 percent of the United States' income, with the top 1 percent earning 24 percent of the income, compared with under 4 percent earned by 15 percent of the population living below the poverty line.

Application: Equitable allocations and equal access

Discussion of discrimination often hinges on a value judgment that individuals ought to be assured access to some commodity. For example, disabled individuals should be assured access to services and the poor should have health care. However, traditional economic theory suggests that, instead of providing such access, these people should be given money to spend as they choose, because providing grants is more efficient than providing access.

As discussed by R. McCain, economists in the first half of the twentieth century generally gave far greater attention to efficiency than to equity in resource allocation. However, in the last half-century, more attention has been directed toward an equitable allocation of resources. McCain attempts to extend this interest in equitable allocations to explain, in terms of economic theory, the intuition that access to commodities might be an entitlement. Entitlement is defined as something that an individual ought to have as a matter of equity. Thus, the theory of equity would support some entitlements. McCain's hypothesis is that neoclassical theory of equity can justify entitlements.

A common result emerging from neoclassical economic theory of fairness is that an equal division of endowments is equitable, but inefficient, and a movement from an equitable allocation to a fair allocation, by some process, improves welfare. As stated by McCain, money compensation for deprivation of access may be equitable and result in a fair allocation only if denial of access does not prevent a household from making a fully informed decision. If access does provide information, then actual access and not merely potential access is a requirement for a fair allocation. For example, excluding a disabled person from access to a lecture on smoking may prevent the individual from making a fully informed decision. When access does provide some information, neoclassical theory of equity can be used to justify entitlements.

Source: R.A. McCain, "Equitable Allocations and the Case for Access," *International Journal of Social Economics* 28 (2001): 831–851.

Summary

1. In partial-equilibrium analysis, only one segment of an economy is analyzed without consideration of possible interactions with other segments. This is in contrast to general-equilibrium analysis, which investigates interactions among agents across market segments.
2. An efficient allocation of commodities is possible by households trading commodities, and an allocation of commodities is said to be Pareto-efficient if no one household can be made better off without making some other household worse off. The necessary condition for such an efficient allocation is that the marginal rates of substitution among all households are equal.
3. The set of Pareto-efficient allocations is represented by the contract curve in an Edgeworth box diagram. At every point on the contract curve, all gains from trade are exhausted.

4. A problem with the Pareto-efficient criterion is it does not result in a complete social ranking of alternative allocations. There are many policies that result in a gain to one agent but a loss to another. For such policies, the Pareto criterion will not aid in determining the social desirability of the policy.
5. As the number of households increases, the process of bartering for commodities becomes increasingly difficult. Since transaction costs escalate with increasing number of households, the competitive price system, where all commodities are valued in the market by their money equivalence, offers a Pareto-efficient mechanism for allocating commodities.
6. The Pareto efficiency of the competitive price system is established by the First Fundamental Theorem of Welfare Economics. Every perfectly competitive allocation is Pareto optimal.
7. The Second Fundamental Theorem of Welfare Economics states that every Pareto-efficient allocation has an associated perfectly competitive set of prices.
8. Walrasian equilibrium in a general equilibrium model is established through a tâtonnement (trial and error) process. At equilibrium in every market, all markets clear, so aggregate demand is equal to aggregate supply.
9. A Pareto-efficient allocation of commodities does result from a Walrasian equilibrium; however, it may not correspond with the optimal social-welfare allocation. A Walrasian equilibrium is based on a given initial allocation of endowments, so for optimal social welfare this distribution of endowments must be optimal.
10. An equitable distribution of initial endowments is where no household prefers any other household's initial endowment. Given an equitable distribution of endowments, Walrasian equilibrium will result in a fair allocation of commodities. In such cases, a state of optimal social welfare may be obtained.
11. Providing equal opportunities for enriching a household's endowments is an equitable distribution of endowments. As indicated by US history, a mating of equal opportunity with free markets can lead toward an optimal social-welfare allocation of commodities.

Key concepts

contract curve, 212
core solution, 211
Edgeworth box, 208
equitable, 226
fair allocation, 226
feasible allocation, 208
First Fundamental Theorem of Welfare Economics, 215
general-equilibrium analysis, 205
Pareto-efficient allocation, 210
Pareto improvement, 211
partial-equilibrium analysis, 205
perfectly competitive price system, 215
price system, 215
pure-exchange economy, 205
Second Fundamental Theorem of Welfare Economics, 215
tâtonnement, 219
Walras' Law, 220

Key equations

$$\mathrm{MRS}_1 = \mathrm{MRS}_2 = \ldots = \mathrm{MRS}_n$$

A necessary condition for a Pareto-efficient allocation of commodities.

$$x_j^R + x_1^F = e_j^R + e_1^F, \quad j = 1, 2$$

An allocation is feasible if aggregate consumption of each commodity is equal to aggregate supply.

$$\mathrm{MRS}_1 = \mathrm{MRS}_2 = \ldots = \mathrm{MRS}_n = p_1/p_2$$

Walrasian equilibrium, where every household's rate of tradeoff equals society's rate of tradeoff.

$$p_1 z_1 + p_2 z_2 = 0$$

Walras' Law, where the value of the aggregate excess demand is zero.

Questions

1. Define each of the following concepts in a pure-exchange economy:
   a. The core solution.
   b. The contract curve.
   c. The set of preferred allocations relative to the initial endowment.
   d. Perfectly competitive allocation.
2. Why could a contract curve be instead called a conflict curve?
3. Outline the meaning of general equilibrium.
4. Why must a perfectly competitive allocation of exchange always lie on the contract curve?
5. The invention of money is one of the major achievements of the human race, for without it the enrichment from expanding trading would be impossible. True or false? Explain.
6. Would it be possible for an equilibrium price to be established in a market even if neither buyers nor sellers know exactly what this price will be? Explain.
7. If the value of the excess demand for $k - 3$ markets is zero, what is the excess demand value in the remaining three markets?
8. Will equal opportunity legislation lead to a Pareto-efficient allocation of resources?
9. Why in this chapter are budget constraints homogeneous of degree zero in prices, but in Chapter 4 they are homogeneous of degree zero in prices and income?
10. If the maximum social-welfare allocation is known, how can a society reach it?

Exercises

It is possible to fly without motors, but not without knowledge and skill.

(Wilbur Wright)

1. Karen has 4 liters of cola and 1 bag of chips. Tim has 1 liter of cola and 2 bags of chips. Given these endowments, Karen's marginal rate of substitution of cola for chips is 3, and Tim's marginal rate of substitution is equal to 1. Draw an Edgeworth box showing the efficiency of this endowment. If it is efficient, explain why. If it is not efficient, explain what exchanges will make both Karen and Tim better off.

2. Laurel and Hardy can exchange fish and chips. Laurel has 2 pounds of fish and no chips, and Hardy has 2 pounds of chips but no fish. Laurel is indifferent between fish and chips, whereas Hardy consumes fish and chips in fixed proportions of 1 fish to 1 chip.

   a. Illustrate the endowment in an Edgeworth box. Draw some representative indifference curves for Laurel and Hardy associated with their preferences and determine the locus of Pareto-efficient allocations.
   b. In a competitive market, if Laurel and Hardy engaged in trading, what would be the equilibrium price ratio. What would be the possible equilibria consumptions for Laurel and Hardy?

3. In a Barbie and Ken economy, investigate the results of exchange given the following preferences:

   a. Neither Barbie nor Ken cares about the other's happiness.
   b. Ken is altruistic and gains some satisfaction from Barbie's welfare.
   c. Ken is envious and loses utility as Barbie becomes better off.

4. An island economy consists of just two households (Robinson, R, and Friday, F) and two commodities (bananas, B, and coconuts, C). Robinson's initial endowment is 3 bananas and 2 coconuts. Friday's initial endowment is only 1 banana but 6 coconuts. Assume Robinson and Friday have the following identical utility functions:

$$U^R(B^R, C^R) = B^R C^R, \qquad U^F(B^F, C^F) = B^F C^F.$$

   a. Draw the associated Edgeworth box.
   b. Draw indifference curves for Robinson and Friday that indicate their allocations with a utility level of 6.
   c. Determine each household's marginal rate of substitution (coconuts for bananas).
   d. Determine the Pareto-efficient allocation condition. On the graph in (a), indicate the locus of points that are Pareto-efficient.
   e. Is the allocation where Robinson obtains 3 bananas and 6 coconuts Pareto-efficient?

f. Determine Robinson's and Friday's consumption bundles in a competitive equilibrium.
g. Determine the relative prices of bananas and coconuts in a competitive equilibrium.

5. Two households A and B have the following utility functions:

$$U^A(x_1^A, x_2^A) = 0.2 \ln x_1^A + 0.8 \ln x_2^A,$$
$$U^B(x_1^B, x_2^B) = \min(x_1^B, x_2^B).$$

Let household A be initially endowed with 0 units of x_1 and 1 unit of x_2, and household B with 1 unit of x_1 and 0 units of x_2. Determine the market-clearing prices and the equilibrium allocation.

6. Assume a two-commodity, two-household pure-exchange economy. Households A and B have the following utility functions:

$$U^A = 0.7 \ln x_1 + 0.3 \ln x_2,$$
$$U^B = 0.6 \ln x_1 + 0.4 \ln x_2.$$

A is endowed with 10 units of x_1 and 2 units of x_2, and B is endowed with 5 units of x_1 and 6 units of x_2.

a. What is the Walrasian equilibrium for this economy?
b. A social planner wishes to implement an allocation that makes the sum of the household's utilities as large as possible at the equilibrium. What is the planner's optimal allocation?

7. In a pure-exchange economy, there are two agents, Barbie, B, and Ken, K, and two commodities, Perrier, W, and Brie, C. Barbie and Ken have preferences represented as

$$U^B = \min(W^B, C^B), \qquad U^K = \min(W^K, C^K).$$

Barbie's initial endowment is 15 units of Perrier and no Brie; Ken's endowment is 10 units of Brie and no Perrier.

a. If Barbie and Ken are price takers, what is the equilibrium allocation?
b. Assume Barbie's endowment is reduced to only 2 units of Perrier, now what is the equilibrium allocation?

8. One trader, Mr Indifferent, regards the two possible consumption commodities as perfect substitutes. The second trader, Mrs Proportion, regards them as perfect complements. Let Mr Indifferent have all of the first commodity and none of the second, so Mrs Proportion has the entire second commodity and none of the first. Determine the equilibrium prices and allocation.

9. In a two-household, two-commodity pure-exchange economy, illustrate graphically that a unique equilibrium may not exist if x_1 is a Giffen good for household A and x_2 is a Giffen good for household B.
10. Illustrate that even if preferences are strictly convex, an equilibrium allocation is not necessarily unique in a two-household, pure-exchange economy.

Internet case studies

1. Discuss the contributions that Nobel Prize-winning economists have made in the area of general-equilibrium analysis.
2. Provide a brief history of the development of Walrasian equilibrium.
3. Discuss the link between Walras' Law and macroeconomic theory.
4. List a number of applications using a pure-exchange model of an economy.

Part III

Producers' rules

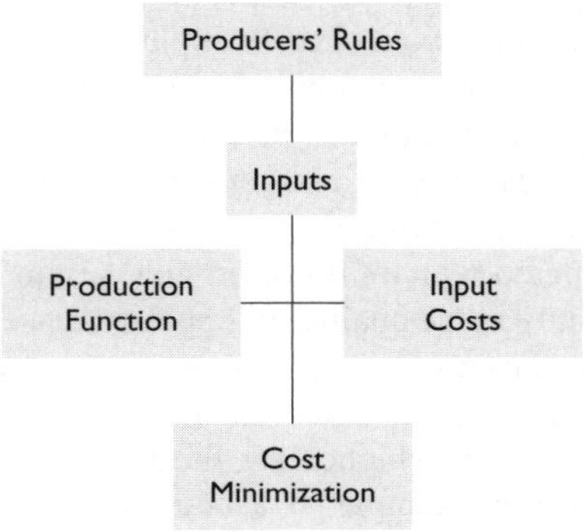

Chapters

The chief business of the American people is business.
(President Calvin Coolidge, 1925)

Translation: All agents are involved with producing commodities.

Decentralized control of resource allocation is made for do-it-yourselfers. They can decide what, how, and when to purchase inputs for producing some outputs for satisfying a want. For example, they can decide what tools are required, and how and when to use the tools for landscaping their yards, cleaning their homes, or repairing their automobiles. However, for a household to be willing to be a do-it-yourselfer, the transaction costs of procuring and combining inputs for producing outputs must be small or zero. A pure-exchange economy, as outlined in Chapter 6, assumes just that: that transaction costs of market exchange are either zero or so small they do not to prevent exchange. Do-it-yourselfers could then purchase commodities in the market and coordinate the combining of these commodities to produce outputs for enhancing utility. However, when the transaction costs of market exchange are high, it may be less costly to coordinate production through a formal organization (firm) than through a market.

These transaction costs are characterized in terms of frequency, uncertainty, and input specialization in production. The more frequently commodities or inputs are combined for the purpose of producing an output, the more the fixed costs of establishing a firm can be spread among the transactions. For example, the thousands of inputs required for assembling automobiles can be combined at a far lower cost by a firm compared with each household acquiring the inputs for automobile assembly.

Higher uncertainty associated with transactions for commodities or inputs creates a more complex contracting environment and associated higher market costs for households. This is compared with a firm offering a certain output from these inputs. For example, the uncertainty in the quality of grapes increases the transaction costs for household winemaking versus purchasing a known varietal wine from a firm.

Finally, input specialization implies that the more a commodity or input is directly made for a particular output, the higher are the transaction costs of discontinuing a marketing relationship. For example, if a household purchased a door panel for assembling a particular make and year of an automobile, and then discontinued the marketing relationship, it would incur high transactions costs when it returned some years later to purchase another door panel for a different make and model year. It is more efficient and less costly for a firm to produce the required door panels during its production of automobiles and then sell the completed automobiles to households.

Thus, firms (which comprise the second basic institution of microeconomic theory) result from transaction costs of market exchange. A **firm** is defined as any agent using economic inputs—such as land, labor, and capital—to produce outputs of goods and services (commodities) sold to households or to other firms (consumers). It is assumed that a firm is able to produce and sell a commodity more efficiently than if the commodity's individual parts were produced and sold separately. This definition of a firm is the minimal requirement for investigating market interactions among households and firms. A complete description of a firm, detailing organizational and management style, is not required here other than stating that firms may be corporations or partnerships, or may represent the productive possibilities of households. Also, firms may include potential productive units that could but are not currently producing products.

Firm. An agent using inputs to produce commodities for consumers. *E.g., a computer manufacturer assembling the drives, memory chips, and other components into a computer for its customers.*

Part 3 is concerned with the rules firms face in combining inputs for producing outputs. In Chapter 7, we address the purely technical relationship of combining these inputs. Such a technical relationship is called a *production function*, which places a constraint on a firm's objective of maximizing profit. We investigate variation in production from changing one input in terms of the *Law of Diminishing Marginal Returns*. When we consider varying more than one input, we examine the production characteristics of substituting one input for another and the effects of proportionally changing all inputs. Based on these characteristics, we can specify alternative production functions. In Chapter 8, we develop the theory of cost, with the objective of determining the conditions for minimizing cost subject to a given level of output. Based on this cost-minimizing objective, we derive the family of short-run and long-run cost curves.

7 Production technology

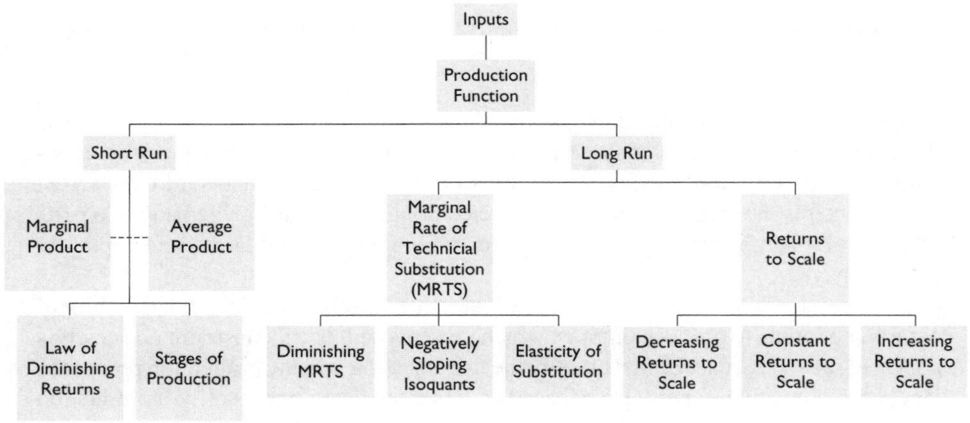

Outline and Conceptual Inquiries

Factors of production dissected

What are all the inputs that go into producing a toothpick?

Defining production constraints: production functions

Application: Origin of the famous Cobb–Douglas production function

Varying one input (short run)

Understanding the law of diminishing marginal returns and stages of production

Can Earth feed the cosmos?

How is your grade-point average affected by this semester's grades?

What stage of production are you in for studying?

Application: Output elasticities and technical efficiency in China's grain production

Considering two variable inputs

Does one cup of skim milk plus two teaspoons melted butter equal one cup of whole milk?

Classifying production functions

Returns to scale: will doubling inputs double output?

If you double all inputs, will output double?

Measuring the elasticity of substitution

Application: Were free and slave labor in the antebellum South perfect substitutes?

Application: Historical note on production functions

Summary

Key concepts

Key equation

Questions

Exercises

Internet case studies

I never saw an ugly thing in my life: for let the form of an object be what it may – light, shade, and perspective will always make it beautiful.

(John Constable)

Translation: Combining inputs results in outputs for increasing consumers' happiness.

A preschooler is connecting dots numbered sequentially on a piece of paper. As she does this, an outline of an elephant suddenly appears on the paper. This preschooler has engaged in **production**: the process of transforming a set of elements into a different set of elements. Examples of production are combining one part oxygen and two parts hydrogen by combustion to produce water, or combining land, labor, and capital to produce hay.

Our aim in this chapter is to investigate this purely technical relationship of combining inputs to produce outputs, which presents a physical constraint on society's ability to satisfy wants. We first classify the factors going into the production process as land, labor, or capital inputs. Then, based on this classification, we derive a production function that establishes a relationship between the production factors and a firm's output. As we investigate effects of variation in one of the production factors, we discuss the Law of Diminishing Marginal Returns and stages of production. Analogous to the discussion of indifference curves (in Chapter 2), we develop the concept of *isoquants,* when two production factors are allowed to vary. We can also substitute one factor for another, and a measure of this ability is the *elasticity of substitution*. The effect of proportional changes in all inputs is called *returns to scale*. Thus, we can classify production functions in terms of their elasticity of substitution and returns to scale attributes.

Production. The process of transferring a set of elements into a different set of elements. *E.g., a bakery combining flour, sugar, oil and other inputs to produce donuts.*

In contrast to utility functions, production functions are measurable. In estimating production functions, applied economists determine for a particular production process whether one input could be substituted for another and what the resulting output would be if all inputs were increased or decreased by some fixed proportion. With this knowledge of the production relationship between inputs and outputs, they can determine the cost of production, the market price, and how much a firm is willing and able to supply, how responsive a firm will be to changes in output and input prices. This knowledge of firms' responsiveness to parameter changes in prices is particularly important in determining the effect of various government policies. For example, how farmers respond to establishing an agricultural support price for crops directly impacts the cost of the program and the effects the program has on farmers' incomes.

Factors of production dissected

Do you realize if it were not for Thomas Edison we would be watching TV by candlelight?
(Al Boliska)

Translation: Like any output, the broadcast of television programs requires inputs (e.g., electricity) for their production.

Jim Fischer, Customer Service Consultant of Volvo Cars of North America, states, "There are on average approximately 9000 individual parts in every Volvo." However, for economic modeling, factors (parts) of production (**inputs**) are generally aggregated into three classifications: land, labor, and capital. This classification allows us to conceptualize simple cases first and then extend the analysis to higher dimensions that are more general (realistic). *Capital inputs* are durable man-made inputs—for example, trucks, buildings, and tools—that are themselves produced goods. (At times, *capital* is used to describe the money used to start up and maintain a firm. To avoid any confusion, we will use the term *financial capital* for this money concept.) *Labor inputs* are the time or service individuals put into production, and *land inputs* or material inputs are all natural resources (e.g., water, oil, and climate). Note that all inputs do not fall uniquely into one of these three classifications. For example, should genetically engineered corn for producing pork be classified as a land or capital input?

What are all the inputs that go into producing a toothpick? Land, labor, and capital, according to our simplifying classifications for producing any product.

Inputs. Factors used in the production of outputs. *E.g., labor used for cutting hair.*

Time also enters the production process. For example, if you state that you want to produce smartphones in the most efficient manner, the time framework must be stated. Is the time framework very short, where the amount of labor and capital for production is fixed? Or is there time to vary labor but not the capital inputs? Economists generally divide time into three periods, based on the ability to vary inputs. The first is the **market period,** where all the inputs in production are fixed; they cannot be changed. For example, in the production of bread, once the bread is placed in the oven, the ingredients are fixed. The second is the **short-run period,** where some inputs are fixed and some inputs are variable. The bread's ingredients are fixed, but the size and type of bread pan are variable. When all inputs are variable, the **long-run period** exists. As you consider what type of bread to bake and when, all inputs are variable.

Market period. All inputs in a production process are fixed. *E.g., the lunch hour for a restaurant.*

Short-run period. Some inputs are fixed and some are variable. *E.g., the number of tables in a restaurant may be fixed, but the owner can vary the number of servers to hire.*

Long-run period. All inputs are variable. *E.g., a new location for a furniture store and a complete turnover of its sales force.*

In terms of actual time, the market-period, short-run, and long-run intervals can vary considerably from one firm to another, depending on the nature of a particular firm. For example, once railroad track is laid, the route the track takes is not easily changed. Thus, a railroad may have some inputs fixed for over 200 hundred years. (In fact, the route of the first railway established in 1758 at Middleton, England, is still currently used.) If the fixed factor is the size of the production facility (plant), then the long run would be how long it takes to change the plant size. One important fixed factor is the owners and managers of a firm: as long as the same owners and managers run the firm, a short-run situation exists. For labor, the long run may be the life of a worker. (As noted by John Maynard Keynes in referring to the macroeconomic long run when prices, wages, and interest rates have all fully adjusted, "in the long run we are all dead.")

This division of time into three periods is a simplification. It would be more reasonable to think there are a number of short-run and long-run stages with intertemporal substitution among the stages. More general models incorporating numerous time stages, called *dynamic models*, are less restrictive in their assumptions. However, for an initial understanding of firm behavior, this more simplified three-period model offers a large number of implications.

Defining production constraints: production functions

I do not even butter my bread. I consider that cooking.

(Katherine Cebrian)

Translation: Buttering bread is a form of production.

The production relation for artichoke dip is

- 1 can artichoke hearts, drained and chopped
- 1 cup mayonnaise
- 1 cup Parmesan cheese
- Garlic and onion powder to taste
- Stir together and bake for one hour at 350 degrees.

In general, firms are interested in turning inputs (the ingredients) into outputs (artichoke dip) with the objective of maximizing profit. Nature imposes technological constraints on firms in the form of restricting how inputs can be turned into outputs. This relationship between inputs and outputs is formalized by a **production function**

$$q = f(K, L, M),$$

where q is the output of a particular commodity [the **total product (TP)**], K is capital, L is labor, and M is land or natural resources.

For example, a shoe manufacturer's output of shoes in a given year is dependent on the amount of capital equipment, labor, and land used. The production function records the condition of many possible ways in which, say, 10,000 shoes could be produced. For any possible combination of capital, labor, and land inputs, the production function records the maximum level of shoe output that can be produced from that combination. In the market period all inputs are fixed, so the level of output cannot be varied. We denote K^o, L^o, and M^o as the fixed levels of capital, labor, and land. The production from these fixed inputs is also fixed at q^o, so

$$q^o = f(K^o, L^o, M^o).$$

If capital and labor could be varied with only land fixed, then a short-run production function would be

$$q = f(K, L, M^o),$$

where it is now possible to vary output by changing either K or L or both K and L. In the long run, all inputs could be varied, so the only restriction on output is technology.

Production function. Restriction on how inputs are transformed into outputs. *E.g., combining various ingredients to make a pizza.*

Total product (TP). Output of a particular commodity. *E.g., the daily output of dresses for a garment manufacturer.*

Thus, the production function represents the set of technically efficient production processes. A production process exhibits **technological efficiency** if it yields the highest level of output for a given set of inputs. As a technical relationship, the production function is void of any economic content. For economists, the technical aspects of production are interesting only as they impact upon the behavior of firms maximizing profit. Generally, the technical aspects of production do impose restrictions on profit, and thus assumptions (axioms) concerning these technical aspects of production are required for developing economic models for explaining and predicting firms' behavior.

Two axioms generally underlie a production function: monotonicity and strict convexity. The *Monotonicity Axiom* implies that if a firm can produce q with a certain level of inputs, it should be able to produce at least q if there exists more of every input. This assumes free disposal of inputs: a profit-maximizing firm will freely dispose of any additional inputs that would cause a decrease in output. As discussed in the following sections, monotonicity implies that all marginal products of the variable inputs are positive at their profit-maximizing level. The *Strict Convexity Axiom*, discussed in the section on isoquant maps and marginal rate of technological substitution, is analogous to the Strict Convexity Axiom in consumer theory.

Technological efficiency. A production process that yields the highest level of output for a given set of inputs. *E.g., a power tool manufacturer employs an engineering firm to design a modern assembly line.*

Application: Origin of the famous Cobb–Douglas production function

The most popular production function used by applied economists is called the Cobb–Douglas function. Considering two inputs, capital and labor, the Cobb–Douglas function may be represented as

$$q = f(K,\ L) = aK^b L^d,$$

where, a, b, and d are all positive constants. As discussed by T.M. Humphrey, this version of the Cobb–Douglas function dates back to 1927, when University of Chicago economist Paul Douglas (1892–1976), on a sabbatical at Amherst, asked mathematics professor Charles Cobb (1875–1949) for help. Douglas required an equation to describe the relationships among manufacturing output, capital input, and labor input for the period 1889–1922. Thus, the Cobb–Douglas function was born.

Or was it? The development of production functions, in general, dates back to at least 1767 when the French physiocrat* A. Turgot (1727–1781) implicitly described total product schedules possessing positive first partial derivatives, positive and then negative second partial derivatives, and positive cross-partial derivatives. Thirty-one years later, Thomas Malthus (1766–1834) presented his famous arithmetic and geometric ratios that imply a logarithmic production function. However, it was Johann Heinrich von Thunen (1783–1850) who was the first to apply differential calculus to productivity theory and probably the first to solve economic optimization problems. He was the first to interpret marginal products as partial derivatives. And it was Thunen who first hypothesized a geometrical series of declining marginal products, implying an exponential production function. In 1850, just before his death, he wrote an equation expressing output per worker as a function of capital per worker. When rearranged, this equation yields the Cobb–Douglas function. So Thunen had discovered the Cobb–Douglas production function over 70 years before it was rediscovered by Cobb and Douglas. Thunen's contributions identify him as the true founder of neoclassical marginal productivity theory. Alfred Marshall (1842–1924) credits Thunen as having the most influence on him in terms of economic theory.

Source: T.M. Humphrey, "Algebraic Production Functions and Their Uses before Cobb–Douglas," *Federal Reserve Bank of Richmond Economic Quarterly* 83 (1997): 51–83.

*Physiocrats lived and worked in France in the middle of the eighteenth century. The word "physiocracy" comes from the Greek *phýsis*, nature, and *krâtos*, power, indicating the importance placed on natural forces. The physiocrats are regarded as the first school of economics. Their intent was to influence the French government's economic policy.

Varying one input (short run)

Marginal product: change in output for an incremental change in an input

> *Whatever you do will be insignificant, but it is very important that you do it.*
>
> (Mahatma Gandhi)

> *Translation: The marginal contribution of an input in production may be insignificant, but in the aggregate all these marginal contributions will significantly impact output.*

Let us first consider variation in only one input. This is a short-run analysis, where all other inputs are held fixed. The change in output, Δq, resulting from a unit change in the one variable input, holding all other inputs constant, is called the **marginal product (MP)** of the variable input. If capital is the one variable input, then the marginal product of capital is

$$\mathrm{MP}_K = \lim_{\Delta K \to 0} \frac{\Delta q}{\Delta K} = \frac{\partial q}{\partial K} = \frac{\partial \mathrm{TP}}{\partial K}.$$

Alternatively, if labor is the one variable input, then the marginal product of labor is

$$\mathrm{MP}_L = \lim_{\Delta L \to 0} \frac{\Delta q}{\Delta L} = \frac{\partial q}{\partial L} = \frac{\partial \mathrm{TP}}{\partial L}.$$

As an example, consider a baker hiring one more unit of labor to transport bread to a market, holding all other inputs constant. The extra output this additional worker produces is the baker's MP of labor. Precisely, MP is the change in output as the change in the variable input goes to zero. MP is analogous to the concept of marginal utility (MU, discussed in Chapter 2), except that MP is not measured on an ordinal scale. Instead, MP is measured on a cardinal scale, the ratio scale.[1] The distances between any levels of MP are of a known size measured in physical quantities (bushels, crates, pounds, etc.). For example, producing one additional automobile with the addition of another worker has meaning (unlike receiving an additional util by consuming another apple, as with MU).

Marginal product (MP). The additional output associated with an additional unit of an input holding all other inputs constant. *E.g., the increase in the volume of groceries sold after adding an additional checker.*

Consider the following cubic production function with labor as the variable input, holding all other inputs fixed:

$$q = 6L^2 - \tfrac{1}{3}L^3.$$

The marginal product of labor for this production function is then

$$\mathrm{MP}_L = 12L - L^2.$$

The graph of this production function along with MP_L is provided in Figure 7.1. Marginal product is the slope of the production function in terms of the one variable input labor. At first, for low levels of labor, total product TP is increasing at an increasing rate. The slope of TP or MP_L is rising. At the point of inflection, the slope is at its maximum, $L = 6$. MP_L is at a maximum:

$$\frac{\partial \mathrm{MP}_L}{\partial L} = 12 - 2L = 0 \Rightarrow L = 6,$$

$$\frac{\partial^2 \mathrm{MP}_L}{\partial L^2} = -2 < 0, \quad \text{maximum}.$$

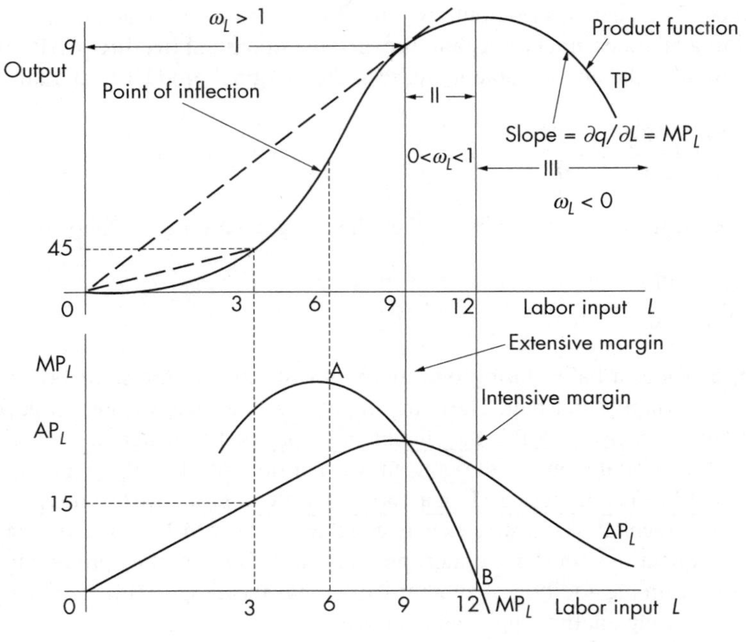

Figure 7.1 **Stages of production and MP_L and AP_L.** The maximum of AP_L divides Stages I and II of production, and where $MP_L = 0$, Stage II ends with the start of Stage III. When AP_L is rising, MP_L is above it; when AP_L is falling, MP_L is below it; and when AP_L is neither rising nor falling, $MP_L = AP_L$.

To the right of maximum MP_L, TP is still increasing, but at a decreasing rate. MP_L is positive, but falling. At maximum TP, the slope of the TP curve is zero, corresponding to $MP_L = 0$:

$$MP_L = 12L - L^2 = 0,$$

$$L(12 - L) = 0 \Rightarrow L = 0 \text{ and } L = 12.$$

Finally, when TP is falling, MP_L is negative. According to the Monotonicity Axiom, given free disposal, a firm will not operate in the negative range of MP_L, so it is generally assumed that $MP_L \geq 0$.

Example 7.1 Deriving marginal products from a Cobb–Douglas production function

For a numerical example of a production function, consider the following Cobb–Douglas production function with capital K and labor L as the two inputs:

$$q = 5K^{1/4}L^{3/4}.$$

The marginal products of capital and labor are then

$$\mathrm{MP}_K = \frac{\partial q}{\partial K} = \tfrac{5}{4}K^{-3/4}L^{3/4} = \tfrac{1}{4}K^{-1}5K^{1/4}L^{3/4} = \tfrac{1}{4}K^{-1}q > 0,$$

$$\mathrm{MP}_L = \frac{\partial q}{\partial L} = \tfrac{15}{4}K^{1/4}L^{-1/4} = \tfrac{3}{4}L^{-1}5K^{1/4}L^{3/4} = \tfrac{3}{4}L^{-1}q > 0.$$

Example 7.2 Deriving average products from a Cobb–Douglas production function

For the same production function as in Example 7.1, $q = 5K^{1/4}L^{3/4}$,

$$\mathrm{AP}_K = q/K = 5K^{1/4}L^{3/4}/K = 5K^{-3/4}L^{3/4} = K^{-1}q > 0,$$

$$\mathrm{AP}_L = q/L = 5K^{1/4}L^{3/4}/L = 5K^{1/4}L^{-1/4} = L^{-1}q > 0.$$

The average products are falling as the inputs increase:

$$\frac{\partial \mathrm{AP}_K}{\partial K} = -\tfrac{3}{4}K^{-1}AP_K = -\tfrac{3}{4}K^{-2}q < 0,$$

$$\frac{\partial \mathrm{AP}_L}{\partial L} = -\tfrac{1}{4}L^{-1}AP_L = -\tfrac{1}{4}L^{-2}q < 0.$$

These falling average products are consistent with the marginal products being less than their respective average products:

$$\mathrm{MP}_K < \mathrm{AP}_K,$$

$$\tfrac{1}{4}K^{-1}q < K^{-1}q,$$

$$\mathrm{MP}_L < \mathrm{AP}_L,$$

$$\tfrac{3}{4}L^{-1}q < L^{-1}q.$$

Average product: output/input

As measured by the US Department of Labor, output per hour of labor for the manufacturing sector increased 4.5 percent in the second quarter of 2010. This measure of productivity, called the *average product (AP)* of an input, is also measured in physical quantities and is defined, for labor, as

$$\mathrm{AP}_L = \frac{q}{L}.$$

In general, **average product (AP)** is output (TP) divided by an input. Thus average product of labor is a measure of the productivity per worker for producing an output. In Figure 7.1, AP_L at first increases, reaches a maximum, and then declines. This results from

$$\mathrm{AP}_L = \frac{q}{L} = \frac{6L^2 - \frac{1}{3}L^3}{L} = 6L - \tfrac{1}{3}L^2,$$

where

$$\frac{\partial \mathrm{AP}_L}{\partial L} = 6 - \frac{2}{3}L = 0 \Rightarrow L = 9,$$

$$\frac{\partial^2 \mathrm{AP}_L}{\partial L^2} = -\frac{2}{3} < 0, \quad \text{maximum.}$$

The productivity of labor, as measured by AP_L, changes as additional workers are employed. This results from the short-run condition that all other inputs remain fixed. At first, with a relatively small number of workers for a large amount of other inputs, adding an additional worker increases the productivity of all the workers; the AP_L increases. However, a point is reached where labor is no longer relatively limited compared with the fixed inputs, so an additional worker will result in AP_L declining. Note that average product will be nonnegative (zero or positive), as long as TP is nonnegative.

Average product (AP). Output divided by an input. *E.g., the average productivity of labor for a power plant is the number of kilowatts generated divided by the number of workers.*

Graphically, we can determine AP_L from the TP curve by considering a line (chord) through the origin. The slope of a chord through the origin is TP divided by labor. Since AP_L is defined as TP divided by labor, the slope of a chord through the origin is the AP_L at a level of labor where the chord intersects TP. As illustrated in Figure 7.1, the slope of the chord through the origin intersecting TP at $L = 3$ is $45/3 = 15 = \mathrm{AP}_L$ at 3 workers. At first, as the number of workers increases, the chord shifts upward and the slope of the chord increases, resulting in increased AP_L. We can continue to shift the chord upward and it will continue to intersect the TP curve until finally it is tangent to the TP curve. At this point, AP_L is at its maximum. If we further increase the slope, the chord will no longer intersect the TP curve. In Figure 7.1, AP_L is at a maximum (the TP curve is tangent with a chord through the origin) at 9 workers. Beyond 9 workers, further increases in labor result in a lower slope for the chord and thus a lower AP_L.

Understanding the law of diminishing marginal returns and stages of production

> *For a successful technology, reality must take precedence over public relations, for Nature cannot be fooled.*
>
> (Richard P. Feynman)

> *Translation: The physical laws of Nature determine the feasible inputs employed for production.*

As the American colonies were first getting established in the seventeenth century, there was a tremendous shortage of labor relative to the land available. The productivity of labor was very high given the relatively large amount of land. This resulted in all sorts of inducements to attract labor to the colonies, including fallacious stories created about how wonderful this new land was. However, severe labor shortages still prevailed, which resulted in forced importation of labor from Africa into slavery. By 1808, this shortage was no longer a major problem and the importation of slaves was discontinued. Although there was an effort in 1859 to reopen the African slave trade, the Civil War prevented it from occurring.

This productivity of labor relative to land in the early years of the American colonies illustrates a firm's cost of producing an output. A firm's costs will depend not only upon the prices it pays for inputs but also on the technology of combining inputs into the output. In the short run, as we saw in Figure 7.1, a firm can change its output by adding variable inputs to fixed inputs. As we have discussed, output may at first increase at an increasing rate. However, given a constant amount of fixed inputs, output will at some point increase at a decreasing rate. This occurs because at first the variable input is limited compared with the fixed input—for example, there might be only a small number of workers for a relatively large fixed area of land. As additional workers are added, their productivity remains very high given the relatively large amount of land and still limited amount of labor. Thus, output TP increases at an increasing rate. However, as more of the variable input is added, it is no longer as limited. Eventually, TP will still be increasing, but at a decreasing rate. MP_L will still be positive, but declining. This is called the **Law of Diminishing Marginal Returns** (or just **diminishing returns**). This law is an engineering law that states as successive units of a variable input, such as labor, are added to a fixed input, such as land, beyond some point the extra or marginal product attributed to each additional unit of the variable input will decline. Specifically,

$$\frac{\partial MP_L}{\partial L} = \frac{\partial^2 q}{\partial L^2} = f_{LL} < 0;$$

beyond some point, the MP of the variable input will begin to decline.

Can Earth feed the cosmos? No, if it was possible, the Law of Diminishing Marginal Returns would be violated and Earth would be invaded by aliens.

Law of Diminishing Marginal Returns. As more of a variable input is added to a constant amount of the fixed inputs, the marginal product of the variable input will eventually decline. *E.g., as more water is added to a plant in a flowerpot, the additional growth in the plant from an additional ounce of water will decline.*

Example 7.3 Law of diminishing marginal returns

From Example 7.1,

$$MP_L = \frac{\partial q}{\partial L} = \frac{15}{4}K^{1/4}L^{-1/4},$$

$$\frac{\partial MP_L}{\partial L} = \frac{\partial^2 q}{\partial L^2} = f_{LL} = -\frac{15}{16}K^{1/4}L^{-5/4} < 0.$$

As labor L increases, the marginal product of labor MP_L declines.

As indicated in Figure 7.1, diminishing marginal returns starts at point A where MP_L is at a maximum, $L = 6$. To the left of point A there are increasing returns and at point A constant returns exist. Between points A and B, where MP_L is declining, diminishing marginal returns exist. To the right of point B, marginal productivity is both diminishing and negative ($MP_L < 0$), which violates the Monotonicity Axiom. Specifically, the MP_L associated with Figure 7.1 is

$$MP_L = 12L - L^2,$$

$$\frac{\partial MP_L}{\partial L} = 12 - 2L.$$

For

$$L < 6, \quad \frac{\partial MP_L}{\partial L} > 0, \quad \text{increasing marginal returns,}$$

$$L = 6, \quad \frac{\partial MP_L}{\partial L} = 0, \quad \text{constant marginal returns,}$$

$$L > 6, \quad \frac{\partial MP_L}{\partial L} < 0, \quad \text{diminishing marginal returns.}$$

The reason the TP curve will at some point increase only at a decreasing rate (concave) is the Law of Diminishing Marginal Returns. Some production functions may not exhibit increasing returns at first. In fact (as examined in Chapter 9), no firm with a profit-maximizing objective will operate in the area of increasing returns or negative returns. Thus, production functions generally will only be concave with diminishing marginal returns throughout the production process. A graphical illustration of a production function characterized by diminishing marginal returns throughout the production process is depicted in Figure 7.2. The production function underlying this figure is

$$q = 10L - \frac{1}{2}L^2,$$

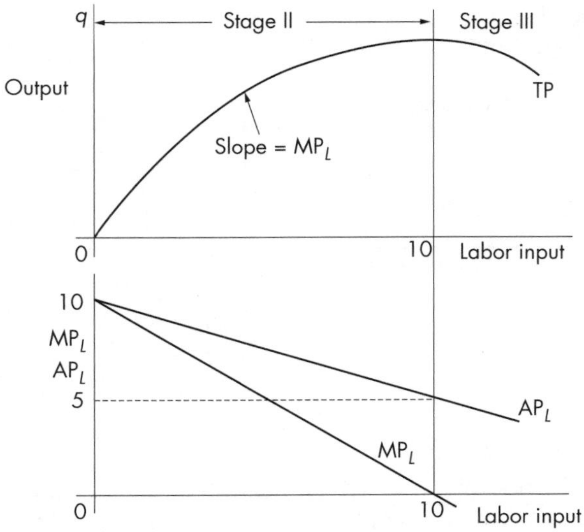

Figure 7.2 **Production function with diminishing marginal returns throughout.** The concave total product curve results in both AP_L and MP_L falling as the variable input, labor, increases.

with

$$MP_L = \frac{\partial q}{\partial L} = 10 - L,$$

$$AP_L = \frac{q}{L} = 10 - \frac{1}{2}L.$$

MP_L and AP_L in this case decline throughout.

The Cobb–Douglas production function can also only exhibit diminishing marginal returns throughout the production process. Furthermore, it can characterize production where all the marginal products are positive. This makes a Cobb–Douglas function very useful for representing firms' technology constraints, given that profit-maximizing firms will only operate in the area of diminishing marginal returns where all marginal products are positive. A Cobb–Douglas production function with these properties is illustrated in Figure 7.3 for a variable level of labor. An example of such a production function is

$$q = 5(K^{\circ})^{1/4}L^{3/4},$$

where capital is fixed at K°; the shapes of MP_L and AP_L are determined by

$$MP_L = \frac{15}{4}(K^{\circ})^{1/4}L^{-1/4} > 0,$$

$$\frac{\partial MP_L}{\partial L} = -\frac{15}{16}(K^{\circ})^{1/4}L^{-5/4} < 0,$$

$$\frac{\partial^2 MP_L}{\partial L^2} = \frac{75}{64}(K^{\circ})^{1/4}L^{-9/4} > 0, \quad \text{minimum},$$

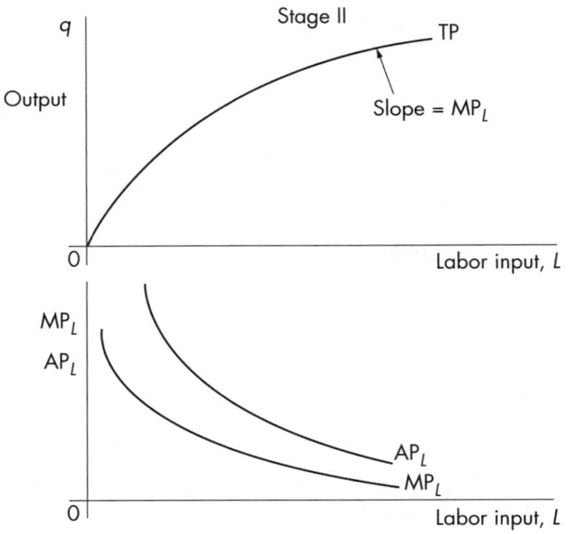

Figure 7.3 **Cobb–Douglas production function with labor as the only variable input.** The concave production technology characterizes Stage II production with diminishing marginal returns and falling average product throughout its range.

$$\mathrm{AP}_L = 5(K^{\circ})^{1/4}L^{-1/4} > 0,$$

$$\frac{\partial \mathrm{AP}_L}{\partial L} = -\frac{5}{4}(K^{\circ})^{1/4}L^{-5/4} < 0,$$

$$\frac{\partial^2 \mathrm{AP}_L}{\partial L^2} = \frac{25}{16}(K^{\circ})^{1/4}L^{-9/4} > 0, \quad \text{minimum.}$$

What is the relationship of marginal product to average product?

In the area of diminishing marginal returns, marginal product can intersect with average product. As indicated in Figure 7.1, this intersection of MP_L and AP_L occurs where AP_L is at a maximum. Note that if the addition to the total, the marginal unit, is greater than the overall average, the average will rise. Specifically, for a production function, if $\mathrm{MP}_L > \mathrm{AP}_L$, then AP_L will increase. If the addition to the total is less than the overall average, then the average will fall: if $\mathrm{MP}_L < \mathrm{AP}_L$, then AP_L will decline. Finally, if the addition to the total is equal to the overall average, the average will neither rise nor fall. At the point when AP_L is a maximum, $\mathrm{MP}_L = \mathrm{AP}_L$ and AP_L is neither rising nor falling. Specifically, if the average is neither rising nor falling, the slope of the average is zero. Taking the derivative of the average results in a relation between the marginal product and average product. The derivative of AP_L is

$$\frac{\partial \mathrm{AP}_L}{\partial L} = \frac{\partial (qL^{-1})}{\partial L} = \frac{\partial q}{\partial L}L^{-1} - qL^{-2}.$$

Multiplying both sides by L gives

$$\frac{\partial \mathrm{AP}_L}{\partial L} L = \frac{\partial q}{\partial L} - \frac{q}{L} = \mathrm{MP}_L - \mathrm{AP}_L.$$

Solving for MP_L yields

$$\mathrm{MP}_L = \mathrm{AP}_L + \frac{\partial \mathrm{AP}_L}{\partial L} L.$$

For the production function illustrated in Figure 7.1,

$$\mathrm{AP}_L = 6L - \frac{1}{3}L^2,$$

$$\frac{\partial \mathrm{AP}_L}{\partial L} = 6 - \frac{2}{3}L,$$

so

$$\mathrm{MP}_L = \left(6L - \frac{1}{3}L^2\right) + \left(6 - \frac{2}{3}L\right)L$$
$$= 12L - L^2.$$

Marginal product is average product plus an adjustment factor $(\partial \mathrm{AP}_L/\partial L)L$. If the slope of AP_L is zero (AP_L is neither rising nor falling), then this adjustment factor is zero, so $\mathrm{MP}_L = \mathrm{AP}_L$. In contrast, if AP_L is rising, $(\partial \mathrm{AP}_L/\partial L)L > 0$, so $\mathrm{MP}_L > \mathrm{AP}_L$. If AP_L is falling, $(\partial \mathrm{AP}_L/\partial L)L < 0$, so $\mathrm{MP}_L < \mathrm{AP}_L$.

How is your grade-point average affected by this semester's grades? Your hard work will payoff in both an increase in human capital and a higher semester's average than your overall average, so your grade-point average will rise.

Example 7.4 How your grade-point average is related to marginal and average units

To see the relationship between the marginal and average units, consider a student's grade-point average. Say a student's overall grade-point average, for all classes taken before this semester, is 2.5 and, for the classes taken this semester, his semester grade-point average is 3.0. This semester grade-point average is the marginal unit. The marginal unit 3.0 is greater than the average unit 2.5, so the student's overall grade-point average improves. If the student only obtained a 2.0 for the semester, his overall average would decline. His overall average will not change if his semester average is equivalent to his overall average.

Example 7.5 Calculating output elasticities

For the specific Cobb–Douglas production function $q = 5K^{1/4}L^{3/4}$ (Example 7.1), the output elasticities for K and L are

$$\omega_K = \frac{\mathrm{MP}_K}{\mathrm{AP}_K} = \frac{\frac{1}{4}K^{-1}q}{q/K} = \frac{1}{4},$$

$$\omega_L = \frac{\mathrm{MP}_L}{\mathrm{AP}_L} = \frac{\frac{3}{4}L^{-1}q}{q/L} = \frac{3}{4}.$$

Output elasticity: MP/AP

Another important relation between an average and marginal product is the output elasticity. An **output elasticity** measures how responsive output is to a change in an input. For example, the output elasticity of labor, denoted ω_L, is defined as the proportionate rate of change in q with respect to L. Given the production function

$$q = f(K, L),$$

the output elasticity of labor is

$$\omega_L = \frac{\partial \ln q}{\partial \ln L} = \frac{\partial q}{\partial L}\frac{L}{q} = \frac{\mathrm{MP}_L}{\mathrm{AP}_L}.$$

As with any elasticity, output elasticity is the marginal unit (slope) weighted by the average unit. As illustrated in Figure 7.1, when $\mathrm{MP}_L > \mathrm{AP}_L$, $\omega_L > 1$; when $0 < \mathrm{MP}_L < \mathrm{AP}_L$, $0 < \omega_L < 1$; and when $\mathrm{MP}_L < 0$, $\omega_L < 0$. Table 7.1 lists estimated output elasticities for baseball wins and attendance with player experience, hitting, and pitching as inputs. In all cases, the output elasticities are between 0 and 1, which indicates the marginal products for these inputs are all positive and less than their associated average products. As an example of the meaning of these elasticities, a 1 percent increase in hitting by players will result in a 0.17 percent increase in attendance.

Table 7.1 Estimated output elasticities for baseball wins and attendance as outputs

Input (Player)	*Output elasticities*	
	Wins	*Attendance*
Experience	0.42	0.44
Hitting	0.11	0.17
Pitching	0.41	0.37

Source: K. Stewart and J.C.H. Jones, "Are Sports Teams Multiproduct Firms?" *Empirical Economics* 39 (2010): 487–514.

Output elasticity, ω_j. The percentage change in output q given a percentage change in input j. *E.g., if output elasticity for capital is ³/₄, a 1 percent increase in capital results in a ³/₄ percent increase in output.*

Stages of production

I think we might be going a bridge too far.

(Sir Frederick Browning)

In 1944, during World War II, the Allied powers attempted to expedite the end of the war by capturing six bridges connecting Holland to Germany. However, this strategy did not reduce the war's duration as much as hoped. In fact, the operation (called the Battle of Arnhem) was considered a defeat. Attempting to capture fewer bridges may have had a greater effect on bringing about the war's end.

Similar to the Allies' determination of how many bridges to take, a firm is interested in determining the profit-maximizing amount of an available input it should employ. As an aid in this determination, we use the technology of production to determine at what stage of production to add a variable input, say labor. The exact profit-maximizing level of labor to hire within this stage depends also on the cost of labor and the price received for the firm's output.

Specifically, we divide the short-run production function into three stages of production. *Stage I* includes the area of increasing returns and extends up to the point where average product reaches a maximum. As illustrated in Figure 7.1, Stage I includes a portion of the marginal product curve that is declining. The distinguishing characteristic of Stage I is that marginal product is greater than average product, so average product is rising. As long as average product is rising, the firm will add additional variable inputs. As an example, if it is profitable to hire a worker at a certain level of average productivity, at fixed prices it will be profitable to hire an additional worker, yielding higher average productivity. In the area of rising average product, the fixed inputs are present in uneconomically large proportion relative to the variable input. The variable input is limited relative to the fixed inputs. As will become more apparent with the introduction of costs (in Chapter 8), a rational profit-maximizing producer would never operate in Stage I of production. If market conditions dictated such a small level of total output, the firm would not produce in the short run, and would produce by using fewer units of the fixed inputs in the long run. In the long run, the fixed inputs become variable. Reduction of the fixed inputs would result in the entire set of product curves shifting to the left, which results in Stage I ending at a lower level of output.

This condition is illustrated in Figure 7.4. The reduction in fixed inputs causes the production function to shift from TP to TP′. This reduces Stage I of production, so a lower level of output and labor hired will not occur in Stage I. Prior to the reduction in fixed inputs, Stage I ends at 9 units of labor associated with the same production function as in Figure 7.1. If a reduction in the fixed input results in the production function

$$q = 2L^2 - \frac{1}{3}L^3,$$

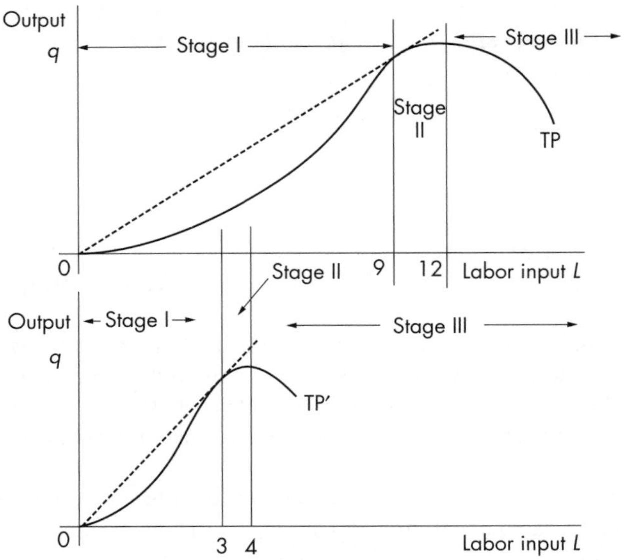

Figure 7.4 **Shifts in stages of production with a reduction in the level of fixed inputs.** As the level of fixed inputs is reduced, the stages of production shift to the left, with Stages II and III occurring at a lower variable input level.

then

$$\text{AP}_L = 2L - \frac{1}{3}L^2,$$

$$\frac{\partial \text{AP}_L}{\partial L} = 2 - \frac{2}{3}L = 0 \Rightarrow L = 3.$$

Now Stage I ends at 3 units of labor instead of 9, allowing a lower level of output and labor hired.

A rational producer will also not operate in *Stage III* of production, defined as the range of negative marginal product for the variable input. In Stage III, TP is actually declining as more of the variable input is added. Figures 7.1, 7.2, and 7.4 illustrate Stage III. Additional units of the variable input in this stage of production actually cause a decline in total output. Even if units of the variable input were free, a rational producer would not employ them beyond the point of zero marginal product. In Stage III, the variable input is combined with the fixed input in uneconomically large proportions. For example, in agriculture, high levels of the variable input, labor, will cause the fixed input, land, to be cultivated too intensively. Indeed, the point of zero MP, for the variable input, is called the *intensive margin*. Similarly, at the point of maximum AP of the variable input, the cultivation of land is extensive, and this point is called the *extensive margin.*

If market conditions dictated an expansion of output beyond the current maximum level based on a given set of fixed inputs, then additional units of the fixed input must be used. This would result in the shifting of the entire production function. In Figure 7.4, expansion of the fixed inputs results in the production function shifting from TP′ to TP, with a corresponding shifting of Stage III to the right and a higher maximum level of output. Specifically, given the production function

$$q = 2L^2 - \frac{1}{3}L^3,$$

$$MP_L = 4L - L^2 = 0 \Rightarrow L = 4.$$

The start of Stage III of production then shifts from $L = 4$ to $L = 12$.

A firm will operate between the extensive and intensive margins, called *Stage II* of production. Within this stage, both AP and MP of the variable input are positive but declining. Also, the output elasticity is between 0 and 1. For example, the output elasticities in Table 7.1 are between 0 and 1, indicating that baseball wins and attendance production are in Stage II of production. In contrast, the output elasticity for the variable input is negative in Stage III and greater than 1 in Stage I. Depending on the firm's cost of variable inputs and price received for its output, the firm will hire some level of the variable input within this Stage II of production. A Cobb–Douglas production function characterizing Stage II is illustrated in Figure 7.3. We will better understand why a firm will not operate in Stages I and III but will operate in Stage II as we next consider production with two variable inputs.

What stage of production are you in for studying? You should be beyond Stage I, somewhere in Stage II. If you are in Stage III, it is time to sleep.

Application: Output elasticities and technical efficiency in China's grain production

As discussed by Yao and Liu, China has only 7 percent of the arable land in the world but has to feed almost one-fourth of the world's population. From 1953 to 1993, cultivated land in China declined by 13 percent. With the continued rise in industrialization and urbanization, this shrinkage of cultivated land may be slowed down but probably not reversed in the near future.

Except for the disastrous years of 1959–1961 (the Great Leap Forward), China has been able to sustain self-sufficiency in food production since 1949. Substituting other inputs for land has allowed per capita food consumption to increase by 1.2 percent annually from 1949 to 1993. For example, fertilizer has increased from 0.5 kg per hectare to 213.4 kg per hectare and the proportion of irrigated land has increased from 8 percent to 51 percent during this time period. However, continued substitution of fertilizer and irrigation for land will eventually cause the marginal product of these inputs to decline. The Law of Diminishing Marginal Returns will retard future output increases. Also, the use of agricultural chemicals is endangering the environment and human health. Thus, further output growth must rely on improvements in technical efficiency.

Yao and Liu estimate a production function along with an inefficiency function to identify the influence inputs will assert on further increases in output (grain production) and the overall efficiency of the agricultural grain sector. Results in terms of output elasticities indicate that land, labor, machinery, fertilizer, and irrigation inputs are all within Stage II of production (Table 7.2). All the inputs are experiencing diminishing marginal productivity.

Table 7.2. Output elasticities for China's grain production

Input	*Elasticities*
Land	0.945
Labor	0.154
Machinery	0.034
Fertilizer	0.341
Irrigation	0.051

Land has the largest impact on output, which is consistent with its relative scarcity. A 1 percent reduction in land will result in a 0.945 percent decline in grain output. Irrigation would have to increase by over 18 percent to offset this loss of land. As indicated by the elasticities, further increases in nonland inputs will have limited success in mitigating agricultural land losses.

In estimating the technical efficiency, Yao and Liu determined that China's grain production is only 64 percent efficient. That is, average grain output falls 36 percent short of the maximum possible level. The authors found that a 1 percent increase in research and development will result in a 4.7 percent improvement in efficiency. (Imperfections in the strains of grain are the most important technical constraint on grain production.) Thus, improved technical efficiency offers greater potential increases in China's grain output than further increases in nonland inputs.

Source: S. Yao and Z. Liu, "Determinants of Grain Production and Technical Efficiency in China," *Journal of Agricultural Economics* 49 (1998): 171–184.

Considering two variable inputs

Headline 2151: Android in running against humanoid for CEO position.

(Michael Wetzstein)

In the process of a firm attempting to minimize cost for a given level of output, it is generally assumed that one input can be substituted for another (an android for a human) and still continue to produce a given level of output. Specifically, it is assumed that a different combination of, say two, inputs will produce the same level of output. For example, in manufacturing microwave ovens, greater use of plastics may be substituted for a reduction in metal with output remaining unchanged.

Recall that indifference curves represent a consumer's preferences for different combinations of two goods with utility remaining constant. Similarly, in production theory, **isoquants** represent different input combinations, or input ratios, that may be used to produce a specified level of output. *Iso* means equal and *quant* stands for quantity, so an isoquant is a locus of points representing the same level of output or equal quantity. For movements along an isoquant, the level of output remains constant and the input ratio changes continuously. Isoquants are the same concept as indifference mapping, with equal utility along the same indifference curve replaced by equal output level along the same isoquant.

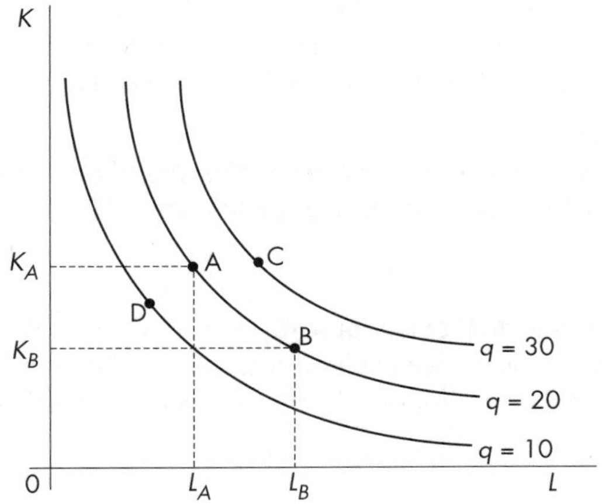

Figure 7.5 **Isoquant map for two variable inputs—capital *K* and labor *L*.** A movement along the isoquant for $q = 20$ from point A to B does not change the output level. However, the input ratio K/L does decline for a movement from A to B. Point C represents an input bundle with $q = 30$ and at point D the output level is $q = 10$.

Isoquant. A locus of points that yield the same level of output. *E.g., substituting renewable for fossil fuels in driving the same pizza delivery route.*

For example, suppose two inputs—capital K and labor L—can be varied in the production of some output. A possible isoquant map for this production process is represented in Figure 7.5. Isoquants are cross-sections of an associated production function $q = f(K, L)$, which represents the technology of producing an output q with the two variable inputs K and L. In Figure 7.5, input bundles (or points) A and B represent different combinations of the capital and labor inputs to produce the same output level, $q = 20$. At point A, input bundle (K_A, L_A) is employed for producing $q = 20$. Increasing the level of labor from L_A to L_B and decreasing the level of capital from K_A to K_B results in input bundle B with the same level of output, $q = 20$. Point C represents an input combination resulting in a higher level of output, $q = 30$, so point C is on a higher isoquant. Finally, point D represents a lower output level combination of the two inputs.

Marginal rate of technical substitution (MRTS)

In Figure 7.5, isoquants are drawn with a negative slope based on the assumption that substituting one input for another can result in output not changing. For example, moving from point B to A, the firm substitutes capital for labor, holding output constant. A measure for this substitution is the **marginal rate of technical substitution (MRTS)**, which is defined as the negative of the slope of an isoquant,

$$\text{MRTS}(K \text{ for } L) = -\frac{dK}{dL}\Big|_{dq=0},$$

and measures how easy it is to substitute one input for another holding output constant. MRTS is similar to the concept of MRS in consumer theory. MRTS measures the reduction in one input per unit increase in the other that is just sufficient to maintain a constant level of output. Put another way, it is the rate at which one variable input is substituted for another variable input, holding output constant.

Does one cup of skim milk plus two teaspoons melted butter equal one cup of whole milk? Yes, skim milk plus butter can substitute for whole milk.

Marginal rate of technical substitution [MRTS(*K* for *L*)]. With a given level of technology, the rate at which a firm can substitute capital for labor, holding output constant. *E.g., if MRTS = 2, then the firm can substitute 2 units of capital for 1 unit of labor without any change in output.*

Example 7.6 Deriving MRTS from a production function

Considering the production function $q = 5K^{1/4}L^{3/4}$ (Example 7.1),

$$\text{MRTS}(K \text{ for } L) = \frac{\text{MP}_L}{\text{MP}_K} = \frac{\frac{3}{4}L^{-1}q}{\frac{1}{4}K^{-1}q} = \frac{3K}{L} > 0.$$

Convex and negatively sloping isoquants

We can establish the underlying assumptions of negatively sloped and convex-to-the-origin isoquants, illustrated in Figure 7.5, by developing the relation between MRTS and the MPs:

$$\text{MRTS}(K \text{ for } L) = \frac{\text{MP}_L}{\text{MP}_K}.$$

We obtain this relationship by taking the total differential of the production function $q = f(K, L)$:

$$\begin{aligned} dq &= \frac{\partial q}{\partial L}dL + \frac{\partial q}{\partial K}dK \\ &= \text{MP}_L dL + \text{MP}_K dK. \end{aligned}$$

Along an isoquant $dq = 0$, output is constant. Thus,

$$0 = \text{MP}_L dL + \text{MP}_K dK,$$

$$\text{MP}_L\, dL = -\text{MP}_K\, dK.$$

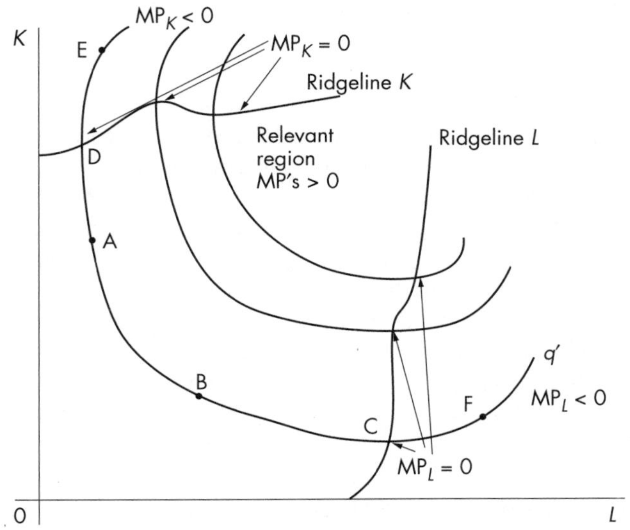

Figure 7.6 **Ridgelines in the isoquant map.** Ridgelines are isoclines representing equal slopes along their length. At every point on ridgeline K, the slope of the isoquant approaches $-\infty$, and at every point on ridgeline L, the isoquants have a zero slope.

Solving for the negative of the slope of the isoquant yields

$$-\frac{dK}{dL}\bigg|_{dq=0} = \frac{\text{MP}_L}{\text{MP}_K} = \text{MRTS}(K \text{ for } L).$$

Along an isoquant, the gain in output from increasing L slightly, $\text{MP}_L dL$, is exactly balanced by the loss in output from a suitable decrease in K, $\text{MP}_K dK$. For isoquants to be negatively sloping, both MP_L and MP_K must be positive. As indicated in Figure 7.6, the ridgelines trace out the boundary in the isoquant map where the marginal products are positive. *Ridgelines* are *isoclines* (equal slopes) where MRTS is either zero or undefined for different levels of output. MRTS is zero where MP_L is zero and is undefined where MP_K is zero. The relevant region is between the two ridgelines, where both MP_L and MP_K are positive. At point C in Figure 7.6, both the slope and MRTS of the isoquant are zero. To the right of C—say point F—labor can no longer be substituted for capital while holding output constant. MP_L is negative, resulting in a negative MRTS and a positively sloping isoquant. The rational, profit-maximizing producer would not operate at a level of labor beyond point C. At point D, both the slope and MRTS are undefined. MP_K is zero. Further increases in capital—say point E—result in negative MP_K.

Diminishing MRTS results in isoquants drawn strictly convex to the origin. This result is analogous to the relationship between MRS and strictly convex indifference curves developed in Chapter 2. For high ratios of K to L, MRTS is large, indicating (with output held constant) that a great deal of capital can be given up if one more unit of labor becomes available.

In Figure 7.6, a movement along the isoquant from point A to B results in MRTS declining due to the convex nature of the isoquants. This assumption of strictly convex isoquants, resulting in diminishing MRTS from point A to B, is related to the Law of Diminishing

Marginal Returns. In the area of diminishing marginal returns (Figure 7.1), an increase in the variable input results in a decrease in its marginal product. Given

$$\text{MRTS}(K \text{ for } L) = \text{MP}_L/\text{MP}_K,$$

a movement from A to B in Figure 7.6 results in an increase in labor with a corresponding decrease in MP_L and a decrease in capital with a corresponding increase in MP_K. Thus, within the area of diminishing marginal returns, a movement from A to B results in MP_L declining, MP_K increasing, and their ratio MRTS declining. A firm will always operate in Stage II of production, which is characterized by diminishing marginal returns, so Stage II of production, for both the variable inputs, is represented by strictly convex isoquants.

In Figure 7.6, for an output level q', a rational producer will only operate somewhere between points D and C. Within this range of a strictly convex, negatively sloping isoquant, the marginal products of both variable inputs are positive and declining as the associated input increases. This is characteristic of Stage II production for both the variable inputs.

Example 7.7 Illustrating diminishing MRTS

Consider the production function from Example 7.1, $q = 5K^{1/4}L^{3/4}$. We determine the diminishing marginal rate of technical substitution or strictly convex isoquants by setting a constant level of output q^o and solving for capital K:

$$q^o = 5K^{1/4}L^{3/4},$$

$$K = \left(\frac{q^o}{5}\right)^4 L^{-3}.$$

Evaluating the derivatives yields

$$\frac{dK}{dL} = -3\left(\frac{q^o}{5}\right)^4 L^{-4} < 0,$$

$$\frac{d^2K}{dL^2} = 12\left(\frac{q^o}{5}\right)^4 L^{-5} > 0.$$

As L increases, MRTS declines.

Stages of production in the isoquant map

We can illustrate the stages of production in the isoquant map by fixing one of the inputs. (Recall that stages of production assume only one variable input.) A situation where the input capital is fixed at some level is indicated by the horizontal line at A in Figure 7.7. In the short run, the firm must operate somewhere on this line. At Stage I, the labor input is small relative to the fixed level of capital. The marginal product of capital and MRTS are negative and the isoquants have positive slopes. At point B, MRTS is undefined, MP_K is zero, and $\text{AP}_L = \text{MP}_L$. This is the demarcation between Stages I and II of production.[2]

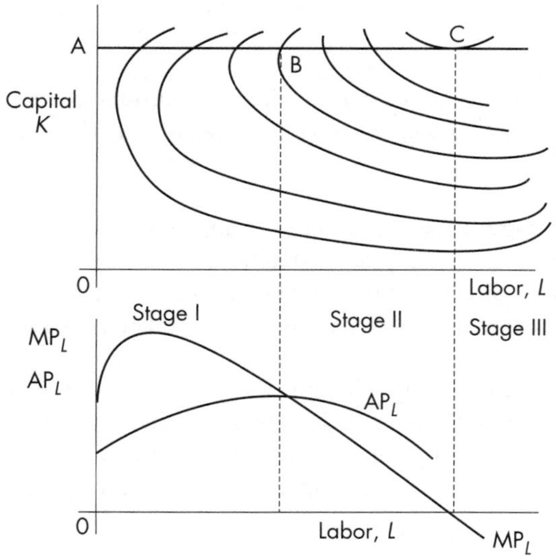

Figure 7.7 **Stages of production in the isoquant map.** For a fixed level of capital at point A, initially the variable input, labor, is in Stage I of production. Increasing labor to point B results in the boundary between Stage I and II. Further increases in labor result in point C, the boundary between Stage II and III.

In Stage II of production, all the isoquants are strictly convex and have negative slopes. At point C, the marginal product of labor is zero, which corresponds to the line of demarcation between Stages II and III.

Classifying production functions

Production functions represent tangible (measurable) productive processes, and thus economists pay more attention to the actual form of these functions than to the form of utility functions. This has resulted in classification of production functions in terms of returns to scale and substitution possibilities as well as empirical estimates of actual production functions. For some production processes, it may be extremely difficult if not impossible to substitute one input for another. (For example, it is generally not wise to substitute one horse for another in the middle of a stream.)

Returns to scale: will doubling inputs double output?

Double your pleasure, double your fun ....

(Wrigley's Doublemint gum ad)

In 1960, Nikita Khrushchev took his shoe off, pounded it on the table at a Union Nations general session, and stated that the USSR would bury the United States economically. As we will see, Khrushchev must have been a strong believer in increasing returns to scale. **Returns to scale** measure how output responds to increases or decreases in all inputs together. This is a long-run concept, since all inputs can vary. As an example, if all inputs are doubled, returns to scale determine whether output will double, less than double, or more than double.

Returns to scale. A measurement of how output changes with a proportionate change in inputs. *E.g., doubling all the ingredients for pancakes will double the pancake batter.*

In many cases, it is difficult to change some inputs at will and thus increase inputs proportionally. An example is in an industry such as agriculture, where environmental conditions not under the firm's control directly impact production. Firms do, however, attempt to control as much of the environmental conditions as feasible. Examples are using greenhouses or applying pesticides.

Assuming it is possible to proportionally change all inputs, a production function can exhibit constant, decreasing, or increasing returns to scale across different output ranges. However, it is generally assumed, for simplicity, that production functions only exhibit either constant, decreasing, or increasing returns to scale. Specifically, given the production function

$$q = f(K, L),$$

an explicit definition of **constant returns to scale** is

$$f(\alpha K, \alpha L) = \alpha f(K, L) = \alpha q, \quad \text{for any } \alpha > 0.$$

If all inputs are multiplied by some positive constant α, then output is multiplied by that constant also. For example, if all inputs are doubled, $\alpha = 2$, then output will also double. If the production function is homogeneous, then a constant returns to scale production function is homogeneous of degree 1 or linear homogeneous in all inputs. Isoquants are radial blowups and equally spaced as output expands (Figure 7.8). Doubling K from 2 to 4 and doubling L from 5 to 10 results in output also doubling from 10 to 20. If doubling your pleasure doubles your fun, then you have a constant returns to scale production function for fun.

Constant returns to scale. A proportional change in inputs results in the same proportional change in output. *E.g., tripling all inputs results in output tripling.*

Decreasing returns to scale occurs if output is increased proportionally less than all inputs:

$$f(\alpha K, \alpha L) < \alpha f(K, L) = \alpha q.$$

For example, doubling all inputs results in less than doubling output, or reducing all inputs by 50 percent results in less than a 50 percent reduction in output. In Figure 7.8, doubling K from 2 to 4 and doubling L from 5 to 10 results in output less than doubling. Here, 4 units of K and 10 units of L produce less than 20 units of output.

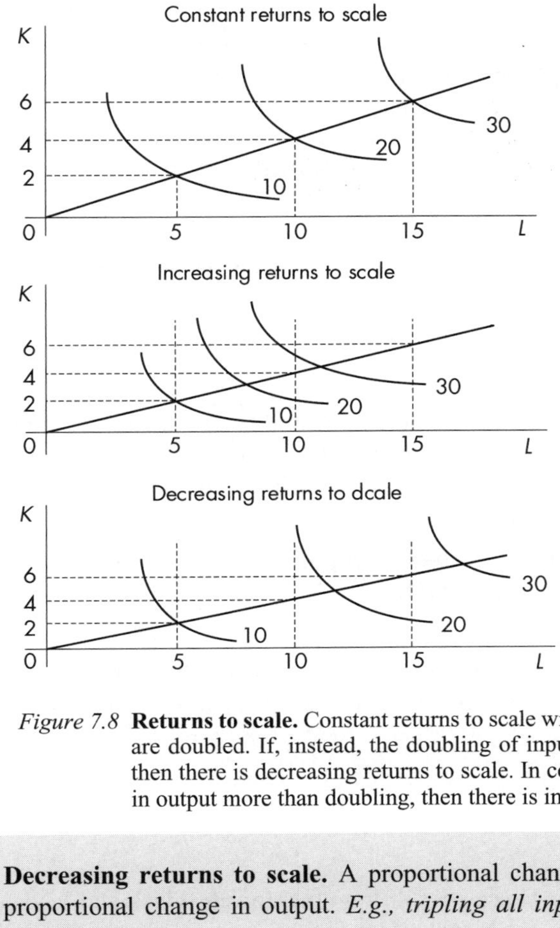

Figure 7.8 **Returns to scale.** Constant returns to scale will result in a doubling of output if inputs are doubled. If, instead, the doubling of inputs results in output less than doubling, then there is decreasing returns to scale. In contrast, if this doubling of inputs results in output more than doubling, then there is increasing returns to scale.

Decreasing returns to scale. A proportional change in inputs results in less of a proportional change in output. *E.g., tripling all inputs results in less than tripling output.*

Example 7.8 Determining returns to scale

Consider the following linear homogeneous production function representing constant returns to scale:

$$q = aK^{1/4}L^{3/4}.$$

Doubling all inputs yields

$$a(2K)^{1/4}(2L)^{3/4} = 2aK^{1/4}L^{3/4} = 2q.$$

Doubling inputs doubles output. In general, if $q = aK^bL^d$, then doubling all inputs yields

$$a(2K)^b(2L)^d = 2^{b+d}q > 2q,$$

for $b+d>1$, increasing returns to scale. If $b+d<1$, then $2^{b+d}q<2q$, indicating decreasing returns to scale. If $b+d=1$, then $2^{b+d}q=2q$, constant returns to scale. For homogeneous production functions, decreasing returns to scale result from the function being homogeneous of degree less than 1, increasing returns to scale result from the function being homogeneous of degree greater than 1, and constant returns to scale result from linear homogeneous production functions.

Increasing returns to scale occurs if output increases more than the proportional increase in inputs:

$$f(\alpha K, \alpha L) > \alpha f(K, L) = \alpha q.$$

For example, again, doubling all inputs results in more than doubling output, or reducing all inputs by 50 percent results in more than a 50 percent reduction in output. In Figure 7.8, doubling K from 2 to 4 and doubling L from 5 to 10 results in output more than doubling. This time, 4 units of K and 10 units of L will produce more than 20 units of output.

If you double all inputs, will output double? Only if the production process is characterized by constant returns to scale.

Increasing returns to scale. A proportional change in inputs results in more than a proportional change in output. *E.g., tripling all inputs results in more than a tripling of output.*

Determinants of returns to scale

Adam Smith established that returns to scale result from two forces: division of labor and managerial difficulties.[3] An increase in all inputs increases the division of labor and results in increased efficiency, so production might more than double. Managerial difficulties result in decreased efficiency, so production might not double. Unfortunately for the former USSR, Khrushchev did not realize the possible inefficiencies associated with large-scale production. The concentration of production in these larger inefficient state enterprises contributed to the USSR imploding in 1991.

The early twentieth century concept of assembly-line mass production is based on division of labor. On the assembly line, each worker has a specialized task to perform for each product being assembled. The worker becomes very skilled at this task, which increases productivity. Automaker Henry Ford is noted for this concept of division of labor and mass production. As a result of division of labor and specialization, Ford experienced increasing returns to scale: doubling all the inputs required for automobile manufacturing resulted in output more than doubling.

One cause of managerial difficulties in mass production is the required stockpiling of parts and supplies. Inventory control must be maintained, where an accounting of spare parts is required. This results in a significant amount of inputs allocated to the storage and accounting of inventories. These managerial difficulties result in decreasing returns to scale. A method that mitigates this decreasing returns to scale from inventory control was developed by Toyota's founder Kiichiro Toyota, who promoted the idea of *just-in-time production.* This concept pulls components to the production line as they are required rather than keeping them in reserve. By 1953, every Toyota laborer was operating an average of from 5 to 10 machines. By 1962, the time it took to change stamping dies was reduced from several hours to 15 minutes. By the 1970s, Toyota's factories were running with just a few hours, rather than a few days, of inventory. Toyota considered the system so powerful that the company deliberately coined difficult and even misleading words to describe it.

Today, firms across the United States are adopting just-in-time production as a method of mitigating inventory decreasing returns to scale. As an example, several of the raw materials, such as gallium arsenide, used in Bell Laboratories are particularly toxic. With a just-in-time delivery system, Bell Labs now uses a process that brings together the much less hazardous chemical constituents of one highly toxic material right at the spot where the combined compound is used. This eliminated the extra inputs required for storing, transporting, and disposing of the hazardous compound—inputs that contribute toward decreasing returns to scale.

One problem with just-in-time production is the increased vulnerability of firms to supply disruptions, such as strikes by labor unions in firms that supply the parts. Without a stockpile of parts, such disruptions could shut down production fairly quickly.

Post-industrial manufacturing is shifting away from mass production of standardized product and evolving toward mass customization—the production of substantial quantities of personalized goods. Called *agile manufacturing,* this results in increasing returns to scale. Agile manufacturing is possible because information about consumers' demands can now be reduced to a series of computer files that are then used for the mass production of customized products. Agile manufacturing can already be found in the computer industry. Over the telephone or Internet, a customer ordering a computer can choose from a variety of microprocessors, memory chips, hard disks, and monitors. In the future, agile manufacturing has the potential of yielding substantial increasing returns to scale in the production of customized consumer products.

As a firm increases in size by increasing all inputs, another possible cause of decreasing returns to scale is the allocation of inputs for environmental and local service projects. As a firm employs more inputs and increases output, it becomes increasingly more exposed to public concerns associated with its production practices. To enhance and maintain goodwill within its community, the firm will allocate additional inputs for environmental and local service projects. This action, although possibly socially beneficial, contributes to decreasing returns to scale. For example, McDonald's once generated over 45 million pounds of polystyrene waste each year. As the public began to protest, McDonald's had to allocate inputs to justify their production practices, resulting in decreasing returns to scale. (Over time McDonald's was finally forced to discontinue the use of polystyrene.)

Returns to scale and stages of production

We determine the relationship between returns to scale and stages of production by assuming a linear homogeneous production function (homogeneous of degree 1), which implies a constant returns to scale production function. Applying Euler's Theorem (see the Mathematical Review) to the production function

$$q = f(K, L),$$

we obtain

$$q = L \cdot \text{MP}_L + K \cdot \text{MP}_K.$$

Note that we assume the degree of homogeneity to be 1 (linear). Dividing by L gives

$$\text{AP}_L = \text{MP}_L + (K/L)\text{MP}_K.$$

Solving for MP_K gives

$$\text{MP}_K = (L/K)(\text{AP}_L - \text{MP}_L).$$

Thus, from Figure 7.1, Stage I is defined as $\text{MP}_L > \text{AP}_L$, which implies $\text{MP}_K < 0$ (as indicated in Figure 7.7). Assuming constant returns to scale, we define the stages of production as

Stage I	$\text{MP}_L > \text{AP}_L > 0$,
	$\text{MP}_K < 0$.
Stage II	$\text{AP}_L > \text{MP}_L > 0$,
	$\text{AP}_K > \text{MP}_K > 0$.
Stage III	$\text{MP}_L < 0$,
	$\text{MP}_K > \text{AP}_K > 0$.

Stages I and III are symmetric for a constant returns to scale production function, and, given the Monotonicity Axiom, the only relevant region for production is Stage II. The Cobb–Douglas production function associated with Figure 7.3 represents a technology consistent with production only in State II.

Measuring the elasticity of substitution

Generally, a firm may compensate for a decrease in the use of one input by an increase in the use of another. For example, a business may decrease the duties of a secretary by using a voice-mail system. As early as the first half of the nineteenth century, Heinrich von Thunen was collecting evidence from his farm in Germany that suggested the ability of one input to compensate for another was significant. Based on his observations, Thunen postulated the principle of substitutability, which states that it is possible to produce a constant output level with a variety of input combinations.

This principle of substitutability is not an economic law, because there are production functions for which inputs are not substitutable. An example is a cake recipe, where the ingredients must be used in a fixed proportion. However, for those functions where inputs are substitutable, the degree inputs that can be substituted for one another is an important technical relationship for producers. Thus, production functions may also be classified in terms of the **elasticity of substitution (ξ)**, which measures how easy it is to substitute one input for another—for example, capital for labor. It determines the shape of a single isoquant.

Elasticity of substitution (ξ). Measures how easy it is to substitute one input (commodity) for another. *E.g., for most, if not all, occupations, it is very easy to substitute women for men.*

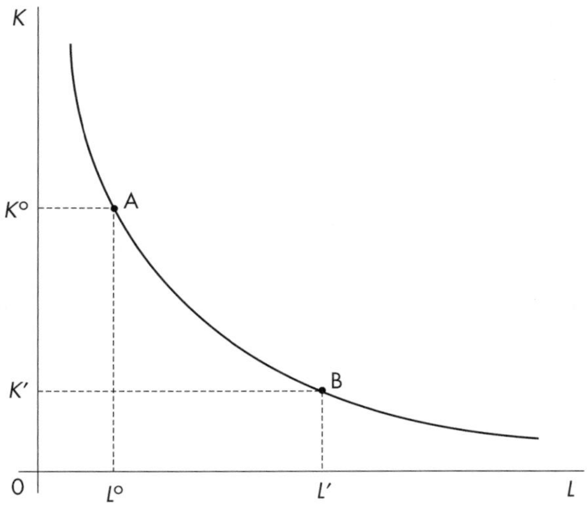

Figure 7.9 **Capital/labor ratio and MRTS, $K^0/L^0 > K'/L'$.** As MRTS declines from point A to B, the capital/labor ratio also declines.

Specifically, in Figure 7.9, consider a movement from A to B, which results in the capital/labor ratio K/L decreasing. A profit-maximizing firm is interested in determining a measure of the ease in which it can substitute K for L. If MRTS does not change at all for changes in K/L, the two inputs are perfect substitutes. Thus, substitution is easy. If MRTS changes rapidly for small changes in K/L, substitution is difficult. If there is an infinite change in MRTS for small changes in K/L (called fixed proportions), substitution is not possible.

A scale-free measure of this responsiveness is provided by the elasticity of substitution ξ. Elasticity of substitution along an isoquant is defined as the percentage change in K/L divided by the percentage change in MRTS:[4]

$$\xi = \lim_{\Delta \mathrm{MRTS} \to 0} \frac{\%\Delta(K/L)}{\%\Delta \mathrm{MRTS}} = \frac{d(K/L)/(K/L)}{d\mathrm{MRTS}/\mathrm{MRTS}} = \frac{d\ln(K/L)}{d\ln \mathrm{MRTS}}.$$

Along a strictly convex isoquant, K/L and MRTS move in the same direction, so the value of ξ is positive. In Figure 7.9, a movement from A to B results in both K/L and MRTS declining, and the relative magnitude of this change is measured by the elasticity of substitution. If ξ is high, MRTS will not change much relative to K/L and the isoquant will be less curved (less strictly convex). A low value of ξ gives rather sharply curved isoquants. In general, it is possible for the elasticity of substitution to vary for movements along an isoquant and as the scale of production changes. However, frequently ξ is assumed constant. Most investigations of production functions have centered on this constant ξ along with assuming constant returns to scale.

Some common constant returns to scale production functions follow.

1 $\xi = \infty$, a *perfect-substitute* technology

$$q = f(K, L) = aK + bL.$$

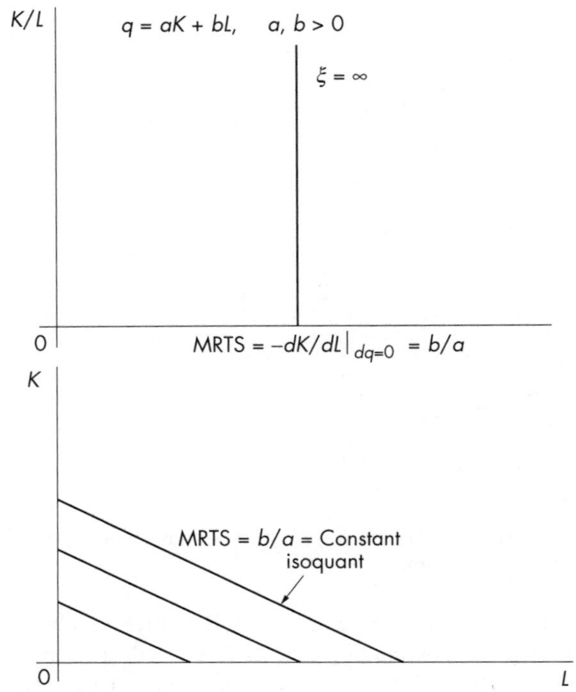

Figure 7.10 **Elasticity of substitution for perfect-substitute technologies.** MRTS is constant for movements along an isoquant characterizing a perfect-substitute technology, so changes in K/L result in no change in MRTS.

A perfect-substitute technology is analogous to perfect substitutes in consumer theory. A production function representing this technology exhibits constant returns to scale:

$$f(\alpha K, \alpha L) = a\alpha K + b\alpha L = \alpha(aK + bL) = \alpha f(K, L).$$

All isoquants for this production function are parallel straight lines with slopes $= -b/a$ (Figure 7.10):

$$\frac{dK}{dL}\bigg|_{dq=0} = -\text{MRTS}(K \text{ for } L) = -\frac{\text{MP}_L}{\text{MP}_K} = -\frac{b}{a}.$$

MRTS is constant, $d\text{MRTS} = 0$, which results in

$$\xi = \frac{d(K/L)/(K/L)}{d\text{MRTS}/\text{MRTS}} = \infty.$$

As illustrated in Figure 7.10, changes in K/L result in no change in MRTS. With perfect substitutes, the marginal products are constants, $\text{MP}_K = a$ and $\text{MP}_L = b$, so there is no diminishing marginal productivity. Production processes characterized by such ease of substitution are rarely encountered in practice. A firm will only use capital or only labor in this case, depending on which input is cheaper per additional increase in output.

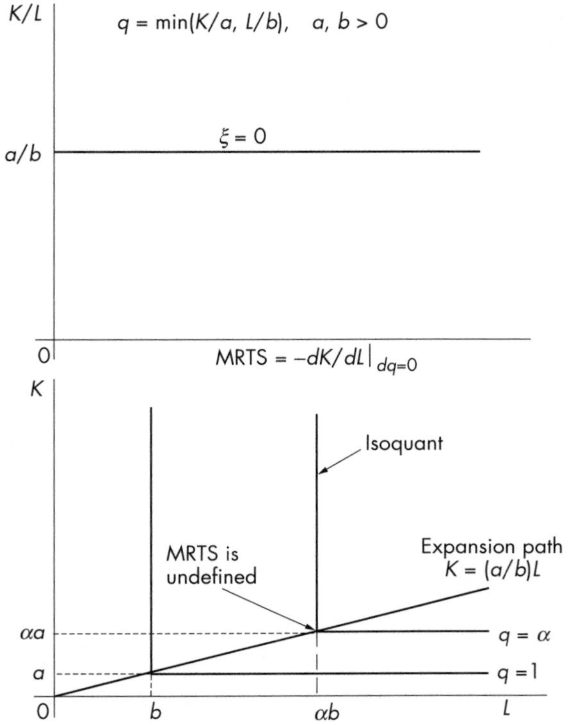

Figure 7.11 **Elasticity of substitution for fixed proportion technologies.** The K/L ratio is fixed, so it is not possible to substitute one input for another.

2 $\xi = 0$, a *fixed-proportion* (or *Leontief*) technology
A production technology that exhibits fixed proportions is

$$q = \min\left(\frac{K}{a}, \frac{L}{b}\right), \quad a, b > 0.$$

This production function also exhibits constant returns to scale:

$$f(\alpha K, \alpha L) = \min\left(\frac{\alpha K}{a}, \frac{\alpha L}{b}\right) = \alpha \min\left(\frac{K}{a}, \frac{L}{b}\right) = \alpha f(K, L), \quad a, b > 0.$$

Fixed-proportion production functions (analogous to perfect complements in consumer theory) are characterized by zero substitution (Figure 7.11). Capital and labor must always be used in a fixed ratio. If a units of K and b units of L are employed, then $q = 1$. If we add more units of L, say αb units, and hold K constant at a, then output remains constant at $q = 1$. Similarly, adding more units of K, holding L constant, does not increase output. The marginal products are constant and zero, but this violates the Monotonicity Axiom and the Law of Diminishing Marginal Returns.

Isoquants for this technology are right-angles as illustrated in Figure 7.11. Note also that these isoquants are not smooth curves; they are kinked. At the kink, MRTS

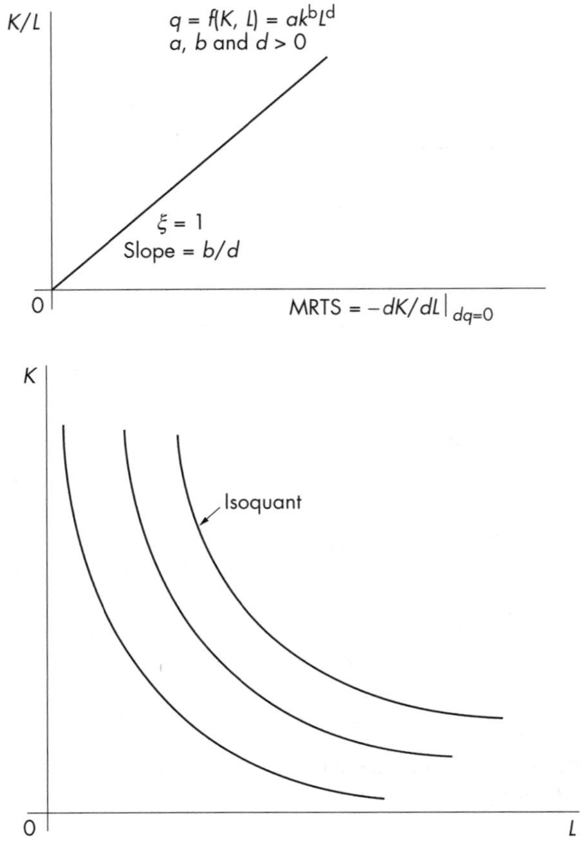

Figure 7.12 **Isoquants for a Cobb–Douglas production function.** For movements along an isoquant representing a Cobb–Douglas technology, MRTS continuously changes. This results in strictly convex isoquants.

is not unique—it can take on an infinite number of positive values—and thus K/L is a constant, $d(K/L) = 0$, which results in $\xi = 0$. The fixed-proportions production function technology has a wide range of applications, including lawn mowing and many cookie recipes.

3 $\xi = 1$, *Cobb–Douglas* technology
Production functions where $\xi = 1$ are Cobb–Douglas production functions. Isoquants for the Cobb–Douglas technology are strictly convex, which assumes diminishing MRTS (Figure 7.12). An example of a Cobb–Douglas production function is

$$q = f(K, L) = aK^bL^d,$$

where a, b, and d are all positive constants. For $b + d = 1$, the Cobb–Douglas function exhibits constant returns to scale:

$$f(\alpha K, \alpha L) = a(\alpha K)^b(\alpha L)^d = a\alpha^{b+d}K^bL^d = \alpha aK^bL^d = \alpha f(K, L).$$

If $b+d>1$, then the production function exhibits increasing returns to scale; if $b+d<1$, then decreasing returns to scale occurs.

The Cobb–Douglas function is quite useful in many applications, because it is linear in logs:

$$\ln q = \ln a + b\ln K + d\ln L.$$

This linear representation is very amenable for econometric analysis. The constants b and d are the output elasticities for capital and labor inputs, respectively:

$$\omega_K = \frac{\partial \ln q}{\partial \ln K} = \frac{\partial q}{\partial K}\frac{K}{q} = \frac{\text{MP}_K}{\text{AP}_K} = b, \text{ output elasticity for capital,}$$

$$\omega_L = \frac{\partial \ln q}{\partial \ln L} = \frac{\partial q}{\partial L}\frac{L}{q} = \frac{\text{MP}_L}{\text{AP}_L} = d, \text{ output elasticity for labor.}$$

Recall that output elasticities measure how responsive output is to a change in an input. If a Cobb–Douglas production function is to represent Stage II of production in both K and L, then the output elasticity parameters b and d are restricted to $0 < (b, d) < 1$. If b is negative, the Cobb–Douglas production function would characterize Stage III for capital. Alternatively, if b is greater than 1, the production function would imply Stage I production for capital. We can estimate these constant output elasticities from actual data and then use such estimates to measure returns to scale.

We determine the elasticity of substitution that equals 1 for a Cobb–Douglas production function by first calculating the marginal products and MRTS, given $q=f(K,L)=aK^bL^d$:

$$\text{MP}_L = dL^{-1}q,$$
$$\text{MP}_K = bK^{-1}q,$$
$$\text{MRTS}(K \text{ for } L) = \text{MP}_L/\text{MP}_K = dK/bL.$$

Solving for the capital/labor ratio yields

$$K/L = (b/d)\,\text{MRTS}(K \text{ for } L).$$

As illustrated in Figure 7.12, K/L is linearly related to MRTS with a slope of b/d and an intercept of zero. Taking the logarithm of both sides

$$\ln(K/L) = \ln(b/d) + \ln \text{MRTS}(K \text{ for } L),$$

yields the elasticity of substitution:

$$\xi = \frac{d(K/L)}{d\text{MRTS}(K \text{ for } L)}\frac{\text{MRTS}(K \text{ for } L)}{K/L} = \frac{d\ln(K/L)}{d\ln \text{MRTS}(K \text{ for } L)} = 1.$$

Example 7.9 Calculating elasticity of substitution for a Cobb–Douglas production function

Given the production function $q = 5K^{1/4}L^{3/4}$, $\omega_K = 1/4$ and $\omega_L = 3/4$, both inputs are in Stage II of production. MRTS(K for L) $= 3K/L$. Solving for the capital/labor ratio K/L and taking the logarithm of both sides gives

$$\ln(K/L) = \ln(1/3) + \ln \text{MRTS}(K \text{ for } L).$$

The elasticity of substitution is

$$\xi = \frac{d(K/L)}{d\text{MRTS}(K \text{ for } L)} \frac{\text{MRTS}(K \text{ for } L)}{K/L} = \frac{d\ln(K/L)}{d\ln \text{MRTS}(K \text{ for } L)} = 1.$$

4 ξ = some positive constant, *constant elasticity of substitution* technology
At times it is desirable to have a general production function that permits ξ to take on any positive value. In such cases, a constant elasticity of substitution (CES) production function can be specified:

$$q = \gamma[\delta K^{-\varsigma} + (1-\delta)L^{-\varsigma}]^{-1/\varsigma},$$

where $\gamma > 0$, $0 \leq \delta \leq 1$, $\varsigma \geq -1$, γ is the efficiency parameter, since it shifts the whole production function, δ is a distribution parameter, and ς is the substitution parameter. The elasticity of substitution is

$$\xi = \frac{1}{1+\varsigma}.$$

The CES production function exhibits constant returns to scale:

$$\begin{aligned} f(\alpha k, \alpha L) &= \gamma[\delta(\alpha k)^{-\varsigma} + (1-\delta)(\alpha L)^{-\varsigma}]^{-1/\varsigma} \\ &= \gamma(\alpha^{-\varsigma})^{-1/\varsigma}[\delta k^{-\varsigma} + (1-\delta)L^{-\varsigma}]^{-1/\varsigma} \\ &= \alpha f(K, L), \ \textit{for any}\ \alpha > 0, \end{aligned}$$

and has generally proved to be useful in empirical studies.

We determine the elasticity of substitution for a CES production function by first calculating the marginal products and MRTS:

$$\begin{aligned} \text{MP}_L &= (-1/\varsigma)\gamma[\delta K^{-\varsigma} + (1-\delta)L^{-\varsigma}]^{-(1/\varsigma)-1}(-\varsigma)(1-\delta)L^{-\varsigma-1} \\ &= (1-\delta)L^{-\varsigma-1}\gamma[\delta K^{-\varsigma} + (1-\delta)L^{-\varsigma}]^{-(1/\varsigma)-1} \\ &= (1-\delta)L^{-\varsigma-1}\gamma^2\gamma^{-1}[\delta K^{-\varsigma} + (1-\delta)L^{-\varsigma}]^{-(1/\varsigma)-1} \\ &= (1-\delta)L^{-\varsigma-1}\gamma^2 q^{-1}. \end{aligned}$$

Similarly,

$$\mathrm{MP}_K = \delta K^{-\varsigma-1}\gamma^2 q^{-1},$$

$$\mathrm{MRTS}(K \text{ for } L) = \frac{\mathrm{MP}_L}{\mathrm{MP}_K} = \frac{1-\delta}{\delta}\frac{K^{\varsigma+1}}{L^{\varsigma+1}}.$$

Solving for the capital/labor ratio K/L yields

$$K/L = \left(\frac{\delta}{1-\delta}\right)^{1/(\varsigma+1)} \mathrm{MRTS}^{1/(\varsigma+1)}.$$

Taking the logarithm of both sides,

$$\ln(K/L) = \frac{1}{\varsigma+1}\ln\left(\frac{\delta}{1-\delta}\right) + \frac{1}{\varsigma+1}\ln \mathrm{MRTS}(K \text{ for } L),$$

yields the elasticity of substitution:

$$\xi = \frac{d(K/L)}{d\mathrm{MRTS}(K \text{ for } L)}\frac{\mathrm{MRTS}(K \text{ for } L)}{K/L} = \frac{d\ln(K/L)}{d\ln \mathrm{MRTS}(K \text{ for } L)} = \frac{1}{\varsigma+1}.$$

Example 7.10 calculating elasticity of substitution for a CES production function

Given the production function $q = 5(0.5K^{-9} + 0.5L^{-9})^{-1/9}$, the elasticity of substitution is

$$\xi = \frac{d(K/L)}{d\mathrm{MRTS}(K \text{ for } L)}\frac{\mathrm{MRTS}(K \text{ for } L)}{K/L} = \frac{d\ln(K/L)}{d\ln \mathrm{MRTS}(K \text{ for } L)} = \frac{1}{\varsigma+1} = \frac{1}{9+1} = 0.1.$$

Application: Were free and slave labor in the antebellum South perfect substitutes?

Large (15 or more slaves) cotton plantations in the antebellum South generally relied on a work gang system of labor. Free labor was not observed working in gangs. Based on this observation, E.B. Field hypothesized that on large plantations free and slave labor were different inputs and thus could not be viewed as perfect substitutes. As a test of this hypothesis, the elasticity of substitution was estimated based on a translog production function (see the next application). Her empirical results support the hypothesis that free and slave labor on large farms were complementary inputs.

Source: E.B. Field, "Free and Slave Labor in the Antebellum South: Perfect Substitutes or Different Inputs?" *Review of Economics and Statistics* 70 (1988): 654–659.

Application: Historical note on production functions

Without history we have no roadmap for the future.

(Rachel Neuwirth)

In the empirical analysis of production, some parametric form (the production function) is assumed. Before computer technology, only the simplest functional forms for production functions could be used for applied research. One popular functional form was the Cobb–Douglas production function. However, by the 1960s, economists started realizing that simple functional forms, including the Cobb–Douglas, could imply strong restrictions on the nature of technology, for example $\xi = 1$. In specifying functional forms for applied production analysis, it is important to choose those that place relatively few prior restrictions on the technology and allow as many relevant effects as possible to be measured. The simple forms—Cobb–Douglas, Leontief, and CES—while convenient for expository purposes, are unlikely to represent production technologies well. Thus, more flexible functional forms for production functions were investigated in the 1970s and 1980s, resulting in the development of the transcendental logarithmic function, translog for short, and the generalized Leontief.

Summary

1. Inputs into production are generally classified as land, labor, or capital. Land inputs are all natural resources; labor inputs are the human services employed in production; and capital inputs are durable man-made inputs.
2. The time required for producing an output is categorized into three periods: market, short-run, and long-run. In a market period, all inputs are fixed; in the short-run period, some inputs are fixed and some are variable; and in the long-run period, all inputs are variable.
3. A production function is a restriction on how inputs may be transformed into outputs. The Monotonicity and Strict Convexity Axioms generally underlie a production function.
4. Marginal product is the additional output received by employing an additional unit of an input holding all other inputs constant. Average product is the average productivity of an input: output divided by input.
5. The Law of Diminishing Marginal Returns states that as more of a variable input is added to a constant amount of the fixed inputs, the marginal product of this variable input will eventually decline.
6. A profit-maximizing firm will operate in Stage II of production, where the marginal products of all inputs are positive. In Stage I (Stage III) of production, the variable input is represented in uneconomical small (large) amounts relative to the fixed inputs.

7. An isoquant is a locus of input combinations representing the same level of output. For movements along an isoquant, the rate at which one input is substituted for another input is called the marginal rate of technical substitution.
8. A production function may be classified in terms of returns to scale and substitution possibilities. Returns to scale measure how output responds to changes in all inputs. Substitution possibilities between two inputs are measured by the elasticity of substitution.
9. Constant returns to scale occurs when multiplying all inputs by a positive constant results in output increasing by this constant times the initial output level. Decreasing (increasing) returns to scale occurs when multiplying all inputs by a positive constant results in output increasing by less than (more than) this constant times the initial output level.
10. Some common production functions used in analytical and empirical investigations are perfect substitutes, fixed proportion (Leontief), Cobb–Douglas, and CES technologies.

Key concepts

average product, 248
constant returns to scale, 264
decreasing returns to scale, 264
elasticity of substitution, 268
firm, 236
increasing returns to scale, 266
inputs, 241
isoquants, 258
Law of Diminishing Marginal Returns, 249
long-run period, 241
marginal product (MP), 245
marginal rate of technical substitution (MRTS), 259
market period, 241
output elasticity, 254
production, 240
production function, 242
returns to scale, 263
short-run period, 241
technological efficiency, 243
total product, 242

Key equation

$$q = f(K, L, M)$$

A production function where output q is a function of the inputs capital K, labor L, and land M.

Questions

1. In an election campaign, assume a political campaign manager has to decide whether to emphasize attack or issues advertisements. Describe the production

function for campaign votes. How might information about this function help the campaign manager to plan strategy?

2. A firm keeps very accurate records on inputs and output. Based on these records, output increased more when the last employee was hired compared with all previous employees. Thus, this last employee must be more productive and should receive a higher wage relative to all the other employees. True or false? Explain.
3. Can you apply marginal productivity theory to the grades you receive in a course? Explain.
4. Thomas Malthus predicted mass starvation because the human population would always grow faster than the increase in food production. Explain this prediction given the Law of Diminishing Marginal Returns.
5. Why does economic theory adopt an assumption of diminishing marginal products when it did not adopt an assumption of diminishing marginal utility?
6. For Inuits, land is abundant relative to people, so the marginal product is less than the average product of labor for hunting. True or false? Explain.
7. In some lesser-developed regions, economists have suggested that removing labor from the land will raise production. Why would economists think such a thing?
8. What implicit assumption of economic theory underlies the conclusion that production occurring on a positively sloped portion of an isoquant curve is irrational?
9. Empirical studies indicate the yield per acre on Japanese farms is generally significantly higher than yields on US farms associated with the same crops. Does this indicate that Japanese farmers are more efficient than US farmers?
10. In a production process, is it possible to have decreasing marginal product in an input and yet increasing returns to scale? Explain.

Exercises

Unless you do your best, the day will come when, tired and hungry, you will halt just short of the goal you desired to reach.

(General George S. Patton)

1. Consider the following production functions:

   i. $q = K^{1/4}L^{1/3}$,
   ii. $q = K^{1/2}L$,
   iii. $q = K^{-1/3}L^{4/3}$,
   iv. $q = K^{1/3}L$,
   v. $q = K^{1/4}L^{-1/4}$,
   vi. $q = K^{1/3}L^{4/3}$,
   vii. $q = 5K^{1/6}L^{3/6}$,
   viii. $q = K^{1/5}L^{1/2}$,
   ix. $q = 4K^{3/4}L^{3/4}$,
   x. $q = K^{1/2}L^{3/2}$.

Answer the following for each function:

a. What are the output elasticities?
b. What is the elasticity of substitution? Explain.
c. What stages of production does the production function represent?
d. What are the returns to scale for the production function?

2. Consider the production function

$$q = K^{1/2}L^{1/2}M^{1/2}.$$

a. What are the output elasticities for the three inputs?
b. What stage of production does the production function represent for M?
c. What is the elasticity of substitution between K and L?
d. What are the returns to scale for this production function?

3. The probability of an automobile accident is a function of a driver's level of caution. Assume there are two drivers with caution levels denoted A and B, and let the probability of avoiding an accident be $\rho(A, B)$. Given that it is not possible to produce an accident avoidance probability greater than 1, determine the shape of isoprobability (isoquant) curves and probability total product curves.

4. Young's Market is producing in the short run with variable labor and some fixed equipment. As the number of workers increases from 1 to 7, the firm's output is 20, 34, 44, 50, 52, 50, and 46.

a. Calculate the marginal and average products of labor.
b. Does this production function exhibit diminishing marginal returns? Explain.
c. Explain possible causes of why the marginal product of labor is negative at the high output levels.

5. A production function is given by $f(K, L) = aK^bL^d$, where K and L are inputs and a, b, and d are parameters.

a. Explain the relationship between stages of production and the parameters.
b. Explain the relationship between returns to scale and the parameters.

6. A transcendental production function is

$$q = f(K, L) = \gamma K^bL^d \exp(aL + oK),$$

where K and L are inputs and γ, a, b, d, and o are parameters. Recall that $\exp(x) = e^x$.

a. Explain the relationship between stages of production and the parameters.
b. Explain the relationship between returns to scale and the parameters.

7. For the CES production function

$$q = (K^{-\varsigma} + L^{-\varsigma})^{-1/\varsigma},$$

show that $K/L = -(\partial K/\partial L)^{\xi}$.

8. Consider the following production functions:

   i. $q = 200K^{0.7}L^{0.8}$,
   ii. $q = 0.5K^{1.5}L^{0.4}$,
   iii. $q = 5K^{0.2}L^{0.6}$,
   iv. $q = 1750K^{0.2}L^{0.8}$.

   Determine which

   a. Do not exhibit decreasing returns to scale.
   b. Contradict the Law of Diminishing Marginal Returns.
   c. Have both decreasing returns to scale and diminishing marginal returns.

9. Consider the following production functions:

   i. $q = 10K^{1/2}L^{1/2}$,
   ii. $q = 2K + 5L$,
   iii. $q = 8KL/(K + L)$,
   iv. $q = K^2L$,
   v. $q = \min(2K, 5L)$.

   For each production function, determine

   a. The firm's MRTS.
   b. The elasticity of substitution.

10. Solve and graph the average and marginal productivity functions for K, given the production function

$$q = KL - K^2,$$

where $L = 5$. At what values of K is $AP_K = 0$? $MP_K = 0$? $AP_K = MP_K$? Where does AP_K reach a maximum value?

Internet case studies

1. Discuss the origin of just-in-time production and how it has affected US manufacturing.
2. List several firms that have adopted agile manufacturing.
3. Who was Leontief and what did he do?
4. Who developed the CES function and how has it been employed?

8 Theory of cost

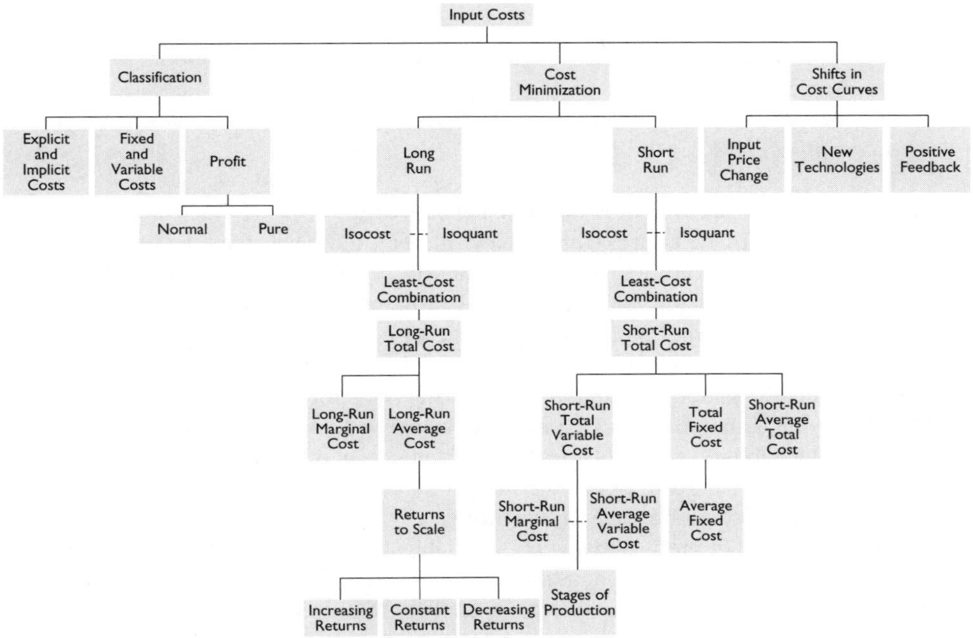

Outline and Conceptual Inquiries

Application: Stakeholder versus shareholder and management ethics

How to classify costs and profits

Explicit and implicit costs

What is the cost of your time in completing a college degree?

Fixed and variable costs

Do you pay both a fixed and variable rate for your monthly cell phone service?

Profits

Determining the cost-minimizing input choice

Long-run costs

How do you produce a low-cost pizza?

Application: Labor unionization and cost of production

Is bigger better?

Application: Economies of scale in electricity production

Is an additional driver's cost of road congestion the same as all the other current drivers?

Short-run costs

Average costs

Marginal cost

Average and marginal cost relationship

Is marginal cost just some adjustment to average cost?

Why will average costs rise with increases in output?

Application: Shapes of the short-run average variable cost curves

How are short- and long-run cost curves related?

Shifting in the cost curves

Input price change

How will marginal cost shift with a change in fixed cost?

New technologies

Accounting is the art of showing a bankrupted firm earning substantial profits.

Translation: For determining a firm's profit, all costs must be considered not just accounting costs.

On a mission to Mars, weight is of prime concern to the crew. If they can determine the least amount of fuel necessary to make it there and back, they will have more weight to allocate toward experiments. Similarly, if firms can determine the least-cost combination of inputs for a given level of output, they will have more dollars to allocate toward profit. With the knowledge of concepts describing the technical aspects of production (Chapter 7), we can discuss how a firm will determine its profit-maximizing combination of output by minimizing costs for this given level of output. The underlying assumption is that a firm's objective is to maximize profit for a given production technology. According to the Austrian school of thought, firms that do not maximize profits are driven out of the market by competitive forces. Thus, the only firms supplying outputs are maximizing profits.

This assumption of profit-maximizing firms deviates from consumer theory, where the problem is maximizing a household's satisfaction, at a given level of income and prices. However, under the three assumptions that prices are fixed, profits are nonstochastic (not random), and firm managers can be controlled by owners, the objective of a profit-maximizing firm is consistent with maximizing the utility of the firm's owners. Specifically, suppose a firm is owned by n households, where ownership means that household j is entitled to a share $\alpha^j \geq 0$ of firm's profit π, $j = 1, \ldots, n$. Household j then receives $\alpha^j \pi$ as its share of profit. All profits are allocated to households, so $\sum_{j=1}^{n} \alpha^j = 1$. Given household j has utility for two commodities x_1 and x_2, $U^j(x_1, x_2)$, the household will attempt to

$$\max U^j(x_1, x_2) \quad \text{s.t. } p_1 x_1^j + p_2 x_2^j = I^j + \alpha^j \pi.$$

The household's income, I^j, is augmented with the household's share of the firm's profit. At fixed prices, higher profit enhances household j's overall wealth and expands its budget set. Thus, all rational owners of a firm, regardless of their utility function, would support the firm's maximizing profits.

Application: Stakeholder versus shareholder and management ethics

As addressed by T. Machan, stakeholder and shareholder perspectives are two theories dominating business ethics. Shareholders hire managers to run the firm with the objective of maximizing profits, while managers are morally responsible for advancing the well-being of stakeholders who are affected by their decisions. These stakeholders are customers, employees, input suppliers, and society as a whole. A shareholder perspective advances the exclusive position that managers should focus solely on maximizing profits. This shareholder perspective is perhaps best summed up by Charles Wilson's (CEO of GM from 1941 to 1953) misquoted statement, "What's good for General Motors is good for the country." Only the government should get involved with other issues concerning fairness and equity. In contrast, a stakeholder perspective holds that corporations were originally created by government (the king), so they are historically an arm of government and thus should be concerned with stakeholder welfare. The middle ground between these two theories is that managers' primary concern should be to maximize profits, but it should not be their exclusive concern. This is consistent with Charles Wilson's actual statement, "What was good for the country was good for General Motors and vice versa." Along with maximizing profits, firms should consider if their actions are in the best interest of America. Depending on which perspective is followed, different policies will result on issues such as insider trading, hostile takeovers, and outsourcing.

Source: T.R. Machan, "Stakeholder vs. Shareholder Theory of the Ethics of Corporate Management," *International Journal of Economics and Business Research* 1 (2009): 12–20.

Profit maximization requires deciding how much output to produce and how much of various inputs to use in producing this output. The constraints on maximizing profit are the technological relation between output and inputs (characterized by a production function), prices of inputs, and the prices of outputs. Determining the profit-maximizing combination of inputs and outputs may be decomposed into two parts. First, a firm will minimize cost for a given level of output, and second, the firm will determine its profit-maximizing output.

To determine this profit-maximizing equilibrium, we will first consider how to produce a given level of output at the least possible cost. Minimizing cost for a given level of output is a necessary condition for profit maximization. If at the supposed profit-maximizing output level costs are not minimized, profits may be further increased by minimizing costs for this level of output. In this chapter, we assume that firms are facing fixed prices for their inputs and outputs. In subsequent chapters, this fixed-price assumption will be relaxed.

Our aim in this chapter is to develop the family of cost curves in both the short and long run, based on the technical relationships between outputs and factors of production. These cost curves incorporate the technology used for producing an output with given input prices. They present all the constraints in production in terms of dollars, so these costs only have to be compared with the output price for determining what profit-maximizing actions a firm should take.

We start this chapter by defining cost. Two general classifications of cost are in terms of who owns the input for which the cost is incurred and is the cost associated with a fixed or variable input. Once we define cost, we give alternative definitions for profits. We then derive the condition for determining the least-cost combination of inputs for a given level of output and illustrate this in an isoquant space. Based on this least-cost determination, we investigate the family of long-run cost curves in terms of returns to scale. We derive short-run cost curves by fixing one of the inputs, and establish the relationships between long-run and short-run cost curves. Then we discuss shifts in cost curves, resulting from a change in input prices, and development of new technologies.

Applied economists estimate cost functions for determining individual firms' supply functions and the shape of the average cost curves. The structure of an industry can be investigated by determining these shapes. For example, economists are interested if an individual firm's average cost curve is flat or declining over a wide range of output. If it is flat, then a number of firms can operate within this industry, each at the lowest level of average cost. In contrast, if average cost is declining over a wide range of output, then only one firm may operate within this industry at a low level of average cost.

How to classify costs and profits

Nothing is particularly hard if you divide it into small parts.

(Henry Ford)

To understand how firms determine their profit-maximizing outputs and inputs, it is useful to divide total cost and profit into a number of classes. These classes provide a structure for investigating how a firm's costs and profit vary with its output. Given this structure, we can determine the outputs and inputs that maximize profits.

Explicit and implicit costs

One of the major concerns of a medical professional (doctor, dentist, veterinarian) in a private practice is the cost if she becomes ill and is unable to work. These costs are not only the overhead costs that are incurred even if the office is closed, but also lost income from not working. In general, a firm's cost of production involves inputs that the firm purchases in the market, such as additional labor or additional capital equipment, plus inputs that the firm already owns, owner's labor, land, or equipment. The costs of employing additional inputs not owned by the firm are called **explicit** (or **expenditure**) **costs**. These include all cash or out-of-pocket expenses incurred in carrying out production. They are the accounting costs for purchased inputs, whether they are fixed or variable. **Implicit costs** (also called **nonexpenditure**, **imputed** or **entrepreneurial costs**) are costs charged to inputs that are owned by the firm.

There is an opportunity cost of using an input in the production of a commodity. This opportunity cost is the loss in benefits that could be obtained by using these inputs in another activity. For example, a building owned by a carpenter that is used for the production of cabinets could instead be rented out as a warehouse. The loss in benefits from not renting the building is the implicit or opportunity cost of the building. The owners of the firm also have an implicit cost associated with the time they devote to a particular production activity. For example, the opportunity cost of a full-time small-business owner is the wage he could have earned in another commercial activity. For example, he could work as a sales representative instead of running his own business. His lost salary as a sales representative is his implicit cost of production for the time he allocates to the business. The **total cost (TC)** of a particular production activity is the sum of explicit plus implicit costs.

What is the cost of your time in completing a college degree? The lost opportunity to gain work experience and income by working is the opportunity cost of completing a college degree.

Explicit (expenditure) costs. Costs of employing inputs not owned by the firm. *E.g., the salary of an employee.*

Implicit (nonexpenditure, imputed, entrepreneurial) costs. Costs charged to inputs owned by the firm. *E.g., the opportunity cost of the time an owner puts into her business.*

Total cost (TC). The sum of explicit and implicit costs. *E.g., the total cost of flying to Europe may be decomposed into the cost of the airfare plus the opportunity cost of the time spent flying.*

Fixed and variable costs

Costs can also be classified according to whether they are fixed or variable.[1] *Fixed costs* are associated with the fixed inputs in production. These are costs that do not vary with changes in output. *Variable costs* are costs associated with variable inputs and do vary with output. Explicit costs may contain both fixed and variable costs. For example, rent paid on the fixed input land is an explicit cost and also a fixed cost. Implicit cost may also contain both fixed and variable costs. For example, land that is owned and allocated to some production activity may be fixed. The owner's labor allocated to the firm may be variable. Thus, **total cost (TC)** is also the sum of both fixed and variable costs. Figure 8.1 illustrates how total cost may be decomposed either in terms of explicit and implicit costs or in terms of fixed and variable costs. Note that in the long run, all inputs are variable, so there are no long-run fixed costs.

Do you pay both a fixed and variable rate for your monthly cellphone service? Generally, yes—this is an example of what is called a two-part tariff (discussed in Chapter 13).

Total cost (TC). The sum of fixed and variable costs. *E.g., on a flight to Europe, the cost of the ticket and opportunity cost of flying are fixed costs, but purchasing any drinks is a variable cost.*

Profits

If you have a sound idea, you can generally find someone willing to back you financially, so money is not an obstacle to making a profit. The obstacle is coming up with the idea and having the energy and enthusiasm to run with it. To determine how to maximize profit with

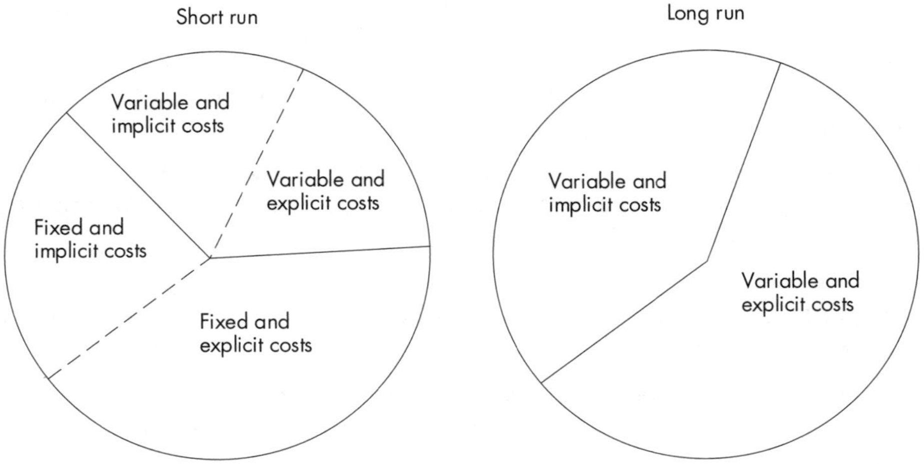

Figure 8.1 **The makeup of total cost in the short and long run.** A circle representing total cost can be formed by summing explicit and implicit costs or summing fixed and variable costs.

some idea, we define profit as either normal or pure. **Normal profit** (also called **necessary**, **ordinary** or **opportunity-cost profit**) is the minimum total return to the inputs necessary to keep a firm in a given production activity.[2] Normal profit equals implicit cost. For example, if implicit cost is the labor the owner of a firm puts into a production activity, this implicit cost is the return necessary to keep the owner from using her labor in another activity. In the long run, if profit is less than implicit cost, the firm may take the inputs it owns and is currently using in this production activity and reallocate them into another activity.

Normal (necessary, ordinary, opportunity-cost) profit. The minimum total return to the inputs necessary to keep a firm in a given production activity. *E.g., if a lawyer could receive a $100,000 salary by working for a law firm, his normal profit from operating his own law firm would be $100,000.*

Pure profit (also called **economic profit**) is defined as total return above total cost. This is in contrast to *business profit*, which does not consider implicit costs so it is just total return minus explicit costs. As discussed in Chapter 9, in the short run, the possibility of earning a pure profit exists but firms will only earn a normal profit in the long run. In the long run, firms have the ability to enter or exit an industry and thus will not operate at a loss or earn a pure profit.

Pure (economic) profit (π). Total revenue minus total cost. *E.g., if a firm earns $500,000 in total revenue and has associated total cost of $450,000, then its pure profit will be $50,000.*

Table 8.1 illustrates the determination of pure profit. Summing all the costs yields a total cost of \$1.3 million. If total revenue is 1 million, then the firm is losing \$300,000. It is operating at a loss, with a negative pure profit of \$300,000. At a revenue level of \$1.3 million, the firm's pure profit is zero. Total revenue just covers the firm's total cost, so the firm is earning a normal profit. A positive pure profit would exist if total revenue could exceed total cost. For example, at \$1.5 million in total revenue, the firm earns a pure profit of \$200,000. That is, it is earning \$200,000 above the minimum total return to the inputs necessary to keep the firm in this production activity.

Table 8.1. A firm's pure profit

Cost			
Fixed			
Explicit	\$100,000		
Implicit	400,000		
Variable			
Explicit	750,000		
Implicit	50,000		
Total cost (TC)	\$1,300,000		
		Pure profit	
Total revenue	\$1,000,000	−\$300,000	
	1,300,000	0	(Normal profit = \$450,000)
	1,500,000	200,000	

Determining the cost-minimizing input choice

A standard argument education opponents use for voting against a property tax proposal for school improvements is that educators are currently spending more than is necessary for providing a quality education. By reallocating resources, they say the cost of schools can be reduced without compromising on quality education. They are generally advocating that schools should first minimize cost for a given level of quality education before requesting any additional financing. We can investigate this cost-minimizing approach for a given level of output (quality education) under two assumptions: there are only two inputs in production (labor and capital), and perfectly competitive input markets exist. As discussed in Chapter 16, perfectly competitive input markets imply that the firm takes input prices as fixed. The supply curves that the firm then faces for these inputs are horizontal (perfectly elastic).

Long-run costs

Isocost

Within the relevant region of the isoquant map, we determine the least-cost combination of inputs for a given level of output by considering the cost of variable inputs. This cost can be represented by **isocost curves**, which are analogous to budget lines in consumer theory. Recall that *iso* means equal, so isocost signifies equal cost. The associated *isocost equation* is represented as

$$\mathrm{TC} = wL + vK,$$

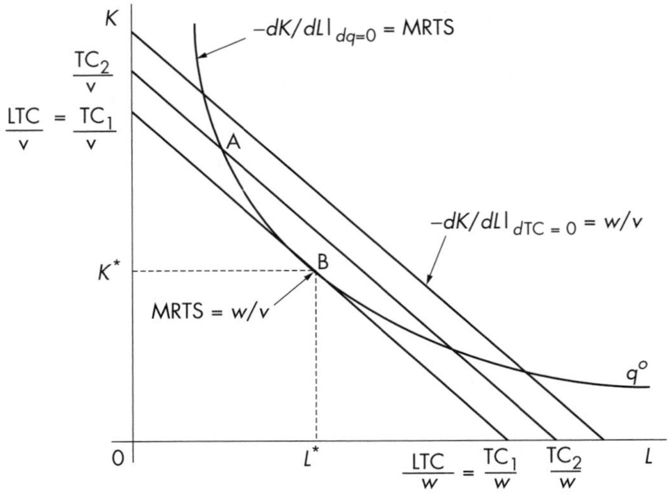

Figure 8.2 **Minimizing cost of a given level of output.** For a given level of output q^o, TC is minimized at point B. At point B, the least-cost combination of inputs is (L^*, K^*) for an output level q^o.

where w is the wage rate of labor and v is the per-unit input price of capital (rent). For a movement along an isocost curve, the firm's cost of production remains fixed.

Isocost curve. A locus of points where the total cost is the same for alternative input combinations. *E.g., the total cost for digging ditches may be the same using 3 backhoes and 6 workers versus 1 backhoe and 25 workers.*

Solving the isocost equation for K,

$$K = -\frac{w}{v}L + \frac{\mathrm{TC}}{v},$$

results in a linear equation with TC/v as the capital (K) intercept and $-w/r$ as the slope. The linear isocost curve associated with this isocost equation is illustrated in Figure 8.2. For a given fixed amount of TC, the intercept TC/v is the amount of capital K that can be purchased if no labor L is purchased. The intercept for labor, TC/w, is the amount of labor that can be hired if no capital is purchased. The slope, $\partial K/\partial L\,|_{dTC=0} = -w/v$ (negative of wages divided by rents) indicates the market rate at which labor can be purchased in place of capital, holding TC constant. This ratio of input prices is called the *economic rate of substitution*. An increase in TC causes a parallel upward shift in the isocost curve, as illustrated in Figure 8.2 for an increase from TC_1 to TC_2.

Example 8.1 Deriving isocost lines

Given $TC_1 = \$10$ with $v = \$2$ and $w = \$5$, the slope of the isocost curve is $dK/dL|_{dTC=0} = -5/2$, with a capital intercept of 5 units and a labor intercept of 2 units. The isocost equation is then

$$TC_1 = 10 = 5L + 2K,$$

or, solving for K,

$$K = -\frac{5}{2}L + \frac{10}{2}.$$

Doubling TC from \$10 to \$20, TC_2, results in the isocost curve shifting upward, with a new capital intercept of 10 units and a labor intercept of 4 units. However, the slope of the isocost curve remains unchanged.

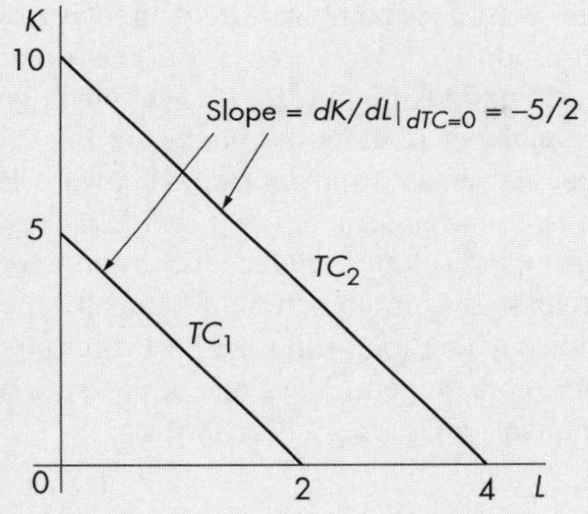

Least-cost combination of inputs

Hiring a boy to do a man's job.

(old adage)

Translation: Price per marginal product for hiring a boy is less than the price per marginal product for hiring a man.

A landscape company is under contract to build a retaining wall for preventing soil erosion from a hill. The firm has the choice of hiring many workers with limited heavy equipment to dig the foundation for this wall or instead hiring fewer workers with more heavy equipment for the same job. Specifically, the profit-maximizing firm is interested in finding the lowest TC for a given level of output, q^o (called **allocative efficiency**). In the long run, this lowest TC is called **long-run total cost (LTC)**:

$$\text{LTC} = \min(wL + vK), \quad \text{s.t. } q^o = f(K, L),$$

where $wL + vK$ is the isocost equation representing the total cost of inputs. A profit-maximizing firm is interested in minimizing this TC, subject to a given level of output. This results in the determination of the least-cost combination of inputs for each possible level of output. The firm can then maximize profits by selecting its optimal level of output.

Allocative efficiency. Employing the least-cost combination of inputs for a given level of output. *E.g., Japanese automobile manufacturers establishing US assembly plants to minimize cost for a given production level.*

Long-run total cost (LTC). Total cost when all inputs are variable. *E.g., the total cost of a bicycle firm opening a store in a college town.*

This cost-minimizing combination of inputs is also illustrated in Figure 8.2. The isoquant represents the given level of output, q^{o}. The objective of the firm is to shift to a lower isocost curve, and thus reduce costs, until the least-cost combination of inputs is obtained for output q^{o}. At a level of TC_2, point A will produce q^{o}. However, a reallocation of inputs along the isoquant can result in a lower TC combination of inputs for q^{o}. Moving down along the isoquant toward point B, output remains unchanged and input prices are fixed, but TC declines. The firm is shifting to lower isocost curves as it moves from A toward B. Also, the input combination is changing. The firm is employing more labor and less capital as it moves from A toward B. At point B, the firm can no longer reduce TC by moving along the isoquant. Thus, point B is the equilibrium least-cost combination of inputs for the output represented by the isoquant q^{o}. This is the point where long-run total costs are minimized, LTC. At point B, the isocost and isoquant curves are tangent. The slope of the isocost curve, $\partial K/\partial L\,|_{dLTC=0}$, is equal to the slope of the isoquant, $\partial K/\partial L\,|_{dq=0}$. Recall that

$$\text{MRTS}(K \text{ for } L) = \frac{\text{MP}_L}{\text{MP}_K} = -\frac{\partial K}{\partial L}\Big|_{dq=0},$$

that is, the marginal rate of technical substitution is equal to the negative of the slope of the isoquant. Thus, at the tangency,

$$\frac{\partial K}{\partial L}\Big|_{d\text{LTC}=0} = \frac{\partial K}{\partial L}\Big|_{dq=0},$$

$$\frac{w}{v} = \frac{\text{MP}_L}{\text{MP}_K} = \text{MRTS}.$$

MRTS equals the input price ratio (the economic rate of substitution). Rearranging terms by dividing through by MP_L and multiplying by v,

$$\frac{w}{\text{MP}_L} = \frac{v}{\text{MP}_K}.$$

At the least-cost combination of inputs, the price per marginal product of each input must be equivalent. Thus, when deciding on the amount of inputs to hire, a firm will attempt to equate the price per marginal product for all of the inputs it purchases. Then the price of an input per additional increase in output is the same for all inputs. Only at point B in Figure 8.2 does this least-cost condition hold. For example, at point A,

$$\frac{w}{v} < \frac{\mathrm{MP}_L}{\mathrm{MP}_K},$$

$$\frac{w}{\mathrm{MP}_L} < \frac{v}{\mathrm{MP}_K}.$$

At A, the cost per marginal product is lower for labor than for capital, so TC may be lowered by substituting labor for capital and moving down along the isoquant to B. At B, L^* units of land and K^* units of capital represent the least-cost combination of inputs for a given level of output. In our example, the landscape firm will arrive at the least-cost combination of labor and heavy equipment by attempting to equate the wage rate per additional output from hiring labor to the rental cost per additional output of renting heavy equipment.

How do you produce a low-cost pizza? Equate the ingredient price per additional increase in taste across all the ingredients, which generally results in using a lot of onions.

Example 8.2 Determining the least-cost combination of inputs

Consider the following cost-minimization problem:

$$\mathrm{LTC} = \min(wL + vK), \ \text{s.t. } q^{\mathrm{o}} = LK,$$

where $wL + vK$ is TC and $q^{\mathrm{o}} = LK$ is the production function representing the technology constraint. The Lagrangian is then

$$\mathcal{L}(L, K, \lambda) = wL + vK + \lambda(q^{\mathrm{o}} - KL).$$

The first-order conditions (FOCs) are

$$\frac{\partial \mathcal{L}}{\partial L} = w - \lambda^* K^* = 0,$$

$$\frac{\partial \mathcal{L}}{\partial K} = v - \lambda^* L^* = 0,$$

$$\frac{\partial \mathcal{L}}{\partial \lambda} = q^{\mathrm{o}} - K^* L^* = 0.$$

Rearranging terms and taking the ratio of the first two FOCs yields

$$\frac{w}{v} = \frac{K^*}{L^*} = \frac{\partial f/\partial L}{\partial f/\partial K} = \frac{\mathrm{MP}_L}{\mathrm{MP}_K} = \mathrm{MRTS}(K \text{ for } L).$$

This is the equation for the expansion path, the locus of points where the isoquant and isocost lines are tangent. Solving for K^*, the expansion-path equation is represented as

$$K^* = \frac{w}{v} L^*.$$

Substituting this expansion-path equation into the constraint and solving for L^* yields

$$q^o - L^*K^* = q^o - L^*\frac{w}{v}L^*$$
$$= q^o - L^{*2}\frac{w}{v} = 0,$$
$$L^{*2} = \frac{q^o v}{w},$$
$$L^* = \left(\frac{q^o v}{w}\right)^{1/2},$$

where L^* denotes the least-cost employment of labor for a given level of output and input prices. This equation is called the *conditional factor demand function* for labor. It is conditional on the given level of output.

Substituting this conditional labor demand function into the expansion-path equation yields the conditional factor demand equation for capital:

$$K^* = \frac{w}{v}L^* = \frac{w}{v}\left(\frac{q^o v}{w}\right)^{1/2} = \left(\frac{q^o w}{v}\right)^{1/2}.$$

Letting $w = \$16$, $v = \$9$, and $q = 144$, the least-cost combination of inputs is

$$L^* = \left(\frac{q^o v}{w}\right)^{1/2} = 9, \quad K^* = \left(\frac{q^o w}{v}\right)^{1/2} = 16.$$

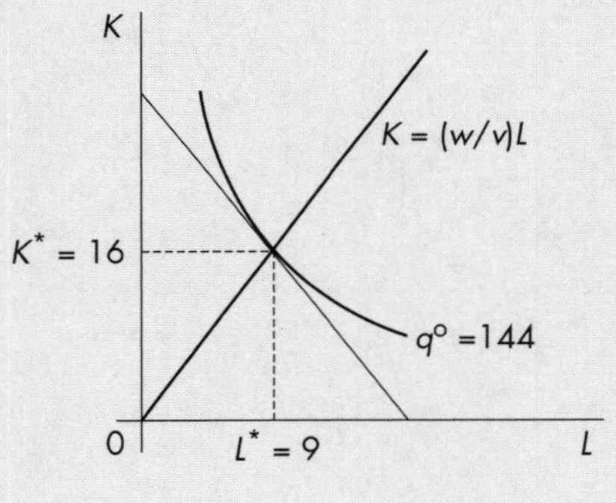

Mathematically, the long-run problem of choosing K and L to minimize cost for a given level of output, q^o, is

$$\text{LTC} = \min_{L,K}(wL + vK) \quad \text{s.t. } q^o = f(K, L).$$

The Lagrangian is

$$\mathcal{L}(L, K, \lambda) = wL + vk + \lambda[q^o - f(K, L)].$$

The FOCs are then

$$\frac{\partial \mathcal{L}}{\partial L} = w - \lambda^* \frac{\partial f}{\partial L} = 0,$$

$$\frac{\partial \mathcal{L}}{\partial K} = v - \lambda^* \frac{\partial f}{\partial K} = 0,$$

$$\frac{\partial \mathcal{L}}{\partial \lambda} = q^{o} - f(K^*, L^*) = 0.$$

Rearranging terms and taking the ratio of the first two FOCs yields

$$\frac{w}{v} = \frac{\partial f/\partial L}{\partial f/\partial K} = \frac{\mathrm{MP}_L}{\mathrm{MP}_K} = \mathrm{MRTS}(K \text{ for } L).$$

Thus, the FOCs yield the same condition for the least-cost combination of inputs, illustrated by point B in Figure 8.2.

Solving for λ^* in the first two FOCs results in

$$\lambda^* = \frac{w}{\mathrm{MP}_L} = \frac{v}{\mathrm{MP}_K}.$$

At the least-cost combination of inputs, λ^* is equal to the additional cost associated with an additional unit increase in output [called the **long-run marginal cost (LMC)**]. The Lagrange multiplier λ^* represents the change in the objective function (LTC) brought about by a relaxation of the constraint ($q = q^{o}$). Thus, $\lambda^* = \mathrm{LMC}$. LMC is the extra long-run cost of producing one more unit of output. The FOCs associated with the Lagrange multiplier state that the additional cost of producing one more unit of output is the same whether it is produced using more capital or more labor.

Long-run marginal cost (LMC). The additional cost associated with an additional unit increase in output when all inputs are variable. *E.g., when a new division within a firm is just starting, the additional cost from increasing its output is long-run marginal cost.*

Application: Labor unionization and cost of production

As discussed by Eberts and Stone, two paradoxes exist in determining the effect of unions on the cost of production. First, productivity increases attributed to unions almost completely offset cost increases from union compensations (union wages). This indicates that the total effect of unionization is small for cost of production but large for labor's influence on output. The paradox is that if unions do have a substantial impact on labor productivity, then they should reduce employment far more than is generally observed. The second paradox involves the work restrictions, including restrictions on firing and number of workers employed, popular in union contracts. Despite complaints by firms that these restrictive employment rules reduce productivity, there is little supporting evidence. In contrast, the overall effect of unions on productivity is generally positive; however, firms complain about these restrictions.

Eberts and Stone offer an explanation of these two paradoxes by identifying three components of a union's effect on cost of production. First is the difference in compensation between union and nonunion workers. Union workers generally command higher wages. The second and third components are the change in technical and allocative efficiency from unionization. Improvements in technical efficiency following unionization may result from improved cooperation between management and workers, reductions in turnover, and a general increase in worker morale. However, unionization is allocative-inefficient. A union restricting a firm's ability to select its preferred employment level results in the firm being unable to operate at the least-cost combination of inputs. Thus, unionization affects cost through changes in allocative efficiency as well as through changes in compensation and production technology.

By considering this allocation effect from unionization, both the paradoxes can be explained. For unions to avoid increasing a firm's costs, it is not enough for the productivity effect to offset the compensation effect. This increase in technical efficiency must also offset the loss in allocation efficiency. Thus, this loss in allocative efficiency is an additional cost of unionization, which explains why firms' cost from unionization may not be small and why firms complain about restrictive union employment rules.

Source: R.W. Eberts and J.A. Stone, "Unionization and Cost of Production: Compensation, Productivity, and Factor-Use Effect," *Journal of Labor Economics* 9 (1991): 171–185.

Expansion path

The locus of points where the isoquant curve and isocost line are tangent is called the *expansion path*.[3] The general form of the expansion path for a cost-minimization problem is illustrated in Figure 8.3, where some level of output can still be produced with zero capital. Generally, an expansion path has a positive slope. An increase in LTC, required for producing a higher level of output, results in both inputs increasing.

Long-run total cost (LTC)

Given the expansion path in Figure 8.3, we can construct the LTC curve by plotting output levels with the corresponding minimal level of long-run cost (Figure 8.4). LTC provides the lowest cost necessary for obtaining a given level of output. Every point on the LTC curve corresponds to a tangency between an isoquant and an isocost line (Figure 8.3). The slope of the LTC curve is LMC, defined as

$$\text{LMC} = \frac{\partial \text{LTC}}{\partial q}.$$

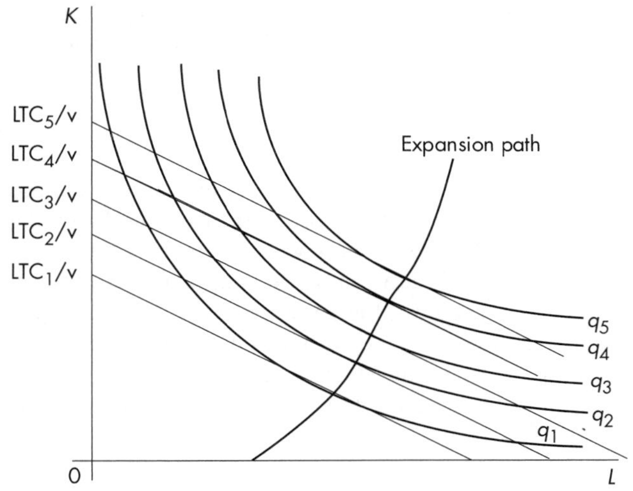

Figure 8.3 **Expansion path.** The locus of points where the isoquant curve and isocost line are tangent represents the minimum long-run cost for obtaining a given level of output.

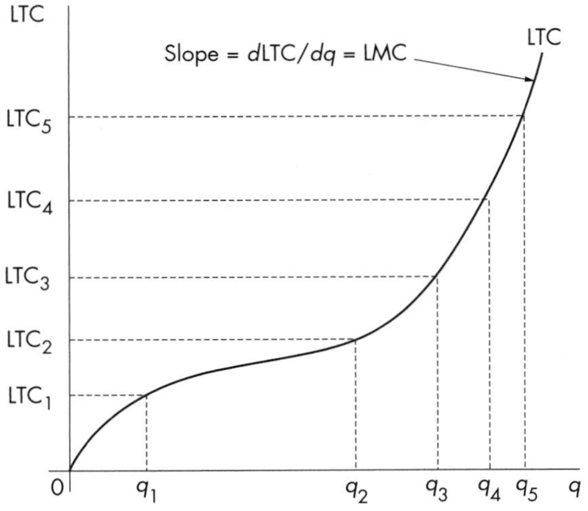

Figure 8.4 **Long-run total cost curve.** The minimum level of long-run cost for given levels of output is represented by the long-run total cost curve.

Also, associated with LTC is **long-run average cost (LAC)**, defined as

$$\mathrm{LAC} = \frac{\mathrm{LTC}}{q}.$$

Long-run average cost (LAC). Long-run total cost divided by output. *E.g., your average cost of electricity usage is your electricity bill divided by the number of kilowatt hours you use.*

Recall from Chapter 7 that average product (AP) of a variable input, for some level of the input, corresponds to the slope of a chord from the origin intersecting the production function at that input level. Similarly, LAC, for some level of output, is the slope of a chord through the origin intersecting the LTC curve at that output level. As illustrated in Figure 8.5, at first as output increases, the chord is tilting downward (the slope is declining), which corresponds to LAC declining. At the tangency of the chord and LTC, LAC is at a minimum, $q = 3$. To the right of the tangency, the chord is tilting upward as q increases, corresponding to LAC increasing. Specifically, we derived the LTC curve in Figure 8.5 given that

$$\text{LTC} = \tfrac{1}{3}q^3 - 2q^2 + 10q.$$

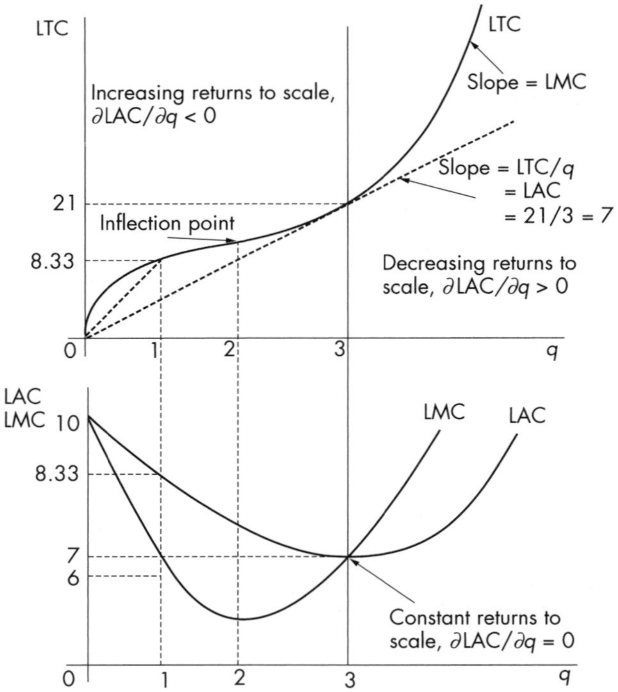

Figure 8.5 **Long-run cost curves.** Increasing returns to scale are associated with LAC declining as output increases. Constant returns to scale occur where the LAC curve is neither declining nor increasing, so LMC = LAC. Decreasing returns to scale are associated with LAC also increasing as output increases.

LMC and LAC are then

$$\text{LMC} = \frac{\partial \text{LTC}}{\partial q} = q^2 - 4q + 10,$$

$$\text{LAC} = \frac{\text{LTC}}{q} = \tfrac{1}{3}q^2 - 2q + 10.$$

The minimum points of LMC and LAC are

$$\frac{\partial \text{LMC}}{\partial q} = 2q - 4 = 0 \Rightarrow q = 2,$$

$$\frac{\partial^2 \text{LMC}}{\partial q^2} = 2 > 0, \quad \text{minimum},$$

$$\frac{\partial \text{LAC}}{\partial q} = \tfrac{2}{3}q - 2 = 0 \Rightarrow q = 3,$$

$$\frac{\partial^2 \text{LAC}}{\partial q^2} = \tfrac{2}{3} > 0, \quad \text{minimum}.$$

This U-shaped characteristic of LAC is due to returns to scale.

Example 8.3 Deriving the LTC curve

Given the conditional factor demand functions in Example 8.2, LTC associated with these least-cost combinations of inputs is

$$\text{LTC} = wL^* + vK^* = w\left(\frac{q^o v}{w}\right)^{1/2} + v\left(\frac{q^o w}{v}\right)^{1/2} = 2(q^o vw)^{1/2}.$$

This represents the minimum long-run cost for producing an output with given prices for the inputs.

As in Example 8.2, letting $w = \$16$, $v = \$9$, and $q = 144$ gives LTC = \$288. Then,

$$\text{LMC} = \partial LTC/\partial q = \lambda^* = (vw/q)^{1/2} = \$1.$$

From Example 8.2, the first two equations in the FOCs yield

$$\lambda^* = w/K^* = v/L^* = \$1.$$

Then,

$$\text{LAC} = \text{LTC}/q = 2(vw/q)^{1/2} = \$2.$$

Also, the LTC curve is concave, given that

$$\partial\text{LMC}/\partial q = -\tfrac{1}{2}(vw)^{1/2}q^{-3/2} < 0.$$

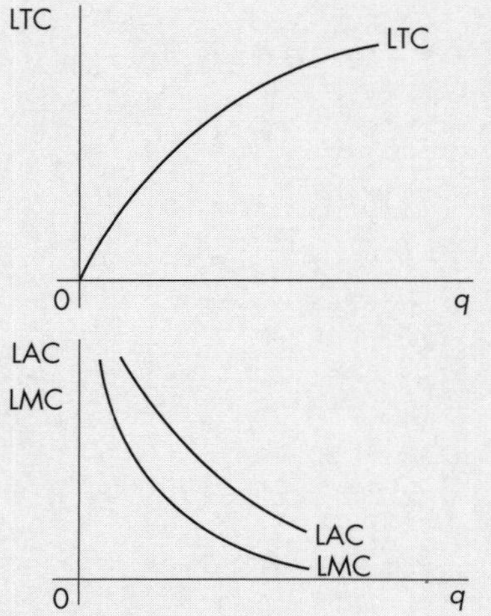

Returns to scale

The concept of returns to scale, developed in Chapter 7, can be directly related to the long-run cost curves. A cost curve may exhibit increasing, decreasing, and/or constant returns to scale. As illustrated in Figure 8.5, increasing returns to scale (also called *economies of scale*) occurs where LAC is declining, $\partial \mathrm{LAC}/\partial q < 0$. Increases in total cost are proportionally smaller than an increase in output. This also corresponds to the concave area of the LTC curve. For example, in this area of increasing returns to scale, a doubling of output results in less than a doubling of LTC. Increasing returns to scale implies that inputs less than double for a doubling of output, which corresponds to LTC also less than doubling for a doubling of output.

Similarly, as illustrated in Figure 8.5, decreasing returns to scale (also called *diseconomies of scale*) occurs where LAC is increasing, $\partial \mathrm{LAC}/\partial q > 0$. Increases in total cost are proportionally larger than an increase in output. This also corresponds to the convex area of the LTC curve. For example, in this area of decreasing returns to scale, a doubling of output results in more than a doubling of LTC. Decreasing returns to scale implies that inputs more than double for a doubling of output, which corresponds to LTC also more than doubling for a doubling of output.

Constant returns to scale (also called *constant economies of scale*) corresponds to $\partial \mathrm{LAC}/\partial q = 0$. Long-run average cost does not change for a given change in output. In Figure 8.5, this corresponds to the minimum point of LAC. If the LTC curve is linear, then constant returns to scale occurs for all levels of output, $\partial \mathrm{LAC}/\partial q = 0$. Such a linear LTC is illustrated in Figure 8.6. The $\partial \mathrm{LAC}/\partial q = 0$, indicating constant returns to scale. For example, a doubling of output results in a doubling of LTC. If $\mathrm{LTC} = 10q$, representing constant returns to scale, then $\mathrm{LMC} = \mathrm{LAC} = 10$. This results in $\partial \mathrm{LMC}/\partial q = \partial \mathrm{LAC}/\partial q = 0$.

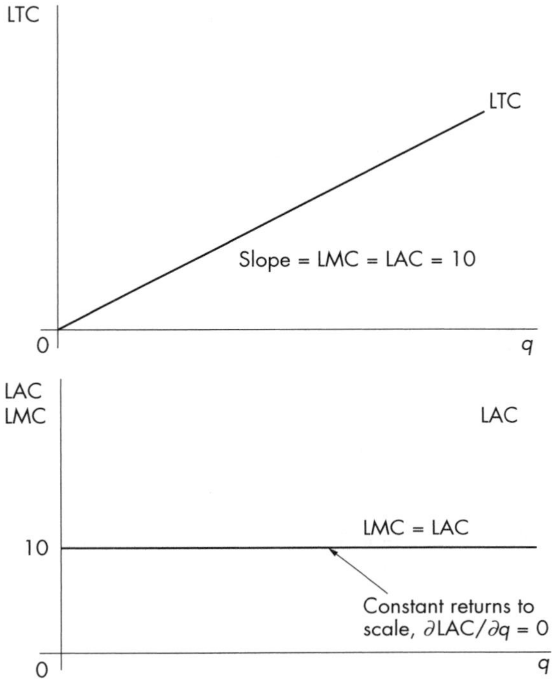

Figure 8.6 **A linear long-run total cost curve representing constant returns to scale.** A linear long-run total cost curve results from constant long-run average cost across all output levels. Long-run marginal cost is then also constant and equal to long-run average costs.

Is bigger better? Bigger is better up to the point of constant returns to scale.

Application: Economies of scale in electricity production

R. Rhine estimates a translog cost function for US electricity production. The objective of his analysis is to determine the economies of scale for utilities within this industry using fossil and nuclear fuels for power generation. Results presented in Figure 8.7 indicate that the long-run average cost curves for both fuels are relatively flat (constant returns to scale). Note that the output and average cost for nuclear fuel generation is higher than for fossil fuel generation. A tradeoff exists in lower average cost of fossil generation and associated increased CO_2 emissions.

Source: R. Rhine, "Economies of Scale and Optimal Capital in Nuclear and Fossil Fuel Electricity Production," *Atlantic Economic Journal* 29 (2001): 203–214.

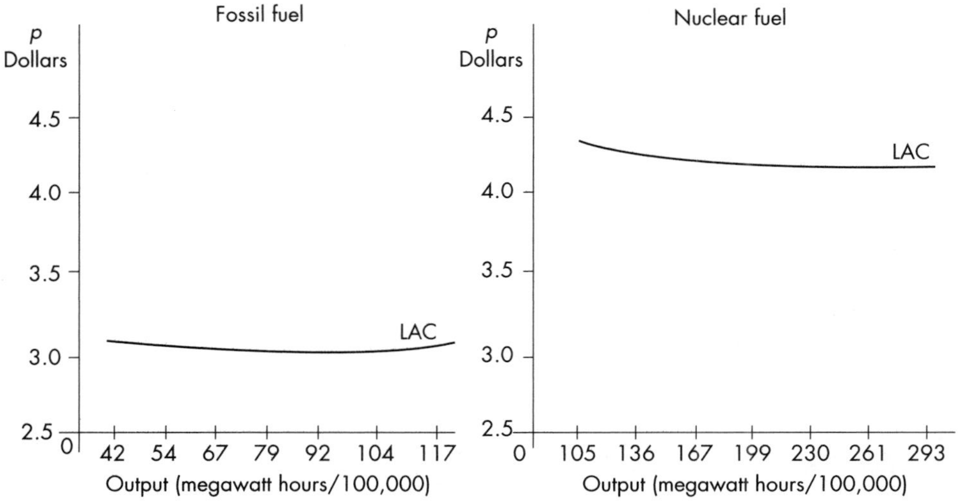

Figure 8.7 **Economies of scale in electricity production.** The LAC curves for both fossil and nuclear fuel power generation are relatively flat, indicating a constant returns to scale production technology.

Average and marginal cost relationship

Average cost is depressed whenever it meets marginal cost.

(Michael Wetzstein)

Translation: Marginal cost equals average cost at average cost's minimum point.

Sometimes, the entrance fee to an amusement park includes the cost for riding any ride. Thus, the marginal cost is zero and the average cost declines as you ride more rides. This illustrates how the relationship between average and marginal units also applies to average and marginal costs. As discussed in Chapter 7 and the Mathematical Review, when a marginal unit is below the average, the average is falling. In Figure 8.5, at first LMC < LAC, so the average is falling. If an average unit is neither rising nor falling, the marginal unit is equal to it (Figure 8.6). Also, in Figure 8.5, at the minimum point of LAC, LMC = LAC. LMC crosses LAC at the minimum point of LAC. Specifically, we can determine the relation between LAC and LMC given that

$$\text{LAC} = \text{LTC}/q = (LTC)q^{-1}.$$

Taking the derivative of LAC with respect to q gives

$$\frac{\partial \text{LAC}}{\partial q} = \frac{q(\partial \text{LTC}/\partial q) - \text{LTC}}{q^2}.$$

Noting that LMC $= \partial \text{LTC}/\partial q$ and rearranging terms,

$$\text{LMC} = \text{LAC} + \frac{\partial \text{LAC}}{\partial q} q.$$

For the LTC illustrated in Figure 8.5,

$$\begin{aligned}\text{LMC} &= (\tfrac{1}{3}q^2 - 2q + 10) + (\tfrac{2}{3}q - 2)q, \\ &= q^2 - 4q + 10.\end{aligned}$$

This is a general relation between marginals and averages. Note that marginal cost is not the cost of producing the last unit of output—the cost of producing the last unit of output is the same as that of producing all the other units of output, which is the average cost of production. Marginal cost is the increase in cost of producing an extra increment of output. Therefore, marginal cost is equal to average cost plus an adjustment factor. The adjustment factor is the additional cost to all factors of production caused by the increase in output. Thus, marginal cost differs from average cost by the per-unit effect on costs of higher output, multiplied by total output. This is the reason marginal quantities are often more useful. If LAC does not vary with output, so that $\partial \text{LAC}/\partial q = 0$, then this adjustment factor is zero. As illustrated in Figure 8.6, LMC is then equal to LAC. If, instead, increasing returns to scale occurs, $\partial \text{LAC}/\partial q < 0$, then LMC $<$ LAC. And if decreasing returns to scale occurs, $\partial \text{LAC}/\partial q > 0$, then LMC $>$ LAC (Figure 8.5).

Is an additional driver's cost of road congestion the same as all the other current drivers? Yes, all of the drivers' additional cost of road congestion, including the additional driver, is the same.

Example 8.4 Illustrating the relationship between marginal and average costs

As an example of the distinction between average and marginal costs, consider the case of road congestion. If a road is not congested, when an additional auto enters there is no effect on the travel time of the other cars already on the road. If the average travel time is 1 hour, then for this clear roadway the marginal time will also be 1 hour. However, assume 100 cars and the addition of another car results in congestion that slows all the other cars by 1 minute. The average travel time is now 61 minutes and the marginal time of travel is the additional car's average travel time, 61 minutes, plus the 1 extra minute imposed on the 100 cars. As indicated by .

$$\text{LMC} = \text{LAC} + \frac{\partial \text{LAC}}{\partial q} q,$$

the marginal travel time is then

$$61 + (1)100 = 161 \text{ minutes}.$$

Short-run costs

Total costs

Upon signing a 5-year lease for their restaurant, the owners of the restaurant have committed themselves to paying a fixed amount in costs regardless of whether they operate or not. This results in a short-run situation where, for short-run profit maximization, the owners will determine the lowest TC for a given level of output and the fixed input (the restaurant). In the short run, this lowest TC is called the **short-run total cost (STC)**. STC, including both explicit and implicit costs, is defined as **short-run total variable cost (STVC)** plus **total fixed cost (TFC)**. Assuming that capital is fixed at K^o (the size of the restaurant) in the short run,

$$\begin{aligned} \mathrm{STC}(K^o) &= \mathrm{STVC}(K^o) + \mathrm{TFC}(K^o), \\ &= \min(wL + vK^o), \end{aligned}$$

subject to a given level of output and where $wL + vK^o$, representing the total cost of the inputs, is the isocost equation. Thus, $\mathrm{STVC}(K^o) = wL^*$ and $\mathrm{TFC}(K^o) = vK^o$, where L^* denotes the level of labor that minimizes costs for a given level of output. TFC represents the explicit and implicit costs that do not vary with output. Even if the firm were to produce nothing, in the short run it must still pay TFC (the rent for the restaurant). As indicated in Figure 8.8, TFC is a horizontal line, showing that, at all output levels, TFC remains the same. STVC represents the explicit and implicit costs that vary directly with output.

> **Short-run total cost (STC).** Short-run total variable cost plus total fixed cost. *E.g., the total cost of operating a bicycle shop given a fixed cost of rent and a variable cost of the total wage bill.*
>
> **Short-run total variable cost (STVC).** Total cost associated with the variable inputs. *E.g., the wage bill.*
>
> **Total fixed cost (TFC).** The total cost for employing the fixed inputs in production. *E.g., the rent paid on a warehouse for storing bicycles.*

In Figure 8.8, STVC at first increases at a decreasing rate and then increases at an increasing rate. As we will demonstrate, this is due to the Law of Diminishing Marginal Returns. STC is the sum of STVC and TFC. From Figure 8.8, the vertical sum of STVC and TFC equals STC. STC and STVC have the same slope at every level of output. STC is higher than STVC by the constant level of TFC across all levels of output. These are referred to as vertically parallel curves. For example, the inflection points of STC and STVC occur at the same output level. Another characteristic of STC and STVC is that they always increase with an increase in output, given that additions to inputs increase output. Only the rate of increase in STC and STVC changes, due to the Law of Diminishing Marginal Returns. We derived the STC, STVC, and TFC curves given

$$\mathrm{STC}(K^o) = \tfrac{2}{3}q^3 - 2q^2 + 6q + \tfrac{8}{3},$$

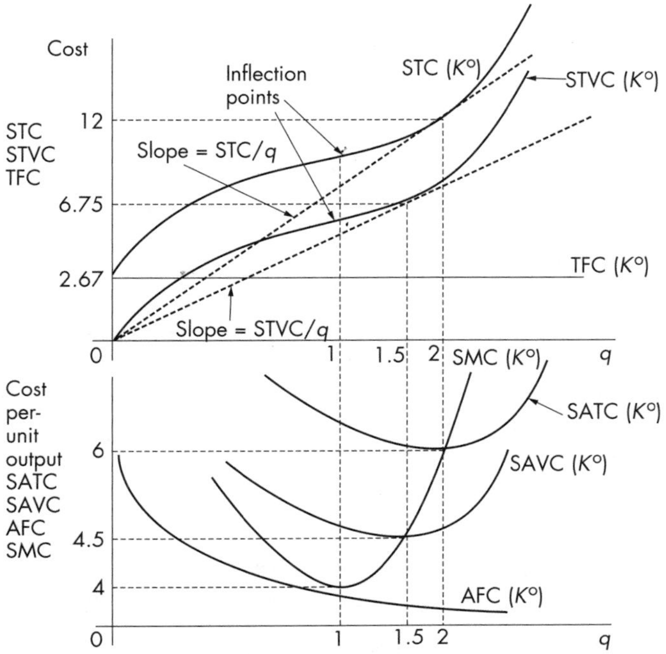

Figure 8.8 **Short-run cost curves.** Short-run total cost is the sum of short-run total variable cost and total fixed cost. Dividing these costs by output results in short-run average total cost equaling short-run average variable cost plus average fixed costs. Short-run marginal cost is the slope of the short-run total cost curve as well as the slope of the short-run total variable cost curve. The short-run average cost curves and the marginal cost curve are U-shaped due to the Law of Diminishing Marginal Returns.

where

$$\text{STVC}(K^{\circ}) = \tfrac{2}{3}q^3 - 2q^2 + 6q \quad \text{and} \quad \text{TFC}(K^{\circ}) = \tfrac{8}{3}.$$

Average costs

Think of parents as being the totals and their offspring the averages and the marginal. This illustrates how short-run costs can be further classified as **short-run average total cost (SATC)**, **short-run average variable cost (SAVC)** and **average fixed cost (AFC)**. We derive all of these average costs by dividing the short-run total cost by output. Specifically, for a fixed level of capital K°,

$$\text{SATC}(K^{\circ}) = \frac{\text{STC}(K^{\circ})}{q} = \text{SAVC}(K^{\circ}) + \text{AFC}(K^{\circ}),$$

where

$$\text{SAVC}(K^{\circ}) = \frac{\text{STVC}(K^{\circ})}{q} \quad \text{and} \quad \text{AFC}(K^{\circ}) = \frac{\text{TFC}(K^{\circ})}{q}.$$

For the cost curves in Figure 8.8,

$$\text{SAVC}(K^o) = \tfrac{2}{3}q^2 - 2q + 6 \quad \text{and} \quad \text{AFC}(K^o) = \frac{\frac{8}{3}}{q},$$

This yields

$$\text{SATC}(K^o) = \tfrac{2}{3}q^2 - 2q + 6 + \frac{\frac{8}{3}}{q}.$$

AFC is continually declining as output increases. However, it is always a positive number, given that TFC is positive and q is nonnegative. As output tends toward zero, AFC approaches infinity, and as output approaches infinity, AFC tends toward zero. Because AFC is always positive but declines as output increases, SATC and SAVC never intersect, but approach each other as output increases.

Short-run average total cost (SATC). Short-run total cost divided by output. *E.g., the total expenses for operating a bicycle stop divided by the number of bicycles sold.*

Short-run average variable cost (SAVC). Short-run total variable cost divided by output. *E.g., the wage bill divided by the number of bicycles sold.*

Average fixed cost (AFC). Total fixed cost divided by output. *E.g., the fixed rent paid on a warehouse for storing bicycles divided by the number of bicycles sold.*

Recall that LAC, for some level of output, corresponds to the slope of a chord from the origin intersecting the LTC curve at that output level. Similarly, SAVC, for some level of output, is the slope of a chord through the origin intersecting the STVC curve at that output level. At first, as output increases, the chord is tilting downward, so the slope is declining, which corresponds to SAVC declining (Figure 8.8). At the tangency of the chord and STVC, SAVC is at a minimum, $q = 1.5$. To the right of the tangency, the chord is tilting upward as output increases, which corresponds to SAVC increasing. As illustrated in Figure 8.8, the U-shaped characteristic of SAVC is due to the Law of Diminishing Marginal Returns.

SATC is the sum of SAVC and AFC. Similar to SAVC, the slope of a chord through the origin intersecting STC is SATC at the output level of the intersection. SATC is also U-shaped due to the Law of Diminishing Marginal Returns and reaches a minimum at the tangency of a chord through the origin and STC, $q = 2$ (Figure 8.8).

For the cost curves in Figure 8.8,

$$\frac{\partial \text{SAVC}}{\partial q} = \tfrac{4}{3}q - 2 = 0 \Rightarrow q = \tfrac{3}{2},$$

$$\frac{\partial^2 \text{SAVC}}{\partial q^2} = \tfrac{4}{3} > 0, \quad \text{minimum},$$

$$\frac{\partial \text{SATC}}{\partial q} = \tfrac{4}{3}q - 2 - \frac{\frac{8}{3}}{q^2} = 0 \Rightarrow q = 2,$$

$$\frac{\partial^2 \text{SATC}}{\partial q^2} = \tfrac{4}{3} + \frac{\frac{16}{3}}{q^3} > 0 \text{ for } q > 0, \quad \text{minimum.}$$

Marginal cost

Short-run marginal cost (SMC) for a fixed level of capital K^{o} is defined as

$$\text{SMC}(K^{\text{o}}) = \lim_{\Delta q \to 0} \frac{\Delta \text{STC}(K^{\text{o}})}{\Delta q} = \frac{\partial \text{STC}(K^{\text{o}})}{\partial q} = \frac{\partial \text{STVC}(K^{\text{o}})}{\partial q}.$$

Recall that STC and STVC are vertically parallel. Due to the Law of Diminishing Marginal Returns, SMC may at first decline, reach a minimum at the point of inflection of STC and STVC, and then rise with increases in output. For the cost curves in Figure 8.8,

$$\text{SMC}(K^{\text{o}}) = 2q^2 - 4q + 6,$$

$$\frac{\partial \text{SMC}}{\partial q} = 4q - 4 = 0 \Rightarrow q = 1,$$

$$\frac{\partial^2 \text{SMC}}{\partial q^2} = 4 > 0, \quad \text{minimum.}$$

Short-run marginal cost (SMC). In the short run, the additional cost associated with an additional increase in output. *E.g., a bicycle shop's additional cost of selling another bicycle.*

Example 8.5 Deriving short-run cost curves

Continuing with the production function $q = LK$ in Example 8.2, assume capital is fixed at K^{o}. In the short run, the firm will determine

$$\text{STC} = \min(wL + vK^{\text{o}}), \text{ s.t. } q = LK^{\text{o}},$$

where only input L is variable. The Lagrangian is then

$$\mathcal{L}(L, \lambda) = wL + vK^{\text{o}} + \lambda(q - LK^{\text{o}}).$$

The FOCs are

$$\frac{\partial \mathcal{L}}{\partial L} = w - \lambda^* K^{\text{o}} = 0,$$

$$\frac{\partial \mathcal{L}}{\partial \lambda} = q - L^* K^{\text{o}} = 0.$$

From these FOCs, SMC $= \lambda^* = w/K^o$. SMC for this technology is constant across output. Solving the second FOC for L^* yields $L^* = q/K^o$, which is called the *conditional short-run demand function* for labor. Substituting this conditional labor demand function into the objective function yields the cost function

$$\text{STC} = wL^* + vK^o = wq/K^o + vK^o,$$

where STVC $= wq/K^o$ and TFC $= vK^o$. The remaining short-run cost functions are

$$\text{SMC} = \frac{\partial \text{STC}}{\partial q} = \frac{\partial \text{STVC}}{\partial q} = \frac{w}{K^o} = \lambda^*,$$

$$\text{SATC} = \frac{\text{STC}}{q} = \frac{w}{K^o} + \frac{vK^o}{q},$$

where SAVC $= w/K^o$ and AFC $= vK^o/q$.

By minimizing STC with respect to the fixed input capital, we derive the LTC function from this STC function:

$$\frac{\partial \text{STC}}{\partial K} = -\frac{wq}{K^2} + v = 0.$$

Solving for K yields the long-run conditional capital demand function:

$$K = (wq/v)^{1/2}.$$

Substituting this long-run demand function into STC results in the same LTC as determined in Example 8.3:

$$\text{LTC} = \frac{wq}{(wq/v)^{1/2}} + v(wq/v)^{1/2} = 2(qwv)^{1/2}.$$

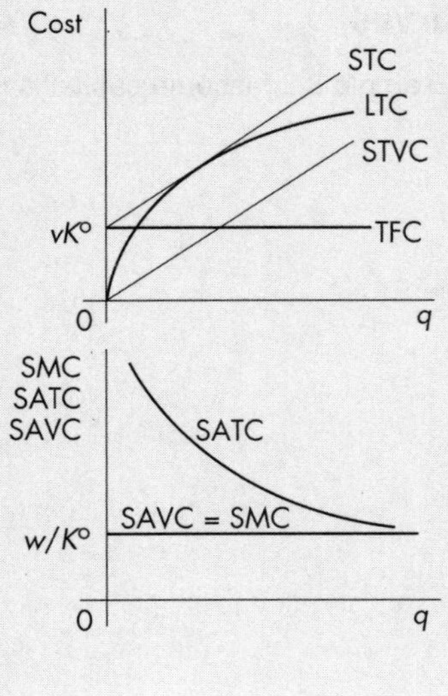

Note that the area under the SMC curve between zero output and some given output (say q_1) is equal to the level of STVC for output q_1. We show this using the fundamental theorem of calculus:

$$\text{STVC}(q_1) = \int_0^{q_1} \text{SMC}(q)dq = \int_0^{q_1} \frac{\partial \text{STVC}(q)}{\partial q} dq$$
$$= \text{STVC}(q_1) - \text{STVC}(0) = \text{STVC}(q_1).$$

At zero output, STVC(0) = 0, variable cost will be zero. For the SMC curve in Figure 8.8,

$$\text{STVC}(1.5) = \int_0^{1.5} \text{SMC}(q)dq = \int_0^{1.5} (2q^2 - 4q + 6)\,dq$$
$$= (\tfrac{2}{3}q^3 - 2q^2 + 6q)\big|_0^{1.5} = \tfrac{2}{3}(1.5)^3 - 2(1.5)^2 + 6(1.5) - 0 = 6.75.$$

Example 8.6 Illustrating STVC as the area under the SMC curve

In Example 8.5, SMC $= w/K^o$. The area under the SMC curve at output level q_1 is the STVC associated with q_1, STVC(q_1):

$$\text{STVC}(q_1) = \int_0^{q_1} \text{SMC}(q)\,dq = \frac{w}{K^o} q_1.$$

Letting $w = 16$, $K^o = 2$, and $q_1 = 8$, then STVC = 64.

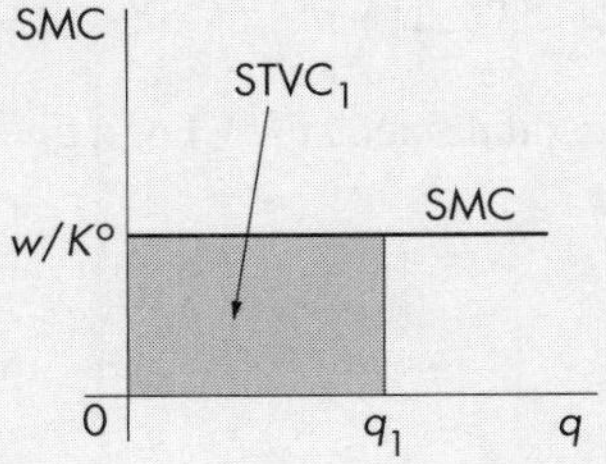

Average and marginal cost relationship

The relationships between average and marginal units again apply to short-run average and marginal costs. As discussed in production theory and the Mathematical Review, when the marginal unit is below the average, the average is falling. In Figure 8.8, at first SMC is below both SATC and SAVC, so the two averages are falling. If the average unit is neither rising nor falling, the marginal unit is equal to it. At the minimum point of SAVC, SMC is equal to it. SMC crosses SAVC at the minimum point of SAVC. At this minimum point, SMC is still below SATC, so SATC continues to fall. SMC and SATC intersect where SATC is at its minimum. Finally, if SMC is above SAVC or SATC, the average is rising. When SMC is rising, STC and STVC are increasing at an increasing rate.

We determine the relationship between the minimum of SATC and SMC or between the minimum of SAVC and SMC in the same way we did in the long-run cost case. For SATC,

$$\text{SMC} = \text{SATC} + \frac{\partial \text{SATC}}{\partial q} q.$$

Is marginal cost just some adjustment to average cost? Yes, the adjustment is the effect a change in output has on the average cost.

Law of diminishing marginal returns and shapes of the short-run cost curves

Short-run cost curves stay in shape with the Law of Diminishing Marginal Returns.
(Michael Wetzstein)

A firm's cost of production depends not only upon the prices of inputs but also on the technology of combining these inputs into an output. In the short run, a firm can change its output by adding variable inputs to the fixed inputs. Recall that the Law of Diminishing Marginal Returns states that at some point when adding additional variable inputs, the marginal product of the variable inputs will decline. This principle describes the physical law of production functions that governs the manner in which all outputs respond when different amounts of variable inputs are added to a constant amount of fixed inputs.

The technology of producing an output directly affects cost of production. In particular, the Law of Diminishing Marginal Returns related to production technology affects the nature of short-run costs. Assuming the production technology exhibits increasing, constant, and diminishing marginal returns, the STC(K°) and STVC(K°) curves increase at a decreasing, constant, and increasing rate, respectively (Figure 8.9). The TFC(K°) curve is constant across output.

Specifically, consider the variable input labor L, with capital fixed at K°. For a given level of output, q°, the short-run cost-minimization problem is

$$\text{STC} = \min_L (wL + vK^\circ) \quad \text{s.t. } q^\circ = q(K^\circ, L).$$

The Lagrangian is then

$$\mathcal{L}(L, \lambda) = wL + vK^\circ + \lambda[q^\circ - q^\circ(K^\circ, L)].$$

The FOCs are

$$\frac{\partial \mathcal{L}}{\partial L} = w - \lambda^* \frac{\partial q}{\partial L} = 0,$$
$$\frac{\partial \mathcal{L}}{\partial \lambda} = q^\circ - q(K^\circ, L^*) = 0.$$

From these FOCs, $\lambda^* = w/\text{MP}_L$ and as a Lagrange multiplier

$$\lambda^* = \frac{\partial \text{STC}(K^\circ)}{\partial q} = \text{SMC}(K^\circ).$$

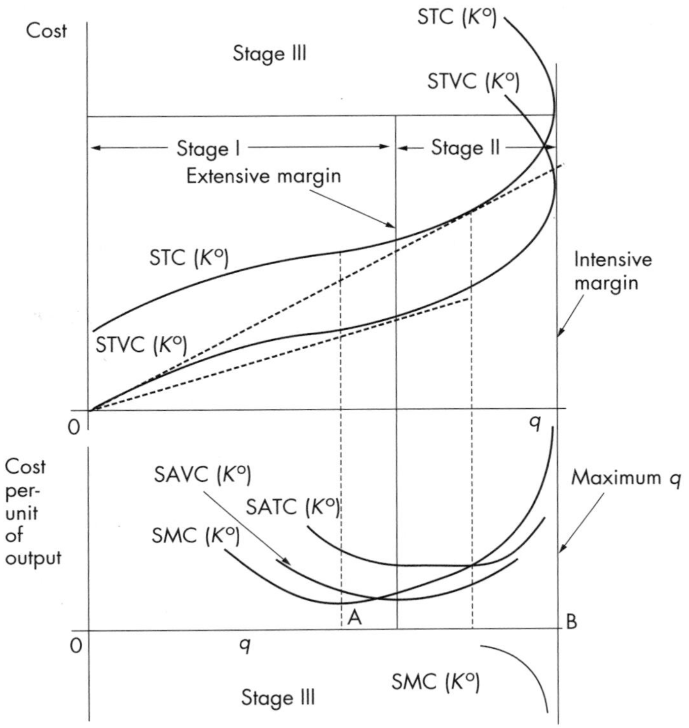

Figure 8.9 **Short-run cost curves and stages of production.** The extensive margin marking the boundary between Stages I and II of production occurs where short-run average variable cost is at a minimum. Maximum output occurs at the intensive margin where short-run marginal cost approaches infinity. Further increases in variable input will reduce output and result in Stage III of production. Stage II of production exists between these extensive and intensive margins.

Thus,

$$\mathrm{SMC}(K^o) = \frac{w}{\mathrm{MP}_L}.$$

As MP_L is increasing, SMC is decreasing. The area to the left of point A in Figure 7.1 represents increasing MP_L, which corresponds to the area to the left of point A in Figure 8.9. As MP_L reaches a maximum (point A in Figure 7.1), SMC reaches a minimum (also point A in Figure 8.9). At the minimum point of SMC, diminishing marginal returns starts. As MP_L declines, the area of diminishing marginal returns, SMC, is increasing. This corresponds to the area to the right of point A in Figures 7.1 and 8.9. Thus, a positively sloping SMC represents diminishing marginal returns, and a negatively sloping SMC curve represents increasing marginal returns. The shape of SMC is determined by the Law of Diminishing Marginal Returns. This law implies that, as output increases, the SMC curve will have a positive slope at some point.

Why will average costs rise with increases in output? The SMC, SAVC, and SATC curves will all eventually rise with increases in output as a result of the Law of Diminishing Marginal Returns.

Stages of production and short-run cost curves

We can also establish a relationship between SAVC and AP_L. When capital is fixed at K^o, $STVC(K^o) = wL^*$, which implies

$$SAVC(K^o) = \frac{wL^*}{q} = \frac{w}{AP_L}.$$

When AP_L is rising, SAVC is falling. Recall that Stage I of production occurs where AP_L is rising in Figure 7.1, which corresponds to SAVC falling in Figure 8.9. The maximum value of AP_L corresponds to the minimum value of SAVC. Finally, where AP_L is decreasing, SAVC is increasing.

In Figure 8.9, the extensive margin (line of demarcation between Stages I and II) is at the minimum point of SAVC. This corresponds to the point of maximum AP_L in Figure 7.1. The intensive margin corresponds to where $MP_L = 0$, point B in Figures 7.1 and 8.9. This results in SMC being undefined, because we cannot divide by zero. However, as MP_L approaches zero, SMC approaches infinity. In Figure 8.9, Stage III of production starts where SMC is undefined. At this intensive margin, output q is at its maximum, as indicated in Figure 7.1, and any further increases in the variable input L will result in a decrease in output. This decline in output as L is further increased results in negative MP_L and SMC, which is characteristic of Stage III production. As illustrated in Figure 8.9, in Stage III, STC and STVC are still increasing, but output is declining. Recall that firms will only operate in Stage II of production, where AP_L is falling for increases in output. This corresponds to where SAVC is rising as output increases. Note that in Stage II of production, SMC is also rising, indicating diminishing marginal returns.

Application: Shapes of the short-run average variable cost curves

As summarized by R. Miller, a number of studies have examined the shapes of SAVC curves for specific industrial plants. They have found that the SAVC curve is very flat and thus coincides with SMC up to some capacity level. This result is not surprising, since firms will not operate in Stage I of production, where SAVC is declining. If there is a binding capacity constraint, they will attempt to operate at capacity or shut down and their SAVC curves will be convex.

In the extreme, the SAVC curve will take on the shape of a reversed letter L (Figure 8.10). The SAVC curve is horizontal until it reaches the capacity level of output, q_C. This occurs when a firm's output is linearly related to a variable input in the short run. Variable cost will then increase in proportion to output, resulting in a horizontal SAVC curve. An example is a manufacturing plant that requires labor in a fixed proportion to its fixed level of machinery. As labor is increased, more machinery can be matched with workers, allowing output to increase in proportion to labor. Once all the machinery is matched with labor (full capacity), any further increases in labor will not expand output, so the SAVC curve becomes vertical.

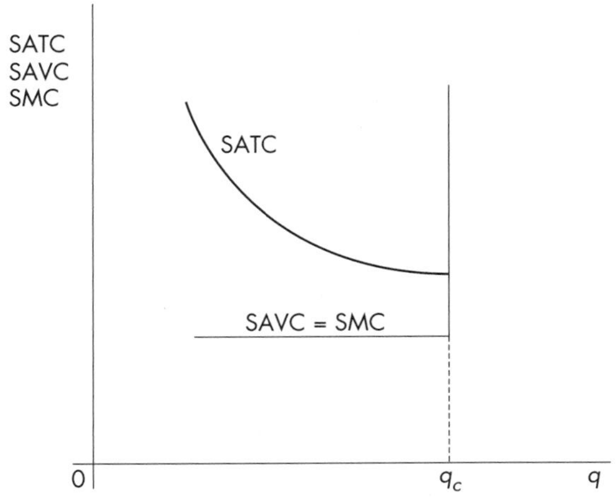

Figure 8.10 **Reversed letter L for the SAVC curve.** For some production technologies, the SAVC curve is horizontal and thus equal to the SMC curve up to some capacity level q_C.

In other firms, such capacity constraints are not binding and output is not linearly related to a variable input. Thus, increases in the variable input will result in diminishing returns, which yields an upward-sloping SMC curve. For example, the output elasticities for United States' baseball and China's grain production, reported in Chapter 7, are all associated with diminishing margin productivity and thus upward-sloping SMC curves.

Source: R.A. Miller, "Ten Cheaper Spades: Production Theory and Cost Curves in the Short Run," *Journal of Economic Education* 31 (2000): 119–130.

Isoquant map and STC

Graphically, we can construct the short-run cost curves by fixing the level of one input in the isoquant map and varying the level of output (Figure 8.11). For example, at the level of output q^1, with capital fixed at K°, the isocost curve associated with $\text{STC}(K^\circ)^1$ represents the minimum cost of producing q^1 with the fixed level of capital K°. In the long run, allowing capital to vary further decreases this short-run minimum cost, represented by the isocost line LTC^1. Because minimizing costs in the short run is a constrained version of long-run minimization, STC cannot be less than LTC. STC will be equal to LTC only where the level of fixed inputs, in this case capital, is the least-cost amount of the input for producing the given level of output. In Figure 8.11, this corresponds to the output level q^2. At q^2, $\text{STC}(K^\circ) = \text{LTC}$.

How are short- and long-run cost curves related?

In general, there are an infinite number of such short-run total cost curves, one for every conceivable level of the fixed input. As the level of capital is varied, a new STC curve is

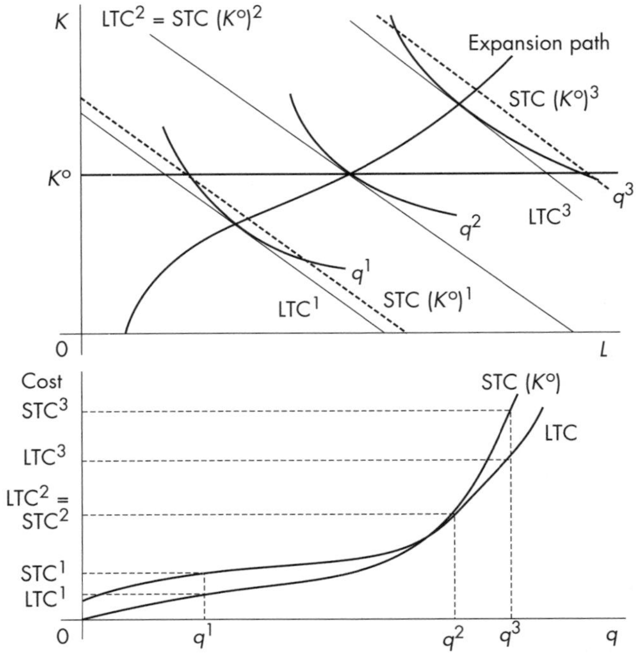

Figure 8.11 **Short-run total cost as a constrained minimization of long-run total cost.** Holding capital fixed at K^o and increasing labor yields the short-run cost-minimizing level of output associated with the short-run total cost curve. Allowing capital as well as labor to vary results in the long-run total cost curve.

traced out, and is tangent to LTC at that level of fixed capital that is the long-run optimal input usage. The envelope of all these cost-minimizing choices is LTC (Figure 8.12). The STC curves for alternative levels of the fixed input capital completely cover the top of the LTC curve and will not dip below it. STC is a constrained cost-minimization version of LTC, constrained by some given level of the fixed input capital, so LTC will never result in a higher cost than STC for a given level of output. Thus, for a level of fixed capital not corresponding to the long-run optimal input usage for a given level of output, STC will result in a higher cost than LTC. STC will only be equal to LTC at the output level where the long-run optimal input usage of capital corresponds to the fixed capital input level associated with the STC. Because STC curves will not dip below the LTC curves, they form an envelope covering the top of the LTC curve.

We derive the long-run average cost (LAC) and long-run marginal cost (LMC) curves from the LTC curve (Figure 8.13). Note that where STC is tangent to LTC, SATC is also tangent to LAC, because the averages are the totals divided by the given level of output. Also, a tangency, by definition, implies that the slopes of STC and LTC are equal at a point of tangency. Thus, as indicated by Figure 8.13, the LMC curve intersects the SMC curves at the output levels where the STC curves are tangent to the LTC curve. Identical to the relation between STC and LTC, SATC curves envelop the top of the LAC curve. SATC cannot be less than LAC for a given level of output, so the SATC curve cannot dip below the LAC curve.

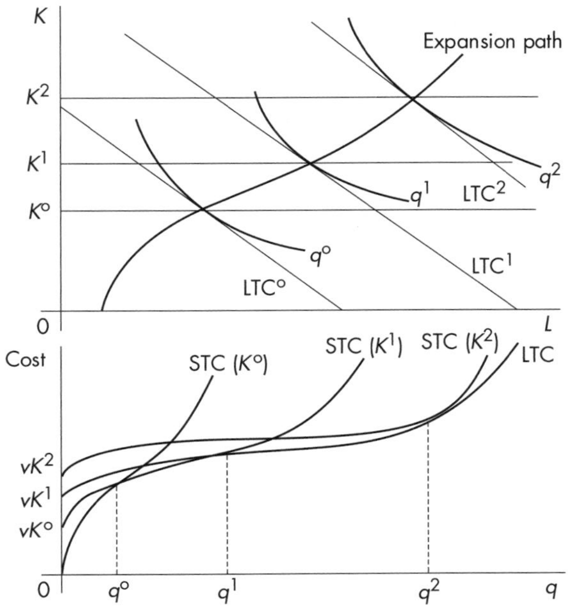

Figure 8.12 **Long-run total cost curve derived from the envelope of the short-run total cost curves.** For alternative levels of the fixed input, capital, a short-run total cost curve may be constructed. The long-run total cost curve is then the envelope of all these short-run total cost curves.

The LMC curve will be horizontal and equal to LAC if the cost curves exhibit constant returns to scale (Figure 8.14). In this case, the minimum points of SATC are tangent to the horizontal LAC curve. In contrast, for both economies and diseconomies of scale, the minima of SATC do not occur at the tangency point with LAC (Figure 8.13).

Example 8.7 Relationships between short- and long-run cost curves

From Example 8.5, we have

$$\text{STC} = \frac{wq}{K^o} + vK^o, \qquad LTC = 2(qwv)^{1/2}.$$

Letting $w = 16$, $v = 9$, and $K^o = 2$ gives

$$\text{STC} = 8q + 18, \qquad \text{LTC} = 24q^{1/2},$$

$$\text{SMC} = 8, \qquad \text{LMC} = 12q^{-1/2},$$

$$\partial\text{SMC}/\partial q = 0, \qquad \partial\text{LMC}/\partial q = -6q^{-3/2},$$

$$\text{SMC} = \text{SAVC}, \qquad \partial^2\text{LMC}/\partial q^2 = 9q^{-5/2} > 0, \text{ minimum},$$

$$\text{SATC} = 8 + 18q^{-1}, \qquad \text{LAC} = 24q^{-1/2},$$

$$\partial\text{SATC}/\partial q = -18q^{-2}, \qquad \partial\text{LAC}/\partial q = -12q^{-3/2},$$

$$\partial^2\text{SATC}/\partial q^2 = 36q^{-3} > 0, \text{ minimum}, \qquad \partial^2\text{LAC}/\partial q^2 = 18q^{-5/2} > 0, \text{ minimum}.$$

At $q = 9/4$, STC = LTC = 36, SATC = LAC = 16, SMC = LMC = 8, and $\partial\text{SATC}/\partial q = \partial\text{LAC}/\partial q = -32/9$.

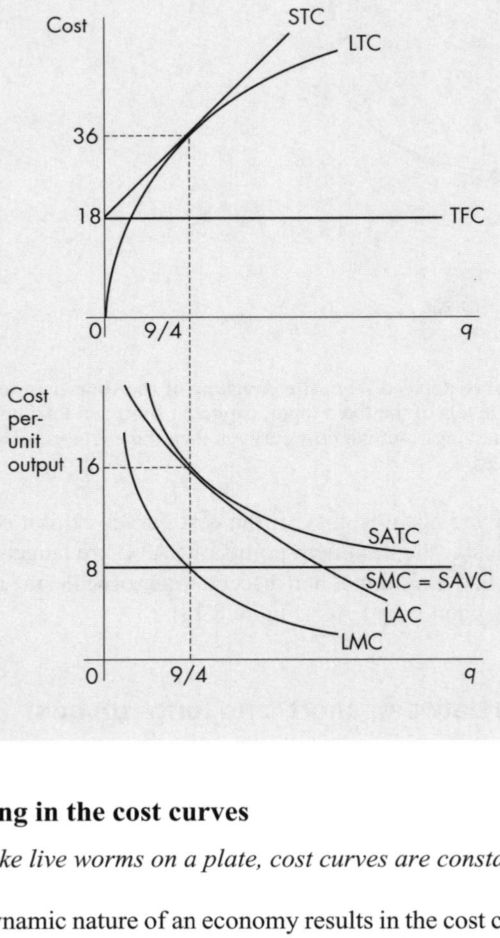

Shifting in the cost curves

Like live worms on a plate, cost curves are constantly shifting (wiggling).

The dynamic nature of an economy results in the cost curves continuously shifting as a result of changes in input prices and new technologies. The cost curves depicted in the figures are just snapshots in time. It is like taking a plate of worms that are wiggling and plunging them into liquid nitrogen (−195.8 °C) and then looking at them.

Input price change

A change in the price of an input will tilt the firm's isocost line, which alters the expansion path. For example, in the long run, an increase in wage rates results in a firm producing

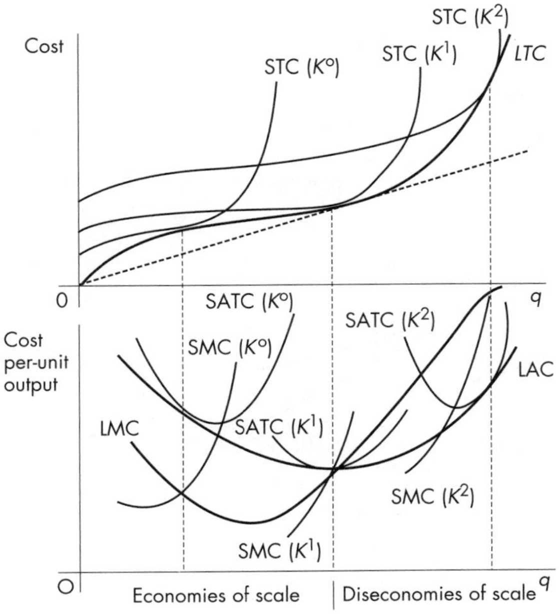

Figure 8.13 **Long-run average cost and long-run marginal cost curves with economies and diseconomies of scale.** Short-run average total cost and long-run average cost curves are tangent at an output where their associated totals are tangent. At these tangencies, the short-run and long-run marginal cost curves interest.

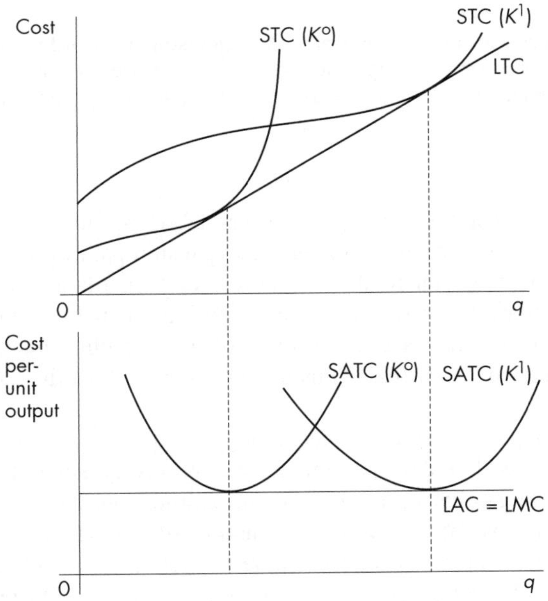

Figure 8.14 **Short-run total cost and long-run total cost curves for a firm facing constant returns to scale.** Given constant returns to scale, the minimum points on the short-run average total cost curves are tangent with a horizontal long-run average and marginal cost curve.

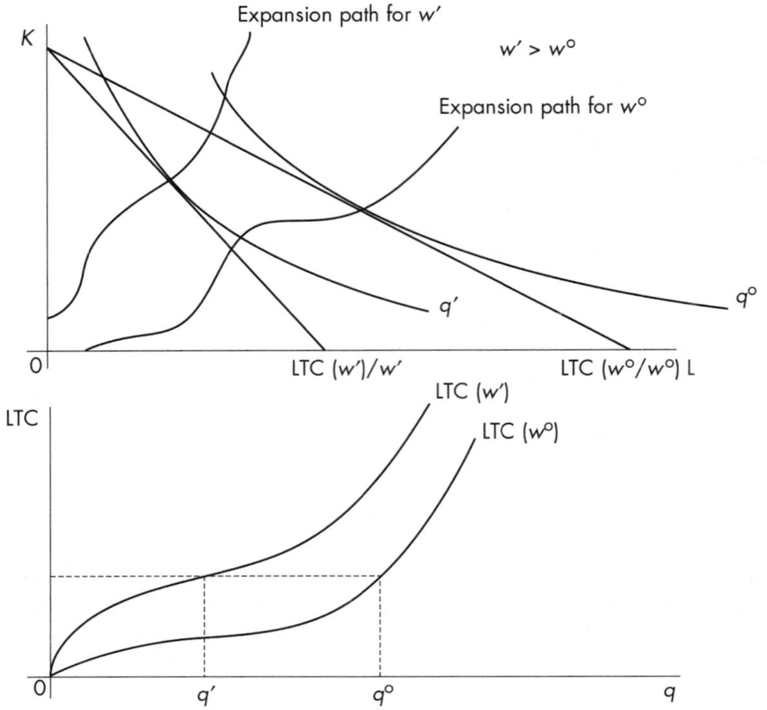

Figure 8.15 **Change in an input price and resulting tilts in the expansion path and the long-run total cost curve.** Increasing the wage rate results in an increase in the minimum cost of producing a given level of output. This results in higher long-run total cost for all output levels.

any output level with relatively more capital and relatively less labor. As illustrated in Figure 8.15, the elasticity of substitution ξ results in the entire expansion path of the firm rotating toward the capital axis. The long-run total cost curve will then tilt to the left (a worm thaws out). For example, recent use of hydraulic fracturing for natural gas in Pennsylvania and West Virginia led to a decrease in the price of gas, which is resulting in utilities substituting natural gas for coal as a fuel. Thus, the cost curves for utilities are shifting to the right.

A more recent example is in cyberspace, information technology. Acquiring information was once very expensive compared with today, particularly for relatively small firms. Modern information technology reduces this cost for small firms and thus the average cost of production. The decrease in cost of obtaining information tilts the LTC to the right, and the cost for a given level of output is reduced more for relatively small sized firms. This may partially explain the breaking apart of big companies. After centuries of firms growing larger, the size of companies in industrial nations began to shrink in the mid-1970s. A contributing factor may be the reduced cost of information for relatively small firms.

Example 8.8 Tilt in the expansion path and LTC from an increase in the price of an input

From Example 8.2, the long-run expansion path is

$$K = \frac{w}{v}L.$$

Letting $w = 16$ and $v = 9$,

$$K = \tfrac{16}{9}L.$$

Increasing the wage rate to $w = 25$, the expansion path tilts upward:

$$K = \tfrac{25}{9}L.$$

From Example 8.3,

$$\text{LTC} = 2(qvw)^{1/2}.$$

At $w = 16$ and $v = 9$,

$$\text{LTC} = 24q^{1/2}.$$

The increase in wages to 25 tilts LTC upward to

$$\text{LTC} = 30q^{1/2}.$$

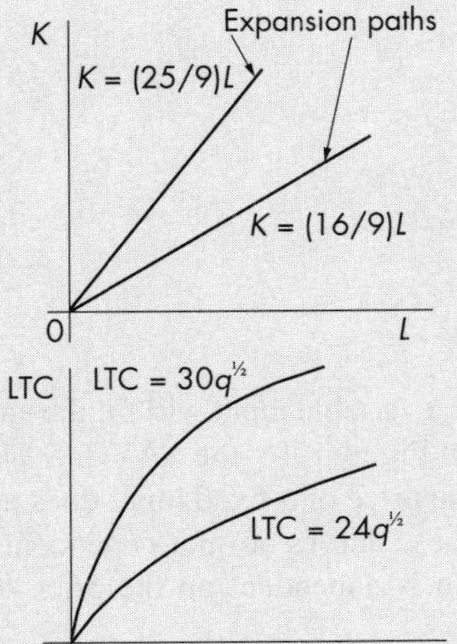

Example 8.9 Shifts in the short-run cost curves given an increase in the price of a variable input

As developed in Example 8.7 for $w = 16$, $r = 9$ and $K^o = 2$, we have

$$\text{STC} = wq/K^o + vK^o,$$

$$\text{STC} = 8q + 18,$$

$$\text{SMC} = 8,$$

$$\text{SATC} = 8 + 18/q.$$

Increasing wages to 20 results in

$$\text{STC}' = 10q + 18,$$

$$\text{SMC}' = 10,$$

$$\text{SATC}' = 10 + 18/q.$$

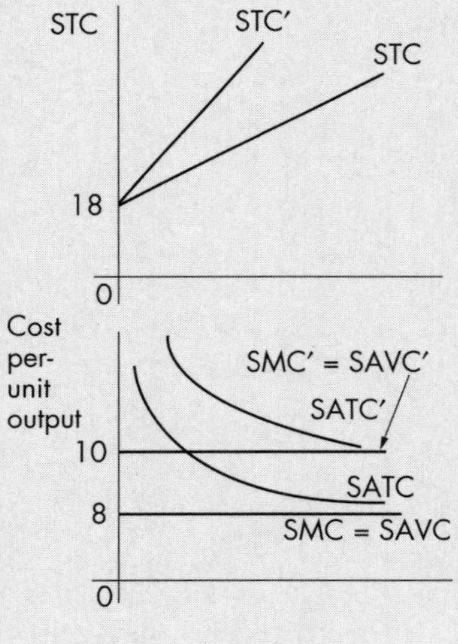

Similarly, in the short run, an increase in the price of a variable input will tilt the short-run total variable cost and total cost curves. As indicated in Figure 8.16, the SAVC, SATC, and SMC curves will also shift. However, an increase in the price of a fixed input does not shift the STVC, SAVC, and SMC curves (Figure 8.17). These curves are not dependent on the price of the fixed input. Only the SATC curve, which is dependent on the price of fixed inputs, shifts.

How will marginal cost shift with a change in fixed cost? Marginal cost will not shift with a change in fixed cost.

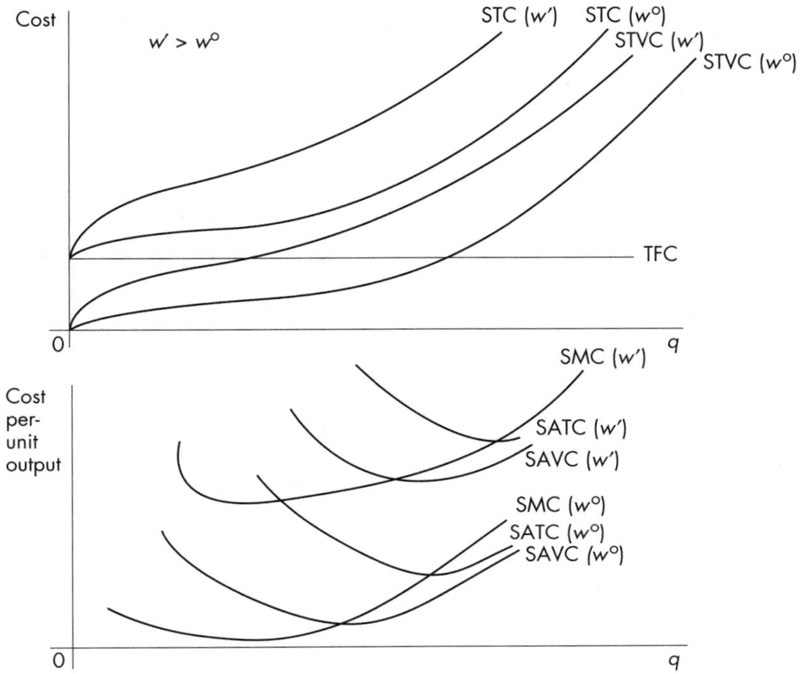

Figure 8.16 **Change in a variable input price and resulting shifts in the short-run cost curves.** An increase in the price of a variable input increases the short-run cost for producing a given level of output. This results in the short-run average total and variable cost curves shifting upward along with short-run marginal cost. However, total fixed cost remains fixed.

Example 8.10 Shifts in the short-run cost curves given an increase in the price of a fixed input

From Example 8.9, we have

$$\text{STC} = wq/K^o + vK^o,$$

$$\text{STC} = 8q + 18,$$

$$\text{SMC} = 8,$$

$$\text{SATC} = 8 + 18/q.$$

Increasing rents to 12 results in

$$\text{STC}' = 8q + 24,$$

$$\text{SMC} = 8,$$

$$\text{SATC}' = 8 + 24/q.$$

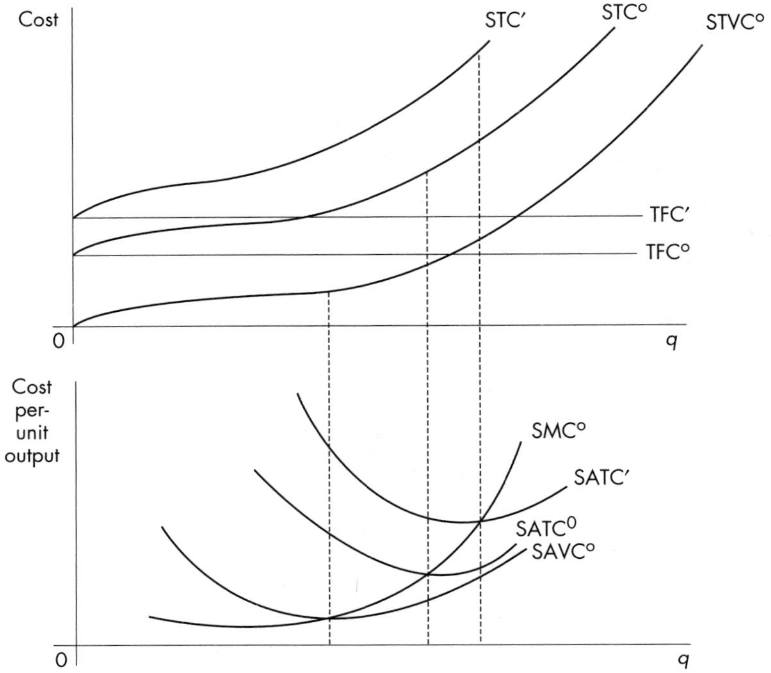

Figure 8.17 **Change in a fixed input price and resulting shifts in the short-run total cost curves.** An increase in total fixed costs does not affect the short-run total variable, average variable, or marginal cost curves. Only the short-run total and average total cost curves shift upward.

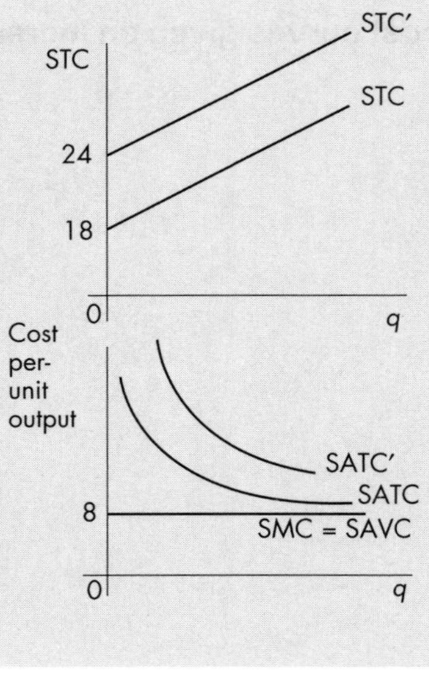

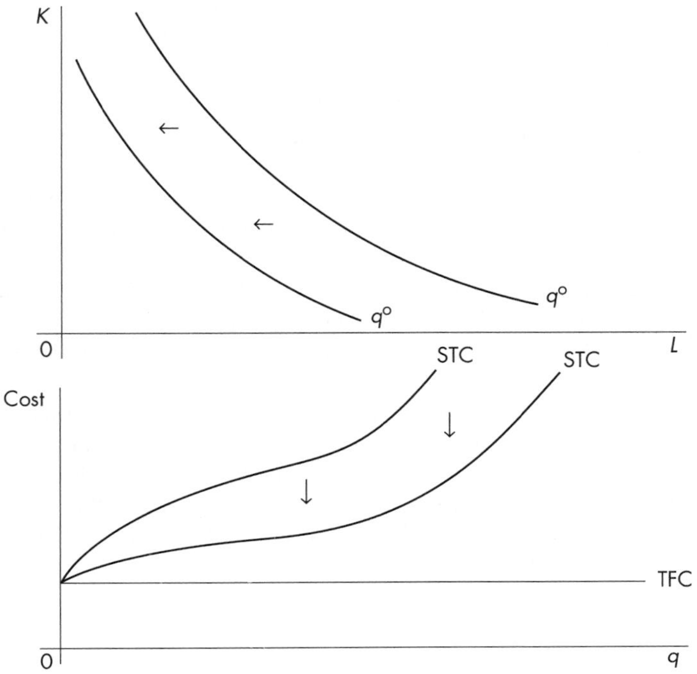

Figure 8.18 **Change in technology causing a tilt in the short-run total cost curve.** An improvement in technology will shift the isoquant inward and thus lower the minimum cost for producing a given level of output. The short-run total cost curve will then tilt downward, representing the lower short-run total cost associated with a given level of output.

New technologies

A second economic change that will cause cost curves to shift is the development of a new technology that alters a firm's production function. This results in the isoquants shifting toward the origin, which causes the cost curves to tilt downward (Figure 8.18).

Positive feedback

An example of the effect new technologies have on total cost curves is the concept of positive feedback. *Positive feedback* is where small chance events in the history of an industry or technology can tilt the competitive balance toward a firm. This may allow the firm to increase output and experience increasing returns to scale. As an example, consider the history of the videocassette recorder. The VCR market started out with two competing formats, VHS and Beta, selling at about the same price. Each format could realize increasing returns to scale from increased output. Large numbers of VHS recorders would encourage video outlets to stock more prerecorded tapes in VHS format. This would enhance the value of owning a VHS recorder, leading to more consumers buying the VHS format. The same would be true for the Beta format. Thus, a small gain in market share would improve the competitive position of one system and help it further increase its lead.

Such a market is initially unstable. It is impossible at the outset to predict which firm (VCR format) would survive. However, by some small event, one company may experience a relative greater increase in sales. In fact, firms will attempt through sales promotion (discussed in Chapter 15) to influence the likelihood of their company experiencing a relatively greater increase in sales. Increased production results in more experience in the processing of the commodity, which lowers the cost of production. Thus, depending on some small events—which companies do try to control—alternative equilibrium solutions are possible.

Positive-feedback economics finds its parallels in modern nonlinear physics.[4] Ferromagnetic materials, spin glasses, solid-state lasers, and other physical systems consisting of mutually reinforcing elements show the same properties as the VCR and other economic examples. They phase-lock into one of many possible configurations. Small perturbations at critical times influence which outcome is selected, and the chosen outcome may not be optimal. Initially, identical firms with significant increasing returns to scale do not necessarily select the same paths, and they will attempt to control which path a market will take. (For example, will the VHS or Beta format become the dominant system?) Although firms attempt to influence the path a market will take, such small events are at times difficult to foresee. For example, influencing the hot toy for Christmas sales is very difficult. To the extent that small events determine the overall path, it is difficult to accurately forecast the effect a new technology will have on a firm's future.

Summary

1. Under the assumptions that prices are fixed, profits are nonstochastic, and firm managers can be controlled by owners, the objective of a profit-maximizing firm is consistent with maximizing the utility of the firm's owners.
2. Total cost may be divided into explicit and implicit costs. Explicit costs are costs of employing inputs not owned by the firm; implicit costs are costs charged to inputs owned by the firm.
3. Total cost may also be divided into fixed and variable costs. Fixed costs are costs associated with the fixed inputs; variable costs are costs that vary with output and are associated with variable inputs.
4. Normal profit is the minimum total return to the inputs necessary to keep a firm in some production activity. Pure profit is total revenue minus total cost. If pure profit is zero, the firm is earning a normal profit. A negative level of pure profit indicates the firm is operating at a loss.
5. An isocost curve represents a locus of points where the total cost is the same for alternative input combinations.
6. The least-cost combination of inputs for a given level of output is determined where the marginal rate of technological substitution is equal to the economic rate of substitution. At this least-cost combination, the price per marginal product for each input is equal to the firm's marginal cost.
7. Increasing (decreasing) returns to scale results when total cost increases proportionally less (more) than an increase in output. Constant returns to scale corresponds to total cost increasing proportionally with output.

8. Short-run total cost is equal to short-run total variable plus total fixed costs. Dividing through by output results in short-run average total cost equaling short-run average variable plus average fixed costs. Short-run marginal cost is the slope of both the short-run total and total variable cost curves.
9. The Law of Diminishing Marginal Returns results in U-shaped short-run average total, average variable and marginal cost curves. Given diminishing marginal returns, Stage II of production corresponds to the situation where short-run marginal cost is rising and above short-run average variable cost. A firm's profit-maximizing level of output will be somewhere within Stage II of production.
10. In the long run, an increase in the price of an input will tilt the long-run total cost curve upward. Similarly, an increase in the price of a variable input will tilt the short-run total variable and total cost curves upward. The tilt in the totals will shift the average and marginal curves upward. Only the curves solely associated with the fixed inputs (total fixed cost and average fixed cost curves) will not shift.
11. An increase in fixed costs shifts the short-run total cost curve upward. The short-run average total cost will then also shift upward; however, the short-run total variable cost, average variable cost, and marginal cost curves do not shift.

Key concepts

Key equations

$$\mathrm{TC} = wL + vK$$

Isocost equation

$$\lambda^* = \frac{w}{\mathrm{MP}_L} = \frac{v}{\mathrm{MP}_K} = \mathrm{LMC}$$

The least-cost combination of inputs is determined by equating the price per marginal product to marginal cost.

$$\text{LMC} = \text{LAC} + \frac{\partial \text{LAC}}{\partial q} q$$

Marginal cost is equal to average cost plus an adjustment factor.

Questions

The harder you work, the luckier you get.

(Plato)

1. Does the shape of an isoquant curve have any bearing on how much a given change in the price of an input changes production costs? Explain.
2. An alumnus bequeaths a plot of land to a university for use as an athletic field. The president states the land did not cost the university anything, so the cost of using the land as an athletic field is zero. What is the cost of this land as an athletic field?
3. If a firm had everywhere-increasing returns to scale, what would happen to its profit if prices remained fixed and it doubled its scale of operations? Based on your answer, will a firm have everywhere-increasing returns to scale?
4. Why can you not tell the shape of the long-run average cost curve from the Law of Diminishing Marginal Returns?
5. Assume production of a product requires two inputs. If the prices of the inputs are equal, then is it correct that the optimal allocation is to employ these inputs in equal amounts? Explain.
6. The addition of the last unit of capital caused output of the firm to increase by 20, whereas the last unit of labor resulted in only a 10-unit increase in output. Thus, capital is more productive than labor and the firm should purchase more capital and hire less labor. True or false? Explain.
7. Explain why cost curves are not just technological data. Why does cost depend on the objectives of a firm and societies' laws?
8. Is a firm's STC curve necessarily rising, or can it have a falling range with increases in output?
9. Is a firm's SATC curve necessarily U-shaped, or can it be rising throughout or falling throughout? What about LAC?
10. Explain why long-run cost curves are envelopes of short-run cost curves.

Exercises

Never, never, never give up.

(Winston Churchill)

1. Consider the following production functions. Given $w = \$1$ and $v = \$2$, find the cost-minimizing input combination to produce 20 units of output for each production function.

   a. $q = 4K^{1/2}L^{1/2}$,

   b. $q = 4K + 7L$,

   c. $q = 10KL/(K + L)$,

   d. $q = K^2L$,

   e. $q = \min(3K, 4L)$.

2. Draw isocost lines for a firm that must pay higher wages for larger purchases of L, but faces a constant price for K. How will the FOCs for cost minimization differ from the case with constant input prices?

3. For a production function with $\xi = 0$, the cost-minimizing input ratio, capital/labor, is a fixed proportion. What are the shapes of the long-run marginal and average cost curves?

4. A perfectly competitive firm has a cost function given by

   $$\text{LTC} = 60q - 18q^2 + 2q^3.$$

   a. What is its total variable cost and total fixed cost?
   b. Graph the marginal and average cost curves.

5. A perfectly competitive firm has a cost function given by

   $$\text{STC} = \tfrac{1}{3}q^3 + 18.$$

   Graph the marginal and average cost curves.

6. Consider the production function $q = K + L$, with input prices $v = 1$ and $w = 2$.

   a. Determine LTC, LMC, and LAC.
   b. If L is fixed at 5, determine STC, STVC, AFC, SMC, SATC, and SAVC.

7. Consider the short-run production function

   $$q = 5L^{1/2},$$

   where the wage rate is 1. Find STC, STVC, SMC, SAVC, and SATC.

8. a. Assume a firm must pay an annual franchise fee, a fixed sum, whether or not it produces any output. How does this fee affect the firm's marginal and average costs?
   b. Instead, assume the firm is charged a fee proportional to its output. Now how does this fee affect the firm's marginal and average costs?
9. Consider the production function

$$q = K^{1/5}L^{2/5}.$$

   a. Derive the short-run total cost curve, where L is fixed.
   b. Derive the short-run average and marginal cost curves.
   c. Derive the long-run total cost curve.
10. Assume a firm's production function is given by

$$q = \min(2K, 4L),$$

and the wage rate is $w = 2$ and the rental rate for capital is $v = 1$.

   a. Calculate the firm's long-run total, average, and marginal cost functions.
   b. In the short run, assume K is fixed at 2 units. Calculate the firm's short-run total, average, and marginal cost functions.
   c. Provide a geometrical representation of the results.

Internet case studies

1. List and define a number of types of profits that economists have developed.
2. How many commodities can you find that have both a fixed and variable cost associated with levels of consumption?
3. Describe a number of positive-feedback systems.

Part IV

Competitive forces

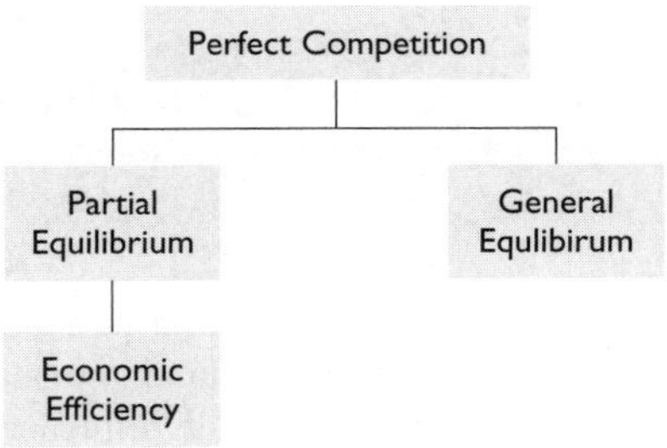

Chapters

We are all in this together. By ourselves.

(John Blog)

Some would argue that markets are vast, poorly understood, and composed of many unpredictable people and firms. Thus, we cannot even know if we are dealing with the partly known, the mainly unknown, or the unknowable. However, economic theory makes markets visible.

The decentralized control of economic activity—where all agents by themselves attempt to maximize their satisfaction—may appear on the surface to involve many unpredictable people. However, just as ecology provides an understanding of equilibrium in an ecological system, economics can explain how this decentralized control achieves market equilibrium. The only signal required for these markets to operate efficiently is the price signal.

Specifically, we can bring together the theories of consumer and producer behavior to develop a theory of how market equilibrium price and quantity for a single commodity are determined. This theory of simultaneous determination of commodity price and quantity is called *commodity-market theory*. A *commodity market* is defined as a collection of agents engaged in transactions regarding the (current or future) exchange of commodities (one of which is typically money). *Agents* are categorized as firms supplying the commodity and consumers demanding the commodity. **Consumers** consist of households, if the commodity is supplied directly to them, or they could also be other firms that purchase the commodity as an input for their production processes.

Consumers. Households or firms purchasing commodities for direct consumption or as inputs in a production process. *E.g., all agents.*

We put the analysis of a commodity market in a partial-equilibrium framework, where markets for all other commodities are assumed constant. We assume that the effects in the market under consideration do not influence any other markets. In Chapter 9, we use partial-equilibrium analysis to determine equilibrium price and output in a single market. This abstraction leads to the development of consumer and producer surplus as welfare measures in Chapter 10. General-equilibrium analysis (Chapter 11) does not make this restrictive assumption.

Pure or *perfect competition* is the main topic of Part 4. We discuss the alternative market structures, *monopoly, monopolistic*, and *oligopoly*, in Parts 5 and 6. Coverage includes price and output determination in these markets and the efficiency of each market structure. Assuming no institutional constraints, such as a legal ceiling price (Chapter 10), firms always have the ability to alter the prices they offer. Furthermore, with incentives, firms will alter prices in response to market supply not equaling market demand.

As we discuss the assumptions underlying the perfectly competitive market in Chapter 9, we discover the *Law of One Price*. Following this discussion, we develop conditions for short-run market equilibrium, based on the market supply and demand curves. We also investigate market demand and supply shifters given specific functional forms for market demand and supply. We then turn to the long-run adjustment and equilibrium conditions in a perfectly competitive market.

In Chapter 10, we investigate economic efficiency, including the concepts of *consumer* and *producer surplus* as measures of efficiency and the efficiency loss, measured by *deadweight loss* in the sum of consumer and producer surplus. We then look at government intervention in markets in terms of ceiling and support prices, commodity taxes, and trade restrictions.

Models developed in the first two chapters of Part 4 are based on partial-equilibrium analysis. In Chapter 11, we investigate the competitive market in a general-equilibrium framework. We develop conditions for efficiency in production, based on the allocation rules of opportunity cost, marginal products, and comparative advantage. We then establish the necessary conditions for efficiency in production and exchange and relate these conditions to a competitive economy.

9 Perfect competition

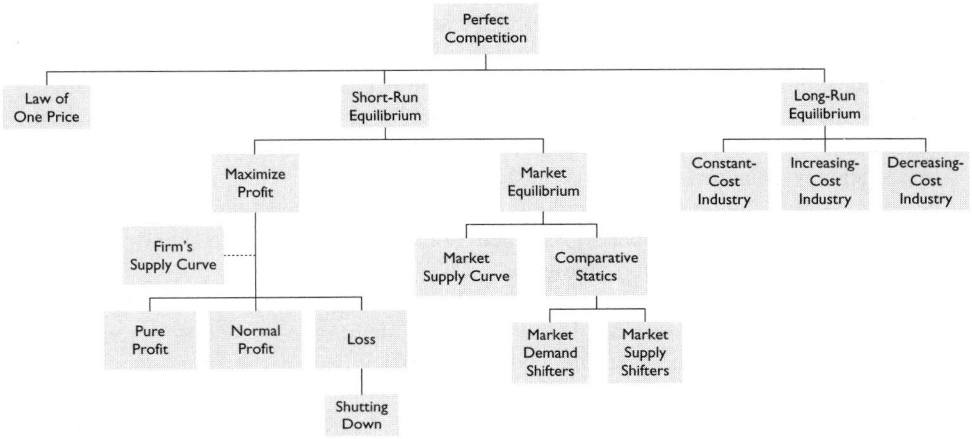

Outline and Conceptual Inquiries

Establishing the Law of One Price
Why will all firms charge the same price without knowingly doing so?

Market period tedium

Understanding the short run
Deriving the market supply curve
Profit potential
How to determine short-run price and output
Establishing market equilibrium
Drawing the individual firm's supply curve
What does the SMC curve tell us?
What does the SATC curve tell us?
Why would a firm ever operate at a loss?
What does the SAVC curve tell us?
What does the AFC curve tell us?
Shifting market demand
Shifting market supply
A market demand and supply shifters model
Application: Food before fuel
Application: Beer tax
Application: Agricultural pesticide cancellation

Long run: removing short-run fixations
Why, in the long run, will revenue never exceed cost?
Long-run cost adjustment
What are the equilibrium conditions?
If the price falls, would a firm ever supply more?
Application: Output tax: who pays the tax?
Application: Should a firm adopt a new technology?

Summary
Key concepts
Key equations
Questions
Exercises
Internet case studies

Competitive forces are economists' dreams and business' nightmares.
(Michael Wetzstein)

A nightmare for a locally owned variety store is for a Wal-Mart to open up next door. Any business would generally suffer a loss in profits if competition from another business was keen. Competition that results in a perfectly competitive market only exists in economists' dreams. Perfect competition is a theoretical extreme; in reality, some markets may approach it, but none ever really obtain it. Even so, as discussed in Chapter 10, economists use the perfectly competitive market model to evaluate the efficiency of actual markets. With perfect competition as the standard, applied economists measure how actual markets and economies with missing markets allocate resources. Based on this comparison, applied economists develop policies and programs to improve resource allocation efficiency.

Our aim in this chapter is to develop the conditions under which a perfectly competitive market structure would exist and then determine the equilibrium market price and output. We then investigate shifts in market demand and supply curves in terms of how a market equilibrium is restored.

The *Law of One Price* is based on the assumption of a perfectly competitive market. The short-run market supply curve is the horizontal summation of individual firms' short-run supply curves. Based on this short-run market supply curve and with a market demand curve, we determine the market equilibrium price and quantity. Given this market equilibrium price, we derive the profit-maximizing output condition of equating marginal cost to marginal revenue for individual firms. At this profit-maximizing output, we investigate conditions for a firm earning a pure profit, earning a normal profit, operating at a loss, or going out of business. We then derive the competitive firm's short-run supply curve. Given specific functional forms for the market demand and supply curves, we develop a model of market demand and supply shifters. We then employ this model in investigating policies of increasing the beer tax, food before fuel, and cancellation of an agricultural pesticide.

We then turn to the long-run competitive equilibrium. We discuss the long-run adjustment to equilibrium by firms freely entering and exiting an *industry* and the phenomenon of cost adjusting to price. We state the conditions for long-run equilibrium and then investigate the effects of a change in market demand for *constant-cost, decreasing-cost,* and *increasing-cost industries*. We conclude by examining the long-run perfectly competitive equilibrium, first with an output tax and then by considering a new technology.

Establishing the Law of One Price

At a local farmers' market with numerous vendors offering fresh tomatoes for sale, an individual vendor has no incentive to alter the price it receives for tomatoes. The vendor can sell all of its tomatoes at the market price, so it has no incentive to reduce the price. However, the vendor will sell few if any tomatoes at a price above the market price. In economics, such a firm is called a price taker and is operating in a **perfectly competitive market** structure. It takes the equilibrium price where supply equals demand as given.

US agricultural production provides a close example of this market structure. Generally, farmers are unable to negotiate with buyers for a higher price for their output, so they take the current market price as given.

Perfectly competitive market. Agents have no incentive to alter the market price they face for a product. *E.g., stock and commodity exchanges.*

The establishment of this competitive price and quantity in a perfectly competitive market is based on certain assumptions. First, it is still assumed that households maximize utility and firms maximize profits. Additional assumptions are as follows:

1. Small size, large numbers. Every firm in the market is so small, relative to the market as a whole, that it cannot exert a perceptible influence on price. Each firm is a price taker.
2. *Homogeneous products* (homogeneous means of uniform structure of the same or a similar kind). All producers sell commodities that are identical with respect to physical characteristics, location, and time of availability. The product of any one seller must be identical in the eyes of the consumer to the product of any other seller.
3. Free mobility of resources. All resources are perfectly mobile. This implies that inputs are not monopolized by an owner or producer, and firms can enter and exit an **industry** without extraordinary costs.
4. Perfect knowledge. Consumers, producers, and resource owners have perfect knowledge concerning the price, physical characteristics, and availability of each commodity. Consumers are fully cognizant of prices, and producers are cognizant of costs as well as prices.
5. Transactions are costless. Agents (buyers and sellers) incur no extraordinary costs in making exchanges.

Given these assumptions, there is only one market price for a commodity. This is called the **Law of One Price**. If the commodity were traded at different prices, buyers would purchase the commodity where it is cheapest and firms would only supply the commodity where it is more expensive. These demand and supply responses would result in an equalization of prices.

Why will all firms charge the same price without knowingly doing so? A large number of small firms are all producing a homogeneous product and facing the same market conditions of perfect knowledge, free entry and exit, and zero transaction costs, so their output and pricing decisions are all the same.

Industry. A group of firms offering the same or like commodities. *E.g., the automobile industry.*

Law of One Price. Given a perfectly competitive market, there is only one market price for a commodity. *E.g., a farmer selling corn is faced with the one market price for corn.*

No market actually fulfills all the assumptions of perfect competition. Therefore, the concept of perfect competition, based on these assumptions, is a theoretical extreme. Similar to the concept of a perfect vacuum or a frictionless state in physics, perfect competition is a model that abstracts from reality and can be used as a basis for evaluating more realistic market structures. Although no market meets all the conditions of perfect competition precisely, some markets come close. For example, in the stock and commodity exchanges in New York and Chicago, there are relatively large numbers of small firms or consumers, and stock or futures contracts represent homogeneous products. Costs of entry and exit into the markets are also low.

Perfect knowledge is the one assumption that generally does not hold in markets. In Chapter 23, we will investigate the market effects of asymmetric information. Even in the stock exchanges, knowledge held by buyers and sellers varies considerably (e.g., insider trading). The very fact there are buyers and sellers of stock suggests there may be a different set of knowledge (predictions) about the future stock price. However, the objectives of agents (households and firms) for investing or divesting in an asset are the major determinants in buying and selling decisions.

Market period tedium

If everything is fixed, nothing moves except boredom.

(Michael Wetzstein)

We begin our study of equilibrium in a perfectly competitive market by considering the market-period, short-run, and long-run assumptions. A market-period equilibrium, illustrated in Figure 9.1, results in no supply response. All inputs are fixed, so a change in price does not result in a change in market supply. An example are wilderness areas (areas untouched by mankind): The supply of wilderness areas is fixed, so an increase in demand results in no supply response. In Figure 9.1, a shift in the demand curve from Q^D to $Q^{D\prime}$ results in the same level of supply, Q^*. The supply curve is perfectly inelastic. This equilibrium condition is generally not very useful, as most markets do exhibit some supply response. In the short run, existing firms can change their quantity supplied, and in the long run, new firms can enter an industry and supply the commodity.

Understanding the short run

Seize any profit now for tomorrow will be too late.

(Michael Wetzstein)

Translation: Firms only earn a pure profit in the short-run.

Georgia peach growers will adjust their supply of peaches according to the market price. If the price for peaches is high in a given week, they will more aggressively pick the fruit. However, in a given growing season, they cannot increase the number of trees. In the short run, the number of firms (trees) in the peach industry is fixed. It is assumed that the cost of new firms entering and existing firms exiting the industry is prohibitive within this short-run time period (season). Although existing firms can only feasibly liquidate their fixed inputs in the long run, they can adjust their supply in response to changing market conditions in the short run. For example, a firm may reduce its supply to zero when facing a low price for its output (peaches).

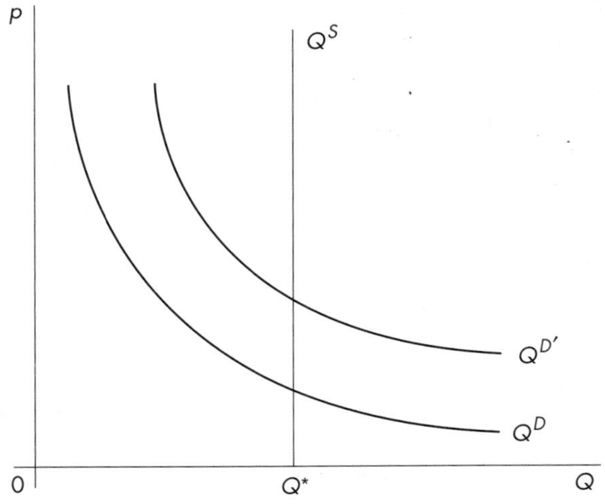

Figure 9.1 **Market-period equilibrium with no supply response.** A perfectly inelastic supply curve results in no supply response from a change in demand. The market equilibrium quantity does not change.

Deriving the market supply curve

Just before a major sporting event, there are usually scalpers selling tickets. The Law of One Price implies that at a given price the scalpers will supply a certain quantity of tickets. At this given price, the sum of all the available tickets across all the scalpers is the total market supply for tickets. We can plot this as a point on the market supply curve for the commodity. Continuously varying the price and summing individual supply across all firms (scalpers), we trace out the **market supply curve** (also called the **industry supply curve**) for the commodity (tickets). Specifically, the short-run market supply curve is the horizontal summation of individual firms' supply curves. As depicted in Figure 9.2 for two firms, the market supply is the horizontal summation of two firms' supply curves. At a price level of p', market supply curve is $Q' = q_1' + q_2'$. In general, the market supply function $Q^S(p)$ is the summation of the supply functions for n individual firms:

$$Q^S(p) = \sum_{j=1}^{n} q_j^S(p),$$

where n is the number of firms in the industry and $q_j^S(p)$ is firm j's supply function.

Market (industry) supply curve. The horizontal summation of individual firms' supply curves. *E.g., the market supply of gasoline at a given price is the sum of each firm's supply at that price.*

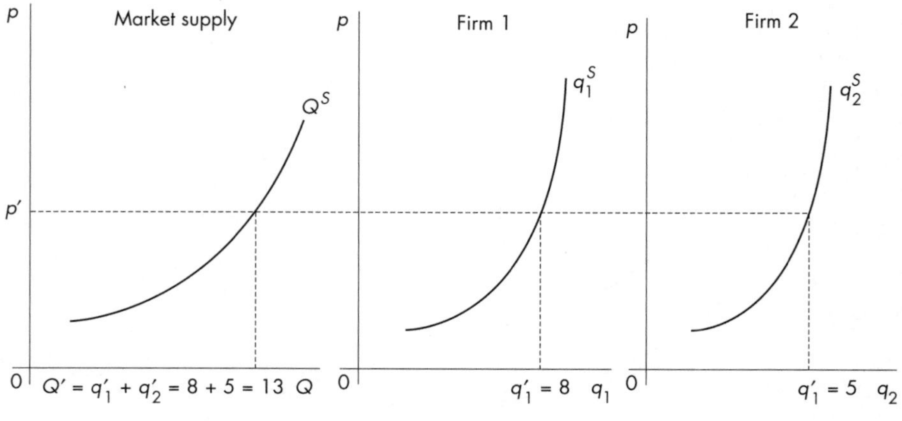

Figure 9.2 **Market supply curve.** The horizontal summation of individual firms' quantity supplied at a given price yields the market supply for this price. Varying the price and summing the individual firms' quantity supplied traces out the market supply curve.

Example 9.1 Deriving market supply

Consider two firms, with firm 1 supplying q_1 and firm 2 supplying q_2. Market supply Q^S is the sum of the two firms' supply. Assume the following individual firm supply functions:

$$q_1^S = -12 + 3p \ (p \geq 4), \quad q_1^S = 0 \ (p < 4),$$
$$q_2^S = -8 + p \ (p \geq 8), \quad q_2^S = 0 \ (p < 8).$$

Market supply is then the horizontal summation of these supply functions:

$$Q^S = q_1^S + q_2^S = (-12 + 3p) + (-8 + p) = -20 + 4p \ (p \geq 8),$$
$$Q^S = -12 + 3p \ (4 \leq p < 8),$$
$$Q^S = 0 \ (p < 4).$$

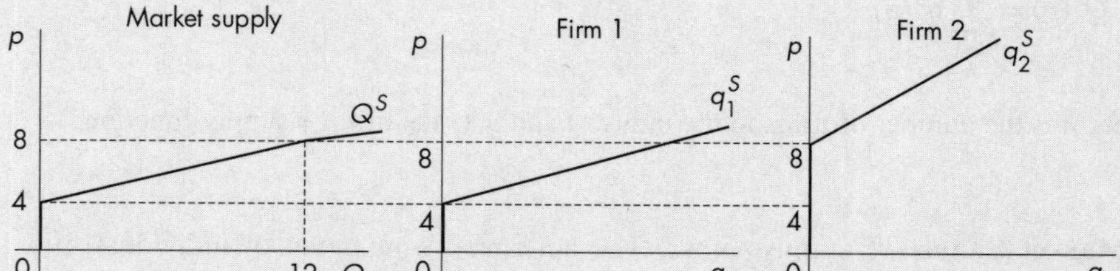

Elasticity of market supply

A measure of the supply response by an industry to a change in output price p is the **elasticity of supply** associated with a market supply function:

$$\varepsilon^S_{Q,p} = \frac{\partial Q}{\partial p}\frac{p}{Q} = \frac{\partial \ln Q}{\partial \ln p}.$$

This is similar to the elasticity of demand, which measures the responsiveness of quantity demanded to a price change. Given that short-run quantity supplied will rise as the output price increases, then $\varepsilon^S_{Q,p} > 0$. Relatively large values of $\varepsilon^S_{Q,p}$ imply that market supply is relatively responsive to a price change, whereas low values indicate that supply is not very responsive. Supply is said to be elastic for $\varepsilon^S_{Q,p} > 1$ and inelastic for $\varepsilon^S_{Q,p} < 1$. For example, researchers estimate the supply elasticity of alternative biofuels (ethanol) at 0.258, inelastic.[1] A 1 percent increase in price will then result in an 0.258 percent increase in fuel ethanol.

Elasticity of supply. The percentage change in quantity supplied given a percentage change in price. *E.g., if the elasticity of supply for apples is 0.6, a 1 percent increase in the price of apples will result in a 0.6 percent increase in the quantity supplied of apples.*

Example 9.2 Determining the elasticity of market supply

As an example of market supply elasticity, consider the quantity of market supply Q^S as an exponential (Cobb–Douglas) function of market price p:

$$Q^S = ap^b,$$

where a and b are positive parameters. Taking the logarithms of both sides,

$$\ln Q^S = \ln a + b \ln p.$$

Then $\varepsilon^S_{Q,p} = \partial \ln Q^S / \partial \ln p = b$.

Profit potential

The objective of a firm is profit maximization, subject to a technology constraint. To meet this objective, every firm faces two important decisions: how much to produce and what price to charge. Profit can be either pure profit or normal profit. Recall from Chapter 8 that short-run pure profit π is total revenue TR minus short-run total cost STC:

$$\pi = \text{TR} - \text{STC},$$

where TR is output price times quantity, pq. Normal profit is the implicit cost of production and occurs when TR = STC. At a level of normal profit, owners of the firm are receiving a return on the inputs they own at a level where there is no tendency for them to employ the inputs in another production activity.

How to determine short-run price and output

To go beyond is as wrong as to fall short.

(Confucius)

Translation: For maximizing profit, overproducing will lead to lost profits the same as will underproduction.

To operate a barber shop, the barber must determine the price of a haircut and how many to give in a week. The price will be based on the current market price. Quantity will depend on the barber's ability to cut hair (technology) and the price of the inputs, which includes the implicit cost of the barber's time. As developed in Chapter 8, the production technology is expressed in STC, where the STC curve is determined given some level of technology and input prices. Thus, for an individual firm's profit-maximization problem, the technology constraint is imbedded in the objective function

$$\max_q \pi = \max_q(\text{TR} - \text{STC}).$$

The first-order condition (FOC) is then

$$\frac{d\pi}{dq} = \frac{d\text{TR}}{dq} - \frac{\partial \text{STC}}{\partial q} = 0,$$

$$\text{MR} - \text{SMC} = 0,$$

where $d\text{TR}/dq$ is defined as marginal revenue MR and $\partial\text{STC}/\partial q = \text{SMC}$. **Marginal revenue** is the change in total revenue for a change in output. Thus, for profit maximization, the firm equates MR to SMC:

$$\text{MR} = \text{SMC}.$$

A firm will adjust output until the marginal increase in revenue, MR, just equals the marginal increase in costs, SMC. The incremental change in profit is zero at MR = SMC. If MR > SMC, then an incremental increase in output will add more to revenue than to cost, and thus profit will increase. Alternatively, if SMC > MR, then an incremental decrease in output will decrease cost more than decrease revenue, and thus also increase profit.

Marginal revenue (MR). The change in total revenue from a change in output. *E.g., the increase in sales a movie theater has from you seeing a movie.*

Under perfect competition, a firm's demand curve is perfectly elastic, $\varepsilon = -\infty$, and thus $p = \text{MR}$. A perfectly competitive firm increasing output does not result in a market price decline, so the additional revenue associated with a unit increase in output is the price per unit, p, that the firm receives. The firm can sell all of the output it wants at a given price. Note that p is **average revenue AR**:

$$\text{AR} = \text{TR}/q = pq/q = p.$$

For a perfectly elastic demand curve, AR is neither rising nor falling; thus, MR is equal to it. The profit-maximizing condition for a perfectly competitive firm is then p = SMC, as illustrated in Figure 9.3. The demand curve facing the competitive firm is horizontal (perfectly elastic): $p_e = \text{AR}_e = \text{MR}_e$. The firm is a price taker. At output level q_e, the firm is maximizing profit, MR = SMC, which corresponds to equality of the slopes associated with the TR and STC curves. At output q', MR > SMC, so this output level is not the profit-maximizing output. Increasing output from q' to q_e results in a change in TR represented by the area $q'\text{AB}q_e$ and the change in STC by represented by $q'\text{EB}q_e$. The difference, EAB, is the increase in pure profit from increasing output. Similarly, at q'', MR < SMC and a decrease in output from q'' to q_e decreases STC by $q_e\text{BD}q''$ but only decreases TR by $q_e\text{BC}q''$. The resulting gain in profit is BDC. To operate at q'' is as wrong as operating at q' in terms of maximizing profit. As long as the TR curve cuts the STC curve, positive pure profits are possible. The shaded area in the figure represents the area where TR > STC. At the points where TR = STC, only normal profits exist; where TR < STC, the firm is operating at a loss.

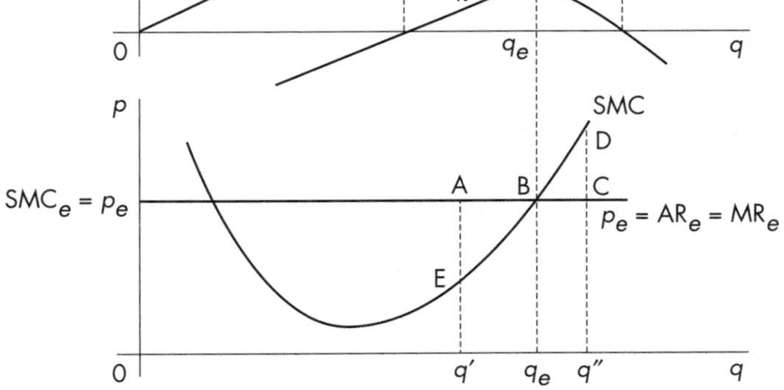

Figure 9.3 **Profit maximization under perfect competition.** When price equals marginal cost, a competitive firm will maximize profit. If price is greater than marginal cost, the firm can increase profit by increasing output and adding more to total revenue than to total cost. Alternatively, if price is less than marginal cost, the firm can increase profit by reducing output and subtracting more from total cost than from total revenue.

Average revenue (AR). Revenue per unit of output. *E.g., the total ticket sales divided by the number of people seeing a movie.*

Establishing market equilibrium

Market equilibrium is established when, at the prevailing price, all producers and all consumers (households and other firms) are satisfied with the amount they are producing or consuming and market demand and market supply are equal (Figure 9.4). In equilibrium, the **market-clearing price** p_e is where quantity demand Q^D is equal to quantity supplied Q^S. If $Q^D > Q^S$, inventories are depleted, resulting in an upward pressure on price. This increase in price tends to dampen quantity demanded and increase quantity supplied, bringing Q^D and Q^S toward equality. Similarly, for $Q^D < Q^S$, inventories expand, triggering price cuts. This decrease in price stimulates quantity demanded and reduces quantity supplied; again bringing Q^D and Q^S toward equality. At p_e, Q_e is supplied and demanded in the market.

Market-clearing price. Market quantity demanded equals quantity supplied. *E.g., the price of lemonade, on a hot day at a park, when the demand for lemonade is equal to the supply.*

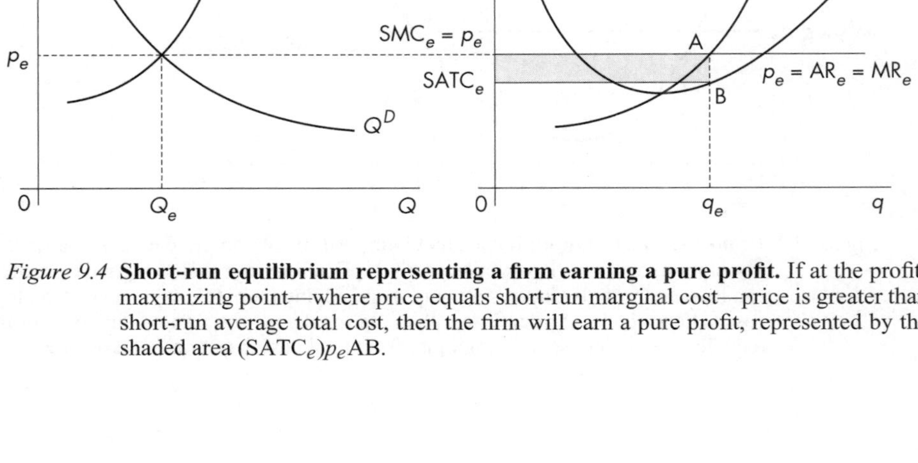

Figure 9.4 **Short-run equilibrium representing a firm earning a pure profit.** If at the profit-maximizing point—where price equals short-run marginal cost—price is greater than short-run average total cost, then the firm will earn a pure profit, represented by the shaded area $(SATC_e)p_eAB$.

Example 9.3 Equating market demand with market supply

Consider the following market demand, Q^D, and market supply, Q^S, functions:

$$Q^D = 10 - 2p,$$

$$Q^S = 5 + 3p.$$

The market-clearing price is determined where quantity demanded is equal to quantity supplied:

$$Q^D = Q^S.$$

Substituting the functions for Q^D and Q^S and solving for p yields the equilibrium price (market-clearing price) p_e:

$$Q_e^D = Q_e^S,$$

$$10 - 2p_e = 5 + 3p_e,$$

$$p_e = 1.$$

Substituting p_e into the market demand, Q^D, or market supply, Q^S, functions, yields the equilibrium output $Q_e = 8$. Perfectly competitive firms will take this equilibrium price as given and base their profit-maximizing level of output on this price.

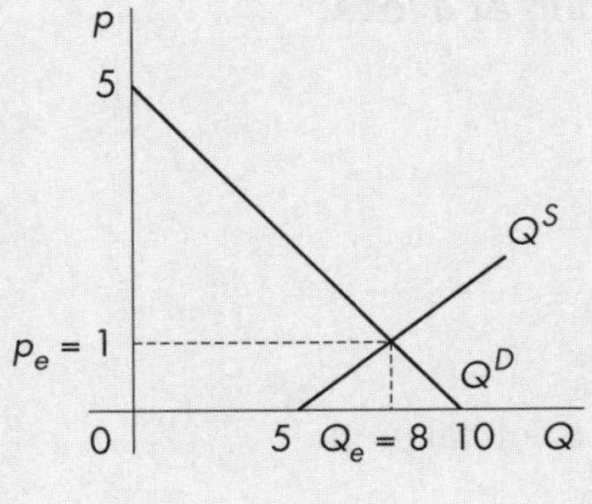

Drawing the individual firm's supply curve

A popcorn farmer in Iowa does not have to determine the price he will charge for his kernels. The market will determine the price per bushel. He does determine how many bushels to sell by increasing production to where the additional cost of production just equals this market price. Based on this equilibrium market-clearing price p_e, perfect competitive individual firms (farmers) determine their profit-maximizing price and output, taking the market-clearing price as given. With MR = SMC as the condition for profit maximization, the SMC curve indicates how much a firm is willing and able to supply (Figure 9.4). The firm equates MR, which for a price-taking firm is equal to p, to SMC in order to maximize profits. MR is equal to p because each individual competitive firm is facing a horizontal perfectly elastic demand curve. Where the equilibrium price p_e intersects the SMC curve, the equilibrium level of the firm's output, q_e, is determined. Thus, as long as the firm is willing to supply a positive level of output, the SMC curve is the firm's supply curve.

What does the SMC curve tell us? It tells us the profit-maximizing level of output.

Pure profit: how sweet it is

When the OPEC oil cartel restricts their world supply of oil, the price of gasoline increases and gas stations earn short-run pure profits, as illustrated in Figure 9.4. Specifically, the SATC curve indicates whether the firm (gas station) is earning a pure profit, or a normal profit, or is operating at a loss. If

$$p > \text{SATC},$$

then a pure profit exists:

$$\pi = \text{TR} - \text{STC} = pq - \text{SATC}q = (p - \text{SATC})q > 0,$$

given $p >$ SATC, TR $= pq$, and STC $=$ SATCq. In Figure 9.4, $p_e >$ SATC$_e$, TR $= p_e q_e$ is represented by the area $0p_e\text{A}q_e$, and STC = SATC$_e q_e$ is the area 0(SATC$_e$)Bq_e. This results in a pure profit represented by the shared area (SATC$_e$)p_eAB.

What does the SATC curve tell us? The SATC curve tells us if a firm is earning a pure profit, or a normal profit, or is operating at a loss.

Normal profit: always in the long run

If instead

$$p_e = \text{SATC}_e,$$

as illustrated in Figure 9.5, a firm would be earning a normal profit:

$$\pi = \text{TR} - \text{STC} = (p - \text{SATC})q = 0.$$

Total revenue TR is represented by the area $0p_e\text{A}q_e$, which is equal to STC represented by the area 0(SATC$_e$)Aq_e, given $p_e =$ SATC$_e$.

Example 9.4 Determining output for a perfectly competitive firm

Consider a perfectly competitive firm facing an output price of $p_e = \$12$ with the following STC function:

$$\text{STC} = q^2 + 10q + 1,$$

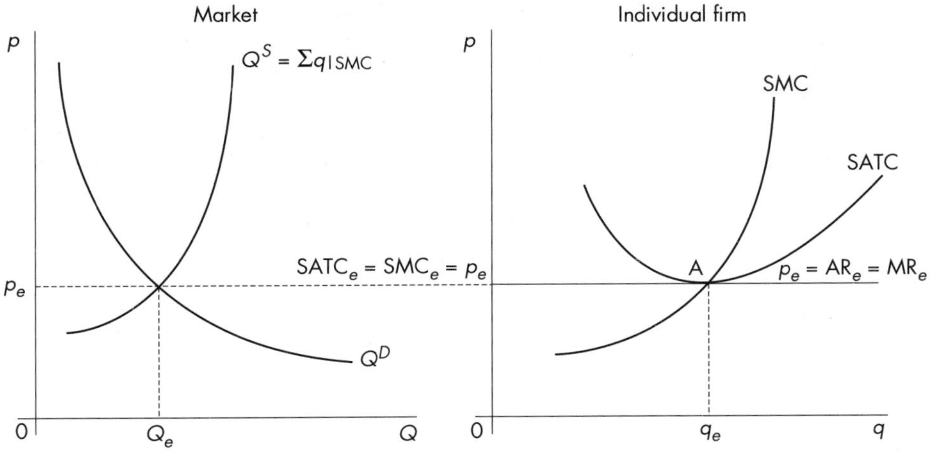

Figure 9.5 **Short-run equilibrium representing a firm earning a normal profit.** If at the profit-maximizing point—where price equals short-run marginal cost—price is equal to short-run average total cost, then the firm will earn a normal profit.

where STVC $= q^2 + 10q$ and TFC $= 1$. The firm's profit-maximizing output is determined by

$$\max_q \pi = \max_q (\text{TR} - \text{STC}) = \max_q [pq - (q^2 + 10q + 1)].$$

The FOC is

$$\frac{d\pi}{dq} = \text{MR} - \text{SMC} = p_e - (2q_e + 10) = 0.$$

Solving for q_e yields the firm's short-run supply function, which indicates how much the firm is willing and able to supply at a given price:

$$q_e = \frac{1}{2}p_e - 5.$$

If the market price facing the firm is $p_e = \$12$, then the firm will supply 1 unit of output, $q_e = 1$. The firm's profit is

$$\pi = pq - \text{STC} = pq - (q^2 + 10q + 1) = 12 - (1 + 10 + 1) = 0.$$

The firm is earning a normal profit: TR $=$ STC.

Suppose the market price falls to \$11; then $q_e = {}^1\!/_2 p_e - 5 = {}^1\!/_2$ and SATC $= \$12.50 > p$, so the firm will operate at a loss:

$$\pi = (11)^1\!/_2 - (1/4 + 5 + 1) = -\$0.75.$$

The loss of \$0.75 is less than the loss of shutting down. If the firm shuts down, it still must pay the TFC = \$1, so the firm will minimize its losses by remaining in business. Price is still above SAVC, $p_e = \$11.00 > \$10.50 = \text{SAVC}$. The firm is able to pay all of its STVC of operating, and still has some revenue left to cover a portion of its TFC. In this case, the firm is able to cover 25 percent of its TFC by staying in business. However, if the price falls below SAVC, the firm is unable to cover even its STVC, so it will minimize its losses by shutting down and incurring a loss equal to TFC.

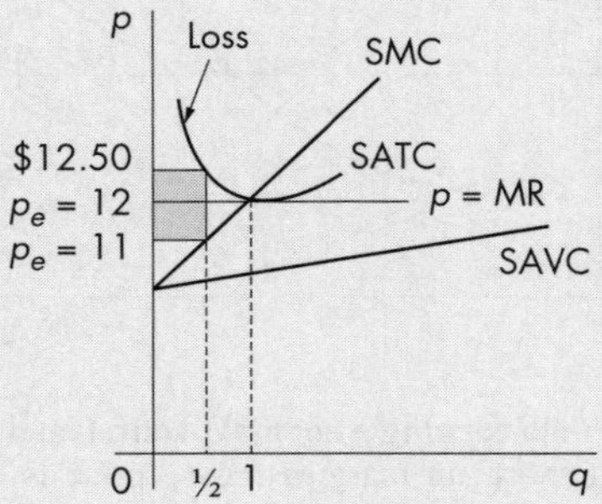

Loss: what to do?

When

$$p < \text{SATC},$$

a firm is operating at a loss:

$$\pi = \text{TR} - \text{STC} = (p - \text{SATC})q < 0.$$

As illustrated in Figure 9.6, TR is the area $0p_e\text{A}q_e$, which is less than STC, represented by the area $0(\text{SATC}_e)\text{B}q_e$. The loss is represented by the shaded area $p_e(\text{SATC}_e)\text{BA}$.

Why would a firm ever operate at a loss? A firm can minimize its losses by continuing to operate if price is greater than short-run average variable cost.

Example 9.5 Illustrating a perfectly competitive firm earning a short-run pure profit

In Example 9.4, if the market price is above SATC, the firm will be earning a pure profit. For example, if $p_e = \$14$, then the firm will supply 2 units of output, given that the firm's short-run supply function is $q_e = p_e/2 - 5$. The firm's pure profit is then

$$\pi = (14)(2) - (4 + 20 + 1) = \$3,$$

where $\text{STC} = q^2 + 10q + 1$, the same as in Example 9.4.

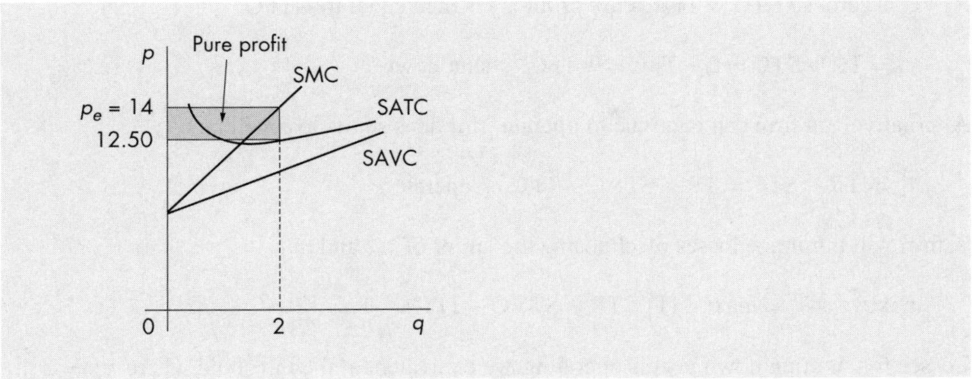

Shutting down: when to do it

Drugstores, gas stations, and convenience stores often stay open late or even operate 24 hours a day. As long as these firms or any firm can cover their variable cost of operation, they will remain open. Once a firm pays all its variable cost, it can then apply any remaining revenue to the fixed operating cost. If it is currently operating at a loss, $p <$ SATC, the profit-maximizing firm may minimize this loss by remaining open. In the long run, firms can eliminate any possibility of operating at a loss by exiting the industry (going out of business). However, in the short run, firms do not have this exiting ability. Their only limited control in minimizing their losses is to determine whether they should operate or shutdown. If a firm shuts down, its output is zero and thus it incurs only fixed cost. At an output level of zero,

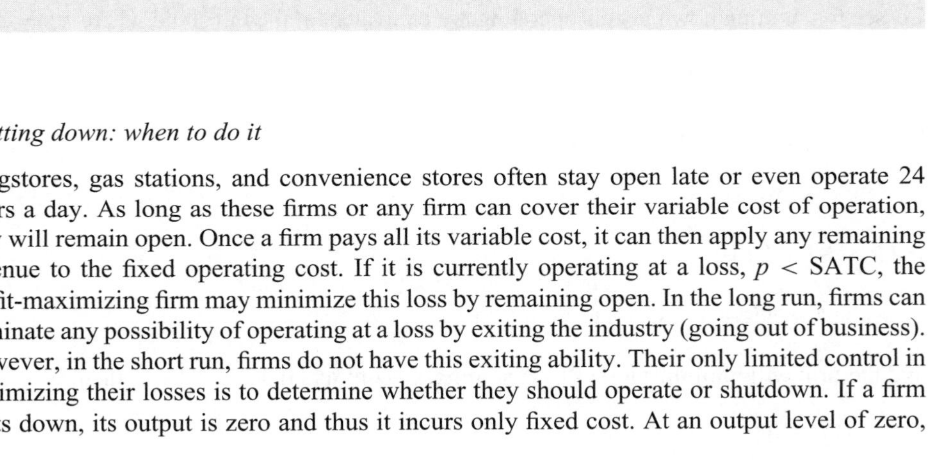

Figure 9.6 **Short-run equilibrium for a firm operating at a loss.** At the profit-maximizing point—where price equals short-run marginal cost—price is less than the short-run average total cost. The firm, if it operates, is operating at a loss, represented by the shaded area.

STVC is zero, so STC = TFC. Pure profit π_S is then equal to −TFC:

$$\pi_S = \text{TR} - \text{STC} = 0 - \text{TFC} = -\text{TFC}, \quad \text{shut down.}$$

Alternatively, a firm can continue to operate. If it does so, its loss will be

$$\pi_O = \text{TR} - \text{STC} = \text{TR} - \text{STVC} - \text{TFC}, \quad \text{operate.}$$

A firm will minimize losses by choosing the larger of π_S and π_O:

$$\max(\pi_S, \pi_O) = \max(-\text{TFC}, \text{TR} - \text{STVC} - \text{TFC}).$$

Losses for shutting down versus operating are equivalent at the threshold where $\pi_S = \pi_O$:

$$-\text{TFC} = \text{TR} - \text{STVC} - \text{TFC}.$$

Simplifying and rearranging terms yields

$$\text{TR} - \text{STVC} = 0.$$

If TR > STVC, then

$$-\text{TFC} < \text{TR} - \text{STVC} - \text{TFC},$$

and the firm will minimize losses by operating. In contrast, if TR < STVC, then

$$-\text{TFC} > \text{TR} - \text{STVC} - \text{TFC},$$

and the firm minimizes losses by shutting down.

This threshold for operating or not may also be stated in terms of per-unit output. Noting that at this threshold

$$\text{TR} - \text{STVC} = pq - \text{SAVC}q = 0,$$

and dividing by q yields

$$p - \text{SAVC} = 0.$$

Thus, if

$$p > \text{SAVC},$$

a firm will minimize losses by continuing to operate, whereas if $p <$ SAVC, it will minimize losses by shutting down. Thus, the SAVC curve indicates whether a firm should operate or not. If the point where price equals SMC is above the SAVC curve, the firm will continue to operate in the short run. Only in the long run, if conditions remain unchanged, will the firm completely suspend operation and exit the industry. With $p >$ SAVC, TR > STVC, so the firm is able to cover (pay) all of its STVC and still have some revenue left to apply toward its TFC. Thus, the firm's losses are less than if it shut down and lost all of the fixed cost.

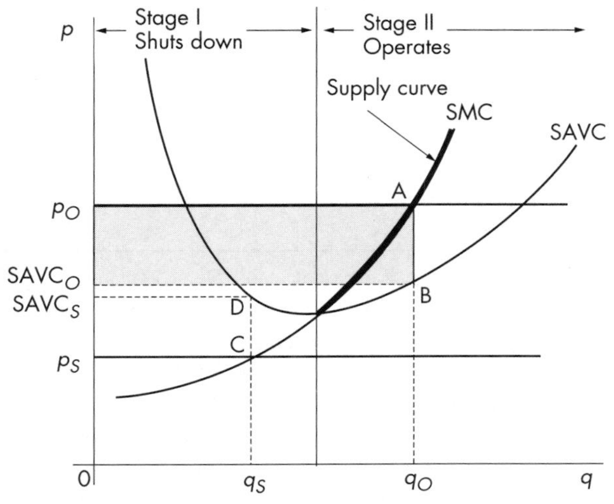

Figure 9.7 **Short-run equilibrium for a firm determining if it should operate or shut down.** In the short run, a firm will only operate in Stage II of production, where price is above short-run average variable cost. Thus, the short-run marginal cost curve above short-run average variable cost is the firm's short-run supply curve.

The role of SAVC in the firm's decision to operate or shut down is illustrated in Figure 9.7. At p_O, TR $= 0p_OAq_O$, which is greater than STVC, represented by the area $0(SAVC_O)Bq_O$. The shaded area $(SAVC_O)p_OAB$ represents revenue above STVC, which can be applied to offset the fixed cost. Thus, the firm will lose this additional revenue $(SAVC_O)p_OAB$, if it shuts down. However, if the price that the firm receives is instead p_S, then TR is represented by the area $0p_SCq_S$ and STVC by the area $0(SAVC_S)Dq_S$. Now the firm is not even covering its variable cost, so, if it operates, its loss is the area $p_S(SAVC_S)DC$ plus TFC. In contrast, if it shuts down, its loss is only TFC. Thus, the firm will minimize its losses by shutting down.

What does the SAVC curve tell us? It tells us if a firm should operate or not.

An example of firms operating where SATC $< p >$ SAVC is the nightly operation of convenience stores and gas stations. The major portion of average variable cost from operating at night is the wage rate for one employee. As long as the firm can cover this variable cost, it will remain open at night. However, in high-crime areas, the cost of crime prevention may result in $p <$ SAVC and the firm closing at dusk. For example, some states require two or more employees to work in a convenience store at night. This increase in SAVC may result in some firms discontinuing their night operations.

Firm's supply curve (SMC above SAVC)

Do not let what you cannot do interfere with what you can do.

(John Wooden)

Specifically, the minimum point of the SAVC curve determines the operating/shutdown condition of the firm. If price is above this minimum, the firm will operate; if price is below this minimum, it will shut down. As illustrated in Figure 9.7, this minimum is the

Table 9.1 Implications of the short-run cost curves

Curve	*Condition*	*Implication*
SMC	SAVC $< p =$ SMC	Supply curve
SATC	$p >$ SATC	Pure profit
	$p =$ SATC	Normal profit
	$p <$ SATC	Loss
SAVC	$p >$ SAVC	Operate
	$p <$ SAVC	Shut down

demarcation between Stage I and Stage II of production. A firm will only operate in Stage II of production. When this profit-maximizing point of price equaling SMC falls below the SAVC curve (Stage I), the firm will shut down. In this case, TR < STVC, so the firm is not able to cover its variable cost of operation. Thus, if it operates, its loss will be all the TFC plus that portion of the STVC not covered by TR. The loss will be less by not producing any output. Only where $p =$ SMC above SAVC will a firm supply a positive level of output. Thus, as illustrated in Figure 9.7, the SMC above the SAVC is the **firm's short-run supply curve,** which indicates how much a firm is willing and able to supply at a given price. In summary, the economic implications from the short-run cost curves are listed in Table 9.1.

Firm's short-run supply curve. How much a firm is willing and able to supply at a given price. *E.g., how much candy a drug store has for sale at a given price.*

We have not yet discussed the average fixed cost (AFC) curve, because it does not aid in determining any short-run decisions facing a firm. In the short run, fixed costs are fixed; since they cannot be altered, firms have no control over them. Similar to your own life, there is little or no value in being concerned about things over which you have no control. So, for short-run maximization of profits, firms are not concerned with fixed costs. These fixed costs are unrecoverable or sunk costs in the short run. Sunk costs are based on past decisions by the firm, such as a decision to invest in a particular piece of equipment. Such decisions and resulting type of fixed inputs do determine the set of choices available to a firm; however, within this set, they do not influence the profit-maximizing choice. As an example, consider a firm whose past decision resulted in obtaining a patent for the manufacture of a certain commodity. This patent opens up a number of opportunities, but the profit-maximizing choice among these opportunities is not determined by ownership of the patent.

What does the AFC curve tell us? It tells us nothing in terms of maximizing short-run profit.

Shifting market demand

Following the infectious disease (anthrax) attacks in New York and Washington DC in September of 2001, there was a large increase in the demand for gasmasks. This change resulted in a shift in the market demand curve for gasmasks, which altered their equilibrium price and quantity. The short-run market equilibrium depends on economic conditions remaining unchanged. Changes in the determinants of market demand, other than price, will shift the demand curve. Recall that a change in the own price of a commodity results in a change in quantity demanded (movement along a demand curve) rather than a shift in demand. Specifically, *market-demand shifters* are changes in consumers' income and preferences, changes in the price of related commodities (substitutes and complements), and changes in population (number of consumers).

Changes that will likely trigger a shift to the right of the market demand curve are an increase in aggregate consumer income, population, or preferences for a commodity; a fall in the price of a complement commodity; or a rise in the price of a substitute. Such a shift will generally occur from these changes unless only a small segment of individual consumers' demands are affected, which causes no perceptible influence on market demand. As illustrated in Figure 9.8, this shift in demand from Q^D to $Q^{D'}$ increases the quantity demanded from Q_e to Q'. Quantity demanded is now greater than quantity supplied, which drives down inventories and exerts an upward pressure on price. This increase in price affects both quantity demanded and quantity supplied of the commodity. First, the rise in price will ration the limited supply and decrease quantity demanded, a movement upward along the demand curve $Q^{D'}$. Quantity demanded will decline from Q'. A reduction in inventories signaling upward pressure on price will also stimulate a supply response by firms. As the price rises, firms will increase output to maintain their profit-maximizing position of equating price to SMC. This increase in output results in a change in quantity supplied (a movement upward along the market supply curve) from Q_e toward Q'_e. The corresponding reduction in quantity demanded and increase in quantity supplied will eliminate the initial excess demand $Q' - Q_e$. A new short-run equilibrium price p'_e will be established, with a corresponding market-clearing quantity Q'_e.

The degree to which price and quantity change as a result of a demand shift depends on the elasticity of supply. As illustrated in Figure 9.9, the more inelastic the supply curve, the less responsive supply is to a shift in demand. A major determinant of supply elasticity is the ability to vary inputs. In a market period, supply is perfectly inelastic, resulting in the absence of a supply response (Figure 9.1). In contrast, if a firm has more time

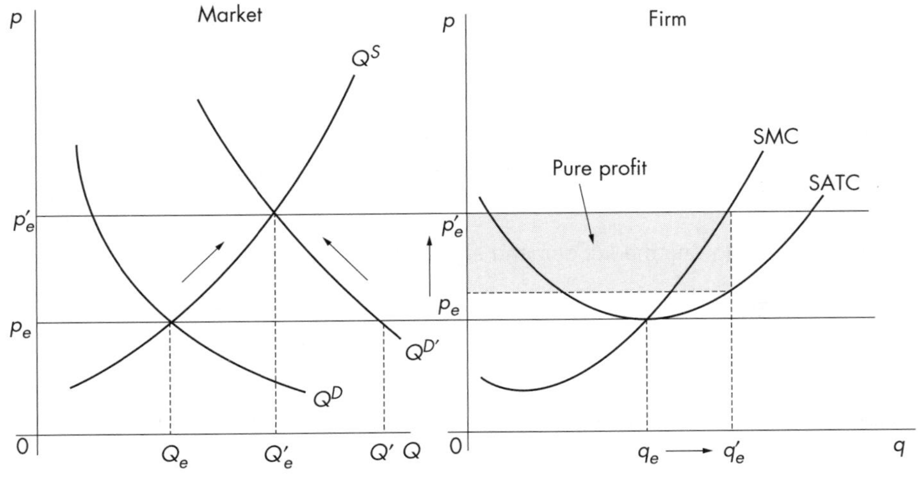

Figure 9.8 **Short-run equilibrium adjustments from an increase in demand.** An upward shift in demand drives the price up. Given the incentive of profit maximizing, firms will respond to this increase in price by increasing output.

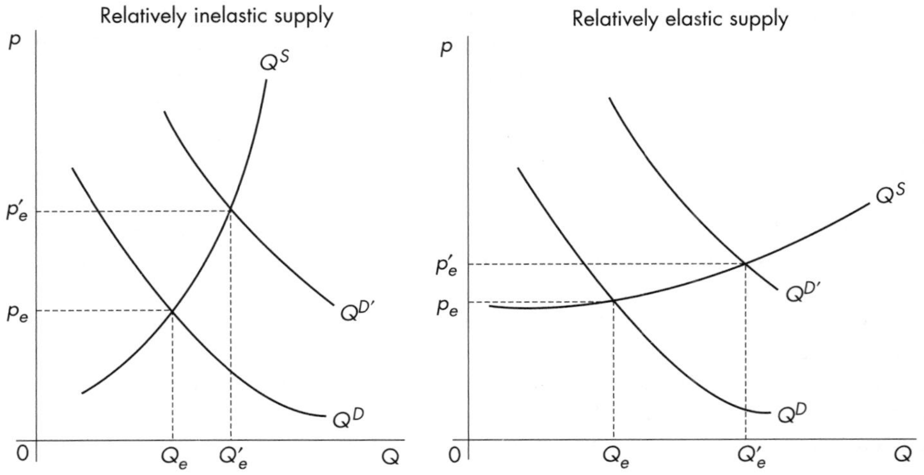

Figure 9.9 **Relative elasticity of supply and demand curve shifts.** The more inelastic the supply curve, the less responsive output is to a change in price.

in which to vary inputs, the supply curve will become more elastic, generating a greater supply response from a shift in demand. Thus, as demonstrated in the section on long-run equilibrium, the long-run supply curve will tend to be relatively more elastic than the short-run supply curve.

The incentive of individual firms within this market to increase output from q_e to q_e' is illustrated by the increase in pure profit (shaded area in Figure 9.8). As illustrated, it is initially assumed that firms are earning a normal profit at the price and output combination p_e and q_e. The increase in price to p_e' and associated output of q_e' from the supply response result in a short-run pure profit for a firm within this industry. This short-run pure profit is represented by the shaded area in Figure 9.8. In this short run, new firms are unable to enter this industry and existing firms cannot be sold; thus, this is a short-run equilibrium condition for existing firms.

Example 9.6 Illustrating short-run market equilibrium with a shift in demand

Consider the following market demand and supply functions:

$$Q^D = 55 - p,$$

$$Q^S = -5 + p.$$

Market equilibrium is established by equating market demand with market supply:

$$Q^D = Q^S,$$

$$55 - p_e = -5 + p_e.$$

Solving for price yields the equilibrium price $p_e = 30$. Substituting this equilibrium price into either the market demand or market supply functions yields the equilibrium market quantity $Q_e = 25$.

If the market demand curve shifts to $Q^{D\prime}$,

$$Q^{D'} = 75 - p,$$

then a new equilibrium price of $p'_e = 40$ and quantity of $Q'_e = 35$ are established. As a result of this increase in market demand and without any supply response, at $p = 30$, $Q^{D'} = 45 > Q^S = 25$. This imbalance of supply and demand causes an upward pressure on price. The increase in price provides incentives for firms to increase their quantity supplied of the commodity and consumers to decrease their quantity demanded.

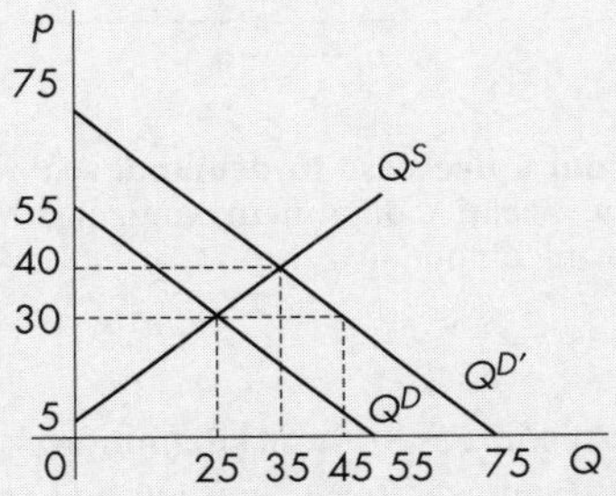

Thus, without intervention from any governmental agencies, the free market will respond to a shift in consumer demand by both rationing quantity supplied and increasing the production of the commodity. This ability of markets to allocate supply without any planning or programs by governmental agencies is what Adam Smith coined the **invisible hand**.[2] This invisible hand also works given a shift to the left of the market demand curve. A decrease in demand—as a result of a loss in aggregate income or population, a decrease in the price of substitute commodities, an increase in price of complements, or a change in preferences away from the commodity—will have the exact reverse effect. For example, the Great Recession decreased the market demand for automobiles. As illustrated in Figure 9.10, this downward shift in demand from Q^D to $Q^{D'}$ decreases the quantity demanded from Q_e to Q'. Quantity demanded is now less than quantity supplied, which increases inventories and exerts a downward pressure on price. This decrease in price affects both quantity demanded and quantity supplied of the commodity. First the fall in price will increase quantity demanded, a movement downward along the demand curve $Q^{D'}$. Quantity demanded will increase from Q' toward Q'_e. A rise in inventories signaling downward pressure on price will also stimulate a supply response by firms. As the price falls, firms will decrease output to maintain their profit-maximizing position of equating price to SMC. This decrease in output results in a change in quantity supplied (a movement downward along the market supply curve) from Q_e toward Q'_e. The corresponding increase in quantity demanded and decrease in quantity supplied will eliminate the initial excess supply $Q_e - Q'$. A new short-run equilibrium price p'_e will then be established, with a corresponding market-clearing quantity Q'_e.

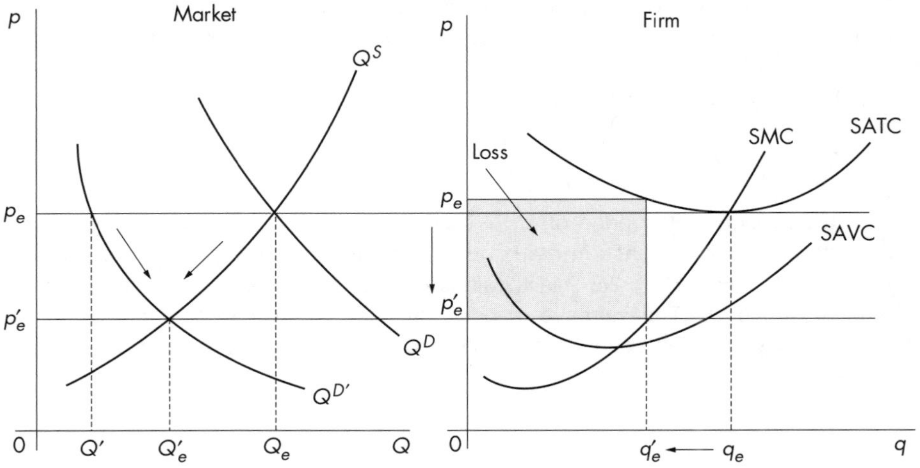

Figure 9.10 **Short-run equilibrium adjustments from a decrease in demand.** A downward shift in demand lowers the price. Given the incentive of profit maximizing, firms will respond to this decline in price by decreasing output.

Invisible hand. The ability of markets to allocate resources without planning or programs by governmental agencies. *E.g., in late spring, market forces will automatically satisfy an increased demand for swimsuits without any governmental planning.*

In an effort to minimize losses, individual firms within this market will decrease output from q_e to q'_e. Price p'_e, where it intersects SMC, is still above SAVC, indicating that a firm will supply a positive level of output even though it is operating at a loss. This loss is illustrated by the firm earning a normal profit with the initial price p_e and the resulting short-run loss as a consequence of the price decline, the shaded area in Figure 9.10. In the short run, existing firms are unable to exit this industry by selling their firms.

Shifting market supply

Just as some changes in demand shift the market demand curve, certain changes in supply will shift the market supply curve. Specifically, *market supply shifters* are a large entrance or exodus of firms into a perfectly competitive industry and any changes in input prices and technology that shift an individual firm's supply curve. For example, the drastic decline in the price of computer microchips resulted in a large increase in the supply of four-function calculators. As with a shift in the market demand curve, the effect of a shift in market supply is dependent on the elasticity of market demand. As illustrated in Figure 9.11, if the market demand curve is relatively elastic, a shift to the right of the market supply curve will not depress output price as much as when the demand curve is relatively inelastic. For example, if in the short run existing firms are earning pure profits, then in the long run new firms will enter this industry. If the market demand curve is relatively elastic, a large increase

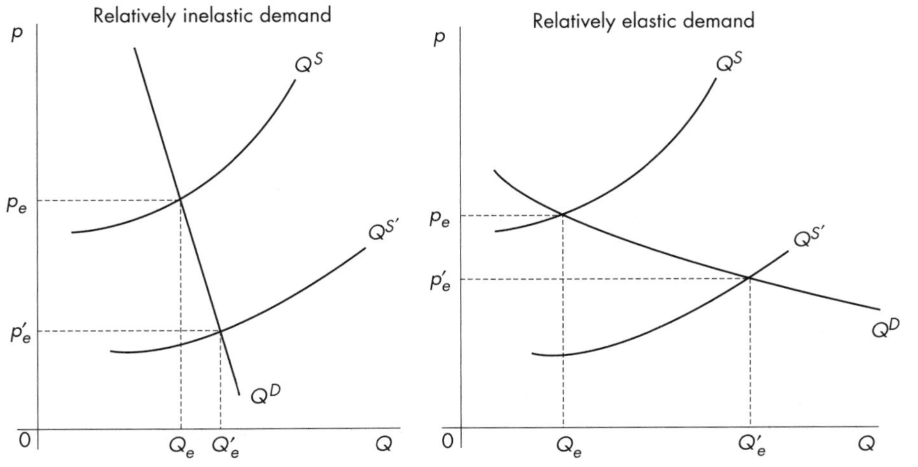

Figure 9.11 **Short-run equilibrium adjustments from an increase in supply.** The more inelastic the demand curve, the more responsive price is to a shift in the supply curve.

in output from new firms entering will not cause a large fall in output price. This relative unresponsiveness of price will slow the erosion of pure profits as new firms enter the industry and will allow a large increase in output. In contrast, with a relatively inelastic market demand curve, a large price decrease will be accompanied by only a small increase in output. The opportunities for pure profits by firms entering the industry will be rapidly eroded away and there will be a relatively modest increase in output.

The influence of demand elasticity on market price and output has implications for technological development in particular industries. If the market demand curve is relatively inelastic, the main benefits from an improvement in technology, resulting in a shift to the right of the market supply curve, will be passed on to consumers in the form of lower prices. In this case, a technology improvement will not stimulate a large increase in quantity demanded. Alternatively, if the market demand curve is relatively elastic, the main impact of technology improvement is manifested in output increases, which directly benefits firms within the industry. Thus, industries with relatively inelastic demand curves may be less likely to invest in technological development.

Example 9.7 Illustrating short-run market equilibrium with a shift in supply

Consider the following market demand and supply functions:

$$Q^D = 55 - p,$$

$$Q^S = -9 + p.$$

Market equilibrium is established by equating market demand with market supply:

$$Q^D = Q^S,$$

$$55 - p_e = -9 + p_e.$$

Solving for price yields the equilibrium price $p_e = 32$. Substituting this equilibrium price into either the market demand or market supply functions yields the equilibrium market quantity, $Q_e = 23$.

If the market supply curve shifts to $Q^{S'}$,

$$Q^{S'} = -5 + p,$$

then a new equilibrium price $p'_e = 30$ and quantity $Q'_e = 25$ are established. As a result of this increase in market supply and without any demand response, at $p = 32$, $Q^D = 23 < Q^{S'} = 27$. This unbalance of supply and demand causes a downward pressure on price. The decrease in price provides incentives for firms to decrease their quantity supplied of the commodity and households to increase their quantity demanded.

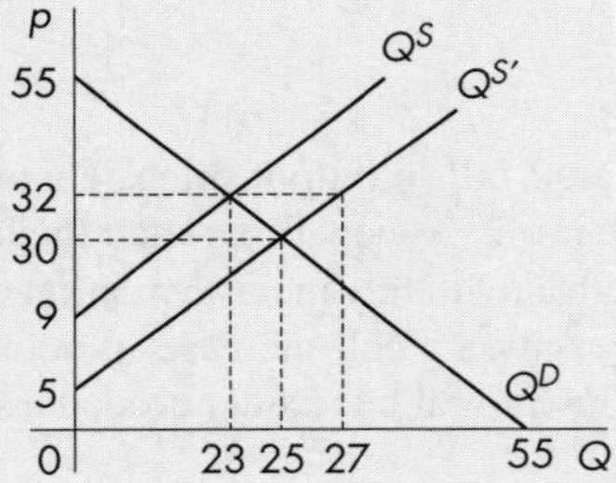

A market demand and supply shifters model

Estimating demand and supply functions by econometric methods, we can determine the market demand and supply elasticities. We can then empirically investigate the market's response to a shift in demand and supply. Such an empirical analysis will provide estimates on the magnitude of changes in price and quantity, given demand and supply shifts. As an application, we will investigate the effects of increases in the price of corn on the food-before-fuel issue, the tax on beer, and the effects of an agricultural pesticide cancellation on a crop.

To investigate the market response, we will assume a Cobb–Douglas market demand function

$$Q^D = ap^b.$$

This is a constant elasticity of demand function, where $b < 0$, with

$$\varepsilon^D_{Q,p} = \frac{\partial \ln Q^D}{\partial \ln p} = b,$$

and a is a constant that shifts the demand curve. We also assume a constant elasticity of supply function

$$Q^S = op^d,$$

where o is a constant that shifts the supply curve. The elasticity of supply is

$$\varepsilon^S_{Q,p} = \frac{\partial \ln Q^S}{\partial \ln p} = d,$$

The model is completed with the following equation, which requires quantity demanded to equal quantity supplied at the equilibrium price p_e:

$$Q^D = Q^S \quad \text{or} \quad ap_e^b = op_e^d.$$

Rearranging terms,

$$\frac{a}{o} = \frac{p_e^d}{p_e^b} = p_e^{d-b}.$$

Solving for p_e yields

$$p_e = (a/o)^{1/(d-b)}.$$

Taking the logarithm of both sides,

$$\begin{aligned}\ln p_e &= \frac{1}{d-b} \ln \frac{a}{o} \\ &= \frac{1}{d-b}(\ln a - \ln o).\end{aligned}$$

This states that

$$\%\Delta p_e = \frac{1}{d-b}(\%\Delta a - \%\Delta o),$$

where Δ represents change. We can now use this model in our applications to investigate the effects of a change in a policy that shifts the demand or supply curves.

Application: Food before fuel

First consider a drastic increase in corn prices as a result of increased fuel ethanol production in 2007. Corn is the major input in US fuel-ethanol production. As a result of a boom in ethanol production, the market demand curve for corn shifted outward by 20 percent. USDA estimates the elasticity of demand $\varepsilon^D_{Q,p} = b$ and the elasticity of supply $\varepsilon^S_{Q,p} = d$ for corn to be -0.91 and 0.23, respectively. If supply were perfectly

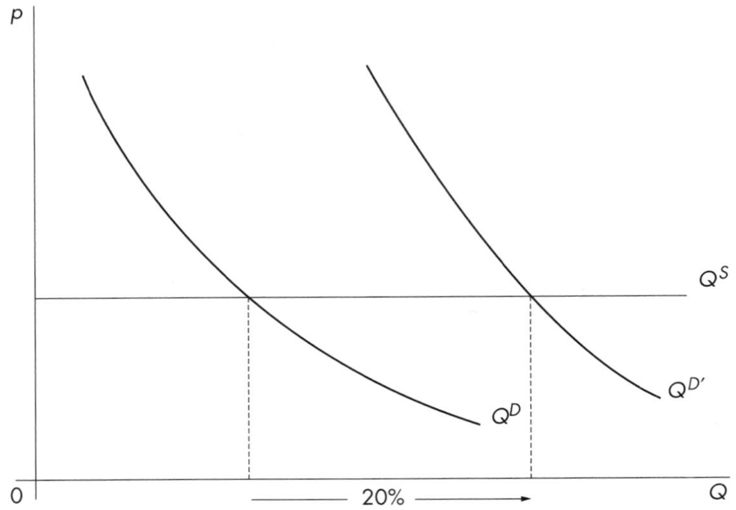

Figure 9.12 **Simple analysis of a demand shift.** Assuming a perfectly elastic supply curve for corn, a shift in demand for corn from increased ethanol production does not change the equilibrium price, so only demand increases.

elastic, quantity of corn would in fact rise by 20 percent (Figure 9.12). However, this analysis is too simple. The supply curve for corn is not perfectly elastic. A corn price rise has a dampening effect on demand (Figure 9.13). Each 1 percent shift outward in the demand curve will cause a 1/1.14 of 1 percent increase in equilibrium price:

$$\%\Delta p_e = [1/(d-b)](1\%) = 1\%/(0.23+0.91) = 1/1.14\%.$$

The boom in ethanol production causes the demand curve to shift outward by 20 percent, so price can be predicted to rise by 0.20(1/1.14) = 17.5 percent. A rise in price by 17.5 percent results in a 0.175(-0.91) = 15.9 percent fall in demand. Thus, a more complete analysis indicates that an increase in corn demand from ethanol production results in a rise in corn consumption of 20 percent. However, the increase in price decreases corn consumption by 15.9 percent. The net result is an increase in corn consumption of 20 percent – 15.9 percent = 4.1 percent.

Source: US Department of Agriculture, "An Analysis of the Effects of an Expansion in Biofuel Demand on U.S. Agriculture," Economic Research Service, May 2007.

Application: Beer tax

As a second application of a demand shift, consider beer excise taxes.* In an effort to increase revenue, reduce driving under the influence of alcohol, and discourage binge

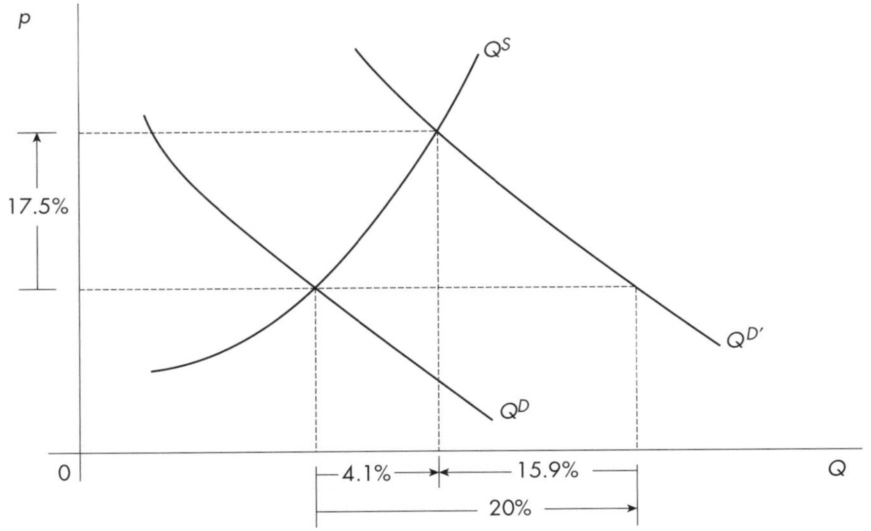

Figure 9.13 **Complete analysis of a demand shift.** An upward shift in the demand curve results in a rise in the price, which stimulates a decline in quantity demanded. So the total effect is mitigated by the price rise.

drinking among college students, various states have considered increasing the excise tax on beer. Saffer and Dave estimated the elasticity of demand for binge drinking, $\varepsilon^D_{Q,p} = b$, to be -0.51 (inelastic). Given this elasticity of demand, we can determine the effect of an excise tax increase, resulting in a 50 percent increase in the market price of beer, on the market price and quantity of bingeing. The excise tax causes the demand curve for beer bingeing to shift downward. Young and Bielinska-Kwapisz's results indicate that the supply of alcohol is perfectly elastic. Given this perfectly elastic supply, the quantity of beer bingeing would fall by $(0.50)(-0.51) = 25.5$ percent (Figure 9.14). There is not a price decline in beer yielding a stimulating effect on demand. Each 1 percent shift inward in the demand curve will cause a $1/(\infty + 0.51)$ of 1 percent decrease in equilibrium price:

$$\%\Delta p_e = [1/(d - b)](1\%) = 1\%/(\infty + 0.51) = 0\%.$$

The excise tax causes the demand curve to shift inward by 25.5 percent and there is no price decline. All of the excise tax is passed onto the students.

Sources: H. Saffer and D. Dave, "Alcohol Advertising and Alcohol Consumption by Adolescents," National Bureau of Economic Research, NBER Working Papers, Number 9676 (May 2003); D. Young and A. Bielinska-Kwapisz, "Alcohol Taxes and Beverage Prices," *National Tax Journal* 55 (2002): 57–74.

*See Chapter 10. An excise tax is a tax per physical unit—for example, a tax per pack of cigarettes, per gallon of motor fuel, or per ounce of alcohol.

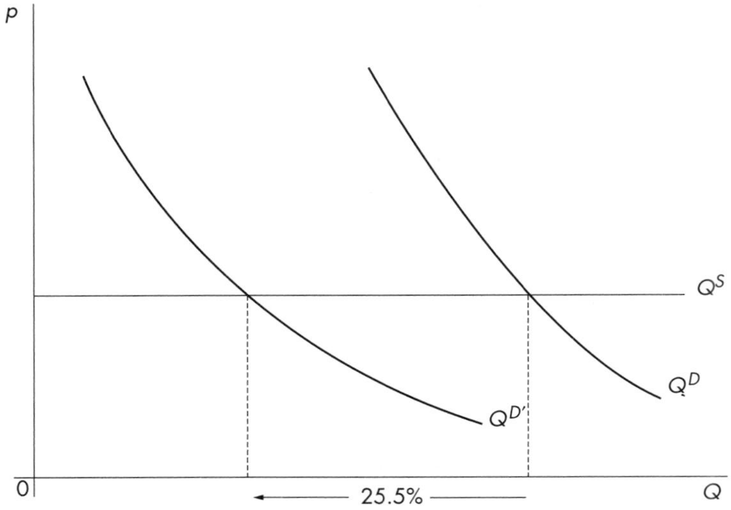

Figure 9.14 **Beer bingeing shift in demand.** A downward shift in the demand curve does not result in a decline in the price, so the total effect is not mitigated by a price decline.

Application: Agricultural pesticide cancellation

As a final application, consider the effects of (Figure 9.15) the cancellation of the glyphosate used in apple production in the West. Cancellation of a pesticide used in agriculture may require the substitution of other more expensive alternative pesticides or other methods of pest control. This increased cost will shift firms' costs upward and thus decreases the supply of the agricultural commodity. For apple production in the West, this increase in cost would result in a decrease in Q^S by 9 percent, $\%\Delta o = -9$ percent, so

$$\%\Delta p_e = [1/(d-b)]9\%.$$

Empirical elasticity estimates are $\varepsilon^D = -0.374$ and $\varepsilon^S = 0.306$ for Western apples. Thus, $1/(d-b) = 1/(0.374 + 0.306) = 1.47$, and

$$\%\Delta p = (1.47)9\% = 13.2\%.$$

Thus, the price of Western apples increases by 13.2 percent, which increases supply by 4.039 percent = (0.132)(0.306). The final result is a 4.961 percent reduction in apple supply.

Source: J. Roosen, "Regulation in Quality Differentiated Markets: Pesticide Cancellations in U.S. Apple Production," *Journal of Agricultural and Applied Economics* 3 (2001): 117–133.

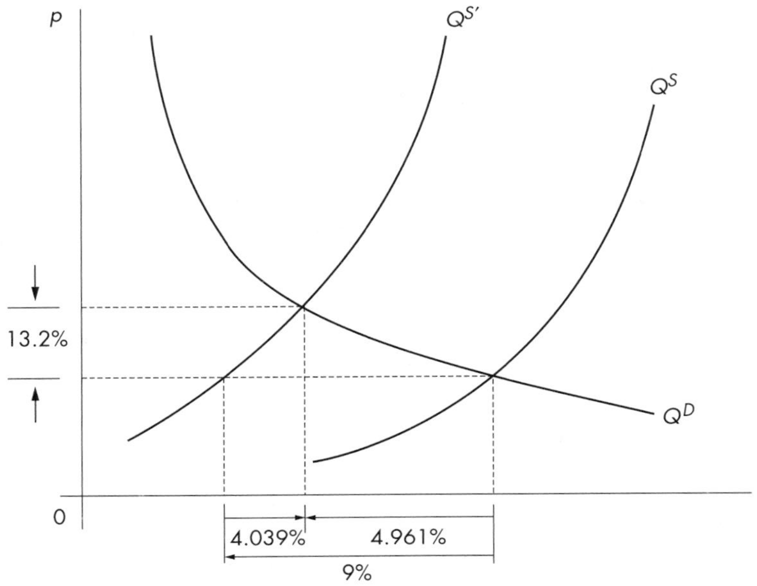

Figure 9.15 **A pesticide cancellation.** An upward shift in the supply curve resulting from a pesticide cancellation causes an increase in the output price, which mitigates the reduction in output.

Long run: removing short-run fixations

If you plan on accomplishing in the long run your goals for the short run, it will be too late.

(Michael Wetzstein)

Translation: Pure profits may only be earned in the short run.

In the 1960s, kiwi fruit producers from New Zealand were earning short-run pure profits by exporting their fruit to the United States. As a result of this profit potential, in 1968, Californian George Tinamidae planted an acre of vineyard land with kiwi vines. By 1980, over 8000 acres in California were devoted to the production of kiwi fruit. This is an example of the long-run response in a perfectly competitive market. In the long run, all inputs can vary, so producers are free to enter or exit an industry. The perfectly competitive model assumes there are no special costs of entering or exiting an industry. Specifically, no barriers to entry exist. For an analysis of the long run, we initially assume a short-run market equilibrium with a representative firm (a New Zealand kiwi fruit producer) earning a pure profit (Figure 9.4). With the assumption of perfect knowledge, all firms have identical cost curves associated with a given level of production, so all current firms within this industry are earning pure profits. In the long run, these short-run pure profits provide incentives for firms to expand their facilities (increase fixed inputs) and for new firms to enter the industry (Californian kiwi fruit producers). This increase in size and number of firms in the industry shifts the market supply curve to the right, resulting in a reduction in the equilibrium price. As the equilibrium price falls, pure profits are reduced, which decreases incentives for existing firms to increase production or new firms to enter into production. As the price continues to fall, pure profits are squeezed further, and when the price falls to where it is equal to SATC, all pure profits are squeezed out and firms earn only normal profits. At this point of normal profits, there is no longer any incentive for firms to further expand production or for new firms to enter. Recall that the definition of a normal profit is the minimum return to inputs necessary to keep a firm in a given production activity. This is the point of long-run equilibrium with price equal to SATC.

Why, in the long run, will revenue never exceed cost? If revenue exceeds cost (pure profit) in the short run, new firms will enter the industry until revenue is equal to cost (normal profit) in the long run.

To confirm this long-run equilibrium position, consider the opposite process of adjustment with firms in the short run operating at a loss (Figure 9.6). For example, in 2009, auto firms experienced substantial losses as a result of the Great Recession. In the long run, firms (auto manufactures) will cut back on production or exit the industry. This will result in the short-run market supply curve shifting to the left, with an associated increase in equilibrium price p_e. This increase in market price reduces the loss of firms remaining in the industry, and when the price rises to SATC, firms will earn normal profits. At normal profits, there is no longer any incentive for firms to exit the industry. The existence of pure profits or losses results in a long-run adjustment characterized by the corresponding entry or exit of resources.

Long-run cost adjustment

Long-run adjustments are also possible in terms of costs. For example, assume that a number of firms enjoy some special advantage—say, a relatively more productive soil. The entry of new firms might push the price down to normal profits for all firms except those with relatively more productive land. The firms with more productive land can continue to reap pure profits in the short run, as indicated in Figure 9.16. However, eventually the profitable land will be sold to new owners. The prospective new owners would be willing to pay more for the land that yields a pure profit compared with land where only normal profits are earned. The increase in cost of the land raises production cost. If the sellers of the more productive land are shrewd bargainers, they will obtain a price that pushes SATC just up to SATC′, the

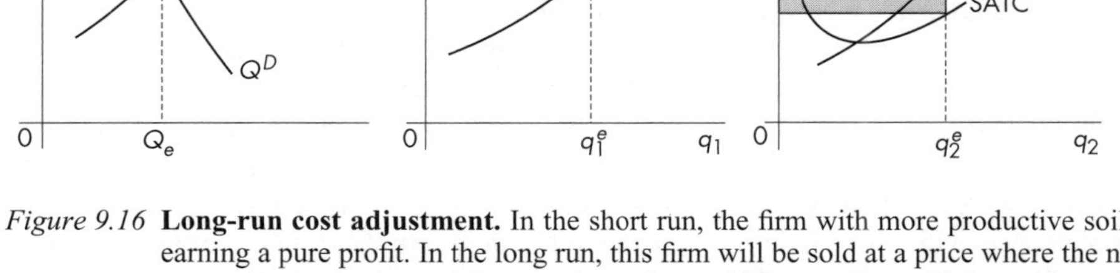

Figure 9.16 **Long-run cost adjustment.** In the short run, the firm with more productive soil is earning a pure profit. In the long run, this firm will be sold at a price where the new owners' output price equals average total cost. This new firm will then only earn a long-run normal profit.

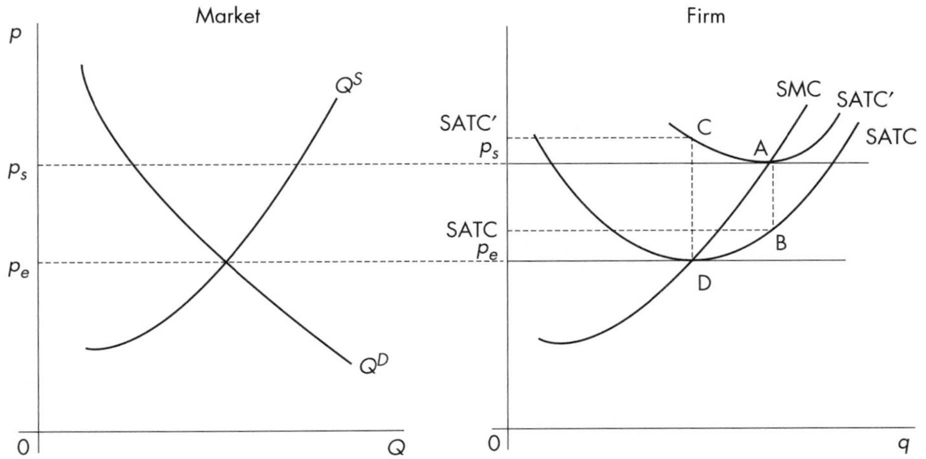

Figure 9.17 **Agricultural support prices.** In the short run, a support price above the equilibrium price p_e results in a short-run pure profit. Land prices increase as a result of this short-run pure profit, so in the long run only a normal profit is earned.

expected future price p_e. Then, in the long run, when the firms are sold, only normal profits will result.

This phenomenon of cost adjusting to price is particularly important in US agricultural policy. As discussed in Chapter 10, the governmentally established support prices increase farm income by creating short-run pure profits for the agricultural firms. As illustrated in Figure 9.17, suppose that prior to any governmental support price, firms are earning normal profits at price p_e. The establishment of a support price p_s, above the equilibrium price p_e, yields a pure profit, represented by the area (SATC)p_sAB. However, over the years, pure profits will be eroded away because of the bidding up of land prices. Eventually, producers are forced back to the same zero pure profit (normal profit) position that existed before the support price policy. Farmers who owned the land during the price rise enjoyed pure profits while they owned the land and will enjoy a capital gain when they sell it. However, the new owners will only receive normal profits at the support price p_S. Efforts to remove the support price meet with a great deal of resistance, because the firms operate at a loss without governmental support. New owners with costs of SATC′ and facing the nonsupport price p_e will experience a loss, represented by the area p_e(SATC′)CD, or will produce nothing and incur a loss of fixed costs. This is potentially a major problem for California marijuana growers. It is currently against the law to grow marijuana, so government enforcement restricts its cultivation. The restrictions lead to higher prices for marijuana and subsequently increased land values where cultivation can be relatively undetected. With pressure to legalize marijuana (a defeated 2010 California ballot initiative), marijuana growers are concerned that they will experience losses with open competition.

Cost adjustments also occur when firms are operating at a loss in the short run. In the long run, owners will sell these losing firms. New owners will not be willing to pay a price for the firms in which they would also operate at a loss. The price of a firm will decline until the new owners receive a normal profit. For example, in the nineteenth century and the first half of the twentieth , an individual could receive from the federal government 160 acres of free land, within the United States, if they were willing to farm on the land for 5 years. Some of these farmers operated at a loss during their tenure on the land. The improvements to the land—including a well, barns, and a house—resulted in the land having some value. However, when the land was sold, the owners could not receive the full price they paid for the improvements, because the farm was operating at a loss. Prospective new owners bid the price of the farm down to where they hoped to realize at least a normal profit. In some cases, the farms passed though a number of owners, with the price of the farm declining at each ownership transaction until an owner could finally earn a normal profit. It is not that previous owners were poor managers, but their SATC's were too high to realize a normal profit. As the farm price declines, SATC shifts downward, reducing losses.

This cost adjustment is also evident in restaurant locations. Original owners may operate at a loss for a number of months, the next owners might last longer, and finally, after the restaurant changes hands a number of times, an owner earns a normal profit. This explains why a restaurant at a given location may change from Mexican to Italian to Chinese.

What are the equilibrium conditions?

Assume that all firms have identical cost (identical knowledge). Long-run equilibrium conditions require every firm to earn exactly a zero pure profit (normal profit). Thus, a perfectly competitive market is in long-run equilibrium if and only if the following conditions hold for every firm within the market:

$$\text{SMC} = \text{SATC} = \text{LMC} = \text{LAC} = p.$$

These conditions imply that a market equilibrium exists where the demand curve for each firm is tangent to its LAC curve at the minimum point (Figure 9.18). Thus, assuming the fixed input is the size of a firm's physical plant, every firm in the industry is driven to the optimum-size plant in the long run. The optimum-size plant occurs at the minimum point of

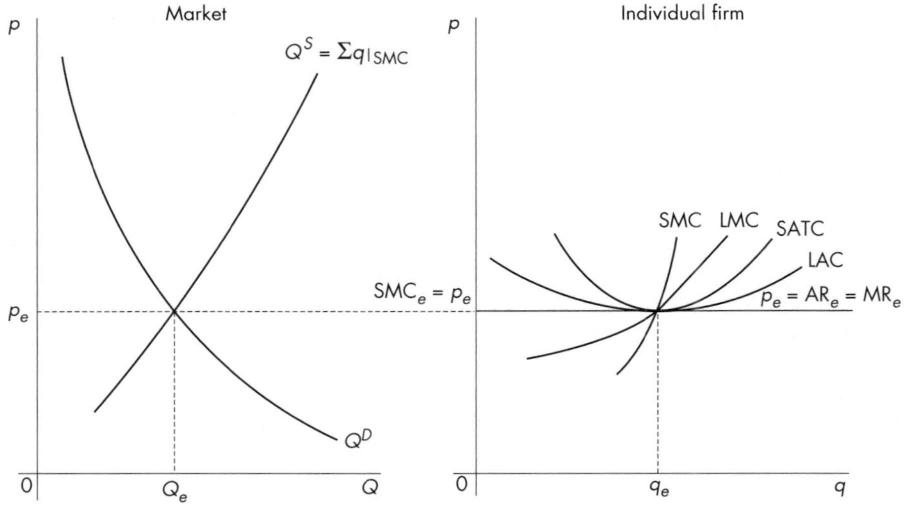

Figure 9.18 **Long-run market equilibrium.** The equilibrium condition in the long run is where $p = \text{SMC} = \text{LMC} = \text{LAC} = \text{SATC}$.

long-run average cost. Also, the firm is operating at full capacity, which is at the minimum of the short-run average total cost curve. Costs per unit of output (average costs) are at a minimum in both the short run and the long run. Thus, the firm is employing the optimum level of its fixed inputs (say, plant size) and within this optimum level is operating at full capacity (minimizing the average costs associated with this size of plant). However, the goal of individual firms is to equate MR to LMC for profit maximization, not to equate price to LAC for zero profits. A consequence of a perfectly competitive firm maximizing profit is the long-run condition of price equaling LAC.

As a demonstration of the necessary and sufficient conditions for this long-run equilibrium of a perfectly competitive market, assume that all firms have the same LAC and that currently the market is in long-run equilibrium. Let the market equilibrium price be p_e and the equilibrium output for each firm be q_e. If there are n firms in the industry, then total industry output is $Q = nq_e$.

If market demand increases, creating an initial disequilibrium, economic forces will work to return the market to equilibrium. As indicated in Figure 9.19, an increase in market demand results in a shift in the demand curve and a short-run increase in price from p_e to p'. Quantity also increases from Q_e to Q_S. Increase in market demand implies a new short-run equilibrium after firms complete their short-run output adjustments to the new demand situation. In the short run, individual firms in this market are now earning a pure profit, which is indicated by the shaded area in Figure 9.19. Short-run pure profits result in new firms entering the industry in the long run. If there are no entry and exit costs, firms will generally only enter an industry when price rises above long-run average cost. If there are entry and exit costs, firms will generally only enter an industry when price rises substantially above long-run average cost. As discussed in Chapter 19, this is called the *hurdle rate*, which is typically three or four times the interest rate on borrowed money.

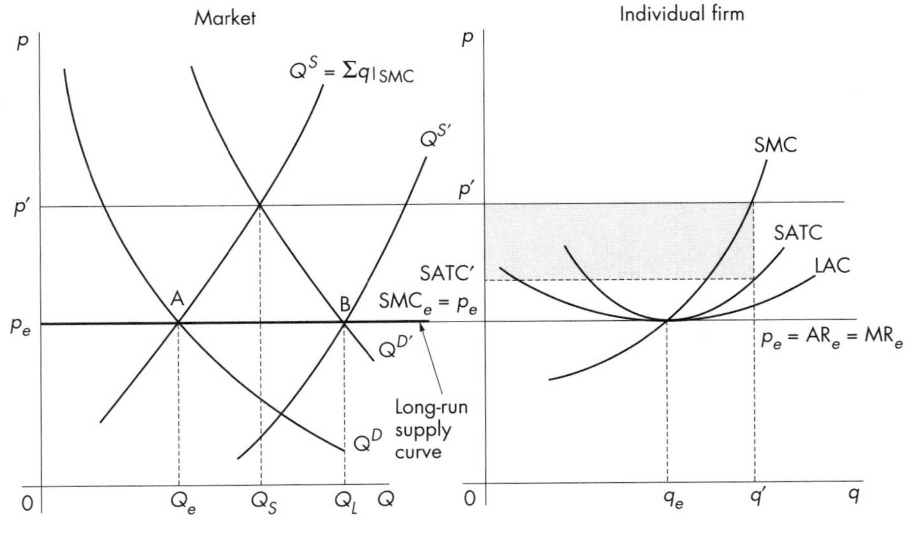

Figure 9.19 **Constant-cost industry.** In the long run, new firms will enter an industry earning short-run pure profits. As these new firms enter, if the cost of production does not change, the long-run market supply curve will be horizontal.

Constant-cost industry

The new long-run equilibrium depends on the effect that new firms entering the industry have on LAC. If we assume that prices of inputs used by the industry remain constant regardless of the amounts of each input demanded, the long-run average cost curve will then be unaffected by the entry and exit of firms. Specifically, we assume that firms within this industry are facing perfectly elastic supply curves for the inputs used in their production. For example, restaurants in one town may not affect the wage rate of labor, so an increase in the demand for labor by restaurants would not affect wages. The long-run average cost curve does not shift as a result of new restaurants entering the industry. An increase in demand for inputs by restaurants results in an increase in the supply without any change in prices. The industry's (restaurants') demand for inputs is so small, relative to the overall market demand for the inputs, that it has no influence on the price of inputs. Thus, as new firms enter and total industry output increases, the average cost of production does not change, and the long-run equilibrium price for this industry is independent of this increase in number of firms and the total industry output. This type of industry is called a **constant-cost industry**. Other examples of constant-cost industries are microbreweries, bookstores, drugstores, tanning salons, and hair salons. These are industries that do not have sufficient demands on inputs to influence input prices.

Constant-cost industry. A market with a horizontal long-run supply curve. *E.g., building new bowling alleys may not affect the cost of construction materials, so an increase in the demand for construction materials by bowling alleys would not affect construction prices.*

Example 9.8 Establishing equilibrium in a constant-cost industry

Assume all firms have the same cost represented by

$$\text{SATC} = q^2 - 2q + 6$$

and face the market demand function

$$Q^D = 110 - 2p.$$

Long-run equilibrium will occur at the minimum of SATC:

$$\partial\text{SATC}/\partial q = 2q_e - 2 = 0.$$

Solving for q results in an output for each firm of $q_e = 1$. At this minimum of SATC, SMC = SATC = p_e. Substituting $q_e = 1$ into SATC yields SATC = $p_e = 5$. Thus, each firm will produce one unit of output and receive \$5 per unit. At $p_e = 5$, the total market demand is $Q_e = 100$. With each firm supplying 1 unit, the number of firms is $n = 100$.

If market demand shifts to the right, resulting in

$$Q^{D'} = 210 - 2p,$$

then firms will be earning pure profits in the short run. In the long run, new firms will enter this industry without any change in costs (constant-cost industry). Firms will continue to enter until all pure profits are squeezed out. Given no change in costs, the minimum point of SATC for existing and new firms remains at $q_e = 1$ and $p_e = 5$. All the increase in demand is satisfied by new firms entering this industry. Total market equilibrium is now $Q_L = 200$, with the number of firms doubling, $n = 200$.

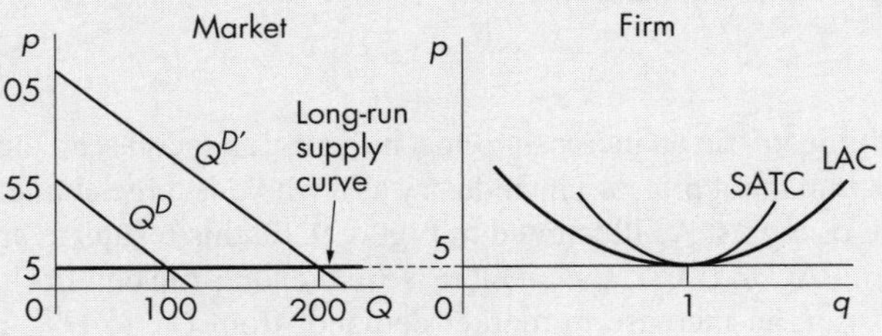

The effect of new firms entering is to shift the short-run supply curve to the right from Q^S to $Q^{S'}$ (Figure 9.19). New firms will continue to enter as long as price is above SATC, indicating the presence of pure profits. This results in price declining from p' back to p_e and output increasing to Q_L. As a result of price declining back to p_e, the long-run market supply curve is horizontal for a constant-cost industry. Note that the new long-run equilibrium corresponds to

$$\text{SMC} = \text{SATC} = \text{LMC} = \text{LAC} = p.$$

This horizontal market supply curve implies a perfectly elastic long-run market supply curve. A shift in market demand will not change the long-run equilibrium price. Firms will enter and exit the industry without any change in short- and long-run costs. However, for some industries, as firms enter and exit, costs will change. Such industries are characterized as increasing- or decreasing-cost industries.

Increasing-cost industry

In an **increasing-cost industry**, long-run equilibrium price is directly related to the number of firms in the industry and to total industry output. Thus, increased demand in the industry leads to increased input prices and associated increased LTC due to increasing industry outputs. For example, an increase in the demand for air travel puts upward pressure on the price of commercial airplanes.

As the number of firms and total output increases, problems of industry concentrations within an area may arise. The upward shift in the LAC curve may then be the result of increased nonpecuniary costs, including air pollution, waste management, or strains on the infrastructure. For example, within an air quality basin, the ambient environment may clean air pollutants resulting from only a few relatively small pulp mills. However, as the number and size of mills increase, the environmental damage may put excessive stress on the environment. If the local air quality authority then imposes instillation of air quality equipment, this will increase firms' cost of production. Another example is a dairy industry that has problems with manure disposal. Increased dairy production may result in increased average cost of manure disposal. Also, the increase in the size and number of firms may require improvements in infrastructure for meeting the higher economic activity. Such improvements may result in higher taxes for the firms, which translate to higher production costs.

Increasing-cost industry. A market with an upward-sloping long-run supply curve. *E.g., the increased demand for construction materials for new home construction results in increased cost for these materials.*

Unlike the constant-cost industry, in an increasing-cost industry, an increase in the demand for inputs will have an effect on input prices. The industry as a whole is large enough to have some influence on the price of inputs. As illustrated in Figure 9.20, this results in an upward shift in the LAC curve, from LAC to LAC′, and an increase in the long-run equilibrium price, from p_e to p'_e. In the short run, an increase in market demand, from Q^D to $Q^{D\prime}$, results in a price rise to p'. The resulting pure profit for an existing firm is then represented by the shaded area. In the long run, this presence of pure profits will attract new firms to enter this market. As new firms enter, the market supply curve shifts to the right, which reduces the market price. However, the associated increase in average cost of production results in LAC increasing to LAC′, so the equilibrium price does not fall back to the initial level p_e. Instead, all pure profits are squeezed out at p'_e, where $p'_e = \text{LAC}'$.

Analogous to the constant-cost industry condition, the long-run market supply curve for an increasing-cost industry is also derived by this shifting of the market demand curve.

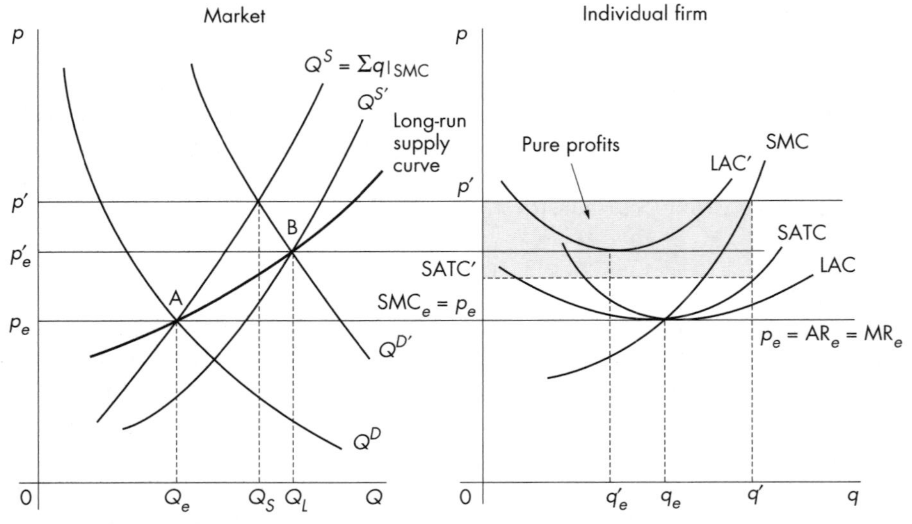

Figure 9.20 **Increasing-cost industry.** In the long run, new firms will enter an industry earning short-run pure profits. As these new firms enter, if the cost of production increases, the long-run market supply curve will have a positive slope.

The increase in cost characteristic of an increasing-cost industry results in a long-run market supply curve with a positive slope (Figure 9.20). However, the long-run market supply curve will still be more elastic than the short-run market supply curve. The facts that existing firms can vary all their inputs and new firms enter the industry provide for a potentially greater flexibility in long-run supply response. For example, the long-run supply elasticity for apples, 0.623, is more elastic than the short-run elasticity of 0.306.[3]

Example 9.9 Establishing equilibrium in an increasing-cost industry

From Example 9.8, assume that the entry of new firms—stimulated by short-run pure profits from a shift in market demand—increases cost. Say this increase in cost results in SATC shifting from

$$\text{SATC} = q^2 - 2q + 6$$

to

$$\text{SATC}' = q^2 - 2q + 7.$$

The minimum point of SATC remains at $q_e = 1$:

$$\partial \text{SATC}/\partial q = 2q - 2 = 0.$$

However, the long-run equilibrium price increases from \$5 to \$6. At a price level of \$6, total market demand is $Q_L = 198$, ($Q_L = 210 - 2p'_e$). The new equilibrium number of firms is now 198 instead of 200 as in a constant-cost industry (Example 9.8). This results in a net loss of two firms.

This is an example of a parallel upward shift in the SATC curve, resulting in no change in the equilibrium output of firms. Alternatively, the SATC curve could also shift upward and to the left or right, resulting in a decrease or increase in individual firms' long-run equilibrium output. The exact nature of the shift in SATC depends on the effect an increase in cost has on the SATC function.

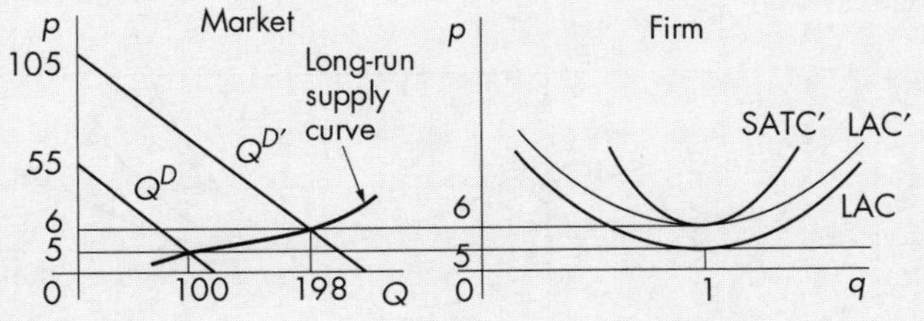

Decreasing-cost industry

A **decreasing-cost industry** results in a long-run equilibrium price that is inversely related to the number of firms in the industry and to total industry output. The US automobile industry from the 1900s through the 1960s is an example. The average price for an automobile declined in terms of real income during this period. The input prices for automobile production declined because the auto industry and various input industries for auto production concentrated in one general area and experienced economies of scale. As a result, a large number of relatively low-cost automobiles were produced. For example, in 1908 the first Model T Ford sold for $950 and during its 19 years of production the price dropped to as low as $250. Nearly 15.5 million Model Ts were sold in the United States.

Another example of a decreasing-cost industry is the handheld calculator. The price of these calculators declined rapidly from the late 1960s to the mid 1980s, with production expanding significantly. In 1969, Sharp's QT-8 four-function calculator sold for $495. By 1978, pocket four-function calculators had become a common household item at a cost of less than $10. A major input in the production of a calculator is the computer chip. As the demand for chips expanded, substantial economies of scale resulted in a reduction in the cost of these chips, and thus the calculator.

For a decreasing-cost industry, increased demand in the industry leads to decreased input prices due to increased industry output. As the demand for inputs increases, the input suppliers may experience economies of scale, resulting in declining average cost of production and price. As illustrated in Figure 9.21, in the short run, an increase in market demand, from Q^D to $Q^{D'}$, results in a price rise to p'. The resulting pure profit for an existing firm is represented by the shaded area. In the long run, the presence of pure profits will attract new firms into this industry. As new firms enter, input prices fall. This results in a downward shift of the LAC curve, from LAC to LAC′, and a decrease in equilibrium price, from p_e to p'_e. For a decreasing-cost industry, the long-run market supply curve has a negative slope. Again, we derive this long-run market supply curve by connecting the long-run equilibrium points resulting from varying market demand.

If the price falls, would a firm ever supply more? In a decreasing-cost industry, an increase in demand can result in a supply response where price falls as supply increases.

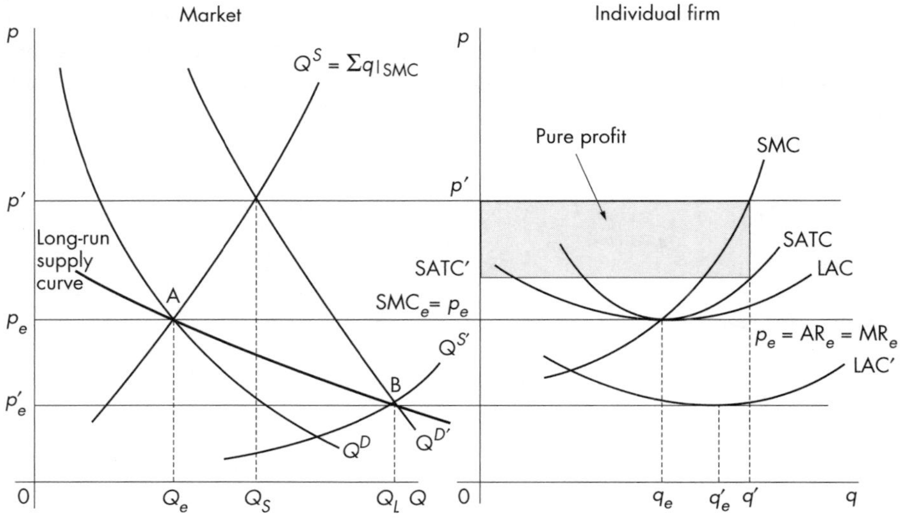

Figure 9.21 **Decreasing-cost industry.** In the long run, new firms will enter an industry earning short-run pure profits. As these new firms enter, if the cost of production decreases, the long-run market supply curve will have a negative slope.

Decreasing-cost industry. A market with a downward-sloping long-run supply curve. *E.g., Flat screen TVs have declined in price with increasing supply as a result of input suppliers experiencing economies of scale.*

Example 9.10 Establishing equilibrium in a decreasing-cost industry

From Example 9.8, assume that the entry of new firms—stimulated by short-run pure profits from a shift in market demand—decreases cost. Say this decrease in cost results in SATC shifting downward from

$$\text{SATC} = q^2 - 2q + 6$$

to

$$\text{SATC}' = q^2 - 2q + 5.$$

Similar to Example 9.9 for an increasing-cost industry, the minimum point of SATC remains at $q_e = 1$:

$$\partial\text{SATC}/\partial q = 2q - 2 = 0.$$

However, the long-run equilibrium price decreases from \$5 to \$4. At a price level of \$4, total market demand is $Q_L = 202$ ($Q_L = 210 - 2p'_e$). The new equilibrium number of firms is now 202 instead of 200 as in a constant-cost industry (Example 9.8). This results in a net gain of two firms.

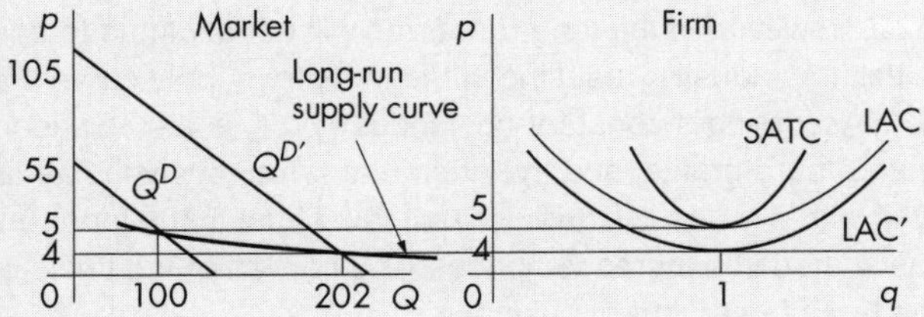

Application: Output tax: who pays the tax?

Analysis of an output tax provides an illustration of the perfectly competitive long-run models. Such models are employed as an aid in understanding how markets react to exogenous shocks such as changes in government polices and environmental conditions. In Figure 9.22,* the output tax increases a firm's cost, resulting in a shift to the left of the supply curve. This increases the price consumers pay, in the short run, from p_e to p_1. Firms receive p_1 but pay a per-unit tax τ, so firms' resulting price is p_S,

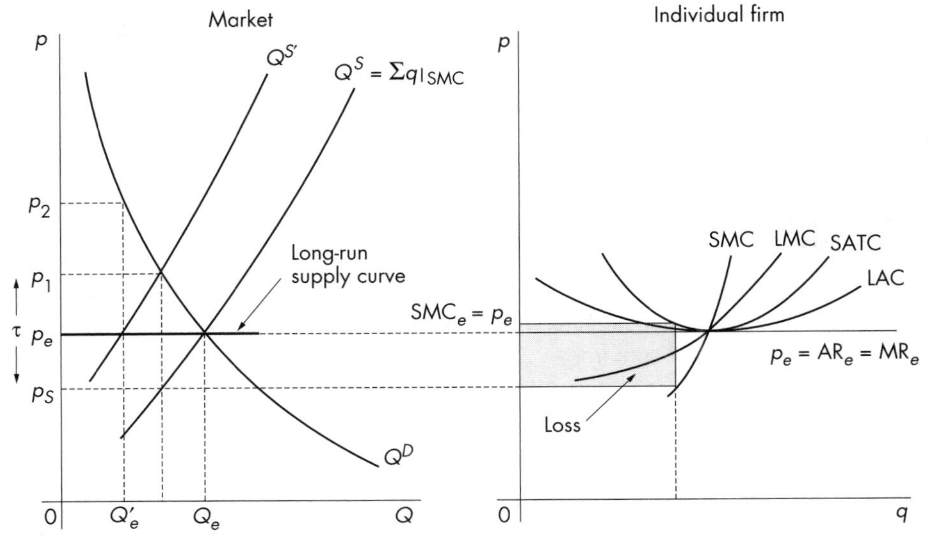

Figure 9.22 **The effect of an output tax.** Assuming a constant-cost industry, imposition of an output tax results in a short-run loss, represented by the shaded area. In the long run, all of the tax is passed on to consumers in the form of higher prices, with firms earning normal profits.

the price net of the tax τ. The tax is then borne partially by consumers and partially by producers. The difference between p_1 and p_S is the amount of tax, τ. The difference $p_1 - p_e$ is the per-unit share borne by consumers, and $p_e - p_S$ is the share borne by the firm.

As a result of the tax, firms in the short run are operating at a loss, as indicated by the shaded area in Figure 9.22. However, in the long run, firms will not continue to operate at a loss. Some firms will exit the industry, resulting in the industry supply curve shifting to the left, from Q^S to $Q^{S'}$. Assuming a constant-cost industry, Q'_e is the new long-run equilibrium quantity with zero pure profits, and the price that firms receive is again p_e. Consumers pay p_2 per unit with $p_2 - p_e = \tau$, the per-unit tax. Thus, in the long run, the entire amount of the tax is shifted into increased prices. The burden of the tax is borne by the consumers and the firms forced out of business.

*See Chapter 10. Output tax is a commodity tax that increases what consumers pay for a commodity above the price firms receive.

Application: Should a firm adopt a new technology?

If it ain't broke, don't fix it.

(Old adage)

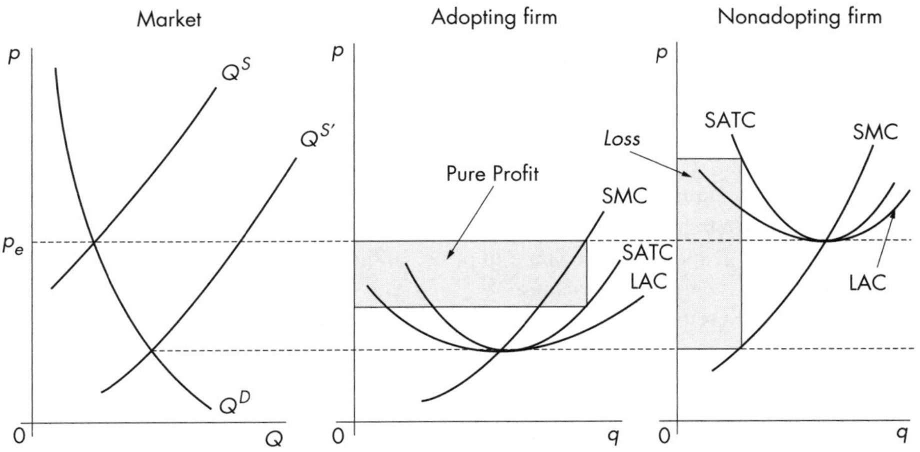

Figure 9.23 **Introduction of a new technology.** Early-adopting firms reap short-run pure profits. After the market price adjusts to the level of long-run average cost of production from the new technology, nonadopting firms operate at a loss.

Consider the introduction of low-cost equipment in a constant-cost industry (Figure 9.23). Suppose a new productive technique is developed that decreases LAC. Initially, the equilibrium price is p_e and a small number of firms adopt this new production technique, which lowers their cost of production. In the short run, these early-adopting firms earn pure profits, which was their motivation for employing this new productive technique. The shaded area in the graph labeled "Adopting Firm," represents this short-run pure profit.

However, as more firms adopt the new technique, the market supply curve shifts to the right, from Q^S to $Q^{S'}$. The equilibrium price will then fall, eventually eliminating any pure profits in the long run. As the equilibrium price falls, firms are rewarded, in the form of short-run pure profits if they adopt this new technique and penalized if they do not adopt it. Nonadopting firms will operate at a loss in the short run and go out of business in the long run. This double-edged sword—reward for adoption and penalty for nonadoption—associated with competition provides a mechanism for the industry adoption of new technologies without governmental agency involvement. Again, this carrot-and-stick result is Adam Smith's invisible hand at work. Nonadopting firms who continue to use the old technique (which is not broken) will go out of business.

In determining the characteristics of early adopters, G.D. Wozniak found that adoption behavior was dependent on an agent's endowment of human capital and investment in adoption information. His results indicate that education and information raise the profitability of early adoption. Adoption behavior was also shown to be positively related to firm size. Producers operating at larger scales of production have a greater incentive to be well informed and thus be early adopters.

Source: G.D. Wozniak, "Human Capital, Information, and the Early Adoption of New Technology," *Journal of Human Resources* 22 (1987): 101–112.

Summary

1. A perfectly competitive market is based on assuming small size and large number of firms, homogeneous products, free mobility of resources, perfect knowledge, and zero transaction costs. These assumptions result in the Law of One Price.
2. The market supply curve is the horizontal summation of individual firms' supply curves. In a market period, the market supply curve is perfectly inelastic, implying no supply response to a change in price. In the short and long run, market supply is responsive to a price change.
3. A profit-maximizing firm will equate marginal revenue to marginal cost for determining its optimal level of output. In a perfectly competitive market, a firm has no influence on output price, so marginal revenue is equal to average revenue (the output price).
4. The short-run marginal cost curve above short-run average variable cost is a perfectly competitive firm's supply curve. It represents how much a firm is willing and able to supply at the current market price.
5. The short-run average total cost curve indicates if a firm is earning a pure profit, normal profit, or operating at a loss. If $p >$ SATC, the firm is earning a pure profit; if $p =$ SATC, it is earning a normal profit; and if $p <$ SATC, it is operating at a loss.
6. The short-run average variable cost curve indicates if a firm should operate or not. If SATC $> p >$ SAVC, then the firm is able to cover all of its variable costs and has some revenue to apply toward its fixed costs. Thus, the firm can minimize its losses by staying in business. In contrast, if price falls below SAVC, then the firm is not able cover all of its variable cost, and thus will incur greater losses by operating. It will minimize its losses by shutting down.
7. Without intervention from any governmental agencies, the free market will respond to an increase in market demand by both rationing quantity supplied and increasing the production of the commodity. In general, markets' response to shifts in demand or supply may be investigated by considering the responsiveness of demand and supply to changes in the market price.
8. In the long run, all inputs can vary, so firms are free to enter and exit an industry. If an industry is experiencing short-run pure profits, in the long run firms will enter this industry. This will result in expanded market output. In contrast, if the industry is experiencing short-run losses, in the long run firms will exit this industry.
9. For a constant-cost industry, the entry or exit of firms does not change the average cost of production, so the long-run market supply curve is perfectly elastic (horizontal). In contrast, for an increasing- (decreasing-) cost industry, the average cost of production rises (declines) with the entry of new firms, so the long-run market supply curve has a positive (negative) slope.

Key concepts

average revenue, 337
consumers, 328
constant-cost industry, 362
decreasing-cost industry, 365
elasticity of supply, 335
firm's short-run supply curve, 346
increasing-cost industry, 363
industry, 331
industry supply curve, 333
invisible hand, 349
Law of One Price, 331
marginal revenue, 336
market-clearing price, 338
market supply curve, 333
perfectly competitive market, 330

Key equations

$$\text{MR} = \text{SMC}$$

Profit-maximizing condition.

$$p > \text{SAVC}$$

Condition for operating.

$$p > \text{SATC}$$

A firm is earning a pure profit.

$$p = \text{SATC}$$

A firm is earning a normal profit.

$$p = \text{SMC} = \text{SATC} = \text{LMC} = \text{LAC}$$

Long-run equilibrium condition.

Questions

Answering the questions is easy. True understanding is difficult.

(Michael Wetzstein)

1. Why do insurance companies continue to peddle automobile policies to potential clients and then state they lose money on every policy they write?
2. Fixed costs are often substantial and real. Why do economists state that firms should disregard these costs in their short-run price and output decisions?
3. Economists state that marginal cost is an operating decision whereas average cost is an investment decision. True or false? Explain.

4. A single farmer is at the mercy of the market because she takes the market price as given. Yet, agricultural prices are very flexible. Explain.
5. If demand for a commodity rises, a short-run effect is an increase in price. Does the reverse hold? That is, if a price rise occurs, can one conclude that demand has increased?
6. Suppose property in an inter-city ghetto was made exempt from property taxes. Would this insure property owners' pure profits? Explain.
7. The market demand for agricultural products is relatively inelastic, whereas many manufactured goods are relatively elastic. Discuss the implication of this statement for a technological improvement in agriculture compared with manufacturing.
8. Why do firms enter an industry when they know in the long-run pure profit will be zero?
9. How is it possible for an industry to be a constant-cost industry when each firm in the industry has increasing marginal costs?
10. Every long-run equilibrium for a firm is also a short-run equilibrium. Is every short-run equilibrium also a long-run equilibrium? Explain.

Exercises

Pride makes us do things well. But it is love that makes us do them to perfection.
(H. Jackson Brown)

1. Assume that 1000 competitive farms produce rice from a fixed amount of land with variable labor. Labor cost required to produce q bushels of rice is $\text{STVC} = \frac{1}{2}q^2$.

   a. Determine a farm's short-run supply curve.
   b. Determine the market supply curve.
   c. Given that the market demand function for rice is $Q^D = 10{,}000 - 1000p$, solve for the equilibrium price and quantity.
   d. What is the equilibrium rent on land?

2. A perfectly competitive firm has a cost function given by

   $$\text{STC}(q) = \tfrac{1}{2}q^2 + 4q + \tfrac{1}{2}.$$

   a. What are its STVC and TFC?
   b. What is its supply curve?
   c. What is the elasticity of supply?
   d. At what output is SATC minimized?
   e. If there are 500 identical firms in this industry, what is the industry's supply curve?
   f. If the market demand function is

   $$Q^D = -100p + 1000,$$

   what are the equilibrium price and quantity?

g. What is the elasticity of market demand at the equilibrium price and quantity?
h. What is the equilibrium level of output for an individual firm?
i. Is a firm in this market earning a pure profit, normal profit, or operating at a loss?

3. Suppose households consider diamonds D and emeralds E as substitutes. Let the supply of both be fixed in the market period at $D = 100$ and $E = 200$. The inverse demand functions for diamonds and emeralds are

$$p_D = 450 - D + \tfrac{1}{2}p_E, p_E = 300 - E + p_D,$$

where p_D and p_E are the respective prices for diamonds and emeralds.
a. What are the equilibrium prices of diamonds and emeralds?
b. Assume that a new discovery of diamonds increases the quantity supplied to 200 units. How will this discovery affect the equilibrium prices?

4. At a market price of \$20 per unit, a firm's short-run total cost function is

$$\text{STC}(q) = 1000 + 10q,$$

and the firm has a capacity to produce 100 units per period.
a. What is the firm's break-even point?
b. What is the profit-maximizing output?

5. A farmer producing two crops, cotton q_C and soybeans q_S, faces infinitely elastic demands for these crops. Prevailing output prices are $p_C = 12$ and $p_S = 24$ for cotton and soybeans, respectively. The farmer's short-run total cost function is

$$\text{STC} = 0.2q_C^2 + 0.3q_S^2 + 600.$$

a. What are the marginal cost functions for q_C and q_S? What are the supply functions?
b. How much q_C and q_S will the farmer produce? What will her profit be?

6. A competitive industry composed of 300 firms is in long-run equilibrium, supplying 2700 units with an equilibrium output price of \$1. Firms within the industry are characterized with three different types of technologies

Number	*Technology*
100	$\text{STVC}_1 = q_1$
100	$\text{STVC}_2 = \frac{1}{10}q_2^2$
100	$\text{STVC}_3 = \frac{1}{2}q_3$ for $q_3 < 10$ and $\text{STC}_3 \to \infty$ for $q_3 \geq 10$.

a. Graph the short-run market supply curve.
b. Assume that market demand shifts, so the new market demand curve is $Q^D = 1200 - 200p$. What are the short-run equilibrium market output and price? What are the outputs of each type of firm?

7. Assume a firm's owners obtain utility from profit and from having the firm engage in socially conscious activities S, such as charitable contributions to local public schools. Derive the FOCs for the firm's utility-maximizing problem. Do these conditions differ from a household's utility-maximizing conditions? Explain.
8. Given the formula for the percentage change in price, assume the quantity of apples demanded Q depends on the price of apples p_a, the price of oranges p_o, and income. The price elasticity of demand for apples is $\varepsilon^D_{Q,pa} = -1.0$ and the cross-price elasticity of demand for apples is $\varepsilon^D_{Q,po} = 1.0$. Associated with these demand elasticities is the income elasticity of demand $\eta_Q = 1/2$ and the short-run elasticity of supply for apples is $\varepsilon^S_{Q,pa} = 2.0$. The price of apples is \$0.50 per pound, the price of oranges is \$1 per pound, and the aggregate household personal income is \$1000 billion. At these prices and income, 4 billion pounds of apples are purchased per year.

   Assuming the price of oranges increases to \$1.50 per pound and personal income increases to \$1100 billion, answer the following:
   a. How will the demand curve for apples shift?
   b. Using the formula in the text for determining the percentage change in equilibrium price, by how much will the price of apples rise in the short run? What will be the new equilibrium price of apples?
   c. What is the final effect of all of these changes in the quantity of apples purchased? How much is purchased?
9. Assume that the long-run total cost function for each firm is

   $$\text{LTC}(q) = q^3 - 4q^2 + 8q.$$

   With the market demand function given by

   $$Q^D = 2000 - 100p,$$

   determine the equilibrium market price and quantity, number of firms in the industry, and each individual firm's output.
10. Assume that a firm can increase its use of an input but cannot decrease it. Illustrate how the marginal cost curve will exhibit a kink at the long-run equilibrium price and quantity. What is the implication of this condition for the relative variability of short-run price and quantity?

Internet case studies

1. Provide a list of constant-, increasing-, and decreasing-cost industries.
2. List the determinants of the elasticity of supply.
3. Determine the hurdle rates for some firms.

10 Economic efficiency

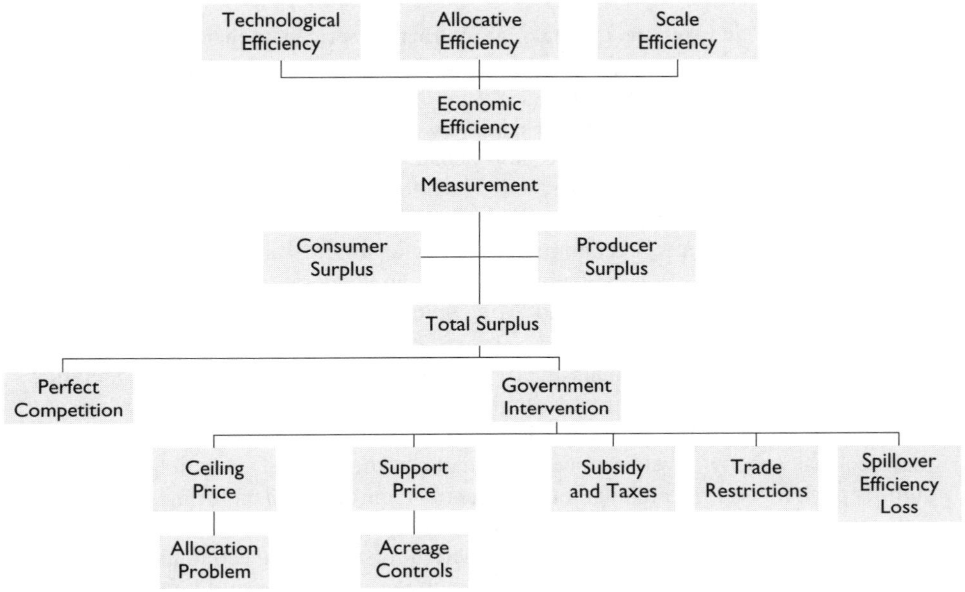

Outline and Conceptual Inquiries

Economic-efficiency criteria

Favorable features of perfect competition

Are you a capitalist?

Unfavorable features of perfect competition

Are you a socialist?

Measuring economic efficiency

Consumers live for consumer surplus

Are you willing to pay more for the pizza than it cost?

Application: The minimum legal drinking age and public health

Producers produce for producer surplus

Total surplus and economic efficiency

Are free markets free of inefficiency?

Government intervention and deadweight loss

Problems with ceiling prices

Is allowing the poor to have affordable housing desirable?

Do you enjoy waiting in lines?

Application: Long-run relation between the black and legal foreign exchange markets

Problems with support prices

Is having an abundance of food desirable?

Price subsidies

Tax

Who pays taxes?

Application: Cigarette taxation

Trade restrictions

Why the big fuss over free trade, anyway?

Application: African famine, made in Europe

Spillover efficiency loss

Do two wrongs make things worse?

Summary

Key concepts

Key equations

Questions

Exercises

Internet case studies

How many economists does it take to change a light bulb? None, if the light bulb required changing, the market would have already done it.

(Pasi Kuoppamäki)

On July 24, 1959, in front of a replica of a suburban American kitchen at the US Trade and Cultural Fair in Sokolniki Park, Moscow, Soviet leader Nikita Khrushchev and Vice President Richard M. Nixon engaged in an impromptu debate about the merits and disadvantages of capitalism and communism. This informal exchange became known as the "Kitchen Debate." The short debate centered on the overall objective of economics to maximize social welfare and which form of economic system has resulted in improving social welfare subject to limited resources.

Underlying this debate is economic efficiency as a necessary condition for maximizing social welfare.[1] In a capitalist system, if an economy or market is operating efficiently, an increase in the demand for a commodity (changing the light bulb) will result in an increase in the market price. This increase in price provides an incentive for firms to increase supply and change the light bulb. If an economy or market is operating inefficiently, the limited resources are not allocated to their most productive markets. This misallocation of resources will reduce the level of commodities available and thus decrease society's welfare (society remains in the dark). This belief in markets' abilities to change a light bulb without any central control versus requiring such control is the marked difference in Nixon's and Khrushchev's viewpoints.

The aim of this chapter is to develop a criterion for measuring economic efficiency. We can then evaluate the perfectly competitive price system in terms of this criterion and governmental intervention into the markets (central control) in terms of its effect on economic efficiency. Given this objective, we define *firm economic efficiency* in terms of *technological, allocative*, and *scale efficiency. Consumer* and *producer surplus* are measures of this economic efficiency, while their sum, *total surplus*, is used as a surrogate for measuring economic efficiency. When total surplus is maximized for a market, that market is considered operating efficiently. As demonstrated in this chapter, a perfectly competitive market will, without any government involvement, maximize this total surplus, and thus, result in economic efficiency.

We introduce the concept of *deadweight loss* as a measure of economic inefficiency. In terms of this deadweight loss, we investigate government-established ceiling prices and the consequent *black market*. We then discuss the alternative forms of government intervention, market price supports, and consider the inefficiencies of these supports along with output controls, particularly employed in the agricultural sector. Even the imposition of a tax can distort prices and result in economic inefficiencies. We derive the deadweight loss associated with *output* and *sales taxes* and show that the amount of the tax borne by firms and consumers depends on the elasticity of supply and demand. We conclude the chapter with a discussion on the inefficiency of trade restrictions, deriving the deadweight loss associated with tariffs and quotas and discussing the market effects of tariffs versus quotas. In conjunction with these trade restrictions, we provide an example of spillover efficiency loss into another market.

The bread and butter of an applied economist's work are in evaluating the effect that various governmental policies and programs have on economic efficiency. Applied economists will estimate the price and other market effects (such as regional production shifts) from various programs in terms of efficiently allocating resources. They suggest changes or alternative policies and programs that may result in the same objectives with an improvement in resource allocation. For example, providing tax breaks for businesses locating in economically depressed areas provides an incentive for businesses to relocate in these areas, which stimulates private job training and employment. Applied economists may compare such a program with an alternative program of using the tax revenue directly for public work training.

Economic-efficiency criteria

To prevent night telegraph operators (brass pounders) from sleeping on the job, operators were required to send a signal over the wires at regular intervals. Thomas Edison, then working as an operator, invented an automated signaling device so he could sleep through his shift rather than spend time awake waiting for a telegraph message. This allowed him to more efficiently allocate his resources. Similarly, a firm that efficiently allocates its resources can improve its position. Incidentally, Edison was caught sleeping and promptly fired.[2]

For **firm economic efficiency** three criteria are required. First is *technological efficiency*, where firms are using production processes that yield the highest output levels for a given set of inputs. As discussed in Chapter 7, it is assumed that all firms are technologically efficient. The second criterion is *allocative efficiency,* where firms minimize costs for a given level of output. Specifically, allocative efficiency requires using the least-cost combination of inputs for a given level of output. The input prices per marginal product of all inputs are equal. Recall from Chapter 8 that for the two-input case of capital K and labor L, this requires

$$\frac{w}{MP_L} = \frac{v}{MP_K}.$$

The third criterion, **scale efficiency,** requires the output price to equal SMC: $p = \text{SMC}$. What consumers or society are willing to pay for an additional unit of output must equal what it cost society to produce this additional unit of output. Output price is how much society is willing to pay for an additional unit of output, and SMC is the cost to society for producing this additional output. If $p > \text{SMC}$, then society is willing to pay more than it cost for additional output, so efficiency is improved if more resources are allocated to the production of this output. Alternatively, if $p < \text{SMC}$, then the reduction in cost from producing less of the output is more than the willingness to pay for the output, so efficiency is improved if fewer resources are allocated to the production of this output.

Firm economic efficiency. A condition where a firm is technological, allocative , and scale-efficient. *E.g., a textile firm that has just modernized its plant has a program for controlling costs within given output levels, and is a price taker in its output markets.*

Scale efficiency. Output price equals marginal cost. *E.g., perfectly competitive markets.*

The perfectly competitive market meets these three criteria for economic efficiency. A necessary condition for a profit-maximizing firm is technical and allocation efficiency, and the competitive firm's perfectly elastic demand curve, where $p = \text{AR} = \text{MR}$, results in the scale-efficiency condition of $p = \text{SMC}$.

Favorable features of perfect competition

When you dance with your customer, let him lead.

(H. Jackson Brown)

Given the economic efficiency of perfect competition, economists frequently use a perfectly competitive industry as a standard for judging other market structures. Economic efficiency in these perfectly competitive industries results in a number of favorable features. First, consumers' preferences are reflected in the marketplace. This is called **consumer sovereignty**. If there is an increase in demand for a commodity, the market price will increase. This increase in price provides incentives for firms to increase output and satisfy the increased demand. This is a very powerful result. No governmental agency is required to determine the level of demand and supply. In a free market, Adam Smith's invisible hand automatically does it. Society's resources are also allocated in the most efficient manner. Firms attempting to satisfy some increase in demand purchase more inputs. Thus, resources naturally flow in the direction of consumer preferences. The invisible hand works again. Finally, assuming flexible input and output prices, full employment of all resources is assured. Individuals (like Nixon) who firmly believe in the free market see these favorable features of perfect competition as very important. Particularly, they see a very limited, if any, role for central government involvement in markets. Instead, decentralizing decisions rests the power of decision making in the hands of those individual agents directly impacted by the decisions. In perfectly competitive markets, firms will respond to consumer preferences, so firms will let consumers lead.

Are you a capitalist? If you believe consumer preferences are reflected in the marketplace, believe in the efficiency of markets, and see only a limited, if any, role for central governmental involvement, then you are a capitalist.

Consumer sovereignty. Consumers' preferences are reflected in the market. *E.g., firms will respond to an increase in consumer preferences for organic foods by increasing the supply.*

Unfavorable features of perfect competition

We live in an age when pizza gets to your home before the police.

(Jeff Marder)

Unfortunately, perfect competition does have some unfavorable features that provide a justification for direct government involvement in markets. As discussed in Part 9, these unfavorable features are generally the result of missing markets for commodities. First, perfect competition results in incomplete reflection of consumers' desires: it does not measure consumers' desire for collective or public goods. As discussed in Chapter 22, *public goods* are commodities where the consumption of the commodity by one consumer does not reduce the consumption of the same commodity for another consumer. For example, national defense is a public good. When an additional consumer is added to a society, it does not reduce the level of national defense for other members of that society. Highways, parks, and income distribution are other examples of public goods. Public goods jointly impact all consumers, whereas private goods only impact the consumer who purchases and consumes the commodity. The joint-impact characteristic of public goods hampers the market's ability to allocate resources for its production. Thus, some consumers may not purchase any amount of a public good, while other consumers do purchase it. However, the nonpurchasers will derive utility from the public good purchased by the other consumers. As discussed in Chapter 22, this is called a *free-rider problem*. By not paying anything for the public good, a consumer receives the good for free. The free-rider problem results in a misallocation of resources, and one justification for government intervention is to correct this misallocation by government supplying public goods. In fact, a major role of government is providing for public goods. For example, a local government will provide police protection. If, as is often the case, the local government is experiencing a large budget shortfall, then cutting the police department's budget may result in the pizza arriving before the police.

A second unfavorable feature of perfect competition is an inadequate measure of social costs and social benefits. A commodity that affects households' utility functions or firms' production functions but is out of the control of the affected household or firm is termed an *externality*. For example, a mill's air pollution that affects a household is an externality. The household has no control over its air quality. The total cost of the mill operation is the mill's production cost plus the social cost of poor air quality. The problem with the presence of externalities is that the market only considers production cost. Without also considering the social cost, resources are potentially misallocated. As discussed in Chapter 21, when externalities exist in an economy, perfect competition provides no method of correcting possible differences between social and private costs resulting from these externalities. Thus, another role for government is to correct any differences between these private and social costs.

Insufficient incentive for progress is a third unfavorable feature of perfect competition. In a system where technological advances can be quickly duplicated by competing firms, there is limited incentive for firms to allocate resources toward innovation with new production techniques and ideas. As a result, government has in many cases provided the resources for research and development in industries that are close to the perfectly competitive model. For example, in the United States, the land grant universities, funded by federal and state governments for agricultural research and education, provide the innovations for the agricultural industry.

These unfavorable features of perfect competition provide a justification for governmental involvement in markets. The level or magnitude of that governmental involvement depends on how much weight is put on the favorable features compared with the unfavorable features of perfect competition. If an individual is a capitalist, she would discount the unfavorable features of perfect competition and advocate a limited role for government (Nixon). In contrast, a socialist sees the unfavorable features of perfect competition as major concerns and suggests a major role for government for correcting these market failures (Khrushchev). The optimal level of governmental involvement may vary from one society to another depending on their desire for private versus public goods. Unfortunately, as indicated by the major shifts in governmental involvement in markets during the twentieth and twenty-first centuries, the optimal level of this involvement is still being determined in many countries around the world. This is particularly true for the former USSR, eastern European countries, and countries in North Africa and the Middle East.

Are you a socialist? If you receive satisfaction from public goods, are concerned about externalities and insufficient incentives for progress, and desire greater governmental involvement in markets, you are a bit more socialistic.

Measuring economic efficiency

Economic efficiency is like May flowers after April showers.

(Michael Wetzstein)

We can use the magnitude or change in consumer and producer surplus as a measure of the economic efficiency of markets. Such measures are particularly important in comparing the economic efficiency of alternative market structures and the change in welfare (surplus) from alternative governmental policies or changes in environmental conditions. Economically efficient benefits in the form of consumer and producer surplus are like May flowers after a market allocates society's resources (April showers).

Consumers live for consumer surplus

When your hair dryer malfunctions and you go to a discount store with a hat on to buy a new one, you may be willing to pay \$20.00 for a new hair dryer. Fortunately, you find just the model you wanted on sale for \$12.95 including any tax. The difference, \$7.05, is your consumer surplus from purchasing the hair dryer. You would have been willing to pay \$7.05 for the ability to purchase the dryer for \$12.95. However, you did not have to pay \$7.05, so it is a surplus or amount that is left over from what you were willing to pay. Specifically, **consumer surplus (CS)** is a measure of the net benefit a consumer receives from being able to purchase a commodity at a particular price. At a fundamental level, only the consumer's preferences matter for measuring a consumer's welfare, but such a measure is difficult to interpret as there is no unique way to measure a consumer's utility. Thus, as an alternative, consumer welfare is measured as the difference between the maximum amount a consumer would be willing to pay and what actually is paid. Measuring consumer welfare in terms of dollars provides a common cardinal scale for comparison across agents in contrast to an ordinal utility scale.

Are you willing to pay more for the pizza than it cost? If you receive any consumer surplus from the pizza, then you are willing to pay more for the pizza than it cost.

Consumer surplus (CS). The net benefit a consumer receives from a commodity. *E.g., you may be willing to pay \$50 for a ticket to the game, but only have to pay \$10. Your consumer surplus is then \$40.*

Formally, the per-unit price of a commodity measures consumers' marginal value of the commodity (the *marginal utility of consumption*). The price of a commodity is a measure of the additional utility consumers receive from consuming an additional unit of a commodity. In other words, price is a monetary measure of how much an additional amount of a commodity is worth to consumers or how much consumers would be willing to pay for the last unit of consumption purchased. Specifically, the total utility or benefit consumers obtain from consuming a commodity at the level Q_e is the area under the market demand curve from zero to Q_e:

$$U(Q_e) = \int_0^{Q_e} p(Q)dQ.$$

In Figure 10.1, this total utility is represented by the area $0ABQ_e$. When we take the derivative of this expression, the price that consumers are willing to pay for the commodity will equal the marginal utility of consumption:

$$\begin{aligned} U'(Q_e) &= p(Q_e) - p(0), \\ &= p_e. \end{aligned}$$

Since consumers are not willing to pay anything for a zero amount of a commodity, $p(0) = 0$. Summing from zero to Q_e the marginal utility of consumption at each incremental level of consumption yields the total utility $U(Q_e)$.

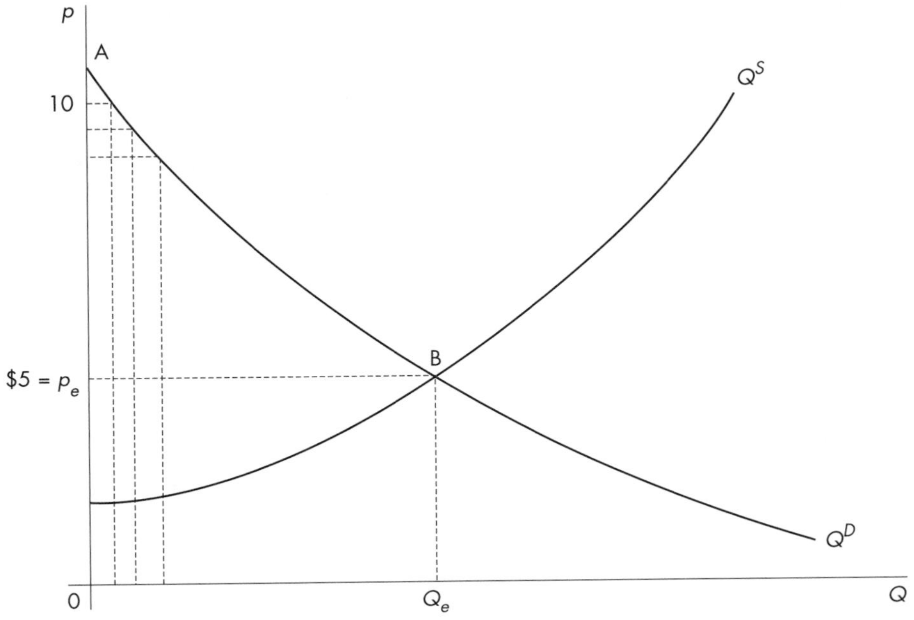

Figure 10.1 **Consumer surplus.** The area below the demand curve above the price represents consumer surplus, area p_eAB. Consumer surplus is the difference between the total benefits from the consumption of Q_e, area 0ABQ$_e$, and the expenditure on the commodity, area 0p_eBQ$_e$.

Consumer surplus measures the difference between the total benefits from the consumption of a commodity and the expenditure on the commodity:

$$\text{CS}(Q_e) = U(Q_e) - p_e Q_e.$$

The area of consumer surplus is illustrated in Figure 10.1. The area $0\text{AB}Q_e$ is the total utility $U(Q_e)$, which consumers receive from consuming Q_e units of the commodity. The actual expenditure for Q_e is the area $0p_e\text{B}Q_e$. $\text{CS}(Q_e)$ is then the difference: $p_e\text{AB} = 0\text{AB}Q_e - 0p_e\text{B}Q_e$. Consumers are willing to pay over \$10 for the first units, but only have to pay the actual market price of \$5. Thus, they receive a surplus of marginal utility, measured as marginal consumer surplus over and above what they pay for these first units. This *marginal consumer surplus* is the difference between the price they are willing to pay (the marginal utility of consumption) and the price they actually pay for the commodity. Given a negatively sloping market demand curve, as quantity demanded increases, the price consumers are willing to pay for an additional unit of a commodity declines. Marginal consumer surplus will also continue to decline. Consumers will continue to purchase the commodity up to Q_e, where the price consumers are willing to pay for additional units is equal to the market price p_e. At this point, marginal consumer surplus is zero and consumers are indifferent in terms of purchasing the commodity or not. Beyond this equilibrium quantity, consumers' willingness to pay is less than the market price p_e, resulting in negative marginal consumer surplus. Consumers will then forgo any additional purchases because such purchases will result in a loss in surplus (welfare). The maximum consumer surplus associated with the market demand curve and p_e is the area below the demand curve above the price, $p_e\text{AB}$.

As illustrated in Figure 10.2, if the equilibrium price increases from p_e to p'_e, the difference in consumers' willingness to pay and what they actually pay (consumer surplus) is reduced (area $p_e p'_e\text{BC}$). Also, the equilibrium level of consumption where marginal consumer surplus is zero is reduced from Q_e to Q'_e, resulting in an additional loss in consumer surplus represented by the area CBD. The total loss in consumer surplus, resulting in a reduction in consumer surplus from $p_e\text{AD}$ to $p'_e\text{AB}$, is then $p_e p'_e\text{BD}$. Similarly, a reduction in price yields an increase

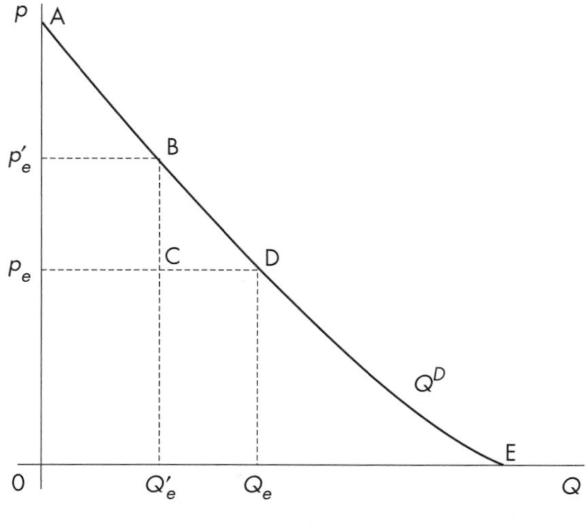

Figure 10.2 **Change in consumer surplus resulting from a price change.** An increase in the price from p_e to p'_e reduces consumer surplus from area $p_e\text{AD}$ to $p'_e\text{AB}$.

in consumer surplus. If the equilibrium price drops from p_e' to p_e, then the increase in consumer surplus is $p_e p_e'$BD.

Example 10.1 Calculating consumer surplus

Consider the demand function

$$Q^D = -2p + 10.$$

Solving for the price yields

$$p = -\tfrac{1}{2}Q + 5.$$

Consumer surplus is the area below the demand curve and above the price. Specifically, as illustrated in the graph, if $p = \$4$, then $Q = 2$. Consumer surplus would then be \$1, which is the area of the triangle with a rise of 5–4 and a run of 2–0. As the price declines from $p = \$4$ to $p = \$2$, consumer surplus increases to \$9. At $p = \$1$, consumer surplus increases to \$16. If the price is \$5 or above, consumer surplus will be zero. Consumers are not willing to purchase any of the commodity at a price of \$5 or more.

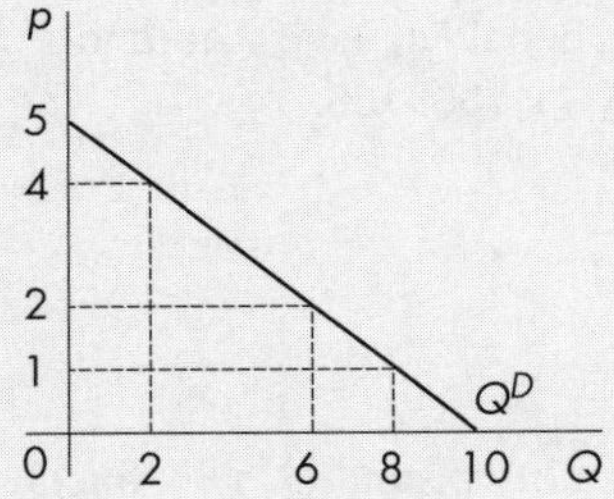

Centrally planned economies will often consider subsidizing the prices on highly inelastic commodities such as food and housing in an effort to boost consumer welfare and maintain order. If they were interested in maximizing consumer welfare for a commodity, the price would be zero and associated consumer surplus (welfare) would be represented by the whole area under the demand curve, 0AE in Figure 10.2. Unfortunately, limited resources prevent society from maximizing consumer surplus across all commodities. This maximizing point only occurs at global bliss (in our dreams). Instead, society must maximize social welfare subject to resource constraints. A necessary condition for maximizing social welfare is for the economy to operate efficiently. An efficient economy requires consideration of not only consumer surplus but also the welfare of producers (producer surplus).

Application: The minimum legal drinking age and public health

In the summer of 2008, over 100 US college presidents called for a reexamination of the minimum legal drinking age. The argument is the current age-21 limit results in more dangerous drinking than would occur if the legal drinking age were lower.

Carpenter and Dobkin summarize a large body of empirical literature, which indicates that setting the minimum legal drinking age at 21 does reduce alcohol consumption and its major harms. However, this finding is not a sufficient justification for the age-21 limit because it does not take into account the benefits (consumer surplus) of alcohol consumption. Thus, when considering at what age to set the minimum legal drinking age, we should determine if the reduction in alcohol-harm offsets the reduction in consumer surplus from preventing individuals from drinking.

Carpenter and Dobkin determine the major individual cost of an additional drink is that it increases the risk of dying. Their estimates indicate that if the drinking age were lowered to 18, there would be an additional 8 deaths per 10,000 person-years for the 18–20 age group. This translates to $15 per driver as the hidden cost of each drink. They also calculated the external costs borne by others at $2.63. These external costs included the risk that an individual will be killed by a drunk driver, that drinkers will commit robbery or assault, and that drinkers will injure themselves and require medical treatment. This indicates that the total cost of a drink is at least $15 plus what the individual paid for the drink. It is unlikely that the average consumer surplus from drinking is this high. Thus, underaged drinkers are not fully aware of the personal costs of their behavior and there is a role for government intervention in setting age limits.

Source: C. Carpenter and C. Dobkin, "The Minimum Legal Drinking Age and Public Health," *Journal of Economic Perspectives* 25 (2011): 133–156.

Producers produce for producer surplus

Producer surplus (PS) at the equilibrium price and quantity p_e and Q_e is defined as pure profit π plus total fixed cost TFC:

$$\text{PS}(Q_e) = \pi + \text{TFC}.$$

Recall that pure profit at the equilibrium price and quantity is

$$\pi = \text{TR}(Q_e) - \text{STC}(Q_e).$$

Producer surplus is then

$$\text{PS}(Q_e) = \text{TR}(Q_e) - \text{STC}(Q_e) + \text{TFC}.$$

Recalling that $\text{STC}(Q_e) = \text{STVC}(Q_e) + \text{TFC}$, we have

$$\text{PS}(Q_e) = \text{TR}(Q_e) - [\text{STVC}(Q_e) + \text{TFC}] + \text{TFC}.$$

This results in

$$\text{PS}(Q_e) = \text{TR}(Q_e) - \text{STVC}(Q_e).$$

Thus, producer surplus is also measured as total revenue minus total variable cost.

Producer surplus (PS). Pure profit plus total fixed cost, which is equivalent to total revenue minus total variable cost. *E.g., if a dentist has variable cost of \$100,000 and revenue of \$250,000, her producer surplus is \$150,000.*

This measure of producer surplus is illustrated in Figure 10.3. Total revenue TR is represented by the area $0p_e\text{A}Q_e$ and STVC by the area $0(\text{SAVC}_e)\text{B}Q_e$. The difference between these areas is $\text{PS}(Q_e)$ [the shaded area $(\text{SAVC}_e)p_e\text{AB}$]. This measure of producer surplus is equivalent to the area below the price p_e and above $\text{SMC}(Q_e)$ (Figure 10.4). Recall from Chapter 8 that the area below the SMC curve is STVC:

$$\int_0^{Q_e} \text{SMC}\, dQ = \text{STVC}(Q_e).$$

Thus, the area above SMC and below price—the producer surplus—is

$$\text{PS}(Q_e) = \text{TR}(Q_e) - \text{STVC}(Q_e),$$

where $\text{TR}(Q_e)$ is the area $0p_e\text{A}Q_e$.

Producer surplus is the difference between the minimum amount at which a firm would be willing to sell a given output, SAVC, and the amount it actually sells the units for, p. Firms are indifferent between selling a unit of output or not when p = SAVC (start of Stage II). At any price above SAVC, firms are earning a per-unit surplus of $p-\text{SAVC}$. This per-unit surplus is the firm's *marginal producer surplus*. Summing this marginal producer surplus for a given output level yields the firm's welfare gain from supplying this output (producer surplus).

As illustrated in Figure 10.5, if the equilibrium price decreases from p_e to p'_e, the difference in the amount that firms are willing to receive for a commodity and what they actually are paid

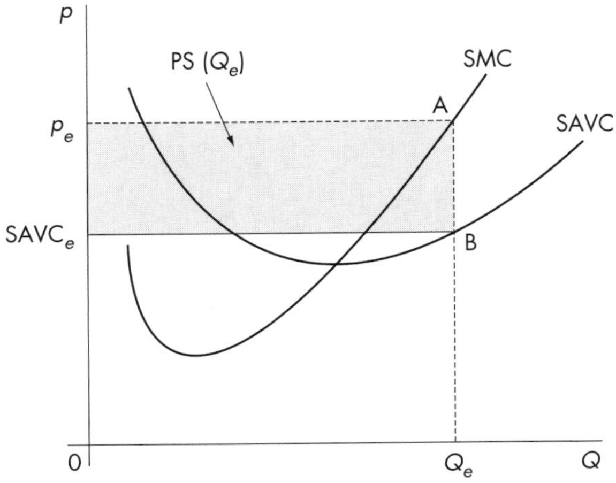

Figure 10.3 **Producer surplus as total revenue minus short-run total variable cost.** The difference between p_e and SAVC_e when multiplied by Q_e is a firm's producer surplus represented by the shaded area.

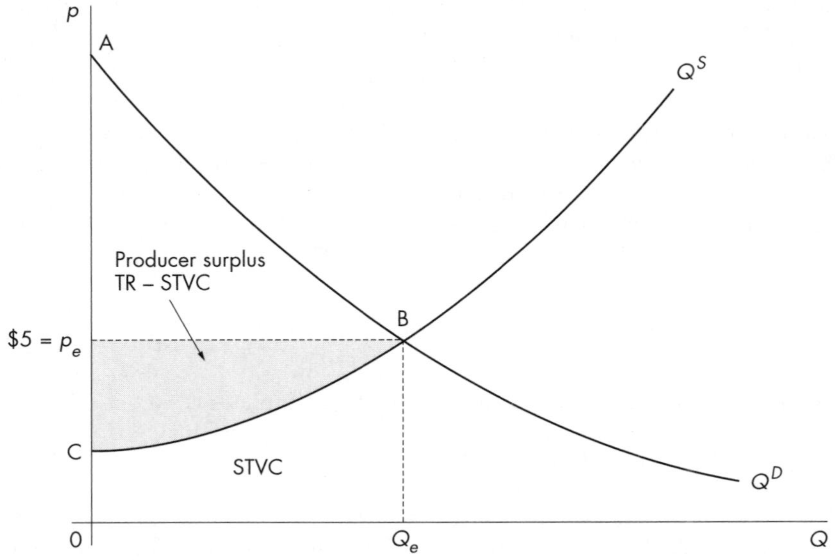

Figure 10.4 **Producer surplus: the area below price and above the marginal cost curve.** Area $0p_eBQ_e$ represents TR and area $0CBQ_e$ represents STVC. The difference, TR – STVC, is the shaded area representing producer surplus, Cp_eB.

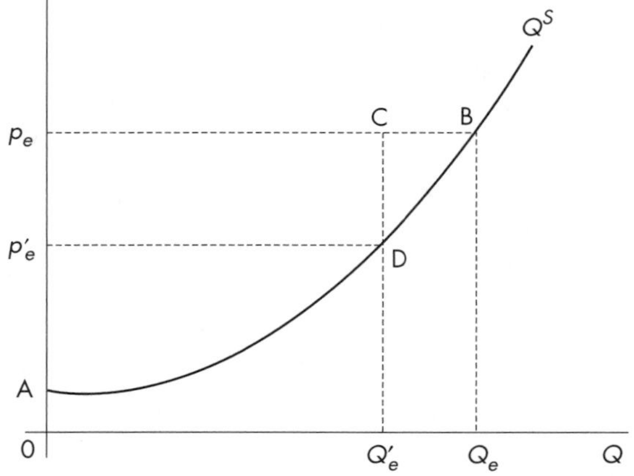

Figure 10.5 **Change in producer surplus resulting from a change in price.** A decrease in the price from p_e to p'_e reduces producer surplus from Ap_eB to Ap'_eD.

(producer surplus) is reduced by the area $p'_e p_e$CD. Also, the equilibrium level of output where marginal producer surplus is zero is reduced from Q_e to Q'_e. This results in an additional loss in producer surplus represented by the area DCB. The total loss in producer surplus is then $p'_e p_e$BD, resulting in a reduction in producer surplus from Ap_eB to Ap'_eD. Similarly, a price enhancement yields an increase in producer surplus. If the equilibrium price increases from p'_e to p_e, then the increase in producer surplus is $p'_e p_e$BD. Examples of price enhancements are government price supports that attempt to increase firms' producer surplus (corporate welfare) by maintaining or enhancing output price. However, such price supports will reduce consumer surplus.

Example 10.2 Calculating producer surplus

Consider the SMC function

$$\text{SMC} = 3 + 3Q.$$

Assuming perfect competition, the condition for maximizing profit is

$$p = \text{SMC},$$
$$p = 3 + 3Q.$$

Solving for Q, the supply function is

$$Q = \tfrac{1}{3}p - 1.$$

Assuming $p >$ SAVC, at $p = \$6$, quantity supplied $Q = 1$, TR $= pQ = \$6$,

$$\text{STVC} = \int_0^1 (3 + 3Q)\,dQ = \left[3Q + \tfrac{3}{2}Q^2\right]_0^1 = 3 + \tfrac{3}{2} = \$4.50,$$

$$\text{PS} = \text{TR} - \text{STVC} = 6 - 4.5 = \$1.50.$$

On doubling the price to $p = \$12$, we have $Q = 3$ and TR $= \$36$, so

$$\text{STVC} = \left[3Q + \tfrac{3}{2}Q^2\right]_0^3 = 9 + \tfrac{27}{2} = \$22.50,$$

$$\text{PS} = 36 - 22.5 = \$13.50.$$

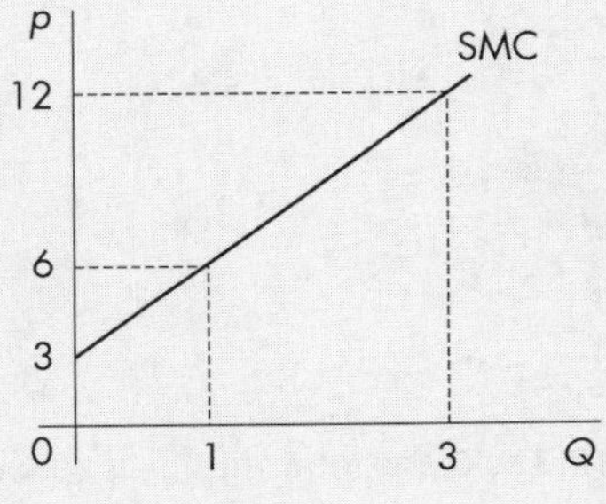

Total surplus and economic efficiency

Generally, government policies affecting the output price (such as a ceiling or support price) or alternative market structures (such as a market with an agent having some monopoly power) will either increase consumer surplus and decrease producer surplus or vice versa. However, such shifts in surplus often come at the price of an overall reduction in the sum of consumer and producer surplus (called *total surplus*). Called **deadweight loss** (or **excess burden**), this is the decrease in total surplus that is not transferred to some other agent. This deadweight loss is a measure of the loss in efficiency associated with a government policy or market structure. Thus, economic efficiency in a market may be defined where the sum of producer and consumer surplus is maximized (where there is no deadweight loss).

Deadweight loss (excess burden). The decrease in total surplus that is not transferred to some other agent. *E.g., the loss in economic efficiency associated with governmentally imposed price controls.*

Example 10.3 Perfect competition maximizes the sum of consumer and producer surplus

Consider the following market demand and supply functions:

$$Q^D = 26 - 2p,$$

$$Q^S = -9 + 3p.$$

Setting $Q^D = Q^S$ results in the perfectly competitive equilibrium price $p_e = 7$ and quantity $Q_e = 12$. Consumer surplus (CS) and producer surplus (PS) are then

$$\text{CS} = (13 - 7)12/2 = \$36,$$

$$\text{PS} = (7 - 3)12/2 = \$24.$$

Summing CS and PS gives the total surplus, \$60.

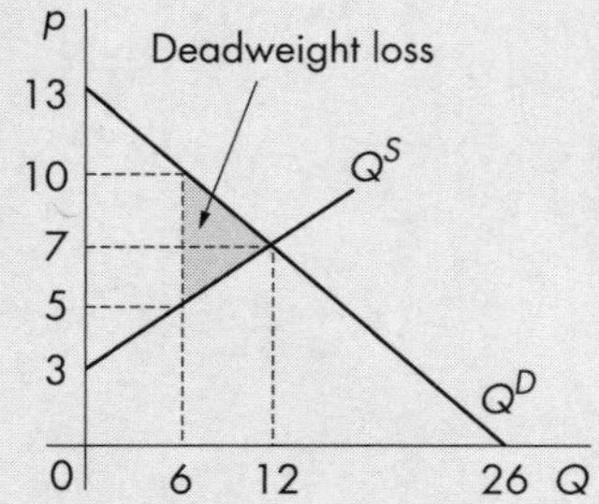

At an output level below the equilibrium of $Q_e = 12$, say 6, the total surplus is reduced. With quantity set at 6 units, the price of \$10 (what consumers are willing to pay for an additional unit of output) is greater than the price of \$5 (what firms are willing to receive for an additional unit of output). This indicates that an enhancement in both consumer and producer surplus is possible by increasing output. However, if output is constrained at 6, a deadweight loss in consumer and producer surplus results. This deadweight loss of \$15 is represented as the shaded area in the above graph.

Alternatively, an output level of 18 can increase the total surplus beyond the perfectly competitive levels. However, this increase comes at a cost of subsidizing both consumers and producers. For example, at a price of \$9, firms will supply an output of 18 and consumers will purchase all this supply only at a price of \$4. At this price of \$9, $Q^S = 18 > Q^D = 8$. Producer surplus, at $p = 9$, is then $(9-3)18/2 = \$54$ and consumer surplus, at $p = 4$, is $(13 - 4)18/2 = \$81$. This yields a total surplus of \$135. Both consumers and firms are better off. However, this requires some central agency to purchase the commodity at \$9 and sell it at \$4. The resulting net loss of \$5 per unit results in a total loss of (\$5)(18) = \$90. Subtracting this loss from the total surplus (\$135) results in only a net surplus of \$45. This is \$15 below the perfectly competitive total surplus of \$60. This net loss of \$15 is represented as the shaded area in the graph below.

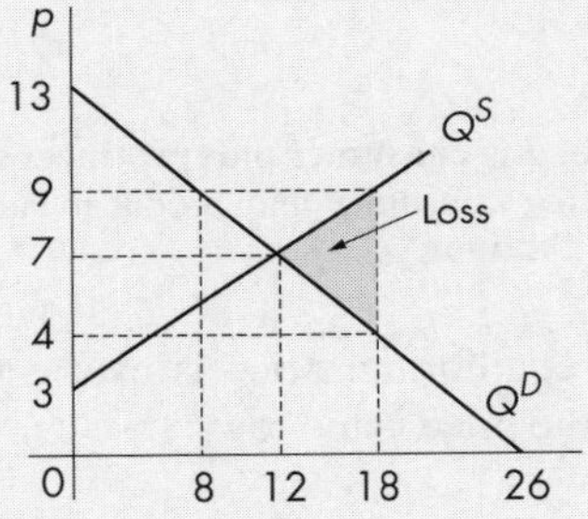

The sum of consumer and producer surplus (total surplus) is maximized in a perfectly competitive market (Figure 10.6). Specifically,

$$\max_Q [\text{CS}(Q) + \text{PS}(Q)] = \max_Q \{[U(Q) - pQ] + [pQ - \text{STVC}(Q)]\}$$

results in the first-order condition (FOC) $U'(Q_e) = \text{SMC}(Q_e)$. Under perfect competition, $p_e = \text{SMC}(Q_e)$, and given $p_e = U'(Q_e)$, the perfectly competitive market is efficient. There is no deadweight loss in a perfectly competitive equilibrium.

Are free markets free of inefficiency? If they are perfectly competitive markets, they are.

Government intervention and deadweight loss

For every action there is an equal and opposite governmental program.

(Bob Wells)

When the market results in some equilibrium set of price and quantity that is not very favorable to some segment of the economy, there often will be pressure from this segment for a governmental policy or program to offset this market effect. Examples are a governmentally

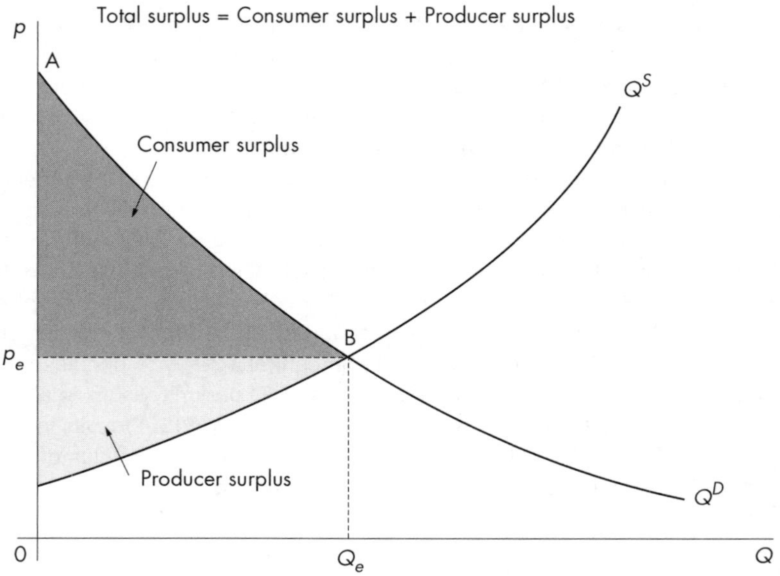

Figure 10.6 **Perfectly competitive equilibrium, maximizing consumer plus producer surplus.** Total surplus, the shaded areas representing consumer and producer surplus, is maximized at the perfectly competitive equilibrium (p_e, Q_e).

imposed ceiling price when some segment feels the equilibrium price is excessive or a governmentally imposed support price when they feel the price is too low.

Problems with ceiling prices

In 1970, as a result of grassroots support from low-income households and student tenants, the Massachusetts legislature passed a law authorizing cities to enact rent control. On January 3, 1997, the Massachusetts legislature enacted the real estate industry law, which killed rent control. Attempts at some form of rent control have been tried in many large cities in the United States with similar results.

Rent control is a form of government intervention into the market called a **ceiling price**. A ceiling price is an established price maximum above which the selling price is not allowed to rise. The effect of a ceiling price on the market for housing is illustrated in Figure 10.7. Price p_e is the free-market price for housing. Without a ceiling price, the quantity supplied of housing is Q_e at p_e. Consumer surplus is represented by the area p_eAB and producer surplus is the area Cp_eB.

Is allowing the poor to have affordable housing desirable? Yes—however, interfering with the price system by imposing a ceiling price may not be the right method for obtaining affordable housing.

Ceiling price. An established price maximum (ceiling) above which the selling price is not allowed to rise. *E.g., ceilings placed on natural gas prices during the 1970s.*

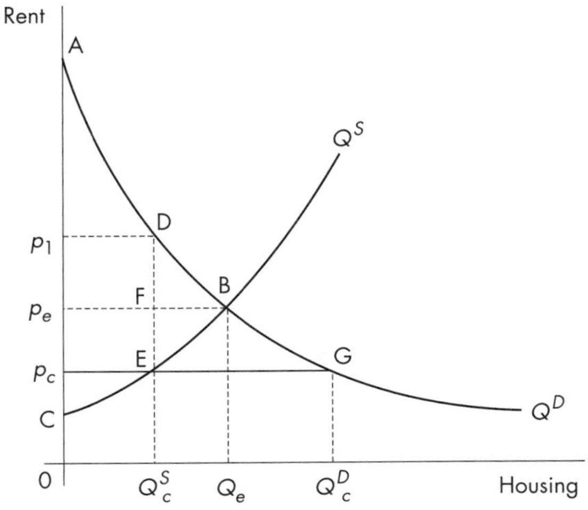

Figure 10.7 **Ceiling Price.** The ceiling price results in quantity demanded exceeding quantity supplied.

Imposing a ceiling price p_c above this market equilibrium price p_e imposes no constraint on the market and thus has no market effect. Only when the ceiling price is set below the free-market price p_e will it affect the market allocation of commodities. With $p_c < p_e$, the market price cannot increase to its free-market level, and this is the objective of the governmental policy. For example, if rents for housing are viewed to be too high, the ceiling price is set lower to reduce these high rents. However, a housing shortage may be the reason for high rents and, as illustrated in Figure 10.7, when the ceiling price p_c reduces quantity supplied from Q_e to Q^S_c and increases quantity demanded to Q^D_c, an even greater housing shortage results.

Consumer surplus with a ceiling price of p_c is p_cADE, and producer surplus is Cp_cE. As a direct result of the ceiling price, there is a loss in efficiency measured by the difference in total surplus under a free market and a market with a ceiling price. This deadweight loss is the area EDB and is a measure of the inefficiency associated with a ceiling price. The pseudo-triangle EDB illustrating deadweight loss appears in many models that result in efficiency loss. These deadweight triangles are called *Harberger triangles*, named after Arnold C. Harberger, who first suggested the triangle method for analyzing deadweight loss.[3]

Note that, as a result of the ceiling price, consumers capture part of the producer surplus, represented by the area $p_c p_e$FE, and consumers lose surplus, represented by the area FDB. If the net effect $p_c p_e$FE – FDB is positive, consumers gain in welfare by taking some of the surplus from the producers. This gain can make ceiling-price legislation very popular among voters even if it results in inefficiencies. This has resulted in rent control being adopted in a number of US cities (over 150 cities in the 1990s).

Politicians who favor ceiling prices may assume that $\varepsilon^S_{Q,p} = 0$, a perfectly inelastic market supply curve, where quantity supplied is not responsive to a price change. In Figure 10.8, consumer surplus at the free-market price is p_eAB and producer surplus is $0p_e$BQ_e. Here a ceiling price p_c results in no efficiency loss, so there is no deadweight loss. Consumers again

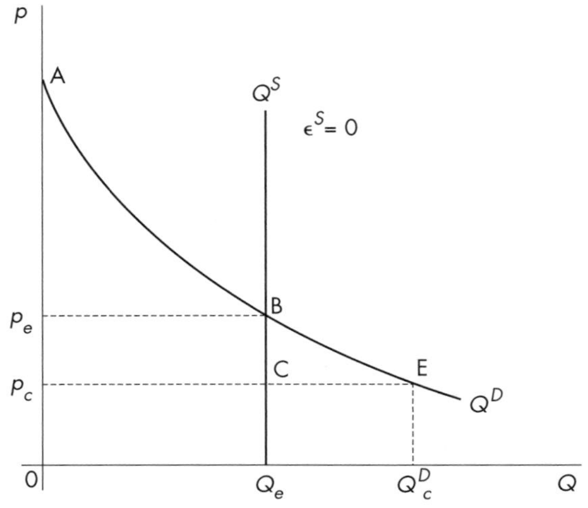

Figure 10.8 **Ceiling price with $\varepsilon^S_{Q,p} = 0$.** The ceiling price p_c results in no efficiency loss. Only some of the surplus, area $p_c p_e$BC, is transferred from the firms to the consumers. However, there is still a loss in satisfaction from consumers who are willing and able to rent $Q_c^D - Q_e$ housing at p_c but are unable to find a vacancy.

capture part of the producer surplus, $p_c p_e$BC, so the effect of the ceiling price is to shift more of the surplus to consumers by taking surplus away from producers.

Although when $\varepsilon^S_{Q,p} = 0$, total surplus remains unchanged, there is still a problem: quantity demanded, Q_c^D, is still greater than quantity supplied, Q_c^S. In Figure 10.7, the difference is $Q_c^D - Q_c^S$, and in Figure 10.8, it is $Q_c^D - Q_e$. Some consumers who are willing and able to rent housing at the ceiling price are unable to find a vacancy. This results in a loss of satisfaction, measured by the consumer surplus that would be gained if Q_c^D housing were supplied. In Figure 10.7, this is the area EDG, and in Figure 10.8, with $\varepsilon^S_{Q,p} = 0$, it is the area CBE. Thus, even if no surplus is lost, by assuming $\varepsilon^S_{Q,p} = 0$, there still is a loss of satisfaction by consumers.

Example 10.4 Ceiling price

Consider again the following market demand and supply functions:

$$Q^D = 26 - 2p,$$

$$Q^S = -9 + 3p.$$

As calculated in Example 10.3, the perfectly competitive equilibrium price and quantity are $p_e = 7$ and $Q_e = 12$, and CS and PS are \$36 and \$24, respectively. The total surplus under perfect competition is then \$60.

Imposing a ceiling price $p_c = 5$ results in $Q_c^D = 16 > Q_c^S = 6$. CS at $p_c = 5$ and $Q = 6$ is $[(13-10)6/2] + (10-5)6 = \$39$. This represents a \$3 increase in CS over the free-market CS of \$36. However, PS declines to $(5-3)6/2 = \$6$, an \$18 decrease from the free-market PS of \$24. The deadweight loss is $(10-5)(12-6)/2 = \$15$. The consumers' portion of the deadweight loss is $(10-7)(12-6)/2 = \$9$. However, consumers capture $(7-5)6 = \$12$ of producer surplus, resulting in the net gain of \$3. At this ceiling price, $Q_c^D > Q_c^S$. Those consumers who would be willing to purchase more of the commodity at $p_c = 5$, but are unable to, have a loss in surplus for this commodity of $(10-5)(16-6)/2 = \$25$. Note that if the ceiling price is removed in the market period, the price increases to \$10 and CS is reduced to $(13-10)6/2 = \$9$, from \$39.

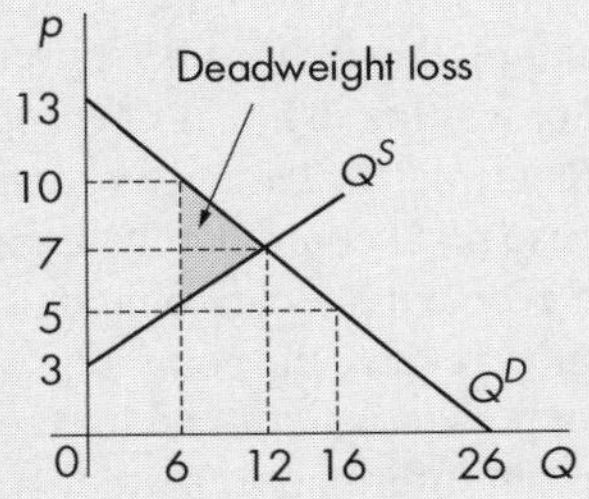

Allocation problem

The reason there is so little crime in Germany is that it is against the law.

(Alex Levin)

Consumers who are unable to purchase the commodity present one of the major problems with a ceiling price policy. The problem is how to allocate the available supply, because a ceiling price results in consumers wanting to purchase more than is being offered for sale. In a free market, this problem does not exist. The market automatically allocates supply in such a way that quantity supplied equals quantity demanded. Again, this is Adam Smith's invisible hand at work. Without a free market, some other mechanism is required for commodity allocation. Generally, this means that a social organization (government) determines the policy for allocation.

For example, during World War II, the US government issued ration stamps for certain commodities, including gasoline and chocolate. Gasoline ration stamps were also printed in 1979, but not issued. Under a ration stamp policy, for consumers to purchase a commodity, they required not only money but also a federal ration stamp. This use of ration stamps results in quantity supplied at the ceiling price to be rationed to the consumers. A problem with ration stamps is determining how many to issue, how to issue them, and who receives them. This generally requires a government agency whose sole purpose is to allocate a commodity—a function the free market does automatically through price signals.

For a ration stamp program to succeed, it must be illegal for consumers to sell their ration stamps to other consumers. Otherwise, the ceiling price would no longer be effective—a consumer would pay the ceiling price plus the cost of the stamp, which is the same as just paying more for the commodity. If a market for buying and selling ration stamps develops, then the governmental issue of such stamps just amounts to a redistribution of income. The effect would be the same as if the government just gave out money instead. In fact, the ability to buy and sell stamps makes the stamps just another form of currency. However, the issuing of ration stamps would generally work well in a very law-abiding society such as Germany.

FIRST-COME-FIRST-SERVED

Without governmental rationing, a ceiling price results in an allocation mechanism called *first-come-first-served.* Those consumers who are first to purchase the commodity are able to purchase it. Once the commodity is exhausted, the remaining consumers who want to purchase the commodity are unable to do so. For example, the United States imposed ceiling prices on gasoline in 1973 and 1979 to prevent rising fuel prices. A major problem with first-come-first-served is waiting lines. Consumers, realizing that supply is limited, will line up to purchase the item before it is gone. This results in lost productivity. Labor waiting in line is not productive. To avoid long lines resulting from the 1973 gasoline price controls, the United States imposed odd–even rationing (only cars with an odd-numbered license plate could purchase gas on an odd-numbered day). First-come-first-served is also not an efficient allocation method in that agents with the greatest willingness to pay will not necessarily receive the commodity.[4] What generally happens is some consumers will pay other consumers to wait in line for them. The effect of this is to raise the price of the commodity. Also, an information market generally develops. People will pay for information as to when and where a certain commodity will be supplied, which also raises the price of the commodity. In some parts of the former USSR, a first-come-first-served allocation mechanism resulted in both a "line waiter" profession and a well-developed information market.

Do you enjoy waiting in lines? If not, you could employ a line waiter to wait in lines for you.

BLACK MARKET

Civil disobedience, championed by David Thoreau (1817–1862) in 1849, is alive and well and has a long history of actually stimulating policy changes. It was employed by the Danish resistance during World War II in the 1940s, by people who opposed McCarthyism in the 1950s, by those fighting South African apartheid in the 1960s, and by antiwar activists in the 1970s. On a more mundane level, civil disobedience can also occur when $Q_c^D > Q_c^S$ (Figure 10.7). There will always be market forces pushing price above the ceiling price. Thus, laws and penalties restricting these market forces are required. However, there will generally be some consumers willing to engage in illegal activities and purchase a commodity above the ceiling price, and some firms willing to supply the commodity at a price above the legal limit. This illegal market, in which a commodity is sold in violation of some law, is called a **black market**. For example, during World War II, price controls on gasoline, meat, and other commodities resulted in a sizable black market. The Office of Price Administration (OPA) Enforcement Office estimated that 15–50 percent of gasoline C coupons (the standard ration coupons available to civilians) were counterfeit, and the National Independent Meat Packers Association claimed that 90 percent of the meat industry operations in the San Antonio region were on the black market. In 1944, 25 percent of New York City residents claimed that they did not even worry about ration stamps or price ceilings when shopping. Currently, in the United States, a considerable black market exists for exotic animals. Endangered species such as the Chinese alligator and Komodo dragon have black market prices of as much as $15,000 and $30,000, respectively. In the world market, the major black market is in weapons and generally among arms dealers, drug-traffickers, terrorists, and other criminals.

Black market. Selling a commodity in violation of some law. *E.g., during World War II, a store selling chocolate without obtaining ration stamps from my unsuspecting mother.*

The black-market price and output, when a ceiling price is established, are illustrated in Figure 10.9. The black-market supply curve is AQ^{SB}. This curve lies to the left of and increases more steeply than the legal-market supply curve Q^S, because sellers incur greater costs and risks in a black market than in a legal market. Higher costs may be in the form of hiding any production or sales or paying government officials not to prosecute them for their illegal activities. The greater the cost of operation in the black market, the steeper will be the supply curve. The black-market demand curve is represented by BQ^{DB}. This curve's lower endpoint is at B rather than at C, because even at the legal ceiling price p_c, some potential buyers will not buy in the black market. They will always obey the laws of the state. Thus, at the ceiling price p_c, quantity demanded in the black market is not the total unsatisfied demand AC, but a smaller quantity AB. The black-market price is p_1, where the black-market demand equals supply. Quantity traded in the black market is $Q_B - Q_c$, and quantity traded in the legal market is Q_c. Total quantity traded is Q_B. As a result of increased supply from the black market, consumer and producer surplus are both increased. In Figure 10.9, consumer surplus is enhanced by the area EDF and producer surplus is increased by the area AEF.

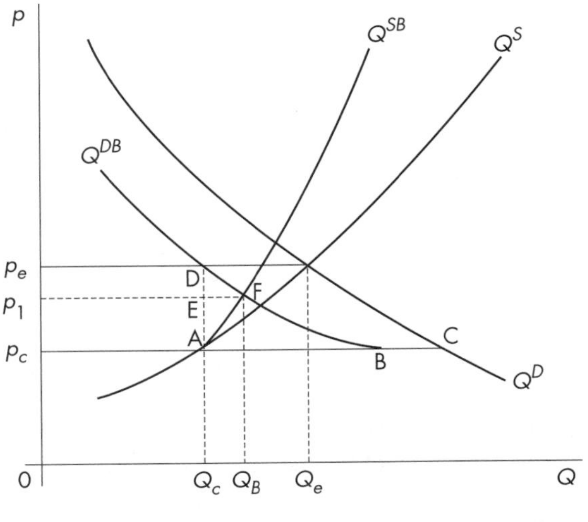

Figure 10.9 **Black-market price and quantity for a ceiling price.** Without a ceiling price, the equilibrium price and quantity are (p_e, Q_e). A ceiling price of p_c results in a black-market price of p_1, with $Q_B - Q_c$ traded in the black market and Q_c traded in the legal market.

This increase in total surplus reduces a portion of the deadweight loss associated with ceiling pricing.

Note that the black-market price may be less than, equal to, or greater than the free-market price p_e, depending on the relative penalties on the consumers and producers trading in the black market. If producers are penalized relatively more than consumers, the black-market supply curve will tilt more to the left and the black-market price will increase. In contrast, if consumers are relatively more penalized, the black-market price will fall as the demand curve shifts to the left.

In centrally planned economies, the black market can constitute a sizeable portion of the economy, and government efforts toward restricting its flow would result in severe welfare losses. However, the lack of free flow of market information, including advertising, would prevent the black-market price and quantity corresponding to the free-market equilibrium.

Example 10.5 The black market

Consider again the following legal-market demand and supply functions:

$$Q^D = 26 - 2p,$$

$$Q^S = -9 + 3p,$$

with the perfectly competitive equilibrium price $p_e = 7$ and quantity $Q_e = 12$. A ceiling price of $p_c = 5$ results in $Q_c^D = 16 > Q_c^S = 6$. Thus, incentives exist for a black market. Given penalties associated with black-market participation, assume that the black-market demand and supply functions are

$$Q^{DB} = 22 - 2p,$$

$$Q^{SB} = 1 + p \quad \text{for} \quad Q > 6.$$

Equating the black-market supply and demand functions and solving for the black-market price p_B yields

$$Q^{DB} = Q^{SB},$$

$$22 - 2p = 1 + p,$$

$$p_B = 7.$$

In this case, the black-market price equals the legal market price. A total of 8 units are supplied: 6 in the legal market and 2 in the black market. From Example 10.4, consumer and producer surpluses in the legal market are still \$39 and \$6, respectively, resulting in a total surplus of \$45. The black market augments this surplus by \$3, with a black-market consumer surplus of $(8 - 7)(8 - 6)/2 = \$1$ and a producer surplus of $(7 - 5)(8 - 6)/2 = \$2$. The sum of the \$45 legal-market ceiling-price total surplus and the \$3 black-market surplus, \$48, is still short of \$60 (the free-market total surplus calculated in Example 10.3).

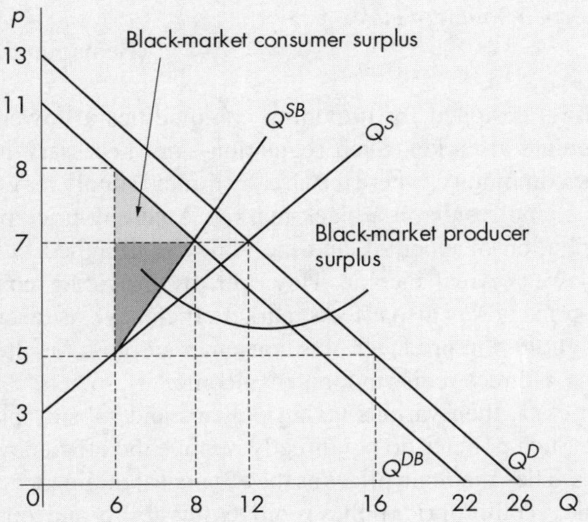

Application: Long-run relation between the black and legal foreign exchange markets

As investigated by M. Bahmani-Oskooee, S. Hegerty, and A. Tanku, governments in many developing counties indulge the existence of a dual exchange rate. To control capital outflows, governments will impose restrictions on the purchase of foreign currencies. Such restrictions may take the form of artificial waiting times and taxes and licensing requirements. These restrictions create an excess demand for foreign currencies, resulting in a parallel market if it is legal or a black market if it is illegal. The interaction of supply and demand in these markets will determine the going market exchange rate for transferring domestic into a foreign currency. Generally, this black-market rate will be higher than the official rate of exchange. The difference (spread) between the two rates (the premium) works as a signal that indicates macroeconomic problems. Thus, a country's central bank will at times adjust the official rate to aid in mitigating the problems. Given these adjustments to the official rate, Bahmani-Oskooee et al. hypothesize that in the long-run the official and black-market rates will converge.

Bahmani-Oskooee et al. used a panel of 25 countries to test this hypothesis. Results support their hypothesis that in the long run the official rate will adjust toward the black-market rate and reach an equilibrium level. The speed of convergence to equilibrium is often higher in the black market, which implies greater efficiency. Thus, any foreign exchange control will only have a short-run impact. The same supply and demand forces that affect the black-market rate will eventually force a government to adjust the official rate, reducing any price premium.

Source: M. Bahmani-Oskooee, S. Hegerty, and A. Tanku, "The Black-Market Exchange Rate versus the Official Rate: Which Rate Fosters the Adjustment Speed in the Monetarist Model?" *Manchester School* 78 (2010): 725–738.

Efficiency versus equity

An ounce of prevention is worth a pound of cure.

(Benjamin Franklin)

In summary, a ceiling-price policy, designed for providing commodities at lower prices, results in the requirement to regulate a market. Such regulation—not necessary in a free market—reduces the supply of the commodity, where the already limited supply may account for a higher-than-acceptable price, and results in a black market. A ceiling-price policy is concerned with equity (the distribution of income), and the policy is designed to provide consumers greater purchasing power or real income. However, by providing consumers additional real income, a ceiling-price policy also affects market efficiency. As discussed, a ceiling price results in a deadweight loss in producer plus consumer surplus. An alternative solution to the equity problem is a direct redistribution of income.[5] If society finds that inequities in income distribution exist, then various taxing policies and subsidy programs can be designed to redistribute it. Such policies do not directly remove the efficiency of free markets in allocating commodities. They maintain prices as the efficient signaling mechanism for allocating resources. In contrast, a ceiling-price policy removes this ability and thus results in inefficiencies.

Once a ceiling price is established and the market reacts by reducing quantity supplied, it becomes politically unpopular to remove the ceiling price. As indicated in Figure 10.7, if the ceiling price were removed, the price would initially rise in the market period to p_1, which is higher than the equilibrium free-market price p_e. Then, as firms adjusted to the removal of the ceiling price, the price would fall to the equilibrium price p_e. However, this initial rise in price after the removal of the ceiling price would reduce consumer surplus from p_cADE to only p_1AD. In centrally planned economics with ceiling prices on many commodities, particularly on food, removal of ceiling prices and subsequent large reductions in consumer surplus has stimulated political unrest and in some cases revolution. By not yielding in the first place to political pressure to establish a ceiling (an ounce of prevention), governments can avoid the highly unpopular act of having to resend it (a pound of cure). However, the short-run benefits of a ceiling price accrue to the current administration, leaving subsequent administrations to deal with the consequences of the inefficiencies from this market intervention.

Problems with support prices

In response to the world depression in the 1930s (called the Great Depression—but, according to my father, it was not so great for the people living at that time), most industrialized countries developed agricultural price-support policies to reduce the volatility of prices for farm products and to increase farm income. A **support price**, the reverse of a ceiling price, is an established price minimum (floor) below which the selling price is not allowed to fall. Setting a support price below the free-market equilibrium price has no effect. Only when the support price is above the free-market price will it have an effect on market allocation. In Figure 10.10, a support price p_s is illustrated, with a free-market equilibrium price p_e and quantity Q_e. Such a support price results in quantity supplied being greater than quantity demanded: $Q_s^S > Q_s^D$. Maintaining this support price requires a government agency to purchase the surplus supply $Q_s^S - Q_s^D$ and keep it out of the market.

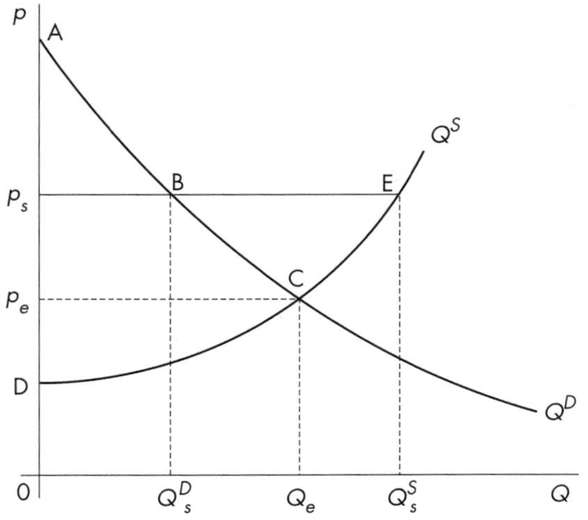

Figure 10.10 **Support price.** The support price results in quantity supplied exceeding quantity demanded.

Support price. An established price minimum (floor) below which the selling price is not allowed to fall. *E.g., the United States currently has a support price for peanuts.*

As a result of a support price, consumer surplus is reduced and producer surplus increased. In Figure 10.10, consumer surplus for the free market is represented by the area p_eAC, with producer surplus represented by the area Dp_eC. The support price increases the commodity price from p_e to p_s and reduces the corresponding consumer surplus to p_sAB. Producer surplus increases from Dp_eC to Dp_sE. A major objective of most support prices is to increase producers' profits. In the figure, producer profits increase by $p_e p_s$EC. Producers capture some of the consumer surplus, $p_e p_s$BC, and receive additional surplus, BEC. The cost to taxpayers is the value of the commodity surplus that must be purchased: the area Q_s^DBEQ_s^S. The support price results in production of the commodity beyond the quantity demanded ($Q_s^S - Q_s^D$). This surplus production is stored, usually with the idea of releasing it in times of drastic reductions in supply. Support prices then result in an economy producing more of a commodity than society demands, which is inefficient.

Example 10.6 Support price

Consider again the following market demand and supply functions:

$$Q^D = 26 - 2p,$$

$$Q^S = -9 + 3p.$$

As calculated in Example 10.3, the perfectly competitive equilibrium price and quantity are $p_e = 7$ and $Q_e = 12$, and consumer surplus (CS) and producer surplus (PS) are \$36 and \$24, respectively. The total surplus under perfect competition is then \$60.

Imposing a support price $p_S = 10$ results in $Q_S^D = 6 < Q_S^S = 21$. CS under this support price is then reduced to $\$9 = (13 - 10)6/2$ and PS is increased to $\$73.50 = (10 - 3)21/2$. Total surplus is then increased to \$82.50, a $\$22.50 = 82.50 - 60$ increase. However, the government must step in and buy up the surplus supply of $15 = 21 - 6$ at the support price of $p_S = 10$. This results in government spending of $\$150 = 15(10)$. The increase in total surplus accrues completely to producers, and the producers also acquire some of the consumer surplus. Producers capture $\$27 = 36 - 9$ of the consumer surplus.

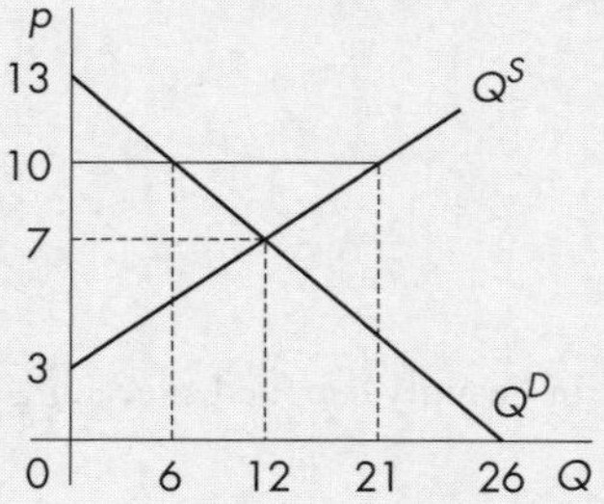

The agricultural production surpluses from support price programs are generally allocated freely to the poor and elderly, donated to lesser developed countries, or given to agricultural producers. These support price programs are inefficient and thus difficult to justify in terms of economics. They are also expensive for governments in terms of having to purchase the surplus, area $Q_s^D\text{BE}Q_s^S$ in Figure 10.10. As a consequence, within the last several decades, we have relied on non-support-price programs such as the free market. Instead of maintaining agricultural surpluses in times of regional reduced supply, demand could be supplied by purchasing agricultural commodities in other regions. The free market would be sufficient to maintain equilibrium between demand and supply. However, in 2007–2008 there was a world shortage of agricultural commodities (particularly corn as a result of its increased use for biofuel). This global shortage of food has resulted in a rethinking of a sole reliance on free markets. Generally, society values having large stores of food to guard against possible unforeseen food shortages and maintaining an agricultural sector capable of feeding its population. For example, Japan, as a nation of islands, maintains a large rice sector rather than relying on imports. China generally avoided the 2007–2008 price spike in food by maintaining a surplus of agricultural commodities. Thus, for national security reasons, nations may attempt to maintain an agricultural sector larger than a free market would provide.

Is having an abundance of food desirable? Yes, societies generally value having a supply of food in excess of what a free market would prescribe.

Acreage controls

It is the opinion of some that crops could be grown on the moon. Which raises the fear that it may not be long before we are paying somebody not to.

(Franklin P. Jones)

The Agricultural Adjustment Act (AAA) in 1933 was one of the first pieces of legislation passed under President Franklin Delano Roosevelt's New Deal program. The AAA attempted to control farm prices by reducing the supply of basic crops (wheat, cotton, rice, tobacco, corn, hogs, and dairy). The AAA empowered the Secretary of Agriculture to fix marketing quotas for the major farm products, to take surplus production off the market, and to reduce production of crops by offering producers payments in return for voluntarily reducing crop acreage. Partly as a result of this act, farm prices increased by 85 percent from 1932 to 1937. However, the Supreme Court declared certain production control features of the AAA unconstitutional.

Such programs as *acreage controls* avoid the problem of surpluses and are designed to raise agricultural prices by limiting the acreage on which certain crops can be grown (in the future, this may include limiting the planet on which a crop can be grown). An example of acreage controls is the US Conservation Reserve Program (CRP), enacted in 1985, which provides payments to farmers to take highly erodible or environmentally sensitive cropland out of production. Currently, approximately 25 percent of US cropland enrolled in the CRP is out of crop production. As illustrated in Figure 10.11, acreage controls are where reduced supply results in the supply curve shifting to the left, to $Q^{S'}$. This decreases quantity and increases price. As a result of acreage controls, consumer surplus is reduced from the area p_eAC to p'AB and producer surplus is increased from the area Dp_eC to Dp'BE. The inefficiency of acreage controls is represented by the deadweight loss, the shaded area EBC, if CRP payments are not considered. This would be the case if farmers were required to reduce output to Q', possibly by some *production quota*. Instead, the CRP works by providing a payment to farmers for restricting output to Q'. The minimum payment would then be BEF, the producer surplus lost from farmers not being allowed to produce at the profit-maximizing output level Q''. In this case of CRP payments, the deadweight loss is BEF. Acreage controls require farmers to take some land out of production with the objective of reducing output. However, producers will generally take marginal, relatively unproductive land out of production and increase their

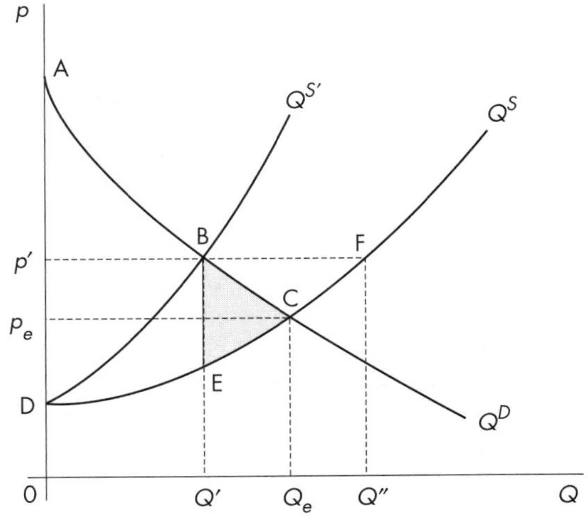

Figure 10.11 **Acreage controls.** The reduction in supply from controlling acreage decreases quantity from Q_e to Q' and increases price from p_e to p'. Consumer surplus is reduced from p_eAC to p'AB, with producer surplus increasing from Dp_eC to Dp'BE.

labor and other variable inputs, including pesticides and fertilizers, in an attempt to maintain production. Thus, the supply curve may not shift to the left as much as the policy intended.

Example 10.7 Acreage controls

Consider again the following market demand and supply functions:

$$Q^D = 26 - 2p,$$

$$Q^S = -9 + 3p.$$

As calculated in Example 10.3, the perfectly competitive equilibrium price and quantity are $p_e = 7$ and $Q_e = 12$, and CS and PS are \$36 and \$24, respectively. The total surplus under perfect competition is then \$60.

Assume that acreage controls shift the market supply curve to the left, so the equilibrium price is \$10. CS under acreage controls is then reduced to $(13 - 10)6/2 = \$9$ and PS is increased to $(10 - 5)6 + (5 - 3)6/2 = \$36$. Deadweight loss is then $(10 - 5)(12 - 6)/2 = \$15$, given production quotas. Producers capture $(10 - 7)6 = \$18$ of the consumer surplus and only lose $(7 - 5)(12 - 6)/2 = \$6$ in deadweight loss. If some type of payment is required to induce firms to restrict output to 6, the payment will be $(10 - 5)(21 - 6)/2 = \$37.50$. Compared with support price, Example 10.6, government spending is less (35 percent less in this case), but the total output is reduced $(21 - 6 = 15)$.

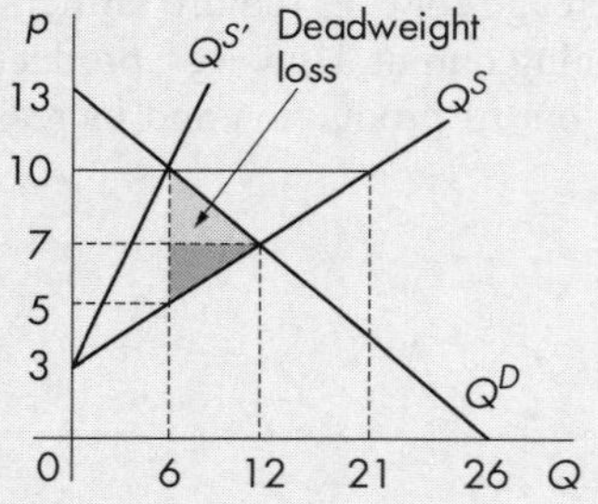

Acreage controls are a specific type of production control where in general the government attempts to restrict supply. Another major use of such controls is on taxicabs in major cities. Such controls generally take the form of limiting the number of medallions, where it is required that each cab have a medallion. As indicated in Figure 10.11, the deadweight loss from such a control is EBC. The rationale for such taxi controls is that the free market is inefficient by not accounting for externalities.[6] Cities without controls and a large number of cab stands and taxicab trips from street hailing, such as New York and Chicago, have experienced oversupply externalities of cabs, with deterioration in driver and vehicle quality. However, the loss in efficiency from a free market must be balanced with externality's costs. In an effort to achieve this balance, cities have adopted various programs, including two-tier control systems, flexible forms of entry control, company-level entry qualifications, geographic restrictions, and service requirements.

Price subsidies

> *The Government's view of the economy could be summed up in a few short phases: If it moves, tax it, if it keeps moving, regulate it and if it stops moving, subsidize it.*
>
> (Ronald Reagan)

Neither price supports nor acreage controls offer much to consumers other than the prospect of spending more and getting less. As policymakers have become more sensitive to consumer complaints, a third instrument (price subsidies) has received increased attention. With a **subsidy (*S*)**, the government generally sets some level for the price that consumers will pay for the commodity and subsidizes firms to the level where they will satisfy the quantity demanded at this price. A per-unit *price subsidy* s in Figure 10.12 promises producers a total subsidy payment S equal to the difference between the subsidized price p_s and the price that consumers pay, p_c. Producers will produce output Q_s^S that decreases price from p_e to p_c for consumers. Producer surplus is increased from the area Cp_eB to Cp_sD, and consumer surplus increases from the area p_eAB to p_cAE. The difference in the price that consumers pay, p_c, and the total price that producers receive, p_s, is the per-unit subsidy paid by the government. The government subsidizes producers by the area p_cp_sDE. The net gain in producer and consumer surplus, the area p_cp_sDBE, is offset by the cost of the subsidy, the area p_cp_sDE. The loss in efficiency is the shaded area BDE. However, in terms of food, increased agricultural production from price subsidies provides an abundant supply of relatively low-cost agricultural products.

Subsidy (*S*). A payment reducing what consumers pay for a commodity below the price firms receive for supplying the commodity. *E.g., bread in many countries is subsidized by the government.*

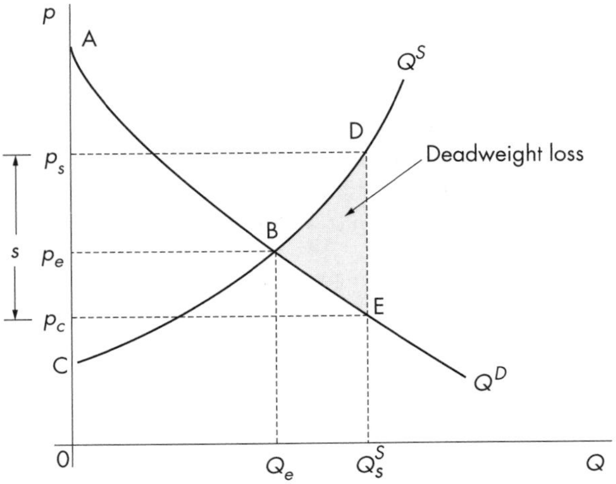

Figure 10.12 **Price subsidy.** Producers receive the price p_S and consumers only pay p_C, with the government paying the difference s. Producer surplus is enhanced, represented by the area p_ep_SDB, and consumer surplus is also increased by the area p_Cp_eBE. The government total subsidy is then p_Cp_SDE, with an associated deadweight loss of BDE.

Similar to ceiling prices, once established, price subsidies are extremely difficult to remove. Firms must cut back on production, given the lower price, say p_c, in Figure 10.12. In the short run, this may result in price dropping to below SAVC for some firms, forcing these firms to shut down. This adjustment process can be quite hard on an economy, if a large share of markets have previously been subsidized and the subsidies are removed all at once. Significant short-run unemployment of resources may occur. However, with governments facing growing budget deficits, they are cutting many social expenditures, including costly food subsidy programs. Such attempts have sparked revolutions within a number of countries.

Example 10.8 Determining the effect a price subsidy has on consumer and producer surplus

Once again, consider the market demand and supply functions

$$Q^D = 26 - 2p,$$
$$Q^S = -9 + 3p.$$

As calculated in Example 10.3, the perfectly competitive equilibrium price and quantity are $p_e = 7$ and $Q_e = 12$, and CS and PS are \$36 and \$24, respectively. The total surplus under perfect competition is then \$60.

A price subsidy for firms results in firms receiving a price of p_c and a per-unit subsidy of s, so their effective price is $(1 + s/p_c)p_c$. The market supply function is then

$$Q^S = -9 + 3(1 + s/p)p.$$

Setting $s = 5$ and equating quantity supplied with demand yields the price that consumers will pay, p_c: $Q^S = Q^D$, $-9 + 3(1 + s/p_c)p_c = 26 - 2p_c$, $-9 + 3p_c + 15 = 26 - 2p_c$, $20 = 5p_c$, $p_c = 4$.

At $p_c = 4$, the equilibrium level of quantity is 18. Firms receive a price of \$9, where the difference in what consumers pay, \$4, and what firms receive, \$9, is the amount of per-unit subsidy, $9 - 4 = \$5$. Consumer surplus is then $(13 - 4)18/2 = \$81$ and producer surplus is $(9 - 3)18/2 = \$54$. Both consumers' and firms' welfare improves with this price subsidy. The total subsidy $S = (9 - 4)18 = \$90$. The efficiency loss is $(9 - 4)(18 - 12)/2 = \$15$.

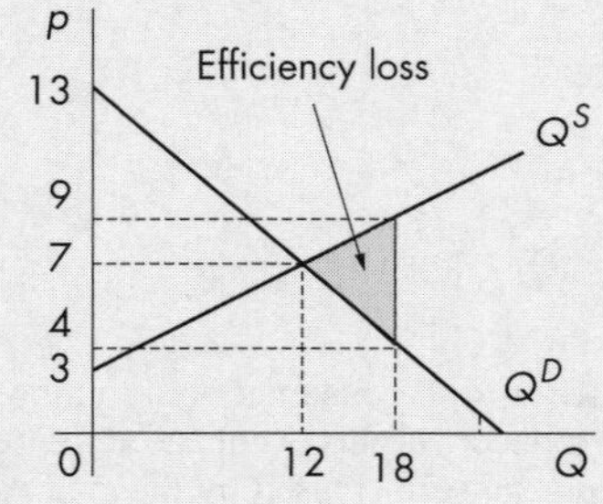

Tax

The government that robs Peter to pay Paul can always depend on the support of Paul.
(George Bernard Shaw)

At one point during the rule of the Egyptian Pharaohs, a tax was imposed on cooking oil. To ensure that citizens were not avoiding the cooking oil tax, scribes (tax collectors) would audit households to ensure that citizens were consuming the proper amounts of cooking oil and not using leavings from other cooking processes as a substitute for the taxed oil. During Julius Caesar's reign in Rome, a 1 percent sales tax was imposed, and during the time of Caesar Augustus the sales tax was 4 percent for slaves and 1 percent for everything else.

The opposite of a price subsidy is a **commodity tax** on a firm's output. This commodity tax may be either an *output tax* (*quantity tax*) such as an *excise tax* or a *sales tax* (value tax or *ad valorem tax*). Excise taxes are generally levied by states on commodities such as cigarettes, motor fuel, distilled spirits, wine, and beer. The term excise tax is redundant, given that *excise* is an old word for tax. Conventionally, an excise tax is a tax per physical unit (per pack of cigarettes, per gallon of motor fuel, or per ounce of alcohol) and varies by state. For example, in 2009, the cigarette excise tax was highest in New York at $4.35 per pack, compared with only $0.30 in Virginia. The sales tax, levied on retail purchases, also varies by state and is another common method for state and local governments to obtain revenue. These two taxes have the effect of increasing the cost to consumers for purchasing a commodity. As illustrated in Figure 10.13 for a sales tax as a percentage of a firm's total sales, this increased cost shifts the supply curve to the left. The per-unit tax τ is then equal to the per-unit price of a commodity times this sales-tax percentage. For example, a 5 percent sales tax on a $1.00 item results in a per-unit tax τ of $0.05. As a result of the sales tax, equilibrium quantity decreases from Q_e to Q_t. Firms receive p_c per unit of output from consumers but have to pay τ per unit in tax, resulting in a net of p_f. Consumer surplus as a result of the tax is reduced

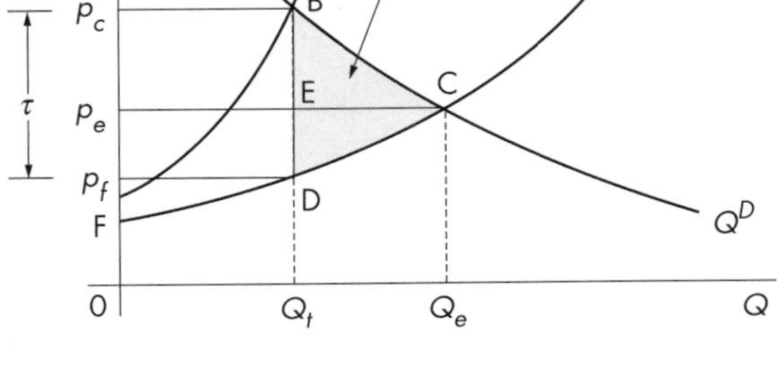

Figure 10.13 **Sales tax τ.** As a result of the sales tax τ, quantity is reduced from Q_e to Q_t and the price that consumers pay is now p_c, with firms receiving a price p_f net of the tax. Consumer surplus is reduced from p_eAC to p_cAB, and producer surplus is reduced from Fp_eC to Fp_fD. The deadweight loss is area DBC.

from the area p_eAC to p_cAB, and producer surplus is reduced from the area Fp_eC to Fp_fD. The government collects the area $p_f p_c$BD in total tax revenue, so the net loss in producer plus consumer surplus is DBC. This is the deadweight loss as a result of the sales tax, that is, the efficiency loss associated with the tax. The tax revenue collected by the government may then be used to finance public goods, including education, roads, health care, and public utilities. As long as the net benefits from these public goods exceed the deadweight loss from the sales tax, welfare is improved as a result of the tax.

Commodity tax (τ). A payment increasing what consumers pay for a commodity above the price firms receive for supplying the commodity. *E.g., all states have an excise tax on gasoline.*

Example 10.9 Determining the share of a sales tax borne by firms and consumers

One last time, consider the market demand and supply functions $Q^D = 26 - 2p$, $Q^S = -9 + 3p$.

As calculated in Example 10.3, the perfectly competitive equilibrium price and quantity are $p_e = 7$ and $Q_e = 12$, and CS and PS are \$36 and \$24, respectively. The total surplus under perfect competition is then \$60.

A sales tax imposed on firms results in firms receiving a price of p_c but having to pay the sales tax, so their net price is $(1 - t)p_c$, where t is the tax rate. Note that $t = \tau/p_c$. The market supply function is then

$$Q^S = -9 + 3(1 - t)p.$$

Setting $t = 1/2$ and equating quantity supplied with demand yields the price that consumers will pay, p_c: $Q^S = Q^D$, $-9 + 3(1 - t)p_c = 26 - 2p_c$, $-9 + \frac{3}{2}p_c = 26 - 2p_c$, $35 = \frac{7}{2}p_c$, $p_c = 10$.

At $p_c = 10$, the equilibrium level of quantity is 6. Firms receive a net price of \$5, where the difference in what consumers pay, \$10, and what firms receive, \$5, is the amount of the tax per unit of output, $10 - 5 = \$5$. Consumer surplus is then reduced to $(13 - 10)6/2 = \$9$ and producer surplus declines to $(5 - 3)6/2 = \$6$. Deadweight loss associated with this sales tax is $(10 - 5)(12 - 6)/2 = \$15$ and the total amount of taxes collected is $(10 - 5)6 = \$30$.

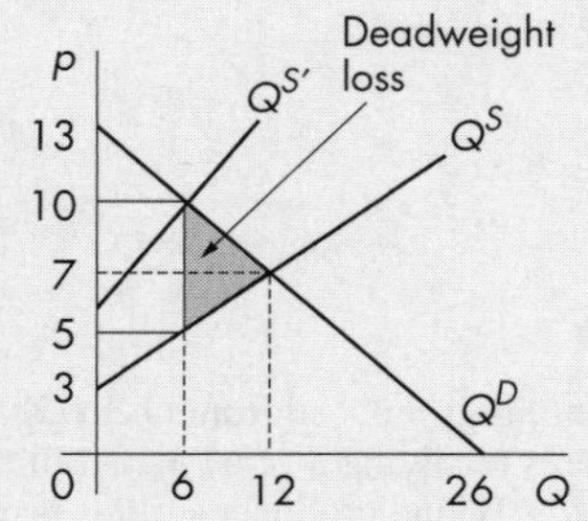

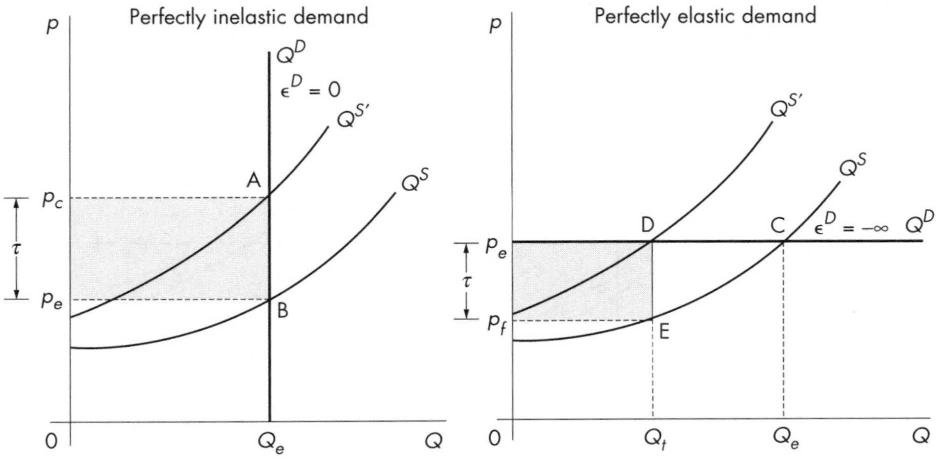

Figure 10.14 **Sales tax with a perfectly inelastic demand curve ($\varepsilon^D = 0$) and a perfectly elastic demand curve ($\varepsilon^D = -\infty$).** A perfectly inelastic demand curve results in all of the tax being shifted to the consumer, area $p_e p_c$AB, with no deadweight loss. In contrast, a perfectly elastic demand curve results in all of the tax being borne by the firm, area $p_f p_e$DE, with deadweight loss EDC.

Note that the sales tax is borne by both consumers and producers, where, as indicated in Figure 10.13, consumers bear the area $p_e p_c$BE and producers bear the area $p_f p_e$ED. The share of the sales tax borne by consumers and producers depends on the elasticities of supply and demand. As illustrated in Figure 10.13, the per-unit tax τ is the difference between the price that consumers pay, p_c, and the net price that firms receive, p_f: $\tau = p_c - p_f$.[7]

If the demand curve is perfectly inelastic, $\varepsilon^D = 0$, then $dp_c/d\tau = 1$ and $dp_f/d\tau = 0$, resulting in the per-unit tax being borne totally by the consumers (Figure 10.14). Alternatively, if demand is perfectly elastic, $\varepsilon^D = -\infty$, then $dp_c/d\tau = 0$ and $dp_f/d\tau = -1$, resulting in the per-unit tax being borne totally by the firms.

In terms of supply, if the supply curve is perfectly inelastic, $\varepsilon^S = 0$, then $dp_c/d\tau = 0$ and $dp_f/d\tau = -1$, resulting in the per-unit tax being borne totally by the firms (Figure 10.15). In the long run, as supply becomes more elastic, producers' share of the sales tax is reduced. If supply is perfectly elastic, $\varepsilon^S = \infty$, then $dp_c/d\tau = 1$ and $dp_f/d\tau = 0$, and all of the tax is shifted to consumers.[8] For $\varepsilon^S = \infty$, producer surplus is zero and the sales tax does not change producer surplus but does reduce consumer surplus from the area p_eFC to p_cFD. All of the tax, the area $p_e p_c$DE, is passed onto the consumers.

Who pays taxes? We all do: a commodity tax is borne by both the seller and buyer of a commodity. The proportion of the tax borne by each depends on the elasticities of supply and demand.

Application: Cigarette taxation

Back in 2009, the single largest federal cigarette tax hike went into effect; the tax per-pack climbed from \$0.39 to \$1.01. Evaluating the impact of a tax increase on cigarette

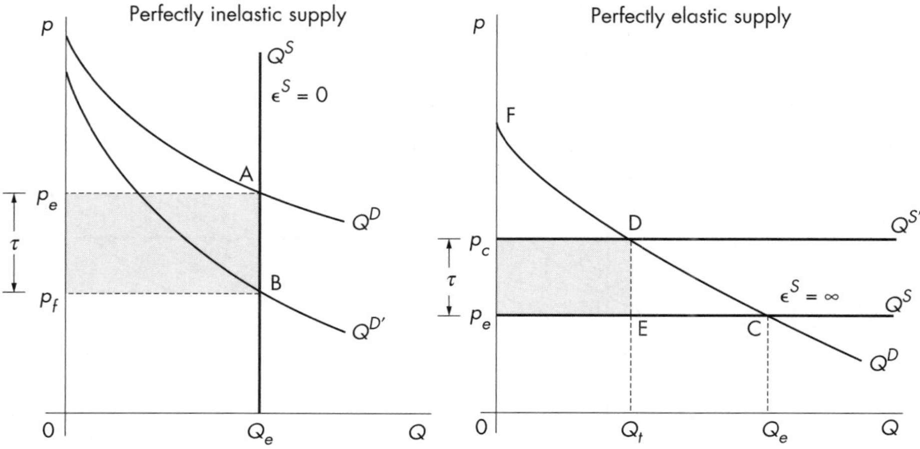

Figure 10.15 **Sales tax with a perfectly inelastic supply curve ($\varepsilon^S = 0$) and a perfectly elastic supply curve ($\varepsilon^S = \infty$).** A perfectly inelastic supply curve results in all of the tax being borne by the firm, area $p_f p_e$AB with no deadweight loss. In contrast, a perfectly elastic supply curve results in all of the tax being shifted to the consumer, area $p_e p_c$DE, with deadweight loss EDC.

consumption, K. Chan and T. Capehart estimated the price elasticity of demand for cigarettes to be −0.26. The addictive power of nicotine limits smokers' ability to reduce consumption. Given this addictive power and the market structure of the cigarette industry, most, if not all, of the tax was passed on to smokers. Based on the elasticity estimate, the federal tax increase on cigarettes will reduce cigarette consumption by 41 percent. Even with highly inelastic demand, large increases in cigarette taxes can significantly reduce consumption. Over 440,000 US smokers quit smoking in 2006 by dying from smoking.

Source: K.K. Chan and T. Capehart, "Health Concerns or Price: Which takes Credit for Declining Cigarette Consumption in the U.S.," *Choices* 19 (2004): 43–46.

Trade restrictions

In December 2011, the US \$0.54 per gallon (\$0.14 per liter) tariff on ethanol was allowed to expire. Such a tariff is likely illegal under World Trade Organization agreements. Brazil, as the major exporter of ethanol, would likely have had success in its case before the WTO to have the US tariff declared illegal and removed. However, Europe still has a \$0.10 per liter tariff on imported ethanol.

In general, international trade restrictions on ethanol and other products, in the form of quotas and tariffs, also result in market inefficiencies. Such restrictions are generally the result of policymakers trying to discourage domestic consumers from purchasing foreign instead of domestic commodities (ethanol). This increases domestic production, which decreases reliance on foreign production. It also maintains foreign currency reserves for the purchase of foreign commodities deemed of higher value by the government. Such trade-restriction policies are costly in the form of market inefficiencies; however, in the name of national security, they are very common.

As an illustration of market inefficiency associated with trade restrictions, consider first a country with an unrestricted free market for a commodity. Assume this country makes up a relatively small portion of world demand and thus has no influence on the world price. Examples are small developing countries that import agricultural commodities such as soybeans and poultry. The equilibria with and without international markets are depicted in Figure 10.16. With no international trade, point D, the country's domestic equilibrium price and quantity are p_e and Q_e, respectively. Assuming the world price p_W is below this domestic price, with international trade, the domestic price will then fall to this world price. This drop in domestic price to the world price increases quantity demanded from Q_e to Q_1 and reduces domestic quantity supplied from Q_e to Q_2. With a domestic supply of Q_2, the excess demand, $Q_1 - Q_2$, is supplied by imports from foreign firms. International trade results in an increase in consumer surplus, represented by the area $p_W p_e$DF, representing a welfare gain for consumers within this country. A portion of this gain in welfare is at the expense of producers within this country and the remaining gain is the pure increase in welfare associated with free trade. The area $p_W p_e$DA is a transfer of some producer surplus from producers to consumers within this country. As a result of free trade, the price that producers receive for their output falls from p_e to p_W, which directly depresses producers' profit, represented by the loss in producer surplus, the area $p_W p_e$DA. This fall in price is a gain for consumers within this country, and they not only gain the entire lost producer surplus but also all of the pure increase in welfare from free trade, the area ADF.

Why the big fuss over free trade, anyway? Free trade results in an efficient allocation of resources.

The introduction of low commodity prices through the opening of domestic markets to international trade can severely harm domestic industries. For example, in a developing country, the flood of cheap agricultural commodities from the United States, supported by the US government's Export Enhancement Program (export subsidy), can retard the development

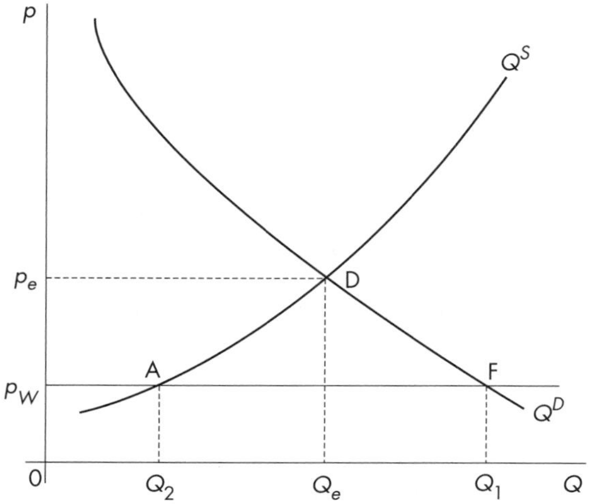

Figure 10.16 **Free trade.** Without trade, the equilibrium price and quantity are p_e and Q_e. Free trade lowers the price to the world price p_W, with Q_2 being supplied domestically and $Q_1 - Q_2$ imported.

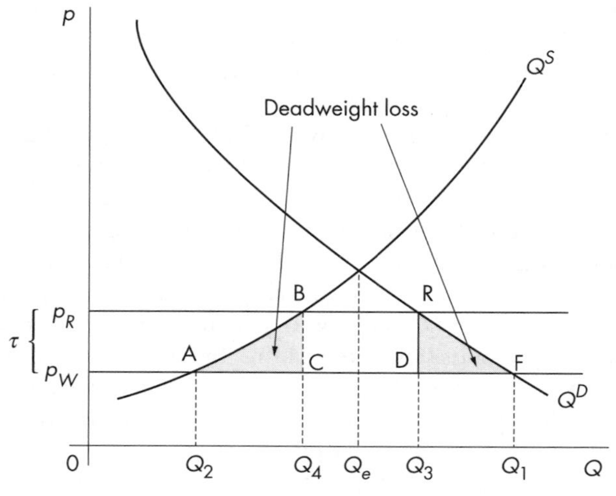

Figure 10.17 **Tariff or quota trade restrictions.** A tariff or quota raising the price from p_W to p_R increases domestic supply from Q_2 to Q_4 and reduces imports from $Q_1 - Q_2$ to $Q_3 - Q_4$. This results in a deadweight loss of ABC plus DRF.

of its own agricultural industry. In an effort to avoid damaging their domestic industries, countries may adopt protectionist policies with programs designed for restricting trade.[9] Historically, the common forms of trade restrictions are in the form of tariffs and quotas. A **tariff** is a tax on imports that directly increases the price of imported commodities. A **quota** is a restriction on the volume of an imported commodity. As illustrated in Figure 10.17, the effects on price and quantity imported are the same for both tariff and quota trade restrictions.

Tariff. Tax on imports. *E.g., the tea tax placed on the American Colonies by England in 1773.*

Quota. Restriction on the volume of a commodity imported. *E.g., the quota on importation of sugar into the United States.*

Example 10.10 Deriving trade restriction inefficiencies

Consider the following domestic supply and demand functions for a country:

$$Q^S = 3p,$$

$$Q^D = 20 - 2p.$$

With no international trade, the equilibrium price and quantity are $p_e = 4$ and $Q_e = 12$, with $(10 - 4)12/2 = \$36$ in consumer surplus and $4(12)/2 = \$24$ in producer surplus. Assuming international trade, with a world price $p_W = 1$, quantity demanded increases to 18 and domestic supply drops to 3. The associated consumer surplus is $(10-1)18/2 =$ \$81, with producer surplus dropping to $1(3)/2 =$ \$1.50.

Imposing a tariff of $\tau = 2$, so the domestic price is now 3, results in a quantity demanded of 14, with a domestic quantity supplied of 9 and the remainder, 5, supplied by foreign producers. With the tariff, consumer surplus is $(10-3)14/2 =$ \$49 and producer surplus is $3(9)/2 =$ \$13.50. Tariff revenue is \$10.00 and deadweight loss is $(3-1)(9-3)/2 + (3-1)(18-14)/2 = (6+4) =$ \$10.

Imposing other trade restrictions, including quotas, yield the same results—except that, with quotas, the \$10 in revenue from the restriction would not flow to the government as is the case for a tariff. Instead, it would be transferred to some other agent such as the foreign supplier of the import.

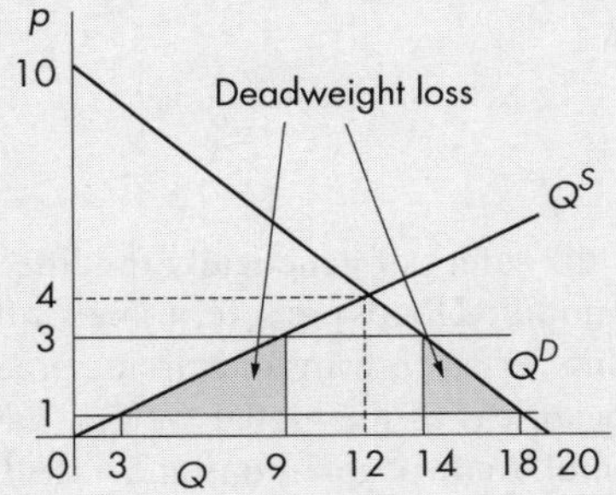

Tariffs

Considering first a tariff of τ per unit of the commodity imported, the price of imports will rise from the world price p_W to the world price plus the tariff: $p_R = p_W + \tau$ (Figure 10.17). Remember that the small size of this country results in its imports having no effect on the world price, so all the tariff is borne by the country's consumers. The world supply curve facing these consumers is perfectly elastic, $\varepsilon^S = \infty$. Consumers facing a higher price, $p_R = p_W + \tau$, will decrease their quantity demanded for the commodity, from Q_1 to Q_3, with an associated welfare loss in consumer surplus, represented by the area $p_W p_R$RF. This loss in consumer surplus is partially offset by a gain in producer surplus. As the trade restriction program was designed to do, the tariff increases the domestic price of the commodity from the world price p_W to $p_R = p_W + \tau$. Domestic producers respond to this enhanced domestic price by increasing quantity supplied from Q_2 to Q_4. This increase in quantity supplied maximizes domestic producers' increase in producer surplus, represented by the area $p_W p_R$BA. The gain in producer surplus is a transfer of some consumer surplus to the producers. An additional amount of lost consumer surplus is transferred from consumers to the government. The government collects the revenue generated from the tariff, which is the tariff τ per unit of the imported commodity times the volume of imports, $Q_3 - Q_4$:

$$\text{Tariff Revenue} = \tau(Q_3 - Q_4).$$

In Figure 10.17, this corresponds to the area CBRD. Not all of the loss in consumer surplus from the trade restriction is transferred; the remainder is deadweight loss. The sum of the deadweight loss areas ABC and DRF is the market inefficiency associated with a tariff.

Quotas

If an import quota is set at the level of imports resulting from levying the tariff, a quota as a trade restriction has a very similar effect as a tariff, $Q_3 - Q_4$ in Figure 10.17. The domestic price, output, and consumption are all the same. This results in the same efficiency loss, represented as the deadweight loss areas ABC and DRF in Figure 10.17. However, with a quota trade restriction, the government does not collect any revenue. The loss in consumer surplus, the area CBRD, is transferred to the agents, who are given the rights to supply $Q_3 - Q_4$ of imports, rather than being transferred to the government as with a tariff. These agents could be the foreign producers or the import agents who purchase foreign commodities for domestic consumption. For example, in the 1980s when the United States negotiated voluntary quotas on importation of Japanese automobiles, the lost consumer surplus was transferred to the Japanese auto manufactures. If the United States had instead negotiated a tariff, this consumer surplus would have transferred as tax revenue to the US Treasury.

Free trade

Currently, there is considerable disagreement over the safety of genetically modified crops. Although many scientists maintain that genetically modified foods are safe, a small influential group of researchers contends that enough uncertainty exists to warrant extreme precaution, even the use of trade restrictions on such foods regardless of the global welfare gains that would occur upon removing the restrictions. In general, trade negotiations under the General Agreement on Tariffs and Trade (GATT) and free-trade zones such as the European Union (EU) and North American Free Trade Agreement (NAFTA) have either eliminated or greatly reduced trade tariffs and quotas. However, governments still attempt various protectionism measures. For example, under the disguise of food safety or environmental protection, a country may refuse entry of foreign commodities (e.g., genetically modified corn) or require expensive testing before entry is allowed. Whether such measures are truly public safety concerns or merely a cover for protectionism is up to the trade negotiators to determine. Such trade restrictions can be investigated with the same model employed for tariffs.

Application: African famine, made in Europe

In 2002, southern Africa suffered its worst drought in a decade. The United Nations World Food Programme estimated that around 13 million people in 6 countries required 1.2 million tons of food aid to avoid famine. However, in the summer of 2002, two countries, Zimbabwe and Zambia, rejected food aid shipments of corn from the United States because some varieties of US corn are genetically modified. Since 1995, farmers in the United States have planted and Americans have consumed genetically engineered corn, soybeans, and cotton. Regulatory authorities in the EU and Japan have also approved genetically modified crops, although European food safety regulators have lost credibility since the "mad cow" crisis of 1996. In 2002, EU Commissioner for Health and Consumer Affairs David Byrne repeatedly stated that, based on 81 independent scientific studies, there is no scientific evidence of added risk to human health or the environment from any of the genetically modified products approved for marketing. However, critics in Europe say this absence of expected or known risks is no longer a sufficient regulatory standard. They argue that powerful new technologies should be kept under wraps until tested for unexpected or unknown risks as well. Unfortunately, testing for something unknown is a logical impossibility.

EU officials may require that genetically modified foods be traced individually through the marketing chain, with legal documentary records to be saved by all producers and handlers for 5 years. African countries do not have the institutional capacity to implement this traceability regulation, so they would have to remain free from genetically modified foods to retain their access to the EU market. Meat products raised with genetically modified feed may also be covered in new EU regulations. Thus, Zambia's rejection of genetically modified corn in food aid shipments was partly based on a fear that if the country lost its "modified-free" animal feed status, meat exports to the EU would decline sharply. By requiring African governments to embrace cautious biosafety regulations, officials in Europe have made it harder for them to accept food aid from the United States. European critics of genetically modified foods did not foresee this potentially deadly spillover effect of their precautionary principles.

Spillover efficiency loss

The "African Famine, Made in Europe" application is a particularly deadly example of the results of *spillover efficiency loss*. A more general economic application is when governments attempt to address higher domestic prices that result from protecting domestic industries by placing ceiling prices on the commodities. For example, many developing countries have ceiling prices on basic commodities such as bread. This introduces further governmental restrictions on the market, with additional cost in terms of market inefficiencies. As these governmental market restrictions expand, the efficiency associated with free markets is further eroded away. The extreme, where most, if not all, markets are severely restricted, yields a centrally planned economy.

In this chapter, we have measured the efficiency loss associated with market interventions in a partial-equilibrium framework. Such measurements only consider the price consequences in one market, ignoring the spillover effects that such price changes have on other markets. As we will discuss in the next chapter, general-equilibrium analysis considers the effects on all markets, given a price change in one market. However, it is not necessary to consider the spillover effects into undistorted free markets when measuring deadweight loss. The price and quantity changes in undistorted free markets do not affect efficiency. In these undistorted free markets, the marginal utility of consumption is equal to the marginal cost of production, so there is no loss in efficiency. In contrast, if one market is affected by some distortion, there may be spillover efficiency losses.

As an example, consider how a tariff on one commodity can spillover into the market for another commodity distorted by a ceiling price. As illustrated in Figure 10.18, in the absence of a tariff on a substitute commodity, a ceiling price will reduce the market price from the free-market equilibrium p_e to the ceiling price p_c. The deadweight loss is then the area EDB. A tariff on a substitute commodity will, by increasing the price of this substitute commodity, shift the demand curve to the right for the ceiling-priced commodity, from Q^D to $Q^{D'}$. The resulting deadweight loss is increased by the area DGHB, so the total efficiency loss from the tariff is the deadweight loss from the commodity with

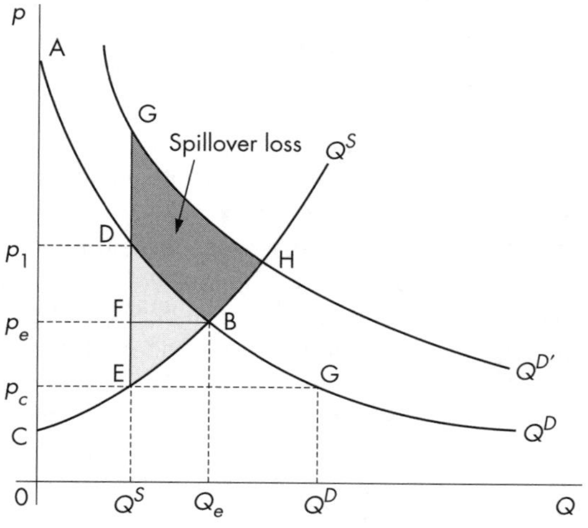

Figure 10.18 **Spillover deadweight loss, ceiling price with a tariff on a substitute commodity.** Imposing a tariff on a substitute commodity increases demand, shifting the demand curve to $Q^{D'}$, which increases the deadweight loss associated with a ceiling price by the area DGHB.

the tariff plus the (spillover) increased efficiency loss associated with the ceiling-price commodity.

Do two wrongs make things worse? Yes, negative spillover effects from a governmental program can cause additional inefficiencies in another market also facing some free-market restrictions.

Summary

1. A firm is economically efficient when it is technologically, allocatively, and scale-efficient. Technological efficiency is when a firm is using the current technology in its production process. Allocative efficiency is when a firm employing the least-cost combination of inputs for a given level of output. Scale efficiency occurs where the output price is equal to the marginal cost of production.
2. A perfectly competitive market meets all three of the criteria for economic efficiency. This results in consumer preferences being reflected in the market, with no governmental agency required to determine the equilibrium level of demand and supply.
3. Unfavorable features of perfect competition are the consequence of missing markets. This results in the perfectly competitive market not efficiently supplying public goods and not accounting for externalities.
4. A measure of market economic efficiency is the total surplus, composed of consumer plus producer surplus. Consumer surplus is the net benefit a consumer receives from a commodity, and producer surplus is pure profit plus total

fixed cost. A perfectly competitive market maximizes this total surplus. There is no deadweight loss.

5. A government-imposed market ceiling price is inefficient in that it creates deadweight loss, requires some type of a commodity allocation system, and results in the creation of a black market.
6. A government-imposed support price is inefficient in that it results in deadweight loss and production surpluses. In agriculture, acreage controls have and are currently being used to reduce production surpluses.
7. Government subsidies result in market inefficiencies in the form of deadweight loss. The adjustment process when these subsidies are removed can be severe on an economy.
8. A commodity tax can be in the form of an output or a sales tax. The amount of a commodity tax borne by consumers versus firms depends on the elasticities of demand and supply. In the extreme, a perfectly elastic supply curve will result in all of the tax being passed on to consumers.
9. Trade restrictions in the form of quotas and tariffs will result in market inefficiencies. Deadweight loss from these restrictions exists in the form of reducing consumer surplus.
10. A price distortion in one market may have spillover efficiency losses in another related market if this other market is also affected by some price distortion.

Key concepts

black market, 394
ceiling price, 390
commodity tax, 405
consumer sovereignty, 378
consumer surplus (CS), 380
deadweight loss, 388
excess burden, 388
firm economic efficiency, 377
producer surplus, 384
quota, 410
scale efficiency, 377
subsidy, 403
support price, 398
tariff, 410

Key equations

$$\text{CS}(Q) = U(Q) - pQ$$

Consumer surplus measures the difference between the total benefits from the consumption of a commodity and the expenditure on the commodity.

$$\text{PS}(Q) = \pi + \text{TFC}$$

Producer surplus is pure profit plus total fixed cost.

Questions

Challenges can be stepping stones or stumbling blocks. It is just a matter of how you view them.

(H. Jackson Brown)

1. A city council is contemplating spending a fixed sum of money on building either a museum or a symphony hall. The council chair is leaning toward supporting the museum because more people will likely attend a museum than attend a symphony. What is the fallacy in the chair's logic?
2. How does the divergence between price and marginal cost affect the way society allocates its resources?
3. Is the objective of maximizing profit part of the dark-side evil empire or a beneficial activity in a free market? Explain.
4. Critics of free markets argue that price as a rationing device discriminates against low-income households. In an effort to mitigate this discrimination, they propose that the government legislate a 50 percent reduction in the prices of all commodities. Would this policy have any effect on the total supply and demand for commodities? Would the policy mitigate this discrimination? Explain.
5. Tony's opportunity cost of time spent waiting in line to purchase gasoline is $20 per hour, and there is a sharp decrease in supply. Would he benefit from imposing price controls on gasoline, resulting in supply being allocated on a first-come-first-served basis? Would an unemployed person benefit?
6. The government should accumulate stockpiles of agricultural goods when crops are plentiful and sell the goods when crops are scarce. This would aid in stabilizing agricultural prices and farm incomes without affecting production. Do you agree or disagree with this statement? Explain.
7. A firm produced 1000 units last year. If a $5 per-unit tax is imposed, the profits of the firm will decline by $5000. True or false? Explain.
8. Consumers have stated that it does not matter what type of tax a government imposes, it will always be paid by the consumers. A tax levied on firms will simply be passed on to consumers in the form of higher prices. Under what market conditions is the consumers' analysis correct?
9. The burden of a commodity tax is shared by producers and consumers. Under what conditions will consumers pay most of the tax? Under what conditions will producers pay most of it? What determines the share of a subsidy that benefits consumers?
10. A tariff to equalize domestic and foreign cost of production is just a subsidy to domestic producers, with the subsidy positively related to an industry's inefficiency. True or false? Explain.

Exercises

Like free trade, the long run is it benefits everyone.

(Henry Hobhouse)

but in the short run, completing the exercises may produce pain.

1. There are ten identical firms producing cosmetics, and the short-run total cost curve for each firm is

$$\text{STC} = 5q^2 + 10q + 25.$$

   a. What is each firm's short-run supply curve? What is the market short-run supply curve?
   b. Calculate the perfectly competitive output and price, given the market demand function

$$Q^D = -2p + 200.$$

   c. Calculate consumer and producer surplus.

2. An accessory belt is a component of an automobile's engine, and without it your \$25,000 car would overheat, resulting in engine failure. A belt currently costs about \$15.00. Estimate your consumer surplus for the belt.
3. A firm has the marginal cost curve shown in the figure.

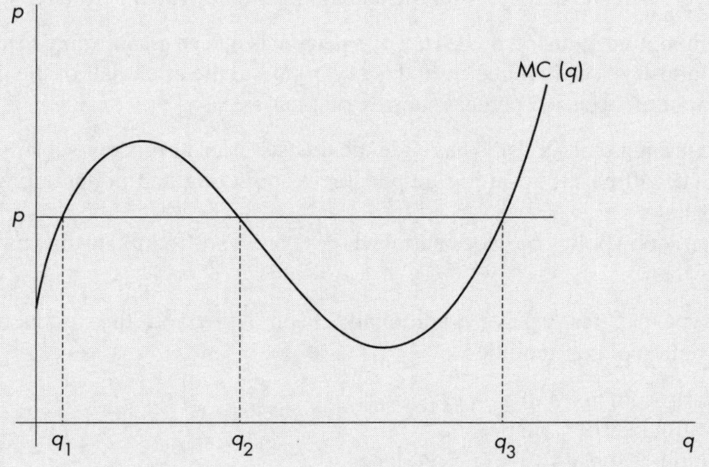

   a. At price p, what are the equilibrium levels of output?
   b. Of the choices in (a), determine the profit-maximizing output level.
   c. Construct the firm's supply curve.

4. Assume that a per-unit subsidy of s dollars is offered to producers of a product. Illustrate graphically how this subsidy affects the sum of consumer and producer surplus. What is the deadweight loss from the subsidy?
5. Suppose the following demand function for illegal drugs:

$$Q^D = 100 - \tfrac{1}{10}p.$$

a. If the Mafia has a constant marginal cost of 200, what will be the equilibrium market price and quantity?
b. Do the dealers (Mafia) or the users care which of the following two penalties is imposed?
   i. Penalty on the dealers resulting in marginal cost increasing to 400.
   ii. Penalty on the users resulting in demand shifting inward to

$$Q^D = 80 - \tfrac{1}{10}p.$$

6. A university parking authority has a policy of rationing the limited supply of parking spaces on its main campus. Parking spaces are classified into two types: perimeter and central. A professor is willing to pay a \$500 premium for a central parking space, whereas a student is only willing to pay a \$100 premium.

   a. Is it a Pareto-efficient allocation if in a lottery the student gets the central space and the professor the perimeter?
   b. Assuming the student could sell the central parking space (either legally or on the black market at zero cost), what would be the price premium for the central parking space, and who parks where?
   c. How does the answer to (b) change if there is no lottery and the professor is given the central space with the student then receiving a perimeter space?

7. In a competitive industry, a sales tax of 5 percent is placed on polluting firms—half of the industry. The revenue from this tax is paid to the other half of the industry, the nonpolluters, as a 5 percent subsidy on their sales.

   a. Assuming that all firms have identical costs prior to this tax-subsidy policy, what will be the resulting output for the polluting and nonpolluting firms? Explain.
   b. Can such a policy be debt-neutral where tax revenues equal subsidy payments? Explain.

8. Four types of taxes have traditionally been levied on the production and consumption of commodities:

   i. Lump-sum taxes of \$$T$ per period.
   ii. Profit taxes of t_p on profits.
   iii. Output taxes of t_o per unit produced.
   iv. Sales taxes of t_s on sales revenue.

   Construct the profit function under each tax assumption and assess its implication for a firm's cost curves and producer surplus.

9. The domestic market supply and demand curves for lemons in a small county are

$$p = 100 + Q^S,$$

$$p = 400 - 2Q^D,$$

where p is the price in cents per pound and Q is the quantity in millions of pounds. The current world price is \$1.20 per pound. The country's congress is considering a tariff of \$0.40 per pound. What domestic price will result if the tariff is imposed? Determine the changes in consumer and producer surplus, government revenue, and any deadweight loss from the tariff.

10. Let the domestic market demand and supply curves for chicken be

$$Q^D = 2500 - 50p, Q^S = 150p - 500.$$

 a. Determine the domestic market equilibrium price and quantity, and calculated consumer and producer surplus at this equilibrium.
 b. Let the world price for chickens be \$5.00. Given free trade, determine the new market equilibrium price and quantity. How many chickens are produced domestically versus imported? What is the resulting consumer and producer surplus?
 c. If a \$5.00 tariff is placed on the importation of chickens, what happens to the domestic price and quantity? Consumer and producer surplus? How much tariff revenue is collected, and what is the deadweight loss?
 d. How does replacing the tariff with a quota, equal to the amount imported under the tariff, affect the results?

Internet case studies

1. Trace the history of Herberger triangles.
2. List the various industries that are currently receiving a government subsidy in the United States.
3. Describe how deficiency payments work for a given agricultural commodity.

11 General competitive equilibrium

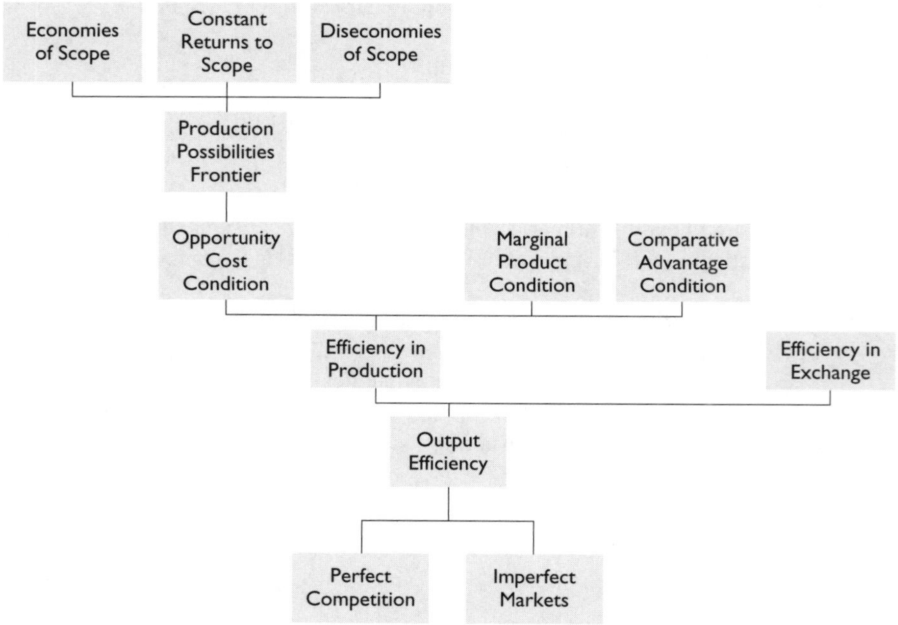

Outline and Conceptual Inquiries

Determining efficiency in production
Allocation Condition 1 (opportunity cost condition)
What is the cost of being inefficient?
What do oil changes and brake repairs have in common?
Application: Economies of scope in endangered-species protection
Allocation Condition 2 (marginal product condition)
Allocation Condition 3 (comparative advantage condition)
Why trade, if you have an absolute advantage?
Application: Comparative advantage and China's export patterns

Determining economic efficiency
If there were only a one-household or homogeneous preferences economy
How would you maximize social welfare?
Deriving Pareto efficiency with more than one type of household preferences
What is the problem when Friday arrives?

Understanding general equilibrium in a competitive economy
Efficiency in production
What is output efficiency?
What is the big deal about free markets?
Optimal reallocation of endowments
Why is a government required?
Application: Distribution and efficiency resolved interdependently

Confronting imperfect markets
What is the problem with imperfect markets?

Summary
Key concepts
Key equations
Questions
Exercises
Internet case studies

> *A central planner does not understand how decentralized decisions determine efficient prices and a marketer does not understand how central control determines them.*
>
> (Michael Wetzstein)

A restriction on the supply of oil will not only cause a rise in the price of oil but also affect the transportation industry through higher fuel prices. This in turn will affect the retail cost of vegetables and may result in an increase in locally grown vegetables. In general, changes in one market will affect demand and supply in other markets. The study of how demand and supply conditions interact in a number of markets and determine the prices of many commodities is called *general-equilibrium analysis*. In general equilibrium, the economy is viewed as a closed and interrelated system where the interactions of all markets determine the equilibrium market prices and quantities. A disturbance in one market generates ripples that spread through many other markets.

A (general) equilibrium model of all markets, where supply and demand for each commodity are equated, will result in necessary conditions for economic efficiency. This equilibrium of supply and demand in all markets is achieved by agents (households and firms) trading commodities, where agents only require knowledge of their own preferences and technologies. Agents will engage in trade until all the gains from trade are exhausted. In Chapter 6, we investigated the basic agent activities of exchange and consumption and outlined competitive equilibrium for a pure-exchange economy. In this chapter, we extend the theory with the addition of a third activity, production. Here, we no longer restrict the supply of commodities to the sum of individual agents' initial endowments. Instead, we allow firms to employ these endowments as inputs into production and produce some outputs that will increase the supply of those commodities.

With the introduction of production, conditions yielding production efficiency are now required for economic efficiency. We first discuss the three allocation conditions for production efficiency. We obtain Allocation Condition 1 (called the *opportunity cost condition*) by deriving the production possibilities frontier, where production must occur for efficiency. We then investigate the relationship of opportunity cost to the production possibilities frontier. In discussing Allocation Condition 2 (the *marginal product condition*), we determine that, for efficiency, inputs should be allocated so that the marginal products in the production of a particular commodity are equal. Finally, we establish Allocation Condition 3 (the *comparative advantage condition*), where for efficient production a firm with the comparative advantage in producing a commodity should produce that commodity.

After we investigate the efficiency in production conditions, we turn the discussion to the conditions for overall economic efficiency. This requires linking producers' efficient production decisions with consumers' preferences. An economy may be production-efficient, but if it is not producing the commodities consumers desire, then it is inefficient. We demonstrate economic efficiency for a one-household economy, determining the maximum level of social welfare. We then turn to efficiency for two or more households and problems encountered with maximizing social welfare in that economy. We establish the link between economic efficiency and a competitive market, and compare the economic efficiency of free markets and centrally planned economies. After reading this chapter, a proponent of central planning should understand how decentralized decisions, only requiring price signals, determine efficient prices. The aim of this chapter is to demonstrate how a perfectly competitive market will result in an efficient allocation of a society's resources.

Based on this link between economic efficiency and competitive markets, applied economists are able to investigate the effects that various policies not only have on the directly affected market but also on related markets. With this general analysis of markets throughout the whole economy, economists can determine the complete impact of policies on an economy. Failure to consider all effects across all markets may result in erroneous analysis and wrong prescriptions for curing market imperfections.

Determining efficiency in production

Follow the production-allocation conditions, and if a society goes hungry, it will at least do it efficiently.

(Michael Wetzstein)

In Chapter 6, we introduced the Edgeworth box for illustrating Pareto-efficient allocations in a two-agent, two-commodity pure-exchange economy. Recall that a Pareto-efficient allocation is an allocation of commodities where it is not possible to make one agent better off without making another agent worse off. We also demonstrated in Chapter 6 how a competitive-price system will yield a Pareto-efficient allocation. We can extend this concept of Pareto efficiency and use the Edgeworth box to discuss production efficiency. Efficiency in production deals with the allocation of resources (inputs) within a specific firm as well as how resources and outputs should be allocated among firms. Generally, an allocation of resources is production-efficient when no reallocation of resources will yield an increase in one commodity without a sacrifice in output from other commodities. The necessary conditions for such an efficient allocation in production may be stated by three allocation conditions. A society fulfilling these three conditions will result in production efficiency even if it is going hungry.

Allocation Condition 1 (opportunity cost condition)

A greeting card manufacture wants to increase its production of Valentine's Day cards. Its opportunity cost for this shift in production is a decrease in its production of birthday cards. In terms of production efficiency, this is the first allocation condition. Specifically, **Allocation Condition 1 (the opportunity cost condition)** states that for production efficiency, no more of one commodity (Valentine's Day cards) can be produced without having to cut back on the production of other commodities (birthday cards). This requires the MRTS for each output to be equal:

$$\text{MRTS}_1 = \text{MRTS}_2 = \ldots = \text{MRTS}_k,$$

where k represents the number of commodities.

Allocation Condition 1 (opportunity cost condition). No more of one output can be produced without having to cut back on the production of other commodities. *E.g., a pizza parlor is Pareto-efficient if increasing the number of pepperoni pizzas results in decreasing the number of cheese and anchovy pizzas.*

As an illustration, consider the optimal choice of inputs for a single firm producing two outputs (fish $\mathcal{F}$ and bread B) with two inputs (capital K and labor L). Assuming limited resources, holding the total quantities of K and L fixed, results in the problem of determining how to efficiently allocate these fixed resources to the production of $\mathcal{F}$ and B. The firm will operate efficiently if it is not possible to reallocate its inputs in such a way that output of $\mathcal{F}$ can be increased without necessarily cutting back on B. In general, a firm with fixed resources has allocated those resources efficiently if it has them fully employed and if the MRTS between the inputs is the same for every output the firm produces.

For example, consider a firm with 100 units of L and 100 units of K using half of each input to produce outputs fish and bread. If the firm employs 50 units of K and 50 units of L in producing fish and $\text{MRTS}_{\mathcal{F}}(K \text{ for } L) = 2$, then the same amount of fish could be produced by employing 48 units of K and 51 units of L (Table 11.1). If the firm employs 50 units of K and 50 units of L to produce bread and $\text{MRTS}_B(K \text{ for } L) = 1$, then the same amount of bread can be produced with 51 units of K and 49 units of L. Thus, the firm can produce the same amount of fish and bread by allocating 48 units of K and 51 units of L to fish production, and 51 units of $K$and 49 units of L to bread production, with 1 unit of K left over. The MRTSs are not equal, so the firm is not operating efficiently. The firm can reallocate inputs and produce the same level of outputs with some resources left over or employ these leftover resources and increase outputs.

Allocation Condition 1 is represented graphically in Figure 11.1. The Edgeworth box shown here is analogous to the box representing the pure-exchange model in Chapter 6 (Figure 6.2). Instead of comparing consumer preference levels with indifference curves, Figure 11.1 compares various output levels for fish and bread with isoquants. Similar to Figure 6.2, Figure 11.1 illustrates that every point inside the box represents a feasible allocation where both resources are fully employed. An allocation where no resources are allocated to fish production (0, 0) and all the resources are devoted to bread production, (100, 100) is a feasible allocation represented, in Figure 11.1, by the origin $0_{\mathcal{F}}$. At this allocation, the output of bread is maximized and no fish is produced. Similarly, at the origin 0_B, the

Table 11.1 Allocation Condition 1 (opportunity cost condition)

Output	*Initial allocation*		*MRTS*	*Reallocation*		*Output*
	Capital K	*Labor L*		*Capital K*	*Labor L*	
Fish	50	50	2/1	48	51	unchanged
Bread	50	50	1/1	51	49	unchanged
Total	100	100		99	100	
Gains from reallocation				1	0	

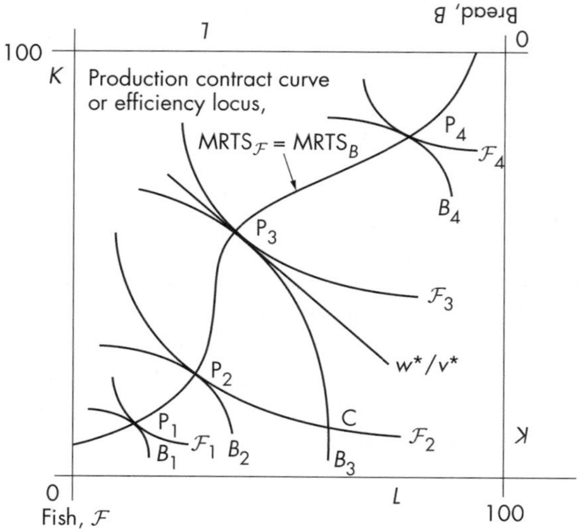

Figure 11.1 **Allocation Condition 1.** The Opportunity Cost Condition for Pareto efficiency (Allocation Condition 1) is $MRTS_{\mathcal{F}} = MRTS_B$, so no more of one commodity can be produced without sacrificing the production of the other commodity.

allocation is (0, 0) toward the production of bread and (100, 100) for fish. Now no bread is produced and the maximum level of fish for this level of inputs is produced. For a movement toward $0_{\mathcal{F}}$, more of the inputs K and L are being allocated toward bread production and less toward fish. Every feasible combination of K and L in the production of fish and bread is represented inside this Edgeworth box. Points outside the box are not feasible, because insufficient levels of K or L, or both, are available. The size of the box is determined by the amount of fixed resources, K and L. An increase in the resources will enlarge the box and allow for the possibility of producing more outputs. (An improvement in the technology of combining resources to produce the outputs will also expand output potential, but not the size of the box.)

Production-efficient allocations are characterized by the *efficiency locus* in Figure 11.1 (also called the **production contract curve**).[1] The production contract curve represents the set of efficient allocations, where at every point on the curve,

$$MRTS_{\mathcal{F}} = MRTS_B.$$

In Figure 11.1, point C is not Pareto-efficient, because it is possible to reallocate the inputs in such a manner that one product can be increased without reducing the other product. For example, moving along the bread isoquant curve toward point P_3, bread production remains unchanged, whereas fish production increases. At point P_3, it is not possible to increase the output of one product without decreasing the output of the other product. Mathematically, the efficiency condition $MRTS_{\mathcal{F}} = MRTS_B$ is determined by maximizing one output while holding the other output constant. This is exactly analogous to the pure-exchange problem of maximizing the utility of one household subject to a given level of utility for the other household.

Production contract curve (efficiency locus). Locus of Pareto-efficient input allocations. *E.g., the fixed amount of labor and ingredients to allocate between producing various combinations of small and extra-large pizzas.*

Example 11.1 Determining the Pareto-efficient input allocations, production contract curve

Consider the following production functions for fish and bread:

$$\mathcal{F} = L_{\mathcal{F}}^{1/5} K_{\mathcal{F}}^{3/5}, \quad B = L_B^{4/5} K_B^{2/5},$$

with $L_{\mathcal{F}} + L_B = 100$ and $K_{\mathcal{F}} + K_B = 50$. The production contract curve or Pareto-efficient set is where

$$\begin{aligned} &\text{MRTS}_{\mathcal{F}}(K \text{ for } L) = \text{MRTS}_B(K \text{ for } L), \\ &\quad K_{\mathcal{F}}/3L_{\mathcal{F}} = 2K_B/L_B. \end{aligned}$$

This condition is determined by maximizing the output of one commodity subject to holding the other output constant. For example, consider maximizing fish output holding the output of bread constant:

$$\max_{\mathcal{F}} L_{\mathcal{F}}^{1/5} K_{\mathcal{F}}^{3/5} \quad \text{s.t.} \quad B = L_B^{4/5} K_B^{2/5}.$$

Noting that $L_B = 100 - L_{\mathcal{F}}$ and $K_B = 50 - K_{\mathcal{F}}$, the Lagrangian for this problem is

$$\mathcal{L}(L_{\mathcal{F}}, K_{\mathcal{F}}, \lambda) = L_{\mathcal{F}}^{1/5} K_{\mathcal{F}}^{3/5} + \lambda\left[B - (100 - L_{\mathcal{F}})^{4/5}(50 - K_{\mathcal{F}})^{2/5}\right].$$

The first-order conditions (FOCs) are then

$$\begin{aligned} \frac{\partial \mathcal{L}}{\partial L_{\mathcal{F}}} &= \frac{1}{5} L_{\mathcal{F}}^{-1} \mathcal{F} + \lambda \frac{4}{5}(100 - L_{\mathcal{F}})^{-1/5}(50 - K_{\mathcal{F}})^{2/5} = 0, \\ \frac{\partial \mathcal{L}}{\partial K_{\mathcal{F}}} &= \frac{3}{5} K_{\mathcal{F}}^{-1} \mathcal{F} + \lambda \frac{2}{5}(100 - L_{\mathcal{F}})^{4/5}(50 - K_{\mathcal{F}})^{-3/5} = 0, \\ \frac{\partial \mathcal{L}}{\partial \lambda} &= B - (100 - L_{\mathcal{F}})^{4/5}(50 - K_{\mathcal{F}})^{2/5} = 0. \end{aligned}$$

Taking the ratio of the first two conditions,

$$\text{MRTS}_{\mathcal{F}}(K \text{ for } L) = \frac{K_{\mathcal{F}}}{3L_{\mathcal{F}}} = \frac{2(50 - K_{\mathcal{F}})}{100 - L_{\mathcal{F}}} = \frac{2K_B}{L_B} = \text{MRTS}_B(K \text{ for } L).$$

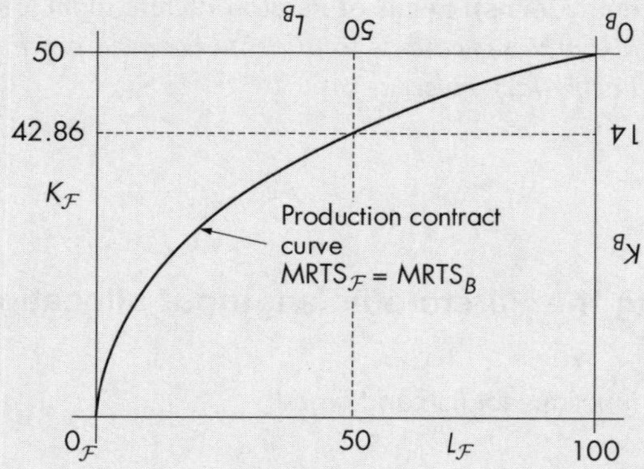

Deriving the production possibilities frontier

In the United States, over 40 percent of all scientists, engineers and technical professionals work in the military defense sector ("guns"). This allocation of talent and intellectual resources could instead be used for other production possibilities ("butter"). Based on the efficiency locus in Figure 11.1, these alternative production possibilities for commodities (guns and butter or fish and bread) can be illustrated by the **production possibilities frontier** (Figure 11.2). This frontier is a mapping of the efficient output levels $\mathcal{F}$ and B for each point on the production contract curve. For the four points labeled P_1, P_2, P_3, and P_4 in Figure 11.1, the corresponding output levels for fish ($\mathcal{F}_1$, $\mathcal{F}_2$, $\mathcal{F}_3$, and $\mathcal{F}_4$) and bread (B_1, B_2, B_3, and B_4)

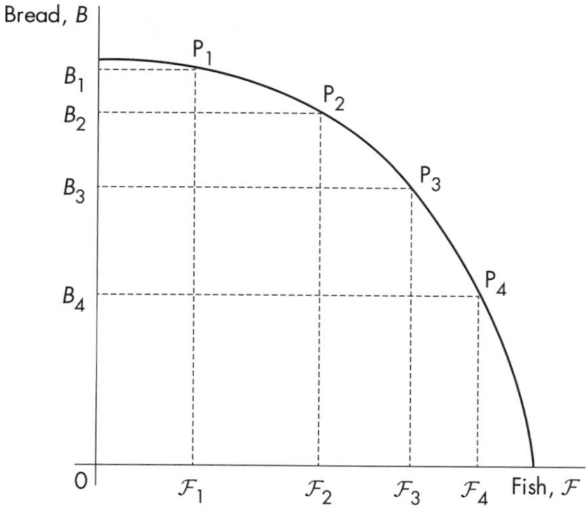

Figure 11.2 **Production possibilities frontier.** On the frontier, the production of fish and bread is Pareto-efficient. It is not possible to increase the production of one commodity without decreasing the production of the other.

are plotted on the horizontal and vertical axes in Figure 11.2. Points on the production possibilities frontier correspond to the tangency of the isoquants along the production contract curve in Figure 11.1 [illustrated by the same labels (P_1, P_2, P_3, and P_4) for both figures]. The output combinations $(\mathcal{F}_1, B_1)$, $(\mathcal{F}_2, B_2)$, $(\mathcal{F}_3, B_3)$, and $(\mathcal{F}_4, B_4)$ associated with (P_1, P_2, P_3, and P_4) are the same for both figures. Every point inside this production possibilities frontier is a feasible allocation corresponding to points inside the Edgeworth box in Figure 11.1. The boundary of the production possibilities frontier represents the efficiency locus (production contract curve) illustrated in Figure 11.1. For given amounts of K and L, the production possibilities frontier indicates the combination of $\mathcal{F}$ and B that can be produced. An increase in the amount of K and L or an improvement in technology will result in the production possibilities frontier shifting outward.

What is the cost of being inefficient? The lost production for satisfying wants is the cost of being inefficient.

Production possibilities frontier. The locus of Pareto-efficient output levels for a given set of inputs and production technology. *E.g., all the combinations of small and extra-large pizzas that could be produced with a fixed amount of ingredients.*

Example 11.2 Determining comparative advantage and the concave production possibilities frontier

Robinson and Friday have the ability to separately produce both fish and bread. However, Robinson, being a land-lover, is more suited for the production of bread. In contrast, Friday is a natural in the water, so her talents lie in fish production. Their production functions for fish $\mathcal{F}$ and bread B using labor (per hour) as the sole input are

$$B_R = 10L_{BR}, \quad \mathcal{F}_R = 5L_{\mathcal{F}R},$$

$$L_{BR} + L_{\mathcal{F}R} = 10,$$

for Robinson, assuming he has 10 hours of available labor, and

$$B_F = 5L_{BF}, \quad \mathcal{F}_F = 10L_{\mathcal{F}F},$$

$$L_{BF} + L_{\mathcal{F}F} = 10,$$

for Friday, also assuming she has 10 hours of total labor available.

Considering Robinson's production functions, we solve for L_B and $L_{\mathcal{F}}$ and substitute the results into his labor/resource constraint to get his production possibilities:

$$\tfrac{1}{10} B_R + \tfrac{1}{5} F_R = 10.$$

Obtained similarly, Friday's production possibilities frontier is

$$\tfrac{1}{5} B_F + \tfrac{1}{10} F_F = 10.$$

From the figures, we see that their combined production possibilities frontier for bread and fish is then concave:

$$B = 150 - \tfrac{1}{2}\,\mathcal{F}_F \quad \text{for} \quad \mathcal{F}_F \leq 100, \mathcal{F}_R = 0,$$

$$\mathcal{F} = 150 - \tfrac{1}{2}\,B_R \quad \text{for} \quad B_R \leq 100, B_F = 0.$$

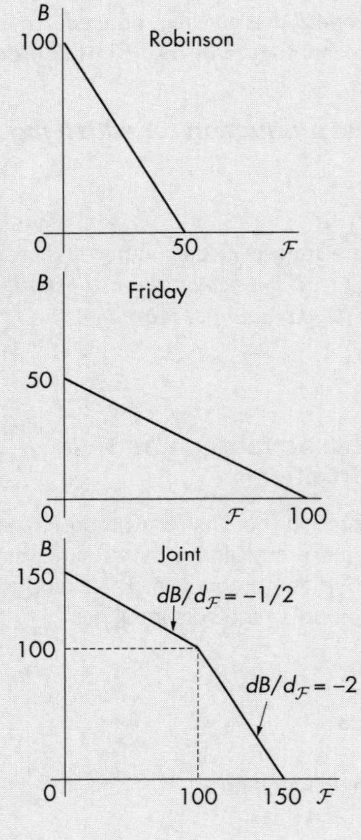

Marginal rate of product transformation

The slope of the production possibilities frontier measures how output $\mathcal{F}$ can be substituted for output B, when the total level of inputs (resources) is held constant. The negative of this slope is called the **marginal rate of product transformation (MRPT)**:

$$\text{MRPT}(B \text{ for } \mathcal{F}) = -\text{slope of the production possibilities frontier}$$

$$= -\left.\frac{dB}{d\mathcal{F}}\right|_{\text{holding inputs constant}}.$$

As indicated, the slope of the production possibilities frontier is negative: $dB/d\mathcal{F}|_{\text{holding inputs constant}} < 0$. Given production efficiency, an increase in one output will require a sacrifice in the other output. Taking the negative of this negative slope yields a positive MRPT.

MRPT measures how much one commodity is sacrificed to produce an additional amount of another commodity. For example, if MRPT(B for $\mathcal{F}$) = 2, then increasing $\mathcal{F}$ by 1 unit will require reducing (sacrificing) two units of B, or increasing B by 2 units will result in a sacrifice of 1 unit of $\mathcal{F}$. At point P_1 in Figure 11.2, the MRPT is a relatively small number, so the sacrifice in B for an additional unit of $\mathcal{F}$ is small. Alternatively, at point P_4, MRPT is a relatively large number, so the sacrifice in B for an additional unit of $\mathcal{F}$ is large. This increase in MRPT as $\mathcal{F}$ increases is due to the concave nature of the production possibility frontier.

Marginal rate of product transformation (MRPT). The rate at which one output can be substituted for another, holding the level of inputs constant. *E.g., the increase in small pizzas when producing one less extra-large pizza.*

Concave production possibilities frontier

The concave shape of the production possibilities frontier in Figure 11.2 is characteristic of most production situations and is based on the technical relationship exhibited by the two outputs. Specifically, we can represent the total cost of producing $\mathcal{F}$ and B by the total cost function TC($\mathcal{F}, B$). Given the fixed level of input supply, cost is constant along the production possibilities frontier. Thus, the total differential of this cost function is

$$d\text{TC} = \frac{\partial \text{TC}}{\partial \mathcal{F}} d\mathcal{F} + \frac{\partial \text{TC}}{\partial B} dB = 0,$$

where $d\text{TC} = 0$ because cost is constant along the production possibilities frontier. Rearranging terms, we have

$$\text{MRPT}(B \text{ for } \mathcal{F}) = -\left.\frac{dB}{d\mathcal{F}}\right|_{d\text{TC}=0} = \frac{\partial \text{TC}/\partial \mathcal{F}}{\partial \text{TC}/\partial B} = \frac{\text{MC}_{\mathcal{F}}}{\text{MC}_B}.$$

In general,

$$\text{MRPT}(q_1, q_2) = \frac{\text{MC}_1}{\text{MC}_2}.$$

We can compare this relation of MRPT equaling the ratio of marginal costs with the allocation of inputs for the production of $\mathcal{F}$ and B by recalling (from Chapter 8) that for one variable input, say labor,

$$\text{MC}_{\mathcal{F}} = \frac{w}{\text{MP}_L|_{\mathcal{F}}},$$

$$\text{MC}_B = \frac{w}{\text{MP}_L|_B},$$

where $MP_L|_{\mathcal{F}}$ is the marginal product of labor in the production of fish and $MP_L|_B$ is the marginal product of labor for the production of bread. Assuming it takes 1 unit of labor to produce 2 units of $\mathcal{F}$, $MP_{\mathcal{F}} = 2$, if the wage rate $w = 1$, then $MC_{\mathcal{F}} = 1/2$. Similarly, say it takes 1 unit of labor to produce 1 unit of B, $MP_B = 1$; then $MC_B = 1$. $MRPT = MC_F/MC_B = 1/2$, which indicates the sacrifice of 2 units of $\mathcal{F}$ to obtain 1 more B. Thus, for a concave production possibilities frontier (as illustrated in Figure 11.2), the ratio of MC_F to MC_B increases as the output of $\mathcal{F}$ increases and B decreases. In the short run, this is the result of the Law of Diminishing Marginal Returns. An increase in $\mathcal{F}$ results in an increase in its SMC, and a decrease in B results in a decrease in its SMC. In the long run, a concave production possibilities frontier will also result if decreasing returns to scale occurs for both outputs. In this case, analogous with the SMC curves, the LMC curves have a positive slope.

As the oldest son in a family of four brothers and a sister and living on a tenant farm during the Great Depression, my father hated farming. As soon as he could, he left the farm and became an industrial engineer working in the military defense sector. In the long run, this is an example of specialized inputs resulting in the production possibilities frontier still being concave even without the assumption of decreasing returns to scale. Specialized inputs exist when some inputs are relatively more suited for production of a particular output. These inputs are said to have a comparative advantage in the production of one output versus another. For example, some inputs are more suited for $\mathcal{F}$ production than for B production. In Figure 11.2, the concave nature of the production possibilities curve implies that increases in $\mathcal{F}$ production require taking inputs out of B production, where they are more suitable, and allocating them to $\mathcal{F}$ production, where they are progressively less suitable. Thus, as the production of $\mathcal{F}$ increases and that of B declines, the marginal cost for $\mathcal{F}$ production increases and the marginal cost for B production decreases, yielding a relatively larger MRPT. For example, consider labor as just one of the inputs. Some individuals may be more specialized in the production of B, for they have a love for baking and take to it naturally. At first, as inputs are taken out of B production and reallocated to $\mathcal{F}$ production, those individuals that do not have a particular love for baking can be allocated to $\mathcal{F}$ production. The loss in B production would be less than if the baking lovers were taken. However, as $\mathcal{F}$ production increases further, the baking lovers will be reallocated to $\mathcal{F}$ production, which will result in a larger sacrifice in B production.

Specialized inputs assume heterogeneous inputs. However, even if inputs are homogeneous, the production possibilities frontier will be concave if production of $\mathcal{F}$ and B use inputs in different proportions or intensities. Different input intensities are represented by nonlinear production contract curves. For example, in Figure 11.3, the production contract curve is bowed above the main diagonal, indicating that the production of $\mathcal{F}$ is relatively more capital-intensive than that of B. If the curve were bowed below the main diagonal, B would be relatively more capital intensive. In general, the production possibilities frontier will be concave if the production contract curve is not linear through the origin of both $\mathcal{F}$ and B. Specifically, consider Figure 11.3, where $\mathcal{F}$ is using a high proportion of capital relative to B. Considering two points P_1 and P_2 on the production contract curve, the weighted average of the two points is represented by the chord connecting the points. Points on this chord result in a lower level of output for both $\mathcal{F}$ and B compared to points on the production contract curve. In terms of the corresponding production possibilities frontier, Figure 11.4, the chord lies in the interior of the mapping that establishes the concave nature of the frontier.

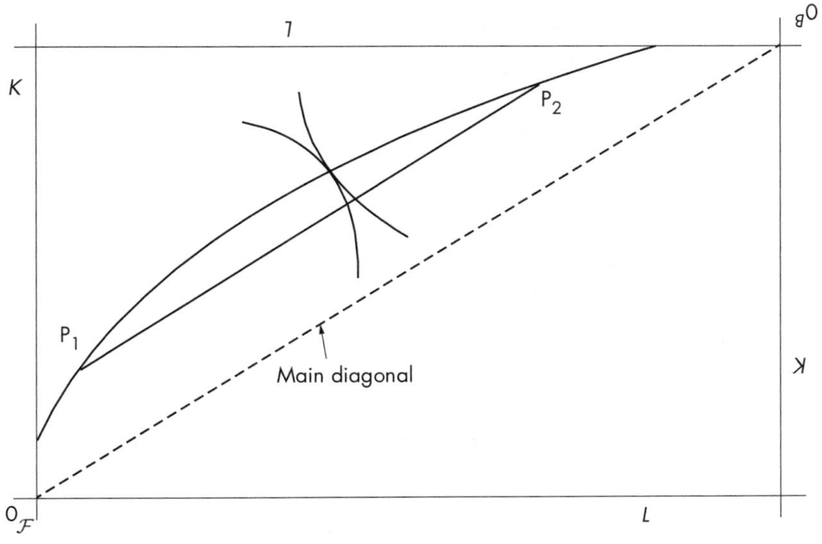

Figure 11.3 **Production contract curve with weighted average of outputs.** Every point on the chord connecting the Pareto-efficient points P_1 and P_2 result in a lower output level, for both outputs, than a point on the contract curve.

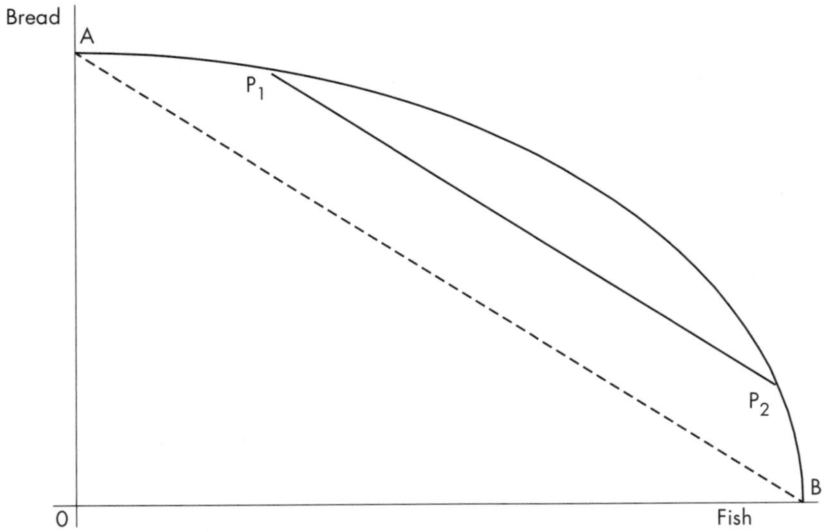

Figure 11.4 **Production possibilities frontier with differing factor intensities.** The chord between P_1 and P_2 lies in the interior of the production possibilities frontier, so every point on this chord represents an inefficient allocation.

Example 11.3 Concave production possibilities frontier, increasing opportunity cost and economies of scope

Consider the following production functions for producing two outputs—fish $\mathcal{F}$ and bread B—with two inputs, K and L:

$$\mathcal{F} = L_{\mathcal{F}}^{1/4} K_{\mathcal{F}}^{1/4},$$

$$B = L_B + K_B,$$

where $L_{\mathcal{F}} + L_B = 10$ is the total amount of labor available and $K_{\mathcal{F}} + K_B = 10$ is the total amount of capital available. The MRTSs for these technologies are

$$\text{MRTS}_{\mathcal{F}}(K \text{ for } L) = K/L,$$

$$\text{MRTS}_B(K \text{ for } L) = 1.$$

To determine the efficiency locus, we equate these MRTSs to get the equation for the production contract curve, $K = L$. Substituting into the production functions for K and solving for L yields

$$L_{\mathcal{F}} = \mathcal{F}^2,$$

$$L_B = B/2.$$

These equations are called the conditional factor demands, conditional on the outputs. We then determine the production possibilities frontier by summing these conditional factor demands and equating the result to the amount of labor available (supply):

$$L_{\mathcal{F}} + L_B = 10,$$

$$\mathcal{F}^2 + B/2 = 10, \text{ production possibilities frontier.}$$

Solving for B, we get

$$B = 20 - 2\mathcal{F}^2.$$

The MRPT $= -dB/d\mathcal{F} = 4\mathcal{F} > 0$ and the $d\text{MRPT}/d\mathcal{F} = 4 > 0$, indicating a concave production possibilities frontier.

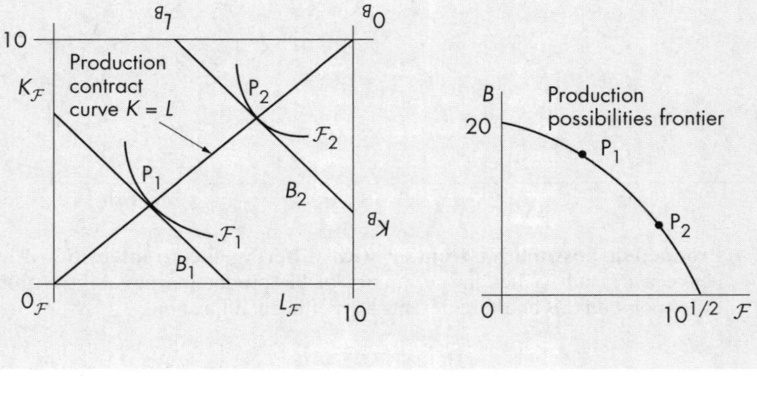

Opportunity costs

The production possibilities frontier illustrates a fundamental condition in economic theory. Assuming that resources are fully employed in the most efficient way, any increase in the production of one commodity, say $\mathcal{F}$, will require the shifting of resources out of the other commodity, in this case B, and vice versa. This sacrifice in the production of some other commodity is the opportunity cost of producing more of the one commodity. The MRPT measures the degree of this opportunity cost. A relatively large MRPT $= -\, dB/d\mathcal{F}|_{d\text{TC}=0}$, indicating a point in a steep portion of a production possibilities frontier (say, point P_4 in Figure 11.2), illustrates a large opportunity cost in increasing $\mathcal{F}$. That is, the sacrifice in B is large relative to the increase in $\mathcal{F}$. In contrast, at a relatively flat portion of the production possibilities frontier (say, point P_1 in Figure 11.2), a lower opportunity cost occurs when resources are shifted from B to $\mathcal{F}$. Moving along the production possibilities frontier from P_1 toward P_2, MRPT increases, representing the increased opportunity cost of increasing $\mathcal{F}$. Similarly, moving along the frontier from P_4 toward P_1, MRPT is decreasing and the opportunity cost of increasing B is increasing. Thus, a concave production possibilities frontier is associated with *increasing opportunity cost.* The more concave the frontier (the greater the rate of change in MRPT), the greater the increase in opportunity cost as one commodity is sacrificed for the production of another. Alternatively, a constant MRPT implies a linear production possibilities frontier and *constant opportunity cost.* Theoretically, if the factor intensities are the same and production functions exhibit increasing returns to scale, then the production possibilities frontier will be convex, which represents *decreasing opportunity cost* as one commodity is substituted for another.

Economies of scope

> *My beauty salon does all my makeup, from washing my hair to trimming my tail.*
>
> (Michael Wetzstein)

Increasing opportunity cost, represented by a concave production possibilities frontier in Figure 11.4, results in the lowest opportunity cost for increasing fish, corresponding to point A. At point A, the production of fish is zero. Similarly, the lowest opportunity cost for producing bread is at point B, where the production of bread is zero. These low levels of opportunity cost result from joint production of fish and bread. In general, a firm incurs production advantages when it produces two or more products. Such joint production can use inputs and technologies common to producing a set of products, so there may be advantages in joint use of inputs, marketing programs, or administration. For example, automobile garages will generally offer a number of automobile services such as brake service, oil changes, and tire rotation rather than, say, only brake service. In fact, unless there are some constraints, such as governmental restrictions preventing joint production, firms will almost always produce more than one product.

Technologies resulting in joint production advantages are called **economies of scope** or **increasing returns to scope**. Economies of scope exist when one firm jointly producing a set of products results in a higher level of output than a set of separate firms each uniquely producing one of the products. Economies of scope results in concave production possibilities curves, where joint production has the advantage of producing more of both outputs with the same resources than two firms producing each product separately.

What do oil changes and brake repairs have in common? The joint production of oil changes and brake repairs has the advantage of producing more of

both with the same resources compared with two firms producing each output separately.

Economics of scope (increasing returns to scope). One firm jointly producing a set of products results in a higher level of output than a set of separate firms each uniquely producing one of the products. *E.g., a supermarket offers a one-stop shop, eliminating the need for multiple stops at a meat market, vegetable stand, dairy, and dry goods store.*

Without these production advantages associated with joint production, the opportunity cost of joint production would be no lower than if one firm specialized in one output and another firm in the other output. Joint production would generate the same output as the two specialized firms. In this case, the production possibilities frontier would be linear, representing constant opportunity cost or **constant returns to scope**. The opportunity cost is constant at all production combinations of the products, so there are no gains from joint production. At point A in Figure 11.4, increasing the production of fish results in MRPT on the concave production possibilities frontier being less than MRPT on the chord between points A and B. Thus, the opportunity cost of producing fish and bread jointly is less than the opportunity cost of specialized production.

Constant returns to scope. No gains from jointly producing products. *E.g., a tomato farm also producing men's white dress shirts.*

Application: Economies of scope in endangered-species protection

In the past, protection of wildlife in the United States had generally focused on individual species, such as the bald eagle and spotted owl, rather than clusters of related species, as evidenced in the Endangered Species Act of 1973. As addressed by A. Ando, this approach does not consider possible economies of scope in protecting a group of related species, although ecologists and conservation biologists have noted the interrelationship among species sharing a habitat. The removal of one species from the endangered species list may require supporting other threatened or endangered species in the habitat. Similarly, protection of one may also protect others.

Ando investigates the hypothesis that economies of scope exist in species protection. Her results support this hypothesis when habitats of species overlap. This consequence of economies of scope in species protection supports a policy to shift protection away from individual species toward species groups. Recent changes in the Endangered Species Act are consistent with this result. Species are now often bundled into multispecies packages during the process of adding species to the endangered and threatened lists.

Source: A.W. Ando, "Economies of Scope in Endangered-Species Protection: Evidence from Interest-Group Behavior," *Journal of Environmental Economics and Management* 41 (2001): 312–332.

Diseconomies of scope

In contrast, decreasing opportunity cost associated with convex production possibilities frontiers, as illustrated in Figure 11.5, characterizes **diseconomies of scope (decreasing returns to scope)**. With diseconomies of scope, the opportunity cost of specialization is lower than the cost of joint production. For example, the joint production of microchips for computers and woodchips for wafer boards has disadvantages in joint production. Microchip manufacturing requires a dust-free production process and woodchip manufacturing generates dust.

As indicated in Figure 11.5, such joint production yields a lower level of joint output compared with separate specialized production. The production possibilities frontier is below the chord connecting points A and B. At point A in Figure 11.5, increasing the production of fish results in MRPT on the convex production possibilities frontier being greater than MRPT on the chord between points A and B. The opportunity cost of producing fish and bread jointly is greater than the opportunity cost of specialized production.

Diseconomies of scope (decreasing returns to scope). One firm jointly producing a set of products results in a lower level of output than a set of separate firms each uniquely producing one of the products. *E.g., one firm jointly involved with Lasik eye surgery and flour milling.*

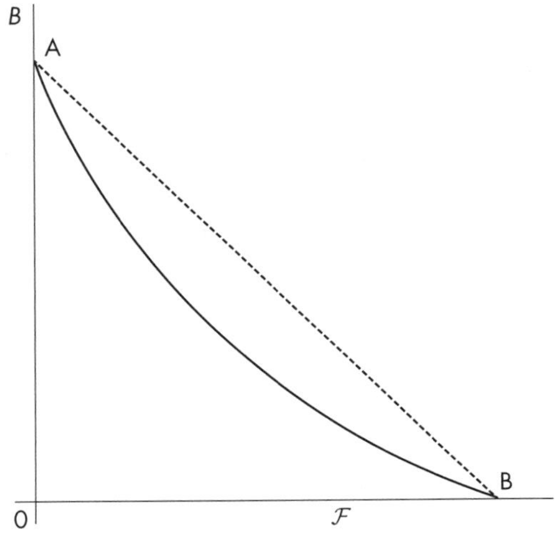

Figure 11.5 **Decreasing returns to scope, decreasing opportunity cost, and convex production possibilities frontier.** The opportunity cost of specialization is lower than the cost of joint production.

Note that there is no direct relationship between economies of scale and economies of scope. Economies of scale is concerned with the output effect of expanding production through increasing all inputs; economies of scope is concerned with the output effect of expanding production through increasing the number of different products produced. They are both related to increasing output, but differ in how output is increased. Returns to scale increases output through input usage and economies of scope increases output through product diversification. For example, both the microchip and woodchip production processes can exhibit increasing returns to scale with decreasing returns to scope.

Example 11.4 Convex production possibilities frontier, decreasing opportunity cost and diseconomies of scope

Consider the following production functions for producing two outputs—fish $\mathcal{F}$ and bread B—with two inputs, K and L:

$$\mathcal{F} = L_{\mathcal{F}} K_{\mathcal{F}},$$
$$B = L_B + K_B,$$

where $L_{\mathcal{F}} + L_B = 10$ is the total amount of labor available and $K_{\mathcal{F}} + K_B = 10$ is the total amount of capital available. The MRTSs for these technologies are

$$\text{MRTS}_{\mathcal{F}}(K \text{ for } L) = K/L.$$
$$\text{MRTS}_B(K \text{ for } L) = 1.$$

To determine the efficiency locus, we equate these MRTSs to get the equation for the production contract curve, $K = L$. Substituting into the production functions for K and solving for L yields

$$L_{\mathcal{F}} = \mathcal{F}^{1/2},$$
$$L_B = B/2.$$

These equations are called the conditional factor demands, conditional on the outputs. We then determine the production possibilities frontier by summing these conditional factor demands and equating the result to the amount of labor available (supply):

$$L_{\mathcal{F}} + L_B = 10,$$
$$\mathcal{F}^{1/2} + B/2 = 10, \quad \text{production possibilities frontier.}$$

Solving for B, we get

$$B = 20 - 2\mathcal{F}^{1/2}.$$

$\text{MRPT} = -dB/d\mathcal{F} = \mathcal{F}^{-1/2} > 0$ and $d\text{MRPT}/d\mathcal{F} = -\frac{1}{2}\mathcal{F}^{-3/2} < 0$, indicating a convex production possibilities frontier.

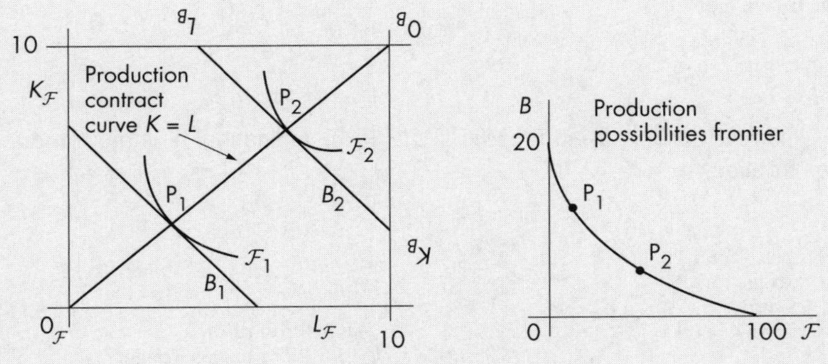

Example 11.5 Linear production possibilities frontier, constant opportunity cost and constant returns to scope

Consider the following production functions for producing two outputs—fish $\mathcal{F}$ and bread B—with two inputs, K and L:

$$\mathcal{F} = L_{\mathcal{F}}^{1/2} K_{\mathcal{F}}^{1/2},$$

$$B = L_B + K_B,$$

where $L_{\mathcal{F}} + L_B = 10$ is the total amount of labor available and $K_{\mathcal{F}} + K_B = 10$ is the total amount of capital available. The MRTSs for these technologies are

$$\text{MRTS}_{\mathcal{F}}(K \text{ for } L) = K/L.$$

$$\text{MRTS}_B(K \text{ for } L) = 1.$$

To determine the efficiency locus, we equate these MRTSs to get the equation for the production contract curve, $K = L$. Substituting into the production functions for K and solving for L yields

$$L_{\mathcal{F}} = \mathcal{F},$$

$$L_B = B/2.$$

These equations are called the conditional factor demands, conditional on the outputs. We then determine the production possibilities frontier by summing these conditional factor demands and equating the result to the amount of labor available (supply):

$$L_{\mathcal{F}} + L_B = 10,$$

$$\mathcal{F} + B/2 = 10, \text{ production possibilities frontier.}$$

Solving for B, we get

$$B = 20 - 2\mathcal{F}.$$

MRPT $= -dB/d\mathcal{F} = 2 > 0$ and $d\text{MRPT}/d\mathcal{F} = 0$, indicating a linear production possibilities frontier.

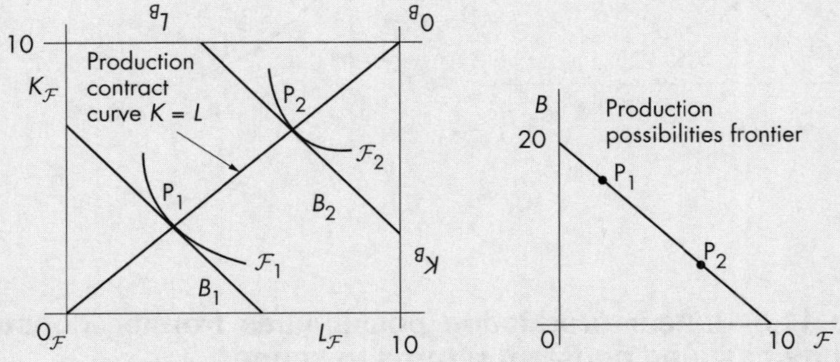

Allocation Condition 2 (marginal product condition)

Suppose Josiah "Jed" Bartlet was running for reelection as president of the United States and had to make a decision on how to allocate his limited campaign resources. He determined it would be more efficient to take resources out of New Hampshire and put them into Ohio in an effort to increase his votes in the Electoral College. If production is to be efficient, resources should be allocated to the point where the marginal product of any resource in the production of a particular commodity (reelection) is the same no matter which firm (state) produces the commodity (electoral votes).

For example, consider two firms (1 and 2) producing the same commodity, say Q, with the following production functions:

$$q_1 = f_1(K_1, L_1),$$
$$q_2 = f_2(K_2, L_2),$$

where the total quantity produced is the sum of individual firms' output, $Q = q_1 + q_2$. Total supplies of labor and capital are given by L and K, so $K_1 + K_2 = K$ and $L_1 + L_2 = L$. An objective of society is to determine the efficient allocation of K and L between the two firms that will maximize output Q:

$$\max Q = \max_{(K_1, L_1, K_2, L_2)} [f_1(K_1,\ L_1) + f_2(K_2,\ L_2)]$$

$$\text{s.t.} \quad K_1 + K_2 = K \quad \text{and} \quad L_1 + L_2 = L.$$

Incorporating the constraints into the objective function by noting that $K_2 = K - K_1$ and $L_2 = L - L_1$ yields

$$\max Q = \max_{(K_1, L_1)} [f_1(K_1, L_1) + f_2(K - K_1, L - L_1)].$$

The FOCs are then

$$\frac{\partial Q}{\partial K_1} = \frac{\partial f_1}{\partial K_1} + \frac{\partial f_2}{\partial K_2}\frac{\partial K_2}{\partial K_1} = \frac{\partial f_1}{\partial K_1} - \frac{\partial f_2}{\partial K_2} = 0,$$

that is,

$$\text{MP}_K|_{\text{firm 1}} - \text{MP}_K|_{\text{firm 2}} = 0,$$

and

$$\frac{\partial Q}{\partial L_1} = \frac{\partial f_1}{\partial L_1} + \frac{\partial f_2}{\partial L_2}\frac{\partial L_2}{\partial L_1} = \frac{\partial f_1}{\partial L_1} - \frac{\partial f_2}{\partial L_2} = 0,$$

that is,

$$\text{MP}_L|_{\text{firm 1}} - \text{MP}_L|_{\text{firm 2}} = 0.$$

Note that $\partial K_2/\partial K_1 = \partial L_2/\partial L_1 = -1$. The FOCs result in $\text{MP}_K|_{\text{firm 1}} = \text{MP}_K|_{\text{firm 2}}$ and $\text{MP}_L|_{\text{firm 1}} = \text{MP}_L|_{\text{firm 2}}$.

In general, for n firms, the FOCs result in **Allocation Condition 2 (the marginal product condition)**:

$$\text{MP}_K|_{\text{firm 1}} = \text{MP}_K|_{\text{firm 2}} = \ldots = \text{MP}_K|_{\text{firm } n},$$

$$\text{MP}_L|_{\text{firm 1}} = \text{MP}_L|_{\text{firm 2}} = \ldots = \text{MP}_L|_{\text{firm } n}.$$

For the labor input with two firms this allocation condition is illustrated in Figure 11.6. If $\text{MP}_L|_{\text{Firm 1}} > \text{MP}_L|_{\text{Firm 2}}$, we can increase the combined output for both the firms, Q, by reallocating the labor inputs. Specifically, we would reduce the amount of labor allocated to firm 2 and increase the amount of labor to firm 1. The area under a marginal product curve is the total amount of output produced.[2] As indicated in Figure 11.6, reducing labor by 1 unit for firm 2 and increasing labor by 1 unit for firm 1 results in a net gain in area under the two curves. The shaded areas in the two graphs represent the change in output, and the shaded area associated with firm 1 is larger than the shaded area for firm 2. This net gain in output represents the increase in output by reallocating the input. We can continue to increase output by shifting the input allocation until the levels of the input used by each firm result in equivalent marginal products.

Allocation Condition 2 (marginal product condition). Resources should be allocated to the point where the marginal product of any resource in the production of a particular commodity is the same no matter which firm produces the commodity.

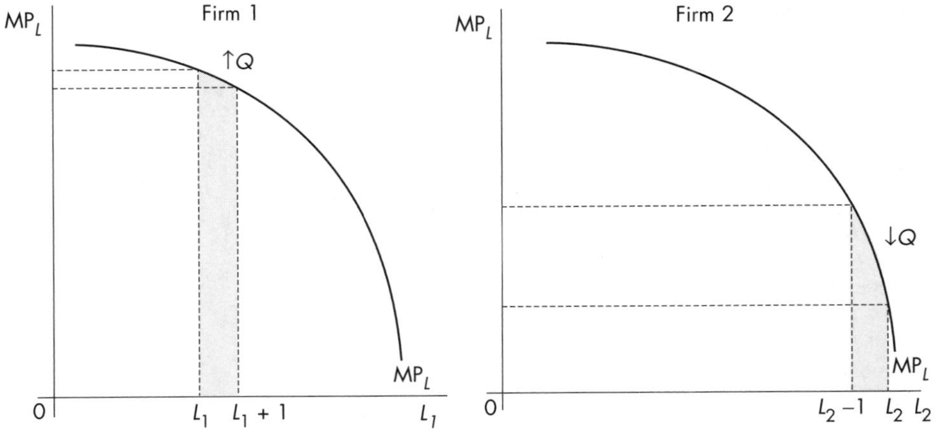

Figure 11.6 **Allocation Condition 2.** The marginal product condition for Pareto efficiency (Allocation Condition 2) is $MP_L|_{\text{Firm 1}} = MP_L|_{\text{Firm 2}}$. With $MP_L|_{\text{Firm 1}} > MP_L|_{\text{Firm 2}}$, output Q can be increased by reallocating labor L from firm 2 to firm 1 until an equality of the MPs is established.

E.g., the additional pizza produced by Pizza Speed from hiring one additional worker should equal the additional pizza produced if Pizza Dash had hired the worker instead.

Example 11.6 Deriving Allocation Condition 2, marginal product condition

Consider an economy with two firms employing labor to produce the same output with technologies represented by the following production functions:

$$q_1 = 10L_1 - \tfrac{1}{2}L_1^2,$$

$$q_2 = 15L_2 - L_2^2,$$

where the subscripts denote firms 1 and 2. Assuming that the supply of labor is fixed at 4 units, $L_1 + L_2 = 4$, we determine the maximum output, $q_1 + q_2 = Q$, by

$$\max Q = \max_{(L_1, L_2)} \left(10L_1 - \tfrac{1}{2}L_1^2 + 15L_2 - L_2^2\right) \quad \text{s.t.} \quad L_1 + L_2 = 4.$$

Incorporating the constraint into the objective function yields

$$\max Q = \max_{L_1} \left[10L_1 - \tfrac{1}{2}L_1^2 + 15(4 - L_1) - (4 - L_1)^2\right].$$

The FOC is then

$$\frac{dQ}{dL_1} = 10 - L_1^* - [15 - 2(4 - L_1^*)] = 0,$$

that is,

$$MP_L|_{\text{Firm 1}} - MP_L|_{\text{Firm 2}} = 0, \text{ Allocation Condition 2.}$$

Solving for L_1^*, the optimal values are $L_1^* = 1$ and $L_2^* = 3$, resulting in $MP_L|_{\text{Firm 1}} = MP_L|_{\text{Firm 2}} = 9$. Optimal output is then $q_1^* = 9.5$, $q_2^* = 36$, so $Q^* = 45.5$.

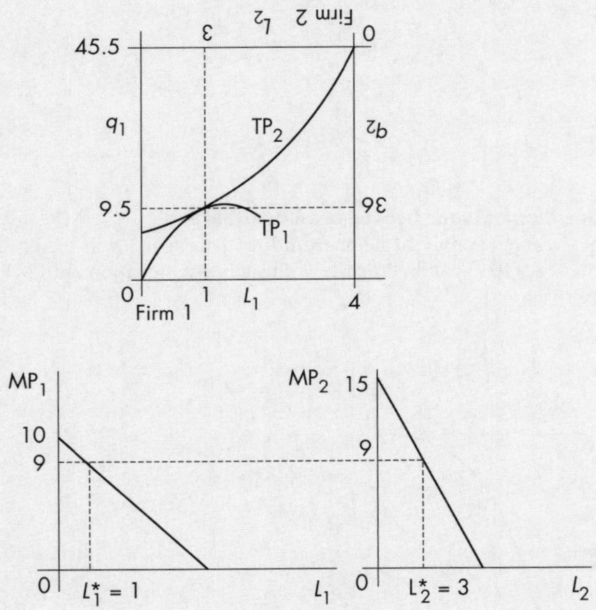

An alternative illustration of Allocation Condition 2 for the production functions of two firms producing the same commodity Q with one variable input labor L is shown in Figure 11.7. For a given level of labor, L°, allocated between the two firms ($L^{\circ} = L_1 + L_2$), the total amount of commodity Q produced is the sum of the two firms' output, $Q = q_1 + q_2$. Note that $MP_L|_{\text{Firm 1}} < MP_L|_{\text{Firm 2}}$, resulting in $Q' = q_1' + q_2'$. Thus, we can increase the total output of Q with the given amount of labor L°, by reallocating labor between the two firms. Specifically, we increase total output by taking labor away from the less productive firm, firm 1, and allocating it to the relatively more productive firm, firm 2. This will enlarge the box vertically, illustrating an increase in total output. Output will continue to increase for the given level of labor, L°, until the production functions are tangent. At this tangency, the marginal products for these two firms will be equal, $MP_L|_{\text{Firm 1}} = MP_L|_{\text{Firm 2}}$. As indicated in Figure 11.8, this results in an efficient allocation of labor for the production of Q, yielding the maximum amount of Q, Q^*, being produced with L° units of labor. Note that Q^* in Figure 11.8

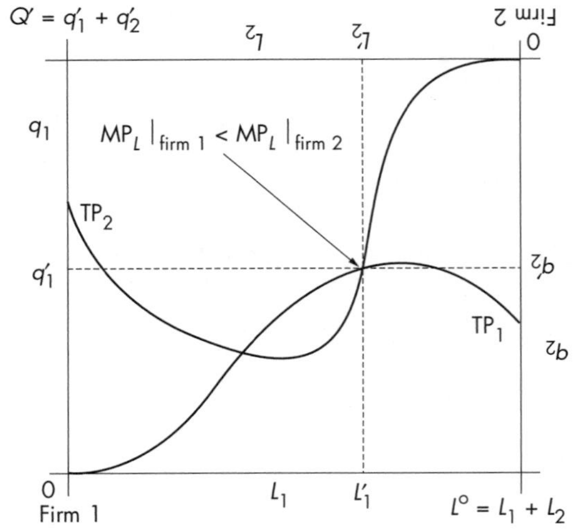

Figure 11.7 **Inefficient allocation of labor between two firms.** $MP_L|_{\text{Firm 1}} < MP_L|_{\text{Firm 2}}$, so a reallocation of the fixed supply of labor from firm 1 to firm 2 will increase output. The Edgeworth box will expand vertically with such a reallocation until $MP_L|_{\text{Firm 1}} = MP_L|_{\text{Firm 2}}$.

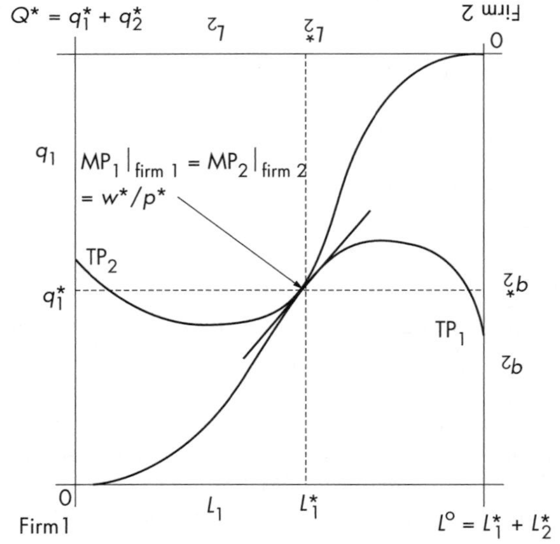

Figure 11.8 **Allocation Condition 2 with an Edgeworth box.** At the Pareto-efficient condition $MP_L|_{\text{Firm 1}} = MP_L|_{\text{Firm 2}}$, the Edgeworth box is as large as it can be vertically without increasing the total amount of labor.

is greater than Q' in Figure 11.7. Output Q^* is the highest level of output possible for a given amount of labor, L^o.

Allocation Condition 3 (comparative advantage condition)

The State Board of Regents with authority over the administration of a state's institutions of higher learning must decide how to allocate resources appropriated by the legislature across the educational institutions offering both undergraduate and graduate degree programs. By equating the sacrifice of undergraduate education for increased graduate education across all institutions, the Regents can efficiently allocate the resources. Specifically, **Allocation Condition 3 (the comparative advantage condition)** states that if two or more firms (higher educational institutions) produce the same outputs (undergraduate and graduate education), then they must operate at points on their respective production possibility frontiers at which their marginal rates of product transformation are equal.

$$\text{MRPT}_{\text{firm } 1} = \text{MRPT}_{\text{firm } 2} = \ldots = \text{MRPT}_{\text{firm } n}.$$

For example, consider two firms each producing fish and bread. The efficient allocation of how much each firm produces of each of the outputs corresponds to where MRPT of firm 1 equals MRPT of firm 2. Figure 11.9 illustrates this Pareto-efficient condition. Within this Edgeworth box, a total amount of 85 and 300 units of fish and bread are produced, respectively. At point A, the MRPT for firm 1 is greater than the MRPT for firm 2. By reallocating the production of outputs between the two firms, we can reduce the total amount of resources employed for producing the given amount of fish and bread. Specifically, moving along firm 2's production possibilities frontier from A toward B, firm 1 produces more bread and less fish while firm 2 produces less bread and more fish. The total level of resources to produce 85 units of fish and 300 units of bread is reduced by a movement from A to B because the production possibilities frontier for firm 1 shifts downward, indicating employment of fewer resources. Only where the MRPTs for the two firms are equal is it impossible to reallocate production in such a way to reduce the resource requirements for the given level of production.

Allocation Condition 3 (comparative advantage condition). If two or more firms produce the same outputs, they must operate at points on their respective production possibility frontiers where their marginal rates of product transformation are equal. *E.g., if two firms are each producing trucks and automobiles, then efficient production requires that the sacrifice in truck production to produce one additional automobile must be the same for both firms.*

Mathematically, we can derive this condition by maximizing the outputs of one firm, holding the level of resources employed by another firm constant. We will continue with the two firms each producing bread B and fish $\mathcal{F}$. We represent the technologies of each firm as $L_1 = f_1(B_1, \mathcal{F}_1)$ and $L_2 = f_2(B_2, \mathcal{F}_2)$, where L_1 and L_2 are the amounts of an input (labor) used in the production of B and $\mathcal{F}$ by each firm. The total amount of bread and fish produced is the sum of the two firms' outputs, $B = B_1 + B_2$ and $\mathcal{F} = \mathcal{F}_1 + \mathcal{F}_2$. The Lagrangian for maximizing firm 1's output of bread and fish, holding firm 2's level of resource (input) constant, is

$$\mathcal{L}(B_1, \mathcal{F}_1, \lambda) = f_1(B_1, \mathcal{F}_1) + \lambda[L_2 - f_2(B_2, \mathcal{F}_2)].$$

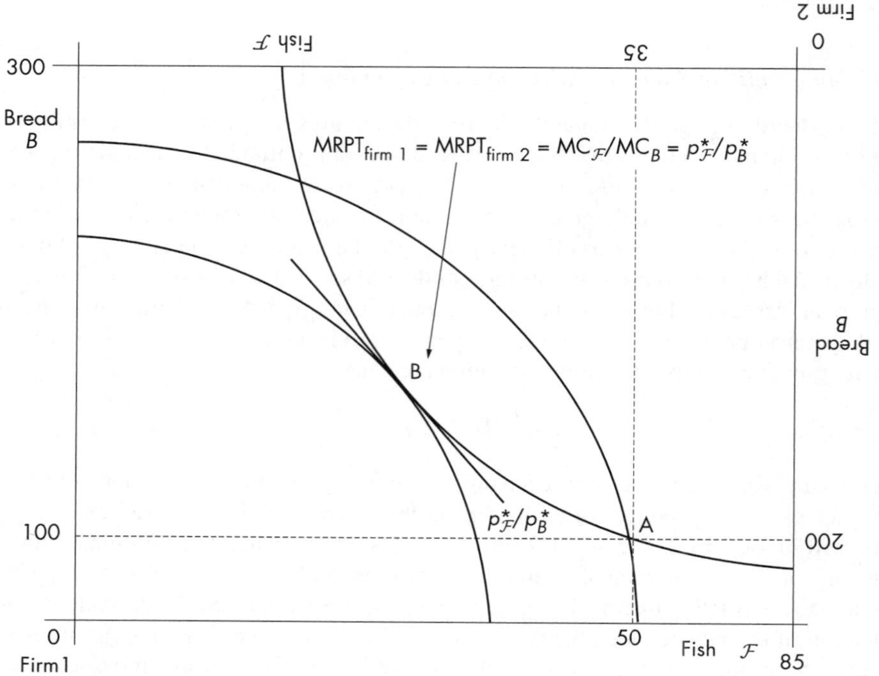

Figure 11.9 **Allocation Condition 3.** The comparative advantage condition (Allocation Condition 3) is $\text{MRPT}_1(B_1 \text{ for } \mathcal{F}_1) = \text{MRPT}_2(B_2 \text{ for } \mathcal{F}_2)$ (point B), so a reallocation of commodities from one firm to the other will not increase the total amount of the commodities produced. At point A, $\text{MRPT}_1 > \text{MRPT}_2$, so a reallocation of commodities, where firm 1 produces more bread and less fish and firm 2 produces more fish and less bread, will increase the total amount of the commodities produced.

The FOCs are

$$\frac{\partial \mathcal{L}}{\partial \mathcal{F}_1} = \frac{\partial L_1}{\partial \mathcal{F}_1} - \lambda \frac{\partial L_2}{\partial \mathcal{F}_2}\frac{\partial \mathcal{F}_2}{\partial \mathcal{F}_1} = 0,$$

$$\frac{\partial \mathcal{L}}{\partial B_1} = \frac{\partial L_1}{\partial B_1} - \lambda \frac{\partial L_2}{\partial B_2}\frac{\partial B_2}{\partial B_1} = 0,$$

$$\frac{\partial \mathcal{L}}{\partial \lambda} = L_2 - f_2(B_2, \mathcal{F}_2) = 0.$$

Note that $\partial \mathcal{F}_2/\partial \mathcal{F}_1 = \partial B_2/\partial B_1 = -1$. Taking the ratio of the first two FOCs results in

$$\frac{\partial L_1/\partial \mathcal{F}_1}{\partial L_1/\partial B_1} = \frac{\partial L_2/\partial \mathcal{F}_2}{\partial L_2/\partial B_2},$$

$\text{MRPT}_1(B_1 \text{ for } \mathcal{F}_1) = \text{MRPT}_2(B_2 \text{ for } \mathcal{F}_2)$, Allocation Condition 3.

Example 11.7 Deriving Allocation Condition 3, comparative advantage condition

Consider the following technologies for two firms, firm 1 and firm 2, each producing two outputs—bread B and fish $\mathcal{F}$—with a single input L:

$$L_1 = B_1^2 + \mathcal{F}_1^2,$$

$$L_2 = 10(B_2^2 + \mathcal{F}_2^2).$$

The total outputs of bread and fish are $B = B_1 + B_2$ and $\mathcal{F} = \mathcal{F}_1 + \mathcal{F}_2$, respectively. The Lagrangian for maximizing firm 1's output, holding firm 2's level of input L_2 constant, is

$$\mathcal{L}(\mathcal{F}_1, B_1, \lambda) = B_1^2 + \mathcal{F}_1^2 + \lambda\left\{L_2 - 10\left[(\mathcal{F} - \mathcal{F}_1)^2 + (B - B_1)^2\right]\right\}.$$

The FOCs are then

$$\partial\mathcal{L}/\partial\mathcal{F}_1 = 2\mathcal{F}_1 + 10\lambda(2)(\mathcal{F} - \mathcal{F}_1) = 0,$$

$$\partial\mathcal{L}/\partial B_1 = 2B_1 + 10\lambda(2)(B - B_1) = 0,$$

$$\partial\mathcal{L}/\partial\lambda = L_2 - 10[(\mathcal{F} - \mathcal{F}_1)^2 + (B - B_1)^2] = 0.$$

Taking the ratio of the first two conditions, we have

$$\text{MRPT}_1(B_1 \text{ for } \mathcal{F}_1) = \frac{\mathcal{F}_1}{B_1} = \frac{\mathcal{F} - \mathcal{F}_1}{B - B_1} = \frac{\mathcal{F}_2}{B_2} = \text{MRPT}_2(B_2 \text{ for } \mathcal{F}_2),$$

Allocation Condition 3.

As an example, let $\mathcal{F}_1 = 7$, $\mathcal{F}_2 = 2$, $B_1 = 3$, and $B_2 = 8$. This implies $\mathcal{F} = 9$, $B = 11$, $L_1 = 58$, and $L_2 = 680$. At this allocation, $\text{MRPT}_1 = 7/3 \neq 2/8 = \text{MRPT}_2$, so an improvement in efficiency is possible. Specifically, holding firm 2's level of input L_2 constant, the same amount of B and $\mathcal{F}$ can be produced by reallocating production with firm 1, using less of the input. From the FOCs,

$$\frac{\mathcal{F}_1}{B_1} = \frac{\mathcal{F} - \mathcal{F}_1}{B - B_1}.$$

Rearranging terms, $B_1 = B\mathcal{F}_1/\mathcal{F} = 11\mathcal{F}_1/9$. Substituting into the third FOC and noting that $L_2 = 680$, we get

$$680 - 10\left[(9 - \mathcal{F}_1)^2 + (11 - 11\mathcal{F}_1/9)^2\right] = 0.$$

$\mathcal{F}_1 = 3.78$ is the solution of this quadratic equation. Then, $B_1 = 11(3.78)/9 = 4.62$, $\mathcal{F}_2 = 9 - 3.78 = 5.22$, and $B_2 = 11 - 4.62 = 6.38$. The input allocation for firm 2 remains the same at $L_2 = 10[(6.38)^2 + (5.22)^2] = 680$, but the amount of input used by firm 1 is reduced from 58 to $(4.62)^2 + (3.78)^2 = 35.63$. The improvement in efficiency is represented by the reduction in resources required to produce 9 units of $\mathcal{F}$ and 11 units of B. This reduction in resources (58 − 35.63 = 22.37) could be allocated for additional production of $\mathcal{F}$ and B or for the production of some other commodities.

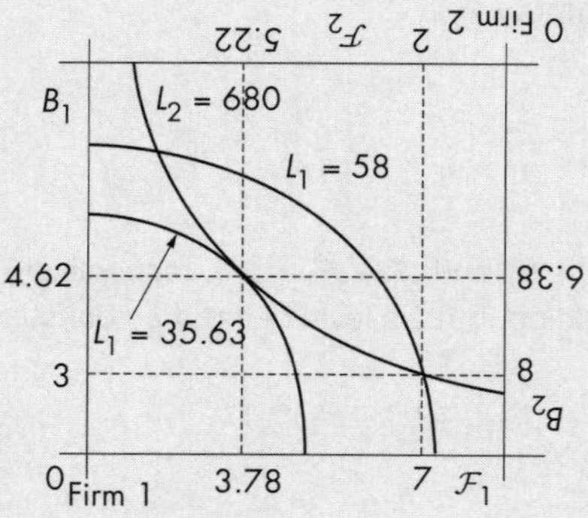

Comparative advantage

David Ricardo (1772–1823), who some consider the Isaac Newton of economics, assumed that international trade determined prices and wages within countries, just as planetary orbits are determined by the sun. In the nineteenth century, when nationalism intervened, economists started believing that each country (planet) could determine their own prices and wages (orbit). In the twentieth century, world conditions reminded economists of the international linkages of prices and wages. Just as physicists learned the limits of mechanics based on idealized assumptions about perfectly elastic and frictionless bodies, economists are learning to look beyond their own countries' borders.

Related to Allocation Condition 3 is the theory of comparative advantage in international trade, first developed by David Ricardo. A country has a **comparative advantage** in commodities that it is relatively more efficient in producing. Efficiency is measured in the sacrifice of other commodities for the production of an additional unit of a commodity. Comparative advantage is in contrast to **absolute advantage**, where a country's cost in terms of input usage, instead of opportunity cost, is used as the measure of advantage. Countries will specialize in producing products for which they have a comparative advantage until their MRPTs are equilibrated. They will then trade with other countries to satisfy consumer demand. For example, in Figure 11.9, the movement from point A to point B results from firm (country) 1 having a comparative advantage in the production of bread and firm (country) 2 a comparative advantage in fish production. As the firms (countries) specialize in the production of the commodity for which they have a comparative advantage, gains from improved efficiency are realized. These gains are the ability to either produce more of both commodities or maintain their current production levels and allocate excess resources to other activities. Thus, total world production will increase. This improved efficiency through comparative advantage and trade is the basis for supporting the idea of reducing trade barriers, such as tariffs and quotas, that constrain free trade.

Why trade, if you have an absolute advantage? There are gains from trade that result in improved efficiency when trading partners specialize in production.

Comparative advantage. The sacrifice in terms of other commodities for the additional production of a commodity is lower for the firm (country) compared with another firm (country). *E.g., Chile has a comparative advantage in the production of wine compared with California. Chilean wine may cost more to produce in terms of inputs, but the opportunity cost of other commodities it could produce is lower.*

Absolute advantage. The input cost for the additional production of a commodity is lower for the firm (country) compared with another firm (country). *E.g., Florida has an absolute advantage in the production of citrus compared with Wisconsin.*

Application: Comparative advantage and China's export patterns

Since China joined the World Trade Organization in 2001, its exports have almost quadrupled. China's share of total world exports grew from under 1 percent in 1980 to over 12 percent in 2010, making China the largest international exporter.

China's economic reforms and its open-door policies have allowed its economy to shift from a heavy-industry-oriented development strategy in a capital-scarce and labor-intensive economy to a comparative advantage strategy. As a labor-abundant underdeveloped country, China appears to have a comparative advantage in the export of labor-intensive products.

Employing an econometric model, C. Yue and P. Hua tested the hypothesis that comparative advantage has resulted in the relative high annual growth in exports. Their results are consistent with this hypothesis. Along with the liberalization of external trade restrictions and exchange controls, China's general export patterns have shifted toward a pattern consistent with comparative advantage. Comparative advantage does explain the level and trend of export patterns in China during its economic transition. The next time you put on a pair of pants, check the label. It could very well state, "Made in China."

Source: C. Yue and P. Hua, "Does Comparative Advantage Explain Export Patterns in China?" *China Economic Review* 13 (2002): 276–296.

Determining economic efficiency

Diner, "Waitress I ordered fish not chicken." Waitress, "But our forte is chicken."

On November 19–23, 1942, in just four days, Soviet forces pinched the German supply lines and surrounded the German Sixth and Fourth Panzer Armies (330,000 troops) in Stalingrad on the Volga River. Hitler ordered supplies airlifted to his surrounded troops. The airlift was Pareto-efficient in terms of production. Unfortunately for the Sixth and Fourth Armies, what they wanted was not supplied. With the coming winter (one of the worst on record), they did not receive sufficient winter uniforms and food. Cold and on the verge of starvation, the German armies surrendered on February 1–2, 1943.

Necessary conditions for **economic efficiency**, with both production and exchange, require all three conditions for production and the one exchange condition to hold (equality of the MRS).[3] These conditions provide for a Pareto-efficient production and exchange of commodities. However, they are not sufficient for achieving economic efficiency. Economic efficiency also requires **output efficiency**, where what firms produce (airlift) is what households (troops) want. As with the airlift, firms may be Pareto-efficient in production, but if they are not producing what households want, the economic system will be inefficient. For example, an economy that concentrates on the efficient production of military commodities at the expense of household items during relative peace is inefficient. This occurred in the former USSR and contributed to its implosion.

Economic efficiency. The three allocation conditions for Pareto efficiency in production are satisfied along with output efficiency. *E.g., perfectly competitive markets.*

Output efficiency. The condition where the MRS for each household equals the MRPT. *E.g., the airlift of commodities during the blockade of Berlin in 1948 and 1949 resulted in an efficient transportation of commodities that the West Berlin citizens required to outlast the blockade.*

This additional necessary condition for economic efficiency, that the right commodities be produced, requires that MRS = MRPT. MRS measures how much a household is willing to substitute one commodity for another, holding utility constant, and MRPT measures the opportunity cost (the sacrifice of another commodity) of producing one more unit of a commodity. If MRS > MRPT, then a household's willingness to substitute one commodity for another is greater than the opportunity cost. Efficiency can then be improved by a reallocation of resources until a household's willingness to pay is equal to the cost of producing any additional unit of a commodity: MRS = MRPT.

If there were only a one-household or homogeneous preferences economy

Robinson Crusoe (1719) by Daniel Defoe is about a mariner, Crusoe, shipwrecked on a Pacific island. He is able to maximize his (social) welfare for 28 years, 2 months and 19 days by equating his MRS to the MRPT. This concept of equating MRS to MRPT is illustrated in Figure 11.10 for the case of a one-household economy (say, only Robinson) or for the case where all households have the same utility function (say, a queen's subjects solely interested in increasing her utility or comrades all working for a common good). Assume this household (or set of households acting as one) produces and consumes two commodities x_1 and x_2 (e.g., fish and bread), with a given level of inputs. In Figure 11.10, the household's preferences, satisfying the preference axioms, for the two commodities are represented by indifference curves superimposed on the household's production possibilities frontier.[4] The household attempts to maximize utility subject to this production possibilities constraint. For example, at commodity bundle A, MRS(x_2 for x_1) > MRPT(x_2 for x_1). The one household can increase its utility by moving down along the production possibilities frontier from A to B. At bundle B, the household is maximizing its utility for this production possibilities frontier, which corresponds to where MRS(x_2 for x_1) = MRPT(x_2 for x_1). This is the economically

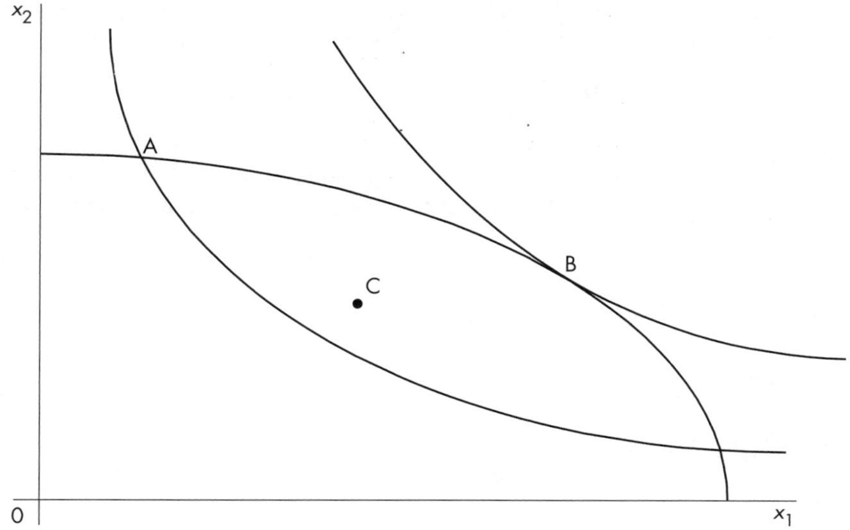

Figure 11.10 **Economic efficiency for a one-household economy.** At the tangency point B, between the production possibilities frontier and the one-household's indifference curve, MRPT = MRS, so the economy is efficient. Also, this Pareto-efficient allocation point B maximizes social welfare for the one-household economy.

efficient commodity bundle (Pareto-efficient allocation) for the economy, and, because there is only one household in this economy, bundle B is also the point where society maximizes social welfare, local bliss. Bundle B is the only point on the production possibilities frontier where there is no other commodity bundle preferred to it. For example, bundle A is Pareto-efficient in terms of production, but there are commodity bundles, such as bundle C, within the production possibilities frontier that are preferred to A. Bundle C is inefficient in terms of production because it is in the interior of the production possibilities frontier. However, the household would prefer the inefficient production of this bundle as opposed to producing a less desirable commodity bundle efficiently. For example, the former USSR may have been efficient in its production of relatively large quantities of military tanks and only a few automobiles (say, point A in the figure), but households within the USSR probably would have preferred an inefficient bundle (point C) with more automobiles and fewer tanks.

How would you maximize social welfare? For a one-household economy, efficiently producing commodities the household desires will maximize social welfare.

Example 11.8 Maximizing social welfare for a one-household economy

Assume Robinson is all alone on an island and states his preferences for commodities x_1 and x_2 as

$$U = x_1^{1/4} x_2.$$

Robinson has the ability to use input L in the production of x_1 and x_2, given the technology represented by the following production possibilities frontier:

$$x_1^2 + x_2^2 = L.$$

Since Robinson is the only consumer, maximizing his utility subject to this production technology is equivalent to maximizing social welfare for society as a whole. The Lagrangian is then

$$\mathcal{L}(x_1, x_2, \lambda) = x_1^{1/4} x_2 + \lambda(L - x_1^2 - x_2^2).$$

The FOCs are

$$\frac{\partial \mathcal{L}}{\partial x_1} = \frac{1}{4}(x_1^*)^{-1} U - 2\lambda x_1^* = 0,$$

$$\frac{\partial \mathcal{L}}{\partial x_2} = (x_2^*)^{-1} U - 2\lambda x_2^* = 0,$$

$$\frac{\partial \mathcal{L}}{\partial \lambda} = L - x_1^2 - x_2^2 = 0.$$

From the first two equations, the condition MRS = MRPT results in

$$\text{MRS}(x_2 \text{ for } x_1) = \frac{x_2^*}{4x_1^*} = \frac{x_1^*}{x_2^*} = \text{MRPT}(x_2 \text{ for } x_1).$$

Rearranging terms,

$$(x_2^*)^2 = 4(x_1^*)^2,$$

$$x_2^* = 2x_1^*.$$

Robinson will consume twice as much of x_2 compared with x_1 in order to maximize utility. If $L = 500$ (the amount of the resource Robinson has available), then, noting that $(x_2^*)^2 = 4(x_1^*)^2$, the production possibilities frontier is

$$(x_1^*)^2 + 4(x_1^*)^2 = 500.$$

Solving for x_1 yields the social welfare maximum outputs:

$$5(x_1^*)^2 = 500,$$

$$(x_1^*)^2 = 100,$$

$$x_1^* = 10 \text{ and } x_2^* = 20.$$

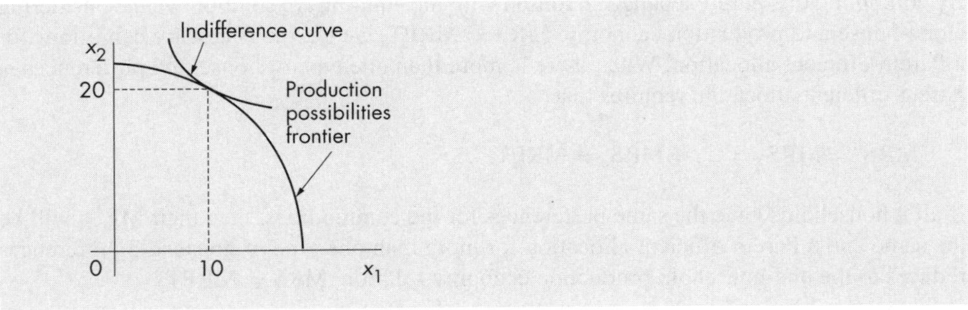

Mathematically, we can derive the output-efficient condition MRS(x_2 for x_1) = MRPT (x_2 for x_1) by maximizing utility subject to a production possibilities constraint. Consider the two commodities x_1 and x_2 with the technology for producing these two commodities from input L represented as a concave production possibilities frontier, $L = f(x_1, x_2)$. Let the household's utility function, which satisfies the four preference axioms, be represented as $U(x_1, x_2)$. The Lagrangian is then

$$\mathcal{L}(x_1, x_2, \lambda) = U(x_1, x_2) + \lambda[L - f(x_1, x_2)].$$

The FOCs are

$$\frac{\partial \mathcal{L}}{\partial x_1} = \frac{\partial U}{\partial x_1} - \lambda \frac{\partial f}{\partial x_1} = 0,$$

$$\frac{\partial \mathcal{L}}{\partial x_2} = \frac{\partial U}{\partial x_2} - \lambda \frac{\partial f}{\partial x_2} = 0,$$

$$\frac{\partial \mathcal{L}}{\partial \lambda} = L - f(x_1, x_2) = 0.$$

Rearranging the first two equations and taking their ratio yields

$$\frac{\partial U/\partial x_1}{\partial U/\partial x_2} = \frac{\partial f/\partial x_1}{\partial f/\partial x_2},$$

$$\text{MRS}(x_2 \text{ for } x_1) = \text{MRPT}(x_2 \text{ for } x_1).$$

At MRS = MRPT, the right commodities, in terms of a household's preferences, are being produced. This corresponds to the Pareto-efficient allocation, which, along with production efficiency, yields economic efficiency.

Deriving Pareto efficiency with more than one type of household preferences

Equating the marginals will get society headed toward global bliss.

(Michael Wetzstein)

In Chapter 6, the general-equilibrium condition for a pure-exchange economy with n households equated the MRS across all the households:

$$\text{MRS}_1 = \text{MRS}_2 = \ldots = \text{MRS}_n.$$

By combining this pure-exchange condition with the equilibrium solution when considering a one-household production economy, MRS = MRPT, we get the necessary conditions for a Pareto-efficient allocation. When there is more than one type of household preferences, a Pareto-efficient allocation requires that

$$\text{MRS}_1 = \text{MRS}_2 = \ldots = \text{MRS}_n = \text{MRPT}.$$

If all n households have the same preferences for the commodities, then their MRSs will be the same and a Pareto-efficient allocation for more than one type of household preferences reduces to the one-household production economy solution, MRS = MRPT.

Two-household economy with heterogeneous preferences

Friday arrives on the island; Robinson is no longer a one-household economy. Assuming that Friday and Robinson have different preferences, we must examine economic efficiency with more than one type of household preferences. As illustrated in Figure 11.11, the Pareto-efficient allocation is where the MRS for Robinson equals the MRS for Friday and both are equal to the MRPT:

$$\text{MRS}_R = \text{MRS}_F = \text{MRPT}.$$

The production-efficient commodities Q_1^* and Q_2^* from the production possibilities frontier form an Edgeworth box. Robinson's indifference map originates from the production

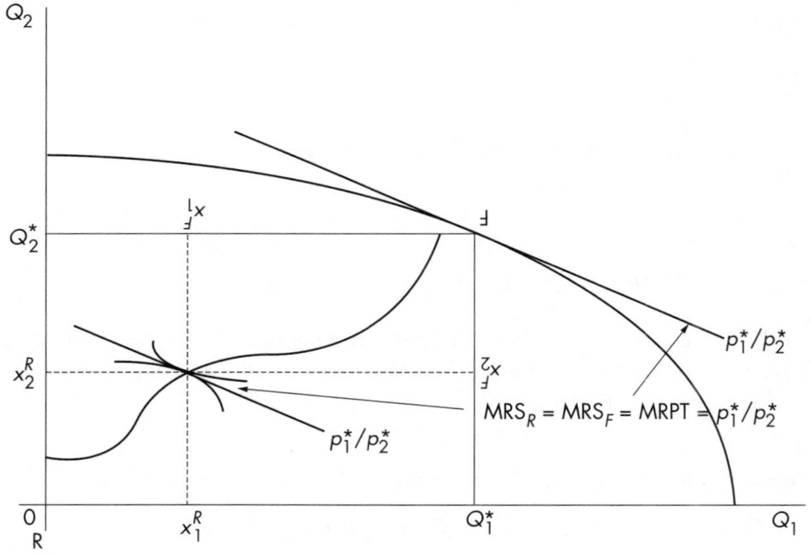

Figure 11.11 **Economic efficiency for a two-household economy.** The Pareto-efficient allocation is $\text{MRS}_R = \text{MRS}_F = \text{MRPT}$. How much households are willing to substitute one commodity for another is just equal to the opportunity cost of substituting one commodity for another. Given production efficiency, this Pareto-efficient allocation yields an economic-efficient allocation of resources.

possibilities frontier point of origin O_R, and Friday's indifference map is rotated 180°, with its origin placed on the production possibilities frontier associated with Q_1^* and Q_2^*. At the point where Robinson's and Friday's MRSs are equal (tangency of the indifference curves) and the MRPT is also equal to their MRSs, a Pareto-efficient allocation exists.

For a demonstration of why this results in a Pareto-efficient allocation, suppose the economy operated where one household's MRS(x_2 for x_1) $= 1 < 2 =$ MRPT(Q_2 for Q_1). The rate at which the household is willing to trade x_2 for x_1 is less than the rate at which Q_2 can be transformed into Q_1. The household is indifferent if 1 unit of x_1 is substituted for 1 unit of x_2. In contrast, in terms of production, 2 units of Q_2 can be produced with a sacrifice of only 1 of Q_1. Thus, it is possible to make this household better off by reallocating the production of Q_1 and Q_2. Producing 2 units of Q_2 by only sacrificing 1 unit of Q_1 will increase the household's utility. The loss in utility of 1 unit of x_1 is offset with only 1 unit of x_2, but the household receives 2 units of x_2, which results in the net increase in satisfaction. This reallocation can continue as long as MRS $\neq$ MRPT. Thus, a Pareto-efficient allocation will occur where the MRS for every household is equal to the MRPT. At this allocation, how much households are willing to substitute one commodity for another is just equal to the opportunity cost in production of substituting one commodity for another.

Example 11.9 Determining economic efficiency for a two-household two-good economy

Suppose Robinson and Friday have the following utility functions and initial endowments of the limited resource L:

$$U^R = x_1^{1/4} x_2, \quad \text{Robinson's utility for commodities } x_1 \text{ and } x_2,$$

$$U^F = x_1 + x_2, \quad \text{Friday's utility for the commodities,}$$

$$e^R = 25 \quad \text{and} \quad e^F = 25,$$

where $e^R + e^F = 50 = L$ and e denotes initial endowment. The production possibilities frontier is

$$Q_1^2 + Q_2^2 = L,$$

where Q_1 and Q_2 equal the total quantities of commodities 1 and 2 produced from resource L. These total quantities (supply) are then allocated to Robinson and Friday, where

$$x_1^R + x_1^F = Q_1,$$

$$x_2^R + x_2^F = Q_2,$$

quantity demanded equals quantity supplied. The condition for a Pareto-efficient allocation is

$$\text{MRS}_R = \text{MRS}_F = \text{MRPT},$$

$$\frac{x_2^{R*}}{4x_1^{R*}} = 1 = \frac{Q_1^*}{Q_2^*},$$

which yields $Q_1^* = Q_2^*$. Given $L = 50$, this results in the optimal production $Q_1^* = Q_2^* = 5$. Robinson and Friday have an equal endowment of resource L, so transforming their endowments into commodities, given $Q_1^* = Q_2^* = 5$, yields the endowments in terms of outputs of $x_1^R = x_1^F = x_2^R = x_2^F = 2.5$. However, at this allocation, $\text{MRS}_R = 1/4 < 1 = \text{MRS}_F$, which is not Pareto-efficient, so utility gains from trading are possible. A Pareto-efficient allocation may be determined by maximizing Robinson's utility subject to Friday's utility. Specifically, Friday's utility is

$$U^F = x_1^F + x_2^F = 5 = (5 - x_1^R) + (5 - x_2^R) \Rightarrow 5 - x_1^R - x_2^R = 0.$$

The Lagrangian is then

$$\mathcal{L}(x_1^R, x_2^R, \lambda) = (x_1^R)^{1/4} x_2^R + \lambda(5 - x_1^R - x_2^R).$$

The FOCs yield $\text{MRS}_R = x_2^{R*}/4x_1^{R*} = 1$. Solving for $x_2^{R*} = 4x_1^{R*}$ (the equation for the contract curve) and substituting into the constraint yields Robinson's efficient allocation, $x_1^{R*} = 1$ and $x_2^{R*} = 4$. Given $x_1^R + x_1^F = Q_1$ and $x_2^R + x_2^F = Q_2$, Friday's efficient allocation is $x_1^{F*} = 4$ and $x_2^{F*} = 1$. This results in $U^R = 4$ and $U^F = 5$.

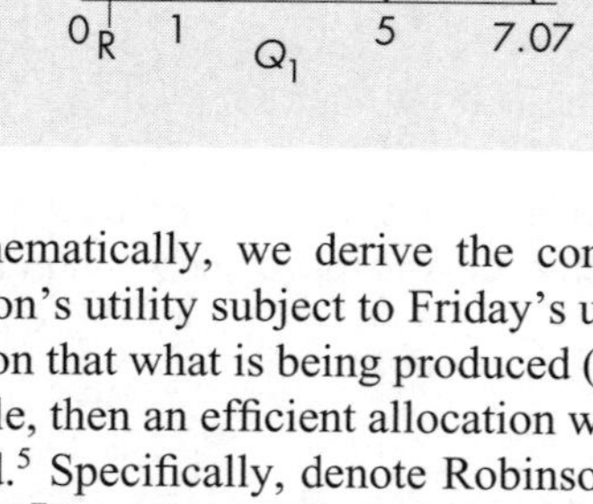

Mathematically, we derive the condition $\text{MRS}_R = \text{MRS}_F = \text{MRPT}$ by maximizing Robinson's utility subject to Friday's utility, the production possibilities constraint, and the condition that what is being produced (supply) must equal demand. If all commodities were desirable, then an efficient allocation would have no excess demand, so supply would equal demand.[5] Specifically, denote Robinson's and Friday's utility functions as $U_R(x_1^R, x_2^R)$ and $U_F(x_1^F, x_2^F)$ and the production possibilities constraint (frontier) as $L = f(Q_1, Q_2)$. For a fixed level of the input L, the economy will supply some combination of Q_1 and Q_2 based on the production possibilities constraint. The supply of Q_1 and Q_2 will then be allocated between

Robinson and Friday:

$$Q_1 = x_1^R + x_1^F,$$
$$Q_2 = x_2^R + x_2^F,$$

quantity supplied will equal quantity demanded. The Lagrangian with four constraints instead of the normal one is

$$\begin{aligned}\mathcal{L}(x_1^R, x_2^R, x_1^F, x_2^F, Q_1, Q_2, \lambda_1, \lambda_2, \lambda_3, \lambda_4) = {} & U_R(x_1^R, x_2^R) + \lambda_1[U_F - U_F(x_1^F, x_2^F)] \\ & + \lambda_2[L - f(Q_1, Q_2)] + \lambda_3(Q_1 - x_1^R - x_1^F) \\ & + \lambda_4(Q_2 - x_2^R - x_2^F).\end{aligned}$$

The FOCs are

$$\left.\begin{aligned}\frac{\partial \mathcal{L}}{\partial x_1^R} &= \frac{\partial U_R}{\partial x_1^R} - \lambda_3 = 0 \Rightarrow \mathrm{MU}_1^R = \lambda_3, \\ \frac{\partial \mathcal{L}}{\partial x_2^R} &= \frac{\partial U_R}{\partial x_2^R} - \lambda_4 = 0 \Rightarrow \mathrm{MU}_2^R = \lambda_4,\end{aligned}\right\} \Rightarrow \frac{\mathrm{MU}_1^R}{\mathrm{MU}_2^R} = \mathrm{MRS}^R = \frac{\lambda_3}{\lambda_4},$$

$$\left.\begin{aligned}\frac{\partial \mathcal{L}}{\partial x_1^F} &= -\lambda_1 \frac{\partial U_F}{\partial x_1^F} - \lambda_3 = 0 \Rightarrow -\lambda_1 \mathrm{MU}_1^F = \lambda_3, \\ \frac{\partial \mathcal{L}}{\partial x_2^F} &= -\lambda_1 \frac{\partial U_F}{\partial x_2^F} - \lambda_4 = 0 \Rightarrow -\lambda_1 \mathrm{MU}_2^F = \lambda_4,\end{aligned}\right\} \Rightarrow \frac{\mathrm{MU}_1^F}{\mathrm{MU}_2^F} = \mathrm{MRS}^F = \frac{\lambda_3}{\lambda_4},$$

$$\left.\begin{aligned}\frac{\partial \mathcal{L}}{\partial Q_1} &= -\lambda_2 \frac{\partial f}{\partial Q_1} + \lambda_3 = 0 \Rightarrow \lambda_2 \frac{\partial f}{\partial Q_1} = \lambda_3, \\ \frac{\partial \mathcal{L}}{\partial Q_2} &= -\lambda_2 \frac{\partial f}{\partial Q_2} + \lambda_4 = 0 \Rightarrow \lambda_2 \frac{\partial f}{\partial Q_2} = \lambda_4.\end{aligned}\right\} \Rightarrow \frac{\partial f/\partial Q_1}{\partial f/\partial Q_2} = \mathrm{MRPT} = \frac{\lambda_3}{\lambda_4},$$

These FOCs yield the Pareto-efficient allocation $\mathrm{MRS}_R = \mathrm{MRS}_F = \mathrm{MRPT}$.

This Pareto-efficient allocation, illustrated in Figure 11.11, is based on a given level of utility for Friday. Changing this level of utility for Friday will result in alternative combinations of Q_1 and Q_2 produced and allocated between Robinson and Friday. As illustrated in Figure 11.12, maximizing Robinson's utility, given U_F° as Friday's level of satisfaction, results in the Pareto-efficient allocation of x_1^R, x_2^R, x_1^F, x_2^F, with Q_1^* and Q_2^* efficiently produced.

Maximizing Robinson's utility, given an alternative level of satisfaction for Friday, say U_F', will result in an alternative Pareto-efficient allocation, $x_1^{R'}$, $x_2^{R'}$, $x_1^{F'}$, $x_2^{F'}$, with Q_1' and Q_2' produced. In general, considering all possible Pareto-efficient allocations, $\mathrm{MRS}_R = \mathrm{MRS}_F = \mathrm{MRPT}$, by varying Friday's utility from consuming zero units of Q_1 and Q_2 to consuming all of Q_1 and Q_2, we obtain a collection of economically efficient utility levels (the contract curve) for both Robinson and Friday. The initial endowment of resources held by Robinson and Friday will determine which of these economically efficient allocations are feasible. For example, if Friday had initially a relatively large share of the resources, then an economically

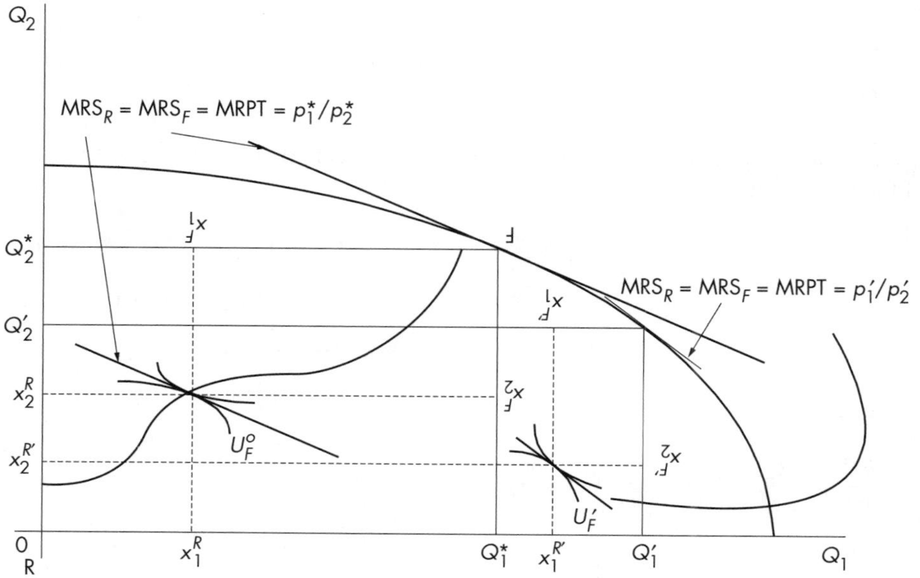

Figure 11.12 **Economic efficiency for alternative utility levels.** Perfectly competitive prices p_1^* and p_2^* correspond to a Pareto-efficient allocation that establishes the economic efficiency of competitive markets. Given a change in the initial endowments, a new Pareto-efficient allocation, $x_1^{R'}$, $x_2^{R'}$, $x_1^{F'}$, $x_2^{F'}$, with Q_1' and Q_2' produced, is obtainable at competitive prices p_1' and p_2'.

efficient allocation resulting in Robinson consuming most of the commodities would not be feasible. As we discuss in the next section, the competitive-price system will yield an economically efficient allocation. However, as discussed in Chapter 6 and further discussed in Chapter 20, the initial allocation of endowments or access to these endowments (equal opportunity) does have social-welfare implications. Even though resources are allocated efficiently, a redistribution of initial endowments may enhance social welfare and thus be socially desirable.

What is the problem when Friday arrives? With two or more households, the initial allocation of endowments also has to be considered for maximizing social welfare.

Example 11.10 Social welfare and an efficient allocation

From Example 11.9, when the initial endowments of resource L were equally allocated so both Robinson and Friday received 25 units each of L, an efficient allocation was $x_1^{R*} = 1$, $x_2^{R*} = 4$, $x_1^{F*} = 4$, and $x_2^{F*} = 1$. This results in $U^R = 4$ and $U^F = 5$. A change in the income distribution between Robinson and Friday by changing the initial endowments will result in an alternative efficient allocation and utility levels. For example, consider the initial endowments $e^R = 30$ and $e^F = 20$.

Transforming their endowments into commodities, given that $Q_1^* = Q_2^*$ still holds, yields $x_1^R = x_2^R = 3$ and $x_1^F = x_2^F = 2$. At this allocation, $MRS_R = 1/4 < 1 = MRS_F$, which is not Pareto-efficient. Maximizing Robinson's utility subject to Friday's utility $U^F = 4$ will result in a Pareto-efficient allocation. Specifically, Friday's utility is

$$U^F = x_1^F + x_2^F = 4 = (5 - x_1^R) + (5 - x_2^R) \Rightarrow 6 - x_1^R - x_2^R = 0.$$

The Lagrangian is then

$$\mathcal{L}(x_1^R, x_2^R, \lambda) = (x_1^R)^{1/4} x_2^R + \lambda(6 - x_1^R - x_2^R).$$

The FOCs yield $MRS_R = x_2^{R*}/4x_1^{R*} = 1$. Solving for $x_2^{R*} = 4x_1^{R*}$, the equation for the contract curve, and substituting into the constraint, yields Robinson's efficient allocations, $x_1^{R*} = 6/5$ and $x_2^{R*} = 24/5$. Given $x_1^R + x_1^F = Q_1$ and $x_2^R + x_2^F = Q_2$, Friday's efficient allocations are $x_1^{F*} = 19/5$ and $x_2^{F*} = 1/5$. This results in $U^R = 5$ and $U^F = 4$. This is a reversal from the equal-endowment utilities presented in Example 11.9. Both allocations are Pareto-efficient.

Understanding general equilibrium in a competitive economy

Decentralized control awarded first place in efficiency.

(Michael Wetzstein)

A perfectly competitive economy assumes that agents (households and producers) take all prices as given. No agent has control over some markets, and thus no agent can influence market prices. In this economy, a general competitive equilibrium is a set of prices (price signals) for both inputs and outputs where quantity demanded equals quantity supplied in all input and output markets, simultaneously. At this set of prices, households maximize utility subject to their initial endowments and firms maximize profit. The set of prices are all the information that is required between the buyers and sellers of commodities.

Efficiency in production

We can establish a relationship between this competitive-equilibrium set of prices and efficiency in production by examining the three allocation conditions. Perfectly competitive pricing provides the necessary conditions for these allocation conditions to hold. Specifically, recall Allocation Condition 1 (Figure 11.1):

$$MRTS_1 = MRTS_2 = \ldots = MRTS_k = w^*/v^* \quad \text{for all } k \text{ commodities,}$$

where the two inputs are labor and capital with a wage rate of w and a rental rate of v. Given perfect competition in the input markets, firms producing these k commodities will equate their MRTS(K for L) to the common input price ratio w^*/v^*, which results in Allocation Condition 1. Thus, in a decentralized tâtonnement process, without any market intervention (as in a central-planning agency), firms will adopt the least-cost combination of inputs for a given level of output given the price signals.

Under Allocation Condition 2 (Figure 11.8), MPs of an input, say labor, are equal for all firms producing the same output Q:

$$\mathrm{MP}_L|_{\text{firm }1} = \mathrm{MP}_L|_{\text{firm }2} = \mathrm{MP}_L|_{\text{firm }3} = \ldots = \mathrm{MP}_L|_{\text{firm }n} = w^*/p^*,$$

where p is the price per unit for output Q. Multiplying both sides by p^* yields $\mathrm{VMP}_L = p^*\,\mathrm{MP}_L = w^*$, where VMP_L is the value of the marginal product for labor. This is the profit-maximizing condition for a perfectly competitive market, where the marginal revenue from hiring an additional worker (VMP_L) is equal to the wage rate w^*. (Refer to Chapter 16 for a more detailed discussion of VMP.) The fixed price signals (w^*, p^*) insure that the MP_L will be the same across all firms producing Q. Thus, again without any market intervention, the free market results in a Pareto-efficient allocation of all the inputs among firms producing the same product. A decentralized decision process yields an efficient resource allocation.

Under Allocation Condition 3 (Figure 11.9),

$$\begin{aligned}\mathrm{MRPT}(q_2 \text{ for } q_1)_{\text{firm }1} &= \mathrm{MRPT}(q_2 \text{ for } q_1)_{\text{firm }2} = \ldots = \mathrm{MRPT}(q_2 \text{ for } q_1)_{\text{firm }n}\\ &= \frac{\mathrm{MC}_1}{\mathrm{MC}_2} = \frac{p_1^*}{p_2^*},\end{aligned}$$

where p_1 and p_2 denote the per-unit prices of outputs q_1 and q_2, respectively. Given perfect competition, all firms face the same set of output prices, which for maximizing profits are set equal to their respective marginal cost of production. Thus, the ratio of marginal costs, MRPT, will be the same for all firms in a perfectly competitive market. This indicates that no firm has a lower sacrifice in the additional production of a commodity than any other firm. Market intervention could not alter the production mix among firms and increase efficiency.

Thus, production is Pareto-efficient under perfect competition without any central decision making. The tâtonnement process based on the decentralized control of households maximizing their utility, given their initial endowments, and firms maximizing profit for a given technology, will result in production efficiency.

What is output efficiency?

> *All progress is based upon a universal innate desire on the part of every organism to live beyond its income.*
>
> (Samuel Butler)
>
> *Translation: In a perfectly competitive price system, an economically efficient allocation of resources results if all agents attempt to maximize their individual happiness.*

If the price ratios associated with households are the same as the price ratios for producers, then (Figure 11.11)

$$\mathrm{MRS}_1 = \mathrm{MRS}_2 = \ldots = \mathrm{MRS}_n = \mathrm{MRPT} = \frac{p_1^*}{p_2^*}.$$

This will be true for any pair of commodities. Thus, the tâtonnement process, through price signals, assures supply and demand will be equalized for all commodities. This results in the market-clearing price, where no excess supply or demand exists (Walrasian equilibrium). Recall that this result is the First Fundamental Theorem of Welfare Economics (discussed in Chapter 6), which states that when the assumptions of perfectly competitive equilibrium hold, every general perfectly competitive equilibrium is efficient in production and results in a Pareto-efficient allocation (output efficiency). The Second Fundamental Theorem of Welfare Economics also holds, given the assumptions of a perfectly competitive equilibrium. That is, every allocation that is efficient in production and could potentially be a Pareto-efficient allocation can be obtained with a general perfectly competitive equilibrium by reallocating initial endowments. Figure 11.12 illustrates the duality of these welfare theorems in a two-household, two-product productive economy. Perfectly competitive prices p_1^* and p_2^* correspond to a Pareto-efficient allocation, which establishes the efficiency of perfectly competitive markets. Given a change in the initial endowments, a new Pareto-efficient allocation, $x_1^{R'}, x_2^{R'}, x_1^{F'}, x_2^{F'}$, with Q_1' and Q_2' produced, is obtainable with perfectly competitive prices p_1' and p_2'.

These dual results provide support for the *laissez-faire* position taken by many economists. Adam Smith's invisible hand of perfectly competitive markets will provide both production efficiency and output efficiency. Society's problem of achieving an economically efficient allocation of resources is decentralized and solved at the individual-agent level. Each household and firm only has to be concerned with its own maximization problem. The only information communicated among agents concerns market prices (price signals). Market prices act as signals in determining the relative scarcity of commodities, and the tâtonnement process results in efficient resource allocation.

What is the big deal about free markets? A perfectly competitive price system will result in an efficient allocation of society's resources.

Optimal reallocation of endowments

> *There is always more misery among the lower classes than there is humanity in the higher.*
>
> (Victor Hugo)
>
> *Translation: There is reluctance on the part of agents with relatively more initial endowments to share with the less endowed. For improving social welfare, a central authority may be required to transfer initial endowments.*

Free markets take the distribution of initial endowments as given, so unless some optimal initial distribution of endowments is mated with competitive markets, social welfare may not be maximized. However, to achieve an optimal initial distribution of endowments, some government authority must be able to identify individual household preferences and endowments. This government authority is some policymaker, social planner, or decision maker with the objective to maximize social welfare. The decision maker is not *paternalistic*, and thus will not undertake actions counter to households' preferences. So that decision makers can properly identify individual preferences and endowments and thus reallocation endowments to improve social welfare, many governmental agencies will require some type of needs evaluation. For example, college financial aid, welfare, and many other public-assistance programs require a completed application designed to reveal an applicant's preferences and endowments.

Why is a government required? A major justification for government is redistribution of the initial endowments for enhancing social welfare.

Application: Distribution and efficiency resolved interdependently

In a study on endowment effects, O'Connor and Muir present a primer on social-welfare maximization that stresses the importance of the interdependency between distribution and efficiency. The Second Fundamental Theorem of Welfare Economics states that a Pareto-efficient allocation can be obtained with a general perfectly competitive equilibrium by reallocating initial endowments. This result is widely employed to motivate the idea of the separability of efficiency and welfare distribution. Specifically, society first determines the distribution of initial endowments and then allows perfectly competitive markets to yield a Pareto-efficient allocation. However, in this two-step process, the distribution of initial endowments is based on the existing set of commodities and prices. A change in endowments will alter the resulting equilibrium allocation of commodities and prices. This change in commodities and prices may require a further shifting of endowments for improving welfare. Thus, welfare distribution of endowments can be only determined simultaneously with equilibrium prices and commodity allocations. Correct prices depend on distributional choices, but distributional choices depend on knowing these correct prices. This is a chicken-and-egg situation: which comes first—the chicken (distribution of endowments) or the egg (Pareto-efficient prices)?

The importance of simultaneously considering distribution and efficiency is particularly significant when a policy results in large endowment shifts. Examples are the privatization of state-owned firms and the transfer of property rights in natural resource conservation and environmental policies. Generally, estimates of consumer and producer surplus are based on the premise of little or no endowment effects. However, particularly in natural resource and environmental policies involving intergenerational rights and endowments, ignoring endowment effects is at best misleading if not erroneous economic analysis. Thus, O'Connor and Muir emphasize the importance of distribution and redistribution of economic opportunity as a primary concern in theoretical and empirical policy analysis.

Source: M. O'Connor and E. Muir, "Endowment Effects in Competitive General Equilibrium: A Primer for Paretian Policy Analyses," *Journal of Income Distribution* 5 (1995): 145–175.

Confronting imperfect markets

When we run on empty, anyone who comes close gets sucked into our lane.

(Michael Wetzstein)

Translation: In a decentralized economic system, any one agent exiting the economy will be replaced with another without complete failure of the economy.

Failure of free markets to achieve efficiency can be due to imperfect competition (Parts 5 and 6), externalities, the supply of public goods, or asymmetric information (Part 9). This inability of free markets alone to maximize social welfare opens the way for governmental programs designed to supplement the market and improve social welfare. A sound understanding of economic theory associated with the general competitive-market equilibrium can guide the development and implementation of effective government programs.

What is the problem with imperfect markets? Free markets may fail to achieve an efficient allocation of resources if there is imperfect competition, externalities, desire for public goods, or asymmetric information.

The opposite of a free market is a *centrally planned economy*, where all aspects of production, distribution, and consumption are based on a governmental plan. An efficient outcome is also possible in a centrally planned economy; however, it requires knowledge of individual household preferences and production possibilities. Such knowledge is difficult and costly to obtain—unless individual preferences and production plans are dictated by some party. However, such dictation is at the expense of individual freedom of expression. Thus, even in centrally planned economies, there still exists a free market, either legal or illegal. The question is what degree of governmental intervention in the free activities of markets is required for improving social welfare?

The general failure of centrally planned socialism in determining efficient resource allocation led to a system of decentralized socialism. Prior to World War II, O. Lange and F. Taylor demonstrated how decentralized socialism can also result in a Pareto-efficient allocation of resources.[6] In this system, the state would own all the capital and rent it out to state-owned, bureaucratically managed, firms. These firms would then be free to maximize profits in a competitively determined labor market. The state would receive all the profit and distribute it to households—in the form of public goods and subsidies—in some equitable form. As in perfect competition, prices would be determined in free markets.

A problem with decentralized socialism is determining the optimal supply of capital. The state would have to make this determination, and there is no invisible hand to reflect households' preferences. Decentralized socialism was only adopted in a limited form after World War II in Eastern Europe. Major problems of allocating capital among firms, political appointment of firm managers, and limited individual incentives resulted in the abandonment of this system in the late 1980s (November 9, 1989: the Berlin Wall came tumbling down).

Socialist societies generally attempt to replace individual incentives to work and invest with social responsibility. These societies put great weight on the common welfare of the whole society. Such a system can work well during national emergencies (such as during wars), where it becomes a social responsibility for all households to work toward ensuring their joint preservation. However, without some common menace, social responsibility wanes as a motivation to work. Thus, some socialist states will manufacture threats, such as happened during the Cultural Revolution in China.

A general problem with relying on a centralized controlled system is the complete system failure that occurs when the control unit fails. Nature has solved this problem through radical decentralization. Cells in a living organism all have the same basic structure, but each type takes on different specialized tasks and performs these tasks autonomously. In the event of a cell failing, its tasks can be taken up by new cells. In an economic system, the free market, with its emphasis on decentralized control, mimics this decentralization found in nature. Human agents are all basically identical and they each take on specialized tasks in the economic system. The failure or exit of any one household or firm will not result in the complete failure of the economic system. Instead, those agents exiting will be replaced by other agents without a perceptible disruption in the economy. This major advantage of decentralization has allowed life to flourish on earth (and other planets?) and allows for a stable and dynamic economic system.

Summary

1. An allocation of resources is production-efficient when no reallocation of resources will yield an increase in one commodity without a sacrifice in output from other commodities.
2. The necessary conditions for efficiency in production are the three allocation conditions concerning the opportunity cost of production (Allocation Condition 1), the marginal product (Allocation Condition 2), and comparative advantage in production (Allocation Condition 3).
3. Allocation Condition 1 (the opportunity cost condition) states that for production efficiency, no more of one commodity can be produced without having to cut back on the production of other commodities.
4. The production possibilities frontier is the locus of Pareto-efficient output levels for a given set of inputs and production technology. The negative of the slope of the production possibilities frontier is the marginal rate of product transformation (MRPT). MRPT measures the rate at which one output can be substituted for another, holding the level of inputs constant.
5. In the short run, concave production possibilities frontiers result from the Law of Diminishing Marginal Returns. In the long run, concave production possibilities frontiers result from specialized input and factor intensities.
6. Economies of scope, yielding a concave production possibilities frontier, occur when one firm jointly producing a set of products results in a higher level of output than a set of separate firms each uniquely producing one of the products.
7. Allocation Condition 2 (the marginal product condition) states that for production efficiency, resources should be allocated to the point where the marginal product of any resource in the production of a particular commodity is the same no matter which firm produces the commodity.
8. Allocation Condition 3 (the comparative advantage condition) states that for production efficiency, if two or more firms produce the same outputs, they must operate at points on their respective production possibilities frontier where their marginal rates of product transformation are equal.
9. The necessary conditions for economic efficiency are the three production-efficiency conditions with the additional condition that what firms produce is what consumers desire (output efficiency). For Pareto-efficient allocation to result in the right commodities being produced, the marginal rate of substitution must be equal to the marginal rate of product transformation.
10. A perfectly competitive market will yield economic efficiency. Market prices are signals for agents to allocate their resources efficiently. Society's problem of efficient allocation of resources is decentralized and solved at the individual-agent level. The only information communicated among agents is market prices.
11. Free markets take the distribution of initial endowments as given, so, unless some optimal initial distribution of endowments is mated with free markets, social welfare may not be maximized. One role for government is to reallocate initial endowments in an effort to enhance social welfare. This requires knowledge

of agents' preferences. Many public-assistance programs designed to reallocate endowments require an application to reveal the household's preferences and endowments.

Key concepts

absolute advantage, 446
Allocation Condition 1, 422
Allocation Condition 2, 439
Allocation Condition 3, 443
comparative advantage, 446
comparative advantage condition, 443
constant returns to scope, 434
decreasing returns to scope, 435
diseconomies of scope, 435
economic efficiency, 448
economies of scope, 433
increasing returns to scope, 433
marginal product condition, 439
marginal rate of product transformation, 428
opportunity cost condition, 422
output efficiency, 448
production contract curve, 424
production possibilities frontier, 426

Key equations

$$\text{MRTS}_1 = \text{MRTS}_2 = \ldots = \text{MRTS}_k$$

Allocation Condition 1.

$$\text{MRPT}(q_2 \text{ for } q_1) = \text{MC}_1/\text{MC}_2$$

The ratio of the marginal costs of producing two outputs with a given level of resources is equal to the marginal rate of product transformation.

$$\text{MP}_L|_{\text{firm } 1} = \text{MP}_L|_{\text{firm } 2} = \ldots = \text{MR}_L|_{\text{firm } n}$$

Allocation Condition 2.

$$\text{MRPT}_{\text{firm } 1} = \text{MRPT}_{\text{firm } 2} = \ldots = \text{MRPT}_{\text{firm } n}$$

Allocation Condition 3.

$$\text{MRS}_1 = \text{MRS}_2 = \ldots = \text{MRS}_n = \text{MRPT}$$

For output efficiency, the amount that consumers are willing to pay for an additional unit of a commodity is equal to the cost of supplying this additional unit.

Questions

Have a warm glow in your heart when you do it right. Just like E.T. in the movie E.T.: the Extra-Terrestrial.

(Michael Wetzstein)

1. What economic facts of life are illustrated by the production possibilities frontier?
2. What would be the shape of a production possibilities frontier for guns and butter when the economy is experiencing increasing returns to scale in both commodities?
3. Discuss the inefficiency associated with the reversal of roles where computer programmers are assigned to clean the building and custodians are assigned to develop computer software.
4. Suppose a fungus is affecting tea plants, requiring more inputs such as labor to grow a pound of tea. How does this affect relative prices and the efficient allocation of coffee and tea? Explain.
5. Why will commodities not be distributed efficiently among consumers if the marginal rate of product transformation is not equal to consumers' marginal rate of substitution? Explain.
6. In Citrusland, the common marginal rate of substitution of lemons for limes is 2 and the marginal rate of product transformation is ½. How should resources be reallocated in this situation? How can this reallocation increase all agents' well-being?
7. What is the free-market mechanism by which consumers' MRS and the producers' MRPT move toward equality? Explain.
8. Discuss the inefficiency of consumers preferring relatively more SUVs and producers instead producing relatively more minivans.
9. Why can feedback effects from one market to another result in a general-equilibrium solution deviating from a partial-equilibrium solution?
10. Scarcity is the cause of the interdependence among agents within an economy. Explain why the economic interdependencies existing within the general-equilibrium model would not exist in the absence of scarcity. Of what significance are the conditions of economic efficiency in a society without scarcity?

Exercises

To think, "I will not think"—This, too, is something in one's thoughts. Simply do not think about not thinking at all.

(Takuan)

1. In Fastfoodsville, the production possibilities frontier for hamburgers H and shakes S is

$$H + 2S = 1200.$$

a. If Douglas prefers eating 2 hamburgers with every shake, how much of each product will be produced?
b. What is the price ratio?

2. Two countries A and B can produce two commodities, apples and oranges, per unit of labor as follows

Country	Apples	Oranges
A	6	24
B	16	32

What is country A's comparative advantage and country B's comparative advantage? Explain.

3. Draw one or more diagrams illustrating each of the following conditions. What do these five conditions establish?

a. The MRS between any two commodities should be the same for any two consumers.
b. The MRTS between any two factors should be the same for any pair of producers (Allocation Condition 1).
c. The MP of a given factor for a given product should be the same for any pair of producers (Allocation Condition 2).
d. The MRPT between any two products should be the same for any pair of producers (Allocation Condition 3).
e. The MRS between any two commodities should be the same as the MRPT between these two commodities for any producer.

4. Consider an economy with two firms and two consumers. Firm 1 is entirely owned by consumer 1, and it produces guns G from oil x, with the production technology $G = 5x$. Firm 2 is entirely owned by consumer 2 and produces butter B from oil x, with technology $B = 2x$. Each consumer owns 20 units of oil. Consumer 1's utility function is $U_1(G_1, B_1) = G_1 B_1^2$ and consumer 2's utility function is $U_2(G_2, B_2) = G_2 B_2$.

a. Find the market-clearing prices for guns, butter, and oil.
b. How many guns and how much butter does each consumer consume?
c. How much oil does each firm use?

5. Suppose Robinson and Friday each have 8 hours of labor to devote to producing either fish $\mathcal{F}$ or bread B. Robinson's utility function is

$$U_R = \mathcal{F}B^3$$

and Friday's is

$$U_F = \mathcal{F}^2 B.$$

Robinson and Friday do not care if they produce fish or bread, and the production functions for each commodity are

$$F = \tfrac{1}{2}\ell_{\mathcal{F}},$$
$$B = 4\ell_B,$$

where $\ell_F + \ell_B = 16$, their combined endowment of labor.

a. What is the equilibrium price ratio $p_{\mathcal{F}}/p_B$?
b. How much $\mathcal{F}$ and B will Robinson and Friday each demand?
c. How should labor be allocated between fish and bread to satisfy the demand?

6. An auto garage offers engine, E, and transmission, T, rebuilding and uses the same facilities and labor for both services. The shop's total cost function is

$$\text{LTC} = E^2 + T^2.$$

Is this total cost function consistent with the presence of increasing or decreasing returns to scale? Economies or diseconomies of scope?

7. In Candyland, there are two regions—Sugar S and Spice H—with chocolate C and gum drops G both produced in each region. The production functions for region Sugar are

$$C_S = \ell_C^{1/2},$$
$$G_S = \ell_G^{1/2},$$

where ℓ_C and ℓ_G are the amounts of labor devoted to C and G production, respectively. Total labor available in region Sugar is 200 units. Similarly, Spice's production functions are

$$C_H = \tfrac{1}{2}\ell_C^{1/2},$$
$$G_H = \tfrac{1}{2}\ell_G^{1/2},$$

where 200 units of labor are also available in Spice.

a. Calculate the production possibilities frontier for regions Sugar and Spice.
b. Assuming labor cannot move from one region to the other, what is the efficient allocation of labor and outputs?

8. An economy with two firms, producing q_1 and q_2, respectively, has the production technologies

$$q_1 + q_2 - \ell_1 = 0,$$
$$q_2 = \ell_2^{1/2},$$

where q_1 and q_2 are outputs and $\ell_1 + \ell_2 = 33$.

a. Derive the production possibilities frontier.
b. Given a social-welfare function $U = q_1 q_2$, determine the optimal levels of q_1 and q_2 and the equilibrium level of prices.

9. Consider a two-consumer (Robinson and Friday) and two-commodity (bread and fish) economy. Let the production possibilities frontier be

$$B = 36 - \mathcal{F},$$

with consumer utility functions

$$U_R = \mathcal{F}_R B_R,$$
$$U_F = \mathcal{F}_F B_F.$$

Assume the initial endowments are $\mathcal{F}_R = 4$, $B_R = 14$, $\mathcal{F}_F = 3$, and $B_F = 15$.

a. Determine the equilibrium allocation of bread and fish.
b. Is this equilibrium efficient?
c. Does this equilibrium maximize social welfare?

10. In Caffeine City, the production functions for tea T and coffee C are

$$T = K^{2/3}L^{1/3},$$
$$C = K^{1/3}L^{2/3}.$$

In its allocation of K and L, the city uses half of K and half of L for tea production and the other half of the inputs for coffee production. In which direction can the city reallocate factors so that both outputs are increased?

Internet case studies

1. Provide examples of both partial- and general-equilibrium analysis.
2. Discuss the contributions that Oskar Lange made to economic theory.
3. Discuss the role of comparative advantage in making business decisions.
4. Make a list of paternalist government policies.

Part V

Monopoly power

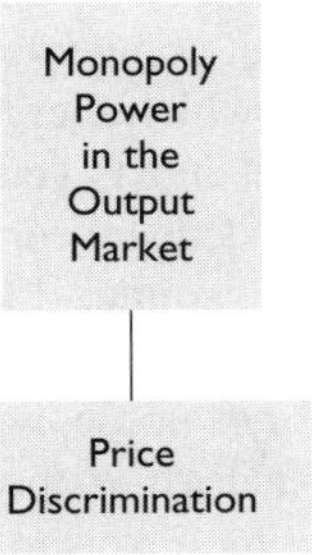

Chapters

Capitalism needs to function like a game of tug-of-war. Two opposing sides need to continually struggle for dominance, but at no time can either side be permitted to walk away with the rope.

(Pete Holiday)

Monopoly power by an agent can take many different forms, but for all forms there is always a desire to control (walking away with the rope). An example of monopoly power on the household level would be a husband denying money to his wife. Even though the wife has a job, the husband (the agent with monopoly power) takes her paycheck and sets a price for all the commodities the wife consumes. The husband captures the wife's entire consumer surplus. At the market level, this monopoly power takes the form of a firm having some control over the market price. This is in contrast to the perfectly competitive assumptions, where all firms are price takers (taking the price they receive for their output as fixed) and all firms within a market produce a homogeneous product. The occurrence of market advertising indicates the presence of heterogeneous (differentiated) products, or at least attempts by firms to create product differentiation. In these markets, firms may attain some control over their output price—they are *price makers* rather than price takers—and the conditions for the Law of One Price fail. The level of control firms can attain over price depends on market conditions associated with the degree of product differentiation, barriers to entry, and the number of firms. Various market structures result, depending on the nature of these conditions.

In Chapters 12 and 13, we consider the market structure of monopoly behavior. Monopoly is the polar case to perfect competition. In a monopoly market, there is a single firm producing a product for which there are no close substitutes. The firm is the industry and thus faces the market demand curve for its price and output decisions. Given the downward-sloping market demand curve, the monopoly has control over the price it receives for its output. For example, if the monopoly reduced its output, the price per unit it would receive for its output would increase.

Monopolies do exist in reality; for example, within a local community, electric, gas, and water companies are generally each a monopoly. Firms with few close substitutes—such as an athletic association offering tickets to a major sporting event, an ice-cream stand on a beach, and a gasoline station on a remote road—can also behave like monopolies. Such firms are said to have some degree of **monopoly power**, defined as the ability to set price above marginal cost. The degree of monopoly power depends on the ability of a firm to profitably set its price above the perfectly competitive price. The fewer the number of close substitutes, the closer a firm is to being a true monopoly. Thus, for a monopoly, the demand for the product must be reasonably independent of the price of other products. Specifically, the cross-price elasticity of demand

$$\varepsilon_{ji} = \frac{dq_j}{dp_i}\frac{p_i}{q_j},$$

which measures the relative responsiveness in the demand for the monopoly product j to changes in the price of commodity i, must be

$$\varepsilon_{ji} < \alpha \quad \text{for all } i \neq j,$$

where α is some arbitrarily small positive number.

Monopoly power. A firm's ability to set price above marginal cost. *E.g., a winery's ability to set a price for its award-wining wine above the marginal cost of production.*

Application: Monopoly power and the United States Post Office

Only the Post Office is allowed to deliver first-class mail, resulting in a monopoly in existence since the founding of the country. The Post Office has always insisted that it requires this protection for maintaining a national service that reaches every American at the same price. However, this Post Office monopoly on delivering letters will likely fade away. The former Postmaster General Marvin Runyon anticipates a world, by 2020, in which paper mail and electronic mail blend together and the Postal Service is a much more automated operation. Through the natural forces of the marketplace, the monopoly power of the Post Office will vanish. By the year 2020, there will be so many ways to communicate, advertise, and ship merchandise that the monopoly power of the Post Office will vanish due to natural market forces. Already, electronic mail is a major factor in communications. For example, it costs over 50 cents to deliver a Social Security check by "snail mail" and just 2 cents electronically. The economics are just too compelling not to drive a change. By 2020, it is likely that millions of Americans will be working at home in virtual companies and small home-based businesses. The Postal Service will have to support this working environment by providing the full array of postal services electronically. However, United Parcel Service, Federal Express, and other carriers will be offering these same or similar services.

In Chapter 12, we first discuss the causes of a monopoly and then determine the profit-maximizing price and output for firms characterized with monopoly power. Using the Lerner Index, a measure of a firm's monopoly power, we investigate the inefficiencies of monopoly power. We also discuss how government may regulate a monopoly in an effort to mitigate welfare losses. Since one type of regulation is to require the monopoly to be a nonprofit organization, we develop a model for nonprofit firms in the Appendix to Chapter 12. Also in the appendix, we discuss behavioral assumptions other than the assumption that firms attempt to maximize profits.

As we have said, a firm with monopoly power has some control over price. Thus, it may be able to enhance profits by *price discrimination,* which exists when a firm can separate the market into two or more segments and offer different prices in each market segment. We investigate this practice in Chapter 13. We define and discuss the alternative types of price discrimination (called first, second and third degrees of price discrimination) in terms of firms' profits, efficiencies, and welfare impacts.

Price discrimination requires developed markets for a commodity, where information on consumer demand for the product exists. In markets lacking this information, a firm may choose to auction its output as an alternative way to enhance profit. In the Appendix to Chapter 13, we discuss the different types of auctions and associated market efficiencies.

12 Monopoly and regulation

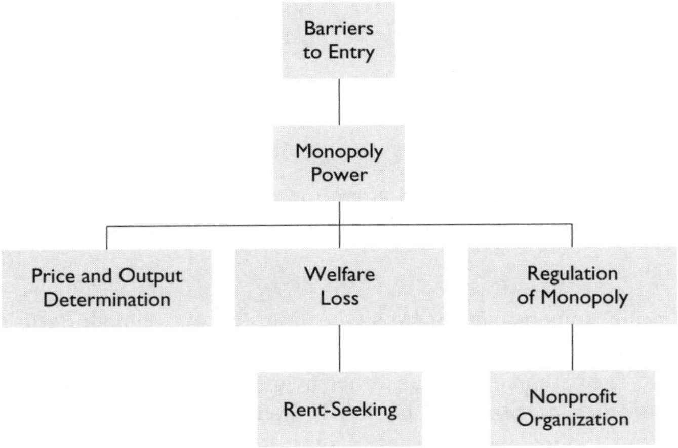

Outline and Conceptual Inquiries

Understanding barriers to entry
What prevents you from establishing a mail service?
Application: The Internet and barriers to entry

Determining the price and output
Does a monopoly charge the highest price it can?
Profit maximization

Calculating the Lerner Index
Application: Is the Lerner Index a practical measure for antitrust enforcement?

Establishing long-run equilibrium

Measuring welfare loss from monopoly power
Rent-seeking behavior
Application: Measurement of real-world distortions
Will taxing a monopoly remove its power?

How to regulate a monopoly
Governmental regulation
Does the government regulate a monopoly or does the monopoly regulate the government?
Application: California regulation of energy and descent into darkness

What are contestable markets?
Does the market regulate a monopoly?

Summary
Key concepts
Key equations
Questions
Exercises
Internet case studies

Appendix to chapter 12

Juggling multiple plants
Why would a firm have multiple plants?

The Earth's environment has a monopoly on life as we know it, so we should learn to work with the environment rather than constantly challenging it.

(Sierra Club)

On a global scale, some scientists are advocating that we regulate Earth's monopoly on our environment by adding nutrients to our oceans to greatly increase the phytoplankton. The carbon dioxide absorbed by the plankton could exceed the harmful level of carbon dioxide produced by the United States from burning fossil fuels. However, before fooling with Mother Nature, the nature of the monopoly and all potential benefits and costs should be fully understood.

The polar extreme of perfect competition is a market with only one firm (Earth) supplying the output (the environment for life). If a firm has no substitutes (competition) for its output, then it is a **monopoly** rather than a perfectly competitive firm. In this chapter, we discuss barriers to entry as the cause of monopolies. We then develop short-run price and output determination for a profit-maximizing monopoly. We derive the relationship of a monopoly's price with the market elasticity of demand and, based on this relationship, develop the *Lerner Index* for measuring the degree of monopoly power.

Monopoly. Only one firm in an industry. *E.g., a local cable TV company.*

Then we investigate the long-run equilibrium for monopolies as well as the opportunity cost of capital as a consequence of monopolies earning only long-run normal profits. Based on this long-run equilibrium, we investigate welfare loss from monopoly power in terms of price not equaling marginal cost, firms operating at less than full capacity, and rent-seeking behavior. We then discuss and evaluate government regulation to correct this potential welfare loss in terms of a market's contestability.

In the chapter's appendix, we develop the conditions for determining the optimal output for each plant for a firm with multiple physical plants. Then, we discuss the determination of price and output for a nonprofit firm as a form of governmental regulation. This nonprofit equilibrium of price and output is based on managers employing their preferences for the firm's decisions. At the end of the appendix, we investigate market-share maximization as an alternative to profit maximization as a firm's motivation.

Our aim in this chapter is to investigate how a firm with monopoly power will misallocate resources and thus is inefficient. To improve efficiency, taxing, regulating, or breaking up monopolies are possible solutions. We hope to provide an understanding of why agents with monopoly power are detrimental to an economy and why the US Justice Department investigates such agents.

Firms with monopoly power have always sparked interest among applied economists. The growth of the industrial state in the nineteenth and twentieth centuries spawned a wealth of investigations by economists into the causes, problems, and potential cures for an economy with monopolies. Their cures have ranged from advocating essentially no cure (e.g., Herbert Spencer, 1820–1903, and William Graham Sumner, 1840–1910) to completely replacing the free market (e.g., Karl Marx, 1818–1883, and Friedrich Engels, 1820–1895). The question that applied economists are now attempting to answer is whether curing the disease (monopoly power) will kill the patient (advancing social welfare). In other words, if the costs of intervening into a market with monopolies (e.g, Microsoft) are more than any benefits received (e.g., advances in computer operating systems), then such intervention is questionable. Thus, applied economists are actively attempting to measure the benefits and cost of various policies designed to promote efficient resource allocation by constraining monopoly-power activities.

Understanding barriers to entry

In April 2000, Judge Thomas Penfield Jackson based his ruling against Microsoft in an antitrust suit on the grounds that the company's monopoly operating system is protected by an "applications barrier to entry" made up of 70,000 Windows-based software programs. The amount it would cost an operating system vendor to create 70,000 applications is prohibitively large. The DC Circuit Court of Appeals overturned the ruling and in November 2001, and without further appeal, the case was settled, with Microsoft agreeing to share its programs with third-party companies. The cause of a monopoly (such as Microsoft) is barriers (obstacles) to entry. If other firms could enter the market, there would likely be no monopoly. **Barriers to entry** are anything that allows existing (incumbent) firms to earn pure profits without threat of entry by other firms. Specifically, barriers to entry are either legal or technical obstacles. One type of *legal monopoly* is established by a state or federal government awarding only one firm an exclusive franchise to provide a commodity. The government may create such a monopoly because there are increasing returns to scale over a wide range of output and thus one firm can supply the market more efficiently than two or more firms. For example, in electric power generation, the LAC curve declines over a wide range of output, which results in one firm's average cost of production being lower than if a number of smaller firms supplied power.

Barriers to entry. Obstacles that allow existing firms to earn pure profits without a threat of entry by other firms. *E.g., only the US Postal Service can legally place a letter in an individual's mailbox.*

Alternatively, if society deems that unrestricted competition among firms in an industry is undesirable, a government may establish a legal monopoly by granting a firm exclusive rights to operate.[1] Patents are examples of this type of legal monopoly. A firm has a *patent monopoly* when a government has conferred to it the exclusive right—through issuance of a patent—to make, use, or vend its own invention or discovery. Firms including IBM, Polaroid, and Xerox have varying degrees of monopoly power through patent protection.

A 1998 decision by the US Court of Appeals for the Federal Circuit, *State Street v. Signature Financial Group,* threw out a judicial rule against business-method patents. A business-method patent is one on a particular method of doing business, such as the concept of frequent-flyer miles. Since *State Street*, the number of applications for class 705 patents (patents on business-related data-processing methods and technologies) increased from 1340 in 1998 to 15,389 in 2009. The controversy surrounding intellectual property rights on business methods is similar to the controversies on software patents and gene patents.

What prevents you from establishing a mail service? The legal barrier to entry prevents you.

Technological barriers to entry may result when a firm's technology results in decreasing LAC over a wide range of output, knowledge of a low-cost productive technique, or control of a strategic resource. Such monopolies are termed **natural monopolies**, because, in contrast to legal monopolies, market forces alone would result in a monopoly. An example of a strategic resource monopoly is China's 95 percent control of rare earth minerals supply (a set of 17 elements in the periodic table). Since the mid-1980s, rare earth minerals started to be used in computers and other electronic products. Chinese leader Deny Xiaoping stated, "The Middle East has oil, but China has rare earth." Similarly, the De Beers Company of South Africa owns over 70 percent of the world's diamond deposits and had contracts with other producers to purchase almost all the total diamond production for sale through its central selling organization. However, in 2000, producers in Russia, Canada, and Australia started to distribute diamonds outside of the De Beers marketing channel, effectively ending De Beers' monopoly.

Sometimes, however, progress can directly impact these natural monopolies. For example, it is currently possible to manufacture diamonds that even jewelers can barely distinguish from naturally occurring diamonds. The cost of this manufacturing process is half the current market price of diamonds. In the near future, DeBeers may not have the level of entry barriers that currently exists. Diamonds may last forever, but not their technological barriers to entry.

Natural monopoly. Market forces result in only one firm in an industry. *E.g., only one airline offering service to a particular community.*

Application: The Internet and barriers to entry

In any economy, the degree of barriers to entry is a major determinant in a firm's level of market share and profit. Exclusivity is rewarded in being able to command and control a market with barriers to entry. The advent of the Internet has removed much of this exclusivity by promoting broad and massive market participation. Command and control markets are being replaced with decentralized control, which is a tenet of perfectly competitive efficiency. The Internet offers a market as a web of interrelationships with low barriers to entry. As the Internet continues to evolve, barriers to entry will further decline, with easy firm entry and consumer participation.

The Internet was developed by the US Department of Defense, with the aid of military contractors and universities, to generate a communication network that could survive a nuclear attack. In 1993, there were 130 websites and less than 2 million hosts (computer Internet links). By 2009, there were 234 million websites and over 700 million hosts. In 2007, over 875 million households shopped by the Internet.

The Internet has grown more rapidly than anyone envisioned. It is removing barriers to entry by opening up new avenues of communications between consumers and firms. A completely new economic system has evolved on the Internet, consisting of low-cost communications with interconnected electronic markets. For example, a US consumer can avoid paying the higher price for a drug offered by a firm with a US patent monopoly by purchasing the drug on the Internet from a foreign supplier. Emerging services and legal frameworks are being developed that promote market efficiency by removing old barriers to entry. On a broader note, the Internet transcends new markets composed of hardware links. People on the Internet respond differently than if they were meeting on the telephone or in person. Thus, a whole new culture, as well as an economic system, is emerging.

Determining the price and output

As with any monopoly, the jury has a right to judge both the law as well as the fact in controversy.

(John Jay)

Translation: A monopoly determines both its output level and per-unit price.

The objective of a monopoly is no different from all other types of firms—they attempt to maximize profits. To maximize profits, monopolies can first determine the profit-maximizing output and then determine from the market demand curve the price required to sell all this output. Alternatively, they can first determine the profit-maximizing price and then from the market demand curve determine the level of output that can be sold at this price. The resulting profit-maximizing price/output combination will be the same regardless of which method is employed. Both are based on a monopoly determining its equilibrium price and output given the market demand curve. This market demand curve is downward-sloping, so if a monopoly reduces output, the price it receives for this output will increase. Unlike a perfectly competitive price-taking firm, a monopoly has control over the market price (is a **price maker**) by varying its output.

Does a monopoly charge the highest price it can? No, the objective of a monopoly is not to charge the highest price but instead to maximize profit.

Price maker. An agent who sets the market price. *E.g., the sole gas station in an isolated town.*

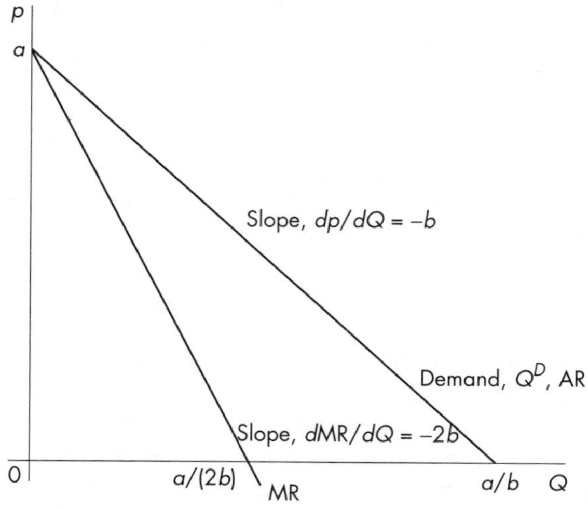

Figure 12.1 **Linear market demand curve.** The marginal revenue curve bisects the linear demand curve and the vertical axis.

Consider the following inverse linear market demand curve:

$$\text{AR} = p = a - bQ,$$

$$\text{TR} = (\text{AR})Q = pQ = aQ - bQ^2,$$

$$\text{MR} = \partial\text{TR}/\partial Q = a - 2bQ,$$

$$= a - bQ - bQ,$$

$$= \text{AR} - bQ,$$

where parameters $a, b > 0$. For a linear demand curve, MR is twice as steep as AR, so it will bisect any horizontal line drawn from the vertical axis to the AR curve. For example, as illustrated in Figure 12.1, the intercept on the horizontal axis is a/b for the AR curve and $a/(2b)$ for the MR curve. The MR intercept on the horizontal axis is half of the AR intercept.

The market demand curve is the monopoly's average revenue. That is, it is the AR (price per unit) that a firm receives for a given level of output. In Figure 12.1, AR is falling as the firm increases output, because consumers are willing and able to purchase more of the commodity at the lower level of AR (price). Falling AR implies that MR is below it. MR is equal to AR plus the adjustment factor, $-bQ$, so, given $-b < 0$ (falling AR), then MR < AR. Recall that MR is the additional revenue associated with an additional unit of output. For a given level of output, MR < AR, because, for a firm to sell an additional unit of output, it must lower its price on all the units to be sold, not just on the additional units. The adjustment factor, $-bQ$, accounts for this condition. For each additional output sold, price falls by $-b$. Multiplying this fall in price by the number of units sold, Q, results in the adjustment to AR for determining MR.

Profit maximization

Mathematically, short-run profit is maximized by

$$\max_Q \pi = \max_Q [\text{TR}(Q) - \text{STC}(Q)].$$

The first-order condition (FOC) is then

$$\frac{\partial \pi}{\partial Q} = \frac{\partial \text{TR}}{\partial Q} - \frac{\partial \text{STC}}{\partial Q} = 0,$$

that is,

$$\text{MR}(Q) - \text{SMC}(Q) = 0.$$

A profit-maximizing monopoly will equate MR to SMC to determine its optimal level of output. As illustrated in Figure 12.2, the profit-maximizing output Q^* corresponds to where MR = SMC. The firm will produce Q^* units of output and, given the market demand curve Q^D, it can sell all of this output at the price p^*. Price p^* corresponds to the level of output Q^* that consumers are willing and able to purchase.

As in perfect competition, the SMC curve for a monopoly determines the profit-maximizing price and output. However, in contrast to perfect competition, the SMC curve above SAVC is not the monopoly's short-run supply curve. Recall that a supply curve illustrates how much a firm is willing and able to supply at a particular price. In Figure 12.2, if the SMC curve for a monopoly is a supply curve, at a price p^* the firm would be willing and able to supply Q' units of output. Although the firm is able to supply Q' at p^*, it is unwilling to do so. The profit-maximizing output is Q^*, and the firm can sell all of this output at the

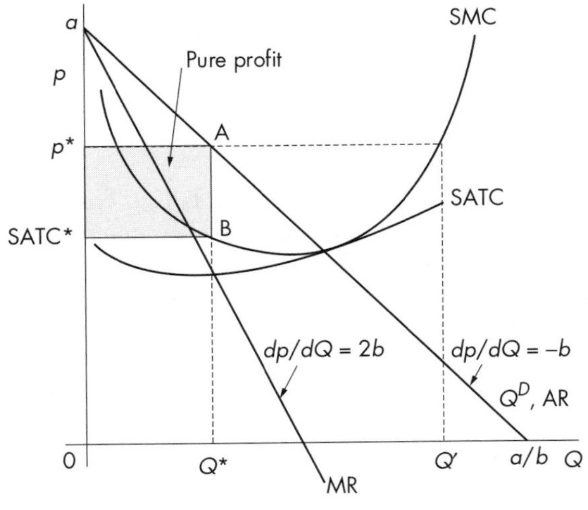

Figure 12.2 **Price and output determination for a monopoly.** The monopoly equates MR to SMC for determining its profit-maximizing output. Given the market demand curve, it can sell all of this output Q^* at price p^*.

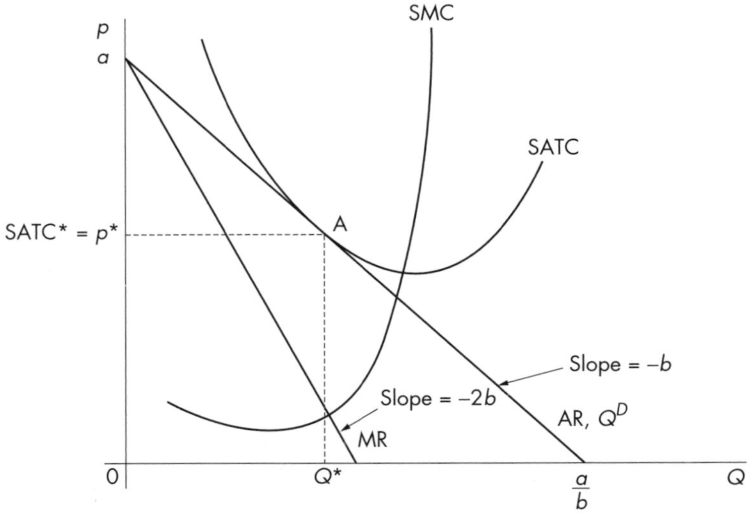

Figure 12.3 **Short-run profit maximization for a monopoly earning a normal profit.** At Q^*, price $p^* = \text{SATC}^*$, so $\text{TR}^* = \text{STC}$.

price p^*. We cannot determine a monopoly's short-run supply curve without requiring some rather restrictive assumptions. Instead, we note that the same factors that shift a monopoly's short-run supply curve also shift the SMC curve in the same direction, so we can think of the SMC curve as a proxy for the supply curve.

Recall that the SATC curve indicates whether a firm is earning a pure profit or a normal profit, or operating at a loss. In Figure 12.2, price p^* is above SATC* for output level Q^*. This indicates that the monopoly is earning a pure profit, represented by the shaded area SATC*p^*AB. The monopoly's TR is represented by the area Op^*AQ* and its STC by the area O(SATC*)BQ*. The difference is pure profit, the shaded area SATC*p^*AB. As illustrated in Figure 12.3, in the short run, a monopoly can also earn only a normal profit, when $p^* =$ SATC*, due to increased input prices, or a decrease in the demand for its output may result in the monopoly only earning a short-run normal profit. In this case, TR* = STC*, represented by the area Op^*AQ*.

In the short run, a monopoly can also operate at a loss if demand falls or costs increase. Home delivery of dairy products is an example where a monopoly in many communities had short-run losses (and in the long run went out of business). A monopoly with short-run losses is illustrated in Figure 12.4, with the losses represented by the shaded area p^*(SATC*)BA. Analogous with a perfectly competitive firm, as long as price is above SAVC, a monopoly will continue to operate in the short run. The monopoly will cover all of its STVC and have some revenue left over for paying a proportion of its TFC. For this condition, the monopoly minimizes its losses by operating. If price falls below SAVC, the monopoly is unable to cover its STVC and will minimize losses by shutting down.

In summary, a monopoly can earn a pure profit or a normal profit, or operate at a loss in the short run. Thus, a firm's level of profit is not an indicator of its degree of monopoly power. As we will see, the percentage markup in price over marginal cost, $(p - \text{SMC})/p$, is the indicator of monopoly power.

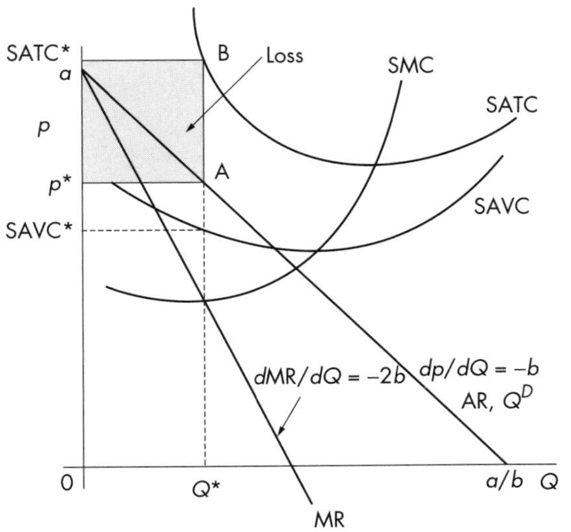

Figure 12.4 **Price and output determination for a monopoly operating at a loss.** At Q^*, $\text{SAVC}^* < p^* < \text{SATC}^*$, so the monopoly is minimizing losses by operating at a loss.

Example 12.1 Calculating profit maximization

Consider the following market demand curve and firm's short-run total cost curve:

$$Q = 11 - \tfrac{1}{5}p,$$

$$\text{STC} = 5Q + 1.$$

Given this market demand, solving for p yields the firm's inverse demand curve

$$p = 55 - 5Q.$$

Profit maximization for this firm is then

$$\begin{aligned}\max_Q \pi &= \max_Q[\text{TR}(Q) - \text{STC}(Q)]\\ &= \max_Q[pQ - (5Q + 1)]\\ &= \max_Q[(55 - 5Q)Q - (5Q + 1)].\end{aligned}$$

The FOC is

$$\frac{\partial \pi}{\partial Q} = 55 - 10Q^* - 5 = 0,$$

that is,

$$\text{MR} - \text{SMC} = 0.$$

Solving this FOC for Q^* gives

$$Q^* = 5, p^* = \$30, \pi^* = \$124.$$

Alternatively, we could determine this profit-maximizing output and price combination by maximizing profit in terms of price:

$$\max_p \pi = \max_p [\text{TR}(Q) - \text{STC}(Q)]$$
$$= \max_p \left[p(11 - \tfrac{1}{5}p) - 5(11 - \tfrac{1}{5}p) - 1\right].$$

The FOC is then

$$\frac{\partial \pi}{\partial q} = 11 - \tfrac{2}{5}p + 1 = 0.$$

Solving for p yields the same profit-maximizing price of \$30.

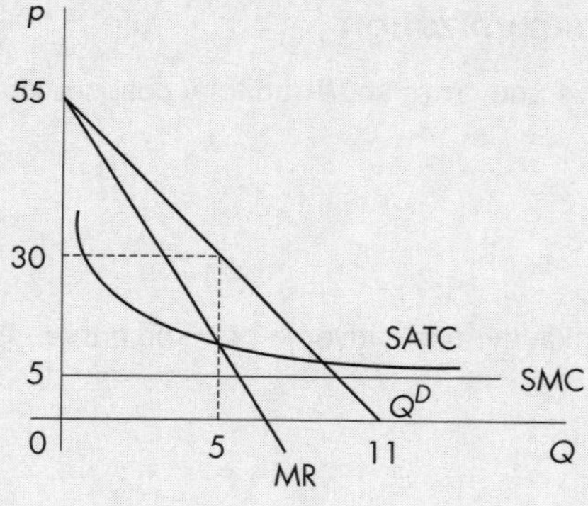

Calculating the Lerner Index

Monopoly power is like coffee—depending on the barriers, it can be strong or weak.
(Michael Wetzstein)

Translation: The degree of monopoly power depends on a firm's elasticity of demand.

An implication of a profit-maximizing firm, regardless of its level of monopoly power, is that it only operates in the elastic portion of the demand curve. Given SMC > 0, a profit-maximizing firm will equate MR $=$ SMC > 0. Using the product rule of differentiation and recalling $TR = pQ$, we find that the relationships of MR to price and to elasticity of market demand are

$$MR = \frac{dTR}{dQ} = p + \frac{\partial p}{\partial Q}Q.$$

In other words, MR is equal to price plus the adjustment factor $(\partial p/\partial Q)Q$. As demonstrated with the linear demand function, for each additional output sold, price falls by $\partial p/\partial Q$. Multiplying this fall in price by the number of units sold, Q, results in the adjustment to AR for determining MR. Factoring out the price from the right-hand side of $MR = p + (\partial p/\partial Q)Q$ yields the relationship between MR and elasticity of demand:

$$\begin{aligned} MR &= p\left(1 + \frac{\partial p}{\partial Q}\frac{Q}{p}\right) \\ &= p\left(1 + \frac{1}{\varepsilon^D}\right), \end{aligned}$$

where $\varepsilon^D = (\partial Q/\partial p)(p/Q)$, the own-price elasticity of demand. For $MR > 0$, $1 + 1/\varepsilon^D > 0$, which implies $\varepsilon^D < -1$ (elastic). If $\varepsilon^D > -1$ (inelastic), then $MR = dTR/dQ < 0$, so a decrease in Q will increase TR. Given $dSTC/dQ > 0$, STC decreases with this decrease in Q, yielding an increase in pure profit. A profit-maximizing firm can continue to reduce Q and increase profit within the inelastic portion of the demand curve. Thus, a firm will reduce output until it is in the elastic portion of the demand curve, where MR = SMC. Table 12.1 summarizes the relationships between demand elasticity and marginal revenue.

Table 12.1. Demand elasticity and marginal revenue

Demand	Marginal Revenue (MR)
Elastic, $\varepsilon^D < -1$	$MR > 0$
Inelastic, $\varepsilon^D > -1$	$MR < 0$
Unitary, $\varepsilon^D = -1$	$MR = 0$

At MR = SMC,

$$MR = p(1 + 1/\varepsilon^D) = SMC.$$

Solving for p gives

$$p = \frac{SMC}{1 + 1/\varepsilon^D}.$$

Under perfect competition, a firm is facing a perfectly elastic demand curve, $\varepsilon^D = -\infty$, so $1/\varepsilon^D = 0$, indicating the condition of $p = \text{SMC}$ for profit maximization. Instead, a monopoly charges a higher price. Since it only operates on the elastic portion of the demand curve ($\varepsilon^D < -1$), $0 < 1 + 1/\varepsilon^D < 1$, so $p > \text{SMC}$.

A measure of the degree of monopoly power is the percentage markup in price over marginal cost $(p - \text{SMC})/p$. Specifically, given

$$p(1 + 1/\varepsilon^D) = \text{SMC},$$

solving for $(p - \text{SMC})/p$ yields the **Lerner Index (L_I)**:

$$p + p/\varepsilon^D = \text{SMC},$$

$$p - \text{SMC} = -p/\varepsilon^D,$$

$$L_I = (p - \text{SMC})/p = -1/\varepsilon^D.$$

The Lerner Index L_I [developed by Abba Lerner (1903–1982) in 1934] varies between 0 and 1 and measures the percentage markup in price due to monopoly power.[2] This relative difference in price and marginal cost is dependent on the elasticity of demand. Under perfect competition, $p = \text{SMC}$, $\varepsilon^D = -\infty$, so $L_I = 0$. The firm is exercising zero monopoly power. Alternatively, if $\varepsilon^D = -1$, then $L_I = 1$, indicating the existence of monopoly power. At $-1 \geq \varepsilon^D > -\infty$, corresponding to $0 < L_I \leq 1$, a relative wedge between price and SMC exists, $p > SMC$. The magnitude of this wedge, and thus the degree of monopoly power, is determined by the elasticity of demand. When the demand curve becomes less elastic, the wedge increases and L_I approaches 1. Recall that a determinant of demand elasticity is the closeness of substitutes, so this wedge for a profit-maximizing firm without close substitutes will be large relative to a firm in a market with many competitors. A monopoly is concerned with the effect a high price has on consumption, when consumers react to a price increase by greatly reducing their demand. Thus, a monopoly will not charge the highest price it can for its output. Instead, it will determine the elasticity of demand for its output and, based on this elasticity, will calculate L_I, the markup of price over marginal cost as a percentage of the price. In practice, the Lerner Index can be difficult to calculate. This is particularly true in industries such as telecommunications where calculating a firm's marginal cost can be difficult.

Lerner Index (L_I). A measure of the degree of monopoly power. *E.g., even for a firm who is the sole producer in an industry, if $L_I = 0$, then it is not exercising any monopoly power.*

Table 12.2 lists measurements of the Lerner Index for the steel and semiconductor industries. The high Lerner Index for Bethlehem steel relative to the other steel firms indicates that Bethlehem exercised a greater degree of monopoly power. Note that the monopoly power in the semiconductor industry is more evenly distributed among the firms.

Table 12.2. Measurements of the Lerner Index for the steel and semiconductor industries

Firm	Lerner Index, 1983–1989
Steel Industry	
Armco	0.063
Bethlehem	0.849
LTV Corporation	0.103
Semiconductor Industry	
Advanced Micro Devices	0.358
Intel Corporation	0.593
Texas Instruments	0.442

Source: J.F. Nieberding, "The Effect of U.S. Antidumping Law on Firms' Market Power: An Empirical Test," *Review of Industrial Organization* 14 (1999): 65–84.

Example 12.2. Lerner Index

From Example 12.1, the profit-maximizing monopoly output and price are $Q^* = 5$ and $p^* = 30$, associated with SMC $= 5$ and $Q = 11 - \frac{1}{5}p$. The elasticity of demand at this profit-maximizing price and output is then

$$\varepsilon^D = \frac{\partial Q}{\partial p}\frac{p^*}{Q^*} = -\frac{1}{5}\frac{30}{5} = -\frac{30}{25} = -\frac{6}{5}.$$

The Lerner Index is

$$L_I = -1/\varepsilon^D = \tfrac{5}{6}.$$

Application: Is the Lerner Index a practical measure of antitrust enforcement?

Addressed by K. Elzinga and D. Mills, economists generally agree that firms have positive price–cost margins ($p >$ SMC). More often than not, firms with Lerner Indices indicating market power are not monopolies in the sense that they constrain output and have little or no competition. Instead, firms' price–cost margins reflect their superior skill, foresight, and industry, which are the result of competition. Large Lerner Indices may also reveal the necessity of covering fixed costs. For example, the cost structure of firms in the technology and pharmaceutical industries requires substantial costs in product development, so marginal cost pricing ($p =$ SMC) is neither feasible nor desirable.

With various potential explanations for a Lerner Index of a given magnitude, it is an unreliable stand-alone indicator of the degree of a firm's market power as a genuine monopoly problem. Thus, its use as a measure of market power in antitrust law is questionable, and as a consequence courts have not embraced the Index as an appropriate indicator of a monopoly. It has, however, influenced merger enforcement, where the relevant question is not whether a firm has market power, but whether a merger would increase this market power.

As summed by K. Elzinga and D. Mills, the legacy of the Lerner Index will not be in its use in antitrust enforcement, but in clarifying the nature of monopoly and emphasizing the implications of departures from perfect competition (p = SMC).

Source: K.G Elzinga and D.E. Mills, "The Lerner Index of Monopoly Power: Origins and Uses," *American Economic Review* 101 (2011): 558–564.

Establishing long-run equilibrium

Even if you are on the right track, you will get run over if you just sit there.

(Will Rogers)

Translation: A firm only has the opportunity of earning a pure profit in the short run.

Long-run equilibrium for a monopoly is illustrated in Figure 12.5. The SATC and LAC curves are tangent at the firm's profit-maximizing output level Q^*, where

$$\text{SMC} = \text{LMC} = \text{MR}.$$

At this equilibrium output and price (Q^*, p^*), the firm is earning a normal profit. In the long run, the firm can only earn a normal profit. If it was earning a pure profit in the short run, when the firm is sold in the long run, the new owners will pay a higher price for the firm than if it was earning only a normal profit. This higher price increases the cost of operation, resulting in an upward shift of the cost curves. Competition for purchasing the firm will result in cost curves for the new owners shifting up to the point of zero pure profit (normal profit). The market price for the firm will increase until, in the long run, all short-run pure profits are squeezed out, p = SATC = LAC.

Even if the firm is not sold, the cost of production (in terms of implicit cost) will increase over time. In the long run, a firm that earned a short-run pure profit will be worth more, say \$100,000. Thus, the owners of the firm have a higher implicit cost of production. Their opportunity cost for operating the firm has increased because they could sell the firm and receive this increase in price (\$100,000) and invest it in another activity. This is called the **opportunity cost of capital**. If the alternative activity had an annual rate of return of, say, 10 percent, then the firm's implicit cost of production would be \$10,000 higher. Short-run pure profit is converted into implicit cost.

Alternatively, if the firm was operating at a loss in the short run, the firm will not be worth as much. Thus, the cost curves will shift downward, resulting in a long-run normal profit.

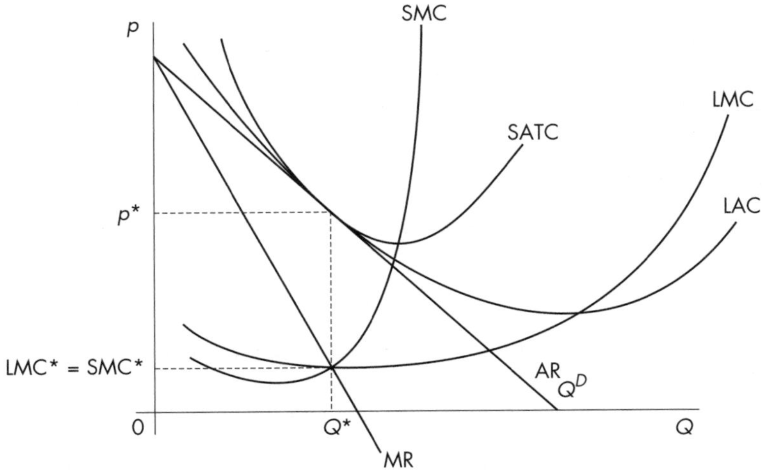

Figure 12.5 **Long-run equilibrium for a monopoly firm.** The SATC and LAC curves are tangent at the firm's profit-maximizing output level Q^*, where MR = LMC = SMC.

Opportunity cost of capital. The profit forgone by not investing financial capital in another activity. *E.g., keeping the equity in your home has an opportunity cost of forgone profit by not investing it in another activity.*

The worth of a monopoly based on its long-run pure-profit potential is called **monopoly rent**. It is the rent that a possible entrant would be willing to pay for the monopoly. For example, if the monopoly was based on a patent, this monopoly rent would be the value of the patent. Given positive monopoly rents, associated opportunity cost exists that when considered result in only long-run normal profits. Without considering that cost adjusts to rents, it is possible to assume that a monopoly will earn a long-run pure profit.

Monopoly rent. The rent an entrant would be willing to pay for a monopoly. *E.g., the amount a food service firm would be willing to pay for the concessions contract at a football stadium.*

The toughest thing about success is that you've got to keep on being a success.
(Irving Berlin)

This fact that cost adjusts to price is particularly important in basic business decision making. Since firms, even those with monopoly power, can only make a pure profit in the short run, owners of firms cannot continue their present activities and expect continued pure profits. If they want to continue to reap a pure profit, they must anticipate market trends so as to sell their firms when conditions are right and be early entrants into markets where firms are earning short-run pure profits. Individuals who can detect market signals for the most profitable timing to enter and exit markets are able to increase their wealth. However, many individuals or firms lack knowledge or are unwilling to act because they can maximize their utility by staying in a particular activity even if it means earning only a normal profit.

Measuring welfare loss from monopoly power

> *Criminal: A person with predatory instincts who has not sufficient capital to form a monopoly.*
>
> (Howard Scott)

As discussed in Chapter 1, the major objective of economics is improving social welfare. Thus, market structures that result in economic inefficiency are considered inferior. Specifically, a monopoly market structure is inferior to a perfectly competitive market structure, based on monopoly's inefficiency.

A monopoly is efficient in terms of both technical and allocative efficiency. A monopoly will produce on the production frontier (technologically efficient) and employ least-cost production (allocatively efficient). However, a monopoly is not scale-efficient. It does not equate price to marginal cost. Thus, the monopoly's long-run equilibrium position is inefficient; it misallocates resources. This inefficiency is characterized by two conditions. First, as indicated in Figure 12.5, $p^* > \text{SMC}^* = \text{LMC}^*$. As discussed in Chapter 10, the price a household pays for a commodity is the marginal utility of consumption, that is, the monetary measure of how much an additional unit of a commodity is worth to the household. Marginal cost is the cost of producing an additional amount of the commodity. Thus, if price is greater than marginal cost (as in the case of monopoly power) society would prefer the firm to increase output. In perfect competition, price is equal to marginal cost. What society is willing to pay for an additional unit of output is equal to what it cost society to produce this additional unit of output. But a monopoly instead restricts output and increases the price, so what society is willing to pay for an additional unit of output is greater than what it cost society to produce this additional unit.

The second inefficiency of a monopoly is that it does not operate at full production capacity. At **full capacity**, the average cost of production is at a minimum, called the *minimum efficient scale*—the average cost of production cannot be lowered by using more or less of any one input. A monopoly does not operate at this minimum point of SATC or LAC. In contrast, a perfectly competitive firm does operate at both minimums. The perfectly competitive long-run equilibrium, corresponding to the minimum point of LAC, is illustrated in Figure 9.18. In contrast, a monopoly's long-run equilibrium, illustrated in Figure 12.5, does not correspond to the minimum point of LAC. For an efficient operation, output should increase to full capacity. The monopoly is not utilizing its inputs in an efficient manner. The fixed costs are spread over too few units of output, resulting in excess capacity and inefficiency.

Full capacity. Average cost of production is at a minimum. *E.g., a movie theater with monopoly power will not set the ticket price so that all the seats are filled. Instead, the theater will increase the ticket price and experience some empty seats (excess capacity).*

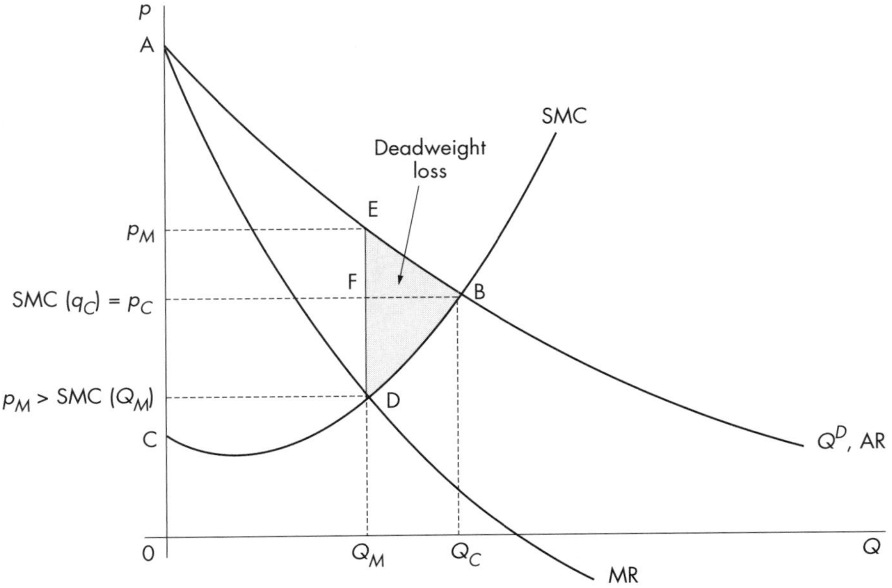

Figure 12.6 **The deadweight loss resulting from monopoly power.** A firm with monopoly power restricts output from Q_C to Q_M and increases price from p_C to p_M. This results in an efficiency loss represented as deadweight loss, the shaded area DEB.

We can represent this inefficiency and associated welfare loss with a monopoly by the deadweight loss in consumer and producer surplus. As illustrated in Figure 12.6, the perfectly competitive equilibrium is (Q_C, p_C). Economic efficiency, measured as the total surplus representing producer plus consumer surplus, is the area CAB, where p_CAB is consumer surplus and Cp_CB is producer surplus. A firm with monopoly power restricts output from Q_C to Q_M, resulting in price increasing from p_C to p_M. Consumer surplus is reduced to p_MAE, with the firm capturing some of the lost consumer surplus, the area p_Cp_MEF. This captured consumer surplus is a measure of the firm's exploitation of consumers. Producer surplus, with monopoly power, is the area Cp_MED. Thus, the efficiency loss in social welfare is the area DEB. This is a deadweight loss resulting from monopoly power, and provides a signal that some governmental intervention may be desirable. However, it does not suggest a particular course of action. The causes of this inefficiency should first be determined, and then a possible set of actions formulated.

Example 12.3 Calculating deadweight loss associated with a monopoly

From Example 12.1, the monopoly's profit-maximization solution is $Q^* = 5$, $p^* = \$30$, with associated $\pi^* = \$124$ and TFC = \$1. Producer surplus is then

$$\text{PS} = \pi + \text{TFC} = 124 + 1 = \$125.$$

This is the area of the rectangle (30 − 5)(5 − 0) = 125. Consumer surplus is

$$CS = (55 - 30)(5 - 0)/2 = 125/2 = \$62.50.$$

Under perfect competition, p = MC = 5, with Q = 10. This results in TR = \$50 and STC = \$51, with $\pi = -1$. Thus, producer surplus is zero:

$$PS = -1 + 1 = 0.$$

Consumer surplus is

$$CS = (55 - 5)(10 - 0)/2 = \$250.$$

Deadweight loss is then the difference between the sum of consumer and producer surplus under perfect competition and this sum under monopoly:

$$\text{deadweight loss} = 250 + 0 - (62.50 + 125) = \$62.50.$$

In the figure, this is represented by the shaded area.

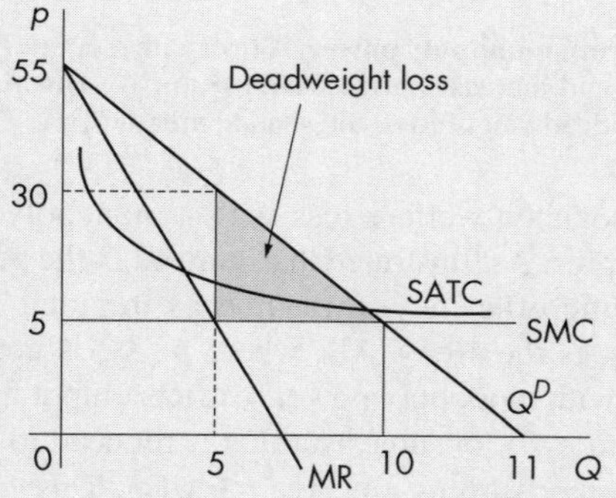

Rent-seeking behavior

Prior to their government bailout in 2008, Fannie Mae and Freddie Mac (government-sponsored firms in the home mortgage market) were among the top Washington lobbying spenders. They spent, in the space of a decade, over \$170 million in lobbying activities. As of 2010, the bailout has cost American taxpayers \$135 billion to pay for losses on defaulted home loans. This illustrates a further efficiency loss associated with a monopoly—expense incurred to obtain and maintain monopoly power (called **rent-seeking behavior**). In this case, *rent* is defined as the monopoly's producer surplus, represented in Figure 12.6 by the area Cp_MED. The potential for obtaining this rent may lead firms to engage in rent-seeking behavior. In general, rent seeking is what economists call the bending of public power for private economic advantage.

Rent-seeking behavior. Expense incurred to obtain and maintain monopoly power. *E.g., the government lobbying that a firm does for maintaining a legal monopoly.*

Firms may incur both strategic expenses in the form of erecting barriers to entry or administrative expenses such as lobbying governmental representatives or legal defense against antitrust actions. In the extreme case of rent-seeking behavior, all monopoly rents will be allocated to this behavior. Assuming that all this rent-seeking behavior is socially wasteful (has no social value), the actual deadweight loss is then represented by the area Cp_MEBD. This represents the producer surplus (rents) plus the deadweight loss DEB. In truth, all rent-seeking behavior is probably not socially wasteful, so including producer surplus as a component of deadweight loss may be used to represent the upward boundary of efficiency loss.

Application: Measurement of real-world distortions

The twisted reality of the real world interferes with the well-oiled economy of theory.
(Michael Wetzstein)

One of the first to estimate the deadweight loss from monopoly power, A.C. Harberger (of Harberger triangles) determined the loss to be only 0.1 percent of total national income. This low result was criticized by G.J. Stigler, partly because Harberger assumed $\varepsilon^D = -1$. Monopolies will operate in a range where $\varepsilon^D < -1$, resulting in more deadweight loss by reducing output and increasing price beyond the point of $\varepsilon^D = -1$. Allowing for $\varepsilon^D < -1$ and addressing other concerns (including rent-seeking behavior), economists have estimated the losses to be up to 7 percent of GNP. These estimates are approximately the same magnitude as or slightly higher than twice the GNP annual growth rate. Thus, there may not be much to be gained by pursuing antimonopoly policies, such as regulation or breaking up of monopolies. The cost of such policies may far exceed the benefits. However, this does not consider the potential future gain in efficiency from the development of an efficient industry. Even a small improvement in efficiency when compounded into the future can have a major affect on an economy. For example, the breakup of AT&T has resulted in a major increase in efficiency for telecommunications. This efficiency gain has resulted in substantial price reductions for consumers and has stimulated innovation. In 1999, the companies created out of AT&T were worth approximately $810 billion, versus $59 billion before the breakup in 1982. This is a 1300 percent increase, compared with a market rise of around 140 percent for IBM, which was not broken up. In 2010, the current AT&T is the seventh largest company in the United States and has reacquired 10 of the 22 companies it lost control of in the 1982 breakup.

Economic theory may indicate a deadweight loss associated with market imperfection, but in the real world the cost of correcting the inefficiency may exceed the benefit. It is up to applied economists to estimate these benefits and costs and recommend what corrective market remedies are required.

Sources: A.C. Harberger, "Monopoly and Resource Allocation," *American Economic Review* 54 (1954) 77–87; G.J. Stigler, "The Statistics of Monopoly and Merger," *Journal of Political Economy* 64 (1956) 33–40.

Taxing rents

One proposed solution for inefficiency in monopoly power is taxing monopoly's profits. Either a **lump-sum tax** or a **profit tax** would reduce monopoly producer surplus. For the lump-sum tax system, we can represent profit as

$$\pi = pQ - \text{STC} - TR_T,$$

where TR_T is the lump-sum tax corresponding to the total tax-revenue collected. The FOC for profit maximization is then

$$\frac{\partial \pi}{\partial Q} = \text{MR} - \text{SMC} = 0.$$

From this FOC, there is no change in the optimal level of output or price, or for determining whether a firm should operate. The level of profit falls by the amount of the increase in the tax. In Figure 12.7, this is illustrated by the upward shift in the TFC and STC curves. However, with no change in the optimal output and price, the inefficiency of the monopoly still exists. Society would still prefer the monopoly to increase output and decrease price. Neither is the problem of resource misallocation solved by a lump-sum tax, because this tax does not affect the allocation of resources. It only affects the distribution of the total economic surplus, by taking some producer surplus away from the monopoly and reallocating it to others in society. Thus, the lump-sum tax is only beneficial if the reallocation of total surplus improves social welfare by redistributing the surplus away from socially wasteful rent-seeking behavior.

Lump-sum tax. A fixed level of tax independent of output level. *E.g., a city liquor license required for selling alcohol.*

Profit tax. A tax on a firm's profit. *E.g., the federal tax on corporate profits.*

Similarly, with a profit tax, there is no change in a monopoly's optimal level of output or price, or for determining whether it should operate. Specifically, we can represent a monopoly's profit with a profit tax as

$$\pi = pQ - \text{STC} - t(pQ - \text{STC}),$$

$$\pi = (1 - t)(pQ - \text{STC}),$$

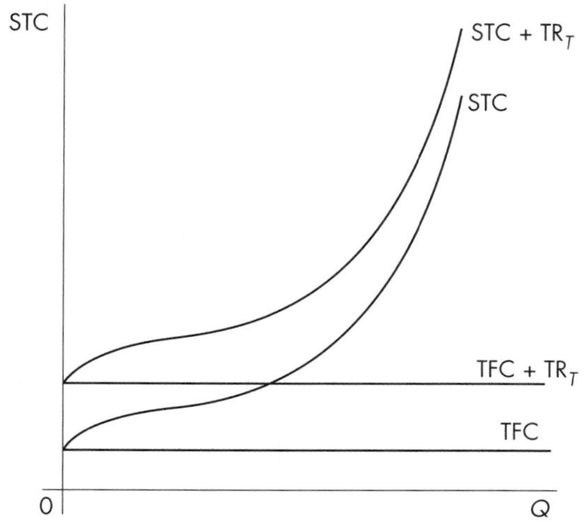

Figure 12.7 **Lump-sum or profit tax.** For both the lump-sum and profit taxes, only the TFC and STC curves shift upward, so such taxes do not affect the firm's profit-maximizing output or price.

where t is some percentage of profit that is taxed. The FOC is then

$$\frac{\partial \pi}{\partial Q} = (1 - t)(\text{MR} - \text{SMC}) = 0,$$

which implies that MR = SMC still remains as the condition for profit maximization. Thus, similar to a lump-sum tax, there is no change in the optimal level of output and price. The level of profit declines by the amount of the increase in the tax. Again, as illustrated in Figure 12.7, this results in an upward shift in the TFC and STC curves. The only difference is that since firms are taxed on a percentage of their profits, the TFC shifts upward for alternative profit levels. Thus, neither lump-sum nor profit taxes cure the ills of monopoly power, but do reduce the ability of a monopoly to engage in socially wasteful rent-seeking behavior.

Will taxing a monopoly remove its power? No, a monopoly will still have control over the output price.

Output and price will change by imposing an output or sales tax. Considering an output tax of τ per unit of output, the firm's profit is

$$\pi = pQ - \text{STC} - \tau Q,$$

The FOC is then

$$\frac{\partial \pi}{\partial Q} = \text{MR} - \text{SMC} - \tau = 0.$$

For a maximum, the second-order condition (SOC) requires $\partial \text{MR}/\partial Q - \partial \text{SMC}/\partial Q < 0$. The effect on output from a change in the tax can be determined by differentiating the FOC with respect to the tax:

$$\frac{\partial \text{MR}}{\partial Q}\frac{\partial Q}{\partial \tau} - \frac{\partial \text{SMC}}{\partial Q}\frac{\partial Q}{\partial \tau} = 1.$$

Solving for $\partial Q/\partial \tau$ yields

$$\frac{\partial Q}{\partial \tau} = \frac{1}{\dfrac{\partial \text{MR}}{\partial Q} - \dfrac{\partial \text{SMC}}{\partial Q}} < 0, \qquad \text{given the SOC.}$$

An increase in the output tax will reduce the firm's output. Given a negatively sloping demand curve, a decline in output will increase the output price. Such a tax has the reverse result of further decreasing the firm's output and increasing price, instead of improving efficiency by increasing output and reducing the price.

Franchise

The City and County of Denver, Colorado, requires three cable channels for public access programming in its franchise agreement with AT&T Broadband. This government issuance of a *franchise* is an alternative pricing policy, generally employed in cable television and radio airwaves markets. The right to be a monopoly within a local market or to control some public domain is sold (franchised), and the proceeds are rebated to the consumers within this market. The rebate is either in the form of tax relief or as provision of some public good. If a competitive auction is used to determine the price of the franchise,[3] then competition will drive up the franchise price to where only a normal profit will be earned by any owners. Government issues of oil leases and timber harvesting on public lands are similar forms of franchising.

However, once a franchise is established, it tends to perpetuate with the same franchise owners in control. Any renegotiation tends to occur without competitive bidding. Thus, as with taxes, an issuance of a franchise does not cure the problems associated with monopoly power. It may not even reduce the ability of the monopoly to engage in rent-seeking behavior unless the franchise is renegotiated with competitive bidding.

How to regulate a monopoly

The point is that you cannot be too greedy.

(Paul Krugman)

In the 1960s the US Justice Department was investigating IBM's dominance of punch-card machines. Until 1968, IBM was a one-stop shop. Customers bought a system from IBM that included the software and maintenance. This bundling of their products was a major barrier to entry for IBM's competitors.[4] The fear of impending antitrust action forced IBM to abandon their bundling practice. Microsoft has also engaged in bundling its products (the Internet browser with the operating system) but, unlike IBM, chose to engage in the antitrust actions.

If a monopoly results in a misallocation of resources, it is inefficient, and regulation may be required. However, prior to regulation, the degree of inefficiency should be determined, because the cost of regulation may exceed any benefits gained. A firm with monopoly power may choose to not exercise its power (called **limit price analysis**), either because they are concerned that restricting output and increasing price will result in other firms entering the market or because they are concerned that they will be regulated. So it may not be in their best interest to be too greedy. Thus, even the *threat* of entry by another firm or the *threat* of regulation may cause a firm expanding output by equating price to marginal cost and, thus, operating efficiency.

Limit price analysis. The threat of governmental regulation or entry by other firms into the market restricts a firm from increasing price above marginal cost. *E.g., an airline may set its price close to marginal cost to avoid other airlines invading its space.*

As an example of limit price analysis, consider the breakfast-cereal industry. In 1995, Kellogg, General Mills, Post, and Quaker Oats controlled over 80 percent of the market. Profits for Kellogg (the market leader) were three times higher than the average profits for all US manufacturers. Cereal prices were also far outpacing inflation for other foods. As a result of this market condition, Congress considered asking the US Attorney General to investigate the cereal industry for antitrust violations. In addition, store-brand and other generic cereals were appearing on the market. Generic cereal makers generally forgo advertising expense (which is approximately 40 percent of the cost for a box of Cheerios), and thus generics cost 30–40 percent less than name-brand cereals. This threat of antitrust actions and the entry of new firms in the industry have resulted in the cereal industry becoming more competitive without governmental regulation.

Governmental regulation

In 1911, the US government succeeded in splitting the oil monopoly created by Standard Oil into 34 companies. A more recent example is the break-up of AT&T into eight companies in 1984 by agreement between AT&T and the US Department of Justice. On June 7, 2000, a US District Court ruled to split the Microsoft Corporation into two smaller companies, one to deal with operating systems and another with the Internet browsers and software applications. However, that ruling was subsequently overturned.

Two main government policies for addressing the inefficiencies of monopoly power are to break up the firm or to regulate it. If the LAC is declining over a wide range of output (a natural monopoly), it may not be feasible to break the monopoly up, and so the government may instead regulate it. Alternatively, if the LAC is relatively flat over a wide range of output, then it may be more efficient to break up the monopoly than to regulate it.

Regulatory policies vary according to the type of government. Socialist governments will tend to regulate through direct government ownership. An example is Indian Airlines, owned by India. In contrast, capitalist governments will tend to establish public utility commissions to oversee private (nongovernment) firms. An example is the electric power companies within the United States, which are privately owned but publicly regulated.

Does the government regulate a monopoly or does the monopoly regulate the government? It depends; the rent-seeking behavior of a monopoly may influence governmental policies more than the governmental regulation influences the monopoly's activities.

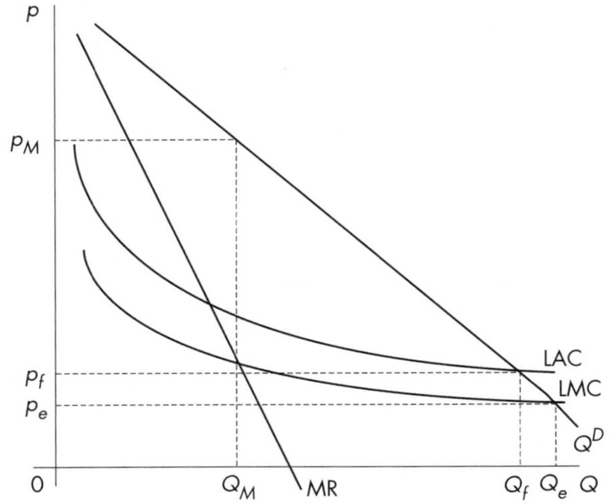

Figure 12.8 **Public utility regulation for a natural monopoly.** Three possible pricing policies for a public utility are monopoly pricing (p_M, Q_M), full-cost pricing (p_f, Q_f) and marginal-cost pricing (p_e, Q_e).

Whether a firm is government-owned or private, a mechanism design is required for determining the government-regulated firm's price and output. As illustrated in Figure 12.8, three major pricing policies exist for price and output determination, where the LAC is drawn only in the portion of increasing returns to scale. (If the demand curve is not in the increasing returns to scale area of LAC, then the appropriate policy may be to break up rather than regulate the monopoly.) The first pricing policy is *monopoly pricing*. In Figure 12.8, this is the unregulated output and price equilibrium (Q_M, p_M). Assuming positive monopoly rents, so $p >$ LAC, the monopoly is earning a long-run pure profit. The monopoly is Pareto-inefficient with this pricing policy, because $p >$ LMC. The Pareto-efficient pricing policy is one that sets $p =$ LMC. This is called *marginal-cost pricing* (Q_e, p_e). A problem with marginal-cost pricing is that the firm will operate at a loss: price p_e is below LAC_e. Many public-utility agencies avoid this problem by allowing the regulated firm to price-discriminate (see Chapter 13), so it can potentially increase its revenue and not operate at a loss.

A public utility agency using marginal-cost pricing is faced with a difficulty in measuring marginal cost versus average cost. Calculating average cost only requires information on the level of total cost and output. Such information is generally available in accounting records, and, if not already provided, can be determined by dividing total cost by output. In contrast, calculating marginal cost requires not only information on the level of total cost, but also information on how total cost is changing for a change in output. The amount by which average cost has to be adjusted must be determined. Information on how costs are changing, given a change in output, is not generally available in accounting records and is relatively difficult to obtain. In both accounting and the popular press, marginal cost is an abstract and theoretical concept. Thus, an alternative, second-best, pricing policy, which most public utilities employ, is called *full-cost pricing* (or *rate-of-return pricing*).[5] As illustrated in Figure 12.8, under full-cost pricing, the public utility agency equates LAC to price (Q_f, p_f): $p =$ LAC. The firm earns a normal profit, and output and price are close to the

Pareto-efficient solution. Also, allowing the firm to price-discriminate may increase output, shifting it closer to the Pareto-efficient marginal-cost pricing solution. Specifically, the public utility agency may allow the firm to provide price discounts to its larger purchasers.[6] This will result in the larger purchasers increasing their purchases, with an associated increase in total consumer surplus. Since the discount is only for the larger purchases, it does not affect the firm's other customers. The largest purchasers will then face a price equal to the firm's marginal cost for the last unit they purchase. This is because if the largest purchaser faced a price greater than marginal cost and the price were lowered, then the purchaser would purchase an extra unit and the seller would sell this extra unit, so both would be better off.

This full-cost pricing policy includes a competitive (fair) return on investment in capital as a constraint on the monopoly's input choice decision. With this constraint, a monopoly's profit-maximizing decision does not yield the same least-cost combination of capital and labor as does the unconstrained decision for the same level of output. The effect is to encourage the monopoly to employ more capital and less labor. Thus, the regulation encourages a monopoly to employ an inefficient capital/labor ratio in an effort to extract more profits under the full-cost pricing constraint.

Application: California regulation of energy and descent into darkness

In response to a recession in the early 1990s, the California legislature removed the full-cost pricing method of regulating prices, where utilities generated electricity and delivered it to customers in exclusive territories over their own power lines. This price-regulated system was replaced with a deregulated system in 1996, where price would theoretically be determined in the free market. Unfortunately, this free-market system was constrained with a complicated set of new regulations and rules. For example, consumer rates were cut 10 percent, and then frozen for five years. Utilities were transformed into middlemen, selling off most of their power plants and buying energy for their customers on the open market. Independent energy marketers could buy power plants and sell electricity directly to users around the state.

This deregulated system created a complex market designed for private manipulation. Increased demand and limited supplies in 2000 resulted in energy sellers around the country dictating and manipulating energy prices. In response, government policymakers attempted to make modifications, but energy sellers devised new methods to exploit the system and run the cost of energy even higher. With retail rates frozen, the soaring price of power was fatal for the utilities. Wholesale power costs for the month of June 2000 topped \$3.6 billion, compared with \$7 billion for all of 1999. That month, the utility company PG&E alone paid roughly \$700 million more for electricity than it could collect from customers. For the first time since World War II, some San Francisco neighborhoods suffered planned blackouts. The state only avoided a major crisis (complete loss of energy) through a costly intervention that put it directly in the power business. California state government spent almost \$8 billion buying power in the first six months of 2001, at higher prices than the end of 2000.

The repercussions of California's descent into darkness tarnished the concept of energy deregulation throughout the United States and exposed massive corporate greed. Energy company lawyers, transcripts of trader conversations gathered by investigators, and interviews with market participants and regulators reveal how the US energy industry cashed in on and contributed to California's energy crisis. Energy companies seized loopholes and local shortages to charge prices hundreds of times higher than normal. Suppliers withheld power from the state's primary market, and sometimes idled power plants to induce shortages and boost prices. Gas companies manipulated supplies and prices, driving up the cost of a main input of electricity.

What is the lesson to be learned here? Whenever there is governmental intervention in the market—regulation or deregulation—care must be taken to consider all the potential positive and negative short- and long-run market effects. With this kind of careful economic analysis, problems like California's energy nightmare can be avoided.

Example 12.4 Government regulation and contestable markets

Consider a monopoly with the following declining long-run average cost function and associated marginal cost function:

$$\text{LAC} = 6 - \tfrac{1}{2}Q,$$

$$\text{LMC} = 6 - Q.$$

Let the inverse demand function for the monopoly's output and the associated marginal revenue function be

$$p = \text{AR} = 9 - 2Q,$$

$$\text{MR} = 9 - 4Q.$$

Based on these costs and demand, the monopoly pricing, full-cost pricing, and marginal-cost pricing schemes are as follows:

Monopoly pricing:

$$\text{LMC} = \text{MR},$$

$$6 - Q_M = 9 - 4Q_M \Rightarrow Q_M = 1, p_M = 7 > \text{LAC} = 6 - \tfrac{1}{2} = 5.5, \pi = 7 - 5.5 = 1.5.$$

Full-cost pricing:

$$\text{LAC} = \text{AR} \Rightarrow \pi = 0,$$

$$6 - \tfrac{1}{2}Q_f = 9 - 2Q_f \Rightarrow Q_f = 2, p_f = 5.$$

Marginal-cost pricing:

$$LMC = AR,$$

$$6 - Q_e = 9 - 2Q_e \Rightarrow Q_e = 3, p_e = 3,$$

$$\pi = 9 - [6 - \tfrac{1}{2}(3)]3 = -4.5.$$

At monopoly pricing, if entry and exit costs are low, a potential entrant can offer a price slightly lower than the monopoly price of 7. The entrant will then capture a large part of the monopoly rent from the incumbent firm. Thus, the monopoly will not set the price at 7 and expect to receive all of the monopoly rent. Instead, the monopoly will expect potential entry and lower its price. A fully contestable market will result in no monopoly rent for a potential entrant to capture. This occurs where p = LAC and coincides with the full-cost pricing scheme of regulation. Thus, regulation may not be necessary in a contestable market.

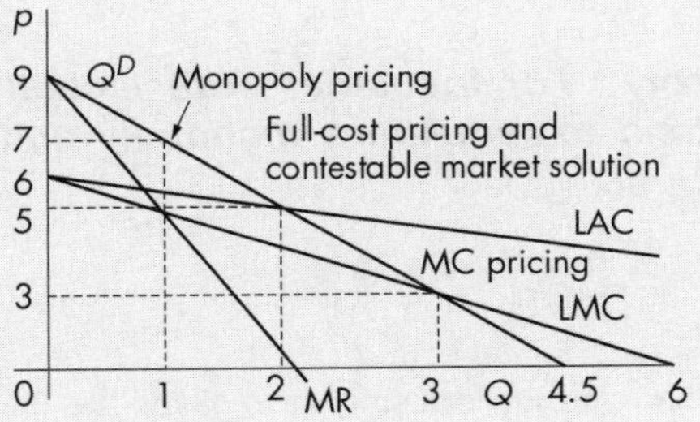

What are contestable markets?

Mortgage brokers who offer potential borrowers alternative loans from a number of financial lending agencies tend to be fly-by-night operations. They are here today, gone tomorrow. With virtually zero sunk cost of operations, they can enter and exit the lending industry at almost zero cost. With zero sunk costs, potential entrant firms could employ hit-and-run tactics. Hit when pure profits exist and run once they are exhausted. Such industries are called **contestable markets**.

Contestable markets. Markets characterized by little or no firm sunk costs, so firms set price equal to average cost to prevent entrant firms employing hit-and run-tactics. *E.g., firms providing services, including accounting and advertising agencies.*

Depending on the contestability of an industry, all natural monopolies may not require regulation. If a monopoly that is earning a pure profit does not have large sunk costs, then barriers to entry would be minor. For example, the monopoly may employ limited capital relative to labor, where the capital (such as computers or office space) is not specific to the production of any particular commodity. Another firm could enter this industry, charge a lower price, and earn a pure profit. Computer software firms are a prime example. Thus, the existing firm will not be able to set a price above average cost. Otherwise, another firm would enter and take over the market by setting a slightly lower price. Even threat of entry by other firms may drive the monopoly's price down toward a price that equals average cost.

This theory of contestable markets indicates, for industries with limited entry and exit costs, that market forces will result in the same outcome as full-cost price regulation. Thus, the requirement to regulate such firms is questionable. In fact, this theory is employed as a justification for deregulation in telecommunications and airlines, and not pursuing regulation with currently unregulated firms such as computer software firms. This is one justification for not breaking up Microsoft.

In June 2011, the US Federal Trade Commission launched an investigation of Google to determine whether or not the search engine was violating antitrust acts. Google holds two-thirds of the US search market and the question is if it is abusing this dominant position. In Google's defense, the contestable markets argument is used, stating, "We face an extremely competitive landscape in which consumers have a multitude of options to access information." They are just "one click away."

Does the market regulate a monopoly? For industries with limited entry and exit costs, market forces will tend to regulate a monopoly and thus, governmental interference is not required.

Summary

1. A monopoly firm is the sole single firm in an industry, so it faces the market demand for its output. It is a price maker rather than a price taker.
2. Barriers to entry are the cause of monopoly power. These barriers prevent other firms from entering into the industry.
3. The objective of a monopoly is generally to maximize profits by setting marginal revenue to marginal cost. In the short run, a firm with monopoly power can earn a pure profit, normal profit, or operate at a loss. In the long run, the monopoly can only earn a normal profit.
4. The Lerner Index measures the percentage markup in price due to monopoly power.
5. Firms exercising monopoly power are inefficient, measured by the deadweight loss. Society would prefer the firm to increase output, lower the price, and operate at full capacity.
6. Taxing monopoly profits does not result in improving monopoly's efficiency, but does reduce the ability of the firm to engage in socially wasteful rent-seeking behavior.
7. Limit price analysis may result in monopolies not exercising their monopoly power, so regulation may not be necessary.
8. It may not be feasible to break up a natural monopoly, so instead some form of regulation may be necessary.
9. Monopoly pricing, marginal-cost pricing, and full-cost pricing are three possible pricing polices available to a regulator.

10. The theory of contestable markets indicates that for industries with limited entry and exist costs, market forces will regulate a monopoly without government intervention.
11. *(Appendix)* A firm with multiple physical plants will maximize profits by equating the marginal cost in each plant to marginal revenue.
12. *(Appendix)* Nonprofit behavior is characteristic of firm managers who either have their own objective of being nonprofit or are required to be nonprofit by a regulator.
13. *(Appendix)* Instead of profit-maximizing behavior, firm managers may be interested in maximizing total revenue either with or without a profit constraint.

Key concepts

barriers to entry, 475
Baumol firm, 515
contestable markets, 499
full capacity, 488
Lerner Index, 484
limit price analysis, 495
lump-sum tax, 492
monopoly, 474
monopoly power, 470
monopoly rent, 487
multiple plants, 506
natural monopolies, 476
nonprofit behavior, 508
opportunity cost of capital, 486
price maker, 477
profit tax, 492
rent-seeking behavior, 490
revenue-maximizing firm, 512

Key equations

$$\mathrm{MR} = \mathrm{SMC}$$

A firm will maximize short-run profit by setting MR equal to SMC.

$$\mathrm{MR} = p + \frac{\partial p}{\partial Q}Q$$

MR is equal to price plus an adjustment factor.

$$\mathrm{MR} = p\left(1 + \frac{1}{\varepsilon^D}\right)$$

For MR to be positive, ε^D must be elastic.

$$L_I = \frac{p - \mathrm{SMC}}{p} = -\frac{1}{\varepsilon^D}$$

The Lerner Index measures the percentage markup in price due to monopoly power.

$$\mathrm{SMC} = \mathrm{LMC} = \mathrm{MR}$$

Long-run equilibrium for a firm is equating SMC and LMC to MR.

$$p = \text{LMC}$$

Marginal-cost pricing for a governmental regulator.

$$p = \text{LAC}$$

Full-cost pricing for a governmental regulator. Also, a contestable market equilibrium solution.

$$\text{MRS}(q_2 \text{ for } q_1) = \frac{\partial U/\partial q_1}{\partial U/\partial q_2} = \frac{\text{SMC}_1 - \text{MR}_1}{\text{SMC}_2 - \text{MR}_2}$$

Nonprofit managers will maximize utility by equating their MRS to the ratio of the SMC net of MR.

$$\text{SMC}_1(q_1) = \ldots = \text{SMC}_n(q_n) = \text{MR}(Q)$$

A firm with multiple physical plants will equate the marginal cost in each plant to the overall marginal revenue.

$$\text{MR} = 0$$

FOC for a revenue-maximizing firm.

Questions

1. A supermarket chain raises its price on a breakfast cereal from \$2.00 a box to \$2.10 and then sells less cereal. Is SMC = MR = 2.10? Explain.
2. A monopoly attempts to set output where price is greater than marginal cost, so to increase profits all that is required is to sell one additional unit at a slightly lower price. What is the fallacy in this argument?
3. Why does monopoly power decrease as elasticity of demand increases in absolute value?
4. Economist M.A. Adelman stated "A useful if not very precise index of the strength of competition … is the resentment of unsuccessful competitors." Analyze his statement in terms of the computer software industry.
5. If the gains to producers from monopoly power could be redistributed to consumers, would the social cost of monopoly power be eliminated? Explain.

6. Why is $p =$ MR socially efficient under perfect competition but not so if a firm has some monopoly power?
7. Is efficiency improved by having a monopolized industry versus no industry at all? Explain.
8. A firm is currently unregulated but believes it will be regulated if its profit becomes too high. Would you expect this firm to minimize cost for a given level of output?
9. When will full-cost pricing of a regulated monopoly cause too high a price in terms of efficiency? Too low a price?
10. It may be rational for a firm not to maximize profits. True or false? Explain.

Exercises

The difference between the impossible and the possible lies in a person's determination.

(Tommy Lasorda)

1. Market demand for a commodity is $Q^D = 12 - p$ and the short-run total cost function for the firm is $\text{STC}(Q) = Q^2 + 1$.

   a. If the firm behaved as a perfectly competitive firm, determine the equilibrium price and quantity.
   b. If instead the firm behaved as a monopoly, what are the equilibrium price and quantity?
   c. How much money would it require for the firm to forgo the monopoly profits and behave instead as a perfectly competitive firm?
   d. How much would consumers be willing to pay the firm to accept competitive profits in place of monopoly profits?

2. Suppose a perfectly competitive industry can produce an output at a constant marginal cost of \$5 per unit. In contrast, a monopoly's marginal cost increases to \$6, because \$1 per unit is paid to government lobbyists for retaining the monopoly's preferred situation. Assume the market demand is

   $$Q^D = 500 - 25p$$

   a. Calculate the perfectly competitive and monopoly outputs and prices.
   b. Calculate the deadweight loss from monopoly power.

3. Suppose a monopoly has the production function

   $$Q = L + K.$$

Let the wage rate be $w = 4$ and the rent on capital be $v = 10$. Assume that the monopoly faces the market demand curve

$$Q^D = 24 - 2p.$$

a. How much output will this firm produce and what price will it set?
b. What is the firm's producer surplus (monopoly rent)?
c. How much labor and capital will be employed?

4. If a monopoly faces a linear demand curve $Q = a - p$ and has constant marginal cost c, show that less than a full change in cost is passed on to consumers. *Hint:* If $p(c)$ is the monopoly price, show that $dp(c)/dc < 1$.

5. A peanut processor produces two joint products, peanuts P and peanut shells S, in a fixed one-to-one proportion. The market demand functions facing these products are

$$Q_P = 220 - 2p_P,$$
$$Q_S = 10 - \tfrac{1}{2}p_S.$$

The firm has $\text{STC}(Q) = 60Q + 2Q^2 + 10$. Determine the profit-maximizing level of production and how much of each product will be sold. What are the profit-maximizing prices?

6. The inverse demand for municipal water in a city is

$$p = 10 - Q,$$

where Q is the number of homes connected and p is the monthly connect charge. The total cost of municipal water is

$$\text{LTC} = 5Q - \tfrac{1}{2}Q^2.$$

a. Is municipal water a natural monopoly? Explain
b. At what output and price level will an unregulated monopoly produce? What is the monopoly's profit?
c. If there is active contestable competition for obtaining a city franchise for providing water service, what will be the franchise fee?
d. What are the socially desirable output and price?
e. What output and price would a regulatory agency set?

7. A monopoly faces the demand curve $Q = 30 - \tfrac{1}{2}p$, and has the following cost function:

$$\text{STC} = Q^2 + 100.$$

a. Find the profit-maximizing output and price and determine the level of profit.
b. Determine the elasticity of demand at the profit-maximizing output.

c. Assume a tax τ on output Q. Find the profit-maximizing level of output in terms of τ. How will output change with a change in τ?

d. What level of tax τ should a government choose if it wishes to extract the maximum tax revenue from this monopoly?

8. The government plans to either tax or subsidize a monopoly facing an inverse demand function $p(Q)$ and a short-run total cost function STC(Q). What tax or subsidy per unit of output would result in the firm acting efficiently?

9. A monopoly faces the inverse demand function $p = 22 - Q$ and a constant average production cost of \$12 per unit.

   a. Graph the average and marginal revenue curves and the average and marginal cost curves. What are the monopoly's profit-maximizing price and quantity? What is the resulting profit? Determine the degree of monopoly power.
   b. A government regulatory agency set a price ceiling of \$14. What quantity will be produced? What will be the firm's profit? How does the degree of monopoly power change?
   c. What price ceiling yields the largest level of output. What is the level of output? What is the firm's profit? How does the degree of monopoly power change?

10. Suppose there are 100 households in a remote Nevada Indian reservation, each with the following demand for telephone service:

$$q = 4 - p.$$

Assume that Nevada Bell's cost of providing telephone service to the reservation is

$$\text{STC} = Q + 200.$$

   a. Under a marginal-cost pricing policy, determine the output and price. What are the level of consumer and producer surplus and the deadweight loss?
   b. Determine the output and price under the full-cost pricing policy. Again, what are the level of consumer and producer surplus and the deadweight loss?
   c. Suppose Nevada Bell is allowed to charge an initial installation fee, but is required to only earn a normal profit and set price using marginal-cost pricing. What will be the fee each household pays? Will all the households be willing to pay this fee?

Internet case studies

1. Is Microsoft a monopoly?
2. Discuss the ethical issue of rent-seeking behavior.
3. Discuss full-cost pricing in terms of regulating environmental issues.

APPENDIX TO CHAPTER 12

Juggling multiple plants

In 2011, the Ford Motor Company had 14 assembly plants in North America—down from 22 in 2002; between 1927 and 1932 it had 38 plants for producing just the Model A. Under some circumstances, a firm may be able to enhance its profit by having more than one physical plant (**multiple plants**). In general, multiple plants can increase short-run profit at a given output level, if the weighted average of the short-run average costs for several plants is less than the short-run average cost for the same total output produced by a single plant. An example is a large corporate farm, where cost constraints prevent the entire farm's acreage being in one contiguous field. Instead, the farm is spread out over many different fields.

Why would a firm have multiple plants? If multiple plants result in enhanced profits by reducing production costs, then a firm will have multiple plants.

To determine the optimal level of production in each physical plant (field), we denote by $\mathrm{STC}_j(q_j)$ the cost function associated with plant j and assume two plants ($j = 1, 2$). The total production is then

$$Q = q_1 + q_2.$$

Thus, a firm maximizes profit by

$$\max_{(q_1,\, q_2)} \pi = \max_{(q_1,\, q_2)} \{\mathrm{TR}(Q) - [\mathrm{STC}_1(q_1) + \mathrm{STC}_2(q_2)]\}.$$

The FOCs are then

$$\frac{\partial \pi}{\partial q_j} = \frac{\partial \mathrm{TR}}{\partial Q}\frac{\partial Q}{\partial q_j} - \frac{\partial \mathrm{STC}_j(q_j)}{\partial q_j} = 0 \quad \text{for all } j = 1,\ 2.$$

Note that $\partial Q/\partial q_j = 1$, $\partial \mathrm{TR}/\partial Q = \mathrm{MR}(Q)$, and $\partial \mathrm{STC}_j(q_j) = \mathrm{SMC}_j(q_j)$, so these FOCs indicate that a firm equates

$$\mathrm{SMC}_1(q_1) = \mathrm{SMC}_2(q_2) = \mathrm{MR}(Q).$$

For maximizing profit, the firm equates the marginal cost in each plant to the overall marginal revenue. For example, if $\mathrm{SMC}_1 < \mathrm{SMC}_2$, the firm could decrease its costs by producing more output in plant 1 and less in plant 2. By equalizing all the SMCs, the firm minimizes costs across all the plants for some given level of output. The firm then determines the profit-maximizing output by equating these equal SMCs across all plants to the common overall MR. In general for n plants, the FOCs are

$$\mathrm{SMC}_1(q_1) = \ldots = \mathrm{SMC}_n(q_n) = \mathrm{MR}(Q).$$

These FOCs for the case of two plants are illustrated in Figure 12A.1. The two marginal cost curves for the plants are summed laterally (horizontally) to obtain an overall output for a given level of marginal cost. The profit-maximizing output is Q^*, of which q_1^* is produced in plant 1 and q_2^* is produced in plant 2. The profit-maximizing price is p^*.

The continuous changing market conditions provide the opportunity for firms to experience short-run pure profit. Firms can earn these profits by adjusting their output among the

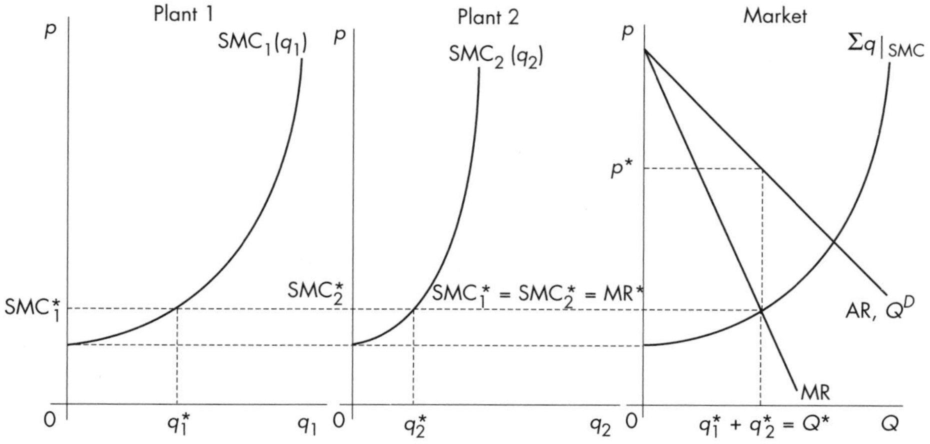

Figure 12A.1 **Multiple plants.** For profit maximization, a firm will equate the SMC in each plant to the overall MR.

different plants in response to anticipated market conditions. Firms that can both anticipate quantity demanded and efficiently supply this demand can earn a short-run pure profit.

Example 12A.1 Determining multi-plant price and output

Consider a firm facing the inverse market demand function

$$p = 10 - \tfrac{1}{2}Q,$$

and operating two plants with output q_1 for plant 1 and q_2 for plant 2. Let the marginal costs for the respective plants be

$$SMC_1 = 1 + 2q_1, \quad SMC_2 = 2 + q_2.$$

The firm will maximize profit by equating the marginal costs in the two plants with overall marginal revenue. Given the market demand function, marginal revenue is

$$MR = 10 - Q.$$

Solving the marginal cost equations for output yields

$$q_1 = \tfrac{1}{2}SMC_1 - \tfrac{1}{2},$$

$$q_2 = SMC_2 - 2.$$

An equation for overall output Q in terms of the plants' marginal cost is

$$Q = q_1 + q_2 = \tfrac{1}{2}SMC_1 - \tfrac{1}{2} + SMC_2 - 2.$$

Substituting the FOC that MR must equal the respective marginal costs yields

$$Q^* = \tfrac{1}{2}(10 - Q^*) - \tfrac{1}{2} + (10 - Q^*) - 2$$

Solving for Q^* yields

$$Q^* = 5, \quad \text{with} \quad p^* = \$7.50, \quad \text{MR}^* = 5, \quad q_1^* = 2, \quad \text{and} \quad q_2^* = 3.$$

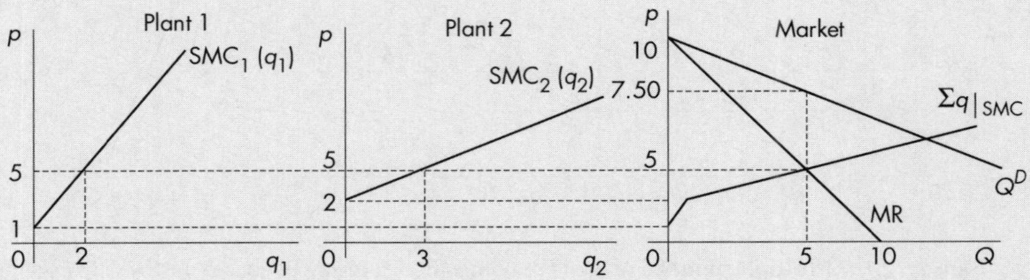

Nonprofit organizations

The People's Republic of China has offered to lend pandas to US zoos for \$10 million over 10 years. A zoo's managers must then determine whether it is worth the cost to develop a panda exhibit given the constraint of facing a full-cost pricing regulation. The zoo can only earn a normal profit. But managers of these zoos have other objectives or goals besides profit maximization. Such *nonprofit behavior* by managers is characteristic of many firms who either have their own constraint of being nonprofit or are regulated by government. Examples of organizations that the government expressly established as nonprofit institutions are religious organizations, many hospitals, and public agencies such as the US Post Office and public radio and television stations.

Is the objective of a nonprofit firm to be nonprofit? No, the objective of a nonprofit firm is to maximize the owners' utility subject to the constraint of being nonprofit.

Managers of these organizations may employ their preferences for the organization's allocating decisions. For example, managers of a zoo may seek input from the public concerning future events sponsored by the zoo, but the final determination is up to the managers. We can address these allocating decisions of nonprofit organization managers by considering an organization producing two outputs q_1 and q_2 and assuming that its managers derive utility from these outputs represented by the utility function $U(q_1, q_2)$. We represent the cost associated with producing q_1 and q_2 by the joint total cost function $\text{STC}(q_1, q_2)$. The managers' budget constraint is that the total cost of producing these outputs must equal the revenue generated from the outputs:

$$\begin{aligned}\text{STC}(q_1, q_2) &= \text{TR}_1 + \text{TR}_2,\\ &= p_1(q_1)q_1 + p_2(q_2)q_2,\end{aligned}$$

where $p_1(q_1)$ and $p_2(q_2)$ are the inverse demand functions for the outputs. The Lagrangian is then

$$\mathcal{L}(q_1, q_2, \lambda) = U(q_1, q_2) + \lambda[STC(q_1, q_2) - p_1(q_1)q_1 - p_2(q_2)q_2].$$

The FOCs are

$$\frac{\partial \mathcal{L}}{\partial q_1} = \frac{\partial U}{\partial q_1} + \lambda(\text{SMC}_1 - \text{MR}_1) = 0,$$

$$\frac{\partial \mathcal{L}}{\partial q_2} = \frac{\partial U}{\partial q_2} + \lambda(\text{SMC}_2 - \text{MR}_2) = 0,$$

$$\frac{\partial \mathcal{L}}{\partial \lambda} = \text{STC}(q_1,\ q_2) - p_1(q_1)q_1 - p_2(q_2)q_2 = 0.$$

Similar to a household problem, taking the ratio of the first two FOCs yields

$$\text{MRS}(q_2 for q_2) = \frac{\partial U/\partial q_1}{\partial U/\partial q_2} = \frac{\text{SMC}_1 - \text{MR}_1}{\text{SMC}_2 - \text{MR}_2}.$$

Managers will maximize their utility by equating their MRS to the ratio of the SMC net of MR. Assuming that managers' preferences satisfy the Nonsatiation Axiom, so the marginal utilities are positive, then, for both outputs, SMC > MR. All profits the organization could earn are evaporated by increasing both outputs above the profit-maximizing levels, where SMC = MR.

The magnitude of the MRS will determine how much the managers will expand output beyond the profit-maximizing level. As MRS(q_2 for q_1) increases, $\text{SMC}_2 - \text{MR}_2$ approaches zero, indicating that the q_2 level of output is relatively near the profit-maximizing level. The extreme case is where $\text{SMC}_2 - \text{MR}_2 = 0$, representing the profit-maximizing level for q_2. This occurs when managers' marginal utility for q_2 is zero. The profits generated by the production of q_2 are then allocated toward increasing the output of q_1. An example of the revenue from one output subsidizing the increased production of another output is collegiate sports. Many universities have a nonprofit athletic association run the collegiate sports program. The major source of revenue is from ticket sales and television revenue of the major sports such as men's football and basketball. This revenue is then used to support the other collegiate programs.

The FOC for a nonprofit organization is illustrated in Figure 12A.2. The budget constraint of $\text{STC} = \text{TR}_1 + \text{TR}_2$ is nonlinear in q_1 and q_2, given that the firm has some monopoly power in the markets for q_1 and q_2. The firm's managers are facing negatively sloping demands for q_1 and q_2. As the output of one commodity increases, its price falls. From the FOC, the utility-maximizing outputs (q_1^*, q_2^*) occur at the tangency of this budget constraint and the indifferent curve, point B. Point A represents the profit-maximizing output (q_1^M, q_2^M). Managers exhaust any profits by expanding output from point A to B. If the managers have no preference for q_2, their indifference curves are vertical and point C represents the utility-maximizing bundle. By maximizing profits for the neutral output q_2, managers will have the maximum revenue over costs to produce more of the desirable output q_1. For example, some nonprofit volunteer firefighter organizations will operate a bar. The profits from the bar are applied to purchase equipment and supplies for fighting fires.

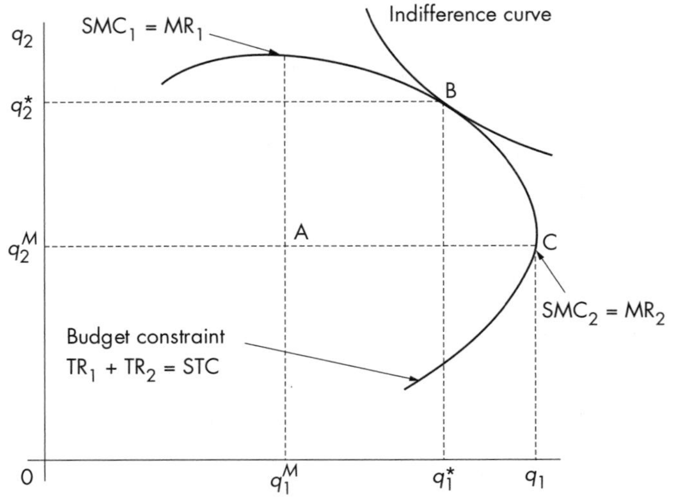

Figure 12A.2 **Nonprofit organization.** A manager will expand output beyond the profit-maximizing point A by allocating all profits to the further production of the outputs. Point B represents such an allocation where a manager has positive preference for both outputs. Point C represents the case where the manager only has preferences for q_1.

Example 12.6. Nonprofit organizations

Consider a nonprofit organization facing the following demand functions for its two outputs q_1 and q_2:

$$q_1 = -2p_1 + 6, q_2 = -2p_2 + 4,$$

with associated short-run total cost of STC $= 2.25 + q_1 + q_2$. Total revenue is then

$$\mathrm{TR}_1 = (3 - \tfrac{1}{2}q_1)q_1,$$

$$\mathrm{TR}_2 = (2 - \tfrac{1}{2}q_2)q_2.$$

First, assume that the organizational preference for these two commodities is viewed as perfect substitutes, represented by the utility function $U(q_1, q_2) = q_1 + q_2$. The organization is interested in maximizing this utility function subject to the constraint of being nonprofit, where total revenue is equal to total cost:

$$\mathrm{TR}_1 + \mathrm{TR}_2 = \mathrm{STC},$$

$$(3 - \tfrac{1}{2}q_1)q_1 + (2 - \tfrac{1}{2}q_2)q_2 = 2.25 + q_1 + q_2.$$

The Lagrangian is then

$$\mathcal{L}(q_1, q_2, \lambda) = q_1 + q_2 + \lambda[(3 - \tfrac{1}{2}q_1)q_1 + (2 - \tfrac{1}{2}q_2)q_2 - 2.25 - q_1 - q_2].$$

The FOCs are

$$\partial\mathcal{L}/\partial q_1 = 1 + \lambda(3 - q_1^* - 1) = 0,$$
$$\partial\mathcal{L}/\partial q_2 = 1 + \lambda(2 - q_2^* - 1) = 0,$$
$$\partial\mathcal{L}/\partial\lambda = (3 - \tfrac{1}{2}q_1^*)q_1^* + (2 - \tfrac{1}{2}q_2^*)q_2^* - 2.25 - q_1^* - q_2^* = 0.$$

From the first two FOCs

$$\text{MRS}(q_2 \text{ for } q_1) = 1 = \frac{2 - q_1^*}{1 - q_2^*} \Rightarrow q_2^* = q_1^* - 1, \quad \text{the expansion path.}$$

Substituting this expansion-path equation into the nonprofit constraint yields

$$3q_1^* - \tfrac{1}{2}(q_1^*)^2 + 2(q_1^* - 1) - \tfrac{1}{2}(q_1^* - 1)^2 - 2.25 - q_1^* - (q_1^* - 1) = 0,$$
$$q_1^* - \tfrac{1}{2}(q_1^*)^2 + 2q_1^* - 2 - \tfrac{1}{2}[(q_1^*)^2 - 2q_1^* + 1] - 1.25 = 0,$$
$$4q_1^* - (q_1^*)^2 - 3.75 = 0 \Rightarrow q_1^* = 2.5, \quad q_2^* = 1.5.$$

Instead, if the firm were to maximize profits,

$$\max_{(q_1,\, q_2)} \pi = \max_{(q_1,\, q_2)} (\text{TR}_1 + \text{TR}_2 - \text{STC})$$
$$= \max_{(q_1,\, q_2)} (3q_1 - \tfrac{1}{2}q_1^2 + 2q_2 - \tfrac{1}{2}q_2^2 - 2.25 - q_1 - q_2).$$

The FOCs are then

$$\partial\pi/\partial q_1 = 3 - q_1^M - 1 = 0 \Rightarrow q_1^M = 2,$$
$$\partial\pi/\partial q_2 = 2 - q_2^M - 1 = 0 \Rightarrow q_2^M = 1.$$

Thus, restricting the firm to a nonprofit status results in both outputs increasing from the profit-maximizing output levels.

Alternatively, if the nonprofit organization only has preferences for one of the commodities, say commodity q_1, with utility $U(q_1) = q_1$, the optimal levels of q_1 and q_2 would then be determined by

$$\mathcal{L}(q_1, q_2, \lambda) = q_1 + \lambda(3q_1 - \tfrac{1}{2}q_1^2 + 2q_2 - \tfrac{1}{2}q_2^2 - 2.25 - q_1 - q_2).$$

The FOCs are

$$\partial\mathcal{L}/\partial q_1 = 1 + \lambda(3 - q_1' - 1) = 0,$$
$$\partial\mathcal{L}/\partial q_2 = \lambda(2 - q_2' - 1) = 0 \Rightarrow q_2' = 1,$$
$$\partial\mathcal{L}/\partial\lambda = 3q_1' - \tfrac{1}{2}(q_1')^2 + 2q_2' - \tfrac{1}{2}(q_2')^2 - 2.25 - q_1' - q_2' = 0.$$

Substituting the optimal solution for q_2, $q_2' = 1$, into the nonprofit constraint results in the solution for q_1:

$$3q_1' - \tfrac{1}{2}(q_1')^2 + 2 - \tfrac{1}{2} - 2.25 - q_1' - 1 = 0,$$

$$2q_1' - \tfrac{1}{2}(q_1')^2 - 1.75 = 0,$$

$$(q_1')^2 - 4q_1' + 3.5 = 0 \Rightarrow q_1' = 2.7.$$

Output q_2 is set at the profit-maximizing level, with all profits diverted to the production of q_1.

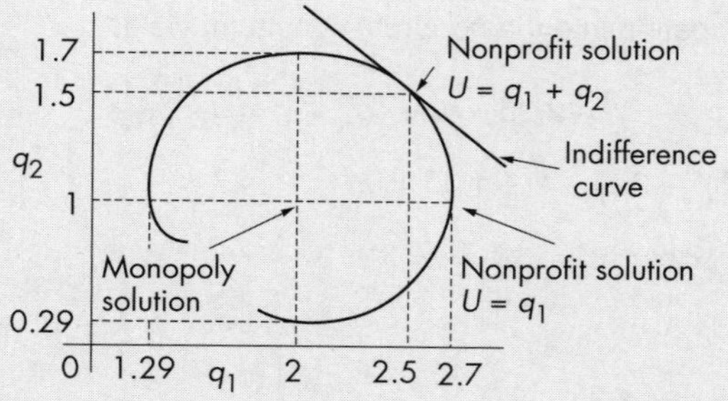

Investigating alternative behavioral assumptions

Damn the profits, full speed ahead to market dominance.

(Michael Wetzstein)

Translation: Maximize total revenue instead of profits.

During the second half of the twentieth century, large discount retail firms entered small local markets and established market dominance. They drove out "mom-and-pop" drugstores and variety stores with low-price volume sales. These discount firms did not employ the profit-maximization paradigm most often used for explaining and predicting firm behavior. Instead, they lowered prices and increased output in an attempt to dominate a local market by capturing most, if not all, of it.

In general, firms may face constraints that result in an alternative behavior dominating profit maximization. An example is the case of contestable markets, where the mere threat of entry by other firms restricts the profit-maximization solution. Other examples are lack of knowledge concerning the marginal cost of production or lack of interest in penetrating and dominating a market.

Revenue maximization

Particularly in the case of a firm interested in maximizing its market share, an alternative behavioral assumption is a *revenue-maximizing firm.* Given an inverse market demand

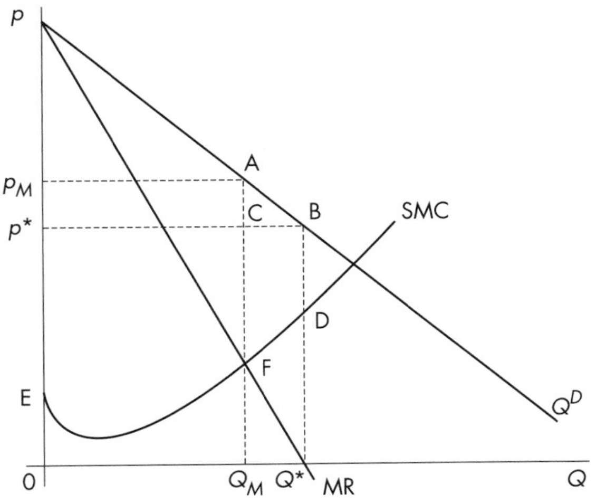

Figure 12A.3 **Revenue-maximizing versus profit-maximizing behavior.** A revenue-maximizing firm equates MR to zero and supplies Q^* units of output at price p^*. This results in a higher output and lower price compared with the profit-maximizing price and output (p_M, Q_M).

function $p(Q)$ where price is a function of output, the optimization problem is

$$\max_Q \mathrm{TR} = \max_Q p(Q)Q.$$

The FOC is then

$$\frac{\partial \mathrm{TR}}{\partial Q} = p + \frac{dp}{dQ}Q^* = 0,$$

that is,

$$\mathrm{MR} = 0.$$

The firm will increase output until an additional unit of output will result in total revenue declining. This revenue-maximizing outcome is illustrated in Figure 12A.3. The optimal level of output for revenue maximization is Q^*, where MR = 0. The firm is able to sell all of this output at the price p^*. This is in contrast to the profit-maximizing solution Q_M with associated price p_M.

As a consequence of revenue maximization, producer surplus must be reduced because the profit-maximizing solution maximizes producer surplus. Any deviation away from this maximum will reduce producer surplus. Producer surplus under revenue maximization is represented by the area Ep^*BD; under profit maximization it is the area Ep_MAF. As a result of shifting from profit maximization to revenue maximization, consumers experience an increase in consumer surplus. They capture some the firm's producer surplus, represented by the area p^*p_MAC, and some of the deadweight loss, the area CAB. This yields a net gain in consumer surplus, the area p^*p_MAB. Although total producer surplus has declined by the difference in the areas p^*p_MAC and FCBD, firms that are interested in revenue maximization consider this position preferable to profit maximization. Thus, overall welfare has improved.

Is a firm's objective to maximize market share or profit? A firm may have the objective of penetrating a market or establishing market dominance, so it may be willing to at least in the short-run sacrifice profit for an increased share of the market.

Example 12A.3 Determining price and output for a revenue-maximizing firm

Consider the following market demand function facing a revenue-maximizing firm:

$$Q = 20 - p.$$

The inverse demand function is

$$p = 20 - Q.$$

Revenue maximization for the firm is then

$$\max_Q \text{TR} = \max_Q p(Q)Q$$
$$= \max_Q (20 - Q)Q.$$

The FOC is

$$\partial\text{TR}/\partial Q = 20 - 2Q^* = 0,$$

that is,

$$\text{MR} = 0.$$

Solving for Q, $Q^* = 10$, with $p^* = 10$. Assuming

$$\text{STC}(Q) = 10 + Q^2,$$
$$\pi^* = p^*Q^* - \text{STC}(Q^*),$$
$$= 100 - 110 = -\$10.$$

Producer surplus is zero and consumer surplus is \$50.

A profit-maximizing firm would equate marginal revenue to marginal cost:

$$\text{MR} = \text{SMC},$$
$$20 - 2Q_M = 2Q_M.$$

Solving for Q, $Q_M = 5$, with $p_M = 15$. This results in a maximum profit of $\pi_M = 75 - 35 =$ \$40.00, producer surplus of \$50.00 and consumer surplus of \$12.50. Total surplus for a revenue-maximizing monopoly is $0+50=\$50.00$, compared with the total surplus for a profit-maximizing monopoly of $50+12.50=\$62.50$.

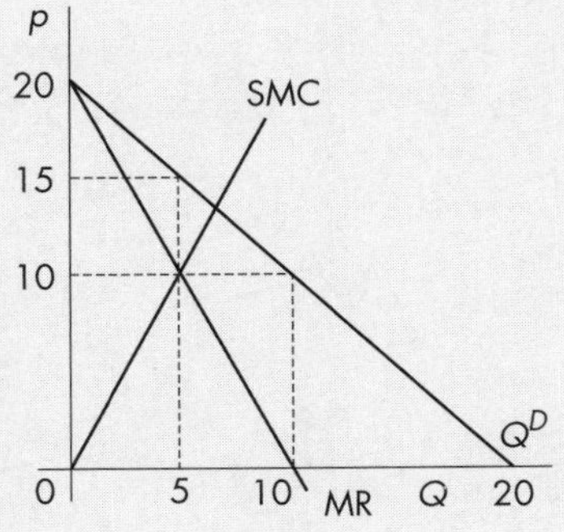

Revenue maximization with a profit constraint

A firm interested in maximizing market share may still require earning some level of short-run profit. Such a firm is referred to as a *Baumol firm.* Owners of such a firm may be interested in appropriating an increased share of the market, but not at the expense of going bankrupt. Thus, the firm may not totally ignore costs in its drive to increase market share. The firm is then constrained in its ability to maximize revenue by the requirement to achieve some profit level. The optimization problem is then

$$\max_Q \text{TR} = \max_Q pQ \quad \text{s.t. } \pi^\text{o} = pQ - \text{STC}(Q),$$

where π^o is some required level of profit. Again, given an inverse market demand curve $p(Q)$, the Lagrangian is

$$\mathcal{L}(Q,\lambda) = p(Q)Q + \lambda[\pi^\text{o} - p(Q)Q + \text{STC}(Q)].$$

The FOCs are then

$$\frac{\partial \mathcal{L}}{\partial Q} = \text{MR} + \lambda'(-\text{MR} + \text{SMC}) = 0,$$

$$\frac{\partial \mathcal{L}}{\partial \lambda} = \pi^\text{o} - p(Q)Q + \text{STC}(Q) = 0.$$

Solving for λ' in the first FOC yields

$$\lambda' = \frac{\text{MR}}{\text{MR} - \text{SMC}}.$$

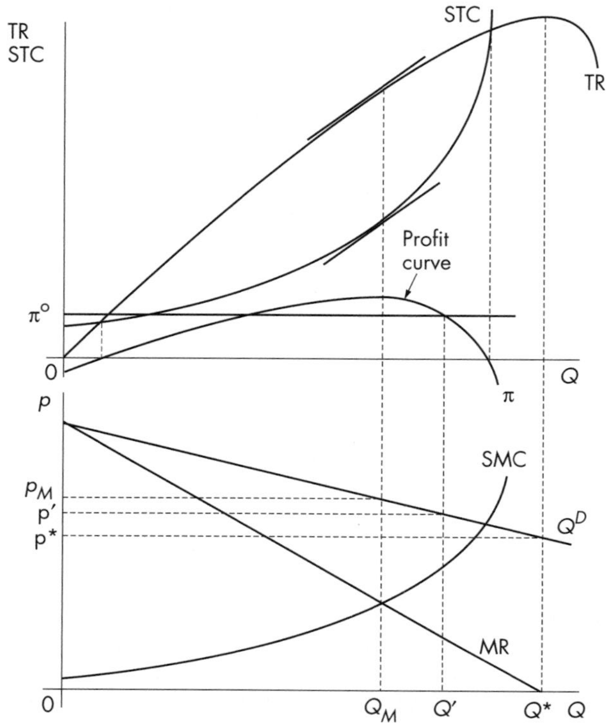

Figure 12A.4 **Revenue maximization constrained by obtaining a given level of profit.** Maximizing revenue for a given profit level π^o results in an output of Q', with an associated price p'.

Recall that the Lagrange multiplier λ' is the derivative of the objective function with respect to the constraint. For maximizing revenue subject to a given level of profit, the Lagrange multiplier is then $\lambda' = \partial \mathrm{TR}/\partial\pi$. When $\lambda' = 0$, total revenue is maximized. This occurs where MR $= 0$. The inverse of λ' is the derivative of profit with respect to total revenue:

$$\frac{1}{\lambda'} = \frac{\partial\pi}{\partial TR} = \frac{\mathrm{MR} - \mathrm{SMC}}{\mathrm{MR}}.$$

When $1/\lambda' = 0$, profit is maximized. This occurs where MR $-$ SMC $= 0$.

This constrained revenue-maximizing solution is illustrated in Figure 12A.4. The unconstrained revenue-maximizing optimal price and output are p^* and Q^*, respectively. At this output level, the firm is operating at a loss, illustrated by the profit curve. Constraining this revenue-maximizing firm to operate at profit level π^o yields the constrained solution p' and Q', resulting in a lower level of total revenue. However, this constrained revenue-maximizing solution still yields a higher level of revenue than does the profit-maximizing level of price and output (p_M, Q_M).

Example 12A.4 Determining price and output for a constrained revenue maximizing firm

Consider the same market demand function as in Example 12A.3. Assume that the firm is interested in maximizing revenue subject to the constraint of profit equaling $22, $\pi^o = 22$. The FOCs for maximizing revenue subject to a given level of profit insure that

$$\pi^o - \text{TR} + \text{STC} = 0.$$

Substituting and solving for Q yields

$$22 - (20 - Q)Q + 10 + Q^2 = 0,$$

$$32 - 20Q + 2Q^2 = 0,$$

$$16 - 10Q + Q^2 = 0,$$

$$(8 - Q)(2 - Q) = 0.$$

The roots are 2 and 8, with 8 yielding a higher level of revenue, so $Q' = 8$, with $p' = 12$.

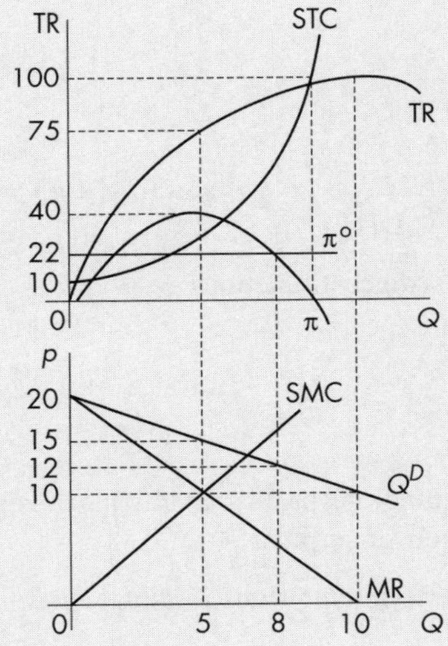

Questions

1. For a multi-plant firm, at each quantity, the marginal cost at plant 1 is 10 percent lower than the marginal cost at plant 2. Total cost will then be minimized if all output is produced at plant 1. True or false? Explain.

2. If a monopoly has two production plants, one of which has rising marginal cost and the other falling marginal cost, it will concentrate all its production in the plant with declining marginal cost. True or false? Explain.
3. Suppose a firm produces identical outputs in two different plants. If the marginal cost at the first plant exceeds the marginal cost at the second plant, how can the firm reduce costs and maintain the same level of output?
4. In the long run, a firm always operates at the minimum level of average costs for the optimally sized plant to produce a given amount of output. True or false? Explain.
5. Authors of textbooks often receive royalties as a percentage of total sales. However, publishers are interested in maximizing profits. Determine the optimal output and price for both an author and a publisher. If an author is interested in lowering the price of her textbook, is she necessarily concerned with students' interests?
6. Suppose a firm is interested in expanding its market share. However, if it expands, it will not be able to maintain the current price so its profits will decline. What should the firm do and why?

Exercises

1. An automobile tire firm has two plants, with $\text{LTC}_1(q_1) = \frac{1}{2}q_1^2$ and $\text{LTC}_2(q_2) = q_2$. If $Q = q_1 + q_2$, what is the cost function for Q, $\text{LTC}(Q)$?
2. Assume a multi-plant firm owns two plants, with cost functions

$$\text{STC}_1 = 2q_1^2 + 30,$$

$$\text{STC}_2 = 5q_2^2 + 10q_2 + 25,$$

and is facing an output price of 20. Determine the profit-maximizing level of outputs for the plants and the firm's total producer surplus.

3. A monopoly has two physical plants with the following short-run total costs:

$$\text{STC}_1 = 4q_1 + 1,$$

$$\text{STC}_2 = 2q_2 + q_2^2 + 1.$$

Its inverse market demand curve is

$$p = 8 - (q_1 + q_2).$$

What is the firm's profit-maximizing level of output in each plant? What market price will it offer?

4. A meat-packing company has three plants for packing meat, with the marginal costs for each plant and demand schedules as shown in the following table:

Output of packaged meat	*Marginal cost ($)*			*Price per packaged meat ($)*
	Plant 1	*Plant 2*	*Plant 3*	
0				
1	28	26	20	96
2	32	28	26	92
3	36	30	32	88
4	40	33	34	84
5	Capacity	Capacity	Capacity	80
6				76
7				72
8				68
9				64
10				60
11				56
12				52

Determine the profit-maximizing price and output and the optimal allocation of output among the three plants.

5. A hospital produces two commodities (quantity q and quality h) and faces infinitely elastic market demands for these commodities. Current prices are $p_q = 12$ and $p_h = 8$. The hospital's short-run total cost function is

$$\text{STC} = 2q^2 + h^2 + 25.$$

a. If the hospital wishes to maximize profits, how much q and h should be produced?
b. Suppose the hospital is managed by a nonprofit organization. The utility function for the management board is

$$U(q, h) = \min(q, h).$$

What levels of q and h will be chosen to maximize the board's utility?

6. In a Baumol firm, the objective is to maximize sales revenue subject to obtaining a given level of profit.

a. Illustrate the equilibrium level of output for such a firm.
b. Contrast the effects of a lump-sum tax, profit tax, output tax, and sales tax on such a firm with the effects of these taxes on a profit-maximizing firm.

7. A revenue-maximizing monopoly requires a profit of at least \$750. The monopoly is facing the inverse demand function $p = 152 - Q$, with STC $= 4Q^2 + 2Q + 250$. Determine the revenue-maximizing optimal price and output subject to this profit constraint and compare the result with the profit-maximizing solution.

13 Price discrimination

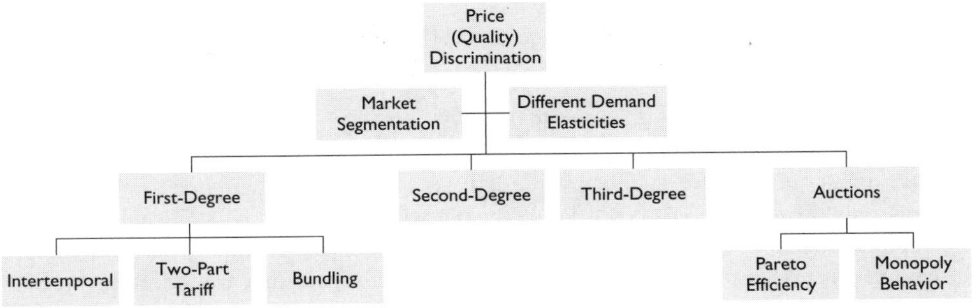

Outline and Conceptual Inquiries

Price-discrimination conditions: no arbitrage and different elasticities
Can you sell your appendectomy to someone else?
Consider first-degree price discrimination
Have you ever been indifferent toward purchasing something?
Application: Intertemporal price discrimination for DVD players
Why are amusement park rides free and park admission prices variable?
Why do automobile companies offer options in packages?
Why practice second-degree price discrimination?
Should you buy the larger size of shampoo or not?
When to third-degree price-discriminate?
Are foreign firms offering lower prices in our market because they want to drive our industries out of business?
Combination of discrimination techniques

Understanding quality discrimination
Application: Sears' drills

Summary
Key concepts
Key equation
Questions
Exercises
Internet case study

Appendix to chapter 13

Auctions
Classification of auctions
Application: A candle auction
When you are the last bidder in an auction, do you only pay the second highest bid?
Mechanism design
Why is it when you win you actually lose?
Application: Avoiding winner's curse
Monopoly behavior
Question
Exercises
Internet case studies

It is illegal to discriminate in terms of education, employment, and in the provision of services on account of race, ethnicity, religion, sex, age, marital status, national origin, ancestry, sexual orientation, disabled veteran status, price, physical or mental disability, learning disability, mental retardation, and criminal records that are not job related.

(City of Boston)

Which item from this list does not belong? That's right, price. Price discrimination is legal, unless it substantially limits competition, and firms will activity price-discriminate in an effort to enhance profits.[1] As discussed in Chapter 12, a firm with monopoly power has some control over the output price when it is facing a negatively sloping demand curve. Thus, it may be possible to increase profits by discriminating among consumers and selling the same product to various customers at different prices. For example, a bar may sell drinks at a lower price per unit during happy hour or a cereal company may offer coupons that reduce the price per unit.

Generally, a firm desires to sell additional output if it can find a way to do so without lowering the price on the units it is currently selling. This is done by separating the market into two or more segments. This separation is called *price discrimination* (or *Ramsey pricing*) and is analogous to a multiproduct firm supplying products in different markets.

Our aim in this chapter is to illustrate how firms are always probing the market for ways to enhance their profits. For a firm's long-run survival, it must constantly devise novel pricing techniques for enhancing profits. Firms who first develop such pricing techniques can earn pure profits, and firms who do not will, in the long run, fail.

We first state the underlying market conditions required for price discrimination. We develop the categories of first-, second-, and third-degree price discrimination and evaluate the efficiency and welfare effects of each type. First-degree price discrimination includes pricing strategies such as the *two-part tariff. Tie-in-sales* and *bundling* are then discussed as an alternative to this type of price discrimination. As with any type of price discrimination, second-degree price discrimination offers potential social benefits in that if a firm did not price-discriminate, it might not be able to produce a desired commodity. Third-degree price discrimination segments the market into, say, a foreign and a domestic market. We then discuss quality discrimination and see that, generally, the same implications associated with price discrimination hold for quality discrimination as well. We conclude the chapter with an appendix on the economics of auctions. When markets are thin, in terms of lacking information on consumer preferences, firms may use auctions to reveal consumer preferences. With these revealed preferences, firms can then determine their price. We discuss and evaluate various types of auctions in terms of firms' potential for maximizing profits and overall welfare effects.

In all large companies, applied economists are actively developing methods for price discrimination. For example, after deregulation of the airline industry in 1978, aviation economists developed all sorts of price discrimination techniques for improving profit such as requiring a Saturday night stay or advanced 14-day bookings. Whether by hiring in-house economists, utilizing outside economic consultants, or devising their own methods, managers will most effectively compete with other firms by practicing price discrimination.

Price-discrimination conditions: no arbitrage and different elasticities

Consider selling your haircut. It is not possible to purchase a haircut in one market and then sell your haircut to someone else in another market. In terms of demand elasticities, if the elasticities associated with the market segments (haircuts) are the same, there does not exist any incentive on part of a firm (barber) to price-discriminate (offer different prices for haircuts), because the profit-maximizing output and price are identical in both markets. Thus, two necessary conditions for price discrimination are the ability to segment the market and the existence of different demand elasticities for each market segment. The ability to segment the market exists if resales become so difficult that it becomes impossible to purchase a commodity in one market and then sell it in another market. When resale is possible, **arbitrage** will eliminate any price discrepancies and the Law of One Price will hold.

Can you sell your appendectomy to someone else? No, it is generally not possible to purchase professional services in one market and then sell them in another market.

Arbitrage. The ability to buy in one market and then sell in another market at a higher price. *E.g., purchasing classic automobiles on the East Coast and then selling them for a higher price in California's Silicon Valley.*

A firm may price-discriminate across any category of consumers, such as income, type of business, quantity purchased, geographic location, time of day, brand name, or age. For example, doctors may charge less for treatment of low-income patients, and a defense contractor will charge the military $500 for a hammer that costs other customers only $20. Depending on how a market can be segmented, economists have categorized these types of price discrimination into first-, second-, and third-degree price discrimination.

Consider first-degree price discrimination

> *At my lemonade stand I used to give the first glass away free and charge the maximum willingness to pay for the second glass. The refill contained the antidote.*
>
> (Emo Phillips)

To obtain the antidote, each consumer will be willing to pay their maximum amount. By selling each antidote to each consumer for his or her maximum willingness to pay, the lemonade stand owner is first-degree price-discriminating. The ultimate in price discrimination—**complete price discrimination**, **perfect price discrimination,** or **first-degree price discrimination**—occurs when it is possible to sell each unit of the product for the maximum price a consumer is willing to pay. Table 13.1 lists the characteristics and examples of first-, second-, and third-degree price discrimination.

Complete, perfect, or first-degree price discrimination. Selling each unit of a commodity for the maximum price a consumer is willing to pay. *E.g., each consumer paying a different price for the same type of automobile.*

Table 13.1 Characteristics of first-, second-, and third-degree price discrimination

	Degree		
Characteristic	*First*	*Second*	*Third*
Output sold to different consumers at different prices (e.g., all forms of price discrimination)	X	X	X
Output sold for the maximum price each consumer is willing to pay (e.g., high-pressure sales, new product pricing)	X		
Price differs across the commodity unit, not across consumers (e.g., cellphone minutes and cereal packaging)		X	
Price differs across consumers, not across commodity unit (e.g., "happy hours," senior discounts, and campus parking).			X

First-degree price discrimination involves tapping the demand curve, as illustrated in Figure 13.1. The first unit of the commodity is sold to a consumer willing to pay the highest price, OA, the second unit to a consumer willing to pay at a slightly lower price, and so on until the demand curve intersects SMC. In this case, the demand or AR curve becomes the MR curve. As the firm increases supply, price declines only for the additional commodity sold, not for all the commodities supplied. (This is in contrast with no price discrimination, where selling an additional unit of output results in not only a lower price for the additional output but also a lower price for all the units sold.) As shown in the figure, the firm equates MR to SMC and supplies a level of output Q_1. This results in TR represented by the area OABQ_1, STC by the area OFEQ_1, and pure profit by the area FABE. Each consumer who purchases the commodity is paying his or her maximum willingness to pay, WTP, for the commodity, and thus receives zero consumer surplus from purchasing the commodity. The area FABE contains the total consumer surplus, for an output level of Q_1, that the firm captures. Since the entire consumer surplus is captured by the firm, all consumers are indifferent between buying the commodity or not.

The lowest price offered by the firm is $p_1 = \text{SMC}(Q_1)$, because the additional revenue generated, p_1, by selling an additional unit of output is just equal to the additional cost, SMC. The last consumer willing to purchase the commodity pays this lowest price, p_1. Consumers who are not willing to pay p_1 do not purchase the commodity. All other consumers who do purchase the commodity pay a price higher than p_1 equivalent to their maximum WTP. Thus, at p_1 and Q_1, what consumers (society) are willing to pay for an additional unit of the commodity is equivalent to what it cost society to produce this

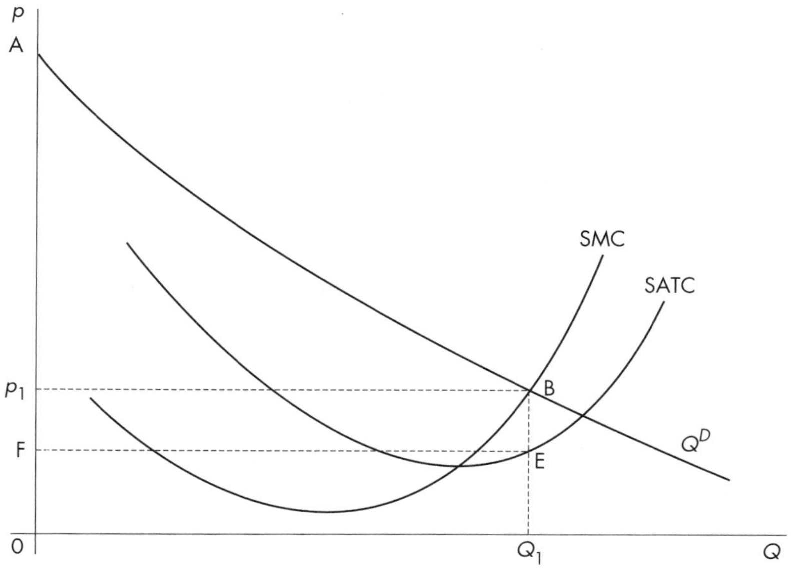

Figure 13.1 **First-degree price discrimination.** For maximizing profit, the firm's lowest price is set equal to the marginal cost, so the firm captures the entire consumer surplus. Profit is then represented by the area FABE, with no deadweight loss.

additional unit, SMC(Q_1). This represents a Pareto-efficient allocation, so with first-degree price discrimination, there is no deadweight loss (inefficiency). However, the distribution of wealth between consumers and owners of firms may be questionable for maximizing social welfare. The firm appropriates the entire consumer surplus, leaving consumers indifferent between consuming the commodity or not.

Have you ever been indifferent toward purchasing something? If the price you pay is equal to the maximum you are willing to pay, then you are indifferent toward purchasing the commodity.

Power corrupts; absolute power is kind of neat.

(John Lehman)

Translation: Monopoly power is inefficient; first-degree price discrimination is efficient.

First-degree price discrimination is difficult to attain. One example is a roadside produce stand where prices vary depending on the type of automobile the consumer is driving and where he is from. A person driving a Lincoln with New York plates will probably pay a premium for boiled peanuts at a roadside stand in Georgia. Another example is high-pressure sales of commodities such as used cars. The initial price is quite high, but the more a consumer balks, indicating she is unwilling to pay the quoted price, the lower the price becomes.

Example 13.1 Calculating first-degree price discrimination

Consider the following market demand function and monopoly's short-run marginal cost function:

$$Q^D = 26 - 2p,$$

$$\text{SMC} = 3 + \tfrac{1}{3}Q^S.$$

Setting $Q^D = Q^S$ results in the perfectly price-discriminating monopoly selling 12 units of output at a price that each consumer is just willing to pay. The firm captures the entire consumer surplus (CS) in addition to the producer surplus (PS):

$$\text{CS} = (13 - 7)12/2 = \$36,$$

$$\text{PS} = (7 - 3)12/2 = \$24.$$

The firm's total surplus is then the sum of CS and PS, \$60, with no deadweight loss.

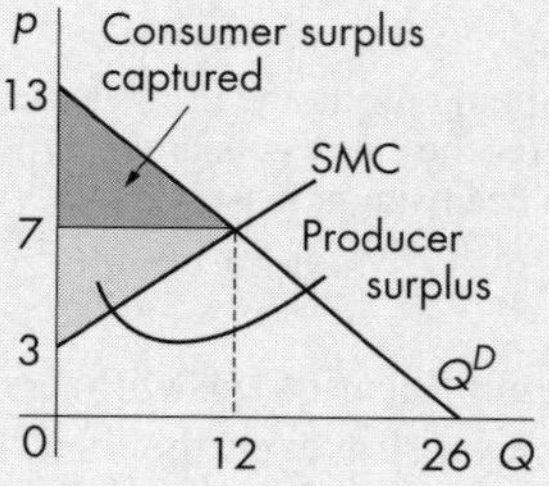

Intertemporal price discrimination

The price to see a first-run movie is initially high. After the movie has run for a number of months, it is released to bargain theaters at a lower price. This type of first-degree price discrimination is called **intertemporal price discrimination**—a product's price is based on different points in time. The price for some new product, such as a tablet computer or a new novel, is initially set high to capture the consumer surplus from those consumers willing to pay the high price rather than waiting. The price is then lowered over time to capture further consumer surplus from those consumers unwilling to pay the high price and willing to wait.

Intertemporal price discrimination. Price discrimination based on different points in time. *E.g., the scalper's price for a ticket to a baseball game will initially be high, but will then decline as the first pitch approaches.*

Application: Intertemporal price discrimination for DVD players

In the 1990s, only consumers with preferences for being one of the first to own a DVD player would actually purchase one and be willing to pay a high price (around $500). These consumers did not have to be convinced why they should purchase one. As the market for first purchasers dried up, the price of DVD players started to decline. The price fell over $200 after two years. By 2001, the average price was just under $200, and at the end of 2002, many DVD players sold for under $100. According to the Consumer Electronics Association, in 2000, nearly 8.7 million DVD players were sold in the United States, and in 2006 this figure increased to 20 million. By 2007, 80 percent of US households had a DVD player. Thus, in 2007, sales declined by 15 percent, with around 10 million sold at an average price of $60. In 2011, most DVD players list for $30–40. Decreasing the price of a commodity over time further taps the market demand curve as consumers require less convincing for their purchases.

Sales of DVD players have now fallen to their lowest level in many years, leading experts to warn that the technology could soon die out. The rising popularity of Internet downloads and digital video recorders have resulted in a switch to watching films and TV series virtually, rather than keeping a hard copy. The trend could see the once-dominant DVD player go the way of the tape, vinyl LP, and VHS players.

Two-part tariffs

In college towns across the United States, student nightclubs will charge an entry fee (cover charge) and then offer drinks at cost. Generally, females are less willing to pay to go to such clubs than males, so the clubs will lower the entrance fee for females. This type of two-part pricing policy, called a **two-part tariff**, is another method of increasing profit through first-degree price discrimination. Consumers pay an entry fee for the right to purchase the commodity being sold. The firm will price-discriminate on entry fees in order to extract as much of a consumer's WTP as possible. The commodity being sold is priced so it will maximize admission subject to the constraint that additional output cannot be sold below cost. This is at $p = \text{SMC}$ and will expand the number of consumers paying entry fees compared with the no price-discrimination condition of $\text{MR} = \text{SMC}$. Another example of a two-part tariff is an amusements park that price-discriminates on entry fees and then offers free rides. The marginal cost of an additional rider is close to zero. Price discrimination on entry fees is achieved through coupons and discounts by age or for membership in certain organizations.

For example, in 1955, Disneyland opened in rural Anaheim, California. In the 1950s and 1960s, Disneyland employed a two-part tariff where an admission price was charged along with a cost for each attraction. Cost of tickets for the attractions varied, with rides like Dumbo costing the least (an A ticket) and rides like Pirates of the Caribbean costing the most (an E ticket). Realizing that the marginal cost of an additional rider was close to zero, Disneyland abandoned the A through E tickets and let consumers ride any of the attractions for free after paying a park entrance fee.

Why are amusement park rides free and park admission prices variable? The marginal cost of an additional rider is close to zero, so rides are free. The park derives its revenue from admission prices and price-discriminates on these admission prices to maximize profit.

Example 13.2 How a two-part tariff works

Consider the following demand functions for two consumers, where we more broadly define a consumer as a certain segment of consumers with some distinguishable common characteristics:

$$q_1 = -2p_1 + 6,$$

$$q_2 = -3p_2 + 9.$$

Assuming SMC = 1, at p = SMC = 1, consumer surplus for consumer 1 is $(3-1)4/2 =$ \$4 and consumer surplus for consumer 2 is $(3-1)6/2 =$ \$6. The firm will then charge an entry fee of \$4 for consumer 1 and \$6 for consumer 2. This will result in a producer surplus of \$10 for the firm, and the consumers will be indifferent whether to consume the commodity or not. The entire total surplus accrues to the firm with no deadweight loss.

Alternatively, assume that the firm is unable to perfectly price-discriminate and instead must charge the same entry fee for both consumers. If the firm charged the higher entry fee of \$6, consumer 1 would not be willing to participate in the market, so the firm would collect only the \$6 entry fee from consumer 2 as its producer surplus. Instead, charging the lower entry fee of \$4 results in both consumers participating and a combined producer surplus for the firm of \$8. Some of the surplus is then transferred from the firm to consumer 2, who was willing to pay \$6 to enter but only has to pay \$4—a gain of \$2. Total surplus remains the same at \$10, so no deadweight loss exists.

However, the firm is not maximizing profits by setting price to marginal cost with an entry fee of \$4. Profits are maximized by setting price above marginal cost with an entry fee equal to the associated consumer surplus of consumer 1:

$$\max_p \pi = \max_p [pq_1 + pq_2 + 2(3-p)q_1/2 - \text{SMC}(q_1 + q_2) - \text{TFC}],$$

where an entry fee $(3-p)/2$ is collected from both consumers and STVC = SMC$(q_1 + q_2)$. Substituting in the demand functions and SMC = 1 results in

$$\max_p \pi = \max_p [(p-1)(6-2p+9-3p) + (3-p)(6-2p) - \text{TFC}].$$

Simplifying,

$$\max_p \pi = \max_p [2(6-2p) + (p-1)(9-3p) - \text{TFC}]$$

$$= \max_p \left[12 - 4p + 12p - 9 - 3p^2 - \text{TFC}\right].$$

The first-order condition (FOC) is

$$\frac{\partial \pi}{\partial p} = 8 - 6p^* = 0 \Rightarrow p^* = \frac{4}{3}, \quad q_1^* = \frac{10}{3}, \quad q_2^* = 5.$$

The entry fee is then $(3 - 4/3)(10/3)½ =$ \$2.78.

Producer surplus is then (4/3 – 1)(25/3) + (3 – 4/3)(10/3) = 75/9 = \$8.33. Consumer 1 pays the entry fee of \$2.78, which exhausts its surplus. Consumer surplus for consumer 2 is (3 – 4/3)5(½) – entry fee = 4.17 – 2.78 = \$1.39. This results in a deadweight loss of 10 – 8.33 – 1.39 = \$0.28.

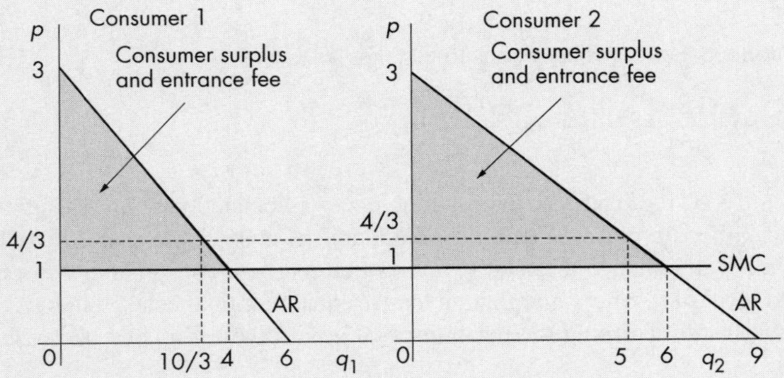

Another example of two-part tariff pricing is automobile rental agencies, which price-discriminate on the fixed daily or weekly fee for renting an automobile and then may or may not have a mileage charge or may include some free fixed mileage limit. This allows an agency to set a higher entry fee while losing fewer consumers who demand lower total miles. The high entry fee captures the consumer surplus of those consumers who have a high demand for the automobile regardless of how many miles they drive, while unlimited mileage captures those consumers with a lower demand.

Two-part tariff. Consumers pay for the ability to purchase a commodity and possibly again for the actual commodity. *E.g., you pay a membership fee for joining a country club in addition to any greens fee.*

A two-part tariff assuming only one consumer is also illustrated in Figure 13.1. In its pricing scheme, the firm sets an entry fee that takes the entire consumer surplus, where $p =$ SMC at p_1, represented by the area p_1AB, and then sets a price of p_1 that results in output Q_1. The firm's profit is then the same as first-degree price discrimination, FABE, and no deadweight loss exists. However, again there may be social-welfare implications from a transfer of surplus from consumers to firms.

With two consumers, the firm can practice perfect price discrimination in the entry fee and again capture the entire consumer surplus. However, if the firm is unable to practice price discrimination, it will only charge one entry fee. The firm will then maximize profits by setting its price above marginal cost, with an entry fee equal to the resulting lowest consumer surplus. With $p >$ MC, a deadweight loss occurs, so the inability to price-discriminate on entry fees results in an inefficient allocation.

We can demonstrate this mathematically by letting $TR_1(p) = pq_1(p)$ and $TR_2(p) = pq_2(p)$ be the total revenues collected from consumers (1 and 2), where $q_j(p), j = 1, 2$, is consumer

j's demand function. We assume that consumer 1 has a lower demand for the commodity than consumer 2. The entry fee, Fee, is then equal to consumer 1's consumer surplus and is a function of p, Fee(p); a price rise (fall) will lower (raise) consumer 1's surplus and hence Fee(p). The firm will then maximize profits by

$$\max_p \pi = \max_p [\text{TR}_1(p) + \text{TR}_2(p) + 2\text{Fee}(p) - \text{STC}],$$

where the firm collects Fee from both consumers. The FOC is

$$\frac{\partial \pi}{\partial p} = \frac{\partial \text{TR}_1}{\partial p} + \frac{\partial \text{TR}_2}{\partial p} + 2\frac{\partial \text{Fee}}{\partial p} - \frac{\partial \text{STC}}{\partial p} = 0.$$

The terms $\partial \text{TR}_1/\partial p + \partial \text{TR}_2/\partial p$ are the marginal revenues associated with increasing the per-unit price p, and $2\partial \text{Fee}/\partial p$ plus $\partial \text{STC}/\partial p$ are the marginal costs. Note that $2\partial \text{Fee}/\partial p < 0$, so an increase in p will enhance the total revenues but decrease consumer 1's surplus and Fee. The optimal level of p, where marginal revenues equal marginal costs, will balance this enhanced revenue from increasing the per-unit price p with the associated decrease in the entry fee, Fee.

When the firm is facing more than two consumers, it must trade off a relatively low entry fee with a higher price versus a high entry fee and price closer to marginal cost. In the case of consumers having similar preferences (demands), the firm will set the price close to marginal cost and extract most of the consumer surplus with a relatively high entry fee. In contrast, when facing consumers with large differences in preferences, the firm will do the reverse: set a low entry fee and extract most of the surplus with price above marginal cost.

Firms will also use a two-part tariff in pricing tie-in sales. **Tie-in sales** are where a firm with monopoly power will require consumers to purchase two or more commodities that are complementary goods. For example, up until the late 1960s, IBM required consumers who purchased an IBM computer to purchase their punch cards. They priced the computer at a perfectly competitive price and then employed monopoly pricing for the punch cards, where MR $=$ SMC $< p$. Thus, this type of two-part tariff will reduce social welfare, and is perhaps why IBM, under Justice Department pressure, stopped the practice. Other examples of tie-in sales are diabetic test kits and computer printers. Firms price the test kits or printers at cost, but they use monopoly pricing in pricing test strips or ink cartridges required for using the machine.[2]

Tie-in sales. A firm requires consumers to purchase two or more commodities that are complementary goods. *E.g., purchasing an Xbox or Wii will require you to purchase games software.*

Bundling

The best car safety device is a rear-view mirror with a cop in it.

(Dudley Moore)

Translation: In terms of bundling commodities, a rear-view mirror with a cop offers a high level of safety.

In many cases, firms are unable to practice first-degree price discrimination because consumer preferences are not completely revealed and the cost of revealing these preferences may be prohibitive. In such cases, the difference in consumers' willingness to pay for commodities and marginal cost of producing the commodities can be exploited by selling commodities in bundles. Such **bundling** exists when a firm requires consumers to purchase a package or set of different commodities rather than some subset of the commodities. For example, many portrait studios will sell a package of photos in different sizes and poses rather than each photo separately. Bundling is a very effective method for enhancing profit when consumers have heterogeneous demands but the firm is unable to effectively separate consumers by their preferences and then price-discriminate. Specifically, bundling is an alternative when firms are unable to perfectly price-discriminate.

Why do automobile companies offer options in packages? Automobile companies are unable to effectively separate consumers by their preferences and then price-discriminate, so they offer options in bundles to enhance their profits.

Bundling. Requiring consumers to purchase a set of commodities rather than some subset of the commodities. *E.g., television cable companies will generally sell a package of channels rather than each channel separately.*

As an example, automobile dealers often offer a package containing a number of options, such as leather seats and antilock brakes. Consumers can purchase the package containing leather seats and antilock brakes; however, they cannot purchase leather seats or antilock brakes separately. Suppose Robinson is willing to pay more for leather seats than Friday, and Friday is willing to pay more for antilock brakes than Robinson. As shown in Table 13.2, if the options were sold separately, the maximum price that could be charged, where both consumers are willing to pay for options, is \$1300 for leather seats and \$1000 for antilock brakes. Revenue would then be \$2300 from each consumer, with TR = \$4600. If the dealer could perfectly price-discriminate and charge each consumer their maximum WTP for each option, then first-degree price discrimination would yield TR = 2000 + 1000 + 1300 + 2500 = \$6800. However, since the dealer cannot do this, it bundles leather seats with anti-lock brakes. Then Robinson is willing to pay \$3000 and Friday \$3800. By charging each consumer \$3000, TR = \$6000, which is greater than the revenue derived from not bundling but lower than the revenue from perfect price discrimination.

Table 13.2 Bundling

	Consumers' maximum willingness to pay (\$)	
	Robinson, R	*Friday, F*
Leather seats	2000	1300
Antilock brakes	1000	2500
Bundling	3000	3800

Table 13.3 Bundling with positively correlated demands

	Consumers' maximum willingness to pay ($)	
	Robinson, R	*Friday, F*
Leather seats	2000	2500
Antilock brakes	1000	1300
Bundling	3000	3800

Bundling is most effective when the demands of the two consumers are negatively correlated; for example, when Robinson has a high WTP for leather seats and a low WTP for antilock brakes and vice versa for Friday. In contrast, if the demands are positively correlated, bundling may not be an effective mechanism for enhancing profits. With the figures in Table 13.3, bundling results in a bundled price of \$3000 and an associated TR of \$6000. This now can be matched by selling leather seating for \$2000 and antilock brakes for \$1000. In this case, bundling is ineffective as a tool for enhancing profit.

Local governments have recently adopted bundling in an effort to entice voters to pass local-option tax measures. Targeting tax revenue to specific projects such as school improvements, a retirement center, a sports complex, or a transit facility improves the likelihood of the tax passing. The negative correlation of these projects makes bundling a very attractive method for funding. If voters had to consider each project separately, the probability of all the projects receiving majority support would decrease.

The advantage of bundling is illustrated in Figure 13.2, where the unbundled monopoly price p_M and output Q_M yield producer surplus represented by the area Ap_MCD, with corresponding consumer surplus p_MBC. Instead if the firm bundled its output, so the consumer no longer has the choice of purchasing the commodity individually, the consumer can only choose to not purchase any of the commodity or some given bundle Q_B. The consumer can then self-select to purchase the bundle or not. Consumer surplus is zero if the bundled commodity is not purchased, so the firm will expand output at price p_M until the consumer is indifferent toward purchasing the bundle or not. At Q_B with price p_M, consumer surplus is $p_M\text{BC} - \text{CEG} = 0$, so the consumer is then indifferent between purchasing the commodity bundle Q_B or not. Producer surplus is then increased by DCEF to Ap_MEF. An example of this type of bundling is the purchasing of a hardware screw. You may only want one screw, but the screws are bundled in a package of a dozen. By selling the screws in bundles, the firm is able to increase its profits. The firm may also offer different-size bundles at different per-unit prices, which is a form of second-degree price discrimination.

Example 13.3 Enhanced profits through bundling

Consider the following market demand and short-run marginal cost functions for a monopoly:

$$Q^D = 10 - p \Rightarrow p = 10 - Q,$$

$$\text{SMC} = \text{SAVC} = 6.$$

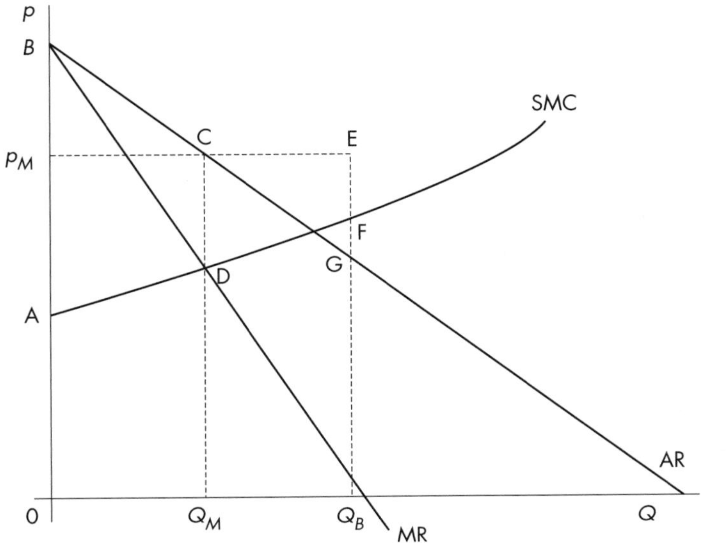

Figure 13.2 **Bundling as a method of firms extracting consumer surplus.** By requiring a consumer to only choose between purchasing the bundle Q_B or not purchasing any of the commodity, the firm is able to increase its profit by DCEF.

If the firm does not bundle its output, then its output price and quantity are determined by

$$MR = SMC,$$

$$10 - 2Q = 6,$$

$$Q_M = 2, \quad p_M = 8.$$

The corresponding consumer and producer surpluses are

$$CS = (10 - 8)2/2 = \$2,$$

$$PS = (8 - 6)2 = 4.$$

Instead, if the firm bundles the commodity and sells it at a per-unit price of 8, where consumer surplus is zero, then the bundled output is determined by

$$\text{unbundled CS} = 2(Q_B - 2)/2.$$

$$Q_B = 4.$$

The firm's producer surplus is then doubled to \$8.

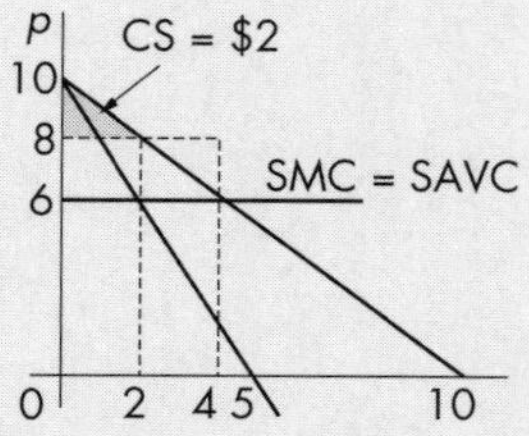

Why practice second-degree price discrimination?

In 2012, the cost of a 1-ounce letter is 28.1¢ using Standard Class (bulk mail), compared with 45¢ for regular First Class mail. This bulk rate discount is an example of second-degree price discrimination and is commonly used by public utilities, where, for example, the per-unit price of electricity often depends on how much is used. Supermarkets also employ second-degree price discrimination by selling items in larger quantities (bulk) for a lower per-unit price. Specifically, **second-degree price discrimination** (also known as **nonlinear pricing**) occurs where a firm with monopoly power sells different units of output for different per-unit prices, and every consumer who buys the same unit amount of the commodity pays the same per-unit price. Price differs across the commodity units and not across consumers. The same price schedule is offered to all consumers and the consumers self-select which price per unit they will pay.

Mixed bundling is an alternative type of bundling associated with second-degree price discrimination. A firm will offer commodities both separately and as a bundle, with the bundled price below the sum of the individual prices. An example is a toy store selling separately swim items such as face masks, fins, and snorkels and then bundling the complete set of swim equipment for one, lower price. Another example is a college athletic association selling season tickets along with separate tickets for each game.

Second-degree price discrimination (nonlinear pricing). A firm sells different units of output at different per-unit prices, and every consumer who buys the same unit quantity of the commodity pays the same per-unit price. *E.g., the price per minute of a long-distance calling card declines as the total number of minutes increases.*

In some cases, it may be possible for a firm with monopoly power to only earn a pure profit if it price-discriminates. As an example, consider second-degree price discrimination where a monopoly establishes two prices for a commodity: a higher per-unit price for the commodity offered in a smaller size and a lower per-unit price for a larger size. As illustrated in Figure 13.3, assume that the monopoly would be operating at a loss if it offered a single (linear) per-unit price for the commodity: the SATC curve does not cross the AR curve at any output level, so no single price will yield a positive pure profit. If, instead, the firm price-discriminates, it will earn a pure profit by selling Q_1 units of the commodity in a smaller unit size at a price of p_1 and $Q_2 - Q_1$ units of the commodity in a larger unit size

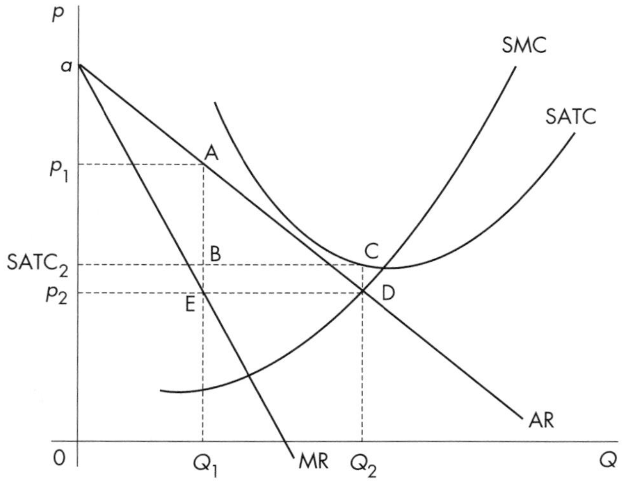

Figure 13.3 **Second-degree price discrimination yielding a pure profit.** No price discrimination at output Q_2 and price p_2 results in the firm operating at a loss, area $p_2(\text{SATC}_2)$CD. By price-discriminating, the firm earns a profit on sales of its smaller-size units, $(\text{SATC}_2)p_1$AB, which is greater than the loss from selling the larger-size units, area EBCD.

at a price of p_2. The pure profit from selling the smaller unit size is represented by the area $(\text{SATC}_2)p_1$AB, which is greater than the loss (negative pure profit) from selling the larger unit size, represented by the area EBCD. Consumers can now consume the commodity that would not be available if the firm did not price-discriminate, and the firm can earn a pure profit. Thus, in this case, both consumers and the firm are better off by price discrimination, implying a Pareto improvement and an associated increase in social welfare. As discussed in Chapter 12, this is one justification for allowing a regulated monopoly to practice price discrimination.

Note that, corresponding to the sale of larger-size units, p_2 is where $p = \text{SMC}$. This assumes that the firm does not practice any other monopolizing behavior besides second-degree price discrimination. The firm then sets $p = \text{SMC}$ for determining the larger-size unit price p_2 and the total amount of the commodity produced, Q_2. Alternatively, if we assume that the firm will engage in further monopolizing behavior, then the firm will not equate $p = \text{SMC}$ for the larger-size unit. Instead, for the two-commodity-size case, the firm will maximize profits for the two alternative size units:

$$\max_{(Q_1,Q_2)} \pi = \max_{(Q_1,Q_2)} [p(Q_1)Q_1 + p(Q_2)(Q_2 - Q_1) - \text{STC}(Q_2)].$$

The FOCs are

$$\frac{\partial \pi}{\partial Q_1} = \text{MR}(Q_1) - p(Q_2) = 0,$$

$$\frac{\partial \pi}{\partial Q_2} = \text{MR}(Q_2) - \frac{\partial p}{\partial Q_2} Q_1 - \text{SMC}(Q_2) = 0.$$

Note that the term $-(\partial p/\partial Q_2)Q_1 > 0$, given that $\partial p/\partial Q_2 < 0$. This is the positive adjustment to MR(Q_2), since marginal revenue only declines for $Q_2 - Q_1$ and not for the small-size unit (Q_1) proportion of the total output Q_2. If the firm did not consider this monopolizing behavior, then the second FOC would be $p_2 = \text{SMC}$. We then determine the optimal level of small-size units Q_1 and associated price p_1 by considering the first FOC, where

$$\text{MR}(Q_1) - p_2 = 0.$$

Solving for Q_1 yields the optimal quantity for the firm to supply in smaller units. The firm can sell this level of output at the price p_1. In Figure 13.3, the maximization problem results in additional revenue above the bulk price p_2 of $(p_1 - p_2)Q_1$, represented by the area p_2p_1AE.

Example 13.4 Determining second-degree price discrimination

Consider the following market demand and short-run total cost functions for a monopoly:

$$Q^D = 17 - \tfrac{1}{2}p \Rightarrow p = 34 - 2Q,$$

$$\text{STC} = Q^2 + 10Q + 50.$$

If the firm does not price-discriminate, its profit-maximizing output and price are determined by

$$\max_Q \pi = \max_Q [pQ - \text{STC}]$$

$$= \max_Q \left[(34 - 2Q)Q - (Q^2 + 10Q + 50)\right].$$

The FOC is then

$$\frac{\partial \pi}{\partial Q} = 34 - 4Q_M - (2Q_M + 10) = 0,$$

that is,

$$\text{MR} - \text{SMC} = 0.$$

Solving for Q_M yields the optimal no-price discriminating quantity, $Q_M = 4$. Substituting this optimal output into the market demand function yields the per-unit price that can be charged for selling all of the output, $p_M = 26$ (the linear price). Pure profit is then $\pi = 104 - 16 - 40 - 50 = -\$2$. The firm will operate at a loss, given $p >$ SAVC $= 14$.

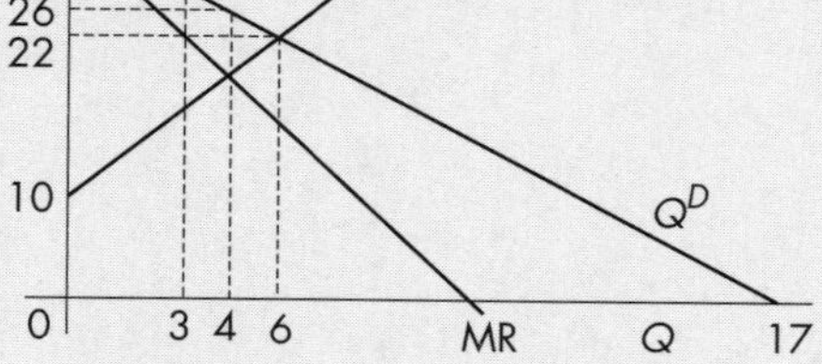

Instead, assume that the firm employs second-degree price discrimination by offering a per-unit price discount for larger-volume purchases (nonlinear pricing). Assume that the firm will set $p = \text{SMC}$ for larger-volume purchases and a higher price for low-volume purchases. Specifically,

$$p = \text{SMC},$$
$$34 - 2Q_2 = 2Q_2 + 10.$$

Solving for Q_2 yields the output level or volume for total purchases, $Q_2 = 6$, with an associated competitive price $p_2 = 22$. The profit-maximizing quantity for the smaller unit, Q_1, is determined by setting this competitive price to MR:

$$22 = 34 - 4Q_1,$$

Solving for Q_1 yields $Q_1 = 3$. From the market demand function, the smaller-unit price is $p_1 = 28$. Thus, 3 units of the commodity are sold in the smaller unit size at $p_1 = 28$ and $(6 - 3) = 3$ units are sold in the larger unit size at a price $p_2 = 22$. Profit is then $\pi = (28)3 + (22)3 - 6^2 - (10)6 - 50 = 150 - 146 = \$4$. The firm is now operating with a pure profit by employing second-degree price discrimination. Note that $\text{CS}_1 = \text{CS}_2 =$ \$9, so the self-selection constraint is satisfied.

Alternatively, assuming that the firm engages in further monopolizing behavior, for the two-commodity-size case,

$$\max_{(Q_1, Q_2)} \pi = \max_{(Q_1, Q_2)} \left[(34 - 2Q_1)Q_1 + (34 - 2Q_2)(Q_2 - Q_1) - (Q_2^2 + 10Q_2 + 50)\right].$$

The FOCs are

$$\frac{\partial \pi}{\partial Q_1} = 34 - 4Q_1 - 34 + 2Q_2 = 0,$$

$$\frac{\partial \pi}{\partial Q_2} = 34 - 4Q_2 + 2Q_1 - 2Q_2 - 10 = 0.$$

Solving for Q_1 and Q_2 yields $Q_1 = 2.4$, $Q_2 = 4.8$, $p_1 = 29.2$, $p_2 = 24.4$, and $\pi = 70.08 + 58.56 - 121.04 = \$7.60$.

Self-selection constraint

One problem with a firm maximizing the smaller-unit revenue (net of revenue from not selling the quantity at the lower price p_2) is that consumers rather than the firm determine who will purchase smaller versus larger sizes of the commodity. There is nothing to prevent a consumer who usually purchases the commodity in bulk from instead purchasing the smaller-size unit. If the firm's price/quantity solution of p_1 and Q_1 yields the unintended result of consumers shifting from purchasing larger-size units to smaller-size units, then this will not be the profit-maximizing solution. The firm instead must determine the optimal price and quantity that will provide an incentive for consumers to purchase the unit size that maximizes the firm's profit. If the consumer surplus for consumers purchasing the larger-size unit is greater than their surplus from purchasing the smaller-size unit, then consumers will self-select and purchase the larger-size unit. Otherwise, self-selection will not occur and the bulk purchasers will switch to purchasing the smaller unit size.

Should you buy the larger size of shampoo or not? If your consumer surplus per unit from purchasing the larger size is greater than the surplus per unit from purchasing the smaller size, then purchase the larger size.

Considering this self-selection constraint on determining the profit-maximizing price and quantity, p_1 and Q_1, the maximization problem is then

$$\max_{Q_1} [p_1(Q_1)Q_1 - p_2Q_1] \quad \text{s.t. } \mathrm{CS}_1 \leq \mathrm{CS}_2,$$

where CS_1 and CS_2 are the bulk consumers' surplus from instead purchasing the smaller unit size and their surplus from purchasing in bulk, respectively. If at the unconstrained optimal solution, where $\mathrm{MR}(Q_1) - p_2 = 0$, the self-selection constraint holds ($\mathrm{CS}_1 \leq \mathrm{CS}_2$), then the firm will maximize profits by setting $\mathrm{MR}(Q_1) = p_2$. If $\mathrm{CS}_1 > \mathrm{CS}_2$, at $\mathrm{MR}(Q_1) = p_2$, then the firm will further increase the price of the smaller-size unit until $\mathrm{CS}_1 = \mathrm{CS}_2$.

For a linear demand curve, the condition $\mathrm{CS}_1 = \mathrm{CS}_2$ corresponds to the revenue-maximizing condition $\mathrm{MR}(Q_1) - p_2 = 0$. We can demonstrate this condition with Figure 13.3. Let $p = a - b\mathrm{Q}$ be the inverse linear demand function faced by the firm. Then

$$\mathrm{CS}_1 = \mathrm{CS}_2,$$
$$\frac{(a - p_1)Q_1}{2} = \frac{(p_1 - p_2)(Q_2 - Q_1)}{2}.$$

Multiplying both sides by 2 and substituting the linear demand function for p_1 and p_2 yields

$$(a - a + bQ_1)Q_1 = [a - bQ_1 - (a - bQ_2)](Q_2 - Q_1),$$
$$bQ_1^2 = b(Q_2 - Q_1)^2,$$
$$Q_1 = Q_2/2.$$

This result is equivalent to the FOC for maximizing revenue, $\mathrm{MR}(Q_1) - p_2 = 0$. Solving for Q_1, by noting that $\mathrm{MR}(Q_1) = a - 2bQ_1$ and $p_2 = a - bQ_2$, yields this equivalence:

$$a - 2bQ_1 - (a - bQ_2) = 0,$$
$$Q_1 = Q_2/2.$$

This equivalence is illustrated in Figure 13.3, where the area $p_1a\mathrm{A}$ representing CS_1 is equivalent to the area EAD representing CS_2 at $\mathrm{MR}(Q_1) - p_2 = 0$. Thus, for a linear demand curve, the self-selection constraint is always satisfied.

When to third-degree price-discriminate?

In October 2001, Bethlehem Steel Corporation (then the United States' third largest steel producer) filed for protection from creditors under Chapter 11 of US bankruptcy laws.

A major cause for this action was an unchecked flow of unfairly traded steel imports into US markets. As a direct result of this trade, Bethlehem put pressure on the federal government to counter this sale of foreign-made steel in the United States below the sale price in the producing country (this is called dumping). Some managers believe that the only reason for a firm to sell its product at a lower price in its foreign market would be to drive competing firms out of business and then exercise monopoly power by increasing price. However, in many cases, the reason the foreign price is lower than the domestic price is that the firm is practicing third-degree price discrimination.

Third-degree price discrimination is a common form of price discrimination, with examples such as senior-citizen discounts, lower prices in foreign versus domestic markets, and "happy hours" at bars. Whenever markets have different demand elasticities and arbitrage among markets is impossible, a firm can engage in third-degree price discrimination. Such price discrimination occurs when a firm with monopoly power sells output to different consumers for different prices, and every unit of output sold to a given category of consumers sells for the same price. For example, in 2012, the nonprofit rate for Standard Class (bulk) mail is 17.2¢, compared with 28.1¢ charged to for-profit consumers. In contrast to second-degree price discrimination, where price differs across the commodity unit (bulk mailings versus individual letters) and not across consumers, in third-degree price discrimination, price differs across consumers (nonprofit versus other consumers) and not across commodity unit.

Are foreign firms offering lower prices in our market because they want to drive our industries out of business? No, foreign firms are attempting to maximize profits by third-degree price discrimination.

Third-degree price discrimination. A firm sells its output at different per-unit prices based on different categories of consumers, and all consumers within a category pay the same price. *E.g., providing discount basketball tickets to college students.*

As an illustration of third-degree price discrimination, let us consider two markets, each with different demand elasticities. Assume that the demand curves are independent, so no leakage exists among markets. Thus, consumers in the market with a lower price cannot resell the product in another market with a higher price. For determining the optimal selling prices and outputs, we let $p_j(q_j)$ be the inverse demand function in the jth market segment and express revenue in the jth market segment by

$$\mathrm{TR}_j(q_j) = p_j(q_j)q_j, \quad j = 1, 2,$$

where q_j is the quantity sold in the jth market segment. Total revenue is then

$$\mathrm{TR}(Q) = \mathrm{TR}_1(q_1) + \mathrm{TR}_2(q_2),$$

where total quantity sold, Q, is

$$Q = q_1 + q_2.$$

Letting STC(Q) be the short-run total cost function, the firm maximizes profits by

$$\max_{(q_1, q_2)} \pi(Q) = \max_{(q_1, q_2)} [\mathrm{TR}_1(q_1) + \mathrm{TR}_2(q_2) - \mathrm{STC}(Q)].$$

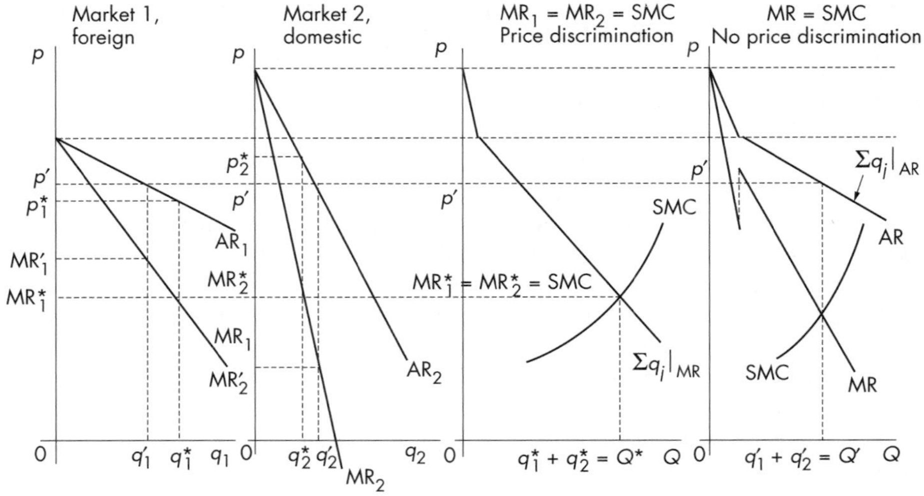

Figure 13.4 **Third-degree price discrimination for two markets.** The firm will maximize profit by equating the marginal revenue in each market to overall marginal cost. This will result in the profit-maximizing prices p_1^* and p_2^* at outputs q_1^* and q_2^*. The overall aggregate output is then $q_1^* + q_2^* = Q^*$.

Partial differentiation yields the FOCs:

$$\frac{\partial \pi}{\partial q_j} = \frac{d\text{TR}_j(q_j)}{dq_j} - \frac{d\text{STC}(Q)}{dQ}\frac{\partial Q}{\partial q_j} = 0 \quad \text{for } j = 1, 2.$$

Note that $\partial Q/\partial q_j = 1$, $d\text{TR}_j/dq_j = \text{MR}_j$, and $d\text{STC}/dQ = \text{SMC}$, so the FOC is $\text{MR}_j = \text{SMC}$ for $j = 1, 2$. If $\text{MR}_1 > \text{MR}_2$, then total revenue and profit can be increased by shifting output from market 2 to market 1. This enhancement in total revenue can continue until the marginal revenues in both markets are equal.

In general, for k markets, $\text{MR}_j(q_j) = \text{SMC}(Q)$ for all k markets. Thus, if a monopoly can divide its market into k independent submarkets, it should divide overall output among the k markets in such a way that it equalizes the marginal revenue obtained in all markets:

$$\text{MR}_1(q_1) = \text{MR}_2(q_2) = \ldots = \text{MR}_k(q_k).$$

This common marginal revenue should be equal to the marginal cost of overall output:

$$\text{MR}_1(q_1) = \text{MR}_2(q_2) = \ldots = \text{MR}_k(q_k) = \text{SMC}(Q).$$

The price charged in each market is determined by substituting the optimal quantity q_j^* into the market's average revenue function $p_j^* = \text{AR}_j(q_j^*)$.

A graphical illustration for two markets (say, foreign and domestic) is provided in Figure 13.4. Consider a level of $\text{MR} = \text{MR}^*$. This value of marginal revenue is attained in both markets if and only if the quantities sold in the two market segments are q_1^* and q_2^*. The remaining FOC requires that this common MR in the two market segments be equated to SMC. This condition determines the optimal (Q, MR) combination. By summing horizontally the MR curves in each of the two markets, we determine the total output for a given level of MR, $\sum q_j|_{\text{MR}}$. Equating $\sum q_j|_{\text{MR}}$ with SMC determines the optimal level of total output, Q^*. Note that the optimal quantities and prices in the two markets are q_1^*, q_2^*, and p_1^*, p_2^*. The optimal price in each market is determined by the demand curve in each market given the optimal output levels.

As illustrated in Figure 13.4, the price is highest in the market segment with the steeply sloped demand function (the domestic market with the more inelastic demand). We can investigate this relation of prices in the separate markets and elasticity by recalling

$$\text{MR}_j(q_j) = p_j\left(1 + \frac{1}{\varepsilon_j^D}\right),$$

where $\varepsilon_j^D = (\partial q_j/\partial p_j)p_j/q_j$ is the own-price elasticity of demand in market j.

We can then relate the prices charged in the separate markets to the own-price elasticities of demand in each of these markets, given that the condition for two markets is $\text{MR}_1 = \text{MR}_2$:

$$p_1\left(1 + \frac{1}{\varepsilon_1^D}\right) = p_2\left(1 + \frac{1}{\varepsilon_2^D}\right),$$

$$\frac{p_1}{p_2} = \frac{1 + 1/\varepsilon_2^D}{1 + 1/\varepsilon_1^D}.$$

This relationship indicates that the prices in any two markets are equivalent if the own-price elasticities of demand are equal. If $\varepsilon_2^D > \varepsilon_1^D$ (demand is more elastic in the foreign market, market 1), then

$$1 + \frac{1}{\varepsilon_2^D} < 1 + \frac{1}{\varepsilon_1^D},$$

which implies

$$p_1/p_2 < 1 \quad \text{or} \quad p_2 > p_1.$$

Thus, the price is higher in the market with the more inelastic demand curve (the domestic market 2). The foreign market, which is more price-sensitive due to a greater degree of competition from other firms (more elastic demand), is charged the lower price. Thus, a foreign firm (say, a steel firm) is not necessarily dumping its product onto the market at unfair prices in an attempt to drive out competition.

In terms of the Lerner Index,

$$\frac{p_1}{p_2} = \frac{1 - L_{I2}}{1 - L_{I1}},$$

where L_{I1} and L_{I2} are the Lerner Indexes in markets 1 and 2, respectively. If market 2 has a greater degree of monopoly power, so $L_{I1} < L_{I2}$, then $p_1 < p_2$.

Whenever the demand is more elastic in one market relative to another and arbitrage is not possible, prices will be lower in this market. For example, demand for movie matinees is more elastic than demand for evening movies. Matinee prices are lower because the opportunity cost of going to a matinee is higher; working and going to school coincide with the matinee time. Similarly, senior citizens and college students are groups with relatively lower incomes, resulting in a more elastic demand for commodities. If a firm is able to segment its market based on these demographics, it can price-discriminate and potentially enhance its profits.

Example 13.5 Determining third-degree price discrimination in two markets

Consider the following demand functions in two separate markets:

$$q_1 = -2p_1 + 6,$$
$$q_2 = -2p_2 + 4.$$

Let the short-run total cost function for this firm be

$$\text{STC} = \tfrac{1}{2} + (q_1 + q_2),$$

and let the total output produced by the firm, Q, be the sum of q_1 and q_2. Solving the demand functions for p_1 and p_2 results in the inverse demand functions for the two markets:

$$p_1 = -\tfrac{1}{2}q_1 + 3,$$
$$p_2 = -\tfrac{1}{2}q_2 + 2.$$

Profit maximization for the firm is then

$$\begin{aligned} \max_{(q_1,q_2)} \pi &= \max_{(q_1,q_2)} (\text{TR} - \text{STC}) \\ &= \max_{(q_1,q_2)} (p_1 q_1 + p_2 q_2 - \text{STC}) \\ &= \max_{(q_1,q_2)} \left[(-\tfrac{1}{2}q_1 + 3)q_1 + (-\tfrac{1}{2}q_2 + 2)q_2 - (\tfrac{1}{2} + q_1 + q_2)\right]. \end{aligned}$$

The FOCs are

$$\frac{\partial \pi}{\partial q_1} = -q_1^* + 3 - 1 = 0,$$

that is,

$$\text{MR}_1 - \text{SMC} = 0,$$

and

$$\frac{\partial \pi}{\partial q_2} = -q_2^* + 2 - 1 = 0,$$

that is,

$$\text{MR}_2 - \text{SMC} = 0.$$

Solving these FOCs for q_1^* and q_2^* yields

$$q_1^* = 3 - 1 = 2,$$
$$q_2^* = 2 - 1 = 1,$$

and, noting that $Q = q_1 + q_2$, then $Q^* = 3$.

Prices in the two markets are then

$$p_1^* = -\tfrac{1}{2}q_1^* + 3 = 2,$$
$$p_2^* = -\tfrac{1}{2}q_2^* + 2 = \tfrac{3}{2},$$

and the elasticities of demand at the optimal levels of output, q_1^* and q_2^*, are

$$\varepsilon_{11}^D = -2(2/2) = -2,$$
$$\varepsilon_{22}^D = -2(3/2) = -3.$$

The price in the more elastic market demand, q_2, is lowest. Profit for the firm is

$$\pi = \text{TR}_1 + \text{TR}_2 - \text{STC}$$
$$= p_1q_1 + p_2q_2 - (\tfrac{1}{2} + Q),$$
$$\pi^* = 4 + \tfrac{3}{2} - \tfrac{7}{2}$$
$$= 2.$$

Consumer surplus in market 1 is $(3-2)2/2 = \$1$ and that in market 2 is $[2-(3/2)]/2 = \$1/4$.

Producer surplus in market 1 is $(2-1)2 = \$2$ and that in market 2 is $[(3/2)-1]1 = \$1/2$.

Deadweight loss in market 1 is $(2-1)(4-2)/2 = \$1$ and that in market 2 is $[(3/2)-1](2-1)/2 = \$1/4$. The total deadweight loss is then $5/4.

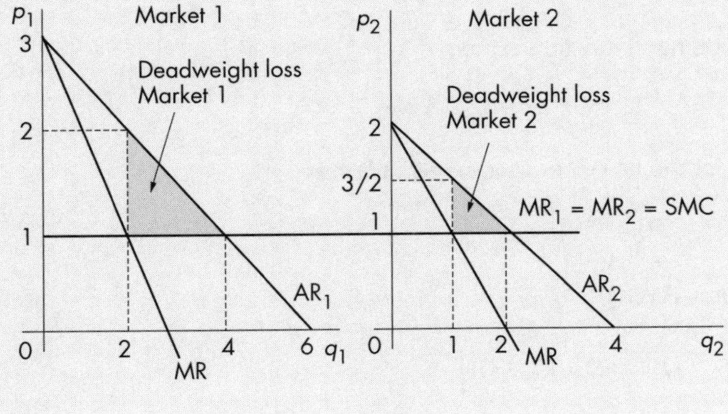

Consider no price discrimination

The relationship between ordinary monopoly (no price discrimination, where full arbitrage exists among consumers) and price discrimination is also illustrated in Figure 13.4. The horizontal summation of the individual market demand curves, $\sum q_j|_{AR}$, is the market demand curve facing the firm if no price discrimination exists. Note the discontinuity of the MR curve associated with this market demand curve. This is due to the kink in the market demand curve. Optimal output is where SMC = MR at output Q' associated with the common price p'. This common price is between the prices charged in the two market segments when price discrimination is practiced. At this common price, the firm sells q_1' in market 1 and q_2' in market 2. Then $MR'_1 > MR'_2$, indicating that the firm could increase profits by practicing price discrimination.

The effect of third-degree price discrimination on social welfare is ambiguous. Social welfare could be enhanced or reduced, depending on consumers' preferences and the wedges between prices and marginal costs. A sufficient condition for welfare to decline is if the total output from price discrimination does not increase.[3] Analogous to second-degree price discrimination, a sufficient condition for a social-welfare gain is if third-degree price discrimination results in satisfying demand in a market where zero output would be supplied with no price discrimination.[4]

For example, prior to airline deregulation, airlines could not compete in terms of price and were required to service certain routes. This resulted in many empty seats on flights and the airlines competing for passengers in terms of service and meals. Since deregulation, airlines compete in terms of price, and by price discrimination generally fill every seat. This has resulted in greatly expanded airline travel, satisfying markets (particularly vacation traveling) that were small or nonexistent before. Thus, social welfare has improved with airline deregulation; however, palatability of airline meals (if even served) is now questionable.

Example 13.6 Consider no price discrimination

Continuing with Example 13.5, if the firm does not price-discriminate, then $p_1 = p_2$ and the firm's demand function is the horizontal summation of the two market demand functions with a common price p:

$$Q = q_1 + q_2 = -2p + 6 - 2p + 4 = -4p + 10.$$

The inverse market demand function is then

$$p = -\tfrac{1}{4}Q + \tfrac{5}{2}.$$

Profit maximization for the no-price-discriminating firm is

$$\begin{aligned}\max_Q \pi &= \max_Q(\text{TR} - \text{STC})\\ &= \max_Q(pq - \text{STC})\\ &= \max_Q\left[(-\tfrac{1}{4}Q + \tfrac{5}{2})Q - (\tfrac{1}{2} + Q)\right].\end{aligned}$$

From Example 13.5,

$$\text{STC} = \tfrac{1}{2} + (q_1 + q_2).$$

The FOC is then

$$\frac{d\pi}{dQ} = -\tfrac{1}{2}Q^* + \tfrac{5}{2} - 1 = 0.$$

Solving for Q^*,

$$Q^* = 3,$$

$$p^* = -\tfrac{1}{4}Q^* + \tfrac{5}{2} = \tfrac{7}{4}.$$

Note that considering the price discrimination prices in Example 13.5, $p_1^* > p^* > p_2^*$.

At $p^* = 7/4$, the total output $Q^* = 3$ is allocated in the two markets based on the individual market demand functions. This results in

$$q_1^* = -2p^* + 6 = \tfrac{5}{2}, \quad q_2^* = -2p^* + 4 = \tfrac{1}{2}.$$

Profit for the no-price-discriminating firm is

$$\pi^* = \tfrac{21}{4} - (\tfrac{1}{2} + 3) = \tfrac{7}{4}.$$

Thus, profit under no price discrimination is less than profit when the firm price-discriminates. Deadweight loss under no price discrimination is $[(7/4) - 1](6 - 3)/2 =$ \$9/8. Thus, deadweight loss under price discrimination, \$5/4 = \$10/8, is higher than that of no price discrimination. This is consistent with the statement that if output remains the same or falls, when a firm practices price discrimination, a social welfare loss occurs.

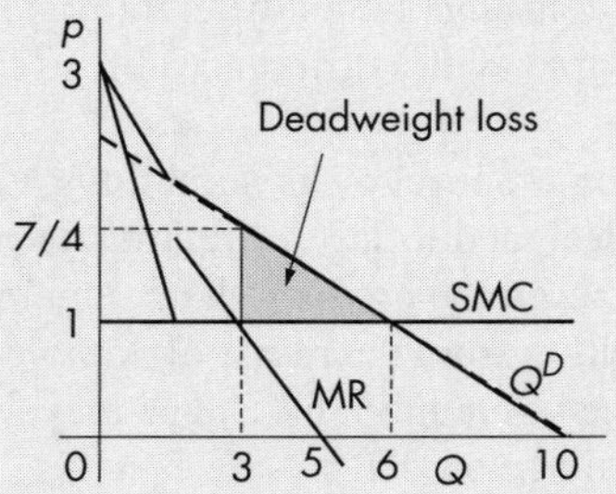

Combination of discrimination techniques

A wise man will make more opportunities than he finds.

(Francis Bacon)

In an effort to earn short-run pure profits, firms will employ combinations of these three price-discrimination techniques, and constantly will be devising new methods for price discrimination. For example the US Post Office uses both second- and third-degree price discrimination in pricing mail delivery. In the long run, costs will adjust to any short-run profits from price discrimination, leading to long-run equilibrium with associated normal profits. Firms failing to engage in this practice of price discrimination will experience declining revenue and be forced out of business.

Analogous to firms, an individual consumer can increase her utility by shifting her consumption patterns and capturing a lower price per unit offered by price-discriminating firms. By altering her pattern of consumption, a consumer is able to recoup some of the surplus appropriated by firms. Unfortunately, firms are generally constantly changing their prices or quantity as market conditions change. For example, candy manufacturers will alter the ounces in different sizes of candy bars, which changes the per-unit price for each size but keep the prices the same. Changes in price discrimination have resulted in a whole industry developing for assisting consumers. For example, travel websites will assist consumers in finding the lowest fares for particular destinations.

Understanding quality discrimination

> *This paperback is very interesting, but I find it will never replace a hardcover book. It makes a very poor doorstop.*
>
> (Alfred Hitchcock)

A manufacturer of DVD players is practicing quality discrimination by offering a range of different physical components and different warranties for its DVDs. A service station is also practicing quality discrimination by offering different grades of gasoline along with full- and self-service islands. Fundamentally, price discrimination and quality discrimination are identical models. Thus, the same implications associated with the various degrees of price discrimination hold for quality discrimination. In quality discrimination, there is a difference in consumers' willingness to pay for a given quality rather than quantity of a commodity.[5] As the examples indicate, a firm can discriminate among consumers with different preferences for product quality. The actual commodity may be the same, with a difference only in service, or the commodity itself may be altered.

Product quality can also take the form of determining the level of its durability. A highly durable product, such as a new consumer appliance designed to last a lifetime, may result in market saturation. Once most consumers have purchased the product, there remains only limited product demand. A firm may also face competition from the resale of durable goods it produced previously. For example, if the product (such as aluminum) can be recycled at a competitive price, the monopoly power of the firm could be eroded away.

There are a number of strategies that firms can use to counter this product durability problem. They can build in planned obsolescence of the product by either marketing an improved version of the product or changing its physical appearance. For example, automobile manufactures generally change their vehicle models' appearance and market the models' improvements on an annual basis. Alternatively, firms may lease their products instead of selling them. Leasing maintains a firm's market power by giving it control over both the new market and the market for resales. Computer software companies generally have licensing agreements preventing the copying of software, but some also will only lease the software through an annual agreement.

Application: Sears' drills

Many firms will practice quality discrimination by offering different qualities of a product to capture differences in consumers' willingness to pay. For example, Sears has different grades for some of its products and labels them "good, better, and best." In terms of power drills, Sears offers hundreds of different drills in different brands. These drills range in price from a 15-amp corded heavy-duty drill for $1399.99 to a 4.8-volt cordless palm drill for $9.25. Adding the option of a warranty doubles the possible different qualities of drills. By tapping into each market niche, firms such as Sears have the potential of extracting additional consumer surplus and thus increasing their profits.

Summary

1. The two conditions for price discrimination are the ability to segment the market and the existence of different demand elasticities for each market segment. Through price discrimination, a firm has the potential of increasing its profit.
2. First-degree price discrimination occurs when it is possible to sell each unit of a product for the maximum price a consumer is willing to pay. One mechanism for obtaining first-degree price discrimination is with a two-part tariff. By first-degree price discriminating on entrance fees, a firm can capture consumers' entire surplus.
3. When a firm is unable to effectively separate consumers by their preferences and then price-discriminate, bundling commodities may offer an alternative to extracting consumers' surplus.
4. Second-degree price discrimination occurs when a firm sells different units of output for different per-unit prices, and every consumer who buys the same unit amount of the commodity pays the same per-unit price.
5. Third-degree price discrimination occurs when a firm sells output to different consumers for different prices, and every unit of output sold to a given category of consumers sells for the same price.
6. A firm can also increase its profits by discriminating among consumers with different preferences for product quality. In quality discrimination, there is a difference in consumers' willingness to pay for a given quality of a commodity. Given this difference, firms can increase their profits by offering a product at different levels of quality.
7. *(Appendix)* An auction can be classified as English, Dutch, or sealed-bid auction. An English auction is a second-bid auction that will result in a Pareto-efficient allocation. A Dutch auction is a first-bid auction that can result in a Pareto-inefficient allocation. A sealed-bid auction is either a first- or second-bid auction where bidders individually submit written bids prior to some deadline.

8. *(Appendix)* A first-bid auction will yield a Pareto-efficient allocation when bidders cannot discern differences in their strategies from other bidders' strategies.
9. *(Appendix)* Winner's curse results when a buyer (seller) with the highest estimated error above (below) the true value of a commodity wins. The optimal strategy for bidders is then to adjust their bids less than their estimated value if they are buyers or more than if they are sellers.
10. *(Appendix)* Monopoly behavior in the form of a reservation price or bidding rings can increase the surplus of agents, but possibly results in market inefficiencies.

Key concepts

affiliated, 561
arbitrage, 523
asymmetric information, 558
auction, 553
bid, 554
bidding rings, 562
bundling, 531
complete price discrimination, 523
Dutch auctions, 554
English auctions, 554
first-bid auction, 555
first-degree price discrimination, 523
intertemporal price discrimination, 526
nonlinear pricing, 534
perfect price discrimination, 523
pool, 562
reservation price, 554
Revenue Equivalence Theorem, 562
sealed bid, 555
sealed-bid auctions, 555
second-bid auction, 555
second-degree price discrimination, 534
thin markets, 553
third-degree price discrimination, 539
tie-in-sales, 530
two-part tariff, 527
Vickrey auction, 555
well-developed markets, 553
winner's curse, 559

Key equation

$$MR_1 = MR_2 = \ldots = MR_k = SMC$$

The FOC for a third-degree price-discriminating firm is equating the marginal revenue in each market to the overall marginal cost.

Questions

Questions are opportunities in work clothes.

(Henry Kaiser)

1. Insurance companies generally have higher premiums for smokers than for nonsmokers. Would this practice be considered price discrimination?

2. Why do camera retailers often sell their cameras at prices very close to the wholesale cost, and then mark up the price of accessories by 100 percent or more?
3. Why would all inefficiencies associated with monopoly power vanish if transaction costs did not exist?
4. Why will pizza shops advertise "buy one large pizza at the regular price and get a second one for only $3.99?"
5. Most private universities charge high tuition but award scholarships to students from low-income families. What are the advantages of this practice compared with charging a uniform tuition for all students?
6. Why might prices in large towns be lower than in smaller communities?
7. Postage for advertisements, newspapers, and magazines is lower than that for first-class letters. Thus, the revenue from first-class letters subsidizes mailing of magazines. True or false? Explain.
8. When seaside resorts raise their rates during the high season and reduce them in the off-season, are they exploiting consumers or promoting a more efficient allocation of resources? Explain.
9. Why does a used-car lot offer the same vehicle for a lower price on the Internet then the sticker price on the windshield?
10. Some consumer groups contend that automobile companies pursue a strategy of planned obsolescence. That is, they produce automobiles that are intended to become obsolete in a few years. Does this strategy make sense for a firm with monopoly power? How might the production of obsolescence depend on the nature of market demand?

Exercises

Nothing takes the place of persistence.

(Calvin Coolidge)

1. You are advising a group of investors who are interested in building a children's gymnastics center. During the peak hours (after school), the demand curve for a child's gymnastic class is

$$q_a = 60 - p_a,$$

where q_a is the size of the fitness center (number of classes offered) and p_a is the cost per class. During off hours, demand consists of only preschool children, so the demand curve shifts downward:

$$q_m = 32 - p_m.$$

Assume the investment is \$12 per class times the number of classes and that operating costs are constant at \$8 per class. How large a gymnastic center would you advise the investors to build, and what prices should be charged for gymnastic classes? [*Hint:* Total cost = $12q_a + 8(q_a + q_m)$.]

2. The willingness to pay for an airline ticket for a business traveler and a tourist are shown in the following table. What pricing policy should this airline adopt to maximize profit?

	Returns (\$)		
	Friday	*Saturday*	*Sunday*
Business	660	600	500
Tourist	300	300	150

3. Let the short-run total cost function for a firm be

$$\text{STC} = \tfrac{1}{4}Q^2 + 2000.$$

The firm supplies output in two regions, where the demand functions are

$$q_1 = 200 - 4p_1, q_2 = 200 - 2p_2.$$

a. If the firm can control supply to each market, how much should it supply and what price should it charge in each market? What is the level of profit?
b. At the equilibrium price and quantity in each market, determine the elasticity of demand in each market.
c. Determine the price and quantity sold in each market if the monopoly is unable to practice price discrimination. What is the resulting profit level?
d. Determine the resulting consumer and producer surplus in (a) and (b). Does price discrimination or no price discrimination yield a higher total surplus and why?

4. A monopoly faces a number of buyers, each of whom has a demand for the monopoly's product represented as $Q = 50 - p$. The monopoly has a constant marginal cost of \$10. The monopoly charges a license fee, which a buyer must pay to be able to purchase, along with a price per unit for each unit of product. What license fee does the monopoly charge?

5. Susan's Orchids sells its output in both the domestic and a foreign market. Agricultural inspection restrictions make purchasing in one market and reselling in the other market illegal. The inverse demand functions associated with each market are

$$p_D = 210 - 2q_D, p_F = 260 - 5q_F.$$

Susan's production process exhibits a constant average cost of \$100 to produce 10 orchids, with a fixed cost of \$5000.

a. What are the profit-maximizing outputs and prices? What is Susan's total profit?
b. What is the price elasticity of demand in the domestic and foreign markets? What is true about the market in which the highest price is charged?
c. Suppose agricultural restrictions are discontinued through trade negotiations, so now anyone can buy and sell orchids in either of the two markets and resell in the other without cost. How many orchids should Susan now sell in each market and at what price? Now that Susan is no longer able to practice price discrimination, how will her profit change? Would she support the agricultural inspection restrictions?

6. A theater with monopoly power is facing a different demand elasticity for its matinees M versus its evening shows E. The theater has costs represented by

$$\text{STC} = 10Q + \tfrac{1}{2}Q^2 + 1000$$

and is facing the following demands:

$$q_M = 100 - 2p_M, q_E = 100 - p_E.$$

a. Determine the profit-maximizing quantities and prices for the matinees and evening shows.
b. Suppose the theater is legally restrained from practicing price discrimination. Calculate the new profit-maximizing quantities and prices, and compare the profit when the theater is allowed to price-discriminate.
c. Would theatergoers prefer the theater to price-discriminate?

7. In the diagram below, Q_M is the profit-maximizing output for a single monopoly with associated price p_M.

a. Assume that instead of charging the one price p_M for all its output, the monopoly sells the first Q_1 units at the per-unit price p_1 and sells the next $Q_M - Q_1$ units at the lower per-unit price p_M. This assumes that the demand curve is unaffected by price discrimination. Compare the total revenue obtained by the sale of Q_M units under second-degree price discrimination with the total revenue resulting from no price discrimination.
b. Show that the monopoly can increase revenue above practicing second-degree price discrimination by further segmenting the market and setting three different prices.
c. What is the profit-maximizing output and total revenue obtained from practicing first-degree price discrimination?

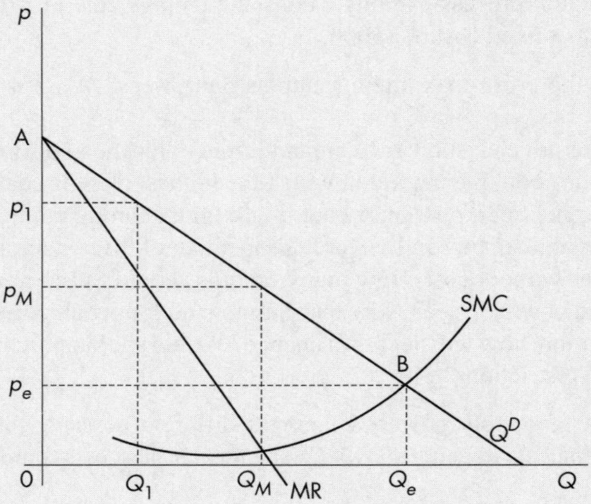

8. Determine the level of output and maximum profit for a first-degree price-discriminating monopoly whose inverse demand and short-run total cost functions are

$$p = 205 - 4Q,$$

$$\text{STC} = 5Q + 8Q^2 + 400.$$

9. Assume that a firm with monopoly power sells toys in catalogs C and retail outlets R. The representative inverse demand functions are

$$p_C = 3 - \tfrac{1}{2}C,$$

$$p_R = 7 - \tfrac{1}{2}R.$$

The firm's short-run total cost function is

$$\text{STC} = 4 + (C + R).$$

a. Determine the profit-maximizing prices and quantities in each market and the corresponding elasticities of demand.
b. If price discrimination is banned, what will happen?

10. As the manager of the country club in a gated community, you must decide on membership dues and greens fees. Potential membership may be divided between 500 avid and 500 passive golfers, with the individual golfer's demand functions

$$q_1 = 8 - p,$$

$$q_2 = 4 - \tfrac{1}{2}p,$$

where q_1 and q_2 are games played per week by the avid and passive golfers, respectively, and p is the greens fee per game. The fixed cost of maintaining the course is $15,000 per week, with zero marginal cost.

a. In an effort to maintain a professional course, you decide to limit membership to only the avid players. However, you are unable to distinguish avid players from passive players. What annual membership dues and greens fees will you set for profit maximization? What is your profit per week?
b. An economic consulting firm advises that you could increase profit by allowing passive players to also become members. What annual membership dues and greens fees would yield the maximum increase in profit? How much does profit increase?

Internet case study

1. List some recent cases of antitrust violations associated with price discrimination.

APPENDIX TO CHAPTER 13

Auctions

It is only an auctioneer who can equally and impartially admire all schools of art.
(Oscar Wilde)

Translation: The auctioneer determines the price for various art forms, which determines an art's value with price as the common standard of measurement.

Law enforcement agencies have property rooms full of stolen or forfeited goods, and the rightful owners are difficult or impossible to identify. Once the merchandise is no longer required as evidence, it must be disposed of. Law enforcement agencies are not in the business to sell commodities, so determining the price for these items and having to then sell them is a problem. One increasingly popular method used by law enforcement agencies is to put the items up for auction on the Internet. Even for agencies whose business it is to buy and sell commodities, auctions may very well be the preferred mechanism for selling their commodities when there is limited market information on demand.

Our previous discussion on price discrimination assumes **well-developed markets** for a commodity with a history of many market transactions providing information on the demand for a commodity. Firms can incorporate these revealed consumers' preferences for the commodity into their price-discriminating decisions. Markets without a history of many market transactions and thus lacking information on consumer preference are called **thin markets**. Examples are unique commodities that are difficult or impossible to duplicate, such as works of art, antiques, oil leases, and unique real estate.

Thin markets require some mechanism for revealing buyers' preferences and then basing the price on the highest willingness to pay. Auctions are one such mechanism. An **auction** is where buyers (households or firms) bid, or state a price they are willing to pay for a commodity. This may be an openly declared bid, available to all buyers and the seller, or a *sealed bid,* where only the seller receives the information. The buyer who offers the highest bid receives the commodity for some price at or below his bid.

Auctions are very popular for selling "priceless" antiques, artworks, and, on the Internet, almost anything. Buyers may also engage in auctioning by soliciting bids from sellers to sell a commodity to the buyer. For example, contractors (sellers) may bid on a construction project for a buyer.

Classification of auctions

In general, an auction can be classified as English, Dutch, or sealed-bid (silent), depending on the auction's mechanism design. An **English auction** is a commonly used auction mechanism where the auctioneer starts with some price. For an agent selling a commodity, this price is a seller's **reservation price**, the lowest price a seller is willing to accept for the commodity. (In contrast, for a buyer offering to purchase a commodity, this price is the maximum price the buyer is willing to pay for the commodity.) In an auction for an agent selling a commodity, buyers openly outcry (bid) their willingness to purchase the commodity at this reservation price. Assuming at least one buyer bids, the auctioneer accepts one of the bids, and then increases the price by some increment and solicits bids from the other buyers at the higher price. As long as at least one buyer makes a bid at the higher price, the auctioneer will continue to increase the price. When no other buyer is willing to make a bid at the auctioneer's higher price, the commodity is sold to the buyer whose last bid was accepted by the auctioneer. This is a fully transparent auction where all bidders' bids are disclosed throughout the whole bidding process. Generally, an auction mechanism is an English auction if it is an iterative price-adjusting process in the direction unfavorable to the bidders.

Application: A candle auction

There are many variations on the English auction designed to shift the market in the direction of one or another agent. In the seventeenth century, the candle auction became popular, where the end of the auction was signaled by the expiration of a candle's flame. This ensured that no-one would know exactly when the auction would end and make a last-minute bid. This prevents auction sniping, where a bidder will place a winning bid at the last possible moment so as not to give others time to respond. Timed online auctions, such as eBay, result in bid sniping, and that is why eBay suggests placing your bid once at your maximum willingness to pay. To avoid auction sniping, some Internet auctions will base the end time of an auction on the degree of last-minute auction activity: heavy bidding near the end delays the ending. An alternative is, instead of a candle, to end the auction at a computer-generated random time.

A **Dutch auction** works in the reverse way. Instead of starting at a seller's reservation price and increasing the price, the auctioneer starts at a price somewhere above the willingness of any buyer to pay for the commodity and then decreases the price. As the price declines, the first buyer willing to purchase the commodity at the current offered price acquires the commodity for that price. A Dutch auction only requires one bid, so it is efficient in terms of auctioning commodities quickly. One problem with the Dutch auction is determining the initial price above buyers' willingness to pay. In particularly thin markets, such as for famous artworks, determining this price may be difficult. Generally, an auction mechanism is a Dutch auction if it is an iterative price-adjusting process in the direction favorable to the bidders.

A **sealed-bid auction** is where bidders submit one bid in a hidden fashion. There is no open outcry. Such auctions are commonly used when it is difficult or undesirable for bidders to simultaneously participate in the auction. Bidders individually submit written bids prior to some deadline. In the case of an auction selling a commodity, these bids are at or above the stated seller's reservation price. In contrast, the bids are below the buyers' reservation price in the case of an auction offering sellers the opportunity to bid on the ability to supply a commodity. At some point past the deadline, the bids are revealed (read) and the buyer (seller) who submitted the highest (lowest) bid purchases (sells) the commodity. An auction where the bid is the commodity's purchased price is called a **first-bid auction**. Sealed bids using first-bid pricing are commonly employed in the awarding of construction contracts, where the construction firm with the lowest bid receives the contract for its bid price. In this case, the construction firm is the seller of the commodity and the auctioneer is representing the buyer.

An important variant of the sealed-bid auction is the **second-bid auction** or **Vickrey auction,** named for the 1996 Nobel Laureate William Vickrey (1914–1996) who was one of the first to theoretically investigate auctions. In a second-bid auction, the buyer with the highest bid wins and receives the auctioned commodity but only has to pay the second-highest bid price. As discussed in the following section, this second-bid mechanism results in agents bidding their true value of the commodity. One of the first uses of the second-bid auction was by stamp collectors (philatelists).

Considering the characteristics of the English, Dutch, first-bid, and second-bid auctions, the English auction is equivalent to a second-bid auction and the Dutch auction is equivalent to a first-bid auction. These auction pairs are equivalent, in that their sets of strategies and mechanisms of transforming strategies into allocations are identical. The English and second-bid auctions are equivalent in assuming that the bidders know their own willingness to pay for the auctioned commodity. With this assumption, a bidder's dominant strategy is to bid until the price exceeds that willingness to pay.[6] The commodity will then be allocated to the one remaining bidder with the highest willingness to pay. The price that this last bidder pays is equal to the second highest valuation plus the auctioneer's incremental increase in the bid price. Auctioneers generally reduce their increment in price as the number of bidders decline. However, they will only reduce the increment to the point where this incremental increase in revenue is equal to the marginal cost in terms of lost revenue from allocating time to continue requesting bids for the current commodity being auctioned instead of moving onto the next commodity up for auction. Assuming this marginal cost is zero, the auctioneer will decrease the increment increase in price to zero. The last bidder, with the highest valuation, will then win the commodity and pay a price equal to the second highest valuation. Thus, the English auction is a second-bid auction.

When you are the last bidder in an auction, do you only pay the second highest bid? Yes, in an English auction, the buyer with the highest bid wins, but pays the second highest bid.

Similarly, Dutch auctions are first-bid auctions, which assume that bidders plan their bids in advance. The only real choice is to select the highest bid that they are willing to pay. However, this highest bid is dependent on what bids the other bidders make. Thus, a bidder's

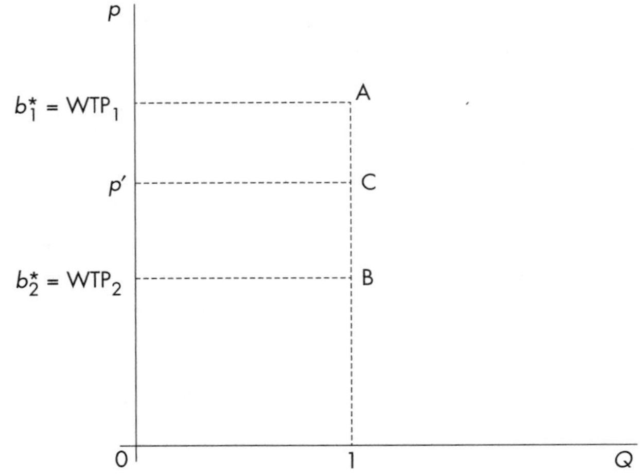

Figure 13A.1 **Pareto efficiency of the buyer with the highest willingness-to-pay receiving the commodity.** In auctioning one unit of commodity Q, bidder 1 has a higher willingness to pay than bidder 2. The Pareto-efficient allocation is then for bidder 1 to receive the commodity.

dominant strategy is dependent on the current information or beliefs the bidder possesses about the other bidders. If she believes the other bidders' willingness to pay is very low, her bid will reflect this belief, resulting in a lower bid. This strategy corresponds to a sealed-bid auction where the first bid is the price for the auctioned commodity. Thus, the Dutch auction is a first-bid auction.

Mechanism design

> *When the leaders choose to make themselves bidders at an auction of popularity their talents, in construction of the state, will be of no service.*
>
> (Edmund Burke)

Because auctions are particular market structures (called mechanism designs), we can investigate them in terms of their Pareto efficiency, and buyers' and sellers' profits.[7] For such an investigation, let us consider two bidders (buyers), with bidder 1 having a higher willingness to pay than bidder 2 for one unit of an auctioned commodity Q. As illustrated in Figure 13A.1, bidder 1's total willingness to pay is WTP_1, represented by the area $O(WTP_1)A1$, and bidder 2's total willingness to pay is WTP_2, represented by the area $O(WTP_2)B1$.

The Pareto-efficient allocation is for bidder 1, with the highest willingness to pay, to receive the commodity. If, instead, bidder 2 received the commodity, a Pareto improvement, where both bidders 1 and 2 could be made better off, is possible. If bidder 2 sells the commodity to bidder 1 at a price between WTP_1 and WTP_2, the welfares of both bidders are improved. For example, at a sale price of p', bidder 1 has a level of consumer surplus represented by the area $p'(WTP_1)AC$ and bidder 2 receives additional income $(WTP_2)p'CB$. The aggregate increase in welfare is represented by the area $(WTP_2)(WTP_1)AB$. In the extreme case, if bidder 1 pays bidder 2 WTP_2 for the commodity, then bidder 2's welfare is unchanged, but bidder 1's welfare increases by the level of consumer surplus $(\text{WTP}_2)(\text{WTP}_1)\text{AB}$. Thus, the Pareto-efficient allocation is for the bidder with the highest willingness to pay to receive the commodity.

Pareto efficiency of second-bid auctions

Bidders' willingness to pay is not generally revealed unless certain design mechanisms, such as auctions, are employed. For an auction to yield a Pareto-efficient allocation, it must be designed to reveal bidders' true willingness to pay. Otherwise, an inefficient allocation may result, with the bidder having the highest willingness to pay not receiving the commodity. To consider the second-bid auction, we let b_1 and b_2 be bidder 1's and bidder 2's respective bids for an auctioned commodity. The expected consumer surplus (payoff) to bidder 1 is then

$$\rho(b_1 \geq b_2)(\text{WTP}_1 - b_2),$$

where ρ denotes probability. This is the probability of bidder 1 having the highest bid. The associated payoff in terms of consumer surplus, $\text{WTP}_1 - b_2$, is the difference between how much bidder 1 is willing to pay and how much he actually pays. Note that if $b_1 < b_2$, then the payoff for bidder 1 is zero, so it is not necessary to add the term associated with $\rho(b_1 < b_2)$.

We determine bidder 1's optimal bid b_1^* by maximizing this expected payoff. If this consumer surplus is positive $(\text{WTP}_1 - b_2 > 0)$, then maximizing the payoff corresponds to maximizing the probability of the payoff, $\rho(b_1 \geq b_2)$. With $\rho(\text{WTP}_1 \geq b_2) = 1$, given $\text{WTP}_1 - b_2 > 0$, the optimal solution is $b_1^* = \text{WTP}_1$. At this optimal solution, $\rho(b_1^* \geq b_2) = 1$. If, instead, $\text{WTP}_1 - b_2 < 0$, then minimizing the probability of the payoff would yield the maximum expected payoff of zero. At $\text{WTP}_1 - b_2 < 0$, $\rho(\text{WTP}_1 \geq b_2) = 0$, so the optimal solution is again $b_1^* = \text{WTP}_1$. Thus, bidder 1's optimal strategy in a second-bid auction is to always reveal his true willingness to pay. Applying the same analysis for bidder 2, she will also always reveal her true willingness to pay in a second-bid auction with her optimal bid of $b_2^* = \text{WTP}_2$.

Generalizing, a second-bid auction results in all bidders setting their bids equal to their willingness to pay. Thus, in a second-bid auction, bidders will reveal their true willingness to pay, which results in a Pareto-efficient allocation. This Pareto-efficient allocation is illustrated in Figure 13A.1. Both bidders 1 and 2 set their bids equal to their willingness to pay, and bidder 1, with the higher willingness to pay, wins and receives the auctioned commodity. Bidder 1 pays b_2^* and receives consumer surplus of $b_2^* b_1^* \text{AB}$ as his payoff.

Inefficiency of first-bid auctions

In contrast, bidders in a first-bid auction may not be so truthful. Thus, it is possible for a first-bid auction to result in the bidder with the highest willingness to pay not receiving the commodity, yielding an inefficient allocation. As we discussed, in a first-bid auction each bidder's optimal bid depends on their beliefs about the value of the other bidders' bids. If his beliefs are incorrect, the bidder with the highest willingness to pay could lose the auctioned commodity.

P. Milgrom provides an example of this inefficiency associated with first-bid auctions.[8] Suppose bidder 1's willingness to pay for a commodity is \$80 and assume he does not know with certainty bidder 2's willingness to pay. Bidder 1 only knows that bidder 2 may be willing to pay \$59 with a 25 percent probability and \$39 with a 75 percent probability. Bidding his true willingness to pay of \$80, bidder 1 will win and receive the commodity at a price of \$80. This results in a zero payoff, where bidder 1's consumer surplus is zero. However, bidder 1 can obtain a positive payoff by bidding slightly more than bidder 2's highest willingness to pay of \$59. For example, if bidder 1 bids \$60, he is still sure of winning, and his payoff is then $80 - 60 = \$20$. Thus, by not bidding his true willingness to pay, bidder 1 can increase his payoff. He is still guaranteed to receive the commodity, and, because he has the highest willingness to pay, a Pareto-efficient allocation still holds. If bidder 1 instead bids \$40, slightly more than bidder 2's lowest bid of \$39, his expected payoff would be maximized at $\frac{3}{4}(80 - 40) = \$30$. Thus, if his belief about bidder 2's strategy is accurate, bidder 1 may maximize his payoff by lowering his bid still further below his true willingness to pay. However, at a bid of \$40, there is no guarantee bidder 1 will receive the commodity. Bidder 2 may bid \$59, and bidder 1, though having the highest willingness to pay, will not be allocated the commodity, yielding an inefficient outcome. This is in contrast with second-bid auctions, which always yield a Pareto-efficient allocation.

The information that bidder 1 has on bidder 2's strategies allows him to increase his payoff relative to bidder 2 and the seller. In general, an agent processing a monopoly on some market information (called **asymmetric information**) can increase her payoff. As discussed in Chapter 23, markets characterized by asymmetric information are generally inefficient. In auction markets, under a first-bid auction, bidders have an incentive to understate their willingness to pay and thus lower their bids. This lower bid results in increased consumer surplus, if they have the highest bid and purchase the commodity at this bid price. The cost of lowering the bid is an increase in the probability of not receiving the auctioned commodity. This payoff—increased consumer surplus with less probability of receiving the commodity as the bid is decreased—is analogous to when a monopoly's price increases, resulting in lower output.[9] Bidders in a first-bid auction will lower their bids until expected payoffs are maximized. Monopolies will increase their price until profits are maximized.

COMMON VALUES

An important case where a first-bid auction does yield a Pareto-efficient allocation, so the highest bid corresponds to the bidder with the highest willingness to pay, is when bidders cannot discern differences in their strategies from other bidders' strategies. In such a case of symmetric information, a Pareto-efficient allocation results. An example is where all bidders have the same common value for the commodity. This is generally the case with contractors bidding for a construction project or petroleum firms bidding on oil leases. The value of being awarded the contract or lease is the resulting potential profit. Assuming the expected profit is the same for all bidders, they will all have the same value for winning the contract.

WINNER'S CURSE

In any auction, the actual value of the commodity may not be known. Each bidder will develop an estimate of its value based on the information they have. For example, contractors will have different estimates of a project's costs, depending on their estimates of the amount of inputs required for the project and estimated project length. Petroleum firms' geologists will have different estimates of the amount of potential oil in an offshore site. These estimates will contain errors, which result in a deviation from the true value of the commodity, WTP. Specifically, let ε_j be the error or deviation from WTP for bidder j. Bidder j's estimated value is then $\widehat{\text{WTP}} = \text{WTP} + \varepsilon_j$. This estimate is unbiased, given that on average a bidder's estimates result in the true value, WTP.

Consider a case where each bidder bids their estimated value, WTP + ε_j. In this case, the bidder with the highest estimated error receives the commodity. If this highest error is positive, the bidder who made this estimate is paying a price above the commodity's true value. This is called the **winner's curse**. Winning indicates that the bidder made the largest error in estimating the value of the commodity.

Why is it when you win you actually lose? You lose when you have made the largest error in estimating the true value of the commodity.

In this case, the optimal strategy for bidders is to bid less than their estimated value. In competitive bidding with common values for the commodity, a bidder will generally win when he overestimates the true value of the commodity. In the case of a contractor, a bidder who underestimates his cost will generally win the contract. All rational utility-maximizing bidders will then adjust their bids for winner's curse. The amount of adjustment depends on the number of bidders. With only a few bidders, the probability of one bidder greatly overestimating the commodity's value is low. When there are a large number of bidders, the probability of one bidder overestimating the commodity's value is high. Thus, bidders should then adjust their bids downward more when faced with a larger number of bidders.

As an example, assume that the estimates for the value of a commodity are uniformly distributed along an interval from 0 to 2WTP, where WTP is still the true value of the commodity. Bidders' estimates are equally likely to take any value along this interval, so the expected value is the true value of the commodity, WTP. This implies an unbiased estimate of the true value. If there is one bidder, the expected value of the highest bid would be WTP. Thus, the one bidder would not adjust his bid downward as a result of winner's curse.

As the number of bidders, n, increases, the value of the highest bid increases. For example, as illustrated in Figure 13A.2, the estimates are arranged as $\widehat{\text{WTP}}_1 < \widehat{\text{WTP}}_2 < \ldots < \widehat{\text{WTP}}_n$, where the subscripts represent bidders. When $n = 2$, the expected value of the highest bid is ⅔(2WTP); when $n = 3$, it is ¾(2WTP). In general, for n bidders, the expected value of the highest bid is $[n/(n + 1)]$(2WTP). A bidder determines his optimal bid by adjusting his estimate of the value of the commodity, $\widehat{\text{WTP}}$, so if it is the highest estimate out of n bidders, he will not bid more on average than the true value, WTP.

We can determine the true value by setting the expected value of the highest bid equal to the bidder's estimated value:

$$\frac{n}{n+1}(2\text{WTP}) = \widehat{\text{WTP}}_n.$$

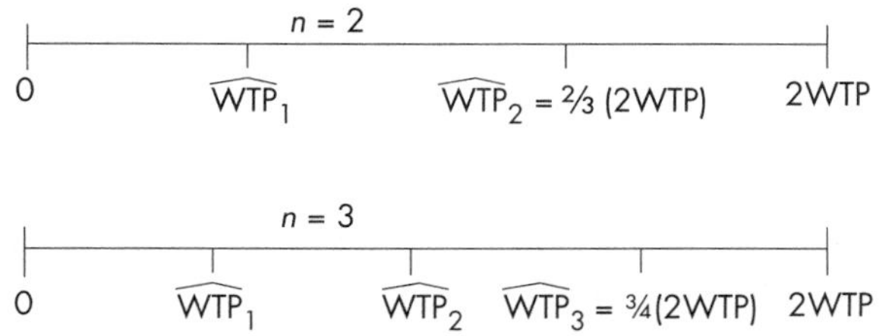

Figure 13A.2 **Expected value of the highest estimated value, $\widehat{\textbf{WTP}}$.** As the number of bidders increases, the highest estimated value of the commodity increases.

Solving for WTP yields

$$\text{WTP} = \frac{\widehat{\text{WTP}}_n(n+1)}{2n}.$$

The bidder's optimal strategy is then to set his bid equal to WTP. Note that

$$\frac{\partial \text{WTP}}{\partial n} = -\frac{\widehat{\text{WTP}}_n}{2n^2} < 0,$$

so an increase in the number of bidders reduces the optimal bid. With all bidders following this strategy, the bidder with the highest willingness to pay will receive the commodity and pay the true value of the commodity WTP.

The ability to reduce the estimation error in determining the value of the auctioned commodity will increase the profit to a bidder. In many industries, where competitive bids are the common form for price determination, the ability of determining accurate estimates is essential for the long-run survival of a firm. Examples are contractors in construction, such as painters, electricians, and plumbers. A painter must do a good job painting, but, possibly even more so, she must be good at bidding for jobs.

Example 13A.1 Determining the optimal bid when adjusting for winner's curse

Assume the estimates for the value of a commodity are uniformly distributed along an interval from zero to 2(WTP). A bidder's optimal bid b^* should correspond to the true value of the auctioned commodity, WTP, assuming that the bidder's estimated value $\widehat{\text{WTP}}$ is the highest among all the bidders, $\widehat{\text{WTP}} = \widehat{\text{WTP}}_n$. This true value and consequently the optimal bid will depend on the number of bidders. Specifically,

$$b^* = \text{WTP} = \frac{\widehat{\text{WTP}}_n(n+1)}{2n}.$$

If, for one bidder, $\widehat{\text{WTP}} = \$50$ and it is the highest bid, then $\widehat{\text{WTP}} = \widehat{\text{WTP}}_n = \$50$. The optimal bids for various number of bidders are shown in the following table:

n	$b^* = \text{WTP}$ (\$)
1	50.00
25	26.00
50	25.50
100	25.25
∞	25.00

As the number of bidders increase, the highest bid converges to the terminal value, 2(WTP), and the optimal bid is then the mean value, WTP. All bidders will adjust their estimates of the mean value $\widehat{\text{WTP}}$ in half and the bidder with the highest estimate of the mean will receive the commodity and pay the determined true value WTP.

Application: Avoiding winner's curse

The importance at being good at bidding was investigated by Kagel and Richard. They found that in first-price common-value auction experiments, super-experienced bidders earned positive profits by setting bids below their WTP and thus avoiding winner's curse. However, they earn less than 50 percent of the optimal profit level associated with the "best response." Satisfying the best response would require winning half as many auctions as were actually won by these super-experienced bidders. For the bidder's prior experience, all bidders participated in four sealed-bid auction sessions preceding the experiments.

Kagel and Richard discuss a number of possibilities why super-experienced bidders continued to receive lower than optimal profits. First, the relatively complicated nature of determining the optimal bid may make it difficult to achieve without colluding. In an experimental setting, colluding is a difficult feat to pull off. However, Kagel and Richard's results indicate that bidders cope quite well with the complexity of bidding strategy by adopting close approximations. Ruling out this first possibility, a second explanation is that overly aggressive bidding was a best response to misguided overbidding of a handful of bidders. However, this also was not the cause, for results indicate asymmetric individual responses. Nor were the possibilities of limited liability for losses in experimental bidding and the thrill of bidding and winning supported by the data.

Kagel and Richard were then left with conjecturing as to why bidders continued to bid more than the best response dictated. In the experiments conducted, best responses were highly variable, sometimes indicating to bid more aggressively and at other times indicating to bid more passively. Thus bidders may have ignored the information content inherent in the feedback once satisfactory profit levels were achieved with their current strategy. In other words, the marginal gain in satisfaction was less than the marginal cost of employing this information.

Source: J.H. Kagel and J. Richard, "Super-Experienced Bidders in First-Price Common-Value Auctions: Rules of Thumb, Nash Equilibrium Bidding, and the Winner's Curse," *Review of Economics and Statistics* 83 (2001): 408–419.

Affiliation

Although only first-bid auctions associated with common values are Pareto-efficient, the expected total surplus is the same as for a second-bid auction. However, the expected payoffs differ under the two types of auctions. This difference is the result of a bidder's increased expected payment in the second-bid auction as her estimate of the commodity's value increases. In a second-bid auction, her payment depends on the estimated value of the commodity by other bidders, which is affiliated with her estimated value. **Affiliation** occurs when a bidder's estimate of the value of a commodity increases as other bidders' estimates also increase. Payments in first-bid auctions are not affected by this affiliation, so they are less effective in extracting surplus from bidders. Thus, sellers have the potential for increasing their profits by using a second-bid auction, which may explain the popularity of second-bid auctions compared with first-bid auctions.

In contrast to affiliated bidders, if each bidder's individual valuation of the commodity is independent of all other bidders and symmetric information exists, then the first-bid and second-bid auctions yield equivalent winning bids. If there is no error in estimating the value of the commodity, then all the bidders would bid the true WTP in both a first- and a second-bid auction. Since the bids are identical in both auctions, the seller's revenue would then be the same under both types of auctions. This is a consequence of the *Revenue Equivalence Theorem,* which states that, given independence of all bidders' strategies, both the second-bid and first-bid auctions yield the same expected profits for every bidder valuation and the same expected revenue for the seller.

Monopoly behavior

Similar to firms with monopoly power, sellers controlling the auction process can institute restrictions on the auction that increase their profits. Such policies generally restrict the auction market, and thus result in inefficient allocations. An example is a seller not selling a commodity if the winning bid is below some reservation price. Not selling the commodity results in an inefficient allocation and can be measured as a deadweight loss in total surplus.

As an example of a reservation-price restriction, consider an auction with two buyers, each with a willingness to pay for the commodity of \$10 at a probability of occurring ¼ of the time and \$50 at a probability of ¾. The possible combinations for bids are (10, 10) with a probability of 1/16, (10, 50) and (50, 10) each with probabilities of 3/16, and (50, 50) with a probability of 9/16. Assuming that the bid increment is \$1, the winning bids in the four combinations are (10, 11, 11, 50). The seller's expected revenue without a reservation price is then

$$(1/16)(10) + (6/16)(11) + (9/16)(50) = (10 + 66 + 450)/16 = 526/16 = \$32.88.$$

If, instead, the seller sets a reservation price of \$50, then 1/16 of the time the seller would not sell the commodity, but 15/16 of the time she would sell it for \$50. The expected revenue is then $(15/16)(50) = \$46.88$. The seller can increase his return by setting a reservation price, and in this case expected revenue is maximized by setting that reservation price at \$50.

Bidding rings

Buyers can also form **bidding rings** (or **pools**), where buyers within the ring do not bid against each other. An appointed buyer will bid on the auctioned commodity, up to the highest willingness to pay of a member in the ring. Members of the ring do not compete in bidding with this appointed buyer. With members not bidding against each other, the winning bid could be lower. If the ring acquires the commodity, then the commodity could be re-auctioned among the members of the ring if it has not already been determined who among the ring gets the commodity. An example of a bidding ring, from the late 1970s to 1997, is 11 wholesale stamp dealers active in New York auction houses.

Bidding rings result in Pareto efficiency, since the buyer with the highest willingness to pay for the commodity wins. However, buyers can capture a large share of the total surplus from the sellers by forming rings. To offset this market advantage of rings, sellers might impose a reservation price. Rings are common in construction projects for which a relatively small number of contractors are bidding. Formal or informal rings are established by contractors, and their rings determine, prior to submitting bids, who will win the contract and at what price. Such rings aid in avoiding problems associated with winner's curse; however, they are, in general, considered in violation of federal and state antitrust laws.

Question

1. A housepainter has a regular contract working for a building contractor. On these jobs, his cost estimates are generally on average correct. When the regular work is slack, he bids competitively for other jobs and the jobs he wins almost always end up costing more than he estimated. Why this difference?

Exercises

1. In an English auction of antiques, there are two bidders, each with values for a lamp of either \$75 or \$50. With a bid increment of \$5, what will be the reservation price for this auction?
2. Suppose n fathers wish to place their child in the last remaining space at a preschool. The preschool opens at 7:30 a.m., and the first father in line will have his child admitted. Each father has to decide when to get in line, and a father who waits t hours incurs a cost ct. Any father showing up after the first father will not stay, so he incurs no waiting cost, $t = 0$. The jth father's monetary utility of placing his child is U^j, and this utility is independently drawn from a uniform distribution [0, 1].

    a. Determine the expected number of hours the first father will wait.
    b. How does this expected number of hours vary with c and n?

Internet case studies

1. Trace the auctioning of a commodity on the Internet.
2. Provide a short biography of William Vickrey.

Part VI

Strategic agent interaction

Game Theory — Imperfect Competition

Chapters

> *When the One Great Scorer comes to write against your name. He marks, not that you won or lost, but how you played the game.*
>
> (Grantland Rice)

What do driving a car, taking a bath with soap, eating fast-food, and taking a cruise all have in common? In all cases, you are consuming a commodity produced by an imperfectly competitive firm. Most real world markets can be classified as **imperfect competition**, somewhere between the polar cases of perfect competition and monopoly. An increase in price in imperfectly competitive markets results in some consumers finding substitutes for a firm's output. Thus, the market faced by these firms is composed of other firms supplying close but not perfect substitutes and satisfying consumer demand. If only very closely related commodities are considered, then the market is narrowly defined, such as a market consisting of only Caribbean cruises. In a broadly defined market, commodities not closely related are also considered as part of the market. An example would be to include all family vacations in the Caribbean market. In general, the definition of such a market should be neither too narrow nor too broad. If it is too narrow, the strategic interaction of firms with other excluded firms would not be considered. Alternatively, if it is too broad, partial-equilibrium analysis of a market yields to general-equilibrium analysis. The gains from a single description of the major interactions among firms within a market are then lost.

Imperfect competition. Markets between the polar cases of perfect competition and monopoly. *E.g., the markets for nearly all the commodities you purchase.*

The appropriate definition of a market depends on the objective of an analysis. For example, consider the fast-food industry. If the objective is investigating the production efficiency of a specific fast-food commodity, say, pizza, then the market could be defined as only firms engaged in pizza production. If, instead, interest is in governmental health regulation of the fast-food industry, then the market will also include all other fast-food firms.

Shirking this issue of appropriately defining a market, we will assume that firms are facing a well-defined market composed of firms producing either homogeneous commodities or a group of differentiated but close substitute products. We further assume that firms within this market have only limited interaction with firms outside it in that they are price takers for prices offered by these outside firms. However, within a market, firms are mutually dependent, and, given this interdependence, the ways in which firms interact with each other define the particular type of imperfectly competitive model. Such interactions can possibly take the form of price, output, or market share competition, as well as competition in terms of product differentiation and selling expenses.

In Chapter 14, we develop the theory of games for modeling these interactions of firms or households. Specifically, the *Prisoners' Dilemma* game is employed for illustrating the conflicts associated with agents' mutual dependence. We then discuss variations on the Prisoners' Dilemma, as well as an alternative set of games involving sequential moves by players (agents). Our aim in this chapter is to investigate how agents interact in making their marketing and production decisions (how they play the game).

In Chapter 15, classical industrial organization models of firm interactions are presented. We investigate the optimal level of advertising, deriving the conditions for optimal advertising and product differentiation based on demand elasticities. We also assess advertising in terms of information versus just persuasion. We then consider monopolistic competition and derive its equilibrium price and output. Next is an investigation into oligopoly market structures, with a discussion of price and output determination as well as the classical oligopoly models of *Cournot*, *Stackelberg*, and *Bertrand*. We discuss both formal cartel arrangements and informal collusion in oligopoly markets. In the appendix, we develop the concept of *product differentiation* in the form of *spatial differentiation* for a linear city.

14 Game theory

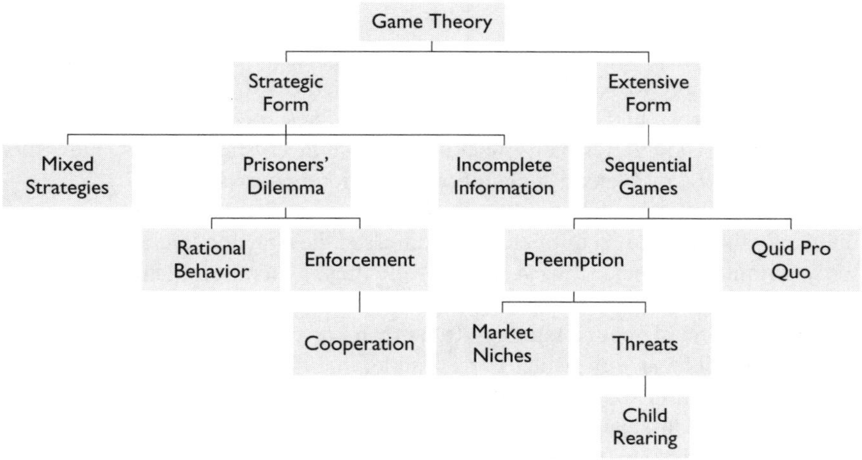

Outline and Conceptual Inquiries

Life is a game in which the rules are constantly changing; nothing spoils a game more than those who take it seriously.

(Quentin Crisp)

Game theory considers situations where instead of agents (households or firms) making decisions as reactions to exogenous prices (dead variables), their decisions are strategic reactions to other agents' actions (live variables). These decisions may be based on astrology, palm readings, telepathy, telekinesis, the aura, crystals, dreams, numerology, and fortune-tellers, or even on some rational decision process.

In previous chapters, the agent's decisions that we discussed generally centered around only the given level of prices. We addressed the strategic interactions of agents in only a limited manner. However, one of the most general problems in economics is outguessing a rival. For example, in firm interactions, a firm seeks to determine its rival's most profitable counterstrategy to its own current policy and then formulates an appropriate defensive measure. For example, in 1996, Pepsi supplied cola aboard Russia's space station *Mir*, so Coca-Cola countered by offering cola aboard the shuttle *Endeavour*. The classical theory of this strategic interaction among firms will be discussed in Chapter 15. In this chapter, we see how the theory of how agents interact (called **game theory**) has extended this classical approach by considering in greater detail the interaction among firms in oligopoly markets.

Game theory. The theory of how agents interact. *E.g., how players play poker.*

Game theory provides an avenue for economists to investigate and develop descriptions of the strategic interaction of agents. **Strategic interdependence** means that each agent's welfare depends not only on her own actions but also on the actions of other agents (**players**). Also, the best actions for her may depend on what she expects the other agents to do. The theory emphasizes the study of rational decision making based on the assumption that agents attempt to maximize utility. Alternatively, agents' behavior could be expanded by considering a sociological, psychological, or biological perspective. Recent progress in game theory has resulted in the ability to view economic behavior as just one special case of game theory. In economics, this strategic interdependence among agents is called **noncooperative game theory**, where binding agreements among agents are not assumed and cooperation may or may not occur among agents as a result of rational decisions. Agents make decisions independently, but there is interdependence among their decisions on the resulting outcome. This is in contrast to **cooperative game theory,** where binding agreements are assumed. Groups of players may enforce cooperative behavior. For example, the interaction of two football teams playing a game is a noncooperative game. In contrast, two people forming a loving relationship to jointly increase their welfare is a cooperative game.

Player. An agent in a game. *E.g., a girl playing the dating game.*

Strategic interdependence. Each agent's welfare depends on the actions of other agents. *E.g., a student's safety in driving to school depends on all the other drivers.*

Noncooperative game theory. A game where binding agreements among agents are not assumed. *E.g., an instructor does not assign students to a group for working on a class project. However, students may decide to form such groups.*

Cooperative game theory. A game where binding agreements among agents exist. *E.g., an instructor assigns students to a group for working on a class project.*

The strategic interdependence of perfectly competitive firms or a monopoly is either minor or nonexistent, so models of perfect competition and monopoly do not require the incorporation of game theory. In contrast, strategic interdependence is a major characteristic of imperfect competition, so game theory has become the foundation of models addressing imperfect-competition firm behavior. Economic models based on game theory are abstractions from the strategic interaction of agents. This abstraction allows tractable interactions, yielding implications and conclusions that can then be used for understanding actual strategic interactions.

In this chapter, we first develop both the strategic and extensive forms of game theory. As we discuss *Prisoners' Dilemma*—the classic example of strategic interaction—we see the difficulties of obtaining a cooperative solution without some binding agreement. However, we show that a cooperative solution may result if the game is played repeatedly. Prisoners' Dilemma games assume that all players move simultaneously. An alternative set of games are *sequential games,* where one player may know other players' choices prior to making a decision. Within the set of sequential games are *preemption games*, where being the first to make a move may have certain advantages. Sometimes a player's first move is to threaten the other players. In this vein, we investigate the consequence of idle threats.

We investigate variations on Prisoners' Dilemma in the chapter's appendix. One game theory model explains why people will generally drive their automobiles right through a green light. Another investigates the Prisoners' Dilemma with incomplete information. We also discuss possible mixed strategies for players to follow. As a final application of game theory, we discuss *quid pro quo,* where issues (games) are not resolved in isolation. The applications of game theory presented in this chapter are just a small sample of the myriad of possible issues that can and have been investigated in a game-theory context.

The game

My work is a game, a very serious game.

(M.C. Escher)

Boxing is the purest form, with only two athletes competing head to head purely with their bodies and minds. One athlete's actions are in direct response to the other athlete's actions.

This interaction among players (athletes) is the foundation of game theory. The **game** is a model representing the strategic interdependence of agents in a particular situation, such as a sport event or a market. This strategic interdependence implies that the optimal actions of a player may depend on what he expects other players will do. Players are the decision makers in a game, with the ability to choose actions within a set of possible actions they may undertake. These players may be individuals or groups of households, firms, governments, animals, or the environment (nature) as a whole. The number of players is finite, and games are characterized by this number of players (for example, a two-player or n-player game). A game-theory model is composed of the players, the rules by which the game is played, the outcome, and the payoffs. Rules involve what, when, and how the game is played. Specifically, rules state what information each player knows before she moves (chooses some action), when a player moves relative to other players, and how players can move (their set of choices). For each possible set of players' actions, there is an outcome and associated payoff for each player. A player's **payoff** is some reward or consequence of playing the game. This payoff may be in the form of a change in (marginal) utility or profit, or some nonmonetary change in satisfaction. It is assumed that payoffs can at least be ranked ordinally in terms of each player's preferences.

Game. A model representing the strategic interdependence of agents. *E.g., regional conflict games that the military plays.*

Payoff. A reward or consequence of playing a game. *E.g., the satisfaction from playing a game, possibly in the form of profits, market share, goodwill, prestige, or fame.*

An example of a game is the hand game, Rock, Paper, Scissors. The rules for this game are that each player simultaneously makes the figure rock, paper, or scissors with one of their hands. The outcome is that rock dominates (crushes) scissors, scissors dominate (cut) paper and paper dominates (smothers) rock. In a two-person game, the player who makes the dominating figure wins the game. When both make the same figure, it's a draw and neither player wins. Players each develop strategies for playing the game, where a **strategy** (also called a **decision rule**) is the set of actions a player may take. A strategy specifies how a player will act in every possible distinguishable circumstance in which he may be placed. For example, how a firm will react to a competitor's possible price changes is the firm's strategy for this competitor's action. In general, a strategy is a player's action plan. In Rock, Paper, Scissors, the strategy is the decision about when to form a rock, paper, or scissors with one's hand. A player's strategy is his complete contingent plan. If it could be written down, any other agent could follow the plan and thus duplicate the player's actions. Thus, a strategy is a player's course of action involving a set of actions (moves) dependent on the actions of the other players. For example, in a more complex game, say, chess, a player's strategy may involve a course of actions (moves) to first put all of her pieces in play, then achieve the advantage by controlling the center of the board, and finally moving forward and taking the opponent's king. Within this strategy, the player develops a specific set of actions for each possible move her opponent could make. Actions implement a given strategy.

Table 14.1 Strategic form for the Rock, Paper, Scissors game

		Player R's strategies		
		Rock	*Scissors*	*Paper*
Player F's Strategies	Rock	(Draw, Draw)	(Win, Loss)	(Loss, Win)
	Scissors	(Loss, Win)	(Draw, Draw)	(Win, Loss)
	Paper	(Win, Loss)	(Loss, Win)	(Draw, Draw)

Note: Within the parentheses, the first payoff is for player F and the second is for player R, (F's payoff, R's payoff).

Strategy (decision rule). A set of actions a player may take specifying how he will act in every possible distinguishable circumstance in which he may be placed. *E.g., a football coach's playbook specifying defensive strategies for each possible offensive strategy an opponent will take.*

Two methods for representing games are **strategic (normal) form** and **extensive form** games. The strategic form lists the set of possible player strategies and associated payoffs in a matrix. Table 14.1 shows the strategic form for the Rock, Paper, Scissors game. The **strategy pairs** consist of the combination of strategies from the two agents. If player F chooses rock and R selects scissors, the strategy pair is (rock, scissors) with the outcome that rock crushes scissors. Player F then wins and player R loses.

These strategies and payoffs are summarized in a **game matrix** (a **payoff matrix**), which lists the payoffs for each player given their strategies. In the strategic form, only the strategies are listed. In contrast, the extensive form provides an extended description of a game by revealing not only the outcomes and payoffs from each set of player strategies but also the possible actions each player can take in response to the other player's moves. A **game tree** is used to represent the extensive form of a game. As illustrated in Figure 14.1 for the Rock, Paper, Scissors game, the game is played from left to right and each node (point) represents a player's decision. These nodes are connected by branches that indicate the actions a player has available at a node.

Strategic (normal) form. A condensed form of a game. *E.g., a listing of possible football plays and associated yardage.*

Extensive form. An extended description of a game. *E.g., in checkers all the possible moves a player can make given all the moves by the other player.*

Strategy pair. A combination of strategies for two players. *E.g., a pitcher throws a fastball and the batter doesn't swing.*

Game or payoff matrix. Lists the payoffs associated with each strategy for each player. *E.g., in baseball, a pitcher has a number of strategies (types of pitches) and the batter has a number of strategies (to swing or not and where to hit the ball). Matching the pitcher's strategies with the batter's yields the payoff matrix.*

Game tree. A figure representing the extensive form of a game. *E.g., Figure 14.1.*

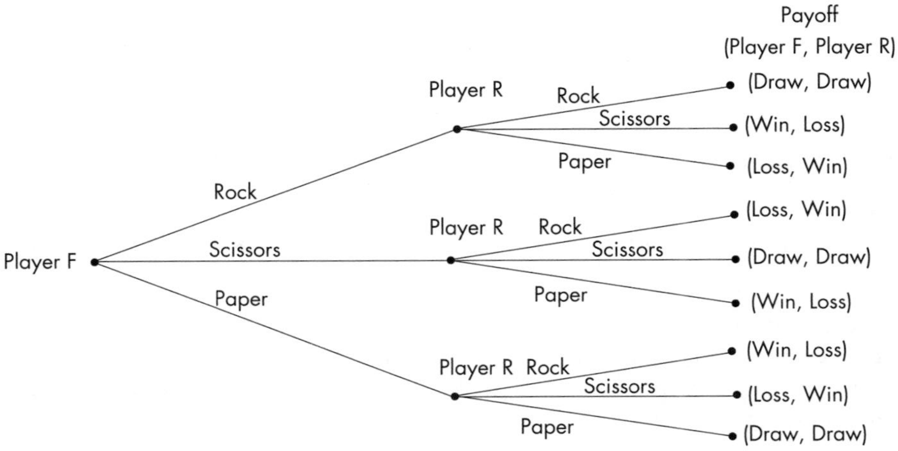

Figure 14.1 **Game tree for Rock, Paper, Scissors game.** This game tree represents the extensive form of a game. If the two players move sequentially, player F moves first, then player R.

The extensive form of a game can be used to model everything in the strategic form plus information about the sequence of actions and what information each player has at each node. Thus, the extensive form contains more detailed information, which may help to eliminate some of the possible equilibrium outcomes. For example, in Figure 14.1, two players F and R have the action choice of making a rock, paper, or scissors. If the two players move sequentially with player F moving first, player R can observe player F's action and always win. As an illustration, if at the initial decision node (also called a **root**), player F chooses rock, then player R—observing player F's choice—will then choose paper. This yields the terminal node with an associated payoff of player F losing and player R winning.

Root. The initial decision node. *E.g., the beginning of the game; the kickoff.*

In this game, sequential moves put the player who moves first at a disadvantage. The other player will always choose an action that results in a win. As a result of this disadvantage, player F will not reveal her action unless player R also reveals his action. When the players thus simultaneously reveal their actions, neither player has any prior information on the actions of the other player—their information set is the same. In a game of simultaneous moves, the game tree can be constructed with either player's actions as the root.

Establishing equilibrium

Recall from Chapter 1 that market equilibrium exists when there is no incentive for agents to change their behavior. This market equilibrium then yields an equilibrium price and quantity. In game theory, a similar equilibrium may exist where players have no incentives to change their strategy. One such equilibrium called the **dominant strategy,** where one strategy is preferred to another no matter what other players do. For example, if a college student plans on going home this weekend regardless of what her roommates do, then going home dominates not going home. When all the players have a dominant strategy, an equilibrium of dominant strategies exists that is determined without a player having to consider the behavior of the other players. However, usually a player must consider other players' strategies and may reduce his set of strategy choices based on rational behavior. By assuming that all players are rational in maximizing utility, a player determines a **rationalizable strategy**. For example, you are willing to fly with an e-ticket because you assume the issuing airline is rational and will let you fly. Generally, players who do not believe in rationalizable strategies will attempt to maximize utility independent of other players. Such players are generally survivalists or hermits.

Dominant strategy. A strategy that is preferred to another strategy no matter what the other players' strategies are. *E.g., studying for an examination dominates not studying regardless of whether the examination is written or oral.*

Rationalizable strategy. One strategy is preferred to another based on the rational behavior of the other players. *E.g., you will accept dollars as payment for services rendered because you know others will also accept these dollars in exchange for commodities.*

A unique equilibrium or a set of equilibria may occur within a set of strategies. Such an equilibrium is called a **Nash equilibrium** after mathematician John Nash (1994 Nobel Laureate), where each player's selected strategy is his or her preferred response to the strategies actually played by all the other players.[1] The strategies are in a state of balance. An equivalent definition of a Nash equilibrium is where each player's belief about the other players' preferred strategies coincides with the actual choice the other players make. There is no incentive on the part of any players to change their choices. In a two-player game, a Nash equilibrium is a pair of player strategies where the strategy of one player is the best strategy when the other player plays his or her best strategy. As illustrated in the following section, not all games have a Nash equilibrium and some games may have a number of Nash equilibria.

Nash equilibrium. Each player's selected strategy is his or her preferred response to the strategies actually played by all the other players. *E.g., if you go to the movies, I will also go.*

Understanding the strategic form

The strategic form of the game is a condensed version of the extensive form. The actions with each player's strategy are not reported in the strategic form (how you play is not reported). Instead, only the possible strategies of each player with associated payoffs (win or lose) are listed. Initially, we assume that both players possess perfect knowledge; each player knows his own payoffs and strategies and the other player's payoffs and strategies. Also, each player knows that the other player knows this. In the strategic form, a player's decision problem is choosing his strategy given the strategies that he believes the other players will choose. Then the players simultaneously choose their strategies, and the payoff for each player is determined.

For example, firms interacting within a market could compete in advertising or jointly advertise in an effort to increase total demand for their products. In most economic situations, agents can jointly or independently influence the total payoff, indicating there is a possibility of cooperation or collusion. **Collusion** is where a joint strategy among a set of players improves their position.

Collusion. A joint strategy among a set of players that improves their payoff. *E.g., two neighbors jointly renting a tiller to till their gardens.*

An example of a strategic interaction among players is the Battle-of-the-Sexes game. The strategic form of this game is presented in Table 14.2, with the payoff matrix composed of (wife's payoff, husband's payoff). The two players are a wife and husband facing the decision of determining what to do on a Saturday night. They have two choices: going to the opera or to the fights. If they both go to the opera (fights) they each receive some positive utility, with the wife's (husband's) level of satisfaction higher than the husband's (wife's). However, if the husband goes to the fights while the wife goes to the opera, they each enjoy their respective activity but not as much as if they went together to either event. In contrast, if the husband goes to the opera and the wife to the fights, they both receive disutility from the experience (the husband finds it difficult to sleep in the opera seats, and the wife is unable to sleep after the fights). As shown in the table, the sum of the payoffs is higher in the two strategy pairs where they go together to the same event compared with each going to a different event.

A result of the payoffs presented in Table 14.2 is the possibility of multiple Nash equilibria. Both going to the opera is a Nash equilibrium, because if either one instead picks fights, their utility is decreased. For example, if the husband picks fights, his utility is reduced from 2 to 1. Similarly, if the wife picks fights, her utility falls from 5 to −7. Likewise, both going to the fights is a Nash equilibrium. If either one instead picks opera, the wife's utility falls from 2 to 1 and the husband's from 5 to −1. In general, even if a Nash equilibrium exists, it may not be unique. As discussed in the appendix to this chapter, this problem of multiple Nash equilibria can be avoided when players choose a strategy mix.

Table 14.2 Battle-of-the-Sexes game

		Husband	
		Opera	*Fights*
Wife	Opera	(5, 2)	(1, 1)
	Fights	(−7, −1)	(2, 5)

Note: The payoffs are (wife's payoff, husband's payoff).

Prisoners' dilemma

> *Man is the only animal that can remain on friendly terms with the victims he intends to eat until he eats them.*
>
> (Samuel Butler)

In 1939, Hitler and Stalin signed a nonaggression pact that divided up Poland; however, in 1941, Hitler attacked Stalin. Strategically interrelated interests such as Hitler's and Stalin's may be represented in terms of the classical **Prisoners' Dilemma** game, developed by A. W. Tucker (1905–1995). In general, the Prisoners' Dilemma game is a situation where two prisoners are accused of a crime. The DA (District Attorney) does not have sufficient evidence to convict them unless at least one of them supplies some supporting testimony. If one prisoner were to testify against the other, conviction would be a certainty. The DA offers each prisoner separately a deal. If one confesses while his accomplice remains silent, the talkative prisoner will receive only 1 year in prison. In contrast, the silent prisoner will be sent up for the maximum of 10 years. If neither confesses, both will be prosecuted on a lesser offense, with a 2-year sentence for both of them. Finally, if both confess, in which case the testimony of neither is essential to the prosecution, both will be convicted of the major offense and sent up for 5 years. As shown in Table 14.3, the payoff matrix is composed of (F's payoff, R's payoff).

Prisoners' Dilemma. A game illustrating the difficulties of obtaining a cooperative solution without some binding agreement. *E.g., an agreement among roommates to clean up after themselves in the kitchen.*

The unique Nash equilibrium to Prisoners' Dilemma is where each prisoner confesses and each is sentenced to 5 years. From Table 14.3, if prisoner R does not confess, prisoner F can increase her payoff by confessing (and thus reducing jail time by 1 year). If prisoner R confesses, prisoner F will again confess, and receive 5 fewer years. Thus, for prisoner F, confessing is always preferred to not confessing. In other words, confessing is the dominant strategy for prisoner F. Similarly, confessing is also the dominant strategy for prisoner R. Thus, the Nash equilibrium is both F and R confessing. No other pair of strategies is in Nash equilibrium, so both confessing dominates all other strategy pairs. If prisoner F does not confess, she will receive 10 years, because prisoner R will believe that if F confesses and he does not confess, then he will receive 10 years. Thus, prisoner R will confess.

This game illustrates the situation, common in economics, where cooperation (not confessing) can improve the welfare of all players. Although the dominant strategy of both

Table 14.3 Prisoners' Dilemma game

		Prisoner R	
		Not confess	*Confess*
Prisoner F	Not confess	(–2, –2)	(–10, –1)
	Confess	(–1, –10)	(–5, –5)

Note: The payoffs are (F's payoff, R's payoff).

prisoners confessing is the Nash equilibrium strategy, it is not the preferred outcome of the players acting jointly. Both prisoners would prefer they jointly do not confess and each receive only 2 years. This is a classic example of rational self-interest behavior not resulting in a social optimum. If the two prisoners could find a way to agree upon this joint strategy of not confessing and, of equal importance, a way to enforce this agreement, both would be better off than when they play the game independently. However, it is still in the interest of both prisoners to secretly break the agreement. The one who breaks the deal and confesses will only receive 1 year, while the other will pay the price of receiving an additional 8 years (2–10). This is an example of a bilateral externality (discussed in Chapter 21); an economic example is the Bertrand model (discussed in Chapter 15).

Why does a district attorney separate prisoners accused of a crime? Separating prisoners prevents them from forming any agreements that will make them better off.

Enforcement

Mexican mafia (La Eme) is a prison-based gang whose members are recruited in prison. Young street-gang members taking their first trip to the penitentiary often join La Eme for the protection it offers in jail. Members of La Eme (or any mafia) will sign an oath of loyalty and silence. Thus, they would never break from a joint optimal solution. This is in contrast to the results in the Prisoners' Dilemma example, where the Nash equilibrium results in confession when the joint optimal solution would be for both prisoners to not confess. For this joint cooperation to result, some type of enforcement is required. Otherwise, there is an incentive on the part of at least one player to break the agreement. One form of enforcement is when the other prisoner has friends in and out of prison (mafia), and it is understood that if word got out that you even considered breaking the agreement, the friends would break you. You would then receive the 10-year prison sentence, unless you also have friends for enforcement.

Why does joining a street gang have advantages? Joining a street gang may give you friends to enforce agreements.

In Table 14.3, the prisoners' decisions highlight the difference between what is best from an individual's point of view and what is best from the point of view of a collective. This conflict endangers almost every form of cooperation. The reward for mutual cooperation is higher than the punishment for mutual defection, but a one-sided defection yields a temptation greater than that reward. This leaves the exploited cooperator with a loser's payoff that is even worse than the punishment for mutual defection. Rankings from temptation through reward and punishment imply that the best move is always to defect, irrespective of the opposing player's move. The logic leads inexorably to mutual defection unless some type of enforcement exists.

Cooperation

> *A person who trusts no one cannot be trusted.*
>
> (Jerome Blattner)

> *Compassion (cooperation) is the keen awareness of the interdependence of all things.*
>
> (Thomas Merton)

In 1997, countries around the world developed the Kyoto Protocol as a first step toward addressing the problem of global warming. As illustrated by this treaty, in general, agents attempt to cooperate, so the previously discussed results of agents defecting from cooperative agreements are generally not observed in societies. Agents often instead cooperate, motivated by feelings of solidarity or altruism. In business agreements, defection is also relatively rare. In fact, in the evolutionary theory of life, cooperation among smaller units leads to the emergence of more complex structures, resulting in multicellular creatures. In this sense, cooperation is as essential for evolution as is competition. In many respects, this is also true for an economy. In fact, cooperation among agents in an economy may be as essential as competition for economic efficiency and enhancing social welfare.

Why are there multicellular creatures? Cooperation among smaller biological units allows multicellular creatures to exist.

A solution consistent with cooperation may result if the Prisoners' Dilemma game is repeatedly played. If one player chooses to defect in one round, then the other player can choose to defect in the next round. In a repeated game, each player has the opportunity to establish a reputation for cooperation and encourage the other player to also cooperate. If a game is repeated an infinite number of times, a cooperative strategy of not confessing may dominate the single-game Nash equilibrium of confessing.

Let us consider first a finite number T of repeated games (a **finitely repeated game**). The last round, T, is the same as playing the game once, so the solution will be the same and both players will defect by confessing. In round $T-1$, there is no reason to cooperate, since they both defected in round T. Thus, in round $T-1$, they both defect. Defection will continue in every round unless there is some way to enforce cooperation on the last round. However, if the game is repeated an infinite number of times (an **infinitely repeated game**), then a player does have a way of influencing the other player's behavior. If one player refuses to cooperate this time, the other player can refuse to cooperate the next time.

Finitely repeated game. A game that is repeated a fixed number of times. *E.g., an instructor allowing only one makeup examination.*

Infinitely repeated game. A game that is repeated forever. *E.g., DNA attempting to replicate itself since the beginning of life.*

Robert Axelrod identifies the optimal strategy for an infinitely repeated game as **tit-for-tat** (also called a **trigger** strategy).[2] In the first round, player F cooperates and does not confess. In every round after, if player R cooperated in the previous round, F cooperates. If player R defected in the previous round, F then defects. This strategy does very well because it offers an immediate punishment for defection and has a forgiving strategy. An application is the carrot-and-stick strategy that underlies most attempts at raising children.

How should you raise your children (or rats)? One method for raising children (or rats) is immediate punishment for bad behavior and immediate award for good behavior.

Tit-for-tat (trigger). A strategy that immediately rewards good behavior and punishes bad behavior. *E.g., horse training or dog obedience school.*

Example 14.1 Prisoner F following a tit-for-tat strategy in Prisoners' Dilemma

Round	*Prisoner F*		*Prisoner R*	
	Strategy	*Payoff*	*Strategy*	*Payoff*
1	Not confess	−2	Not confess	−2
2	Not confess	−10	Confess	−1
3	Confess	−5	Confess	−5
4	Confess	−1	Not confess	−10
5	Not confess	−2	Not confess	−2

Prisoner F starts out not confessing, and will stay with the strategy of not confessing as long as R does not confess. However, if R confesses, then F will confess, which provides immediate punishment to R. As long as R confesses, F will punish R. However, if R does not confess, then F in the immediate next round will reward R by also not confessing. Prisoner R will soon learn that cooperating minimizes his losses (prison terms). Thus, both players' optimal strategy is to cooperate and not confess.

An alternative strategy is **win-stay/lose-shift**. If a player wins with a chosen strategy, she keeps the same strategy for the next round. If she loses, she changes to an alternative strategy. This strategy is similar to the tit-for-tat strategy in terms of preventing exploiters from invading a cooperative society. It will provide incentives for any exploiter to cooperate. **Exploiters** in a cooperative society are players who attempt to maximize their payoff given the strategies of the other players. It does not matter to exploiters if their strategy results in cooperation or not. They are only interested in maximizing their payoff. However, this win-stay/lose-shift strategy fares poorly among noncooperators. Against persistent defectors, a player employing the win-stay/lose-shift strategy tries every second round to resume cooperation. In animal psychology, this win-stay/lose-shift strategy is viewed as fundamental. A rat is ready to repeat an action that brings reward and will tend to drop behavior that has painful consequences.

Win-stay/lose-shift. If a player wins, the strategy is retained on the next round; if a player loses, the strategy is changed on the next round. *E.g., when driving, you may continue to exceed the speed limit until you get caught. Once caught, you may drive the rest of the way at the speed limit.*

Exploiters. Players who invade a cooperative society and attempt to maximize their payoff given the strategies of the other players. *E.g., Hitler.*

Example 14.2 Prisoner F following a win-stay/lose-shift strategy in Prisoners' Dilemma when facing an exploiter

Round	*Prisoner F*		*Prisoner R*		
	Strategy	*Payoff*	*Strategy*	*Payoff*	
1	Not confess	−10	Confess	−1	
2	Confess	−5	Confess	−5	
3	Not confess	−10	Confess	−1	} Average prison term 3 years
4	Confess	−5	Confess	−5	
5	Not confess	−10	Confess	−1	
6	Not confess	−2	Not confess	−2	} Average prison term 2 years
7	Not confess	−2	Not confess	−2	
8	Not confess	−2	Not confess	−2	

Prisoner F starts out not confessing; however, R, the exploiter, will confess. Prisoner F loses, so in the second round confesses and R also confesses. Prisoner F again loses, so in the third round shifts to not confessing; R exploits this by confessing. This results in F again shifting and R, the exploiter, continuing to confess in the fourth round. Prisoner F then loses and shifts to not confessing in the fifth round. A cycle is now established, with F shifting between each round and R always confessing. However, now R realizes this cycle, and on average he will lose 3 each round by maintaining it. If R did not confess each round, he would only lose 2. Thus, the exploiter would cooperate on the first round by not confessing and always not confess on the subsequent rounds. This will result in both players cooperating by not confessing.

Example 14.3 Prisoner F following a win-stay/lose-shift strategy versus a tit-for-tat strategy in Prisoners' Dilemma when facing a noncooperator

Round	*Win-stay/lose-shift strategy for F*				*Tit-for-tat strategy for F*			
	Prisoner F		*Prisoner R*		*Prisoner F*		*Prisoner R*	
	Strategy	*Payoff*	*Strategy*	*Payoff*	*Strategy*	*Payoff*	*Strategy*	*Payoff*
1	Not confess	−10	Confess	−1	Not confess	−10	Confess	−1
2	Confess	−5	Confess	−5	Confess	−5	Confess	−5
3	Not confess	−10	Confess	−1	Confess	−5	Confess	−5
4	Confess	−5	Confess	−5	Confess	−5	Confess	−5

Prisoner F starts out not confessing; however, R, the noncooperator, will always confess. With F following a win-stay/lose-shift strategy, F will shift after each round, because R refuses to cooperate. This results in higher losses for F compared with R. If, instead, F follows a tit-for-tat strategy, F will only not confess on the first round and then follow the noncooperator R by confessing. After the first round, this results in the same losses for F as R, and less of a loss for F than with the win-stay/lose-shift strategy.

Application: Game theory is not for playing games

As one of the three game theorists to share the 1994 Nobel Prize in economics, Reinhard Selten stated, "Game theory is for proving theorems, not for playing games." The best way to play a game depends on how others actually play, not on how some theory dictates that rational individuals should play.

Nash equilibrium is the foundation of game theory and one of the most popular theoretical underpinnings of economics. For example, in industrial organization, virtually all recent theoretical developments are applications of game theory. Game theory appears to have matured in the last 50 years, with orderly classifications and refined versions of basic approaches. As stated by Goeree and Holt, "It is hard not to notice parallels with theology, and the highly mathematical nature of the developments makes this work about as inaccessible to mainstream economists as medieval treatises on theology would have been to the general public."

Unfortunately, experimental evidence of actual agents' behavior does not always support the theoretical result that agent behavior will converge to Nash predictions. As a demonstration of this divergence, Goeree and Holt present contradictions between theory and behavior for each major classification of games.

As an illustration, let us consider the one-shot Traveler's Dilemma game, one of the contradictions presented by Goeree and Holt. In this game, two players independently and simultaneously choose integer numbers within the interval 180–300. Both players are paid the lower of the two numbers, plus an amount $I > 1$ is transferred from the player with the higher number to the player with the lower number. With $I > 1$, the best response is to undercut the other player's decision by 1, so the upper bound of 300 is never a best response. A rational player will then assign a probability of 0 to a choice of 300, but with 299 now the upper bound, it too will be ruled out by a rational player. Such rational behavior will continue until only the lower bound 180 survives this iterated deletion process. This results in 180 as the unique Nash equilibrium.

The contradiction of this Nash equilibrium with actual behavior is based on the idea that when the cost, $2I$, of having the high number is low, the penalty from choosing the high number is so small that attempting to undercut the other player is not of much value. The cost of picking a high number when the other player picks low is minimal; however, picking high when the other player also chooses high has the potential of a large payoff. In other words, downside loss is low and upside gain is potentially very high. However, for a large penalty, the cost of not undercutting the other player is high, so then one should pick low. This results in the hypothesis that actual behavior could be well away from the Nash equilibrium of 180 for low levels of *I* but consistent with the Nash equilibrium for high levels. As a test of this hypothesis, Goeree and Holt asked 25 pairs of students to play the game with $I = 5$ and with $I = 180$. The results were consistent with the hypothesis. Close to 80 percent of the players chose the Nash equilibrium $I = 180$, with an average of 201. However, approximately the same percentage chose the highest possible number, 300, with an average of 280, for the low penalty of 5. These opposite polar results of Nash equilibrium and actual behavior for a low penalty does not disappear or diminish over time when players play the game repeatedly and thus have an opportunity to learn. Game theory is unable to explain the data associated with the penalty/reward parameter effect on average payoffs.

As discussed by Goeree and Holt, economists are starting to explain such contradictions using computer simulations and theoretical analyses of learning and decision error processes. In reality, your best strategies should be based on how others actually play, not on some game theoretic result.

Source: J.K. Goeree and C.A. Holt, "Ten Little Treasures of Game Theory and Ten Intuitive Contradictions," *American Economic Review* 91 (2001): 1402–1422.

How to play sequential games

Skate to where the puck is going to be, not where it has been.

(Wayne Gretzky)

In early 2003, World Chess Champion Garry Kasparov tied (3 to 3) with the computer chess champion Deep Junior, which can evaluate 3 million moves per second using an algorithm based on sequential game theory. The programs are designed to look ahead and reason back. In chess, first the player with the white pieces makes a move then the player with black pieces. This is called a **sequential game**, or **dynamic game**, where one player may know the other player's choice before she has to make a choice (a hockey player will know where the puck is going to be before he skates to it). Many economic games have this structure. For example, a monopolist may determine consumer demand prior to producing an output, or a buyer knows the sticker price on a new automobile before making an offer.

Sequential (dynamic) game. In making a choice of strategies, a player already knows the other player's choice. *E.g., in labor union negotiations, first management makes an offer and then the union responds to this offer.*

As an example of a sequential game, consider again the Battle-of-the-Sexes game in Table 14.2. Recall that the couple is considering their leisure activity for this coming weekend. The husband prefers going to the fights while the wife prefers the opera. However, they both prefer spending their leisure activity together. This results in two pure-strategy Nash equilibria (both going to the opera or both going to the fights) if both players reveal their

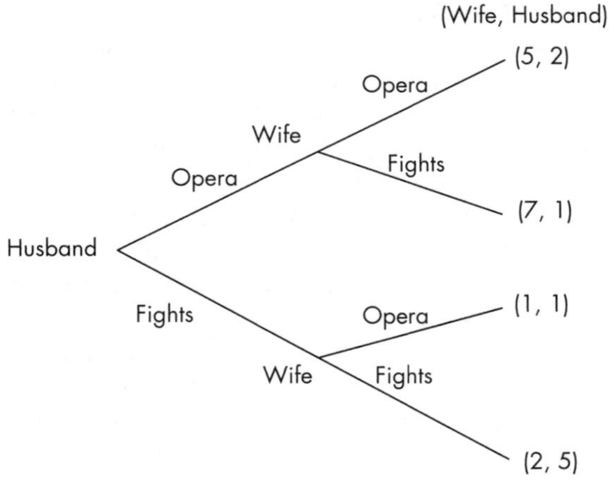

Figure 14.2 **A game tree for the Battle-of-the-Sexes game.** In this sequential game, the husband moves first, then the wife. The Nash-equilibrium outcome for this game is the couple going to the fights.

choices simultaneously. Instead, let us suppose that the husband chooses first and then the wife. The game tree outlining this sequence of choices is illustrated in Figure 14.2.

This game tree is a description of the game in extensive form and indicates the dynamic structure of the game, where some choices are made before others. Once a choice has been made, the players are in a subgame consisting of the strategies and payoffs available to them from then on. If the husband picks opera, the subgame is for the wife to choose. If she picks opera also, the husband ends with a payoff of 2 and the wife with a payoff of 5. If the husband picks the fights, it is optimal for the wife to also pick the fights. The resulting payoffs are 5 for the husband and 2 for the wife. For the husband (the first player), 5 is greater than 2, so the equilibrium for this sequential game is for the couple to go to the fights. This is one of the Nash equilibria in the strategic form of the game, Table 14.2. Both going to the fights is not only an overall equilibrium, but also an equilibrium in each of the subgames. A Nash equilibrium with this property is known as a *subgame perfect Nash equilibrium.*

The unique equilibrium of both going to the fights is conditional on who makes the first choice. If, instead, the wife made the first move, the alternative Nash equilibrium, both going to the opera, would be the unique solution of this sequential game. Thus, this strategy pair of opera and fights is really a subset of a larger game involving the strategies of moving first or second. We use a technique called **backward induction** to determining a subgame perfect Nash equilibrium, by working backward toward the root in a game tree. Once the game is understood through this backward induction, the players play it forwards. Thus, it is perfectly true, as philosophers say, that life must be understood backwards. But they forget that it must be lived forwards.

Backward induction. In a game tree, the equilibrium strategies are determined by working backward toward the root. *E.g., given the answer to a mathematics problem, it may be easier to find the solution by working backward from the answer.*

To apply backward induction, we first determine the optimal actions at the last decision nodes that result in the terminal nodes. We then determine the optimal action at the next to last decision nodes, assuming that optimal actions will follow at the last decision nodes. We continue this backward process until the root node is reached. Backward induction implicitly assumes that a player's strategy will consist of optimal actions at every node in the game tree. This assumption is called the **principle of sequential rationality**. At any point in the game tree, a player's strategy should consist of optimal actions from that point on, given the other players' strategies.

Principle of sequential rationality. At any point in a game tree, a player's strategy is consistent with future optimal actions. *E.g., getting plenty of sleep before an examination is consistent with having the energy for an optimal performance on an examination.*

Applying backward induction to the Battle-of-the-Sexes game, the last decision nodes are the wife's, where at each node she has the decision to go to the opera or the fights. For the node resulting from the husband choosing fights, the wife's decision is to choose fights, with payoffs of 2 for the wife and 5 for the husband. Similarly, for the node resulting from the husband choosing opera, the wife's decision is to choose opera, with payoffs of 5 for the wife and 2 for the husband. Given that the optimal actions have been determined at the last decision nodes, we can construct a reduced game tree, illustrated in Figure 14.3. The process is then continued by considering the next-to-last decision nodes, which in this case is the one root node. At this root node, the husband decides between going to the opera or the fights, given the actions that will follow at the next decision node. The husband will then choose fights with a payoff of 5 for him and 2 for his wife, which is the subgame perfect Nash equilibrium.

Who should make the first move on a date? You. Whoever makes the first move on a date sets the tone for the rest of the date.

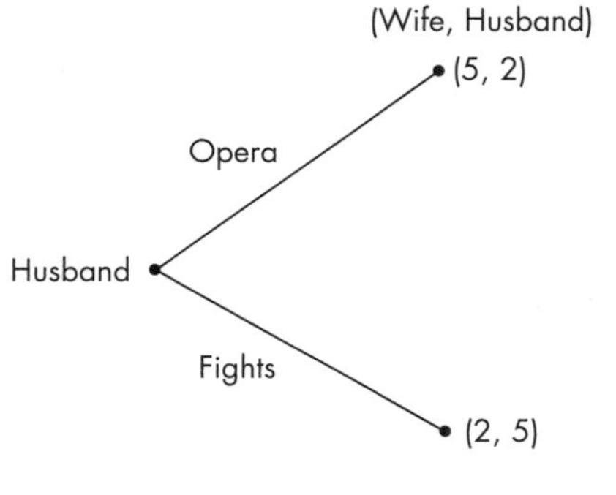

Figure 14.3 **Reduced game tree for Battle-of-the-Sexes.** By backward induction, the wife's optimal actions have been determined for each possible choice of the husband.

Preemption games

> *The best defense is a strong offense.*
>
> (Jack Dempsey)
>
> *Translation: There are advantages to moving first.*

The Battle-of-the-Sexes game illustrates the advantage of moving first. In many economic game theory models, firms who act first have an advantage. Such games are called **preemption games**, where strategic precommitments can affect future payoffs. For example, a firm adopting a relatively large production capacity in a new market can saturate the market and thus make it difficult for ensuing firms to enter. Any economies of scale associated with this production can be achieved with this large capacity, so the firm moving first has the potential of lower average production costs. This ability to first seize a market depends on the market's contestability. If the market is contestable, potential entrant firms can practice hit-and-run entry, which will mitigate any advantages of moving first. Governments concerned with the ability of firms to saturate a market and forestall entry of other firms have attempted to place restrictions on such behavior. As an example of the benefits of temporary protection, President Reagan placed a five-year tariff on motorcycles to rescue the domestic motorcycle company Harley-Davidson. The company used the opportunity to retool and become once again competitive.

When would you advocate tariffs and quotas? In an effort to prevent large foreign firms from displacing domestic supply, you may advocate trade restrictions in the form of tariffs and quotas.

> **Preemption game.** A game where agents moving first have an advantage. *E.g., an automobile dealer setting the initial sticker price for an automobile.*

An example of a preemption game is provided in Table 14.4. Firms 1 and 2 are faced with the choice of entering or not entering a market. The market is not large enough for both to enter, so, if they both enter, they will each experience losses in payoff of −5. If neither firm enters the market, both payoffs are 0. The two pure-strategy Nash equilibria are for one firm to enter and the other not. Thus, whichever firm moves firsts and enters the market will receive a positive payoff of 10, and the other firm will not enter and will receive a 0 payoff. The strategy for firms is then to be the first to enter the market. If one of the firms is a foreign firm and has some advantages of being first to enter a domestic market, the domestic government may attempt to restrict that entry to enable the domestic firm to enter first. Once the domestic firm enters, the foreign firm no longer has an incentive to enter.

Table 14.4 Preemption game

		Firm 2	
		Entry	*No entry*
Firm 1	Entry	(–5, –5)	(10, 0)
	No entry	(0, 10)	(0, 0)

Note: The payoffs are (firm 1, firm 2).

Market niches

Preemption games can also help us understand discount stores' location strategies. In the United States, small towns generally only have sufficient populations to support one major discount store such as Kmart, Target, or Wal-Mart. The first discount firm to establish a store in the town drives out any preexisting local nondiscount competition and then has a local monopoly. As the country gets saturated with these discount stores, opportunities to establish local monopolies decline. Then the discount firms will attempt to fill a **market niche** instead. For example, Target stores cater to upper-middle-income households. Similarly, once a discount store enters a local market, existing nondiscount stores will attempt to adjust their market in an effort to find a market niche not covered by the discounts.

For nondiscount stores, price-competing with a discount store is generally not an optimal choice. As implied in Table 14.5, a chain of discount stores will generally, by economies to scale, have lower average costs than a single nondiscount store. Thus, if the nondiscount store attempts to compete by lowering its price, the discount store will also lower its price. This results in losses for the nondiscount store, −5, while the discount store still remains profitable. As indicated in the table, the dominant strategy for the nondiscount store is to maintain its high price. The strategy for the discount firm is then to enter and offer slightly lower prices than the nondiscount store. The nondiscount store can then either develop a niche market around the discount store or eventually go out of business.

Why should a nondiscount store not lower prices when a discount store enters the market? A chain discount store will generally have lower average costs than a single nondiscount store, so competing with a discount store on prices will result in a loss for the nondiscount store.

In general, producers will also attempt to occupy every market niche to keep potential entrants from gaining access into a market. Through research and development, a firm will endeavor to supply a complete range of a particular product to cover every niche.[3] For example, in the market for toothbrushes, a firm will attempt to supply every type of brush from a baby's to a denture brush.

Market niche. A segment of the market that demands a commodity that is slightly differentiated from other commodities. *E.g., the market for luxury automobiles such as Lincoln Continentals.*

Table 14.5 Discount entry

		Discount firm	
		Entry	*No entry*
Incumbent nondiscount firm	Accommodate High price	(–1, 20)	(10, 0)
	Fight Low price	(–5, 5)	(5, 0)

Note: The payoffs are (nondiscount firm, discount firm).

Table 14.6 Market niches

		Firm 2	
		Niche C	*Niche H*
Firm 1	Niche C	(–10, –10)	(15, 5)
	Niche H	(5, 15)	(–5, –5)

Note: The payoffs are (firm 1, firm 2).

As an illustration of competition for market niches, let us consider two firms entertaining entry into a market for a commodity, say, breakfast cereals with two niches, sweet cereals C and healthy cereals H. The payoff matrix is provided in Table 14.6. This payoff matrix is of the same form as the Battle-of-the-Sexes payoff matrix in Table 14.2. Thus, if both firms move simultaneously, two Nash equilibria result, with each firm picking a different market niche. As in Figures 14.2 and 14.3, whichever firm moves first will capture the preferred market niche and receive the higher payoff. To be first, the firm must make a commitment, either by actually providing the product first or by advertising in advance that it will supply the product for the preferred niche. If there are large sunk costs associated with this commitment, then the other firm (say, firm 2) will realize that firm 1 is in fact committed to the preferred product niche C and may then accede and supply in niche H.

Threats

> *Go after a man's weakness, and never, ever, threaten unless you're going to follow through, because if you don't, the next time you won't be taken seriously.*
>
> (Roy M. Cohn)

Instead of making a commitment to supply in the preferred niche market C and incurring sunk cost, firm 1 could attempt to just threaten firm 2. For example, firm 1 could threaten firm 2 by just stating it will produce in niche C regardless of what firm 2 does. However, firm 2 has to believe the threat to acquiesce. One way to make a credible threat is to make the commitment in sunk cost. Or, firm 1 could attempt to mislead firm 2 into believing it is making a commitment to niche C when in fact it is not. This assumes asymmetric information.[4] An example of misleading one's rivals is the liberation of Europe in World War II. The Allies intentionally misled the Germans about their intended landing site of Normandy, France.

Idle or **empty threats** will not succeed in inducing a player to select some action. As an example, consider two competing firms advertising. The payoff matrix, in Table 14.7, represents the returns from the firms' choices of either advertising or not. The pure-strategy Nash equilibrium is for firm 1 to advertise and firm 2 not to advertise. Firm 1's advertising has a relatively large impact on the returns for the two firms. As such, at least in terms of advertising, firm 1 is the dominant firm in this industry. Despite firm 1's dominance, firm 2's advertising does positively affect firm 1's returns, by possibly expanding the total market in which the products are being advertised. In this case, advertising is not drawing sales from one firm to another but instead is making the product known to consumers, which enlarges both firms' markets. Thus, firm 1 would prefer firm 2 to also advertise; however, the added expense of advertising by firm 2 is not covered by its returns: Firm 2's payoff declines from 30 to 15 if it also advertises. However, even considering the dominance of firm 1, it cannot

Table 14.7 Idle threats

		Firm 2	
		Advertising	*No advertising*
Firm 1	Advertising	(65, 15)	(50, 30)
	No advertising	(20, –5)	(10, 5)

Note: The payoffs are (firm 1, firm 2).

threaten not to advertise in order to induce firm 2 into advertising. Threats will not work, because, no matter which choice firm 2 makes, firm 1's dominant strategy and its subgame perfect Nash equilibrium is to advertise. Firm 2 will realize that if firm 1 is rational, it will always advertise, so a threat of not advertising by firm 1 is not credible. It does not carry any weight (commitment). The subgame perfect Nash equilibrium results in a selection of a Nash equilibrium obtained by removing the strategies involving idle threats. It is very important to always be willing and able to carry out a threat.

Idle (empty) threat. Threat by an agent who has no commitment to follow through. *E.g., Britain's threat to declare war on Germany if it invaded Czechoslovakia.*

Child rearing

> *Children might or might not be a blessing, but to create them and then fail them is surely damnation.*
>
> (Lois McMaster Bujold)

If one player derives satisfaction from penalizing the other, then threats made by the player will be credible. The more credible the threat, the more likely it will be acted upon. An example is child rearing. Through reward and punishment, a parent derives satisfaction of good behavior from a child. Figure 14.4 shows a game tree representing the interactions of a parent and child. In this sequential game, the child selects her behavior and then the parent chooses to reward or punish it. The pure Nash equilibrium is a badly behaved child rewarded, where the subgame perfect Nash equilibrium is for the parent to always reward. If the child believes that the parent will always reward any behavior, it will choose bad behavior. In contrast, if the child is under the impression that the parent will punish bad behavior even if it hurts the parent, then a threat by the parent will not be idle. In Figure 14.4, the parent will not reward bad behavior even considering the parent's payoff increases from 35 to 40. The subgame perfect Nash equilibria are now for the parent to reward good behavior and punish bad. The child will then realize bad behavior will result in punishment with an associated zero payoff. Thus, with the threat, the child will select good behavior over bad and increase her payoff from 0 to 15.

When punishing a child, why does a parent say, "this will hurt me more than it will hurt you?" A parent does not want to punish the child, but realizes if he does not, the child will engage in bad behavior.

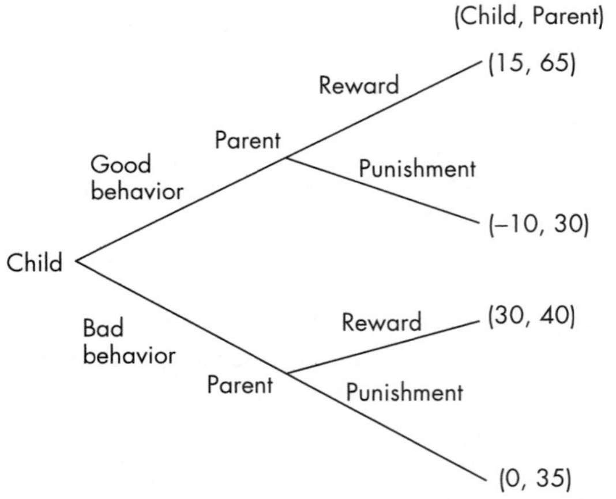

Figure 14.4 **A game tree for child rearing.** In this sequential game, the child moves first, then the parent. The Nash-equilibrium outcome for this game is a badly behaved child rewarded unless the parent's threat is not idle.

In general, this example of parent/child interaction is a principal/agent model, where the principal is the parent and the child is the agent.[5] The principal is attempting to provide incentives, both positive and negative, to elicit the correct behavior from the agent. In a repeated game, consistent behavior on the part of a principal can dominate inconsistent behavior. For example, if a parent is consistent in following through with any threats, the child will realize that the probability of punishment for bad behavior is high and correct her bad behavior. Establishing a reputation of always being committed to any threats can lead to cooperation by the other player.

In the Prisoners' Dilemma game, an example of consistent behavior is where a tit-for-tat strategy is consistently played. Unless these incentives (threats) are taken seriously, the agent will not select the principal's desirable actions. For example, suppose a Tea Party governor relaxes regulatory constraints on small business by not enforcing various environmental regulations. The threat of enforcement exists, but it is an idle threat. If a proenvironmental governor is elected, the threat will become credible and firms will likely comply with the regulations.

Summary

1. A game is a model representing the strategic interdependence of agents (players) in a particular situation. Two methods for representing a game are strategic- and extensive-form games. The extensive form models everything in the strategic form plus additional information that may aid in eliminating certain outcomes from consideration.
2. The classic example of a simultaneous game is Prisoners' Dilemma, which illustrates how cooperation can improve the welfare of all agents. Generally, to

facilitate cooperation, some type of enforcement is required that rewards good behavior and punishes bad behavior.

3. In many economic situations, agents interact by moving sequentially rather than simultaneously. A game tree may be used to describe the extensive form of these sequential games. Backward induction is used for determining the solutions.
4. The agent who acts first generally has the advantage. Games that model such behavior are called preemption games and may be used for describing firm entry into a market, market niches, and threats.
5. *(Appendix)* In many economic situations, the optimal solution is to prevent other players from predicting your strategy. Thus, mixed strategies can often improve a player's payoff.
6. *(Appendix)* Games with incomplete agent information as a result of some information asymmetries are called Bayesian games. Similar to mixed-strategy games, probabilities associated with payoffs are used for determining solutions.
7. *(Appendix)* Single issues represented by one game are not often resolved in isolation from other decisions. Generally, a multitude of issues and decisions require determining a joint outcome. A method for resolving these issues is quid pro quo—something for something else.

Key concepts

backward induction, 582
Bayesian game, 597
Bayesian Nash equilibrium, 597
collusion, 574
complete information game, 597
cooperative game theory, 568
decision rule, 570
dominant strategy, 572
dynamic game, 581
empty threats, 586
exploiters, 578
extensive form, 571
finitely repeated game, 577
game, 569
game matrix, 571
game theory, 568
game tree, 571
idle threats, 586
imperfect competition, 565
imperfect information game, 597
infinitely repeated game, 577
iterated deletion, 596
market niche, 585
maximin strategy, 594
mixed strategies, 594
Nash equilibrium, 573
noncooperative game theory, 568
payoff, 570
payoff matrix, 571
perfect information game, 597
player, 568
preemption games, 584
principle of sequential rationality, 583
Prisoners' Dilemma, 575
pure Nash equilibrium, 593
pure strategies, 593
quid pro quo, 598
rationalizable strategy, 573
root, 572
security value, 594
sequential games, 581
strategic form, 571
strategic interdependence, 568
strategy, 570
strategy pairs, 571
tit-for-tat, 577
trembling hand game, 596
trembling-hand Nash equilibrium, 596
trigger, 577
win-stay/lose-shift, 578

Questions

Success comes before work only in the dictionary.

(Vidal Sassoon)

1. A rule for meetings, either explicit or implicit, is that a meeting will not start until everyone is present and latecomers will not incur any penalty. What is the dominant strategy?
2. What is a tit-for-tat strategy? Why is it a rational strategy for the infinitely repeated Prisoners' Dilemma game?
3. Every Nash equilibrium is Pareto-optimal. True or false? Explain.
4. Why is there always a unique Nash equilibrium when all players have a dominant strategy?
5. In terms of output price, what is the dominant strategy available to a perfectly competitive firm?
6. Why might games played repeatedly yield different results than games played only once?

Exercises

The more you sweat in training, the less you will bleed in battle.

(US Navy Seals)

1. *It is better that ten guilty escape than one innocent suffer (Sir William Blackstone).* You are one of 12 jurors contemplating your verdict on a criminal case. The jurors will vote by secret ballot; a unanimous vote is required for conviction. Based on all the evidence you have heard, you estimate the probability of the accused being guilty at 80 percent. Your valuation of the four possible outcomes (conviction or acquittal of an actually guilty or an actually innocent person) is as follows:

		Outcome of trial	
		Convicted	Acquitted
Reality	Guilty	1	–10
	Innocent	–100	1

   a. Show your dominant strategy is to vote for acquittal.
   b. How high must your estimate of the probability of guilt be before your dominant strategy will become voting for conviction?

2. Two electronic firms, Gadget and Remote, are planning to market a new system for home entertainment. Each firm can develop either a high-quality system (H),

or a low-quality system (L). Market research indicates that the resulting profits for each firm given the alternative strategies are as follows:

		Firm Remote H	L
Firm	H	(15, 15)	(25, 20)
Gadget	L	(20, 30)	(10, 10)

a. If both firms make their decisions simultaneously and follow maximin strategies, what will the outcome be (a maximin strategy is defined in the appendix to this chapter)?
b. Assume Gadget has a head start on planning, and thus can commit first. What will be the outcome? If, instead, Remote has the head start, what will be the outcome?
c. Getting a head start is costly because speeding up planning has associated additional cost. Consider a two-stage game in which first each firm decides how much money to allocate toward speeding up its planning, and then it announces which product it will produce. Which firm will spend more to speed up its planning? How much will it spend? Should the other firm spend anything to speed up its planning? Explain.

3. Illustrate with a payoff matrix how the following statement is false:

"A foreign firm competing in price with a domestic firm in the domestic market suffers from facing a quota."

4. Chris is negotiating the sale of a fishing boat to Judy, where the negotiations will last one or two rounds. In the first round, Chris offers to sell the boat at price p_1. If Judy accepts his offer, then Chris receives a payoff p_1 and Judy a payoff of WTP $- p_1$, where WTP is Judy's willingness to pay for the boat. Chris does not know Judy's WTP with certainty. He only knows with equal probability that it is either 3 or 4. If Judy refuses Chris' first offer, then Chris will make a second offer p_2 in round two. If Judy accepts this second offer, then Chris receives a payoff p_2 and Judy a payoff $1/4$ (WTP $- p_2$). If Judy refuses the second offer, then bargaining ends with Chris receiving a payoff of 1 and Judy a payoff of 0. If Judy is indifferent between accepting or rejecting an offer, she will accept it.

a. For this sale, illustrate the extensive-form game.
b. Determine the unique Nash equilibrium.

5. Consider the following payoff matrix:

		Friday 1	2	3	4
Robinson	1	(–50, –50)	(–50, 1)	(0, 0)	(50, 2)
	2	(50, 2)	(50, –25)	(1, 0)	(–50, –50)

a. If the game is played only once, what strategy should Friday choose if she cannot engage in any pregame conversation with Robinson?
b. What are all the pure-strategy Nash equilibria for this game?
c. Is your choice for Friday in (a) one of the Nash-equilibrium strategies? Is it a rational strategy?
d. Assume pregame conversation is allowed. Would you expect Friday to alter her choice in (a)?

6. The bucks of some mammals, such as deer, conflict with other bucks over the opportunity to mate with a doe. In such conflicts a buck can fight the other buck or retreat if his rival starts to fight. The following expected payoff matrix for two bucks indicates that if a buck fights and the other buck also fights, both are seriously injured in battle:

		Buck B	
		Fight	Retreat
Buck A	Fight	(–8, –8)	(5, 0)
	Retreat	(0, 5)	(1, 1)

Instead, if he fights and the other buck retreats, he gets to mate with the doe. If both bucks retreat at any threat of a fight, the doe may choose one of them or just wander off.

a. Assume that a buck cannot determine whether a rival will fight or retreat. The payoff to adopting either strategy depends on the proportion of the other bucks that will fight or retreat. Explain why there will not be an equilibrium where all bucks will fight or they all retreat.
b. Develop an equation to indicate that when the proportion of the male deer population that will fight is α, the payoff to fighting is the same as the payoff to retreating.
c. Solve this equation for the value of α, so the aggressors are as well off as sissies.

7. The Prisoners' Dilemma game indicates that pregame discussions can result in both players improving their payoff once the game is played. This result is not always the case when the possibility of threats exists. Consider the following game between two grocery stores, where a supermarket is attempting to force a "mom-and-pop" grocery out of business. To do so, the supermarket could open a store right next door to the mom-and-pop grocery, but it would prefer that Mom and Pop just close down. The payoff matrix is as follows:

		Mom-and-pop grocery	
		Stay	Exit
Supermarket	No entry	(4, 2)	(5, 0)
	Entry	(2, –5)	(3, –10)

a. Determine the Nash equilibrium.
b. What threat could the supermarket use if it could talk with Mom prior to the game?
c. How could Mom and Pop respond?

8. Overexploitation of a common-property resource belonging to a number of agents is a major problem in a number of industries such as fishing, logging, and oil extraction. Analyze this overexploitation problem in a Prisoners' Dilemma framework.
9. Carly, C, Katherine, K, and Erica, E, are playing Paintball. From fixed positions, they shoot a paintball at each other. When one is hit by the paintball, she is out of the game, and the one remaining without being hit wins. The game is started by drawing straws to see who shoots first. It is common knowledge that Carly is a crack shot who always hits her target. Katherine hits her target 80 percent of the time and Erica only 50 percent. Determine the expected probability of each player winning.
10. Two siblings, Sara and Brian, must determine how to divide \$10 their Uncle Tony gave them for Christmas. Sara will be the first to suggest how the gift should be divided. However, if Brian rejects Sara's suggestion, their father will recommend that Brian suggest an alternative division. However, their father will also punish them for not getting along by taking half of the money. If Sara rejects Brian's offer, their father will again take half of the remaining money away and then recommend that Sara make another suggestion. If Brian rejects Sara's second suggestion, their father will be totally disgusted with them and take the entire gift away. Realizing what their father will do, how will Sara and Brian divide up the gift? Is there an advantage to making the first suggestion?

Internet case studies

1. Provide a list of various academic disciplines that have employed game theory. How has game theory been employed in these disciplines?
2. Write a case study on a firm that uses a market niche to increase profits.
3. Play the Prisoners' Dilemma game online.

APPENDIX TO CHAPTER 14

Using mixed strategies

I retain my attraction by at certain moments being warm and fuzzy and at others being cold and prickly.

(Michael Wetzstein)

Translation: By mixing strategies, a player can increase her expected payoff.

Von Neumann (1903–1957) and Morgenstern (1902–1977) developed the idea of mixed strategies as opposed to pure strategies.[6] **Pure strategies** are deterministic, where for some strategy set, a player has a 100 percent probability of selecting a strategy given the strategy of his opponent. An example is the game in Table 14.2; each strategy picked by the couple was a pure strategy. The Nash equilibria associated with these strategies are called **pure Nash equilibria**. At times, your optimal solution is to prevent other players from predicting your strategy. One way to do this is to randomly choose strategies, that is, to use **mixed strategies**.

How should you play the Rock, Paper, Scissors game? Can randomly selecting your course of actions improve your happiness? In the Rock, Paper, Scissors game, you do not want the other player to determine any pattern to your selections, so randomly selecting your course of actions can improve your payoff (happiness) unless you can make your selection based on determining a pattern to the other player's selections.

As an example, consider the payoff matrix in Table 14A.1, which represents the percentage of votes cast between Republican and Democratic presidential candidates. Each political party has two strategies: run an attack campaign against the other party's candidate or run on the issues. Neither of these two strategies represents a Nash equilibrium for the political parties. For example, if Democrats employ the attack strategy, Republicans can also pick the attack strategy and win 78 percent of the vote. The Democrats would then switch to the issue strategy and increase their voter percentage to 70 percent. Republicans would then switch to the issues strategy. This creates no resulting pure Nash equilibrium. Thus, no pair of strategies results in a Nash-equilibrium solution. Both parties have an incentive to change their strategy, given the strategy of the other.[7]

Suppose the Republicans employ a mixed instead of a pure strategy. For example, say one-third of the time Republicans pick the attack strategy and two-thirds of the time they pick the issues strategy. If the Democrats employ the attack strategy, the expected voter percentage for Republicans is

$$\tfrac{1}{3}(78) + \tfrac{2}{3}(24) = 26 + 16 = 42.$$

If the Democrats employ the issues strategy, Republicans' voter percentage is

$$\tfrac{1}{3}(30) + \tfrac{2}{3}(90) = 10 + 60 = 70.$$

If the Republicans are interested in maximizing their lowest expected voter percentage, they can employ a **maximin strategy**, which maximizes the minimum, or **security value,** for a

Table 14A.1 Mixed strategies

		Democrats' strategies	
		Attack	*Issues*
Republicans' strategies	Attack	(78, 22)	(30, 70)
	Issues	(24, 76)	(90, 10)

Note: The payoffs are (Republicans' percent of ballots cast, Democrats' percent of ballots cast)

given strategy. This maximin mixed strategy results where the expected voter percentage is the same for whichever strategy the Democrats pick. Letting ρ be the Republicans' probability of picking the attack strategy, with $1-\rho$ the probability of their picking the issues strategy, the expected payoffs are then equal when

$$\begin{array}{ccc}\text{Republicans' expected payoff} & & \text{Republicans' expected payoff}\\ \text{if Democrats pick attack} & = & \text{if Democrats pick issues}\end{array}$$

$$\rho(78)+(1-\rho)(24)=\rho(30)+(1-\rho)(90).$$

Solving for ρ,

$$78\rho-24\rho-30\rho+90\rho+24-90=0,$$

$$\rho^*=66/114=0.58.$$

With this maximin mixed strategy, Republicans receive an expected voter percentage of 55.3 percent, with Democrats being indifferent to employing either the pure strategy of attack or issues. Thus, when a pure strategy results in a disequilibrium, a mixed strategy could yield a Nash equilibrium.

Application: Mixed strategy and speeding tickets

As discussed by Kim and Kim, one of the most famous policy recommendations suggested by game theorists is by G. Tsebelis. His results indicate that an increase in fines for speeding is not a viable policy tool for decreasing drivers' speed. This is because interactions between police and drivers are characterized as a mixed-strategy game. In such a game between police and a driver, the probability of a driver getting caught speeding is not decreased by increasing the speeding fine. This probability of getting caught is only dependent on the probability of the police being on the road. Thus, the equilibrium solution is for drivers not to consider the level of a speeding fine when determining to speed or not.

However, as noted by Kim and Kim, this game theory result is inconsistent with common sense and the real world. Drivers will slow down as speeding fines increase. Using a system dynamics model for a mixed-strategy game and assuming expected utility maximization on the part of both police and drivers, they show that it takes a very long time for the Tsebelis equilibrium to occur. Thus, we should not depend on the equilibrium for choosing driver actions. In terms of policy, increasing speeding fines will in the short run result in drivers reducing their speed.

Sources: D-H. Kim and D. Kim, "A System Dynamics Model for a Mixed-Strategy Game Between Police and Driver," *System Dynamics Review* 13 (1997): 33–52; G. Tsebelis, "The Abuse of Probability in Political Analysis: The Robinson Crusoe Fallacy," *American Political Science Review* 83 (1989): 77–91.

Rational behavior

In Table 14.3, the dominant strategy for both prisoners of confessing is determined by each prisoner without regard to the behavior of the other prisoner. The other player could be irrational by not attempting to maximize utility, but this would not affect the other player's decision. However, usually when determining a strategy, a player must consider other players' rationality and employ an **iterated deletion** method to reduce his strategy choices. For example, when driving an automobile, you generally assume that other drivers are rational and will obey specific driving rules. Based on this, you further assume that they will stop at red lights, so your strategy will be to drive through an intersection when you have a green light. You determine this strategy by continuing to delete the irrational behavior of drivers driving through a red light.

Why do you drive through a green light? Assuming other drivers are rational, you drive through a green light.

In driver education courses, drivers are taught to "drive defensively," implying that not all drivers are rational all the time and even rational drivers make mistakes. Thus, although the selected driving strategy is to generally assume rationality on the part of other drivers, irrational behavior is always possible. Games that incorporate the possibility of players making a mistake are called **trembling hand games**. The equilibrium associated with such games (e.g., defensive driving) is called a **trembling-hand Nash equilibrium**.

A slight modification of the Prisoners' Dilemma will illustrate the iterated deletion method for determining a strategy. Say, Prisoner F is the DA's daughter, so if the two prisoners do not confess to the crime, the DA will let her go with no jail time. This modification is presented in Table 14A.2. Prisoner R's dominant strategy is still confessing, regardless of the rationality of prisoner F. However, if prisoner R confesses, then prisoner F should also confess, but if prisoner R does not confess, then prisoner F should not confess. Prisoner F's strategy choice now depends on prisoner R's actions. A unique strategy for prisoner F does not exist unless prisoner F considers the rationality of prisoner R. The rational choice for prisoner R is to confess, so if prisoner F assumes that prisoner R is rational, then prisoner F will also confess. Prisoner F's strategy is based on the assumption that prisoner R is rational and that prisoner F knows prisoner R is rational. Prisoner F deleted the dominant strategy of prisoner R not confessing, so that with this deletion, only one strategy choice remains for prisoner R. This illustrates, the iterated deletion method may require only one iteration to reduce the choice down to one strategy. For games with more than two strategies for players, a number of iterations may be required.

In general, if all players are rational and all players know that all other players are rational, then, by iterative deletion, a player will delete all possible strategies of the other players that

Table 14A.2 Prisoners' Dilemma with Prisoner F as the DA's daughter

		Prisoner R	
		Not confess	*Confess*
Prisoner F	Not confess	(0, –2)	(–10, –1)
	Confess	(–1, –10)	(–5, –5)

Note: The payoffs are (F's payoff, B's payoff).

are irrational. The strategies resulting from an iterative deletion process are rationalizable strategies. Within these rationalizable strategies are the Nash equilibria for the game, where the players are correct in their conjectures concerning other players' rationality.

Incomplete-information games

A key component of the Allied victory in World War II was the British capture of a German Naval Enigma machine that allowed the Allies to decode German U-boat activities. With this decoded information, the British were able to employ counterstrategies to known German strategies. For example, the British were able to locate and sink cargo ships and tankers that were supplying U-boats in the South Atlantic. This ability to break the German codes is an example of asymmetric information, where one player has more information than another. For example, a used car dealer will generally have more information about a particular vehicle than a potential buyer. A buyer might not know with certainty the actual condition of a vehicle, which will directly affect the payoffs of the car dealer and the buyer. The buyer may only know with some probability the actual condition. This problem of incomplete or asymmetric information can be solved as an *imperfect-information game* (called a **Bayesian game**). In contrast, games where players have perfect knowledge about each other's strategies and payoffs are called **perfect-information** or **complete-information games**.

As an example of a Bayesian game, let us reconsider the Prisoners' Dilemma game with prisoner F again as the DA's daughter. Assume now that prisoner F has imperfect information on prisoner R's preferences, but prisoner F does know with some probability prisoner R's preferences. For example, with probability ρ, prisoner F knows prisoner R's preferences are those listed in Table 14A.2, and with probability $1-\rho$, prisoner R does not want to cooperate with the DA and confess. Assume that cooperating with the DA is equivalent to an additional 10 years in jail. The strategic form of this game is presented in Table 14A.3.

We determine the Nash equilibrium (called a *Bayesian Nash equilibrium* in this case) by first considering prisoner R's dominant strategies, given the two possible payoffs associated with probabilities ρ and $1-\rho$. If prisoner R has preferences with probability ρ, type 1, his dominant strategy is to confess. In contrast, for preferences associated with probability $1-\rho$, type 2, prisoner R's dominant strategy is not to confess. Given these dominant strategies for prisoner R, prisoner F's strategy is to confess if prisoner R's preferences are of type 1 and not

Table 14A.3 Prisoners' Dilemma with Prisoner F as the DA's daughter and possessing incomplete information

		Prisoner R		
		Not confess	*Confess*	
			Type 1 with probability ρ	*Type 2 with probability* $1-\rho$
Prisoner F	Not confess	(0, –2)	(–10, –1)	(–10, –11)
	Confess	(–1, –10)	(–5, –5)	(–5, –15)

Note: The payoffs are (F's payoff, R's payoff).

confess if prisoner R's preferences are type 2. Thus, prisoner F will confess if her confession payoff given prisoner R is type 1, -5ρ, plus her confession payoff given prisoner R is type 2, $-1(1-\rho)$, is greater than her payoff of not confessing given prisoner R is type 1, -10ρ, plus her payoff of not confessing given prisoner R is type 2, $0(1-\rho)$:

$$-5\rho - 1(1-\rho) > -10\rho + 0(1-\rho),$$
$$-5\rho - 1 + \rho > -10\rho,$$
$$\rho > 1/6.$$

She will not confess if $\rho < 1/6$. She is indifferent if $\rho = 1/6$. Note the similarities between the Bayesian Nash Equilibrium and mixed strategies. For example, both rely on probabilities of payoffs, and the optimal strategy is an expected value based on these probabilities.

Quid pro quo

A compromise is the art of dividing a cake in such a way that everyone believes he has the biggest piece.

(Paul Gauguin)

In the effort to change the name of the then Washington National Airport to Ronald Reagan National Airport for former President Reagan's 87th birthday (in 1998), the Democrats proposed a quid pro quo of also naming the Justice Department headquarters for former Attorney General Robert F. Kennedy. Often a single issue (naming a facility) represented by a payoff matrix or a game tree cannot be resolved in isolation from other issues. Instead, a multitude of issues exist requiring a joint outcome. For example, in trade negotiations, countries will generally not negotiate one commodity at a time but instead consider a whole group of commodities simultaneously. In fact, because considering a combination of issues can benefit one or more players and harm others, negotiations many times start with what issues will be negotiated. For example, the Paris Peace Accords to end the Vietnam War started with negotiating the shape of the table that negotiators would sit around.

Why did the United States and Vietnam argue over the shape of the table for peace negotiations? In an effort to achieve a negotiation advantage, the United States and Vietnam argued over the shape of the table and who should sit around it.

Resolving multiple issues requiring a joint outcome often requires **quid pro quo** (something for something else). As an example, consider two politicians each with a favorite earmark (bill or provision) that particularly benefits their home district. Politician F favors an earmark that provides for constructing a bridge in her district and politician R favors a military earmark procuring equipment from a firm in his district. The payoff matrices for each earmark are shown in Table 14A.4. As indicated, politician F's dominant strategy is to support the bridge construction earmark, and politician R's dominant strategy is to support the military equipment earmark. In contrast, politician R's dominant strategy is not to support the bridge earmark and politician F's dominant strategy is to not support the military earmark. The total payoff for the two politicians is the sum of the payoffs, 20 + 50, for both bills (70, 70).

Table 14A.4 Quid pro quo

Bridge Earmark

		Politician R	
		Supporting	*Not supporting*
Politician F	Supporting	(100, 10)	(50, 20)
	Not supporting	(–10, 5)	(–20, 30)

Military Procurement Earmark

		Politician R	
		Supporting	*Not supporting*
Politician F	Supporting	(10, 100)	(5, –10)
	Not supporting	(20, 50)	(30, –20)

Note: The payoffs are (politician F, politician R).

Neither politician supports the other's earmark, which decreases the likelihood of passage. Thus, politician F wants politician R's support and vice versa. The solution is for each politician to support the other's earmark, quid pro quo. Linking the two bills into one negotiation improves the payoffs, 100 + 10, for both politicians (110, 110). Negotiators who understand these interactions can effectively bundle the interests of diverse agents and reach a common compromise.

Application: Quid pro quo? China's investment-for-resource swaps in Africa

In 2006, China rolled out its "Go Out" strategy that promotes Chinese investments abroad and mobilizes China's banking sector to facilitate international capital flows and mergers to seek natural resources. This Go Out policy resulted in 750 Chinese firms operating in 50 African countries. China is a new investor in Africa. As investigated by Chan-Fishel and Lawson, these investments are undertaken by state-owned firms and state-controlled banks. This has resulted in the charge that China is using aid in a quid pro quo policy to access Africa's natural resources. It is offering infrastructure investments in exchange for access to natural resources. An example is in Angola, where, shortly after a China infrastructure loan to repair railways and construct new government offices, Angola did not renew French-based offshore oil licenses and instead gave them to China. Other examples are in Nigeria, Uganda, and Zimbabwe. In 2006, just after oil was discovered in Uganda, China started a number of infrastructure projects there.

As noted by Chan-Fishel and Lawson, China is not the only country involved with such quid pro quo practices. India, Malaysia, and South Korea have all been involved. In fact, Western countries have operated with quid pro quo for decades. Adjustments imposed by the World Bank have had the effect of aid-for-resources (quid pro quo). To receive financing from the World Bank, a developing country is required to liberalize its economy. This clears the path for Western companies to invest in Africa's natural resource sectors.

Source: M. Chan-Fishel and R. Lawson, "Quid Pro Quo? China's Investment-for-Resource Swaps in Africa," *Development* 50 (2007): 63–68.

Questions

1. In Table 14.3, if both prisoners followed the cautious approach by using the maximin strategy, what would be the resulting equilibrium? Is this a Nash equilibrium?
2. If Prisoner F (the DA's daughter) in Table 14A.2 follows the cautious maximin strategy, would she have to follow the iterated deletion method to arrive at her preferred strategy of confessing? Explain.
3. Why may the Bayesian Nash equilibrium in Table 14A.3 differ from the equilibrium associated with Prisoner F employing the cautious maximin strategy.
4. In Table 14.4, if firm 1 knows that firm 2 will follow a cautious maximin strategy, what should it do?

Exercises

1. Illustrate the payoff matrix for a two-person Rock, Paper, Scissors game, and show that it does not have an equilibrium strategy pair. If the two players both follow a mixed strategy of choosing each strategy with a probability of one-third, what is the payoff for each player?
2. Russell and Earl are playing a number-matching game. Each selects 1, 2, or 3. If the numbers match, Russell pays Earl \$6. If they differ, Earl pays Russell \$2.

   a. Describe the payoff matrix for this game and show that it does not possess a Nash-equilibrium strategy pair.
   b. Show that with mixed strategies this game does have an equilibrium if each player plays each number with a probability of one-third. What is the payoff for this game?

3. Bubba and Billy are playing chicken. Bubba speeds his hot rod south down a one-lane dirt road and Billy speeds his hot rod north along the same single-lane road. Each has two strategies: stay on the road or swerve. If one player chooses to swerve, he loses face and if both swerve, they both lose face. However, if both choose to stay, they both die. The payoff matrix is as follows:

		Billy	
		Stay	Swerve
Bubba	Stay	(–5, –5)	(2, –2)
	Swerve	(–2, 2)	(–1, –1)

a. Find all pure-strategy equilibria.
b. Find all mixed-strategy equilibria.
c. What is the probability that both will survive?

4. Two Plains Native Americans may either cooperate in hunting a buffalo or individually trap prairie dogs. The payoff matrix for hunting is as follows:

		Indian B	
		Hunt buffalo	Trap prairie dogs
Indian A	Hunt buffalo	(10, 10)	(0, 1)
	Trap prairie dogs	(1, 0)	(1, 1)

a. Determine all the Nash equilibria.
b. Assume A knows that B is employing a mixed strategy between hunting buffalo and trapping prairie dogs. How will B's probability of hunting buffalo influence A's optimal strategy?
c. Suppose a hunting party is organized with n Native Americans. The complete hunting party must cooperate for hunting buffalo. If all the other $n-1$ Native Americans adopt the same mixed strategy as Native American B, how will their probability of hunting buffalo influence A's optimal strategy? (This exercise illustrates how the probability for cooperation declines as the number of agents increases.)

15 Industrial organization

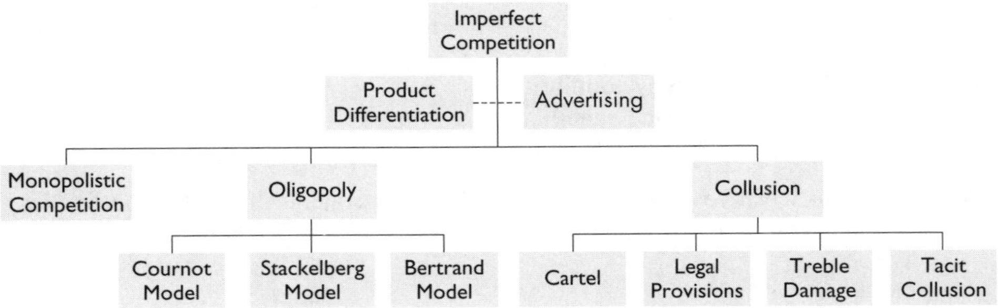

Outline and Conceptual Inquiries

Interested in profits? Then consider product differentiation

Why does every member in your economics class probably have a different type of toothbrush?

Application: Production differentiation at the movies

Advantages of advertising (selling cost)

Determining profit maximization

Assessing advertising

Should you let advertising change your preferences?

Application: Web 2.0 and citizen review sites

Monopolistic competition ills

Does monopolistic competition lead to a large number of sick firms?

Determining short- and long-run equilibrium under monopolistic competition

Application: Moneylenders and bankers

Understanding oligopolies

Determining price and output

Cournot model: commercial real estate

Are Cournot firms zombies?

Stackelberg model: Microsoft

Do you respond to some stimulus?

Collusion: OPEC

Bertrand model: Airlines

Do firms really compete over price?

Generalized oligopoly models

Collusion in oligopoly markets: fair-trade pricing

Application: OPEC cartel

Legal provisions: pollution standards

Is collusion among firms allowed?

Summary

Key concepts

Key equations

Questions

Exercises

Internet case studies

Appendix to chapter 15

Spatial differentiation: gas stations

Perfectly competitive location

Why do different fast-food restaurants always seem to locate in the same vicinity?

Determining the profit-maximizing price

Application: Is zoning "creeping socialism?"

Treble-damage model

Tacit collusion: beat any price

What is the real reason firms advertise that they will match any of their competitors' prices?

Price leadership: New York City banks

Questions

Exercises

Internet case study

You can tell the ideals of a nation by its advertisements.

(Norman Douglas)

Steve Jobs, the co-founder, chairman, and chief executive officer of Apple, was a master at product differentiation. Jobs and his Apple design team were always steps ahead of their competition in product design (examples are the Apple II, Mac, iPhone, and iPad). Firms such as Apple with some degree of monopoly power can control their product price and influence their output by advertising and differentiating their product. The resulting enhanced profit is not necessarily caused by advertising and product differentiation. Profits may be high because the product coincidentally was offered in the right place at the right time. (An example is a firm selling iodine tablets for radiation after the Japanese Fukushima Daiichi nuclear power meltdown in 2011.) However, in general, improvements in effective marketing can boost profit significantly. Marketing efficiency of a firm may be characterized in terms of attempting to satisfy customer preferences by acquiring information on these preferences, determining competing firms' strategies, and then efficiently allocating marketing resources.

Applied economists are actively working either within firms or as consultants to provide empirical analysis on market efficiency. For example, economists provide market share movement analysis, mapping of alternative marketing strategies, sales force size and productivity determination, advertising expenses and mix optimization, and sales analysis and targeting. Economic consulting firms will even develop a quantitative measure of alternative marketing strategies and provide scores indicating which strategy action yields the most profit enhancement. The scores can then be employed by a firm's management to allocate resources where the largest payoff in terms of profits will occur. Management will then attempt to equate marginal revenue with margin cost in marketing its output.

The degree of monopoly power and how firms interact determine these strategies offered by applied economists. For example, firms facing markets with a relatively large number of competitors will have a different set of strategies than firms in markets with only a small number of rivals. Thus, alternative economic models for developing strategies are employed, based on the degree of monopoly power and firm interactions.

For determining economic efficiency, we contrast these imperfectly competitive models of firm behavior with the perfectly competitive and monopoly models. The standard for judging these imperfectly competitive markets is perfect competition. As discussed in Chapter 11, a perfectly competitive market is Pareto-efficient. Perfectly competitive equilibrium occurs where price equals marginal cost and firms operate at full capacity (at the minimum point of average total cost). However, there are some desirable features of imperfect competition. For example, consumers may desire firms to product-differentiate, advertise, and innovate—all of which have limits under perfect competition. Under perfect competition, the characteristics of homogeneous products and perfect knowledge preclude firms from advertising and innovating.

Our aim in this chapter is to investigate how price, output, sales promotion, and product differentiation are determined under various market conditions. We begin with product differentiation, presenting a model determining the optimal level of product differentiation and advertising (selling expenses). We then assess advertising for its information versus persuasive characteristics.

Following this assessment of advertising, we examine the classical models of monopolistic competition and oligopolies. In the discussion of classical oligopoly, we first develop the Cournot model, which assumes that firms do not realize that their individual output decisions affect the output decisions of their competitors. In the Stackelberg model, one firm does realize the interdependence of output decisions and determines its optimal output decision based on this realization. In this context, we also consider the Stackelberg disequilibrium, where each firm realizes output interdependence but believes that other firms do not. The final classical oligopoly model is the Bertrand model, which assumes that firms compete in terms of price rather than through output. After developing the equilibrium conditions for the Bertrand model, we contrast these with the Cournot conditions.

In the final section of this chapter, we investigate the economics of collusion in oligopoly markets, with the OPEC oil cartel as an application. We also briefly discuss formal cartel arrangements and legal provisions. In the Appendix to the chapter, we develop a spatial differentiation model for a linear city with firms located on one main street. After deriving the conditions for an optimal location of the competitive firms, we contrast these conditions with the socially optimal location. We also discuss informal tacit collusion, including price leadership models.

Interested in profits? Then consider product differentiation

People can have the Model T in any color, so long as it is black.

(Henry Ford)

Henry Ford may not have been interested in product differentiation, but today firms are constantly attempting to distinguish their product in an effort to enhance profits (Apple). For example, toothbrushes come in a wide variety of sizes, shapes, colors, textures, and motors (electric toothbrushes). Even the bristles are different: some are concave, others convex, and some are soft on the outside and hard on the inside while others are just the reverse. This wide range of **product differentiation** offers consumers a great deal of choice in determining their optimal selection. However, determining the various different markets for toothbrushes is difficult, though it could be argued that caricature (cartoon) children's toothbrushes should be separate from adult brushes or that there is a separate market for electric toothbrushes. Demand for product differentiation is derived by consumers receiving some level of utility for having products differentiated. Firms respond to this demand by differentiating their products, possibly by quality and style, guarantees and warranties, services provided, and location of sales. This product differentiation by firms may be either real or imaginary. How differentiated a product is lies in the eyes of the beholder.

Why does every member in your economics class probably have a different type of toothbrush? Firms will attempt to maximize profits by offering a number of products that are only slightly differentiated from other products.

Product differentiation ($\mathcal{D}$). Commodities closely related, but not identical. *E.g., different makes and models of automobiles.*

The heterogeneous nature of products due to product differentiation provides firms with some degree of monopoly power. Individual firms are then facing a downward-sloping demand curve for their product. There is no longer a market with firms producing identical products. Instead, there are a group of firms producing a number of closely related but not identical products. Thus, the Law of One Price for a market no longer exists. It is replaced with each firm having a partial monopoly and setting its own price.

Application: Production differentiation at the movies

As discussed by Sedgwick, in 1946, box-office revenue from motion pictures represented 1.1 percent of US total personal consumption expenditure and fell to only 0.2 percent by 1965. Motion pictures do not contribute a great deal to national income, but they do attract a large number of consumers. In 1946, 4.5 billion movie tickets were sold (33 visits per capita). Going to the movies then fell to a low point of 0.82 billion in 1972, followed by a gentle recovery, with 1.4 billion (4.8 per capita) in 2009. During this time, the mode of film consumption diversified from the movie theater alone to home viewing on television. Video, cable, satellite dishes, and the Internet have further invaded the movie theater's market.

Extreme product differentiation exists in motion pictures, with audiences being attracted to particular genres. In the early years, westerns and musicals were in high demand; recently rock and roll, sex, and violence are popular. Sedgwick employs the concepts of horizontal and vertical product differentiation in analyzing motion pictures. For commodities composed of characteristics, they are vertically differentiated if one contains more of some or all of the characteristics and horizontally differentiated if one contains more of some but fewer of other characteristics. Motion picture producers have recognized a number of quite clearly differentiated groups of viewers and differentiated their films both vertically and horizontally to satisfy the demands of each group. In terms of horizontal differentiation, the *Motion Picture Guide* has 170 distinct genre categories for films. In terms of vertical differentiation, quality differences exist within each genre. As illustrated by Sedgwick, in 1952 of the 20 westerns listed among the top revenue earners, *High Noon* was ranked above *Bend in the River*, which was ranked above *Westward the Women*. Films such as *Gone with the Wind* (1939), *The Sound of Music* (1965), *Titanic* (1998), and *Avatar* (2009) are extreme examples of vertical differentiation.

Source: J. Sedgwick, "Product Differentiation at the Movies: Hollywood, 1946 to 1965," *Journal of Economic History* 62 (2002): 676–705.

Advantages of advertising (selling cost)

The Federal Trade Commission's Cigarette Report for 2006 indicates that the five largest cigarette manufacturers spent \$12.49 billion on advertising and promotional expenditures in

2006, a 4.7 percent decline from 2005. Cigarette sales fell from 354.6 billion in 2005 to 350.6 billion in 2006.

By offering a differentiated product, a cigarette company (or any other firm) can enhance its profit by undertaking selling cost. **Selling costs** (also called **information differentiation**) are marketing expenditures including advertising, merchandising, sales promotion, and public relations aimed at adapting the buyer to the product. This distinguishes them from production costs, which are designed to adapt the product to the buyer. Thus, firms advertise to shift the market demand for their commodity upward, which increases market share and short-run pure profits. For example, by advertising "only one per customer" or "while supplies last," a firm may stimulate demand for its product. A firm's advertising objective is to convince consumers that its product is not sharply differentiated from competing products yet is somehow superior. When deciding on the optimal strategy to pursue, a firm will weigh the additional revenues generated by such shifts in the demand curve against the cost of differentiating its product.

Selling costs (information differentiation). Marketing expenditures aimed at adopting the buyer to the product. *E.g., a beer commercial that shows the popular jet set drinks this brand of beer.*

Determining profit maximization

Assume that costs and revenue depend on $\mathcal{D}$, a dollar measure of the extent of product differentiation; A, a measure of advertising expenditures; and q, which is output. Letting $q = q(p, \mathcal{D}, A)$ be the demand function for a firm's output, the objective of the firm is to maximize profit by varying p, $\mathcal{D}$, and A:

$$\begin{aligned}\max \pi(p, \mathcal{D}, A) &= \max(\text{TR} - \text{STC})\\ &= \max\{pq(p, \mathcal{D}, A) - \text{STC}[q(p, \mathcal{D}, A)] - \mathcal{D} - A\}.\end{aligned}$$

The first-order conditions (FOCs) are then

$$\frac{\partial \pi}{\partial p} = q + p\frac{\partial q}{\partial p} - \text{SMC}\frac{\partial q}{\partial p} = 0,$$

$$\frac{\partial \pi}{\partial \mathcal{D}} = p\frac{\partial q}{\partial \mathcal{D}} - \text{SMC}\frac{\partial q}{\partial \mathcal{D}} - 1 = 0,$$

$$\frac{\partial \pi}{\partial A} = p\frac{\partial q}{\partial A} - \text{SMC}\frac{\partial q}{\partial A} - 1 = 0.$$

Solving these FOCs for SMC and specifying them in terms of elasticities yields

$$\text{SMC} = \frac{q}{\partial q/\partial p} + p = \frac{p}{(\partial q/\partial p)(p/q)} + p = p\left(\frac{1}{\varepsilon_p^D} + 1\right),$$

$$\text{SMC} = -\frac{1}{\partial q/\partial \mathcal{D}} + p = -\frac{\mathcal{D}}{q(\partial q/\partial \mathcal{D})(\mathcal{D}/q)} + p = -\frac{\mathcal{D}}{q\varepsilon_{\mathcal{D}}^D} + p,$$

$$\text{SMC} = -\frac{1}{\partial q/\partial A} + p = -\frac{A}{q(\partial q/\partial A)(A/q)} + p = -\frac{A}{q\varepsilon_A^D} + p,$$

where ε_p^D, $\varepsilon_{\mathcal{D}}^D$, and ε_A^D are the price, product differentiation, and advertising elasticities of demand, respectively. Recall that $\varepsilon_p^D < 0$. Also, $\varepsilon_{\mathcal{D}}^D > 0$ and $\varepsilon_A^D > 0$, otherwise a corner solution would result with $A = \mathcal{D} = 0$.

Equating the SMC equations for price and advertising and solving for the advertising/sales ratio A/pq yields

$$p\left(\frac{1}{\varepsilon_p^D} + 1\right) = -\frac{A}{q\varepsilon_A^D} + p,$$

$$\frac{p}{\varepsilon_p^D} = -\frac{A}{q\varepsilon_A^D},$$

$$\frac{A}{pq} = -\frac{\varepsilon_A^D}{\varepsilon_p^D}.$$

A firm's optimal advertising/sales ratio is equal to the negative of the ratio of demand elasticities with respect to price and advertising. Similarly, a firm's optimal product differentiation/sales ratio is equal to the negative of the ratio of demand elasticities with respect to price and product differentiation:

$$\frac{\mathcal{D}}{pq} = -\frac{\varepsilon_{\mathcal{D}}^D}{\varepsilon_p^D}.$$

These conditions (called the *Dorfman-Steiner conditions*) state that the optimal levels of product differentiation and advertising per unit of sales depend on the respective elasticity relative to the negative of the demand price elasticity. For a given demand price elasticity, the more responsive (more elastic) output is to either product differentiation or advertising, the more a firm will engage in these activities. Recall that firms operate in the elastic portion of the demand curve, $-\infty \leq \varepsilon_p^D < -1$. The price elasticity of demand dampens the response of output to product differentiation and advertising. This reduces the amount of expenditure per unit of sales on these items. In the extreme, the optimal level of product differentiation and advertising for a perfectly competitive firm, with $\varepsilon_p^D = -\infty$, is $D = A = 0$. A perfectly competitive firm has no incentive to engage in product differentiation or advertising. In contrast, a revenue-maximizing firm with $\varepsilon_p^D = -1$ will consider the total response in output to a change in either product differentiation or advertising.

In general, for profit maximization, marginal revenue from each activity must equal marginal cost for that activity. For example, as indicated by these FOCs, a firm will produce additional advertising messages up to the point at which the marginal revenue from the additional demand generated by a message is equal to the message's marginal cost. Messages that spark the greatest reaction from consumers will receive a larger share of expenditures.

Firms generally will engage in both product differentiation and advertising, which indicates at least some positive increment to profit for these two activities. In fact, advertising services is a major industry within the United States, accounting for 2–3 percent of the US GNP. However, determining the marginal revenue for each activity is difficult because the market for advertising messages is not separated from the market for the commodity. For example, beer is a joint product where beer and advertising for beer are both produced. Firms that do not account for this joint production and contributing all of any increase in revenue to advertising will overinvest in advertising. Firms must remember that the commodity itself has some value, so some individuals will consume the product regardless of the level of advertising. The marginal revenue being generated by advertising reflects consumers' willingness to pay for both the commodities being purchased and for the information provided by the advertising.

> *Be neither too remote nor too familiar.*
>
> (Charles, Prince of Wales)

In terms of product differentiation, firms will differentiate their products to soften price competition. As discussed in Chapter 14, by differentiating their products, firms can possibly satisfy a market niche, and thus create monopoly power with the potential of increasing profit. However, firms generally do not seek this maximum level of product differentiation. Instead, they offer products that are not too different from their competitors' products yet have some unique features. For example, a soap manufacturer may claim that its soap will not only get you clean but also make you beautiful. This idea of not maximizing product differentiation is related to the Law of the Obvious: Better to be a half-step ahead and understood than a whole step and ignored.

Example 15.1 Calculating the optimal level of output, product differentiation, and advertising

Consider the following TR and STC functions:

$$\mathrm{TR} = 14q + 20\mathcal{D} + 20A - 5q^2 - 3\mathcal{D}^2 - 3A^2,$$

$$\mathrm{STC} = -2q - 8\mathcal{D} - 10A + 3q^2 + 4\mathcal{D}^2 + 2A^2 + 50.$$

Profit is then

$$\pi = \mathrm{TR} - \mathrm{STC} = 16q + 28\mathcal{D} + 30A - 8q^2 - 7\mathcal{D}^2 - 5A^2 - 50.$$

The FOCs for profit maximization are

$$\partial\pi/\partial q = 16 - 16q^* = 0 \Rightarrow q^* = 1,$$

$$\partial\pi/\partial \mathcal{D} = 28 - 14\mathcal{D}^* = 0 \Rightarrow \mathcal{D}^* = 2,$$

$$\partial\pi/\partial A = 30 - 10A^* = 0 \Rightarrow A^* = 3.$$

Assessing advertising

> *Chess is as elaborate a waste of human intelligence as you can find outside an advertising agency.*
>
> (Raymond Chandler)

In general, it is not possible to determine the overall social value or loss associated with advertising. Advertising is not a composite commodity where prices associated with all forms of advertising move together. Thus, empirical evidence on the precise effect of advertising in general is not available. An economic assessment is only undertaken when advertising is disaggregated across types and commodities. Such disaggregation has yielded some implications. Specifically, advertising can affect choices among commodities that are close substitutes, but it may or may not have any effect on overall consumption choices. For example, cigarette advertising can have a major effect on consumers' choice of brands. However, there is little evidence that cigarette advertising has increased the demand (consumption choice) for cigarettes among adults. In terms of youth, evidence does suggest that Camel advertising (Joe Camel) directed toward youth had increased the demand among youth. This advertising campaign was so successful that anti-smoking groups sued R.J. Reynolds (the manufacture of Camels) to discontinue the Joe Camel advertising campaign. In 1997, the suit was settled out of court and R.J. Reynolds voluntarily ended its Joe Camel ads.

The advertisement is the most truthful part of a newspaper.

(Thomas Jefferson)

Two major types of advertising are informational advertising and persuasive advertising.

Informational advertising educates consumers by providing information on product price, location, and characteristics. This can make markets more efficient by reducing consumers' search cost and enabling them to make rational choices. Informational advertising is generally found in newspapers, such as weekly grocery ads. By familiarizing consumers with products, this type of advertising broadens the market for commodities, which results in economies of scale and more efficient markets. For example, advertising has decreased the price of eyeglasses and contact lenses. Advertising also encourages competition by exposing consumers to competing products and enabling firms to gain market acceptance for new products more rapidly than they could without advertising.

Persuasive advertising is where a firm is attempting to modify consumers' preferences by creating wants that result in a distortion of natural preference patterns. Little information concerning the product is generally provided. Television advertising is generally of the persuasive type. Persuasive advertising can encourage artificial product differentiation among commodities that are physically similar. Persuasive advertising among competing firms tends to have a canceling effect (examples are colas and detergents). This duplication of effort results in a waste of resources, inefficiencies, higher production costs, and higher prices, so any real economies of scale may be lost. Also, persuasive advertising facilitates concentration of monopoly power because large firms can usually afford continuous heavy advertising whereas new or smaller firms cannot.

Should you let advertising change your preferences? If advertising yields new information about a commodity, you may benefit from letting the advertising change your preferences. If advertising is instead just persuasive, then the resulting distortion in your natural preferences may not be desirable.

A censor is a person who knows more than he thinks you ought to.

(Lawrence J. Peter)

The National Advertising Division of the Council of Better Business Bureaus was created by the advertising community in 1971 to provide a system of voluntary self-regulation, minimize government intervention, and foster public confidence in the credibility of advertising. As a result, advertisers, advertising agencies, and consumers rely on this division to maintain high standards of principles in advertising. By 2010, over 3800 advertising cases had been successfully handled through this self-regulatory process. This has reduced the inefficiencies associated with advertising and mitigated the pressure for government regulation. A problem with any type of regulation is determining what is true and false in advertising and who should determine it. Documentation supporting advertising claims and litigation costs associated with regulation may increase product price. Also, laws governing regulation must be enforced, which require governmental appropriations.

Application: Web 2.0 and citizen review sites

In primitive times, with Web 1.0, we posted words and pictures on our websites. Today, with Web 2.0, we provide material including citizen review sites. Websites offer the collective recommendations of many customers. We no longer have to solely rely on the promotions of firms. Instead, sites such as TripAdviser for vacations, Yelp for restaurants, IMDb for movies, Edmunds for cars, Amazon for books, and RateBeer for beers offer customer ratings, potentially supplanting firm promotions. This is a sobering development for firm advertising. Firms are no longer the sole source of their product promotion. Consumers are now efficiently communicating among themselves.

But what about fraudulent reviews? Phony reviews can poison the review sites. This results in firms using fake names to post positive reviews for their own products and negative reviews for their competitors' products. This is called astroturfing (fake grass roots). To counter astroturfing, citizen review sites (e.g., Amazon) encourage reviewers to use their real names . Some sites (Yelp and TripAdviser) hire staff and develop software to remove bogus reviews.

Source: D. Pogue, "Critical Mass: How to Maintain the Power of Online Reviews," *Scientific American* (June 2011): 36.

Monopolistic competition ills

The competition is eating me alive.

(Michael Wetzstein)

Service stations, convenience stores, and fast-food franchises are characterized by product differentiation, a relatively large number of firms, and easy entry into the market. Such market structures were first described by Edward H. Chamberlin (1899–1967) in 1933 as **monopolistic competition**. The key difference between perfect competition and monopolistic competition is that product differentiation is in the eye of the beholder (buyer). Monopolistically competitive firms produce heterogeneous (similar but not identical) products with relatively easy entry into the industry. Products may be differentiated by brand name, color of package, location of the seller, customer service, or credit conditions. This results in each firm having a partial monopoly of its own differentiated product, and thus it is possible to have wide differences among firms in price, output, and firm profit.

Does monopolistic competition lead to a large number of sick firms? Yes, each firm experiences a low volume of sales associated with a low profit margin (they are sick firms).

Monopolistic competition. Firms within a market producing heterogeneous products with relatively easy entry into this market. *E.g., gift and souvenir shops outside a national park.*

Because each firm has a partial monopoly, each has its own output demand curve. These demand curves are downward-sloping, indicating that a seller can increase its price without losing all of its sales. Also, there is no industry supply curve. The whole concept of an industry becomes somewhat clouded and vague in monopolistic competition as a result of product differentiation. Instead, a product group exists where the products of competitors are close but not perfect substitutes. Elasticity will vary inversely with the degree of product differentiation. The smaller the degree of product differentiation and the greater the number of sellers, the closer the market will be to perfect competition.

In contrast to perfect competition, sellers under monopolistic competition can vary the nature of their product and employ product promotion as well as change their output to influence profit. These features make the monopolistic-competition model very useful for describing decentralized allocations in the presence of producing with excess capacity. Recall from Chapter 12 that a monopoly produces with excess capacity but, unlike monopolistic competition, allocation decisions are centralized into one firm. In contrast, perfectly competitive allocation decisions are decentralized into many firms. However, perfectly competitive firms are operating at the minimum point of long-run average cost, and thus are at full (rather than excess) capacity. Monopolistic competition focuses the market implications of operating with excess capacity without the worry of strategic interactions among firms.

Determining short- and long-run equilibrium under monopolistic competition

Assume that all firms have essentially identical demand and cost functions. The demand curves are also assumed to be linear and the price received by each seller is a function of the quantities sold by each of the n firms within the industry. The inverse demand function for firm j is then

$$p_j = a - bq_j - d \sum_{\substack{i=1, \\ i \neq j}}^{n} q_i, j = 1,\ 2,\ \ldots,\ n.$$

Firm j's demand curve is dependent on the level of demand associated with its $n-1$ competitors, $\sum_{i=1, i\neq j}^{n} q_i$. The partial derivative $\partial p_j/\partial q_i = -d < 0$, but is numerically small in absolute value.

The effect of a quantity change on the part of one of the firm's competitors is spread over all of its $n-1$ competitors.

Firm j's total cost function is represented as $\text{STC}(q_j)$ for all $j = 1, 2, \ldots, n$. Given that d is numerically small, the effect is then negligible from a firm's change in output upon the price of any particular competitor. Thus, the firm acts as if its actions have no effect upon its competitors. Assuming that the profit function for firm j is

$$\pi_j = q_j\left(a - bq_j - d\sum_{\substack{i=1,\\ i\neq j}}^{n} q_i\right) - \mathrm{STC}(q_j),$$

the firm equates MR to SMC on the assumption that the output levels of its competitors remain unchanged:

$$\mathrm{MR}(Q_j) = a - 2bq_j - d\sum_{\substack{i=1,\\ i\neq j}}^{n} q_i = \mathrm{SMC}(q_j).$$

With identical demand and cost functions (a symmetry assumption), if it is profitable for one firm to make a particular move, it is profitable for all firms. Thus, firms will not move along the inverse demand curve

$$p_j = a - bq_j - d\sum_{\substack{i=1,\\ i\neq j}}^{n} q_i, j = 1,\ 2,\ \ldots,\ n,$$

but instead along the following demand curve where $q_j = q_i$:

$$p_j = a - [b + (n-1)d]q_j.$$

The actual or effective inverse demand curve the firms are facing has a steeper slope, $-[b + (n-1)d]$, than the inverse demand curve the firms believe they are facing with a slope of $-b$. Firms determine their profit-maximizing output level, assuming that total output only changes by their small output change. However, they do not realize that their individual profit-maximizing decisions will be replicated by all the other firms within this market, causing a change in total output beyond their small output change.

These two demand functions are shown in Figure 15.1. The effective demand curve Q^D is where a firm's competitors' prices are always the same as its and thus is more steeply sloping then the demand curve Q^d where competitors' prices remain fixed. Also depicted in Figure 15.1 is the firm's SMC curve. Given these demand curves and the SMC curve, the equilibrium price and output can be determined by first assuming the firm is selling q^o units of output at the market price of p^o. This price and output combination is not the profit-maximization combination. The firm determines its profit-maximizing output and associated price by setting its SMC equal to MR. For determination of marginal revenue, the firm assumes that any change in its price will not be followed by the other firms. The Q^d demand curve then becomes the relevant demand curve for the firm, and it attempts to operate as a monopoly given this demand curve. The firm assumes that profit is then maximized at an output q^1 with price p^1. However, all firms follow this same logic and take the same action, because by assumption they all have the same information and the same motivation. As a result, the actual movement in price is downward on the Q^D demand curve rather than the Q^d curve. At this new price p^1, the output sold by each firm is only q^2.

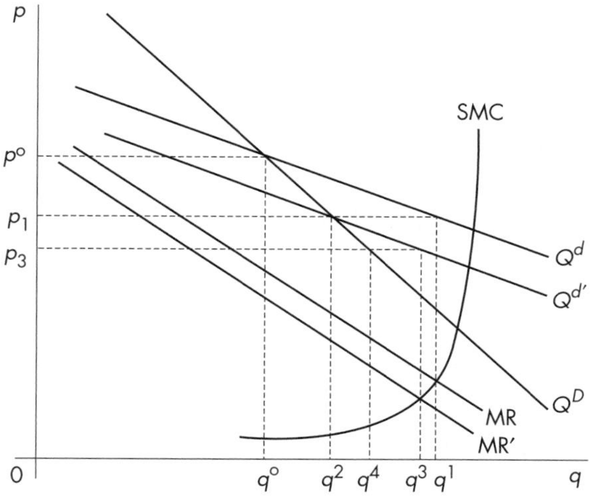

Figure 15.1 **Short-run output and price determination for a monopolistically competitive firm.** The firm determines its profit-maximizing output q^1 and price p^1 by setting SMC equal to MR associated with the Q^d demand curve. All firms take this same action, resulting in only q^2 units of output sold.

At (p^1, q^2), the Q^d demand curve shifts down to $Q^{d'}$ resulting from the increase in supply by the firm's competitors. The firm then adjusts its price and output, given that it believes it is facing this new demand $Q^{d'}$, by determining the associated marginal revenue MR′. Setting SMC equal to MR′, the firm expects to sell q^3 at a price of p^3, but only sells q^4 associated with the Q^D demand curve.

As illustrated in Figure 15.2, this output and price adjustment continues until output q_e and price p_e are reached. This equilibrium price and output combination is where the perceived marginal revenue MR equals SMC at the intersection of the two demand curves. The firm's profit position at this equilibrium depends upon the relationship between the short-run average total cost of production and the two demand curves. Figure 15.2 illustrates the firm earning a normal profit, but the firm can also earn a short-run pure profit or operate at a loss. The long-run equilibrium position is also illustrated in Figure 15.2. In this equilibrium position, the long-run average cost curve LAC is tangent to the Q^d curve at the output q_e and price p_e where the Q^d and Q^D curves intersect.

As with monopoly and perfectly competitive market structures, a long-run pure profit for monopolistically competitive firms will be zero. In the short run, monopolistically competitive firms earning pure profits will attract new firms supplying similar products. Consumers will perceive these new products as possible substitutes, so the demand curves for the original firms will shift downward and eventually squeeze out any pure profits. Also, as with monopoly and perfect competition, in the long run, costs will also adjust and squeeze profits. However, as indicated in Figure 15.2, production is not at the minimum of LAC, $p >$ LMC, so there is deadweight loss in consumer and producer surplus. However, because firms only have a partial monopoly, their aggregate level of output will be greater than that for a pure monopoly. In Figure 15.2, the Q^D demand curve cuts above the short-run average total cost curve, creating an area where a monopoly can earn a short-run pure profit by reducing output to within

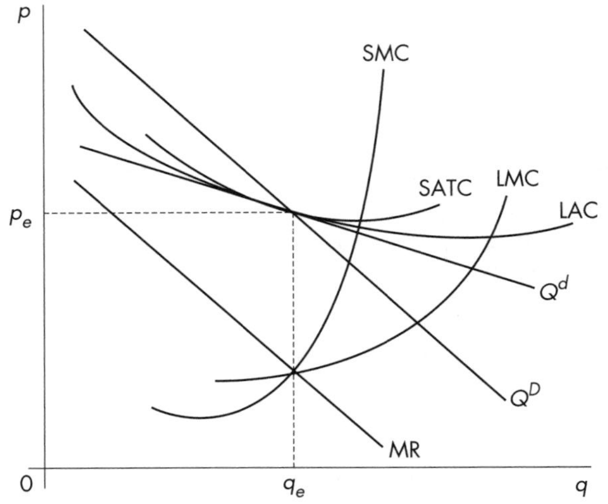

Figure 15.2 **Long-run equilibrium for a monopolistically competitive firm.** In the long run, the firm will only earn a normal profit where the equilibrium price p_e equals SATC = LAC.

this area. Thus, monopolistically competitive firms' level of resource misallocation is less than if a monopoly was the sole supplier in the industry. Also, consumers may view the greater degree of product differentiation (more choices) as a desirable characteristic, which mitigates this inefficiency.

Example 15.2 Determining the output and price for a monopolistically competitive firm

Consider an industry comprising 497 firms, with each firm facing the following inverse demand and cost functions:

$$p_j = 12 - 2q_j - \sum_{\substack{i=1,\\ i \neq j}}^{497} q_i, j = 1, 2, \ldots, 497.$$

$$\text{MC}_j = 5.$$

Firm j's marginal revenue is then

$$\text{MR}_j = 12 - 4q_j - \sum_{\substack{i=1,\\ i \neq j}}^{497} q_i, j = 1, 2, \ldots, 497.$$

In equilibrium, $q_j = q_i$, so

$$\text{MR}_j = 12 - 500q_j.$$

Profit maximization results in $\mathrm{MR}_j = \mathrm{MC}_j$:

$$12 - 500q_j^* = 5.$$

Solving for q_j yields the equilibrium level of output for each firm:

$$q_j^* = 7/500.$$

The effective inverse demand function is

$$p_j = 12 - (2 + 496)q_j.$$

Equilibrium price is then

$$p_j^* = 12 - 498(7/500) = 5.03.$$

At this equilibrium, the Q^d curve is

$$p_j = 12 - 2q_j - 496(7/500)$$
$$= 5.06 - 2q_j.$$

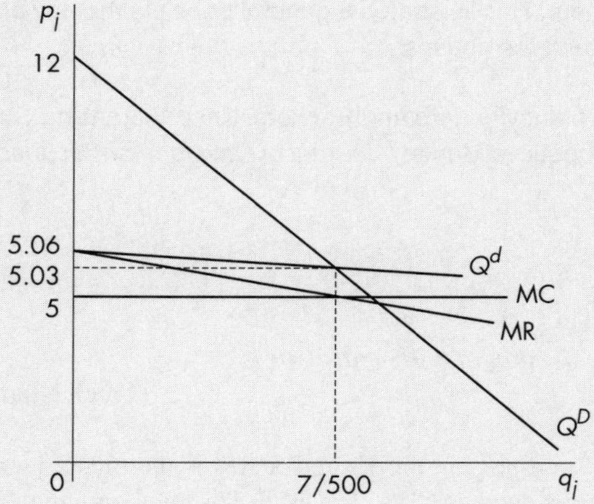

Application: Moneylenders and bankers

The poor in many underdeveloped countries rely heavily on private moneylenders and not on sources of institutional finance. Governmental institutions for enforcing money lending contracts are generally not well developed, so a significant cost of obtaining a loan is the direct cost of enforcing the contract. Once a borrower has been screened and accepted by a given moneylender, other moneylenders are an imperfect substitute. With free entry into money lending, the market is monopolistically competitive. If the marginal cost of moneylenders increases, then the equilibrium interest rate will increase.

Hoff and Stiglitz offer three models demonstrating how a subsidy lowering the private opportunity cost of funds to moneylenders may cause the marginal cost of moneylending to rise and increase the interest rate. First, economies of scale in terms of lending-transactions costs and a subsidy inducing new entry result in each moneylender cutting back on loans and thus in rising marginal cost and interest rate. Second, this increase in entry adversely affects borrowers' incentives to repay, which increases each moneylender's enforcement cost. Borrowers may perceive that if they default on one moneylender, it will be less difficult to find another one. Third, enforcement of a contract is ensured through a combination of collection effort by a moneylender and reputation effects that punish defaulters. Reputation effects are only as strong as the information flows that support them. The informal exchange of information about each borrower's credit history is less complete as the number of moneylenders increase, resulting in increased marginal cost for moneylenders.

The results of these models aid in determining the impact that subsidies to rural credit have in developing countries. On the surface, economic intuition suggests that an increase in government-subsidized credit should trickle down to borrowers in the form of lower interest rates. In contrast, Hoff and Stiglitz's models indicate this may not be true and thus provide support for the view that increased access to financial capital by the poor requires lending directly to them. This illustrates a general principle that to correct a market failure one must understand the causes.

Source: K. Hoff and J.E. Stiglitz, "Moneylenders and Bankers: Price-Increasing Subsidies in a Monopolistically Competitive Market," *Journal of Development Economics* 55 (1998): 485–518.

Understanding oligopolies

We are here to awaken from the illusion of our separateness.

(Thich Nhat Hanh)

A major market characterized as an oligopoly in the United States is the media landscape. This market is dominated by giant firms such as CBS, The Walt Disney Company, General Electric, News Corporation, Time Warner, and Viacom. To a large extent, these firms furnish your television programs, movies, videos, radio shows, music, and books. In general, an **oligopolistic market** is characterized by the existence of a relatively small number of sellers with interdependence among sellers. These firms are producing either a homogeneous product (called *perfect oligopoly*) or heterogeneous products (*imperfect oligopoly*). An example of a homogeneous oligopoly market is the steel industry. The automobile, cigarette, gasoline, and cola industries are heterogeneous markets. If there are two sellers, it is called a **duopoly**.

The relatively small number of sellers in an oligopolistic market is the result of barriers to entry, which may result from product differentiation, economies of scale, control over indispensable resources, or exclusive franchises. Product differentiation in the face of uncertainty may result in brand identification, where it is difficult for new firms to break through this attachment. Economies of scale may result where total market size permits only a few optimally sized plants. Control over indispensable resources prevents entry on technological grounds, and exclusive franchises present legal barriers to entry. In addition to few firms, barriers to entry, and economies of scale, oligopolistic markets are characterized by mutual dependence. It is necessary for each firm to consider the reactions of its competitors (awaken from any illusion of separateness).

Oligopolistic market. A market comprised of a relatively small number of interdependent firms. *E.g., the markets for electronic products such as TVs, DVDs, and cameras.*

Duopoly. A market composed of two firms. *E.g., the market for satellite television reception is composed of DirecTV and Dish Network.*

Determining price and output

Whether oligopolistic firms attempt to maximize profit or have some other objective, they must determine an associated price and output policy based on some objective. A firm may have a pricing policy that results in less-than-maximum profit to discourage potential entrants. (This is an example of contestable markets where even the threat of entry will prevent firms from maximizing profit.) Thus, instead of maximizing profit, a firm might attempt to maximize sales in an effort to maintain control over a share of the market.

To determine price and output of an oligopolistic firm, let us consider a duopolist market selling an undifferentiated product (*perfect duopolist*). In terms of politics, this may be the two political parties, Democrats and Republicans, selling alternative solutions for providing public goods. Let p denote a common selling price, and q_1 and q_2 the outputs of the first and second firms, respectively. We determine this common selling price p by the total market output of the two firms, Q, where $q_1 + q_2 = Q$. Then $p = p(Q)$. An increase in either output will result in a decrease in the price:

$$\frac{\partial p}{\partial q_1} < 0, \frac{\partial p}{\partial q_2} < 0.$$

Total revenue for the jth firm is then

$$\text{TR}_j = p(Q)q_j, \quad j = 1, 2,$$

and total cost for the jth firm is $\text{TC}_j(q_j)$. Assuming that the firms' objectives are to maximize their own profits, the profit for each firm is

$$\max_{q_j} \pi_j = \max_{q_j} \left[p(Q)q_j - \text{TC}(q_j)\right], j = 1,\ 2.$$

Firm j's profit depends on the amount of output chosen by the other firm, so firm j must predict the other firm's output decision. If one firm changes its output, the other firm may react to this change in output by adjusting its output. This is just the sort of consideration that goes into game theory discussed in Chapter 14. Each player (firm) must predict the strategies of the other players. This is a one-shot game where the profit of firm j is its payoff and the strategy set of firm j is the possible outputs it can produce. An equilibrium is then a set of outputs (q_1^*, q_2^*) in which each firm is choosing its profit-maximizing output level, given its beliefs about the other firm's choice, and each firm's belief about the other firm's choice is actually correct. Recall from Chapter 14 that this is called a Nash equilibrium.

Assuming an interior optimum for each firm, the FOC for firm 1 using the product rule for differentiation is

$$\frac{\partial \pi_1}{\partial q_1} = p(Q^*) + \frac{\partial p(Q)}{\partial q_1} q_1^* - \mathrm{MC}_1(q_1^*) = 0.$$

Employing the chain rule for the second term on the right-hand side, where Q is a function of q_1 and q_2 and q_2 is a function of q_1, yields

$$\frac{\partial p(Q)}{\partial q_1} = \frac{\partial p(Q)}{\partial Q}\frac{\partial Q}{\partial q_1} + \frac{\partial p(Q)}{\partial Q}\frac{\partial Q}{\partial q_2}\frac{\partial q_2}{\partial q_1}.$$

This results in

$$\frac{\partial \pi_1}{\partial q_1} = p(Q^*) + \frac{\partial p(Q)}{\partial Q}\left(\frac{\partial Q}{\partial q_1} + \frac{\partial Q}{\partial q_2}\frac{\partial q_2}{\partial q_1}\right) q_1^* - \mathrm{MC}_1(q_1^*) = 0.$$

Note that $\partial Q/\partial q_1 = \partial Q/\partial q_2 = 1$, so

$$\frac{\partial \pi_1}{\partial q_1} = p(Q^*) + \left(\frac{\partial p(Q)}{\partial Q} + \frac{\partial p(Q)}{\partial Q}\frac{\partial q_2}{\partial q_1}\right) q_1^* - \mathrm{MC}_1(q_1^*) = 0.$$

The FOC for firm 2 is then

$$\begin{aligned}\frac{\partial \pi_2}{\partial q_2} &= p(Q^*) + \frac{\partial p(Q)}{\partial Q}\left(\frac{\partial Q}{\partial q_2} + \frac{\partial Q}{\partial q_1}\frac{\partial q_1}{\partial q_2}\right) q_2^* - \mathrm{MC}_2(q_2^*) \\ &= p(Q^*) + \left(\frac{\partial p(Q)}{\partial Q} + \frac{\partial p(Q)}{\partial Q}\frac{\partial q_1}{\partial q_2}\right) q_2^* - \mathrm{MC}_2(q_2^*) = 0.\end{aligned}$$

To solve these FOCs for the optimal levels of outputs, q_1^* and q_2^*, the functional forms of $\partial q_2/\partial q_1$ and $\partial q_1/\partial q_2$ are required. These derivatives are called **conjectural variations**. They represent one firm's conjecture or expectation of how the other firm's output will alter as a result of its own change in output. A variety of different duopoly models result, depending on what economic assumptions are made regarding these conjectural variations. We will investigate a number of these models.

Conjectural variation. A firm's expectation of how another firm's action (output) will change as a result of its own actions (change in output). *E.g., how an automobile dealership expanding its business expects its competitor to react.*

Cournot model: commercial real estate

First let us consider the **Cournot model** developed by the French mathematician Antoine Augustin Cournot (1801–1877) in 1838. This model assumes that the conjectural variations are zero:

$$\frac{\partial q_2}{\partial q_1} = \frac{\partial q_1}{\partial q_2} = 0.$$

A firm, setting its own output, assumes that the other firm's output will not change, and the firms make their independent output decisions simultaneously. The simultaneous output decision by firms is directly related to the Nash equilibrium associated with simultaneous-moves games in Chapter 14. For example, a firm may determine its output capacity without regard to the capacity of other firms. Firms do not realize the interdependence of their output decisions in their attempts at maximizing profit. Thus, the Cournot duopoly solution implies that each firm equates its own MR to MC without regard to any possible reaction by the other firm:

$$p(Q^*) + \frac{\partial p(Q)}{\partial Q} q_j^* - \mathrm{MC}_j(q_j^*) = 0, \quad j = 1,\ 2.$$

Note that even with zero conjectural variations, the solution for (q_1, q_2) still involves the simultaneous solution of each firm's FOC. Firms may not *realize* their decisions affect their competitor, but, given the output price is determined by each firm's output level, their decisions *do* affect the other firm's output determination.

Are Cournot firms zombies? Yes they are, in terms of not responding to the environment by basing their output decisions on other firms' output decisions.

Cournot model. An oligopoly model that assumes firms base their output decisions on zero conjectural variations. *E.g., a building contractor, building homes in response to an increase in demand, not realizing other contractors will also respond to this demand.*

An example of Cournot firms is the commercial real estate market in large metropolitan cities. When the market for commercial real estate is very tight, characterized by limited supply of commercial buildings, the price per square foot for office space increases. This increase in price stimulates speculative building of office space by a number of firms. However, each individual firm does not consider the effect on its total revenue of other firms building office space. Thus, when all the additional office space becomes available, the market is flooded and the price drops. This result is magnified when the high price for office space is during an economic boom period in the city's cyclical economy. If the city's economy is in a slump (say, from the Great Recession) when the office space becomes available, the price drop can be substantial.

How the Cournot model, perfect competition, and monopoly are related

Factoring out $p(Q^*)$ from the FOC for profit maximization, $\partial\pi_j/\partial q_j = 0$, $j = 1, 2$, and multiplying the second term by $1 = Q^*/Q^*$ yields

$$p(Q^*)\left[1 + \frac{\partial p(Q)}{\partial Q}\frac{Q^*}{p(Q^*)}\frac{q_j^*}{Q^*}\right] = \mathrm{MC}_j(q_j^*), \quad j = 1,\ 2.$$

Since elasticity of demand $\varepsilon^D = (\partial Q/\partial p)p^*/Q^* < 0$,

$$p(Q^*)\left(1 + \frac{\alpha_j}{\varepsilon^D}\right) = \mathrm{MC}_j(q_j^*),$$

$$p(Q^*)\left(1 + \frac{1}{\varepsilon^D/\alpha_j}\right) = \mathrm{MC}_j(q_j^*),$$

where $\alpha_j = q_j/Q$ is the share of total output by firm j. If there is only one firm in this industry, then $\alpha_j = 1$ and the FOCs reduce to the monopoly solution.[1] As the number of firms increase, each firm's share of total output, α_j, declines, resulting in ε^D/α_j decreasing toward $-\infty$. Firms are facing a more elastic demand curve as the number of firms increases. In the limit as the number of firms approaches infinity, the perfectly competitive solution $p = \mathrm{MC}$ results. At this perfectly competitive solution, the Cournot assumption of zero conjectural variations is correct. Firms assume that their decisions will not have any influence on the market, and their assumptions are correct.

As an example of price and output determination by Cournot firms, consider the inverse linear market demand function for a duopoly market:

$$p = a - b(Q), \quad a > 0, \quad b > 0,$$

where $Q = q_1 + q_2$, the combined output of the two firms. Let the cost functions for these firms be

$$\mathrm{STC}_1 = cq_1 + \mathrm{TFC},$$

$$\mathrm{STC}_2 = cq_2 + \mathrm{TFC},$$

where $c > 0$ and $a > c$. Note that c represents a constant SMC = SAVC. With a greater than the firms' SAVC, they will each supply a positive level of output.

Assuming that each firm maximizes profit,

$$\max_{q_j} \pi_j = \max_{q_j} \left\{[a - b(q_1 + q_2)]q_j - cq_j - \mathrm{TFC}\right\}, \quad j = 1,\ 2,$$

the FOC for firm 1 is then

$$\frac{\partial \pi_1}{\partial q_1} = a - b(q_1 + q_2) - bq_1 - b\frac{\partial q_2}{\partial q_1}q_1 - c = 0.$$

The corresponding FOC for firm 2 is

$$\frac{\partial \pi_2}{\partial q_2} = a - b(q_1 + q_2) - bq_2 - b\frac{\partial q_1}{\partial q_2}q_2 - c = 0.$$

Since Cournot firms' conjectural variations are both zero, firm 1's FOC reduces to

$$a - b(q_1 + q_2) - bq_1 - c = 0.$$

Solving for q_1 gives

$$q_1 = \frac{a - c - bq_2}{2b}.$$

This is firm 1's **reaction function**, which states how firm 1's output changes (reacts) when firm 2's output changes.

Reaction function. How one firm reacts to a change in another firm's action (output). *E.g., how an automobile dealership reacts to its competitor's expanding its facilities.*

Similarly, firm 2's reaction function is

$$q_2 = \frac{a - c - bq_1}{2b}.$$

These reaction functions are illustrated in Figure 15.3, with the Cournot equilibrium level of outputs for firms 1 and 2 resulting at their intersection. This Nash equilibrium can be found by substituting firm 2's reaction function into firm 1's and solving for q_1:

$$q_1 = \frac{a - c - bq_2}{2b}$$

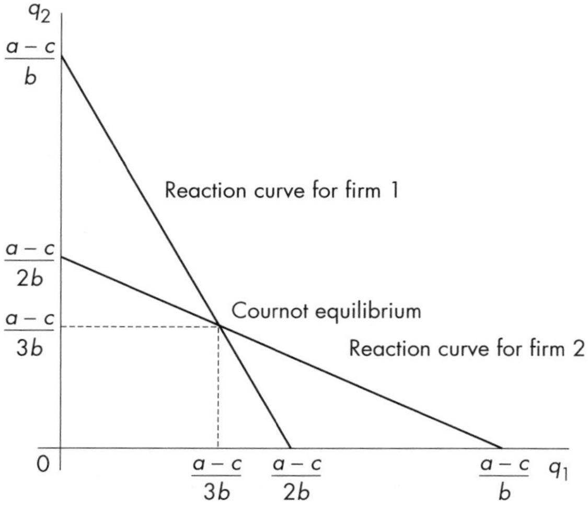

Figure 15.3 **Cournot equilibrium.** The intersection of the firms' reaction curves determine the Cournot equilibrium outputs $q_1^C = q_2^C = (a - c)/3b$.

$$= \frac{a - c - b(a - c - bq_1)/2b}{2b}$$
$$= \frac{2a - 2c - a + c + bq_1}{4b}$$
$$= \frac{a - c}{4b} + \frac{q_1}{4},$$
$$q_1^C = \frac{a - c}{3b}.$$

Substituting this equilibrium level of output q_1^C into firm 2's reaction functions yields the Nash equilibrium output for firm 2:

$$q_2^C = \frac{a - c - bq_1^C}{2b}$$
$$= \frac{a - c - b(a - c)/3b}{2b}$$
$$= \frac{a - c}{3b} = q_1^C.$$

Market output Q^C and price p^C are then

$$Q^C = \frac{2(a - c)}{3b},$$
$$p^C = a - b(Q^C)$$
$$= a - 2b\frac{a - c}{3b}$$
$$= \frac{3a - 2a + 2c}{3}$$
$$= \frac{a + 2c}{3}.$$

Deriving isoprofit curves

The dynamics of the Cournot approach can be analyzed using reaction curves that show the optimal profit-maximizing output for each firm, given the output of the competitor. Consider some profit level for firm 1:

$$\pi_1^{\text{o}} = [a - b(q_1 + q_2)]q_1 - cq_1 - \text{TFC}$$
$$= aq_1 - bq_1^2 - q_1q_2 - cq_1 - \text{TFC}.$$

This is the equation for firm 1's isoprofit curve for π_1^{o} level of profit. An **isoprofit curve** represents an equal level of profit for alternative levels of a firm's output. As illustrated in Figure 15.4, the isoprofit curves radiate out from firm 1's monopoly solution. When firm 2's output is zero, firm 1 is the sole supplier and, as a monopoly, will maximize profit at $Q = q_1 = (a - c)/2b$. This represents the highest possible level of profit for firm 1. As firm 2

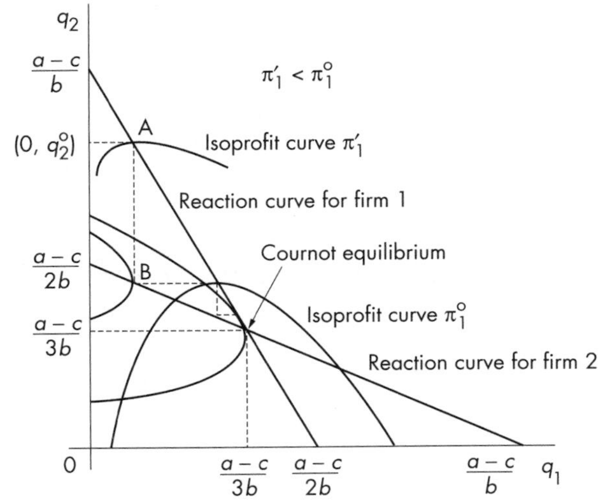

Figure 15.4 **Dynamic adjustments to the Cournot equilibrium.** Each firm will react by adjusting its output to the other firm's output according to its reaction curve. This adjustment by both firms continues until the Cournot equilibrium is reached.

increases its output from zero, profit for firm 1 declines. This is illustrated by isoprofit curves with lower levels of profit as q_2 increases.

Isoprofit curve. A curve representing an equal level of profit for alternative levels of a firm's output. *E.g., if a steel company experiences a loss in sales but profits remain the same, the firm is then moving along its isoprofit curve.*

Firm 1 will maximize its profit for a given level of q_2 by shifting to the isoprofit curve with the highest profit. As illustrated in Figure 15.4, the isoprofit curve tangent to the constraint of firm 2's output equaling q_2^o is firm 1's profit-maximizing level given q_2^o. At this point of tangency, the slope of the lowest possible isoprofit curve, representing the highest possible profit, is equal to the zero slope of the constraint. The FOC for maximizing profit, given firm 2's level of output, yields firm 1's reaction curve which passes through all the tangency points of the isoprofit curves and firm 2's output constraint.

Similarly, firm 2 will maximize its profit for a given level of firm 1's output. Firm 2's isoprofit curves radiate out from its monopoly solution, with profit declining as q_1 increases. The maximum profit level for firm 2, given some output level for firm 1, is where the isoprofit curve is vertical and tangent to the constraint of firm 1's output. Firm 2's reaction curve passes through this tangency.

Given these isoprofit and reaction curves, firm 1 will react to firm 2's output level q_2^o, resulting in a movement to point A. Firm 2 will then react to this positive output level by firm 1 by decreasing output, yielding point B. These Cournot firms have no capacity for learning, so the adjustment process continues until the Cournot equilibrium is established.

Example 15.3 Determining the Cournot, Stackelberg, and Collusion equilibria

Given the linear demand and cost functions

$$p = a - b(q_1 + q_2),$$
$$\text{STC}_j = cq_j + \text{TFC}, \quad j = 1, 2,$$

let $a = 14$, $b = 1$, $c = 2$, and TFC $= 5$. The Cournot reaction functions are then

$$q_1 = \frac{a - c - bq_2}{2b} = 6 - \tfrac{1}{2}q_2,$$
$$q_2 = \frac{a - c - bq_1}{2b} = 6 - \tfrac{1}{2}q_1.$$

Nash equilibrium outputs and price are

$$q_2^C = q_1^C = \frac{a - c}{3b} = 4,$$
$$Q^C = \frac{2(a - c)}{3b} = 8,$$
$$p^C = \frac{a + 2c}{3} = \$6.$$

Cournot firms' profits are

$$\pi_j^C = p^C p_j^C - cq_j^C - \text{TFC} = 24 - 13 = \$11, \quad j = 1, 2.$$

If firm 1 is a Stackelberg leader and firm 2 a Cournot follower, then

$$q_1^S = \frac{a - c}{2b} = 6,$$
$$q_2^S = \frac{a - c}{4b} = 3,$$
$$p^S = a - b(q_1^S + q_2^S) = 14 - 9 = \$5.$$

Profits are then

$$\pi_1^S = p^S q_1^S - cq_1^S - \text{TFC} = 30 - 12 - 5 = \$13,$$
$$\pi_2^S = p^S q_2^S - cq_2^S - \text{TFC} = 15 - 6 - 5 = \$4.$$

With both firms acting as leaders, $q_1 = q_2 = (a - c)/(2b) = 6$ and $p = \$2$, with profit equaling $-\$5$ for each firm.

If the two firms collude, then (joint output) price and profit are

$$Q^M = \frac{a-c}{2b} = 6,\ p^M = \$8,\ \pi^M = 48 - 12 - 10 = \$26.$$

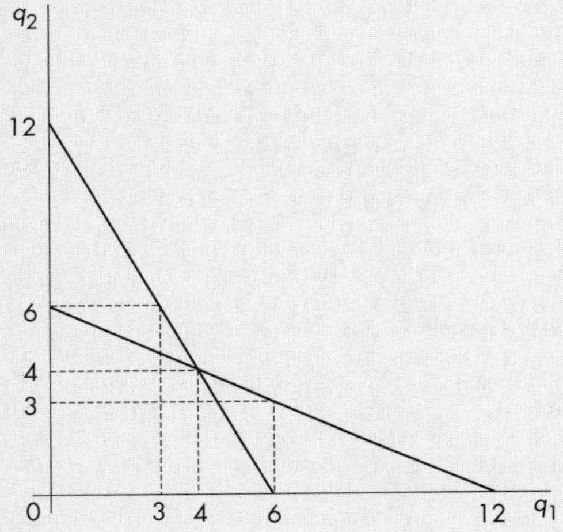

Stackelberg model: Microsoft

The **Stackelberg model**, developed by the German economist Heinrich von Stackelberg (1905–1946), is a duopoly quantity leadership model where one firm (the leader) takes the likely response of the competitor (the follower) into consideration when maximizing profit. Specifically, the model allows for the leader to have a nonzero conjectural variation on the follower. A follower behaves exactly as a Cournot firm, so its conjectural variation is still zero. The leader then takes advantage of the assumption that the other firm is behaving as a follower. This is a sequential game theory problem where the leader has the advantage of moving first. Industries with one dominant large firm and a number of smaller firms are examples of markets with possible Stackelberg characteristics. For example, in the personal computer operating systems industry, Microsoft is the dominant leader firm, with a number of smaller follower firms.

Do you respond to some stimulus? If you base your decisions on the likely decision of others, then you have Stackelberg characteristics and respond to a stimulus.

Stackelberg model. A duopoly quantity leadership model where one firm (the leader) takes the likely response of the competitor (the follower) into consideration when maximizing profit. *E.g., Potter's firm and George Bailey's Building and Loan in the movie* It's a Wonderful Life.

As an example of the Stackelberg model, let us consider the Cournot linear demand function example, with firm 1 as the leader and firm 2 as the follower. Suppose firm 1 believes that firm 2 would react along the Cournot reaction curve

$$q_2 = (a - c - bq_1)/2b.$$

Firm 1's conjectural variation is then

$$\frac{\partial q_2}{\partial q_1} = \frac{-b}{2b} = -\frac{1}{2}.$$

Given the FOC associated with firm 1,

$$\frac{\partial \pi_1}{\partial q_1} = a - b(q_1 + q_2) - bq_1 - b\frac{\partial q_2}{\partial q_1}q_1 - c = 0,$$

and substituting in the conjectural variation yields

$$\frac{\partial \pi_1}{\partial q_1} = a - b(q_1 + q_2) - bq_1 + \tfrac{1}{2}bq_1 - c = 0$$

The reaction curve for firm 1 is then

$$a - bq_1 - bq_2 - bq_1 + \tfrac{1}{2}bq_1 - c = 0,$$

$$\tfrac{3}{2}bq_1 = a - c - bq_2,$$

$$q_1 = \frac{a - c - bq_2}{\tfrac{3}{2}b}.$$

The way we calculated firm 1's conjectural variation and substituting it into firm 1's FOC is the same as maximizing firm 1's profit subject to firm 2's reaction function. In a sequential game, this corresponds to firm 1 setting its output first. Firm 1 will set its output level by considering how firm 2 will react to it. Given firm 2's reaction function, we can determine the subgame perfect Nash equilibrium for firm 1. Specifically,

$$\max_{q_1} \pi_1 = \max_{q_1} \{[a - b(q_1 + q_2)]q_1 - cq_1 - \text{TFC}\}$$

subject to

$$q_2 = \frac{a - c - bq_1}{2b}.$$

Substituting the constraint into the objective function results in the same FOC for firm 1:

$$\max_{q_1} \pi_1 = \max_{q_1} \left\{ \left[a - b\left(q_1 + \frac{a - c - bq_1}{2b} \right) \right] q_1 - cq_1 - \text{TFC} \right\},$$

$$\frac{\partial \pi_1}{\partial q_1} = a - 2bq_1 - (a - c - 2bq_1)\left(\frac{b}{2b}\right) - c = 0$$

$$a - 2bq_1 - bq_2 + \tfrac{1}{2}bq_1 - c = 0,$$

$$a - b(q_1 + q_2) - bq_1 + \tfrac{1}{2}bq_1 - c = 0.$$

The outcome for both firms then depends on the behavior of firm 2. If firm 2 is using the Cournot reaction curve, as firm 1 believes, then the solution is the Stackelberg equilibrium for firm 1:

$$q_1^S = \frac{a-c}{2b},$$

$$q_2^S = \frac{a-c}{4b}.$$

This solution is derived from the FOCs of profit maximization (the reaction functions) for the two firms. Equating these FOCs yields

$$\begin{aligned}
a - b(q_1+q_2) - bq_1 + \tfrac{1}{2}bq_1 - c &= a - b(q_1+q_2) - bq_2 - c \\
-bq_1 + \tfrac{1}{2}bq_1 &= -bq_2, \\
\tfrac{1}{2}bq_1 &= bq_2, \\
\tfrac{1}{2}q_1 &= q_2.
\end{aligned}$$

Substituting this solution into firm 1's reaction function results in the solution for firm 1:

$$\begin{aligned}
a - b(q_1 + \tfrac{1}{2}q_1) - \tfrac{1}{2}bq_1 - c &= 0, \\
a - bq_1 - \tfrac{1}{2}bq_1 - \tfrac{1}{2}bq_1 - c &= 0, \\
a - 2bq_1 - c &= 0, \\
q_1^S &= \frac{a-c}{2b}.
\end{aligned}$$

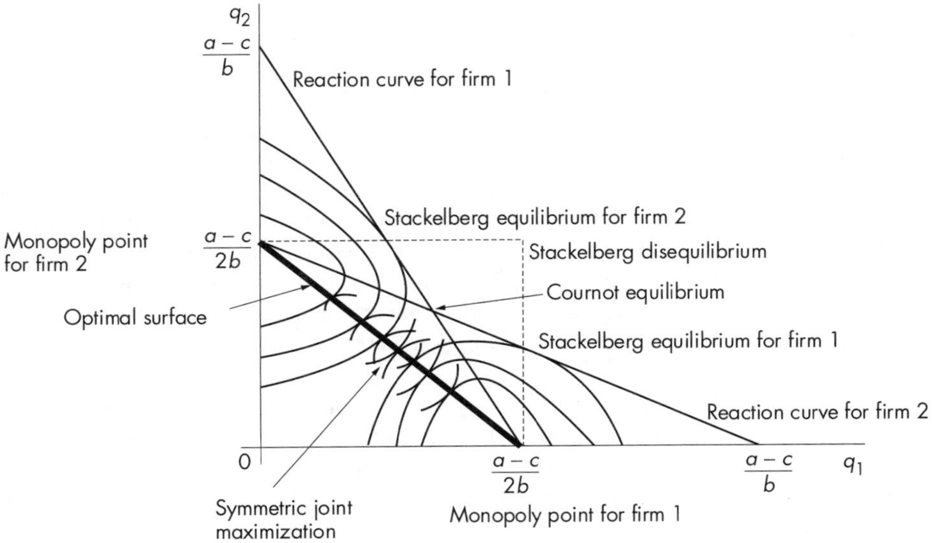

Figure 15.5 **Stackelberg equilibrium and disequilibrium.** Stackelberg equilibria are obtained where the Stackelberg firm's isoprofit curve is tangent to the Cournot firm's reaction curve. If both firms behave as Stackelberg firms, then the Stackelberg disequilibrium results.

Noting that $q_2^S = \frac{1}{2}q_1^S$, then

$$q_2^S = \frac{a - c}{4b}.$$

This results in firm 1 earning a higher profit and firm 2 earning a lower profit than at the Cournot equilibrium. As illustrated in Figure 15.5, firm 1 maximizes profit subject to firm 2's reaction curve. This results in a tangency of firm 1's isoprofit curve with firm 2's reaction function. Firm 1 is able to increase its profit with the knowledge of firm 2's reaction function. Similarly, as illustrated in Figure 15.5, if firm 2 is the Stackelberg firm, facing Cournot firm 1, then the equilibrium output and profit levels are reversed.

Example 15.4 Using game theory in determining Cournot and Stackelberg payoffs

Examples of Cournot and Stackelberg equilibria are provided in Example 15.3, with associated profits for each type of firm depending on the strategic interaction of the two firms. In a game theoretical framework, these profits for each firm can be considered the payoffs of being a follower or a leader. This results in the following payoff matrix:

		Firm 2	
		Leader	Follower
Firm 1	Leader	(–5, –5)	(13, 4)
	Follower	(4, 13)	(11, 11)

Note: Payoffs are (firm 1, firm 2).

Two Nash equilibria result, with one firm being a follower associated with the other firm as the leader. For example, if firm 1 is the leader with firm 2 as the follower, then firm 1 receives the Stackelberg leader profit of \$13 and firm 2 receives a profit of \$4. There is no incentive for either firm to change its strategy. At these two Nash equilibria, if a leader switched to be a follower, its profit would fall from \$13 to \$11. Similarly, if a follower became a leader, it would operate in the red, with a profit of −\$5. The Cournot presumption of both firms as followers yielding profits of \$11 each is a disequilibrium result. Both firms could improve their individual profits by unilaterally becoming a leader. As Stackelberg firms, they would realize that the other firm is a follower and maximize profit subject to the follower's reaction function. However, if both firms become Stackelberg firms, this would result in Stackelberg disequilibrium,with a negative profit of \$5 each.

If we extend the game to include the possibility of the firms colluding, then a joint profit of \$26 results (see Example 15.3 for the calculation of this joint profit). If each firm receives at least \$13, which results in profit being evenly divided, they will both receive the same profit as a Stackelberg leader. However, unless the collusion can be enforced, there will be a profit incentive for either firm to increase its profit. This assumes that the other firm abides by the agreement and does not increase its output.

Example 15.5 Sequential game for Cournot and Stackelberg behaviors

In Example 15.4, two Nash equilibria resulted when each firm was either a follower or a leader. Which of these Nash equilibria will become the subgame perfect Nash equilibrium may depend on which firm is willing and able to act first. For example, say firm 1 acts first and becomes either a follower or a leader. Given firm 1's choice, firm 2 then determines its optimal choice of becoming a follower or a leader. The game tree for this sequential game is as follows:

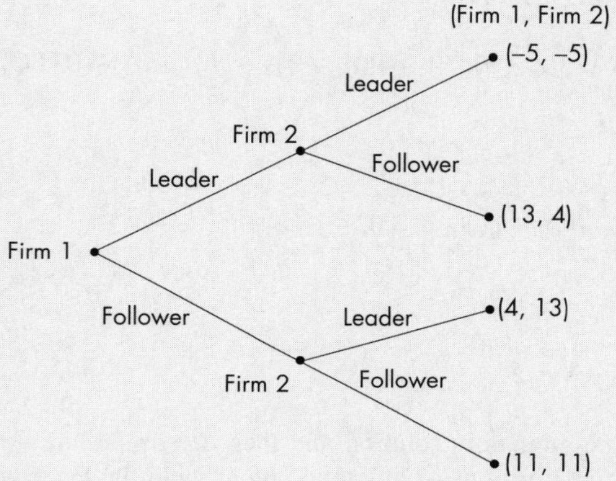

Using backward induction, firm 2's optimal actions are to be a follower if firm 1 is a leader and a leader if firm 1 is a follower. This results in the following reduced game tree.

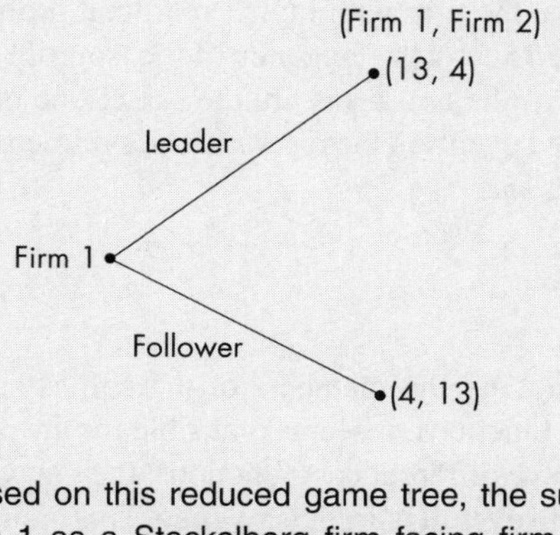

Based on this reduced game tree, the subgame perfect Nash equilibrium solution is firm 1 as a Stackelberg firm facing firm 2 as a Cournot firm. By acting first, firm 1 is able to secure a preferred market position. Game trees similar to this are applied for investigating various types of marketing strategies. Examples are establishment of market niches and an incumbent firm accommodating versus fighting a potential firm entering its market.

Stackelberg disequilibrium

Suppose that firm 2 is using the Stackelberg reaction curve instead of the Cournot reaction curve, so each firm incorrectly believes the other is a follower using the naive Cournot assumption. The firms each set their output at $(a-c)/2b$, expecting that their competitor will be a follower and set its output at $(a-c)/4b$. The result is *Stackelberg disequilibrium*, illustrated in Figure 15.5. Both firms earn lower profit than the Cournot equilibrium.

Collusion: OPEC

Rather than attempt to guess reactions of competing firms, firms can increase their profit by colluding and maximizing joint profit, as follows:

$$\max_{(q_1,q_2)} \pi = \max_{(q_1,q_2)} (\pi_1 + \pi_2) = \max_{(q_1,q_2)} \{[a - b(q_1+q_2)](q_1+q_2) - c(q_1+q_2) - 2\text{TFC}\}.$$

The FOCs are

$$\frac{\partial \pi}{\partial q_1} = \frac{\partial \pi}{\partial q_2} = a - b(q_1+q_2) - b(q_1+q_2) - c = 0.$$

Solving for $Q = q_1 + q_2$ gives

$$Q = (q_1+q_2) = (a-c)/2b.$$

Firms set total output equal to the monopoly solution and then determine how to divide this output among them. Alternative divisions of this total output yield the Pareto-optimal surface in Figure 15.5. At any point not on this optimal surface, one firm can be made better off without making the other firm worse off. On this optimal surface, one firm cannot be made better off without making the other firm worse off. For the firms to be on the optimal surface, their marginal profits $\partial\pi/\partial q_j$ must be equal. If they are not equal, then joint profit could be increased by shifting production toward the firm with higher marginal profit. This equality of marginal profit is illustrated in Figure 15.5 by the tangency of the isoprofit curves along the optimal surface. Given that the costs of the two firms are the same, one possible division would be for the total output to be divided evenly. This results in the symmetric joint maximization position (also illustrated in Figure 15.5)

$$q_1 = q_2 = \frac{a-c}{4b}.$$

How this maximum joint profit is distributed among the members of the collusion is not determined. If the producers have identical cost functions, it seems plausible for the profit to be evenly distributed. In contrast, if producers have different cost functions, they may divide up output based on equating their marginal costs to overall marginal revenue. This is similar to the discussion in Chapter 12 of a multi-plant firm determining the profit-maximizing output in each of its plants. However, a decision on how to allocate the resulting profit is still required. Ultimately, the allocation depends upon the bargaining power of the firms, which leads to the game theory discussed in Chapter 14.

Although collusion offers the highest joint profit for the firms, a firm can increase its individual profit if the other firm does not deviate from the agreed-upon output limits. This is called *cheating* and, as illustrated in Figure 15.5, each firm has a profit incentive to cheat. For example, suppose that the firms agree to evenly divide the total monopoly output. If firm 1 assumes that firm 2 will abide by this agreement, then firm 1 can increase its output and shift to lower isoprofit curves, yielding higher profit. Firm 2 has an equal incentive to cheat by also increasing output. Both firms now believe that the other firm's output decision is independent of theirs, which is the underlying assumption of the Cournot model. Thus, the collusion collapses (when firms increase their output) in a failed attempt to further increase their individual profit.

Bertrand model: Airlines

Cournot and Stackelberg models assume that firms determine their output and, based on the total output supplied, the market determines the price. However, in many markets, the reverse behavior is observed: firms determine their price and the market then determines quantity sold. Examples are commercial airlines in pricing tickets, hotels in setting room rates, and automobile firms in setting sticker prices for their vehicles. A model incorporating this pricing behavior is the **Bertrand model**, named after the French mathematician Joseph Bertrand (1822–1900), who proposed the model as an alternative to the Cournot model. Similar to the Cournot model, the Bertrand model assumes simultaneous instead of sequential decision making. For the Bertrand model, this results in a Nash-equilibrium set of prices for the firms.

Do firms really compete over price? Yes, for many industries, including new books, haircuts, and bar drinks, firms compete over the sales price.

> **Bertrand model.** An oligopoly model that assumes firms base their price decisions on zero conjectural variations on prices. *E.g., a travel agency setting a price for an Asian tour.*

Perfect oligopoly: construction firms

In the Bertrand model, assuming homogeneous products (perfect oligopoly), each firm has an incentive to undercut the price of its competitors and thus capture all the sales. A firm will undercut its competitors' prices as long as its price remains above marginal cost. If all firms have identical marginal costs, then any firm setting a price higher than marginal costs will be undercut by another firm offering a slightly lower price. Thus, the perfectly competitive solution that yields a Pareto-efficient allocation will exist with each firm setting price equal to marginal cost. With as few as two firms, this result is a consequence of the firms setting their bid price equal to marginal cost. The firms are in effect auctioning off their output in a first-bid common-value auction, which yields a Pareto-efficient allocation.

Note that this Bertrand-model Pareto-efficient solution for as few as two firms contrasts with the Cournot solution. Only when the number of firms approaches infinity will the Cournot model yield a Pareto-efficient solution. Thus, efficiency depends on how firms strategically interact. The Bertrand, Cournot, and Stackelberg models illustrate how equilibrium outcomes and efficiency in an oligopolistic industry depend on the type of strategic interaction engaged in by firms.

Imperfect oligopoly: hotels

The preceding Bertrand solution only holds for a perfect oligopoly. If consumers perceive differences among the products offered by firms, then product differentiation exists. Thus, an imperfect oligopoly market exists, with each firm having some monopoly power. With this monopoly power, a profit-maximizing firm will set price in excess of marginal cost and thus operate inefficiently.

Specifically, consider two firms each with constant marginal cost c. The demand for firm j's output is

$$q_j = q_j(p_1, p_2), \quad j = 1, 2,$$

where an increase in p_1 lowers quantity demanded of q_1 and raises q_2, with $\partial q_1/\partial p_1 < 0$ and $\partial q_2/\partial p_1 > 0$, whereas an increase in p_2 has the reverse effect, with $\partial q_1/\partial p_2 > 0$ and $\partial q_2/\partial p_2 < 0$. Each product is a gross substitute of the other. In the Bertrand model, each firm takes its competitor's price as given for maximizing profit:

$$\begin{aligned}\max_{p_j} \pi_j &= \max_{p_j} \left[p_j q_j(p_1, p_2) - c q_j(p_1, p_2) - \text{TFC}\right] \\ &= \max_{p_j} \left[(p_j - c) q_j(p_1, p_2) - \text{TFC}\right], \quad j = 1, 2,\end{aligned}$$

where c is constant marginal cost. Thus, in an imperfect-oligopolistic market characterized by product differentiation, equilibrium prices will be set above marginal cost, resulting in an inefficient allocation.

As an example, consider again two firms 1 and 2 and assume that each firm faces the following linear demand functions:

$$\begin{aligned}q_1 &= a - bp_1 + dp_2, \\ q_2 &= a - bp_2 + dp_1,\end{aligned}$$

where outputs q_1 and q_2 are substitutes (but not perfect substitutes), so some degree of product differentiation exists. In this Bertrand model, each firm attempts to maximize profit by choosing its own price, given that the price of its competitor does not change. For simplicity, assume firms have zero cost, so firm 1's profit-maximization problem reduces to maximizing total revenue:

$$\max_{p_1} \pi_1 = \max_{p_1} [p_1(a - bp_1 + dp_2)].$$

The FOC is then

$$\frac{\partial \pi}{\partial p_1} = a - 2bp_1 + dp_2 = 0.$$

Solving for p_1 results in firm 1's reaction function to a change in firm 2's price:

$$p_1 = \frac{a}{2b} + \frac{d}{2b} p_2.$$

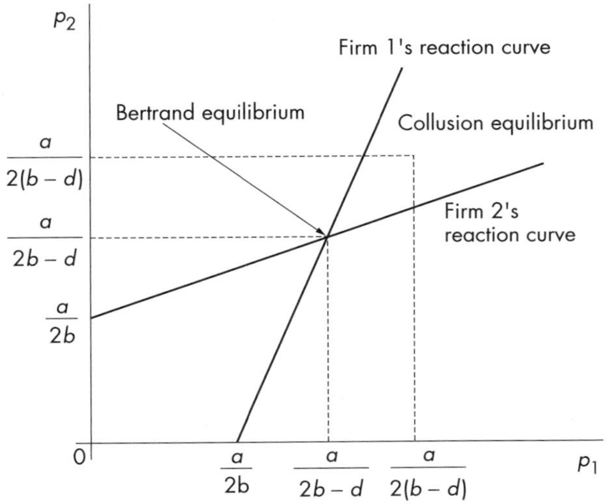

Figure 15.6 **Bertrand equilibrium.** The intersection of the firms' reaction curves determine the Bertrand equilibrium prices $p_1^* = p_2^* = a/(2b-d)$.

Similarly, maximizing profit for firm 2, holding firm 1's price constant, yields firm 2's reaction function:

$$p_2 = \frac{a}{2b} + \frac{d}{2b}p_1.$$

These reaction functions are illustrated in Figure 15.6, with the Bertrand equilibrium corresponding to where they intersect. Thus, the equilibrium prices are determined by solving simultaneously the two reaction functions. Setting the reaction functions in implicit form and equating yields

$$a - 2bp_1^* + dp_2^* = a - 2bp_2^* + dp_1^* = 0,$$
$$p_1^* = p_2^*.$$

Substituting the equality of prices into either of the firms' reaction functions and solving for price results in the equilibrium prices:

$$p_1^* = p_2^* = \frac{a}{2b-d} > \mathrm{AC} = \mathrm{MC} = c = 0.$$

The firms will maximize profits by setting price above marginal cost, and at $p_1^* = p_2^*$ an equilibrium is obtained.

Collusion: auction bidding rings

As with the Cournot model, firms can improve their Bertrand profits by colluding. Instead of setting their prices independently, they collude and jointly determine the same price.

Maximizing joint profit yields

$$\max_p \pi = \max_p(\pi_1 + \pi_2) = \max_p [2p(a - bp + dp)].$$

The FOC is then

$$\frac{d\pi}{dp} = 2a - 4bp^J + 4dp^J = 0,$$

so

$$p^J = \frac{a}{2(b-d)}.$$

This results in the firms jointly increasing their prices and associated profit.

As discussed in Chapter 14, repeatedly played games can be directly applied to firm behavior involving strategic interactions. For example, the Bertrand model in game theory yields the same results as the Prisoners' Dilemma game when it also is played repeatedly. The assumptions of the Bertrand model result in the impossibility of collusion over a finite time period. In contrast, over a horizon of infinitely repeated games, no final period exists, which prevents punishment in ensuing rounds. Thus, as in the Prisoners' Dilemma, cooperation can be the optimal strategy. As discussed in the Appendix to this chapter, this type of cooperation is termed tacit collusion. Firms behave as a cartel without ever developing a joint marketing strategy.

Example 15.5 Calculating a Bertrand equilibrium

Consider the following demand functions:

$$q_1 = a - bp_1 + dp_2,$$

$$q_2 = a - bp_2 + dp_1,$$

where $a = 18$, $b = 2$, and $d = 1$, with zero marginal costs. The Bertrand equilibrium prices are then

$$p_1^* = p_2^* = \frac{a}{2b - d} = \$6.$$

The equilibrium quantities are $q_1^* = q_2^* = 18 - 2(6) + 6 = 12$. Bertrand profits, assuming zero cost of production, are then $\pi_1^* = \pi_2^* = p_1^* q_1^* = p_2^* q_2^* = 6(12) = \$72.00$.

Maximizing joint profit, the price is

$$p_1^* = p_2^* = \frac{a}{2(b-d)} = \$9,$$

with each firm producing $q_1^J = q_2^J = 18 - 2(9) + 9 = 9$. Profits for the two colluding firms are then $\pi_1^J = \pi_2^J = 9(9) = \$81$.

A firm can increase its profit if it defects from this joint production and maximizes profit, given that the other firm maintains the joint price of \$9. If the defecting firm is firm 1, we have

$$\max \pi_1 = \max (p_1 q_1) \ \text{ s.t. } q_1 = 18 - 2p_1 + 9 = 27 - 2p_1.$$

Substituting the constraint into the objective function gives

$$\max_{p_1} \pi_1 = \max_{p_1} [p_1 (27 - 2p_1)] = \max_{p_1} \left(27p_1 - 2p_1^2\right).$$

The FOC is then

$$\partial \pi / \partial p_1 = 27 - 4p_1 = 0 \Rightarrow p_1^D = 27/4 = \$6.75,$$

where p_1^D is the optimal price for the defector. At this optimal price, $q_1^D = 18 - 2(6.75) + 9 = 13.50$ and $\pi_1^D = 6.75(13.50) = \$91.13$. Firm 2's output and profit associated with firm 1 defecting are $q_2 = 18 - 2(9) + 6.75 = 6.75$ and $\pi_2 = 9(6.75) = \$60.75$. This potential increase in profit from defecting provides an incentive to defect. However, if both firms defect, then a tâtonnement process will result in the Bertrand equilibrium of $p_1^* = p_2^* = \$6$ with $q_1^* = q_2^* = 12$ and a profit of \$72.00 each.

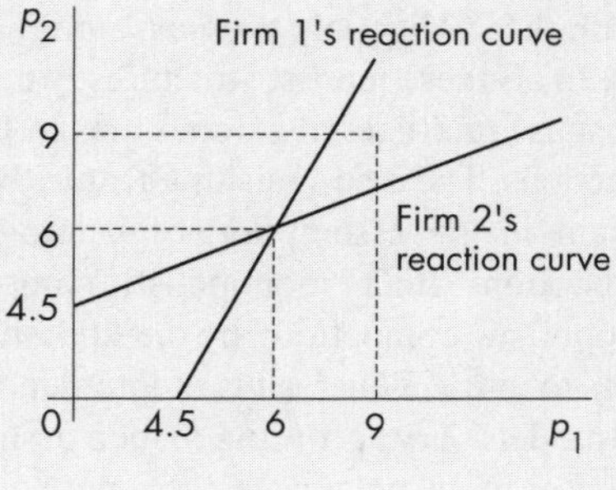

Example 15.6 Bertrand payoffs

In economics, one application of the Prisoners' Dilemma game is the Bertrand equilibrium. This application may be demonstrated by recalling Example 15.5, where the prices, outputs, and profits for the Bertrand firms operating independently, jointly, and also defecting are calculated. Using these profits as payoffs in a Prisoners' Dilemma game with strategies of defecting and collusion, the resulting payoff matrix is

		Firm 2	
		Defect	Collusion
Firm 1	Defect	(\$72, \$72)	(\$91.13, \$60.75)
	Collusion	(\$60.75, \$91.13)	(\$81, \$81)

Note: The payoffs are (firm 1, firm 2).

This results in the classic Prisoners' Dilemma game, where the dominant strategy for both firms is to defect. However, as discussed in Chapter 14 for firms (players) competing (playing) an infinite number of times, the possibility of retaliation exists. This may then result in firms colluding.

Generalized oligopoly models

Other combinations of assumptions exist concerning firms' actions, reactions, and conjectures about other firms' behavior. Furthermore, there are decision variables besides output and price, including advertising expenditures, market shares, and new-market penetration. In each case, an alternative model of firms' interaction would be required. The major difficulty with these models is determining the conjectural variations. There is no general agreement among economists that any existing oligopoly model is appropriate for analyzing firms' behavior in a specific industry. Thus, it is difficult to predict the equilibrium solution for a particular oligopolistic market. Economic models are generally weak in predicting the expected reactions of individual agents to market prices, output and input levels, shifts in demand and supply, technological change, and variations in tax rates. Thus, economists have developed models that do not focus on these reactions, and then measure the conjectural variation terms. As discussed in Chapter 14, one approach is to consider these interactions by employing game-theory models.

A summary of the characteristics associated with these oligopoly models, along with the other market structures, is provided in Table 15.1. In all these market structures, we assume transaction costs to be small or zero. When we discuss multilateral externalities in Chapter 21, we will relax this assumption of costless transactions. The distinguishing feature between perfect competition and monopolistic competition is the assumption of heterogeneous products—resulting in advertising and product promotion—under monopolistic competition. Oligopolistic markets are distinguished from monopolistic competition by their relative large size and small number as a consequence of barriers to entry. This results in interdependence among firms within oligopoly markets. Oligopoly models vary according to their assumption concerning how firms respond to this interdependence. In the polar case, the monopoly is the industry.

In reality, markets for differentiated products represent a continuum across these market structures. For applied research, an economist will investigate the characteristics of a particular market and select the appropriate market model with modifications to use for analysis.

Collusion in oligopoly markets: fair-trade pricing

I want either less corruption, or more chance to participate in it.

(Ashleigh Brilliant)

The idea of oligopoly firms engaged in collusive production or pricing agreements has always existed in economics. Generally, there is an incentive for the members of a collusive arrangement (called a **cartel**) to cheat. We can apply game theory to investigating the behavior of firms involved with collusive arrangements to better understand the consequences of various behaviors (strategies). For example, consider the payoff matrix in Table 15.2.

Table 15.1 Market structures

Characteristic	*Market*					
	Perfect competition	*Monopolistic competition*	*Oligopoly*			*Monopoly*
			Cournot	*Stackelberg*	*Bertrand*	
Number of firms	Many	Many	Few	Few	Few	One
Firm size	Small	Small	Large	Large	Large	Large
Product differentiation	No	High	Possible	Possible	Possible	Absolute
Demand elasticity	Perfectly elastic	Perceived elastic, effectively inelastic	Inelastic	Inelastic	Inelastic	Inelastic
Sales promotion	No	Yes	Yes	Yes	Yes	No
Barriers to entry	No	No	Yes	Yes	Yes	Yes
Perfect knowledge of output and price signals	Yes	No	No	No	No	Yes
Firm interdependence	No	Yes	Yes	Yes	Yes	No
Conjectural variations	Zero	Zero	Zero	Nonzero	Zero	—
Costless transactions	Yes	Yes	Yes	Yes	Yes	Yes
Profit condition	$p = \text{MC}$	MR = MC, perceived demand	MR = MC	MR = MC	MR = MC	MR = MC
Efficiency	Yes	No, but product differentiation	Yes, as number of firms increases	No	Yes, for homogeneous products	No

The establishment of a cartel by these two firms will yield a payoff of 10 for each firm. However, this is not a pure Nash-equilibrium outcome. Each member can cheat by defecting from the cartel and increase its payoff. For example, if firm 2 defects while firm 1 remains loyal, then firm 2's payoff increases to 15 and firm 1's payoff is reduced to 3. Thus, there is an incentive for both firms to cheat and defect, which results in a payoff of 5 for each firm. For this reason, it is generally thought that cartels are inherently unstable in the absence of some binding constraints on the participants. Economists have suggested that the purpose of many government regulatory agencies and minimum-price laws (such as "fair-trade" pricing) is to institutionalize cartels to prevent cheating. Yet, even without some binding constraints, the long-run viability of a cartel may be supported by the establishment of a firm's reputation for cooperation and encouraging other firms to also cooperate. With repeated opportunities for showing this cooperation through regular cartel meetings on price and output determination, a cooperative equilibrium may result.[2]

Table 15.2. Cartel

		Firm 2	
		Collusion	*Defect*
Firm 1	Collusion	(10, 10), cartel	(3, 15)
	Defect	(15, 3)	(5, 5)

Note: The payoffs are (firm 1, firm 2).

Cartel. A collusive agreement among agents. *E.g., two firms agreeing not to compete in each other's market.*

Application: OPEC cartel

As an example of the instability associated with cartels, consider the Organization of Petroleum Exporting Countries (OPEC) oil cartel established in September 1960 by five founding nations: Iran, Iraq, Kuwait, Saudi Arabia, and Venezuela. Eight other nations joined later: Qatar (1961), Indonesia (1962), Libya (1962), United Arab Emirates (1967), Algeria (1969), Nigeria (1971), Ecuador (1973), and Gabon (1973, associate member). OPEC's objective is to coordinate and unify petroleum policies among member countries in an effort to secure fair and stable prices for petroleum producers; to offer an efficient, economic, and regular supply of petroleum to consuming nations; and to ensure a fair return on capital to those investing in the industry.

The consequence of a group of firms (or countries in the case of OPEC) forming a cartel is illustrated in Figure 15.7. We initially assume the oil-producing countries are earning normal profits in a perfectly competitive market at price and output levels p_e and Q_e. This was generally the case for the oil-producing countries in the 1960s. In the early 1970s, OPEC member countries took control of their domestic petroleum industries and finally gained the monopoly power to influence world oil prices. This required an agreement on cutting back on the total amount of oil produced by the cartel members and resulted in the Arab oil embargo in 1973 (with crude oil prices increasing approximately 50 percent).

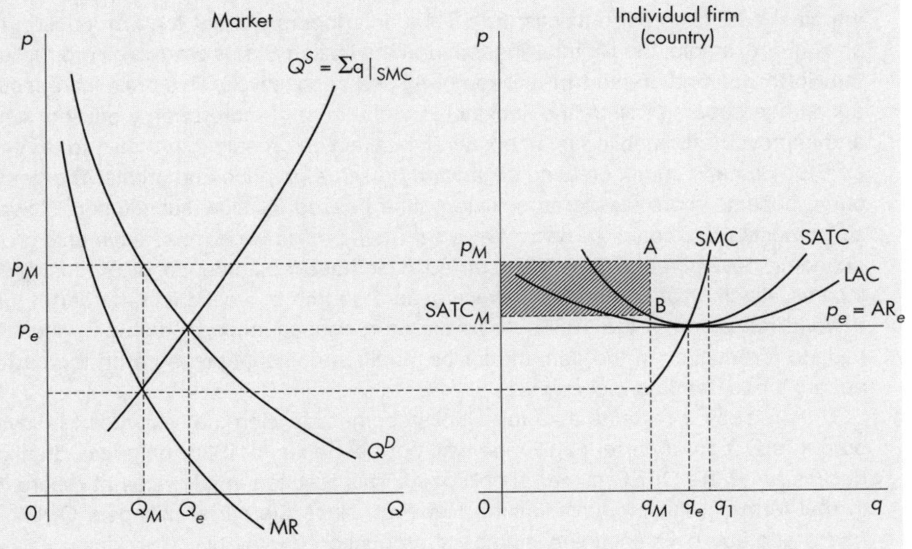

Figure 15.7 **OPEC countries and cartels.** The perfectly competitive market price and output are p_e and Q_e, with each country producing output q_e. Forming a cartel, market output is restricted to Q_M, with a rise in price to p_M. At an output of q_M, each country is earning a pure profit represented by the shaded area $(SATC_M)p_M$AB.

The maximum level of profit for the cartel would be the monopoly price and output level (p_M, Q_M). This increase in price results in increased profits for members of the cartel. However, an agreement on how much each country must cut back on production is required. One method is to have the cartel act like a multi-plant firm, where each plant in this case is a country. Thus, the cartel would equate short-run marginal cost for each country to overall marginal revenue:

$$MR = SMC_1 = SMC_2 = \ldots = SMC_n,$$

where n is the number of countries. This will result in maximum profit for the cartel, and then all that has to be determined is how to divide up this profit. As a result of member countries cutting back on production, oil prices peaked in the early 1980s. Instead of equating each country's marginal cost to marginal revenue, oil production was greatly curtailed by the Iranian revolution and the Iraq–Iran war.

An OPEC country is now earning a pure profit from oil production, represented by the shaded area $(SATC_M)p_M AB$ in Figure 15.7. Given this pure profit, the countries were interested in economic development projects such as roads, hospitals, new schools, and other industries. Thus, they use the revenue from oil production as a form of income to secure loans for these projects.

The increased price of oil in the 1970s and 1980s stimulated other countries (firms) to start supplying oil. **Interlopers**, who can supply oil but are not members of the cartel, will respond to the increase in price from p_e to p_M by setting price, p_M, equal to marginal cost for profit maximization. Thus, interlopers will set their production level at q_1. For example, the United Kingdom and the United States started oil production in the North Sea and on the North Slope of Alaska, respectively. This price increase also encouraged users of oil to find substitutes in the form of more energy-efficient homes and improved automobile fuel economy. These actions resulted in a shift to the left of OPEC's demand curve, creating downward pressure on price and profits. The demand curve became more elastic as sufficient time passed to allow substitution. However, since most OPEC countries have to maintain their profit level to make payments on their economic development loans, they started to increase the amount of oil production. The income elasticity of demand for oil was also a source of weakening the cartel, given a world recession in the 1980s—partially as a consequence of high oil prices. This caused a reduction in the demand for oil, putting additional pressure on the cartel to absorb these demand reductions.

Thus, unless a cartel is able to establish some provision that enforces the level of output reduction, a cartel equilibrium will not be stable. In 1986, oil prices drastically declined and the OPEC oil cartel collapsed. This resulted in oil prices at record lows in real terms (adjusting for inflation). However, since the cartel collapse, OPEC has had a strategy of maintaining members' production quotas by constraining capacity. With the world demand for oil continuing to rise, OPEC's limited capacity is resulting in rising oil prices. Though capacity constraints, OPEC is able to maintain high oil prices during strong world demand for oil. However, this is resulting in very volatile oil prices. During global economic expansion (say, in 2004–2008), the demand for oil increases and limited OPEC capacity prevents the cartel from increasing supply to satisfy this demand—leading to high oil prices. In contrast, during global economic contraction, OPEC members will not cut back on supply—leading to a fall in oil prices. During the Great Recession of 2008–2010, oil prices dropped significantly. With OPEC's current policy of using capacity as a vehicle for maintaining the cartel, volatility in oil prices is likely to continue unless alternative sources of energy are developed.

Interloper. A firm who markets the commodity but is not a member of the cartel. *E.g., a supplier of illegal drugs who is not a member of the street gang that controls the local drug market.*

Legal provisions: pollution standards

In some regions or industries, **antitrust** restrictions attempt to make cartels illegal, whereas in others, cartels are actively supported by governments. For example, within the United States, for certain industries, Section 1 of the Sherman Antitrust Act (1890) prohibits contracts, combinations, or conspiracies in restraint of trade. Section 2 of the act declares that it is unlawful for any person to monopolize, attempt to monopolize, or conspire to monopolize trade. Also, the Clayton Act (1914) prohibits price discrimination where this substantially lessens competition or creates a monopoly in any line of commerce. The Federal Trade Commission (FTC) Act (1914) supplements the Sherman and Clayton Acts and fosters competition by prohibiting unfair and anticompetitive practices such as deceptive advertising and labeling. Either the government or private agencies, including firms and households, can bring suit against a cartel. However, a number of US industries are not covered by these acts. For example, by the Capper–Volstead Act (1922), agriculture is not included under the antitrust acts. Also, Section 7 of the Taft–Hartley Act (1935) allows labor unions, which are a type of collusive activity, to form.[3] In terms of export markets, the Webb–Pomerene Act (1918) allows price fixing and other forms of collusion for exporting commodities.

Is collusion among firms allowed? Depending on the particular industry and type of collusion, it may be allowed for some firm's activities and not for others.

Antitrust. Prohibiting the establishment and operation of cartels. *E.g., the dissolution of Standard Oil in 1904.*

As an example of a legal provision that implicitly establishes a cartel, consider a law that imposes a standard limit on the level of pollution (or some other externality[4]) that a firm emits. If the level of pollution is directly related to the level of output, then the standard limits the total output of the industry, which results in firms earning short-run pure profits and often forces the industry into a cartel. As an example, consider the timber industry, where the externality is the destruction of forests. As we will discuss in Chapter 21, an alternative policy would be to tax firms according to their level of pollution. However, since taxing results in short-run losses for firms, firms have an incentive to lobby for pollution standards as opposed to taxes. This may be one reason the mechanism of standards is generally employed instead of taxes in the United States.

Summary

1. Product differentiation is in the eyes of the beholder, so it may be real or imaginary. Firms may differentiate their products by quality and style, guarantees and warranties, services provided, and location of sales.
2. Given the ability of product differentiation, firms have an incentive to undertake selling costs. Selling costs are marketing expenditures aimed at adopting the buyer to the product. For profit maximization, the marginal revenue derived from selling costs must equal the marginal cost. Similarly, the marginal revenue from product differentiation must equal the marginal cost for profit maximization.
3. The two major types of advertising are informational and persuasive. Informational advertising educates consumers about firms' products and prices. Persuasive advertising is when a firm attempts to modify consumers' preferences.

4. Monopolistic competition is a market structure characterized by a relatively large number of firms with each firm able to practice some form of product differentiation. In contrast, an oligopolistic market is characterized by the existence of a relatively small number of sellers with interdependence among sellers.
5. The Cournot model assumes that oligopolistic firms do not realize the interdependence of their decisions with their competitor's decisions. In contrast, the Stackelberg model assumes that one firm is a leader and takes the likely response of a competitor, the follower, into consideration.
6. The Cournot and Stackelberg models assume that firms determine their output, and, based on the total output supplied, the market determines the price. Alternatively, the Bertrand model assumes the reverse behavior, where firms determine their price and the market then determines quantity sold.
7. A major cartel influencing world oil prices is the OPEC cartel. This cartel is not backed by any legal provisions, so it has a history of instability in its efforts to boost the price of crude oil.
8. *(Appendix)* Product differentiation in terms of location is called spatial differentiation. Even if the products are identical, a firm's location can differentiate its product from its competitors.
9. *(Appendix)* The necessary and sufficient conditions for the perfectly competitive equilibrium location for two firms are when the two firms locate at the same place and have no incentive to change locations.
10. *(Appendix)* Within the United States, certain industries are prohibited from colluding, and treble damages may be assessed for illegal pricing practices. However, assessing these damages may not yield the efficiency results that the US Department of Justice enforcing the antitrust acts would yield.
11. *(Appendix)* When firms are unable to explicitly collude, they may attempt tacit collusion. For example, they may offer the same price for their commodities. This common price may then be altered by a price leader without any formal explicit, colluding mechanism.

Key concepts

antitrust, 640
Bertrand model, 631
cartel, 636
cheating, 631
combative advertising, 644
conjectural variations, 618
Cournot model, 619
dominant firm, 657
duopoly, 616
information differentiation, 606
interloper, 640
isoprofit curve, 622
monopolistic competition, 610
oligopolistic market, 616
price leadership, 656
price war, 654
product differentiation, 604
reaction function, 621
selling cost, 606
spatial differentiation, 646
Stackelberg model, 625
Sweezy's kinked demand, 654
tacit collusion, 653
treble damage, 651

Key equations

$$\frac{\partial \text{TR}}{\partial q} - \frac{\partial \text{STC}}{\partial q} = 0$$

The optimal level of output is determined by setting marginal revenue equal to marginal cost of output.

$$\frac{\partial \text{TR}}{\partial \mathcal{D}} - \frac{\partial \text{STC}}{\partial \mathcal{D}} = 0$$

The optimal level of product differentiation is determined by setting marginal revenue equal to marginal cost of product differentiation.

$$\frac{\partial \text{TR}}{\partial A} - \frac{\partial \text{STC}}{\partial A} = 0$$

The optimal level of advertising is determined by setting marginal revenue equal to marginal cost of advertising.

$$\text{MR} = \text{SMC}_1 = \text{SMC}_2 = \ldots = \text{SMC}_n$$

A cartel with n firms (countries) will maximize the cartel's profits by equating MR to each of the member's short-run marginal cost.

Questions

1. Product demand observed by a perfect competitor and demand as viewed by a firm with monopoly power are quite different. Thus, product differentiation is out of the question for one and may be essential for the other. True or false? Explain.
2. Automobile companies will advertise cash rebates for purchasing a certain make or model of a car. Why don't they just lower the price of the car?
3. The level of advertising a firm engages in is likely to vary inversely with the real differences in its product. Why?
4. Service stations under the same company in a city cannot be considered to be monopolistically competitive, because each only supplies a small part of the total gasoline market and all sell the same product. True or false? Explain.
5. Monopolistic competition leads to waste through the unnecessary proliferation of real or imagined differences among varieties of a commodity. True or false? Explain.
6. In terms of monopolistic competition, why are there gas stations dotting the highways and consumers stating that all these stations are not required?
7. In the monopolistic-competition model, each firm behaves as a Cournot firm toward other firms but as a Stackelberg firm toward consumers. True or false? Explain.

8. My father, Eugene, grew up on an Iowa farm during the Great Depression and remembers having to kill baby pigs. Waste of this kind is inconsistent with profit-maximizing behavior. Do you agree or disagree with this statement? Explain.
9. Why has the OPEC oil cartel succeeded in raising prices substantially, while the following cartels have not?

   Intergovernmental Council of Nations Exporting Copper (CIPEC), a copper cartel
   International Bauxite Association (IBA), a bauxite cartel
   International Coffee Organization, a coffee cartel
   Union of Nations Exporting Bananas (UPEB), a banana cartel

10. Some economists argue that regulation can actually create cartels instead of controlling them. A group of competitors can act as a monopoly by becoming regulated and using the regulatory process to increase producer surplus. Why might a firm prefer regulation versus competition?

Exercises

Many of life's failures are people who did not realize how close they were to success when they gave up.

(Thomas Edison)

1. Assume that a firm with monopoly power has a demand function where quantity demanded depends not only on the market price p, but also on the firm's level of advertising A. Let the inverse demand function be

   $$p = 53 - 2Q + 2A^{1/2}.$$

   The firm's short-run total cost function is

   $$\text{STC} = 2Q^2 + 5Q + A + 10.$$

   a. First, assume that the firm does not engage in any advertising, so $A = 0$. What will be the output and corresponding price for a profit-maximizing firm? What will be the firm's profit?
   b. Rework (a), this time assuming that the firm determines both its profit-maximizing output and level of advertising.
2. Advertising by two firms might cancel each other's effect on demand. If this is the case, then advertising increases costs without any effect on sales, so the level of profit for both firms falls (this is called combative advertising). Show how a Prisoners' Dilemma might arise among firms making decisions on combative advertising. Indicate how profits may be enhanced if advertising in the industry

were completely banned. How does this result apply to the current restriction on cigarette advertising?

3. Suppose two duopolists produce differentiated commodities with zero cost. In equilibrium, the prices each obtain depend on the output quantities of each commodity, given the following inverse demand functions:

$$p_1 = 10 - q_1 - \tfrac{1}{2}q_2,$$

$$p_2 = 10 - q_2 - \tfrac{1}{2}q_1.$$

   Provide the Cournot, Stackelberg, and Bertrand equilibriums.

4. Two firms in a market produce identical products at a cost $\text{STC}(q_j) = \frac{1}{2}q_j^2 + \frac{1}{16}$, $j = 1$ and 2. The firms are facing the inverse market demand function $p = 1 - (q_1 + q_2)$. Compute the Cournot equilibrium.

5. Duopolist 1 is producing a differentiated product and facing the inverse demand function

$$p_1 = 200 - 4q_1 - 2q_2,$$

   with a cost function $\text{STC} = 5q_1^2 + 500$. Duopolist 2's objective is to maintain a constant one-third market share. Determine the optimal price and output for duopolist 1 and its level of profit. What is the output level for duopolist 2?

6. Consider a duopoly with product differentiation in which the demand and cost functions are

$$q_1 = 15 - 2p_1 + p_2, \quad \text{STC}_1 = 5q_1 + 10,$$

$$q_2 = 16 + p_1 - 2p_2, \quad \text{STC}_2 = 2q_2 + 5.$$

   Determine the Bertrand equilibrium.

7. Consider two Bertrand firms each with constant marginal and average cost. Let $\text{MC}_1 = 5.1$ be firm 1's marginal cost and $\text{MC}_2 = 3$ be firm 2's marginal cost. The two firms are facing the same market demand for their output,

$$Q = 100 - 5p,$$

   where $Q = q_1 + q_2$, with price changing in 0.1 intervals.

   a. Determine the equilibrium market price, outputs, and profits for each firm.
   b. Is this equilibrium market price Pareto-efficient?

8. Firms 1 and 2 are facing the market inverse demand curve $p = 1 - q_1 - q_2$, with zero costs. Each believes that whatever price it sets will be matched exactly by the other firm, resulting in each firm receiving a one-half share of the market. What are the market equilibrium output and price and how does this equilibrium compare with a monopoly (collusive) equilibrium?

9. The world's supply of kryptonite is controlled by 10 firms, each having 10,000 grams of this potent mineral. The market demand for kryptonite is

$$Q^D = 5000 - 1000p,$$

where p is the price per gram.

a. If all firms could collude and set the price of kryptonite, what price would they set and how much of their supply would they sell?
b. Why is the price computed in (a) an unstable equilibrium?

10. Suppose that a number of firms are facing the same short-run total cost function

$$\text{STC}_j = 1 + q_j + q_j^2$$

and that the inverse market demand is $p = 6 - \frac{1}{5}Q$.

a. Assuming that the firms are all earning normal profits, what is the competitive-equilibrium market price, quantity, and number of firms, n?
b. Assume that these n firms collude and establish a cartel. Determine the market price and quantity, and the amount each firm produces. What is each firm's profit?
c. What would be an interloper's output and profit, given that it could sell any output level at the cartel price?

Internet case studies

1. Write a case study on a particular government antitrust action against a firm. Why was the firm investigated for antitrust violations? Under what sections of the antitrust legislation was the firm in possible violation? What was the final resolution of the governmental actions?
2. Document the actions of a particular cartel. How and when did the firms organize and what were their objectives? How effective was the cartel in meeting these objectives? What was the consequence on markets as a result of the cartel?
3. On a time line, document the history of OPEC and the associate price of crude oil.

APPENDIX TO CHAPTER 15

Spatial differentiation: gas stations

A major form of product differentiation is product location, called **spatial differentiation**. Even if the products are identical, a firm's location can differentiate its product from its competitors, and the firm may then be able to charge a higher price and enhance its profit. In this case, the three ingredients for business success are location, location, location.

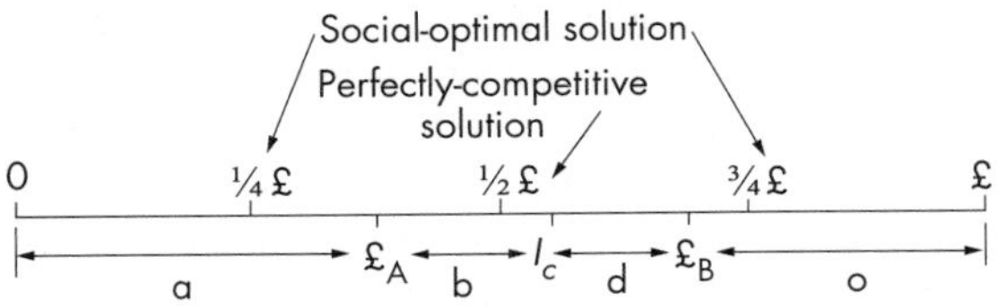

Figure 15A.1 **Product differentiation by location (spatial).** For a linear city of length £, the perfectly competitive solution is for the two firms to locate at the midpoint (city center). In contrast, the socially optimal solution is for the two firms to locate one-fourth of the way at either end of the city, 1/4£, 3/4£.

As an example, consider a linear city with one main street of length £. Along this street, consumers are uniformly distributed with a density of 1, and each consumer purchases 1 unit of output. Each consumer's transportation cost is c per unit of length from a store. Two stores selling the identical commodity, at zero cost, locate at distances $£_A$ and $£_B$ along the street (Figure 15A.1). Let p_A denote the per-unit price for the store located at $£_A$ and p_B the per-unit price for the store located at distance $£_B$. A consumer located at distance I_c will incur a total cost of purchasing the commodity at store $£_A$ of $p_A + c(I_c - £_A)$, where $c(I_c - £_A)$ is the total transportation cost, and a cost of purchasing at store $£_B$ of $p_B + c(£_B - I_c)$. Assuming that at distance I_c, these total costs are the same, so that this consumer is indifferent regarding which store to choose, then

$$p_A + c(I_c - £_A) = p_B + c(£_B - I_c).$$

Solving for I_c yields

$$I_c - £_A = \frac{p_B - p_A}{c} + £_B - I_c,$$

$$I_c = \frac{p_B - p_A}{2c} + \frac{£_A + £_B}{2}.$$

As this point of indifference shifts toward $£_A$, p_A increases, resulting in a smaller market for store $£_A$. As I_c shifts toward $£_B$, p_B increases, resulting in a smaller market for store $£_B$. Also, if $£_A = £_B$, the stores are located directly across the street from each other. This implies no product differentiation, so the commodities in the two stores are perfect substitutes. The point of consumer indifference, I_c, coincides with the stores' location, so $£_A = £_B = I_c$. Thus, $p_A = p_B$. This condition of $£_A = £_B$ is a necessary condition for a perfectly competitive solution.

Perfectly competitive location

Fast-food franchises will generally all locate at the same point within a town or on a highway (fast-food oasis). Similarly, gas stations will tend to be bundled together at one exit rather than be dispersed along a lonely interstate. (There always appear to be a lot of gas stations except when you are low on gas.) This phenomenon is a result of perfectly competitive equilibrium. The necessary and sufficient conditions for the perfectly competitive equilibrium are when the two stores locate at the same location, $£_A = £_B$, and have no incentive to change locations.

For example, say $£_A = 1/4£$; then, if $£_B$ is just to the right of $£_A$, store $£_B$ will capture $3/4£$ of the market and store $£_A$ will only capture $1/4£$ of the market. However, the store $£_A$ will realize this potential gain by the other store and shift its planned location further down the street. Store $£_B$ will then do the same, and this leapfrogging will continue until there is no gain from doing so. This occurs where both stores locate at the city center, $1/2£$. Now with both at the city center, if one store shifts to the right or left, its market share will decline. Locating at the city center is the perfectly competitive equilibrium.

Why do different fast food restaurants always seem to locate in the same vicinity? All firms, in an effort to maximize profit, will locate in an area with the highest market demand. This will result in the firms locating in the same area.

In contrast, if the stores locate at the opposite ends of the street, maximal product differentiation exists. This corresponds to $£_A = 0$, $£_B = £$, and I_c will be at the city center, $I_c = 1/2£$, if $p_A = p_B$.

Determining the profit-maximizing price

We determine the profit-maximizing price for store $£_A$ by

$$\begin{aligned}\max_{p_A} \pi_A &= \max_{p_A} [p_A(£_A + I_c - £_A)] = \max_{p_A} [p_A I_c] \\ &= \max_{p_A} \left[p_A\left(\frac{p_B - p_A}{2c} + \frac{£_A + £_B}{2}\right)\right].\end{aligned}$$

and that for store $£_B$ by

$$\begin{aligned}\max_{p_B} \pi_B &= \max_{p_B} [p_B(£ - £_B + £_B - I_c)] = \max_{p_B} [p_B(£ - I_c)] \\ &= \max_{p_B} \left[p_B\left(£ - \frac{p_B - p_A}{2c} - \frac{£_A + £_B}{2}\right)\right].\end{aligned}$$

The FOCs are then

$$\begin{aligned}\frac{\partial \pi}{\partial p_A} &= \frac{p_B^* - 2p_A^*}{2c} + \frac{£_A + £_B}{2} = 0, \\ \frac{\partial \pi}{\partial p_B} &= £ - \frac{2p_B^* - p_A^*}{2c} - \frac{£_A + £_B}{2} = 0.\end{aligned}$$

We determine the profit-maximizing prices p_A^* and p_B^* by solving these two FOCs for p_A^* and p_B^*. From the first FOC, we have

$$\frac{p_B^*}{2c} = \frac{p_A^*}{c} - \frac{£_A + £_B}{2}.$$

Substituting into the second FOC gives

$$£ - \frac{2p_A^*}{c} + £_A + £_B + \frac{p_A^*}{2c} - \frac{£_A + £_B}{2} = 0.$$

Solving for p_A^* yields

$$£ - \frac{3p_A^*}{2c} + \frac{£_A + £_B}{2} = 0,$$

$$p_A^* = \tfrac{c}{3}(£_A + £_B + 2£).$$

By substituting p_A^* into one of the FOCs (say, the first FOC), we can determine the profit-maximizing price for store $£_B$

$$\frac{\partial \pi}{\partial p_A} = \frac{p_B^* - 2p_A^*}{2c} + \frac{£_A + £_B}{2} = 0,$$

$$p_B^* = 2p_A^* - (£_A + £_B)c,$$

$$p_B^* = \frac{2c}{3}(£_A + £_B + 2£) - (£_A + £_B)c,$$

$$p_B^* = \frac{c}{3}[4£ - (£_A + £_B)],$$

As indicated by these price functions,

$$p_A^* = \frac{c}{3}(£_A + £_B + 2£),$$

$$p_B^* = \frac{c}{3}[4£ - (£_A + £_B)],$$

the prices for the two stores will be the same only when each store receives one-half of the market, $\frac{1}{2}£$. This will occur if both stores locate at the city center, $\frac{1}{2}£$; if they locate at opposite ends of the street (e.g., $£_A = 0$ and $£_B = £$); or if they locate one-fourth and three-fourths of the way up the street (e.g., $£_A = \frac{1}{4}£$ and $£_B = \frac{3}{4}£$).

As illustrated in Figure 15A.1, stores locating at $\frac{1}{4}£$ and $\frac{3}{4}£$ result in no consumers having to travel more than one-fourth of the street length to purchase a commodity. This is the socially optimal location for the stores, where the total travel cost TC for the consumers is minimized. Specifically,

$$\min_{(a,b,d,o)} \text{TC} = \min_{(a,b,d,o)} \left(\int_0^a cdc + \int_0^b cdc + \int_0^d cdc + \int_0^o cdc \right)$$

$$= \min_{(a,b,d,o)} \left(\frac{a^2 + b^2 + d^2 + o^2}{2} \right) \quad \text{s.t. } a + b + d + o = £.$$

The Lagrangian is then

$$\mathcal{L}(a, b, d, o, \lambda) = \frac{a^2 + b^2 + d^2 + o^2}{2} + \lambda(£ - a - b - d - o).$$

The FOCs are

$$\partial\mathcal{L}/\partial a = a^* - \lambda^* = 0,$$

$$\partial\mathcal{L}/\partial b = b^* - \lambda^* = 0,$$

$$\partial\mathcal{L}/\partial d = d^* - \lambda^* = 0,$$

$$\partial\mathcal{L}/\partial o = o^* - \lambda^* = 0,$$

$$\partial\mathcal{L}/\partial\lambda = \pounds - a^* - b^* - d^* - o^* = 0.$$

From these FOCs, $a^* = b^* = d^* = o^* = \lambda^*$, and, given the last FOC,

$$\pounds - 4\lambda^* = 0 \Rightarrow \lambda^* = {}^1\!/_4\pounds = a^* = b^* = d^* = o^*.$$

Thus, the social optimal solution is to locate the stores at distances $^1/_4\pounds$ and $^3/_4\pounds$. However, recall that the perfectly competitive equilibrium is for both stores to locate at the city center, $^1/_2\pounds$. (Society would prefer having gas stations dispersed along a highway rather than all bundled together at one exit.) This deviation in perfect competition and the socially optimal solution is one justification for government intervention, such as zoning laws, to correct market failure.

Example 15A.1 Product differentiation by location (spatial)

If we let each consumer's transportation cost per unit of length be $c = 1$ and the total length of the main street be $\pounds = 1$, then the optimal price functions derived from the two stores' profit-maximizing conditions are

$$p_A^* = \tfrac{1}{3}(\pounds_B + \pounds_A + 2),$$

$$p_B^* = \tfrac{1}{3}[4 - (\pounds_B + \pounds_A)].$$

Different locations of the two stores will result in the following pricing and profits for the stores:

0	⅛	¼	⅜	½	¾	1	p_A	p_B	π_A	π_B
$\pounds_A$				l_c		$\pounds_B$	1	1	0.50	0.50
				$\pounds_A, \pounds_B$			1	1	0.50	0.50
		$\pounds_A$		l_c	$\pounds_B$		1	1	0.50	0.50
$\pounds_A$	l_c	$\pounds_B$					0.75	1.25	0.09	1.09
		$\pounds_A$	l_c	$\pounds_B$			0.92	1.08	0.34	0.68
$\pounds_A, \pounds_B$							–	1.33	0	1.33

The polar ($\pounds_A = 0$, $\pounds_B = \pounds$), perfectly competitive, and socially optimal solutions all result in the same prices and profits for the two stores. However, the polar and socially optimal solutions are unstable, assuming the firms have not yet determined their store locations. The only equilibrium solution is the perfectly competitive solution, where both stores locate at the city center, $^1/_2$£. However, given established fixed locations, prices and profit will vary depending on the spatial differentiation of the stores. With one store located at the end of the street, $£_A = 0$, and the other store located at $£_B = {}^1/_4$, the store at $£_B$ has a location advantage. Its commodity is differentiated from $£_A$ in terms of lower transportation costs for 7/8 of the consumers. Thus, store $£_B$ can charge a high price, and short-run pure profit is above the profit of store $£_A$. This advantage in location is also apparent at $£_A = {}^1/_4$ and $£_B = {}^1/_2$. Here, the store at $£_A$ has increased its profit by shifting from $£_A = 0$ to $£_A = {}^1/_4$ and the store at $£_B$ has experienced a loss in profit. A monopoly position for the store at $£_B$ is $£_A = 0$ and $£_B$ approaches zero. Given $£_A = 0$, as $£_B$ approaches zero, the store at $£_B$ will capture the whole market and maximize its profit.

Application: Is zoning "creeping socialism?"

Socialism is defined as government ownership of the means of production. With the exception of natural monopolies, such as municipal sewers and water, socialism within the United States is not widespread. Instead, governments have relied on regulation to correct market inefficiencies. If this regulation is socialism, then zoning (or more generally urban planning) represents creeping socialism since the 1920s. As addressed by R. O'Toole, urban planning has recently accelerated and is now running rather than creeping. He concludes that zoning laws have become increasingly restrictive over the years and that they are a threat to freedom of choice, private property rights, mobility, and local governance.

But how does urban planning in general and zoning in particular affect urban growth? D. da Mata et al. have developed a model to explain urban growth. Their results indicate that increases in rural population, improvements in interregional transportation, and education level of the labor force have strong positive impacts on urban growth. In contrast, crime and violence impinge negatively on growth. In terms of zoning laws, urban areas with more restrictive zoning laws have higher growth rates. Their results indicate that correcting market inefficiencies will improve efficiency and thus social welfare.

Sources: R. O'Toole, "Is Urban Planning 'Creeping Socialism?'" *Independent Review* 4 (2000): 501–516; D. da Mata, U. Deichmann, J.V. Henderson, S.V Lall, and H.G Wang, "Determinants of City Growth in Brazil," The World Bank, Policy Research Working Paper Series, 3723 (2005).

Treble-damage model

Both the Sherman and Clayton antitrust acts allow private lawsuits by households and firms to collect up to three times the damages (**treble damage**) they sustained from illegal price setting. Such private antitrust lawsuits represent a very large percentage of antitrust cases. Annually, since the 1960s, private antitrust cases have represented over 90 percent of all antitrust cases. A large portion of interfirm legal disputes have been private antitrust suits. The incentive of collecting treble damages induces agents (firms and households) to reveal any illegal pricing practices by other agents and provides the government with an army of private watchdogs over antitrust activities.

S. Salant developed a model of cartel pricing behavior facing treble damages if detected.[5] Assume that a group of firms form a cartel with STC(Q), and face an inverse market demand function $p(Q)$. The cartel's profit-maximizing price with no threat of an antitrust lawsuit is determined by

$$\max_{Q} \pi = \max_{Q} [p(Q)Q - \text{STC}(Q)].$$

The FOC is then

$$\text{MR}_M = \text{SMC}_M.$$

This results in the cartel's monopoly power price p_M and output Q_M. The cartel operates inefficiently by restricting output and increasing price compared with the perfectly competitive solution.

When the cartel price is illegally set equal to the monopoly price, agents (other firms and households) affected by this illegal price may take legal action. Let the probability of the agents' winning the suit be ρ, with an award of $s_w[p_M Q_M - \text{STC}(Q_M)]$. If the damaged parties are awarded the full amount under the law, then $s_w = 300$ percent, so $0 < s_w \leq 300$ percent, where s_w is the percentage of pure profit awarded.

Accounting for these potential damages, the cartel's profit-maximization problem is then

$$\begin{aligned} \max_{Q} \pi &= \max_{Q} \{p(Q)Q - \text{STC}(Q) - \rho s_w[p(Q)Q - \text{STC}(Q)]\} \\ &= \max_{Q} \{(1 - \rho s_w)[p(Q)Q - \text{STC}(Q)]\}. \end{aligned}$$

The expected percentage of profit awarded, ρs_w, is equivalent to a profit tax t, $\rho s_w = t$. Analogous to a profit tax, the award does not address the problem of resource misallocation; the inefficient level of output and price still exists. Thus, private antitrust lawsuits may not yield the same efficiency results as would occur if the US Department of Justice enforced the antitrust acts. The Justice Department's antitrust actions may prevent the firms from jointly exercising monopoly power. This result assumes that the cartel's profit, after paying the award for damages, is still positive, and thus above the zero-profit perfectly competitive solution. If $\rho s_w > 1$, then profits are negative and there is no incentive for the firms to establish a cartel. The increased probability of paying large fines for illegal collusive activities resulting from private litigation will deter such inefficient activities. Thus, private antitrust litigation is an important component of antitrust enforcement.

Example 15A.2 Private antitrust litigation

Consider a group of firms who form a cartel with a constant marginal cost of \$5 and facing the market demand function

$$Q(p) = 15 - p.$$

With no possibility of antitrust litigation, the cartel's profit-maximizing price and output are determined by

$$\max_Q \pi = \max_Q [(15 - Q)Q - 5Q - \text{TFC}].$$

The FOC is then

$$\partial \pi / \partial Q = 15 - 2Q_M - 5 = 0.$$

Solving for Q_M yields the monopoly quantity $Q_M = 5$, with corresponding price $p_M = 10$. The monopoly profit is then \$25.00 – TFC, yielding a producer surplus of \$25.00.

The potential of private antitrust litigation will reduce this cartel's profit. The degree of profit reduction depends on the magnitude of the probability of being fined and the amount of the fine. The cartel's problem is then

$$\max_Q \pi = \max_Q \{(1 - \rho s_W)[(15 - Q)Q - 5Q - \text{TFC}]\}.$$

This results in the same optimal price and output of $p_M = 10$ and $Q_M = 5$, under the assumption of no potential for litigation. The resulting producer surplus will be determined by the magnitude of ρs_W.

	Cartel's producer surplus			
Award percent of profit	Probability of a fine, ρ			
	0	1/5	1/10	1/25
0%	25	25	25	25
100%	25	20	22.5	24
200%	25	15	20	23
300%	25	10	17.5	22

Tacit collusion: beat any price

When firms are unable to explicitly collude but realize that strategic interactions exist, they may attempt to collude covertly. This is called **tacit collusion,** where firms implicitly collude by developing a joint marketing strategy. For example, a store advertising that it will beat

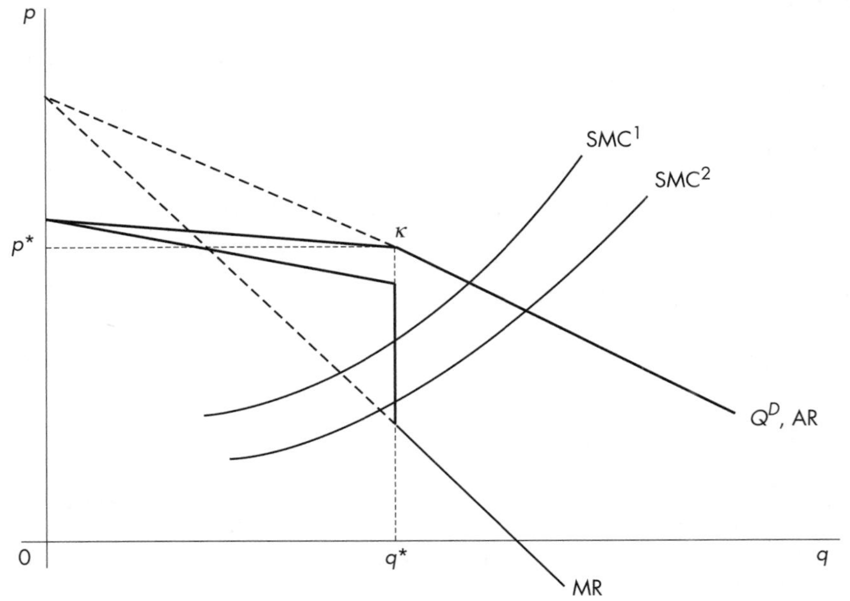

Figure 15A.2 **Sweezy's kinked demand curve.** Alternative levels of marginal cost will result in the same price and associated output (p^*, q^*).

any price offered by a competitor is sending a market signal to its competitors: either match my price or you may suffer a large loss in sales. Enforcing this policy requires information on competitors' prices. Customers provide this information by reporting (spying on) cheating competitors who offer lower prices. Thus, stores will tend to offer the same items at the same price and compete instead on other grounds such as service, availability, and advertising.

This type of firm behavior was modeled in 1939 by P.W. Sweezy (1910–2004) and called *Sweezy's kinked demand curve*.[6] As indicated in Figure 15A.2, different levels of costs do not result in market price variations. The optimal price and quantity (p^*, q^*) are the same for the two different levels of SMC: SMC^1 and SMC^2. This results from a kink in the demand curve at point κ (κ for kinked). At the kink, the demand curve (AR curve) is not smooth, implying that the slope at κ is not unique. The kink in AR corresponds to a kink in TR (recall that TR is AR times q) and thus the slope of TR, MR, is not unique at κ. This results in the range of values for MR at κ.

What is the real reason firms advertise that they will match any of their competitors' prices? This is a form of tacit collusion used to maintain or increase industry profits.

Sweezy's kinked demand curve illustrates how firms' behavior results in firms offering the same price for their output. The firms' managers believe that if they decrease their price, other firms will follow. Firms are concerned that reducing price may cause a **price war**, where all firms attempt to undercut their competitors' prices, resulting in a major decline in price. Such price wars occur at times with gasoline service stations located at adjacent corners of a highway intersection. Thus, firms' believe that their demand curves are relatively inelastic for price decreases. In other words, a price decrease will not increase sales volume sufficiently to increase profits, because other firms will follow. However, owners also believe that if they increase the price, other firms will not increase their prices and their volume of sales will fall off, resulting in decreased profits. Thus, firms do not react to changes in the cost of production. For example, in Figure 15A.2, SMC^1 and SMC^2 result in the same level of output q^* and price p^*.

In terms of the price conjectural variations, Sweezy's kinked demand curves imply

$$dp_2/dp_1 = 0 \quad \text{if } dp_1 \text{ is positive (firm 1 increases price),}$$

$$dp_2/dp_1 = 1 \quad \text{if } dp_1 \text{ is negative (firm 1 decreases price),}$$

where dp_2/dp_1 is firm 1's conjecture about the rate of change in firm 2's price with respect to changes in firm 1's price.

Note that Sweezy's kinked demand curve is not a true equilibrium model, because it does not determine both price and output. It only states that if the output is at some level, then there is a kink in the demand at that point. The model does not determine where the kink will be. Furthermore, the model does not provide any conditions for how the price will change. However, as illustrated for two firms in Table 15A.1, a price increase by all firms can increase all firms' profits. Firms maintaining the same marketing strategy of beating any competitor's price exclude the possibility of price differences among them. A Nash equilibrium then results in both firms increasing price.

Table 15A.1. Tacit collusion

		Firm 2	
		Price decrease	*Price increase*
Firm 1	Price decrease	(−2, −2)	(5, −6)
	Price increase	(−6, 5)	(2, 2)

Note: The payoffs are (firm 1, firm 2).

Example 15A.3 Deriving Sweezy's kinked demand curve

Consider a firm facing the following demand relation:

$$q = 20 - 4p \quad \text{for } 0 \leq q \leq 4,$$

$$q = 12 - 2p \quad \text{for } 4 \leq q \leq 12.$$

This demand relation is associated with a kinked demand curve, where the kink κ occurs at $q = 4$ and $p = 4$. The elasticity of demand at the kink varies depending on whether the price change is positive or negative. For a positive change (a price increase), the elasticity of demand is

$$\varepsilon^D = \frac{dq}{dp}\frac{p}{q} = -4(4/4) = -4.$$

The elasticity of demand for a negative price change (declining price) is

$$\varepsilon^D = -2(4/4) = -2.$$

Note that demand is elastic regardless of the direction the price change takes. However, it is more elastic for a price increase. Marginal revenue associated with the demand relation is

$$\text{MR} = -\tfrac{1}{2}q + 5 \quad \text{for } 0 \le q \le 4,$$

$$\text{MR} = -q + 6 \quad \text{for } 4 \le q \le 12.$$

At $q = 4$, MR $= 3$ for the function where $0 \le q \le 4$ and MR $= 2$ for the function where $4 \le q \le 12$. Assuming a constant SMC, SMC can range from 2 to 3 without any change in the equilibrium output or price.

An increase in price from \$4 to \$4.50 will result in a decrease in q of 2. At $p = 4.50$, $q = 20 - 4(4.50) = 2$, so $2 - 4 = -2$. TR at $p = 4$ and $q = 4$ is \$16 and at $p = 4.50$ and $q = 2$, it is \$9. This results in a TR loss of \$7. Assuming SMC $= 2$, STC will decline by \$4, given a drop in output of 2. This results in a net loss of \$3 if the firm raises its price. Similarly, a decrease in price from \$4 to \$3.50 results in an increase in q of 1. At $p = 3.50$, $q = 12 - 2(3.50) = 5$, and $5 - 4 = 1$. The change in TR is $(3.50)5 - 16 = \$1.50$. Given a decrease in price, TR is enhanced if elasticity is elastic. However, STC increases by \$2, resulting in a net loss of \$0.50. Thus, firms will not vary their prices.

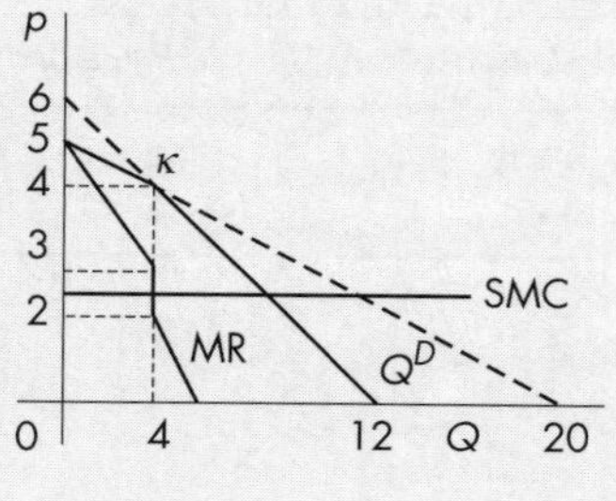

Price leadership: New York City banks

For tacit collusion, some type of implied signaling arrangement is required for a simultaneous increase in price. Price leadership provides such a mechanism. In a **price leadership** market, one firm (or a group of firms) is considered the leader in pricing, and all other firms will adjust prices when the leader does. The price leader signals to firms when the right time for increasing prices has arrived. Examples of price leadership firms are the big-box retailers (KMart, Target, and Walmart) and the New York City banks in the commercial banking industry.

As an example, consider a market composed of a single price leader along with a number of other firms (followers), who match their prices to the price set by this price leader (Figure 15A.3). The demand curve Q^D represents the total market demand facing all the firms (the price leader plus the followers), and the supply curve Q_F^S represents the horizontal

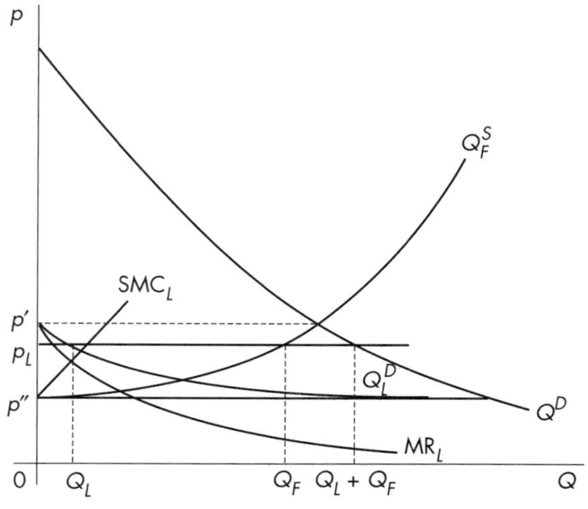

Figure 15A.3 **Price leadership.** The demand curve facing the price leader, Q_L^D, is determined by subtracting the followers' supply curves from the total market demand Q^D. Based on this demand curve Q_L^D, the price leader determines its profit-maximizing price and quantity (p_L, Q_L).

summation of the follower firms' short-run marginal cost curves. The price leader takes the level of all the follower firms' supply at each price and subtracts this supply from the quantity demanded at each price. The *residual demand curve*, represented as the demand curve Q_L^D, is the demand curve that the price leader is facing. Note that at a price above p', all of the demand is satisfied by the follower firms, so the price leader will not supply any output. At a price below p'', $p <$ SAVC for all the firms, including the price leader, so no firm is willing to supply a positive level of output. For determining its optimal output Q_L, the price leader sets marginal revenue, associated with its Q_L^D demand curve, equal to SMC$_L$. The price at which the price leader can sell all of this output is then p_L. The followers match this price p_L and together are willing to supply Q_F of the output. Thus, supply is equal to market demand at p_L, with Q_L supplied by the price leader and Q_F by all the follower firms.

The price leader is generally a **dominant firm** within a market. In this case, changes in output by the price leader will have a major effect on the market price. Thus, this firm has a greater potential of penalizing any firm not following its price change. For example, OPEC is the price leader in the supply of crude oil, and, within OPEC, Saudi Arabia is the price leader. How a particular price leader is determined or how a leader maintains leadership are important questions, which this model does not address.

Example 15A.4 Price leadership

Consider the following supply function (based on the horizontal summation of the follower firms' SMC curves) and market demand function:

$$Q_F^S = -4 + 2p,$$

$$Q^D = 20 - 2p,$$

Subtracting the follower firms' supply function from the market demand function yields the price leader's demand function:

$$Q_L^D = Q^D - Q_F^S = 20 - 2p + 4 - 2p = 24 - 4p.$$

Solving for p results in the price leader's AR function:

$$p = AR = 6 - \tfrac{1}{4}Q_L.$$

Multiplying both sides by Q_L and taking the derivative yields the price leader's MR function:

$$\text{TR}_L = pQ_L = 6Q_L - \tfrac{1}{4}Q_L^2 \Rightarrow \text{MR}_L = \frac{d\text{TR}_L}{dQ_L} = 6 - \tfrac{1}{2}Q_L.$$

Assuming that the price leader's short-run marginal cost function is

$$SMC_L = 2 + \tfrac{3}{2}Q_L$$

and then equating $\text{MR}_L = \text{SMC}_L$ results in the price leader's profit-maximizing output level:

$$6 - \tfrac{1}{2}Q_L = 2 + \tfrac{3}{2}Q_L \Rightarrow Q_L = 2.$$

The price leader will sell all of this output at a price

$$p = 6 - \tfrac{1}{4}Q_L = 11/2.$$

The follower firms will match this price and together supply

$$Q_F^S = -4 + 2(11/2) = 7.$$

Total supply is then

$$Q_L + Q_F = Q = 9.$$

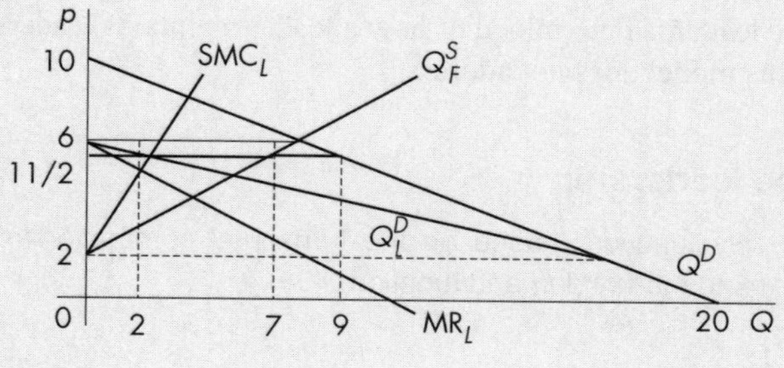

Questions

1. Why do banks announce a prime interest rate and change it only occasionally?
2. In Breakdown City, auto shops have formed an association and have agreed to post a schedule of minimum hourly labor charged for repair work. How is this action of benefit to each shop? Why will they not have to police this agreement? Explain.
3. Could an oligopoly that does not alter its price when demand shifts still be maximizing profit? Explain.
4. Is the kinked demand curve an objective fact of the marketplace or a subjective phenomenon in the mind of each oligopoly? Explain.

Exercises

1. Potential consumers of ice cream are uniformly distributed along a mile-long ocean beach, and these consumers will go to the nearest vendor to purchase their ice cream. All vendors sell their ice cream at the same price, and if more than one vendor is at the same location, their business is evenly split.

   a. For a game in which two ice cream vendors pick their locations simultaneously, show that there is a unique pure-strategy Nash equilibrium.
   b. Show that with three vendors, no pure-strategy Nash equilibrium exists.

2. Suppose there are three independent counties (A, B, and C) where a state solid waste dump may be located. The counties are all in a row alphabetically and none wants the dump located within itself or in an adjacent county. Each county is willing to pay \$20 to keep the dump from being located within itself. Their willingness to pay to keep the dump out of an adjacent county is shown in the following table:

County	Willingness to pay
A	10
B	6
C	0

   a. In terms of efficiency, where should the dump be located?
   b. Assume that the counties could freely negotiate over the location of the dump by providing compensation for counties harmed by the dump location. Determine the equilibrium level of compensation and the location of the dump.

3. Suppose that the demand for crude oil is given by

   $$Q^D = 4000 - 100p,$$

where Q^D is the quantity of oil and p is the per-unit price. Also, assume that there are 100 identical producers of crude oil, each with marginal cost

$$\text{SMC} = \tfrac{1}{2}q + 10,$$

where q is a firm's output.

a. Assuming that each producer is a price taker, calculate the market supply curve and the market equilibrium price and quantity.
b. Suppose that a virtually infinite supply of crude oil is discovered by a potential price-leader firm and that this oil can be produced at a constant average and marginal cost of $10. Assuming that the supply behavior of the competitive fringe is not changed by this discovery, how much should the price leader produce for profit maximization? What will be the market price and quantity?

Internet case study

1. Compare and contrast Sweezy's kinked demand curve with a game-theory approach that also models oligopoly behavior of price rigidity.

Part VII

Input markets

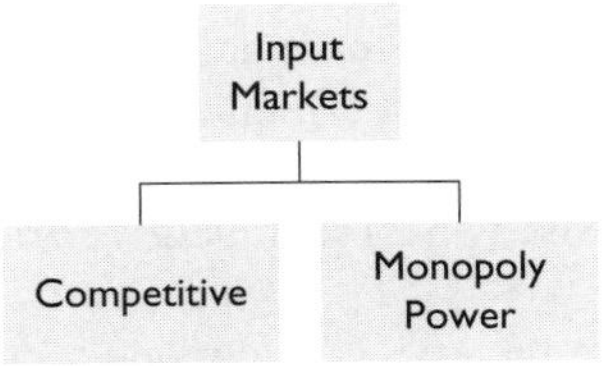

Chapters

> *A recession is when your neighbor is out of work. A depression is when you are out of work.*
>
> (Harry Truman)

Why study input markets? When you are in the unemployment line, at least you will understand why you are there. Input prices paid to inputs—in particular, wages and salaries of workers—are directly tied to their market demand and supply. When we understand how the market demand and supply for inputs are determined, we can also understand how firms determine when to hire and replace inputs. With this understanding, we can evaluate the economic efficiency of various tools firms use to increase their profit by employing inputs. In some cases, these tools result in firms exploiting owners of the inputs. When this happens, various countermeasures are employed by owners of inputs, in particular labor. With knowledge about this interaction between the demanders and suppliers of inputs, we gain insights into the current love/hate relationship between labor and management.

Firms in their production processes are generally not self-sufficient in supplying inputs (factors of production) for producing their outputs. Some inputs they own—such as the owner's labor and some capital equipment and resources (such as land)—but other inputs—such as workers' labor—must be purchased in the market. The optimal amount of inputs to purchase is assumed to be based on least-cost production, a necessary condition for profit maximization. In Chapters 16 and 17, we determine the optimal level of inputs to be purchased.

Specifically, we develop market demand and supply for inputs in a perfectly competitive market. We place particular attention on the labor market, deriving the market supply curve for labor in the first section of Chapter 16. Based on this market supply curve, we define *economic rent* and relate that to a single-tax scheme and *Ricardian rent*. We then discuss the marginal productivity theory of input demand and investigate the comparative statics of input demand as well as the responsiveness of input demand to input price changes. We determine the perfectly competitive equilibrium input price and, based on this competitive price, a firm's profit-maximizing level of the input.

In Chapter 17, we evaluate the effect of monopoly power in input markets (called *monopsony power*) relative to the perfectly competitive market. We discuss the inefficiency of monopsony power and input-wage discrimination. Then we investigate cases of monopoly in the supply of inputs and a bilateral monopoly (where a monopsony is facing a monopoly). In light of all this, we then discuss labor unions' objectives and associated wage offers.

16 Competitive input markets

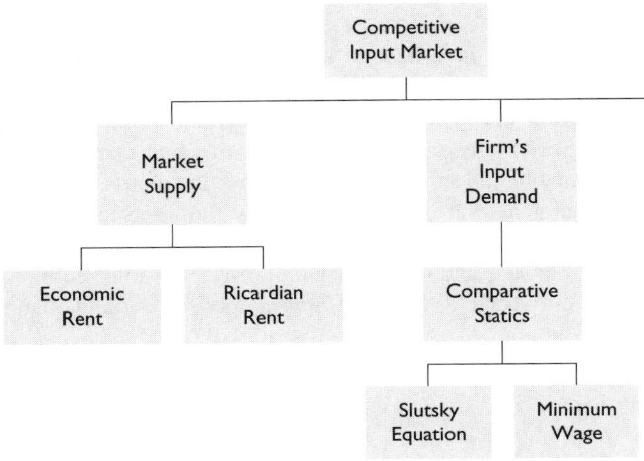

Outline and Conceptual Inquiries

Deriving the market supply curve for labor
- **Application: Implications of restricting US immigration on farm labor supply**

Understanding economic rent
- *Do you have high or low economic rent?*

Land rent: the Henry George single-tax scheme
- *Should only land be taxed?*
- **Application: Optimal commodity taxes based on rents**

Ricardian rent: input demand is a derived demand from the output market
- *Do high store rents result in high product prices?*

Marginal productivity theory of factor demand
One-variable-input case: $VMP_L = w$ as the labor demand function
Two-variable-input case: deriving input demands from VMP's functions
- **Application: Firm hierarchies and wage rates**

Establishing perfectly competitive equilibrium in the factor market

Summary
Key concepts
Key equations
Questions
Exercises
Internet case studies

Appendix to chapter 16

Investigating comparative statics of input demand
One-variable-input case
Two-variable-input case: substitution effect
- *Do firms substitute one input for another given an input price change?*
- *Will a firm alter its output given an input price change?*

Responsiveness of demand to input price change
- **Application: Minimum wage**
- *Are you affected by the minimum wage?*
- *Should teenagers be in favor or opposed to an increase in the minimum wage?*

Questions
Exercises
Internet case study

The male is a domestic animal which can be trained to do most things.
(Jilly Cooper)

In its 60-team roster, a National Football League franchise will pay a minimum rookie salary of \$355,000 annually in 2012. If the rookie does not get hurt, with additional training, his salary can increase into the millions. In general, firms will employ inputs (factors of production) in the production of an output with the objective of maximizing profit. To determine the profit-maximizing level of an input, the associated cost per unit (implicit or explicit) of each input is required. In a free-market economy, this cost per unit is determined by the supply and demand for the inputs. For example, perfect competition in a factor market is characterized by the intersection of factor market supply and demand curves (Figure 16.1), where X is the total market quantity of an input (rookie football players) and v is the per-unit price. The intersection of the market supply and demand curves yields the equilibrium input price v_e and quantity of the input X_e.

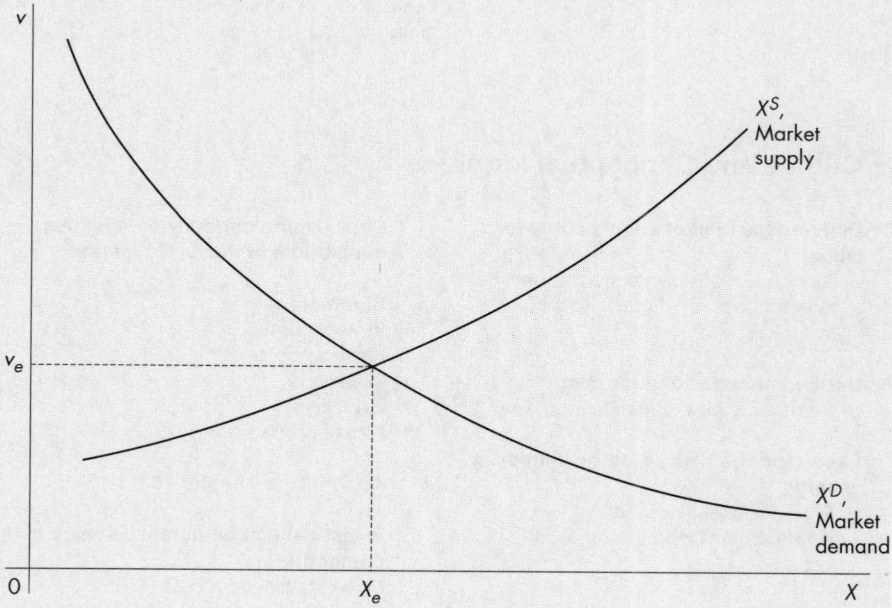

Figure 16.1 **Factor market under perfect competition.** The interaction of factor market supply and demand curves determines the equilibrium factor price and quantity.

Inputs are supplied by resource owners—agents who either own land and capital or supply their labor as inputs into production.

Intuitively, we assume that the input supply curve is upward-sloping: an increase in the input price v results in an increase in quantity supplied of input X. In contrast, the input demand curve would then be downward-sloping: a decrease in v yields an increase in quantity demanded for X. This demand curve is a derived demand based on firms' objective of maximizing profit. We assume that firms hire land, labor, and capital to produce a profit-maximizing output and that the quantities hired depend on the level of output.

In this chapter, we investigate theoretically the above intuitive discussion of the market demand and supply for inputs, particularly for the labor market. We first derive the input market supply curve for labor as the horizontal summation of individual workers' supply curves. We then evaluate this input market supply curve for various inputs in terms of the surplus benefits (called *economic rent*) that it provides to the suppliers of the input. Based on this economic rent, we investigate Henry George's single-tax scheme. We then develop *Ricardian rent* as an important predecessor to marginal analysis based on profit maximization. In our subsequent discussion of the input demand curve, we derive the comparative statics of an input demand curve in terms of the substitution and output effects. We illustrate this responsiveness of input demand to input price changes with the minimum wage. Based on the aggregation of individual firms' demand for the input, we develop the competitive input market equilibrium. Given this market equilibrium price, we determine firms' optimal profit-maximizing level of the input.

Our aim in this chapter is to investigate the perfectly competitive input market. Economists use this competitive input market as the standard for measuring input market efficiency. As discussed in Chapter 17, any monopoly power in the input market is judged against the Pareto-efficient allocation resulting from a perfectly competitive input market.

Deriving the market supply curve for labor

Regardless of what firm you work for, never forget the most important product you are selling is yourself.

(Jack Brown)

In perfectly competitive markets, the determination of wage rates and employment levels depends directly on the labor market supply curve. Based on individual workers' labor supply curves (Chapter 4), we can derive the **labor market supply curve**. Specifically, this curve is the horizontal summation of individual workers' supply curves. This summation is illustrated in Figure 16.2 for two workers, where ℓ_1 and ℓ_2 are worker 1's and worker 2's supplies, respectively. The wage rate is w and X is the total amount of labor supplied in the market. Both workers are facing the same wage rate, and it is assumed that they take this wage rate as given (they do not negotiate a wage).[1] As derived in Chapter 4, the individual labor supply curves will have a positive slope when the income effect does not fully offset the substitution effect. Otherwise, an individual labor supply curve will be backward-bending (generally only at high wage rates). When the individual labor supply curves have positive slopes, at a given wage rate w', each worker is then willing and able to supply a given level of labor services. As illustrated in Figure 16.2, at w', workers 1 and 2 are willing to

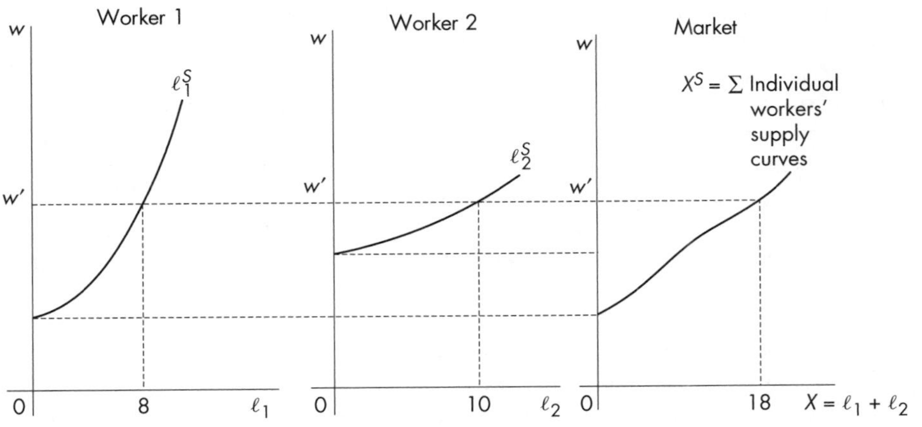

Figure 16.2 **Market supply curve for labor.** The labor market supply curve is the horizontal summation of individual workers' supply curves.

supply 8 and 10 units of labor (say, hours per day), respectively. The market supply curve for this labor is then the sum of the hours ($8 + 10 = 18$). As the wage rate increases, each worker is willing to supply more labor services, and thus the sum of labor supplied will increase. Even if some of the workers have backward-bending labor supply curves, the market supply will likely still be positively sloping. However, if (as was the case in the early part of the twentieth century) a substantial number of workers have a backward-bending supply curve, then the market supply curve may also be backward-bending. (In the early twentieth century, as wages increased, the average work week declined to around 40 hours per week.)

Labor market supply curve. The horizontal summation of individual workers' labor supply curves. *E.g., the sum of all the hours computer programmers are willing and able to work at a given wage.*

Example 16.1. Deriving the labor market supply curve

Consider the following two individual workers' labor supply functions:

$$\ell_1^S = -5 + w,$$

$$\ell_2^S = -16 + 2w.$$

The labor market supply curve is then the sum of these two workers' supply functions:

$$X^S = \ell_1^S + \ell_2^S = -5 + w + (-16 + 2w)$$
$$= -21 + 3w \quad \text{for } X \geq 3,$$
$$X^S = -5 + w \quad \text{for } 0 < X < 3.$$

At $w = 8$, worker 1 is willing to supply 3 units (hours) of labor, while worker 2 is unwilling to supply any hours. The total market supply is then 3 hours. At $w = 10$, 5 and 4 hours will be supplied by workers 1 and 2, respectively, with a total market supply of 9 hours.

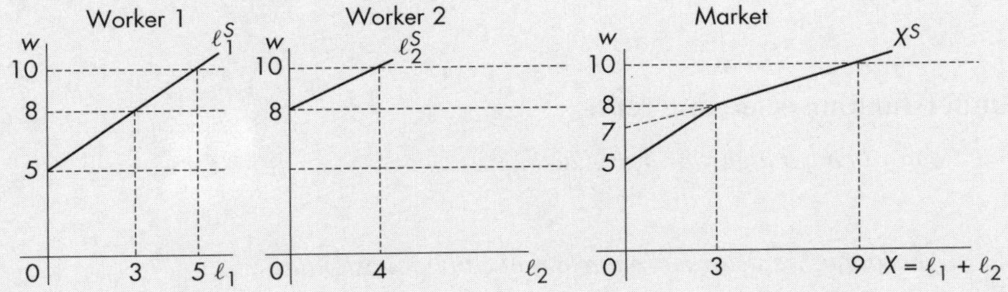

Mathematically, the labor market supply function for two workers is the sum of each worker's individual labor supply functions:

$$\ell_1^S = \ell_1(w), \quad \ell_2^S = \ell_2(w).$$

The total labor market supply is then the sum of the amounts supplied by the two workers:

$$X^S = \ell_1^S + \ell_2^S.$$

Application: Implications of restricting US immigration on farm labor supply

As a result of failed legislation and the September 11 attacks, the United States has primarily focused on border security in an effort to reduce illegal immigration. Such efforts directly restrict the market supply of farm labor. To investigate the effects of this border security on labor supply, Devadoss and Luckstead have developed a trade and illegal immigration model that analyzes the impacts of increased border security on farm labor and commodity markets. Their theoretical results indicate that increased resource allocation to border control constricts the flow of illegal labor, but also reduces commodity trade. Utilizing an econometric model, results indicate that a 10 percent increase in spending on border control curbs the quantity of illegal farm labor by almost 9000 workers and reduces commodity trade by approximately $180 million. This translates to US agricultural exports to Mexico declining by 5 percent. A distinct tradeoff exists between a reduction in illegal labor flow and commodity trade. Reduction in immigrant workforce does have adverse implications for US agriculture. Thus, Devadoss and Luckstead conclude that immigration reform that develops a guest-worker program will allow a supply of farm labor for crop production. Such a program will have a positive impact on agricultural production and profitability, along with reducing the cost of agricultural products to consumers.

Source: S. Devadoss and J. Luckstead, "Implications of Immigration Policies for the U.S. Farm Sector and Workforce," *Economic Inquiry* 49 (2011): 857–875.

Understanding economic rent

I enjoy being a highly overpaid actor.

(Roger Moore)

Translation: An actor's economic rent can be substantial.

In the nineteenth century, there was no cause dearer to the hearts of oppressed tenants than the promise that rent would be abolished in a communist state. These tenants, along with lawyers and politicians, thought of economic rent as solely what is paid by the tenant to the landlord. If nothing is paid, then there is no rent. However, Henry George (1839–1897) and his followers knew that rent is a naturally occurring surplus. It is the potential return arising solely from use of a particular site. Anyone who has use of that site has access to its economic rent. It cannot be abolished by any law or destroyed by agreements between landlords and tenants. The most that can occur is that the potential is not tapped, which is a deadweight loss. Specifically, the concept of **economic rent**, based on factor supply, is defined as the portion of total payments to a factor that is in excess of what is required to keep the factor in its current occupation. Economic rent is the same concept as producer surplus (discussed in Chapter 10), except that the surplus accrues to the factor. From Figure 16.3, the total dollar amount necessary to retain the level X_e in this occupation is given by the area $0ABX_e$.

As we will discuss in Chapter 17, if firms could perfectly discriminate among factor suppliers, total payment would be $0ABX_e$. Perfectly competitive markets, however, do not work in this manner. All similar inputs are paid the same price. However, some factor owners would settle for less, which leads to economic rent. For example, in terms of labor, a worker receiving a wage rate of \$25 per hour may be willing to work for only \$20 per hour. The \$5 difference is a per-hour surplus (economic rent) accruing to the worker. In Figure 16.3, total factor payments are $0v_eBX_e$. Subtracting the area necessary to retain the level X_e in this occupation, $0ABX_e$, from the total factor payments, $0v_eBX_e$ results in economic rent, Av_eB.

Do you have high or low economic rent? If you can offer a relatively unique service that is in high demand (acting), then your economic rent will be very high. In contrast, if you offer common services that are not in high demand, then your economic rent will be very low.

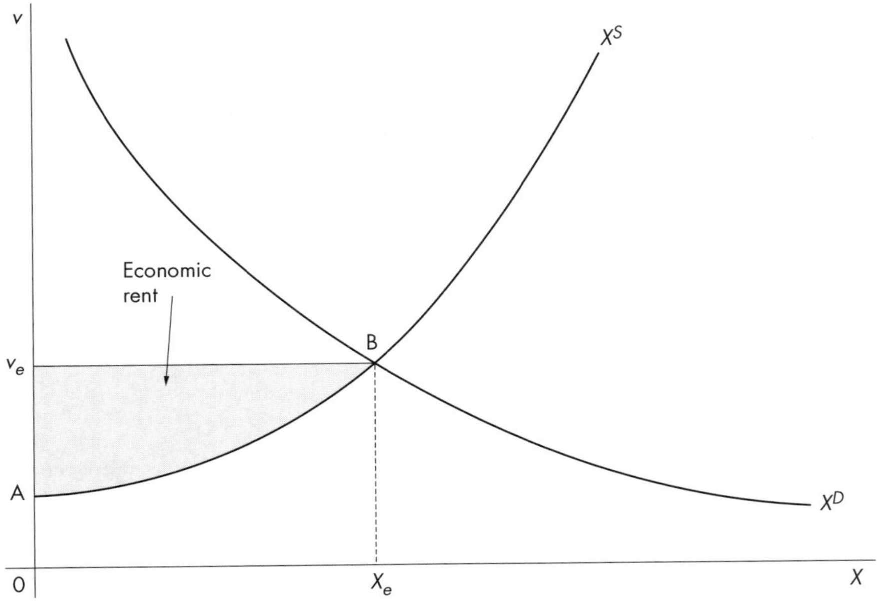

Figure 16.3 **Economic rent.** The area below the wage rate and above the supply curve represents economic rent.

Economic rent. The portion of total payment to a factor that is in excess of what is required to keep the factor in its current occupation. *E.g., if a baseball player plays the game solely for the love of the game, his whole salary is economic rent.*

Economic rent and opportunity cost

Secretaries have numerous employment opportunities at approximately the same wage, so their opportunity cost for working at a particular place is large relative to their wage rate. Any factor of production that has many alternative uses will have a very elastic supply curve for one type of employment. This factor can receive almost as high a price elsewhere, so quantity supplied will be reduced sharply for a small decline in factor price. As illustrated in Figure 16.4, economic rent is small for factors with this very elastic supply. The factor earns only slightly in excess of what it might earn elsewhere (opportunity cost). This opportunity cost is represented by the area $0ABX_e$, leaving very little economic rent, area Av_eB. For the labor market, the wage rate is just above the wage at which a worker would just be willing to supply his or her labor services (called the **reservation wage**). Thus, a worker's opportunity cost is high, resulting in low economic rent. This low economic rent results in workers stating it is hardly worth their time to work. A decline in wages can then result in this opportunity cost exceeding the income from working and thus result in a decline in the number of workers. This high opportunity cost results in the supply of workers being very responsive to a change in wages. In the extreme, a perfectly elastic supply curve

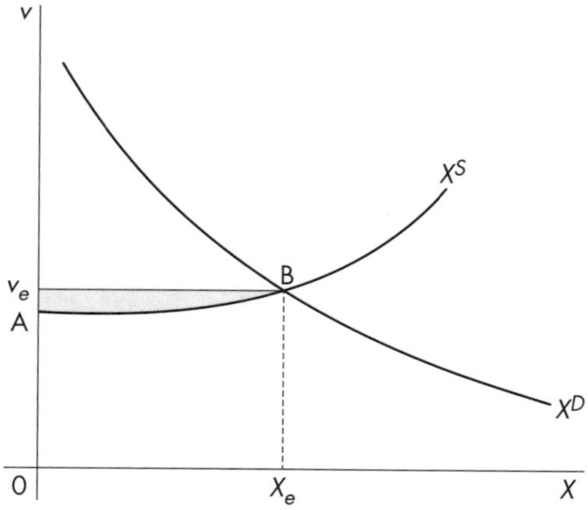

Figure 16.4 **Low level of economic rent associated with an elastic market supply curve.** The factor price is just above the reservation price. A decline in the factor price can then result in the opportunity cost exceeding the revenue generated from supplying the factor.

results in zero economic rent accruing to the factor, so the reservation wage (in general, called the reservation price) is equal to the wage rate. The opportunity cost is then equal to the total factor payments, making a factor owner indifferent between supplying the factor or not.

Reservation wage. The lowest wage a worker is willing to accept to work in a given occupation. *E.g., an electrician may be willing to work at a wage below the union wage rate.*

In contrast, professional football players generally have limited opportunities at approximately the same wage. Their wage rate is substantially above the wage at which they would just be willing to supply their labor services (reservation wage), so their economic rent is relatively large (Figure 16.5). A decrease in a football player's wage will have limited impact on decreasing supply (relatively inelastic supply). Some football players would be willing to play football for free. Alternative earning possibilities (opportunity cost) of football players are generally quite low, so a large part of their wage is economic rent. In Figure 16.5, the opportunity cost is ABX_e, with the shaded area representing economic rent. As the labor-supply curve becomes more inelastic, the opportunity cost declines with an associated increase in economic rent.

Land rent: the Henry George single-tax scheme

Henry George (1839–1897) applied the idea of large economic rents accruing to owners of factors with highly inelastic supply curves to land. He assumed that land is in fixed supply (perfectly inelastic). In Figure 16.6, no matter what the level of demand, the supply of land

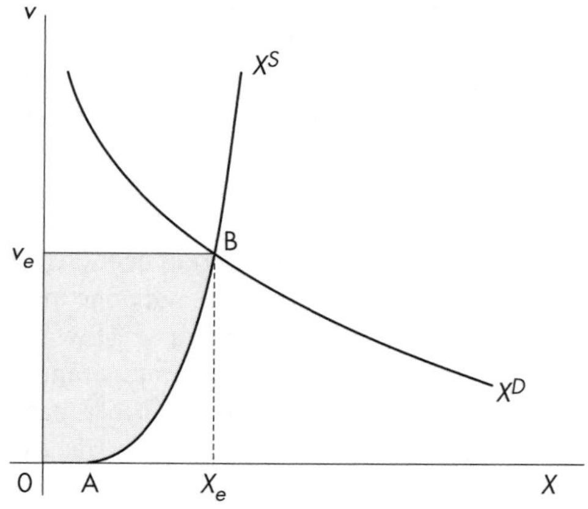

Figure 16.5 **Economic rent associated with an inelastic supply curve.** The factor price is substantially above the reservation wage of supplying the factor, so a decline in the factor price will have limited impact on the factor supply.

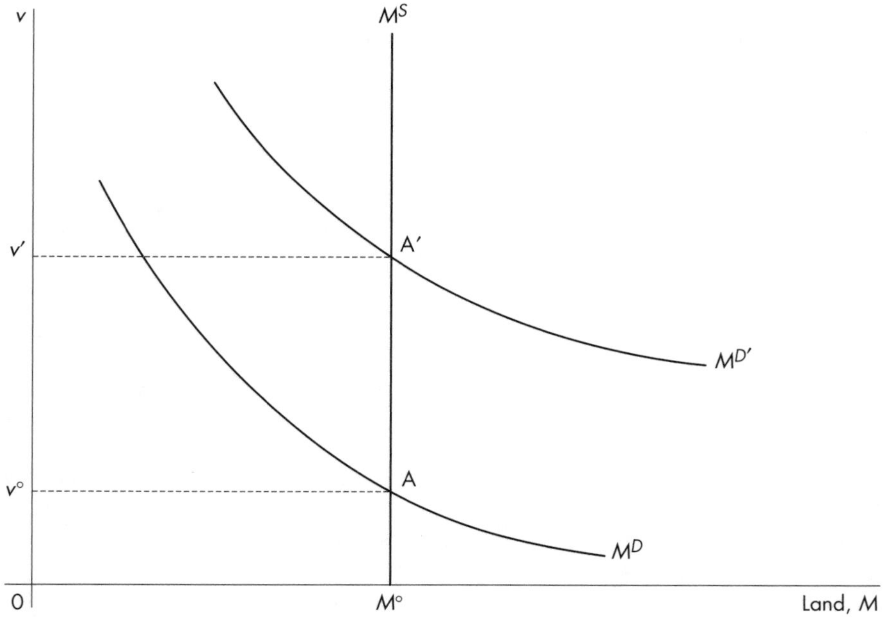

Figure 16.6 **Land rent.** If the supply curve for land is perfectly inelastic, there is no supply response to a change in factor price.

is fixed at M^o. Given the demand curve M^D, a return (economic rent) to the landowners is $0v^oAM^o$. With the demand curve $M^{D'}$, return is $0v'A'M^o$. Thus, an increase in the demand for land has no effect other than to enrich the landowners. Henry George proposed that those rents accruing to such fortunate landowners be taxed at a very high level because this taxation would have no effect on the quantity of land provided. He assumed a zero supply response, so a tax on land would not create inefficiencies. Note that there is no deadweight loss in Figure 16.6 from a tax causing a shift in demand from $M^{D'}$ to M^D. Given no deadweight loss, some proponents of this *Henry George Theory* even suggested this should be the only method of tax collection.[2]

This type of *single-tax scheme* may be worth considering in an agrarian economy where all land is of the same type yielding the same productivity. When land has only one main use, the opportunity cost is near zero, resulting in a highly inelastic supply curve. However, for most other economies, there are multiple uses for land, such as for residential, commercial, or industrial development. Thus, an opportunity cost exists for using land in a particular activity, which creates inefficiencies associated with the single-tax scheme. The deadweight loss associated with these inefficiencies is investigated in Chapter 10.

Should only land be taxed? No, such a single-tax scheme distorts the market for land, which results in an inefficient land allocation.

Example 16.2 Calculating economic rent

Consider the following inverse input market demand and supply functions:

$$v = 10 - X^D, \quad \text{input demand,}$$

$$v = 2 + X^S, \quad \text{input supply.}$$

Equating demand with supply and solving for X,

$$10 - X = 2 + X,$$

$$X_e = 4, \; v_e = 6.$$

Economic rent is then the area below the equilibrium price and above the supply curve, $(6-2)(4-0)/2 = \$8$. Consumer surplus is also $(10-6)(4-0)/2 = \$8$. Recall that consumer surplus, which flows to the firm employing this input, is the area below the demand curve and above the equilibrium price.

Instead, if the market supply curve were perfectly elastic, for example $v = 6$, then economic rent would be zero. The reservation price to retain the level X_e in this market would equal the price of the input, v_e. In contrast, if the market supply curve were perfectly inelastic, for example $X^S = 4$, then economic rent would be $6(4) = \$24$.

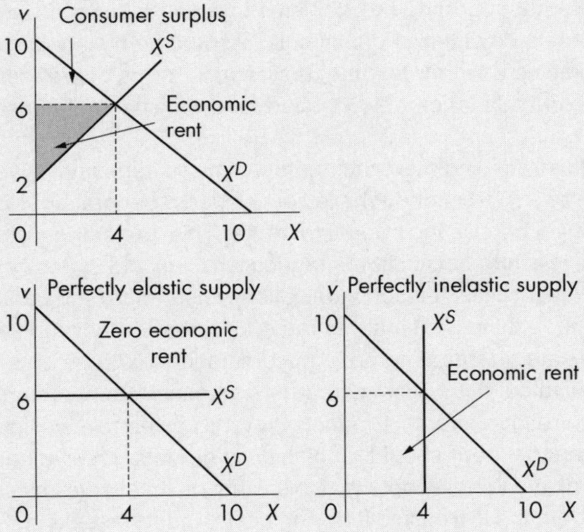

It might be feasible to tax other factors used in a production activity where alternative uses are slight. For example, a high tax rate on professional sports players would have little or no effect on the number and quality of professional players. Such a tax would not greatly distort the market allocations (there would be little if any deadweight loss), plus disadvantaged youth will not see sports as a substitute for education in achieving success. An example of such a tax is the Major League Baseball competitive balance tax. Instituted in 2002, the tax is intended to reduce players' salaries, with the tax revenue being used to support ball clubs with relatively fewer resources.

Application: Optimal commodity taxes based on rents

In general, economic rents are created from a number of economic and natural patterns, so attempts to tax them can have varying efficiency effects. Taxes on sectors with resource rents (called Ricardian rents and discussed in the next section) generally are nondistorting. However, taxes on monopolies can act as a tax on a tax (the monopoly markup) and reduce efficiency. Taxes on regulated sectors with rent-seeking behavior may even improve efficiency. As outlined by Perroni and Whalley, the size, nature, and distribution of rents affect both the costs of taxes and the optimal rate structures.

The Henry George Theory suggests for an industry with a relatively fixed factor, such as land, that a tax will have limited resource-distorting effects. In contrast, under imperfect competition, the optimal tax rates tend to be inversely proportional to the degree of monopoly power. The greater the markup of price above marginal cost, the larger will be the distortion associated with a tax. The reverse is true for rent-seeking firms, where a tax reduces the rent available for wasteful rent seeking. Thus, as addressed by Perroni and Whalley, an appropriate commodity tax design given all these types of rents and rent-supporting mechanisms involves a tradeoff between preferences-related and rent-related effects. For example, resource rents are largest in the agricultural sector, suggesting a higher tax rate; however, in terms of preferences, consumers generally desire an abundance of low-priced food, which is not consistent with a high tax.

Based on the objective of determining a tax rate that maximizes consumer's welfare given a tax revenue requirement, Perroni and Whalley developed a general-equilibrium tax model for the Canadian economy incorporating rents. This general-equilibrium model is composed of five sectors: agricultural (agriculture, mining, forestry, and fishing), manufacturing, utilities (utilities, telecommunications, insurance, and banking), transportation, and other. The resulting optimal tax rates for each sector are listed in Table 16.1. Their results indicate a large difference in commodity tax rates by sector. The resulting higher optimal rates in the agricultural and transportation sectors are characterized by relative high resource rents. Products currently given relative light tax treatment for equity reasons (e.g., food) should on efficiency grounds receive harsher tax treatments. Finally, Perroni and Whalley note that this variation in tax rates by sector is amplified when one considers the increasing lobbying costs and rent seeking.

Table 16.1. Optimal tax rates by sector

Agricultural	59%
Manufacturing	32%
Utilities	48%
Transportation	61%
Other	38%

Source: C. Perroni and J. Whalley, "Rents and the Cost and Optimal Design of Commodity Taxes," *Review of Economics and Statistics* 80 (1998): 357–364.

Ricardian rent: input demand is a derived demand from the output market

Oil prices have fallen lately. We include this news for the benefit of gas stations, which otherwise would not learn of it for six months.

(William D. Tammeus)

Even agricultural land parcels range from very fertile (low cost of production) to rather poor quality (high-cost) land. Thus, there is a supply response associated with land that restricts the application of an efficient single tax on land. Based on this observation, David Ricardo (1772–1823) made one of the most important conclusions in classical economics. More fertile land tends to command a higher rent. Ricardo's analysis assumed many parcels of land of varying productive quality for growing wheat, resulting in a range of production costs for firms. As an example, in Figure 16.7, three levels of firms' SATC and SMC curves are illustrated, along with the market demand and supply curves for wheat. The market for wheat determines the equilibrium price for wheat. At this equilibrium, an owner of a low-cost land parcel earns a relatively large pure profit with $p >$ SATC. Considering this profit as a

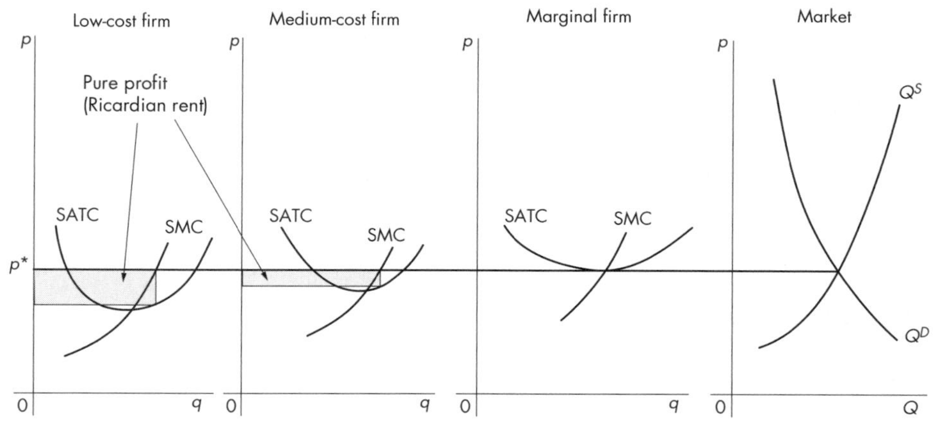

Figure 16.7 **Ricardian rent.** A low-cost firm earns higher pure profit (Ricardian rent) relative to the medium-cost and marginal firms. The marginal firm earns only a normal profit, so firms with higher cost than this marginal firm will have no incentive to enter this market.

return to land, the low-cost firm is earning relatively high rents (**Ricardian rent**) for its land. A medium-cost firm earns less profit (Ricardian rent). Price is still greater than SATC, but it is not as great as for the low-cost firm. In contrast, the marginal firm is earning a zero pure profit (Ricardian rent), p = SATC. Any additional parcels of land brought into wheat production will result in a loss, so there is no incentive for these parcels to be brought into production. The presence or absence of Ricardian rent in a market works toward allocating resources to their most efficient use.

Ricardian rent. Profit accruing to an input. *E.g., the profit a collegiate athletic association makes from its student athletes.*

Ricardo's analysis indicates how the demand for land is a demand derived from the output market. The level of the market demand curve for output determines how much land can be profitably cultivated and how much profit in the form of Ricardian rent will be generated. His theory explains why some firms earn a pure profit in competitive markets: when managerial ability, location, or land fertility differ.

For example, a favorably situated store (firm) will earn positive pure profits, while stores at the margin earn only normal profits. But it is not the store's cost of production (cost of petroleum)—for example, the rent it pays for a particular location—that determines the store's output prices (price of gasoline). Output prices are determined by the market demand and supply curves for these outputs. Those prices, in turn, determine profit (Ricardian rent). Thus, in a perfectly competitive output market, it is not true that a store can offer lower prices because it does not have to pay "high downtown rents." If its rent is lower than downtown, the store may earn a short-run pure profit. But in the long run, the store will only experience a normal profit, as any pure profit gets capitalized into the firm's costs. Thus, the store's prices may be less, but it is not because their rent is less. Output prices are determined in the markets for these outputs, not by the cost of production.

Do high store rents result in high product prices? No, in a perfectly competitive market, rents do not determine product prices. The market supply and demand determine a product's price.

Marginal productivity theory of factor demand

Pleasure in the job puts perfection in the work.

(Aristotle)

"Political Economy, you think, is an enquiry into the nature and causes of wealth—I think it should rather be called an enquiry into the laws which determine the division of produce of industry amongst the classes that concur in its formation. No law can be laid down respecting quantity, but a tolerably correct one can be laid down respecting proportions. Every day I am more satisfied that the former enquiry is vain and delusive, and the latter the only true object of the science."[3]

Ricardian rent theory was an important predecessor to the development of economic theory based on marginal analysis derived from profit maximization. This is particularly true in terms of the theory associated with factor demand. A firm's demand for a factor is based on the firm's attempt to maximize profits. The differences in a firm's demand for factors determine at what proportions these factors are used in production.

One-variable-input case: $VMP_L = w$ as the labor demand function

To see that factor demand is a derived demand from profit maximization, let us first consider a production function with only labor L as the variable input, $q = f(L)$. Assume that output is sold in a perfectly competitive market at a price per unit p and that the firm can hire all the labor it wants at the prevailing wage rate w. Because we assume perfect competition in the output market, the firm's output market demand curve is perfectly elastic. The firm has no control over the output price p. Because the firm is able to hire all the labor it wants at a wage rate w, it is also facing a perfectly elastic labor supply curve. The firm takes the wage rate as given. The firm's profit-maximizing objective is then

$$\max_{(q,L)} \pi = \max_{(q,L)} (pq - wL - \text{TFC}) \quad \text{s.t. } q = f(L).$$

Incorporating the production function into the firm's profit-maximizing objective function yields

$$\max_{L} \pi = \max_{L} [pf(L) - wL - \text{TFC}],$$

where $pf(L)$ is total revenue as a function of the level of labor L employed and wL is the firm's total variable cost (wage bill). The first-order condition (FOC) is then

$$\frac{d\pi}{dL} = p\frac{df(L)}{dL} - w = 0,$$

or

$$p\text{MP}_L = w.$$

Recall from Chapter 7 that $df(L)/dL = \text{MP}_L$, the marginal product of labor. Here, the term $p\text{MP}_L$ is called the **value of the marginal product** of L, VMP_L. In a perfectly competitive output market, VMP_L is the additional revenue received by hiring an additional unit of L. Marginal product measures the additional output from employing an additional unit of an input. How much this additional unit is worth (valued) is determined by multiplying this additional output by a measure of its per-unit value. In a perfectly competitive output market, the output price is the measurement for per-unit value. Thus, price times marginal product is the value of the marginal product, that is, the value of the additional output generated from employing an additional unit of an input.

Value of the marginal product (VMP). Output price times the marginal product. *E.g., the increase in the volume of groceries sold times price is a supermarket's value of the marginal product of having an additional clerk.*

Example 16.3 Derived demand for labor as the only variable input

Consider the following production function and associated profit equation:

$$q = L^{1/2},$$

$$\pi = pL^{1/2} - wL - \text{TFC}.$$

Maximizing profit with respect to the variable labor input results in

$$\frac{d\pi}{dL} = \tfrac{1}{2}pL^{*-1/2} - w = 0,$$

that is,

$$\text{VMP}_L - w = 0.$$

Solving for L^* yields the derived demand function for labor:

$$\tfrac{1}{2}pL^{*-1/2} = w,$$

$$L^{*-1/2} = 2w/p,$$

$$L^* = (p/2w)^2.$$

This labor demand function has a negative slope,

$$\partial L/\partial w = -p^2/(2w^3) < 0,$$

and is convex,

$$\partial^2 L/\partial w^2 = 3p^2/(2w^4) > 0.$$

Given $p = 2$ and $w = 1$, for profit maximization the firm will hire 1 unit of labor, $L^* = 1$. VMP_L at this equilibrium is \$1, which is equal to the wage rate of \$1. If TFC = 1, then $\pi = 2(1) - 1 - 1 = 0$ (a normal profit). Instead, if the firm only hired a quarter-time worker, $L = 1/4$, then $\text{VMP}_L = 2 > w = 1$, and $\pi = 2(1/4)^{1/2} - 1/4 - 1 = -1/4$. VMP $> w$, so the firm can increase its profit by hiring the worker full time. If $L = 4$, then $\text{VMP}_L = 1/2 < w = 1$, so $\pi = 2(2) - 4 - 1 = -1$. VMP $< w$, so the firm can increase its profit by reducing the amount of workers it is employing. Reducing the number of workers results in STC falling more than TR, which increases the profit.

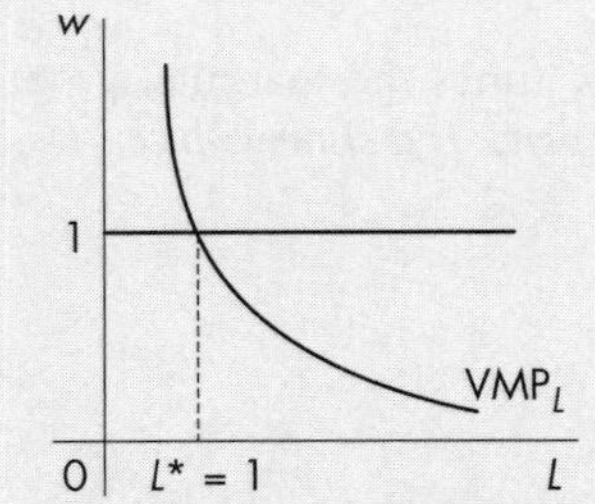

This FOC for profit maximization results in a tangency point A in Figure 16.8 between an isoprofit line and the production function, where $\text{VMP}_L = w$. An **isoprofit line** represents a locus of points where the level of profit is the same. For movements along an isoprofit line, profit remains constant. An upward shift in an isoprofit line represents an increase in profit. We develop the isoprofit line from the isoprofit equation for a given level of profit:

$$\pi^* = pq - wL - \text{TFC},$$

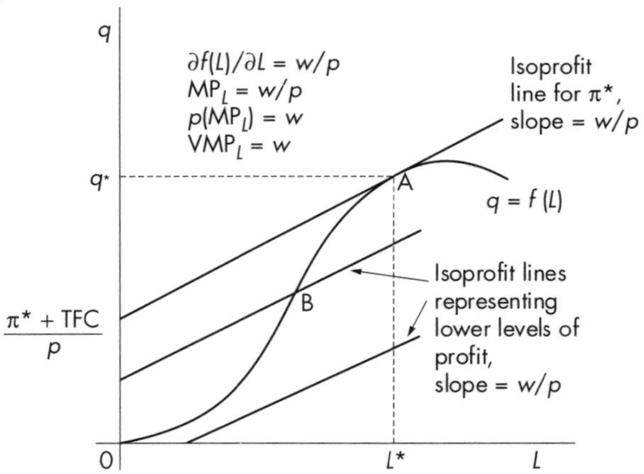

Figure 16.8 **Isoprofit lines and production functions.** Profits are maximized for a given production technology at the tangency between the isoprofit line and the production function. At this tangency, $\text{VMP}_L = w$, which results in L^* as the profit-maximizing level for labor.

where π^* represents some constant level of profit. Solving for q yields

$$q = \frac{\pi^* + \text{TFC}}{p} + \frac{w}{p}L.$$

As illustrated in Figure 16.8, the slope of the isoprofit line is $dq/dL = w/p$. At the tangency point A, the slopes of the isoprofit line and the production function are equal. Since the slope of the production function is $\text{MP}_L = dq/dL$, at this tangency $w/p = \text{MP}_L$. Multiplying through by p yields the FOC for profit maximization, $w = p\text{MP}_L = \text{VMP}_L$.

Isoprofit line. A locus of points where the level of pure profit is the same for various levels of a variable input. *E.g., the level of profit may be the same for a large supermarket with many clerks as for a small mom and pop grocery.*

This FOC for profit maximization states that the isoprofit line tangent to the production function will maximize profit subject to the production function. This tangency condition for profit maximization is termed **price efficiency**. Price efficiency requires both allocative and scale efficiency. As discussed in Chapter 10, allocative efficiency occurs where the ratio of marginal products of inputs equals the ratio of the input prices, and scale efficiency is where marginal cost equals output price. Overall economic efficiency for a firm is established when both price efficiency and technical efficiency exist (Figure 16.9). A firm is technically efficient when it is using the current technology for producing its output—that is, it is on the production frontier of the production process. At point B in Figure 16.8, the firm is technically efficient but not price-efficient. Moving up along the production function, the firm shifts to a higher isoprofit line, representing a higher level of profit. At the tangency point A, the firm can no longer remain on the production function constraint and further increase profit. Thus, the firm has reached the highest isoprofit line possible and maximizes profits for this technology. At this point A, the firm is also price-efficient.

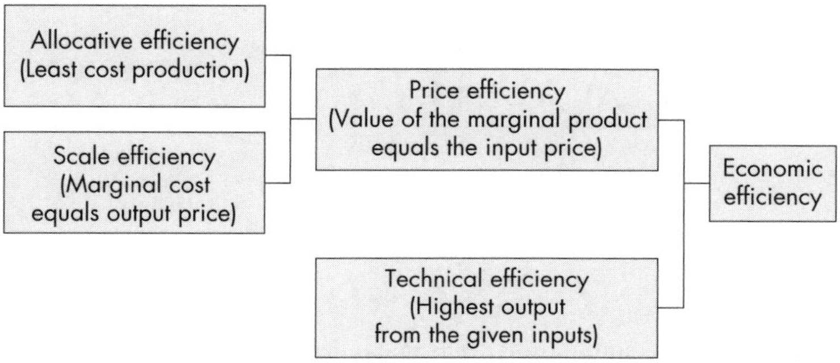

Figure 16.9 **Flowchart illustrating the different types of efficiencies for a firm.** If a firm is allocative and scale-efficient, then it is said to be price-efficient. If a firm is both price-efficient and technically efficient, then it has achieved economic efficiency.

Price efficiency. When a firm is both allocatively and scale-efficient. *E.g., an Amish farm minimizing cost for a given level of output and equating its marginal cost to the output price is price-efficient. However, it is not necessarily using the current technology for production, so it is not technically efficient.*

As illustrated in Figure 16.10, at the equilibrium wage w^*, the value of the marginal product of labor VMP_L equals the wage rate w^*. If only L' workers are hired instead, then profit could be enhanced by increasing the amount of labor. Increasing labor from L' to L^* results in additional revenue of $L'\text{AB}L^*$, with associated cost of $L'\text{CB}L^*$. The additional revenue is greater than the additional cost, so profit increases by CAB. Alternatively, at L'', decreasing the amount of labor to L^* results in revenue falling by $L^*\text{B}L''$, with cost declining even more, $L^*\text{BD}L''$. The reduction in cost is more than the loss in revenue, so profit will increase by the area $\text{BD}L''$. At point B, where $\text{VMP} = w^*$, the firm maximizes profits.

For the case of one variable input, the VMP_L curve is the labor demand curve. Solving the FOC, $w = \text{VMP}_L$, for L results in the firm's input demand function for labor, $L = L(p, w)$. This demand for labor is directly derived from the FOC, and the output price p is a determinant of this input demand.

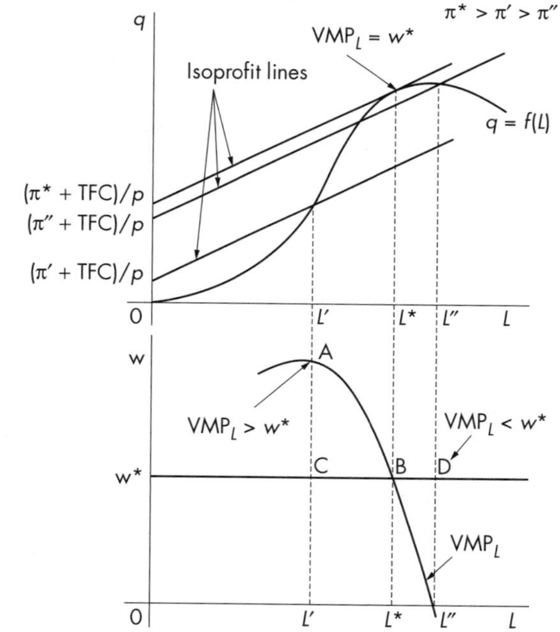

Figure 16.10 **The first-order condition for profit maximization in the input market for a perfectly competitive firm in both the input and output markets.** As labor is increased from L' to L^*, the firm's profit is enhanced by the area CAB. Beyond L^*, further increases in labor will result in profit declining. At L'', profit is lower than at L^*. The loss in profit from L^* to L'' is represented by the area $\text{BD}L''$.

Two-variable-input case: deriving input demands from VMP's functions

Let us extend the analysis to two variable inputs by allowing both capital K and labor L to vary. The production function with these two variable inputs is $q = f(K, L)$, where q, K, and L are all traded in perfectly competitive markets at prices p, v, and w, respectively. The problem facing a profit-maximizing firm with this production function is

$$\max_{(L,\,K)} \pi = [pf(K, L) - vK - wL - \text{TFC}].$$

The FOCs are then

$$\frac{\partial \pi}{\partial L} = p\text{MP}_L - w = 0,$$
$$\frac{\partial \pi}{\partial K} = pMP_K - v = 0.$$

From these FOCs, $v = p\text{MP}_K = \text{VMP}_K$ and $w = p\text{MP}_L = \text{VMP}_L$. The FOC for labor is illustrated in Figure 16.10. At L', $\text{VMP}_L > w^*$; the addition to revenue for an increase in labor is greater than the additional cost, so profit is enhanced by increasing labor. In contrast, at L'', $\text{VMP}_L < w^*$; the loss in revenue for a decrease in labor is less than the loss in cost, so profit is enhanced by decreasing labor. At $\text{VMP}_L = w^*$, point B, profits are maximized. Similarly, changing capital around the optimal level will result in a decline in profit, so, for both variable inputs, the firm will equate the VMP for the variable input to the associated input price as a necessary condition for profit maximization.

We can generalize this result for k inputs, where for each input the FOC for profit maximization is to set the VMP for an input equal to its associated price. Specifically, $\text{VMP}_j = v_j, j = 1, \ldots, k$, where v_j denotes the input price for input x_j. Solving these FOCs simultaneously for the k inputs yields the input demand functions $x_j = x_j(p, v_1, \ldots, v_k)$. Note that, in contrast to the one-input case, with two or more inputs, the VMP curves are not the input demand curves. For example, in the two-variable case, solving $w = \text{VMP}_L$ for L yields $L = f_L(p, w, K)$, which is not the input demand function for labor. We obtain the input demand function for labor by solving simultaneously the FOCs, resulting in $L = L(p, w, v)$.

Figure 16.11 illustrates this difference in the demand curve for an input and the associated VMP curves for the two variable inputs labor and capital. VMP_L depends on the level of capital also employed. An increase in the amount of capital employed will enhance the productivity of labor, so the VMP_L curve will shift upward. This is illustrated in the figure by a shift in VMP_L from $\text{VMP}_L|_{K^o}$ to $\text{VMP}_L|_{K'}$, given an increase in capital from K^o to K'. A decrease in the wage rate from w^o to w' results in $\text{VMP}_L|_{K^o} > w'$, so the firm will hire more workers. This increase in labor will result in VMP_K increasing, so $\text{VMP}_K > v$. In response, the firm will purchase more capital, which shifts the VMP_L curve upward from $\text{VMP}_L|_{K^o}$ to $\text{VMP}_L|_{K'}$. The new equilibrium level of labor L' associated with w' is where $w' = \text{VMP}_L|_{K'}$. The demand curve for labor then intersects the initial wage/labor level (w^o, L^o) and the new level (w', L'). This labor demand curve is more elastic than the VMP_L curves because the level of capital is allowed to vary along the labor demand curve. In contrast, for a given VMP_L curve, capital is fixed. Only where the demand curve intersects a VMP_L will this fixed level of capital for a given VMP_L curve correspond to the optimal level.

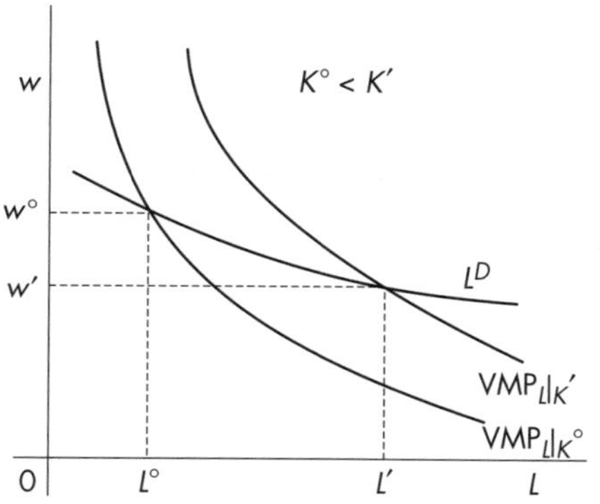

Figure 16.11 **The labor demand curve with variable capital.** If capital is fixed at K^o, then the $VMP_L|_{K^o}$ curve is the firm's labor demand curve. However, allowing capital to vary, the firm will adjust both capital and labor, given a change in the wage rate. This results in a more elastic labor demand curve L^D.

Example 16.4 Derived input demand with two variable inputs

Consider the following production function with labor and capital as the variable inputs:

$$q = L^{1/4}K^{1/4}.$$

Profit maximization, subject to this production function constraint, is

$$\max_{(L,\,K)} \pi = \max_{(L,\,K)} \left[pL^{1/4}K^{1/4} - vK - wL - \text{TFC}\right].$$

The FOCs are then

$$\partial\pi/\partial L = \tfrac{1}{4}pL^{*-3/4}K^{*1/4} - w = 0,$$
$$\partial\pi/\partial K = \tfrac{1}{4}pL^{*1/4}K^{*-3/4} - v = 0.$$

These two FOCs imply that

$$w = \tfrac{1}{4}pL^{*-3/4}K^{*1/4} = \text{VMP}_L,$$
$$v = \tfrac{1}{4}pL^{*1/4}K^{*-3/4} = \text{VMP}_K.$$

Taking the ratio, the economic rate of substitution is equal to MRTS(K for L):

$$\frac{w}{v} = \frac{\tfrac{1}{4}pL^{*-3/4}K^{*1/4}}{\tfrac{1}{4}pL^{*1/4}K^{*-3/4}} = \frac{K^*}{L^*} = \text{MRTS}(K \text{ for } L).$$

Solving for K^* yields the expansion-path equation, $K^* = (w/v)L^*$. Substituting this expansion path into the first FOC and solving for L^* yields the derived factor demand function for labor:

$$\tfrac{1}{4}pL^{*-3/4}K^{*1/4} - w = \tfrac{1}{4}pL^{*-3/4}\left[(w/v)L^*\right]^{1/4} - w$$
$$= \tfrac{1}{4}pL^{*-1/2}(w/v)^{1/4} - w = 0.$$

Solving for L^* yields

$$L^* = \left(\frac{p}{4w^{3/4}v^{1/4}}\right)^2 = \frac{p^2}{16w^{3/2}v^{1/2}}, \qquad \text{derived demand function for labor.}$$

We obtain the derived demand function for capital by substituting this labor demand function into the expansion path:

$$K^* = \frac{w}{v}\frac{p^2}{16w^{3/2}v^{1/2}} = \frac{p^2}{16w^{1/2}v^{3/2}}, \qquad \text{derived demand function for capital.}$$

Letting $p = 2$, $v = w = 1$, then $L^* = K^* = 1/4 = 0.25$. Instead, if $w = 2$, then $L^* = 0.09$ and $K^* = 0.18$.

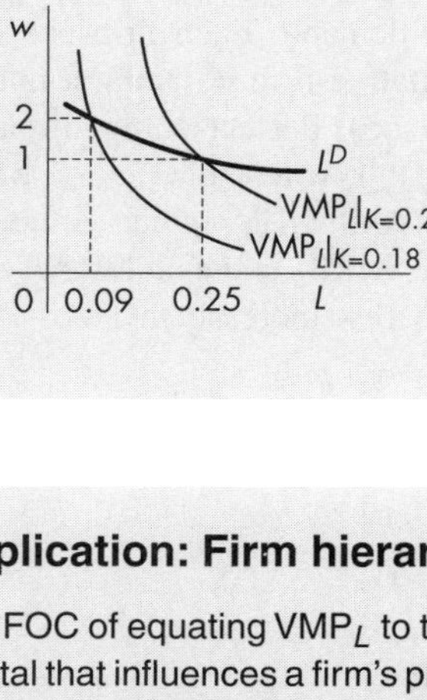

Application: Firm hierarchies and wage rates

The FOC of equating VMP_L to the wage rate is based on labor processing some human capital that influences a firm's productivity. As an alternative to this human-capital theory, economists have considered a jobs-based approach that focuses on the connection between jobs and wages. One jobs-based theory is the hierarchy theory, which analyzes management structure based on a pyramid of levels and a span of control, or the number of direct subordinates a manager has, at each level.

As a test of the ability of this hierarchy theory to explain wage rates, K.J. Meagher developed an econometric model with determinants representing the position a worker is in a firm's pyramid as explanatory variables. Human-capital determinants such as education and experience were also incorporated into the model. The results indicate that wages are nondecreasing as the number of levels below a worker increases. Hierarchical position has no effect on wages in small hierarchies (less than two levels).

With three or more levels, an increase by 1 in the number of levels below a worker increases wages by 10 percent, or, as the model indicates, is equivalent to over two extra years of education. Meagher explains this higher wage by the higher productivity resulting from control over subordinates. Thus, wages should be thought of as the joint outcome of a worker's skills (human capital) and the job that the worker holds.

Source: K.J. Meagher, "The Impact of Hierarchies on Wages," *Journal of Economic Behavior and Organization* 45 (2001): 441–458.

Establishing perfectly competitive equilibrium in the factor market

Why will I not hire your son? We are in equilibrium, that is why.

(Michael Wetzstein)

In 2008, there were 4.3 million secretaries and administrative assistants within the United States. This is one of the largest job categories, and the market is characteristic of a perfectly competitive factor market. As illustrated in Figure 16.12, a perfectly competitive factor market is characterized by many buyers and many sellers of the input, labor (secretaries). No single employer or employee can influence the wage rate. The wage rate w_e is determined in the market through the free interaction of supply and demand. Each firm can hire all the labor it wants at the market wage w_e, so the representative firm is facing a horizontal labor supply curve (perfectly elastic supply curve, $\varepsilon^S = \infty$). Perfect competition in the output market results in $p = \text{MR}$. Thus, $p\text{MP}_L = \text{MR}(\text{MP}_L)$, where $\text{pMP}_L = \text{VMP}_L$ and $\text{MR}(\text{MP}_L)$ is defined as **marginal revenue product** for labor, MRP_L, which is the change in total revenue resulting from a unit change in labor. Here, MRP_L is the additional revenue received from increasing labor and measures how much this increase in labor is worth to the firm:

$$\frac{\partial \text{TR}}{\partial L} = \frac{\partial \text{TR}}{\partial q}\frac{\partial q}{\partial L} = \text{MR}(\text{MP}_L) = \text{MRP}_L.$$

Marginal revenue product (MRP). The change in total revenue resulting from a change in an input. *E.g., the increase in receipts from a restaurant hiring an additional server.*

As illustrated in Figure 16.13, if there is imperfect competition in the output market, then $p > \text{MR} = \text{SMC}$ and $p\text{MP}_L = \text{VMP}_L > \text{MRP}_L = \text{MR}(\text{MP}_L)$. Specifically, recalling that MR may be expressed in terms of the elasticity of demand ε^D,

$$\text{MR} = p\left(1 + \frac{1}{\varepsilon^D}\right),$$

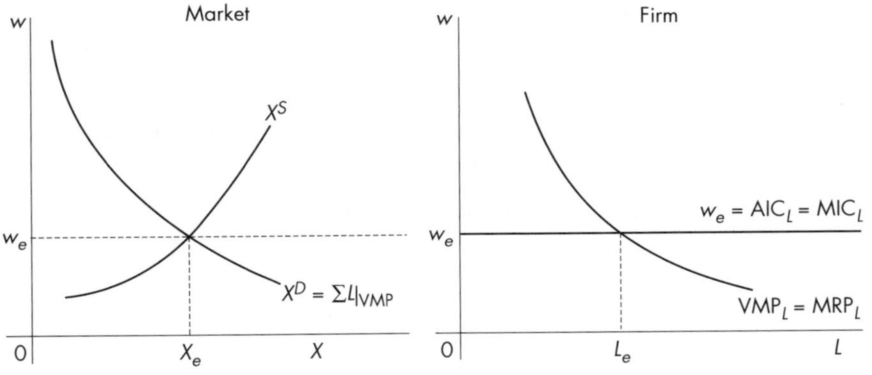

Figure 16.12 **Perfect competition in both the factor and output markets.** The intersection of the labor market demand and supply curves determines the equilibrium wage rate faced by a representative firm. At this market wage rate, the firm will then maximize profit by employing L_e workers.

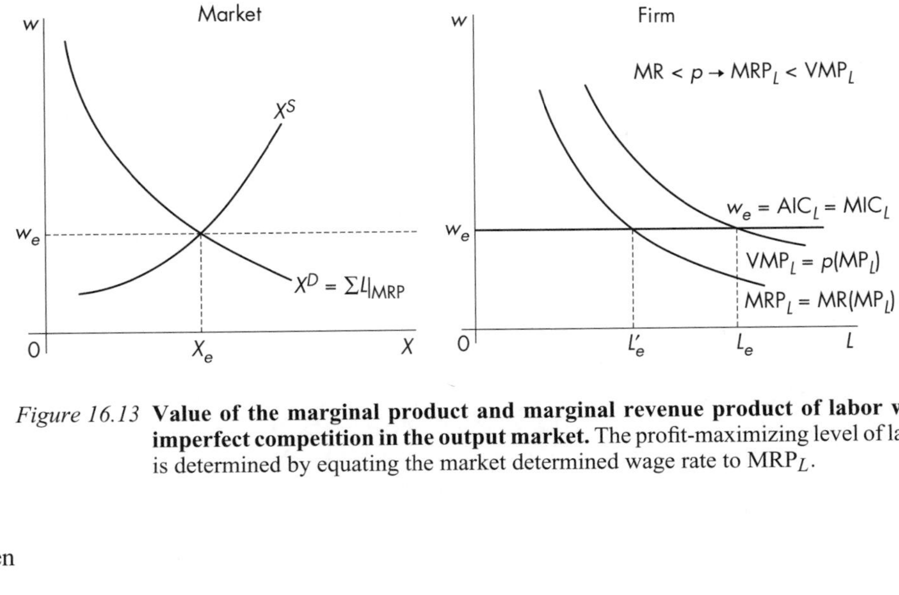

Figure 16.13 **Value of the marginal product and marginal revenue product of labor with imperfect competition in the output market.** The profit-maximizing level of labor is determined by equating the market determined wage rate to MRP_L.

then

$$\begin{aligned}\text{MRP}_L &= p\left(1+\frac{1}{\varepsilon^D}\right)\text{MP}_L\\ &= \left(1+\frac{1}{\varepsilon^D}\right)p\text{MP}_L = \left(1+\frac{1}{\varepsilon^D}\right)\text{VMP}_L.\end{aligned}$$

Given that a profit-maximizing firm only operates in the elastic region of the demand curve, then $\varepsilon^D < -1$, resulting in $1 \geq 1 + 1/\varepsilon^D > 0$. As the elasticity of demand tends toward negative infinity (perfectly elastic, $\varepsilon^D = -\infty$, a perfectly competitive market), $1/\varepsilon^D$ will approach zero, where $\text{MRP}_L = \text{VMP}_L$. Otherwise, for any firm facing a downward-sloping market demand curve (indicating at least some monopoly power), $\text{MRP}_L < \text{VMP}_L$.

Example 16.5. Calculating the marginal revenue product and value of the marginal product for labor

A firm is facing the following market demand function for its output,

$$p = 20 - Q^D,$$

and is constrained by the production function

$$Q = 4L^{1/2}.$$

The firm's MR is then

$$\text{MR} = 20 - 2Q,$$

and in terms of the labor input it is

$$\text{MR} = 20 - 2(4L^{1/2}) = 20 - 8L^{1/2}.$$

The marginal product of labor is

$$\text{MP}_L = 2L^{-1/2}.$$

The marginal revenue product of labor is then

$$\text{MRP}_L = \text{MR}(\text{MP}_L) = (20 - 8L^{1/2})2L^{-1/2} = 40L^{-1/2} - 16.$$

The derivatives of MRP_L are

$$d\text{MRP}_L/dL = -20L^{-3/2} < 0,$$

$$d^2\text{MRP}_L/dL^2 = 30L^{-5/2} > 0.$$

Assuming that the firm's SMC function is

$$\text{SMC} = Q,$$

the market price, where MR = SMC, is then $p = 40/3$. Given this price, the firm's value of the marginal product of labor is

$$\text{VMP}_L = p\text{MP}_L = (40/3)(2L^{-1/2}) = (80/3)L^{-1/2},$$

with

$$dVMP_L/dL = -(40/3)L^{-3/2} < 0,$$

$$d^2VMP_L/dL^2 = 60L^{-5/2} > 0.$$

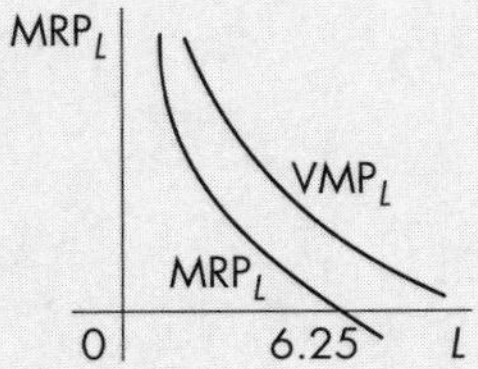

In general, the profit-maximizing problem for a firm facing a competitive wage rate w_e is

$$\max_L \pi = \max_L [pf(L) - wL - \text{TFC}],$$

where $pf(L)$ is total revenue as a function of the level of labor employed and wL is the firm's total variable cost (wage bill). The FOC is then

$$\frac{d\pi}{dL} = \text{MR}(\text{MP}_L) - w_e = 0,$$

that is,

$$\text{MRP}_L - w_e = 0.$$

As illustrated in Figure 16.12, if the firm is also in a perfectly competitive market for its output, then $p = \text{MR}$, resulting in $\text{MRP}_L = \text{VMP}_L$. In contrast, as illustrated in Figure 16.13, if the firm has some monopoly power in its output market, then $p > \text{MR}$, yielding $\text{MRP}_L < \text{VMP}_L$. In both cases, the market for labor is assumed to be perfectly competitive with the wage rate determined by the intersection of the market demand and supply curves for labor. The firm will take this competitive wage rate as given and equate it to its MRP_L. As indicated in Figure 16.12, if the firm is facing a competitive output price, then it will hire L_e workers at w_e. Instead, as indicated in Figure 16.13, if the firm has some monopoly power in the output market, then, by restricting its output, it will hire less labor, L'_e.

Example 16.6. Determining labor demand under perfect competition in both the output and input markets

Consider again the production function from Example 16.4, $q = 4L^{1/2}$, and let output price $p = 10$ and input price $w = 4$. Output price p and wage w are fixed, representing perfect competition in both the output and input markets. The objective of the firm is to maximize profit:

$$\max_{(q,\,L)} \pi = \max_{(q,\,L)} (pq - wL) \qquad \text{s.t. } q = 4L^{1/2}.$$

Substituting the constraint into the objective function yields

$$\max_{L} \pi = \max_{L} \left(p4L^{1/2} - wL\right).$$

The FOC is then

$$\frac{d\pi}{dL} = 2pL^{*-1/2} - w = 0.$$

The term $2pL^{*-1/2}$ is VMP_L and w is AIC_L, which, in the case of perfect competition in the input market for labor, is equal to MIC_L. Solving for L gives

$$L^{*-1/2} = w/2p,$$

$$L^* = (2p/w)^2.$$

This is the input demand function for labor. Substituting the values for the output price and the wage rate results in $L^* = 25$. The firm will hire 25 workers, given $p = 10$ and $w = 4$.

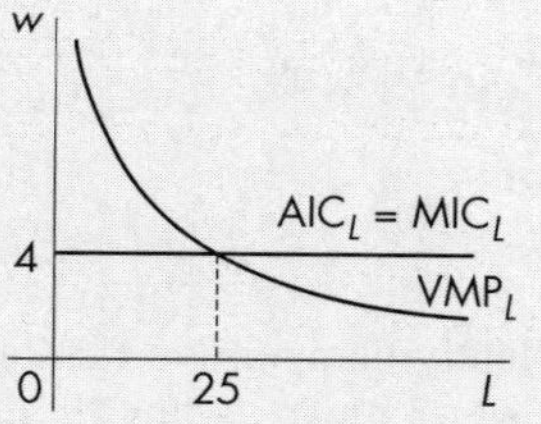

The horizontal supply curve for labor is called the **average input cost** (or **average expenditure**) curve for labor (AIC_L). It is **total input cost** (or **total expenditure**) of labor (TIC_L), in this case the wage bill (wL), divided by labor:

$$\text{AIC}_L = wL/L = w.$$

In other words, AIC_L is the average cost per worker, which is the worker's wage rate w. Associated with this AIC_L is the **marginal input cost** (or **marginal expenditure**) of labor, MIC_L, which is defined as

$$\text{MIC}_L = \frac{\partial(wL)}{\partial L},$$

the addition to total input cost from hiring an additional unit of labor. Note that when AIC_L is neither rising nor falling, MIC_L is equal to it. This result is the consequence of the general relationship between averages and marginal units. If the average unit is neither rising nor falling, then the marginal unit will be equal to it. The same relationship holds for AIC and MIC as for average and marginal cost (see Chapter 8).

Average input cost (AIC). The per-unit cost of a given amount of an input. *E.g., the average cost of labor for an automobile repair shop is the total cost of wages divided by the number of workers.*

Total input cost (TIC). The total cost of employing a given level of an input. *E.g., a restaurant's bill for the food it purchases.*

Marginal input cost (MIC). The addition to total input cost from employing an additional unit of an input. *E.g., the increase in total costs from a restaurant hiring an additional server.*

Example 16.7. Determining labor demand under imperfect competition in the output market and perfect competition in the input market

From Example 16.5, the $MRP_L = 40L^{-1/2} - 16$. Assuming again that the perfectly competitive wage rate $w = 4$, the firm will maximize profit by setting MRP_L equal to this wage rate:

$$MRP_L = w,$$

$$40L^{-1/2} - 16 = 4.$$

Solving for L yields

$$L'_e = 4.$$

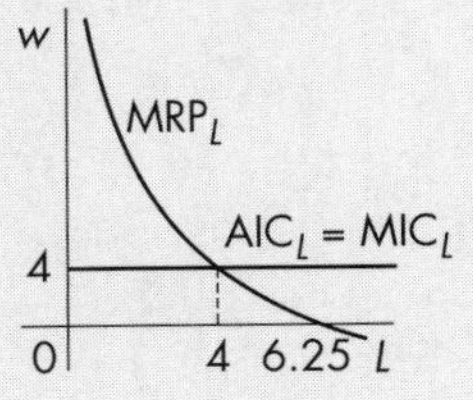

Summary

1. The market supply curve for labor is derived by the horizontal summation of individual workers' supply curves.
2. Economic rent is that portion of total payment to a factor that is in excess of what is required to keep the factor in its current occupation. The price at which a factor is just willing supply is called the reservation price.
3. A firm will employ the profit-maximizing level of a variable input where the VMP of the input is set equal to its price. This corresponds to the tangency of the isoprofit line with the production function.
4. For one variable input, the VMP curve is the firm's demand curve for the input. For two or more inputs, the VMP functions are solved simultaneously for the input demand functions.
5. A perfectly competitive input market is characterized by many buyers and sellers of an input. Each firm can buy (hire) all the inputs it wants at the market price (wage). Each supplier of the input can offer as much of the input it wants at the given price (wage).
6. *(Appendix)* The total effect of an input price change may be decomposed into the substitution and output effects. The substitution effect measures a change in the level of an input given a change in its price, holding output constant. The output effect is the change in level of an input when the output changes as a result of a change in the input price.
7. *(Appendix)* The minimum wage is a price floor below which the wage rate cannot fall. If the minimum wage is below the equilibrium wage rate, it has no effect on the market. However, if it is set above this equilibrium wage rate, it will influence the market level of the input. The actual effect is an empirical question.

Key concepts

average input cost (AIC), 688
economic rent, 668
isoprofit line, 678
labor market supply curve, 665
marginal input cost (MIC), 688
marginal revenue product (MRP), 684
minimum wage, 699
output effect, 695
price efficiency, 679
reservation wage, 669
Ricardian rent, 675
substitution effect, 695
total input cost (TIC), 688
value of the marginal product (VMP), 677

Key equations

$$\text{VMP}_L = w$$

The profit-maximization condition for a perfectly competitive firm in the output market is to equate the value of the marginal product for a variable input (labor) to its associated price (wage).

$$\mathrm{MRP}_L = w$$

The profit-maximization condition for a firm is to equate the marginal revenue product for a variable input (labor) to its associated price (wage).

$$\frac{\partial L}{\partial w} = \frac{\partial L}{\partial w}\bigg|_{dq=0} + \frac{\partial L}{\partial q}\frac{\partial q}{\partial w} < 0$$

The total effect on an input (labor) from its own price (wage) change may be decomposed into the substitution and output effects.

Questions

A person's mind stretched by a question never regains its original dimension.
(Oliver Wendell Holmes)

1. A convenience store near a college campus has high prices because it pays higher rents. True or false? Explain.
2. Rock musicians sometimes earn over $10 million per year. Explain this large income in terms of economic rent?
3. Why does a military draft cause wars to be too cheap?
4. What is the decision rule for the employment of a particular input to a production process? How does this depend on the supply and demand conditions in the output market?
5. Wage rates are high in New York City compared with the rest of the United States, but so are living costs. This indicates that labor is more productive in New York City than in the other US cities. Explain.
6. Firms should pay a worker according to her marginal productivity. If the last worker has a marginal product of 5 units and these 5 units have a total market value of $100, then the worker's payment should be $100. Any payment less than $100 entails exploitation. Is there any validity in this statement? Explain.
7. A general definition of unemployment is workers willing and able to work at the going wage but unable to find employment. Does the equilibrium wage rate in a competitive labor market generate full employment? Explain.
8. Why would a firm that is losing money hire another worker?
9. In recent years, college tuition costs have risen faster than the general price level; however, college professors' salaries have failed to keep pace with the price level. Why?
10. If the United States opened its borders and allowed any immigrant into the country, who would be the winners? The losers?

Exercises

A trained mind can grasp anything. It can dive deep into the subtlest subject and understand even transcendental exercises.

(Michael Wetzstein)

1. Given $w = 10$, determine the economic rent for each of the following individual labor supply functions:

   a. $\ell = w + 4$;
   b. $\ell = 14$ (perfectly inelastic supply);
   c. $\ell = 140/w$ (backward-bending labor supply).

2. In terms of Ricardian rent, a low-cost firm and marginal firm have the following short-run total-cost curves:

$$\text{STC}_1 = q_1^2 + q_1 + 1,$$

$$\text{STC}_2 = q_2^2 + q_2 + 4.$$

   a. Which cost curve represents the low-cost firm and which represents the marginal firm?
   b. Determine the Ricardian rent for each firm.

3. A travel company has only one variable input, labor. The company's production function for providing travel services is

$$q = 10L^{1/2}.$$

   If the average price of travel services is \$8 and the wage rate is \$20, determine the number of workers the firm will hire.

4. Suppose that a perfectly competitive firm produces an output employing labor and capital and sells its output at price p and hires labor and rents capital at w and v, respectively. Assume that a payroll tax of t percent of total payroll costs is instituted.

   a. Determine and interpret the FOCs for this profit-maximizing firm.
   b. Show how the quantities of labor and capital employed will vary with the tax rate.

5. The stock-adjustment model is one method for modeling a firm's decision to hire workers. This model assumes that the change in labor employed $(L_j - L_{j-1})$ between, say, months is proportional to the difference between the firm's optimal level of workers, L_j^*, and the actual level of workers last month, L_{j-1}:

$$L_j - L_{j-1} = \alpha\left(L_j^* - L_{j-1}\right),$$

   where $0 < \alpha < 1$.

Suppose that a firm has production function $q = L^{1/2}$ and short-run total cost function $\text{STC}(q) = 100 + q^2$.

a. If the output price $p = 10$, determine the optimal level of workers hired.
b. Suppose that in the first month the firm employed 10 workers, $L_1 = 10$. With $\alpha = 1/2$, how many workers will be hired each month for the next 3 months?

6. A land baron has three farms (A, B, and C) differing in fertility. The productivity of the three farms with one to three workers is listed in the following table:

Number of workers	*Level of output*		
	Farm A	*Farm B*	*Farm C*
1	8	6	3
2	15	9	5
3	19	11	6

This table indicates that if one worker is hired for each farm—a total of three workers—then total output will be $8 + 6 + 3 = 17$. If, instead, the farm C worker is shifted to farm A, then the total output will be $15 + 6 = 21$.

a. If the land baron has four workers available, what would be the most productive allocation of labor and how much would be produced? What is the marginal product of the last worker?
b. If the output is sold in a perfectly competitive market at a price per unit of \$1, what will be the wage rate? Given that TFC is \$6, determine the profit for this landowner.

7. An African colonial cattle ranch has a production function

$$q = (KL)^{1/2},$$

and, in the short run, $K = 25$ and $v = \$1$ per unit of capital.

a. If the rancher can hire African cowboys at a wage of \$1, what is the ranch's short-run supply curve?
b. Suppose there is a revolution and the colonial government is replaced with a socialist government that collectivizes the ranch. The ranch is now managed by the cowboys, who pay the socialist government rent for the capital equipment. The cowboys are egalitarian, so they share the net revenue, the excess of total revenue over capital cost equally. Their objective is then to maximize average net revenue per cowboy. What is the cowboys' short-run supply curve?
c. Graph the two short-run curves and explain their differences.

8. Graph isocost curves for a firm that pays higher prices for larger purchases of x_1, but faces a constant price for x_2. How will the FOCs for cost minimization differ?

9. Consider the following production functions:

   i. $q = L^{1/3}K^{1/3}$;
   ii. $q = L^{2/3}K^{2/3}$.

   a. Derive the demand functions for L and K as functions of p, v, and w.
   b. Are the demand functions downward-sloping?

10. A perfectly competitive input market is composed of 1000 workers. Each worker has the following supply function for work:

$$L_j^S = -12 + 2w, \quad j = 1, 2, \ldots, 1000.$$

There are 500 firms in this labor market, each with the labor demand function

$$L_j^D = 16 - w, \quad j = 1, 2, \ldots, 500.$$

   a. Calculate the equilibrium wage rate.
   b. Determine the labor supply curve facing any one firm.
   c. At the equilibrium wage rate, determine the elasticity of market supply and the elasticity of supply facing any one firm.

Internet case studies

1. Establish a link between the single-tax theory of Henry George and environmental preservation.
2. Outline two major theories developed by David Ricardo and the impact that these theories have had on economic thought.

APPENDIX TO CHAPTER 16

Investigating comparative statics of input demand

Applied economists employ comparative statics analysis to determine the market effects of wage-rate changes on firms' hiring decisions. For example, the flood of European emigration to America during the nineteenth century had a destabilizing effect on wages. Applied economists can determine the direction and magnitude of such effects using comparative statics analysis. Specifically, comparative statics may be employed for determining the slope of the input demand curves. Intuitively, the slope of the demand curve for an input—say labor—is negative, $\partial L/\partial w < 0$. An increase in wages would tend to dampen a firm's demand for the input. By varying the parameter w (comparative statics), economists can investigate the conditions underlying this negative slope.

One-variable-input case

First let us consider the case with a single variable input (say, labor). Recall that in Stage II of production, MP_L decreases as L increases. VMP is MP times a fixed price p, so VMP_L will also decrease as L increases. The demand curve for one variable input is its VMP curve, so $\partial L/\partial w < 0$. A decrease in w results in an increase in L. Specifically, allowing both w and L to vary, the total differential of $w = pMP_L$ is

$$dw = p\frac{\partial MP_L}{\partial L}\frac{\partial L}{\partial w}dw.$$

Note that MP_L is a function of L and L is a function of w. The functional relationship results in the chain rule. Dividing by dw gives

$$1 = p\frac{\partial MP_L}{\partial L}\frac{\partial L}{\partial w}.$$

Solving for $\partial L/\partial w$ yields

$$\frac{\partial L}{\partial w} = \frac{1}{p\partial MP_L/\partial L}.$$

If $\partial MP_L/\partial L < 0$, which is true for Stage II production, then $\partial L/\partial w < 0$. Given that the production function is characterized by the Law of Diminishing Marginal Returns in Stage II, a firm's demand curve for the one variable input has a negative slope.

Two-variable-input case: substitution effect

Once, when crossing the border between the United States and Mexico, I observed a trench being excavated. On the US side, a backhoe with three workers was being used; on the Mexican side, only workers with picks and shovels were used. This difference is due to the change in the ratio of input prices as you walk across the border. Specifically, a relative price change with two or more variable inputs creates the possibility for a firm to substitute inputs. This is analogous to households substituting commodities when the relative prices of these commodities vary. Recall from Chapter 4 that with use of the Slutsky equation, the total effect on household demand from a commodity price change can be decomposed into the substitution and income effects. A similar Slutsky decomposition exists for a firm's input demand. The total effect on labor demand from a change in w is decomposed into the **substitution effect** and the **output effect**:

$$\text{total effect } (\partial L/\partial w) = \text{substitution effect} + \text{output effect}.$$

Substitution effect

In Figure 16A.1, if output q is held constant at q_1, there will be a tendency to substitute L for K in the productive process given a decrease in w (waking across the border from the United States into Mexico). This is illustrated by a movement from A to B. As discussed in Chapter 8, the FOCs for cost minimization require that MRTS $= w/v$. A decrease in w results

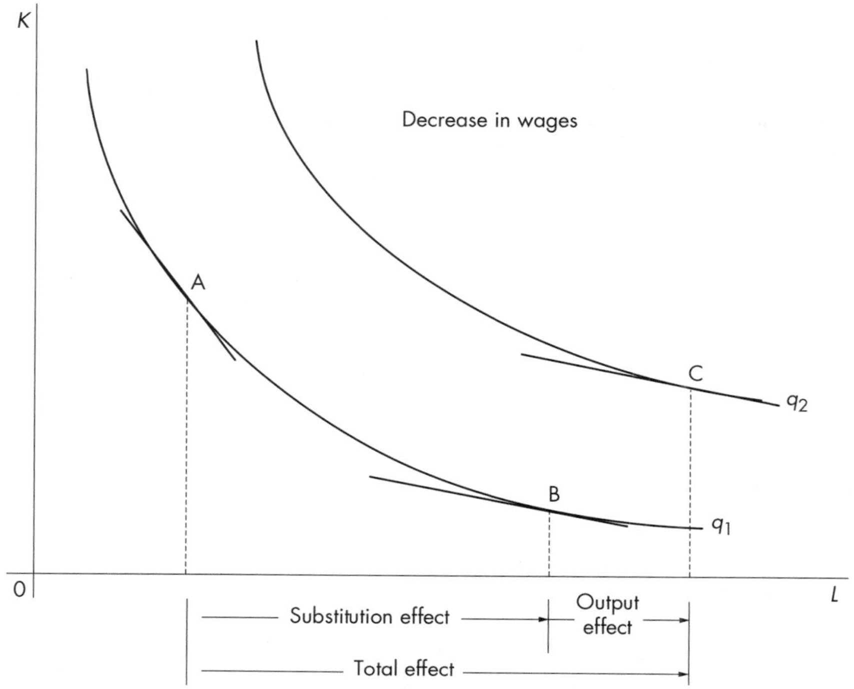

Figure 16A.1 **Substitution and output effects in production.** The total effect of a price change may be decomposed into the substitution and output effects. Given an initial input allocation at A, a wage rate decline results in a substitution effect represented by the movement from A to B plus the output effect, a movement from B to C.

in a movement from A to B, so, due to diminishing MRTS, this substitution effect must be negative:

$$\text{substitution effect} = \left.\frac{\partial L}{\partial w}\right|_{q=q_1} < 0.$$

This is analogous to the substitution effect in consumer theory.

Do firms substitute one input for another given an input price change? Unless the production technology represents fixed proportions, firms can and will substitute one input for another, given an input price change.

Output effect

Next consider the output effect. Generally, a decrease in wages will result in a change in output q. Thus, it is not correct to hold q constant. Considering this change in q (the output effect), the analogy to the household's utility-maximization problem breaks down. The reason is that consumers have budget constraints that firms do not. Firms produce as much as the

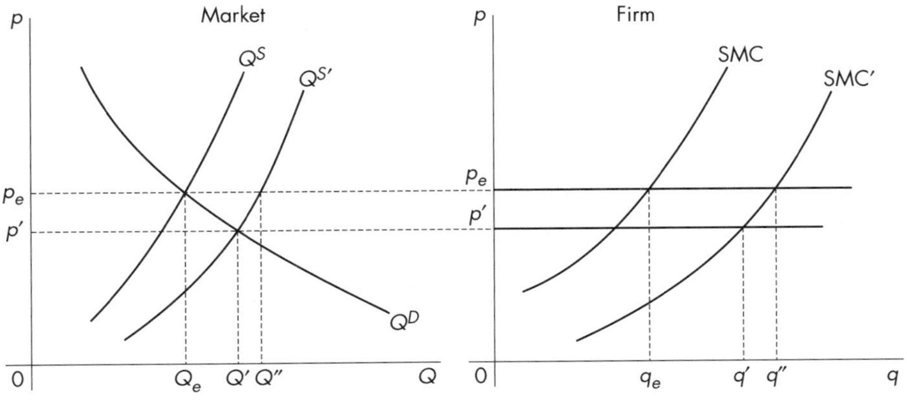

Figure 16A.2 **A decrease in input price shifts the short-run marginal cost curve from SMC to SMC′, which increases the firm's output.** Given a negatively sloping market demand curve, a decline in the input price results in a firm's output increasing from q_e to q'.

available demand allows, with the objective of maximizing profits. Consumers attempt to maximize utility given a budget constraint.

The effect on output from an input price change requires investigating a firm's profit-maximizing output decisions. A decrease in w will shift the firm's expansion path, and thus all cost curves will shift, including short-run marginal cost. As illustrated in Figure 16A.2, the short-run marginal cost curve will shift from SMC to SMC′. This will result in the market supply curve shifting from Q^S to $Q^{S'}$. If market demand were unresponsive to this market supply shift (perfectly elastic), then market output would increase from Q_e to Q'' and individual firms would increase their output from q_e to q''. Instead, market demand is generally negatively sloping, so market price will then decline, from p_e to p', which dampens the increase in output. Output only increases from Q_e to Q' for the market as a whole and from q_e to q' for individual firms. The effect is still an increase in output, so $\partial q/\partial w < 0$. This increase in output will cause even more labor to be demanded, given that $\partial L/\partial q > 0$ in Stage II of production. The output effect is then

$$\text{output effect} = \frac{\partial L}{\partial q}\frac{\partial q}{\partial w} < 0.$$

Will a firm alter its output given an input price change? If the input price change shifts the firm's marginal cost curve, then the firm will alter its output given this price change.

Thus, the substitution and output effects will move the input choice to point C in Figure 16A.1. Both effects work to increase L in response to a decrease in w. Similarly, substitution and output effects will both result in a decrease in L from an increase in w. Combining the substitution and output effects gives the total effect:

$$\text{total effect} = \text{substitution effect} + \text{output effect} < 0.$$

$$\frac{\partial L}{\partial w} = \left.\frac{\partial L}{\partial w}\right|_{dq=0} + \frac{\partial L}{\partial q}\frac{\partial q}{\partial w} < 0.$$

Any firm's demand curve for a factor of production will be negatively sloping, which implies a negatively sloping market demand curve for the factor. Specifically, the market demand curve for an input is the horizontal summation of individual firms' demand curves for that input. This is analogous to the horizontal summation of individual households' demand curves for deriving the market demand curve for a firm's output. In general, both firms and households may have a demand for the same item. Firms will demand the item as an input into production of an output, and households will use the item directly as a commodity for enhancing their welfare. Examples of items used by both firms and households are electricity, water, gasoline, and ice cream. In general, unless the item is specific for a given task, both households and firms could have a demand for it.

Example 16A.1 Inversely related input demand and input prices for the two-input case

Consider the derived input demand functions from Example 16.4:

$$L^* = \frac{p^2}{16w^{3/2}v^{1/2}},$$

$$K^* = \frac{p^2}{16w^{1/2}v^{3/2}}.$$

The response of labor and capital to a change in their own price is

$$\frac{\partial L}{\partial w} = \frac{-\frac{3}{2}p^2}{16w^{5/2}v^{1/2}} < 0,$$

$$\frac{\partial K}{\partial v} = \frac{-\frac{3}{2}p^2}{16w^{1/2}v^{5/2}} < 0.$$

Responsiveness of demand to input price change

As we just saw, an increase in w results in a decrease in L. The magnitude of this response depends on the size of the substitution and output effects. In the short run, the substitution effect will tend to be small relative to the long run because firms do not have as much time to adjust to an input price change. For example, in the short run, a farmer, faced with an increase in the price of water, may substitute other inputs, such as pesticides, to maintain yields. In the long run, the farmer could also adjust the amount of acreage devoted to his crop to maintain overall production. Thus, the substitution effect will tend to be larger in magnitude over the long run. Compared with the short-run input demand curve, this will result in a more elastic long-run demand curve for inputs. This degree of substitution will vary by industries and depends on the elasticity of substitution ξ. For firms within an industry where $\xi = 0$ (fixed proportions), no substitution is possible, so the substitution effect is zero.

In contrast, if the elasticity of substitution is relatively large, firms could make substitutions with relative ease, implying a relatively large substitution effect.

The output effect will also tend to be smaller in the short run than in the long run because firms and households have limited time to adjust. In the long run, two forces will tend to result in a larger output effect. First, the firm's long-run marginal cost curves will be more elastic than the short-run curves in terms of changes in input prices. The more responsive marginal cost is to an input price change, the larger will be the output effect. Second, the market demand curve will become more elastic as households have more time to adjust to the increase in supply and reduced price. The more elastic the market demand curve, the larger will be the output effect.

The magnitude of this output effect will also vary by the type of industry. For example, in the restaurant industry, a large part of a restaurant's cost is labor, so an increase in wages will result in a large increase in the restaurant's marginal costs. This upward shift in marginal cost, combined with the relatively elastic market demand for restaurants, will result in a relatively large output effect. In contrast, self-service service stations, especially pay-at-the-pump stations, have by design a very small part of their costs associated with labor. For these firms, an increase in labor costs will not result in a large shift upward in the marginal cost curve. Marginal cost is relatively inelastic to a wage change. Also, the market demand for gasoline is relatively inelastic, so the output effect will be relatively small.

Application: Minimum wage

> *In all recorded history there has not been one economist who has had to worry about where the next meal would come from.*
>
> (Peter Drucker)

As an application of the substitution and output effects, consider the minimum wage. The **minimum wage** is a price floor (discussed in Chapter 10) below which the wage rate cannot fall. If the minimum wage is below the equilibrium wage rate, then it has no effect on the market. However, if it is set above this equilibrium wage rate, then it will have an influence on the market level of the input. In the United States, a national minimum wage of $0.25 per hour was established by Fair Labor Standards Act of 1938. Since then, the minimum wage has increased in response to general inflation and changing social values.

The effect of a minimum wage on the market for unskilled labor is illustrated in Figure 16A.3. In the absence of a minimum wage, the equilibrium wage rate and unskilled labor hired are w_e and X_e. If imposing a minimum wage increases the wage rate from w_e to w_M, the result is a decrease in the number of unskilled workers hired from X_e to X_M and an increase in the number of unskilled workers willing to work at w_M, X_W. Thus, the quantity supplied, X_W, is greater than the quantity demanded, X_M, which results in an employment gap (unemployment), $X_W - X_M$. The elasticities of supply and demand will determine the magnitude of this gap. If the demand and supply curves are relatively inelastic, this gap will be small. The size of this gap is an empirical question. In fact, there is probably no issue that has received more investigation by economists than minimum-wage policy. The only real consensus is that an increase in the minimum wage will result in a higher wage for unskilled workers who were earning a wage below this new minimum and are able to keep their jobs after the increase becomes effective. However, in other labor markets where an increase in the minimum wage is below the current market wage rate, an increase in the minimum wage may have little if any employment effects.

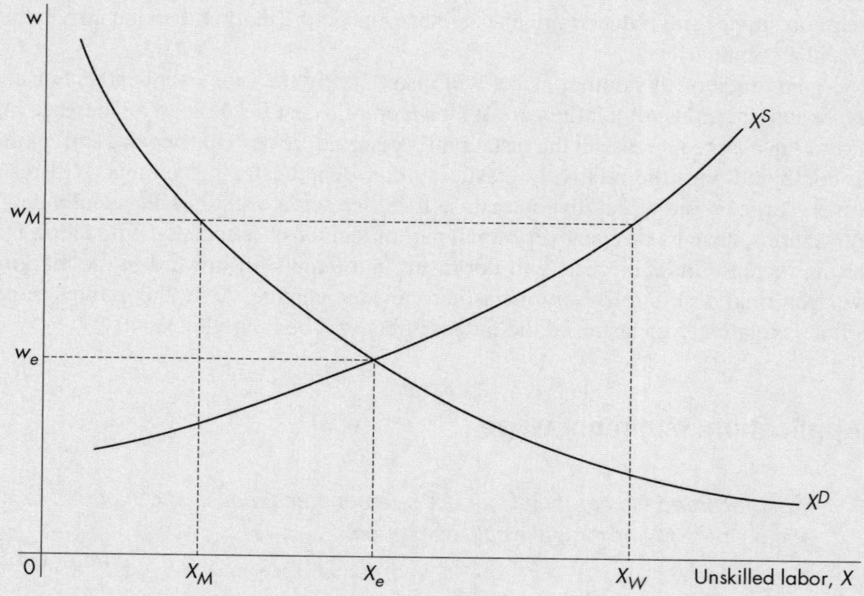

Figure 16A.3 **Minimum wage in the market for unskilled labor.** A minimum wage of w_M increases the wage rate from w_e to w_M, which decreases the quantity demanded for workers from X_e to X_M and increases the quantity supplied from X_e to X_W.

Assuming the minimum wage does increase the wages that a firm must pay unskilled workers, the substitution and output effects of this increase are illustrated in Figure 16A.4. As a result of this increase in unskilled workers' wages, a firm will have an incentive to substitute skilled labor for unskilled labor and decrease output. As illustrated in the figure, an increase in unskilled workers' wages from w_e to w_M results in a movement from point A to point C. The substitution of skilled labor for unskilled labor is one reason why skilled labor unions are in favor of the minimum wage. The minimum wage in Mexico is considerably lower than in the United Sates, which explains the many unskilled Mexican workers with picks and shovels versus the few skilled US workers with a backhoe digging the trench at the border.

Are you affected by the minimum wage? Yes, even given you are earning a wage above the minimum, if your labor can be substituted for minimum-wage earners, then you are affected by the minimum wage.

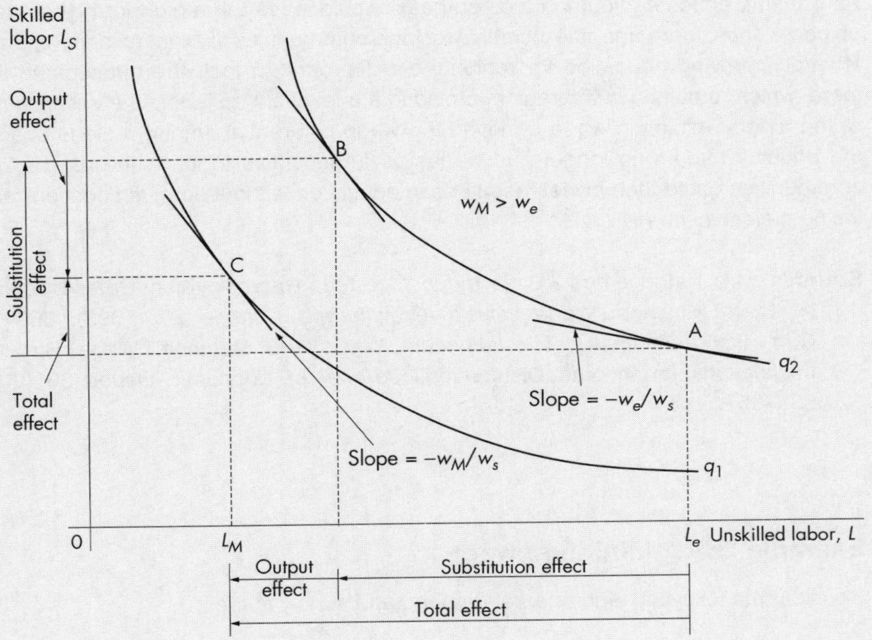

Figure 16A.4 **Total effect of an increase in unskilled wages resulting from an increase in the minimum wage.** Increasing the minimum wage from w_e to w_M results in reducing the employment of unskilled workers from L_e to L_M and increasing the employment of skilled workers.

Teenage unemployment

Empirical evidence indicates that an increase in the minimum wage may adversely affect teenage employment. Particularly hard hit are disadvantaged teenage groups. Given some on-the-job experience, adults who did not finish high school are far less adversely affected by increases in the minimum wage. However, disadvantaged teenagers have very limited skills in terms of formal education and limited, if any, on-the-job training. Furthermore, these individuals are generally not able to commute to areas where employment opportunities are at or above the minimum wage.

Should teenagers be in favor or opposed to an increase in the minimum wage? If they have a job and are able to keep it after the increase, they should favor an increase in the minimum wage; otherwise, they should oppose it.

Regional economic development

In terms of regional economic development, a minimum wage can have significant positive effects. For example, in the United States prior to the first minimum-wage act in 1938, wages in the southeastern United States were significantly lower than in the north.

As a result, educated youth in the southeast would leave the region for higher wages up north. Thus, there was little incentive for local communities to allocate more resources toward improving education for regional development. In fact, the uneducated labor force, which remained in the region, provided a pool of cheap labor. The establishment of the federal minimum wage removed the wage differential among regions and thus the educated youth no longer had wages as an incentive to leave the region. Local communities could then invest resources in education without so much concern about losing their investment.

Sources: M.D. Patridge and J.S. Partridge, "Are Teen Unemployment Rates Influenced by State Minimum Wage Laws?" *Growth and Change* 29 (1998): 359–382. O.M. Levin-Waldman, "The Minimum Wage and Regional Wage Structure: Implications for Income Distribution," *Journal of Economic Issues* 36 (2002): 635–657.

Example 16A.2 Minimum wage

Consider the following labor market demand and supply curves:

$$X^D = 14 - 2w,$$

$$X^S = -1 + w.$$

Equating demand with supply yields the equilibrium wage rate w_e and employment level X_e:

$$X^D = X^S,$$

$$14 - 2w = -1 + w,$$

$$w_e = 5, X_e = 4.$$

Imposing a minimum wage of \$6 reduces the demand for labor by 2, $X^D = 2$, and increases the supply of labor by 1, $X^S = 5$. The resulting level of unemployment is 3.

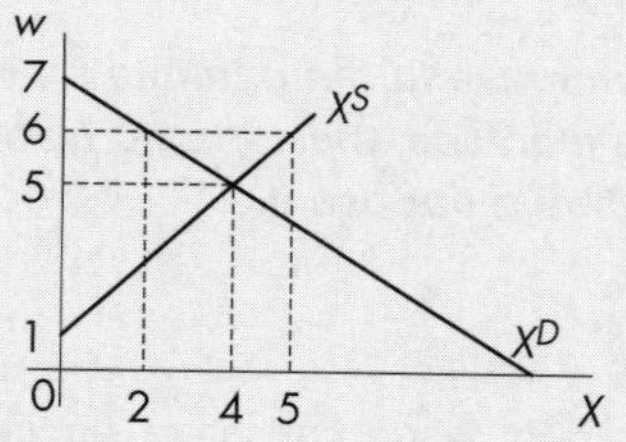

Questions

1. Compare and contrast the effects of agricultural support prices and the minimum-wage laws.
2. The government can legislate a minimum wage, but cannot force employers to hire unprofitable workers. Thus, minimum wages increase unemployment among low-wage workers. True or false? Explain.
3. Minimum-wage laws tend to protect highly skilled workers from competition from unskilled workers. How is this statement correct if the existence of unemployment lowers wages?
4. What is the effect of the minimum wage on the supply of illegal aliens in the United States? Explain.
5. Poverty and unemployment may be eliminated through the minimum wage. An increased minimum wage gives workers more purchasing power, which increases demand for commodities. This increase in demand creates more employment. True or false? Explain.

Exercises

1. The derived demand function for labor, given the production function $q = L^{1/4}K^{1/4}$, is

$$L(p, v, w) = \left(\tfrac{1}{4}p\right)^2 v^{-1/2} w^{-3/2}$$

(see Example 16.4). The supply function for q and the labor demand function conditional on this output q are

$$q(p, v, w) = \tfrac{1}{4}pv^{-1/2}w^{-1/2},$$
$$L(v, w, q) = v^{1/2}w^{-1/2}q^2.$$

Based on this production technology, verify the Slutsky equation

$$\frac{\partial L}{\partial w} = \left.\frac{\partial L}{\partial w}\right|_{dq=0} + \frac{\partial L}{\partial q}\frac{\partial q}{\partial w} < 0.$$

2. Consider the following input market demand and supply functions:

$$X^D = 10 - v,$$
$$X^S = v.$$

a. Determine the market equilibrium input price and quantity.
b. Calculate the economic rent and consumer surplus.
c. Suppose that a minimum price of $v = 6$ is imposed by the government. What is the new equilibrium level of X? What is the level of unemployed input, and the new levels of economic rent, consumer surplus, and deadweight loss?

3. An increase in the minimum wage raises a firm's relative demand for skilled labor versus unskilled. Will it also increase the absolute demand for skilled labor, if skilled and unskilled workers are perfect complements? What if they are perfect substitutes? What assumptions are skilled trade unions implying when they support raising the minimum wage?

Internet case study

1. List the arguments for and against the minimum wage.

17 Monopoly power in input markets

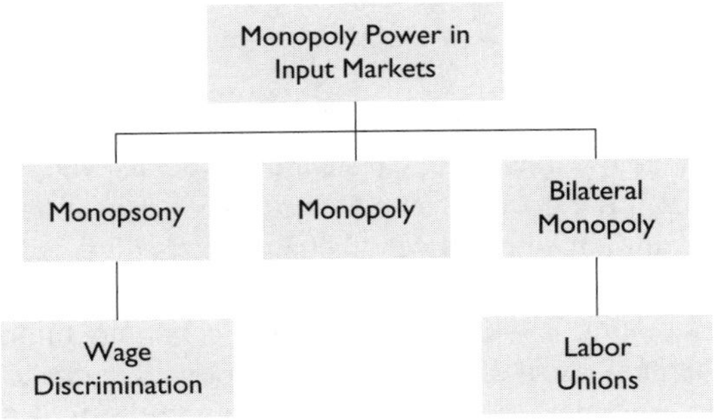

Outline and Conceptual Inquiries

The rights and interests of the laboring man will be protected and cared for not by our labor agitators, but by the Christian men to whom God in his infinite wisdom has given control of property interests of the country, and upon the successful management of which so much remains.

(George Baer)

Firm owners in the nineteenth century felt they had a God-given right to exercise monopoly power on their workers. They were the aristocrats who ran not only industry and commerce but also the government. As a result of their monopoly power in the input market, called **monopsony power**, factor markets diverged from the perfectly competitive assumption developed in Chapter 16. In the input market, **monopsony**, a single buyer for an input, is the polar case of perfect competition. An example is a mining firm in a company town. If you are to be employed in this town, you will work for the mine. Other examples are a southern plantation prior to the Civil War and, in agricultural regions, a single food-processing plant dominating employment for many miles around. A firm that is a major but not the sole employer is called an **oligopsony**. Examples are a number of textile companies in a small town or a university in a college town. It is also possible for a supplier of the input to possess monopoly power. For example, in some labor markets, a labor union may have monopoly power.

Monopsony power. A buyer of an input has some control over the price of the input. *E.g., a sawmill in a local community determining the price for timber.*

Monopsony. Only a single buyer for an input. *E.g., the US Post Office hiring mail carriers.*

Oligopsony. A buyer in a market with only a few other buyers. *E.g., a small number of lumber mills in a valley.*

Our aim in this chapter is to determine the efficiency loss associated with monopoly and monopsony power in a factor market. To do so, we must first determine firms' input pricing and employment decisions under various assumptions concerning buyers' monopsony power and suppliers' monopoly power. As in Chapter 16, the focus of this investigation is on the labor market. We first derive a monopsony's profit-maximizing wage rate and level of employment. The general condition that a firm equates its marginal revenue to marginal cost for profit maximization still holds. However, in this case, marginal revenue and marginal cost are measured as the additional worker hired rather than the additional output produced. We illustrate the inefficiency of monopsony pricing by the deadweight loss in total surplus. In our discussion, we see that monopoly in the supply of inputs is the same as a monopoly supplying any output, discussed in Chapter 12. With knowledge gained about monopsony and monopoly input pricing, we investigate a monopoly facing a monopsony, called a *bilateral monopoly*. We then discuss labor unions as cartels with the potential of exerting monopoly power, in terms of their objectives and effectiveness. Similar to output-price discrimination, a monopsony may wage-discriminate. We discuss first-, second- and third-degree wage discrimination in the Appendix to this chapter.

The rise of monopsony power directed toward labor in the nineteenth century and the emergence of labor unions to counter this power is an ongoing topic of research. Applied economists working for monopsonies are constantly devising new approaches to determine the factor supplier's reservation price (wage). Similarly, economists for factor suppliers are always devising methods for determining the demanders' reservation price.

Determining the monopsony wage and employment

Australia's Medicare, Canada's Medicare, and the United Kingdom's National Health Service are single-payer universal health-care systems, where the government is the only buyer of health-care services. Such conditions are characteristic of firms with monopsony power in the labor market (doctor services) facing an upward-sloping supply curve for labor.

Analogous to a monopoly facing the market demand curve, a monopsony, as the sole employer of the input, faces the market supply curve. Thus, for a monopsony to hire an additional input (say, labor), the price (wage rate) has to increase not just for the additional input (worker) but for all inputs (workers). So the marginal input cost (MIC) curve is upward-sloping and lies above the supply curve. For example, given a linear inverse market labor supply curve, the firm's average input cost, AIC, is

$$\mathrm{AIC}_L = w = a + bL, \quad \text{with } b > 0;$$

then $\partial w/\partial L = b > 0$. For the firm to hire an additional worker, wages for all workers must increase by b. Given that the total input cost, TIC, is

$$\mathrm{TIC}_L = (\mathrm{AIC}_L)L = aL + bL^2,$$

the marginal input cost is then

$$\mathrm{MIC}_L = \frac{\partial \mathrm{TIC}_L}{\partial L} = a + 2bL,$$

$$\frac{\partial \mathrm{MIC}_L}{\partial L} = 2b > 0.$$

For a linear supply curve, the MIC curve is twice as steep as the AIC curve and thus bisects this AIC curve and the vertical axis.

This effect of imperfect competition in a labor market (monopsony power) is illustrated in Figure 17.1. A monopsony who hires a relatively large share of the available employees faces an upward-sloping average input cost curve (supply curve) for labor, the AIC_L curve. AIC_L (wages) is a function of the number of workers hired, $w(L)$. Increasing the number of workers, L, then requires increasing wages, $\partial w(L)/\partial L > 0$. In other words, for the firm to hire an additional worker, it must increase the wage rate. This corresponds to moving to a higher point on the AIC_L curve. The monopsony will pay a higher wage not only to the additional

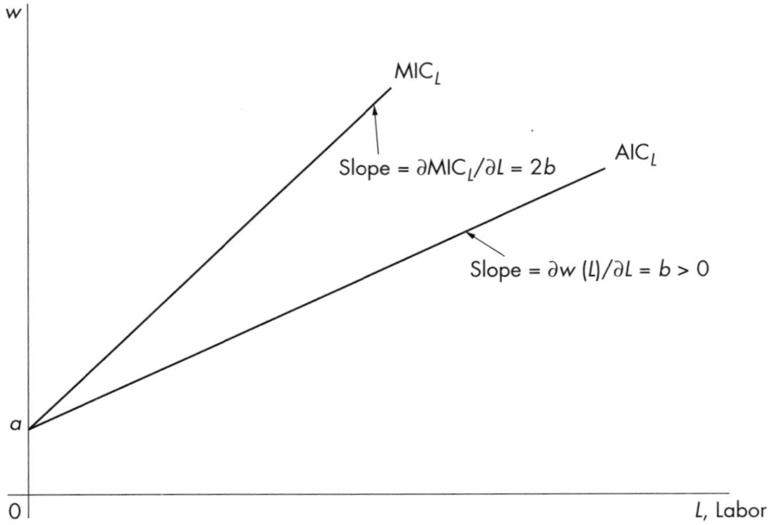

Figure 17.1 **Monopsony power in the labor market resulting in $\mathrm{MIC}_L > \mathrm{AIC}_L$.** For a monopsony to hire an additional worker, it must increase the wage rate not only for this additional worker but for all the workers. This results in $\mathrm{MIC}_L > \mathrm{AIC}_L$.

worker but also to those workers already employed. Specifically, $\mathrm{TIC}_L = w(L)L$. Using the product rule to take the derivative with respect to L yields

$$\mathrm{MIC}_L = \frac{\partial[w(L)L]}{\partial L} = w + L\frac{\partial w}{\partial L} = \mathrm{AIC}_L + L\frac{\partial w}{\partial L}.$$

That is, the marginal input cost for labor (MIC_L) is equal to AIC_L plus an adjustment factor $L\partial w/\partial L$. This adjustment factor accounts for having to pay a higher wage to those workers already employed.

Under perfect competition in the factor market, this adjustment factor is zero, $\partial w/\partial L = 0$, so the marginal cost of hiring one more worker is the market wage w. With perfect competition in the factor market, the firm takes the wage rate as given. For a firm with monopsony power, this adjustment factor is positive, $L\partial w/\partial L > 0$, so the marginal input cost of hiring an additional worker (MIC_L) is greater than the wage rate (AIC_L). Recall that if the marginal unit (in this case MIC_L) is greater than the average unit (AIC_L), the average is rising. This relation between MIC_L and AIC_L is illustrated in Figure 17.1. AIC_L is rising, $\partial w/\partial L > 0$, so the adjustment is positive. This results in $\mathrm{MIC}_L > \mathrm{AIC}_L$.

In terms of elasticity of supply, $\varepsilon^S = (\partial L^S/\partial w)(w/L^S)$, we represent MIC_L as

$$\mathrm{MIC}_L = \frac{\partial(wL)}{\partial L} = w + L\frac{\partial w}{\partial L} = w\left(1 + \frac{1}{\varepsilon^S}\right) = \mathrm{AIC}_L\left(1 + \frac{1}{\varepsilon^S}\right).$$

When supply is perfectly elastic ($\varepsilon^S = \infty$), the supply curve is horizontal and $\mathrm{MIC}_L = \mathrm{AIC}_L$ (the firm is a perfectly competitive employer of labor). In contrast, when a firm is facing an upward-sloping supply curve, $0 < \varepsilon^S < \infty$, the potential for monopsony power exists with $\text{MIC}_L > \text{AIC}_L$.

How monopsonies maximize profit

There is no way of keeping profits up, but by keeping wages down.

(David Ricardo)

Suppose that a firm with monopsony power in both of its two variable inputs L and K is interested in maximizing profits,

$$\max_{(q,L,K)} \pi = \max_{(q,L,K)} [pq - w(L)L - v(K)K - \text{TFC}],$$

subject to a production function

$$q = f(L, K).$$

Forming the Lagrangian, we have

$$\mathcal{L}(q, L, K, \lambda) = pq - w(L)L - v(K)K - \text{TFC} - \lambda[q - f(L, K)].$$

The first-order conditions (FOCs) are

$$\frac{\partial \mathcal{L}}{\partial q} = \text{MR} - \lambda^* = 0,$$

$$\frac{\partial \mathcal{L}}{\partial L} = -\text{MIC}_L + \lambda^* \text{MP}_L = 0,$$

$$\frac{\partial \mathcal{L}}{\partial K} = -\text{MIC}_K + \lambda^* \text{MP}_K = 0,$$

$$\frac{\partial \mathcal{L}}{\partial \lambda} = q - f(L, K) = 0.$$

As developed in Chapter 12, $\text{MR} = p + (\partial p/\partial q)q$. If there is perfect competition in the output market, then $\partial p/\partial q = 0$ and $\text{MR} = p$. Otherwise, the firm also has some monopoly power in its output market, so $\text{MR} < p$. The first FOC indicates that $\text{MR} = \lambda^*$. Substituting $\text{MR} = \lambda^*$ into the next two FOCs yields the conditions for profit maximization:

$$\text{MIC}_L = \text{MRP}_L,$$

$$\text{MIC}_K = \text{MRP}_K.$$

As defined in Chapter 16, $\text{MR}(\text{MP}_L) = \text{MRP}_L$, the marginal revenue product of labor. Similarly, $\text{MR}(\text{MP}_K) = \text{MRP}_K$, the marginal revenue product of capital.

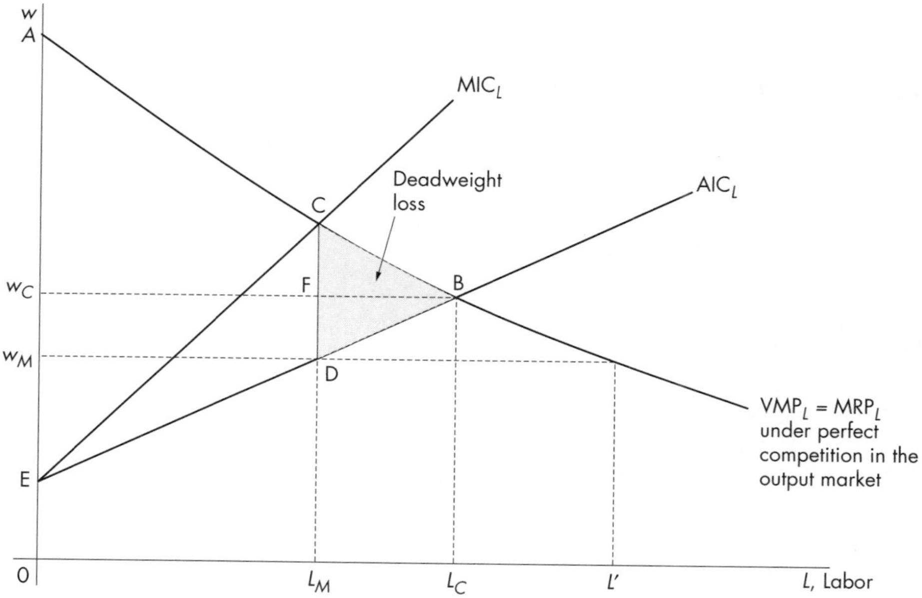

Figure 17.2 **Comparison of perfect competition and monopsony wage rate and labor employment.** By restricting the amount of labor employed from the perfectly competitive level L_C to L_M and reducing the wage rate offered from the perfectly competitive wage w_C to w_M, the monopsony is inefficient. This inefficiency is represented by the deadweight loss, the shaded area DCB.

As indicated in Figure 17.2, the FOCs imply that a monopsony has restricted labor and decreased wages compared with the perfectly competitive market solution. The monopsony firm equates MIC_L to MRP_L for determining the profit-maximizing level of labor, L_M. We obtain the wage rate necessary to acquire this level of labor, w_M, by moving up to the AIC_L curve and across. A perfectly competitive market equilibrium corresponds to where $\text{AIC}_L = \text{MRP}_L$. The competitive equilibrium input price and level of input are then w_C and L_C, respectively, compared with a monopsony, where $L_C > L_M$ and $w_C > w_M$. To keep profits up, a monopsony will keep wages down.

Does a monopsony offer the lowest wage it can? No, a monopsony does restrict the employment of labor and reduces the wage rate, but it does not offer the lowest wage it can. Instead, it offers a wage that will maximize its profit.

In the case of monopsony power, the MRP_L curve is not the labor demand curve of the firm. As illustrated in Figure 17.2, if the MRP_L curve were the demand curve, at w_M the monopsony would be willing to hire L' workers, but instead it is only willing to hire L_M. (Recall from Chapter 16 that the MRP is only the input demand curve for a perfectly competitive firm for a single variable input.) This fact that the MRP_L curve is not the demand curve for a monopsony is analogous to the fact that the MC curve is not the supply curve for a monopoly as discussed in Chapter 12. In both cases, the firm will instead restrict the market allocation to maximize profit. A monopoly restricts the output and increases the output price, and a monopsony restricts the input and decreases the input price.

Example 17.1 Determining the input price and employment for a firm with monopsony power

Suppose that a monopsony has the production function $q = 48L - L^2$. Assume the firm is facing an output price $p = 6$ and that its total wage bill for labor (total input cost for labor) is $\text{TIC}_L = 6L^2$. Output price is constant, which implies perfect competition in the output market. The objective of the monopsony is to maximize profits:

$$\max_{(q,\,L)} \pi = \max_{(q,\,L)} (pq - \text{TIC}_L) \quad \text{s.t. } q = 48L - L^2.$$

Substituting the production function, output price, and the function for TIC_L into the objective function results in

$$\max_L \pi = \max_L \left[6\left(48L - L^2\right) - 6L^2\right].$$

The FOC is then

$$\frac{d\pi}{dL} = 6(48 - 2L_M) - 12L_M = 0.$$

$\text{MRP}_L = 6(48 - 2L_M)$ and $\text{MIC}_L = 12L_M$. Solving for L_M gives

$$L_M = 12.$$

The monopsony wage is $w_M = 72$. We determine this wage, which is AIC_L, by noting that $\text{AIC}_L = 6L$. We also note that the MIC curve is twice as steep as the linear AIC curve. Given a linear AIC curve, the MIC curve bisects this AIC curve and the vertical axis.

Note that the Lerner Index for this monopsony is

$$L_I = (144 - 72)/72 = 1.$$

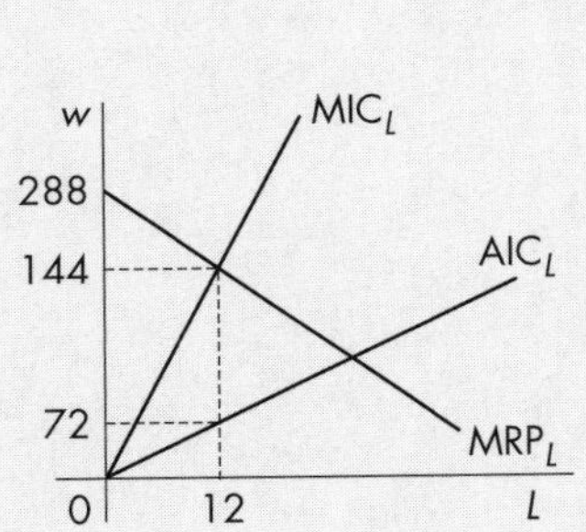

Example 17.2 Comparing perfect competition and monopsony input price and employment

Continuing with Example 17.1, we determine the perfectly competitive equilibrium wage and number of workers hired (w_C, L_C) by equating MRP_L to AIC_L:

$$6(48 - 2L) = 6L.$$

Solving for L,

$$L_C = 16.$$

The wage or AIC_L under perfect competition is then $w_C = 96$.

Under perfect competition, the consumer surplus accruing to the firm employing labor as an input is

$$\text{consumer surplus} = (288 - 96)16/2 = \$1536.$$

Economic rent under perfect competition is

$$\text{economic rent} = (96)(16)/2 = \$768.$$

In contrast, with monopsony power, consumer surplus increases to

$$\text{consumer surplus} = [(288 - 144)12/2] + (144 - 72)12 = \$1728,$$

and economic rent decreases to

$$\text{economic rent} = (72)(12)/2 = \$432.$$

This results in a deadweight loss of $(1536 + 768 - 1728 - 432) = \$144$.

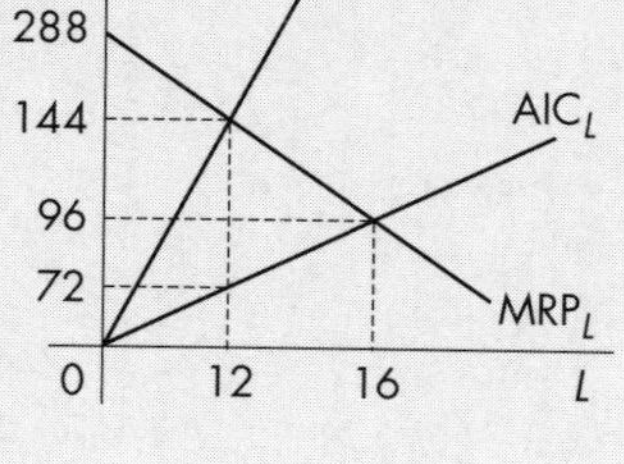

Understanding the inefficient monopsony market

> *Current poverty is unlike that of the past centuries. It is not the result of natural scarcity, but of a set of priorities imposed upon the rest of the world by the rich. Consequently, the modern poor are not pitied, but written off as trash.*
>
> (John Berger)

The monopsony's profit-maximizing solution is to restrict the number of workers and decrease the wage rate compared with the perfectly competitive market solution. This results in an inefficient solution where $w = \text{AIC}_L < \text{MRP}_L$. MRP is the additional revenue or benefit to society from hiring an additional worker and w is the cost of hiring this additional worker. The benefits are thus greater than the cost, so society would prefer the firm to increase employment. In contrast, the perfectly competitive solution is $w = \text{MRP}_L$, indicating that the additional benefits just equal the additional cost.

We can illustrate this inefficiency in a monopsony market by the net loss in consumer surplus and economic rent. In a perfectly competitive input market, the sum of consumer surplus and economic rent is maximized. Specifically,

$$\max_L(\text{consumer surplus} + \text{economic rent})$$

$$= \max_L\left[(\text{TR} - wL) + \left(wL - \int_0^L \text{AIC}_L dL\right)\right]$$

$$= \max_L\left(\text{TR} - \int_0^L \text{AIC}_L dL\right)$$

$$= \max_L\left[pq(L) - \int_0^L \text{AIC}_L dL\right].$$

The FOC results in $\text{MRP}_L = \text{AIC}_L$. A perfectly competitive input market will result in $\text{MIC}_L = \text{AIC}_L = \text{MRP}_L$, which maximizes the sum of consumer surplus and economic rent. By not equating AIC_L to MRP_L, the monopsony is not maximizing this sum of the surpluses and thus is inefficient.

This inefficiency is illustrated in Figure 17.2. Under perfect competition, consumer surplus is the area w_CAB and economic rent is the area Ew_CB. A monopsony restricts the amount of the input employed, which results in the input price falling to w_M. Consumer surplus increases to the area w_MACD, which captures some of the perfect-competition economic rent, the area $w_M w_C$FD. This is a measure of the level of exploitation by the monopsony. In terms of the labor market, this is a measure of how the firm is exploiting the labor class. Thus, economic rent is reduced to the area Ew_MD. The efficiency loss resulting from monopsony power is represented by the deadweight loss, the shaded area DCB. In markets where firms are exploiting labor by exercising a great deal of monopsony power, poverty is not a result of national resource scarcity but is caused by the rich exploiting the poor.

A firm with monopsony power in its input market reacts much the same as a firm with monopoly power in its output market. In both cases, the firm has control over its market, by reacting to either consumer demand for a monopoly or input supply for a monopsony. Both types of firms restrict the market allocation compared with the perfectly competitive solution.

Deriving the Lerner Index

As with monopoly power, a Lerner Index exists for measuring the degree of monopsony power. This index measures the relative wedge between wages w and MRP_L. Specifically, given

$$\text{MIC}_L = w\left(1 + \frac{1}{\varepsilon^S}\right),$$

at the optimal level of profits,

$$\text{MRP}_L = w\left(1 + \frac{1}{\varepsilon^S}\right).$$

Solving for $1/\varepsilon^S$ yields a Lerner Index

$$L_I = \frac{\text{MRP}_L - w}{w} = \frac{1}{\varepsilon^S}.$$

Thus, the difference between MRP_L and w provides a measure of monopsony power. Specifically, it is the percentage markdown due to monopsony power. If $\text{MRP}_L = w$, then $L_I = 0$, and the firm is not exercising any monopsony power. If there are few alternatives for employment, then the supply curve for labor becomes more inelastic, the wedge between MRP_L and w increases, and L_I increases, indicating a greater degree of monopsony power.

Monopsony power is particularly prevalent where the cost for workers relocating or computing to alternative employment is high. As these costs are reduced, the monopsony power of firms declines. For example, first the automobile and then the interstate highway system greatly increased the mobility of workers, removing the monopsony power of many company towns. Regional public transit systems that allow intercity workers to be employed outside the city decrease intercity monopsony power of firms. The Internet is currently greatly reducing the monopsony power of firms by giving many people the ability to work from home and thus enlarging employment opportunities. In contrast, the sustained high unemployment levels after the Great Recession are partially caused by unemployed households unable to accept employment requiring them to relocate. The collapse of the housing market prevents households from selling their houses and relocating without incurring high relocation costs. Such constraints on household mobility support firms' local monopsony power.

Application: Monopsony power in major league baseball

Mullin and Dunn utilized baseball card prices to measure the star quality (charisma) of major league baseball players. Based on this star quality measure and player productivity, they measured players' MRP and examined monopsonistic exploitation. Using an econometric model, Mullin and Dunn estimated each player's MRP and compared it with his salary. Table 17.1 lists their estimated MRPs, salaries, and Lerner indexes. These estimates indicate that hitters are far more exploited than pitchers. Pitchers are close to the competitive salary level, whereas a greater level of monopsony power is being excised with hitters. However, salary is not the only cost that a ball team incurs in hiring players. Considering other costs, say, the cost of supporting the Minor League teams for developing Major League players, would reduce these estimated degrees of monopsony power.

Table 17.1. Marginal revenue product, salary, and Lerner Index for major league baseball

Player	*Marginal revenue product (MRP) (average)*	*Salary (average)*	*Lerner Index*
American League	2,622,000	1,033,000	1.5
National League	2,498,000	996,000	1.5
Hitters	3,407,000	1,007,000	2.4
Pitchers	1,393,000	1,028,000	0.3

Source: C.J. Mullin and L.F. Dunn, "Using Baseball Card Prices to Measure Star Quality and Monopsony," *Economic Inquiry* 40 (2002): 620–632.

Application: Teachers face monopsony power

A teacher shortage within the United States has existed for well over half a century. When labor shortages persist, monopsony power as a cause is hypothesized. As a test of this hypothesis, S. Kitae used an index to measure monopsony power facing the US teacher labor market. Results reveal that the index is substantially higher in the teacher labor market relative to other comparable labor markets. Thus, this supports the hypothesis that monopsony power is a cause of the teacher shortage.

Source: S. Kitae, "The Monopsony Power in the US Teacher Labor Market," *Empirical Economics Letters* 7 (2008): 553–559.

Monopoly in the supply of inputs

Every advance in this half-century: Social Security, civil rights, Medicare, aid to education ... one after another—came with the support and leadership of American Labor.

(Jimmy Carter)

Suppliers of the input form a cartel and exercise some degree of monopoly power. The objective of this cartel will vary depending on the nature of the input. For example, labor unions may be more interested in maximizing the wages of current union membership or increasing the size of the union rather than maximizing the union's economic rent (equating marginal cost to marginal revenue). However, it is generally assumed that a sole

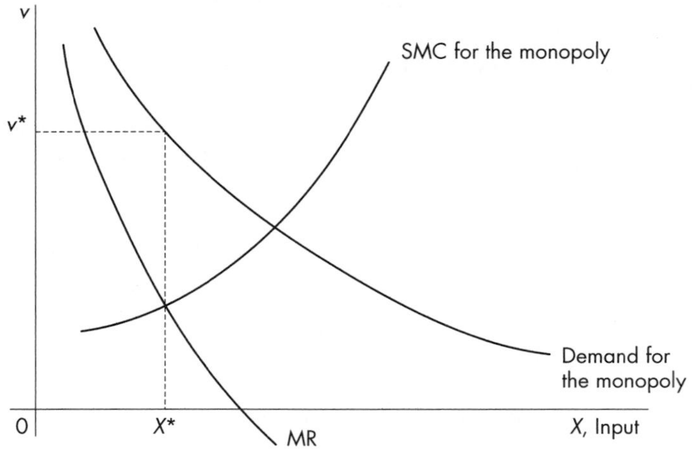

Figure 17.3 **Monopoly in the input market.** The monopoly equates SMC to MR to determine its profit-maximizing supply of factor X.

supplier of an input (other than labor) will attempt to maximize economic rent (profit). The supplier's output is an input used by another firm. Thus, the monopoly models for output and price determination discussed in Chapters 12 and 13 are applicable here. As discussed in Chapter 12, a monopoly will generally restrict output below and increase price above the perfectly competitive equilibrium. This same monopoly solution for a firm with monopoly power in the input market is illustrated in Figure 17.3. The monopoly is facing the market demand for its output, which is the horizontal summation of all the firms' derived demand for the output supplied by this monopoly. Given an SMC curve, the input monopoly will equate SMC to the MR associated with this market demand and determine its profit-maximizing output X^*. The firm will then determine the price v^* at which it can sell all of this output from the market demand curve. As discussed in Chapter 13, the input monopoly can practice price discrimination and any other (legal?) practices in an effort to enhance profit. Similarly, if there are a number of suppliers of an input, alternative game-theory models may describe their strategic interactions.

What is bilateral monopoly and bargaining?

Under capitalism, man exploits man. Under communism, it is just the opposite.

(John Kenneth Galbraith)

Translation: A monopsony attempts to exploit labor and a labor union attempts to exploit firms.

In 1981, after the Professional Air Traffic Controllers Organization (PATCO) went on strike, President Reagan fired 11,359 controllers. It was not until August 1993 that President Clinton signed an Executive Order lifting the ban on the rehiring of the controllers. By 2006, only 846 controllers had been rehired. The Federal Aviation Administration (FAA) was sued by PATCO for age discrimination in hiring back the controllers. It goes without saying that the PATCO strike marked a turning point in labor relations.

This scenario is an example of a **bilateral monopoly,** where a monopoly supplier of an input (traffic controllers) sells its input (labor) to a monopsony buyer (FAA). (*Bilateral oligopoly*, where a set of oligopoly firms supply to oligopsony firms, can also exist.) Other examples of bilateral monopoly power are the NFL players and owners; the US Postal Service and the National Postal Handlers Union; and a textile firm and the Union of Needletrades, Industrial, and Textile Employees (UNITE). Also, a bureau or government-sponsored nongovernmental organization (NGO) and its government review group may be considered a bilateral monopoly. A *bureau* or an NGO are defined as nonprofit organizations that are financed by a periodic appropriation, and the employees do not appropriate any part of the difference between revenues and costs as personal income. A bilateral monopoly exists when a bureau or NGO sell their services only to the government and the government buys this service only from the bureau or NGO.

Bilateral monopoly. A monopoly selling its output to a monopsony. *E.g., the US Department of Defense and a military arms manufacturing firm.*

The case of a bilateral monopoly for an input X is illustrated in Figure 17.4. The curve labeled X^D is either the VMP_X or MRP_X, curve, according to whether the final output produced by this input is sold under conditions of perfect competition or monopoly. The MRP_X curve represents how much the monopsony is willing to pay per unit for a given level of the input. This directly corresponds to the AR curve for the monopoly. Thus, the MRP_X for a monopsony is the monopoly's AR curve. Although a monopoly has no supply curve, if a monopoly were constrained to sell at competitive prices (rather than where SMC = MR), then the upward-sloping portion of the monopoly's SMC curve above its SAVC would indicate the amounts that would be supplied. The SMC curve then represents how much the monopoly is willing to supply at a given wage. Again, this directly corresponds to the AIC_X curve for the monopsony.

The monopsony solution is X_M and v_M, where the monopsony equates MRP_X to MIC_X. Ignoring the monopsony power of the buyer and considering only the monopoly power of the seller, we see that the monopoly's profit-maximizing output and price are X_U and v_U, where the monopoly equates MR to SMC. The buyer and seller are, in general, close to agreement on the amount of input to hire. The objective of both is to restrict output from the perfectly competitive solution. Thus, their equilibrium levels of the input are often the same or close, as indicated in Figure 17.4. For example, professional football players are in general agreement with team owners on the number of players for each team. However, there is an inherent conflict on the wage rate. The input price offered by the monopoly, v_U, is considerably higher than the price offered by the monopsony, v_M. Given only one buyer and one seller of the input, they will reach some agreement, but it is impossible to determine the actual price that will be established without knowing the bargaining strengths and skills of each firm. We could only make assumptions and incorporate them into a game-theory model to determine the optimal strategies for the agents.

Until the 1990s, labor fared well in bargaining situations. Afterward, labor influence has generally declined. For example, the bargaining in the 1990s between Caterpillar and the United Auto Workers, along with 6- and 17-month strikes, resulted in very limited gains

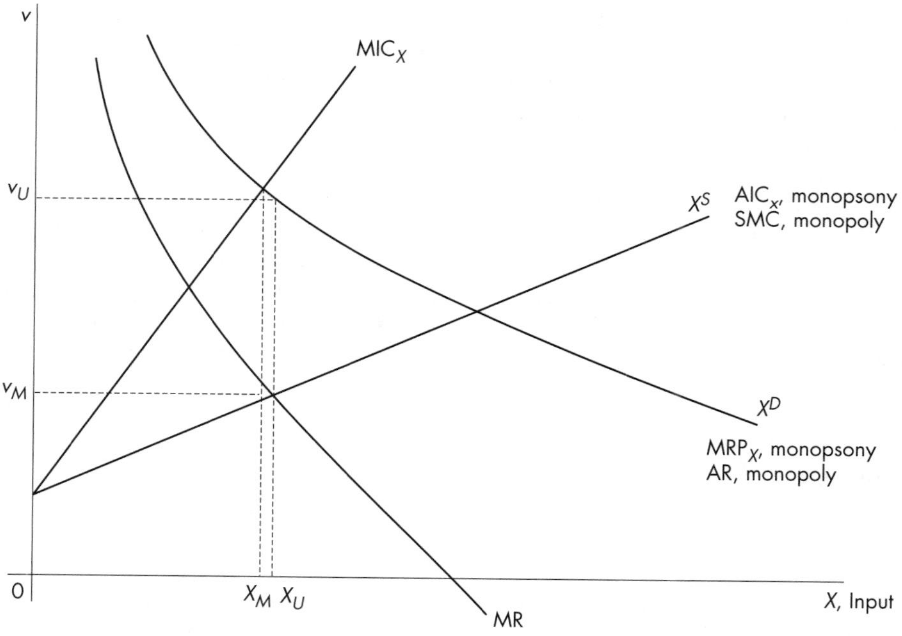

Figure 17.4 **Bilateral monopoly.** The monopsony's input price and the level of the input it is willing to hire are v_M and X_M. In contrast, the monopoly's price and level of input it is willing to offer are v_U and X_U.

by the union. The now famous bargaining phase between President Reagan and PATCO resulted in the controllers losing not only all their demands but also their jobs. Unions have been facing increased opposition and loss of bargaining rights. An example is the governor of Wisconsin in 2011 removing such rights from public employees. In contrast, the United Parcel Service (UPS) and Teamsters Union negotiations (with a strike in 1997) resulted in more full-time employees. Numerous negotiations between the baseball players' union and team owners (with 8 strikes in a span of 12 years) diminished the popularity of the sport, with long-term damage to both players and owners. As a result, there has been no talk of strikes this century. In general, monopsony buying power may be partially or entirely negated by the countervailing monopoly selling power.

Can unions improve efficiency? If unions can counter the monopsony power of firms with a resulting increase in wages and number of workers hired, then unions can result in improved efficiency.

Example 17.3. Bilateral monopoly

Let a monopsony's production function and a monopoly's marginal cost function be

$$q = 60X - \tfrac{1}{2}X^2,$$

$$SMC_X = X,$$

where SMC_X corresponds to the monopsony's AIC_X. Total input cost for the monopsony is then

$$TIC_X = vX = X^2.$$

Assuming that the monopsony attempts to maximize profits,

$$\max_{(q,X)} \pi = \max_{(q,X)} (TR - TIC_X)$$
$$= \max_{(q,X)} \left(pq - X^2\right)$$
$$= \max_{(X)} \left[p\left(60X - \tfrac{1}{2}X^2\right) - X^2\right].$$

The FOC is then

$$\frac{d\pi}{dX} = p(60 - X_M) - 2X_M = 0,$$

that is,

$$MRP_X - MIC_X = 0.$$

Solving for X_M gives

$$60p - pX_M - 2X_M = 0,$$
$$X_M(p+2) = 60p,$$
$$X_M = 60p/(p+2).$$

If $p = 1$, then $X_M = 20$. The monopsony's input price v_M is determined by how much it must offer to purchase X_M inputs. This is based on the AIC_X curve, as follows:

$$AIC_X = TIC_X/X = X,$$
$$v_M = X_M = 20.$$

The Lerner Index associated with this monopsony price is $L_{IM} = (40 - 20)/20 = 1$.

As for the monopoly, it attempts to maximize profit, given its demand curve, which is the monopsony's MRP_X curve:

$$AR = v_U = MRP_X = p(60 - X).$$

At $p=1$, $AR = 60 - X$ and $TR = (60 - X)X$, which results in $MR = 60 - 2X$. Equating MR to the monopoly's SMC curve results in the equilibrium solution for the monopoly:

$$MR = SMC,$$

$$60 - 2X = X,$$

$$X_U = 20.$$

The monopoly's price is determined by the AR curve:

$$v_U = AR = 60 - X_U,$$

$$v_U = 40.$$

The Lerner Index for this monopoly price is $L_{IU} = (40 - 20)/40 = 1/2$.

In this case, the equilibrium level of the input is the same for both the monopsony and the monopoly. However, their equilibrium level of price is not the same, $v_M < v_U$. Through negotiations, as the price converges from these two extreme levels and the input increases, the two Lerner Indices approach zero. The countervailing monopoly selling power will offset the monopsony buying power, which results in a more efficient input allocation. This is an example of a violation of the Theory of the Second Best, discussed in Chapter 20. Basically, this theory suggests that removing one source of monopoly power will improve efficiency. This example illustrates how it is possible for the reverse to occur. Allowing monopoly power in the face of monopsony power may in some cases improve efficiency.

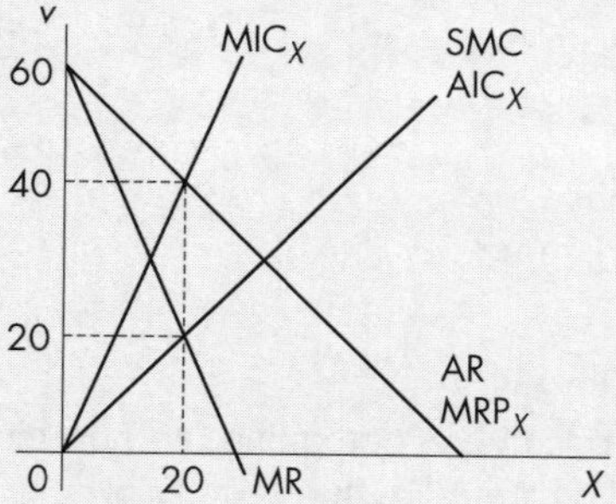

Application: Bilateral monopoly in Canadian chicken markets

J.P. Gervais and S. Devadoss hypothesize that processors and producers of chickens in Ontario represent a bilateral monopoly, where the equilibrium price of chickens depends on a coefficient of bargaining power. Considering the stochastic properties of price and cost data, the hypothesis of equal bargaining strengths between processors and producers in Ontario over the period 1997–2002 is rejected. Chicken processors had greater bargaining power than producers.

Source: J.-P. Gervais and S. Devadoss, "Estimating Bargaining Strengths of Canadian Chicken Producers and Processors Using a Bilateral Monopoly Framework," *Agribusiness* 22 (2006): 159–173.

Labor unions

A **labor union** is a cartel of workers with the objective of promoting the interests of the union membership. The objective of a union varies a great deal depending on the desires of the membership or the union bosses. Some unions are solely interested in improving working conditions and benefits of their members; others may have social goals or a political agenda. In the past, unions have advocated the establishment of a communist or socialist state. However, most unions within the United States are mainly interested in improving members' benefits.

Labor union. A cartel of workers with the objective of promoting the interest of the union membership. *E.g., the United Auto Workers.*

Unions' influence over wages.

Union gives strength.

(Aesop's Fables)

Translated: Unions can counter monopsony power.

A labor union does not try to maximize wages, because then only a few workers would be hired. It also does not encourage firms to hire as many workers as possible, because then the wage rate would be very low or zero. Instead, a general objective of a labor union may be to increase the wages of union members.

Wages are determined by forces of supply and demand, similar to prices in an output market. Thus, for a union to modify wages, it must in some way modify or change the market for labor. There are three general methods by which this can be done. The first is to increase the demand for labor. This method is probably the most desirable, because it results in more workers being hired at an increased wage. However, this method is also the most difficult, because in general unions have little influence over the demand for labor. One way unions attempt to increase labor demand is to increase the demand for the final product. For example, union advertising encourages consumers to buy union-made products. Specifically, the Union Label and Service Trades Department of the AFL-CIO (founded in 1909), promotes products and services produced in the United States by union members. Unions have also supported garment labeling requirements. For example, all garments made in the United States are required to have the label "Made in the USA." In recent years, unions have supported laws for protective tariffs or quotas on imports and lobbied against free-trade agreements, including the North American Free Trade Agreement. (However, limiting imports has the effect of limiting exports, which can curtail labor employment.)

Increasing the productivity of labor will also increase the demand for labor. To increase labor productivity, unions promote improved working conditions, shortened work weeks, and employee education. Negotiating over job descriptions may also increase or at least maintain the demand for labor. This may lead to *featherbedding*, which is an attempt by unions to create or maintain jobs that employers claim are not really necessary. An example is the job of a fireman on a railroad, when all the locomotives are powered by diesel. Such make-work schemes are not very successful, because they result in unnecessary production costs. High costs may in the long run result in higher output prices, which lead to consumers finding substitute commodities, which results in a decline in demand for union labor.

A second method for increasing wages is to reduce the supply of labor. Unions are generally more successful with this method. This is particularly true among the craft unions representing skilled trades. *Skilled unions* can control supply by controlling entry into the training or apprenticeship program and requiring that employees have a certificate or license bearing witness of successful completion of the program. Power to license is generally in the hands of the union, giving them power to restrict labor supply.

Reducing the supply of labor has the effect of shifting the supply curve for labor to the left of what it would be with free entry. This increases union wages and reduces the number of workers employed. Trade unions and professional associations have utilized this technique with a high degree of success, because the reduced number of workers does not, at least in the short run, harm established members. However, individuals who could obtain higher incomes if they were allowed to enter the union are harmed, and consumers are harmed by paying more for services rendered.

The third method is bargaining for higher wages. This method is generally utilized by unskilled or semiskilled workers, including teamsters, steel workers, and auto workers. The goal is to bring all workers in the industry into union membership. *Semiskilled* and *unskilled unions* are unable to restrict the supply of workers by licensing. This differs from the way skilled unions use licensing, controlling entry into the training program, and requiring a license for working. Instead, semiskilled and unskilled unions will attempt to establish a *closed shop,* where all the workers in a firm or even the industry must belong to the union. The union then represents all the workers and negotiates with management. It is important for the union to require that all workers join the union, otherwise a worker could be an interloper—not join, save any union dues, and still reap any benefits from union negotiation.[1]

Unions' objectives

In 1912, the Industrial Workers of the World (the Wobblies) organized a strike against the textile mills in Lawrence, Massachusetts. This strike started when the mill owners, responding to a state legislature action reducing the work week from 54 to 52 hours, cut wages by 3.5 percent. The move produced a strike of 50,000 textile workers that included arrests, police and militia attacks, and broad public support for the strikers. An enraged public protest finally forced the mill owners not only to restore the pay cuts but to increase the workers' wages beyond the monopsony wage rate and hire more workers.

To analyze this strike and other monopsony and union negotiations, let us consider first a monopsony buyer of labor services confronting a large number of independent sellers of

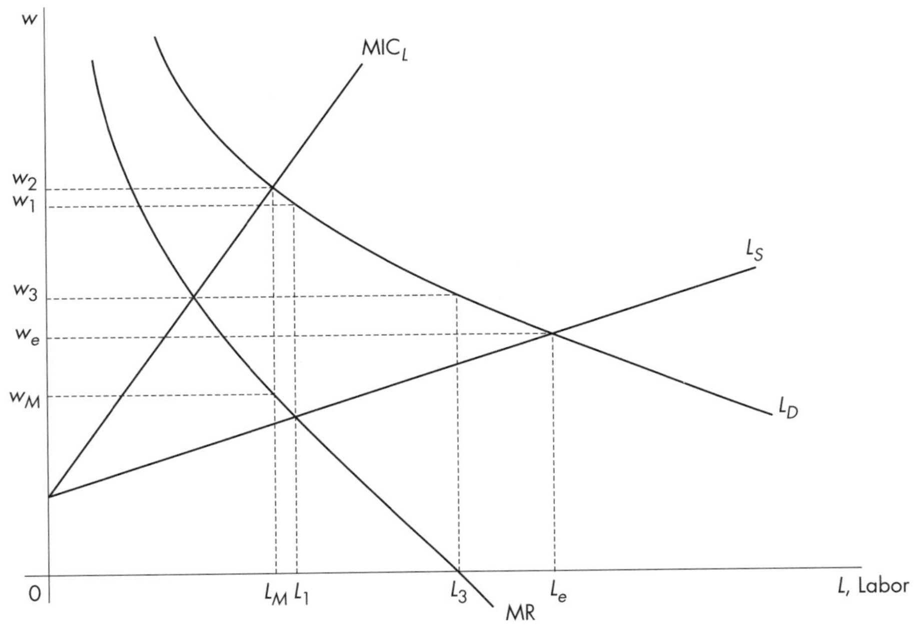

Figure 17.5 **Labor union's objectives.** The highest possible wage rate consistent with the monopsony level of labor employment is w_2. Alternatively, labor will maximize its profits (economic rent) by offering L_1 workers at a wage rate of w_1, or it can maximize the wage bill where MR = 0 by offering L_3 workers at a wage rate of w_3. Labor may also choose to employ the highest level of workers, L_e, at the perfectly competitive wage rate of w_e.

these services. In Figure 17.5, this results in the equilibrium level of labor L_M and wage w_M. Now, we let a union (the Wobblies) organize and become the sole supplier of labor services to the monopsonist. If the union is powerful enough to enforce any wage rate that it establishes and if the objective of the union is to maximize its economic rent, then it will seek a wage rate of w_1 at an employment level of L_1. However, the union may have other objectives. For example, the union may prefer to obtain the highest possible wage rate consistent with the initial level of employment L_M, w_2. Alternatively, the union may seek the largest wage bill (total revenue for the union). Maximizing the wage bill corresponds to where MR = 0, so the union would offer L_3 workers at a wage rate of w_3. However, at these wages (w_2, w_1, w_3), an excess supply of labor exists. More workers are willing to supply their labor than the available demand. Thus, for the union to obtain these higher wages, it must restrict the supply of labor. In contrast, this excess supply of workers vanishes if the union's interests are to employ the highest level of laborers at a wage above w_M. This results in the perfectly competitive solution of L_e workers at a wage rate of w_e.

Does a union offer the highest wage it can? No, a union may instead offer the highest wage for a given level of employment, or it may have the objective of obtaining the highest wage bill or employment given the current wage.

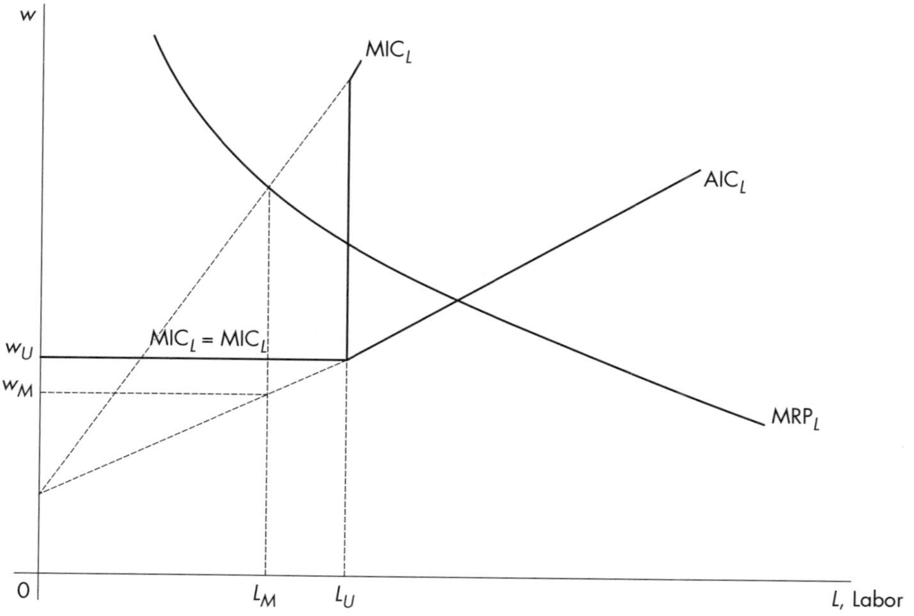

Figure 17.6 **Labor union's wage and employment.** At a union wage of w_U, the firm can hire all the labor it wants at this wage up to L_U. Beyond L_U, the firm must offer a higher wage if it wants to hire more workers. A profit-maximizing firm will equate MRP_L to MIC_L and hire L_U workers at a wage of w_U.

As illustrated in Figure 17.5, the introduction of a labor union into a previously monopsonized labor market may possibly result in a higher level of employment as well as in a higher wage rate. For example, if a union is successful at increasing the wage above the monopsony wage of w_M, say w_U in Figure 17.6, then the firm can hire all the labor it wants at this wage up to L_U. AIC_L is horizontal along this level of labor, so MIC_L is equal to it. At L_U, the AIC_L curve is kinked and the MIC_L curve shifts up to its previous level. Thus, in the short run, the firm will hire L_U workers, which is greater than L_M, and offer a wage w_U, which is higher than the monopsony wage w_M. This short-run result is a win/win situation for the union. It got the firm to not only offer a higher wage but also to be willing to hire more workers.[2]

Example 17.4 Labor union's objectives

Consider the following functions:

$$\text{SMC} = \text{AIC}_L = L,$$

$$\text{AR} = \text{MRP}_L = 60 - 2L.$$

The associated MIC_L and MR functions are

$$MIC_L = 2L,$$

$$MR = 60 - 4L.$$

The monopsony wage rate and employment level are determined by

$$MIC_L = MRP_L,$$

$$2L = 60 - 2L.$$

Solving for L results in the monopsony employment level of $L_M = 15$. The monopsony can then offer a wage rate of only $w_M = 15$ and obtain this employment level given $w = AIC = L$. However, at this level of employment, the union would negotiate for a wage of $w_2 = 30$. This wage represents the maximum a monopsony is willing to pay, $MRP_L = 60 - 2L$, for an employment level of 15.

If the labor union is interested in maximizing its economic rent, we set

$$SMC = MR,$$

$$L = 60 - 4L.$$

Solving for L, the union is willing to offer an $L_1 = 12$ employment level at a wage $w_1 = 36$, determined by the maximum that the monopsony is willing to pay, $MRP_L = 60 - 2L$.

Instead, if the union is interested in maximizing the wage bill, we set

$$MR = 60 - 4L = 0.$$

This will result in the union offering an $L_3 = 15$ employment level at a wage again determined by the monopsony's maximum willingness to pay, $w_3 = 30$.

Alternatively, we can determine the maximum employment level, given the union's supply curve (which corresponds to the perfectly competitive solution), by setting SMC = AR:

$$L = 60 - 2L.$$

The solution is $L_e = 20$, with an associated wage of $w_e = 20$.

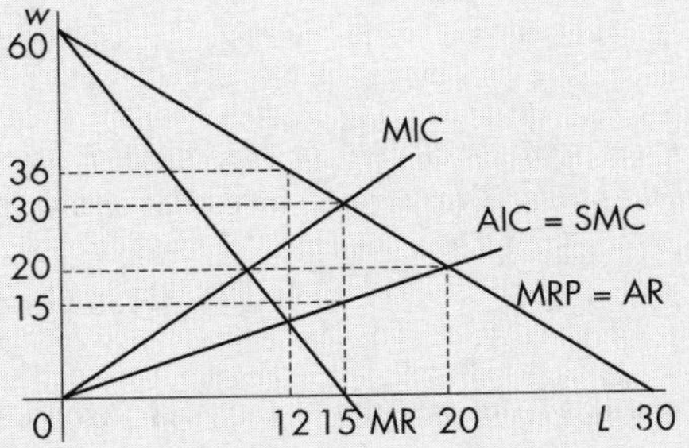

Long-run consequences

> *Fathers send their children to college either because they went to college or because they did not.*
>
> (L.L. Hendren)

Eighty movies were shot in Boston, Massachusetts, from 1995 to 2000, but in the following two years, only 15 films were made there. In the spring of 2000, following complaints from studios that the union had forced them to hire more crew members than needed in exchange for labor peace during filming, a federal investigation found that union movie contracts from Boston Teamsters Local 25 had guaranteed union members 25 hours of overtime each week. Thus, location managers shifted a significant amount of production away from the Boston area to less expensive countries such as Canada, Australia, and New Zealand and to Pittsburgh, Toronto, and other cities made to look like Boston. It was not until 2007 when a newly elected president of Local 25 established a degree of professionalism that Boston restored its movie industry. By 2010, over 400 movies had been shot in Boston.

This example illustrates that in the long run unions may not be able to maintain higher wages and higher level of employment. The firm's cost curves will shift upward as a result of this higher cost. If this upward pressure on costs results in increased prices, consumers might substitute other commodities for the firm's output, which shifts the firm's demand curve for its output and inputs downward. The result will be downward pressure on wages and labor layoffs. An example is the long-run adjustment of the US auto industry in the 1970s. Large wage hikes in the 1970s, not generally associated with increased productivity, pushed the prices of US automobiles to a point where they were no longer competitive with foreign manufacturers (mainly Japanese). This resulted in households substituting foreign cars for American cars and precipitated high levels of unemployment among US auto workers.

Firms may attempt to mitigate this higher cost by seeking other regions for their manufacturing operations (possibly international outsourcing) with lower, nonunion labor costs. This results in a loss of union employment and a reduction in wages. The shifting of manufacturing from the US unionized north to the southeast in the mid-twentieth century is an example. The current trend is for US manufacturers to locate just across the Mexican border, where labor costs and environmental restrictions are relatively low.

These long-run consequences of outsourcing indicate that having a union card is no guarantee of long-run relative high wages. If you are among the early members of a union that was successful in raising wages, you may benefit; however, encourage your children to go to college. These relative high-paying union jobs may not last into the next generation of workers.

Labor strikes

> *I tell you, sir, the only safeguard of order and discipline in the modern world is a standardized worker with interchangeable parts. That would solve the entire problem of management.*
>
> (Jean Giraudoux)

The Haymarket explosion of May 4, 1886 resulted from a strike at the McCormick Reaper works in Chicago. Four strikers were killed by police; in reprisal, a group of anarchists threw a bomb that killed several policemen. The police then opened fire, killing four more strikers and wounding 200 more.

A major tool that unions have in labor negotiations is the threat of striking. *Labor strikes* can take a number of forms, from actual walking out and picketing to a worker slowdown, lasting for years or only a few minutes. In all cases, a major objective of strikes is to show management how the union can and will cause a significant loss in a firm's revenue. However, a union is in a symbiotic relationship with management, it is not in the general interest of the union to bankrupt a firm.

A union must have the ability to severely curtail output in order to have the power of inflicting damaging losses upon management and shareholders. Generally, in oligopolistic industries with large factories producing a large share of a firm's output, by picketing the limited entry and exit locations, a strike can shut down a factory and prevent nonstriking workers from crossing the picket lines. Thus, a strike or the threat of a strike can be a very effective tool in labor negotiations. However, in a perfectly competitive industry, such as agriculture where a relatively large number of firms produce in a large number of open fields, the effectiveness of strikes as a tool for labor negotiation is severely limited. A union would probably not have the resources to prevent production in all the fields, and therefore could possibly only restrict industry output rather than shut it down.

Specifically, in the agricultural sector, migrant farm workers have organized into a union and have attempted to use strikes as a tool for increasing wages. The demand for migrant farm workers only exists during harvest, so migrant farm workers have attempted to increase wages by striking at harvest. The goal of the strike is to significantly reduce production to the point where firms are operating at a loss. However, as previously stated, it is difficult to prevent all the farms from harvesting their output with substitute labor, so it is generally not possible for strikers to accomplish this goal. In fact, a situation may result where the union's actions reduce the supply of output to the point that market price, along with profits for the firms, increases. In this case, the union has forced the firms into a cartel situation where they earn pure profits. Thus, instead of forcing firms to increase wages, so that workers will come back to work, the union has provided incentives for the firms to not agree with union demands. This result occurred when the United Farm Workers in California went on strike in 1979 against the California lettuce growers. Studies indicate that the lettuce growers, in general, did actually benefit from the strike.[3] As a result of the limited success of their strikes, the United Farm Workers instead attempted to increase wages by shifting the demand curve for lettuce outward. For example, they created a union label and encouraged restaurants and households to only purchase union-labeled lettuce.

Should a union strike during peak production? No, unless it has other objectives besides increasing wages.

A union often does have other objectives besides increasing wages in the short run. For example, a strike can provide a great deal of public exposure to the problems facing workers. This could then result in government policies addressing these problems. For example, the National Association for the Advancement of Colored People supported the Montgomery Bus Boycott led by Martin Luther King, Jr from 1955 to 1956 (381 days) along with various subsequent marches, including the massive voting rights protest in Birmingham, Alabama, and the 250,000-people march on Washington, DC. These boycotts and marches resulted in the landmark 1964 Civil Rights Act and the 1965 Voting Rights Act.

This labor unrest has resulted in the wage rate in some markets being determined by more than the market demand and supply curves. Firms may offer higher wages out of fairness to workers, so they can have a better standard of living. Without a better standard of living, workers may not be as productive. This higher wage is explained by *efficiency wage theory*: increased labor productivity pays for the higher wages.

Application: Coal miners' strikes

In his book *Soft Coal, Hard Choices*, Price Fishback provides an economic evaluation of coal miners' relationship with the coal firms and the unions. In particular, he evaluates the question of what the miners gained from strikes. He concludes that miners generally gained higher wages in the year following the strike, but the gains came at a high cost. For every day on strike, a miner lost about a half-day's earnings. Comparing the wage gains with lost strike days, the miners lost almost $2 (in 1967 dollars) for every day they struck. If the strike was for union recognition, winning this recognition resulted in a $156 annual increase in earnings. However, such strikes were less than 44 percent effective and tended to last 100 days or longer. This cost miners almost $200 in lost earnings. The expected net gains from winning union recognition are not positive until almost three years after recognition. In general, the monetary (pecuniary) returns from strikes were negative, but, for some localized unions, strikes may very well have resulted in positive returns.

Considering the additional nonpecuniary benefits from strikes, the gains from strikes were generally positive. The recognition of unions representing miners resulted in labor having a larger voice in management. For example, with union representation, grievance mechanisms were established. This provided miners the ability to issue complaints without fear of being fired. Also, the solidarity of workers resulting from comradeship in striking influenced politicians to enact prolabor legislation. However, it should not be forgotten that these positive gains came after an early history of violence. From 1890 to 1909, there were nearly 300 individuals killed from strike-related activities in the United States.

Source: P. Fishback, *Soft Coal, Hard Choices: The Economic Welfare of Bituminous Coal Miners, 1890–1930*. New York: Oxford University Press (1992).

Summary

1. For a monopsony to hire another worker, it must not only offer this new worker a higher wage, but also increase the wages for all its workers. Thus, the additional cost of hiring this worker, the marginal input cost, is greater than the wage rate.
2. The Lerner Index for determining the degree of monopsony power measures the relative wedge between an input price and the marginal revenue product.
3. A firm with monopsony power will maximize profit by restricting the amount of the input purchased and lowering the input price. This results in an inefficient

allocation where the wage rate is less than the marginal revenue product. Analogous to monopoly power, this inefficiency is measured by the deadweight loss in consumer surplus and economic rent.

4. A bilateral monopoly exists when a monopsony faces a monopoly. Both will attempt to restrict the market allocation, so there is generally limited conflict in determining this allocation. However, there is generally a large wedge between the price the monopoly is offering to sell and the price the monopsony is willing to pay. The bargaining strengths and skills of the agents will determine the outcome.
5. Labor unions generally have more control over the supply of labor than over its demand. The objectives of unions vary depending on the preferences of their members. For example, unions may be interested in maximizing the number of workers above some monopsony wage rate, maximizing the union's economic rent, or maximizing the total wage receipts.
6. Labor strikes can take a number of forms, from worker stoppages to worker slowdowns. However, for a strike to be effective, it must curtail output to the point that the firm currently suffers losses or has the prospect of future losses.
7. *(Appendix)* Profits for a monopsony may be enhanced if the firm can practice input-price discrimination. Depending on the ability to segment the input market, an input-price-discriminating monopsony can practice first-, second- and third-degree price discrimination.
8. *(Appendix)* Under third-degree input-price discrimination, a monopsony will equate the marginal input cost in each input market to its marginal revenue product. The more inelastic the supply curve in a market, the lower will be the price offered by the monopsony.

Key concepts

Key equations

$$\text{MIC}_L = \text{AIC}_L + L\frac{\partial w}{\partial L}$$

Marginal input cost equals average input cost (price) plus an adjustment factor.

$$\text{MIC} = \text{MRP}$$

For profit maximization, a firm will equate marginal input cost to marginal revenue product.

$$\text{MIC}_1 = \text{MIC}_2 = \ldots = \text{MIC}_k = \text{MRP}$$

Under third-degree input-price discrimination, a firm will maximize profits by equating the marginal input cost in each input market to its marginal revenue product.

Questions

1. If all jobs were the same, everyone would earn the same wage. True or false? Explain.
2. Why is the cost of an additional employee hired by a monopsony greater than the employee's wage?
3. Is it to the advantage of employers to pay the lowest wage possible? Explain.
4. A monopsony hires labor for less than the competitive wage. What type of inefficiency will this use of monopsony power cause? How would your answer change if the monopsony in the labor market were also a monopoly in the output market?
5. What is the impact of the interstate highway and regional transit systems on monopsony power?
6. Why do many colleges pay low wages for student labor? Would the situation likely change if students unionized? Explain.
7. Would a labor union negotiating for higher wages prefer that the firm's output demand be relatively elastic or inelastic? Explain.
8. As capital accumulates, does the bargaining power of workers increase or decrease? Explain.
9. Strikes are totally unproductive, so they should be outlawed. True or false? Explain.
10. A minimum wage may increase employment. True or false? Explain.

Exercises

Exercising your way to better mental health: combat stress, fight depression, and improve your overall mood and self-concept with these simple exercises.

(Larry M. Leith)

1. Ms Exploiter owns a large textile factory in a small, remote county. Her factory is the only source of employment for most of the county, and thus she has monopsony power. The supply curve for textile workers is

$$L = 160w,$$

where L is the number of workers hired and w is their hourly wage. Assume that Ms Exploiter's labor demand (MRP for garment workers) is

$$L = 1600 - 80\text{MRP}_L.$$

   a. How many workers will she hire to maximize profit and what wage will she pay?
   b. Suppose that the government implements a minimum wage covering all textile workers at \$8 per hour. How many workers will Ms Exploiter hire and what will be the level of unemployment?
   c. Compare the difference in deadweight loss between the monopsony and minimum wage equilibria.
   d. Graph the results of (a)–(c).
   e. How does a minimum wage imposed under monopsony compare with a minimum wage imposed under perfect competition?

2. A high school requires a security system to prevent any unauthorized activities, so it decides on hiring security guards G and renting cameras C. A level of security S is then obtained, given

$$S = (GC)^{1/2}.$$

The minimum level of security required is $S = 12$.

   a. Wages for the guards are $w = 20$ and cameras rent for $v = 20$. What is the least-cost combination of guards and cameras and what is this minimum cost?
   b. Suppose that the high school is the only employer of security guards and that the supply curve for guards is

$$G = 2.58w.$$

   Now what is the least-cost combination of guards and cameras and what is the minimum cost? What is the wage rate of the security guards?

3. Suppose that duopsonists in a labor market have the production functions

$$q_1 = L_1 - \tfrac{1}{2}L_1^2,$$

$$q_2 = L_2 - \tfrac{1}{2}L_2^2,$$

where $Q = q_1 + q_2$ and the associated output price is 1. Let the inverse labor supply function be $w = \frac{1}{4}(L_1 + L_2)$. Determine the Cournot equilibrium for L_1 and L_2.

4. A buyer for a firm's input X has the demand function

$$X = 366 - v,$$

where v is the price per unit of the input. The supply function for X is

$$X = v.$$

   a. Determine the price and amount of X employed under conditions of monopoly, monopsony, and perfectly competitive markets.
   b. Calculate the deadweight loss associated with the monopoly, monopsony, and perfectly competitive markets.

5. Assume that the production of output q requires capital K, where the supply curve for K is

$$K^S = v$$

and the demand curve for K is

$$K^D = 24 - v,$$

with v as the rental rate of K.

   a. How many units of capital will a perfectly competitive market, monopsony, and monopoly employ and what will be their associated rental rates?
   b. Assuming that the total fixed cost of the capital owners is equal to their economic rent under a perfectly competitive market and that the total fixed cost of the producers of q is equal to their consumer surplus under a perfectly competitive market, determine the profits for the firms under each market structure.

6. Given a pure-exchange general-equilibrium model, illustrate and discuss the condition of a bilateral monopoly and relate it to the bilateral monopoly model in partial equilibrium.

7. A firm has the following demand function for labor:

$$L^D = 29 - \tfrac{1}{2}w,$$

where w is the wage rate. The supply for labor is

$$L^S = 4 + 2w.$$

   a. Determine the solutions that prevail under conditions of perfectly competitive markets, monopsony, and a revenue-maximizing union.
   b. Graph the results of (a).
   c. Calculate the deadweight loss associated with the three market structures.

8. The buyer and seller for a bilateral monopoly have the following production functions, respectively:

$$q_1 = 270q_2 - 2q_2^2,$$

$$K = \tfrac{1}{4}q_2^2.$$

Assume that the price of q_1 is 3 and the price of K is 6.

a. Determine the values of q_2 and p_2 for the buyer and seller under monopoly, monopsony, and perfectly competitive markets.
b. Determine the limits for price bargaining, assuming that the buyer's lower limit is the monopoly solution and the seller's upper limit is the monopsony solution.
c. Calculate the deadweight loss associated with each market structure.

9. Let the demand and supply functions for labor be, respectively,

$$L^D = -w + 6,$$

$$L^S = w.$$

a. Determine a labor union's wage and number of workers to be supplied if its objective is to maximize the union's total revenue.
b. Calculate the economic rent and consumer surplus.
c. Determine the wage and number of workers to be hired for a monopsonist interested in maximizing profits.
d. Calculate the economic rent and consumer surplus for the optimal solution in (c).
e. Calculate the Lerner Index for both the union and monopsonist wage rates.

10. a. If a union desires to maximize the total wage bill, what wage rate will it demand?
b. If unemployed workers were paid unemployment insurance at the level of A per worker and the union now desired to maximize the sum of the wage bill and the total amount of unemployment compensation, what wage rate would it demand?

Internet case studies

1. Provide one list of industries with closed shops and another list with open shops. What are the similarities among the industries within the lists?
2. Provide a brief history of the US labor movement and the role of the federal government.

APPENDIX TO CHAPTER 17

Monopsony wage discrimination

Any man who pays more for labor than the lowest sum he can get men for is robbing his stockholders. If he can secure men for $6 and pays more, he is stealing from the company.

(Stockholder of American Woolen)

Translation: Unless a manager actively practices wage discrimination, he is not maximizing profit.

In 2002, two trucking company owners stated, "Paying each coal truck driver 25 percent of the money generated by his rig makes more sense for the driver and the company than paying hourly wages." However, United Mine Worker President Cecil Roberts disagreed, comparing the practice to the piecemeal wage discrimination coal companies used in the early twentieth century. Back then, most coal miners (called tonnage men) were paid piecemeal to avoid shirking.[4] The union ended this wage discrimination and released coal miners from the grip of the coal barons; however, firms are always developing new methods of wage discrimination to improve their profits.

Similar to price discrimination associated with a firm having monopoly power in the output market (discussed in Chapter 13), a firm with monopsony power in the input market might increase its profits by practicing *wage discrimination*. However, such wage discrimination is in many cases illegal. For example, in the United States, it is illegal to discriminate by age, gender, religion, or national origin. Also, labor unions will attempt to prevent firms from practicing various types of wage discrimination. For example, a firm may discriminate by offering lower wages and fewer benefits for part-time employment, and labor unions may attempt to equalize this wage disparity.

Why do firms wage-discriminate? Firms wage-discriminate to enhance profits.

The conditions that allow a firm to practice wage discrimination or, in general, input-price discrimination are analogous to those for price discrimination in the output market. Specifically, the elasticity of supply among different labor markets must be different and there can be no leakages among markets. Workers must have different preferences for working in this industry and they can only participate in one market.

The three degrees of output price discrimination also apply to wage discrimination. **First-degree wage discrimination** (or **perfect wage discrimination**) is where a firm offers the lowest possible wage for each unit of labor. This lowest wage is the employee's **reservation wage**, which is no more than the employee could receive at an alternative source of employment. Thus, all of the economic rent is captured by the firm.

In Figure 17.2, the first unit of labor will be offered at a wage of 0E and the firm will receive the surplus of EA. The firm will offer the next unit of labor at a slightly higher wage, given that the increase in the reservation wage, AIC_L, is positively sloped. For each additional worker that the firm hires, the firm offers the worker her reservation wage. At the no-wage-discrimination level L_M, the firm still receives a positive surplus of DC for that unit of labor. Now a no-wage-discrimination firm will not hire labor beyond L_M, because if it hires an additional worker, it must offer a higher wage not only to the additional worker but to all the workers hired, and this would lower profits.

In contrast, a wage-discriminating firm can offer an additional worker a higher wage without increasing the wages of all the previously hired workers. Thus, the wage-discriminating firm will continue to hire as long as a positive surplus is received for each additional unit of labor hired. In Figure 17.2, this additional surplus is exhausted at employment level L_C where the marginal revenue product for hiring an additional unit of labor is just equal to workers' reservation wage rate: $MRP_L = AIC_L$.

Example 17A.1 Determining first-degree wage discrimination

From Examples 17.1 and 17.2,

$$MRP_L = 288 - 12L,$$

$$AIC_L = 6L.$$

A perfect wage-discriminating firm will equate MRP_L to AIC_L:

$$288 - 12L = 6L.$$

Solving for L gives

$$L_C = 16.$$

The firm will hire 16 workers, which corresponds to the competitive employment level. However, the firm will pay workers only their reservation wage and capture the entire surplus. Thus, economic rent is zero and consumer surplus, represented by the shaded area, is (288)16/2 = \$2304.

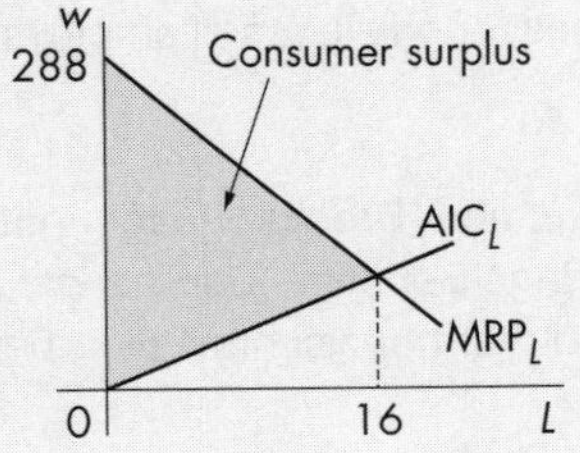

Note that, just as with perfect price discrimination, there is no deadweight loss associated with perfect wage discrimination, and thus the firm is efficient. However, the shifting of the surplus from labor to the owners of a firm would be distasteful to labor and may not improve social welfare.

Generally, firms will attempt to perfectly wage-discriminate by varying pay increases across employees. An example is university faculty members, where salary increases are partially based on the ability of a faculty member to be hired at another institution. This type of wage discrimination works particularly well when employees are performing essentially different tasks. In contrast, where workers perform the same task, perfect wage discrimination may not be worth the cost of workers rebelling over such discrimination. In this case, firms may employ **second-degree wage discrimination**, where workers of the same class or type receive different wages based on their level of effort. Workers with different opportunity cost for working will put forth a different level of effort.[5] Similar to second-degree output price discrimination, second-degree wage discrimination has a self-selection constraint. Here, an employee can self-select his or her level of effort. For example, workers of the same gender may receive different wage increases (merit raises) based on how hard they work. Another type of second-degree wage discrimination is piecemeal pay, where workers are paid according to the amount of a certain activity completed rather than an hourly wage. An employee can then self-select how much of the activity he or she wants to complete. For example, migrant farm workers are usually paid according to how many bushels of the harvested crop they are able to pick. This type of second-degree price discrimination avoids the problem of labor's demand for equal pay for equal work.

Application: Input discrimination in nonwage benefits

To increase profits, firms often employ wage-discriminating practices in nonwage benefits. For example, subsidized childcare increases the compensation of mothers with children relative to those without. However, such practices are not allowed if an employer wants a tax deduction on its nonwage benefits to employees. For example, Section 105 of the Internal Revenue Code stipulates that an employer's self-insured health insurance plan is tax-deductible only if it nondiscriminates among its employees in offering the plan. Nondiscrimination benefit rules increase firms' costs of mixing workers with different preferred benefits, so firms will circumvent these rules by practicing third-degree wage discrimination. For example, firms will hire anomalous workers (employees whose benefit preferences differ from the general employees) on a part-time basis.*

Older workers are also protected from third-degree wage discrimination by the Federal Government Age Discrimination in Employment Act (ADEA). This law makes it unlawful for an employer to fire, fail to hire, or discriminate against an older worker with respect to his or her compensation, terms, conditions, or privileges of employment. Protection under this law begins at age 40.

*In an article by William Carrington, Kristin McCue, and Brooks Pierce entitled "Nondiscrimination Rules and the Distribution of Fringe Benefits" (*Journal of Labor Economics* 20 (2002): S5–S33), it is demonstrated that nondiscrimination benefit rules do alter firms' compensation practices.

Third-degree wage discrimination is when firms pay a different wage across types or classes of workers. The wage is the same within a particular class, but differs across classes. The different classes represent different markets, so, assuming that the elasticity of supply is different in each market, the firm can increase profits by wage-discriminating.

As an illustration of third-degree wage discrimination, consider two labor markets each with different supply elasticities, such as senior citizens or nonseniors, illegal aliens or legal residents, and young adults or adults. In these markets, the supply curve for young adults may be more elastic than that of the general population of employees; they may have a higher opportunity cost for working, so they are relatively more responsive to a change in wages. In contrast, seniors and illegal aliens may have more inelastic supply curves; their opportunity cost for working is very low, so they will be willing to work at most any wage. In our example, we assume that no leakages exist among markets. For example, senior citizens will not dye their hair and undergo facelifts.

We determine the optimal wages and employment levels by letting $w_j(L_j)$ be the inverse supply function in the jth labor market ($j = 1, 2$) and express the total wage bill in this market by

$$\text{TIC}_j(L_j) = w_j(L_j)L_j,$$

where L_j is the level of employment in the jth labor market. Total input cost is then $\text{TIC}(L) = \text{TIC}_1(L_1) + \text{TIC}_2(L_2)$, where $L = L_1 + L_2$. Letting $\text{TR}(L)$ be the total revenue function, the monopsony maximizes profits by

$$\max_{(L_1, L_2)} \pi = \max_{(L_1, L_2)} [\text{TR}(L) - \text{TIC}_1(L_1) - \text{TIC}_2(L_2)].$$

Partial differentiation yields the FOCs

$$\frac{\partial \pi}{\partial L_j} = \frac{d\text{TR}}{dL}\frac{\partial L}{\partial L_j} - \frac{d\text{TIC}_j}{dL_j} = 0 \quad \text{for } j = 1,\ 2,$$

$$\text{MRP} = \text{MIC}_1 = \text{MIC}_2,$$

or in general for k labor markets, $\text{MRP}(L) = \text{MIC}_j(L_j)$, for $j = 1, \ldots, k$. Note that $\partial L/\partial L_j = 1$. Thus, if a monopsony can divide its labor market into k independent sub-markets, then it should divide overall employment among the k labor markets in such a way that it equalizes the marginal input cost in all labor markets. This common marginal input cost should be equal to the marginal revenue product for the total labor force. We determine the wages paid in all labor markets by substituting the optimal level of employment in the jth market, L_j^*, into average input cost $w_j^* = \text{AIC}_j(L_j^*)$.

Figure 17A.1 illustrates the case of two labor markets, where the level of marginal input cost (MIC^*) is attained in both labor markets if and only if the levels of employment in the

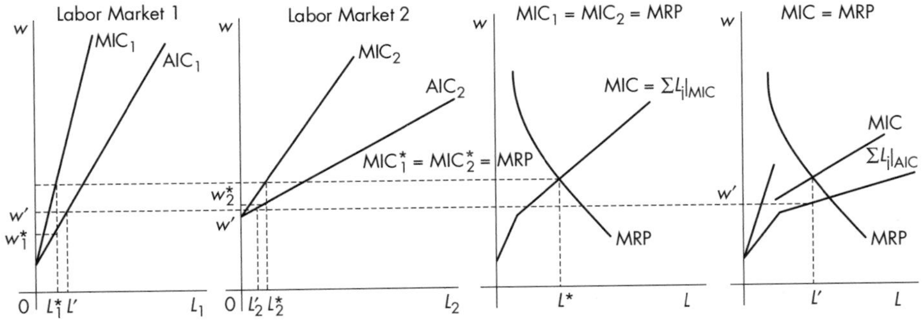

Figure 17A.1 **Third-degree wage discrimination in two labor markets.** The optimal level of workers to hire in each market and wage rates offered are determined by equating the MIC in each market to the MRP. This results in a total of L^* workers hired, with L_1^* workers in market 1 and L_2^* workers in market 2. Wage rates are w_1^* in market 1 and w_2^* in market 2. If the firm is unable to practice wage discrimination, it will hire a total of L' workers, with L_1' workers in market 1 and L_2' workers in market 2. The common wage rate in the two markets is then w'.

two markets are L_1^* and L_2^*. MIC equals MIC* in both labor markets only if total employment is $L^* = L_1^* + L_2^*$.

The remaining FOC requires that this common MIC in the two labor markets be equated to MRP. This condition determines the optimal (L, MIC) combination, which is given by the intersection of the MRP and the horizontal summation of the marginal input cost curves, $\sum L_j|_{\mathrm{MIC}}$. Note that the optimal employment levels and wages in the two markets are L_1^*, L_2^* and w_1^*, w_2^*.

The optimal levels of wages are determined by the wage rate necessary to hire L_1^* and L_2^* workers in the two respective markets. As illustrated in Figure 17A.1, the wage is highest in the labor market with the more elastic supply. We determine this elasticity of supply by considering

$$\mathrm{MIC}_j(L_j) = w_j\left(1 + \frac{1}{\varepsilon_j^S}\right),$$

where ε_j^S is the elasticity of labor supply in the jth labor market, $\partial \ln L_j^S / \partial \ln w_j$. The wages offered in the two separate labor markets may be related to the own-wage elasticities of supply in each of these markets given the condition

$$\mathrm{MIC}_1 = \mathrm{MIC}_2,$$

$$w_1\left(1 + \frac{1}{\varepsilon_1^S}\right) = w_2\left(1 + \frac{1}{\varepsilon_2^S}\right),$$

$$\frac{w_1}{w_2} = \frac{1 + 1/\varepsilon_2^S}{1 + 1/\varepsilon_1^S}.$$

This relationship indicates that the wages in any two labor markets are equal to one another if and only if the own-wage elasticities of supply are equal. If $\varepsilon_2^S > \varepsilon_1^S$ (supply is more inelastic in market 1), then

$$1 + \frac{1}{\varepsilon_2^S} < 1 + \frac{1}{\varepsilon_1^S},$$

which implies

$$w_1/w_2 < 1 \quad \text{or} \quad w_2 > w_1.$$

Thus, the wage is higher in the market with the more elastic supply. The market that is more wage-sensitive and thus has more elastic supply is offered the higher wage. In the other market, workers (senior citizens and illegal aliens) are "happy" to work and thus are offered lower wages.

In terms of the Lerner Index,

$$\frac{w_1}{w_2} = \frac{1 + L_{I2}}{1 + L_{I1}},$$

where L_{I1} and L_{I2} are the Lerner Indices in markets 1 and 2, respectively. If market 1 has a greater degree of monopsony power, so $L_{I1} > L_{I2}$, then $w_1 < w_2$.

Example 17A.2 Determination of third-degree wage discrimination

Consider the following supply functions in two separate labor markets:

$$L_1 = -2 + w_1,$$
$$L_2 = -10 + 2w_2.$$

Let the total revenue function for labor be

$$\text{TR}_L = 28L - L^2,$$

where $L = L_1 + L_2$. Solving the supply functions for w_1 and w_2 results in the inverse supply functions for the two markets:

$$w_1 = L_1 + 2,$$
$$w_2 = \tfrac{1}{2}L_2 + 5.$$

Profit maximization for the firm is

$$\max_{(L_1,\, L_2)} \pi = \max_{(L_1,\, L_2)} (TR_L - TIC_L) = \max_{(L_1,\, L_2)} (TR_L - w_1 L_1 - w_2 L_2)$$
$$= \max_{(L_1,\, L_2)} \left[\left(28L - L^2\right) - (L_1 + 2)\, L_1 - \left(\tfrac{1}{2}L_2 + 5\right) L_2\right].$$

The FOCs are

$$\frac{\partial \pi}{\partial L_1} = (28 - 2L^*) - (2L_1^* + 2) = 0,$$

that is,

$$\text{MRP}_L - \text{MIC}_1 = 0,$$
$$\frac{\partial \pi}{\partial L_2} = (28 - 2L^*) - (L_2^* + 5) = 0,$$

that is,

$$\text{MRP}_L - \text{MIC}_2 = 0.$$

The FOCs imply $\text{MRP}_L = \text{MIC}_1 = \text{MIC}_2$. We determine the optimal levels of employment within each market by first solving the marginal input costs for labor:

$$L_1 = -1 + \tfrac{1}{2}\text{MIC},$$
$$L_2 = -5 + \text{MIC}.$$

Summing over labor,

$$L = L_1 + L_2 = -6 + \frac{3}{2}\text{MIC}.$$

Solving for MIC and equating with MRP yields the optimal level of employment for each market:

$$\text{MIC}_L = \text{MRP}_L,$$

$$4 + \tfrac{2}{3}L^* = 28 - 2L^*,$$

$$L^* = 9, \quad \text{MIC} = 10, \quad L_1^* = 4, \quad L_2^* = 5, \quad w_1^* = 6, \quad w_2^* = 7.5.$$

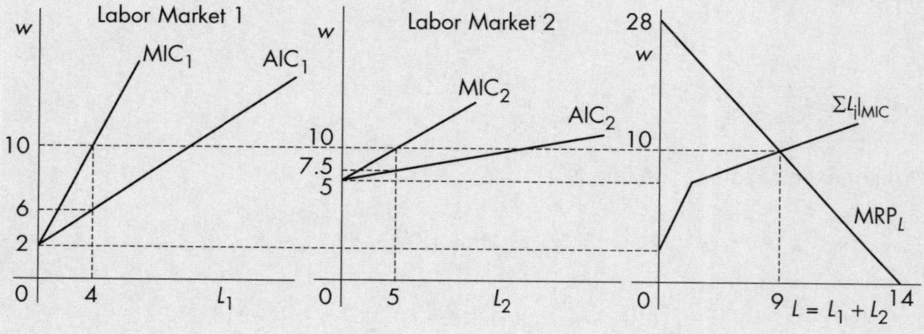

Example 17A.3 Calculating Lerner Indices and supply elasticities under third-degree wage discrimination

The supply functions and profit-maximizing wages and employment levels in the two markets from Example 17A.2 are

$$L_1 = -2 + w_1, L_2 = -10 + 2w_2, w_1^* = 6, L_1^* = 4, w_2^* = 7.5, L_2^* = 5.$$

In the two labor markets, the elasticities of supply and the Lerner Indices at these optimal employment levels are

$$\varepsilon_1^S = \frac{dL_1}{dw_1}\frac{w_1^*}{L_1^*} = \frac{3}{2}, \qquad L_{I1}^* = \frac{2}{3},$$

$$\varepsilon_2^S = \frac{dL_2}{dw_2}\frac{w_2^*}{L_2^*} = 3, \qquad L_{I2}^* = \frac{1}{3}.$$

Market 2 has the more elastic labor supply curve, which corresponds to a lower Lerner Index and higher wage.

The relation of ordinary monopsony (no-wage discrimination) and wage discrimination is also illustrated in Figure 17A.1. If no wage discrimination exists, then horizontally summing the individual labor market supply curves, $\sum_j L_j \Big|_{AIC}$, yields the market supply curve facing the firm. To the left of the kink in the market supply curve, only workers in market 1 will supply labor. To the right of this kink, both labor markets will offer workers. Because of this kink, the associated MIC curve is discontinuous.

Optimal employment is where MIC = MRP at the employment level L' associated with the common wage w'. This common wage is between the wages charged in the two market segments when third-degree wage discrimination is practiced. At this common wage, the firm offers to employ L_1' in labor market 1 and L_2' in labor market 2. $\text{MIC'}_1 > \text{MIC'}_2$, indicating that the firm could increase profits by practicing wage discrimination. Profit could be enhanced by offering higher wages and thus increasing employment of labor in the low-MIC market and by reducing employment, which lowers wages, in the high-MIC market.

Depending on the wedge between the wage and marginal revenue product, the direction in which welfare changes as a result of third-degree wage discrimination is ambiguous. However, a sufficient condition for welfare to fall is if the total employment from wage discrimination does not increase.[6] Analogous to price discrimination in the output market, a sufficient condition for a welfare gain is if wage discrimination results in employing a segment of the labor market that would not be employed in the absence of wage discrimination.

Similar to output price discrimination, profit-maximizing firms with monopsony power will employ combinations of these three wage-discrimination techniques and will constantly be devising new methods. In the long run, cost will adjust to any short-run profits from wage discrimination, leading to long-run equilibrium with associated normal profits. Firms failing to engage in this practice of wage discrimination will, in the long run, experience declining revenue and be forced out of business unless barriers to entry are maintained.

Workers can increase their welfare by shifting their labor supply given this wage discrimination and possibly capture a higher wage. By organizing into unions, workers may be able to recoup some of the surplus appropriated by firms. Such countervailing monopoly power by unions facing monopsony power can improve the welfare of society as a whole.

Example 17A.4. Monopsony with no wage discrimination

Consider the supply functions from Example 17A.2. If the monopsony does not practice wage discrimination, it will then face the horizontal summation of these supply functions. Specifically, labor supply functions in the two labor markets are

$$L_1 = -2 + w,$$

$$L_2 = -10 + 2w.$$

Summing, we have

$$L = L_1 + L_2 = -2 + w - 10 + 2w = -12 + 3w.$$

Solving for w, which is AIC_L, gives

$$w = 4 + \tfrac{1}{3}L.$$

Total input cost (TIC_L) is average input cost multiplied by L, and taking the derivative of TIC_L yields

$$MIC_L = 4 + \tfrac{2}{3}L.$$

Note that MIC_L is twice as steep as AIC_L. For a linear AIC curve, the associated MIC curve bisects this AIC and the vertical axis. Equating MIC_L to MRP_L (determined in Example 17A.2) yields the profit-maximizing level of labor to employ with no wage discrimination:

$$MRP_L = MIC_L,$$

$$28 - 2L' = 4 + \tfrac{2}{3}L',$$

$$L' = 9, w' = 7, L_1' = 5, L_2' = 4.$$

Note that the wage is between the two different wages under wage discrimination (Example 17A.2): $w_1^* < w' < w_2^*$. Total employment remains unchanged whether the firm practices third-degree wage discrimination or not. However, by employing wage discrimination, the firm increases its profit by increasing its hiring in labor market 2 and offsetting this increase by a decrease in hiring in market 1.

Profit for the monopsony with no wage discrimination is

$$\pi = TR - TIC = (28L - L^2) - wL = 28(9) - 9^2 - 7(9) = 108.$$

For the monopsony with third-degree wage discrimination from Example 17A.2, profit is

$$\pi = TR - TIC = (28L - L^2) - w_1L_1 - w_2L_2 = 28(9) - 9^2 - 6(4) - 7.5(5) = 109.5.$$

Thus, profits are lower under no wage discrimination than under third-degree wage discrimination. The Lerner Indices in the absence of wage discrimination are $L_{l1}' = L_{l2}' = (10 - 7)/7 = 3/7$. Comparing these with the Lerner Indices under wage discrimination (Examples 17A.2 and 7A.3), $L_{l2}^* < L_{l1}' = L_{l2}' < L_{l1}^*$. Thus, wage discrimination results in a greater degree of monopsony power in market 1 and a lesser degree in market 2.

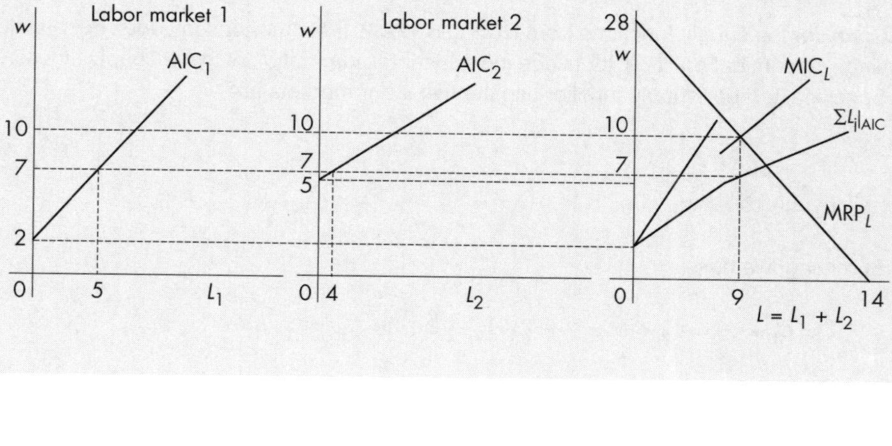

Application: Racial wage discrimination in the trucking industry

The Motor Carrier Act of 1980 provided the legislative power to end four decades of trucking regulation. Prior to this act, for-hire carriers whose sole line of business was freight carriage were the major beneficiaries of being able to exercise monopoly power from regulation. This resulted in pure profits for these carriers and corresponding high wages for drivers. Private carriers that transported their own goods were largely exempt from the regulation, so the act did not directly affect their profits.

As outlined by Agesa and Brown, the lack of product market competition of for-hire regulation allowed carriers and unions to wage-discriminate and pass the cost on to consumers. In this case, employer discrimination is highly dependent on the product market. This discrimination was supported by the International Brotherhood of Teamsters union, which had a history of minority exclusion.

Agesa and Brown investigated racial wage discrimination by examining the for-hire and private carrier sectors prior to and following regulatory reform. By estimating truck drivers' earnings by sector, regulatory regime, and racial group, they captured indirect and direct employer and union discrimination in a sector and regime. Their results indicate that during regulation, the wages of white for-hire carriers were 27 percent higher than for their minority counterparts. Union discrimination accounted for only 7 percent of this wage discrimination, while employer discrimination accounted for 63 percent. The remainder is explained as differences in attributes. Following deregulation, the racial wage gap in the for-hire carrier sector decreased to 10 percent, with union discrimination and employer discrimination accounting for 10 percent and 30 percent, respectively. Although the union's discriminatory practices did not change much, employers greatly reduced their level of discrimination, with a more competitive product market resulting from deregulation. Agesa and Brown concluded that increased efficiency from deregulation has resulted in decreased employer discrimination. Their results provide empirical evidence that enhanced product market competition can reduce employer discrimination, which diminishes the requirement for direct government market intervention to mitigate racial and other illegal wage discrimination.

Source: J. Agesa and A. Brown, "Regulation, Unionization, and Racial Wage Discrimination: An Analysis of the Trucking Industry," *American Journal of Economics and Sociology* 57 (1998): 285–305.

Questions

1. Why might an international corporation with identical plants in different countries pay different wage rates to workers in various countries even if their skill levels are the same?
2. A master's degree may on average increase the lifetime earnings of a male by less than it increases the lifetime earnings of a female. Why?

3. If each input receives a payment equivalent to its marginal revenue product, will there be any inefficiency? Will the resulting distribution of income be socially optimal? Explain.
4. What are the differences in inputs employed, prices, surpluses, and welfare implications among a perfectly competitive input market, a monopsony market, and a perfect input price-discriminating monopsony market.

Exercises

1. Consider a firm that has a monopoly in its output market and is a perfectly price-discriminating monopsony in its input market. The production function $Q = {}^1\!/_2 L$, the inverse demand function $p = 50 - 2Q$, and the inverse supply function $w = 1 + L$.
   a. Determine the optimal levels of Q, L, w, and p.
   b. What are the welfare implications of output level Q and employment L?
2. Given that $q = 5X - \frac{1}{2}X^2$, the output price for q is $p = 2$, and the supply function is $X = \frac{1}{3}v$, compare price and output decisions of a revenue-maximizing supplier of X facing a perfectly price-discriminating monopsonist.
3. Consider the situation of a slave who is unable to supply labor in the market. Assume that his master provides a fixed subsistence level of food and shelter along with a wage.
   a. What would be the wage rate offered by the master? What wage rate would the slave prefer? What is the deadweight loss?
   b. When would it be in the interest of the master to free her slave and pay him a wage?
4. Suppose that a logging company is the only employer of labor in an area. The supply curve for female workers is

$$L_F = 400w_F$$

and that for male workers is

$$L_M = 100w_M + 200,$$

where w_F and w_M are the hourly wage rates paid to female and male workers, respectively. Assume that the firm sells its lumber in a perfectly competitive market at \$2 per unit and that each worker hired (both male and female) can harvest 4 units per hour.

a. If the firm wishes to maximize profits, how many female and male workers should be hired and what will be the wage rates for female and male workers? What will be the firm's level of profit?
b. If the firm is constrained by market forces to pay all workers the same wage, how will the results compare with those in (a).

Internet case study

1. Outline the economic arguments for and against equal pay for equal value.

Part VIII

Risky world and intertemporal choices

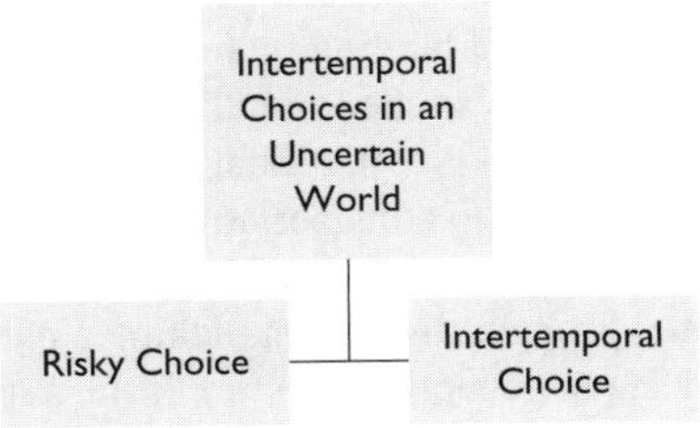

Chapters

In the real world, the rearview mirror is always clearer than the windshield.
(Warren Buffet)

The previous chapters have outlined constrained versions of our dream optimal allocation decisions. These were certain states, where there was no risk or uncertainty and resources were unlimited over time. The only constraint was that some central authority determines the level of resources available in each time period. Any resources unused in a current period could not be saved and used to augment the future resource base. The discussion in these chapters centered on determining the terms of trade (prices) for commodities in a dream market and how households maximize utility for a given income or firms maximize profit with a given technology. Implicit assumptions underlying these chapters were that no uncertainty existed in terms of trade, incomes, preferences, nature of commodities, or technology, and that choices and consequential outcomes only occurred in the current time period. The outcomes of any decision were known in advance with certainty and only influenced current satisfaction.

This assumption of a certain world is unrepresentative of any real-world economy and would certainly be a world without the pleasure and disappointment of surprises. The assumption of only the current time period is also generally unrepresentative (except for some thrill-seekers who live only for the moment). In reality, current consumption and investment decisions are generally based on an expected return in future periods.

Therefore, in Part 8, we consider agents' decision rules in a more realistic environment of risk and uncertainty. *Risk* and *uncertainty* exist when agents (households and firms) do not have full prior information concerning the outcomes of decisions. *Risk* is involved when the probability of each outcome is known. An example is tossing a coin; there is a 50 percent probability of it landing on heads and a 50 percent probability of it landing on tails. *Uncertainty* exists when not all outcomes following a decision are known, and, even for those that are known, probabilities associated with the outcomes are unknown. Agents must then try to consider all the possible outcomes and estimate the probabilities of each. For example, a football coach has to consider all the possible outcomes and the associated probabilities when picking a particular play. What makes football, other games, and life in general interesting is the inability to predict surprises.

We investigate risky choices and risk aversion in Chapter 18 by first defining probability and stating the *Independence Axiom*, which states that what does not happen should not affect a household's risky choice. Given this Independence Axiom, we develop the concept of an expected utility function. We also discuss risk preferences and insurance as a mechanism for risk sharing. Based on an expected utility function, we derive the utility-maximizing commodity bundle.

In Chapter 19, we investigate the optimal level for purchasing commodities or inputs in a current time period, with expected satisfaction from these purchases possibly occurring in both the current and future time periods. We first determine the optimal level of real-capital inputs owned by a household or firm. We develop a life-cycle model where current decisions are dependent on future and past levels of real capital. We then discuss human capital, using a household's objectives to determine the optimal level of human-capital investment. Within this discussion of human capital, we address the *Separation Theorem*, which states that households can separate human-capital decisions from consumption decisions. We then consider discounting future costs and returns as a method of determining the present value of net returns (profits) from a capital item.

18 Risky choice and risk aversion

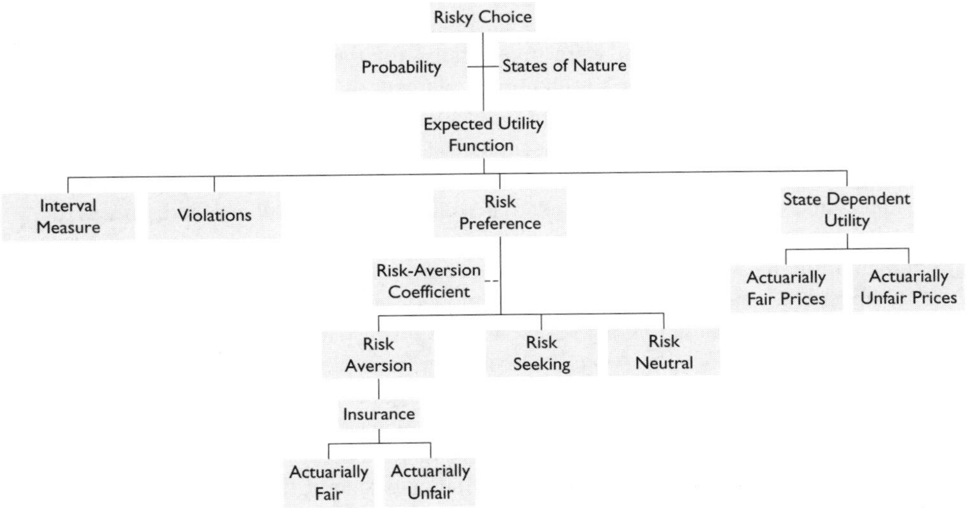

Outline and Conceptual Inquiries

Understanding probability

Subjective probability: good guess

What is the probability that you will read this chapter?

Objective probability: frequency of occurrence

What is the probability that you will take a bath tonight?

Mutually exclusive probabilities

States of nature

Can you be at two places at once?

Deriving the expected utility function

Application: Expected tornado hit and demand for shelters

Risk preference

Are you a risk taker, or do you purchase insurance?

Risk aversion: school principals

Risk seeking: self-employed

Risk neutrality: government

Are zombies risk-neutral?

Certainty equivalent

Why have insurance?

Optimal level of insurance

How much insurance should you purchase?

Application: Elderly willingness to pay for Medicare

Actuarially favorable outcomes

Calculating the risk-aversion coefficient

What is your number?

Application: Precautionary principle

Should it be policy first, then science? Or science first, then policy?

State-dependent utility

Actuarially fair prices: fully insure

Actuarially unfair prices: accept some risk

Risk seeking

Summary

Key concepts

Key equations

Questions

Exercises

Internet case studies

Appendix to chapter 18

Interval measurement of utility

Linear transformations

Violations of expected utility

Allais's Paradox

Machina's Paradox

If you cannot go to the football game, would you watch it on television?

St Petersburg Paradox

Should you always play the lottery?

Questions

Internet case study

Nothing is certain but uncertainty.

(Pliny the Elder)

In 1995 and 1996, at least 67 employees (including 45 officers) of the Sacramento, California Police Department were investigated for their alleged involvement in a pyramid scheme. This scheme resulted in 6.7 percent of those who joined receiving a 700 percent return on their investment ($3500 on a $500 investment) as long as 93.3 percent received nothing. A pyramid scheme is a fraudulent system of making money that requires an infinite stream of new investors for success. Recruits give money to recruiters and then enlist fresh recruits to give them money. Such a scheme is called a pyramid scheme because it is the shape of a pyramid. If a pyramid were started by a conman at the top with 10 recruits underneath him, then 100 underneath the 10, then 1000 underneath them, and so on, the pyramid would involve 10 billion agents in just 10 layers and one conman on top. Compare this result with the Earth's population of only about 7 billion people. A similar scam is a Ponzi scheme, named after Charles Ponzi, who defrauded people in the 1920s by getting people to invest in something for a guaranteed rate of return and using the money of later investors to pay off the earlier ones. In 2009, Bernard Madoff pleaded guilty to 11 federal felonies and admitted to turning his wealth-management business into a Ponzi scheme that defrauded thousands of investors of billions of dollars. What is the lesson? Beware of any high certain rate of return. Nothing is certain but uncertainty.

The general theory of agent choice under certainty, developed in previous chapters, cannot be employed for investigating optimal decisions given risky outcomes. The actual outcomes that occur in an uncertain world depend on their probability of occurring. Based on both *subjective* and *objective probabilities*, we define risky alternatives (called *states of nature*) in this chapter. Given alterative states of nature, we define the *Independence Axiom*, which precludes states that will not happen from impacting household preferences. Given this Independence Axiom, we develop the expected utility function as an interval measure of utility. We then define households' risk preferences in terms of *risk-averse, risk-seeking,* and *risk-neutral preferences*. Given a household's risk preference, we develop the concept of *certainty equivalent* along with its implications for insurance. We also develop the concepts of actuarially fair insurance and asymmetric information associated with insurance. We end the chapter with a discussion of *state dependent utility,* where the first-order conditions (FOCs) for expected utility maximization are derived for a household with risk-averse preferences facing actuarially fair and unfair markets. In the Appendix to the chapter, we discuss the interval measurement of utility along with violations of expected utility, including the Allais, Machina, and St Petersburg paradoxes.

Our aim in this chapter is to introduce the concepts of risk and uncertainty and investigate the impacts that they have on agents' decisions. Expected utility is extensively used by applied economists as a tool for investigating this impact. When issues of risk and uncertainty are relevant for decision making—such as evaluating consumers' demand for insurance—an applied economist will usually turn to expected utility as a tool for developing possible solutions.

Understanding probability

> *I despise life insurance agents because they argue that I shall someday die, which is not true.*
>
> (Stephen Leacock, died March 28, 1944)

A household's decision regarding going to a movie this weekend has some probability associated with it. Even if the household plans to go, something unexpected may occur and it may not go. The household will not go to the movie if its opportunity cost of going rises to the point where the cost of going outweighs the benefit. As the household's opportunity cost increases, the probability of going to a movie decreases. **Probability** is a measure of the likelihood that an outcome will occur. An **outcome** could be some level of income, amount or quality of a commodity, or a change in price. If an outcome cannot happen, its probability is 0; if an outcome is certain to occur, its probability is 1. In the previous chapters, we assumed that the probabilities of all possible outcomes were either 0 or 1. All possible outcomes were certain to occur. Relaxing this assumption allows the probability of an outcome to range from 0 to 1.

Probability (ρ). The likelihood that an outcome will occur. *E.g., the likelihood (probability) of you attending the next class lecture may be 80 percent.*

Outcome. A particular result when undertaking some action. *E.g., the vast knowledge you will gain from attending your next class lecture.*

Subjective probability: good guess

The probability of going to the movies in the future is a type of probability called *subjective probability*, where a household has a perception that an event (going to the movies) will occur. A household's perception is based on the conditions of current market prices, its preferences, and its income. Any changes in these conditions will alter the household's perceptions, and households with different preferences will have different perceptions. This results in different subjective probabilities by individual households through time and across various households.

What is the probability that you will read this chapter? The probability that you will read this chapter depends on current conditions. If current conditions are right (a test tomorrow), the probability may be very high that you will read at least part of this chapter.

Objective probability: frequency of occurrence

> *The odds against there being a bomb on a plane are a million to one, and against two bombs a million times a million to one. Next time you fly, cut the odds and take a bomb.*
>
> (Benny Hill)

Another type of probability is *objective probability*, the frequency with which certain outcomes will occur. From past experiences, the objective probability of an outcome can be measured. For example, if it is observed over some time interval that a household goes to the movies on weekends 13 times in 1 year, then the frequency of going to the movies is once every 4 weeks. The probability of going to the movie on any weekend is then $1/4$ or 25 percent. This is an objective probability, measured by the frequency of occurrence, and depends on past household behavior. The past frequency of a bomb on a plane is a million to one. However, this frequency (probability) will not change by you taking a bomb.

What is the probability that you will take a bath tonight? If you were a homesteader in the nineteenth century and it were a Saturday night, then the objective probability is close to 100 percent.

Mutually exclusive probabilities

Both subjective and objective probabilities are mutually exclusive—only one outcome will occur. For example, a household will either go to the movies this coming weekend or not. The probabilities associated with each possible outcome thus always sum up to 1. If $1/4$ is the probability that the household goes to the movies, then $3/4$ is the probability that it will not. These two possible outcomes exhaust all possible outcomes and, given the mutually exclusive nature of these probabilities, the probabilities sum to 1. In general, assuming a finite number of outcomes, k,

$$\sum_{j=1}^{k} \rho_j = 1,$$

where ρ_j is the probability of outcome j occurring.

States of nature

Do not count your chickens before they are hatched.

(Aesop's Fables)

Translation: The state of nature for a chicken to hatch from each egg is not 100 percent.

In making future consumption plans, a household will consider the probability of possible outcomes. In determining the probabilities of these outcomes, the household may use a combination of both subjective and objective probabilities. The household is then faced with choosing alternatives with uncertain outcomes by means of known probabilities. Each risky alternative is called a **state of nature** or **lottery**, N, defined as a set of probabilities, summing to 1, with a probability assigned to each outcome. For example, the state of nature associated with our household movie choice is $(1/4, 3/4)$. If the probability of going to the movies is $3/4$ and that of not going is $1/4$, then the state of nature is reversed $(3/4, 1/4)$. In general, a state of nature is a set of probabilities associated with all k outcomes.

State of nature. A set of probabilities associated with all possible outcomes. *E.g., if there is a $2/3$ probability of you studying and then a $1/3$ probability of you going out, the state of nature is $(2/3, 1/3)$.*

Consistent with previous chapters, we assume that households are rational when facing these states of nature, with a preference relation $\succsim$. Outcomes could be in any form, including consumption bundles, money, or an opportunity to participate in another state of nature (called a *compound lottery*).

There is a fundamental difference between commodities and states of nature. Commodities can and generally are consumed jointly. Examples are driving and listening to the radio or drinking and driving (not a recommended method for maximizing utility). In contrast, states of nature, by their definition of being mutually exclusive, cannot be consumed jointly. Either one state of nature exists or another, but two or more states of nature cannot exist at the same time (except possibly in the movies or in our dreams). For example, a household cannot have a 25 percent probability of going to the movies and a 75 percent probability of going to the movies at the same time.

Can you be at two places at once? No, you cannot experience two different states of nature at the same time (except in science fiction or your dreams).

This idea of being unable to jointly consume two or more states of nature is a fundamental assumption of many theories dealing with choice under uncertainty, and is summarized by the following **Independence Axiom**.

Independence Axiom

If N, N', and N'' are states of nature, then $N \succsim N'$ if and only if

$$\rho N + (1-\rho)N'' \succsim \rho N' + (1-\rho)N''.$$

The preference that a household has for one state of nature N over another state N' should be independent from other states of nature, say N''. This other state of nature N should be irrelevant to a household's choice between N and N'. In other words, what does not happen should not affect the level of preferences between two possible states of nature. For example, assume that N is a state of nature where the probability of getting a cola drink is 1, N' is a state where getting an un-cola drink has a probability of 1, and N'' is a state where getting water has a probability of 1. Then the amount of water a household may receive should not influence the preferences for cola or un-cola. The household does not end up with any water, so it should not influence the choice between cola and un-cola. Under these alternative states, only one of the three possible states will occur. Either the household will receive cola, un-cola, or water, but it will not jointly receive these drinks. The preference between cola and un-cola should not be influenced by the amount of water in another state of nature. However, increasing the amount of water in N will influence the preference between cola and water and the preference between un-cola and water.

Independence Axiom. The preference that a household has for one state of nature over another state is independent from other states of nature. *E.g., the preferences associated with a $^2/_3$ probability of studying and a $^1/_3$ probability of going out versus a $^3/_5$ probability of studying and a $^2/_5$ probability of going out are independent of a $^3/_4$ probability of studying and a $^1/_4$ probability of going out.*

Deriving the expected utility function

What makes something special is not just what you have to gain, but what you feel there is to lose.

(Andre Agassi)

Suppose that the probability of a candidate for governor supporting environmental issues once elected (state of nature) varies by candidate. Only one state of nature will actually occur; however, there is a probability associated with which state of nature will occur. The utility of environmentalists will vary depending on which state of nature occurs (which candidate gets elected). The average (expected) utility from the election will then be the sum of the utilities for each candidate weighted by the associated probability of being elected. Based on the Independence Axiom, the utility function for choice under uncertainty is additive for consumption in each possible state of nature. That is, for all possible states of nature, utility from consumption in one state of nature is added to the utility from consumption in another state. This is called an **expected utility function** (also called the **von Neumann–Morgenstern utility function**).

Specifically, for two possible states of nature, the expected utility function is

$$U(\vec{x}_1, \vec{x}_2, \rho_1, \rho_2) = \rho_1 U(\vec{x}_1) + \rho_2 U(\vec{x}_2),$$

where U is the utility function associated with contingent commodity bundles $\vec{x}_1$ and $\vec{x}_2$ consumed in states of nature 1 and 2, respectively, and ρ_1 and ρ_2 are the respective probabilities of the states of nature occurring. Note that $\rho_1 + \rho_2 = 1$. A **contingent commodity** is a commodity whose level of consumption depends on which state of nature occurs. Thus, the expected utility function is the weighted sum of the utility from consumption in the states of nature, where the weights are the probabilities of the states occurring. If only one of the states of nature occurs, say state 1, then $\rho_1 = 1$ and $\rho_2 = 0$, and the utility function reduces to

$$U = U(\vec{x}_1).$$

This is the standard utility function that we used in the previous chapters, with certainty assumed. With uncertainty, the probabilities are $0 < (\rho_1,\ \rho_2) < 1$, and the utility function represents the average or expected utility, given the alternative possible states of nature.

Expected (von Neumann–Morgenstern) utility function. The weighted average of utility obtained from alternative states of nature. *E.g., if one state of nature involves going home for the weekend and the other involves staying at school to study, then the utility associated with these two possible states is their weighted average, where the weights are the probability of going home or staying at school.*

Contingent commodity. A commodity whose level of consumption depends on which state of nature occurs. *E.g., the amount of popcorn you consume depends on whether you go to the movies or not.*

Application: Expected tornado hit and demand for shelters

Dorothy and Toto in the movie *The Wizard of Oz* (1939) were lucky; on April 27, 2011 a real F5 tornado hit Tuscaloosa, Alabama, killing hundreds and caused more damage than any other tornado in US history. Particularly hard hit were people in mobile homes as opposed to those in homes with foundations.

Based on an expected utility function, Sutter and Poitras examined the response of housing choice to tornado risk. The vulnerability of mobile home parks, combined with their growing share of the US housing market, has led to proposed mandates for community shelters in these parks. However, expected utility theory suggests that households should account for tornado risk in their housing choice. Sutter and Poitras tested for an effect of tornado risk on mobile-home demand using cross-sectional state data, as well as data from counties in three tornado-prone states. Their results indicate that people do respond to tornado risk: each expected annual state tornado death per million residents reduces demand for mobile homes by 3 percent.

Source: D. Sutter and M. Poitras, "Do People Respond to Low Probability Risks? Evidence from Tornado Risk and Manufactured Homes," *Journal of Risk and Uncertainty* 40 (2010): 181–196.

Risk preference

Behold the turtle. He makes progress only when he sticks his neck out.
(James Bryant Conant)

Translation: Life is full of uncertainty, so in order to enjoy it you must accept some risk.

Driving your car when the fuel tank is nearly empty carries some probability of running out of gas before stopping at a service station. Thus, the state of nature associated with a 90 percent probability of stopping for gas at the next service station may not be certain. Instead, you may run out of gas first, so the probability may be only 50 percent. This variability in the outcomes of some state of nature when the probability of each outcome is known is called **risk**. Generally, the statistical concept of variance is employed as a measure for risk. *Variance* is a measure of the spread of a probability distribution, so it measures the variability in outcomes. The greater the variance and thus variability in outcomes, the greater is the risk. For example, for a salaried employee, the state of nature associated with receiving a fixed salary per month is risk-free. It has no variability, no risk, and a variance of 0. In contrast, an employee working on commission, say, based on sales, has some risk; his monthly salary can vary. The larger the variability in salary, possibly measured in terms of its variance, the greater the risk. In general, unless compensated for this exposure to risk, households appear to have an aversion to risk. In an effort to reduce this risk exposure, they will attempt to shift risk onto another agent. The common practice of purchasing insurance is a form of shifting risk, and its prevalence suggests that risk aversion is common among not only households but also firms.

Are you a risk taker, or do you purchase insurance? If you voluntarily purchase insurance, then you are averse to risk.

Risk. Variability in the outcomes associated with a state of nature. *E.g., you may plan on either going out or studying tonight, but you may instead get sick.*

Risk aversion: school principals

Most people would rather be certain they are miserable than risk being happy.
(Robert N. Anthony)

In a game of tossing a coin, if it is heads, then a household will receive \$5 and if it is tails, then the household must pay \$5. The expected value of the game is then

$$\tfrac{1}{2}(5) + \tfrac{1}{2}(-5) = 0,$$

which is called actuarially fair. **Actuarially fair games** are games in which the expected values are zero or the cost of playing a game is equivalent to the game's expected value. If, instead, the payoff for heads is increased to \$15, the expected value is now

$$\tfrac{1}{2}(15) + \tfrac{1}{2}(-5) = 5.$$

A \$5 cost of playing the game would reduce the expected payoff to zero, which is then actuarially fair. In terms of risk preferences, a household has **risk-averse preferences** if it refuses to play actuarially fair games. Thus, a risk-averse household would generally refuse to play these games unless there is some utility (e.g., personal pleasure) in the actual process of playing and the potential loss from paying is relatively small. It would prefer its correct certain (miserable?) state to a risky state with a possible loss in happiness. Some individuals do play actuarially unfair games, where the expected value is negative. For some individuals who play slot machines or state lotteries, the fun of playing and dreams of winning yield utility in excess of the small cost of playing. Examples of risk-averse preferences are school principals and providers of vaccines. School principals in planning playgrounds tend to focus on providing equipment that minimizes the risk of injury, so teeter-totters are generally not provided. Health officials are risk averse in advocating childhood vaccines that minimize the risk of a childhood pandemic.

Actuarially fair games. The cost of playing the game is equivalent to the game's expected value. *E.g., in blackjack, a player who is able to count the cards can increase the expected returns to the point they equal the cost of playing.*

Risk-averse preferences. A household who will not play actuarially fair games. *E.g., a sales associate who prefers a fixed salary compared to a commission based on the level of sales.*

Concave utility function

In automobile sales, a salesperson generally works on some commission (about 4–8 percent) where his salary is dependent on the level of his sales. However, risk-averse households would generally prefer a certain salary versus a variable salary based on sales with an expected value equivalent to the certainty salary. A risk-averse household will not play actuarially fair games because for this household winning the game increases utility by a lesser degree than losing reduces it. Such a household prefers its current level of wealth over the variance in wealth associated with an actuarially fair game even though the payoffs, in terms of resulting expected wealth, are the same.

Mathematically, for two possible states of nature, risk aversion may be stated as

$$U(\rho_1 W_1 + \rho_2 W_2) > \rho_1 U(W_1) + \rho_2 U(W_2),$$

where W_1 and W_2 are the levels of wealth resulting from possible outcomes 1 and 2, respectively. The level of utility associated with the expected wealth, $U(\rho_1 W_1 + \rho_2 W_2)$, is greater than for the state of nature resulting in the expected utility of wealth, $\rho_1 U(W_1) + \rho_2 U(W_2)$. If the outcomes were an employee's salary, then a risk-averse employee would prefer the state of nature with the certain salary, resulting in $U(\rho_1 W_1 + \rho_2 W_2)$, over the uncertain salary with an expected utility level of $\rho_1 U(W_1) + \rho_2 U(W_2)$. This inequality is called *Jensen's inequality*, and it defines a concave function illustrated in Figure 18.1. A zero level of wealth corresponding to $U = 0$ results from a positive linear transformation of the expected utility function (see the Appendix to this chapter). Due to the concave nature of the utility function, the weighted average of the wealth levels W_1 and W_2 yields a lower expected utility of wealth, $\rho_1 U(W_1) + \rho_2 U(W_2)$, than the utility of the expected wealth, $U(\rho_1 W_1 + \rho_2 W_2)$. Note that the weights are the probabilities of wealth levels W_1 and W_2 occurring, $\rho_1 + \rho_2 = 1$, and, from Figure 18.1, in this case, $\rho_1 > \rho_2$. Thus, risk aversion is equivalent to a concave expected utility function, which implies a diminishing marginal utility of wealth, $\partial^2 U/\partial W^2 < 0$. As wealth increases, the marginal utility of wealth declines.

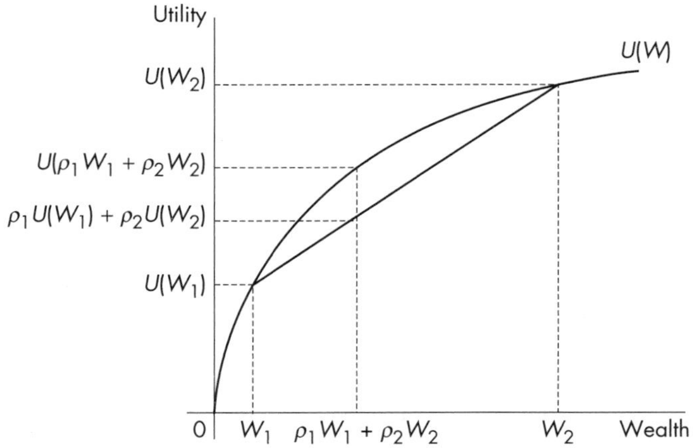

Figure 18.1 **Risk-averse preferences.** Risk aversion is equivalent to a concave expected utility function, which implies diminishing marginal utility of wealth.

Example 18.1 Illustrating risk-averse preferences

Consider two uncertain outcomes having a 50 percent probability of occurring, with outcomes $W_1 = 2$ and $W_2 = 4$. Assume that a household has the following expected utility function:

$$U(W) = 10W - W^2.$$

The household will be risk-averse if

$$U\left(\tfrac{1}{2}W_1 + \tfrac{1}{2}W_2\right) > \tfrac{1}{2}U(W_1) + \tfrac{1}{2}U(W_2).$$

Evaluating this inequality yields

$$U\left[\tfrac{1}{2}(2) + \tfrac{1}{2}(4)\right] > \tfrac{1}{2}U(2) + \tfrac{1}{2}U(4),$$
$$U(3) > \tfrac{1}{2}(16) + \tfrac{1}{2}(24),$$
$$21 > 20.$$

This inequality indicates that the household is risk-averse, represented by a concave expected utility function. Note that the second partial derivative $\partial^2 U/\partial W^2 = -2 < 0$, which indicates diminishing marginal utility of wealth.

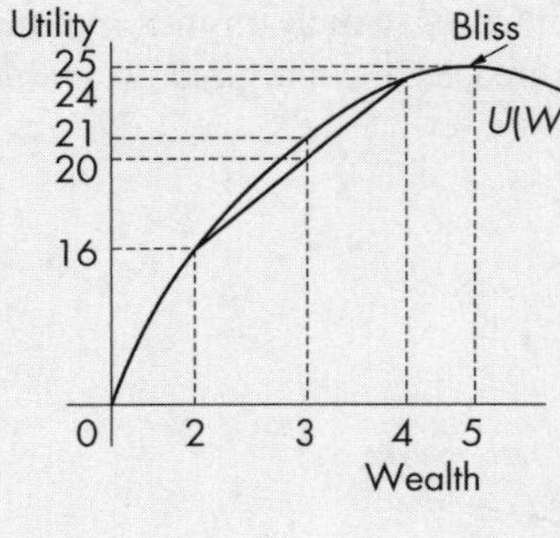

Risk seeking: self-employed

Some research indicates that sensation seeking may be attributed to a genetic bottleneck in the thalamus (the clearinghouse in the forebrain where most sensory data are collected and then sent to the cerebral cortex for processing). A blockage in the thalamus results in the brain being under-stimulated, starved of impressions from the outside world. It is thought that sensation seekers learn to compensate for this under-stimulation. They have found that engaging in risky activities stimulates them and they get pleasure from it. Thus, some individuals may have **risk-seeking preferences** (also called **risk-loving preferences**). These individuals prefer a random distribution of wealth over its expected value. For example, in addition to the possibility of earning higher incomes, some individuals prefer the challenge of facing uncertain income compared with the more mundane guaranteed salary. Such individuals gravitate toward occupations with more variable income streams. Examples are being self-employed, day-trading stocks, or working as a commodities trader. Some individuals are not only risk seeking in terms of their wealth, but also in life itself. Examples are race-car drivers, soldiers in special military forces, and criminals. Generally, most individuals do not have such extreme risk-seeking preferences. However, at least for small potential losses in income, many households have some risk-seeking characteristics. For example, many households engage in gambling, either by playing the lottery or by other forms of wagering. Overall, households do not have a genetic bottleneck in the thalamus, so they are generally risk-averse when it comes to relatively large potential losses.

Risk-seeking (risk-loving) preferences. A household who will play actuarially fair games. *E.g., a sales representative who prefers a commission based on the level of sales over a fixed salary.*

Mathematically, risk seeking reverses the inequality for risk aversion. For two possible states of nature, risk-seeking preferences are defined as

$$U(\rho_1 W_1 + \rho_2 W_2) < \rho_1 U(W_1) + \rho_2 U(W_2).$$

As illustrated in Figure 18.2, for risk-seeking preferences, the expected utility function is now convex. Due to the convex nature of the utility function, the weighted average of wealth levels W_1 and W_2 yields a higher expected utility of wealth, $\rho_1 U(W_1) + \rho_2 U(W_2)$, than the utility of the expected wealth, $U(\rho_1 W_1 + \rho_2 W_2)$. Thus, risk seeking is equivalent to a convex expected utility function, which implies an increasing marginal utility of wealth, $\partial^2 U/\partial W^2 > 0$. As wealth increases, the marginal utility of wealth increases.

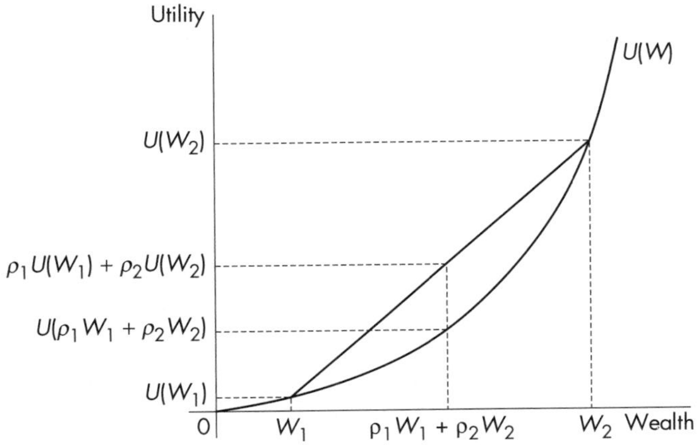

Figure 18.2 **Risk-seeking preferences.** Risk seeking is equivalent to a convex expected utility function, which implies increasing marginal utility of wealth.

Example 18.2 Illustrating risk-seeking preferences

As in Example 18.1, consider two uncertain outcomes, each having a 50 percent probability of occurring, with the outcomes $W_1 = 2$ and $W_2 = 4$. However, this time assume a different expected utility function,

$$U(W) = 10W + W^2.$$

The household will be risk seeking if

$$U\left(\tfrac{1}{2}W_1 + \tfrac{1}{2}W_2\right) < \tfrac{1}{2}U(W_1) + \tfrac{1}{2}U(W_2).$$

Evaluating this inequality yields

$$U\left[\tfrac{1}{2}(2) + \tfrac{1}{2}(4)\right] < \tfrac{1}{2}U(2) + \tfrac{1}{2}U(4)$$

$$U(3) < \tfrac{1}{2}(24) + \tfrac{1}{2}(56)$$

$$39 < 40.$$

This inequality indicates that the household is risk seeking, represented by a convex expected utility function. Note that the second derivative $\partial^2 U/\partial W^2 = 2 > 0$, which implies increasing marginal utility of wealth.

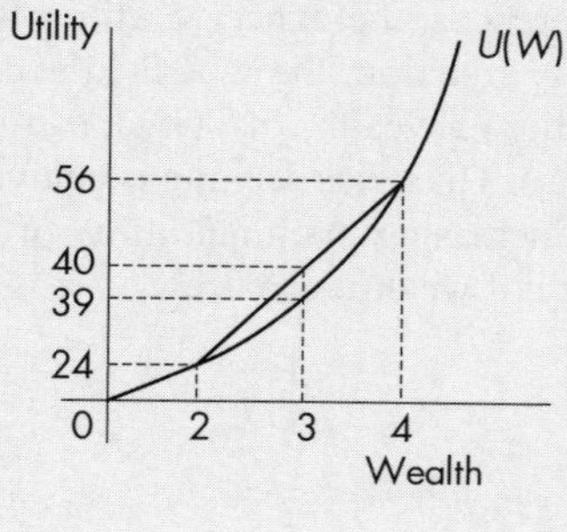

Risk neutrality: government

Intermediate between risk aversion and risk seeking is the linear expected utility function representing risk-neutral preference. Households with **risk-neutral preferences** are not concerned with the variation in wealth. Their only concern is the expected value of wealth. A risk-neutral household is indifferent between receiving a certain income versus an uncertain income, provided that the expected income from the uncertain outcome is equivalent to the certain income. A risk-neutral household is indifferent among all alternatives with the same expected value of wealth. An example of risk-neutral preferences is the *Arrow-Lind Theorem*, which states that government should be risk-neutral. This assumes that government can transfer risk through their ability to distribute losses over a large population so the per capita loss for each household is small. Also, the government's risk portfolio is diversified—it can pool a large number of risks—so its risk for any one outcome is negated.

Are zombies risk-neutral? No, zombies would be indifferent not only toward receiving certain versus uncertain expected income, but also to the level of wealth.

Risk-neutral preferences. A household who is indifferent between playing an actuarially fair game or not. *E.g., a sales representative who is indifferent between a commission and a fixed salary.*

Example 18.3 Illustrating risk-neutral preferences

As in Examples 18.1 and 18.2, consider again two uncertain outcomes each having a 50 percent probability of occurring with outcomes $W_1 = 2$ and $W_2 = 4$. This time, assume that a household has the linear expected utility function

$$U(W) = 10W.$$

The household will be risk-neutral if

$$U\left(\tfrac{1}{2}W_1 + \tfrac{1}{2}W_2\right) = \tfrac{1}{2}U(W_1) + \tfrac{1}{2}U(W_2).$$

Evaluating this equality yields

$$U\left[\tfrac{1}{2}(2) + \tfrac{1}{2}(4)\right] = \tfrac{1}{2}U(2) + \tfrac{1}{2}U(4),$$

$$U(3) = \tfrac{1}{2}(20) + \tfrac{1}{2}(40),$$

$$30 = 30.$$

The equality indicates that the household is risk-neutral, represented by a linear expected utility function. Note that the second derivative $\partial^2 U/\partial W^2 = 0$, which implies constant marginal utility of wealth.

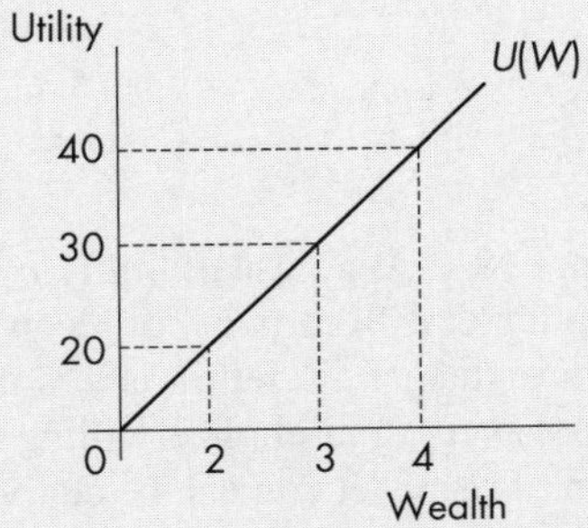

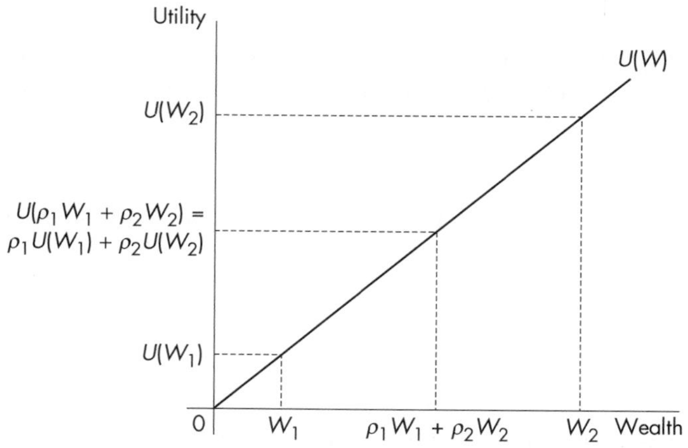

Figure 18.3 **Risk-neutral preferences.** Risk neutrality is equivalent to a linear expected utility function, which implies constant marginal utility of wealth.

Considering two outcomes, a household is considered risk-neutral when the utility of expected wealth is equal to the expected utility of wealth:

$$U(\rho_1 W_1 + \rho_2 W_2) = \rho_1 U(W_1) + \rho_2 U(W_2).$$

Risk-neutral preferences are depicted in Figure 18.3, where the expected utility function is now linear. Due to the linear nature of the utility function, the weighted average of wealth levels W_1 and W_2 yields the same expected utility of wealth, $\rho_1 U(W_1) + \rho_2 U(W_2)$, as the utility of the expected wealth, $U(\rho_1 W_1 + \rho_2 W_2)$. Thus, risk-neutral preferences are equivalent to a linear expected utility function, which implies a constant marginal utility of wealth, $\partial^2 U/\partial W^2 = 0$. Marginal utility is constant at all levels of wealth.

Certainty equivalent

Another popular method for measuring risk aversion is the certainty equivalent. The **certainty equivalent (*C*)** is the amount of return a household would receive from a certain outcome, so it is indifferent between a risky outcome and this certain outcome. Specifically, given two uncertain outcomes,

$$U(C) = \rho_1 U(W_1) + \rho_2 U(W_2).$$

The certainty-equivalence concept is illustrated in Figure 18.4. At a level of utility $\rho_1 U(W_1) + \rho_2 U(W_2)$, the household is indifferent between receiving C with certainty or receiving the risky outcome $\rho_1 W_1 + \rho_2 W_2$. As illustrated in the figure, the certain return is less than the risky outcome, $C < \rho_1 W_1 + \rho_2 W_2$. This implies that a risk-averse household is willing to trade some expected return for certainty. Thus, the definition of risk aversion can be equivalently defined as $C < \rho_1 W_1 + \rho_2 W_2$. The inequality sign is reversed for risk-seeking preferences, and the inequality becomes an equality for risk-neutral preferences.

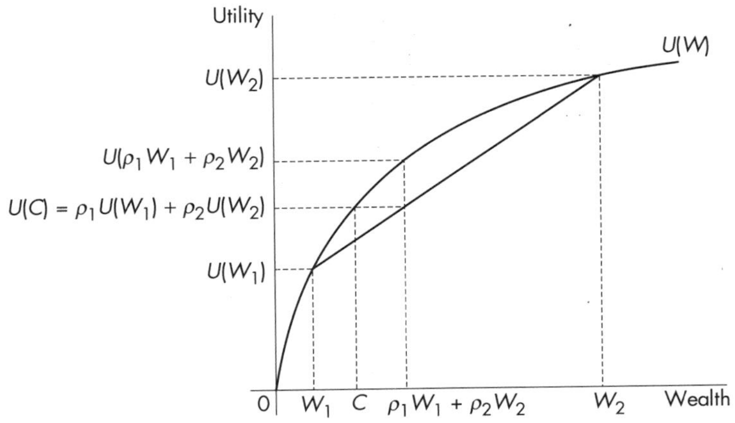

Figure 18.4 **Risk aversion and certainty equivalence.** The household is indifferent between receiving C with certainty or receiving the risky state of nature $(\rho_1 W_1 + \rho_2 W_2)$. For risk-averse preferences, $C < \rho_1 W_1 + \rho_2 W_2$.

Certainty equivalent (C). The amount of return C that a household would receive from a certain outcome so that it is indifferent between a risky outcome and this certain outcome. *E.g., the level of a fixed salary a sales representative would receive for her to be indifferent between receiving a commission or receiving this fixed salary.*

Example 18.4. Calculating the certainty equivalent

Considering the risk-averse preferences in Example 18.1, the expected utility function is

$$U(W) = 10W - W^2,$$

with a utility level of 20 associated with an expected utility of wealth of $\frac{1}{2}U(W_1) + \frac{1}{2}U(W_2)$. Setting this expected utility function equal to 20 and solving for W yields the certainty-equivalent level of wealth C. Specifically,

$$20 = 10W - W^2.$$

Solving using the quadratic formula yields $C = 2.76$. Note that $C = 2.76 < 3$, indicating that the household has risk-averse preferences.

For the risk-seeking preferences in Example 18.2, we determine the certainty equivalent by setting the expected utility of wealth, 40, equal to the expected utility function:

$$40 = 10W + W^2.$$

Solving for W results in the certainty-equivalent wealth level of 3.06. Since $C = 3.06 > 3$, the household is risk-seeking.

Finally, for the risk-neutral preferences in Example 18.3, the certainty equivalent is equal to the expected utility function of 3.

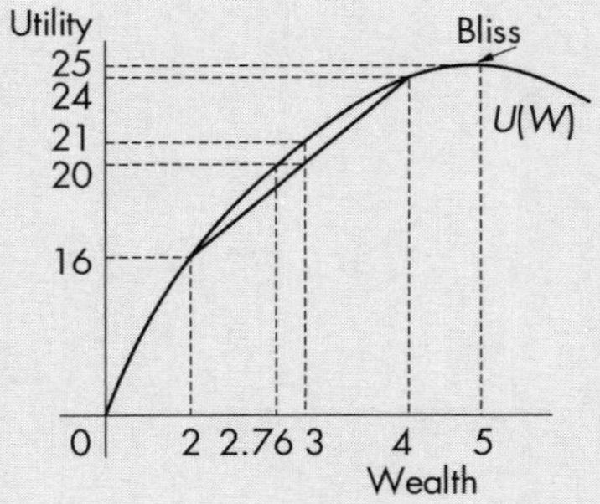

Why have insurance?

Insurance: A bet you make with someone that you will die sooner than later.

(Michael Wetzstein)

Insurance companies first developed in the United States around the end of the eighteenth century. By 1841, there were 131 mutual and stock fire and marine insurance companies, with a number of these companies also writing life insurance policies. From this modest beginning, insurance companies have developed to where one can acquire an insurance policy against almost any risky outcome. Certainty equivalence, where risk-averse households are willing to trade some expected return for certainty, underlies the functioning of insurance. Households are willing to pay to avoid risky outcomes. The maximum amount that they are willing to pay is the difference between expected wealth and the certainty equivalent of wealth, $(\rho_1 W_1 + \rho_2 W_2) - C$. They would not be willing to pay more than this difference, because this would result in a loss of utility. They will be willing to pay less than this amount, in the form of insurance premiums, to avoid the risky outcome and insure a given level of wealth. For example, households are willing to purchase homeowner insurance to avoid the possible loss in wealth from a burglary.

Optimal level of insurance

We can determine a household's optimal level of insurance A^* by assuming that the household has initial level of wealth W and faces the risk of sustaining a loss D with probability ρ. The household can reduce the amount of the loss by purchasing insurance A at a cost of p per unit decrease in D (per-unit insurance premium). Purchasing a level of insurance A will then reduce the loss from D to $D - A$. If the outcome results in no loss occurring, then the household's wealth is

$$W - pA,$$

the initial wealth W minus the total cost of the insurance, pA. If a loss occurs, the household's wealth level is then

$$W - pA - (D - A),$$

the initial wealth W minus the total cost of the insurance, pA, and the net loss, $D - A$. The household's expected wealth is then

$$(1 - \rho)(W - pA) + \rho[W - pA - (D - A)],$$

which reduces to

$$W - pA - \rho(D - A).$$

Although any expected utility function representing risk-averse preference can be employed, for simplicity, assume the following logarithmic expected utility function:

$$U = (1 - \rho)\ln(W - pA) + \rho \ln[W - pA - (D - A)].$$

Note that

$$\frac{\partial U}{\partial W} = \frac{1 - \rho}{W - pA} + \frac{\rho}{W - pA - (D - A)},$$

$$\frac{\partial^2 U}{\partial W^2} = -\frac{1 - \rho}{(W - pA)^2} - \frac{\rho}{[W - pA - (D - A)]^2},$$

representing the diminishing marginal utility of wealth condition for risk aversion. We can then determine the efficient level of insurance A^* by maximizing this expected utility function:

$$\max_A U = \max_A \{(1 - \rho)\ln(W - pA) + \rho \ln[W - pA - (D - A)]\}.$$

The first-order condition (FOC) is

$$\frac{\partial U}{\partial A} = -p(1 - \rho)(W - pA)^{-1} + \rho(1 - p)[W - pA - (D - A)]^{-1} = 0.$$

Example 18.5 Determining actuarially fair insurance

Assume an initial wealth of \$100,000 and a 5 percent probability of incurring a \$10,000 loss. Given the risk-averse expected utility function

$$U = 0.95\ln(100{,}000 - 0.05A) + 0.05\ln[100{,}000 - 0.05A - (10{,}000 - A)],$$

the optimal level of insurance is $A^* = 10{,}000$ with a premium of $pA^* = 0.05(10{,}000) = 500$. The household's wealth is then \$99,500.

Actuarially fair insurance

Assume that the price of insurance is *actuarially fair*, so the insurance company has zero administrative costs, resulting in only claim costs. The insurance premium, pA, would then be equal to the company's cost of claims, ρA. Thus, $p = \rho$, and the FOC becomes

$$-\rho(1-\rho)(W-\rho A)^{-1} + \rho(1-\rho)[W-\rho A-(D-A)]^{-1} = 0,$$

$$(W-\rho A)^{-1} = [W-\rho A-(D-A)]^{-1}.$$

The equality will hold when $A^* = D$. If the insurance is actuarially fair, a risk-averse household maximizing expected utility will fully insure against all losses. Note that the household's wealth is then $W - pA$, regardless if the loss D occurs. This wealth is equivalent to the household's expected wealth

$$W - pA^* - \rho(D - A^*).$$

Actuarially unfavorable insurance

In general, as a result of asymmetric information, insurance is *actuarially unfavorable* rather than fair.[1] For example, an insurer does not know whether you habitually take your keys out of the ignition switch or not. Because insurance is actuarially unfavorable, the premium paid by the household will be higher than the expected loss, $pA > \rho D$. Thus, the household's wealth with insurance will be less than its expected wealth:

$$W - pA^* < W - \rho D.$$

In this case, the household will not fully insure against all losses, but instead will be willing to accept some risk. Actuarially unfavorable insurance implies $p > \rho$, given $A \leq D$. A rational household will not over-insure. Specifically, rearranging the FOC gives

$$\frac{p(1-\rho)}{\rho(1-p)} = \frac{W-pA}{W-pA-(D-A)} > 1.$$

With $p > \rho$, the ratio $p(1-\rho)/\rho(1-p) > 1$, which yields the inequality.

The more the insurance is actuarially unfavorable, the less insurance will be purchased. However, as long as this difference between premium and expected loss, $pA - \rho A$, is below the maximum amount that a household is willing to pay for avoiding risky outcomes [the difference between expected wealth and the certainty equivalent of wealth, $(W - \rho D) - C$], it will purchase the insurance:

$$pA - \rho D < W - \rho D - C,$$

$$pA < W - C.$$

In other words, for a household to be willing to purchase insurance, the insurance premium must be less than the difference in initial risky wealth and the certainty equivalence. If premiums are in excess of this difference, the household will not purchase the insurance.

How much insurance should you purchase? If the insurance is actuarially fair, you should fully insure against all losses. If it is actuarially unfavorable, you should insure for less than your losses and assume some of the risk.

As an example, farmers are generally reluctant to purchase crop insurance against crop losses from adverse weather. The premiums for such insurance are generally based on the current prices for determining the loss value of the crop. However, any upward price response, given the decline in yield, will mitigate any losses. This can result in premiums exceeding expected losses to the point where crop insurance is not purchased.

Application: Elderly willingness to pay for Medicare

For the elderly, medical expenses are the largest single source of stochastic financial expenses. Although most hospital expenses are paid by Medicare, 26 percent of physicians' care and over 50 percent of nursing home expenses are not covered. Approximately 13 percent of the elderly spend over 20 percent of their income on health care. Thus, the elderly are not fully insured against the loss of health, and most rely on savings to cover the uninsured risk.

Levin hypothesized that, given this condition of being partially self-insured, the elderly will not dissave after retirement but instead maintain their savings as a precaution against possible large uninsured medical expenses. As test of this hypothesis, Levin developed an econometric model for estimating the relationship between purchases of actuarially unfair health insurance and the ability of the elderly to self-insure. Empirical results support his hypothesis of the elderly not dissaving after retirement. The results also indicate that medical insurance is a normal good where a $1000 increase in wealth causes an elder to spend an additional $0.23 on health insurance. As economic theory would suggest, the elderly do determine their level of health insurance based on their wealth.

Source: L. Levin, "Demand for Health Insurance and Precautionary Motives for Savings among the Elderly," *Journal of Public Economics* 57 (1995): 337–367.

Example 18.6 Actuarially unfavorable insurance

As assumed in Example 18.5, let the initial wealth be $100,000, with a 5 percent probability of incurring a $10,000 loss. However, now also assume $p = 5.1$ percent $> \rho$, indicating actuarially unfavorable insurance. The FOC is then

$$\frac{p(1-\rho)}{\rho(1-p)} = \frac{W - pA}{W - pA - (D - A)} > 1,$$

$$\frac{5.1\%(1-5\%)}{5\%(1-5.1\%)} = \frac{100{,}000 - 5.1\%A}{100{,}000 - 5.1\%A - (10{,}000 - A)},$$

$$\frac{0.048}{0.047} = \frac{100{,}000 - 0.051A}{90{,}000 + 0.949A},$$

$$1.02(90{,}000 + 0.949A) = 100{,}000 - 0.051A,$$

$$-8200 + 1.02A = 0,$$
$$A^* = \$8039.$$

Thus, the household will only insure \$8039 of the \$10,000 in possible damages, or approximately 80 percent.

Increasing the price of the insurance from 5.1 percent to 5.2 percent results in

$$\frac{5.2\%(1-5\%)}{5\%(1-5.2\%)} = \frac{100{,}000 - 5.2\%A}{100{,}000 - 5.2\%A - (10{,}000 - A)},$$
$$\frac{0.049}{0.047} = \frac{100{,}000 - 0.052A}{90{,}000 + 0.948A},$$
$$1.04\,(90{,}000 + 0.948A) = 100{,}000 - 0.052A,$$
$$-6400 + 1.04A = 0,$$
$$A^* = \$6154.$$

An increase in the premiums reduces the amount a household is willing to insure.

Actuarially favorable outcomes

If your life is free of failures, you are not taking enough risks.

(Jackson Brown, Jr)

If an uncertain state is actuarially favorable, a risk-averse household will also accept some risk. A life free of failures will then not maximize utility. **Actuarially favorable** outcomes are assets where the expected value is positive or the cost of the asset is less than the asset's expected value. An **asset** is the title to receive commodities or monetary returns at some period in time. If the returns are in the form of commodities, the asset is called a *real asset*; assets yielding monetary returns are called *financial assets*. An example of a real asset is a stamping machine (the asset) for fabricating automobile fenders (the commodity). A financial asset could be stock in a company providing a monetary return in the form of dividends.

Asset. The title to receive commodities or monetary returns at some period in time. *E.g., your high school diploma.*

Actuarially favorable. The cost of an asset is less than the asset's expected value. *E.g., a United States Savings Bond.*

We can demonstrate this willingness of households to take on some risk by considering two assets, one certain, or risk free, and the other risky. (A *risk-free asset* is one that pays a certain fixed return. In general, US Treasury bills are considered a risk-free asset.) Let r_C be the rate of return for the certain asset and let r_1 and r_2 be two possible rates of return on the risky asset. The probability of r_1 occurring is ρ, so $1-\rho$ is the probability of outcome r_2. Assume that the mean return of the risky asset exceeds the return of the certain asset:

$$\rho r_1 + (1-\rho)r_2 > r_C.$$

Otherwise, risk-averse households would never invest in the risky asset. Let α_R and α_C denote the proportions of wealth invested in the risky and certain assets, respectively. Assume that all of the wealth is invested in these two assets, so $\alpha_R + \alpha_C = 1$.

The objective of a household is determining the optimal amounts of wealth to invest in the two assets. The household has a probability ρ of earning a $\alpha_R W r_1 + \alpha_C W r_C$ return and a probability of $1-\rho$ of earning $\alpha_R W r_2 + \alpha_C W r_C$ return. Assuming a logarithmic expected utility function, a household is interested in maximizing its return for a given level of wealth:

$$\max_{(\alpha_R,\alpha_C)} [\rho \ln(\alpha_R W r_1 + \alpha_C W r_C) + (1-\rho)\ln(\alpha_R W r_2 + \alpha_C W r_C)] \quad \text{s.t.} \quad \alpha_R + \alpha_C = 1,$$

$$\max_{(\alpha_R,\alpha_C)} [\rho \ln W + \rho \ln(\alpha_R r_1 + \alpha_C r_C) + \ln W - \rho \ln W + (1-\rho)\ln(\alpha_R r_2 + \alpha_C r_C)]$$

$$\text{s.t.} \quad \alpha_R + \alpha_C = 1.$$

Taking a linear transformation by subtracting ln W (see the Appendix to this chapter), yields

$$\max_{(\alpha_R,\,\alpha_C)} [\rho \ln(\alpha_R r_1 + \alpha_C r_C) + (1-\rho)\ln(\alpha_R r_2 + \alpha_C r_C)] \quad \text{s.t.} \quad \alpha_R + \alpha_C = 1.$$

Incorporating the constraint into the expected utility function yields

$$\max_{\alpha_R} \{\rho \ln[\alpha_R r_1 + (1-\alpha_R) r_C] + (1-\rho)\ln[\alpha_R r_2 + (1-\alpha_R) r_C]\}.$$

The FOC is then

$$\frac{\rho(r_1 - r_C)}{\alpha_R(r_1 - r_C) + r_C} + \frac{(1-\rho)(r_2 - r_C)}{\alpha_R(r_2 - r_C) + r_C} = 0.$$

Assume that the household is unwilling to take any risk, so $\alpha_R = 0$. The FOC then reduces to

$$\rho(r_1 - r_C) + (1-\rho)(r_2 - r_C) = 0,$$

$$\rho r_1 - \rho r_C + (1-\rho) r_2 - (1-\rho) r_C = 0,$$

$$\rho r_1 + (1-\rho) r_2 - r_C = 0,$$

$$\rho r_1 + (1-\rho) r_2 = r_C.$$

If the expected rate of return on the risky asset is the same as the certain return, then, by the definition of risk aversion, a risk-averse household will not invest in the risky asset. When the expected rate of return is greater than the certain return, $\alpha_R > 0$, risk-averse households will accept some risk. At the point where returns are greater than the certain return for all possible outcomes, $\alpha_R = 1$, households will invest only in the risky asset. For the two possible outcomes, this occurs where both r_1 and r_2 are greater than r_C.

This example of a risk-averse household willing to accept some risk is an exercise in diversification. In general, considering many assets, as long as the assets are not perfectly correlated, there are some gains from diversification. Households will have a portfolio of assets for maximizing their expected utility. The overall riskiness of this portfolio depends on their degree of risk aversion. In general, the greater the degree of risk aversion, the less risky will be the portfolio.

Example 18.7 Actuarially favorable risk

Consider two assets: one with a certain return of 5 percent and a risky asset with a 30 percent probability of a 2 percent return and a 70 percent probability of a 10 percent return. Given a logarithmic expected utility function and an initial wealth level of \$100,000, the FOC is

$$\frac{\rho(r_1 - r_C)}{\alpha_R(r_1 - r_C) + r_C} + \frac{(1-\rho)(r_2 - r_C)}{\alpha_R(r_2 - r_C) + r_C} = 0,$$

$$\frac{30\%(2\% - 5\%)}{\alpha_R(2\% - 5\%) + 5\%} + \frac{70\%(10\% - 5\%)}{\alpha_R(10\% - 5\%) + 5\%} = 0,$$

$$\frac{-0.009}{-0.03\alpha_R + 5\%} + \frac{0.035}{0.05\alpha_R + 5\%} = 0,$$

$$-0.009(0.05\alpha_R + 0.05) + 0.035(-0.03\alpha_R + 0.05) = 0,$$

$$-0.00045\alpha_R - 0.00045 - 0.00105\alpha_R + 0.00175 = 0,$$

$$0.0015\alpha_R = 0.0013,$$

$$\alpha_R = 86.67\%.$$

Approximately 87 percent of the risk-averse household's wealth is in the risky asset. Given initial wealth of \$100,000, \$86,667 will be allocated to the risky asset.

Calculating the risk-aversion coefficient

Sister, before you marry him, you better make sure you have a risk-aversion coefficient of a boxer.

(Michael Wetzstein)

Translation: Her risk-aversion coefficient better be very low, for this is a high-risk marriage.

A measure of the degree of risk aversion is the *Arrow–Pratt risk-aversion coefficient* υ, which is defined in terms of the expected utility function and is based on the curvature of the latter:

$$\upsilon = -\frac{U''}{U'},$$

Recall that for a risk-neutral household, the expected utility function is linear, so $U'' = 0$, which results in $\upsilon = 0$. A risk-averse household will have a concave utility function, indicated by $U'' < 0$. The more risk-averse a household, the more concave is the function, and thus the larger will be $-U''$ and υ. Thus, the larger υ is, the more risk-averse is the household. For an extremely risk-averse household, $\upsilon = \infty$. Note that the partial derivative $U' > 0$. Such households will always fully insure against any risk, regardless of the price. Examples are an individual with a major depressive disorder who will not get out of bed or individuals with a particular phobia such as flying or driving. Similarly, a risk-seeking household will have a convex expected utility function with $U'' > 0$. The risk-aversion coefficient is then negative, and the more negative it is, the more risk-seeking the household is. For an extremely risk-seeking household, $\upsilon = -\infty$. Such households would not insure against any risk. An example is a suicide bomber.

What is your number? The higher your number, the more risk-averse you are. My number is five.

Example 18.8 Measuring risk-aversion coefficients for various expected utility functions

If $U = \ln W$, then $U' = 1/W$, $U'' = -1/W^2$, and $\upsilon = 1/W$, indicating that risk aversion decreases with increased wealth.

If $U = W^2$, then $U' = 2W$, $U'' = 2$, and $\upsilon = -1/W$, indicating that risk seeking decreases with increased in wealth.

If $U = W$, then $U' = 1$, $U'' = 0$, and $\upsilon = 0$, indicating risk-neutral preferences all along the linear utility curve.

If $U = W^{1/2}$, then $U' = \frac{1}{2}W^{-1/2}$, $U'' = -\frac{1}{4} W^{-3/2}$, and $\upsilon = \frac{1}{2}W^{-1}$, indicating that risk aversion decreases with increased wealth.

If $U = -1/W$, $U' = 1/W^2$, $U'' = -2/W^3$, and $\upsilon = 2/W$, indicating that risk aversion decreases with increased wealth.

If $U = e^{2W}$, then $U' = 2e^{2W}$, $U'' = 4e^{2W}$, and $\upsilon = -2$, indicating constant risk seeking with increasing wealth.

If $U = -e^{-2W}$, then $U' = 2e^{-2W}$, $U'' = -4e^{-2W}$, and $\upsilon = 2$, indicating constant risk aversion with increasing wealth.

Example 18.9 Effect of risk aversion on portfolio selection

As in Example 18.7, consider two assets: one with a certain return of 5 percent and a risky asset with a 30 percent probability of a 2 percent return and a 70 percent probability of a 10 percent return. With initial wealth still at \$100,000, the risk-aversion coefficient for a household, given a utility function

$$U = -e^{-\upsilon W},$$

is υ.

The expected utility function is then

$$U = 30\%\left(-\exp\left\{-\upsilon\left[\alpha_R W r_1 + (1-\alpha_R)\, W r_C\right]\right\}\right)$$
$$+ 70\%\left(-\exp\left\{-\upsilon\left[\alpha_R W r_2 + (1-\alpha_R)\, W r_C\right]\right\}\right).$$

Maximizing this expected utility function with respect to α_R, the FOC is

$$30\% \upsilon (r_1 - r_C) \exp\{-\upsilon [\alpha_R W r_1 + (1 - \alpha_R) W r_C]\}$$
$$+ 70\% \upsilon (r_2 - r_C) \exp\{-\upsilon [\alpha_R W r_2 + (1 - \alpha_R) W r_C]\} = 0.$$

Rearranging terms gives

$$\frac{-30\%(r_1 - r_C)}{70\%(r_2 - r_C)} = \frac{\exp(-\upsilon \alpha_R W r_2)}{\exp(-\upsilon \alpha_R W r_1)}.$$

Substituting in values for the rates of return and taking the logarithm of both sides yields

$$0.257 = \exp(-\upsilon \alpha_R W 8\%),$$
$$\upsilon \alpha_R W 8\% = 1.358,$$
$$\alpha_R = 1.358/(\upsilon W 8\%).$$

Assuming two risk-aversion coefficients $\upsilon = 0.001$ and $\upsilon = 0.0005$, $\alpha_R = 17$ percent and 34 percent, respectively. A decrease in the risk-aversion coefficient results in a portfolio with greater risk.

Note that the second derivative U'' is divided by U', so the risk-aversion coefficient will not vary by a linear transformation of the utility function (see the Appendix to this chapter). Given the linear transformation $V = aU + b$,

$$V' = aU',$$
$$V'' = aU'',$$
$$\upsilon = -U''/U' = -V''/V'.$$

Employing the risk-aversion coefficient as a measure of risk aversion provides a comparison across household wealth levels. Generally, it is assumed that wealthier households are willing to take more risk than less-wealthy households. Thus, as a household's wealth increases, the risk-aversion coefficient declines, $\partial \upsilon / \partial W < 0$. An example of a utility function representing decreasing risk aversion is

$$U = \ln W,$$

where the risk-aversion coefficient is $\upsilon = 1/W$. As wealth increases, the aversion to risk declines, $\partial \upsilon / \partial W = -1/W^2 < 0$. However, not all utility functions represent decreasing risk aversion. Examples of decreasing, increasing, and constant risk aversion as wealth increases are provided in Example 18.8.

Example 18.10 Demonstrating how the risk-aversion coefficient is unaffected by a linear transformation of the utility function

Consider the following linear transformation of the utility function $U = \ln W$:

$$V(U) = 2U + 5.$$

From Example 8.8, the risk-aversion coefficient for $U = \ln W$ is $\upsilon = 1/W$. The risk-aversion coefficient for $V(U)$ is the same:

$$V'(U) = 2/W,$$
$$V''(U) = -2/W^2,$$
$$\upsilon = 1/W.$$

The risk-aversion coefficient can also be employed for a comparison of risk preferences across households. For example, given two households R and F, household R would be more risk-averse than household F if $\upsilon_R > \upsilon_F$ for all levels of household wealth. This allows a partial ordering of households' preferences from those households who least prefer a risky outcome to those households who are less averse to the risky outcome. However, it is not a complete ordering. If, for example, $\upsilon_R > \upsilon_F$ for some but not all levels of wealth, then it is not possible to state that household R is more risk-averse than household F.

Application: Precautionary principle

The world is increasingly faced with serious problems, including release of genetically modified crops, global warming, and loss of biodiversity. As a result, some politicians and consumer groups are taking an extreme risk-averse position to any activity and insisting on using the *precautionary principle*. This principle states when an activity raises the threat of harm to human health or the environment, precautionary measures should be taken even if some cause-and-effect relationships are not fully established scientifically. For example, the government should ban the use of genetically modified crops even if scientific evidence does not indicate any danger to human health or the environment. This extreme risk-averse position puts constraints on markets and stifles innovation. For example, applying the precautionary principle to the discovery of controlled fires would have prevented the use of this method.

The precautionary principle has been adopted into law in the European Union. Within the United States, less risk-averse regulations are in force. For example, the Food Quality Protection Act of 1996 overseeing pesticide residues in food sets the standard of reasonable certainty that no harm will result from aggregate exposure to pesticide residue. This act is based on science first, then policy. Before any activity can be withheld from the market, human health and environmental impact assessments must indicate harm will result. In contrast, the more risk-averse precautionary principle places policy first, then science. Do not allow the activity until it has been shown that no harm will result. The magnitude of current world problems is causing agents to become more risk-averse, so they are tending to shift their support more toward the precautionary principle. For example, although the US Chamber of Commerce opposes the adoption of the precautionary principle, the city of San Francisco, California, in 2003 was the first to adopt it within the United States.

Should it be policy first, then science? Or science first, then policy? If you are extremely risk-averse and thus support the precautionary principle, then you say policy first, then science.

State-dependent utility

A household may derive utility not only from the monetary returns, but also from the states of nature that underlie them, called **state-dependent utility**. Given this expected utility function for a household, we can determine the utility-maximizing state of nature subject to a constraint on wealth. Assume that a household has a choice of two states of nature. For example, state 1 could be running its own business and state 2 could be having a position in a large international firm. Associated with each state is a set (bundle) of contingent commodities, where each set is available only if the particular state occurs. By representing these commodity bundles in terms of monetary values (W_1 and W_2), we can determine the level of wealth required for obtaining the alternative bundles. Like all commodities, contingent commodities have an associated price. This price is the cost of a particular uncertain state of nature occurring with certainty, so that the associated contingent commodities may be received. An example is a political lobbyist's expenditures on legislators to assure the passage of some legislation.

State-dependent utility. A household derives utility not only from the monetary returns, but also from the states of nature that underlie them.

Let p_1 and p_2 be the price of receiving contingent commodities associated with states 1 and 2, respectively. In purchasing one of these alternative contingent commodities, the household is constrained by a given level of initial wealth W. Thus, the household's contingent budget constraint is

$$p_1 W_1 + p_2 W_2 = W.$$

Recall that only bundle W_1 or bundle W_2 can occur and be consumed. The price ratio p_1/p_2 indicates the market tradeoff between states 1 and 2. It measures the rate at which contingent commodities in state 2 can be substituted for contingent commodities in state 1, holding the level of initial wealth constant. For example, if $p_1/p_2 = 1/3$, then a decrease of \$1 in wealth in state 2 would yield an increase of \$3 of wealth in state 1, holding the initial level of wealth constant.

Actuarially fair prices: fully insure

Assume that prices p_1 and p_2 are actuarially fair and that the market for contingent commodities within alternative states is active, with many buyers and sellers (called *well-developed markets*).[2] If state 1 occurs with probability ρ and state 2 with probability $1-\rho$, then the market will reveal these probabilities: $p_1=\rho$ and $p_2=1-\rho$.

Assuming the Independence Axiom and that the household expects state 1 to occur with probability ρ, the expected utility associated with the two contingent commodity bundles is

$$U(W_1, W_2) = \rho U(W_1) + (1-\rho)U(W_2).$$

The household will attempt to maximize this expected utility, given its budget constraint. The Lagrangian for this problem is then

$$\mathcal{L}(W_1, W_2, \lambda) = \rho U(W_1) + (1-\rho)U(W_2) + \lambda(W - p_1W_1 - p_2W_2).$$

The FOCs are

$$\frac{\partial \mathcal{L}}{\partial W_1} = \rho U'\left(W_1^*\right) - \lambda^* p_1 = 0,$$

$$\frac{\partial \mathcal{L}}{\partial W_2} = (1-\rho)U'\left(W_2^*\right) - \lambda^* p_2 = 0,$$

$$\frac{\partial \mathcal{L}}{\partial \lambda} = W - p_1W_1^* - p_2W_2^* = 0.$$

From these FOCs, we obtain

$$\text{MRS}(W_2 \text{for } W_1) = \frac{\rho U'(W_1^*)}{(1-\rho)U'(W_2^*)} = \frac{p_1}{p_2}.$$

Assuming actuarially fair markets for contingent commodities,

$$\text{MRS}(W_2 \text{for } W_1) = \frac{\rho U'(W_1^*)}{(1-\rho)U'(W_2^*)} = \frac{\rho}{1-\rho} = \frac{p_1}{p_2},$$

$$\frac{U'(W_1^*)}{U'(W_2^*)} = 1,$$

which results in $U'(W_1^*) = U'(W_2^*)$, so $W_1^* = W_2^*$. Thus, a risk-averse household facing actuarially fair markets will be willing to pay for facing a state with certainty where the final level of wealth is the same regardless of which state occurs. An example is the market for insurance, where the price for achieving a given state is the insurance premium and the contingent commodity is the contingent insurance claim. With actuarially fair insurance markets, risk-averse households will fully insure against possible losses. They will purchase insurance up to the point where the level of wealth is the same regardless of whether the state of nature involves a loss.

This efficient level of wealth is illustrated in Figure 18.5. The axes measure wealth for the two alternative states, and the certainty line is a 45° line from the origin. This line measures the same level of wealth regardless of which state of nature occurs. Indifference curves measure

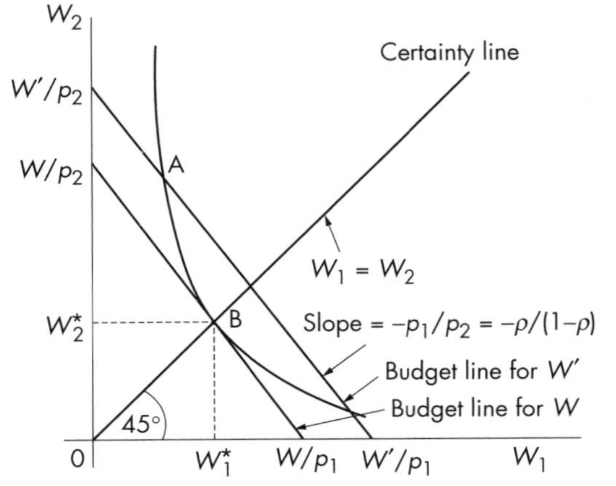

Figure 18.5 **Risk aversion in state-dependent utility.** For a household to be willing to accept some uncertainty, say point A, it would have to be given additional wealth, represented by the upward shift in the budget line from W to W'.

the equivalent level of expected utility to the certainty level associated with the certainty line. Points not on the certainty line represent utility levels associated with some uncertainty in which state of nature will occur. A household's budget constraint is represented by the budget line W. Every point on the budget line represents the actuarially fair probability of the two states of nature occurring. A risk-averse household is unwilling to play an actuarially fair game, so movements off the certainty line on the budget line will result in lower levels of utility. For a risk-averse household to be willing to accept some risk, they must be compensated in the form of additional wealth. As an example, for a household to be willing to accept some uncertainty, say point A, where $W_1 < W_2$, it would have to be given additional wealth represented by the upward shift in the budget line from W to W'. This additional wealth, $W' - W$, is called a *risk premium*, the extra return to compensate for the risk. Thus, a risk-averse household has indifference curves that are convex to the origin. Point A is unobtainable with initial wealth W. However, at point A,

$$\text{MRS}(W_2 \text{ for } W_1) = \frac{\rho U'(W_1^*)}{(1-\rho)U'(W_2^*)} > \frac{p_1}{p_2},$$

the household can maintain the same level of utility, but requiring less initial wealth, by moving down along the indifference curve. This decrease in required initial wealth continues until point B, where the wealth levels of the states are equal, is reached on the certainty line.

Example 18.11 Risk-averse preferences for contingent commodities

Consider two states of nature, where state 1 is some accident, such as a fire, and state 2 is no accident. Denote $\rho = 1/4$ as the probability of state 1 occurring, so the probability of state 2 is $1 - \rho = 3/4$. Assume that a household's initial wealth is \$100,000 and that markets are actuarially fair, so prices reflect the probabilities of the states occurring. Given a risk-averse household with a logarithmic expected utility function, the utility-maximizing problem is

$$\max U(W_1, W_2) = \max\left(\tfrac{1}{4}\ln W_1 + \tfrac{3}{4}\ln W_2\right) \quad \text{s.t. } \tfrac{1}{4}W_1 + \tfrac{3}{4}W_2 = 100{,}000.$$

The Lagrangian is then

$$\mathcal{L}(W_1, W_2, \lambda) = \tfrac{1}{4}\ln W_1 + \tfrac{3}{4}\ln W_2 + \lambda\left(100{,}000 - \tfrac{1}{4}W_1 - \tfrac{3}{4}W_2\right).$$

The FOCs are

$$\partial\mathcal{L}/\partial W_1 = \tfrac{1}{4}(1/W_1^*) - \tfrac{1}{4}\lambda^* = 0,$$
$$\partial\mathcal{L}/\partial W_2 = \tfrac{3}{4}(1/W_2^*) - \tfrac{3}{4}\lambda^* = 0,$$
$$\partial\mathcal{L}/\partial\lambda = 100{,}000 - \tfrac{1}{4}W_1^* - \tfrac{3}{4}W_2^* = 0.$$

Solving these FOCs results in $W_1^* = W_2^* = 100{,}000$.

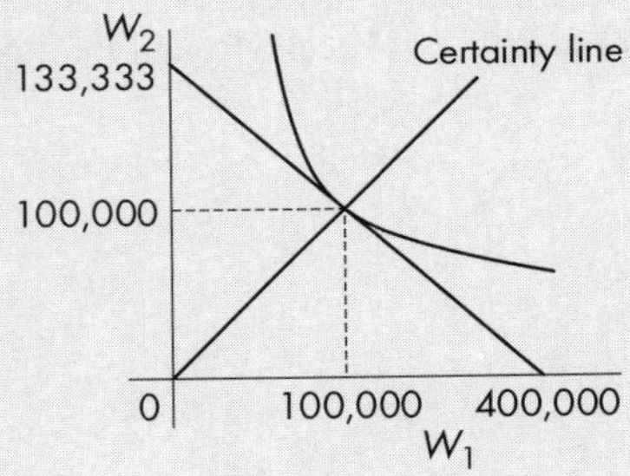

Example 18.12 Risk-averse preferences and insurance

Continuing with Example 18.11, suppose that a household is facing a risky choice with a 75 percent probability of state 2 with a contingent commodity of \$120,000 and a 25 percent probability of receiving \$40,000 with state 1. A risk-averse household with a logarithmic expected utility function will receive a level of utility equaling

$$U = \tfrac{1}{4}\ln(40{,}000) + \tfrac{3}{4}\ln(120{,}000) = 2.65 + 8.77 = 11.42.$$

If the household purchased an actuarially fair insurance policy that transfers \$20,000 when state 2 occurs to \$60,000 when state 1 occurs, its utility will increase to

$$U = \tfrac{1}{4}\ln(100{,}000) + \tfrac{3}{4}\ln(100{,}000) = \ln(100{,}000) = 11.51.$$

The cost of the insurance is \$20,000 if state 2 occurs, but it returns \$60, 000 (80,000 – 20,000 = 60,000) when state 1 occurs. The premium is 25 percent of the \$80,000 policy claim.

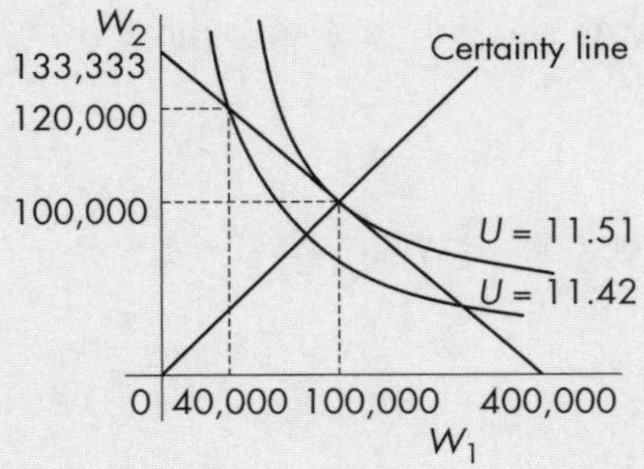

Actuarially unfair prices: accept some risk

If the market is *actuarially unfair*, then a risk-averse household may choose to accept some risk. For example, consider an unfair price ratio of $p_1/p_2 < \rho/(1-\rho)$. Recall that, from the FOCs for expected utility maximization,

$$\text{MRS}(W_2 \text{ for } W_1) = \frac{\rho U'(W_1^*)}{(1-\rho)U'(W_2^*)} = \frac{p_1}{p_2}.$$

Assuming the actuarially unfair condition $p_1/p_2 < \rho/(1-\rho)$,

$$\text{MRS}(W_2 \text{ for } W_1) = \frac{\rho U'(W_1^*)}{(1-\rho)U'(W_2^*)} = \frac{\rho}{1-\rho} < \frac{p_1}{p_2},$$

$$\frac{U'(W_1^*)}{U'(W_2^*)} < 1.$$

This results in $U'(W_1^*) < U'(W_2^*)$, so, assuming diminishing marginal utility of income, $W_1^* > W_2^*$. Thus, a risk-averse household facing actuarially unfair markets will be willing to accept some risk, since the relative price of W_1 is low compared with the actuarially fair price ratio. This result is illustrated in Figure 18.6. The low price $p_1'/p_2' < \rho/(1-\rho)$ results in the budget line tilting outward, which establishes a tangency with the indifference curve to the right of the certainty line. This results in the risky outcome of $W_1^* > W_2^*$.

Example 18.13 Actuarially unfair markets

Continuing again with Example 18.11, consider the actuarially unfair prices $p_1' = 1/5 =$ and $p_2' = 4/5$, so $p_1'/p_2' = 1/4 < p_1/p_2 = \rho/(1-\rho) = 1/3$. Assuming again a risk-averse

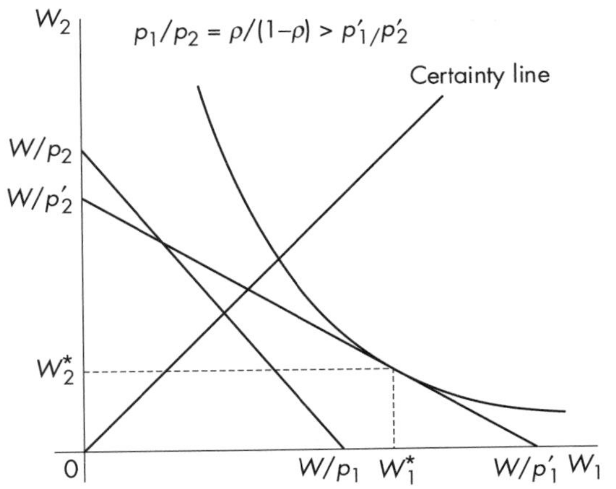

Figure 18.6 **Actuarially unfair markets.** A risk-averse household facing actuarially unfair markets is willing to accept some risk.

household with a logarithmic expected utility function, the utility-maximizing problem is now

$$\max U(W_1, W_2) = \max\left(\tfrac{1}{4}\ln W_1 + \tfrac{3}{4}\ln W_2\right) \quad \text{s.t. } \tfrac{1}{5}W_1 + \tfrac{4}{5}W_2 = 100{,}000.$$

The Lagrangian is then

$$\mathcal{L}(W_1, W_2, \lambda) = \tfrac{1}{4}\ln W_1 + \tfrac{3}{4}\ln W_2 + \lambda\left(100{,}000 - \tfrac{1}{5}W_1 - \tfrac{4}{5}W_2\right).$$

The FOCs are

$$\partial\mathcal{L}/\partial W_1 = \tfrac{1}{4}(1/W_1^*) - \tfrac{1}{5}\lambda^* = 0,$$
$$\partial\mathcal{L}/\partial W_2 = \tfrac{3}{4}(1/W_2^*) - \tfrac{4}{5}\lambda^* = 0,$$
$$\partial\mathcal{L}/\partial\lambda = 100,000 - \tfrac{1}{5}W_1^* - \tfrac{4}{5}W_2^* = 0.$$

Solving these FOCs yields

$$\text{MRS}(W_2 \text{for } W_1) = W_2^*/3W_1^* = \tfrac{1}{4}.$$

Solving for W_2^*,

$$W_2^* = \tfrac{3}{4}W_1^*,$$

and substituting into the budget constraint yields

$$100,000 - \tfrac{1}{5}W_1^* - \tfrac{4}{5}(\tfrac{3}{4}W_1^*) = 0,$$

$$\tfrac{4}{5}W_1^* = 100,000.$$

Thus, the optimum contingent commodities $W_1^* = \$125,000$ and $W_2^* = \$93,750$.

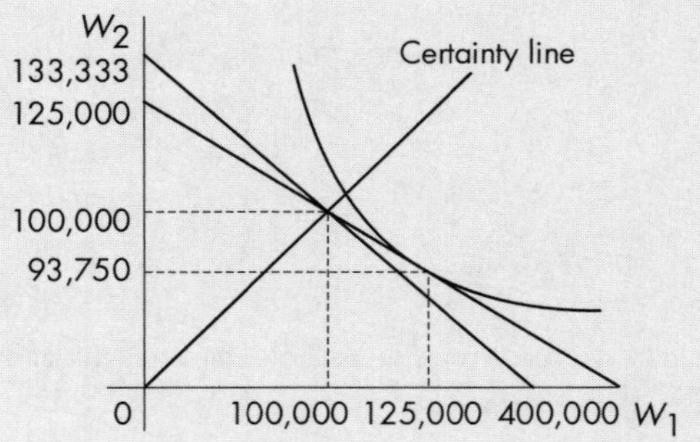

Risk seeking

As illustrated in Figure 18.7, a risky outcome will also result if a household is risk-seeking. The risk-seeking household's indifference curves are concave from the origin, which implies that the expected value for a certain outcome must be higher than any risky outcome before the household will be indifferent between the outcomes. This results in a corner solution, point A, where the household prefers the outcome with greater risk.

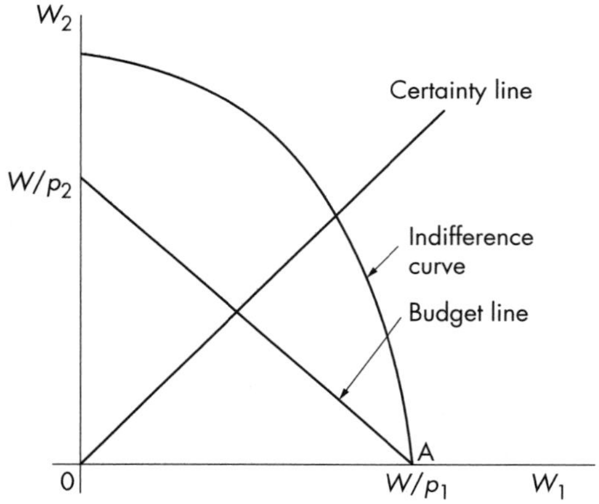

Figure 18.7 **Risk-seeking preferences for contingent commodities.** The household's indifference curves are concave from the origin. This implies that the expected value for a certain outcome must be higher than any risky outcome before the household will be indifferent between the outcomes.

Example 18.14 Risk-seeking preferences for contingent commodities

Continuing with Example 18.11, consider two states of nature, where state 1 is some accident, such as a fire, and state 2 is the absence of this accident. Denote $\rho = 1/4$ as the probability of state 1 occurring, so the probability of state 2 is $1 - \rho = 3/4$. Assume that a household's initial wealth is $100,000 and markets are actuarially fair, so prices reflect the probabilities of the states occurring. Now, given a risk-seeking household with the following expected utility function, the utility-maximizing problem is

$$\max U(W_1, W_2) = \max\left(\tfrac{1}{4}W_1^2 + \tfrac{3}{4}W_2^2\right) \quad \text{s.t. } \tfrac{1}{4}W_1 + \tfrac{3}{4}W_2 = 100,000.$$

The risk-seeking household will minimize utility with the certainty outcome of $W_1 = W_2 =$ $100,000 and maximize utility with the risky outcome of a 25 percent chance of receiving $400,000 and a 75 percent chance of receiving nothing.

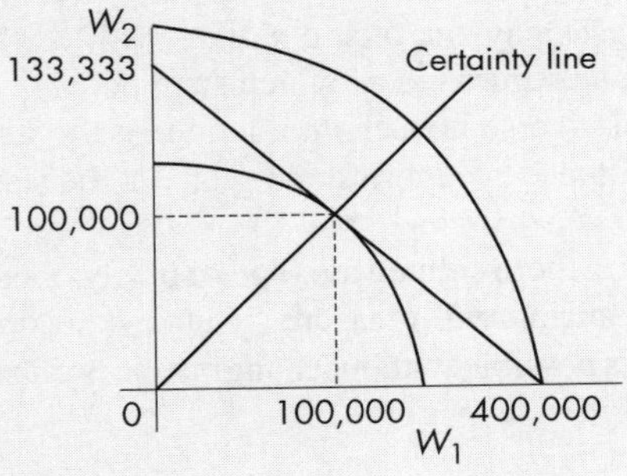

Summary

1. Probability is a measure of the likelihood that an outcome will occur, and can be classified as subjective and objective. Subjective probability is where a household has a perception that an event may occur; objective probability is the frequency with which an outcome will occur.
2. In making future consumption plans, it is assumed that households must choose among alternatives with outcomes of known probabilities. These outcomes result in contingent commodities whose consumption levels depend on which state of nature occurs.
3. The ranges of risk preferences for households are classified as risk-averse, risk-seeking, and risk-neutral. Risk-averse preferences are associated with concave utility functions, which imply diminishing marginal utility of wealth. Risk-seeking preferences are associated with convex utility functions, and linear utility functions result from risk-neutral preferences.

4. The certainty equivalent is the amount of return that a household would receive from a certain outcome so that it is indifferent between a risky outcome and this certain outcome. An implication of certainty equivalence is that risk-averse households are willing to trade some expected return for certainty.
5. If insurance is actuarially fair, a risk-averse household attempting to maximize expected utility will fully insure against all losses. In contrast, with actuarially unfair insurance, a household will not fully insure and thus will be willing to accept some risk.
6. For actuarially favorable outcomes, a risk-averse household will accept some risk. The degree of risk a household is willing to accept is generally greater the less risk-averse a household is.
7. A measure of the degree of risk aversion is the Arrow–Pratt risk-aversion coefficient, which is based on the curvature of the expected utility function. The larger the risk-aversion coefficient, the more risk-averse is a household.
8. A household's expected utility function is used to determine the utility-maximizing state of nature for a given level of wealth. A risk-averse household facing actuarially fair markets will be willing to pay for facing a state with certainty where the final level of wealth is the same regardless of which state occurs.
9. If the market is actuarially unfair, a risk-averse household may choose to accept some risk. A risk-seeking household will also accept risk and seek out the state of nature with the greatest risk.
10. *(Appendix)* An expected utility function is the weighted average of utility obtained from alternative states of nature. It is an interval measure of utility, so only a linear, not a monotonic, transformation is possible without changing the preference ordering.

Key concepts

Key equations

$$U(\vec{x}_1, \vec{x}_2, \rho_1, \rho_2) = \rho_1 U(\vec{x}_1) + \rho_2 U(\vec{x}_2)$$

An expected utility function is the weighted sum of the utility from consumption in the states of nature.

$$U(\rho_1 W_1 + \rho_2 W_2) > \rho_1 U(W_1) + \rho_2 U(W_2)$$

Risk aversion is where the level of utility associated with the expected wealth is greater than the expected utility of wealth.

$$U(\rho_1 W_1 + \rho_2 W_2) < \rho_1 U(W_1) + \rho_2 U(W_2)$$

Risk seeking is where the level of utility associated with the expected wealth is less than the expected utility of wealth.

$$U(\rho_1 W_1 + \rho_2 W_2) = \rho_1 U(W_1) + \rho_2 U(W_2)$$

Risk neutrality is where the level of utility associated with the expected wealth is equal to the expected utility of wealth.

$$U(C) = \rho_1 U(W_1) + \rho_2 U(W_2)$$

Certainty equivalent is the amount of return that a household would receive from a certain outcome so that it is indifferent between a risky outcome and this certain outcome.

$$pA < W - C$$

For a household to be willing to purchase insurance, the insurance premium must be less than the difference in initial risky wealth and the certainty equivalent.

$$\upsilon = -U''/U'$$

The risk-aversion coefficient is based on the curvature of the expected utility function.

Questions

1. If the marginal utility of a household's income decreases as its income increases, would you expect the household to be willing to make a bet where the chance of winning \$100 is exactly the same as the chance of losing \$100? Why or why not?

2. Managers often receive liberal severance pay provisions in their contracts (called "golden parachutes"). Why would owners of a firm offer such provisions?
3. Will a risk-neutral household play a lottery where the probability of losing \$1 is 0.99999 and the probability of winning \$100,000 is 0.00001? How about a risk-averse household? A risk-seeking household?
4. Why do households purchase cruise insurance when the premium paid exceeds the expected value of missing the cruise?
5. A small rural hospital's survival depends on the health of its only ailing doctor and whether it receives a state grant. What are the mutually exclusive states of nature that this hospital should be concerned about?
6. In a state lottery, each ticket costs \$1, with a probability of 0.9 of receiving the \$1 back and 0.1 of winning \$1.20. If a risk-averse household can purchase insurance against a loss from the lottery, how much would it be willing to pay?
7. Why does the assumption of diminishing marginal utility of wealth imply risk aversion?
8. Why does the demand for insurance imply risk aversion?
9. What risk preferences are airline ticket counters, banks, and post offices assuming by having a single line facing multiple servers?

Exercises

When you make a mistake, don't look back at it long. Take the reason of the thing into your mind and then look forward. Mistakes are lessons of wisdom.

(Hugh White)

1. A peach grower in Georgia is considering installing irrigation in his orchard. With the irrigation system, his profit π will be \$500 per acre, with an annual cost for irrigation of \$100. Without irrigation, his profit is only \$300 in a bad-weather season, but in a normal-weather year it will be equivalent to the \$500 per acre with irrigation. Assume that he is risk-neutral with the objective of maximizing expected profits.

   a. On average, if the grower believes there is a 70 percent probability of a normal-weather year, should he install an irrigation system?
   b. What would the probability of a normal-weather year be if he was indifferent between installing irrigation or not?
   c. Assuming the probabilities in (a) and that he is risk-averse, how much would he have to pay in lost profit to maintain a constant level of profit?

2. Gale, a high roller, places an even bet of \$50,000 on the Atlanta Braves winning the World Series. If she has a logarithmic utility function in terms of wealth and her current wealth is \$200,000, what is her minimum belief on the probability of the Braves winning?

3. Suppose there is a 50 percent probability of a major earthquake in California. A homeowner with a logarithmic utility function in terms of wealth and a current wealth of \$500,000 will suffer a \$200,000 loss from the quake.

   a. Determine the cost of actuarially fair insurance.
   b. Will the homeowner purchase the fair insurance?
   c. What is the maximum administration cost that the homeowner would be willing to pay for purchasing the insurance?

4. Marj is planning on flying with Fly-A-Wreck Airlines to collect on a \$2 million sweepstake. She values her life at \$1 million with a logarithmic utility function and values the outcome of dying in a plane crash at zero.

   a. If there is a 20 percent probability of losing her life, what is the expected value of the flight?
   b. Assume Marj could purchase flight insurance against the possible loss of life. At an actuarially fair premium, will she purchase the insurance?
   c. If the fair insurance policy only covers two-thirds of the loss, will she purchase the policy?

5. a. For the following expected utility functions, determine if the household is risk-averse, risk-neutral, or risk-seeking:

      i. $U = 5\ln W$;
      ii. $U = W^3$;
      iii. $U = W^{1/4}$;
      iv. $U = e^{W/10,000}$;
      v. $U = -e^{-W/10,000}$;
      vi. $U = 50,000 + W$.

   b. Assume that the households in (a) have current wealth of \$100,000. The households are offered a 0.6 probability of increasing their wealth to \$150,000. However, there is a 0.4 probability of their wealth declining to \$50,000. Which households will take the offer?
   c. If they must take the offer, which households would be willing to purchase insurance and how much will each be willing to pay?

6. For the expected utility function $U = W^{1/2}$, calculate the certainty equivalent and expected value for the equally likely gamble of receiving a payoff of 4 or 16 and instead receiving 16 and 36. Interpret these results.
7. Anthony is an extremely risk-averse individual with a utility function for two states of nature represented by $U = \min(W_1, W_2)$, where W_1 and W_2 are contingent commodities. Graph the indifference curves for Anthony and show that, regardless of the associated prices (actuarially fair or unfair), he will always fully insure. How risk-averse is Anthony?
8. Erick, an astronomer, is considering two mutually exclusive career paths: either becoming an Earth-bound astronomer or becoming an astronaut and observing the heavens from space. The Earth-bound career pays I_E = \$100,000 annually; the astronaut career, which has a 10 percent chance of Erick becoming stranded in

space, pays I_S annually. Erick's preferences can be represented by the following utility function:

$$U = 1 - \frac{100{,}000}{I_j} - \alpha, \quad j = E, S,$$

where $\alpha = 0$ if he is not stranded and $\alpha = 1$ if he is stranded.

a. What is the level of utility from being an Earth-bound observer?
b. What is the expected utility in terms of I_S from being an astronaut?
c. Determine the risk premium that Erick requires for becoming an astronaut.

9. Paul is interested in hiring a computer programmer for his firm. He can either search for a potential employee himself or hire a headhunter firm to find the employee for him. If he searches himself, there is a 30 percent chance of not hiring the right person for the job. In contrast, the headhunter will always find the right match. If the right person is not found for the job, the value of the programming is only \$5000, compared with \$40,000 for the right person. Paul's risk aversion is represented by a logarithmic utility function. What is the maximum amount Paul would be willing to pay the headhunter?
10. Sixteen-year-old Mark is faced with two states of nature. State 1 is no auto accident, with a $1/3$ probability of occurring, and state 2 is an accident. The actuarially unfair prices that Mark is facing are $p_1 = 1/4$ and $p_2 = 3/4$ for states 1 and 2, respectively. Assume that Mark's risk-averse preferences are represented by $U = W^{1/2}$ and that his initial wealth is \$84,000. Determine the optimum contingent commodities for Mark.

Internet case studies

1. How many definitions of probability can you come up with?
2. List some available tools and techniques for managing risk?
3. Outline the general debate on Social Security in terms of being actuarially fair.
4. Discuss a number of "golden parachutes" used for reducing the risks of firm managers.

APPENDIX TO CHAPTER 18

Interval measurement of utility

In contrast with certainty utility functions, which are ordinal measures of utility, expected utility measures utility on an interval scale. Thus, unlike certainty utility functions, changes in the marginal utilities of expected utility do represent changes in preferences. Specifically,

$$\mathrm{MU}_1 = \frac{\partial}{\partial \vec{x}_1} U(\vec{x}_1, \vec{x}_2, \rho_1, \rho_2) = \rho_1 \frac{\partial U}{\partial \vec{x}_1}$$

represents the change in utility from a change in the consumption bundle $\vec{x}_1$. Thus, any monotonic transformation of an expected utility function may not yield the same measure of household preferences. The reason for this result is that the Independence Axiom may be violated by a monotonic transformation.

As an example, consider the following expected utility function:

$$U(\vec{x}_1, \vec{x}_2, \rho_1, \rho_2) = \rho_1 \ln \vec{x}_1 + \rho_2 \ln \vec{x}_2.$$

The marginal utilities associated with this function are

$$\mathrm{MU}_1 = \frac{\rho_1}{\vec{x}_1}, \mathrm{MU}_2 = \frac{\rho_2}{\vec{x}_2}.$$

Taking a monotonic transformation in the form of the antilog on both sides of the utility function yields

$$V(\vec{x}_1, \vec{x}_2, \rho_1, \rho_2) = \vec{x}_1^{\rho_1} \vec{x}_2^{\rho_2}.$$

The resulting marginal utilities are

$$\mathrm{MU}_1 = \rho_1 \vec{x}_1^{\rho_1 - 1} \vec{x}_2^{\rho_2}, \mathrm{MU}_2 = \rho_2 \vec{x}_1^{\rho_1} \vec{x}_2^{\rho_2 - 1}.$$

Now the amount of $\vec{x}_2$ that the household would receive under state 2 does influence the household's preferences for state 1 associated with $\vec{x}_1$. Similarly, the amount of $\vec{x}_1$ that the household would receive under state 1 also influences the household's preferences for state 2 associated with $\vec{x}_2$. This transformation violates the Independence Axiom.

Linear transformations

Transformations that do not violate the Independence Axiom are *increasing linear transformations* (also called *positive affine transformations*). An increasing linear transformation is written in the form

$$V(U) = aU + b, \quad a > 0.$$

As an example, consider again the expected utility function

$$U(\vec{x}_1, \vec{x}_2, \rho_1, \rho_2) = \rho_1 \ln \vec{x}_1 + \rho_2 \ln \vec{x}_2.$$

A linear transformation is then

$$V(U) = a\rho_1 \ln \vec{x}_1 + a\rho_2 \ln \vec{x}_2 + b.$$

The marginal utilities associated with this function are

$$\mathrm{MU}_1 = \frac{a\rho_1}{\vec{x}_1}, \mathrm{MU}_2 = \frac{a\rho_2}{\vec{x}_2},$$

which do not violate the Independent Axiom.

The interval measure of utility implies that differences in utility across states of nature are important, given expected utility functions. For example, denoting outcomes as U_1, U_2, U_3, and U_4, their differences

$$U_1 - U_2 > U_3 - U_4$$

imply that a household prefers the difference between utilities 1 and 2 over the difference between 3 and 4. This is in contrast with a certain preference ordering (discussed in Chapter 2), where households cannot determine the magnitude of a change in satisfaction between two commodity bundles.

Example 18A.1 Positive linear transformation

An example of a positive linear transformation is the temperature scale, where a linear transformation converts degrees Fahrenheit, °F, to degrees Celsius, °C:

$$°C = \tfrac{5}{9}(°F - 32°).$$

Violations of expected utility

Expected utility is a convenient representation of households' preferences when faced with uncertainty. This is why it is used throughout economic theory, yielding positive as well as normative implications. However, expected utility is not universal in offering reasonable explanations of household behavior.

Allais's Paradox

One example of possible household behavior that violates expected utility is called the **Allais Paradox**, developed by M. Allais (1911–2010), 1988 Nobel laureate in economics. As an example, consider three possible monetary outcomes or prizes. First prize is \$1.5 million, second prize is \$0.1 million, and the third outcome is not winning, with a monetary outcome of zero. In this game, a household is faced with two possible states of nature:

$$N_1 = (0, 1, 0), \text{ receiving \$0.1 million with certainty,}$$

and

$$N_2 = (0.1, 0.85, 0.05).$$

Generally, households would take the certainty choice of receiving \$0.1 million over the 10 percent probability of receiving 15 times more, but also facing a 5 percent risk of winning nothing. Thus, $N_1 \succ N_2$. However, this preference choice is not consistent with expected utility. Assuming these prizes represent monetary payoffs in utility, the expected utilities from the two states of nature are

$$U_1 = \$0.1,$$
$$U_2 = (0.1)1.5 + (0.85)0.1 + (0.05)0$$
$$= 0.15 + 0.085 + 0 = \$0.235,$$

which implies $N_2 \succ N_1$. Thus, expected utility implies that the household would choose N_2 over N_1 when it is very plausible that households would choose the certainty state of nature N_1.

Machina's Paradox

Another paradox associated with expected utility is **Machina's Paradox.** As an example, consider a college student with three possible outcomes: attending the college football post-season bowl game, watching the game on TV, or going to the movies. Suppose that the student's highest preference is attending the football game, followed by watching it on TV, and followed by going to the movies. One state of nature is a 99.9 percent probability of attending the bowl game associated with a 0.1 percent probability of watching it on TV. A second state of nature again has a 99.9 percent probability of attending the game with a 0.1 percent probability of going to the movies. Under the Independence Axiom, the student would choose the first state of nature over the second. However, at least some students (households) may find it perfectly rational to choose the second state of nature. The student may be disappointed about not attending the bowl game and feel that watching it on TV would only reinforce the disappointment. Thus, what could have occurred affects the household's utility and choices, which violates the Independence Axiom.

If you cannot go to the football game, would you watch it on television? Most individuals would (I would), but some would not. For the individuals that would not watch it because they are disappointed about not attending the game, their preferences violate the Independence Axiom.

As these paradoxes illustrate, sometimes household preferences violate the Independence Axiom and thus limit the usefulness of expected utility as a model of preferences. However, analogous to the Giffen Paradox in the aggregate investigation of markets, expected utility can be assumed to represent household preferences. Economists are interested in the investigation of resource allocation within an economy, which requires abstraction to form general assumptions on household preferences. It is reserved for the discipline of psychology to further our understanding of an individual person's rational choice facing alternative states of nature. As an example, households are at times affected by the *Law of Small Numbers (hasty generalization)*, where they reach a conclusion based on insufficient evidence. They make a hasty conclusion without considering all of the information. Such hasty generalizations can be a basis for prejudices, where generalizations regarding a large group are based on a small number of individuals in that group. Alternatively, after a traffic accident, individuals will tend to overstate the likelihood that they will have an accident. These subjective probabilities are then based on the state of nature for which they are determined. It is difficult for households to form subjective probabilities, which leads to biases in their determination.

St Petersburg Paradox

By definition, risk-averse households will not play actuarially fair games, and under some conditions may not even play games with positive expected payoffs. An example of households not playing a game with positive expected payoffs is the *St Petersburg Paradox,* first investigated by the mathematician Daniel Bernoulli (1700–1782) in the eighteenth century. As a demonstration of this paradox, consider tossing a coin until a tail appears. If a tail first appears on the jth toss, the household receives $\$2^j$. For example, if a tail occurs on the first toss, the payoff is $2^1 = 2$. If a tail first occurs on the second toss, the payoff is $2^2 = 4$, and so on. A feature of this game is the infinite number of possible outcomes. At least theoretically, a coin can be tossed forever and never result in a tail. However, the probability of not getting a tail until the jth toss declines exponentially. Specifically, the probability of getting a tail for the first time in the jth toss is $(^1\!/_2)^j$. It is the probability of getting $j-1$ heads and a tail. For example, the probability of getting the first tail after the fifth toss is the probability of tossing a coin five times and getting four heads and then 1 tail:

$$\underbrace{\left(\tfrac{1}{2}\right)\left(\tfrac{1}{2}\right)\left(\tfrac{1}{2}\right)\left(\tfrac{1}{2}\right)}_{j-1 \text{ heads}}\left(\tfrac{1}{2}\right) = \left(\tfrac{1}{2}\right)^5 = 3.125\%.$$

The expected value of this St Petersburg Paradox game is then

$$\sum_{j=1}^{\infty} 2^j \left(\tfrac{1}{2}\right)^j = \sum_{j=1}^{\infty} 1^j = \infty.$$

An actuarially fair outcome for this game would require setting the price for playing the game at infinity. However, no risk-averse household would be willing to pay anything close to infinity for the right to pay the game. It is highly unlikely that a risk-averse household would pay all of its wealth or even \$100 for the right to play the game, even though the expected payoff of infinity would be far greater. The unbounded payoff as the number of tosses goes to infinity is the condition that causes this paradox.

Should you always play the lottery? No, if you are risk-averse, you will not play an actuarially fair lottery and may not even play a lottery with positive expected payoffs.

Placing an upper bound on the payoff avoids problems like the St Petersburg Paradox. This assumes some level of payoff (global bliss point) where any additional payoff will not result in further increases in utility. For example, assume that the bliss point is \$300 million, which is possible in some of the big multistate lotteries. Assuming that winning a lottery is heavenly, then any payoff greater than \$300 million would not yield any further increase in utility. In terms of the St Petersburg Paradox, 2^{28} is approximately \$300 million, thus the expected payoff from playing the game is \$28, which is the actuarially fair cost of playing.

Questions

1. Which of the following utility functions are expected utility functions? Which are positive affine transformations of another one?

   a. $U = x_1 x_2^{-\rho}$;

b. $U = \rho \ln x_1 + (1 - \rho) \ln x_2$;
c. $U = a + b[\rho x_1 + (1 - \rho)x_2]$;
d. $U = \rho x_1 + (1 - \rho)x_2^2$;
e. $U = \rho x_1^2 + (1 - \rho)x_2^2$;
f. $U = \rho(-e^{-x_1}) + (1 - \rho)(-e^{-x_2})$;
g. $U = \rho x_1 + (1 - \rho)x_2$;
h. $U = [\rho x_1 + (1 - \rho)x_2]^2$.

Internet case study

1. Discuss the concept of a rational household in terms of the Allais and St Petersburg paradoxes.

19 Intertemporal choice and capital decisions

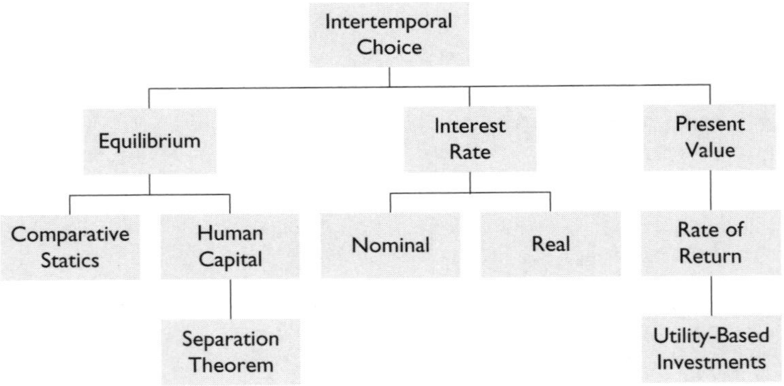

Outline and Conceptual Inquiries

Intertemporal choice
Understanding intertemporal indifference curves
Are you patient or impatient?
Intertemporal budget constraint
Establishing an equilibrium
Are you a lender, a borrower, or a Polonius?

Developing human capital
Maximizing utility with no financial markets: a developing country
Maximizing utility with financial markets (the Separation Theorem)
Why do college students shop at electronic stores and boutiques?

Determination of the Interest Rate *i*
Real interest rate (rate of return) versus nominal interest rate

Discounting the future
Discounting in a two-period model
Is a dollar forthcoming a year from now worth as much as a dollar today?
Application: Consumer discount rates for energy-using durables

Multi-period discounting
Maximizing present value
Application: Public disaster compensation funds
Infinite horizon
Net present value (NPV)
Application: Avoiding real estate bubbles

Summary
Key concepts
Key equations
Questions
Exercises
Internet case study

Appendix to chapter 19

Comparative statics: interest rate change
Adjusted Slutsky equation
Will a borrower always decrease consumption given a rise in interest rates?
Application: Taxation on interest income
Will a tax-rate reduction on interest income increase savings?

Rate of return: telemarketing fraud
Uncertain investment decisions: the value of waiting
Does the ability to wait have value?

Utility-based investments: jewelry investments
Is purchasing a diamond necessarily a rational investment?

Intertemporal choice and behavioral economics
Questions
Exercises
Internet case studies

The dynamics of capitalism is postponement of enjoyment to the constantly postponed future.

(Norman O. Brown)

In Charles Dickens' short fiction *A Christmas Carol*, Ebenezer Scrooge represents evil nineteenth-century capitalism, where the objective was maximizing income by always postponing all the enjoyment in life. This is an extreme representation of intertemporal choice. Generally, agents (even Scrooge at the end) will postpone some but not all enjoyment for increased future enjoyment. An example is how a student expects to have a greater potential for future happiness by investing now in education. In general, every utility-maximizing agent has a plan for the future. Without a future plan, happenstance determines destinations. In an attempt to determine its own optimal destination, an agent will investigate the optimal levels of durable commodities (for consumers) and real-capital inputs (for firms).

The marginal input cost faced by a firm (discussed in previous chapters) is dependent on the nature of an input. Inputs may be broadly classified as nondurable and durable. **Nondurable inputs** are exhausted in the current production period, and thus are unavailable for future production. All inputs employed for only the current production period are considered nondurable. For example, an hour of labor hired is exhausted in the current production period, so this hour cannot also be used in future production. A capital item such as a truck rented only for a current production period is considered a nondurable input. The level of nondurable inputs is measured as a *flow*, which, like a river, may rise or fall over a period of time.

Nondurable inputs (commodities). Commodities that are exhausted in the current production period. *E.g., eating a candy bar.*

In contrast, **durable inputs** are inputs owned by a firm that may not be exhausted in the current production period and thus can continue contributing toward future production. Such inputs are generally called *real capital* or *real assets* for physical capital and **human capital** for owners' own labor and skills devoted to a firm. By using the term *real*, we make the distinction between *financial capital* such as money, stocks, or bonds, and physical capital such as buildings or machinery. Durable inputs are purchased with the intention of using them for a sustained period of time. The returns from the durable input item are then returns not only from current production but also from future production. Thus, to determine the cost of a durable input, we must consider not only the returns in the current period but the returns over the total useful life of the inputs. Durable inputs are measured as a *stock*. Over a period of time, the level of a durable input does not vary, and provides a flow of services through time.

Durable inputs (commodities). Commodities that may not be exhausted in the current production process. *E.g., an automobile.*

Human capital. An individual's abilities and knowledge. *E.g., a physician has a level of abilities and knowledge to treat patients.*

Our aim in this chapter is to investigate the intertemporal choices of expenditures among time periods. We consider the impatient and patient preferences of consumers in making intertemporal choices and the equilibrium allocation of current and future consumption. Within our discussion of a consumer's optimal level of human capital, we present the Separation Theorem, which allows human-capital decisions to be considered separately from consumption decisions. Given the Separation Theorem, we address the implication of this optimal investment in human capital. We then determine the interest rates in terms of the real rate versus the nominal rate of interest. Given the real rate, we use present-value analysis to discount future costs and returns from a capital investment.

In the Appendix to the chapter, we investigate comparative statics in the interest rate and the adjusted Slutsky equation measuring the substitution and income effect of an interest rate change. We also discuss investment decisions given uncertain and irreversible investments resulting in positive option values, along with utility-based investments.

The theoretical development of intertemporal choice and capital decisions results in two major implications for applied economic analysis. First is the Separation Theorem, which states that in well-developed financial markets investment capital decisions can be considered separate from consumption decisions that potentially result in improving welfare. Particularly in developing countries, applied economists will aid in shaping policies and programs that result in financial markets that enable households and firms to separate their investment and consumption decisions. The second major implication is the theoretical development of investment decisions under uncertainty. Applied economists are employing a theory of real capital option value for determining when to undertake an investment. Failure to consider this investment option value often leads to non-optimal investment decisions.

Intertemporal choice

As John Maynard Keynes said, in the long run we are all dead. Some individuals, including drug addicts and doomsayers, consider this long run to be tomorrow, so they are only concerned with present consumption and resource allocation. Any future returns are discounted to zero and have no value. However, most households and firms are concerned with the future, so they consider the future flow of consumption and returns to determine their current consumption and resource allocations. For example, a student will invest currently in human capital with the expectation of receiving a future return on this investment. To determine the optimal level of real capital inputs (capital *stocks*), agents calculate the value of future returns (capital *flow*) associated with the capital input. The element of time is directly involved in this determination. Remember, you cannot escape the responsibility of tomorrow by evading it today.

Generally, future returns are uncertain and a decision to invest in a capital input today has associated costs that cannot be recovered once incurred (called **sunk cost** or historical cost). For example, once a new car has been purchased and driven off a dealer's lot, it is considered a used car and not worth as much as a new one. The decision to purchase this new car results in an irreversible sunk cost, which is the difference between the new purchase price and its value as a used car.

Sunk cost. Cost that cannot be recovered once incurred. *E.g., the price of a new pair of pants minus any garage-sale value.*

Sunk cost is the actual cost incurred for employing an input in a particular production process. Since a nondurable input is completely exhausted in the current production period, its future market value is zero. Thus, the sunk cost for a nondurable input is the total cost for the input. For example, the sunk cost of engaging in advertising is the expenditures for this advertising. In contrast, since a durable input continues to contribute toward future production periods, it may have some future market value. Thus, the sunk cost for a durable input may be less than the total cost for the input. We determine its sunk cost by deducting any remaining market value from its total cost. For example, the sunk cost for purchasing an automobile is not its purchase price, but its decline in market value.

Sunk costs can be avoided or delayed by postponing a decision to purchase a capital input. The decision is generally not whether to purchase the input or not, but whether to purchase it today or at some future time. Such decisions are called **intertemporal choice**, where choices of consumption are made over time.

Intertemporal choice. Consumption choices made over time. *E.g., waiting until Saturday to do grocery shopping for the week.*

We may investigate intertemporal choice by considering two time periods, where an agent's decision is choosing the optimal level of expenditures between these time periods. The agent could be a firm with the choice of determining the level of capital expenditures or a household determining the optimal level of consumption. We can think of the commodity as a composite commodity with an associated price set at 1 for both time periods. Let us say the agent is a consumer who will receive income I_1 in period 1 and I_2 in period 2. This is the consumer's endowment, which can be allocated to current or future consumption. Consumption within these two time periods is dependent on this endowment. The consumption and saving decisions during a given time period are the result of *a life-cycle model*, a planning process that considers simultaneously both time periods, where the consumption and saving decisions for a given time period are dependent on future and past income (endowment) levels. For example, a college student with a current low income level may have a high level of consumption (purchasing quality audio systems) because she expects higher income levels after graduation. In general, the life-cycle model accounts for a household smoothing out consumption over a lifetime, so the household is a borrower during household formation and a lender once established (to save for retirement).

The consumer's maximizing-utility problem over these two time periods is to determine the optimal level of consumption and saving (or borrowing) in each period subject to the given endowment. This utility-maximizing solution may result in the consumer saving in period 1 to yield a higher level of consumption in period 2. Or the consumer may borrow in period 1 and consume more in this current period. The preferences of the consumer for future consumption as opposed to current consumption will determine whether she saves, borrows, or just spends all of her current income in each time period.

Understanding intertemporal indifference curves

We spend the first half of our lives wasting our health to gain wealth, and the second half of our lives spending our wealth to regain our health.

(Voltaire)

Translation: Movement along an intertemporal indifference curve.

Using x_1 and x_2 to represent current consumption (time period 1) and future consumption (time period 2), respectively, we can represent the consumer's preferences for these commodities by the utility function

$$U(x_1, x_2).$$

Assuming that this utility function represents diminishing marginal rate of substitution characterized by strictly convex indifference curves, we illustrate *intertemporal indifference curves* in Figure 19.1. Recall that the marginal rate of substitution MRS(x_2 for x_1) measures how much a consumer is willing to substitute commodity x_2 for x_1. In the case of consumption in two time periods, MRS(x_2 for x_1) measures how much the consumer is willing to substitute future consumption x_2 for current consumption x_1.

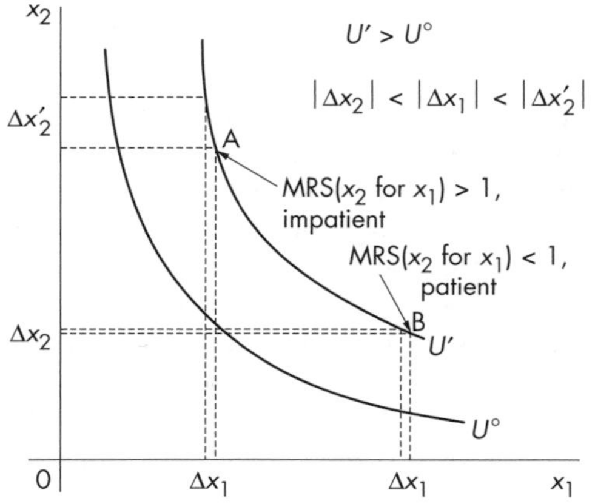

Figure 19.1 **Intertemporal indifference curves representing diminishing marginal rate of time preference.** At point A, for the consumer to be willing to give up some x_1, she would have to be compensated with relatively more of x_2. The consumer is then said to be impatient. If the consumer is patient, he is willing to postpone current consumption for less additional consumption in the future, point B.

This rate of substitution across time periods is called the **marginal rate of time preference**. If MRS(x_2 for x_1) > 1, then, for the consumer to be willing to give up some of x_1, he would have to be compensated with relatively more of x_2. This occurs at point A in Figure 19.1, where $|\Delta x_1| < |\Delta x_2'|$. In this case, the consumer is said to be **impatient**—where he prefers current consumption to postponing consumption into the future. In contrast, a consumer is said to be **patient** if he is willing to postpone some current consumption even for less of it in the future, point B in Figure 19.1. At point B, $|\Delta x_1| > |\Delta x_2|$ and MRS(x_2 for x_1) < 1. In general, most consumers are impatient. Impatient preferences imply discounting future utility, which assumes that a dollar forthcoming a year from now is not worth as much as a dollar today.

Are you patient or impatient? If you are not a squirrel, you are probably impatient. Squirrels are patient; in the winter, they are often unable to find all the nuts they buried in the fall.

Marginal rate of time preference. The rate at which a consumer is willing to substitute future consumption for current consumption. *E.g., the rate at which an employee is willing to invest in a retirement plan.*

Impatient. Consumer preference of preferring current consumption to postponing consumption into the future. *E.g., given the uncertainly of a dress still being on sale tomorrow, you decide to purchase it today.*

Patient. Willing to postpone some current consumption even for less of it in the future. *E.g., parents who are willing to sacrifice a great deal of current consumption so that their children will have a better future.*

Example 19.1 Intertemporal strictly convex preferences

Consider the intertemporal utility function $U = x_1 x_2$. The marginal rate of time preference is

$$\text{MRS}(x_2 \text{ for } x_1) = x_2/x_1.$$

Setting the utility function equal to some constant U^o, so $dU = 0$, gives

$$U^o = x_1 x_2.$$

Solving for x_2 yields

$$x_2 = U^o/x_1.$$

Evaluating the derivatives, we have

$$-\text{MRS} = \left.\frac{dx_2}{dx_1}\right|_{U=U^o} = -\frac{U^o}{x_1^2} < 0,$$

$$-\frac{d\text{MRS}}{dx_1} = \frac{d^2x_2}{dx_1^2}\Big|_{U=U^o} = \frac{2U^o}{x_1^3} > 0.$$

This implies that $d\text{MRS}/dx_1 < 0$. An increase in x_1 results in MRS declining, diminishing MRS (strictly convex preferences).

If current and present consumption are equal ($x_1 = x_2$), then the consumer is neither impatient nor patient but instead has *neutral time preferences.* If $x_1 > x_2$, then the consumer is patient, and if $x_1 < x_2$, then the consumer is impatient. For example, if $x_1 = x_2 = 4$, then $U = 16$ and the consumer is neither impatient nor patient. Instead, if $x_1 = 8$ and $x_2 = 2$, then the consumer still has a utility level of 16, but is patient. If the reverse occurs, with $x_1 = 2$ and $x_2 = 8$, then utility is again 16, but the consumer is now impatient.

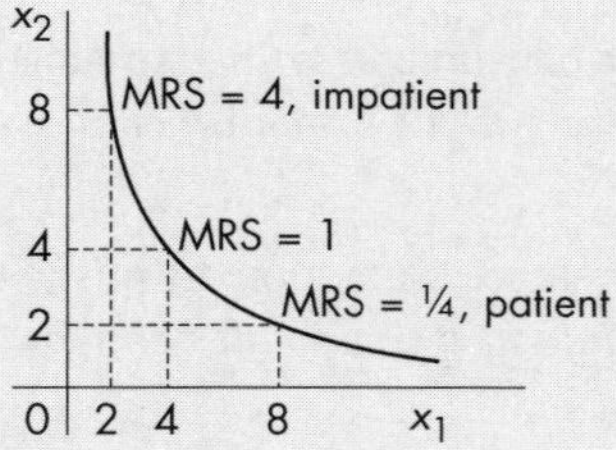

Intertemporal budget constraint

Whether impatient or patient, a consumer will face a budget constraint with fixed endowment e and prices in each of the two periods. This intertemporal budget constraint represents the tradeoff between current and future consumption. A consumer can substitute future for current consumption by borrowing income at an **interest rate *i***, or forego current consumption for future consumption by lending income at the same interest rate. With levels of income I_1 and I_2 for the two periods and the price for the commodity at 1, the intertemporal budget constraint is

$$x_2 = I_2 + (1 + i)(I_1 - x_1).$$

The level of consumption in period 2, x_2, depends on the income received in period 2, I_2, and on the remaining income from period 1. If $I_1 - x_1 > 0$, then the consumer did not spend all of her income in period 1 and has some residual income (savings), the difference $I_1 - x_1$, left over for spending in period 2. If the consumer lends this residual at a rate of interest i, then in period 2, she will not only have the residual $I_1 - x_1$ but also the interest on the loan of $i(I_1 - x_1)$. The residual income plus interest on the loan will augment her income in period 2. Instead, if she spends more than her income in period 1, so $I_1 - x_1 < 0$, she can borrow income at a rate i to increase her current consumption. This results in a reduction in income available in period 2 of $(1 + i)(I_1 - x_1) < 0$. Thus, available income in period 2 is less than I_2. If $I_1 - x_1 = 0$, then $I_2 - x_2 = 0$ and the consumer is neither a borrower nor a lender.

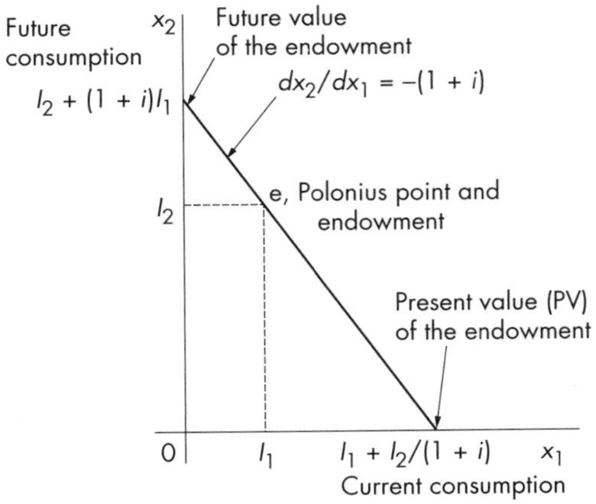

Figure 19.2 **Intertemoral budget constraint.** This budget constraint represents the trade-off between current and future consumption. Points on the constraint to the left of point e are possible if the consumer saves in period 1. Points to the right of point e represent borrowing in period 1.

This is called the *Polonius point* from Shakespeare's play *Hamlet*, where Polonius told his son, "Neither a borrower nor a lender be."

Interest rate (i). The rate at which agents can borrow and lend money. *E.g., the rate of interest you are paying on your credit card balance.*

This intertemporal budget constraint is illustrated in Figure 19.2. Point e is the Polonius point representing the consumer's endowment in terms of current and future consumption. An increase in the endowment will shift the budget constraint outward and increase the possible feasible allocations available to the consumer.

The intercepts are determined by considering zero consumption of x_1 or x_2. If no x_1 is consumed, then the consumer will lend out all of her income in period 1 and have $I_2 + (1+i)I_1$ of income to consume in period 2. This is the future value of the endowment and is represented as the x_2 intercept in Figure 19.2. Alternatively, if she plans to not consume any of the commodity in period 2, then she will borrow income $PV_2 = I_2/(1+i)$ from period 2 for consuming in period 1. The consumer is not able to borrow the full amount of income in period 2, I_2, because she must pay interest on the borrowed income, iPV_2. The amount she can borrow, PV_2, plus interest iPV_2 is then equal to I_2:

$$PV_2(1+i) = I_2.$$

Solving for PV_2 yields

$$PV_2 = I_2/(1+i).$$

PV_2 is called the **present value** of I_2. It is the value of I_2 if it is received in period 1 instead of period 2. Total income in period 1 with zero consumption in period 2 is then

$$I_1 + PV_2 = I_1 + I_2/(1+i).$$

This is the present value of the endowment and is represented as the x_1 intercept in Figure 19.2.

Present value (PV). The current value of an item received in some future time period. *E.g., given a 5 percent annual interest rate, receiving* \$100 *a year from now is worth* $(100/1.05) = \$95.24$ *today.*

The slope of the budget constraint is $dx_2/dx_1|_{de=0} = -(1+i)$, which is the negative of the time rate of substituting future consumption for present consumption. If the consumer gives up 1 unit of x_1, she can increase future consumption x_2 by $1+i$. This is the savings from not consuming the 1 unit plus the interest received from lending the 1 unit of income. Alternatively, if the consumer consumes one more unit of current consumption x_1, she must give up $1+i$ units of future consumption.

Example 19.2 Graphing an intertemporal budget constraint

Consider the following values for the intertemporal budget constraint:

$$x_2 = I_2 + (1+i)(I_1 - x_1),$$

$I_1 = \$10$, $I_2 = \$8$, and $i = 5$ percent. This constraint assumes that the price for the commodity is 1 in both the current and future periods. Based on these values, the future value of the endowment is

$$I_2 + (1+i)I_1 = 8 + (1.05)10 = \$18.50$$

and the present value of the endowment is

$$I_1 + I_2/(1+i) = 10 + 8/(1.05) = \$17.62.$$

The slope of the budget constraint is $-(1+i) = -1.05$.

An increase in the future income from \$8 to \$10 will shift the budget constraint outward. This results in new intercepts for the future and present values of the endowment:

$$I_2 + (1+i)I_1 = 10 + (1.05)10 = \$20.50, \quad \text{future value},$$

$$I_1 + I_2/(1+i) = 10 + 10/(1.05) = \$19.52, \quad \text{present value}.$$

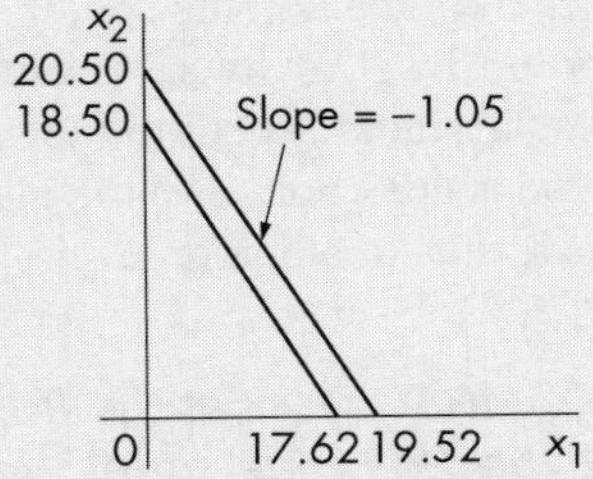

Establishing an equilibrium

Lenders look at "the three Cs" when deciding to extend credit to borrowers: character, capital, and capacity. To assess character, they investigate borrowers' credit history in terms of repayment of loans. Borrowers' assets in the form of property, savings, and investments provide a measure of financial capital. Salary, job security, and living expenses indicate borrowers' capacity for repaying a loan.

Assuming that these three Cs are not a constraint on borrowing, the Lagrangian for maximizing intertemporal utility subject to the budget constraint is

$$\mathcal{L}(x_1, x_2, \lambda) = U(x_1, x_2) + \lambda[x_2 - I_2 - (1+i)(I_1 - x_1)].$$

The first-order conditions (FOCs) are

$$\frac{\partial \mathcal{L}}{\partial x_1} = \frac{\partial U}{\partial x_1} + \lambda(1+i) = 0,$$

$$\frac{\partial \mathcal{L}}{\partial x_2} = \frac{\partial U}{\partial x_2} + \lambda = 0,$$

$$\frac{\partial \mathcal{L}}{\partial \lambda} = x_2^* - I_2 - (1+i)\left(I_1 - x_1^*\right) = 0.$$

Taking the ratio of the first two FOCs yields

$$\text{MRS}(x_2 \text{for } x_1) = \frac{\partial U/\partial x_1}{\partial U/\partial x_2} = 1 + i > 1.$$

Given a positive interest rate i, a consumer will be impatient. The equilibrium levels of current and future consumption occur where the marginal rate of time preference is set equal to the time rate of substituting future consumption for current consumption. Superimposing the intertemporal budget constraint (Figure 19.2) with the indifference curves (Figure 19.1) illustrates this equilibrium condition. As illustrated in Figures 19.3 (for a borrower) and 19.4 (for a lender), the tangency between the indifference curve and the budget constraint represents the equilibrium condition where the consumer maximizes utility for her given budget. In Figure 19.3, bundle A represents the equilibrium combination of current and future consumption. The consumer will consume x_1^* in current consumption and x_2^* in future consumption. In order to consume these levels, she borrows income $x_1^* - I_1$ to augment her current income of I_1. Thus, consumption of x_1 increases from the Polonius point I_1 to x_1^*. Borrowing on future consumption results in the equilibrium level of future consumption $x_2^* < I_2$. The reverse occurs for a lender. In Figure 19.4, a lender's equilibrium current consumption x_1^* is less than the Polonius point I_1. The lender does not consume all of her current income, and lends out the remainder, $I_1 - x_1^*$. This results in a higher level of future consumption x_2^* than the Polonius point I_2.

Are you a lender, a borrower, or a Polonius? If your MRS < 1 + i at the Polonius point, you are a lender; if your MRS > 1 + i at the Polonius point, you are a borrower, and if MRS = 1 + i at the Polonius point, neither a borrower nor lender be.

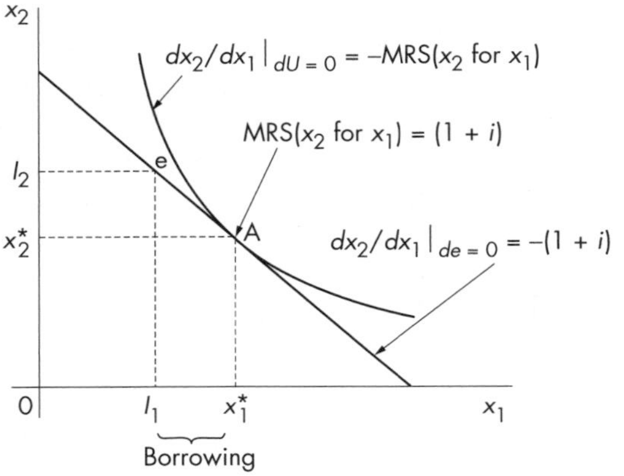

Figure 19.3 **Equilibrium for a borrower.** The tangency at point A between the indifference curve and the budget constraint represents the equilibrium condition where the consumer maximizes utility for her given budget. The equilibrium levels of consumption are x_1^* and x_2^*, resulting in the consumer borrowing $x_1^* - I_1$ in income.

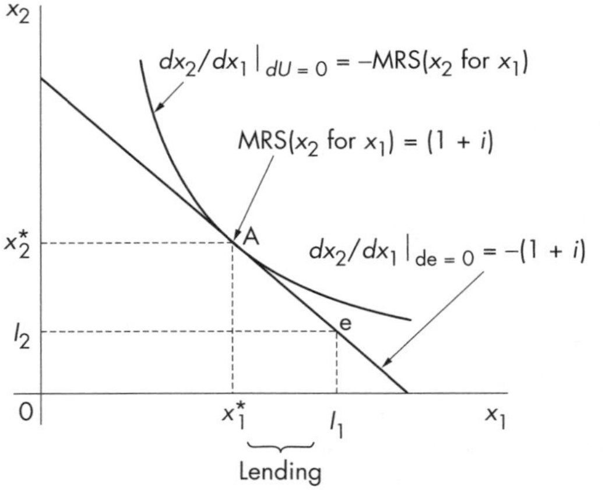

Figure 19.4 **Equilibrium for a lender.** The tangency at point A between the indifference curve and the budget constraint represents the equilibrium condition where the consumer maximizes utility for her given budget. The equilibrium levels of consumption are x_1^* and x_2^*, resulting in the consumer lending $I_1 - x_1^*$ in income.

Example 19.3 Calculating equilibrium levels of current and future consumption for a lender

Consider again the utility function in Example 19.1 and the intertemporal budget constraint in Example 19.2:

$$U(x_1, x_2) = x_1 x_2,$$
$$x_2 = I_2 + (1+i)(I_1 - x_1)$$
$$= 8 + 1.05(10 - x_1).$$

The Lagrangian for maximizing this utility function, subject to the budget constraint, is

$$\mathcal{L}(x_1, x_2, \lambda) = x_1 x_2 + \lambda[x_2 - 8 - 1.05(10 - x_1)].$$

The FOCs are then

$$\partial\mathcal{L}/\partial x_1 = x_2^* + 1.05\lambda^* = 0,$$
$$\partial\mathcal{L}/\partial x_2 = x_1^* + \lambda^* = 0,$$
$$\partial\mathcal{L}/\partial\lambda = x_2^* - 8 - 1.05(10 - x_1^*) = 0.$$

From the first two FOCs, $x_2^*/1.05 = -\lambda^*$ and $x_1^* = -\lambda^*$, so $x_2^* = 1.05x_1^*$. Substituting this result into the constraint (the last FOC) yields the equilibrium levels of x_1 and x_2:

$$x_2^* - 8 - 1.05(10 - x_1^*) = 0,$$
$$1.05x_1^* - 8 - 10.50 + 1.05x_1^* = 0.$$

Solving for x_1^*, the equilibrium level of current consumption is

$$2.10x_1^* - 18.50 = 0,$$
$$x_1^* = 8.81.$$

Given the result from the first two FOCs, $x_2^* = 9.25$.

The preferences for this consumer are to spend \$8.81 on current consumption out of the \$10 in current income. The residual consumption, \$1.19, is then lent out, allowing for increased consumption in the future. As determined in Example 19.1, MRS(x_2 for x_1) = x_2/x_1. At the equilibrium consumption levels, MRS(x_2 for x_1) = 9.25/8.81 > 1, indicating that the consumer is impatient.

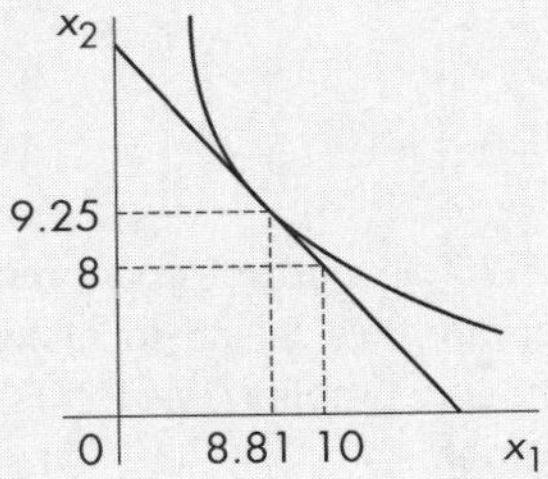

Example 19.4 Calculating equilibrium levels of current and future consumption for a borrower

In relation to Example 19.3, consider a change in consumer preferences toward current consumption. Such a change would result in greater weight being placed on current consumption within the utility function. Specifically, consider the utility function $U(x_1, x_2) = x_1^2 x_2$. The Lagrangian for maximizing this utility function, subject to the same budget constraint as in Example 19.3, is

$$\mathcal{L}(x_1, x_2, \lambda) = x_1^2 x_2 + \lambda[x_2 - 8 - 1.05(10 - x_1)].$$

The FOCs are then

$$\partial\mathcal{L}/\partial x_1 = 2x_1^* x_2^* + 1.05\lambda^* = 0,$$
$$\partial\mathcal{L}/\partial x_2 = x_1^{*2} + \lambda^* = 0,$$
$$\partial\mathcal{L}/\partial\lambda = x_2^* - 8 - 1.05(10 - x_1^*) = 0.$$

From the first two FOCs, the marginal rate of time preference is equal to the time rate of substituting future consumption for present consumption:

$$\text{MRS}(x_2 \text{ for } x_1) = 2x_2^*/x_1^* = 1.05.$$

Solving for x_2^* gives

$$x_2^* = (1.05/2)x_1^*,$$

and substituting into the constraint yields

$$x_2^* - 8 - 1.05(10 - x_1^*) = 0,$$
$$(1.05/2)x_1^* - 8 - 10.50 + 1.05x_1^* = 0.$$

Solving for x_1^*, the equilibrium level of current consumption is

$$(3/2)(1.05)x_1^* - 18.50 = 0,$$
$$x_1^* = 11.75.$$

Given the result from the first two FOCs, $x_2^* = 6.17$.

The preferences for this consumer are to spend \$11.75 on current consumption out of only \$10 in current income. Thus, the consumer borrows \$1.75 to allow for consumption above its current income. At this equilibrium consumption level, MRS(x_2 for x_1) $= 2(6.17)/11.75 > 1$, indicating an impatient consumer.

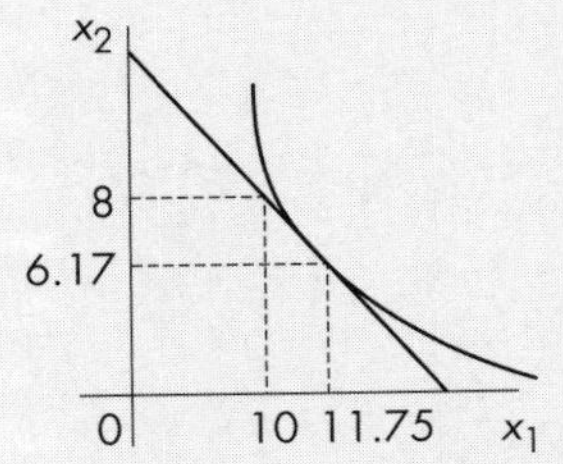

Developing human capital

Education is the best provision for old age.

(Aristotle)

Adam Smith was the first to compare an educated worker to an expensive machine. The skills embodied in a worker (human capital) can be rented out to employers, and the higher the level of these skills, the higher is the expected rent. Thus, the returns on investment in human capital are a higher level of earnings and greater job satisfaction over a worker's lifetime. By investing in human capital, workers can increase their productivity and enhance future wage rates.[1] A worker's productivity is determined by his or her level of human capital. The higher the level of human capital, the more productive the worker generally is. Human capital is made up of many characteristics, from physical to mental abilities. Each individual is endowed with a set of human-capital characteristics and has the ability to augment them. Investments in training and education, both formal and informal, will increase a worker's human capital and productivity. A degree or certificate for completing a specific educational or training program can be used as a signal (discussed in Chapter 23) of increased productivity and thus a justification for a higher wage. Experience obtained from on-the-job training will also increase a worker's human capital. This experience may be considered an investment in human capital if the wage rate is lower than alternative opportunities and results in a future higher wage.

Augmenting human capital involves both the explicit cost of any formal education and training programs and the opportunity cost of lost income and leisure from reallocating time toward human-capital improvements. Using analysis similar to that for determining the optimal levels of current and future consumption, the cost of human capital involves decreasing current consumption with the expectation of enhanced future income (prepare now to satisfy tomorrow's wants).

Maximizing utility with no financial markets: a developing country

The United Nations Food and Agricultural Organization (FAO) estimated in 2010 that over 13.6 percent of the world's population (mostly women and children) are undernourished. Access to food for the poor in developing countries is not related to food production but rather to the lack of markets. Noticeably missing is the financial market. Without a financial market, households are unable to borrow to obtain an adequate diet or to invest in human capital.

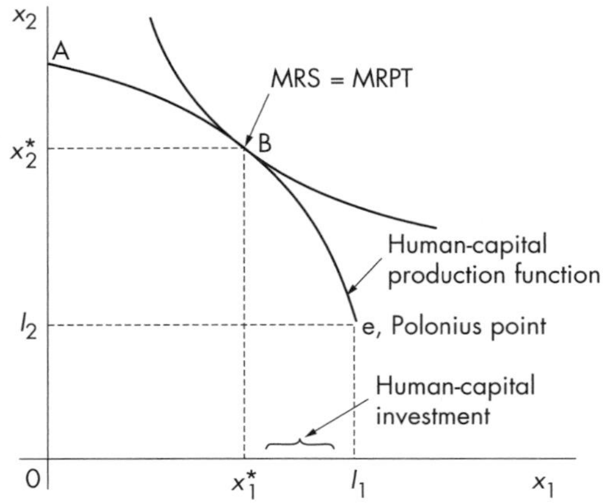

Figure 19.5 **Investment in human capital.** The optimal level of consumption and investment in human capital is point B, where the indifference curve is tangent to the human capital production function. At this tangency, x_1^* and x_2^* will be consumed, with $I_1 - x_1^*$ invested in human capital.

Specifically, the objective of a consumer is to determine the optimal level of human-capital investment. As illustrated in Figure 19.5, a consumer is initially endowed with income I_1 in the current period and income I_2 in the future period. By allocating some current income toward human-capital investment, the consumer can increase future income. This relationship between human-capital investment and enhanced future income is called the **human-capital production function**. A rational consumer will attempt to first invest in human-capital characteristics that will yield the highest increase in future income and then in characteristics with less potential income enhancement. This implies that the human-capital production function exhibits diminishing marginal returns from human-capital investment. That is, each additional unit of human-capital investment enhances future income by a smaller amount, illustrated in Figure 19.5. The increase in human-capital investment increases future income at a decreasing rate, which yields a concave human-capital production function. Note that if zero human capital is produced, then the levels of income in the two periods will remain at the Polonius point e. Alternatively, if all current income is allocated toward human-capital investment, then income available for current consumption is zero and the maximum amount of future income, point A, will result.

Human-capital production function. A function describing how investment in human capital enhances future income. *E.g., a function representing how investing in a college degree increases future earnings potential.*

As further illustrated in Figure 19.5, we determine the optimal levels of consumption and investment in human capital using intertemporal preferences for current and future consumption. A condition for obtaining these optimal levels is the tangency between the indifference curve and the human-capital production function. At this tangency,

$$\text{MRS}(x_2 \text{ for } x_1) = \text{MRPT}(x_2 \text{ for } x_1),$$

which occurs at point B. The optimal level of current consumption is x_1^* out of current income I_1. The remaining income $(I_1 - x_1^*)$ is the optimal level of investment in human capital. This investment in human capital increases future income by $x_2^* - I_2$, resulting in x_2^* as the optimal level of future consumption. Thus, a new Polonius point, point B, results and, if no borrowing or lending occurs, point B represents the equilibrium allocation. Point B is on a higher intertemporal indifference curve than point e, so utility is enhanced by investing in human capital.

Mathematically, the condition MRS = MRPT can be derived by maximizing intertemporal utility subject to a human-capital production function constraint. Let $f(x_1, x_2) = 0$ represent a concave human capital production function, where an investment in human capital reduces x_1 and increases x_2. The Lagrangian is then

$$\mathcal{L}(x_1, x_2, \lambda) = U(x_1, x_2) + \lambda f(x_1, x_2).$$

The FOCs are

$$\frac{\partial \mathcal{L}}{\partial x_1} = \frac{\partial U}{\partial x_1} + \lambda \frac{\partial f}{\partial x_1} = 0,$$

$$\frac{\partial \mathcal{L}}{\partial x_2} = \frac{\partial U}{\partial x_2} + \lambda \frac{\partial f}{\partial x_2} = 0,$$

$$\frac{\partial \mathcal{L}}{\partial \lambda} = f(x_1, x_2) = 0.$$

Rearranging the first two FOCs and taking the ratio yields

$$\frac{\partial U/\partial x_1}{\partial U/\partial x_2} = \frac{\partial f/\partial x_1}{\partial f/\partial x_2},$$

$$\text{MRS}(x_2 \text{ for } x_1) = \text{MRPT}(x_2 \text{ for } x_1).$$

At MRS = MRPT, the optimal level of human capital is being produced efficiently.

Example 19.5 Determining the optimal level of human capital investment with no financial markets

Suppose that a consumer's intertemporal preference for consumption is

$$U = x_1^{1/2} x_2.$$

The consumer receives current income of \$12, which increases to \$15 in the future time period, and faces the human-capital production function

$$4x_1^2 + x_2^2 = 801,$$

where 801 represents the value of the Polonius point on the production function, $4(12^2) + 15^2 = 801$. Maximizing utility subject to the production function yields the Lagrangian

$$\mathcal{L}(x_1, x_2, \lambda) = x_1^{1/2} x_2 + \lambda\left(801 - 4x_1^2 - x_2^2\right).$$

The FOCs are then

$$\partial\mathcal{L}/\partial x_1 = \tfrac{1}{2} x_1^{*-1} U - 8\lambda^* x_1^* = 0,$$
$$\partial\mathcal{L}/\partial x_2 = x_2^{*-1} U - 2\lambda^* x_2^* = 0,$$
$$\partial\mathcal{L}/\partial\lambda = 801 - 4x_1^{*2} - x_2^{*2} = 0.$$

From the first two FOCs, the condition MRS = MRPT results in

$$\text{MRS}(x_2 \text{ for } x_1) = x_2^*/2x_1^* = 4x_1^*/x_2^* = \text{MRPT}(x_2 \text{ for } x_1).$$

Rearranging terms,

$$x_2^{*2} = 8x_1^{*2}.$$

Substituting into the human-capital production function yields

$$4x_1^{*2} + 8x_1^{*2} = 801.$$

Solving for x_1 results in

$$12x_1^{*2} = 801,$$
$$x_1^{*2} = 66.75,$$
$$x_1^* = 8.17, \quad x_2^* = 23.11.$$

The optimal level of investment in human capital is then \$3.83, yielding an increase in future consumption of $23.11 - 15 = \$8.11$.

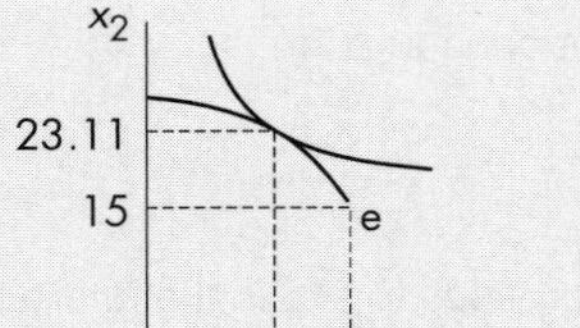

Maximizing utility with financial markets (the Separation Theorem)

As previously stated, financial markets are still a major constraint on the economic development of many developing countries. However, financial markets within developing countries continue to grow. This is good news for emerging market economies, given the growing body of evidence indicating that financial-sector development contributes significantly to economic growth. Global finance has led to a strong increase in world welfare. This link between finance markets and welfare is illustrated in Figure 19.6. Point B is the equilibrium point if there is no borrowing or lending (no financial markets). With financial markets allowing borrowing and lending, the consumer can increase her choice of current and future consumption levels and thus possibly enhance satisfaction. Recall that the intertemporal budget constraint passing through the Polonius point with a slope of $-(1+i)$ specifies the available borrowing and lending options. This is illustrated by the budget constraint I' in Figure 19.6. However, this does not include the possibility of enhancing human capital. By investing in human capital, the consumer's Polonius point moves up along the human-capital production function, which shifts the budget constraint outward from I' toward I''. The consumer will continue to invest in human capital and move up along the human-capital production function as long as the budget constraint continues to shift outward. At the tangency of the human-capital production function with the budget constraint, point D, any further increases in human capital will cause the budget constraint to reverse direction and start to shift down. Thus, in terms of increasing utility, point D represents the highest constraint. Budget constraint I'' dominates all the other budget constraints intersecting the human-capital production function. At point D, the optimal level of human capital investment is $I_1 - x_1'$, which yields the largest feasible set of consumption opportunities.

Given this budget constraint I'', we can determine the optimal level of current and future consumption by borrowing or lending. In Figure 19.6, this occurs at point F, where x_1'' is consumed in the current period by borrowing $x_1'' - I_1$ and x_2'' is consumed in the future period. An example is a college student who borrows to increase current consumption while furthering his education. The student takes out student loans while in school with the expectation of

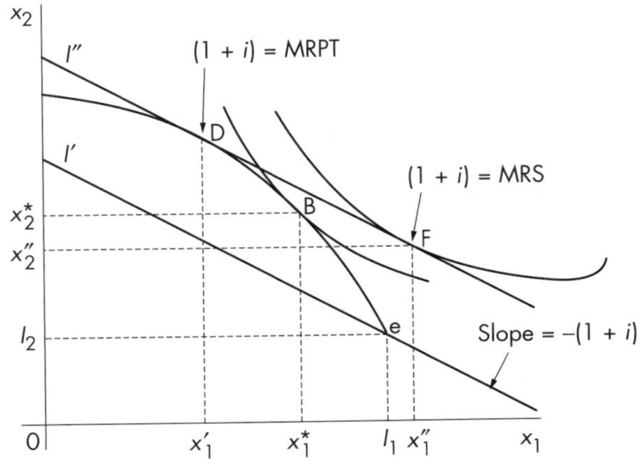

Figure 19.6 **Separation of human capital and consumption decisions.** Allowing for borrowing and lending, point D yields the optimal level of human-capital investment, $I_1 - x_1'$. Point F, where the indifference curve is tangent to the budget constraint, yields the optimal level of current and future consumption, x_1'' and x_2''.

paying these off once he graduates and starts earning an income. One of the objectives is to ensure a comfortable standard of living as a student, and this is accomplished by evening out the difference in income during and after a student's education.

The ability to borrow and lend money separates the level of human-capital investment from the decision of optimal consumption across time periods. This was not the case when this ability to borrow and lend was not considered. As illustrated in Figure 19.6, we determined the consumer's level of human-capital investment with no financial markets by the tangency between the indifference curve and the production function, resulting in allocation (x_1^*, x_2^*). Thus, the consumer's preferences directly determined the level of human-capital investment. In contrast, with financial markets, we apply the Separation Theorem and separate the human-capital decision from a consumer's preference for consumption. The **Separation Theorem** states that the existence of markets, in this case a financial market, allows a consumer to separate production decisions (production of human capital) from consumption decisions. As we have said, in developing countries, financial markets are generally not well developed, so such a separation of decisions is not possible. In cases where a consumer is currently at a subsistence level of living and has no discretionary income to allocate toward investing in human capital, this may lead to an under-investment in human capital. Thus, establishing financial markets that allow consumers to borrow and lend can have a major impact on economic development.

Why do college students shop at electronic stores and boutiques? Financial capital markets allow college students to separate their human-capital decisions (to attend college) from their consumption decisions, so they need not forgo certain consumption items for an education.

Separation Theorem. The existence of markets allows agents to separate production decisions from consumption decisions. *E.g., given an investor's ability to borrow and lend based on his preferences, the optimal allocation of risky assets can be determined without knowledge of the investor's preferences.*

Example 19.6 Separation Theorem in the optimal determination of human-capital investment and consumption

Consider again the human-capital production function from Example 19.5:

$$4x_1^2 + x_2^2 = 801.$$

Under the Separation Theorem, we first maximize the intertemporal budget constraint independent of the utility:

$$\max_{(I_1, I_2)} I = \max_{(I_1, I_2)} [(1+i)I_1 + I_2] = \max_{(x_1, x_2)} [(1+i)x_1 + x_2]$$

subject to the production function. The Lagrangian is

$$\mathcal{L}(x_1, x_2, \lambda) = (1+i)x_1 + x_2 + \lambda\left(801 - 4x_1^2 - x_2^2\right).$$

The FOCs are then

$$\partial \mathcal{L}/\partial x_1 = (1+i) - 8\lambda^* x_1^* = 0,$$
$$\partial \mathcal{L}/\partial x_2 = 1 - 2\lambda^* x_2^* = 0,$$
$$\partial \mathcal{L}/\partial \lambda = 801 - 4x_1^{*2} - x_2^{*2} = 0.$$

Rearranging the first two FOCs and taking their ratio yields

$$1 + i = 4x_1^*/x_2^* = \text{MRPT}(x_1 \text{ for } x_2).$$

Solving for x_2^* and substituting into the constraint yields the optimal level of human-capital investment:

$$x_2^* = \frac{4x_1^*}{1+i},$$
$$801 - 4x_1^{*2} - \left(\frac{4x_1^*}{1+i}\right)^2 = 0,$$
$$4x_1^{*2}\left[1 + \frac{4}{(1+i)^2}\right] = 801,$$
$$x_1^{*2} = \frac{200.25(1+i)^2}{(1+i)^2 + 4}.$$

Assuming that the interest rate i is 5 percent, then $x_1^* = 6.58$, $x_2^* = 25.06$. In Example 19.5, $I_1 = 12$, so the optimal level of investment in human capital is \$5.42 and the maximum endowment

$$I'' = (1+i)6.58 + 25.06 = 6.91 + 25.06 = 31.97.$$

We can now maximize utility, given I'' and the utility function in Example 19.5:

$$\mathcal{L}(x_1, x_2, \lambda) = x_1^{1/2} x_2 + \lambda(31.97 - 1.05x_1 - x_2).$$

The FOCs are then

$$\partial \mathcal{L}/\partial x_1 = ½ x_1^{''-1} U - 1.05\lambda'' = 0,$$
$$\partial \mathcal{L}/\partial x_2 = x_2^{''-1} U - \lambda'' = 0,$$
$$\partial \mathcal{L}/\partial \lambda = 31.97 - 1.05x_1'' - x_2'' = 0.$$

Rearranging the first two FOCs and taking the ratio yields

$$x_2''/2x_1'' = 1.05.$$

Solving for x_2 and substituting into the constraint yields

$$x_2'' = 2.1x_1'',$$
$$31.97 - 1.05x_1'' - 2.1x_1'' = 0,$$
$$x_1'' = 31.97/3.15 = 10.15, \quad x_2'' = 21.31.$$

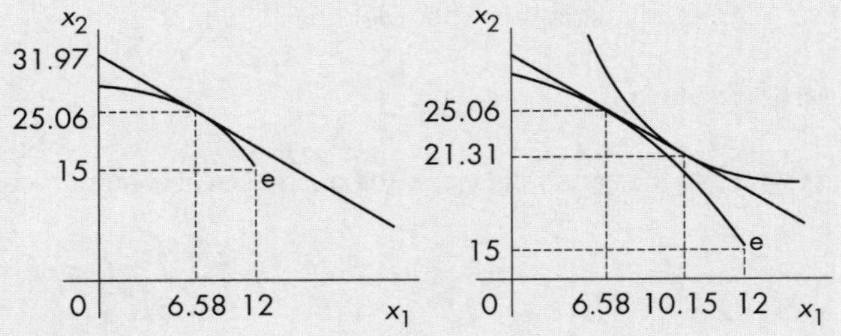

The separation theorem applies to all situations faced by both households and firms where markets allow optimal investment decisions to be separated from consumption or production decisions. With well-developed financial markets complementing markets for commodities, economic efficiency can be enhanced. As further discussed in Part 9, since missing markets do not result in a Pareto-efficient allocation, they reduce social welfare.

Mathematically, under the Separation Theorem, we can first maximize the endowment subject to the human-capital production function and then maximize utility subject to this maximum obtainable endowment. Recall that the intertemporal budget constraint is

$$I = (1+i)I_1 + I_2 = (1+i)x_1 + x_2,$$

and the human-capital production function in implicit form is

$$f(x_1, x_2) = 0.$$

Maximizing I subject to $f(x_1, x_2) = 0$ results in the Lagrangian

$$\mathcal{L}(x_1, x_2, \lambda) = (1+i)x_1 + x_2 + \lambda f(x_1, x_2).$$

The FOCs are

$$\frac{\partial \mathcal{L}}{\partial x_1} = (1+i) + \lambda^* \frac{\partial f}{\partial x_1} = 0,$$
$$\frac{\partial \mathcal{L}}{\partial x_2} = 1 + \lambda^* \frac{\partial f}{\partial x_2} = 0,$$
$$\frac{\partial \mathcal{L}}{\partial \lambda} = f(x_1, x_2) = 0.$$

Rearranging the first two FOCs and taking their ratio yields

$$1+i=\frac{\partial f/\partial x_1}{\partial f/\partial x_2}=\text{MRPT}\,(x_2 \text{ for } x_1).$$

Thus, as indicated in Figure 19.6, where the slope of the budget constraint is tangent with the production function, the endowment I is maximized. This results in the maximum level of I, I'', and the optimal level of human-capital investment associated with point D.

We can now maximize utility given this maximum level of I, I''. The appropriate Lagrangian is

$$\mathcal{L}(x_1,x_2,\lambda)=U(x_1,x_2)+\lambda\left[I''-(1+i)x_1-x_2\right].$$

The FOCs are then

$$\frac{\partial\mathcal{L}}{\partial x_1}=\frac{\partial U}{\partial x_1}-\lambda''(1+i)=0,$$

$$\frac{\partial\mathcal{L}}{\partial x_2}=\frac{\partial U}{\partial x_2}-\lambda''=0,$$

$$\frac{\partial\mathcal{L}}{\partial \lambda}=I''-(1+i)x_1-x_2=0.$$

Rearranging the first two FOCs and taking their ratio yields

$$\frac{\partial U/\partial x_1}{\partial U/\partial x_2}=1+i,$$

$$\text{MRS}\,(x_2 \text{ for } x_1)=1+i.$$

As indicated in Figure 19.6, this occurs at the tangency of the budget constraint and the indifference curve, indicating the optimal current and future consumption levels (x_1'', x_2'').

Determination of the interest rate *i*

To raise or lower interest rates? That is a question for the Federal Reserve Chairman. Will the rates respond? A question for the market.

(Michael Wetzstein)

Translation: The equilibrium market rate of interest is determined by the intersection of the demand and supply curve.

For the 2011–12 academic year, interest rates on federal subsidized education loans declined. Students who took out a Stafford Loan for the 2011–12 academic year received an interest rate of 3.4 percent, which is 1.1 percent less than the previous year.[2] Thus, in contrast to our preceding development of intertemporal choice, the interest rate is not fixed at some given level that borrowers and lenders use in making their intertemporal consumption decisions. In this regard, an interest rate corresponds to a market-determined price for an exchange of commodities at a point in time. It is directly associated with the price in a market, where trades are made across the two periods. However, it is implicitly assumed that neither a borrower (such as a student) nor a lender has control over the interest rate. They both are interest-rate takers.

We determine this market price between the two periods and its correspondence with the interest rate by considering the intertemporal budget constraint,

$$x_2 = I_2 + (1+i)(I_1 - x_1).$$

Rearranging this budget constraint by placing both current and future consumption levels (x_1, x_2) on the left-hand side yields

$$(1+i)x_1 + x_2 = (1+i)I_1 + I_2 = I.$$

Since I is the future value of the endowment, the budget constraint in this form is represented in the future value. In terms of market prices, if p_1 represents the commodity price in the current period and p_2 is price in the future period, then

$$p_1 x_1 + p_2 x_2 = (1+i)I_1 + I_2.$$

In this future-value form of the budget constraint, the price of future consumption is set $p_2 = 1$ and the current price $p_1 = 1+i$. In other words, the value of the current price in the future is its current value, which is 1, plus the interest rate i. Given these prices, the time rate of substituting future consumption for current consumption is then the ratio of these prices, $p_1/p_2 = 1+i$. Specifically,

$$\left.\frac{dx_2}{dx_1}\right|_{dI=0} = -\frac{p_1}{p_2} = -(1+i).$$

Figure 19.2 along with subsequent figures illustrate this price ratio.

Alternatively, we may express the budget constraint in present-value form by dividing the future value budget constraint by $1+i$:

$$x_1 + \frac{x_2}{1+i} = I_1 + \frac{I_2}{1+i}.$$

The current price is now $p_1 = 1$ and the future price is discounted, $p_2 = 1/(1+i)$. This present-value form of the budget constraint reverses the time rate of substitution. It measures the time rate of substituting current consumption for future consumption:

$$\left.\frac{dx_1}{dx_2}\right|_{dI=0} = -\frac{p_2}{p_1} = -\frac{1}{1+i}.$$

The present-value form of the budget constraint may be visualized by reversing the axes in Figure 19.2.

We determine the equilibrium-market price of future goods, $p_2 = 1/(1+i)$, and thus the interest rate i, in the same manner as any price. The intersection of the market supply (Q_2^S) and market demand (Q_2^D) curves for future consumption will determine this equilibrium interest rate. An increase in the price of future consumption (a fall in i) will provide an incentive for firms to supply more in the future. As illustrated in Figure 19.7, this results in a positively sloping supply curve, which in the short-run assumes diminishing marginal returns

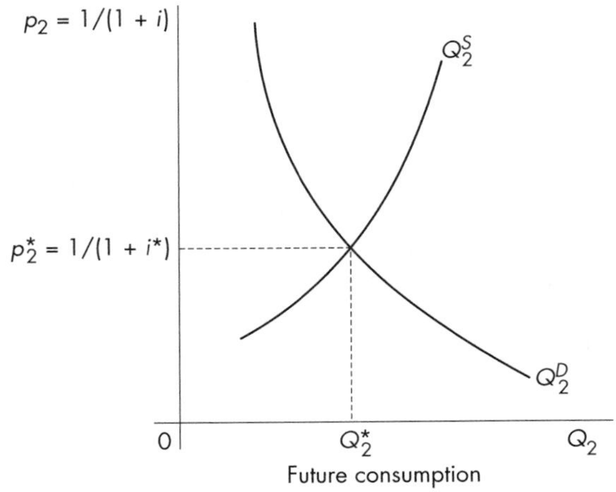

Figure 19.7 **Equilibrium interest rate for future consumption.** The intersection of market supply and demand curves for future consumption determines the equilibrium level of the interest rate i.

in producing future consumption. Given a relative increase in the price of future consumption, firms will allocate additional resources toward supplying the future commodity by producing more capital inputs and less of the current commodity. As illustrated in Figure 19.7, the market equilibrium is (p_2^*, i^*), associated with a negatively sloping market demand curve for future consumption. This assumes that as the price of future consumption increases (i falls), consumers will consume less in the future.

There are a number of factors that affect this equilibrium i, i^*. First, the ability to use some capital today to produce a higher level of possible consumption in the future could be enhanced through technological progress. The result is an outward shift in the supply curve and a resulting higher equilibrium interest rate. This result does occur, given that producers would be willing and able to pay a higher rate of compensation for the use of the foregone current consumption.

Another important factor is risk. With uncertainty about the future period, consumers may be more reluctant to postpone consumption, and thus require higher compensation for foregoing current consumption. Specifically, in the future period, they may not be sure they will receive the expected level of consumption. Lower future expectations will result in a downward shift in the demand curve for future consumption and a lower equilibrium price and associated higher i^*. The more unsure consumers are, the more they have to be compensated by higher interest rates.

A third factor is consumers' underlying rate of time preference. For example, for consumers who place more value on future consumption, the demand for future consumption will increase, with an associated increase in price and corresponding fall in the interest rate.

Real interest rate (rate of return) versus nominal interest rate

In 1981, interest rates were in double digits. Lenders could sit back and savor the income from their FDIC-insured CDs earning 15 percent and United States Treasury Bills earning

14 percent. In 2010, interest rates were at record lows. Borrowers were enthusiastic about low rates of interest: 3.4 percent on student loans and 10 percent on outstanding credit card balances. Lenders unable or unwilling to eat into their principal reduced their spending (tightened their belts). However, in reality, these lenders were suffering from money illusion. The high interest payments in the 1980s were never real payments at all. A lender spending his or her 15 percent interest in 1981 was eating into principal. With 1981 inflation at 9.4 percent, those lenders spending all 15 percent (nominal) interest were allowing the real value of their principal to drop by 9.4 percent. They were dipping into their principal just as much as lenders in 2010 (with little or no inflation) that spent more than their interest income.

In general, the market interest rate illustrated in Figure 19.7 is highly correlated with the expected rate of inflation. The market equilibrium interest rate in Figure 19.7 assumes that prices in the two periods remain constant (zero inflation), so residual consumption in the current period $(I_1 - x_1)$ allows the consumer to purchase $(1+i)(I_1 - x_1)$ units of consumption in the future.

We can relax this assumption of zero inflation by assuming some positive rate of increase in prices from the current to the future period. Let α denote this rate of increased prices and continue to assume that the current period price is 1. The future price is then $p_2 = 1+\alpha$. Substituting this inflation adjustment into the intertemporal budget constraint and solving for x_2 yields

$$\begin{aligned} p_1x_1 + p_2x_2 &= (1+i)I_1 + I_2, \\ (1+i)x_1 + (1+\alpha)x_2 &= (1+i)I_1 + I_2, \\ x_2 &= \frac{1+i}{1+\alpha}(I_1 - x_1) + \frac{I_2}{1+\alpha}. \end{aligned}$$

Considering the possibility of inflation, we weight the residual consumption in the current period, $I_1 - x_1$, and income in the future period, I_2, by the level of inflation $1+\alpha$. This results in the **real interest rate** (**rate of return** or **discount rate**) r and real income $I_2/(1+\alpha)$. Real income adjusts future income by the rate of inflation and measures the consumer's purchasing power. The higher the rate of inflation, the lower is a consumer's future purchasing power for a given level of future income. The rate of return is defined as

$$1+r = \frac{1+i}{1+\alpha},$$

and it measures how much additional consumption a consumer will receive in the future if the consumer reduces her current consumption by a marginal unit. The real interest rate is the rate in terms of a bundle of commodities. In contrast, $1+i$ measures the additional future income that the consumer would receive for a marginal reduction in current consumption. If the level of inflation is zero, $\alpha = 0$, then $r = i$ and additional future income will exactly purchase the additional consumption. In general, the interest rate observed in the market is determined by both the real interest rate r and the expected inflation rate, α. (The term *expected* is used because generally the rate of inflation from the current to the future period is not known with certainty.) This observed market interest rate i is called the **nominal rate of interest.** The nominal interest rate is the rate in terms of money. With the presence of inflation, consumers and firms expect to be compensated for the effect of inflation on future ability to purchase commodities. Solving for the real interest rate r in the previous equation provides an explicit relation between the real, r, and nominal, i, interest rates

$$r = \frac{1+i}{1+\alpha} - 1$$
$$= \frac{i-\alpha}{1+\alpha}.$$

If the expected rate of inflation α is relatively small, then the real interest rate may be approximated by

$$r = i - \alpha,$$

the nominal rate minus the inflation rate.[3] For example, if inflation is 6 percent with an associated 10 percent nominal rate of interest, then the real rate of interest would be approximately 4 percent. Compare this with the exact measure for the real interest rate:

$$r = \frac{i-\alpha}{1+\alpha} = \frac{10\% - 6\%}{1+6\%} = \frac{0.04}{1.06} = 3.77\%.$$

Thus, the additional consumption a consumer can consume in the future period for a marginal reduction in current consumption is approximately 4 percent.

Rate of return (discount rate or real interest rate) (*r*). Nominal interest rate adjusted for expected inflation rate. *E.g., the real interest rate you are paying on your credit card balance is the interest rate that the bank charges minus the inflation rate divided by the level of inflation.*

Nominal rate of interest (*i*). Observed market interest rate. *E.g., the rate of interest you are charged on your credit card balance.*

Figure 19.8 illustrates the historical pattern (1949–2010) of the real and nominal rates of return for the prime interest rate.[4] Of particular note is how the prime interest rate generally corresponds to the rate of inflation, whereas the real interest rate is generally inversely related with inflation. Also, the deflation (decline in prices) in 1949 and the Great Recession of 2009 resulted in the real interest rate exceeding the nominal rate.

Discounting the future

Economists are concerned about using conventional discounting techniques to value public benefits over hundreds of years, where tradeoffs are evaluated across multiple generations. On the basis of equity, lower discount rates or even no discounting, $r = 0$, should be used to compare the value of costs and benefits across generations. Such an argument may apply regarding the use of discount rates for complex projections of global warming and loss of biodiversity. However, for inter-generational comparisons over a period of less than

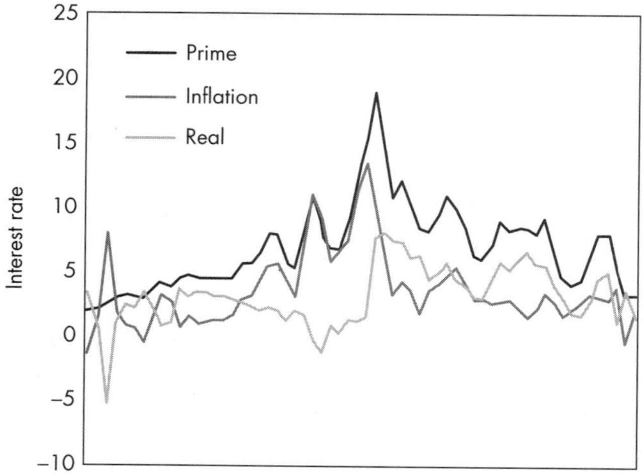

Figure 19.8 **Historical patterns of nominal and real interest rates.** The prime interest rate (a nominal rate) from 1949 to 2010 adjusted for inflation yields the real prime interest rate.
(*Source:* Federal Reserve Board.)

100 years, discounting the future benefits and cost of a durable commodity or a capital asset is consistent with the impatient preferences of agents.

The decision whether to purchase a durable commodity or capital asset is dependent on the costs and benefits derived from the item. In general, there is an initial purchase price for, say, a capital input, and then benefits are received and costs incurred as the capital input is used over time. This requires a method for comparing dollars received over different time periods. Such a comparison is required because agents are assumed to be impatient. A dollar forthcoming a year from now is not worth as much as a dollar today. Also, a dollar received today can be used immediately. Thus, there is an opportunity cost of not receiving the dollar until some future time period. This opportunity cost must be taken into account when comparing dollars received over different time periods. The real interest rate is a measure of this opportunity cost. A dollar received today can be invested and can earn an annual rate of return r; so, in a year from now, it will be worth $1+r$. The value $1+r$ is the price of a dollar in the current period relative to its price in the future period.

Discounting in a two-period model

The opportunity cost of consumption is observed in the future-value budget constraint associated with two-period models:

$$(1+r)x_1 + x_2 = I,$$

where the future price of current consumption is $1+r$ and the future price of future consumption is 1. Dividing through by $1+r$ yields the present-value budget constraint:

$$x_1 + \frac{x_2}{1+r} = \frac{I}{1+r},$$

where $I/(1+r)$ is the present value of the income. The current price is now equal to 1 and the future price is discounted $1/(1+r)$, where the rate of return r is called the **discount rate**. The discounted future price is the amount of money that if invested at a rate of return r would grow to exactly \$1 in the future period. For example, if the annual rate of return is 5 percent, then the present value of \$1 received in a year is $1/(1.05) = 0.95$. If \$0.95 were invested in the current period at a 5 percent rate or return, it would be worth \$1 a year from now. For most analyses, presenting prices in present instead of future value is very convenient. For example, generally, the cost of a capital asset is paid at the time of purchase and the future benefits are then discounted back to the purchase date for comparison. The rate used for discounting varies depending on the objective and (risk) preferences of agents. For economic analysis of loan applications, banks will typically use the long term (30-year) US Treasury bond rate.

Is a dollar forthcoming a year from now worth as much as a dollar today? No, it is only worth 1/(1 + r).

Discount rate (r). Rate of return used to compare the value of a dollar received sometime in the future to a dollar received today. *E.g., as the risk of receiving a dollar one year from now increases, an increased discount rate will reflect this increased risk.*

Application: Consumer discount rates for energy-using durables

In considering the purchase of an energy-using durable, such as a home air conditioner, we generally consider both the initial purchase price (capital cost) and operating costs over time. Operating costs depend on the amount of utilization. If a household plans on using the durable commodity a great deal, say a household in Phoenix using an air conditioner all year round, then operating costs weigh heavy in the decision. For many energy-using durables, a large tradeoff exists in capital costs and operating cost. For example, the purchase price of a more energy-efficient air conditioner may be higher, but the overall operating cost will be lower. For major appliances such as air conditioners, refrigerators, and dryers, the energy costs (operation costs) as well as the purchase price (capital cost) are required by law to be listed.

In the short run, a consumer may not be able to change the durable commodity currently being used (the capital stock is fixed), but could change the utilization of the commodity. For example, when facing a large increase in electrical rates, a household may not be able in the short run to replace the existing air conditioner with a more efficient one, but could decrease its use. However, in the long run, a household can trade off higher initial capital costs (buying a new unit) against a reduction in operating costs. Which type of appliance to purchase depends on a household's discount rate. If the discount rate is high, a household will heavily discount any future earning and tend toward a less energy-efficient appliance. Thus, any energy conservation through improved technology might not be very successful. If lower rates are used in engineering calculations, then forecasts of household demand for energy-efficient appliances will be biased. Also, if an individual household's discount rate is higher than the social rate, then an inefficient level of energy-efficient appliances will be purchased.

R. Hartmen and M. Doane estimated the individual household's discount rate for weatherization investments to be greater than 26 percent for low-income households. This substantially exceeds values used in engineering to determine life-cycle costs in evaluating the tradeoff between increased energy conservation and lower operating cost against higher initial capital costs. Thus, forecasts of consumer demand for energy-efficient appliances may be too optimistic. Also, some economists have noted a defective telescopic faculty in households' decisions involving discounting. Households tend to have a higher discount rate compared with the socially determined market rate. This divergence between individual households' discount rates and the social discount can be narrowed by a subsidy on initial capital costs. Such a subsidy in the form of a tax credit is currently available for electric cars.

Source: R.S. Hartmen and M.J. Doane, "Household Discount Rates Revisited," *Energy Journal* 7 (1986): 139–148.

Multi-period discounting

Assuming that the utility for being reincarnated is $U = 1$, a newborn baby's discounted present value for being reincarnated after living an expected life of 70 years, at a 10 percent discount rate, is zero. He is not at all interested in being reincarnated. However, assuming the same expected life and discount rate, his 60-year-old grandmother has a positive present value for being reincarnated of $1/(1.1)^{10} = 0.39$. As one grows old, the present value of reincarnation increases.

Specifically, extending the concept of present value to more than two time periods involves discounting all the future periods back to the current period. For example, in a three-period model, the \$1 price in the current period does not require discounting, so it remains \$1. The \$1 price in the second period discounted to the current period is, as before, $1/(1+r)$. Continuing, a price of \$1 in the third period can be first discounted to the second period, which is $1/(1+r)$. This is how much the price must be in the second period to be equal to \$1 in the third period, or it is the price of third-period consumption in terms of second-period dollars. Further discounting, the third-period price so it is in terms of current prices involves dividing again by $1/(1+r)$. This results in $1/(1+r)^2$, which is what the price must be in the current period for it to be \$1 in the third period. Each additional dollar spent on consumption in the third period costs the consumer $1/(1+r)^2$ dollars in the current period. For example, with $r = 5$ percent, \$1 in the third period discounted back to the current period is

$$\frac{1}{(1.05)^2} = 0.91.$$

On an annual basis, receiving \$0.91 now is equivalent to receiving \$1 three years from now at a 5 percent rate of return. The budget constraint for a three-period model with constant interest rate r is then

$$x_1 + \frac{x_2}{1+r} + \frac{x_3}{(1+r)^2} = I_1 + \frac{I_2}{1+r} + \frac{I_3}{(1+r)^2}.$$

In general, for T time periods, the budget constraint with a constant rate of return is

$$x_1 + \frac{x_2}{1+r} + \ldots + \frac{x_T}{(1+r)^{T-1}} = I_1 + \frac{I_2}{1+r} + \ldots + \frac{I_T}{(1+r)^{T-1}},$$

that is,

$$\sum_{j=1}^{T} \frac{x_j}{(1+r)^{j-1}} = \sum_{j=1}^{T} \frac{I_j}{(1+r)^{j-1}}.$$

As an example, in 1626, Peter Minuit bought Manhattan Island from the Native Americans for around 60 Dutch guilders. Sixty guilders in 1626 were worth approximately 1.5 pounds of silver. Assuming this is troy weight of 12 ounces to a pound and silver today sells for around \$35.00 per ounce, Manhattan Island cost Minuit \$630. The 2010 market value for Manhattan Island is \$133 billion (New York City, Department of Finance Annual Report). Assuming that 25 percent of this market value is land value (\$33.25 billion), Minuit's investment in Manhattan increased in value at an annual rate of 4.7 percent. The present value of \$33.25 billion discounted 384 years at a 4.7 percent discount rate is approximately 60 guilders. Minuit would probably have been better off investing in something else with a higher rate of return.

Table 19.1 shows the present value of \$1 received in a number of time periods with various rates of return. At a 5 percent rate of return, the present value of receiving \$1 in 10 years is \$0.71. In other words, receiving \$0.71 now is equivalent to receiving \$1 ten years from now. As the time for receiving the \$1 increases, the opportunity cost increases, so a delay in receiving the \$1 from 10 years to 30 years results in a decline in present value to \$0.23. Note that the higher the rate of return, the greater is the future discount. At a 15 percent discount rate, the present value of receiving \$1 in 30 years is only \$0.02, compared with \$0.74 at a 1 percent discount rate.

Also illustrated in Table 19.1 is the *Rule of 72*,which provides the approximate number of years (exact for a 10 percent rate of return) required to double your money at a given interest rate or, equivalently, for the present value to decrease by one-half. Specifically, the Rule of 72 is

$$\text{years to double your money} = 0.72/r.$$

As indicated in the table, for $r = 10$ percent, it will take 7.2 years for \$0.50 to double to \$1. Equivalently, the present value is half of the dollar received in 7.2 years. For any other rate

Table 19.1 Present value of \$1 received in year j at a rate of return (discount rate) r

	Year j						
Rate of return (discount rate) r	1	2	5	7.2	10	20	30
1%	\$0.99	\$0.98	\$0.95	\$0.93	\$0.91	\$0.82	\$0.74
2%	\$0.98	0.96	0.91	0.87	0.82	0.67	0.55
5%	\$0.95	0.91	0.78	0.70	0.71	0.38	0.23
8%	\$0.93	0.86	0.68	0.57	0.46	0.21	0.10
10%	\$0.91	0.83	0.62	0.50	0.39	0.15	0.06
15%	\$0.87	0.77	0.50	0.37	0.25	0.06	0.02

of return, the Rule of 72 is only an approximation. For example, at $r = 8$ percent, it will take 9.01 years $[0.50 = (1.08)^{-9.01}]$ for your money to double rather than the Rule of 72 approximation of 9 years (72/8). The Rule of 72 is quite accurate for rates of return below 20 percent; however, at higher rates, the error starts to become significant.

Maximizing present value

Analogous to maximizing utility when considering only a single time period, a household that can freely borrow and lend at a given rate of return r would prefer an income stream with a higher present value, as illustrated in Figure 19.9. Given an initial intertemporal budget constraint PV°, with the x_1 intercept representing the present value of the endowment $I_1 + I_2/(1 + r)$, a household maximizes utility at point A. At this equilibrium, the consumer consumes x_1^* units of current consumption and x_2^* units of future consumption. If an increase in the present value of the endowment shifts the intertemporal budget constraint outward from PV° to PV′, a household free to borrow and lend can then consume any combination of current and future consumption on this new budget line PV′. For any given level of x_1, the household now has the income to consume more of x_2 relative to the initial budget constraint. For example, at x_1^*, the household can consume x_2' units of future consumption, compared with only x_2^* units at the initial budget constraint. Thus, at any level of x_1, the household will prefer the present value of income PV′ over PV°. This enhanced present value of income, PV′, is then said to dominate the initial present value of income, PV°. For preferences represented by the intertemporal indifference curve in Figure 19.9, the household can increase satisfaction relative to the initial budget constraint by choosing an allocation between points B and C on the PV′ budget constraint.

Households use the dominance of a higher present value over all lower present values when choosing among investment options. **Investments** could be the purchase of real capital inputs (real assets) used by firms for producing outputs, or durable commodities and human capital purchased by households. (Recall that durable commodities are commodities that are useful

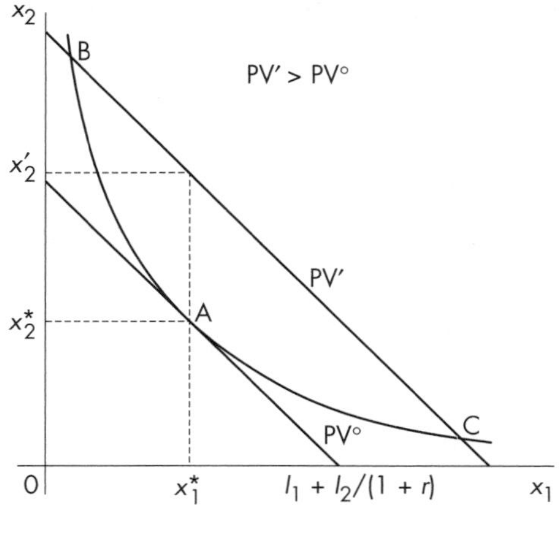

Figure 19.9 **Increase in the present value of income improves satisfaction.** An increase in the present value of the endowment will shift the budget constraint outward from PV° to PV′. The present value of income PV′ dominates the initial present value PV°, so the consumer can increase her satisfaction relative to PV°.

for more than one time period.) These investments will yield a flow of benefits measured as monetary returns over the life of the asset. For example, the value of the increase in productivity per time period from purchasing a capital input is a firm's investment benefits, and the willingness to pay per time period for owning a consumer appliance would be a household's benefits from purchasing an appliance. Let TR_j denote this total benefit (revenue) in time period j, where $j = 1, 2, \ldots, T$, and T is the number of time periods. To compare investment options yielding different levels of revenue across time periods, we calculate each option's present value PV:

$$PV = TR_1 + \frac{TR_2}{1+r} + \frac{TR_3}{(1+r)^2} + \ldots + \frac{TR_T}{(1+r)^{T-1}} + \frac{SV}{(1+r)^T}$$

$$= \sum_{j=1}^{T} \frac{TR_j}{(1+r)^{j-1}} + \frac{SV}{(1+r)^T},$$

where SV is the **salvage value** at the end of the investment. For example, if the asset is an automobile, the salvage value is the net return (profit) from selling the used automobile.

Investment. Purchase of a capital item. *E.g., expenses incurred by a student for improving her human capital.*

Salvage value. The value of a capital item at the end of the production process. *E.g., the value of laying hens when they are culled from egg production.*

Assuming the costs of investments are the same, the asset with the highest present value will yield the highest return over the duration of the investment. Denoting by PV_A, PV_B, and PV_C the present values of three possible investment options, a utility function may be represented as

$$U = \max(PV_A, PV_B, PV_C).$$

For example, if $PV_A = 10$, $PV_B = 15$, and $PV_C = 12$, then utility will be maximized with investment option B.

Example 19.7 Net present value (NPV) criterion for a two-period model

Consider a firm having two investment options, A and B. The fixed cost for investment A is \$100 and that for B is \$150. Investment A yields net benefits of \$50 in the current period and \$75 in the future period, and investment B yields \$10 in the current period and \$170 in the future period. Assuming that the rate of return is zero (there is no discounting of future returns), the costs and benefits are directly summed:

$$NPV_A = -100 + 50 + 75 = \$25,$$

$$NPV_B = -150 + 10 + 170 = \$30.$$

With a zero rate of return, investment B yields a higher net present value, indicating that it is the preferred option.

Considering instead a positive rate of return of 10 percent,

$$NPV_A = -100 + 50 + 75/(1.1) = \$18.18,$$

$$NPV_B = -150 + 10 + 170/(1.1) = \$14.54.$$

Now investment A is the preferred option. The relatively large return in the future period from investing in B is discounted to the point where investment B is no longer as attractive as A.

Application: Public disaster compensation funds

The September 11th Victim Compensation Fund and the Gulf Spill Compensation Fund are designed to provide an alternative to the risk, expense, and delay inherent in civil litigation by offering victims an opportunity to receive inexpensive and predictable resolution of claims. This compensation fund mechanism is designed to avoid cases such as the resolution of asbestos claims that resulted in the longest tort litigation in US history. The issue is that common law adjudication, an individual case-by-case mechanism of problem solving, is ill-suited for addressing a public disaster that involves billions of dollars. Such individual adjudication is inefficient, inconsistent, and fails to deter agent misconduct. The compensation funds are designed to compensate any individual or the personal representative of a deceased individual who suffered a loss as a result of the public disaster. In general, monetary awards are offset (reduced) by any life insurance and other collateral source compensation, including pensions. Present-value analysis is used for evaluating the future payments from these collateral-source offsets. This allows for the appropriate discounting of the amount actually deducted from a victim's award.

Specifically in terms of the September 11th Compensation Fund, the Department of Justice used three blended after-tax discount rates to compute the present value of the award and then adjusted this discount rate to reflect current yields on mid- to long-term US Treasury securities. The actual compensation that a victim received was the economic loss (based on discounted lost earnings) plus noneconomic losses (pain, emotional suffering, loss of enjoyment of life, and mental anguish) minus the discounted collateral-source compensation. The noneconomic losses were \$250,000 plus an additional \$50,000 for the spouse and each dependent of the deceased victim.

Victims will compare the present value of a compensation fund award with the expected present value of an award from taking civil litigation instead. Risk-neutral victims would select whichever alternative yielded the highest expected value; risk-averse victims would only select the expected present value from a civil litigation if it were higher than the fund's award by some risk premium.

Infinite horizon

> *What some call health, if purchased by perpetual anxiety about diet, isn't much better than tedious disease.*
>
> (Alexander Pope)

> *Translation: Heaven and Hell are both perpetuities, but one has a positive and the other has a negative present value.*

A special case of evaluating the present value of an asset is where the time periods approach infinity, $T \to \infty$. When the returns are the same in each time period, an investment with an infinite horizon is called a perpetuity (or a *consol*). Specifically, for constant returns of TR per period, then the present value is

$$\mathrm{PV} = \frac{\mathrm{TR}}{1+r} + \frac{\mathrm{TR}}{(1+r)^2} + \ldots,$$

where the returns start in the second period. We can simplify this perpetuity by first factoring out $1/(1+r)$:

$$\mathrm{PV} = \frac{1}{1+r}\left\{\mathrm{TR} + \left[\frac{\mathrm{TR}}{1+r} + \frac{\mathrm{TR}}{(1+r)^2} + \ldots\right]\right\}.$$

The terms in the square brackets represent PV:

$$\mathrm{PV} = \frac{1}{1+r}(\mathrm{TR} + \mathrm{PV}),$$

$$\frac{\mathrm{TR} + \mathrm{PV}}{\mathrm{PV}} = 1+r.$$

Solving for PV yields

$$\mathrm{PV} = \frac{\mathrm{TR}}{r}.$$

Thus, we determine the present value of a perpetuity yielding TR per period by dividing the yield TR by the rate of return r. Present value is the amount required at rate of return r to receive a return per period, TR, forever. For example, given $r = 5$ percent, receiving \$100 per period forever is worth $100/0.05 = \$2000$ today. That is, \$2000 would return \$100 annually at a 5 percent rate of return forever. An increase in the rate of return will lower the present value of the perpetuity. For example, if the rate of return increased from 5 percent to 10 percent, receiving \$100 forever would be worth $100/0.1 = \$1000$ today. Thus, with a 10 percent rate of return, only \$1000 is required to receive \$100 forever.

The perpetuity is used as an approximation to the present value of a stream of returns over a finite number of years (called an *annuity*). For example, consider a finite, 30-year time interval. At a 10 percent rate of return, the present value of the perpetuity is, as calculated above, \$1000. In contrast, the present value of the annuity for 30 years is

$$\mathrm{PV} = 100/(1.1) + 100/(1.1)^2 + 100/(1.1)^3 + \ldots + 100/(1.1)^{30} = \$942.69.$$

Using the perpetuity formula as an approximation results in only a $(1000/942.69) - 100$ percent $= 6$ percent overestimate of the present value of the annuity.

Calculating the PV for 30 years is a little more difficult than calculating a perpetuity, but a financial calculator or a spreadsheet will do the task easily. Without these tools, the perpetuity formula gives an approximation for the finite stream of returns that is closer to the actual value when the rate of return and number of years are relatively large. For example, for a 30-year annuity with a 5 percent rate of return, the calculated PV is

$$PV = 100/(1.05) + 100/(1.05)^2 + 100/(1.05)^3 + \ldots + 100/(1.05)^{30} = \$1537.25.$$

The perpetuity value is \$2000, a (2000/1537.25) – 100 percent = 30 percent overestimation of the present value. For a finite stream of only 10 years with a 10 percent rate of return, the calculated PV is

$$PV = 100/(1.1) + 100/(1.1)^2 + 100/(1.1)^3 + \ldots + 100/(1.1)^{10} = \$614.46.$$

Here, the perpetuity value of \$1000 overestimates the present value of the annuity by (1000/614.46) – 100 percent = 63 percent.

Net present value (NPV)

> *If you can show a positive net present value to your banker, she may just give you that loan for that overpriced pickup truck.*
>
> (Michael Wetzstein)

A student says, "It would seem to me what you paid for it, less what you have depreciated it on your taxes, would equal its net present value, presuming you do not still owe on it. Am I close, or is the NPV what you can sell it for?" Neither. *Net present value* (NPV) is the value today of a future payment (present value of revenues minus present value of costs). Generally, investment costs also vary and may consist of an initial fixed cost, TFC, to acquire a capital input or durable commodity and then some variable costs incurred during each time period over the length of the investment. To illustrate, we let $STVC_j$ denote the level of variable cost in time period j. For example, for the cost of owning an automobile, there is the initial purchased cost and then variable costs of fuel and repairs in each time period over the life of the automobile. Subtracting these costs incurred in each time period from the benefits derived results in the net benefits per time period. Discounting these future net benefits to the present yields NPV:

$$NPV = -TFC + \frac{TR_2 - STVC_2}{1+r} + \frac{TR_3 - STVC_3}{(1+r)^2} + \ldots + \frac{TR_T - STVC_T}{(1+r)^{T-1}} + \frac{SV}{(1+r)^T},$$

where it is assumed that the flow of net benefits starts in the second time period. Assuming that this flow of future net benefits is known with certainty, the option with the highest NPV should be undertaken first. Further, assuming the investment options are independent, all options with NPV > 0 should be purchased. By assuming independence, we are assuming that undertaking any of the investment options does not change the NPV of the other remaining options. This **net present value criterion** for purchasing an asset when NPV > 0 is generally equivalent to the economic condition of equating marginal costs to marginal benefits.

Benefits from an investment are the change in overall returns, and costs are the associated change in cost. A net present value greater than zero then corresponds to marginal benefits exceeding marginal costs.

Net present value criterion. A condition for undertaking an investment if the net present value is positive and known with certainty. *E.g., if the net present value for a rental property is positive with certainty, purchase the property.*

Application: Avoiding real estate bubbles

A real estate bubble is an economic price bubble that occurs periodically in markets. It results when prices rapidly increase until they reach unsustainable levels relative to incomes. This is then followed by a drastic decline in prices.

In terms of the 2007 US real estate bubble, the Federal Reserve Chairman Alan Greenspan in 2005 stated that "at a minimum, there's little 'froth'." He added, "It's hard not to see that there are a lot of local bubbles." When prices continued to rise, he indicated that bubbles usually could not be detected unit after they popped. From 2006 to 2011, home prices in Merced, California fell 70 percent. With proper evaluation of real estate, we personally can avoid these bubbles.

A perpetuity is often used in real estate to determine the value of a property. The annual net income or the net cash flow of a property is determined and then the market value of the property is determined by the interest rate (called the cap rate). This assumes that the current income from the property continues in perpetuity and increases with inflation. It also assumes that when the property is sold, the new owners will apply the same perpetuity valuation approach. Investing with this perpetuity approach in determining market value will aid in not becoming a victim of a bubble. However, the key is correctly predicting the net cash flow into perpetuity.

In terms of purchasing a home, there is generally no net cash flow, but the general rule- of-thumb is not to exceed 25 percent of your net (take-home) income. With this 25 percent of income as the net cash flow, we can use a perpetuity to determine the price to pay for a home and we can ride out housing market bubbles.

Summary

1. Determining the optimal level of capital inputs requires calculating the value of future returns associated with the capital input.
2. An impatient agent prefers current consumption to postponing consumption into the future. A patient agent is willing to postpone some current consumption for less of it in the future.

3. The Polonius point is where an agent is neither a borrower nor a lender but is consuming all of the income endowed within a time period during the time period.
4. The equilibrium levels of current and future consumption occur where the marginal rate of time preference is set equal to the time rate of substituting future consumption for current consumption.
5. With no financial markets, consumers' optimal levels of consumption and investment in human capital are determined by the tangency between the indifference curve and the human-capital production function.
6. The ability to borrow and lend money separates the level of human-capital investment from the decision of optimal consumption across time periods. Such a separation is an application of the Separation Theorem.
7. The intersection of the supply and demand curves for future consumption will determine the equilibrium interest rate.
8. The observed market interest rate is called the nominal interest rate and is determined by both the real interest rate and the expected rate of inflation. This real interest rate (rate of return) is the rate of interest adjusted for the rate of inflation.
9. Discounting allows for comparing future costs and returns with current costs and returns.
10. An agent would prefer an income stream with a higher present value.
11. The present value of a perpetuity yielding a return per time period is determined by dividing this return by the rate of return.
12. The net present value of an investment option is the discounted benefits and costs of the option. If the future net benefits are known with certainty, then the option with the highest NPV should be undertaken first and all independent options with NPV > 0 should be undertaken.
13. *(Appendix)* The discounted present value of future income is the value of this future income if it is instead received in the current period.
14. *(Appendix)* A lender is always a lender for any increase in interest rates. A borrower is always a borrower for any decrease in interest rates.
15. *(Appendix)* The no-arbitrage condition is the application of the Law of One Price to investment decisions. Identical assets must yield the same rate of return.
16. *(Appendix)* With uncertainty, sunk cost, and postponement, a hurdle rate triggers an investment decision. This hurdle rate may require that the present value of benefits exceed the costs by two or three times before an asset will be purchased.
17. *(Appendix)* The option of making an investment decision has some value (option value), which is lost once the decision to invest is undertaken. Considering this option value results in a positive hurdle rate, so ENPV must be greater than the option value before investment should occur.
18. *(Appendix)* For utility-based investments, the rate of return is composed of the utility rate of return plus the appreciation rate of return.

Key concepts

appreciation, 845
call option, 842
consol, 825
discount rate, 819
durable input (commodity), 793
human capital, 793
human-capital production function, 806
hurdle rate, 842
hyperbolic discounting, 845
impatient, 797
interest rate, 798
intertemporal choice, 795
investment, 822
liquidity, 841
marginal rate of time preference, 797
net present value criterion, 826
nominal interest rate, 816
nondurable input (commodity), 793
option value, 843
patient, 797
present value (PV), 800
rate of return, 816
real option value, 843
real interest rate, 816
riskless arbitrage, 841
salvage value, 823
Separation Theorem, 810
sunk cost, 795

Key equations

$$x_2 = I_2 + (1+i)(I_1 - x_1)$$

Intertemporal budget constraint.

$$\text{MRS}(x_2 \text{ for } x_1) = \frac{\partial U/\partial x_1}{\partial U/\partial x_2} = 1 + i$$

The equilibrium levels of current and future consumption occur where the marginal rate of time preference is set equal to the time rate of substituting future consumption for current consumption.

$$\text{MRS}(x_2 \text{ for } x_1) = \text{MRPT}(x_2 \text{ for } x_1)$$

For the case of no financial markets, intertemporal utility is maximized where the marginal rate of time preference is equal to the marginal rate of product transformation.

$$\text{MRS}(x_2 \text{ for } x_1) = \text{MRPT}(x_2 \text{ for } x_1) = 1 + i$$

For the case with financial markets, intertemporal utility is maximized where the marginal rate of time preference and the marginal rate of product transformation are both set equal to the time rate of substituting future consumption for current consumption.

$$1 + r = \frac{1+i}{1+\alpha}$$

The additional consumption that a consumer will receive in the future if the consumer reduces its current consumption by a marginal unit is equal to the additional future income the consumer would receive for this marginal reduction in current consumption divided by the future price level.

$$\mathrm{PV} = \mathrm{TR}/r$$

The present value of a perpetuity yielding TR per period is determined by dividing this return by the rate of return.

$$\frac{\partial x_1}{\partial i} = \left.\frac{\partial x_1}{\partial i}\right|_{dU=0} + (I_1 - x_1)\frac{\partial x_1}{\partial I}$$

Adjusted Slutsky equation for a change in the interest rate.

$$r = \frac{U + \mathrm{TR}}{p}$$

For utility-based investments, the rate of return is equal to the monetary value of utility from owning the capital commodity plus the amount of appreciation divided by the purchase price.

Questions

Oh, the difference between nearly right and exactly right.

(H. Jackson Brown)

1. Your boss tells you in a very perturbed tone, "I don't care what you learned in economics. If you don't include all our sunk costs in your analysis, I'll fire you." Are sunk costs now relevant in your decision making? Explain.
2. Labor is generally measured in labor hours and capital in terms of dollars. Why the difference?
3. A consumer with neutral time preferences views no difference among the same commodities available at different times. True or false? Explain.
4. Can you explain why most students enter college immediately after graduating from high school?
5. Under what conditions could a rational individual be simultaneously an investor and a borrower?
6. In developing countries, food is both an investment good and a consumption good. Why?
7. Discuss the three prices of capital: rental rate, rate of return, and interest rate.
8. Why can large corporations borrow money at a lower interest rate than households?
9. How can furniture stores advertise no payments on any furniture purchases for 18 months? This deal seems too good to pass up. Is it?
10. How can automobile companies offer automobile loans at below the market interest rate?

Exercises

One finds life through conquering the fear of death within one's mind. Make a go-for-broke charge and conquer the exercises with one decisive slash.

(Togo Shigekata)

1. Assume

$$U(x_1, x_2) = x_1^{1/2} + x_2^{1/2}(1+i)^{-1}.$$

a. Demonstrate that this utility function exhibits impatient preferences.

b. Maximize this utility function subject to the wealth constraint

$$W = x_1 + x_2,$$

where $W = 10$ and $i = 10$ percent.

2. Given $I_1 = 8$, $I_2 = 10$, and $i = 5$ percent, graph the intertemporal budget constraint. How does a 25 percent tax placed on income in period 2 affect this budget constraint? Graph the result.

3. The husband states, "I will not sell it; I want to save it. It's not worth much now, but in 30 years it may be worth three times as much." What should his wife say? Explain.

4. A firm has two investment options. Option 1 will yield a net return of \$1000 in the first year followed by \$5000 in the second year and then \$10,000 in the third year. Option 2 will yield a constant \$5000 over the 3-year period.

a. At a 5 percent discount rate, which option should the firm undertake?

b. With a possible downturn in the economy likely, leading to uncertainty associated with these net returns, the firm has revised its discount rate upward to 15 percent. Now which option should the firm undertake?

5. To sell your home, you are willing to make a loan to the buyer. The buyer agrees to pay you only the interest due on the loan for the next 4 years, with a balloon payment in the 5th year representing the sale price of the house. If the selling price of the house is \$150,000, at a 6 percent interest rate, what would be the present value of this balloon payment?

6. A furniture store offers no payments on any furniture purchases for 18 months. By charging a monthly interest rate of 1 percent and being able to borrow money at a 0.5 percent monthly rate, over the 18 months, how much would a store make in interest on a \$2000 purchase?

7. Assuming a 10 percent interest rate and no taxation effects, what is the optimal option in the following cases?

a. A \$1500 rebate at purchase, or 5 percent financing for 1 year on a \$30,000 SUV.

b. Taking a one-time cash payment of \$250 million in a lottery, or \$30 million annually for the next 50 years.
c. Going to graduate school for 4 years at an income of \$10,000 and after graduating earning \$60,000 per year for 6 years and then \$100,000 per year for the next 30 years, or no graduate school and earning \$30,000 per year for 5 years and then \$75,000 for the next 35 years.

8. You are deciding whether to buy or lease a \$30,000 automobile. A 3-year lease will cost you \$6000 per year. If you instead purchased the automobile, the automobile will be worth \$20,000 at the end of 3 years. Assume your discount rate is 10 percent.

   a. Should you buy or lease the automobile?
   b. Suppose that if you lease, at the end of the 3-year lease you will again lease another automobile for 3 years at \$6000 per year. Instead, if you purchase the automobile, you will drive it for 6 years and then sell it for \$10,000. Now should you buy or lease?
   c. Based on these results, develop some general rule for when you should lease versus purchase automobiles.

9. Erick's goal is to retire after working 40 years with a retirement income equaling 60 percent of his last year's salary. His starting salary is \$30,000, with an annual pay increase of 4 percent.

   a. If he can earn a 10 percent return on any savings, what percent of his annual salary should he save for achieving this goal?
   b. How does this percentage change if he only earns a 5 percent return on savings?

10. Assuming a rate of return r, what is the present value of a perpetuity yielding TR per period? What is the present value of this perpetuity if it does not start until T periods from now? Based on these answers, develop an equation for the present value of an annuity paying TR per year for T periods.

Internet case study

1. Provide a list of other examples of the Separation Theorem.

APPENDIX TO CHAPTER 19

Comparative statics: interest rate change

The Federal Reserve Board Regulation DD: Truth in Saving Section 230.5 states that a consumer (lender) must receive advanced notice from the depository institution (borrower) of any interest rate change. Changing the interest rate will tilt the budget constraint (illustrated in Figures 19A.1 and 19A.2) and result in a new equilibrium bundle of current and future

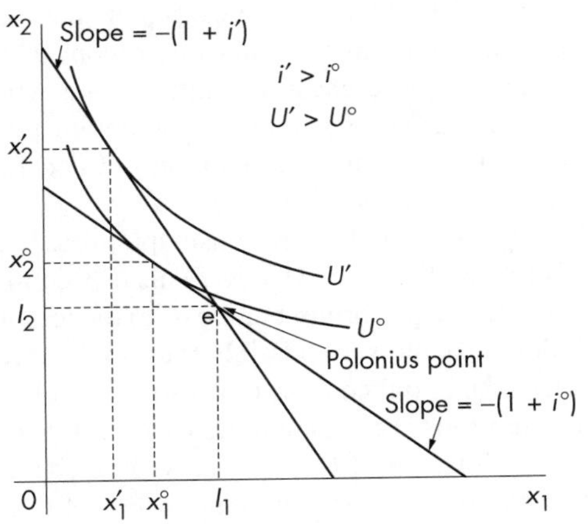

Figure 19A.1 **Interest rate increase with lender decreasing current consumption.** An interest rate increase from i^{o} to i' results in current consumption declining from x_1^{o} to x_1' and future consumption increasing from x_2^{o} to x_2'.

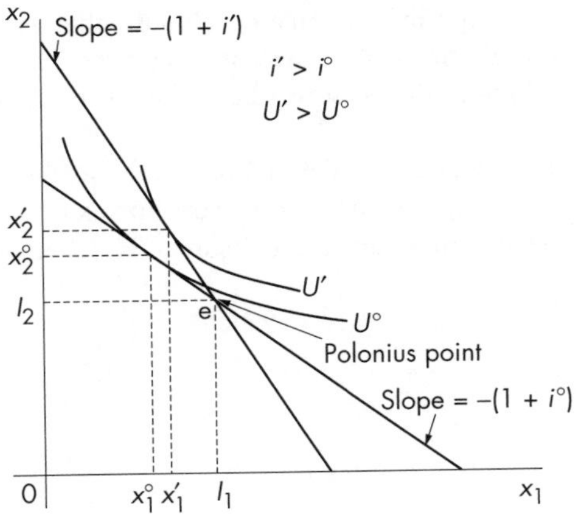

Figure 19A.2 **Interest rate increase with lender increasing both current and future consumption.** An increase in the interest rate from i^{o} to i' results in current consumption increasing from x_1^{o} to x_1' and future consumption also increasing from x_2^{o} to x_2'.

consumption. This tilt rotates around the Polonius point, because, whatever the interest rate, the consumer can follow Polonius and neither borrow nor lend. Figure 19A.1 illustrates this tilt for an increase in the interest rate from i^{o} to i'. Recall that the slope of the budget constraint is $-(1+i)$. As the interest rate increases, the slope of the budget constraint is then larger in absolute value, so the budget constraint becomes steeper. As a result of this increase in the interest rate, an increase in savings by reducing current consumption will yield a higher level of future consumption.

The change in the interest rate results in a new equilibrium mix of current and future consumption. For example, as indicated in Figures 19A.1, if the interest rate increases and the consumer is a lender, the level of current consumption falls and future consumption increases. Alternatively, depending on the consumer's preferences, this interest rate increase for a lender can result in current consumption increasing and future consumption falling, remaining unchanged or also increasing. Figure 19A.2 illustrates both current and future consumption increasing for a lender facing an increase in the interest rate.

For all these possible new equilibrium mixes of current and future consumption associated with a lender's increase in the interest rate, a lender will remain a lender. This is because the Weak Revealed Preference Axiom requires a lender's equilibrium bundle be to the left of the Polonius point. Bundles to the right of the Polonius point were possible prior to the interest rate increase and were not chosen by the lender. The initial equilibrium is still possible after the interest rate increase, so the new equilibrium must be a bundle that was not possible prior to the rate change. As indicated in Figures 19A.1 and 19A.2, the only area where this can occur is to the left of the Polonius point, resulting in the lender being better off from an interest rate increase.

Just as a lender is always a lender for an interest rate increase, a borrower is always a borrower for an interest rate decline. Again, this is because the Weak Revealed Preference Axiom requires a borrower's equilibrium bundle be to the right of the Polonius point. A decline in the interest rate cannot result in a new equilibrium that existed prior to the interest rate decrease and was not chosen by the borrower. The initial equilibrium is still possible after the interest rate decline, so the new equilibrium must be a bundle that was not possible prior to the rate change. As indicated in Figure 19A.3, the only area where this can occur is to the right of the Polonius point, resulting in the borrower being better off from an interest rate decrease.

Similar to the lender equilibrium mix, this change in the interest rate results in a new equilibrium mix of current and future consumption for a borrower. For example, as indicated in Figure 19A.3, if the interest rate declines and the consumer is a borrower,

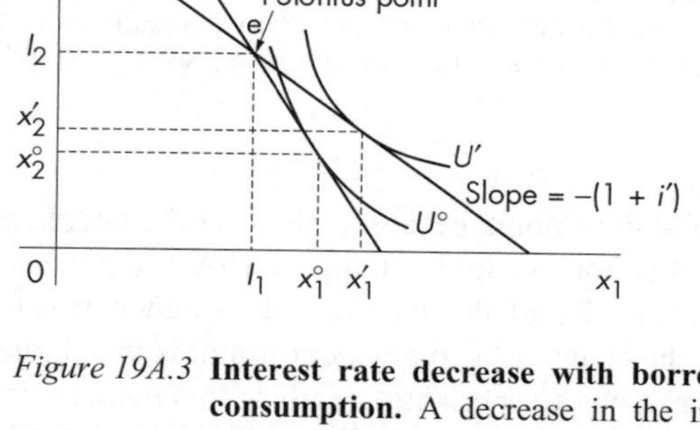

Figure 19A.3 **Interest rate decrease with borrower increasing both current and future consumption.** A decrease in the interest rate from i^{o} to i' results in current consumption increasing from x_1^{o} to x_1' as well as future consumption increasing from x_2^{o} to x_2'.

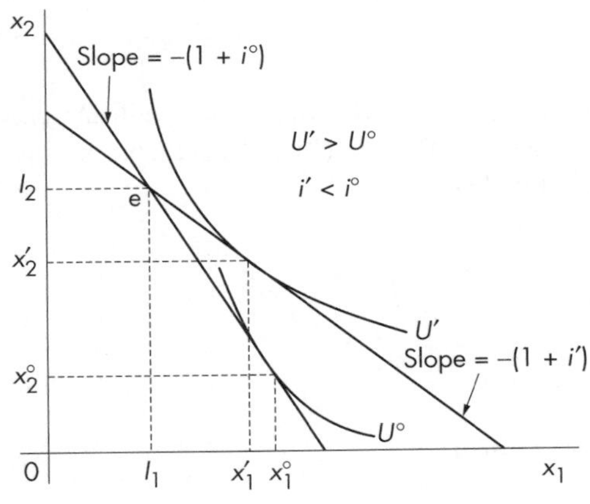

Figure 19A.4 **Interest rate decrease with borrower decreasing current consumption and increasing future consumption.** A decrease in the interest rate from i^{o} to i' results in current consumption decreasing from x_1^{o} to x_1' and future consumption increasing from x_2^{o} to x_2'.

the level of both current and future consumption increases. Alternatively, depending on the consumer's preferences, this interest-rate decrease for a borrower can result instead in current consumption increasing and future consumption falling, remaining unchanged, or also increasing. An example of current consumption falling with future consumption increasing for a borrower facing a decrease in the interest rate is illustrated in Figure 19A.4.

Adjusted Slutsky equation

The effect of a change in the interest rate on the equilibrium mix of current and future consumption (for both borrowers and lenders) can be decomposed using the adjusted Slutsky equation. This decomposition, into income and substitution effects, is the same as a change in wages discussed in Chapter 4. In this case, the adjusted Slutsky equation considers an additional income effect when the interest rate is changed. For example, a rise in the interest rate for a lender will result in potentially a higher level of income in the future. An adjustment to the income component of the Slutsky equation is then required to account for this change in potential income when the interest rate changes.

Considering the effect of a change in the interest rate on current consumption of x_1, the adjustment is

$$\frac{\partial x_1}{\partial I}\frac{\partial I}{\partial i},$$

where I is the total potential future value of income,

$$I = (1 + i)I_1 + I_2.$$

This is the change in current consumption when income changes, $\partial x_1/\partial I$, times the change in potential income with an interest rate change, $\partial I/\partial i$. Taking the derivative of I with respect to i yields the change in potential income with a rate change:

$$\partial I/\partial i = I_1.$$

For example, if the interest rate increases by 1 percent, potential income will increase by I_1(1 percent). Thus, the adjustment to the income effect is $(\partial x_1/\partial I)I_1$. Incorporating this adjustment into the standard Slutsky equation yields

$$\frac{\partial x_1}{\partial i} = \left.\frac{\partial x_1}{\partial i}\right|_{dU=0} - \frac{\partial x_1}{\partial I}x_1 + \frac{\partial x_1}{\partial I}I_1$$

$$= \left.\frac{\partial x_1}{\partial i}\right|_{dU=0} + (I_1 - x_1)\frac{\partial x_1}{\partial I}$$

total effect = substitution effect + income effect.

As discussed in Chapter 4, the substitution effect is always negative. In this intertemporal case, as the interest rate increases (holding utility constant), current consumption x_1 declines. As illustrated in Figure 19A.5, the substitution effect is negative for an increase in the interest rate from i^o to i'. Holding utility constant at U^o, an increase in the interest rate results in an upward movement along the indifference curve, from bundle A to bundle B. As a result of the rate increase, the consumer decreases current consumption x_1 from x_1^o to x_1'. Thus, the substitution effect is negative, $(\partial x_1/\partial i)|_{dU=0} < 0$.

We can investigate the sign of the income effect by assuming that current consumption is a normal good, so $\partial x_1/\partial I > 0$. An increase in income results in current consumption increasing. The sign of the income effect will now depend on whether the consumer is a lender $(I_1 - x_1 > 0)$ or borrower $(I_1 - x_1 < 0)$. As indicated in Figure 19A.6, the income effect will be negative and reinforce the negative substitution effect if the consumer is a borrower. Specifically, the initial equilibrium is at point A associated with interest rate i^o. An increase in the interest rate from i^o to i' results in point C as the new equilibrium point. An increase

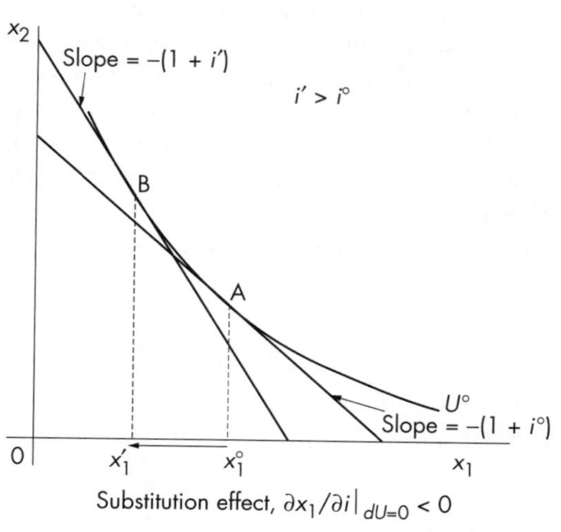

Figure 19A.5 **Negative substitution effect.** An increase in the interest rate holding utility constant will result in a decline in current consumption from x_1^o to x_1'.

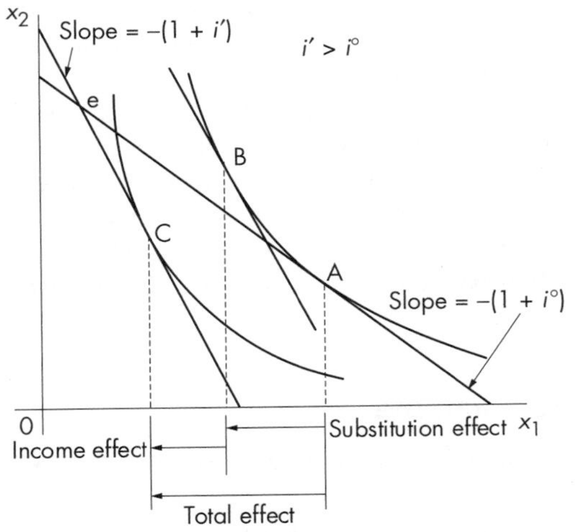

Figure 19A.6 **Adjusted Slutsky equation for a borrower facing an increase in the interest rate.** For a borrower with current consumption as a normal good, an increase in the interest rate will always lower current consumption.

in the interest rate reduces current consumption. This total effect of a movement from A to C may be decomposed into the substitution and income effects. Holding utility constant, the substitution effect is illustrated by a movement from A to B, a decline in current consumption. This decline in current consumption is reinforced by the income effect, a movement from B to C. As illustrated in the figure for a borrower with current consumption a normal good, an increase in the interest rate will always result in lower current consumption (Table 19A.1).

Will a borrower always decrease current consumption given a rise in interest rates? Yes, given current consumption is a normal good.

In contrast, the income effect with an increase in interest rate for a lender will be positive and will dampen or offset the negative substitution effect. The lender's total effect will result in either a decrease in current consumption when the income effect does not totally offset the

Table 19A.1 Summary of effects of interest-rate changes on borrowers and lenders

Agent	*Change in interest rate*	*Results*	
Lender	Increase	Always a lender	
Borrower	Decrease	Always a borrower	
Assume that current consumption is a normal good, $\partial x_1/\partial I > 0$			
Borrower	Increase	Negative income effect reinforces the substitution effect	Current consumption decreases
	Decrease	Negative income effect reinforces the substitution effect	Current consumption increases
Lender	Increase/decrease	Positive income effect dampens or offsets the substitution effect	Current consumption result is ambiguous

negative substitution effect or an increase in current consumption when the income effect is greater than the absolute value of the substitution effect. This increase in lender's current consumption may result because the lender is receiving so much more income in the future that his preferences are to increase current consumption.

This same reasoning for an increase in the interest rate also applies to a decrease in the interest rate. Retaining the assumption of a normal good for x_1, a borrower will always increase consumption for a decline in interest rate. In contrast, for a lender, the total effect is ambiguous. Current consumption may increase, decline, or remain unchanged for a lender. For example, the lender may have some target level of future income, possibly required for retirement. A decline in the interest rate will then require increased savings and thus decrease current consumption to meet this target.

Application: Taxation on interest income

As an application of the adjusted Slutsky equation, consider taxation on interest income. Politicians have debated for decades the effect that a reduction in the tax rate on interest income would have on savings. Some claim that such a reduction would provide a strong incentive toward increased savings, while others contend that it would have little or no impact on savings. We can investigate the effect of removing the tax on interest income by using the adjusted Slutsky equation. Consider first the intertemporal budget constraint given a tax on interest income at a rate t:

$$x_2 = I_2 + [1 + (1 - t)\, i](I_1 - x_1),$$

where the amount of tax collected is $ti(I_1 - x_1)$. The slope of the budget constraint is now $-[1 + (1 - t)i]$ instead of $-(1 + i)$. Prior to the tax, a marginal decrease in current consumption increased future consumption by $1 + i$. Now, with the tax, future consumption only increases by $[1 + (1 - t)i]$. Some of the interest income $i(I_1 - x_1)$ earned for future consumption is now reallocated to satisfy the tax obligation. Instead of the full interest income $i(I_1 - x_1)$ being available for future consumption, only $(1 - t)i(I_1 - x_1)$ is available. For example, if the tax rate is 25 percent on interest income, then $t = 25$ percent and only 75 percent of the interest income is available for future consumption. We illustrate intertemporal budget constraints considering both a tax and no tax on interest income in Figure 19A.7. Both constraints pass through the endowment point e and are the same to the right of the endowment where the consumer would be a borrower. Only when a consumer is a lender who incurs interest income would the constraints with and without the tax diverge. As a result of the tax, the budget constraint is kinked and tilts downward from the endowment. This further restricts the choices of current and future consumption available to the consumer. Reducing the tax on interest income will tilt the budget constraint associated with the tax upward toward the zero-tax constraint. This will expand the consumption choices available to the consumer. However, if the consumer is a borrower who incurs no interest income, this expanded choice has no effect on the optimal allocation of consumption. The tangency between the intertemporal budget constraint and the indifference curve occurs to the right of the endowment point e for a borrower and is unaffected by the tax decrease. In contrast, a lender's optimal choice is affected. For a lender, the change in the optimal level of current and future consumption and the corresponding savings in current income depend on the

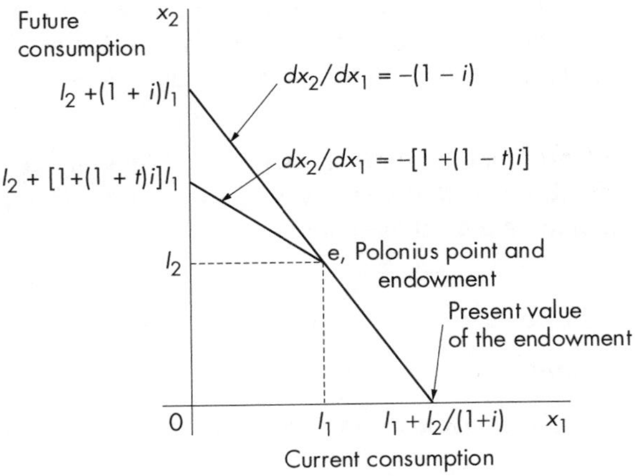

Figure 19A.7 **Intertemporal budget constraint with a tax on interest income.** A tax on interest income results in the budget constraint having a kink at the endowment point e. This tax further restricts the choices of current and future consumption.

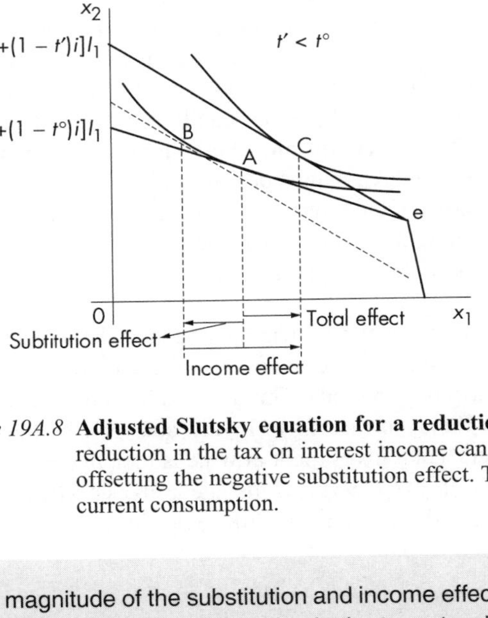

Figure 19A.8 **Adjusted Slutsky equation for a reduction in the interest income tax rate.** A reduction in the tax on interest income can result in the income effect completely offsetting the negative substitution effect. This would then result in an increase in current consumption.

relative magnitude of the substitution and income effects. As illustrated in Figure 19A.8, the substitution effect from a decline in the tax rate will decrease current consumption and thus stimulate increased savings. However, the income effect can mitigate this savings stimulus and may actually, as illustrated in the figure, completely offset the substitution effect. In this case, savings could actually decline. Thus, it is not possible to make a definitive statement concerning how a reduction in a tax on interest income would affect savings. Economists are mixed in their views of whether savings will increase as a result of a decline in the tax on interest income. Empirical estimates do indicate that the tax rate will affect a household's portfolio of savings. Holdings of heavily taxed assets, such as interest-bearing accounts, decline as a share of savings with an increase in the tax rate.

Will a tax-rate reduction on interest income increase savings? Theoretically, a reduction in the tax on interest income will increase savings only if the income effect does not completely offset the substitution effect.

Rate of return: telemarketing fraud

Believing in the no-arbitrage condition, I invested my life savings with the nice man who just rang my doorbell.

(Michael Wetzstein)

Translation: Markets will result in the same equilibrium rate of return for all investments.

If there was no uncertainty in future net benefits, the estimated annual \$40 billion in telemarketing fraud, estimated by the American Association of Retired People (AARP), would not exist. Such marketing would result in the same rate of return as US Treasury bonds. The criterion for choosing alternative investments based on net present value assumes that the rates of return for these investments are the same. Assuming no uncertainty in future net benefits, the financial market will result in the same equilibrium rate of return for all investments. This is called the **no-arbitrage condition**, where there are no opportunities of purchasing one asset by selling another and realizing a positive gain in returns. No arbitrage is the application to investment decisions of the Law of One Price, discussed in Chapter 9. If two investments are identical except that one has a higher rate of return than the other, then no consumer will be willing to purchase the low-yielding asset. Thus, all assets must yield the same rate of return.

Consider the choice of investing in a rare bottle of wine or a security bond. The rare bottle of wine has a current period price p_1 and a future price p_2, and there are no other returns (including dividends) between the two time periods. The bond yields a rate of return r over the two time periods. Suppose that the agent has \$1 to invest, and let x be the number of bottles of wine that can be purchased. Total investment in wine is then $p_1x = 1$ or $x = 1/p_1$. In the future time period, wine is worth $p_2x = p_2/p_1$. If the agent invests \$1 in a bond, then it will be worth $1 + r$ in the future period. In equilibrium, the \$1 of investment will have the same rate of return for both assets, so

$$p_2/p_1 = 1 + r.$$

If conditions result in the rates of return deviating from this equality, then arbitrage will take place and restore the equilibrium. For example, if

$$p_2/p_1 < 1 + r,$$

then agents holding wine in the current period will sell and purchase bonds. Selling one bottle of wine in the current period and investing in bonds yields $p_1(1 + r)$ returns in the future period, compared with only p_2 returns from instead keeping the bottle. Note that, given the above inequality, $p_1(1+r) > p_2$. The agent can then in the future repurchase the bottle of wine and have some remaining additional revenue. This is known as *riskless arbitrage*, where a guaranteed gain exists by selling one asset and buying another. Given that agents are willing to engage in riskless arbitrage, financial markets will tend toward a no-arbitrage equilibrium.

The equilibrium is restored by tâtonnement in the normal demand and supply market framework. In the above example, agents will attempt to sell wine and purchase bonds. This will result in an increase in both the supply of wine and the demand for bonds. This increase in supply of wine will depress its current price p_1 and increase the price of bonds by r falling until equilibrium is restored:

$$p_2/p_1 = 1+r.$$

We can establish the relationship between this equilibrium and present value by multiplying the equality by p_1 and dividing by $1+r$:

$$p_1 = p_2/(1+r).$$

Thus, the current price of an asset is its present value.

As with any commodity, the Law of One Price does not hold when alternative assets possess varying characteristics. For example, the rate of return will not necessarily be the same if the selling costs (cost of liquidating an asset) differ among alternative assets,[5] which they tend to do. The degree of selling expenses is measured by the *liquidity* of the asset. An asset is very liquid if the selling costs are minimal. Alternatively, an asset with relatively large selling costs has a low level of liquidity. An example of a highly liquid asset is money in a checking account, where the only cost of selling the asset involves using your debit card. In contrast, investments in real estate have a very low level of liquidity; the cost of liquidating real estate is relatively high. The rate of return may then vary when taking into account the liquidity of an asset. In general, the lower the level of liquidity, the higher the rate of return. Higher returns must offset the higher cost of liquidating the asset.

Uncertainty in the net benefits from alternative investment decisions can also affect the rate of return. In general, the greater the risk of an investment, the higher the rate of return that is required to attract buyers. We outlined investment decision rules under risk in Chapter 18 and now extend those rules.

Uncertain investment decisions: the value of waiting

> *Never do today what you can put off till tomorrow. Delay may give a clearer light as to what is best to be done.*
>
> (Aaron Burr)

When deciding when to purchase a certain make and model of automobile, it may be worthwhile to delay the purchase until the uncertainty concerning its reliability is revealed. Generally, investment decisions are characterized by uncertainty. The actual benefits and costs from a decision are not known with certainty, and forecasting ability is generally limited beyond one or two periods into the future. For example, the destruction of tropical rain forests for current increased agricultural production has associated uncertain environmental costs, including global warming and decreased biodiversity. Given uncertain net present values, the expected value of the net present value, ENPV, can be used. The criterion is then to purchase all options where ENPV > 0. However, as discussed in Chapter 18, this criterion does not consider the uncertainty of investment options. A particular investment option may result in ENPV > 0, but with a relatively large variance. If an agent is then risk-averse, alternative risk-averse criteria may be employed.

Irreversible investments

Once the toothpaste is out of the tube, it is hard to get it back in.

(H.R. Haldeman)

You will know when global warming has occurred when Las Vegas hotels advertise ocean views. On a planetary scale, investments resulting in CO_2 emissions and new land cultivations have the sunk costs of global warming and deforestation. Such investments, like extracting toothpaste, are not easily reversible once undertaken. With uncertainty, concern for the ability to reverse an investment decision may exist. After purchasing an asset, it is possible, given uncertainty, that net present value is less than zero. In such a case, it would be optimal to reverse the investment by selling the asset. Such a reversal is possible when there are no sunk costs associated with the investment. (Recall that sunk costs cannot be recovered.) However, some sunk costs generally exist with the purchase of any asset.

Due to sunk costs, asset purchases are partially or completely irreversible. Once the decision is made to purchase, it is costly to reverse. Thus, the criterion to purchase all options where ENPV > 0 may not be correct given the characteristic of irreversibility. The uncertainty of future net present value may result in a negative net present value, and assets with high sunk costs cannot be sold without the investment suffering some loss. Thus, in the case of relatively high sunk costs, expected net present value may have to be substantially higher than zero before an asset is purchased. This wedge between ENPV $= 0$ and the positive ENPV that will trigger a purchase is called the *hurdle rate*, which is the ratio of expected net discounted benefits to costs. For many firms, this hurdle rate is where the present value of benefits is two to three times cost before the firm will purchase an asset. The discount rate used for calculating net present value varies, but is typically around 7–8 percent. A rule-of-thumb that some companies use in investment decisions is to undertake an investment only if it results in a \$1 back each year for every \$2 spent initially. Approximating this return into perpetuity at an 8 percent discount rate, the present value of the returns is $1/0.08 = 12.5$. This results in a hurdle rate of $12.5/2 = 625$ percent. The expected net present value of benefits has to be over six times the initial cost.

The uncertainty characteristic of investments may affect not only the choice of assets but also the timing of when to purchase. By postponing a purchase, new information that impacts purchase choice may become available. Generally, the decision is not whether to purchase an asset but when to do so. One problem with net present value analysis is that it assumes that an irreversible decision, such as an automobile purchase, is a now-or-never proposition. The analysis does not consider the decision to postpone an investment. However, the ability to delay is a very important element of most investment decisions. For example, should you cut the rain forest today or let it stand?

The opportunity to make an irreversible investment decision has some value. This investment option of making a decision is analogous to a financial call option. A *call option* gives an investor the right, but not an obligation, to buy an asset by a certain date for a certain price. The decision can be made at some future time. When an irreversible decision is made (exercised), the option is lost. The possibility of waiting for new information that may impact the decision is lost. Thus, this idea of keeping your options open has some value. For example, you may be willing to pay more for an audio receiver with five channels allowing for a home theater system. The five channels provide the option of possibly later purchasing compatible components for the theater system. This **option value** is an opportunity cost that should be included as part of the cost of investment. Including this option value results in a positive hurdle rate, with the following criterion for when to purchase an asset:

$$\text{ENPV} > \text{option value}.$$

Thus, the expected present value of benefits must not only exceed cost but also cover the value of retaining the option to invest. For example, the possibility that new information will reveal that a rain forest species can be used to cure AIDS may change a decision that may have made this species extinct (clearing the rain forest).

Does the ability to wait have value? Yes, there is an option value of waiting before taking some action.

Two-period models

When it is not necessary to make a decision, it is necessary not to make a decision.
(Lord Falkland)

We will investigate this *real option value* (the term *real* is added to distinguish it from financial options) in a two-period model.[6] Consider a firm determining whether it should mine gold. The investment in mining equipment is completely irreversible; once it is acquired and put into operation at the mine site, the cost of removing the equipment is prohibitive. Currently, the annual net benefit from mining is \$10, but next year it will change, with probability ρ it will rise to \$15 and with probability $1 - \rho$ it will fall to \$5. The net benefits will then remain at this new level. The decision is to either start mining now or wait until the next period to see if the resource price goes up or down. Assuming a 10 percent rate of return, an initial investment of \$100, and $\rho = 1/2$, the expected net present value of mining now, with an expected future net benefit of \$10, is

$$\text{ENPV} = -100 + \sum_{j=0}^{\infty} \frac{10}{(1.1)^j} = -100 + \frac{10}{1 - 1/1.1}$$
$$= -100 + 110 = 10.^7$$

The expected net present value is positive, so consider mining now. However, this analysis ignores the opportunity cost of mining now rather than waiting and keeping the option of not mining open until the next period price is revealed. By delaying mining one period, it will only be optimal to invest in mining if net benefits increase to \$15. This results in

$$\text{ENPV} = \frac{0.5}{1.1}\left(-100 + \sum_{j=0}^{\infty} \frac{15}{(1.1)^j}\right) = 29.54.$$

Expected net present value is higher when the decision is delayed, so it is optimal to wait. In the second period, if annual net benefits increase to \$15, then the firm should exercise the option and start mining. Instead, if the net benefits fall to \$5, then it should not exercise the option. The value of the option to wait is the difference between the two ENPVs (29.54 − 10), \$19.54. The firm would be willing to pay \$19.54 more for the opportunity to delay mining. Note that if the choice was to mine only in the first period or not at all, there would be no option value, and the ENPV = 10 indicates to start mining. Irreversibility and ability to delay mining result in a positive option value. Anticipated competitive entry into the market by other firms or mineral leases about to expire result in greater cost of delaying, and thus irreversibility will affect the investment decision to a lesser degree.

An alternative model is to consider uncertainty over the cost of an asset, for example, the cost of a nuclear power plant or the cost of developing alternative-fueled vehicles. Assume that the net benefit of the resource is constant at \$10, but the investment cost is uncertain. This investment cost may be uncertain because of input prices fluctuating over time or government regulation changing unpredictably. Uncertainty of this type has the same effect on the investment decision as uncertainty over the future value of net benefits. It creates an opportunity cost of investing now rather than waiting for new information.

As an example, suppose that investment costs are \$100 today but next year they will increase to \$150 or decrease to \$50, each with probability of ½. If the firm invests today, the ENPV will be

$$\text{ENPV} = -100 + 110 = \$10.$$

Alternatively, if the firm waits one period, then it will be optimal to invest only if investment costs fall to \$50:

$$\text{ENPV} = (0.5/1.1)(-50 + 110) = \$27.27.$$

Thus, waiting is preferable to investing now.

Utility-based investments: jewelry investments

Diamonds, an investment that lasts forever?

(Michael Wetzstein)

Assets generally yield returns in the form of both monetary returns and utility from owning the asset. For example, a farmer may receive increased revenue from purchasing a new tractor as the result of improved productivity. But he may also receive utility from owning a new tractor by showing it off to his neighbors. This increase in utility from purchasing an asset may be small and insignificant or quite significant. For example, a new vacuum cleaner may not yield a significant increase in utility compared with the increase in labor productivity. In contrast, a new house generally provides the household a significant amount of utility. In cases where the utility from purchasing an asset is significant, the value of this increased satisfaction along with monetary returns from owning the asset should be considered when evaluating its benefits and costs.

Is purchasing a diamond necessarily a rational investment? If you only consider the monetary returns, probably not. But if you also consider the utility from owning the diamond (and showing it off), it may then be a worthwhile investment.

As an example, consider the monetary returns and utility associated with purchasing a house. Monetary returns are in the form of increased value called *appreciation*. Generally, through time, a house will appreciate and the owner can sell it for more than the purchase price. Along with the house appreciating, the owner is receiving utility by living in the house. Putting a monetary value on this utility can be difficult and involves a number of assumptions. One method is to find a surrogate for this utility that has an associate monetary value. For example, renters' utility from renting a house can serve as a surrogate for home owners' utility. The rent that renters pay can then be used as the monetary value of the utility received from purchasing a house.

Let U denote the annual rent for a house and TR the amount of appreciation over 1 year of ownership (net of all expenses for maintenance and repairs). Total benefit from purchasing the house is then $U + \text{TR}$. The rate of return r for a year of ownership is then this total benefit divided by the purchase price p:

$$r = \frac{U + \text{TR}}{p}.$$

This total rate of return is composed of the utility rate of return U/p and the appreciation rate of return TR/p. In equilibrium, this rate of return will equal the rates of return on other assets. The appreciation rate of return will, however, be less than this equilibrium rate r. In terms of only the financial increase in an investment, TR/p, investing in assets that have no utility rate of return will yield a higher rate of return. Generally, the purchase of assets with a relatively high utility rate of return (e.g., artworks and jewelry) solely as a financial investment will not yield as high a return compared with other investments and thus would not be an optimal choice. Only if relatively high value is placed on the utility derived from owning the asset will they possibly be an optimal choice.

Intertemporal choice and behavioral economics

Intertemporal behavior can be inconsistent with rational behavior (time-consistent behavior) when households discount outcomes in the short run more than for outcomes in the long run (called **hyperbolic discounting**). Time-consistent behavior is when a household prefers one commodity bundle $\vec{x}_1$ over another $\vec{x}_2$ regardless of when on some time interval the preferences are determined. If $\vec{x}_1 \succ \vec{x}_2$ in year one, then, for time-consistent behavior, in say year four, the preference relation must still hold: $\vec{x}_1 \succ \vec{x}_2$. The preference ordering does not change. With hyperbolic discounting, the discounted returns fall very rapidly for small delay periods, but then fall slowly for longer delay periods. With hyperbolic discounting, a reversal in the preference ordering occurs. In year one, $\vec{x}_1 \succ \vec{x}_2$, but in year four, $\vec{x}_2 \succ \vec{x}_1$. As an example, consider a drug addict who prefers one fix today instead of two fixes tomorrow, but prefers two fixes one year plus one day to one fix one year from now. The drug addict is present-biased by discounting the short run more than the long run. It turns out that such hyperbolic discounting is not at all unusual and is even observed in animal behavior studies. It is able to explain revealed preferences that are inconsistent with assuming a constant discount rate. Discounting may actually be a preference that is influenced by a household's expectations, endowments, tastes, and prices. This leads to some economists questioning whether discounting actually describes what people do when they make intertemporal choices.

Example 19A.1 Hyperbolic discounting

Assume that a household is faced with the choice of receiving $50 now or $75 one year from now. At a 10 percent discount rate, the household will prefer waiting:

$$50 < \frac{75}{1+0.10} = 68.19,$$

$$\frac{68.19}{50} = 1.36 > 1.$$

This preference still holds if the choice is postponed for four years:

$$\frac{50}{(1+0.10)^4} < \frac{75}{(1+0.10)^5},$$

$$\frac{50}{(1+0.10)^4} < \frac{1}{(1+0.10)^4}\frac{75}{1+0.10},$$

$$34.15 < 46.57,$$

$$46.57/34.15 = 1.36 > 1.$$

The preference ordering remains unchanged, so the household displays time-consistent behavior.

In contrast, some households may prefer receiving $50 now over waiting for $75 a year from now, but their preferences reverse if the choice is postponed. Such hyperbolic behavior may be illustrated by assuming that a household still has a 10 percent discount rate for the future choice but now has a 60 percent discount rate for the near-term choice. This results in a near-term preference order reversal

$$50 > 75/(1+0.6) = 46.88,$$

$$46.88/50 = 0.94 < 1.$$

Questions

1. A higher interest rate will result in both a borrower increasing current consumption and a lender decreasing current consumption. True, false, or partly true and partly false?
2. After my dad's heart failure, my time preference for present over future consumption increased. Is this rational? Explain.
3. In some countries, a higher income tax rate is applied to unearned income compared with earned income. What is the effect on investment in human capital relative to physical capital?

Exercises

1. Illustrate the adjusted Slutsky equation for a lender, where an increase in the interest rate will increase the consumption of x_1.
2. Investment in a vineyard will not yield a positive return until the 5th year after establishment. The initial start-up cost is $2000 per acre, with an annual maintenance cost of $200 per acre during the first 4 years of establishment. In the 5th year, the grape harvest will yield an annual net return of $500 per acre for its remaining 20-year life.

   a. At a 10 percent discount rate, should this vineyard investment be undertaken?
   b. Unfortunately, blight is threatening the grape orchards, resulting in a 1 percent probability that in the first year your orchards would have to be destroyed. Should you start your vineyard now, or delay starting until next year when there is no longer a threat of blight?

Internet case studies

1. Discuss the no-arbitrage condition and riskless arbitrage in terms of commodity market calls and puts.
2. Make a list of articles that investigate the irreversibility of investments caused by environmental impacts.

Part IX

Missing markets

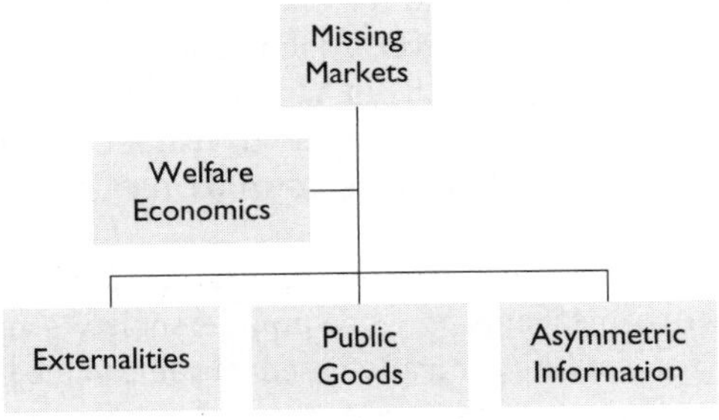

Chapters

Achieving a market for every commodity is like heading toward heaven. Everyone wants to go there, but not too soon.

(Michael Wetzstein)

Spaceships in *Star Trek: Deep Space Nine* routinely take shortcuts between far parts of the universe by traveling through wormholes. Theoretically possible, according to Einstein's General Theory of Relativity, a wormhole is a kind of space–time tunnel. Physicists, to no avail, have attempted to construct them mathematically without breaking any laws of physics. Economists have had far more success in theoretically constructing and then actually building economic wormholes between the economy and missing markets to improve social welfare. An economic wormhole is a market solution that addresses the allocation problem of a nonmarket commodity. An example is agents trading pollution permits in a market. The wormhole translates an environmental issue into economic terms.

Such wormholes would not be required if markets existed for all commodities that consumers demand. With no missing markets, freely operating markets not only would be Pareto-efficient but also would yield a socially optimal allocation of society's limited resources.[1] Unfortunately, markets do not exist for all commodities that consumers demand. For example, the government has to play the role of Robin Hood because no markets exist for achieving the social optimal distribution of income.

Markets are generally missing for externalities (Chapter 21), public goods (Chapter 22), and information (Chapter 23). As a result of these missing markets, signals in the form of market prices do not exist to reveal consumer preferences for society's allocation of resources. However, establishing markets where they do not exist to provide price signals generally results in harming some agents. These agents have adjusted their utility-maximizing allocations based on missing markets, so establishing a market may reduce their satisfaction. In other words, they may want to go to heaven, but not too soon.

This lack of price signals for revealing consumer preference has resulted in the design of alternative mechanisms to determine society's optimal allocation of resources. These mechanisms are generally based on some value judgment concerning society's preferences. The economic theory supporting these mechanism designs is termed *welfare economics*, and allocations based on these mechanism designs are called *constrained* or *second-best Pareto-optimal allocations*. Second-best mechanisms are generally solutions offered by a governmental agency, although households and firms may also offer second-best mechanisms. Unfortunately, government agencies are unable to obtain agents' private information, such as consumers' preferences, so their solutions for these market failures may or may not result in improving social welfare. As outlined in Chapter 20, if market failure occurs, where some of the assumptions of the welfare theorems do not hold, then a market equilibrium will not necessarily yield a Pareto-optimal allocation. It is then up to applied economists to find and develop mechanism designs, such as wormholes between the economy and missing markets, that improve social welfare.

In Chapter 20, we investigate the concepts of welfare economics by first constructing a social-welfare function based on the assumption that individual consumers' utility functions can be measured on a cardinal scale. We then state *Arrow's Impossibility Theorem,* which indicates the impossibility of deriving a social-welfare function, given consumers' ordinal preference ranking and based on some reasonable assumptions concerning social preference ranking. Because we cannot derive a social-welfare function without revealed knowledge of consumers' cardinal utility ranking, we investigate alternative mechanisms for making social choice. We then discuss the four general categories of market failure (monopoly power, externalities, public goods, and asymmetric information) in terms of constraining mechanisms designed for improving social welfare.

Each of the remaining chapters in Part 9 investigates one particular missing market. First, in Chapter 21, we address externalities and evaluate the inefficiencies associated with externalities and the mechanisms that have been designed for resolving these inefficiencies. The issues associated with providing public goods are the topics of Chapter 22. We first define public goods in relation to private goods and then address the *free-rider problem* associated with providing public goods. We then discuss the Pareto-efficient conditions for a public good and the second-best Pareto-optimal mechanism designs. In Chapter 23, we consider problems associated with markets possessing asymmetric information. We also discuss *adverse selection* and *moral hazard* associated with asymmetric information. We then develop a *principal-agent model* to illustrate possible market inefficiencies and mechanisms for correcting these inefficiencies.

20 Welfare economics

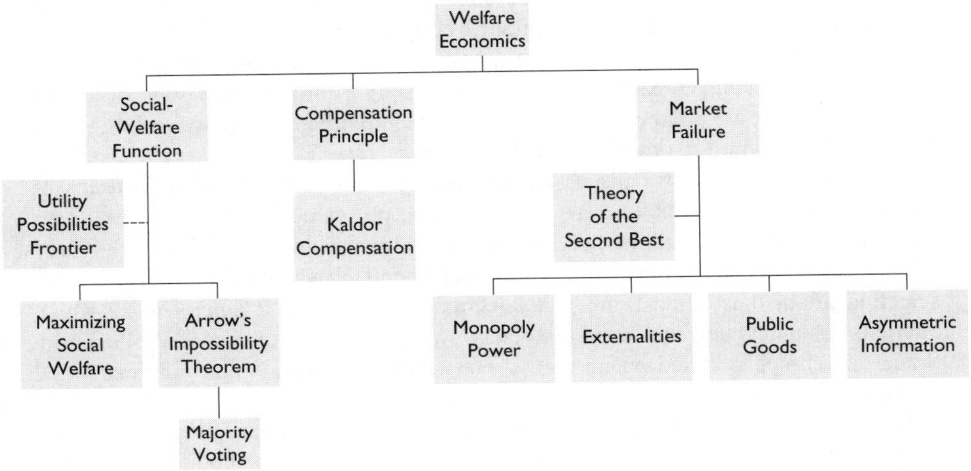

Outline and Conceptual Inquiries

A man [economist] who knows the price of everything and the value of nothing.
(Oscar Wilde)

On a June morning, an employee gives birth in a restroom at her workplace. Later that day, her fellow workers find her infant's body in a dumpster behind the business. At the same time, an infant born three months premature and weighing less than a pound is in an intensive care unit staying alive only with the finest state-of-the-art equipment. These are polar extremes of how much individual agents are willing to pay for (value) a commodity (keeping an infant alive).

In previous chapters, we discussed the value of commodities solely in terms of individual agent's satisfaction. To include society's value of commodities under alternative resource allocations directly involves **welfare economics**, which is the study of all feasible allocations of resources for a society and the establishment of criteria for selecting among these allocations. This selection is called *Public Choice Theory*, which attempts to understand and explain society's actual choice for resource allocation. Since this choice is based on normative economics involving value judgments and various agents having conflicting value judgments, it is difficult to establish a socially optimal allocation. However, even if these differing value judgments prevent a socially optimal allocation, the theory of welfare economics provides a method for delineating the important conceptual issues facing all societies. With such a description of issues, the winners and losers from a particular reallocation of resources can be determined.

Welfare economics. The study of criteria for a society's selection among feasible allocations of resources. *E.g., who should stay at home and who should go to war.*

Our aim in this chapter is to investigate how economic theory attempts to reconcile individual decentralized resource allocation with the overall social values of a society. This reconciliation may be accomplished with a social-welfare function, requiring a cardinal measure of individual consumer preferences. In this chapter, we maximize the welfare function subject to a *utility possibilities frontier* based on individual consumers' preferences. Then we specify and compare alternative egalitarian social-welfare functions. We discuss *Arrow's Impossibility Theorem,* which indicates that a social-welfare function is impossible given consumers' ordinal ranking of utility and based on some reasonable assumptions concerning society's social rankings. Because we cannot determine a social ranking based on individual consumers' ordinal preferences, we evaluate the idea of majority voting as a **second-best Pareto-optimal allocation.** At the end of the chapter, we discuss causes of market failure, such as monopoly power, externalities, public goods, and asymmetric information as potential constraints on improving social welfare.

Second-best Pareto-optimal allocations. Allocations based on mechanisms (besides price signals) designed for improving society's allocation of resources. *E.g., placing a tax on emitters of noxious gases.*

In the Appendix to this chapter, we investigate the *compensation principle* as an alternative to developing a social-welfare function. We also demonstrate the *Theory of the Second Best* by showing how any policy designed for improving social welfare that only corrects some constraints may not result in a social-welfare improvement.

Because economists are unable to specify a social-welfare function, a complete army—rather than a handful (five)—of applied economists is required to develop and direct mechanism designs for filling in the economic gaps resulting from missing markets. The objective of each mechanism is to yield an incremental improvement in social welfare. The tâtonnement process of these mechanisms will then move a society toward maximizing social welfare.

Deriving a social-welfare function

From each, according to his ability; to each, according to his need.

(Karl Marx)

This quote is a social-welfare criterion that history has shown to be very difficult, if not impossible, to implement. Using the very broad definition of social welfare as a level of happiness for society as a whole, a measure of this happiness is required to determine the socially optimal allocation of resources. Such a measure for determining how well-off agents are in a society requires a set of welfare criteria. Much of the research on the formulation of welfare criteria and their implications for economic policy has relied on the Pareto-allocation criterion. A *Pareto criterion* is a value judgment based on unanimity rule. If one agent could be made better off without reducing the welfare of others, then social welfare could be improved by the allocation that makes this one agent better off. Since no one agent is made worse off and at least one agent is made better off, it is assumed, given the independence of utility functions, that all agents would support the Pareto criterion. As outlined in Chapters 6 and 11, a Pareto-optimal allocation yields an efficient allocation of resources and thus is a necessary condition for a social optimum. However, many decisions on allocation result in an improvement of one agent's utility at the expense of other agents. For example, a redistribution of endowments from taxing wealthy households and providing government-subsidized housing for poor households may increase social welfare but cannot be justified by the Pareto criterion. Thus, a fundamental inadequacy of the Pareto welfare criterion is its inability to yield a complete ranking of all social states within an economy.

Thus, the Pareto criterion is useless in the context of many policy propositions, so additional welfare criteria are necessary to determine if these policies will improve social welfare. These additional welfare criteria may result in a **social-welfare function**, which is a utility function for society that provides a method for aggregating individual consumers' utilities and thus orders commodity bundles for a society.

Is a social-welfare function only an economic illusion? Yes, as we will demonstrate with Arrow's Impossibility Theorem, such a function can order commodity bundles for a society only under some rather unreasonable assumptions.

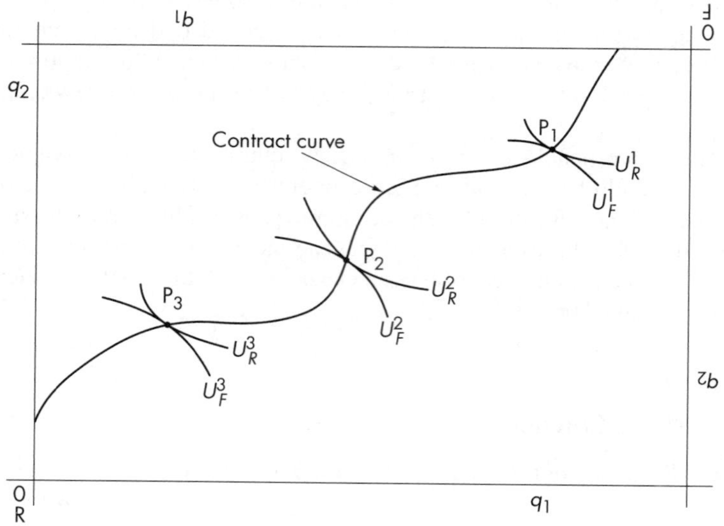

Figure 20.1 **Contract curve for a two-consumer, two-commodity pure-exchange economy.** Every point on the contract curve is Pareto-efficient and represents tangencies of Friday's and Robinson's indifference curves.

Social-welfare function. A function that orders commodity bundles for a society. *E.g., a dictator's utility function would be the social-welfare function for her country.*

To investigate a social-welfare function, a comparison of individual consumers' utilities is generally required, and thus it is assumed that utility functions can be measured on a cardinal scale. Specifically, in contrast to the assumptions outlined in Chapter 2, it is assumed that preference relations are based on a cardinal measure of the difference between commodity bundles. Under this assumption, taking a monotonic transformation of the utility function will change the preference relationships.

Revising the pure-exchange economy

Consider first a pure-exchange economy we developed in Chapter 6. The two-consumer (Friday and Robinson), two-commodity (q_1 and q_2) economy is illustrated in Figure 20.1. In the figure, only those points on the contract curve can be considered as possible candidates for a social optimum. For example, points P_1, P_2, and P_3 on the contract curve represent the tangencies of Friday's and Robinson's indifference curves. Any point off this contract curve is not Pareto-efficient, so it is possible to increase the welfare of one consumer without reducing the welfare of the other. From the contract curve in Figure 20.1, we can derive a utility possibilities frontier, which is theoretically similar in construction to the production possibilities frontier (Chapter 11). The **utility possibilities frontier**, illustrated in Figure 20.2, is a mapping of the Pareto-efficient utilities for Robinson, R, and Friday, F, corresponding

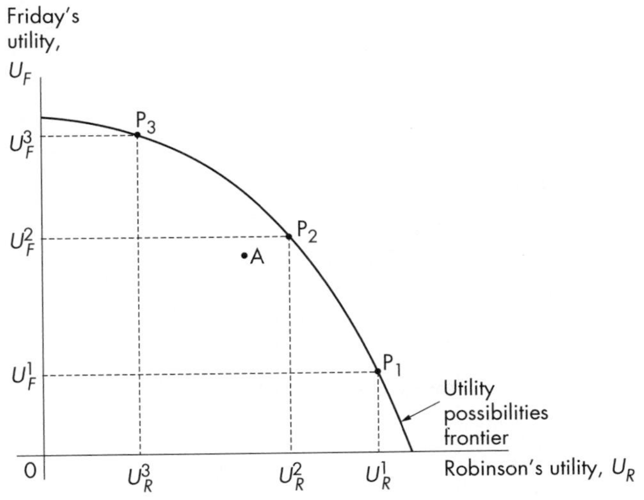

Figure 20.2 **Utility possibilities frontier.** Every point on the utility possibilities frontier represents a point on the contract curve. Feasible allocations inside the Edgeworth box are associated with points inside the utility possibilities frontier.

to each point on the contract curve. For the three points labeled P_1, P_2, and P_3 in Figure 20.1, the corresponding utility levels for Robinson (U_R^1, U_R^2, and U_R^3) and Friday (U_F^1, U_F^2, and U_F^3) are plotted on the horizontal and vertical axes, respectively, in Figure 20.2. Points on the utility possibilities frontier correspond to the tangency of the indifference curves along the contract curve in Figure 20.1. The utility combinations (U_R^1, U_F^1), (U_R^2, U_F^2), and (U_R^3, U_F^3) associated with P_1, P_2, and P_3 are the same for both figures. Every point inside this utility possibilities frontier is a feasible allocation corresponding to points inside the Edgeworth box of Figure 20.1. The boundary of the utility possibilities frontier represents the efficiency locus (contract curve) in Figure 20.1. For a given amount of q_1 and q_2, the utility possibilities frontier indicates the combination of U_R and U_F that can be obtained. Note that an increase in the amounts of q_1 and q_2 will result in the utility possibilities frontier shifting outward.

Utility possibilities frontier. The locus of Pareto-efficient utility levels for a given set of outputs. *E.g., the different levels of satisfaction two children receive for various shares of milk and cookies.*

With increasing opportunity cost, which yields a concave utility possibilities frontier, the sacrifice in Friday's utility increases for an additional unit increase in Robinson's utility. However, although a monotonic transformation of an agent's utility function preserves the preference ordering, it can result in opportunity cost switching from increasing to decreasing. This is one basis for the assumption of measuring utility on a cardinal scale, analogous to output.

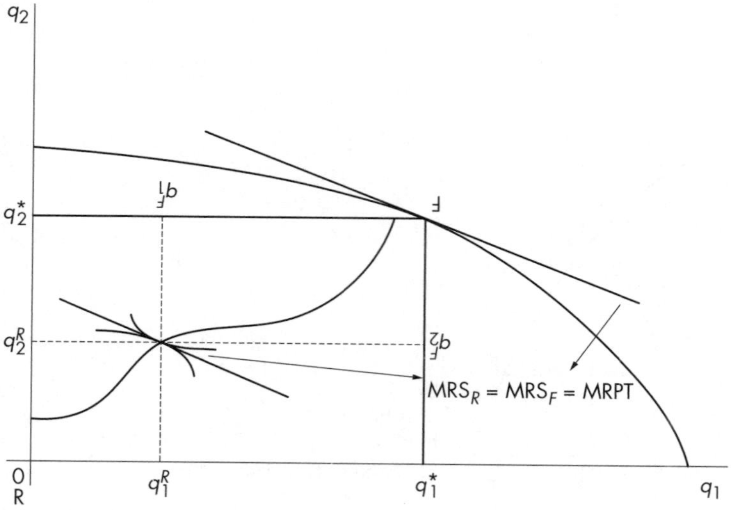

Figure 20.3 **Efficiency in production and exchange for a two-consumer economy.** A Pareto-optimal solution exists where Robinson's and Friday's MRSs are equal to the MRPT.

Considering production and exchange

We can also derive a utility possibilities frontier in a general equilibrium context by considering production. As developed in Chapter 11, the efficiency condition, illustrated in Figure 20.3, is based on a given level of utility for Friday. Changing this level of utility for Friday will result in alternative combinations of q_1 and q_2 produced and allocated between Robinson and Friday. As illustrated in Figure 20.4, maximizing Robinson's utility given U_F^o as Friday's level of satisfaction results in the Pareto-efficient allocation of $(q_1^R, q_2^R, q_1^F, q_2^F)$, with q_1^* and q_2^* efficiently produced. With an alternative level of satisfaction for Friday, say U_F', maximizing Robinson's utility will result in an alternative Pareto-efficient allocation $(q_1^{R'}, q_2^{R'}, q_1^{F'}, q_2^{F'})$, with q_1' and q_2' produced. In general, considering all possible Pareto-efficient allocations ($MRS_R = MRS_F = MRPT$), we obtain a collection of Pareto-efficient utility levels for both Robinson and Friday by varying Friday's utility from zero to the level where Robinson's utility would be zero. Plotting these Pareto-efficient utility combinations yields a utility possibilities frontier (Figure 20.2). For an economy with production, every utility bundle on this frontier represents a Pareto-efficient allocation where not only $MRS_R = MRS_F$ but also $MRS_R = MRS_F = MRPT$. A utility bundle in the interior of this frontier, say point A, is not Pareto-optimal. At point A, it is possible to increase either Robinson's or Friday's utility without decreasing the other consumer's utility. In contrast, on the frontier, say at point P_1, Friday's utility cannot be increased without reducing Robinson's utility. Thus, at P_1, the utility combination and any other utility bundle on the frontier are Pareto-optimal. The initial endowment of resources held by Robinson and Friday will determine the agent's location on the frontier. If Robinson has a proportionally larger share of the initial resources, utility bundle P_1 may result. A reversal of endowments may yield a higher utility level for Friday, such as bundle P_3.

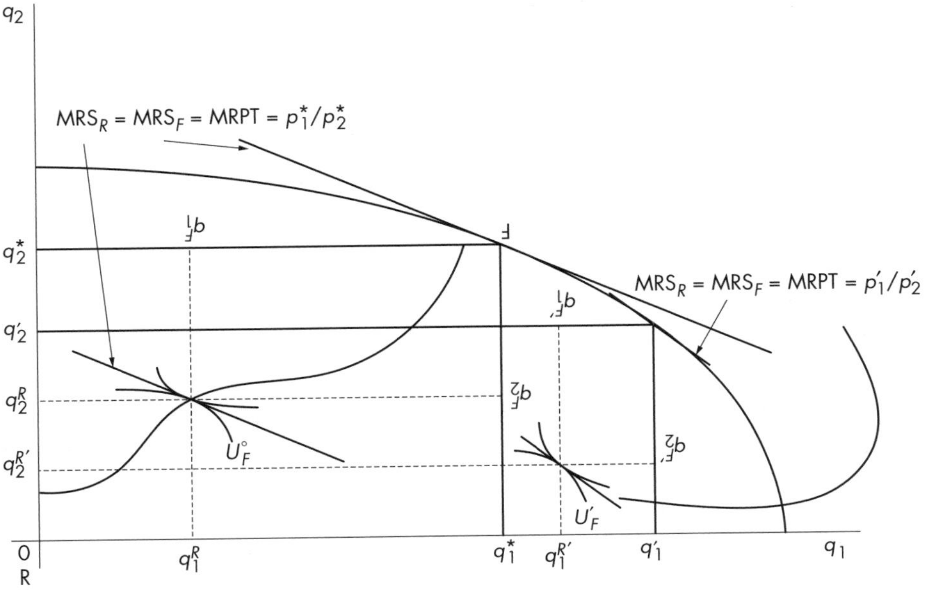

Figure 20.4 **Efficiency in production and exchange for alternative utility levels.** Within the production possibilities frontier, at each level of Friday's utility, a Pareto-optimal solution exists.

Example 20.1 Deriving a utility possibilities frontier in a pure-exchange economy

Analogous to Example 11.2 for a production possibilities frontier, we may derive a utility possibilities frontier. To do so, we equate the MRSs from utility functions instead of the MRTSs from production functions. Specifically, for a two-consumer economy, let Friday's and Robinson's utility functions be

$$U_F = q_1 + q_2,$$

$$U_R = q_1^{1/4} q_2^{1/4},$$

where $q_1^R + q_1^F = 16$ is the total amount of commodity q_1 available and $q_2^R + q_2^F = 16$ is the total amount of q_2 available. The MRSs are

$$\text{MRS}_F(q_2 \text{ for } q_1) = 1,$$

$$\text{MRS}_R(q_2 \text{ for } q_1) = q_2/q_1.$$

Equating these MRSs to determine the efficiency locus yields the equation for the contract curve, $q_1 = q_2$. Substituting into the utility functions for R and F and solving for

q_1 yields

$$q_1^F = \tfrac{1}{2}U_F,$$
$$q_1^R = U_R^2.$$

These equations are called the *Hicksian* or *compensated demand functions.* We then determine the utility possibilities frontier by summing these Hicksian demand functions and equating the result to the total amount of commodity q_1 available:

$$q_1^F + q_1^R = 16,$$
$$\tfrac{1}{2}U_F + U_R^2 = 16, \qquad \text{utility possibilities frontier.}$$

Note that $dU_F/dU_R = -4U_R$ and $d^2U_F/dU_R^2 = -4 < 0$, indicating that the utility possibilities frontier is a negatively sloped concave function. However, taking a monotonic transformation of Robinson's utility by raising it to the fourth power, so that $U_R = q_1q_2$, results in a convex utility possibilities frontier. Specifically, the monotonic transformation does not change $\mathrm{MRS}_R(q_2 \text{ for } q_1) = q_2/q_1$. However, Robinson's Hicksian demand function is now $q_1^R = U_R^{1/2}$. This results in the utility possibilities frontier

$$\tfrac{1}{2}U_F + U_R^{1/2} = 16,$$

which is a convex function given that

$$dU_F/dU_R = -U_R^{-1/2} \quad \text{and} \quad d^2U_F/dU_R^2 = \tfrac{1}{2}U_R^{-3/2} > 0.$$

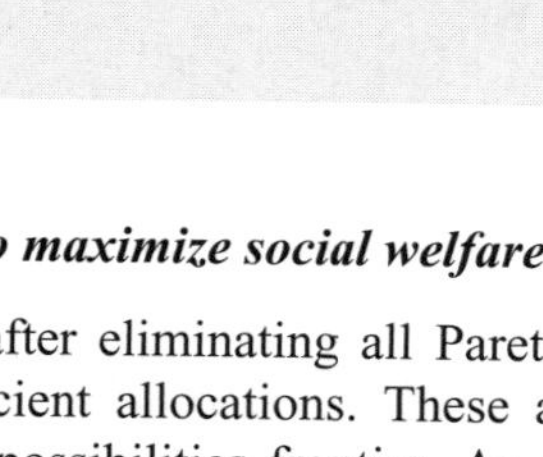

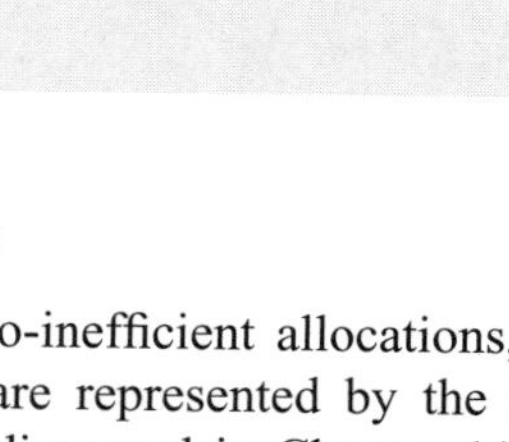

How to maximize social welfare

Even after eliminating all Pareto-inefficient allocations, there remain an infinite number of efficient allocations. These are represented by the infinite number of points on the utility possibilities frontier. As discussed in Chapter 11, the First Fundamental Theorem of Welfare Economics states that a perfectly competitive equilibrium will result in a Pareto-efficient allocation. Depending on the initial distribution of endowments, a perfectly competitive equilibrium can occur at any point on the utility possibilities frontier. A free-market criterion states that the perfectly competitive solution occurring at any point on the utility possibilities frontier is equitable. Thus, any Pareto-efficient outcome is a fair allocation that will then lead to maximizing social welfare.[1] It rewards consumers who are able and willing to work hard. In terms of equity, this assumes that all consumers have an equal opportunity to succeed if they are willing to put forth the effort. For example, in the nineteenth and twentieth centuries, America was the land of opportunity where anyone who had the willingness to work could succeed. Thus, regardless of the level of their other endowments, the opportunity exists for any consumer to succeed—so all you have to do is work hard and you will be successful.

However, equal opportunity may not exist in every consumer's endowment, so the allocation resulting from a perfectly competitive equilibrium may not be equitable. Not all consumers may have the same opportunities. Thus, society may redistribute income (initial endowments) among consumers in an effort to achieve equity. Once equity is achieved, the competitive market will yield a Walrasian equilibrium that is Pareto-efficient. Such a resulting fair allocation is both equitable and Pareto-efficient, and in this sense can be considered a point of optimal social welfare. Achieving equity may take the form of redistributing income by taxing the wealthy and giving the tax revenue to the poor (the government plays Robin Hood), providing commodities to the poor (e.g., Medicaid or surplus food from agricultural support programs), or market regulation (e.g., rent control or agricultural price supports). Efforts by governments to achieve a more equitable allocation are costly in terms of possibly generating inefficiencies within an economy. For example, the government playing Robin Hood dampens the incentive to work and invest, and often directs resources toward tax avoidance.

We can use the concept of a social-welfare function as a method for determining the socially optimal allocation among points on a utility possibilities frontier. With a social-welfare function, we can determine the point that maximizes social welfare in terms of both equity and efficiency criteria. Assuming that the government is not paternalistic, this function would generally depend on the welfare (utility) of the agents within an economy.[2] The government would then maximize social welfare subject to the utility possibilities frontier.

For example, consider the following social-welfare function $\mho$ for an economy consisting of two consumers (Robinson, R, and Friday, F):

$$\mho = \mho(U_R, U_F).$$

Assuming a diminishing marginal rate of substitution between consumer utilities, we can determine convex **social indifference** or **isowelfare curves**. This assumption implies that society has *inequality aversion*, where (holding social welfare constant) the more satisfaction Robinson has, the less society is willing to give up Friday's utility for one more unit of Robinson's utility. As illustrated in Figure 20.5, the tangency between a social indifference curve and the utility possibilities frontier results in the maximum level of social welfare. Point P_2 is the only point on the utility possibilities frontier where there is no other point preferred to it. For example, point P_3 is Pareto-efficient, but there are points, such as A, within the utility possibilities frontier that are preferred to P_3. Even though point A is Pareto-inefficient (it is in the interior of the utility possibilities frontier), society prefers it over the Pareto-efficient point P_3. Using the maximum level of social welfare, point P_2, we then determine the optimal allocation of commodities in the Edgeworth box (Figure 20.1) for a pure-exchange economy, or the production possibilities frontier (Figure 20.3) for a production and exchange economy.

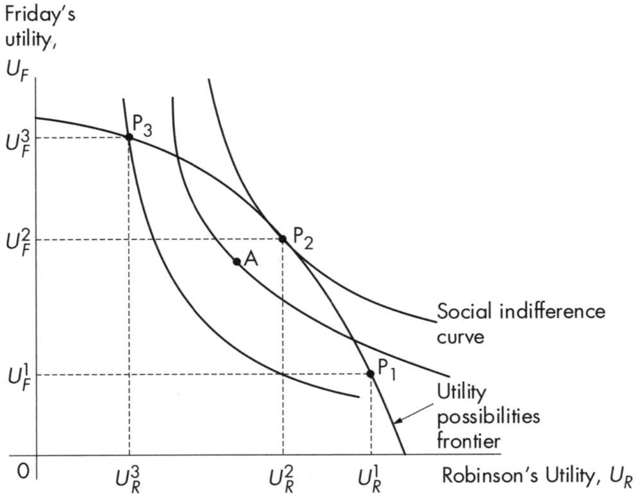

Figure 20.5 **Maximizing social welfare.** At point P_2, social welfare is maximized for the given utility possibilities frontier.

Social indifference (isowelfare) curves. A locus of points that yield the same level of social welfare. *E.g., social welfare remains unchanged when the benefits to water-skiers from building a reservoir are offset by the harm to river rafters.*

Example 20.2 Maximizing social welfare assuming a social-diminishing marginal rate of substitution between consumers' utilities

Consider the concave utility possibilities frontier derived in Example 20.1,

$$\tfrac{1}{2}U_F + U_R^2 = 16,$$

associated with a social-welfare function of the form $\mho = U_R U_F$. The Lagrangian for maximizing social welfare subject to the utility possibilities frontier is

$$\mathcal{L}(U_R, U_F, \lambda) = U_R U_F + \lambda\left(16 - \tfrac{1}{2}U_F - U_R^2\right).$$

The first-order conditions (FOCs) are then

$$\partial\mathcal{L}/\partial U_R = U_F^* - 2\lambda^* U_R^* = 0,$$

$$\partial\mathcal{L}/\partial U_F = U_R^* - \tfrac{1}{2}\lambda^* = 0,$$

$$\partial\mathcal{L}/\partial\lambda \ = 16 - \tfrac{1}{2}U_F^* - U_R^{*2} = 0.$$

This results in MRS(F for R) $= U_F^*/U_R^* = 4U_R^*$, which implies $U_F^* = 4U_R^{*2}$. Substituting this result into the utility possibilities frontier yields the social-welfare maximizing level of utilities $U_F^* = 21.3$ and $U_R^* = 2.3$.

Substituting these optimal levels of utility into the Hicksian demand functions from Example 20.1 yields the optimal allocation of outputs q_1 and q_2:

$$q_1^{F*} = \tfrac{1}{2}U_F^* = 10.7, \quad q_2^{F*} = 10.7,$$

$$q_1^{R*} = U_R^{*2} = 5.3, \quad q_2^{R*} = 5.3.$$

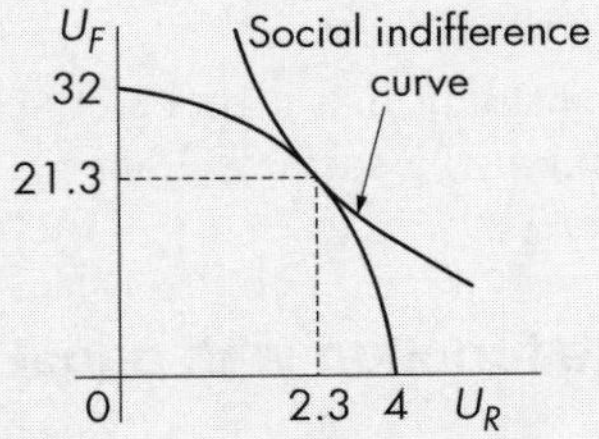

Shapes of isowelfare curves

The law, in its majestic equality, forbids the rich as well as the poor to sleep under bridges, to beg in the streets and to steal bread.

(Anatole France)

Translation: Because the allocation of initial endowments is not equitable, equality under the law will not necessarily improve social welfare.

A social-welfare function represents society's preferences for particular Pareto-efficient points on a utility possibilities frontier. Similar to individual consumer preference functions, the various social preferences may be represented by social indifference curves taking on various shapes. These shapes (and thus social preferences) are generally based on some equitable allocation among the Pareto-efficient allocations. The comparison of alternative Pareto-efficient points requires value judgments concerning the tradeoff among consumer utilities. Therefore, there can be no one definition for equity. Thus, the social indifference curves will take on a number of forms depending on which criterion (value judgment) is employed for determining an equitable allocation. We will discuss two such criteria: the egalitarian and utilitarian.

Egalitarian: households?

Je veux que les paysans mettent la poule au pot tous les dimanches.

(King Henry IV of France)

Translation: I want there to be no peasant in my realm so poor that he will not have a chicken in his pot every Sunday.

Egalitarianism can take two forms. One *egalitarian criterion* allocates each consumer an equal amount of each commodity (a chicken in every pot, a house for every household, a car in every driveway). In terms of our Robinson and Friday two-commodity economy, this egalitarian criterion sets $q_1^R = q_1^F$ and $q_2^R = q_2^F$. In a pure-exchange economy, Robinson and Friday would split the total endowment of each commodity in half. Unless Robinson and Friday have identical utility functions (which is unlikely), the level of utility achieved by them will not be the same. But their utility levels are not a factor in this egalitarian equity. Thus, in terms of a social-welfare function, social preferences for Robinson's or Friday's utilities are identical and are perfect substitutes as long as commodities are allocated equally between them. A relevant social-welfare function for this type of egalitarianism is then

$$\mho(U_R, U_F) = U_R + U_F \quad \text{s.t. } q_1^R = q_1^F \text{ and } q_2^R = q_2^F.$$

Maximizing this welfare function with the additional constraint that it be Pareto-efficient in terms of a utility possibilities frontier will result in maximizing social welfare.

Example 20.3 An egalitarian social-welfare function with equal commodities

Consider the utility functions for Robinson and Friday from Example 20.1:

$$U_F = q_1 + q_2,$$

$$U_R = q_1^{1/4} q_2^{1/4},$$

where $q_1^R + q_1^F = 16$ is the total amount of commodity q_1 available and $q_2^R + q_2^F = 16$ is the total amount of q_2 available. In this pure-exchange economy, an egalitarian allocation is $q_1^R = q_1^F$ and $q_2^R = q_2^F$. Substituting this allocation into the total amount of q_1 and q_2 available results in $q_1^R = q_1^F = q_2^R = q_2^F = 8$ as the solution. The resulting utility levels are $U_R = 2.83$ and $U_F = 16$.

Alternatively, we may derive the solution by

$$\max \mho = \max(U_R + U_F) \text{s.t. } q_1^R = q_1^F,\ q_2^R = q_2^F, \text{ and } \tfrac{1}{2}U_F + U_R^2 = 16,$$

where the last constraint is the concave utility possibilities frontier from Example 20.1. Substituting the egalitarian constraints into both the objective function and the utility possibilities frontier yields

$$\max_{(q_1,\, q_2)} \mho = \max_{(q_1,\, q_2)} \left(q_1^{1/4} q_2^{1/4} + q_1 + q_2\right) \quad \text{s.t.} \tfrac{1}{2}(q_1 + q_2) + \left(q_1^{1/4} q_2^{1/4}\right)^2 = 16,$$

where a distinction between commodities consumed by Robinson and Friday is no longer required, so the superscripts R and F are dropped. The Lagrangian for this problem is

$$\mathcal{L}(q_1, q_2, \lambda) = q_1^{1/4} q_2^{1/4} + q_1 + q_2 - \lambda\left[\tfrac{1}{2}(q_1 + q_2) + \left(q_1^{1/4} q_2^{1/4}\right)^2 - 16\right].$$

The FOCs are then

$$\partial \mathcal{L}/\partial q_1 = \tfrac{1}{4} q_1^{-1} U_R + 1 - \tfrac{1}{2}\lambda - 2\lambda U_R \tfrac{1}{4} q_1^{-1} U_R = 0,$$

$$\partial \mathcal{L}/\partial q_2 = \tfrac{1}{4} q_2^{-1} U_R + 1 - \tfrac{1}{2}\lambda - 2\lambda U_R \tfrac{1}{4} q_2^{-1} U_R = 0,$$

$$\partial \mathcal{L}/\partial \lambda = \tfrac{1}{2}(q_1 + q_2) + \left(q_1^{1/4} q_2^{1/4}\right)^2 - 16 = 0.$$

Rearranging the first two FOCs and taking their ratio yields

$$\frac{q_1^{-1}(\frac{1}{4}U_R - \frac{1}{2}\lambda U_R^2)}{q_2^{-1}(\frac{1}{4}U_R - \frac{1}{2}\lambda U_R^2)} = \frac{q_1^{-1}}{q_2^{-1}} = \frac{\frac{1}{2}\lambda - 1}{\frac{1}{2}\lambda - 1} = 1.$$

This results in $q_1^R = q_2^R$ and $q_1^F = q_2^F$ and, given $q_1^R = q_1^F$ and $q_2^R = q_2^F$, implies

$$q_1^R = q_1^F = q_2^R = q_2^F = 8.$$

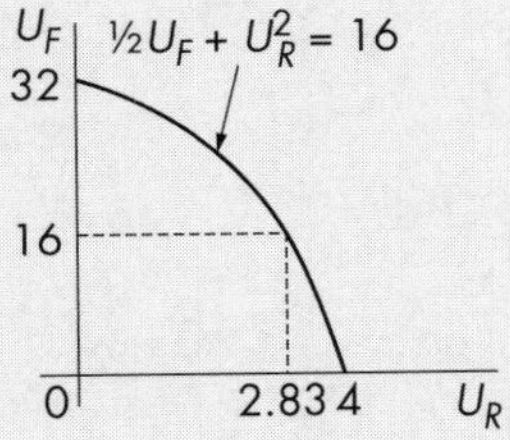

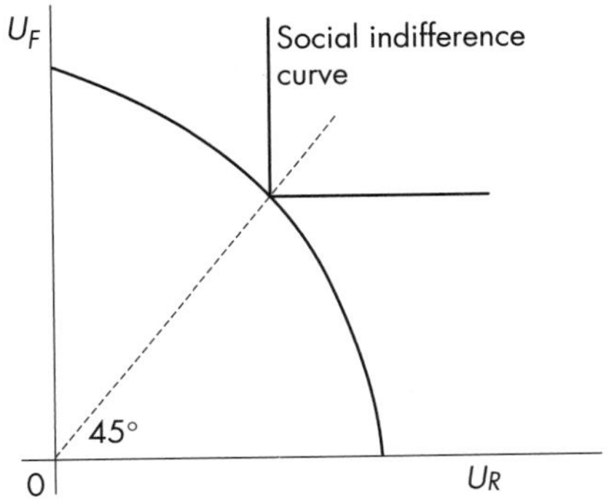

Figure 20.6 **Rawlsian social-welfare function.** The most equitable allocation maximizes the utility of the least well-off consumer.

The second type of egalitarian criterion is an allocation of commodities resulting in the equality of utilities across all consumers. For Robinson and Friday, this criterion sets $U_R = U_F$. A social-welfare function resulting in the equality of utilities is the *Rawlsian criterion*, which states that the most equitable allocation maximizes the utility of the least-well-off consumer in society. For Robinson and Friday, the Rawlsian criterion is

$$\mho(U_R, U_F) = \min(U_{R,}, U_F).$$

The maximum level of social welfare given a specific utility possibilities frontier is $U_R = U_F$ on the Pareto-efficient utility possibilities frontier (Figure 20.6). Unless Robinson and Friday have the same utility functions, equality of utilities will not result in Robinson and Friday each receiving the same commodity allocation.

Example 20.4 An egalitarian social-welfare function with equal utilities, Rawlsian criterion

A Rawlsian social-welfare function for Robinson and Friday is

$$\mho = \min(U_R, U_F).$$

The expansion path for this function is where $U_R = U_F$.

Considering the utility possibilities frontier from Example 20.1,

$$\tfrac{1}{2}U_F + U_R^2 = 16,$$

and substituting the expansion path into the frontier results in $U_R = U_F = 3.76$. Assuming a pure-exchange economy with total endowments of 16 for both q_1 and q_2, the commodity allocations among Robinson and Friday are

$$q_1^R = 14.14, \quad q_1^F = 1.88,$$

$$q_2^R = 14.14, \quad q_2^F = 1.88.$$

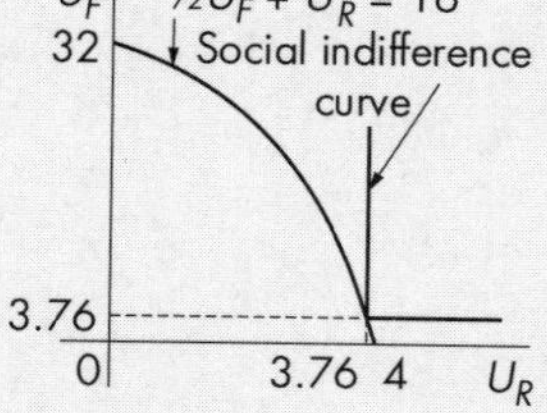

Application: Egalitarian households

Participation of women in the labor force in the United States increased rapidly during and after World War II; however, for approximately 30 years, there was no corresponding rise in men's participation in homemaking. Generally, childcare continued to be viewed as women's responsibility even if she also worked outside the home. In the late 1970s, employed wives spent approximately 26 hours per week on housework, compared with 52 hours for full-time homemakers. However, husbands only devoted approximately 11 hours per week to housework, so employed women had far less leisure time than their husbands. In general, households were not egalitarian.

A number of theories exist for explaining this lack of egalitarianism. In the 1960s, resource theory focused on the fact that the spouse with accumulation of resources exercised monopoly power on the other. At the end of the twentieth century, comparative advantage emerged as an alternative theory. By allocating tasks according to comparative advantage, overall household welfare increased. This theory assumes that division of labor is entirely rational, so women just choose less leisure time than men. However, many economists were uncomfortable with this explanation and proposed the social environment as an additional constraint on maximizing household welfare. Social environment includes beliefs and attitudes concerning appropriate division of labor.

To understand these beliefs and attitudes, in 2002, Davis and Greenstein surveyed 17,636 individuals in 28 countries who were either married or cohabiting with a significant other. Understanding the social environment of couples cohabiting is becoming important with the changing social structure of a family. In 2006, households with married couples slipped just below 50 percent. Results indicated that men overall spend 9 hours a week on housework, compared with women spending over 20 hours. This implies that there is still a gender norm, with women doing more housework than men regardless of union type. However, there is a marriage effect. Marriage has a traditionalizing effect on couples—even with egalitarian couples. Regardless of a couple's relative earnings or work hours, cohabiting males spend more time at housework than their married counterparts, while the opposite holds for women. Married women spend more time at housework than their cohabiting counterparts.

Davis and Greenstein also found that men with higher earnings than their partners did less housework than men with lower relative incomes. Higher earnings may be leveraged to bargain for less housework.

Source: S.N. Davis and T.N. Greenstein, "Effects of Union Type on Division of Household Labor: Do Cohabiting Men Really Perform More Housework?" *Journal of Family Issues* 28 (2007): 1246–1272.

Utilitarian: dropping the atomic bombs on Japan

> *You are my slave, because my gain is greater than your loss of freedom.*
>
> (Michael Wetzstein)

The *utilitarian criterion* maximizes the sum of consumers' utility. This criterion was formally developed by Bentham and provided the initial impetus to utility theory. For Robinson and

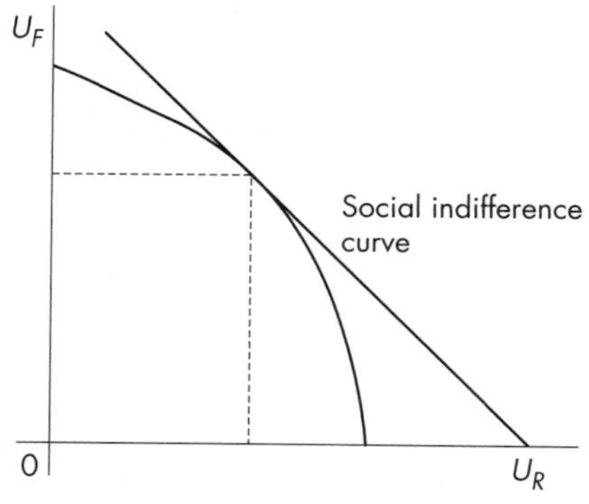

Figure 20.7 **Benthamite (classical utilitarian) social-welfare function.** Maximizing the sum of consumers' utility subject to a utility possibilities frontier will maximize social welfare.

Friday, the criterion is

$$\mho(U_R, U_F) = U_R + U_F,$$

which is called the *classical utilitarian* or *Benthamite welfare function,* and is maximized subject to a utility possibilities frontier (Figure 20.7). Under the utilitarian criterion, increases or decreases in individual consumers' utility directly results in identical changes in social welfare. Also, only total utility is relevant, so the utilitarian criterion does not consider the distribution of utility. As long as the social gain is larger than the social loss, it makes no difference that the consumer who gains in utility may already be happier than the other consumer. Unless the utility functions of individual consumers are close to being identical, the utilitarian criteria can result in substantial differences in consumers' utility (a slave owner versus a slave).

Although ethics teaches that virtue is its own reward, the classical utilitarian function teaches that reward is its own virtue. Only the total level of utility is important. By incorporating some virtue (morality) into the classical utilitarian function, we get a generalization of this function, which is the weighted sum of the utilities:

$$\mho(U_R, U_F) = \alpha_R U_R + \alpha_F U_F, \quad \alpha_R + \alpha_F = 1.$$

The weights (α_R, α_F) indicate how important each consumer's utility is to overall social welfare. For example, the utility of an individual such as Mother Teresa will be weighted higher than that of a child sex offender or, during World War II, American lives were weighted higher than the lives of Japanese. In Figure 20.7, the utilitarian social-welfare optimal allocation is the tangency between the social indifference curve and the utility possibilities curve. Depending on the weights associated with individual consumers' utility, any Pareto-efficient point on the utility possibilities frontier could be a social-welfare maximum.

In summary, the more egalitarian a society is, the more social indifference curves will approach right angles, indicating that the society is more concerned with equity issues of distribution. For a utilitarian society that is indifferent to distribution, the curves are

Table 20.1 Criteria for maximizing social welfare

Criteria	*Description*
Free-market	Any market outcome is equitable, given equal opportunity
Utilitarian	Maximize the weighted sum of consumers' utilities
Egalitarian:	
Equal distribution	Equal amount of commodities across all consumers
Rawlsian	Maximize the utility of the least-well-off consumer

more linear, showing that the society simply maximizes the sum of utilities. The free-market criterion does not weight each consumer's utilities, so it cannot be represented by a social welfare function. Instead, given equal opportunity, all Pareto-efficient outcomes are considered equitable and the markets will then yield a fair allocation that maximizes social welfare. Table 20.1 lists the alternative criteria for maximizing social welfare where the free market criterion is the least concerned with equity followed by the utilitarian criterion with the egalitarian criteria the most concerned with equity.

What type of society do you live in? If you live in the United States, where the variation of commodity bundle allocations per agent is much wider than other developed countries, you live in a utilitarian society.

Example 20.5 Utilitarian criteria

The Lagrangian for maximizing

$$\mho = U_R + U_F$$

subject to the concave utility possibilities frontier in Example 20.1 is

$$\mathcal{L}(U_R, U_F, \lambda) = U_R + U_F - \lambda\left(\tfrac{1}{2}U_F + U_R^2 - 16\right).$$

The FOCs are then

$$\partial\mathcal{L}/\partial U_R = 1 - 2\lambda^* U_R^* = 0,$$

$$\partial\mathcal{L}/\partial U_F = 1 - \tfrac{1}{2}\lambda^* = 0,$$

$$\partial\mathcal{L}/\partial\lambda \;\; = \tfrac{1}{2}U_F^* + U_R^{*2} - 16 = 0.$$

The second FOC results in $\lambda = 2$, then, from the first FOC, $U_R^* = 1/4$. Incorporating Robinson's utility level into the last FOC yields $U_F^* = 31.88$. The allocation of commodities, for a pure-exchange economy, with total endowments of 16 for both q_1 and q_2 are then

$$q_1^R = 0.06, \quad q_1^F = 15.94,$$

$$q_2^R = 0.06, \quad q_2^F = 15.94.$$

This result illustrates how the distribution of utility is not a determinant in the utilitarian criteria. The consumer who receives more enjoyment from consumption will receive more of the commodities.

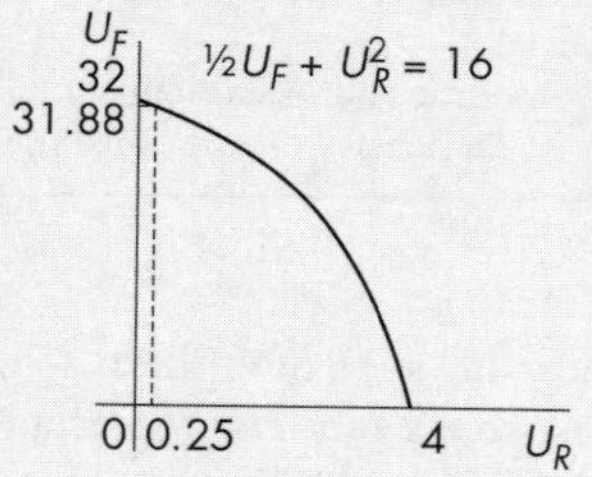

Arrow's impossibility theorem

A problem in maximizing social welfare is how to establish this social-welfare function. A welfare function based on individual consumer preferences would be desirable, assuming social welfare is to reflect some aggregate consumer preferences. For example, we could determine a social-welfare ranking of toys by two toddlers given that the toddlers will both want the same toy. However, because preference ranking by consumers is generally only ordinal, there is not sufficient information to determine a reasonable social-preference ranking of choices. There are numerous examples where, due to the ordinal preference ranking among individuals, an aggregate ranking is impossible. A classical example is the Battle of the Sexes game discussed in Chapter 14; the couple cannot jointly (socially) rank their preferences for opera or fights. **Arrow's Impossibility Theorem** states explicitly that it is impossible to establish a reasonable social preference ranking based solely on individual ordinal preference rankings.

Arrow's Impossibility Theorem. A social preference ranking satisfying a set of reasonable axioms is impossible, given an ordinal ranking of individual agent preferences. *E.g., a five-member household cannot use social preference ranking to determine which movie they will rent for Friday night.*

As an illustration of Arrow's theorem, suppose that there are several feasible social states, and it is assumed that each individual in society can ordinally rank these states as to their desirability. To derive a social-welfare function, there must exist a ranking of these states on a society-wide scale that considers these individual preferences fairly. Let us consider just three possible social states (A, B, and C). For example, these states could be sending a human to Mars (and back), building and equipping 10 new aircraft carrier task forces, or providing universal health care (all costing around \$1 trillion each). (Of course, the states could be less dramatic: for example, build a new school, civic center, or court house.) Arrow's Impossibility Theorem states that a reasonable social ranking of these three states cannot exist based only on how individual agents ordinally rank these states. A reasonable social ranking may be stated with the following axioms relating individual consumers' preferences:

1 **Completeness.** The social ranking must rank all social states. Either $A \succ B$, $B \succ A$, or $A \sim B$ for any two states. This axiom is identical to the Completeness Axiom for individual preference ordering.
2 **Transitivity.** Society's social ranking must be transitive. Given three social states, A, B, and C, if $A \succ B$ and $B \succ C$, then $A \succ C$. This axiom is identical to the Transitivity Axiom for individual preference ordering.
3 **Pareto.** If every consumer prefers A to B, then A is preferable in a social ranking. This also holds for the other two pairs (A, C) and (B, C). This axiom is identical to a Pareto improvement, discussed in Chapter 6.
4 **Nondictatorial.** One consumer's preferences should not determine society's preferences. There is no agent paternalism.
5 **Pairwise independence.** Society's social ranking between A and B should depend only on individual preferences between A and B, not on individual preferences for some other social state, say state C. This axiom is identical to the Independence Axiom for individual preference ordering of states of nature.

We can now state Arrow's Impossibility Theorem more formally:

Arrow's Impossibility Theorem

A social preference ranking satisfying these five axioms is impossible, given an ordinal ranking of individual agent preferences.

This theorem implies that there is no way to aggregate agents' ordinal preferences into a social preference ranking without relaxing one of these axioms.

These axioms may seem a reasonable set of conditions for democratically choosing among social states. However, Arrow demonstrated that it is impossible to socially choose among all possible sets of alternatives without violating at least one of the axioms. No general social ranking, given ordinal agent preferences and obeying axioms 1 through 5, exists. Thus, social choice must be unreasonable if based on agents' ordinal preference ranking.

How are society's preferences for commodities ranked? They are ranked unreasonably if based on agents' ordinal preference ranking.

What is wrong with majority voting?

To see that Arrow's Impossibility Theorem holds, let us consider majority voting, an important social preference **mechanism design** (a set of rules governing the procedures for social [collective] choice). Majority voting satisfies both the Pareto Axiom and the Nondictatorial Axiom, so it is sensitive to each individual agent's preferences. Also, it can be shown by *May's Theorem* that majority voting is symmetric among agents, which means that it treats all agents the same and all agents have just one vote. It is also neutral among alternatives, by not making a distinction among alternatives a priori. However, majority rule can lead to a pattern of social choices that is not transitive even though every voter has ordinal and transitive preferences. Thus, it violates Axiom 2.

Mechanism design. A method for eliciting agent's preferences for collective decisions. *E.g., the design of procedures for environmental standards or the writing of an insurance policy where an insurer's level of precaution is unobservable.*

The law is not justice. It is a very imperfect mechanism. If you press exactly the right buttons and are also lucky, justice may show up in the answer. A mechanism is all the law was ever intended to be.

(Raymond Chandler)

As an illustration, consider the ballot in Table 20.2 among three voters: Robinson, Friday, and Simpson (Bart). The voters' preferences are as follows:

Robinson and Simpson prefer alternative A to B.

Robinson and Friday prefer alternative B to C.

Friday and Simpson prefer alternative C to A.

Thus, the majority (two) prefers A to B and B to C, but the majority also prefers C to A. Thus, majority voting results in a cyclical pattern that is intransitive. This is called the *Condorcet Paradox*, which presents a major problem for group decision making.

Does majority voting result in a preference ordering of society's alternatives? No, majority voting can result in a cyclical pattern of preferences, which will not result in any social preference ordering.

Next let us consider the case where each voter must vote for just one alternative. As illustrated in panel (a) of Table 20.3, the ordinal preference ranking in Table 20.2 results in a three-way tie. All three alternatives receive equal votes. However, if one of the alternatives is removed, then a clear winner results. As illustrated in panel (b), when alternative C is removed, alternative A receives a majority vote. Here, Axiom 5 is violated.

We see this violation of Axiom 5 often in US presidential elections, where a third-party candidate has determined the outcome. A recent example is the 2000 election, where Vice

Table 20.2 Condorcet paradox

Voters	*Preferences for alternatives*		
	A	*B*	C
Robinson	3	2	1
Friday	1	3	2
Simpson	2	1	3

The ordinal preference ranking is: 3 (highest), 2 (next highest), and 1 (last).

Table 20.3 Pairwise independence

Voters	*Panel (a)*			*Panel (b)*	
	Votes for alternatives			*Votes for alternatives*	
	A	*B*	*C*	*A*	*B*
Robinson	1			1	
Friday		1			1
Simpson	1		1	1	
Total	1	1	1	2	1

President Al Gore lost the election to George Walker Bush, partly as a result of Ralph Nader's candidacy.

Thus, the development of a social-welfare function requires more than just an ordinal ranking of individual consumer preferences. It requires a comparison of utilities across consumers on a cardinal scale.[3] For example, one reason why a third party can influence the results of an election is that no weight is given to the intensity of voters' desires. However, intensity of desires is a utility measure that can only be measured on at least a cardinal scale. The magnitude or intensity of an individual voter's desires is not known when she votes. However, allowing voters an ordinal preference ranking (Table 20.2), instead of voting for just one vote (Table 20.3) does elicit additional information on the voter's preference. This may result in a social ranking more consistent with a majority of the electorate. New voting machines, being put into place after the 2000 presidential election, have the capability to allow voters to ordinally rank candidates. Called instantaneous voting, such a procedure has not yet been widely adopted, but offers the potential of further revealing voters' preferences and mitigating any strategic voting, discussed next.

Strategic voting

Nobody speaks the truth when there is something they must have.

(Elizabeth Bowen)

A problem with allowing ordinal ranking of candidates (or any other choices) is the possibility of strategic voting. *Strategic voting* is where an agent does not reveal her true preferences but instead votes to enhance the outcome in her favor. This is a game-theory strategy that is particularly effective when the number of voters is relatively small or a strategic-voting coalition can be formed. One form of strategic voting is for an agent, say Friday, to rank her first choice the highest, and then rank the other alternatives inversely to the expected outcome. Thus, Friday would rank the alternative expected to be in close competition with her first choice last, suppressing the competitive threat.

Strategic voting is illustrated in Table 20.4 for determining the social ranking of four alternatives. In panel (a), alternative A, which was not Friday's top choice, comes out on top. However, as illustrated in panel (b), Friday can change the outcome by ranking alternative A low (strategic voting). Now Friday's top choice, alternative B, comes out on top as the social choice. Judges in the Olympic Games have been accused of practicing this type of strategic voting.

Table 20.4 Strategic voting

Voters	Panel (a)				Panel (b)			
	Preferences for alternatives				*Preferences for alternatives*			
	A	*B*	*C*	*D*	*A*	*B*	*C*	*D*
Robinson	4	3	2	1	4	3	2	1
Friday	3	4	1	2	1	4	2	3
Simpson	4	3	1	2	4	3	1	2
Total	11	10	4	5	9	10	5	6

The ordinal preference ranking is 4 (highest), 3 (next highest), 2 (next), 1 (last).

Can your optimal revealed preferences deviate from your true preferences? Yes, if your true preferences result in a less desirable outcome compared with revealing some other preference, then your optimal revealed preferences will deviate from these true preferences.

A method for removing this potential of strategic voting is *sequential voting.* In sequential voting, the lowest-ranking alternative after each vote is dropped and another vote is then taken on the remaining alternatives. In panel (b) of Table 20.4, alternative C only received a rating of 5. Dropping this alternative from the list yields individual preference ranking for three alternatives listed in panel (a) of Table 20.5. Now alternative D received the lowest ranking. Dropping alternative D and re-voting on alternatives A and B yields the outcome in panel (b). From panel (b), alternative A is still selected even given strategic voting by Friday. Sequential voting is used to elect the Speaker of the House in the US House of Representatives. Employing sequential voting also allows for a social ranking of alternatives based on the Pairwise Independence Axiom. Implementing such as process for US presidential elections would probably have changed a number of outcomes. By adopting instantaneous voting, where voters rank their choices, the low-ranking alternatives could be automatically dropped until only two alternatives are left. Given these two remaining alternatives, a president with the majority of support would then be elected.

Table 20.5 Sequential voting

Voters	Panel (a)			Panel (b)	
	Preferences for alternatives			*Preferences for alternatives*	
	A	*B*	*D*	*A*	*B*
Robinson	3	2	1	2	1
Friday	1	3	2	1	2
Simpson	3	2	1	2	1
Total	7	7	4	5	4

This result from Arrow's Impossibility Theorem illustrates that a confederation of individuals forming a society should not be expected to behave with the same coherence as would be expected from an individual. What Arrow's Theorem implies is that the institutional detail and procedures of a political process (mechanism design) cannot be neglected. Thus, it is not surprising that those academic disciplines that complement economics, such as political science and psychology, have evolved to address the process of group choice. In general, these academic disciplines attempt to determine the intensities of individual and group desires and formulate policies and rules for group choice and actions. As demonstrated by the Condorcet Paradox and the quid pro quo example in Chapter 14, an agenda that determines which alternatives are first considered will affect social choice.

Application: Nonpartisan blanket primaries

Nonpartisan blanket primaries (also called Louisiana primaries, Cajun primaries, or jungle primaries) are elections where all candidates for an office run in the same primary regardless of political party (nonpartisan). The top two candidates receiving the most votes go onto a second round of voting where the candidate with the majority vote wins the election. It is then possible for two candidates from the same party to advance to the second round. Such sequential voting is becoming increasingly popular in the US states. Louisiana was first to adopt the mechanism in 1976 for US House and Senate elections. In 2010, a proposition passed to adopt nonpartisan blanket primaries in California.

These blanket primaries are not a true sequential voting mechanism since only one iteration is carried out, yielding the top two candidates. This results in different outcomes if one party has more candidates than another, resulting in vote splitting among the candidates within the same party. For example, consider an election with four Democrats and two Republicans running in a nonpartisan blanket primary. If the primary election results in the four Democrats jointly receiving 60 percent of the vote (with 15 percent each) and the two Republicans then jointly receiving 40 percent (with 20 percent each), only the two Republicans would advance to the second round. Instead, having additional iterations would result in a different outcome. However, this requires additional elections that are expensive and likely cause voter fatigue. Using instantaneous voting where voters ordinally rank candidates would avoid such problems.

Market failure

It is error alone which needs the support of government. Truth can stand by itself.
(Thomas Jefferson)

Translation: Government involvement in markets is required only when markets fail.

Suppose some process for group decision does exist for determining the optimal social choice. Then a naive solution, based on the Second Fundamental Theorem of Welfare Economics, would advocate allowing markets the freedom to obtain this social optimal given a reallocation of endowments. Unfortunately, this solution is based on the properties of a perfectly competitive equilibrium, an extreme theoretical case of resource allocation, which does not generally hold for any society. When the properties of a perfectly competitive equilibrium do not hold, the resulting equilibrium is not efficient, so **market failure** occurs. In general, conditions causing market failure are classified into four categories: monopoly power, externalities, public goods and asymmetric information.

Market failure. An economic failure (that occurs) when the resulting market equilibrium is not efficient. *E.g., when a power company sets its price above marginal cost.*

As discussed in Chapters 12, 13, and 17, monopoly power exists when one or a number of agents (suppliers or demanders of a commodity) exert some market power in determining prices. As discussed in Chapter 21, an externality is an interaction among agents that is not adequately reflected in market prices—the effects on agents are external to the market. Air pollution is the classic example of an externality (a negative externality given it decreases an agent's utility.) A public good (discussed in Chapter 22) is where one individual's consumption of a commodity does not decrease the ability of another individual to consume it. Examples are national defense, income distribution, and street lights. Finally, asymmetric information (Chapter 23) is when the perfectly competitive assumption of all agents having complete information about commodities offered in the market does not hold. Incomplete information can exist when the cost of verifying information about a commodity may not be universal across all buyers and sellers. For example, sellers of used automobiles may have information about the quality of various automobiles that may be difficult (costly) for potential buyers to acquire. When there is asymmetry in information, buyers may purchase a product in excess of a given quality.

> *A government is not only established for the prevention of mutual crime and fostering exchange, but also for noble actions.*
>
> (Aristotle)

> *Translation: Governments are established for improving social welfare by correcting market failures.*

The existence of monopoly power, externalities, public goods, and asymmetric information is justification for the establishment of governments to provide mechanisms to address resulting market failures. Governments can regulate firms with the objectives of mitigating monopoly power and negative externalities, and governments can provide for public goods either by direct production or by private incentives (wormholes). Also, governments can generate information, aid in its dissemination, and mandate that information be provided in an effort to reduce asymmetric information. The more a government must intervene in the marketplace to correct these failures, the less dependent will the economy be on freely operating markets. In some societies, these market failures appear quite large, and thus freely operating markets are severely limited. This is true in many centrally planned economies, where the government determines what and how to produce as well as who should receive the commodities produced. Even within the United States, which generally relies on free markets to allocate resources and outputs, there is always a question concerning the level of government intervention. Many environmental regulations directly limit the inputs that firms can use in their production decisions. For example, local zoning ordinances may restrict a firm's use of inputs that generate noise, smoke, or odors.

Why have a government? To address market failures caused by the existence of monopoly power, externalities, public goods and asymmetric information.

Summary

1. A measure of social welfare based on a Pareto criterion implies unanimity rule. Given a Pareto criterion, an allocation where agents must be made no worse off and at least one agent made better is required for improving social welfare.
2. The utility possibilities frontier is a mapping of the Pareto-efficient utilities for agents corresponding to each point on a contract curve.
3. A social-welfare function represents society's preferences for particular Pareto-efficient points on a utility possibilities frontier.
4. An egalitarian social-welfare function can be where either the total endowment of commodities is allocated equally among all the agents or the allocation of commodities makes all agents' utilities equal. In contrast, the utilitarian criterion maximizes some weighted sum of all agents' utilities.
5. Arrow's Impossibility Theorem states that it is impossible to establish a reasonable social preference ranking based solely on individual ordinal preference rankings.
6. Majority voting, a mechanism design for determining social choice, can result in a social preference ranking that is not transitive.
7. By not revealing his or her true preferences, an agent can employ strategic voting to potentially alter a social choice toward improving his or her satisfaction. Sequential voting is a method that counters some forms of strategic voting.
8. Conditions resulting in market failure are classified into four categories: monopoly power, externalities, public goods, and asymmetric information.
9. *(Appendix)* The compensation principle is a revealed preference approach that does not rely on specifying a welfare function to measure changes in social welfare.
10. *(Appendix)* The Theory of the Second Best states that social welfare can be improved even if market impediments exist in some markets by fostering perfectly competitive markets in other markets. This second-best solution does not generally hold when markets are interconnected.

Key concepts

Arrow's Impossibility Theorem, 870
compensation principle, 882
first-best solution, 887
isowelfare curve, 861
Kaldor compensation, 883
market failure, 876
mechanism design, 871
second-best, 887
Pareto-optimal allocation, 854
single-peaked preferences, 881
social indifference curve, 861
social-welfare function, 855
strong compensation test, 883
Theory of the Second Best, 887
utility bundle, 882
utility possibilities frontier, 856
weak compensation test, 884
welfare economics, 854

Key equations

$$\mho(U_R, U_F) = \min(U_{R,}, U_F)$$

The Rawlsian criterion for social welfare.

$$\mho(U_R, U_F) = U_R + U_F$$

The Benthamite welfare function.

Questions

1. It is nonsense to seek the greatest good for the greatest number of people. True or false? Explain.
2. One possible social ordering is to put the titles of all possible alternatives in a big drum, draw the titles at random, and use the order of drawing to determine the social ordering. Which of the assumptions associated with Arrow's Impossibility Theorem are satisfied and which are violated by this social ranking?
3. Why has the determination of income distribution always been a major interest of economists?
4. We cannot expect governmental decisions to result in maximizing social welfare, because such decisions are made on the basis of majority-rule voting. Do you agree or disagree with this statement? Explain.
5. In 1863, John Stuart Mill stated something like the following: "Each individual's happiness is a good to that individual and the general happiness, thus, a good to the aggregate of all persons." Explain.

6. In the movie *Star Trek IV: The Voyage Home*, Mr Spock states something like this: "The needs of the many outweigh the needs of the few." Is this statement justifiable in terms of Pareto-efficiency criteria? Explain.
7. Society should attempt to equalize economic opportunity instead of income. True or false? Explain.
8. What is your criterion of fairness in the distribution of income? Does it result in any conflict with Pareto efficiency? Explain.
9. Why does one vote per individual interfere with Pareto efficiency?
10. Adam Smith stated, "The pursuit of private gain leads to public benefit." Explain under what conditions this is not true.

Exercises

These problems are bicycles for the mind. They may not take you anywhere, but they tune up the brain power that can.

(Michael Wetzstein)

1. Assume the following production possibilities frontier:

$$X = q_1^2 + q_2^2,$$

where $X = 500$.

   a. What is MRPT(q_2 for q_1)?
   b. Assuming only one consumer in this economy with MRS(q_2 for q_1) $= 2$, what is the efficient allocation? Does this allocation maximize social welfare?

2. The utility possibilities frontier for agents A and B is $U_A + 2U_B = 120$.

   a. Graph this utility frontier.
   b. Given the *Nietzschian social-welfare function* $\mho(U_A, U_B) = \max(U_A, U_B)$, what is the maximum level of U_A and U_B?
   c. Now consider a Rawlsian criterion $\mho(U_A, U_B) = \min(U_A, U_B)$. What is the maximum level of U_A and U_B now?
   d. If social welfare is given by $\mho(U_A, U_B) = U_A^{1/2} U_B^{1/2}$, what is the maximum level of U_A and U_B?
   e. Illustrate the three social maxima on the graph in (a).

3. In the table below, the rankings of the Three Stooges are listed for three options. A ranking of 3 indicates that 3 is preferred over 2 and 1, and 2 is preferred over 1.

   a. Show that majority-rule voting results in intransitive social choices.
   b. Explain how this intransitivity may be eliminated if the Stooges could buy or sell their votes.

Stooges	*Option*		
	A	*B*	*C*
Larry	3	2	1
Moe	2	1	3
Curly	1	3	2

4. Consider a central authority who has Q units of a commodity to allocate among two consumers, with utility functions $U_j(x_j) = x_j^{1/2}, j = 1, 2$, and $Q = x_1 + x_2$. The central authority allocates the commodity to maximize the sum of consumers' utilities, $U(Q) = \sum_j U_j$.
   a. Derive the equilibrium allocation for the consumers (x_1^*, x_2^*) as a function of Q, and determine the optimal value for $U(Q)$.
   b. Let $p(Q) = U'(Q)$. Show that if (x_1^*, x_2^*) is the optimal allocation of the commodity given available quantity Q, then $p(Q) = U_j'(x_j^*)$ for $j = 1, 2$ with $x_j^* > 0$.
   c. Demonstrate that if the two consumers maximize utility facing a price for the commodity of $p(Q)$, then the aggregate demand for the commodity is exactly Q.
5. Two sailors, A and B, are marooned on an island with 200 pounds of sea rations, R. The utility functions for sailors A and B are

   $$U_A = R_A^{1/2}, \qquad U_B = \tfrac{1}{2} R_B^{1/2},$$

   where $R_A + R_B = 200$.
   a. If the ration is allocated equally between the sailors, how much utility will each receive?
   b. How should the rations be allocated between the sailors to assure equality of utility?
   c. Assume that the sailors develop the social-welfare function

   $$\mho = R_A^2 R_B.$$

   How will the ration now be allocated for maximizing social welfare?
6. An economy has the following production possibilities frontier for two commodities:

   $$B^2 + \mathcal{F}^2 = 288.$$

   In this economy, the preferences for the two consumers (R and F) are represented as

   $$U^R = (B_R \mathcal{F}_R)^{1/2}, \qquad U^F = B_F \mathcal{F}_F.$$

Given the social-welfare function $\mho = U^R U^F$, determine the allocation of B and $\mathcal{F}$ between R and F.

7. A social-welfare function for two commodities is $\mho = 2(q_1 + 2)q_2$ and the economy's production possibilities frontier is $2q_1 + 4q_2 - 12 = 0$. Determine the social maximum values for q_1 and q_2.
8. Use a two-agent, general equilibrium model to illustrate a situation in which there will be two equilibria when the assumption of a concave utility possibilities frontier is relaxed.
9. The social states for two agents with utility functions $U^B = x_1x_2$ and $U^C = x_1x_2$ are shown in the following table:

States	*Bonnie*		*Clyde*	
	x_1	x_2	x_1	x_2
A	5	5	5	5
B	2	14	12	3
C	5	4	6	6

Provide a social ranking of these states. What criteria did you use for this ranking?

10. Suppose that alternatives A, B, and C in Table 20.2 represent levels of spending for some public good (say, education) where A < B < C.
    a. Graph the table with preferences for the agents on the vertical axis and spending levels A, B and C on the horizontal axis.
    b. Which agents have a single-peaked level of preferences? Which agent has multiple peaks?
    c. Show that if instead the multiple-peaked agent had single-peaked preferences represented as C ≻ B ≻ A, then the Condorcet Paradox does not hold. This is called *single-peaked preferences*, where given agents with these preferences majority voting is transitive (the Condorcet Paradox does not hold).

Internet case studies

1. Outline the contributions of Public Choice Theory to neoclassical microeconomic theory.
2. Provide a brief outline of Marquis de Condorcet's (1743–1794) philosophy.
3. Outline the use of gasoline rationing during World War II.
4. Provide a list of strategic-voting methods that have been employed.

APPENDIX TO CHAPTER 20

Understanding the compensation principle

Any change, even a change for the better, is always accompanied by drawbacks and discomforts.

(Arnold Bennett)

Translation: Generally changes result in non-Pareto improvements.

The welfare function discussed in the chapter and the compensation principle are two distinct approaches to the problem of measuring welfare. A welfare-function approach is generally required if the objective is to determine the maximum social-welfare point on a utility possibilities frontier. However, in reality, many problems involve choosing between points on the frontier, where different points result from different policies. For example, damming a river may increase the satisfaction of households who enjoy waterskiing but decrease utility for households who enjoy white-water rafting. A social-welfare function could be used for determining the preferred policy (building the dam or not). Alternatively, a revealed preference approach (called the **compensation principle**) that does not rely on specifying a welfare function could be employed.

To explain the compensation principle, let us consider an initial point (*utility bundle*), A, on the utility possibilities curve U^{o} for Friday and Robinson (Figure 20A.1). As a result of some policy action, the utility possibilities curve shifts to U', with an associated new utility bundle B. As indicated in the figure, utility bundle B is preferred to A by both agents, which indicates a Pareto improvement. Thus, any policy that moves society from A to B should be undertaken, since the utilities of both agents are enhanced. For example, a policy of having everybody drive on the same side of the road (e.g., their right side) generally results in increasing all agents' utility.

Unfortunately, not all policies have such win/win outcomes for the agents. In fact, normally, some agents may prefer B to A and some A to B. An example is the effect on waterskiers' and rafters' utility from constructing a dam. In such non-Pareto-improvement cases, we can use the compensation principle to determine the social choice between

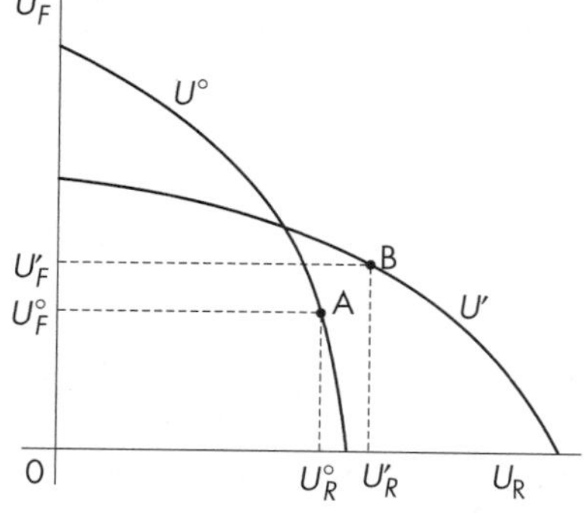

Figure 20A.1 **Pareto-improvement policy move.** Assume as a result of a policy action the utility possibilities frontier shifts from U^{o} to U'. The resulting utility bundle B is a Pareto improvement over the initial bundle A.

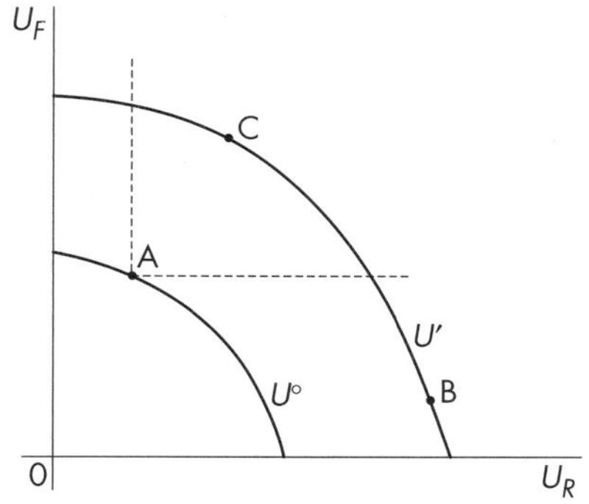

Figure 20A.2 **Strong compensation test.** Given any utility bundle associated with utility possibilities frontier U^o, say A, and a policy resulting in bundle B, then Robinson is better off but Friday is worse off. It is then possible to compensate Friday for her loss by moving from B to C.

policy actions, where one policy could be maintaining the status quo (not building the dam). To illustrate let us consider a policy resulting in the outward shift in the utility possibilities curve from U^o to U' (Figure 20A.2). Given a social-welfare function, the relaxation of the utility possibilities constraint from U^o to U' would increase welfare. Thus, the policy should be adopted (build the dam). Using what is called the strong compensation test in place of a social-welfare function, the same conclusion in terms of policy adoption will result (build the dam).

The *strong compensation test* is stated as follows:

Strong compensation test

Given *any* utility bundle A associated with U^o, if adopting a policy results in at least one utility bundle C being preferred to A by both agents, then social welfare is improved by adopting the policy.

This strong compensation test is illustrated in Figure 20A.2. All feasible utility bundles associated with U^o are represented by the area under U^o. At every one of these feasible utility bundles, it is possible to increase one or both agents' utility by adopting a policy yielding U'. Wherever the initial utility bundle A is in the feasible area under U^o, it is possible to adopt a policy yielding U' and compensate any agents harmed by the policy in such a way as to make both agents better off. As illustrated in the figure, if A is the initial utility bundle and a policy results in B, Robinson is made better off by the policy but Friday is worse off (not a Pareto improvement). However, it is possible to monetarily compensate Friday, resulting in a movement to C, which results in both agents being better off. This type of compensation is termed *Kaldor compensation.* If Friday is actually compensated, then both agents' utilities are improved with the policy and the policy should be undertaken.

If you are compensated for your loss, can social welfare then improve? Yes, if you are compensated such that no agent is made worse off and at least one agent is made better off, then social welfare is improved.

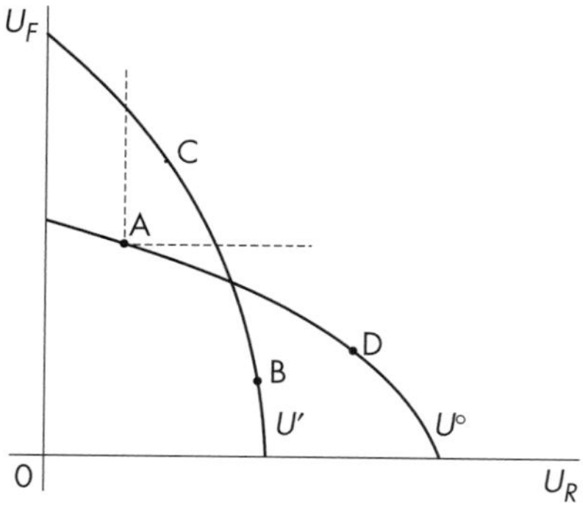

Figure 20A.3 **Weak compensation test.** Given utility bundle A and a policy resulting in bundle B, then Robinson is better off but Friday is worse off. It is possible to compensate Friday for her loss by moving from B to C.

Not all policies result in a utility possibilities frontier that includes all the feasible utility bundles prior to the policy. Graphically, this is illustrated in Figure 20A.3 by the utility possibilities frontiers crossing. In this case, the strong compensation test does not hold. For example, at utility bundle D associated with frontier U°, there is no utility bundle associated with frontier U' that is Pareto-preferred. If there was a utility bundle associated with frontier U', then it would be possible to compensate any agents harmed by adoption of the policy associated with U'. In the figure, for any utility bundle on the portion of frontier U° below U', utility bundles associated with frontier U' exist that are Pareto-preferred to the bundle on U°. For example, consider the initial utility bundle A associated with U° and a policy action that results in B associated with U'. Now a Pareto improvement can result at bundle C if Friday is Kaldor-compensated for the loss of utility. This is an example of the *weak compensation test,* stated as follows:

Weak compensation test

Given utility bundle A associated with U°, if adopting a policy results in at least one utility bundle C being preferred to A by both agents, then social welfare is improved by adopting the policy.

For both of these compensation tests, the question of whether compensation is carried out is really a question about equity. The welfare theorems demonstrate that the question of equity can be separated from the question of allocative efficiency. The compensation criterion is concerned solely with allocative efficiency, and the question of equity can best be handled by alternative mechanisms such as redistribution taxation. A policy change is an improvement if those who gain evaluate their gains at a higher figure than the value that the losers set upon their losses.

In 1941, Tobor Scitovsky (1910–2002) noted a problem with the Kaldor compensation criteria. In Figure 20A.4, A and B are not comparable. Neither the strong nor the weak compensation test can reveal anything about the relative desirability of A versus B. Also, considering Figure 20A.5, B is preferred to A in terms of the weak compensation criterion, because C is Pareto-preferable to A. For example, building the dam, resulting in a movement

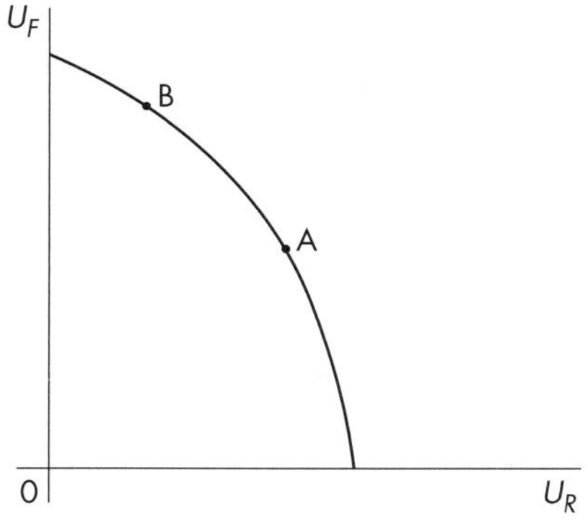

Figure 20A.4 **Failure of the Kaldor compensation criteria in ranking outcomes.** Neither the strong nor weak compensation tests can reveal anything concerning the desirability of A over B.

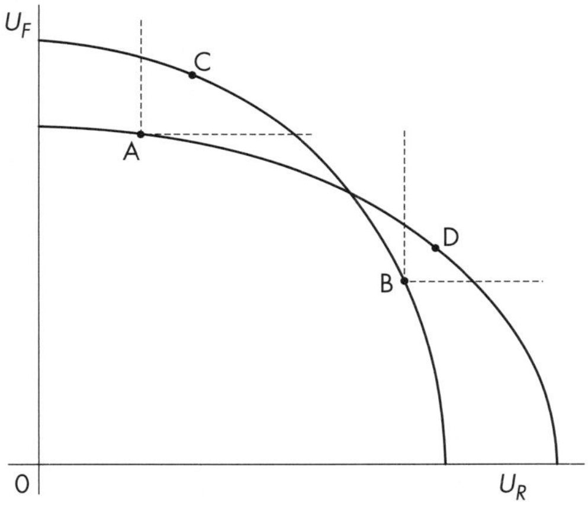

Figure 20A.5 **Compensation paradox.** The weak compensation test results in B preferred to A but also A preferred to B.

from A to B, results in improved utility for waterskier Robinson but decreased utility for rafter Friday. If Friday could be compensated for her loss, both agents' utility would increase to point C. However, A is also preferred to B, because D is Pareto-preferred to B. If the dam is not built, Robinson can be compensated for his loss, resulting in point D, which is Pareto-preferred to building the dam, point B. This paradox is the main defect of the compensation criterion; nevertheless, the compensation tests are the basis of most applied welfare analysis.

These tests do not resolve the basic problem of interpersonal preferences required to evaluate a policy change that is not Pareto-optimal. Specifically, they assume that the marginal utility of income for all agents is the same whether they are poor or rich. This assumption generally does not hold, given that a dollar is not equally valuable to everyone.

A comparison based on monetary compensation is thus biased. For example, a gain of $100 may be only a minimal gain hardly noticed by a wealthy individual. In contrast, a loss of $25 may mean a great deal to a poor individual. However, these tests would conclude that there is a net gain in welfare. Furthermore, the criteria implicitly base recommendations on agents' relative willingness and ability to pay, which assumes a given distribution of income.

As discussed in the previous chapters, changes in consumer surplus as a result of policy alterations are used as measures of willingness to pay. Comparing these changes for policy analysis is a compensation-type criterion, and thus the same problems associated with these compensation tests are associated with consumer surplus analysis. Despite this shortcoming, it is often useful to apply these tests and determine consumer and producer surplus for measuring the change in welfare resulting from alternative policies.

Application: Counting losses in natural resource damages

In assessing natural resource damage, such as the 2011 BP Gulf oil spill, applied economists apply a Kaldor compensation framework. First, the payment just sufficient to compensate an agent for the natural resource damage is determined, and then damages are aggregated across agents to determine the total value of damages. Besides the problems inherent in determining the level of compensation for an individual agent, determining who should be counted in the aggregation of households is questionable. Total damages can be reduced through identifying types of agents who benefit from the damage and establishing criteria for excluding agents who claim to be harmed by natural resource injury.

Based on welfare economics, A. Randall critically examined claims concerning offsetting benefits and justifications for excluding damages claimed on behalf of certain types of agents. Specifically, four claims were investigated: (1) rubberneckers who receive benefits from observing natural resource injury or clean-up operations; (2) claims on behalf of agents who were unaware of the natural resource damage; (3) agents whose behavior is inconsistent with individual utility-maximizing; and (4) altruists who have an unselfish interest in the welfare of others.

In evaluating these four claims, Randall concluded that the claim for rubberneckers enjoying benefits that partially offset welfare losses is implausible. There is no sound reason for society to honor such claims. The investment in human capital (gathering information and learning) as a motive for rubbernecking is more plausible than rubbernecking for immediate pleasure. Also, utilitarianism censors certain preferences as unacceptable. If there are rubberneckers who are willing to pay for more disasters, society should not count these benefits when assessing natural resources damages. However, the second claim of considering damage associated with agents who were unaware of the damage is plausible. The adage "what you do not know cannot hurt you" is flawed. When an injury is real, awareness is not a prerequisite for harm. An example is provided by Randall: murder is harmless to the victim if performed so the victim dies unaware. If ignorance of an injury is a sufficient condition for harmlessness, then harm can be minimized by maximizing ignorance. This suggests that the flow of information following a natural resource injury should be minimized, which is not welfare-enhancing. There is also little justification for excluding agents whose behavior is inconsistent with individual utility-maximizing. Preferences based on ethical principles and choices to participate in collective efforts to provide public goods may not be consistent in terms of maximizing an individual agent's utility in isolation, but may still be consistent in terms of maximizing social welfare.

Randall concluded that full compensation is warranted for altruists if the actual victims of the natural resource damages are not compensated at all. However, if victims are fully compensated, then altruists should not be compensated. As noted by Randall, the correct response of an altruist to the question "What compensation do you require, knowing that victims are fully compensated?" is zero.

Source: A. Randall, "Whose Losses Count? Examining Some Claims about Aggregation Rules for Natural Resources Damages," *Contemporary Economic Policy* 15 (1997): 88–97.

Theory of the Second Best

We will not be satisfied with perfect competition in some markets; our objective is perfect competition for all.

(Michael Wetzstein)

The four general types of impediments to perfect competition—monopoly power, externalities, public goods, and asymmetric information—are generally present in many economic systems. Given some market impediments, a perfectly competitive price system in other markets will thus be unable to generate a Pareto-optimal allocation of resources. Some policymakers have contended that a perfectly competitive price system should still be advocated for some sectors of the economy even if impediments remain in other sectors. By fostering perfectly competitive markets in these sectors, the Pareto conditions for allocation efficiency would at least be satisfied in some markets. This reasoning is a second-best solution to the problem of optimal allocation. A *first-best solution* is where an optimal allocation of resources is only constrained by technology. A *second-best solution* involves other constraints on resource allocation, such as the four general impediments. According to the **Theory of the Second Best,** this second best solution should be adopted. Unfortunately, this Theory of the Second Best generally is not correct.

In 1956, R. Lipsey and K. Lancaster determined that if certain constraints within an economic system prevent some of the Pareto conditions from holding, then, given these constraints, it will generally not be preferred to have the Pareto conditions hold elsewhere.[4] Requiring more but still not all of the Pareto-optimality conditions to hold is not necessarily preferable than having fewer hold. Thus, each individual situation associated with an impediment must be analyzed, rather than drawing one policy recommendation incorporating all impediment situations.

As an example, suppose that there are three commodities q_1, q_2 and y produced with one input X, where the market for y exhibits some impediments. According to the Theory of the Second Best, households will maximize their satisfaction if the remaining commodities are sold at perfectly competitive prices where prices equal marginal costs. Lipsey and Lancaster concluded that this theory is not necessarily correct.

To illustration the failure of the Theory of the Second Best, let us consider the case of one household (or a number of consumers all with the same utility function) with the input X a numeraire commodity, so its price $v = 1$. This household maximizes utility subject to a production possibilities frontier $X = f(q_1, q_2, y)$, and with $v = 1$ this is the total cost of producing the outputs. The household is then faced with

$$\max U(q_1, q_2, y) \quad \text{s.t.} f(q_1, q_2, y) - X = 0.$$

The Lagrangian is then

$$\mathcal{L}(q_1, q_2, y, \lambda) = U(q_1, q_2, y) + \lambda [f(q_1, q_2, y) - X].$$

The FOCs are

$$\frac{\partial \mathcal{L}}{\partial q_1} = \text{MU}_1 + \lambda \text{MC}_1 = 0,$$

$$\frac{\partial \mathcal{L}}{\partial q_2} = \text{MU}_2 + \lambda \text{MC}_2 = 0,$$

$$\frac{\partial \mathcal{L}}{\partial y} = \text{MU}_y + \lambda \text{MC}_y = 0,$$

$$\frac{\partial \mathcal{L}}{\partial \lambda} = f(q_1, q_2, y) - X = 0.$$

Thus,

$$\text{MRS}(q_2 \text{ for } q_1) = \frac{\text{MU}_1}{\text{MU}_2} = \frac{\text{MC}_1}{\text{MC}_2} = \text{MRPT}(q_2 \text{ for } q_1),$$

$$\text{MRS}(q_2 \text{ for } y) = \frac{\text{MU}_y}{\text{MU}_2} = \frac{\text{MC}_y}{\text{MC}_2} = \text{MRPT}(q_2 \text{ for } y).$$

Each MRS equals the respective MRPT. Now suppose that y is not sold at MC. A constraint that expresses this is $\text{MU}_y = a\text{MC}_y$, where $a \neq \text{MU}_2/\text{MC}_2$. The Lagrangian for maximizing $U(q_1, q_2, y)$ subject to this new constraint and the production possibilities frontier $f(q_1, q_2, y) - X = 0$ is

$$\mathcal{L}(q_1, q_2, y, \lambda_1, \lambda_2) = U(q_1, q_2, y) + \lambda_1 [f(x_1, x_2, y) - X] + \lambda_2 \left(\text{MU}_y - a\text{MC}_y\right).$$

The FOCs are

$$\frac{\partial\mathcal{L}}{\partial q_1} = \mathrm{MU}_1 + \lambda_1\mathrm{MC}_1 + \lambda_2\left(\frac{\partial\mathrm{MU}_y}{\partial q_1} - a\frac{\partial\mathrm{MC}_y}{\partial q_1}\right) = 0,$$

$$\frac{\partial\mathcal{L}}{\partial q_2} = \mathrm{MU}_2 + \lambda_1\mathrm{MC}_2 + \lambda_2\left(\frac{\partial\mathrm{MU}_y}{\partial q_2} - a\frac{\partial\mathrm{MC}_y}{\partial q_2}\right) = 0,$$

$$\frac{\partial\mathcal{L}}{\partial y} = \mathrm{MU}_y + \lambda_1\mathrm{MC}_y + \lambda_2\left(\frac{\partial\mathrm{MU}_y}{\partial y} - a\frac{\partial\mathrm{MC}_y}{\partial y}\right) = 0,$$

$$\frac{\partial\mathcal{L}}{\partial\lambda_1} = f(x_1, x_2, y) - X = 0,$$

$$\frac{\partial\mathcal{L}}{\partial\lambda_2} = \mathrm{MU}_y - a\mathrm{MC}_y = 0.$$

Solving for the marginal rate of substitution MRS(q_2 for q_1),

$$\mathrm{MRS}(q_2 \text{ for } q_1) = \frac{\mathrm{MU}_1}{\mathrm{MU}_2} = \frac{\lambda_1\mathrm{MC}_1 + \lambda_2(\partial\mathrm{MU}_y/\partial q_1 - a\partial\mathrm{MC}_y/\partial q_1)}{\lambda_1\mathrm{MC}_2 + \lambda_2(\partial\mathrm{MU}_y/\partial q_2 - a\partial\mathrm{MC}_y/\partial q_2)}$$

$$\neq \mathrm{MRPT}(q_2 \text{ for } q_1).$$

Thus, we cannot infer that the MRS for q_1 and q_2 should equal $\mathrm{MC}_1/\mathrm{MC}_2 = \mathrm{MRPT}(q_2$ for $q_1)$. If some distortion where $p_1 \neq \mathrm{MC}_1$ or $p_2 \neq \mathrm{MC}_2$ is removed in the economy, we cannot argued that society will be better off if other distortions such as $p_y \neq \mathrm{MC}_y$ are present. Only when the second cross-partials ($\partial\mathrm{MU}_y/\partial q_1$, $\partial\mathrm{MC}_y/\partial q_1$, $\partial\mathrm{MU}_y/\partial q_2$, $\partial\mathrm{MC}_y/\partial q_2$) are all equal to zero will a more efficient allocation result by a removal of a distortion in markets for q_1 or q_2. Specifically, this would occur if the commodities are not closely related as complements or substitutes.

These FOCs are illustrated in Figure 20A.6 for two commodities q_1 and q_2. In the absence of market failure for commodity y, the only constraint on social welfare is the production possibilities frontier. In the figure, maximum social welfare will then occur where a social indifference curve is just tangent to this possibilities frontier, point A. In contrast, point A is not obtainable if there is some market impediment for commodity y, implying an additional constraint on the economic system. Representing this additional constraint as a line below point A, a production-efficient point is then point D. However, given this impediment, social welfare is maximized at point C. The inefficient point C is preferable to the efficient point D. Thus, given some market impediment for commodity y, a policy advocating perfect competition in the markets for commodities q_1 and q_2 leading to production efficiency may not be a social-welfare improvement.

In societies where consumers and producers depend substantially or completely on markets for providing the commodities consumed and produced, the interconnected markets will result in nonzero cross-partials. Free markets take this interconnectedness into account through price signals in the allocation of scarce resources and will theoretically yield a Pareto-efficient allocation. However, market failures will disrupt this efficient allocation, possibly requiring government intervention into the market. Investigating the Theory of the Second Best indicates that the correct government policies to address these market failures must

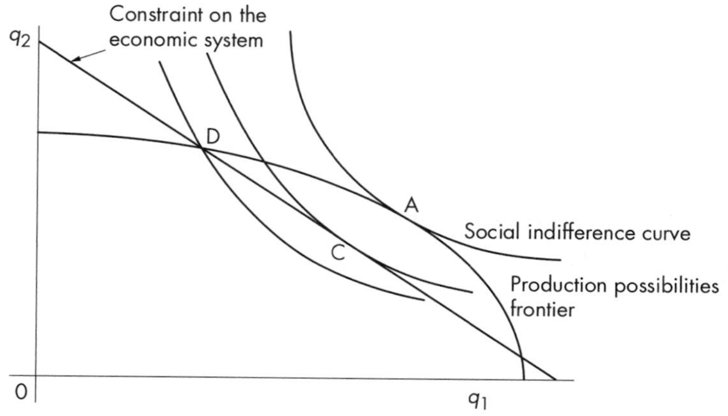

Figure 20A.6 **Theory of the Second Best.** Maximizing social welfare subject to only a production possibilities frontier occurs at point A. Let the constraint on the economic system preventing the attainment of point A be some market impediment. This market-impediment constraint results in a Pareto-efficient production point D, which does not coincide with the maximum social-welfare point C.

be based on the entire interconnectedness of markets. Policies that only address a subset of markets may have undesirable consequences.

Are free-market zealots correct? No, they are not correct if they advocate perfect competition in one sector of an economy when there is still market failure in another sector.

Whether such second-best perfectly competitive solutions are optimal will depend on the particular situation and on the nature of the constraints present in the economic system. With knowledge of society's preferences and technology, it may in fact be possible to derive some optimal departures from perfectly competitive pricing. Governmental policy departures from free markets, such as environmental protection, antitrust legislation, and provision of public goods and market information, may yield welfare improvements relative to the free market. The failure of the Theory of the Second Best implies that assessing the full consequence of a policy requires considering the policy effect across all markets, given market interconnectedness.

Example 20A.1 Theory of the Second Best

Consider the following utility function composed of three commodities q_1, q_2, and y, for an economy with either one household or all households with the same preferences:

$$U = q_1 q_2^2 y.$$

The production possibilities frontier is

$$q_1^2 + q_2^2 + y^2 = 16.$$

Maximizing utility subject to this frontier yields the Lagrangian

$$\mathcal{L}(q_1, q_2, y, \lambda) = q_1 q_2^2 y + \lambda\left(16 - q_1^2 - q_2^2 - y^2\right).$$

The FOCs are then

$$\partial\mathcal{L}/\partial q_1 = q_2^{*2} y^* - 2\lambda q_1^* = 0,$$

$$\partial\mathcal{L}/\partial q_2 = 2q_1^* q_2^* y^* - 2\lambda q_2^* = 0,$$

$$\partial\mathcal{L}/\partial y = q_1^* q_2^{*2} - 2\lambda y^* = 0,$$

$$\partial\mathcal{L}/\partial\lambda = 16 - q_1^{*2} - q_2^{*2} - y^{*2} = 0.$$

These FOCs imply

$$\text{MRS}(q_2 \text{ for } q_1) = \frac{q_2^*}{2q_1^*} = \frac{q_1^*}{q_2^*} = \text{ MRPT}(q_2 \text{ for } q_1) \Rightarrow q_2^* = 2^{1/2} q_1^{*2},$$

$$\text{MRS}(y \text{ for } q_1) = \frac{y^*}{q_1^*} = \frac{q_1^*}{y^*} = \text{ MRPT}(y \text{ for } q_1) \Rightarrow y^* = q_1^*.$$

Substituting the functions for q_2 and y into the last FOC and solving for q_1 yields

$$16 - q_1^{*2} - q_2^{*2} - y^{*2} = 0,$$
$$16 - q_1^{*2} - 2q_1^{*2} - q_1^{*2} = 0,$$
$$4q_1^{*2} = 16 \Rightarrow q_1^* = 2, y^* = 2, q_2^* = \left(2^{1/2}\right)2 = 2.83, U^* = 32.$$

Now consider the following additional constraint resulting from some market failure for y, $q_1 q_2^2 = 2y$. The Lagrangian for this problem with two constraints is

$$\mathcal{L}(q_1, q_2, y, \lambda_1, \lambda_2) = q_1 q_2^2 y + \lambda_1\left(16 - q_1^2 - q_2^2 - y^2\right) + \lambda_2\left(q_1 q_2^2 - 2y\right).$$

The FOCs are now

$$\partial\mathcal{L}/\partial q_1 = q_2^{*2} y^* - 2\lambda_1^* q_1^* + \lambda_2^* q_2^{*2} = 0,$$
$$\partial\mathcal{L}/\partial q_2 = 2q_1^* q_2^* y^* - 2\lambda_1^* q_2^* + 2\lambda_2^* q_1^* q_2^* = 0,$$
$$\partial\mathcal{L}/\partial y = q_1^* q_2^{*2} - 2\lambda_1^* y^* - 2\lambda_2^* = 0,$$
$$\partial\mathcal{L}/\partial\lambda_1 = 16 - q_1^{*2} - q_2^{*2} - y^{*2} = 0,$$
$$\partial\mathcal{L}/\partial\lambda_2 = q_1^* q_2^{*2} - 2y^* = 0.$$

These FOCs imply

$$\text{MRS}(q_2 \text{ for } q_1) = \frac{q_2^*}{2q_1^*} = \frac{2\lambda_1^* q_1^* - \lambda_2^* q_2^{*2}}{2\lambda_1^* q_2^* - 2\lambda_2^* q_1^* q_2^*}.$$

Thus, MRS is not equal to MRPT. We get the solution for these FOCs with five equations and five unknowns by first solving the second FOC for q_1 and the first and fifth FOCs for q_2^2:

$$q_1^* = \frac{\lambda_1^*}{y^* + \lambda_2^*}, \qquad \text{2nd FOC,}$$

$$q_2^{*2} = \frac{2\lambda_1^* q_1^*}{y^* + \lambda_2^*} = 2q_1^{*2}, \qquad \text{1st FOC,}$$

$$q_2^{*2} = \frac{2y^*}{q_1^*} = 2q_1^{*2} \Rightarrow q_1^* = y^{*1/3}, \qquad \text{5th FOC.}$$

Thus, $q_1^{*2} = y^{*2/3}$ and $q_2^{*2} = 2y^{*2/3}$. We then find the optimal value for y by substituting these results into the production possibilities frontier:

$$q_1^{*2} + q_2^{*2} + y^{*2} = y^{*2/3} + 2y^{*2/3} + y^{*2} = 16 \Rightarrow y^* = 3.10,$$

which results in $q_1^* = 1.46$ and $q_2^* = 2.06$, with $U^* = 19.21$. Note that, due to the additional constraint, the level of utility declined from $U = 32$ to $U = 19.21$.

Requiring production efficiency in markets for q_1 and q_2, given the condition of market failure for y, results in the following conditions:

$$q_1^2 + q_2^2 + y^2 = 16, \qquad q_1 q_2^2 = 2y.$$

Considering the value of $y = 2$, then $q_1 = 0.34$ and $q_2 = 3.43$, with $U = 8$.

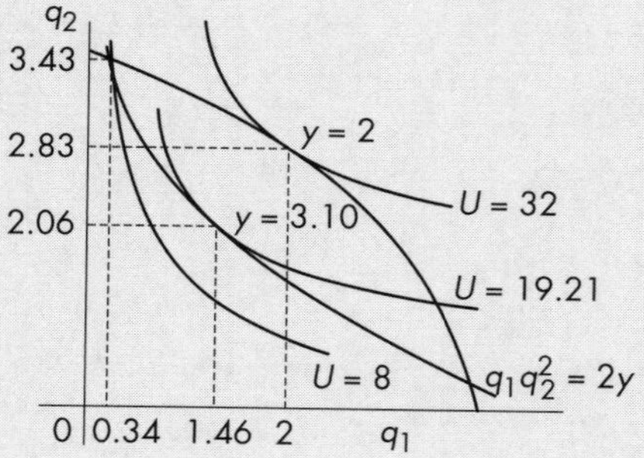

Application: Following directions

The calculus underlying this failure of the Theory of the Second Best may be a little complex, but, as discussed by P. Dorman, all FOCs represent only a set of commands. Each FOC (equimarginal condition) can be viewed as an instruction to be followed, just as you would follow your GPS driving instructions to get to a party: "after the third light, turn right, go three blocks, turn left and the party is then at the second house on the left." The most efficient route is to follow all the GPS instructions correctly (a Pareto-efficient allocation). The failure of the Theory of the Second Best states that if all the instructions are followed but one (e.g., turning left rather than right), then you will end up far from the party. Even having correct instructions (perfectly competitive price signals) in all but one case will not get you to the party. In an effort to correct this wrong turn, it is necessary to violate additional instructions. One bad turn requires another.

The failure of the Theory of the Second Best prevents economists from considering one market at a time. An example provided by Dorman is the automobile industry. Even if there is no market failure in the automobile market, it may still be desirable for government to regulate fuel efficiency. If the price of gasoline is below its marginal cost, so that the Pareto conditions in the petroleum market are not satisfied, then regulation requiring a higher level of fuel efficiency than consumers demand at the low gas prices may improve social welfare. In general, many mechanism designs for improving social welfare are in response to the failure of the Theory of the Second Best. Economists and policymakers develop mechanism designs in markets to offset the inefficient allocations generated in other markets.

Source: P. Dorman, "Waiting for an Echo: The Revolution in General Equilibrium Theory and the Paralysis in Introductory Economics," *Review of Radical Political Economics* 33 (2001): 325–333.

Questions

1. Under what conditions is perfect competition neither feasible nor desirable in a particular market? If it is feasible and desirable in a market, will it improve social welfare to foster perfect competition in these markets?
2. Explain how the conditions of economic efficiency can be satisfied when all industries are monopolies. How is this explanation related to the Theory of the Second Best?
3. Under what conditions is partial-equilibrium analysis possibly more appropriate than general-equilibrium analysis? Do these conditions support the implications resulting from the Theory of the Second Best?

Exercises

1. Volunteers in the military are willing to accept a 1/1000 risk of death in combat if their combat pay is $10,000. What is their combined willingness to be compensated to accept the loss of one casually?

2. Assume a two-agent economy with utility for each agent varying, according to the following table, by the type of society they are in:

Society	*Utility 1*	*Utility 2*
A	100	100
B	5	205

The agents do not know which utility level they will receive in the two societies A and B.

a. If an agent prefers living in a Rawlsian society, in which society would it choose to reside? What if the agent has utilitarian social preferences?
b. If an agent is risk-neutral, what would the probability of receiving utility 2 in society B have to be before he would prefer society B to A?

3. Assume that U^o and U' are two utility possibilities frontiers with associated Pareto-efficient allocations (utility bundles) of A for U^o and B for U'. Show graphically that it is possible for U' to pass the strong compensation test over U^o, but in terms of the utilitarian criterion be socially undesirable.

Internet case study

1. Provide a list of Nicholas Kaldor's (1908–1986) accomplishments.

21 Externalities

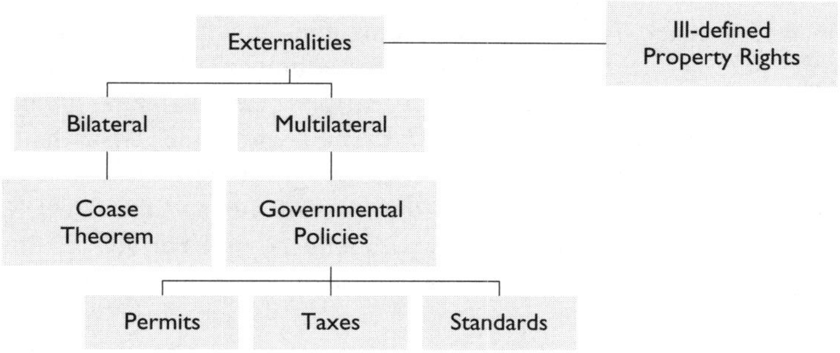

Outline and Conceptual Inquiries

Defining externalities
Is a capital crime an externality?

Understanding property rights
Who has property rights?
Application: Oyster industry

Bilateral externalities
Independent decision making
Why do polluters pollute?
Dependent (joint) decision making
Is joining rather than fighting a polluter socially desirable?
Resolving externality inefficiency
When will free markets resolve externality inefficiencies?

Multilateral externalities

Governmental policies
Permit system: CO_2
What has happened to property rights when you obtain a hunting license?
Application: The NO_x budget program
Taxes and standards (quotas): air quality standards
Application: Establishing a fat tax to reduce obesity
Application: Gamifying instead of taxing to internalize negative externalities
Stock externalities: global warming
Firms' preference
Would a firm prefer standards or taxes?

Summary
Key concepts
Key equations
Questions
Exercises
Internet case studies

Appendix to chapter 21

Common property
What is a cause of species extinction?
Application: Fish populations

Questions
Exercise
Internet case study

I shot an arrow into the air, and it stuck.

(Belfast Graffito)

Emissions from one automobile are generally low, relative to an industrial (e.g., coal power plant) smokestack. However, aggregating emissions from millions of vehicles results in the automobile being the largest air polluter. Driving an automobile is probably a household's most polluting activity. Efforts since 1970 have greatly reduced typical vehicle emissions. However, by 2007, the number of miles driven had increased by 150 percent, which offset the benefits of controlling emissions. Since 2007, the miles driven has started to decline due to the rising cost of fuel and the Great Recession. This decline in vehicle emissions coupled with reduced miles driven results in major reductions in on-road automobile pollutants; yielding significant improvements in air quality.

The cause of this automobile pollution is a major market failure in the presence of an externality (pollution) resulting from missing markets. With missing markets, signals in the form of market prices do not exist to reveal consumer preferences for society's allocation of resources. As discussed in this chapter, if well-defined property rights existed, markets would generally occur for externalities. This would reduce the necessity of mechanisms designed to correct externality-generated inefficiencies. Thus, one role for government is providing a legal system (mechanism design) to support well-defined property rights for all of society's resources.

In this chapter, we first investigate property rights and the consequences of externalities resulting from ill-defined property rights. We then broadly classify externalities as either bilateral or multilateral. We discuss the inefficiencies associated with *bilateral externalities* and address enforceable property rights (given the *Coase Theorem*) as a means for resolving these inefficiencies. The Coase Theorem states that if a market can be created for an externality, an efficient outcome will result regardless of how well-defined property rights are allocated.

We then investigate markets where the Coase Theorem does not hold. First, we discuss the issue of *multilateral externalities* (with the general case of common property addressed in the Appendix to the chapter). Then we evaluate governmental policies involving quotas, taxes, and fostering markets for externalities (eliminating missing markets) as tools for addressing market inefficiencies. Through these policies, governmental agencies develop mechanisms that assign property rights and regulate agent behavior, enforcing the policies through penalties for noncompliance and dividends for compliance. However, government mechanisms may not always result in improving social welfare. Such mechanisms can only result in alternative second-best Pareto-efficient allocations. The opportunity cost of allocating resources toward establishing and maintaining mechanisms may exceed the cost of inefficiency associated with some externalities. As further developed in this chapter, the existence of this opportunity cost implies that there are still externalities at some allocation where social welfare is maximized.

Applied economists are active in estimating these costs and associated benefits of alternative mechanisms for addressing externalities. Thus, our aim in this chapter is not to determine the least-cost allocation for removing an externality. Instead, the objective is to understand why ill-defined property rights result in missing markets for commodities and resulting externalities. We then can determine the optimal level of an externality and minimum cost of achieving a given externality level.

Defining externalities

Have you ever noticed the people who are late are often so much jollier than the people who have waited for them?

(E.V. Lucas)

You experience an externality when having to slow down as soon as a driver in front of you slows to look at a traffic accident. Specifically, an **externality (z)** is present whenever some agent's (say, R's) utility or production technology includes commodities whose amounts are determined by other agents without particular attention to the effect on R's welfare. This definition rules out any market-price effects on agents' utility or production, called **pecuniary externalities**, which arise when the external effect is transmitted through price changes. A pecuniary externality does not cause a market failure. For example, suppose that a new firm enters a market and drives up the rental price of land. The land market provides a mechanism by which the parties can bid for land, and the resulting prices will reflect the value of land in its various uses. Without pecuniary externalities, the price signals would fail to sustain an efficient allocation.

Furthermore, consumers relying on firms for the supply of commodities are not externalities. For example, there is no externality in you relying on a farmer for food. Farmers do not determine how much each individual household will consume. Deliberately affecting the welfare of others is also not an externality. For example, deliberate criminal actions against agents are not externalities. However, waiting for someone who is not particularly concerned about your welfare is an externality.

Is a capital crime an externality? It depends on the intent: first-degree intentional homicide is not an externality, but first-degree reckless homicide is.

Externality (z). An agent's utility includes commodities whose amounts are determined by other agents who pay no particular attention to the effect on the agent's welfare. *E.g., a firm discharging sulfur dioxide into the atmosphere that affects nearby households' living.*

Pecuniary externalities. External effects transmitted through changes in prices. *E.g., a freeze in Florida resulting in a sharp increase in the price of orange juice is not an externality on consumers of orange juice.*

Understanding property rights

The meek shall inherit the Earth, but not its mineral rights.

(Albert Einstein)

In October 1990, plaintiff Richard Lee Mann, on his own private property, shot a red wolf that he deemed a threat to his cattle. The federal government prosecuted Mann under the Endangered Species Act (ESA) and he pleaded guilty. This case led to the passage in 1995 of a North Carolina bill entitled "An Act to Allow the Trapping and Killing of Red Wolves by Owners of Private Land." This State law directly conflicted with the federal regulations of the ESA. The US Court of Appeals, 4th Circuit, June 6, 2000 upheld the regulation as a valid exercise of federal power under the Commerce Clause. However, anti-wolf fever has continued with further killings—in 2010, only 130 wild red wolves roamed northeastern North Carolina.

Property rights are a bundle of entitlements defining an owner's rights, privileges, and limitations (not killing red wolves) for use of a resource. For example, in many cities, owning a plot of land may give you the entitlement to build a house but not to drill a well. These entitlements very considerably, from being very restrictive in a planned community to having essentially no restrictions in some rural areas. Regardless of the nature of entitlements, a well-defined structure of property rights will provide incentives for the efficient allocation of resources. For example, the following list is one set of well-defined **private-property rights** that result in a Pareto-efficient allocation:

1 *Universality*. All resources are privately owned and all entitlements completely specified.
2 *Exclusivity*. All benefits and costs accrued from owning and employing resources accrue to the owner.
3 *Transferability*. All property rights are transferable from one owner to another in a voluntary exchange.
4 *Enforceability*. Property rights are secure from involuntary seizure or encroachment by others.

In previous chapters, we implicitly assumed that well-defined property rights existed. Given these well-defined property rights, we demonstrated that perfectly competitive markets yield an efficient-price system for resource allocation. Such a system is where producers maximize their profits and households maximize their utility, given their respective resource constraints and current state of technology.

Property rights. A bundle of entitlements. *E.g., ownership of a residential real estate lot allows you to place a home, but not a commercial establishment, on the property.*

Private property rights. Property entitlements vested with individual agents. *E.g., private ownership of natural resources and capital goods.*

Unfortunately, the presence of externalities violates this assumption of well-defined property rights. For example, building a cabin that blocks the neighbor's view of the lake results in a cost that accrues to the neighbor. With externalities, household preferences for commodities are not defined solely over the bundle of commodities that it has ability to choose. Instead, some commodities over which the household has no control (called *consumption externalities*) affect preferences. Similarly, the assumption of firms freely choosing inputs is also violated with the presence of *production externalities*. Generally, consumption or production externalities exist when agents (households and firms) are directly affected by the actions (external effects) of other agents. Examples are the presence of other vehicles on a congested highway or the sight of a neighbor's flower garden. Highway congestion is an example of a **negative externality,** and a flower garden is an example of a **positive externality**. When such externalities exist, the perfectly competitive equilibrium does not correspond to a Pareto-optimal allocation.

Negative externality. Negative external effects. *E.g., a roommate's untidiness.*

Positive externality. Positive external effects. *E.g., a roommate's tidiness.*

A **common property** resource exists when no individual agent has property entitlements and thus an agent cannot employ the resource for individual gain. The economic inefficiency of common property is developed in the Appendix to this chapter. In a communist economy, all society's resources are considered common property. In a centrally planned socialist economy, the state (government) has the property entitlements and controls property (resource) allocation for the common good of society. In a free-market economy, property entitlements are vested privately with individual agents, leading to private property as the dominant form of property rights.

Who has property rights? If it is private property, then the entitlements are vested with the owner of the property; if it is common property, then the entitlements are vested with all members of the society.

Common property. A resource owned in common by all the agents in an economy. *E.g., whales in the open seas.*

Application: Oyster industry

Following a brief larva stage (spat), an oyster connects permanently to a firm subaqueous material such as a rock or shell (cultch). The permanent connection prevents oysters from migrating, so oysters can become private property in terms of who owns their sea-floor area. This has resulted in private property-right structures, based on lease holdings, characterizing one type of property rights in the US Atlantic and Gulf oyster industry. Common property is the other property-right structure.

A problem with the common property structure is that oyster harvesting generally removes cultch. Unless the cultch is replaced, oyster production in a harvested area is greatly diminished. Common property provides little in the way of incentives to replenish the cultch. Also, overcrowding of oyster vessels in these common areas results in congestion and the harvest of immature oysters. These problems, which yield inefficiencies, suggest that private property may offer a more efficient alternative. In the case of migratory species (most fish and birds), enforcement problems may make private property rights inefficient. However, for nonmigratory species (oysters), property rights could yield an efficient allocation.

Agnello and Donnelley investigated the influence that common property versus private property rights have on the oyster industry's economic efficiency. Their empirical findings suggest that private property rights in general yield a significant increase in efficiency. Common property rights are associated with low productivity resulting from limited cultch replenishment, congestion, overexploitation, and governmental restrictions. The estimated magnitude of this inefficiency, in terms of the elasticity of labor productivity with respect to private property rights, is 0.608. A 10 percent increase in private property rights is expected to increase the average product of labor by 6.08 percent. Given this elasticity and the 10 percent increase in private property rights, Agnello and Donnelley estimated that the average product of labor would increase by 338 pounds per worker, resulting in an average income enhancement of $179 per worker.

Source: R.J. Agnello and L.P. Donnelley, "Property Rights and Efficiency in the Oyster Industry," *Journal of Law and Economics* 18 (1975): 521–533.

Bilateral externalities

A person who states he sleeps like a baby usually does not have one.

(Leo J. Burke)

Translation: The baby is a source of a bilateral externality that affects a person's sleep (global bliss?).

A **bilateral externality** is where one agent's utility or profit is affected by another agent's actions. These agents could be two firms with their production technologies linked. The firms could be producing either the same or different outputs. For example, the firms could be a chemical plant and a kayak rental company located on the same river or an apple orchard and honey producer. Alternatively, the agents could be two households or one firm and a household—for example, two households living in a duplex where one household enjoys loud music, or a firm with a security umbrella that encompasses a household's property. For expository purposes, we will assume that the agents are firms, with one firm experiencing a negative externality from the other; however, the ensuing analysis holds for any firm/household combination.

Bilateral externality. Two agents with one agent's utility affected by the other agent's actions. *E.g., your roommate's constant singing affects your happiness in either a positive or negative way.*

Rather than well-defined property rights, assume that firm 1's short-run total cost function is a function of marketable output q_1 and a nonmarket output (externality) z, $\text{STC}_1(q_1, z)$. For example, q_1 could be the production of processed chicken and z the associated river

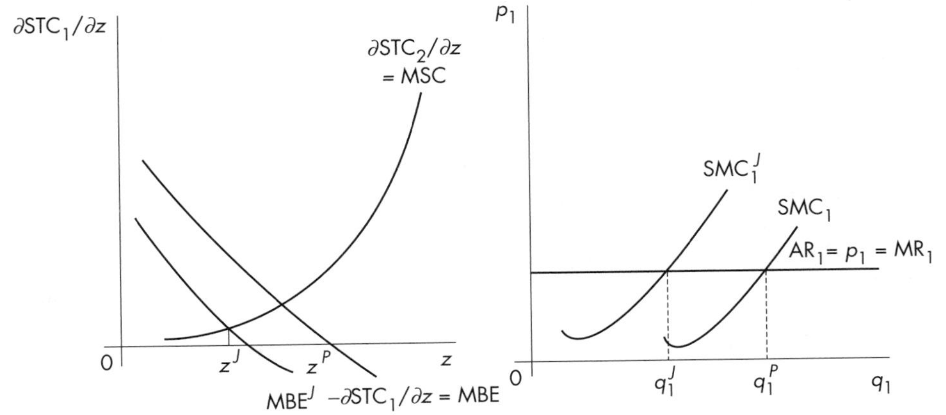

Figure 21.1 **Negative externality.** The optimal level of the externality z is lower under joint decision making (z^J, q_1^J) than under private decision making (z^P, q_1^J).

water pollution. Assuming State II of production for q_1, the associated marginal cost curve, $\partial \text{STC}_1/\partial q_1 = \text{SMC}_1 > 0$, has a positive slope, $\partial \text{SMC}_1/\partial q_1 > 0$. For the externality z, $\partial \text{STC}_1/\partial z < 0$; increasing the externality z will decrease the cost of production. This represents a marginal benefit to the firm. For illustration purposes, define this marginal benefit as the **marginal benefit of the externality (MBE)**:

$$\text{MBE} = -\frac{\partial \text{STC}_1}{\partial z} > 0.$$

The associated MBE curve is illustrated in Figure 21.1, given the Law of Diminishing Marginal Returns. As z increases, MBE declines. Given a missing market for z, there is no positive market price for z, so a profit-maximizing firm would produce where $\partial \text{STC}_1/\partial z = 0$. An increase in costs with no associated change in revenue will decrease profit. The level of z that minimizes costs is then where $\partial \text{STC}_1/\partial z = 0$.

Marginal benefit of the externality (MBE). A decrease in the cost of production when employing more of the externality. *E.g., increasing the level of water pollution lowers the cost of producing chemical dyes.*

Assume that firm 2's short-run total cost function is directly affected by firm 1's nonmarket output z, $\text{STC}_2(q_2, z)$, where q_2 denotes firm 2's marketable output, kayak rentals. Firm 2's cost of producing q_2 is directly affected by the amount of z that firm 1 produces. A negative externality implies $\partial \text{STC}_2/\partial z > 0$; an increase in z increases STC_2 and depresses profit. The partial $\partial \text{STC}_2/\partial z > 0$ is called the **marginal social cost (MSC)** of the externality.

Marginal social cost (MSC). An increase in a negative externality increases the cost of an agent affected by the externality. *E.g., increased water pollution increases the cost of kayak rentals.*

The MSC curve for an externality is illustrated in Figure 21.1. The positive slope associated with MSC indicates that as z increases, the marginal social cost increases, $\partial \text{MSC}/\partial z > 0$ and $\partial^2 \text{MSC}/\partial z^2 > 0$. Firm 2's costs are increased by an increase in z at an increasing rate. For example, the river may be able to assimilate initial increases in water pollution, so the MSC of water pollution for, say, kayaking is low. However, as water pollution increases, the capacity of the river for assimilating pollution may be exceeded, resulting in the marginal cost for the kayak firm increasing at an increasing rate.

Independent decision making

In its profit maximization, firm 1 has control over both q_1 and z, so

$$\max_{(q_1,z)} \pi_1 = \max_{(q_1,z)} [p_1 q_1 - \text{STC}_1(q_1, z)],$$

where p_1 is the per-unit price that firm 1 receives for its output q_1. Since z is a nonmarket output, there is no associated market price. The first-order conditions (FOCs) are then

$$\frac{\partial \pi_1}{\partial q_1} = p_1 - \text{SMC}_1(q_1, z) = 0,$$

$$\frac{\partial \pi_1}{\partial z} = -\frac{\partial \text{STC}_1(q_1, z)}{\partial z} = 0.$$

The first FOC is discussed in Chapter 9 and illustrated in Figure 21.1. The second condition establishes the cost-minimizing level of z as a necessary condition for profit maximization. The level of the externality z should be adjusted to the point where the additional reduction in cost of generating an additional unit of z is zero. Solving these FOCs simultaneously for z and q_1 results in their optimal levels z^P and q_1^P. Figure 21.1 illustrates this optimal solution, where z^P is associated with $-\partial \text{STC}_1/\partial z = \text{MBE} = 0$ and q_1^P with $\text{SMC}_1 = p_1$.

For profit maximization, firm 2 only has control over its output q_2, but the production of q_2 is influenced by the externality z, so

$$\max_{q_2} \pi_2 = \max_{q_2} [p_2 q_2 - \text{STC}_2(q_2, z)],$$

where p_2 is the per-unit price of q_2. The FOC is then

$$\frac{\partial \pi_2}{\partial q_2} = p_2 - \text{SMC}_2(q_2, z) = 0.$$

Again, this establishes price equaling marginal cost as a condition for profit maximization.

The externality results from firm 2 having no control over z, which affects its production. Firm 1 controls the level of z and has no incentive to consider the effect z has on firm 2's production. When firm 2's additional social cost MSC associated with firm 1's pollution z is not considered by firm 1, an inefficient high level of pollution may result. At z^P in Figure 21.1, MSC > MBE, so decreasing z will subtract more from cost than from benefits. Thus, not considering the additional social costs or benefits from an externality generally results in an inefficient allocation of resources.

Why do polluters pollute? Polluters have no incentive to consider the consequences of their pollution.

Dependent (joint) decision making

Like other airports, Albany International Airport in New York maintains a noise abatement program designed to reduce the impact of aircraft noise on the community. As an aid in remedying current and future noise impact, residential properties within the airport's noise footprint are eligible for purchase. This program amounts to internalizing the social costs of a negative externality (noise) into the agent's (airport) decisions. Such internalization results in a Pareto-efficient allocation of resources.

In terms of firms 1 and 2, this internalization of social costs results in firm 1 taking into consideration the impact of its production decisions on firm 2's production possibilities. With this consideration, the output z is now no longer an externality. All the effects of z are now internalized into firm 1's production decisions, which is accomplished by maximizing the joint profit of the two firms ($\pi = \pi_1 + \pi_2$). This is equivalent to the two firms merging to form one firm that produces marketable outputs q_1 and q_2, with associated prices p_1 and p_2 along with the nonmarket output z. With joint action, there is no longer an externality; the additional social costs are now internalized within this one firm.

Mathematically, joint profit maximization is

$$\max_{(q_1,q_2,z)} (\pi_1 + \pi_2) = \max_{(q_1,q_2,z)} [p_1q_1 + p_2q_2 - \text{STC}_1(q_1, z) - \text{STC}_2(q_2, z)].$$

The FOCs are

$$\frac{\partial \pi}{\partial q_1} = p_1 - \text{SMC}_1^J(q_1, z) = 0,$$

$$\frac{\partial \pi}{\partial q_2} = p_2 - \text{SMC}_2^J(q_2, z) = 0,$$

$$\frac{\partial \pi}{\partial z} = -\frac{\partial \text{STC}_1(q_1, z)}{\partial z} - \frac{\partial \text{STC}_2(q_2, z)}{\partial z} = 0,$$

where SMC_j^J is the short-run marginal-joint cost of producing $q_j, j = 1, 2$. The first two FOCs are the same as when the firms act privately. A perfectly competitive firm equates price to marginal cost. Under joint action, the optimal levels of q_1 and q_2, denoted q_1^J and q_2^J, are where price is equated with marginal cost. For a negative externality, $q_1^J < q_1^P$, given that z increases costs for producing q_2. The last FOC differs from the independent conditions where the firms act privately. Now the optimal levels of q_1, q_2, and z depend on the effect of z on firm 2's costs. The partial derivative $\partial \text{STC}_2(q_2, z)/\partial z$, which is marginal social cost, enters into the calculus.

Is joining rather than fighting a polluter socially desirable? Yes, by joining the polluter, there is no longer an externality, and the additional social costs from pollution are internalized within a joint-decision process.

Figure 21.1 illustrates the optimal levels of z and $q_1(z^J, q_1^J)$. Instead of setting $\partial \mathrm{STC}_1/\partial z$ equal to zero, as in the case of independence among the firms, joint production sets the $-\partial \mathrm{STC}_1/\partial z$ equal to the marginal social cost:

$$-\frac{\partial \mathrm{STC}_1(q_1, z)}{\partial z} = \frac{\partial \mathrm{STC}_2(q_2, z)}{\partial z},$$

$$\mathrm{MBE}^J = \mathrm{MSC},$$

where MBE^J is the *marginal joint benefit of the externality* from joint production of q_1 and q_2. The joint action will result in firm 1 decreasing the level of z below the point where $\mathrm{MBE} = 0$. The marginal social cost derived from firm 2, $\partial \mathrm{STC}_2(q_2, z)/\partial z$, is now internalized into the decision process. The difference between the private and joint-optimal solution is illustrated in Figure 21.1. The optimal level of z decreases from z^P to z^J, along with a decrease in the optimal level of output from q_1^P to q_1^J. Firm 1's short-run marginal cost of producing q_1 shifts to the left from SMC_1 to SMC_1^J, given the increased cost associated with internalizing the production of z. Similarly, firm 1's marginal benefit of the externality shifts to the left to MBE^J, given the decrease in q_1. Through internalization, firm 1 pays a cost for producing z. At the Pareto-efficient level of z, z^J, the amount firm 1 is willing to pay for producing an additional unit of z is equal to firm 2's additional costs associated with this additional production of z. Note that if firm 2's cost of producing q_2 is independent of z, then no externality exists. Firm 2's cost associated with z is then zero, so firm 1 will again equate the additional cost of producing an additional unit of z to zero.

Example 21.1 Bilateral externality

Consider firm 1, with the short-run total cost function

$$\mathrm{STC}_1 = -5z + z^2 - zq_1 + q_1^2 + 10,$$

facing a perfectly competitive per-unit price for q_1 of $p_1 = 2$. The short-run marginal cost is then $\mathrm{SMC}_1 = -z + 2q_1$ and the marginal cost of the externality is $\mathrm{MBE} = 5 - 2z + q_1$. Profits are maximized by

$$\max_{(q_1, z)} \pi_1 = \max_{(q_1, z)} \left[2q_1 - \left(-5z + z^2 - zq_1 + q_1^2 + 10\right)\right].$$

The FOCs for profit maximization are

$$\partial \pi_1/\partial q_1 = 2 + z^P - 2q_1^P = 0 \Rightarrow q_1^P = 1 + \tfrac{1}{2}z^P,$$

$$\partial \pi_1/\partial z = 5 - 2z^P + q_1^P = 0.$$

Solving the first FOC for q_1^P and substituting it for q_1^P in the second FOC yields $z^P = 4$ and $q_1^P = 3$. This is the private-market solution, where firm 1 does not consider the possible effects of z on the other agent. This private-market solution results in $SMC_1 = -4 + 2q_1$ and $MBE = 8 - 2z$.

Assume that z enters firm 2's cost of production as follows:

$$STC_2 = 3z + 20q_2 + 10.$$

Taking the partial derivative of STC_2 with respect to z yields

$$MSC = \partial STC_2/\partial z = 3 > 0.$$

An increase in z results in firm 2's short-run total cost increasing. Firm 2 suffers from firm 1's production of z. This negative externality is not considered by firm 1 in choosing its profit-maximizing level of z. We determine firm 2's losses from z through maximizing the joint profit:

$$\max_{(q_1,q_2,z)} (\pi_1 + \pi_2) = \max_{(q_1,q_2,z)} \Big[2q_1 + p_2 q_2 - \left(-5z + z^2 - zq_1 + q_1^2 + 10\right) - (3z + 20q_2 + 10)\Big].$$

The FOCs are then

$$\partial\pi/\partial q_1 = 2 + z^J - 2q_1^J = 0 \Rightarrow q_1^J = 1 + \tfrac{1}{2}z^J,$$

$$\partial\pi/\partial z = 5 - 2z^J + q_1^J - 3 = 0,$$

$$\partial\pi/\partial q_2 = p_2 - 20 = 0.$$

Solving these FOCs for z^J and q_1^J yields $z^J = 2$ and $q_1^J = 2$. Note that the optimal level of z declines from 4 to 2, reflecting the negative benefits of z on firm 2's cost of production. The short-run marginal-joint cost function for q_1 is now $SMC_1^J = -2 + 2q_1$ and $MBE^J = 7 - 2z$.

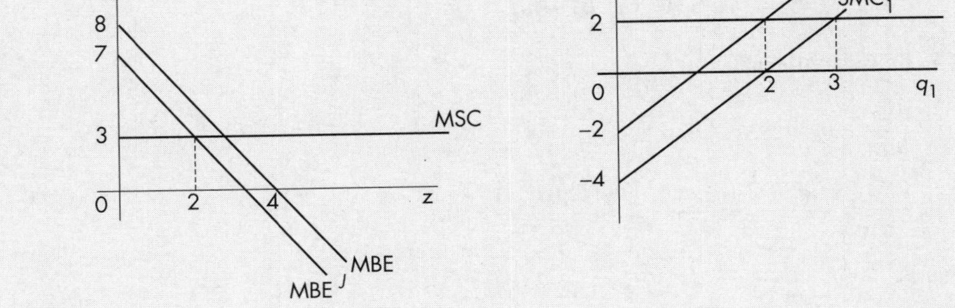

Resolving externality inefficiency

Brass bands are all very well in their place, outdoors and several miles away.
(Sir Thomas Beecham)

In 2006, the Oakland International Airport provided \$5 million for installation of new soundproofing windows at local area schools to counter takeoff and landing noise. Such solutions to externality inefficiencies are possible when conditions allow agents to negotiate an optimal solution. Providing favorable negotiating conditions is a major approach to mitigate inefficiencies associated with externalities. Based on these negotiations, a market for an externality is then established.

For example, suppose for a negative externality z that enforceable property rights are established where firm 2 is assigned the rights to the production level of z (noise). Thus, firm 1 is unable to produce z without firm 2's approval. We denote by Fee the total price (fee) for z units that firm 2 charges firm 1. For profit maximization, firm 2 will determine the level of Fee where firm 1 is indifferent between paying Fee and producing z units of the externality or not producing any of the externality. If firm 2 charged a price below Fee, firm 1 would still produce z units. However, an increase in Fee would enhance firm 2's profits without changing the level of z. Increasing Fee transfers some of firm 1's producer surplus in the production of z to firm 2. Thus, firm 2 will increase Fee to the point where the entire producer surplus from producing z units is absorbed by Fee. At this point, firm 1 is indifferent between paying Fee and producing z units or not producing any z. Mathematically, this occurs where

$$\pi_1(q_1, z) - \text{Fee} = \pi_1\left(q_1^0, 0\right),$$

$$p_1 q_1 - \text{STC}_1(q_1, z) - \text{Fee} = p_1 q_1^0 - \text{STC}_1\left(q_1^0, 0\right),$$

with q_1^0 representing the optimal level of output given $z = 0$.

Firm 2 will then maximize profits subject to the level of Fee where firm 1 is indifferent:

$$\max_{(q_2, z)} \pi_2 = \max_{(q_2, z)} [p_2 q_2 + \text{Fee} - \text{STC}_2(q_2, z)]$$

$$\text{s.t. } p_1 q_1 - \text{STC}_1(q_1, z) - \text{Fee} = p_1 q_1^0 - \text{STC}_1\left(q_1^0, 0\right).$$

Solving for Fee in the constraint and substituting into the objective function yields

$$\max_{(q_2, z)} \pi_2 = \max_{(q_2, z)} \left[p_2 q_2 - \text{STC}_2(q_2, z) - \text{STC}_1(q_1, z) + \text{STC}_1\left(q_1^0, 0\right) + p_1 q_1 - p_1 q_1^0\right].$$

The FOCs are then

$$\frac{\partial \pi_2}{\partial q_2} = p_2 - \text{SMC}_2^J = 0,$$

$$\frac{\partial \pi_2}{\partial z} = -\frac{\partial \text{STC}_2(q_2, z)}{\partial z} - \frac{\partial \text{STC}_1(q_1, z)}{\partial z} = 0,$$

that is,

$$-\text{MSC} + \text{MBE}^J = 0.$$

The optimal levels for q_2 and z are the same solutions as in the joint production, z^J and q_2^J.

Given this charge, Fee, for producing z^J units of a negative externality, firm 1's profit-maximizing problem is

$$\max_{q_1} \pi_1 = \max_{q_1} \left[p_1 q_1 - \text{STC}_1\left(q_1, z^J\right) - \text{Fee}\right].$$

The FOC is then

$$\frac{\partial \pi_1}{\partial q_1} = p_1 - \text{SMC}_1^J = 0.$$

Note that these three FOCs are identical to the FOCs for joint-profit maximization. By assigning a property right to z, a market is created for z. This market allows a firm to charge a price for its production of z. The resulting solution is the same optimal solution obtained under joint action, z^J. In fact, as demonstrated by R. Coase and stated as the **Coase Theorem,** if trade of an externality can occur (a market exists), then bargaining will lead to an efficient outcome no matter how property rights are allocated. This assumes that there are no transaction costs associated with bargaining. Any asymmetry in information between the buyer and seller can cause transaction costs, which will not result in an efficient outcome no matter how property rights are allocated. Specifically, suppose that firm 1 now has the property rights to produce as much of the externality z as it desires. In the absence of any trading, firm 1will select the private level of z, z^P. Firm 2 will offer to pay firm 1 to move from firm 1's private solution z^P to the joint-optimal solution z^J.

When will free markets resolve externality inefficiencies? Given well-defined property rights and assuming few if any transaction costs that allow a market to develop, this market will resolve any externality inefficiencies.

> **Coase Theorem.** If a market can be established for an externality, an efficient outcome will result regardless of how property rights are allocated. *E.g., with two roommates, if the externality is loud music, the roommate who has the property rights to the noise level will receive a payment. If this roommate is the generator of the music, she will receive a payment for toning down the music. If the other roommate has the property rights, she will receive payment for allowing a certain level of music.*

Specifically, firm 1 will be indifferent between producing an alternative level of z and receiving S as payment from firm 2 or producing z^P and receiving no payment:

$$\pi_1(q_1, z) + S = \pi_1\left(q_1^P, z^P\right),$$

$$p_1 q_1 - \text{STC}_1(q_1, z) + S = p_1 q_1^P - \text{STC}_1\left(q_1^P, z^P\right).$$

Firm 2 will then maximize profits, subject to the level of S where firm 1 is indifferent:

$$\max_{(q_2, z)} \pi_2 = \max_{(q_2, z)} \left[p_2 q_2 - S - \text{STC}_2(q_2, z)\right]$$

$$\text{s.t. } p_1 q_1 - \text{STC}_1(q_1, z) + S = p_1 q_1^P - \text{STC}_1\left(q_1^P, z^P\right).$$

Solving for S in the constraint and substituting into the objective function yields

$$\max_{(q_2,z)} \pi_2 = \max_{(q_2,z)} \left[p_2 q_2 - \text{STC}_2(q_2,z) - \text{STC}_1(q_1,z) + \text{STC}_1\left(q_1^P, z^P\right) + p_1 q_1 - p_1 q_1^P\right].$$

The FOCs are then

$$\frac{\partial \pi_2}{\partial q_2} = p_2 - \text{SMC}_2^J = 0,$$

$$\frac{\partial \pi_2}{\partial z} = -\frac{\partial \text{STC}_2(q_2,z)}{\partial z} - \frac{\partial \text{STC}_1(q_1,z)}{\partial z} = 0.$$

Again, the optimal levels for q_2 and z are the same solutions as in the joint production, z^J and q_2^J.

Firm 1's profit-maximizing problem is

$$\max_{q_1} \pi_1 = \max_{q_1} \left[p_1 q_1 - \text{STC}_1\left(q_1, z^J\right) + S\right].$$

The FOC is then

$$\frac{\partial \pi_1}{\partial q_1} = p_1 - \text{SMC}_1^J = 0.$$

This is exactly the same optimal result when the property rights are controlled by firm 2 or with joint production. Given well-defined property rights and that agents can bargain with essentially zero transaction costs, the resulting solution will be Pareto-efficient. In practice, it is rare to find externalities with these characteristics. Normally, a profit incentive exists either to internalize the externality by merging or to establish a market for the externality. Thus, market forces tend to remove any possible existence of a bilateral externality.

There are, however, distributional effects that depend on the assignment of property rights. Property rights are a form of initial endowments, which do have market value. For example, even though the Coase Theorem states that the optimal levels of z, q_1, and q_2 remain unaffected by the property-rights assignment, the resulting profit levels of the firms are affected. When an agent is bestowed the property right, its benefits will not decrease and the potential exists for enhancing benefits. Greater control over property rights improves the bargaining power of an agent and hence potential rewards. Thus, the distribution of benefits can change with the assignment of property rights. A market with well-defined property rights and essentially zero transaction costs will provide a Pareto-optimal allocation, but any improvement in social welfare is dependent on the equity impacts of the resulting allocation.

Example 21.2 Coase Theorem

Profits for firm 1 under the alternative scenarios in Example 21.1 are as follows:

For the private solution, where $q_1^P = 3$ and $z^P = 4$,

$$\pi_1\left(q_1^P, z^P\right) = p_1 q_1^P - \text{STC}_1\left(q_1^P, z^P\right)$$
$$= 2(3) - \left[-5(4) + 4^2 - 4(3) + 3^2 + 10\right] = 2(3) - 3 = 3.$$

For the joint solution with a negative externality, where $q_1^J = 2$ and $z^J = 2$,

$$\pi_1\left(q_1^J, z^J\right) = p_1 q_1^J - \text{STC}_1\left(q_1^J, z^J\right)$$
$$= 2(2) - \left[-5(2) + 2^2 - 2(2) + 2^2 + 10\right] = 2(2) - 4 = 0.$$

The profit for firm 1, given the restriction that it cannot produce any z, is determined by setting $z = z^0 = 0$:

$$\max_{q_1} \pi_1(q_1, 0) = \max_{q_1}[2q_1 - \text{STC}_1(q_1, 0)] = \max_{q_1}\left[2q_1 - q_1^2 - 10\right].$$

The FOC yields $q_1^0 = 1$ and $\pi_1 = -9$.

If firm 2 is assigned the property rights for z and is able to exercise all of the associated bargaining power, then it will extract the entire producer surplus associated with z from firm 1:

$$\text{Fee} = \pi_1\left(q_1^J, z^J\right) - \pi_1\left(q_1^0, 0\right) = 0 - (-9) = 9.$$

Firm 2 will receive \$9 and let firm 1 produce 2 units of z. Firm 1 will then operate at a loss of \$9, equivalent to the $z = 0$ restriction.

If, instead, firm 1 is assigned the property rights for z, then firm 1 will maximize its producer surplus associated with z:

$$S = \pi_1\left(q_1^P, z^P\right) - \pi_1\left(q_1^J, z^J\right) = 3 - 0 = 3.$$

Firm 1 will receive \$3 from firm 2 to reduce its level of z from 4 to 2. Note that this payment of \$3 is the difference between its unrestricted private level of z and the social level of z.

Multilateral externalities

Laugh and the world laughs with you, snore and you sleep alone.

(Anthony Burgess)

Translation: Your laughing is a positive externality to all who come in contact with you.

For the 2008 Summer Olympic Games, Beijing, China restricted vehicle use, decreased coal combustion, and closed some pollution-emitting factories. This resulted in a significant reduction in PAHs (polycyclic aromatic hydrocarbons) that result from combustion. If the Olympic air quality control measured continued, it would cut in half the lifetime risk of lung cancer for Beijing's residents.

This example of externalities (PAHs) being generated and affected by numerous agents (households) illustrates **multilateral externalities,** which are far more common than bilateral externalities. Numerous agents create transaction costs associated with ill-defined property rights, and these obstruct the market from internalizing externalities. The Coase Theorem no longer holds given these transaction costs. Thus, efforts to internalize these externalities may require some type of government intervention into markets.

Multilateral externalities. Externalities affecting numerous agents. *E.g., a group of rowdy spectators at a soccer match.*

Governmental policies

Do not throw away the dishes with the dishwater.

(Old Adage)

Translation: The market inefficiencies associated with externalities should not preclude use of markets in an efficient allocation solution.

Government actions to mitigate the inefficient exploitation of resources have taken a number of forms. One policy is to instill some form of private property rights on a common property resource. For example, in the western United States, the common property problem of livestock overgrazing was addressed by issuing grazing permits. Ranchers who own grazing permits are allowed to use public rangeland for a set fee. The original grazing permits issued by state and federal agencies were freely given to ranchers. Thus, the common property of public lands was transferred to private ownership. Without a permit, one could not use the public land for its major (and in many cases only) use, grazing. These permits then acquired a market value through their incorporation into the land value of the ranch holding the permits. This policy of granting private property rights to common property may result in improving economic efficiency; however, it does raise equity issues in terms of enhancing ranchers' endowments at the expense of other agents.

Permit system: CO_2

The Kyoto Protocol treaty became effective in 2005 and established emissions trading as a mechanism to address climate change. The objective was to reduce overall greenhouse gases by 5.2 percent in 2012 compared with the 1990 levels. Target levels of percent emission reduction for each country were established and countries were given allowances (permits) to emit greenhouse gases. In response to the treaty, the European Union designed a permit trading mechanism that allows countries to trade their permits. Countries can meet their targets by cutting emissions themselves or by trading emissions permits with other countries.

A country with emissions over its permits can purchase a permit from a country with emissions under its permit level.

This trading of emission permits represents a governmental management tool for a common property ("natural" carbon dioxide atmospheric levels). The government controls the resource and establishes barriers preventing agents from extracting the resource unless licensed by the government. For example, the government may issue a **permit** to extract a certain quantity and/or size of a resource. Fishing and hunting licenses are examples. These licenses may dictate the quantity or type of game that can be extracted, along with the time of season. A permit system can also be employed for reducing a firm's undesirable emissions that adversely affect air and water quality. Prior to generating a negative externality, say, carbon dioxide, a firm would be required to obtain a permit. The number of permits can be limited to achieve some target level, for example, permits for hunting grizzly bear to achieve a target population level, or per-unit emissions permits to maintain a certain level of air quality.

What has happened to property rights when you obtain a hunting license? The property right to an animal has transferred from common ownership to you.

Permit. Permission to extract a certain quantity of a resource. *E.g., a permit to log a certain section of a US National Forest.*

The allocation of permits transfers certain property rights to the permit holder. In the case of a hunting permit, the hunter pays for this transfer of the property right. In terms of firms generating some negative externality, they may be issued permits at or below their historical emissions level, given they possess a history of quasi-property rights to emission releases. The allowance to trade (buy and sell) permits, called *marketable permits,* creates a market for the permits, with an associated equilibrium price. If a firm's marginal cost of reducing emissions is greater than the market price for a permit to release emissions, it would minimize cost by purchasing the permit and releasing emissions. In contrast, if its marginal cost of reducing emissions is less than the market price for a permit to release emissions, it would minimize cost by selling permits and reducing its emissions. In equilibrium, each firm's marginal cost of reducing emissions would be equal to the market price for permits.

Specifically, let us consider two firms engaged in generating a negative externality. Let z_1 and z_2 represent the emission levels of firms 1 and 2, respectively, with associated short-run total cost functions $\text{STC}_1(q_1, z_1)$ and $\text{STC}_2(q_2, z_2)$. Assume that a target level of total emissions z^J is established, so $z^J = z_1 + z_2$. We determine the minimum cost of achieving emissions level z^J by

$$\min_{(z_1,z_2)} TC = \min_{(z_1,z_2)} [STC_1(q_1, z_1) + STC_2(q_2, z_2)] \quad \text{s.t. } z^J = z_1 + z_2,$$

where TC is the total cost of reduced emissions. The Lagrangian is then

$$\mathcal{L}(z_1, z_2, \lambda) = STC_1(q_1, z_1) + STC_2(q_2, z_2) - \lambda\left(z^J - z_1 - z_2\right).$$

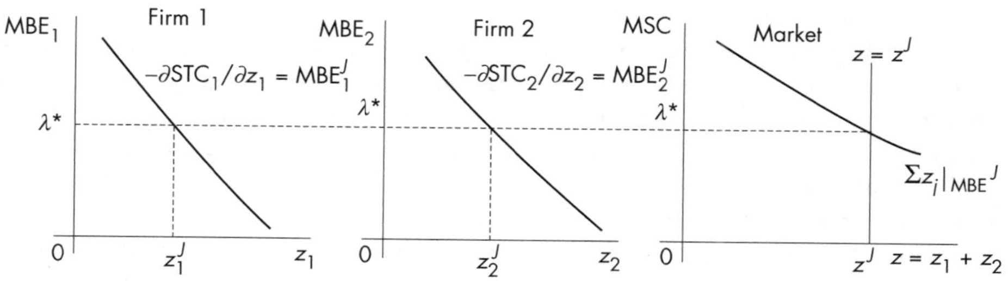

Figure 21.2 **Minimum cost of achieving a given emission level.** Equating each of the firm's marginal benefit of emissions to marginal social cost yields the optimal level of emissions for each firm (z_1^J, z_2^J).

The FOCs are

$$\frac{\partial \mathcal{L}}{\partial z_1} = \frac{\partial \mathrm{STC}_1(q_1, z_1)}{\partial z_1} + \lambda^J = 0,$$
$$= -MBE_1^J + \lambda^J = 0,$$

$$\frac{\partial \mathcal{L}}{\partial z_2} = \frac{\partial \mathrm{STC}_2(q_2, z_2)}{\partial z_2} + \lambda^J = 0,$$
$$= -MBE_2^J + \lambda^J = 0,$$

$$\frac{\partial \mathcal{L}}{\partial \lambda} = z^J - z_1^J - z_2^J = 0.$$

The minimum-cost condition of achieving a z^J level of emissions is $\mathrm{MBE}_1^J = \mathrm{MBE}_2^J = \lambda^J$. Firms' short-run marginal benefits of emissions are set equal to λ^J. In this case, the Lagrange multiplier is the marginal social cost of combined emissions by the two firms, $\lambda^J = \partial\mathrm{TC}/\partial z$. Setting this equal to each firm's MBE^J yields the minimum cost of establishing a z^J level of emissions. This result is illustrated in Figure 21.2. The target level z^J is obtained at minimum cost with firms 1 and 2 generating z_1^J and z_2^J emissions, respectively.

Example 21.3 Deriving the minimum cost for a given level of emissions

Consider the following short-run total cost functions for firms 1 and 2 engaged in generating negative externalities z_1 and z_2, respectively:

$$\mathrm{STC}_1 = -6z_1 + z_1^2 + q_1^2 + 10,$$

$$\mathrm{STC}_2 = -10z_2 + z_2^2 + q_2^2 + 10.$$

We determine the minimum cost of achieving emission level z^J by

$$\min_{(z_1,z_2)} \mathrm{TC} = \min_{(z_1,z_2)} (\mathrm{STC}_1 + \mathrm{STC}_2) \quad \text{s.t. } z^J = z_1 + z_2$$

$$= \min_{(z_1,z_2)} \left(-6z_1 + z_1^2 + q_1^2 + 10 - 10z_2 + z_2^2 + q_2^2 + 10\right) \quad \text{s.t. } z^J = z_1 + z_2.$$

The Lagrangian is then

$$\mathcal{L}(z_1, z_2, \lambda) = -6z_1 + z_1^2 + q_1^2 + 10 - 10z_2 + z_2^2 + q_2^2 + 10 - \lambda\left(z^J - z_1 - z_2\right).$$

The FOCs are

$$\partial\mathcal{L}/\partial z_1 = -6 + 2z_1^J + \lambda^J = 0 \Rightarrow z_1^J = 3 - \tfrac{1}{2}\lambda^J,$$

$$\partial\mathcal{L}/\partial z_2 = -10 + 2z_2^J + \lambda^J = 0 \Rightarrow z_2^J = 5 - \tfrac{1}{2}\lambda^J,$$

$$\partial\mathcal{L}/\partial\lambda = z^J - z_1^J - z_2^J = 0,$$

$$z^J - \left(3 - \tfrac{1}{2}\lambda^J\right) - \left(5 - \tfrac{1}{2}\lambda^J\right) = 0 \Rightarrow \lambda^J = 8 - z^J.$$

Letting $z^J = 6 \Rightarrow \lambda^J = 2$, $z_1^J = 2$ and $z_2^J = 4$.

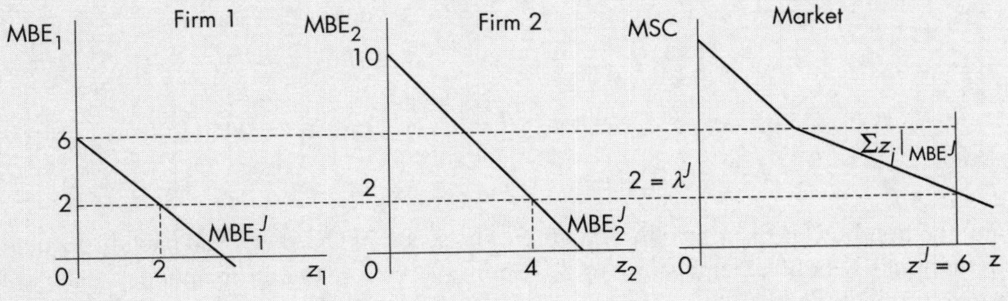

Establishing a marketable permit system achieves this minimum social cost of emissions. Let p_z represent the per-unit equilibrium price of a permit and z_1^0 and z_2^0 the initial level of permits for firms 1 and 2, respectively, where $z^J = z_1^0 + z_2^0$. With $j = 1, 2$ representing either of the firms, each firm will maximize profits as follows:

$$\max_{(q_j,z_j)} \pi_j = \max_{(q_j,z_j)} \left[p_j q_j - \mathrm{STC}_j\left(q_j, z_j\right) + p_z\left(z_j^0 - z_j\right)\right], \quad j = 1, 2.$$

Note that when $z_j^0 - z_j < 0$, the firm is using more permits then it was allocated, so it will acquire additional permits in the amount of $z_j - z_j^0$ at a per-unit price p_z. In contrast, if $z_j^0 - z_j > 0$, the firm is not using all of its permit allocation and will then sell $z_j^0 - z_j$ at a

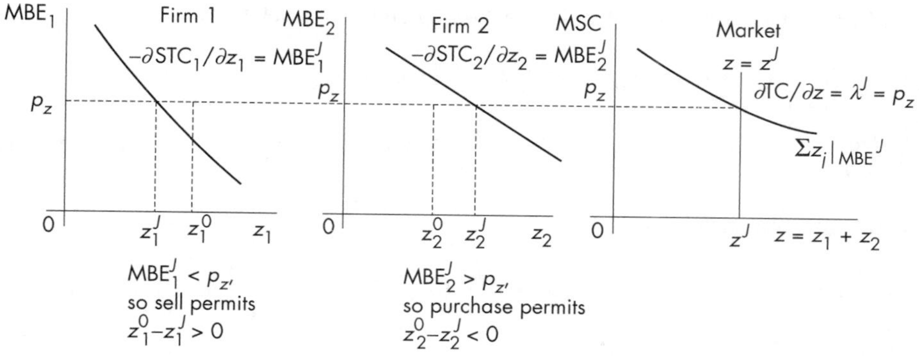

Figure 21.3 **Minimum cost of achieving a given emission level with marketable permits.** Minimum cost for a given level of emissions z^J results if firm 1 sells $z_1^0 - z_1^J$ permits to firm 2 at price p_z.

per-unit price p_z. The FOCs are then

$$\frac{\partial \pi_j}{\partial q_j} = p_j - \text{SMC}_j^J(q_j, z_j) = 0,$$

$$\frac{\partial \pi_j}{\partial z_j} = -\frac{\partial \text{STC}_j(q_j, z_j)}{\partial z_j} - p_z = 0,$$

that is,

$$\text{MBE}_j^J - p_z = 0, \quad j = 1, 2.$$

Again, the first FOC is discussed in Chapter 9. The second FOC states that each firm equates their marginal benefit of emissions to p_z. Setting $p_z = \lambda^J$, this corresponds to the cost-minimization solution of achieving emission reduction (z_1^J, z_2^J), illustrated in Figure 21.3. Also illustrated in the figure, the target level of z^J is obtained at minimum cost with firms 1 and 2 generating z_1^J and z_2^J emissions, respectively. At these minimum emission levels, $\text{MBE}_1^J = \text{MBE}_2^J = \lambda^J = p_z$ and $z_1^J + z_2^J = z_1^0 + z_2^0 = z^J$. The initial level of permits for firm 1, z_1^0, exceeds z_1^J, resulting in $z_1^0 - z_1^J > 0$, which implies $\text{MBE}_1^J < p_z$. So firm 1 sells $z_1^0 - z_1^J$ permits. Firm 2 purchases these permits from firm 1, so it can increase its emissions level from z_2^0 to z_2^J.

A major limitation of this marketable permit system exists when the spatial distribution of the externality generated by all the firms is not uniform. If the agents who are being affected by the externalities are not uniformly affected by each firm, then the permit system will result in some agents receiving even more of the externality. For example, assume that households of type A are only affected by firm 1's emissions and households of type B only by firm 2's emissions. As illustrated in Figure 21.3, firm 1 sells permits to firm 2. Thus, from the initial emission levels (z_1^0, z_2^0), emissions for type A households are reduced at the expense of type B households, who receive a higher emission level. Although the emission level is now generated at minimum cost, the distribution of the resulting emissions may not be optimal.

Example 21.4 Deriving the minimum social cost with a permit system

Continuing with the same cost functions as in Example 21.3 an emission level of $z^J = 6$ yields a price for the permits, p_z, equal to the multiplier $\lambda^J = 2$.

Profit maximization is then

$$\max_{(q_1, z_1)} \pi_1 = \max_{(q_1, z_1)} \left[pq_1 - \left(-6z_1 + z_1^2 + q_1^2 + 10\right) + p_z\left(z_1^0 - z_1\right)\right],$$

$$\max_{(q_2, z_2)} \pi_2 = \max_{(q_2, z_2)} \left[pq_2 - \left(-10z_2 + z_2^2 + q_2^2 + 10\right) + p_z\left(z_2^0 - z_2\right)\right].$$

The FOCs are

$$\partial \pi_1/\partial q_1 = p - 2q_1^* = 0,$$

$$\partial \pi_1/\partial z_1 = 6 - 2z_1^J - p_z = 0,$$

$$\partial \pi_2/\partial q_2 = p - 2q_2^* = 0,$$

$$\partial \pi_2/\partial z_2 = 10 - 2z_2^J - p_z = 0.$$

For $p = 30$, $q_1^* = q_2^* = 15$. At $p_z = 2$, the optimal solution for z_1 and z_2 is the same as in Example 21.3, where costs are minimized for a given level of emissions. Specifically, $z_1^J = 2$ and $z_2^J = 4$. Letting the initial allocation of permits be $z_1^0 = z_2^0 = 3$, then $z_1^0 - z_1^J = 1 > 0$ and $z_2^0 - z_2^J = -1 < 0$. Firm 1 will sell 1 permit to firm 2. Comparing the costs of the allocation $z_1^0 = z_2^0 = 3$ with the solution with permits $z_1^J = 2$ and $z_2^J = 4$ yields

$$\text{STC}_1^0 = -6(3) + 3^2 + 15^2 + 10 = 226$$

$$< \text{STC}_1^J = -6(2) + 2^2 + 15^2 + 10 = 227,$$

$$\text{STC}_2^0 = -10(3) + 3^2 + 15^2 + 10 = 214$$

$$> \text{STC}_2^J = -10(4) + 4^2 + 15^2 + 10 = 211,$$

$$\text{TC}^0 = \text{STC}_1^0 + \text{STC}_2^0 = 226 + 214 = 440$$

$$> \text{TC}^J = \text{STC}_1^J + \text{STC}_2^J = 227 + 211 = 438.$$

The permit system lowers the total cost for a given level of emissions.

Application: The NO_X Budget Program

The NO_X Budget Program (NBP) is an emissions (NO_X) trading program associated with electric power plants in 19 eastern US states. NO_X emissions cause production of ozone, which is linked to increased respiratory ailments, reduced lung capacity, and ecological degradation. NBP is designed to help Northeastern and Mid-Atlantic States attain federal ozone standards. Although some states contribute more than others to ozone nonattainment, the NBP applies uniform stringency across all 19 states. A pollution permit can be used to offset a ton of NO_X emissions regardless of where the emissions occur. The NBP required major reductions in NO_X emissions, with a deadline for full compliance of May 2004. Firms then had the choice of purchasing permits to offset emissions, install NO_X control technologies, or reduce production during the ozone season.

The NBP was introduced following a restructuring of the electricity industry. Up until the mid 1990s, US electricity was predominately generated by vertically integrated public utilities. Regulators set electricity rates so the utility could earn normal profits (see Chapter 12). Large discrepancies in electricity rates across states suggested restructuring the industry by replacing regulation with free markets. By 2001, 19 states with high electricity rates passed restructuring legislation. The California electricity crisis effectively stopped this restructuring (see the Application in Chapter 12).

In light of this restructuring and NBP, Fowlie investigated emission trading, restructuring, and investment in pollution abatement. Using data from the NBP, she estimated an econometric model of the NO_X compliance decision. The model allows firms with different economic regulation to weigh their compliance decisions. Results indicate that deregulated utilities were less likely to adopt NO_X control technologies compared with regulated or publicly owned utilities. As a consequence, a larger share of the permitted pollution is being emitted in states where air quality problems are more severe.

Source: M. Fowlie, "Emissions Trading, Electricity Restructuring, and Investment in Pollution Abatement," *American Economic Review* 100 (2010): 837–869.

Taxes and standards (quotas): air quality standards

The US Environmental Protection Agency has set national air quality standards for six common pollutants (carbon monoxide, 9 parts per million (ppm); ozone, 0.075 ppm; lead, 1.5 micrograms per cubic meter ($\mu g/m^3$); nitrogen dioxide, 0.053 ppm; particulate matter, 15 $\mu g/m^3$; and sulfur dioxide, 0.03 ppm). Despite improvements in air quality over the last 30 years, millions of people still live in countries with unhealthy air for one or more of these six pollutants.

If general knowledge exists of which firms can efficiently reduce a negative externality relative to other firms, then direct taxes or standards may be employed. Direct taxes on negative externalities have the theoretical foundation of the agent (say, a firm) receiving an inefficient price for the negative externality it is generating. With ill-defined property rights, such as the common property of air quality, firms would receive a zero price for the generation of emissions. An efficient price would be a tax-equivalent to the marginal social cost of the negative externality. Then the profit-maximizing problem for firm j is

$$\max_{(q_j, z_j)} \pi_j = \max_{(q_j, z_j)} \left[p_j q_j - \mathrm{STC}_j\left(q_j, z_j\right) - \tau_j z_j\right],$$

where τ_j is a per-unit tax for firm j on the negative externality z. Potentially, firms with differing production capabilities for efficiently reducing the negative externality would face different tax levels. On a practical level, the tax would generally be the same for firms with like production technologies within the same industry and causing similar harm to other agents.

Assuming a constant tax level across two firms, τ, the FOCs are then

$$\frac{\partial \pi_j}{\partial q_j} = p_j - SMC_j^J\left(q_j, z_j\right) = 0,$$

$$\frac{\partial \pi_j}{\partial z_j} = -\frac{\partial STC_j(q_j, z_j)}{\partial z_j} - \tau = 0,$$

that is,

$$\mathrm{MBE}_j^J - \tau = 0, \quad j = 1, 2.$$

Again, the first FOC is discussed in Chapter 9. The second FOC states that firm j equates its marginal benefit of emission to τ. Equating the tax τ to MSC_j will yield an efficient level of emission generation by each firm, z_j^J. This solution is illustrated in Figure 21.4. As illustrated in Figure 21.1, if there is only one agent—in this case firm 2—being affected by firm j's emissions, then $\tau = \partial \mathrm{STC}_2/\partial z_j$. In such cases, given well-defined property rights, the Coase Theorem would apply and no government-established price for the market would be required for efficiency. However, as the number of agents increases, even with well-defined property rights, the transaction costs of determining who are being affected by a negative externality increases. Thus, a government mechanism design in the form of an emissions tax may be socially desirable. Such a tax, equivalent to MSC, is called a **Pigouvian tax** after Arthur Pigou (1877–1959).

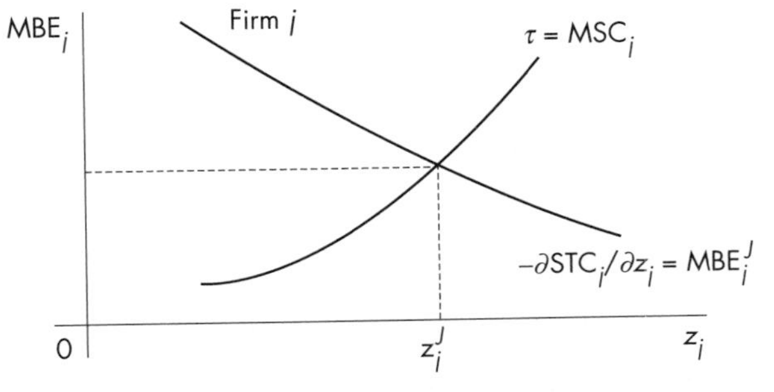

Figure 21.4 **Pigouvian tax on emissions.** Setting a tax per unit on emissions to the marginal-social cost of emissions will yield the optimal level of emissions z_j^J.

Pigouvian tax. A tax on a negative externality. *E.g., a per-unit tax on CO_2 emissions.*

Example 21.5 Deriving a Pigouvian tax

From Example 21.1, consider firm 1 with the following the short-run total cost function:

$$\text{STC}_1 = -5z + z^2 - zq_1 + q_1^2 + 10.$$

In addition, assume that the firm also must pay a per-unit tax τ on emission level z. Assume that $\tau = 3$ and that the firm is facing a perfectly competitive per-unit price for q_1 of $p_1 = 2$. Profits are then maximized by

$$\max_{(q_1,z)} \pi_1 = \max_{(q_1,z)} \left[2q_1 - \left(-5z + z^2 - zq_1 + q_1^2 + 10 + 3z\right)\right].$$

The FOCs for profit maximization yield

$$\partial\pi_1/\partial q_1 = 2 + z^J - 2q_1^J = 0 \Rightarrow q_1^J = 1 + \tfrac{1}{2}z^J,$$

$$\partial\pi_1/\partial z = 5 - 2z^J + q_1^J - 3 = 0.$$

Solving the first FOC for q_1^J and substituting the result into the second FOC yields $z^J = 2$ and $q_1^J = 2$. As shown in Example 21.1, without the emission tax, firm 1 does not consider the possible effects of z on other agents, which results in $z^P = 4$ and $q_1^P = 3$.

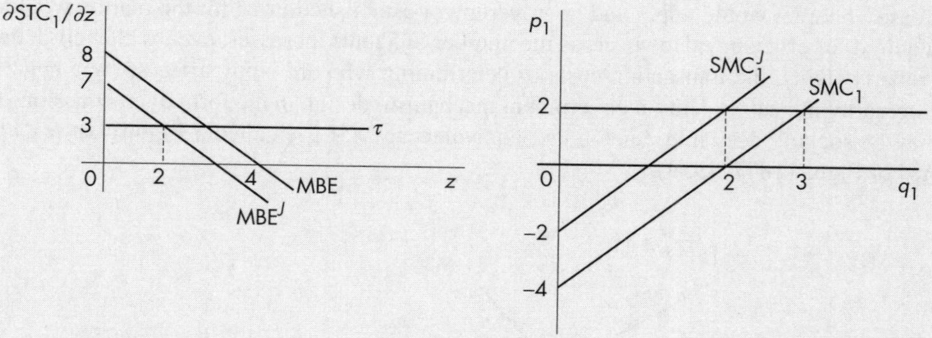

Application: Establishing a fat tax to reduce obesity

In October 2011, Denmark became the first country to impose a Pigouvian tax on saturated fat in foods, with Finland and Romania seriously considering it. The Danish tax is 16 Danish krøner per kilogram of saturated fat in foods with more than 2.3 percent saturated fat, which is approximately $1.30 per pound. The tax is based on the amount of fat used to produce the food, not the amount in the final product. The tax would then add approximately $0.40 to the price of a hamburger, with the objective of increasing life expectancy. Denmark also has higher taxes on sodas, cigarettes, and alcohol beyond that required by the European Union, and it has recently increased taxes on ice cream, chocolate, and sweets by 25 percent.

Are such Pigouvian fat taxes effective? Clark and Dittrich provide insights into this question by examining three alternative types of fat taxes. They conclude that all types of fat taxes lack sufficient specificity in targeting obesity and may under some circumstances lead to increased obesity. Thus, caution is suggested in using taxes to reduce obesity and promote healthy outcomes.

The most commonly advocated fat tax in the literature is the composite commodity fat tax. A food group (composite) is taxed based on the average fat content of food composite. Such a tax could cause a household to increase its fat intake by switching to higher-fat foods within the food composite. An example is ice cream, where low-fat ice cream and high-fat ice cream are in the same food composite. Prior to the tax, households may be willing to pay a premium for low-fat ice cream, but with the tax they will then substitute high-fat ice cream, given their limited budget.

An alternative is a nutrient tax with all foods taxed according to their fat content. An example is the current Danish fat tax. However, a tax on fat alone may not reduce caloric intake as households substitute other commodities high in sugar or salt. Obesity (or poor health in general) is not simply the result of fat intake. This is why Denmark has imposed taxes on other commodities high in sugar. Thus, a nutritional-index fat tax is proposed that taxes a food based on a health impact index. The problem lies in developing such an index that would vary by age, gender, and race. Such a complex index would be costly to develop and require constant modification. As a result, Clark and Dittrich do not recommend the use of a tax to promote healthy outcomes.

The alternative is to promote healthy diets through education so households will tend to voluntarily adopt healthy life styles.

Source: J. Clark and O. Dittrich, "Alternative Fat Taxes to Control Obesity," *International Advances in Economic Research* 16 (2011): 388–394.

Application: Gamifying instead of taxing to internalize negative externalities

A major negative externality is automobile traffic violations. Speeding and driving through red lights are socially inefficient by adversely affecting other drivers. Such driving externalities are generally internalized by randomly taxing violators—issuing moving traffic fines. With the advent of road intersection cameras, the probability of being taxed for a negative traffic externality approaches one. As an alternative to a penalty (stick) for internalizing the externality, G. Zichermann and J. Linder advocate a reward (carrot) for not generating it. Instead of the camera being used solely for issuing tickets, it is also used for rewarding good driving. The camera records drivers driving at or under the speed limit, and they are then entered into a lottery to win a portion of the revenue collected from traffic fines (taxes). This is an example of gamification, which is a process of using game thinking and game mechanics to engage users and solve problems.

Source: G. Zichermann and J. Linder, *Game-Based Marketing*, Hoboken, NJ: Wiley (2010).

Assuming that general knowledge exists of which firms can efficiently reduce a negative externality relative to other firms, Pigouvian taxes directly associated with a possible spatial MSC would not have the spatial distribution limitation associated with a permit system. Aside from the problem of acquiring this general knowledge for implementation, Pigouvian taxes are Lindahl taxes and thus face the same limitations.[1] Mainly, agents facing a higher tax rate relative to others may not respond well to the tax-discriminating nature of Pigouvian taxes. However, a major problem with a Pigouvian tax is its indirect method of reducing a negative externality versus the direct method of setting some quota (called an **emissions standard**).

Emissions standard. A quota on the level of emissions. *E.g., restricting the level of* CO_2 *emissions.*

Setting emissions standards directly reduces the level of a negative externality to some stated level. In contrast, a tax requires firms to consider the effect of the tax on their profits and adjust the level of emissions accordingly. In a dynamic setting where the MSC is continuously changing, adjusting the emission standards to these changes will yield a direct short-run response of establishing the desired emissions level whereas changing the tax rate may not. The short-run MBE curve may be rather inelastic to the change in a tax, resulting in less than the desired reduction in emissions. The desired level of emissions may not be obtained until the long run, and by then the MSC may have changed. This difference in the long-run versus short-run adjustments is illustrated in Figure 21.5. An upward shift in the MSC curve to MSC′, indicating a higher marginal social cost at all levels of emissions, warrants a reduction in emissions from z^0 to z''. Changing the emission standards from z^0 to z'' will directly produce this desired effect. The firm's response is not dependent on the elasticity of the MBE^J curve. However, the effect of emissions from a tax change does depend on the elasticity of the MBE^J curve. In the short run, an increase in the tax from τ^0 to τ'' only results in a decrease in emissions from z^0 to z'. Only in the long run will the emissions fall to z''. Thus, a system of taxes requires additional knowledge concerning the long- and short-run response of firms' emissions to tax changes.

An example of taxes versus standards is maintaining air quality within an air basin (such as the Los Angeles area). Changing weather conditions will affect the air quality on a daily basis. An inversion layer, where the ambient air temperature increases with altitude, traps air pollution within the basin, potentially resulting in poor air quality. Announcing stricter

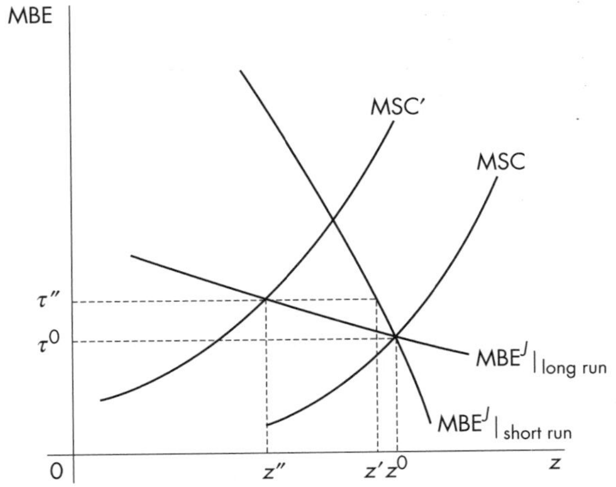

Figure 21.5 **Standards versus taxes with long-run and short-run adjustments.** For an optimal level of emissions z'', resulting from a shift in MSC to MSC$'$, changing the emission standards from z^0 to z'' will directly produce the desired effort. In contrast, an emissions tax of τ'' in the short run will reduce emissions to $z' > z''$. Only in the long run will the tax result in z'' emissions.

emission standards when such weather conditions occur (such as limiting vehicle traffic, factory production, and outdoor activities) would directly mitigate the problem. Announcing an increase in emission taxes may not have such immediate effects.

In contrast, when the MSC curve is relatively static (does not shift), a tax will minimize firms' cost relative to a standard. An example is water quality, where the socially desirable level of effluent remains relatively constant. As previously derived, one of the FOCs for two firms maximizing profits given a negative externality tax is

$$-\frac{\partial \mathrm{STC}_1(q_1, z_1)}{\partial z_1} = -\frac{\partial \mathrm{STC}_2(q_2, z_2)}{\partial z_2} = \tau,$$

that is,

$$\mathrm{MBE}_1^J = \mathrm{MBE}_2^J = \tau.$$

This condition is demonstrated graphically in Figure 21.6 for two firms located relatively close to each other, so the MSC is the same regardless of which firm changes its effluent level. As indicated in the figure, the cost-minimizing levels of effluents are z_1^J and z_2^J for firms 1 and 2, respectively. Only if MBE^J is the same for both firms will $z_1^J = z_2^J$. For example, in the figure $z_1^J < z_2^J$, given that $\mathrm{MBE}_1^J < \mathrm{MBE}_2^J$ for all levels of z. Thus, taxation offers a lower cost for reducing a given level of effluent compared with setting the same emission standard for both firms. Only if $\mathrm{MBE}_1^J = \mathrm{MBE}_2^J$, resulting in the minimum-cost solution of $z_1^J = z_2^J$, will setting the same emissions standards result in the cost not being higher than taxing effluents.

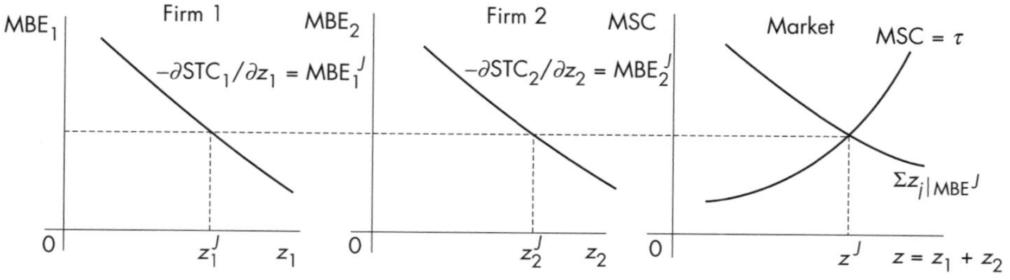

Figure 21.6 **Minimum cost of achieving a given effluent level with a Pigouvian tax.** An effluent tax of τ results in the minimum cost of achieving a given level of effluent with firms 1 and 2 producing z_1^J and z_2^J effluents, respectively.

Example 21.6 Comparing emission standards versus Pigouvian taxes

Continuing with the same cost functions for firms 1 and 2 as in Example 21.3, consider imposing a per-unit tax $\tau = 2$. Profit maximization is then

$$\max_{(q_1, z_1)} \pi_1 = \max_{(q_1, z_1)} \left[pq_1 - \left(-6z_1 + z_1^2 + q_1^2 + 10 + \tau z_1 \right) \right],$$

$$\max_{(q_2, z_2)} \pi_2 = \max_{(q_2, z_2)} \left[pq_2 - \left(-10z_2 + z_2^2 + q_1^2 + 10 + \tau z_2 \right) \right].$$

The FOCs are

$$\partial \pi_1 / \partial q_1 = p - 2q_1^* = 0,$$

$$\partial \pi_1 / \partial z_1 = 6 - 2z_1^J - \tau = 0,$$

$$\partial \pi_2 / \partial q_2 = p - 2q_2^* = 0,$$

$$\partial \pi_2 / \partial z_2 = 10 - 2z_2^J - \tau = 0.$$

For $p = 30$, $q_1^* = q_2^* = 15$. At $\tau = 2$, the optimal solution for z_1 and z_2 is the same as in Example 21.3, where costs are minimized for a given level of emissions. Specifically, $z_1^J = 2$ and $z_2^J = 4$. Instead, imposing a standard on both firms of $z_1^0 = z_2^0 = 3$ results in the following cost comparison:

$$\text{STC}_1^S = -6(3) + 3^2 + 15^2 + 10 = 226$$
$$< \text{STC}_1^J = -6(2) + 2^2 + 15^2 + 10 = 227,$$

$$\text{STC}_2^S = -10(3) + 3^2 + 15^2 + 10 = 214$$
$$> \text{STC}_2^J = -10(4) + 4^2 + 15^2 + 10 = 211,$$

$$TC^S = STC_1^S + STC_2^S = 226 + 214 = 440$$
$$> TC^J = STC_1^J + STC_2^J = 227 + 211 = 438,$$

where the superscript S indicates an emissions standard. Similar to a permit system, taxes lower the total cost for a given level of emissions compared with standards.

Stock externalities: global warming

The above taxes-versus-standards analyses are associated with an externality at one point in time. Such analyses are useful for controlling an externality at a given time period that has no future cumulative effects. An example is local air quality, which will change with varying weather conditions but not cumulate over time. In contrast are *stock externalities,* which are externalities that can accumulate over time. Global warming results from the accumulation of atmospheric CO_2 and other gases which are major stock externalities. Other stock externalities are salt accumulations in estuaries and heavy metals, such as cadmium, in drinking water. Economic analysis of these stock externalities requires a dynamic analysis where an agent's current actions contribute to the future accumulation of a stock externality. This future externality accumulation results in agents' (households, firms, and government) uncertainty concerning the marginal social benefits from reducing the externality. With price-based policies, including taxes and marketable permits, a market for the stock externality is created that provides information on the evolution of both the stock and costs. This ability to learn by observing agents' reactions to changing prices is a *learning curve*, which provides valuable information on agent responsiveness in reducing the externality. Creating such a learning curve with a market results in the efficiency of taxes or marketable permits over standards (quotas).

Firms' preference

The nice thing about standards is that there are so many of them to choose from.
(Andrew S. Tanenbaum)

Translation: Rent-seeking firms can influence legislation toward their advantage.

Firms' preference for emission standards versus taxes depends on which mechanism yields a higher profit for a given level of emissions. For example, if emission standards directly limit total output, firms may prefer such standards to a Pigouvian tax. As indicated in Figure 21.7, the standards may provide a cartel situation, which can result in improved profit. Prior to any standards, let the perfectly competitive equilibrium price and output be (p_e, q_e). With the imposition of standards, the socially optimal output declines to q_s and the price increases to p_s, resulting in a net gain in producer surplus of $p_e p_s$AC − DCB. Alternatively, imposition of a tax that reduces the output price to p' with the same output q_s results in a loss in producer surplus of $p' p_e$BD. In this case, firms have incentives to support emission standards versus Pigouvian taxes.

Would a firm prefer standards or taxes? Whichever enhances, maintains, or diminishes the least profit is preferred.

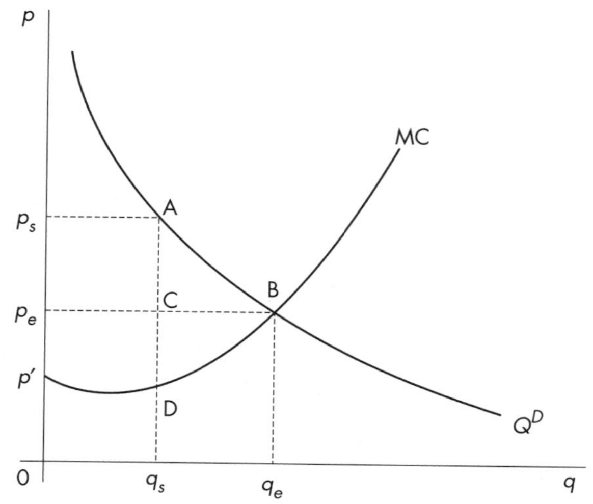

Figure 21.7 **Producer surplus for standards versus taxes.** If a decrease in output from q_e to q_s corresponds to a reduction in emissions, then emission standards will increase the price of output from p_e to p_s. This yields a net gain in producer surplus of $p_e p_s$AC − DCB. Instead, an emission tax yielding the same reduction in output q_s reduces producer surplus by $p' p_e$BD.

Summary

1. An externality is present whenever an agent's utility includes commodities whose amounts are determined by other agents without any attention to the effects on the agent's welfare.
2. Property rights are a bundle of entitlements defining an owner's rights, privileges, and limitations for use of a resource. Two major classifications of property rights are common property and private property.
3. Given a bilateral externality, independent decision making results in the marginal benefit of the externality equaling zero for the agent generating the externality. In contrast, dependent or joint decision making results in marginal-joint benefit of the externality equaling marginal social cost for a negative externality.
4. The Coase Theorem states that if a market can be established for an externality, then bargaining will result in an efficient outcome no matter how property rights are allocated. However, there are welfare effects that depend on the assignment of these property rights.
5. Multilateral externalities exist when externalities affect numerous agents. Efforts to internalize these externalities may require some type of governmental mechanism design.
6. A governmental permit system transfers certain property rights to the permit holder. Such permits are a second-best Pareto-efficient mechanism for preventing

over-exploitation of a resource. A major limitation of a permit system exists when the spatial distribution of the externality is not uniform.

7. An efficient price for an externality is a Pigouvian tax equivalent to the marginal social cost of the negative externality. A major problem with a Pigouvian tax is its indirect method of reducing a negative externality.
8. When marginal social cost is continuously changing through time, adjusting the emission standards to these changes will yield a direct response for establishing the desired emission level. Changing the tax rate instead may not yield the desired response.
9. Agents' preference for emission standards versus taxes depends on which mechanism yields a higher level of satisfaction for a given level of emission.
10. *(Appendix)* Common property exists when all agents can use a resource without having to pay for it. This results in agents not considering the full cost of the resource stock, resulting in over-exploitation of the resource.

Key concepts

bilateral externalities, 900
Coase Theorem, 907
common property, 899
emissions standard, 920
externality, 897
marginal benefit of the externality (MBE), 901
marginal social cost (MSC), 901
multilateral externalities, 910
negative externality, 899
pecuniary externalities, 897
permit, 911
Pigouvian tax, 917
positive externality, 899
private property rights, 898
property rights, 898

Key equations

$$\frac{\partial \pi_1}{\partial z} = -\frac{\partial STC_1(q_1, z)}{\partial z} = 0$$

A FOC for a profit-maximizing firm that generates an externality and does not consider the effect of this externality on other agents.

$$\frac{\partial \pi_1}{\partial z} = -\frac{\partial STC_1(q_1, z)}{\partial z} - \frac{\partial STC_2(q_2, z)}{\partial z} = 0$$

A FOC for a profit-maximizing firm that generates an externality and does consider the effect of this externality on another agent.

$$\text{MBE}^J = \text{MSC}$$

For a negative externality, the efficient solution is determined where the marginal joint benefit of the externality is set equal to the marginal social cost.

$$\mathrm{MBE}_1^J = \mathrm{MBE}_2^J$$

The FOC for minimizing cost for achieving a given level of emissions.

$$\mathrm{MBE}_j^J - p_z = 0$$

Under a permit system for a negative externality, the efficient solution is for firms to equate their marginal joint benefit of the externality to the per-unit equilibrium price of the permit.

$$\mathrm{MBE}_j^J - \tau = 0$$

Under a Pigouvian tax for a negative externality, the efficient solution is for firms to equate their marginal joint benefit of the externality to the per-unit tax.

$$\mathrm{MBE}_1^J = \mathrm{MBE}_2^J = \tau$$

Under a Pigouvian tax, the FOC for two firms minimizing cost for achieving a given level of emissions.

Questions

1. Consider a society where there are no individual property rights. Would it be possible to have a free-market economy? Explain.
2. Two types of legal assignment of property rights concerning product safety are *caveat emptor*, let the buyer beware, and *caveat vendor*, let the seller beware. Discuss the Pareto-efficiency and welfare effects of these rights given the Coase Theorem.
3. Ten people are having dinner together at an expensive restaurant and agree to divide the total bill equally among them. What is the additional cost to any one of them of ordering an appetizer for $10? Explain why this may be an inefficient allocation of expenses.
4. Is economic efficiency a positive externality as a result of perfectly competitive firms' maximizing profit? Explain.
5. What are the externalities associated with a firm's rent-seeking behavior?
6. Why might a free market result in less than the Pareto-efficient level of recycling commodities such as tires and batteries?
7. Increasingly, the property rights to smoke in public places have shifted from smokers to nonsmokers. Has this shift in property rights resulted in no change in the equilibrium solution? Explain in terms of the Coase Theorem.

8. The Coase Theorem proves that government should not become involved in pollution-control regulations. True or false? Explain.
9. Are there any problems with requiring deposits on automobiles as a solution to abandoned automobiles? Explain.
10. In an effort to provide incentives for farmers to internalize externalities, activities including soil-erosion control are tied to agricultural support-price programs. This amounts to a subsidy for farmers to internalize their externalities. In general, and for agriculture in particular, what is the major problem of subsidizing versus taxing firms that generating negative externalities?

Exercises

Education's purpose is to replace an empty mind with an open one.

(Malcolm S. Forbes)

1. Hazel and Bernice are roommates. Hazel prefers staying up late whereas Bernice prefers her beauty sleep. Each month, Hazel and Bernice each receive the same living allowance from a scholarship. Draw an Edgeworth box depicting the possible allocation of allowances and hours of lights on. Note that both must be affected by the same number of hours the lights are on, but they can receive a different proportion of the total living allowance.

   a. Assume that the dorm's policy is that one roommate must have the other's permission to stay up late. Label the initial endowment point in the graph for this case. Draw the highest indifference curves that Hazel and Bernice can possibly achieve without any trade. Shade in all of the allocations that would make both roommates better off than the initial endowments.
   b. If the dorm has no policy on staying up late (so a roommate's permission is not required), indicate the initial endowment point and shade in all of the allocations that would make both roommates better off.
   c. Under the policy of needing a roommate's permission to stay up late, what is the highest level of utility Bernice can achieve? What is the highest level Hazel can achieve? Under the lack of a policy, what are the two utility levels?
   d. Assume Bernice is indifferent to how late Hazel stays up. Draw a new Edgeworth box representing this change in preferences and answer (a)–(c).
   e. Which property-right distribution does Hazel prefer? Which one does Bernice prefer? What is the intuition behind these results?

2. A firm's marginal cost is $MC = 0.4q$ and it faces a perfectly competitive price of \$20 for its output.

   a. What is the firm's output level?
   b. Assume the firm is polluting the air and the Environmental Protection Agency estimates the social marginal cost of production to be $MC_S = 0.5q$. If the

market price is still \$20, what is the socially optimal level of production for the firm? What should the level of a government excise tax be to bring about this optimal level of production?

3. Oscar Madison and Felix Unger are the odd couple living together in an apartment. Oscar is generally a slob, and Felix is a neat freak. However, as much as he would like, Felix cannot clean Oscar's bedroom. Assume that it would take 4 hours per day to clean his room. Oscar's marginal cost per hour of cleaning is \$20 for the first hour, increasing by \$20 for each additional hour. Felix receives marginal benefits from Oscar's clean bedroom of \$60 for the first hour, decreasing by \$20 for each additional hour.

   a. Determine the optimal number of hours Oscar's bedroom is cleaned per day.
   b. If it is possible to hire a maid at \$20 per hour, how many hours would Felix hire, assuming that the maid charges by the hour?
   c. Instead of hiring a maid, would Felix be willing to pay \$70 per day to have Oscar move out?

4. Two textile mills, located across a river from each other, are polluting the river. The marginal costs of pollution reduction for each firm are

$$\text{MCE}_1 = 4E_1 + 4,$$

$$\text{MCE}_2 = \tfrac{4}{3}E_2 + \tfrac{4}{3},$$

where E is the reduction in pollution from unregulated levels. The associated marginal social benefit is estimated to be

$$\text{MSB} = 10 - E,$$

where $E = E_1 + E_2$.

   a. What is the socially optimal level of water-pollution reduction?
   b. What level of per-unit pollution tax τ will achieve this optimal level of pollution reduction. What is each firm's level of pollution reduction? What is the total variable cost for pollution reduction?
   c. If, instead, the government imposed a standard requiring each firm to equally reduce the level of pollution to achieve the socially optimal solution in (a), what are the costs for each firm?
   d. What is the cost to society for using standards versus taxes?

5. Two firms have cost functions

$$\text{STC}_1 = 5q_1^2 + 400,$$

$$\text{STC}_2 = 5q_2^2 + 10q_1 + 1000,$$

where firm 1's output positively affects firm 2's cost.

The two operate in perfectly competitive markets facing output prices of $p_1 = 100$ and $p_2 = 200$.

a. Determine the profit-maximizing outputs and profits for these firms operating independently.
b. Determine the socially optimal levels of output and profit. Is it in the firms' interest to operate at these levels?

6. Two polluters have marginal benefit of pollution functions

$$\text{MBE}_1 = 9 - z_1,$$

$$\text{MBE}_2 = 6 - z_2.$$

a. Determine the unregulated level of pollution.
b. If a per-unit pollution tax of $\tau = 2$ is imposed, what are the levels of emissions?
c. At what price for a marketable pollution permit will total pollution be limited to 7 units? Assuming that the permits are initially evenly divided, who will sell their permits and who will buy them?

7. Drinkit City generates 70 million beverage containers annually. The marginal social cost for disposing of these containers in a landfill is

$$\text{MSC}_L = 0.04 + 0.01Q_L,$$

where Q_L is measured in millions of containers. If, instead, these containers are recycled, the marginal social cost for recycling is

$$\text{MSC}_R = 0.02 + 0.02Q_R,$$

where again quantity Q_R is measured in millions of containers.

a. Determine the cost-minimizing allocation between landfill and recycling.
b. What is the social optimal level for a beverage-container deposit?

8. A certain agricultural crop has the inverse market demand function

$$p = 30 - Q,$$

and an aggregate marginal cost function of

$$MC = Q.$$

a. Determine the competitive-equilibrium price and quantity, along with the producer surplus.
b. Suppose that soil erosion results in the following marginal social cost function

$$\text{MC}_S = \tfrac{3}{2}Q.$$

What is the Pareto-efficient level of output and price, along with the producer surplus? What is the cost to farmers if they internalize the soil-erosion externality?

c. As an incentive for farms to internalize this negative externality, the government establishes a support price of $p = 21$. Will farmers accept this subsidy and internalize the soil-erosion externality?

9. Consider two MBE functions,

$$MBE_1 = 100/z_1,$$

$$MBE_2 = 50 - 5z_2.$$

a. Which function results in MBE decreasing at a decreasing rate as emissions increase?
b. Which function can result in a zero level of emissions?
c. Graph the functions.

10. Two polluting firms have the STC curves

$$STC_1 = 2z_1^2 - 24z_1,$$

$$STC_2 = z_2^2 - 10z_2.$$

a. For each firm, determine its private optimal level for the externality.
b. Assume that firm 1's negative externality is twice as harmful as firm 2's and that society wishes to reduce the combined harmful effects to 8 units, so $2z_1 + z_2 = 8$. Determine the appropriate level of taxes for the two firms and the associated externalities.

Internet case studies

1. Critique the conditions that violate the Coase Theorem. Do you believe in it?
2. For a selected resource, such as water, air, or food, determine the associated health standards and how they vary across states or countries.
3. List the major world externalities, both positive and negative.
4. Determine the social cost for a particular negative externality.
5. Determine the social benefit for a particular positive externality.
6. Provide a case study of a Pigouvian tax used to internalize a negative externality.
7. Discuss the conflicting issues associated with the forfeiture of individual property rights for protecting environmental quality.

APPENDIX TO CHAPTER 21

Common property

Individual people do not own the atmosphere, oceans, wild animals, most rivers and lakes, and some land parcels (Antarctica). These resources are common property, held in common by

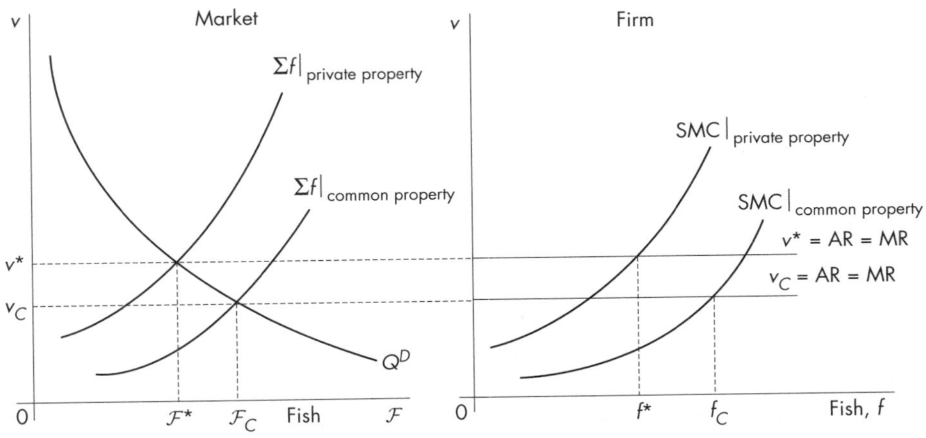

Figure 21A.1 **Common versus private property equilibrium.** When a resource is held in common, the cost of reducing the stock of the resource is not considered. Not considering this cost results in a higher level of resource extraction, $\mathcal{F}_C > \mathcal{F}^*$.

all agents, so no one agent has any rights to control the use of these resources. Common property resources have the characteristic of free (open) access. All agents (households and firms) can use these resources without paying for them. Property rights for common property either do not exist or if they exist are not enforced. When property rights are not well defined, the Coase Theorem does not hold and an inefficient-market allocation may result.

With well-defined private property rights, firms (agents) have control over a resource and can exercise barriers preventing other firms (agents) from accessing the resource. In the case of monopolies, one firm has control over the whole supply of the resource. For example, China has close to a monopoly on rare-earth minerals. In competitive markets, each firm has control over some subset of the total resource supply and, with the barrier of property rights, can prevent other firms' access. These barriers allow a firm to appropriate the value of the resource. Having exclusive access to the resource has some value, so selling a unit of the resource will diminish the total resource stock and thus its value. This reduction in value is part of the cost associated with supplying the resource and should be considered in the determination of profit maximization. For profit maximization, perfectly competitive firms will equate the price received for the resource (say, fish), v, to the associated short-run marginal cost, $\text{SMC}|_{\text{private property}}$ (Figure 21A.1). This results in a Pareto-efficient market supply F* with associated price v^*.

With common property, no firm can erect barriers to prevent other firms from accessing the resource. Access is free (open) to all firms. Thus, maintaining and conserving the resource has no value to any of the firms. If the firm does not access and exploit the resource, another firm will, so firms will not consider the value of the resource stock in their determination of profit maximization. The cost of reducing this resource stock is not considered. The result is a lower per-unit cost of the resource sold, indicated as $\text{SMC}|_{\text{common property}}$ in Figure 21A.1. This lower cost shifts the market supply curve to the right, increasing the total supply of the resource from the efficient level of $\mathcal{F}^*$ to $\mathcal{F}_C$. The resulting inefficient common property solution is a result of not considering the social cost of reducing the total resource stock. The resource stock has value, but not considering the effect of a reduction in this value (social cost) when a unit of the resource is extracted results in the inefficiency of the common property solution.

A major implication of this common property solution is the possibility of premature exhaustion of the resource stock. With the value of the resource stock not being considered, firms may continue to exploit a resource until it is exhausted. For example, the hairy mammoth in the Arctic region may have been hunted to extinction by man. Although Japanese scientists are attempting to recreate the mammoth through genetic re-engineering, if the value of the stock of mammoths had been considered, extinction may not have occurred. (And Japanese scientists could reallocate their limited resources to other problems.) Many wild animal populations serve as more recent examples of common property resource. Unless some form of control is established, where the value of animals' existence is considered, animals—such as whales, marine fisheries, and range animals—run the risk of becoming extinct.

What is a cause of species extinction? Not considering the value of maintaining a sustainable population of a common-property species may lead to its extinction.

> *The animals of the planet are in desperate peril. Without free animal life we will lose the spiritual equivalent of oxygen.*
>
> (Alice Walker)

Ownership of private property is not a necessary condition for the value of a resource stock to be considered in agents' decisions. A society's customs and habits may include this value even in an environment of common property. For example, a village with common property grazing around the village may be very efficient in the use of the common property, with customs and tradition dictating the efficient level of livestock to graze. A Peace Corps volunteer who advocates breaking up the common property into privately owned parcels may lead the community into inefficiencies. For example, the spatial distribution of rainfall may be the original reason for grazing in common. Breaking up the common property into privately owned parcels may restrict grazing to parcels that do not receive sufficient year-round moisture—an inefficient allocation of resources.

Example 21A.1 Common property

Consider first a common property resource, where no firm has barriers preventing other firms from accessing the resource. Let a representative perfectly competitive firm possess the short-run total cost curve

$$\text{STC}|_{\text{common}} = 6f^2 + \text{TFC},$$

where f is quantity of fish caught. Given that the market price for this resource is $v = 144$, we determine the private profit-maximizing solution by

$$\max_f \pi|_{\text{common}} = \max_f \left(144f - 6f^2 - \text{TFC}\right).$$

The FOC is then

$$\frac{\partial \pi|_{\text{common}}}{\partial f} = 144 - 12f_C = 0 \Rightarrow f_C = 12.$$

In contrast, if the firm had control over the resource, then the value of resource stock would be considered. Let $72f$ represent the total value of this resource stock; then the loss in value from a small decrease in the stock is the marginal cost of \$72. The firm's total cost is then

$$\text{STC}|_{\text{private}} = 6f^2 + 72f + \text{TFC},$$

and profits are determined by

$$\max_f \pi|_{\text{private}} = \max_f \left(144f - 6f^2 - 72f - \text{TFC}\right).$$

The FOC is

$$\frac{\partial \pi|_{\text{private}}}{\partial f} = 144 - 12f^* - 72 = 0 \Rightarrow f^* = 6.$$

Taking into consideration the value of the resource stock results in a reduction in the exploitation of the resource.

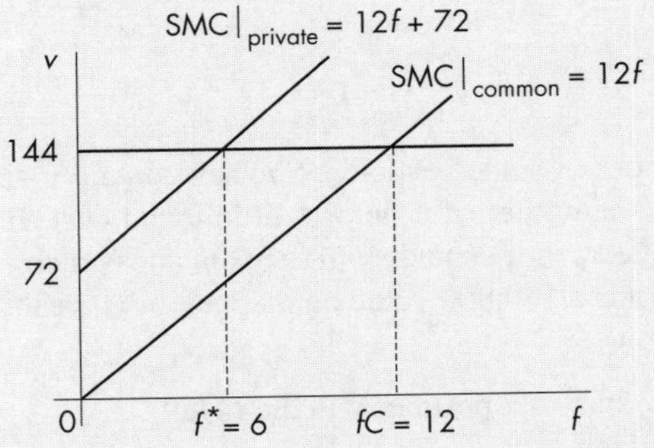

Application: Fish populations

In 2011, fish accounted for approximately 15 percent of the world's average animal protein consumption. Fish is the fastest-growing source of food in the developing world, and the consumption of fish has doubled since the 1950s, resulting in a drastic depletion of fishery stocks. Over 30 percent of fish populations are overexploited, depleted, or recovering. As a result fish species will be disappearing from the market and disputes among countries over fishing rights will intensify. This directly impacts countries' food security, nutrition, and wealth.

There are growing legal efforts to enforce current controls on the fisheries sector by trade measures and against illegal, unreported, and unregulated fishing. However, it is still projected that fishery stocks will continue to decline, but possibly at a slower rate. As a result of declining stocks and growing demand, applied economists estimate that fish prices on average will raise by 10 percent in the best-case scenario and possibly 50 percent in a worst-case scenario. It is predicted that aquiculture (fish farming) will respond to this rise in price by increasing world fish production. The degree of response will determine how high prices will rise and the impact it has on fishery stocks and social welfare.

Questions

1. Everybody's property is nobody's property. Explain.
2. What is a major determinant of species extinction?

Exercise

1. A farmer is deciding how to dispose of some pesticide. She can contain it safely at a cost of $7800, or bury it in the corner of a field at little or no cost. If she chooses this second option, in 10 years the pesticide will seep out and contaminate a neighbor's well. The neighbor puts a $20,000 value on the well in 10 years and he has a discount rate of 10 percent.
   a. Is it efficient for the farmer to bury her pesticides in the field?
   b. Is burying the pesticides equitable?
   c. Is burying the pesticides sustainable?

Internet case study

1. Investigate the different management policies for the sustainability of property held in common. In particular, compare and contrast traditional African management practices with private property policies.

22 Public goods

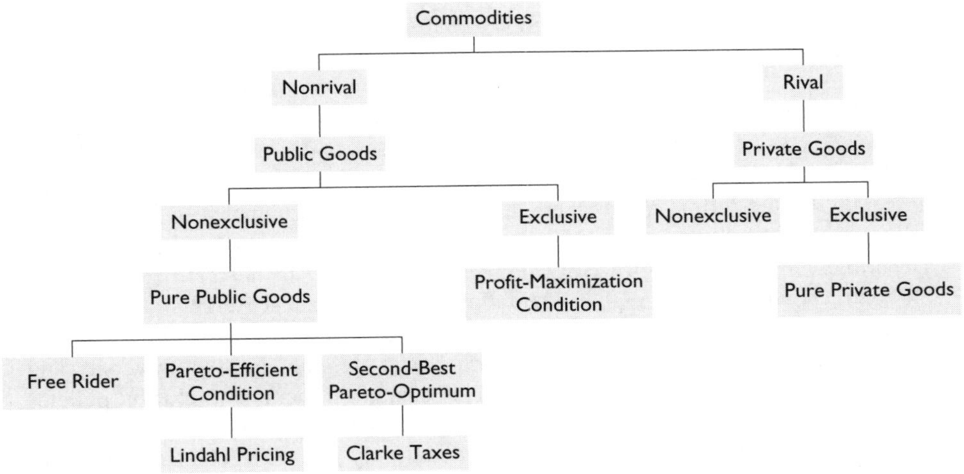

Outline and Conceptual Inquiries

Understanding rivalry and exclusive good characteristics

Nonrival but exclusive commodities (public goods): toll bridges

When will a firm sell you a video versus rent it to you?

Application: The phantom profits of the opera

Free-rider problem: public broadcasting

Why pay when you could ride for free?

Application: The union free-rider problem

Pareto-efficient conditions for pure public goods

Clarke tax

Application: Pigou and Clarke join hands

Summary

Key concepts

Key equation

Questions

Exercises

Internet case studies

The true meaning of life is to plant trees, under whose shade you do not expect to sit.

(Nelson Henderson)

Translation: Providing a public good from which all agents will derive satisfaction increases social welfare.

In February 1990, Georgia Southern University broke off its relationship with Forest Heights Country Club after a black faculty member was denied membership. At the time, Forest Heights had never allowed a black person to become a member, but the university hosted formal events there and the golf team participated in the Schenkel Invitational and paid the club $3200 annually to practice there. In April 1992, the US Department of Education, Office of Civil Rights, instructed the university to terminate all contracts with Forest Heights. The fallout prompted Forest Heights to rethink its member exclusion policies and allow black membership. In 1993, the Office of Civil Rights freed the university to contract with Forest Heights, and the university and country club resumed their relationship. This change in member exclusion policies shifted the country club from beings a public good to more of a pure public good.

In previous chapters, we generally considered only *private goods*—commodities consumed individually by consumers. One consumer's consumption of such a commodity precludes other consumers' consumption. In this chapter, we consider *nonrival* commodities, a major class of commodities where one consumer's consumption of a commodity does not preclude other consumers' consumption. These commodities (called *public goods*) are goods where there is no congestion. For example, one consumer's satisfaction from breathing clean air does not rival (compete with) other consumers gaining pleasure by also breathing the air.

We first define public and private goods in terms of their rivalry and exclusive characteristics. We then investigate exclusive but nonrival commodities and the condition for renting instead of selling nonrival commodities. We address the *free-rider problem* associated with public goods in a game-theory framework and develop Pareto-efficient conditions for allocating public goods. We discuss how to obtain this Pareto-efficient allocation when markets can be developed to establish prices for public goods (called *Lindahl prices*). In conclusion, we discuss the *Clarke tax,* which provides a second-best Pareto-efficient mechanism for allocating public goods.

Our aim in this chapter is to understand the distinguishing characteristics between private and public goods and why a free market (decentralized control) will not result in a Pareto-efficient allocation of public goods. This fact leaves applied economists with the task of developing various mechanisms for determining the optimal allocation of resources to the production of public goods.

Understanding rivalry and exclusive good characteristics

If all the vehicles in the United States are placed end to end, it would probably be Labor Day Weekend.

(Doug Larson)

A **public good** is a *nonrival commodity,* where one consumer's consumption does not reduce the amount available to other consumers. Nonrival commodities exist when the marginal cost of another consumer consuming the commodity is zero. In contrast, a **private good** is a *rival commodity* (also called a *depletable* or *diminishable commodity*), where each additional unit consumed by one consumer results in less of the commodity being available for other consumers. For a rival commodity, congestion is so severe that only one consumer can consume the commodity.

Public good. A nonrival commodity, where one consumer's consumption of a commodity does not preclude other consumers from consuming it. *E.g., the Internet.*

Private good. A rival commodity, where each additional unit consumed by one consumer results in less of the commodity available for other consumers. *E.g., a candy bar.*

Both public and private goods are further classified based on their exclusiveness. An *exclusive commodity* has the characteristic that other consumers can be excluded from consuming the commodity. In contrast, a *nonexclusive commodity* is where either it is illegal to exclude other consumers from consuming the commodity or the cost of exclusion is prohibitive. **Pure private goods** are distinguished from private goods by their exclusiveness: private goods are all rival commodities, and pure private goods have the additional criterion of being exclusive. Similarly, public goods are all nonrival, and **pure public goods** have the additional criterion of nonexclusive. If consumption of a nonexclusive commodity also does not deplete the commodity for other consumers (a nondepletable commodity), the commodity is a pure public good. Pure public goods are a specific type of externality that affects all consumers in an economy. If one consumer is to consume a certain amount of a pure public good, then all consumers will consume that same level.

Pure private good. A rival and exclusive commodity. *E.g., a candy bar.*

Pure public good. A nonrival and nonexclusive commodity. *E.g., the Bill of Rights.*

Examples of commodities possessing characteristics of rivalry and exclusiveness are provided in Table 22.1. An exclusive commodity, such as food, with high congestion costs associated with rivalry is a pure private good. The cost of an additional unit of the commodity is nonzero. In a free-market economy, such pure private commodities are generally provided by firms. The table also shows that a private good, such as fire protection, can also be a nonexclusive commodity. In contrast, public goods with zero congestion costs are nonrival, so an additional consumer does not add any additional cost for providing commodities. For exclusive public goods, consumers can be excluded unless, for example, they pay an entrance price (subscription fee, toll, or ticket), and the marginal cost of an additional subscriber is zero. (Exclusion can also be based on some nonprice criteria such as gender, race, national origin, or social status. However, in the United States, such criteria are generally illegal.) In free markets, public goods can be privately produced by firms (such as movie

Table 22.1. Rivalry and exclusiveness in commodities

Exclusive	*Rivalry*	
	Yes: Private good	*No: Public good*
Yes	**Pure private goods:** Food, clothing, private services	**Public goods:** Coded TV broadcasts, toll roads and bridges, movie theaters, private clubs, trains
No	**Private goods:** Public education and health, fire and police protection	**Pure public goods:** Street lights, national defense, roadways, parks, air quality, ozone layer, lighthouses

theaters) or publicly produced by governmental agencies (such as toll roads and bridges). Nonexclusive pure public goods (such as street lights) are generally provided solely by government agencies.

Distinctions among rival, nonrival, exclusive, and nonexclusive commodities are in terms of the degree to which a commodity falls in one category or another. For example, fire and police protection could be considered pure public goods for a community if protection is at a level where the marginal cost of an additional consumer is near zero. As the number of consumers increases with an associated increase in marginal cost, fire and police protection would then become more rival commodities. Similarly, increased highway congestion at some point will raise the marginal cost of highway commuting, which increases the degree of rivalry on roads (Labor Day Weekend). Finally, consumer preferences for a public commodity are not always positive. Bad public commodities (called *public bads*) also exist. Examples are environmental degradation (including air and water pollution), global warming, and species extinction.

Nonrival but exclusive commodities (public goods): toll bridges

Anyone can be a member of our club as long as they are a white male.

(Michael Wetzstein)

In 1731, books were very expensive, and only the very wealthy could afford them. Thus, some printers (one of them being Benjamin Franklin) known as the Leather Apron Club (printers' aprons at that time were made of leather) started the first lending library, open to everyone. They pooled their money and purchased books, which people could borrow. Books are nonrival and exclusive commodities. Today, the same nonrival characteristics of certain commodities allow public libraries to share books and electronic media such as tapes, CDs, and DVDs; video outlets to share (for some rental fee) videos and electronic games; and equipment rental firms to rent a variety of items from backhoes and party supplies.

To investigate market sharing associated with nonrival but exclusive commodities, let us first consider the case of a firm offering the commodity assuming that no sharing exists. Let $p(q)$ be the inverse demand function with associated constant marginal and average cost of c. The firm's profit-maximizing problem is then

$$\max_q [p(q)q - cq].$$

Now, if consumers rent the commodity instead of purchasing, the level of consumption y will be greater than the level of production. For example, more videos will be watched than produced. Let α be the number of times each commodity is shared by a consumer, so the level of consumption is $y = \alpha q$.

Assuming that all the commodities are only rented, the rental price would be $p(y)$, along with some positive transactions cost c_t of renting versus owning the commodity. Purchasing a commodity reduces the transaction costs involved with renting. (This is the major reason why many households purchase rather than rent lawn mowers.) The marginal consumers, with zero consumer surplus, would be willing to pay $p(y)$ to rent the commodity minus this transaction cost, $p(y) - c_t$. Further assuming that there are α of these marginal consumers sharing one commodity, the per-unit price that the firm receives is α times $p(y) - c_t$:

$$\alpha[p(y) - c_t] = \alpha[p(\alpha q) - c_t].$$

The firm's profit-maximizing problem for renting the commodity is then

$$\max_q \{\alpha[p(\alpha q) - c_t]q - cq\},$$

$$\max_q \left\{p(\alpha q)\alpha q - \left(\frac{c}{\alpha} + c_t\right)\alpha q\right\},$$

$$\max_y \left\{p(y)y - \left(\frac{c}{\alpha} + c_t\right)y\right\}.$$

Comparing this profit-maximizing problem for producing and then renting the output versus the maximizing problem associated with producing and then selling the output, the only difference is in the marginal costs. The marginal cost for selling the commodity is c; the marginal cost associated with producing the commodity for renting is $(c/\alpha) + c_t$. Thus, profits will be higher for renting if the marginal cost for production associated with renting is lower than the marginal cost for selling:

$$\frac{c}{\alpha} + c_t < c.$$

This condition for renting versus selling a commodity is illustrated in Figure 22.1. Assume that the demand for renting is the same as purchasing, so both can be represented by the same demand curve. For profit maximization, the firm will equate MR to MC. As illustrated in the figure, marginal cost for renting is lower than the marginal cost for selling the commodity. Thus, the firm will set a rental price of p_R^*, and y^* of the commodity will be consumed. If the firm sold the product, then the price and quantity sold would be p^* and q^*. If the marginal cost from renting is less than the marginal cost from selling, then the profits from renting, $\pi[(c/\alpha) + c_t]$, are higher than for selling $\pi(c)$. The more a product is characterized as a nonrival, the higher will be the number of times each product is shared with consumers, α. As α increases, the marginal cost of renting falls relative to selling, and thus enhances the profitability of renting versus selling the product.

As α approaches infinity, the condition for renting instead of selling the commodity is then $c_t < c$. The firm will then rent the commodity instead of selling it, when the marginal cost of production is greater than the consumers' transactions costs of renting instead of owning the commodity. For example, the transactions cost for newly released videos is

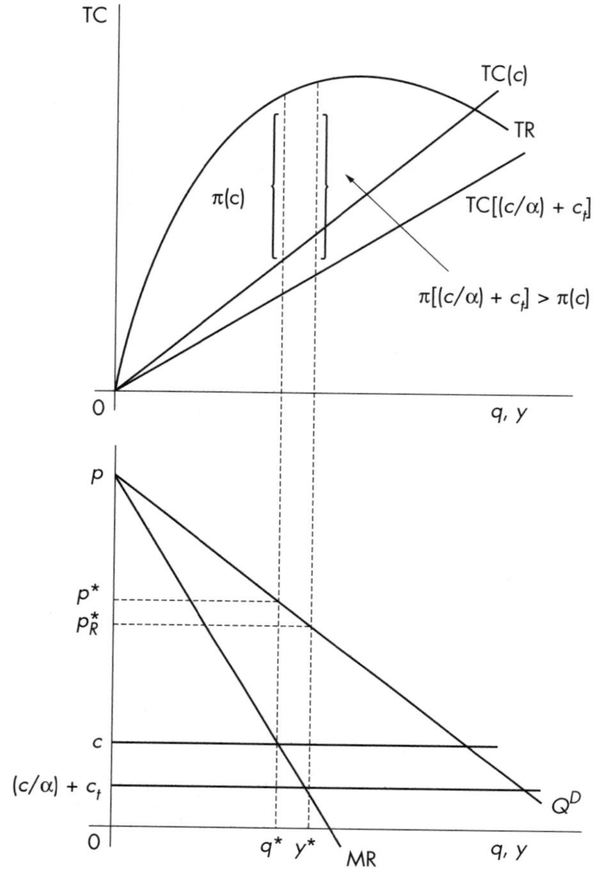

Figure 22.1 **Renting versus selling a product.** The marginal cost of renting is lower than the marginal cost of selling, so the firm facing the same demand curve for renting versus purchasing will rent the output y^* at price p_R^*.

relatively low compared with the marginal cost, so consumers generally will rent new releases. In contrast, the marginal selling cost of used videos (salvage value) is relatively low, so consumers may instead purchase the video rather than rent it.

When will a firm sell you a video versus rent it to you? A firm will generally sell you previously viewed videos and rent you new releases.

Application: The phantom profits of the opera

Within the United States, classical performing arts (ballet, opera, and symphony) are owned by consumers of the arts. Consumers making their own consumption are a type of nonprofit organization. However, the arts are a nonrival commodity, which the owners can exclude others from consuming.

As indicated by J. Kuan, some researchers have concluded that the performing arts are not driven by profit maximization and thus many are inefficient in that they do not attempt to minimize costs or employ the current state of technology. Considering the arts as a nonrival good produced by the consumers of the arts, Kuan demonstrated that the performing arts are able to achieve first-best Pareto-efficient outcomes (are economically efficient). The performing arts are managed by high-demand consumers of the arts who have well-defined utility-maximizing objectives. These "elitist socialites" will engage in price-discrimination practices to extract the total consumer surplus from the other, lower-demanding consumers. In attempting to fill empty seats with the highest-paying customers, they will price-discriminate by seat location. An upper-upper balcony seat (the "nose-bleed" section) sells at a bargain price, whereas a center orchestra seat goes at a premium. This level of price discrimination is the envy of every profit-maximizing cinema owner. However, nonprofit firms providing nonrival but exclusive goods require some type of organization for high-demand consumers to aggregate their utility functions, resolve the free-rider problem, and develop mechanisms for extracting low demanders' surplus. High society with its rules and incentives provides such an organization.

Source: J. Kuan, "The Phantom Profits of the Opera: Nonprofit Ownership in the Arts as a Make-Buy Decision," *Journal of Law, Economics, and Organization* 17 (2001): 507–520.

Example 22.1 Determining price and output for nonrival but exclusive commodities

Consider the following inverse demand curve for a commodity:

$$p = 10 - q/100,$$

with an associated constant marginal cost of 4. A firm's profit-maximizing problem is then

$$\max_q \pi(q) = \max_q [(10 - q/100)q - 4q].$$

The first-order condition (FOC) is

$$\partial\pi/\partial q = 10 - q/50 - 4 = 0,$$

resulting in $q^* = 300$, $p^* = 7$, and producer surplus

$$\text{PS}^* = 7(300) - 4(300) = \$900.$$

If the number of times the commodity is shared is $\alpha = 100$, then the level of consumption is $y = 100q$. With a transactions cost of $c_t = 1$, the firm's profit-maximizing problem for renting the commodity is then

$$\max_y \pi(y) = \max_y [(10 - y/100)y - (4/100 + 1)y].$$

The FOC is

$$\partial\pi/\partial y = 10 - y/50 - 1.04 = 0,$$

resulting in $y^* = 448$, $p_R^* = 5.52$, $PS_R^* = 5.52(448) - 1.04(448) = \$2007.04$. Thus, the firm increases profit by producing 4.48 units and renting each unit 100 times. This results from the marginal cost of production associated with renting being lower than the marginal cost for selling:

$$4/100 + 1 < 4,$$
$$1.04 < 4.$$

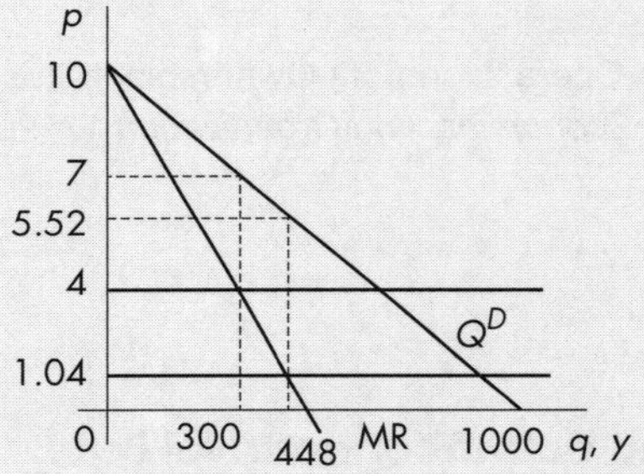

Free-rider problem: public broadcasting

My view of the ball game is just fine up in this here tree.

(Michael Wetzstein)

For years, the Public Broadcasting System (PBS) had relied on its one major source of funding, "from viewers like you." A major problem with this system of voluntary contributions is that fewer than 4 out of 100 hundred viewers normally contribute. In 2010, PBS estimated that approximately 171.3 million people watched PBS, with only about 5.5 million contributing and 165.8 million noncontributors getting a "free ride."

The problem is that the nondepletable and nonexclusive characteristics of a pure public good (such as PBS) result in each consumer's purchase of the commodity providing utility not only directly to this consumer but also to all other consumers. If consumers only consider their own utility in purchasing the commodity and not the effects that such purchases have on all other consumers, externalities are present. Consumers then have an incentive to let other consumers purchase the public good and receive utility from it without any cost. This condition is called the free-rider problem. A **free rider** is a consumer who cannot be excluded

Table 22.2 Free-rider problem for a clean kitchen as the public good

		Roommate 2	
		Clean	*Do not clean*
Roommate 1	Clean	(50, 50)	(−25, 120)
	Do not clean	(120, −25)	(0, 0)

Note: The payoffs are (roommate 1, roommate 2).

from receiving the benefits of a nondepletable commodity and who is unwilling to pay his portion of the cost (a non-PBS member viewing a PBS program or my watching the game in a tree). By not cooperating and paying his portion of the cost associated with the public good, the free rider gains.

Free rider. A consumer who cannot be excluded from receiving the benefits of a nonrival commodity and who is unwilling to pay her portion of the cost. *E.g., a student in a class group project who chooses not to participate but receives the same grade as all the others in the group.*

This free-rider problem is another form of the Prisoners' Dilemma game. As an illustration, assume two roommates with the public good of a clean kitchen (Table 22.2). If they cooperate and both agree to share in the labor of cleaning, their payoffs are 50 each. These payoffs could be in monetary units or some other measurement. However, by not cooperating, becoming a free rider, and letting the other roommate clean, the free rider can increase her payoff from 50 to 120. The Nash-equilibrium result is both attempting to be free riders (not cooperating), resulting in a dirty kitchen.

Generally, in the case of a small number of agents with limited or no transaction costs, the Coase Theorem applies and this externality problem is resolved. However, as the number of agents increases, a Coasian solution is generally not possible. With a large number of agents, it is generally easy to be a free rider and let the other agents assume the cost of providing a public good.

Why pay when you could ride for free? When there are only a small number of agents, you may be able to ride for free now, but they will catch you in the future (repeated game). If there are a large number of agents, have a nice ride.

Application: The union free-rider problem

In the United States, states are allowed to pass right-to-work (RTW) laws. Under these laws, employers covered by a union agreement cannot be required to join the union. In states without RTW laws, employees can be required to join the union. In 2000, around

8 percent of US private sector employees were covered by labor union agreements but were not union members (free riders). These free riders do not have to pay union dues (approximately 1.25 percent of wages) and are not obliged to participate in strikes. As the number of free riders increase, the less effective is the union. The most effective method to deter free riding is negotiating different wage settlements for members and nonmembers. However, this is illegal under federal law. A second-best method that unions use to discourage free riding is offering member-only benefits. For example, firms may allow unions to participate in the decision process of training program allocations, which the union can then use to confer wage advantages for its members. The union benefits the firm by promoting efficiency and in return is given the privilege of differentially rewarding the members (quid pro quo).

O. Eren examined the membership wage premium among private sector union employees. He investigated membership effects over the wage distribution in an econometric model. His estimates support the hypothesis that firms with unions do discriminate in favor of union members. This discrimination is lowest for high wage earners, reflecting a lower relative cost of membership for this group than for lower paid workers. Overall, results indicate that members do earn 9.4 percent more than comparable covered nonmembers.

Source: O. Eren, "Does Membership Pay Off for Covered Workers? A Distributional Analysis of the Free Rider Problem," *Industrial and Labor Relations Review* 62 (2009): 367–380.

Pareto-efficient conditions for pure public goods

If God had really intended people to fly, he would make it easier to get to the airport.

(George Winters)

Translation: An inefficient level of the public good (transportation to the airport) exists.

A small child requires a costly operation to repair her heart, but her single mother cannot afford it. A neighbor steps in and asks all the other neighbors to donate what they can for the child's operation. The resulting sum of these donations covers the surgery costs, and the child is saved. This scenario represents an efficient allocation of a pure public good (the child's operation), where the sum of each agent's (a neighbor's) willingness to pay is equal to the cost of the public good (the operation). The perfectly competitive solution would have resulted in the mother not being able to purchase the operation and the child dying.

Not accounting for the positive externalities on the neighbors is the cause of this market failure. Specifically, recall from Chapter 11 that a Pareto-efficient allocation condition for consumer 1 considering purchasing commodities x_1 and y is

$$\text{MRPT}(x_1 \text{ for } y) = \text{MRS}_1(x_1 \text{ for } y),$$

$$\frac{\text{MC}_y}{\text{MC}_1} = \frac{\partial U_1/\partial y}{\partial U_1/\partial x_1},$$

where MRPT denotes the marginal rate of product transformation and MRS is the marginal rate of substitution. Letting x_1 and y be a private good and a pure public good, respectively, the $\text{MRS}_1(x_1 \text{ for } y)$ is how much consumer 1 is willing to sacrifice of the private good x_1 for one more unit of the pure public good y. $\text{MRS}_1(x_1 \text{ for } y)$ is consumer 1's maximum willingness to pay, or the reservation price, for the pure public good. However, this condition does not consider the externalities associated with the pure public good. With these externalities, society's maximum willingness to pay (MRS_S) is higher, given that the pure public good y provides the same positive benefits to other consumers:

$$\text{MRPT}(x_1 \text{ for } y) = \text{MRS}_1(x_1 \text{ for } y) < \text{MRS}_S(x_1 \text{ for } y).$$

Thus, the level of the pure public good provided in a perfectly competitive market is below the socially efficient solution.

We can develop the Pareto-efficient condition for a pure public good supplanting the inefficient condition, $\text{MRPT} = \text{MRS}_1$, by considering a two-consumer economy with purchasing decisions of x_1 and y. Again let y be the amount of the pure public good and x_1 and x_2 the amounts of the private good associated with consumers 1 and 2, respectively. Note that there is no subscript on y. Both consumers consume the same amount of y, and y is nondepletable. However, they may consume different amounts of the private commodity, so $x_1 + x_2 = Q$, where Q is the total amount of the commodity produced.

We can describe the technological possibilities of this economy by the production possibilities frontier, $f(Q, y) = 0$. The welfare-maximization problem is then

$$\max_{(x_1, x_2, y)} \mho[U_1(x_1, y), U_2(x_2, y)] \qquad \text{s.t.} f(Q, y) = 0,$$

where U_1 and U_2 are the utility functions for consumers 1 and 2, respectively and $\mho$ is some social-welfare function. Forming the Lagrangian, we have

$$\mathcal{L}(x_1, x_2, y, \lambda) = \mho[U_1(x_1, y), U_2(x_2, y)] - \lambda f(Q, y),$$

The FOCs are then

$$\frac{\partial \mathcal{L}}{\partial x_1} = \frac{\partial \mho}{\partial U_1}\frac{\partial U_1}{\partial x_1} - \lambda \frac{\partial f}{\partial Q}\frac{\partial Q}{\partial x_1} = 0,$$

$$\frac{\partial \mathcal{L}}{\partial x_2} = \frac{\partial \mho}{\partial U_2}\frac{\partial U_2}{\partial x_2} - \lambda \frac{\partial f}{\partial Q}\frac{\partial Q}{\partial x_2} = 0,$$

$$\frac{\partial \mathcal{L}}{\partial y} = \frac{\partial \mho}{\partial U_1}\frac{\partial U_1}{\partial y} + \frac{\partial \mho}{\partial U_2}\frac{\partial U_2}{\partial y} - \lambda \frac{\partial f}{\partial y} = 0,$$

$$\frac{\partial \mathcal{L}}{\partial \lambda} = f(Q, y) = 0.$$

Note that $\partial Q/\partial x_1 = \partial Q/\partial x_2 = 1$, given $Q = x_1 + x_2$. Solving for the Lagrange multiplier and equating yields

$$\frac{\dfrac{\partial \mho}{\partial U_1}\dfrac{\partial U_1}{\partial y} + \dfrac{\partial \mho}{\partial U_2}\dfrac{\partial U_2}{\partial y}}{\dfrac{\partial f}{\partial y}} = \frac{\dfrac{\partial \mho}{\partial U_1}\dfrac{\partial U_1}{\partial x_1}}{\dfrac{\partial f}{\partial Q}} = \frac{\dfrac{\partial \mho}{\partial U_2}\dfrac{\partial U_2}{\partial x_2}}{\dfrac{\partial f}{\partial Q}}.$$

The last equality establishes

$$\frac{\partial \mho}{\partial U_1}\frac{\partial U_1}{\partial x_1} = \frac{\partial \mho}{\partial U_2}\frac{\partial U_2}{\partial x_2}.$$

The marginal gain in welfare associated with additional consumption of commodity Q by a consumer must be equal for all consumers. If this were not the case, then it would be possible to reallocate Q among the consumers in a way that increases social welfare. Cross-multiplying the first equality given in the above equation yields

$$\frac{\dfrac{\partial \mho}{\partial U_1}\dfrac{\partial U_1}{\partial y}}{\dfrac{\partial \mho}{\partial U_1}\dfrac{\partial U_1}{\partial x_1}} + \frac{\dfrac{\partial \mho}{\partial U_2}\dfrac{\partial U_2}{\partial y}}{\dfrac{\partial \mho}{\partial U_2}\dfrac{\partial U_2}{\partial x_2}} = \frac{\dfrac{\partial f}{\partial y}}{\dfrac{\partial f}{\partial Q}},$$

$$\frac{\dfrac{\partial U_1}{\partial y}}{\dfrac{\partial U_1}{\partial x_1}} + \frac{\dfrac{\partial U_2}{\partial y}}{\dfrac{\partial U_2}{\partial x_2}} = \frac{\dfrac{\partial f}{\partial y}}{\dfrac{\partial f}{\partial Q}}.$$

The first term is consumer 1's $\text{MRS}_1(x_1 \text{ for } y)$ and the second term is consumer 2's $\text{MRS}_2(x_2 \text{ for } y)$. The term on the right-hand side is the $\text{MRPT}(Q \text{ for } y)$ between the public and private good. Thus, the condition for Pareto efficiency is

$$\text{MRS}_1 + \text{MRS}_2 = \text{MRPT}.$$

In general, this condition for Pareto efficiency differs from the condition characterizing a perfectly competitive solution. Instead of the perfectly competitive condition

$$\text{MRS}_1 = \text{MRS}_2 = \ldots = \text{MRS}_n = \text{MRPT for } n \text{ consumers},$$

the Pareto-efficient condition is

$$\text{MRS}_S = \sum_{j=1}^{n} \text{MRS}_j = \text{MRS}_1 + \text{MRS}_2 + \ldots + \text{MRS}_n = \text{MRPT}.$$

The sum of the neighbors' willingness to pay (MRS_S) equated to the cost of the operation (MRPT) results in a Pareto-efficient allocation of the pure public good (the operation). A more mundane example is of a home theater system costing \$5000, with 100 sorority sisters each willing to pay \$50. Individually, no one sister would purchase the system, but collectively the Pareto-efficient response would be to purchase it.

MRS_S is the sum of the individual consumers' MRS, so it accounts for the benefits all the consumers receive from the pure public good. We then equated this MRS_S to the MRPT to determine the Pareto-efficient level of resource allocation. The individual consumers' $MRS(x_j \text{ for } y)$ are each consumer's reservation price, or maximum willingness to pay, for the pure public good.

We can relate this concept of $MRS(x_j \text{ for } y)$ as a consumer's reservation price for y to the market price for y, p_y, by letting the price of Q be a numeraire, so $p_Q = 1$. For utility maximization, the consumer sets $MRS(x_j \text{ for } y) = p_y/p_Q$. Then, for $p_Q = 1$, a consumer's reservation price is equal to the market price: $MRS(x_j \text{ for } y) = p_y$. Thus, for a pure public good, summing these reservation prices yields the total per-unit price that society is willing to pay for the pure public good y. Equating this total per-unit price to the cost of supplying one more unit, $MRPT(Q \text{ for } y)$, yields a Pareto-efficient allocation.

Consumers paying their reservation price per unit for the pure public good is one Pareto-efficient outcome. This yields a marked distinction for efficiency between private and pure public goods. For a private good, all consumers consume different amounts of the commodity (say, a candy bar) but pay the same market price. For a pure public good all consumers consume the same amount of the commodity (say, national defense) but pay different prices. This distinction is illustrated in Figures 22.2 and 22.3. The market demand curve for a private good is the horizontal summation of the individual consumers' demand curves for the private good. Treating the reservation price $MRS(y \text{ for } x_j)$ as the price of the private good Q, the Pareto-efficient allocation is for both consumers to pay the same price:

$$MRS_1(y \text{ for } x_1) = MRS_2(y \text{ for } x_2) = MRPT(y \text{ for } Q).$$

From Figure 22.2, at this price, 10 and 8 units of Q are demanded by consumers 1 and 2, respectively. This yields a total market demand of 18. These individual demand curves are based on the preference orderings of the consumers, which are represented by indifference curves.

Example 22.2 Horizontal summation for a private good

Consider the demand functions $x_1 = 16 - 2p$ and $x_2 = 20 - 2p$ for two consumers. Let the price of all other commodities equal 1 (composite commodity), so MRS $= p$. If $Q = x_1 + x_2$ is a private good supplied by a perfectly competitive market with MC $= {}^1/_2Q$, then the equilibrium level of quantity and price will be determined by the horizontal summation of the demand functions. Specifically,

$$Q = x_1 + x_2 = (16 - 2p) + (20 - 2p) = 36 - 4p.$$

Solving for $p =$ AR,

$$p = 9 - \tfrac{1}{4}Q.$$

For perfectly competitive profit maximization, AR = MC,

$$9 - \tfrac{1}{4}Q^* = \tfrac{1}{2}Q^*.$$

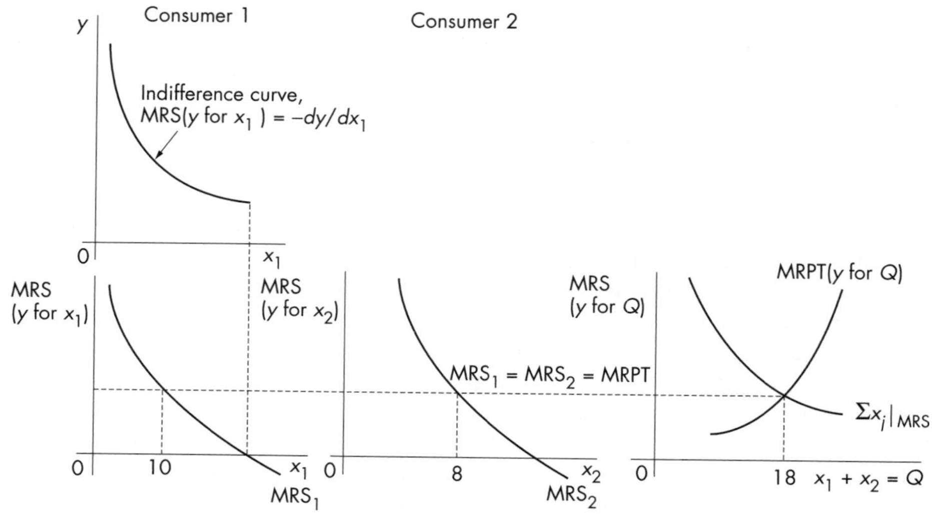

Figure 22.2 **Horizontal summation of the demand curves for a private good.** For a private good, consumers pay the same price per unit for the commodity but consume different amounts.

Note that MRPT = MC/1, given that the composite commodity price is the numeraire. Solving for Q, $Q^* = 12$, $p^* = 6$, $x_1^* = 4$, and $x_2^* = 8$. All consumers are faced with this same price but consume different amounts.

For a public commodity, each consumer consumes the same amount of the commodity but at a different price. We derive the market demand curve by vertically summing the individual consumers' demand curves, as shown in Figure 22.3. Consumer 1's $\text{MRS}_1(x_1 \text{ for } y) = 4$ and consumers 2's $\text{MRS}_2(x_2 \text{ for } y) = 1$. The Pareto-efficient allocation is where

$$\text{MRS}_1\,(x_1 \text{ for } y) + \text{MRS}_2\,(x_2 \text{ for } y) = \text{MRPT}\,(Q \text{ for } y).$$

If the price of Q is the numeraire, $p_Q = 1$, then the ratio $p_y/p_Q = 4 = \text{MRS}_1(x_1 \text{ for } y)$ and $p_y/p_Q = 1 = \text{MRS}_2(x_2 \text{ for } y)$. Consumer 1 pays \$4 per unit for the pure public good and

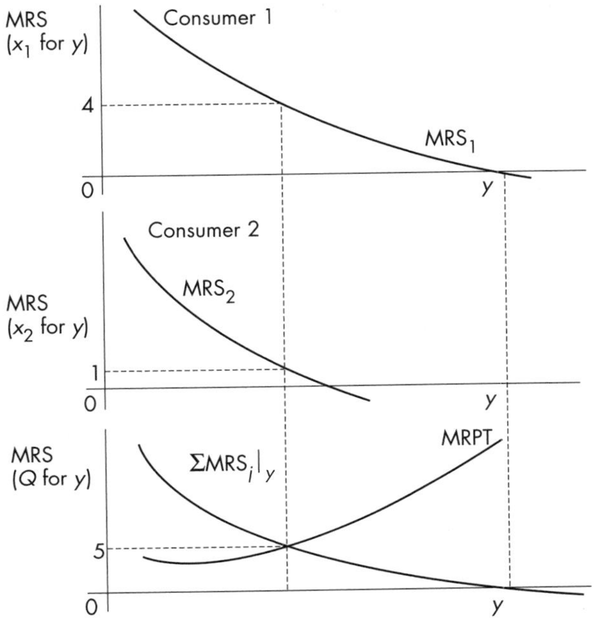

Figure 22.3 **Vertical summation of the demand curves for a pure public good.** For a pure public good, all consumers receive the same quantity of the commodity but pay a different price.

consumer 2 pays \$1, but they each consume the same amount. The total amount paid is \$5 for the purchase of the pure public good.

Example 22.3 Vertical summation for a public good

Assume that Q in Example 22.2 is a public instead of a private good. Now the Pareto-efficient allocation is for all consumers to consume the same level of Q but pay different prices. This results in the vertical summation of the inverse demand functions $p_1 = 8 - {}^1\!/_2 Q$ and $p_2 = 10 - {}^1\!/_2 Q$.

Assume a composite commodity, where all other commodities are represented by a price equal to 1. Thus, $\text{MRS}_1 = p_1$ and $\text{MRS}_2 = p_2$.

The vertical summation yields

$$\text{AR} = \sum_j p_j = p_1 + p_2 = 18 - Q.$$

Perfectly competitive equilibrium, where AR = MR = MC, is then

$$18 - Q^* = \tfrac{1}{2} Q^*.$$

Note that MRPT = MC/1, given that the composite commodity price is the numeraire. The equilibrium is then $Q^* = 12$, $p_1^* = 2$, and $p_2^* = 4$.

All consumers consume the same amount but pay different prices.

Consumer surplus for both consumers is $36 each and producer surplus is also $36. The total surplus is then 3(36) = $108.

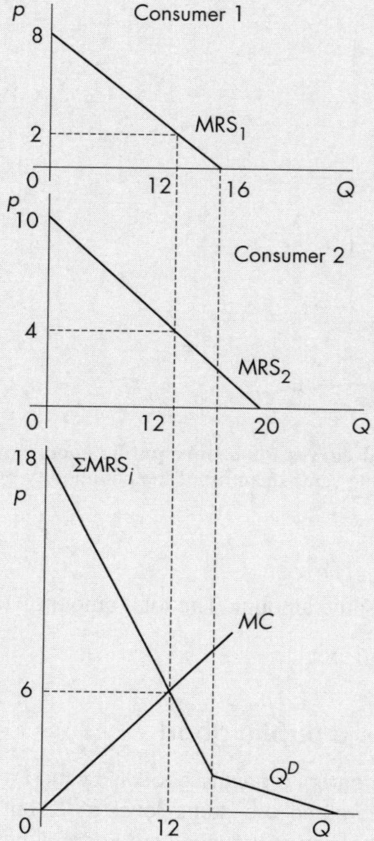

Example 22.4 Pure public good provided in a private good market

In Example 22.3, if the pure public good is instead provided in a private good market, the horizontal summation of the demand curves result in the solution of Example 22.2: $p^* = 6$, $x_1^* = 4$, and $x_2^* = 8$. However, consumer 1 can become a free rider and not purchase any of the pure public good. Now only consumer 2's demand for the commodity enters the market, so

$$Q = x_2 = 20 - 2p.$$

Solving for price

$$p = 10 - \tfrac{1}{2}Q,$$

and equating to MC $= {}^1\!/_2 Q$ yields

$$10 - \tfrac{1}{2}Q = \tfrac{1}{2}Q;$$

$Q^* = 10$ and $p^* = 5$.

Consumer 1's consumer surplus is $8(16)/2 - 3(6)/2 = \$55$, and consumer 2's consumer surplus is $5(10)/2 = \$25$. The firm's producer surplus is \$25. This results in a total surplus of \$105, which is less than the total surplus from a vertical summation of demand curves (Example 22.3) of \$108. A deadweight loss of \$3 then occurs as a result of treating the pure public good as a private good.

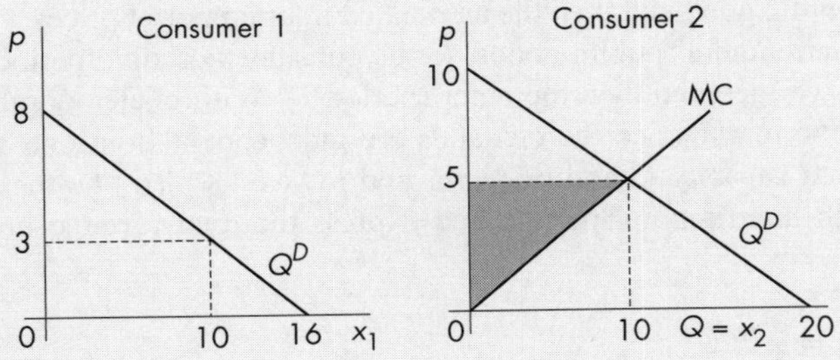

One solution for the inefficiency of perfectly competitive markets in providing for pure public goods is to establish another market that will account for the externalities associated with public goods. We offered such a solution in Chapter 21, where a market for permits could be established to yield a second-best Pareto-efficient allocation. This market solution may or may not be feasible, depending on the nature of the inefficiency. A market solution works well when a commodity can be segmented so that a proportion of the property rights for the commodity can be transferred from the public to a private agent. The market-permit system is one case where this market solution can be feasible. Permits transfer a proportion of a common property commodity to a private agent. However, it is not as attractive for correcting the public goods allocation problem. The nonrival and nonexclusive characteristics of a pure public good prevent the segmenting of the commodity. For example, an individual household cannot purchase a proportion of national defense. To establish such a market (a *Lindahl market*) for a pure public good, each consumer would have to voluntarily reveal and pay their reservation price (their **Lindahl price**) per unit for the pure public good (as they do for PBS programming?). Summing these reservation prices and equating the sum to the MRPT would then determine the efficient allocation of the pure public good. Such markets generally are not feasible, mainly as a consequence of the free-rider problem. Consumers' dominant strategy is to understate their preferences (by discounting their Lindahl prices) and rely on other consumers to pay a larger share for pure public goods. The nonexclusive characteristic of pure public goods fosters this free-rider strategy.

Lindahl price. Each agent's per-unit reservation price for a pure public good. *E.g., the per-unit price you are willing to pay each time you tune into National Public Radio.*

When a public good is available across time, households may have different demands for the good depending on the time consumed. The demand may be high during a certain time or day of the week. Public transportation, roads, and electricity have peak loads during daytime. Amusement parks and vacation resorts have peak periods on holidays or weekends. In such cases of differences in intertemporal demands, Lindahl pricing can result in a Pareto-efficient level of output. Here, output is measured as the capacity limit on the public good. Free riders are not a problem with intertemporal public goods because the difference in the demand for the public good at different times is revealed. Instead of different demands for the same public good, the demand for the public good can differ by time of day, season, or year. The problem is then to determine the Pareto-efficient level of output (capacity) for the public good and then the associated intertemporal prices.

As an illustration of intertemporal public goods, let us consider two time periods, with one (period 1) having a lower demand then the other (period 2). With intetemporal goods, no leakages exist among the markets, so the demands are independent from one another. For determining the optimal capacity Q and prices p_1 and p_2, we let $p_j(Q)$ be the inverse demand function in the jth intertimporal period, and express the total revenue in the jth period by

$$\mathrm{TR}_j(Q) = p_j(Q)Q, \quad j = 1, 2.$$

Overall total revenue is then

$$\mathrm{TR}(Q) = \mathrm{TR}_1(Q) + \mathrm{TR}_2(Q).$$

Letting STC(Q) be the short-run total cost function representing operating and increased capacity costs, the firm or government agency's profit function is

$$\pi(Q) = \mathrm{TR}_1(Q) + \mathrm{TR}_2(Q) - \mathrm{STC}(Q).$$

Assume that the firm is either regulated or has the objective to determine the Pareto-efficient level of capacity, so it does not exercise any monopoly power.[1] The FOC is then

$$\frac{\partial \pi}{\partial Q} = \frac{dTR_1(Q)}{dQ} + \frac{dTR_2(Q)}{dQ} - \frac{dSTC(Q)}{dQ} = 0.$$

Note that $d\mathrm{TR}_j/dQ = \mathrm{MR}_j = p_j$ and $d\mathrm{STC}/dQ = \mathrm{SMC}$, so the FOC is $p_1 + p_2 = \mathrm{SMC}$. The firm will vertically sum the intertemporal demand curves and equate the sum to the marginal cost of capacity.

In general, for k intertemporal periods, the efficient level of capacity is determined by

$$p_1(Q) + p_2(Q) + \ldots + p_k(Q) = \text{SMC}(Q).$$

The price charged in each intertemporal period is determined by substituting the optimal capacity Q^* into the intertemporal average revenue functions $p_j^* = \text{AR}_j(Q^*)$.

A graphical illustration for two intertemporal periods (say, peak-load and off-peak electrical power demand) is provided in Figure 22.4. Summing the average revenue curves vertically yields the marginal benefits of increasing capacity. Equating this marginal benefit to the marginal cost of increasing capacity determines the optimal capacity level Q^*. Based on this optimal capacity, the optimal prices p_1^* and p_2^* in the two periods are determined. The optimal price in each period is determined by the demand curve in each period given the optimal capacity level.

As illustrated in Figure 22.4, the price is highest in the peak-load period 2: $p_2^* > p_1^*$. It is also possible that the optimal capacity is not fully used during the off-peak period. As illustrated in the figure, if $\text{MC}_{\text{capacity}}$ shifts downward to $\text{MC'}_{\text{capacity}}$, then the optimal capacity

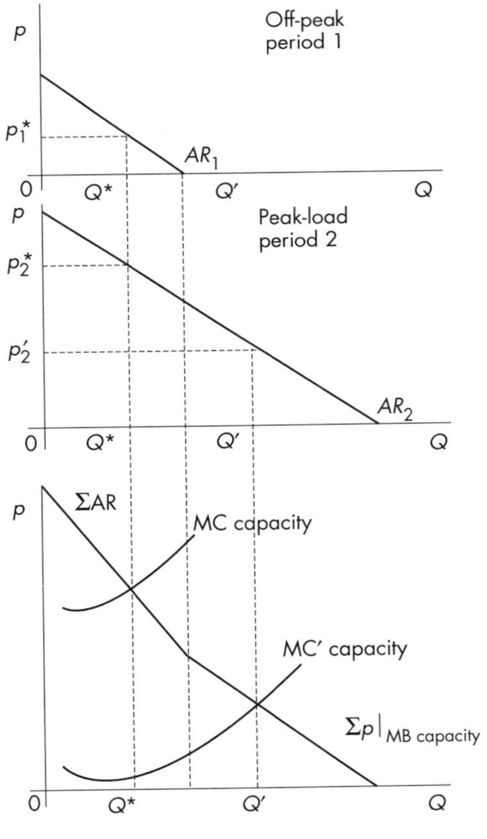

Figure 22.4 **Peak-load pricing.** The capacity of the public good is determined by vertically summing the intertemporal demand curves and equating the sum to the marginal cost of capacity. This results in the higher intertemporal demand (period 2) paying a higher price for the public good.

Q' is not fully utilized in period 1. An example is driving a lonely highway late at night. At Q', capacity is fully supported by the peak-load demand.

Example 22.5 Determining the optimal capacity in intertemporal markets

Considering Example 22.3, assume that consumer 1 is composed of the off-peak consumers and consumer 2 is made up of the peak-load consumers. Given $MC = {}^{1}/_{2}Q$, the optimal level of capacity is then 12, with a peak-load price $p_2 = 4$ and an off-peak price $p_1 = 2$. If, instead, marginal cost shifts to $MC' = (1/18)Q$, then capacity is only determined in the peak-load period with $p_2 = 10 - {}^{1}/_{2}Q$. The Pareto-efficient capacity level is then determined by

$$p_2 = 10 - \tfrac{1}{2}Q' = (1/18)\,Q',$$
$$10 - (10/18)\,Q' = 0,$$
$$Q' = 18.$$

There is excess capacity in the off-peak period, so the price is $p_1 = 0$ and all the capacity is supported by the peak-load demand at a price $p_2 = 1$.

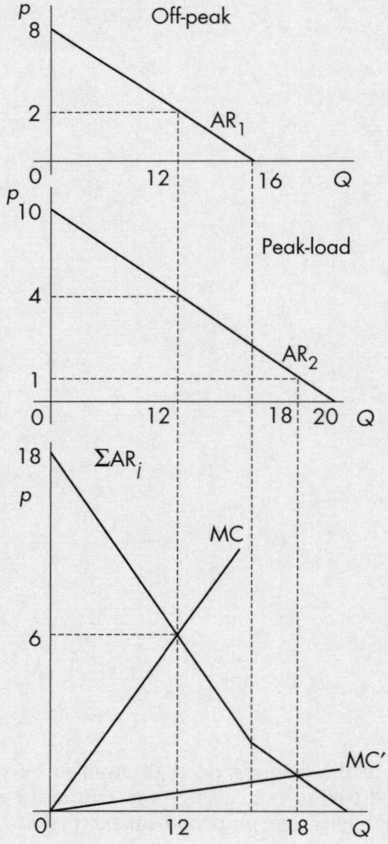

With intertemporal markets, consumers reveal their demands, so free riders are not a problem and a Pareto-efficient allocation is possible. However, when consumers are not differentiated by time or some other distinction, free riders can prevent obtaining a Pareto-efficient allocation. One solution to this problem is for government to impose a per-unit tax on each consumer equivalent to their respective reservation prices. However, unlike reservation prices for private and intertemporal public goods, these Lindahl prices are not revealed in the market. Consumers cannot adjust their level of consumption unilaterally, which destroys the possibility of a market for pure public goods, and a governmental agency has no feasible mechanism for determining each consumer's willingness to pay. Thus, to impose such a tax, the governmental agency must perfectly price-discriminate among consumers. As discussed in Chapter 13, such price-discrimination systems are difficult to achieve. Even if it were feasible to determine consumers' Lindahl prices and perfectly price discriminate, consumers might object to paying differentially per unit for pure public goods. They might be more inclined to support funding for pure public goods based on ability to pay rather than willingness to pay. Many public health and housing agencies base their fees and rents on ability to pay (level of initial endowments). In general, pure public goods are financed by taxes based on income and wealth. As opposed to decentralized control for the allocation of private goods, some type of centralized control is then required for public good allocations. The determination of the types, amounts, and funding for pure public goods may then be based on some mechanism design, discussed in Chapter 20. In general, such mechanism designs attempt to determine the intensities of individual and group desires and formulate a mechanism composed of policies and rules for group choice and actions. The Clarke tax is one such mechanism, where, under some rather restrictive conditions, the tax provides incentives for consumers to reveal their true preferences for a social choice.

Clarke tax

Please no more taxes, I will tell you the truth.

(Michael Wetzstein)

Translation: A Clarke tax will result in agents telling the truth and only pivotal agents will have to pay a tax.

Eliciting truthful preferences for pure public goods can mitigate the misallocation of governments' taxing, spending, and regulatory authorities by overcoming the free-rider problem. Proponents of the Clarke tax mechanism, based on a second-bid auction, claim that the tax mechanism will not completely cure the cancer (free riders) by yielding a Pareto-efficient allocation, but has the potential to treat the symptoms.

As an illustration, consider a group of consumers jointly deciding on the purchase of a pure public good. If purchased, every consumer will pay a predetermined amount for purchasing the good. An example is an appliance, such as a flat screen TV in a dormitory. Let c_j be this predetermined amount for consumer j, and summing over all consumers equals the cost of the pure public good. Consumers will then state how much they are willing to pay toward purchasing the pure public good. The difference between consumer j's willingness to pay, WTP_j, and the predetermined amount is the net benefit NB_j:

$$\mathrm{NB}_j = \mathrm{WTP}_j - c_j.$$

If the sum of net benefits over all consumers is positive, then the pure public good should be purchased.

The problem is designing a mechanism that provides an incentive for consumers to reveal their true net benefit for the pure public good instead of revealing an exaggerated figure in an attempt to influence this social choice. However, an exaggeration is only of concern if it affects the social choice. For example, say consumer j attempted to be a free rider by stating a value of zero, yielding a net benefit of $-c_j$. If the sum of net benefits over all consumers is still positive, then this free rider does not influence the social choice, so it is of no concern. Only consumers whose exaggeration will affect the social choice are of concern. Such consumers are called *pivotal consumers*, where their net benefit determines whether the sum of net benefits is positive or negative. In the extreme, all the consumers could be pivotal consumers or none could be pivotal. It is possible that any one consumer could be pivotal, so ensuring that all potential pivotal consumers have the right incentives corresponds to ensuring that all consumers reveal their true preferences.

When a social choice is changed by a pivotal consumer, this adversely affects the other consumers. For example, if the other consumers have positive net benefits for a pure public good and the pivotal consumer's negative net benefit resulted in not purchasing the good, then all the other consumers are made worse off. A measure for how much the other consumers, in aggregate, are worse off from not purchasing the pure public good is the sum of the net benefits excluding the pivotal consumer, say consumer 1:

$$\tau_1 = \sum_{j \neq 1}^{n} \text{NB}_j > 0.$$

Similarly, if the other consumers have negative net benefits for the pure public good and the pivotal consumer's positive net benefit resulted in purchasing the commodity, then all the other consumers are again made worse off. The measure for how much the other consumers, in aggregate, are worse off from purchasing the pure public good is the negative of the sum of the net benefits excluding the pivotal consumer, say consumer 1:

$$\tau_1 = -\sum_{j \neq 1}^{n} \text{NB}_j > 0.$$

Analogous to imposing a Pigouvian tax on negative externalities (discussed in Chapter 21), the pivotal consumer is taxed by the amount he or she harms the other consumers, τ_1. Such a tax is called a *Clarke tax*, which is paid by all the pivotal consumers, resulting in these consumers having the incentive to reveal their true preferences for the pure public good. The Clarke tax mechanism is a second-bid, sealed-bid auction for a pure public good. A pivotal consumer's tax is equal to the second-highest valuation, which is the sum of all the other consumers' net benefits. Note that the benefits from the tax revenue cannot be distributed to the other consumers in a manner that influences the other consumers' net benefit for the pure public good. Furthermore, consumers facing a higher tax rate relative to others may not respond well to the tax-discriminating nature of the Clarke tax.

One problem with the Clarke tax is that it is not necessarily Pareto-efficient. The predetermined payment may result in some cases where a group of consumers has negative net benefits for the pure public good even when the sum of net benefits is positive.

Purchasing the pure public good will then harm these consumers and thus not result in a Pareto improvement. Instead, some type of compensation principle (discussed in Chapter 20) would be required to justify the social-welfare benefits of a Clarke tax.

Example 22.6 Clarke tax

Consider an economy with three consumers (Friday, Robinson, and Simpson) who must decided on purchasing some pure public good at a cost of $900. Before determining if they should purchase the good or not, they agree to evenly split the cost, so each will pay $300. As indicated in the table below, Friday places a high value on the pure public good, well in excess of the $300 predetermined cost. In contrast, Robinson and Simpson do not value the good above this predetermined cost. Thus, if they voted to purchase the pure public good, the majority (two out of three) would vote not to purchase the good. However, the sum of net benefits is positive, $50, indicating that in aggregate they receive a positive value from purchasing the pure public good. This difference in outcomes results from the sum of net benefits considering the intensity of consumers' preferences for the good and thus giving more weight to consumers with stronger preferences for or against the pure public good. In contrast, one vote per consumer implicitly assumes that the intensity of preferences is the same for all consumers.

Consumer	*Cost ($)*	*Value ($)*	*Net benefit ($)*	*Clarke Tax ($)*
Friday	300	700	400	350
Robinson	300	150	−150	0
Simpson	300	100	−200	0

The sum of net benefits excluding Friday is −$350, indicating that Friday is a pivotal consumer. Without considering Friday's preferences, the pure public good would not be purchased. Considering Friday's preferences, the pure public good is purchased and both Robinson and Simpson are harmed by the purchase in the combined amount of $350. The Clarke tax on the pivotal consumer, Friday, is then $350. After Friday pays this tax, her value from the purchase of the pure public good is reduced from $400 to $50. Friday has no incentive to exaggerate her value for the pure public good above $700, because, at her evaluation, the good is purchased. She also has no incentive to reduce her value for the good, because a reduction in her evaluation decreases the probability of the pure public good being purchased and does not change the tax she has to pay. It is in her interest to reveal her true evaluation of the pure public good.

In contrast, Robinson and Simpson are not pivotal consumers. The sum of net benefits excluding either Robinson's or Simpson's net benefits is still positive. The pure public good is still purchased even if Robinson's or Simpson's net benefits are not considered. However, both Robinson and Simpson are made worse off by the purchase of the pure public good. Purchasing the pure public good is not a Pareto-optimal move. If, for example, Robinson exaggerated his valuation in order to prevent the pure public good from being purchased, he would become a pivotal consumer and face paying a Clarke tax. Robinson would have to set his net benefit at less than −$200 to ensure that the pure public good is not purchased. He would then face a Clarke tax equal to the sum of the other net benefits ($200 = 400 − 200). By exaggerating his value for the pure public good, resulting in it not being purchased, Robinson saves the loss in net benefit of $150 if it was purchased, but pays $200 for this savings. Robinson lost more, $50, by exaggerating rather than revealing his true valuation.

Similar to Robinson, Simpson will minimize his losses by revealing his true valuation. Exaggerating to the point of becoming a pivotal consumer by setting his net benefit at less than −$250, Simpson pays a Clarke tax of $250 to save $200 in losses from the purchase of the pure public good. Like Robinson, Simpson lost more, $50, by exaggerating rather than revealing his true valuation. Thus, the Clarke tax provides incentives for all three consumers to reveal their true evaluation of the pure public good.

Application: Pigou and Clarke join hands

In the absence of public goods and externalities, perfectly competitive markets are incentive compatible. Both households and firms optimize their trades with prices as signals. None of the agents have any incentive to misrepresent their true preferences. This results in a Pareto-optimal allocation of resources. The invisible hand steers an economy toward Pareto efficiency.

As addressed by H. Sinn, a Pigouvian tax can provide the correct incentives to reduce a negative externality (e.g., waste-water discharge from cattle slaughterhouses), which results in achieving some environmental quality standard. However, a Pigouvian tax does not incorporate victims' preference for clean water. The appropriate level of the tax and environmental standard are unknown. This makes it impossible to design a pure price mechanism to fully solve the environmental problem.

One solution proposed by Sinn is to combine a Clarke tax with this Pigouvian tax. The two taxes are complementary, with the Clarke tax inducing the victims to reveal their preferences and the Pigouvian tax providing correct incentives for the polluters to mitigate environmental degradation. Two invisible hands join in solving the environmental inefficiency. Sinn demonstrates how this Clarke and Pigouvian taxation mechanism provides a practical solution to market failure. However, as with any incentive mechanism, possible problems of collusion between agents and the costs of agents disclosing their preferences must be resolved before such a mechanism is adopted. With such problems, government mechanism designs may fail to efficiently allocate resources. This has resulted in the proposition of advocating greater tolerance for market failure. However, as addressed by Sinn, a reverse proposition also exists. Requiring Pareto efficiency for a government mechanism design for a public good, which a free market cannot achieve, would be utopian. Thus, economists should concentrate on the development of market-oriented mechanisms (wormholes) that minimize the inefficiencies associated with missing markets. One such mechanism may be a Clarke and Pigouvian taxation wormhole.

Source: H. Sinn, "Pigou and Clarke Join Hands," *Public Choice* 75 (1993): 79–91.

Summary

1. Pure public goods are nonexclusive and nonrival commodities; pure private goods are exclusive and rival commodities. A commodity is nonexclusive when it is not possible to exclude other consumers from consuming the commodity. A rival commodity is where each additional unit consumed by one consumer results in less of the commodity available for other consumers.
2. The nonrival characteristics of a commodity allow the possibility of sharing the commodity among consumers. For a public good (exclusive but nonrival), as the number of times each commodity is shared increases, the firm will tend to rent the commodity instead of selling it. Specifically, when the marginal cost of production is greater than the consumers' transaction costs of renting instead of owning, the firm will generally rent instead of selling the commodity.
3. A free rider is an agent who cannot be excluded from receiving the benefits of a nondepletable commodity and who is unwilling to pay his portion of the cost.
4. The Pareto-efficiency condition for a pure public good is to set the sum of consumers' MRS to the MRPT. This is in contrast to the Pareto-efficient condition for a private good of equating each consumer's MRS to the MRPT.
5. Mechanisms designed for determining group choice generally attempt to uncover the intensities of individual and group desires. One such mechanism is the Clarke tax, where pivotal consumers are provided an incentive to reveal their true preferences.
6. For intertemporal public goods, free riders are not a problem because the difference in demand occurring at different times are revealed.

Key concepts

free rider, 942
Lindahl price, 951
private good, 937
public good, 937
pure private good, 937
pure public good, 937

Key equation

$$\begin{aligned}\mathrm{MRS}_S &= \sum_{j=1}^{n} \mathrm{MRS}_j = \mathrm{MRS}_1 + \mathrm{MRS}_2 + \ldots + \mathrm{MRS}_n \\ &= \mathrm{MRPT}\end{aligned}$$

The social marginal rate of substitution for a pure public good is the sum of consumers' marginal rates of substitution. The Pareto-efficient level of the pure public good is then determined by equating this social marginal rate of substitution to the marginal rate of product transformation.

Questions

1. Determine whether each of the following commodities is generally a pure private, private, pure public, or public good:
    a. Drinking water;
    b. Electricity;
    c. Internet service;
    d. Elementary schooling;
    e. University education;
    f. Toll bridges;
    g. Medicare services;
    h. Library books;
    i. Heavy machinery rental;
    j. National Public Radio reception;
    k. US Coast Guard rescue service;
    l. A country's embassy services;
    m. Household thermostat setting.
2. Explain the difference among local, national, and international public goods. What is the importance of this distinction for mechanisms designed with the aim of providing public goods?
3. Few resource-related decisions are truly private. True or false? Explain.
4. Some individuals think it is okay to be illegally connected to cable TV so they do not pay any monthly charges, but would never consider shoplifting? Why?
5. Why do video stores allow you to keep a video rental for a number of days without additional charges?
6. Students are often assigned to work in groups for class projects. Why does this generally result in one or two students expending most of the effort and the other students not contributing their fair share of the effort? What are some remedies?
7. Relatively little air-pollution abatement is purchased in unregulated markets, so is it reasonable to conclude that there is little demand for it? How about buggy whips? Explain.
8. Externalities in the consumption of medical services are cited as a cause of the market under-producing the socially optimal level of these services. What evidence can be used to determine the validity of this statement?
9. Externalities associated with public goods can be corrected by either the government directly supplying the commodity or the government subsidizing the supply. Provide an example of each method.
10. Why is the Clarke tax not generally adopted for determining the level of expenditure on public goods?

Exercises

It is exercise alone that supports the spirits and keeps the mind in vigor.

(Cicero)

1. The Parking Services Department on a small college campus has control of 1000 student parking spaces. The annual demand for these spaces, as a function of the price p for a parking permit, is

$$Q^D = 2000 - 20p.$$

   a. If Parking Services wants to set a Pareto-efficient price but believing that a parking space is a rival good, what price will it set?
   b. Following a survey, Parking Services determines that a parking space is a nonrival good, with the number of times it is shared, α, a function of the price:

$$\alpha = 20 - \tfrac{1}{2}p.$$

   With this information, what is the profit-maximizing price of a permit, and how many students will share a parking space?
   c. Determine the consumer and producer surplus for the rival versus the nonrival assumptions. Will Parking Services set a policy of issuing more permits than there are spaces? If so, will students overall like this policy?

2. Suppose that it costs \$50,000 per day to construct and maintain a bridge. Ten thousand drivers are willing to pay \$4 each in toll to cross the bridge and another 10,000 are willing to pay \$2.

   a. Assuming that it is not possible to price-discriminate, will a private firm build and operate the bridge? If so, what toll would it charge?
   b. Should some government agency build and operate the bridge? If so, what toll would it charge?
   c. How do your answers to (a) and (b) change if it is possible to price-discriminate? (Some common forms of price discrimination are discounts to commuters and higher tolls based on the number of axles a vehicle has.)

3. Dylan, Natalie, and Alex have the following demand schedules for a commodity:

	Quantity		
Price	*Dylan*	*Natalie*	*Alex*
1	10	8	6
2	9	7	5
3	8	6	4
4	7	5	3
5	6	4	2

	Quantity		
Price	*Dylan*	*Natalie*	*Alex*
6	5	3	1
7	4	2	0
8	3	1	0
9	2	0	0
10	1	0	0

a. Assuming that the commodity is a private good, determine the market demand schedule.
b. Answer (a) if instead the commodity is a public good.
c. Given the following supply schedule, determine the optimal level of quantity if the commodity is a public good:

Price	*Quantity supplied*
24	13
21	11
18	9
15	7
12	5
9	3
6	1
4	0
2	0
1	0

4. In Itchville, there are three types of consumers: Human, Klingon, and Vulcan. Their inverse demand curves for mosquito control C are

$$p_1 = 300 - C, \quad p_2 = 400 - 2C, \quad p_3 = 500 - C.$$

Assume that mosquito control is a pure public good that can be produced at a constant marginal cost of \$400.

a. What is the optimal level of mosquito control?
b. How much mosquito control would a perfectly competitive market provide?
c. How much of a subsidy would be required for each consumer to yield a Pareto-efficient allocation of the public good in a perfectly competitive market? Will a subsidy provided to the firm producing the public good result in the same Pareto-efficient outcome?

5. One hundred households are located around a lake, with each household having a neighbor on either side of them. Every household has the same preferences and consumes only one commodity, but each household is envious of the consumption by the household on its left. Specifically, $U(C, L) = C - L^2$, where C is a household's own consumption and L is consumption by the household on its left.

   a. What is the optimal level of consumption if all households consume the same amount?
   b. If every household is consuming 1 unit, can any two households make themselves better off by either redistributing consumption between them or throwing some away?
   c. How about a group of three people?
   d. How large is the smallest group that could cooperate to benefit all of its members?

6. The production possibilities frontier for an economy that produces one public good y and one private good Q is

   $$y^2 + Q^2 = 320{,}000.$$

   This economy has 100 households with identical preferences for the public and private good given by

   $$U = x_j y, \quad j = 1, 2, \ldots, 100, \qquad \text{where } Q = \sum_{j=1}^{100} x_j.$$

   a. Determine the optimal levels of Q and y.
   b. If the markets for the private and public goods are perfectly competitive, determine the levels produced.

7. Assume that there are two groups of property owners in Los Alamos, New Mexico. Group 1 is composed of home owners with the following demand function for a regional fire-protection program:

   $$q_1 = 40 - p$$

   Commercial real estate owners comprise group 2, with a fire-program demand function

   $$q_2 = 50 - p.$$

   Let the marginal cost associated with regional fire protection be 30.

   a. Determine the optimal level of regional fire protection and the corresponding Lindahl prices. How much does the fire program cost and how is it allocated between the two groups?
   b. If fire protection were instead left to the individual groups, what would be the level of protection and who would likely be the free riders?

8. Suppose that there are two types of consumers in a community. Their inverse demand curves for a public good are

$$p_1 = 16 - y, \quad p_2 = 20 - y.$$

Assume that this pure public good can be produced at MC $= y$.

   a. How much would a perfectly competitive market provide and which type of consumer will purchase it?
   b. For the consumer purchasing the commodity in (a), how much of a subsidy S would be required for the level of the commodity purchased to be equal to the Pareto-efficient allocation? Does it make a difference if this subsidy is provided to the firm producing the commodity or the consumer purchasing the commodity?

9. Three astronauts are determining what items to bring and share on a mission to Mars. Weight is a big factor on such a mission, so each astronaut is given a fixed allocation for any items she wants to bring. For items to be shared among all three, they have decided to deduct the weight equally from each of their weight allocations.

   a. One particular item they are considering sharing is a DVD player, which weighs 3 pounds. In terms of weight, astronaut 1 places a value for the DVD player at 1.5, astronaut 2 a value of 1.25, and astronaut 3 (an android) a value of 0. Would a majority vote result in bringing the DVD player to Mars?
   b. Determine how a Clarke tax will change the solution in (a). What is the level of the tax, and who pays?

10. A soft drink firm has the option of selling its refreshments in either disposable or reusable containers. The inverse demand function for these containers is

$$p = 5 - (q/400),$$

and the firm is facing a constant marginal cost of $c = 1/3$ with an additional transactions cost only for the reusable containers of $c_t = 2/3$. The reusable containers can be used 10 times, so $\alpha = 10$.

   a. Why will the firm not use reusable containers for its soft drinks?
   b. How much of a firm subsidy would be required for the firm to switch to reusable containers?
   c. Given the minimum subsidy required for switching, what would be the reduction in the number of containers used by switching to reusables?
   d. Instead of a subsidy, how much of a tax would be required for the firm to switch to reusable containers? What would be the reduction in the number of containers used by this switching?

Internet case studies

1. Discuss a number of successful techniques that public goods organizations use to overcome the free-rider problem.
2. Contrast the concepts of willingness to pay with ability to pay in terms of funding public goods.
3. Discuss the prospects of demand-revealing mechanisms, such as the Clarke tax, becoming relevant policy tools for public decision making.

23 Asymmetric information

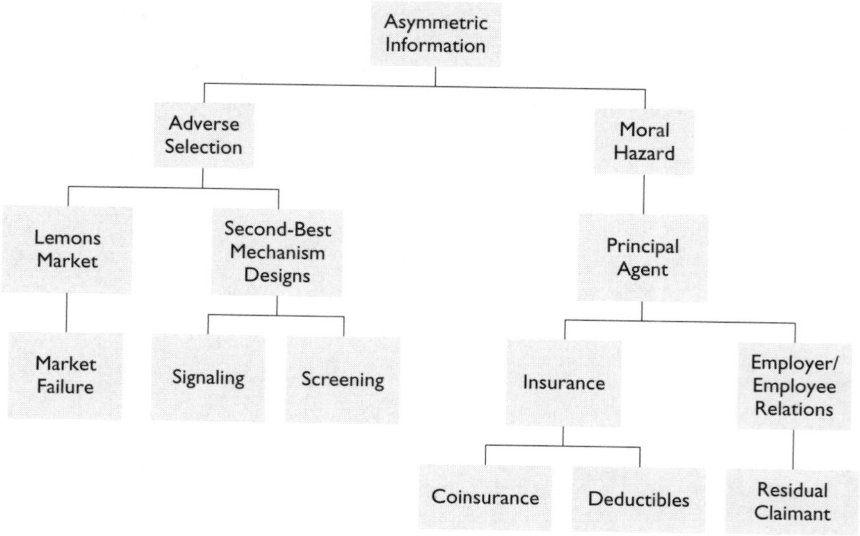

Outline and Conceptual Inquiries

Understanding adverse selection

Lemons market: used cars

Should you purchase a used vehicle?

Application: Commercial real estate leasing

Finding second-best mechanism designs

Is a salesperson's advice valuable?

Application: The GED signal

Is it efficient to screen before purchasing?

What are principal-agent models?

Pareto efficiency with no moral hazard: *Nineteen Eighty-Four*

Insurance market with no moral hazard

Insurance and moral hazard

Why can't you insure your car for 100 percent of a loss?

Employer and employee relations

When the cat's away, will the mice play?

Application: The incorruptible cashier

Pareto efficiency with no moral hazard

Inefficiency with moral hazard

Why are fast-food outlets independently owned and operated?

Application: Sharecropping

Why does an accused felon not flee?

Why are some interns not paid or are paid a low wage?

Summary

Key concepts

Key equations

Questions

Exercises

Internet case studies

Scienta est potentia.

(Francis Bacon)

Translation: Knowledge is power. Possessing a monopoly on market information can increase an agent's satisfaction.

Managers (insiders) of firms can increase their profit by taking actions based on insider information (information that is not available to the public). If insiders obtain positive (negative) information about a company, they buy (sell) the company's stock with the expectation that the stock's price will rise (fall) when the positive (negative) information is publically announced. Such insider trading of securities, where asymmetric information exists between the insider and the general public, is illegal.[1] However, incorporating information not known by all agents in market pricing is generally legal—legal, but unethical. When selling a commodity, agents are not legally required to provide full disclosure of information on a commodity. An example is running the following ad:

For Sale: Parachute. Only used once, never opened, small stain.

Let the buyer beware.

Prior to this chapter, we have generally implicitly assumed or explicitly stated symmetry in market information as a characteristic of market structure. We have assumed that all agents had costless access to this information, so symmetry in the market existed, with both buyers and sellers having the same market information.

For example, one of the explicit characteristics of perfect competition is agents' perfect knowledge.

In general, market information is costly, and this cost may vary between buyers and sellers, resulting in **asymmetric information** held by agents. One set of agents—say sellers—may be more knowledgeable about a commodity (parachute) than another set—say buyers. Information cost may vary among agents as a result of differences in education and experience about the commodity. Examples are a firm possessing limited information about a potential worker's abilities, a used car buyer not having the complete repair and maintenance history on an auto, and an insurance company not knowing the risky behavior of a potential insurer.

Asymmetric information. Market information varies across agents. *E.g., the seller of a house may have more knowledge about its condition than a buyer.*

When commodities are homogeneous and their characteristics are readily available, the cost of determining these characteristics is small, so the assumption of market symmetry would generally hold. For example, symmetric information generally holds for the commodity futures market, where, except for delivery dates, all futures contracts on the same commodity have identical characteristics. In contrast, asymmetric information will generally exist for heterogeneous commodities with characteristics that are costly to determine. An example is the vehicle market, where the condition of a vehicle is difficult to determine without costly testing. The heterogeneous nature of used vehicles prevents a general determination of a vehicle's condition based on examination of other like vehicles. A major consequence of this asymmetric information is the possible disappearance of markets. Missing markets then result in an inefficient allocation of resources.

Our aim in this chapter is to demonstrate how missing markets and associated efficiency losses result in the presence of asymmetric information. This asymmetry in information generates two types of outcomes: *adverse selection* and *moral hazard*. We first address adverse selection, where one agent's decision depends on unobservable characteristics that adversely affect other agents. We use the used-automobile market to illustrate the missing market and resulting market inefficiencies associated with adverse selection. We then discuss the mechanisms of *signaling* and *screening* as second-best Pareto-efficient mechanisms for addressing these inefficiencies. This is followed by a discussion of moral hazard, where a contract is signed among agents, with one agent being dependent on the unobservable actions of other agents. Using a *principal-agent model*, we derive the inefficient level of precaution taken by agents, which results from the principal being unable to observe the agents' actions (moral hazard). We then evaluate mechanisms (such as coinsurance) designed to address the inefficiencies associated with moral hazard.

Asymmetric information is a relatively new area for applied economic analysis. In 1970, George A. Akerlof, who earned the 2001 Nobel Prize for economics, was the first to address the problems and solutions associated with adverse selection. Knowledge of moral hazard has been around since the advent of insurance in the eighteenth century. However, only recently have applied economists investigated the ramifications of moral hazard on economic efficiency. Novel solutions addressing moral hazard—particularly in terms of employer and employee relations—are continuously being offered.

Understanding adverse selection

The secret is to become wise before you get old.

(O.H. Jackson Brown)

Translation: By becoming wise before you get old, you can reduce the level of market adverse selection.

Governor Earl Warren of California was appointed US Supreme Court Chief Justice by President Dwight Eisenhower in 1953 and served until 1969. By 1956, Chief Justice Warren's judicial options indicated he was in the process of transforming the court into a platform for a libertarian activist approach to public law and personal rights far beyond the Eisenhower brand of progressive Republicanism. Chief Justice Warren brought constitutional revolution in the application of the Bill of Rights and the Civil War amendments to the states. This resulted in the liberalization of the right to foreign travel, to vote, to run for office, to fair representation, to "one person, one vote," and to an elevated commitment to freedom of expression. It also resulted in the distribution of "Impeach Earl Warren" bumper stickers and Warren Impeachment Kits. One of President Eisenhower's biggest disappointments was the appointment of Earl Warren. This is an example of market adverse selection resulting from asymmetric information. Information on Earl Warren's character was hidden, which resulted in market adverse selection.

Asymmetric information in a market can result in market inefficiencies. If information concerning the characteristics of a commodity (Earl Warren) is not freely available, inefficient allocations may result. One type of asymmetric information is called **adverse selection** (also called **hidden information**), where an informed agent's decision depends on unobservable characteristics that adversely affect uninformed agents. The classic example (developed by Akerlof) is the market for used cars. Assume that used cars can be grouped by quality into two groups. Within each group, the used cars are homogeneous and are associated with a single price. Comparing vehicles between the groups, they are heterogeneous in quality and thus are not valued by identical prices. In a free (symmetric) information case, the two heterogeneous groups of commodities (used cars) would have separate markets with associated prices p_1 and p_2.

Adverse selection (hidden information). An informed agent's decision depends on unobservable characteristics that adversely affect uninformed agents. *E.g., a buyer of a piano does not possess information that a seller has on the condition of the strings and sound board.*

Lemons market: used cars

Generally, sellers of a used car, through experience, know the vehicle's history and thus can determine its market price at zero or very minimal cost. In contrast, buyers do not have this experience, so the cost of determining this information for each group of used cars is prohibitive. Without this information, buyers may base their market-price determination on the average quality of used cars available. This asymmetry in information results in buyers only willing to pay up to the average price of used cars available, μ_p, and at this average price sellers would be willing to supply only

$$Q^s = \sum_{p_j \le \mu_p} q_j(p_j),$$

where $q_j(p_j)$ is the supply of used cars in group j. The above-average used cars, associated with $p_j > \mu_p$, will not be offered for sale. Sellers would be unwilling to supply their cars for less than the vehicle's market value. Buyers realize that the above-average used cars will not enter the market at the average price μ_p, so the average quality of used cars offered in the market is less than the average quality of used cars available. They will then adjust downward their willingness to pay for used cars offered in the market. Then only sellers who value their cars below this new lower price will supply vehicles, so the average quality of used cars offered in the market will once again decline. This tâtonnement process will continue until only the lowest-quality group of used cars are offered and sold in the market. When only the lowest-quality group is offered for sale, any asymmetry in information vanishes. With symmetric information, buyers' and sellers' expected prices match and only a market for the lowest-quality group exists. The missing markets for the other quality groups of used cars represent market failure. These lowest-quality cars are popularly referred to as lemons, so this market failure associated with adverse selection is called the *lemons problem.*

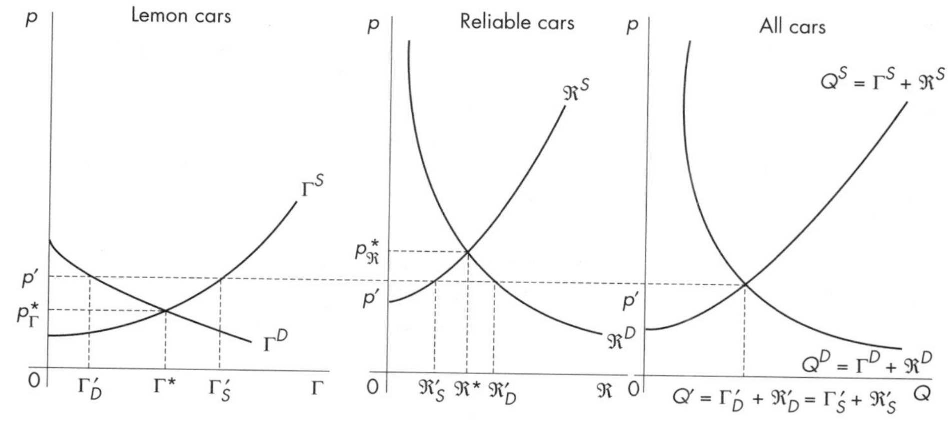

Figure 23.1 **Lemons problem.** When quality discrimination is possible, an efficient allocation results with Γ^* lemon and $\Re^*$ reliable cars traded. Without the ability to discriminate by quality, only a lemon market for cars will remain, with a missing market for reliable cars.

In Figure 23.1, the lemons problem is illustrated for two quality groups of used vehicles, reliable cars, $\Re$, and lemons, Γ. Curves Γ^S and $\Re^S$ are the supply curves for lemons and reliable cars, respectively. The supply curve for reliable cars is above the lemons curve, indicating that sellers of reliable used cars are only willing to supply these higher-valued vehicles at prices above the lemon cars. The demand curves for lemons and reliable cars are represented by Γ^D and $\Re^D$, respectively. Buyers are willing to pay a higher price for reliable cars compared with lemons, so the reliable demand curve is above the lemon demand. Given free information, the market is able to discriminate between these two types of quality cars, so market clearing prices exist for both the reliable and lemon automobile markets. The equilibrium price and quality for reliable cars are then $p^*_\Re$ and $\Re^*$ and for the lemons they are p^*_Γ and Γ^*.

Asymmetric information in the form of adverse selection prevents buyers from freely distinguishing reliable cars from lemons. Buyers may know the proportions of automobiles that are reliable and those that are lemons, but are unable to distinguish the quality of a given automobile. The overall market demand Q^D facing the sellers will then be the horizontal sum of lemon and reliable demand curves. Similarly, the total supply of cars Q^S is the horizontal sum of the lemon and reliable supply curves. The resulting equilibrium price and quantity are p' and Q'. This loss in the ability of the market to distinguish between reliable and lemon cars results in the number of lemons offered on the market increasing from Γ^* to Γ'_S and the number of reliable cars declining from $\Re^*$ to $\Re'_S$. In contrast, the demand for lemons decreases from Γ^* to Γ'_D and the demand for reliable cars increases from $\Re^*$ to $\Re'_D$. This imbalance within the two markets will result in some buyers who expect to receive a reliable car instead receiving a lemon. As buyers realize that the ratio of reliable to lemon cars is declining in the market, they will adjust their expected quality downward. Participation in the number of buyers wanting a reliable car will decline as the expectation of obtaining a reliable car in the market decreases. The resulting downward shift in the demand curve further drives reliable cars out of the market, which further erodes the demand for reliable cars. This tâtonnement process will continue until buyers only expect lemons to be supplied, so their market demand curve is Γ^D. Such a market will then supply Γ^* automobiles at a price of p_Γ^*, and a missing market will exist for the reliable cars. The market is unable to allocate both the supply of reliable and lemon cars efficiently to buyers. It is unable to price-discriminate across quality differences. An efficient allocation would result in such quality discrimination, and buyers would have the market choice of purchasing either reliable or lemon cars. Without this market ability to quality-discriminate, some buyers may by chance purchase a reliable car, but these may not be the buyers with the highest willingness to pay. Failure of the market to allocate commodities based on willingness to pay results in an inefficient allocation.[2]

Should you purchase a used vehicle? Yes, but very warily.

Example 23.1 Lemons problem

Consider the following demand and supply functions for lemons, Γ, and reliable cars, $\Re$:

$$\Gamma^D = 55 - 2p_\Gamma, \quad \Re^D = 130 - p_\Re,$$

$$\Gamma^S = p_\Gamma - 5, \quad \Re^S = p_\Re - 10,$$

where the superscripts D and S refer to demand and supply, and the subscripts Γ and $\Re$ to lemons and reliable cars, respectively. With free information, the following equilibrium prices and quantities are established in the markets:

$$\Gamma^D = \Gamma^S \Rightarrow p_\Gamma = 20, \quad \Gamma^* = 15,$$

$$\Re^D = \Re^S \Rightarrow p_\Re = 70, \quad \Re^* = 60.$$

With asymmetric information in the form of adverse selection, where buyers do not have the same information on the reliability of a vehicle as a seller, the markets for lemons and reliable cars collapse into one market. Summation across quantity of the demand and supply functions, yields the aggregate demand and supply functions

$$Q^D = 0 + \Re^D = 130 - p \qquad \text{for } p > 27.5,$$

$$Q^D = \Gamma^D + \Re^D = (55 - 2p) + (130 - p) = 185 - 3p \qquad \text{for } 0 < p < 27.5,$$

$$Q^S = \Gamma^S + \Re^S = (p - 5) + (p - 10) = 2p - 15 \qquad \text{for } p \geq 10,$$

$$Q^S = \Gamma^S + 0 = p - 5 \qquad \text{for } 5 < p < 10.$$

Note that the absence of subscripts on p results from the markets collapsing into one market. Equilibrium for this combined market is then

$$Q^D = Q^S,$$

$$0 + \Re^D = \Gamma^S + \Re^S \Rightarrow p' = 48.33, \quad Q' = 81.67.$$

For the lemon and reliable markets, a price of p' results in $\Gamma^{D\prime} = 0$, $\Gamma^{S\prime} = 43.33$, $\Re^{D\prime} = 81.67$, and $\Re^{S\prime} = 38.33$. This imbalance of demand for reliable and lemon cars compared with the supply is a consequence of the lemons problem and will result in only a market for lemons, with a missing market for reliable cars.

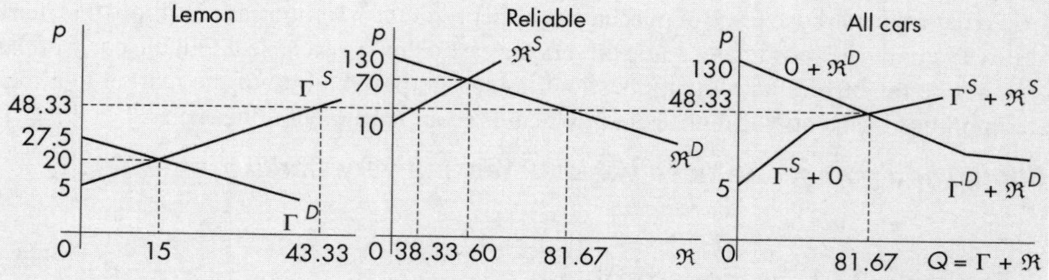

The cause of this missing market and associated inefficient allocation of resources is an externality between sellers of reliable and lemon cars. As illustrated in Figure 23.1, as the number of sellers offering lemons increases, buyers' expectations regarding the quality of vehicles in the market is affected, so the price that buyers are willing to pay declines. This lower price adversely affects sellers of reliable cars by preventing them from selling their vehicles and thus improving efficiency. The externality between sellers for reliable cars and lemons has distributional implications as well. Owners of lemons may receive more than their automobile is worth and owners of reliable cars less. Buyers processing limited information generally benefit sellers of lemon products.

Used car markets are one example of market failure in the presence of adverse selection. The problem of adverse selection exists in other markets as well. For example, in the insurance market, buyers of insurance know more about their general health than any insurance company. Unhealthy consumers are more likely to buy insurance, because healthy consumers will find the cost of insurance too high. Similar to the used car market, the tâtonnement process will continue until only the unhealthy consumers purchase insurance, which will make selling insurance unprofitable. Another example is the labor market, where workers' potential productivity is unobservable by a hiring firm but the workers themselves know their productive capabilities. Again, the tâtonnement process will result in only the less productive workers being hired. This market failure resulting from adverse selection explains why a new automobile declines in value once it is driven off the lot, why insurance is so high for a previously uninsured driver or a person with no medical history, and why starting salaries are low with a potential for frequent raises once hired.

Application: Commercial real estate leasing

A major issue in leasing is the renter's private information on the potential usage of the leased property. This asymmetric information on the renter's expected intensity of property utilization is an issue in determining the type of lease offered by a landlord. In general, partly depending on expected intensity of property utilization, a gross lease or a net lease is offered. In a gross lease, the landlord pays all operating expenses, including utilities, property taxes, maintenance, and repair. In a net lease, the renter pays some or all of the operating expenses. Both net and gross leases are widely utilized. This observed use of both leasing types raises questions addressed by R. Mooradian and S. Yang as to the determinants of landlord and renter choice between leasing types and how gross leases are structured and priced if landlords are unable to determine renters' intensity of property utilization.

One explanation for the use of gross leases is the presence of economies of scale associated with landlords providing operating management and maintenance services. With these economies, a landlord can provide management and services at a lower cost than renters. Landlord provision of services also mitigates contracting problems and reduces negative externalities among tenants of multitenant retail properties. Thus, two opposing forces—asymmetric information and economies of scale—dictate which type of lease option will be offered.

Mooradian and Yang determined that the type of lease offered reflects the relative power of the landlord. In a competitive market, the cost savings from shifting maintenance to the landlord with a gross lease mitigates the asymmetric information problem. The lower cost is passed on to the renter, which results in a greater proportion of renters selecting a gross lease even given the cost of being pooled with higher-intensity renters. However, in a monopolistically competitive market, all of the cost savings in economies of scale do not accrue to the renters, so the degree of mitigating the asymmetric information problem is less.

Applying this conclusion to the commercial real estate market, Mooradian and Yang suggest that for retail properties (including shopping centers) where tenants are in close proximity to each other (possibly leasing a fraction of the total space), a net leasing agreement would be cost-prohibitive. Thus, even with asymmetric information and different intensities of utilization among renters, a gross lease would generally be used. In contrast, for agricultural and industrial properties, there are few if any economies of scale for a gross lease, so net leasing would generally be observed.

Source: R.M. Mooradian and S.X. Yang, "Commercial Real Estate Leading, Asymmetric Information, and Monopolistic Competition," *Real Estate Economics* 30 (2002): 293–315.

Finding second-best mechanism designs

On March 23, 2010 President Obama signed legislation to overhaul the United States' health care system and guarantee access to medical insurance for millions of Americans. Prior to this legislation, around 40 million Americans were completely uninsured and millions of others had inadequate coverage. Opponents of the legislation are against a provision requiring that people purchase insurance and contend that the provision is unconstitutional. However, such a provision can avoid the inefficiencies of adverse selection in health care. By making the purchase of insurance compulsory, unhealthy citizens benefit from insurance premiums below their expected health costs and healthy citizens can purchase insurance at lower rates. Such a governmental policy is called *cross-subsidization*, where healthy consumers pay a portion of the health care for unhealthy consumers. This is one justification in favor of Medicare for the elderly. By providing insurance for all the elderly, adverse selection is eliminated. However, without knowing agents' private information, obtaining the Pareto-optimal allocation is not possible. Acquiring such information is costly, so only a constrained or second-best Pareto optimum can be obtained.

In general, insurance companies can avoid adverse selection by offering group health insurance plans at places of employment. This type of group insurance is called *pooling*, where both healthy and unhealthy consumers are pooled together. The insurance premiums are then based on the average cost of health care and adverse selection is eliminated by requiring all employees to participate.

Government agencies can also improve the functioning of markets by providing free information or requiring product information prior to sale. Many government agencies provide information useful for making market decisions. Examples of free information are diverse, from the US State Department cautioning tourists visiting a particular region to the USDA publishing situation and outlooks for agricultural commodities. An example of requiring product information is the Food and Drug Administration's requirement for food labeling on processed foods.

Signaling: Warranty

A lie told often enough becomes the truth.

(Vladimir Ilyich Lenin)

Buyers and sellers can both potentially benefit from creating markets that were missing as a consequence of adverse selection. This provides incentives for developing market mechanisms to mitigate market failure associated with adverse selection. Mechanisms that transfer information from the informed agent to the uninformed agent are called **signaling**. A naive type of signal on the part of a buyer is to ask the sellers the quality of a commodity—for example, asking a used car dealer the condition of a car. The cost of such a signal could be very high if the signal is inaccurate and the commodity is purchased. This is an example of a particularly *weak signal*, where the cost of providing a signal is the same for all sellers regardless of the quality of their product. Appearance can be another weak signal when the cost is the same for all agents. Nothing succeeds like the appearance of success. A *strong signal* must have an associated lower cost for sellers offering relatively high-quality commodities compared with the cost for sellers offering poor-quality commodities. Examples of strong signals used by firms are reputation and standardization. Firms offering higher-quality commodities have an advantage over other firms in establishing a reputation for quality. For example, construction subcontractors can provide a signal for quality construction by developing a list of satisfied customers that a potential customer can contact. Generally, painters, plumbers, and roofers will develop such lists for signaling. Even some used car sales representatives can develop a reputation for quality used vehicles.

Is a salesperson's advice valuable? A salesperson's cost of providing advice is close to zero and the same regardless of a product's quality, so take this advice with a grain of salt. Many salespeople hope that enough lying will cause the customer to become a believer.

Signaling. A transfer of information from the informed agent to the uninformed agent. *E.g., a car dealership may advertise that it is the number-one seller of automobiles, which implies a signal that this is the preferred place to purchase an auto.*

One problem with reputation as a signaling device is the delay associated with establishing a reputation. This problem may be partially avoided by supplementing reputation with guarantees and warranties as explicit signals of product quality. For example, with mounting problems such as sticky accelerator pedals and a brake-system glitch, in 2010 Toyota lost a significant amount of its reputation for manufacturing top-quality automobiles. In response, Toyota included a complimentary worry-free maintenance plan with the purchase or lease of a new car. As another example, restaurant food at tourist locations can be poor because the transient nature of consumers does not allow reputation to play a role. In response to this problem, the travel industry will publish restaurant guides, which provide signals to potential consumers.

Such signals are useful in cases where buyers lack information on the quality of some commodity that they do not purchase on a regular basis. For regularly purchased commodities that vary in quality, firms will attempt to standardize the commodities they are offering to signal quality. For example, a fruit and vegetable wholesaler will attempt to always offer the same quality of produce. Through standardization, sellers send a strong signal that buyers can expect quality produce from them. Some firms will even advertise such standardization as a market signal. For example, Holiday Inn had an advertising campaign stating "No surprises if you stay at one of our motels."

In general, a signaling mechanism will be employed by informed agents. These agents are not always the seller. For example, the agent could be an antique dealer purchasing items for his shop. Through experience, this dealer will have a greater knowledge about the market than sellers. A reputable dealer could then employ signaling mechanisms to separate him from disreputable dealers, such as disreputable antique dealers of the past, who would offer to clean the attic for a household in exchange for all of its contents and thus acquire valuable antiques at very low cost from the attic contents.

The concept of signals in a labor market context was first developed by Michael Spence, who earned the 2001 Nobel Prize for economics with George A. Akerlof. A strong signal of a person's labor productivity is education. Education generally does improve a person's productivity; however, even if it did not, it would still be a strong signal of productivity. Any admission requirements to a university or college will only result in higher-quality individuals entering the institution. "Quality in, quality out" is the signal to employers. Consumers, firms, and government agencies have also used gender, race, color, religion, and national origin as signals for labor productivity but these signals, besides being illegal in the United States, are generally weak. Exceptions are when insurance companies target insurance rates by such characteristics as age and gender. Some segments of society may feel that the use of such discriminatory signals is morally wrong and thus should be illegal. Economic theory does not pass judgment on the morality of these signals, but it does provide a framework for determining the economic consequences of restricting such signals. Theory would indicate that a government restriction on one signal would result in firms adopting related signaling mechanisms to maintain profits.

For the used car market, reliable car dealers will be able to offer signals—say, in the form of warranties—at a lower cost than lemon dealers, as illustrated in Figure 23.2. This lower warranty cost will result in the lemon dealers being unable to compete in offering warranties. Thus, only reliable dealers offer warranties. Through these signals (warranties), the market for used vehicles can now be separated into two markets: lemons and reliable cars. The market equilibrium for lemons is Pareto-efficient by corresponding to the free-information equilibrium (p_Γ^*, Γ^*). The market supply and demand curves for lemons did not shift, and introduction of a signal for reliable cars has established a separate market for lemons.

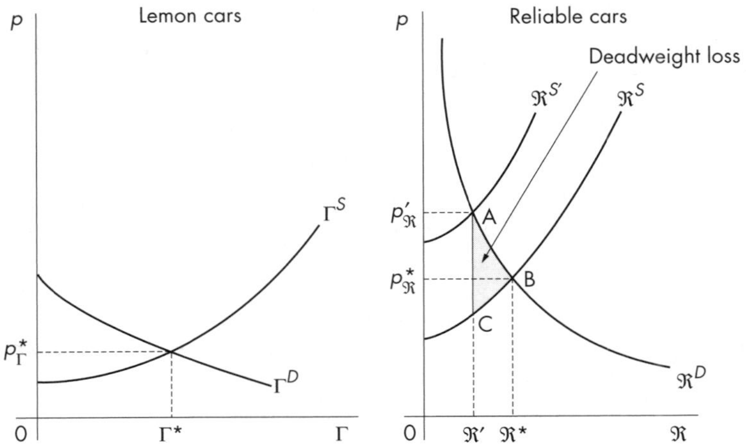

Figure 23.2 **Signaling.** The market for lemon cars is still Pareto-efficient and now, with signals, a market for reliable cars can be established. Due to the cost of signals, the reliable market is associated with deadweight loss, area CAB, so it is a second-best Pareto-efficient outcome.

In contrast, the market supply curve for reliable cars shifts up from $\Re^S$ to $\Re^{S\prime}$, representing the increased cost associated with offering warranties. As a result of this supply shift, the equilibrium quantity of reliable cars, $\Re'$, is below the free-information quantity of $\Re^*$ and the equilibrium price $p'_\Re$ is above the free-information price $p^*_\Re$. This results in a deadweight loss associated with the signal represented by the area CAB. Such a market equilibrium is called a *separating equilibrium*, given that it segments the pooled market for lemons and reliable cars into two markets. However, this is only a second-best Pareto-efficient outcome because, in markets with free information, sellers do not incur the extra expense of signals. There is a deadweight loss of removing the inefficiency associated with the asymmetric-information externality. Note that this deadweight loss is the cost of removing the externality and is a loss in both producer and consumer surplus. Thus, similar to the effects of a sales or output tax (discussed in Chapter 10), both buyers and sellers will pay for the cost of the signal. The proportion of costs paid by buyers and sellers depends on the relative elasticities of supply and demand for reliable cars. In the long run, as the elasticity of supply becomes more elastic, a larger proportion of the signal cost is passed on to the buyers.

Example 23.2 Signaling

Continuing with Example 23.1, assume that a strong signal by sellers of reliable cars costs \$60 per vehicle sold. This results in the following modified supply function for reliable cars, with the demand function for reliable cars and supply and demand functions for lemons remaining unchanged:

$$p_\Re = 10 + \Re^{S'} + 60.$$

The separating-equilibrium price and quantity established in the market for lemons corresponds to the free-information equilibrium

$$\Gamma^D = \Gamma^S \Rightarrow p_\Gamma = 20, \Gamma^* = 15.$$

Considering the shift in the supply curve for reliable cars resulting from the introduction of signals, the equilibrium price and quantity for reliable cars are now

$$\Re^D = \Re^{S'} \Rightarrow p' = 100, \Re^{S'} = 30,$$

compared with the free-information equilibrium price and quantity $p_\Re = 70$ and $\Re^S = 60$. The deadweight loss associated with the signal is $(80)(30)/2 = \$1200$, where the buyers' portion of the loss is \$450 and the sellers' portion is \$750.

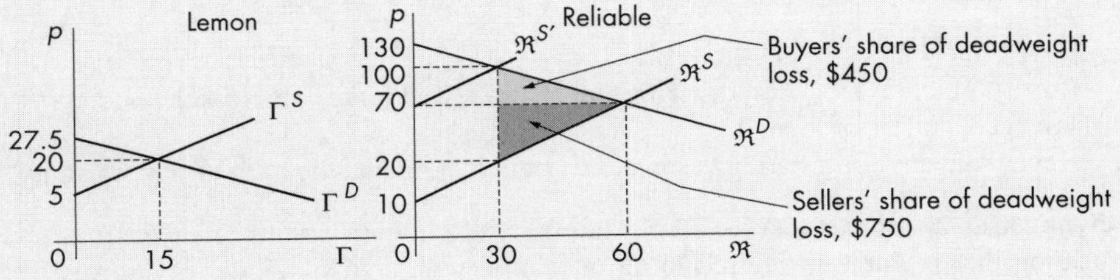

Application: The GED signal

The General Education Development (GED) credential was introduced in 1942 as a method for veterans without a high school diploma to earn high school certification. Today, the GED has evolved as the primary method for high school dropouts to receive certification. The GED examination is composed of a five-test battery covering literature and the arts, mathematics, writing, social studies, and science. In 2008, around 500,000 high school dropouts passed the test, representing 12 percent of annual high school graduates.

The economic returns to a GED can be examined given the diverse productivity level of the dropouts. The higher productivity dropouts can use the GED as a signal of their productivity to employers and receive a higher wage rate. A separating equilibrium for GED versus non-GED acquisition will exist if the expected net benefit of GED acquisition is positive for higher-productivity dropouts and negative for lower-productivity dropouts. Estimating this difference in net benefits, M. Clark and D. Jaeger found that foreign-born men with a GED who received all of their formal education abroad earn significantly more than either foreign-education high school dropouts or graduates. In contrast, US-native GED recipients earn less than high school graduates but significantly more than dropouts.

Source: M.A. Clark and D.A. Jaeger, "Natives, the Foreign-Born and High School Equivalents: New Evidence on the Returns to the GED," *Journal of Population Economics* 19 (2006): 769–793.

Screening: car inspections

> *Nobody believes the official spokesman, but everybody trusts an unidentified source.*
>
> (Ron Nesen)
>
> *Translation: Do not rely on the signals from a seller or buyer; instead obtain information from another source.*

The following are the top three techniques to prevent used car scams:

1. Have a mechanic inspect the vehicle.
2. Run a Vehicle History Report. This report will reveal if the vehicle was flooded, rebuilt, salvaged, stolen, or totaled.
3. Never sign anything stating "as is, no warranty." Obtain at least a 30-day warranty.

Symmetric information associated with free information results in a Pareto-efficient allocation that is Pareto-preferred to an allocation with signals. However, signals can be a second-best Pareto-efficient outcome if they result in a separating equilibrium, which improves efficiency. Unfortunately, not all signals do this. Weak signals resulting in a *pooling equilibrium*, where signals of different quality sellers cannot be differentiated, do not separate the markets, so market efficiency is not improved. In such markets, buyers may attempt to distinguish or screen the various commodities offered on the market. **Screening** exists when a buyer employs a mechanism for sorting the commodities offered by sellers. Examples of screening are a buyer having a used car inspected prior to purchase or an employer offering internships prior to employment. In general, screening is employed by the uninformed agent, which can be either a buyer or a seller. For example, price discrimination, discussed in Chapter 13, is a form of screening where the seller does not have information on buyers' willingness to pay for the commodity. By screening buyers based on their characteristics, sellers can create separate markets and practice price discrimination.

Screening. An agent employs a mechanism for sorting commodities. *E.g., a high school senior will determine which university to attend by gaining information about each institution under consideration.*

In some cases, buyers rely on a third party for screening. For example, a consumer may acquire their dentist, house painter, doctor, or maid through a recommendation from another consumer or through a firm that screens commodities and then sells the information to potential buyers. For example, the magazine *Consumer Reports* is in the business of screening commodities. Major third parties for screening are government agencies providing

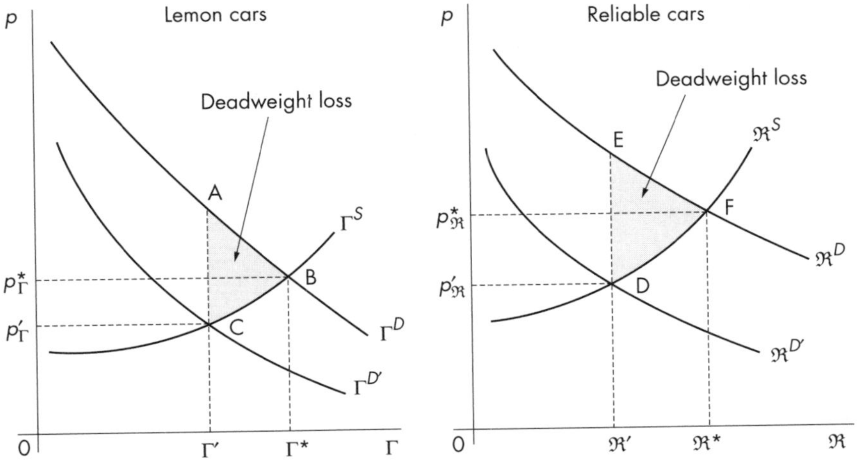

Figure 23.3 **Screening.** The second-best Pareto-efficient outcome of screening results in a separating equilibrium, but with output and prices (Γ', p'_Γ) and $(\mathfrak{R}', p'_\mathfrak{R})$ lower than the free-information equilibrium (Γ^*, p_Γ^*) and $(\mathfrak{R}^*, p_\mathfrak{R}^*)$. The deadweight loss associated with screening is represented by the shaded areas.

market information. An example is a California regulation requiring restaurants with 20 or more locations to provide calorie counts for menu items.

For an illustration of screening, let us consider again the used car market, where potential buyers may screen vehicles by having them inspected. As illustrated in Figure 23.3, the cost of screening will shift the demand for both lemons and reliable cars downward, from Γ^D to $\Gamma^{D'}$ for the lemons market and from $\mathfrak{R}^D$ to $\mathfrak{R}^{D'}$ for the reliable car market. The resulting separating-equilibrium prices, p'_Γ and $p'_\mathfrak{R}$, are lower than the free-information equilibrium prices, p_Γ^* and $p_\mathfrak{R}^*$, and the separating-equilibrium quantities Γ' and $\mathfrak{R}'$ are lower than the free-information equilibrium quantities Γ^* and $\mathfrak{R}^*$. The cost of screening is the sum of deadweight losses in the lemons market (the shaded area CAB) and the reliable market (the shaded area DEF).

Both signaling and screening have the potential for reducing asymmetric information and yielding a second-best Pareto-efficient outcome. In both cases, there is a cost of reducing this asymmetric-information externality. This cost of signals or screening may offset any market efficiency gains, so they may or may not improve social welfare.

Is it efficient to screen before purchasing? If the additional benefit from screening is greater than the any additional cost, then further screening is warranted.

Example 23.3. Screening

Continuing again with Example 23.1, suppose that buyers engage in screening, with vehicle inspection of $6 per vehicle sold. This inspection cost applies to all vehicles, resulting in the following modified demand functions for lemons and reliable cars, with the supply functions remaining unchanged:

$$p_\Gamma = 27.5 - \tfrac{1}{2}\Gamma^{D'} - 6,$$

$$p_\mathfrak{R} = 130 - \mathfrak{R}^{D'} - 6.$$

The separating-equilibrium price and quantity established in the markets for lemons and reliable cars are then

$$\Gamma^{D'} = \Gamma^S \rightarrow p' = 16,\ \Gamma' = 11,$$

$$\mathfrak{R}^{D'} = \mathfrak{R}^S \rightarrow p' = 67, \mathfrak{R}' = 57.$$

The deadweight loss associated with screening is the sum of the losses in the two markets:

$$[(6)(4)/2] + [(6)(3)/2] = 12 + 9 = \$21.$$

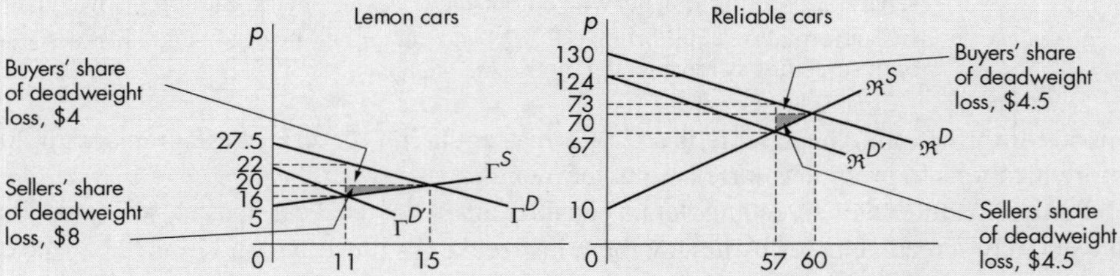

What are principal-agent models?

In all large corporations, there is a pervasive fear that someone somewhere is having fun with a computer on company time. Networks help alleviate that fear.

(John C. Dvorak)

The Indian Removal Act of 1830 was designed to relocate all eastern Indian tribes west of the Mississippi by exchanging their land for land in the West. A pledge was made with the Indians to enact the policy on a strictly voluntary basis. However, nearly all relocations were carried out under duress or wars. For example, the Cherokee were forced on the Trail of Tears death march to the West in 1838. The ever-broken treaties by the US government with Indian tribes resulted from another form of asymmetric information, called moral hazard. The concept of moral hazard developed from the study of the insurance market. An insurer has no control over the policyholder not taking precautions toward reducing the probability of an insured event from occurring. The term **moral hazard** (also called **hidden actions**) is derived from the condition that a policyholder may take the wrong (immoral) action by not taking proper precautions. For example, an auto insurance firm has no control over the hidden action of a policyholder leaving the car keys in an unlocked car. In contrast to adverse selection, which exists at the time when buyers purchase a commodity from sellers, moral hazard lasts over the life of some established agreement. Moral hazard may result if the purchase of a commodity

(Indian treaty) establishes future returns or utility of an agent (Indians) being dependent on the actions of another agent (US government).

Moral hazard (hidden actions). The actions of an agent affecting another agent (the principal) are hidden from the principal. *E.g., the preparation that an instructor puts into a lecture is not observed by the students.*

Moral hazard is not restricted to issuance of insurance. It generally exists whenever one agent (called the **principal**) depends on another agent (called the agent) to undertake some actions. If the agent's actions are hidden from the principal, then asymmetric information is present in the form of moral hazard and market inefficiencies may result. In general, contracts establishing such dependence are designed to mitigate potential moral hazard problems. Problems in designing contracts result from this **principal-agent problem**. Examples are owners of a firm who are unable to observe a manager's work ethic, an instructor's inability to observe how hard a student is actually studying, or an owner of a broken-down car unable to observe a mechanic's efforts at repairs. In all these examples, agents have the ability to hide actions, so the principals are faced with a principal-agent problem. The uninformed principal wants to provide the informed agent with efficient incentives for fulfilling the contract.

Principal. An agent who depends on another agent to undertake some actions. *E.g., a doctor depending on her receptionist to act professionally.*

Principal-agent problem. A problem of moral hazard when the principal depends on an agent to undertake some actions. *E.g., a receptionist who does not act professionally when interacting with patients.*

Pareto efficiency with no moral hazard: Nineteen Eighty-Four

In George Orwell's novel *Nineteen Eighty-Four*, Big Brother's Ingsoc (English Socialism) Party developed the use of technology to monitor the lives of its citizens through surveillance, propaganda, and brainwashing. In so doing, the Party removed moral hazard from society and established Pareto efficiency; however, social welfare was far from maximized.

As an illustration of no moral hazard, assume that agents face an expected loss associated with some event. Examples are losses from fire damage to their business or an auto accident. Without any insurance, consumers (households and firms) face the full cost of some negative event, which reduces their welfare. They can mitigate this negative impact of the event by taking precaution. An increase in the level of precaution can both reduce the likelihood of the event occurring and the magnitude of the loss when the event does occur. An objective of a consumer is to determine the optimal level of precaution P. Similar to cost functions discussed in Chapter 8, assume that the total cost of precaution at first increases at a decreasing rate and then increases at an increasing rate with the level of precaution (Figure 23.4). A basic level of precaution offers a great deal of protection with little increase in cost. Examples are driving with traffic instead of against it, locking your car when shopping, or buckling your seat belt. At this basic level of precaution, precaution costs are increasing, but at a decreasing rate.

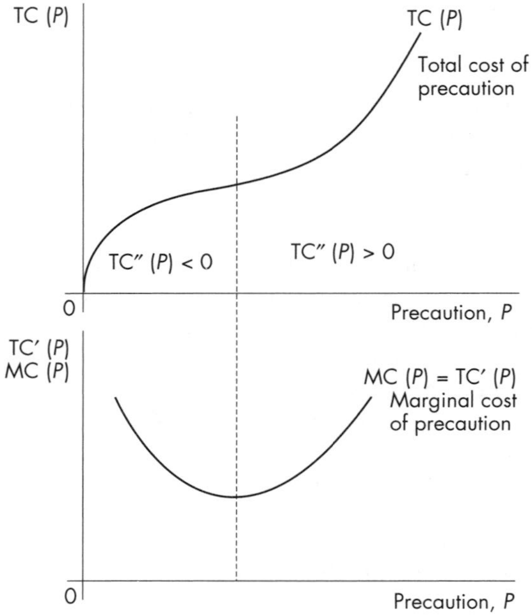

Figure 23.4 **Total and marginal cost curves for precaution.** At first the total cost of precaution may increase at a decreasing rate. However, at some point, total cost of precaution will increase at an increasing rate.

However, at some point, an additional level of precaution will result in costs increasing at an increasing rate. Specifically, if $\mathrm{TC}(P)$ is the total cost function for precaution, then $\mathrm{TC}'(P) > 0$ and at first $\mathrm{TC}''(P) < 0$ but at some precaution level $\mathrm{TC}''(P) > 0$. For example, at first a great deal of fire protection can be purchased with a small investment in a smoke detector. For additional protection, fire extinguishers can be purchased at a higher cost per unit, followed by a sprinkler system at an even higher cost per unit.

Associated with a given level of precaution is an expected loss. This expected loss is the probability of the event occurring times the total loss. For example, at a given level of precaution, if the probability of a fire in a given time period is one in a thousand (1/1000) and the loss from such a fire is \$100,000, then the expected loss per period is \$100. This expected loss is a cost incurred by the consumer that can be reduced by the level of precaution. Let $\mathrm{EL}(P)$ represent such an expected loss function with $\mathrm{EL}'(P) < 0$. As illustrated in Figure 23.5, it is assumed that for an additional unit of precaution, the additional reduction in expected loss decreases, $\mathrm{EL}''(P) > 0$. This assumes, for a given expenditure, that the consumer will first employ types of precaution that offer a relatively larger reduction in losses. For example, the first unit of fire protection, such as a number of smoke detectors, reduces the expected loss more than instead spending the same amount on fire extinguishers.

The objective of a consumer is determining the efficient level of precaution that minimizes overall cost (the sum of expected losses and the cost of precaution):

$$\min_P [EL(P) + TC(P)].$$

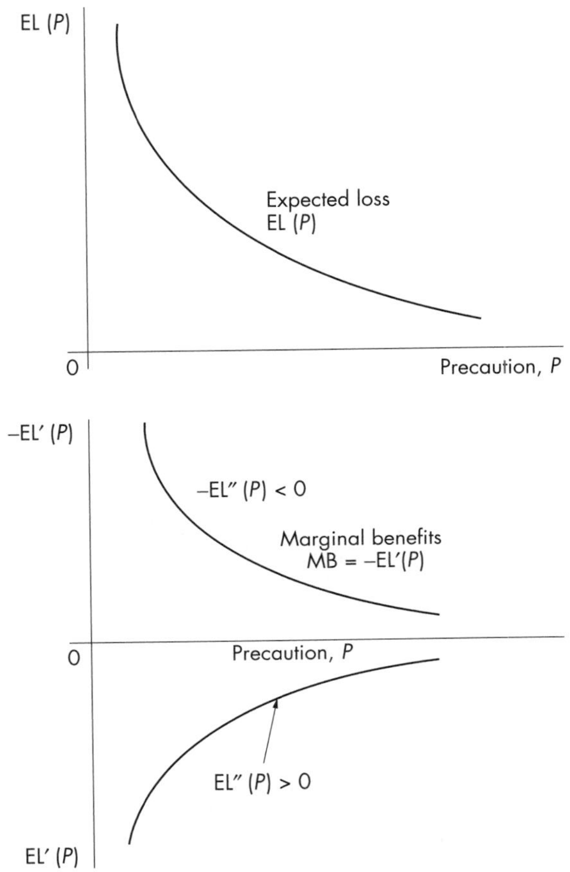

Figure 23.5 **Expected losses.** As the level of precaution increases, the expected loss decreases.

The first-order condition (FOC) is then

$$TC'(P) = -\text{EL}'(P),$$

where TC′(P) is the marginal cost MC(P) and –EL′(P) is the marginal benefit of precaution MB(P). This marginal benefit is the reduction in expected losses associated with an increase in precaution. Recall that EL′(P) < 0, so the marginal benefit, –EL′(P), is positive (Figure 23.5). The optimal level of precaution P^* is where marginal cost equals marginal benefit. If marginal benefit is greater than marginal cost, an increase in precaution will reduce EL(P) more than the increase in TC(P), so overall costs fall. Similarly, if marginal benefit is less than marginal cost, a decrease in precaution will reduce TC(P) by more than the increase in EL, so overall cost will again fall.

This optimal level of precaution is illustrated in Figure 23.6. The positively sloping marginal precaution-cost curve represents the assumption of increasing per-unit precaution cost, and the negative marginal precaution-benefit curve represents the assumption of decreasing reduction in expected loss as precaution increases. At P^*, where marginal benefit

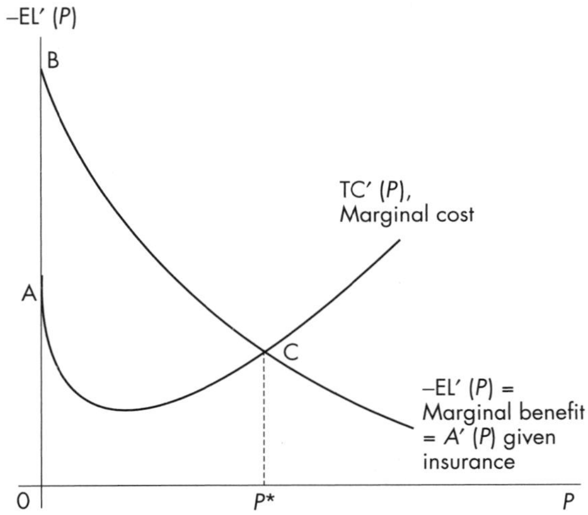

Figure 23.6 **Pareto-efficient precaution level with no moral hazard.** At point C, the marginal benefit equals the marginal cost of precaution, resulting in the efficient level of precaution P^*.

equals marginal cost, overall costs are minimized. To the left (right) of P^*, marginal benefit is greater (less) than marginal cost, so the consumer has an incentive to increase (decrease) precaution.

Example 23.4 Determining the efficient level of precaution

Assume that the total cost of precaution may be represented as

$$TC(P) = 80P - 12P^2 + \tfrac{2}{3}P^3$$

and expected loss as

$$\text{EL}(P) = 1000 - 80P + 2P^2,$$

where P is the level of precaution. The FOC for minimizing the sum of expected loss and cost of precaution is then

$$TC'(P) = -\text{EL}'(P),$$

$$\text{MC}(P) = \text{MB}(P),$$

$$80 - 24P + 2P^2 = -(-80 + 4P).$$

Solving for P results in the Pareto-efficient level of precaution $P^* = 10$.

With an actuarially fair insurance policy with no moral hazard, the insurance policy would yield the same efficient level of precaution $P^* = 10$. However, the presence of moral hazard results in the inefficient level of precaution $P = 0$. The resulting deadweight loss is $(1000 - 400) - (267 - 0) = \$333$.

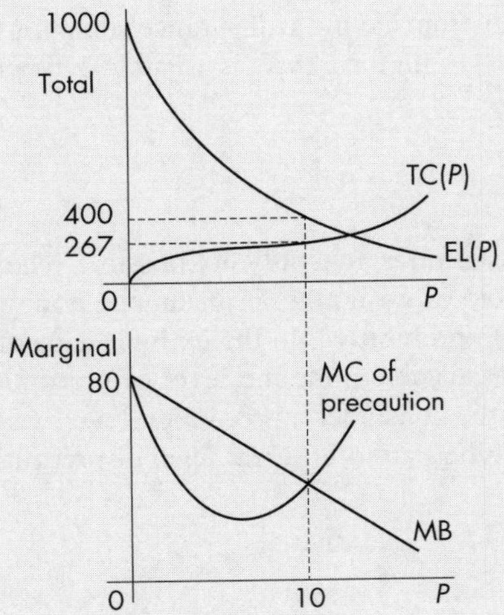

Insurance market with no moral hazard

As discussed in Chapter 18, a risk-averse agent will not voluntarily take on additional risk and will seek out opportunities for avoiding risk. The advent of insurance allows an agent to shift this risk of a negative event onto another agent (an insurance company). In the event of a loss, such as a flood, an insurance company compensates the agent for the loss. Assume that the contract (policy) between the principal (the insurance company) and the agent (consumer) is actuarially fair insurance. If the consumer can purchase insurance covering the full expected loss for a given level of precaution, then the consumer no longer suffers a loss from a negative event, EL = 0. However, the consumer must pay the premium, which, for actuarially fair insurance, is equal to EL. Assuming no moral hazard, the insurance company will want to design a policy where the expected payout varies by the level of precaution a consumer takes. The premiums would be higher for a low level of precaution by a consumer and decline as the level of precaution increases. Let $A(P)$ represent this insurance premium, so $A'(P) < 0$. Analogous to EL, $A''(P) > 0$.

The consumer is still faced with the problem of determining the optimal level of precaution that minimizes the overall cost of taking precaution and now paying the insurance premium:

$$\min_{P} [TC(P) + A(P)].$$

The FOC is then

$$TC'(P) = -A'(P).$$

The consumer equates the marginal precaution cost, $TC'(P)$, to the marginal precaution benefit, $-A'(P)$. This marginal precaution benefit is the additional savings in premium costs from an additional increase in precaution. As illustrated in Figure 23.6, with no moral hazard and actuarially fair insurance, this results in the same level of precaution as in the no-insurance case. In general, assuming agents gain some utility from having an insurance company assume the risk (assuming agents are risk averse) then P^*, with insurance, is a Pareto-efficient level of precaution.

Insurance and moral hazard

Unfortunately, this Pareto-efficient level of precaution is generally not possible. The hidden level of precaution by consumers makes the cost of designing an insurance policy where premiums are based on every level of precaution prohibitive. In the extreme case of moral hazard, where the insurance company cannot at all determine the level of precaution, the insurance premium would not be a function of the consumer's precaution level. Assuming that the insurance company sets the premium at the Pareto-efficient level of precaution P^*, the consumer will

$$\min_P [TC(P) + A(P^*)].$$

The optimal solution is for the consumer to not take any precaution, $P = 0$. The zero level of precaution increases the risk of the negative event occurring, resulting in the insurance company having to pay higher-than-expected claims. This is the root of the terminology "moral hazard" for the insurance company (the principal). Unless the insurance company can design policies that provide incentives for consumers taking precaution, a tâtonnement process will result in no insurance company being able to pay all its claims from revenue generated by premiums. The inefficiency of zero precaution associated with moral hazard is represented by the deadweight loss, the area ABC in Figure 23.6.

Why can't you insure your car for 100 percent of a loss? Insurance companies are unable to observe your level of precaution, so they cannot design a policy to cover 100 percent of your possible loss.

The tâtonnement process toward an equilibrium can also result in instances where agents are over-insured. For example, due to falling property values or a failing business, an agent may realize that the level of insurance is more than the property is worth. If this information is hidden from the insurance company (a case of adverse selection), then the hidden action of not taking any precautions to prevent fire or even causing the business to burn down can increase returns. The business insurance is worth more than the property. For this reason, in fire investigations, the owners are always suspects. Another extreme case of moral hazard is first-degree murder for the insurance money. From an economic standpoint, these examples represent cases where both adverse selection and moral hazard coexist.

Coinsurance

The deadweight loss associated with moral hazard can be reduced by inducing consumers to take some precaution. One type of inducement, employed by many health insurance companies, is called *coinsurance*. Policies with coinsurance provisions require the consumer to pay some percentage of the cost, so the insurance company pays less than 100 percent of

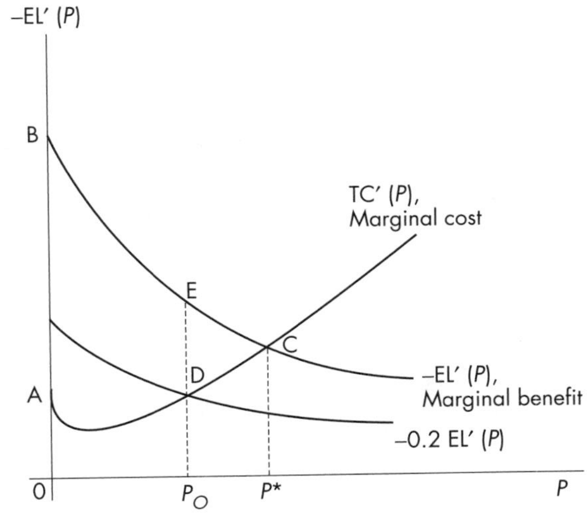

Figure 23.7 **Coinsurance.** Moral hazard results in a deadweight loss represented by the area ABC. With coinsurance, the second-best Pareto-efficient precaution level P_O results. Deadweight loss is then reduced to the area DEC.

the loss. The actual percentage paid varies, but a common rate is for an insurance company to pay 80 percent and consumers the remaining 20 percent. As the percentage of the loss a consumer pays increases, less of the risk is shifted to the insurance company and the consumer is more willing to take precaution. Consumers will tend to seek lower-cost treatments rather than alternative higher-cost treatments. For example, a consumer may take over-the-counter drugs for treating the symptoms of a cold rather than going to a medical doctor. If, for example, the consumer does pay 20 percent of the cost along with a fixed premium A, then it will

$$\min_P [0.2\text{EL}(P) + TC(P) + A].$$

The FOC is then

$$-0.2\text{EL}'(P) = TC'(P).$$

As illustrated in Figure 23.7, the marginal benefit curve tilts downward and intersects the marginal cost curve at the second-best Pareto-efficient equilibrium level of precaution $P_O > 0$. The deadweight loss is then reduced from the area ABC to DEC. Note that only when moral hazard can be eliminated will a Pareto-efficient solution P^* exist.

Example 23.5 Coinsurance

Assume the same total cost of precaution function as in Example 23.4,

$$TC(P) = 80P - 12P^2 + \tfrac{2}{3}P^3,$$

and expected loss

$$EL(P) = 1000 - 80P + 2P^2,$$

where P is the level of precaution. Assuming that the consumer pays 20 percent of this total expected loss, her loss function is now

$$0.2EL(P) = 200 - 16P + 0.4P^2.$$

Given a fixed cost of insurance A the FOC for minimizing the sum of expected loss and cost of precaution is

$$TC'(P) = -0.2EL'(P),$$

$$MC(P) = 0.2MB(P),$$

$$80 - 24P + 2P^2 = -(-16 + 0.8P).$$

Solving for P results in the inefficient level of precaution $P_O = 7$. The deadweight loss associated with $P_O = 7$ is (538 – 400) – (267 – 201) = \$72. This second-best Pareto-efficient allocation results in a decrease in deadweight loss of (333 – 72) = \$261 from the zero level of precaution.

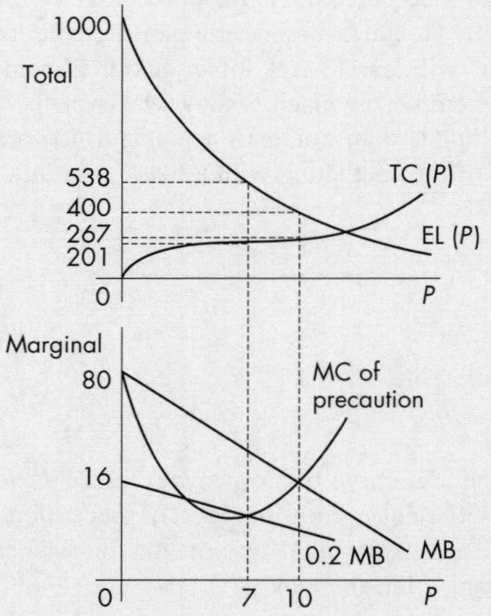

Deductibles

Writing insurance policies with deductibles is another option that insurance companies employ for increasing agents' precaution level. *Deductibles* require agents to incur all the loss up to some dollar limit. For example, if an auto insurance policy has a \$500 deductible provision, then the first \$500 in damages is paid by the car owner, with the insurance company paying any remaining damages. Generally, the higher the deductible, the lower will be the insurance premiums. Insurance companies will incorporate deductibles into their policies when agents' basic level of precaution is so low that insurance companies cannot earn normal profits. For example, without some deductible for auto insurance, our roadways could take on a bumper-car atmosphere, resulting in dramatic insurance premium increases with few if any consumers then willing to be insured.

With the deductible provision, the optimal level of precaution for a consumer is determined by

$$\min\left\{\min_P [TC(P) + EL(P)], D_A\right\},$$

where D_A is the level of the deductible. The maximum cost that a consumer will incur is the deductible D_A. However, if the overall cost of precaution plus expected losses is less than D_A, then a consumer can lower his cost below D_A. The FOC for minimizing cost is then

$$TC'(P) = -EL'(P),$$

if $D_A > \min[\text{TC}(P) + \text{EL}(P)]$, yielding the optimal level of precaution P^* (Figure 23.6). If $D_A < \min[\text{TC}(P) + \text{EL}(P)]$, then a zero level of precaution, $P^* = 0$, is the optimal level. With D_A as the lowest possible level of cost, expenditures on precaution will not result in any additional benefits.

Deductibles allow consumers to insure against large losses, but be responsible for any relatively small expected losses below a deductible. This result of consumers taking some level of precaution reduces the deadweight loss associated with moral hazard. As D_A increases, this deadweight loss is reduced, as consumers will likely choose the no-insurance level of precaution P^*. Consumers who are more willing to take risk will self-insure by seeking higher insurance deductibles. However, with increases in D_A, risk-averse consumers are worse off since they are less able to shift this risk to another agent (the insurer).

Other options available to insurance companies for increasing agents' precaution level are combinations of coinsurance and deductibles and subsidizing preventive care. Health insurance policies will generally have both deductibles and coinsurance provisions, and they may also offer preventive care such as annual physical examinations and routine blood tests at reduced cost. For example, under the 2010 US health care reform bill, health insurance plans must provide recommended preventive care services without cost-sharing (co-pays or deductibles).

Example 23.6 Deductibles

Assume the same total cost of precaution function as in Example 23.4,

$$TC(P) = 80P - 12P^2 + \tfrac{2}{3}P^3,$$

and expected loss

$$EL(P) = 1000 - 80P + 2P^2,$$

where P is the level of precaution. The optimal level of precaution with no insurance is then $P^* = 10$. This yields $TC(P^*) = 400$ and $EL(P^*) = 267$, with sum \$667. If the deductible is less than \$667, the consumer will choose a zero level of precaution with a corresponding deadweight loss of \$333. In contrast, for a deductible greater than \$667, the consumer will self-insure with $P^* = 10$.

Employer and employee relations

If I worked as much as others, I would do as little as they.

(Michael Wetzstein)

Translation: Generally all employees engage in shirking unless in Orwell's 1984 world.

Although first applied to the insurance market, moral hazard exists whenever asymmetric information in the form of hidden actions is prevalent in a principal-agent agreement. For example, moral hazard can exist between an employer (the principal) and an employee (the agent). Unless an employer can constantly monitor the productivity of employees, employees can engage in leisure while working (called **shirking**) by reducing their level of effort. For example, surfing the Internet by employees has become a major form of shirking. The asymmetric information on the level of employees' productivity creates inefficiencies. An objective of employers is designing contracts that provide employee incentives directed at improving productivity and reducing shirking. In the past, military commanders reduced shirking during a battle by providing alcohol just prior to a conflict (fighting drunk) and then killing anyone found shirking (turning and running).

When the cat's away, will the mice play? Yes, they will have the run of the house.

Shirking. Employees engaging in leisure while working. *E.g., Thomas Edison sleeping during his night shift as a telegraph operator.*

Application: The incorruptible cashier

As outlined by D.J. Boorstin, it was not until the 1880s that the cash register was employed for registering sales. Prior to this date, few merchants had an accurate record of sales. Salesclerks were instructed to record every transaction into a daybook (even if a fire broke out). However, it was easy for clerks to shirk. Negligence, illiteracy, and laziness made owners' records incomplete. Pilfering was common, especially where salesclerks made change from their own pockets or an open cashbox.

The invention of the cash register, patented in 1879 by James Ritty (and called Ritty's Incorruptible Cashier), became the answer to this shirking problem. After Ritty sold the patent for \$1000, the new owners added a cash drawer and a bell that rang every time the drawer was opened. The cash register would display the amount of each sale, require the clerk to record the sale for access to the cash drawer, and keep track of all transactions. The bell, which announced the ringing up of a sale, transformed a private transaction into a public announcement, which greatly reduced the ability of a salesclerk to shirk. It is not surprising that when the clerks were presented with the cash register, they resented it, considering it a slur on their character. This resulted in limited adoption. In 1884, John Henry Patterson purchased the shaky company for $6500—far in excess of its value—and the cash register finally emerged as an accepted tool for transactions.

Patterson employed novel sales strategies that resulted in the establishment of the National Cash Register Company. He opened training schools for salespersons and organized revival meetings. At these schools and meetings, salespersons were taught high-pressure sales methods and proper appearance. Patterson initiated sales quotas and sales territories, which properly channeled rivalry among salespersons and developed goodwill. He provided company recreation rooms, banquets, picnics, and concerts, and he landscaped the factory grounds into an industrial garden. Today, cash registers are common, but the bell is gone.

Source: D.J. Boorstin, *The Americans: The Democratic Experience*, New York: Random House (1973).

Pareto efficiency with no moral hazard

If you are not fired with enthusiasm, you will be fired with enthusiasm.

(Vince Lombardi)

Many times when talking to a company representative on the telephone, the conversation may be recorded. Such recordings offer a mechanism for an employer to monitor an employee's effort (1984). The major incentive for employees' effort is the compensation they receive for supplying their labor, in the form of wage income. Assuming symmetric information (no moral hazard), we can determine the Pareto-efficient level of employee effort E^* by considering the employer's objective function and an employee's participation constraint. No moral hazard implies that an employer can observe an employee's level of effort. In addition, let us assume that the employer determines the labor contract and the employee can then either accept or reject the contract. An employer is concerned with productivity of an employee, denoted by the production function $q = f(E)$, where q is some output level. Given a per-unit output price p and the wage rate based on an employee's effort $w(E)$, the employer's objective is maximizing profit from this employee:

$$\max_E [pf(E) - w(E)E].$$

The employee has a cost of increasing effort in the form of total opportunity cost from lost shirking, $\mathrm{TC}_E(E)$. Let $\mathrm{MC}_E(E)$ denote the marginal cost of effort, so $\mathrm{MC}_E(E) = \partial \mathrm{TC}_E(E)/\partial E$. In general, as illustrated in Figure 23.8, this marginal opportunity cost is U-shaped. The marginal cost of effort may at first decline. For very low levels of effort (to the left of E_M), additional effort results in the marginal cost of effort declining. They are spending so much time shirking, a little additional effort results in lower marginal opportunity cost. In contrast,

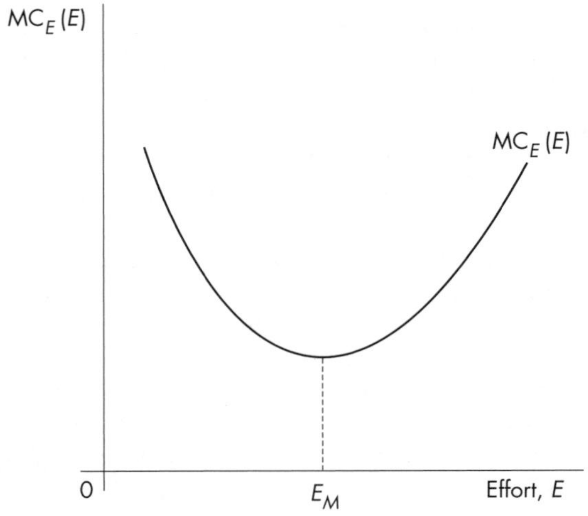

Figure 23.8 **Employee's marginal opportunity cost of effort.** This U-shaped cost curve results from marginal cost of effort declining for low levels of effort. An employee is spending so much time shirking that a little additional effort results in lower marginal opportunity cost.

at relatively higher effort levels (to the right of E_M), any additional effort raises this marginal opportunity cost. The employee's payoff for E level of effort is the difference between wage income $w(E)E$ and total opportunity cost $\text{TC}_E(E)$:

$$w(E)E - TC_E(E).$$

Instead of working for this particular employer, the employee could be engaged in other activities, including being employed by another employer, being self-employed, or being immersed in total leisure. Assume that the next-highest payoff from these alternatives is U^o. The employee will be willing to work for an employer if the payoff is at least as great as U^o. Specifically, if

$$w(E)E - TC_E(E) \geq U^o,$$

then U^o is called the *reservation-utility level* and the equation is called the *participation constraint.* The employer must pay at least the level U^o if he expects to hire the employee. The employer's objective is then

$$\max_E \pi = \max_E [pf(E) - w(E)E],$$

subject to

$$w(E)E - TC_E(E) = U^o.$$

The constraint is an equality because if $w(E)E - \text{TC}_E(E) > U^o$, then the employer could lower wages and still hire the employee. Substituting the constraint into the objective function yields

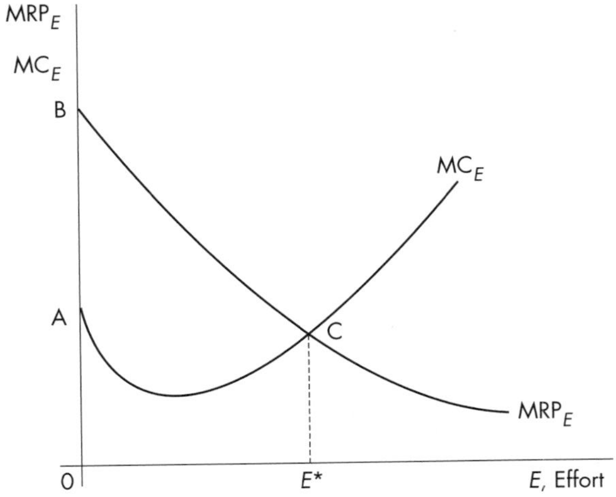

Figure 23.9 **Pareto-efficient level of effort for a risk-averse employee.** The employer equates the marginal revenue product of labor, MRP_E, to the marginal opportunity cost of effort, MC_E, for determining the optimal level of employee effort.

$$\max_E \left[pf(E) - TC_E(E) - U^{\circ}\right].$$

The FOC is then

$$MRP_E = MC_E.$$

For profit maximization, the employer will equate the marginal revenue product of an employee's effort, MRP_E, to the employee's marginal opportunity cost of effort, MC_E. Solving this FOC for E results in the Pareto-efficient level of employee effort E^*. This Pareto-efficient allocation is illustrated in Figure 23.9, where MRP_E is equated to MC_E. Note that this result corresponds to the perfectly competitive equilibrium in the factor markets discussed in Chapter 16.[3]

The compensation scheme necessary for obtaining employee-effort level E^* is where the level of compensation just equals the reservation-utility level plus the employee's cost of effort:

$$w(E)E = U^{\circ} + TC_E(E).$$

If the employer is risk-neutral and the employee risk-averse, then the employer will fully insure the employee against any wage risk. Thus, the employer will offer a fixed wage rate $w^* = w(E^*)$.[4] The optimal contract when effort is observable both specifies the Pareto-efficient effort level E^* and fully insures a risk-averse employee against income losses. In contrast, when the employee is also risk-neutral, insurance is not necessary, so any compensation scheme where wages are a function of profits, with

$$w(\pi)E = U^{\circ} + TC_E(\pi),$$

will be efficient.

Example 23.7 Pareto-optimal contract when effort is observable

Suppose that the output price $p=1$, the employer's production function is

$$f(E)=20E-\tfrac{1}{4}E^2,$$

and the employer is facing a participation constraint

$$w(E)E-E^2=U^o.$$

Note that $w(E)E$ is the total wage compensation and E^2 is the employee's total opportunity cost of effort. The employer's objective is

$$\max_E\left[20E-\tfrac{1}{4}E^2-w(E)E\right]\quad \text{s.t. } w(E)E-E^2=U^o.$$

Incorporating the constraint into the objective function yields

$$\max_E\left[20E-\tfrac{1}{4}E^2-E^2-U^o\right].$$

The FOC is then

$$\text{MRP}_E=\text{MC}_E,$$

$$20-\tfrac{1}{2}E^*=2E^*.$$

Solving for E yields $E^*=8$. Assuming that the reservation utility $U^o=0$ and the employee is risk-averse, then, given the constraint, the equilibrium wage $w^*=8$.

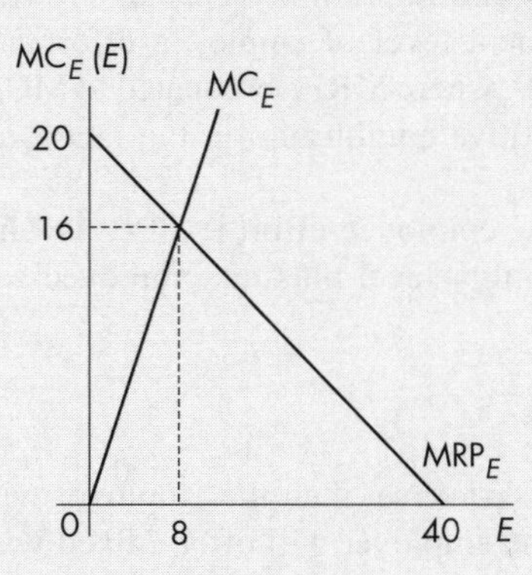

Inefficiency with moral hazard

> *Anyone can do any amount of work provided it is not the work he is supposed to be doing at the moment.*
>
> (Robert Benchley)

Translation: Without proper monitoring, employees can still be working but not doing the work they should be doing.

On October 11, 1867, at Fort Leavenworth, Brevet Major General George Armstrong Custer, Lieutenant Colonel, 7th US Cavalry, was found guilty on a number of charges and sentenced to suspension from rank and command for one year and forfeiture of his pay. The first charge was absence without leave from his command. General Custer was shirking. On July 15, 1867, he had been absent from his command without proper authority and had traveled to Fort Harker, Kansas (to visit his wife)—a distance of 275 miles—when his command was expected to be actively engaged against hostile Indians. His army career ended on June 25, 1876, with his death at the Battle of Little Big Horn. Not being able to observe General Custer's actions (the presence of moral hazard) resulted in his court martial and possibly in the United States' loss at Little Big Horn.

In many cases, the cost of monitoring effort prohibits constantly observing an employee's (General Custer's) level of effort (unless it is Orwell's 1984). For example, an employer is generally unable to observe a night clerk at a convenience store or a truck driver for a furniture company. When effort is not observable, the Pareto-efficient effort level comes in conflict with the result of full insurance. The only method for increasing employee effort is relating wages to the firm's profit. The random nature of profit results in the employee assuming some uninsured risk. Such conflicts create inefficiencies unless the employee is risk-neutral. A risk-neutral employee is only concerned with expected profit. He would not be concerned with any random nature of profit and thus is indifferent with taking uncertain profit in replace of a certain wage.

Example 23.8 Unobservable effort and no incentive-compatibility constraint

If an employer cannot observe an employee's effort and does not consider the incentive-compatibility constraint, then the employee will minimize effort. Continuing with Example 23.7, the minimum effort for the employee is zero, $E = 0$. This results in a deadweight loss of $(20 - 0)8/2 = \$80$.

In contrast, when an employee is risk-averse, the increased share of profit relative to a certain wage does affect the employee. Incentives for increased effort are directly associated with an employee's cost of increased risk. This results in an additional constraint on the employer. The employer not only maximizes profit subject to the participation constraint

$$w(E)E - TC_E(E) \geq U^o,$$

but also is subject to an *incentive-compatibility constraint*, where they must offer a compensation scheme that gives an employee an incentive to choose the required effort level. When the employer can directly observe employees' efforts, employees will put forth the required level of effort, regardless of their desire. In contrast, when effort is not directly observable, employees can shirk by not putting forth the required level of effort. To avoid such shirking, employers must offer a compensation scheme to induce the employee to offer E^* units of effort, determined by setting the employee's payoff associated with E^* at least as great as the payoff for any other level of effort:

$$w(E^*)E^* - TC_E(E^*) \geq w(E)E - TC_E(E)$$

for all levels of effort E. At any wage below this constraint, the employee will shirk by not putting in the effort E^*. In the extreme case, not considering this incentive-compatibility constraint results in an employee seeking an effort level independent of his wages. In this case, the employee would minimize his total effort

$$\min_E TC_E(E).$$

The optimal solution is for the employee to totally shirk and not exert any effort, so $E = 0$. This zero level of effort is analogous to the zero level of precaution associated with insurance, illustrated in Figure 23.6. Again, this is the root of the terminology "moral hazard," where in this case the employer is the principal. Unless the employer can design contracts that provide incentives for employees to choose effort, a tâtonnement process will result in a zero level of effort. The inefficiency of $E = 0$ associated with moral hazard is represented by the deadweight loss, the area ABC in Figure 23.9.

Designing employment contracts with compensation mechanisms that take into consideration this incentive-compatibility constraint will provide incentives for employees to increase their work efforts. This will reduce the inefficiency associated with wages not directly linked with the level of effort. However, such contracts will be second-best Pareto-efficient allocations since they still result in the risk-averse employee not being fully insured. Only with symmetric information associated with no hidden action on the part of the agent (the employee) will a Pareto-efficient allocation exist.

Residual claimant: a franchise

> *There are an enormous number of managers who have retired on the job.*
>
> (Peter F. Drucker)
>
> *Translation: Lack of incentives can result in managers shirking rather than working.*

Large poultry enterprises (integrators) use residual claimant production contracts with independent farmers to raise chickens. By having the farmers assume the risk of raising the chickens, farmers will have incentives to take the necessary effort in preventing disease and other possible adverse effects on the chickens. In the United States, 98.9 percent of chicken broiler farmers operate under production contracts—there has not been an open market for broilers since the 1950s. The poultry farmers do not own chickens; they only raise them for the integrators. The production contracts are used to control how growers raise chickens.

In poultry contracting, the farmers are the residual claimant to the output. This is an example of a second-best Pareto-efficient compensation scheme incorporating incentive compatibility. A **residual claimant** is an agent (farmer) who receives the payoff from the output after any fees are paid to a principal (poultry integrator). This is a type of *fixed-fee contract* where the principal receives a fixed amount (Fee) and the agent receives the remaining (residual) returns. An employee as the residual claimant will maximize her payoff by equating the marginal revenue product of the employee's effort to the employee's marginal opportunity cost of effort. Examples of residual claimant contracts are franchises and employee buyouts.

The employee (or manager) pays the employer (or owner) a lump sum for the right to operate an enterprise. In such cases, the employer is using a two-part tariff price-discrimination scheme, discussed in Chapter 13. Fast-food enterprises are a typical example of franchising. The owner of a fast-food establishment pays the parent company a fixed fee for the right to operate the enterprise (*franchise*). In the case of **employee buyouts**, employees purchase the company from the owners. If the owners have control in writing the contract, they will set the fee where an employee is indifferent between the incomes received from this activity versus an alternative activity:

$$w(E^*)E^* - TC_E(E^*) - \text{Fee} = w(E)E - TC_E(E),$$

where Fee is the fee paid to the owners.

Residual claimant. The agent who receives the payoff from the output after any fees have been paid to a principal. *E.g., a newspaper boy who purchases the papers from the newspaper and then receives all the revenue from selling them.*

Employee buyout. Employees purchasing a company from the owners. *E.g., Publix Super Markets employees purchasing the store's stock, so it is now an employee-owned company.*

In both the franchise and employee buyout cases, the employees become the residual claimant and their compensation is now dependent on the profits of the firm minus the lump sum payment to the owners. Employees are now the owners, so they accrue both the economic rent from effort and, as owners (employers), the consumer surplus. Specifically, the employees' objective is to maximize consumer surplus plus economic rent minus the franchise fee:

$$\max_E \,[pf(E) - TC_E(E) - \text{Fee}].$$

The FOC is then

$$\text{MRP}_E = MC_E.$$

Although marginal benefit equals marginal cost, risk-averse employees are not able to fully insure against losses. This results in a second-best Pareto-efficient allocation.

Such residual-claimant contracts are very popular when the employees are able to take precautions and reduce possible losses in profits at a lower cost than the owners. For example, managers of a fast-food enterprise can, at a far lower cost than the owners, expend effort in hiring more highly motivated employees and thus avoid profit losses from less well-motivated employees. The managers located at the establishment are able to manage the profit risks far more effectively than an absentee owner.

Why are fast-food outlets independently owned and operated? The owners of these outlets, managing on site, are able to take precautions and reduce losses in profits at a lower cost than remote managing at a corporate headquarters.

Example 23.9 Residual claimant

Using the same production function and participation constraint as in Example 23.7, and again letting the output price $p = 1$, the agent's objective is to

$$\max_{E} \left[20E - \tfrac{1}{4}E^2 - E^2 - \text{Fee} \right],$$

where Fee is the franchise fee. The FOC is the same as in Example 23.7, so $E^* = 8$. If the principal sets a franchise fee of Fee = \$80, he can extract all the agent's surplus, so the agent's profit is $\pi = 0$. The principal's profit is the franchise fee of \$80.

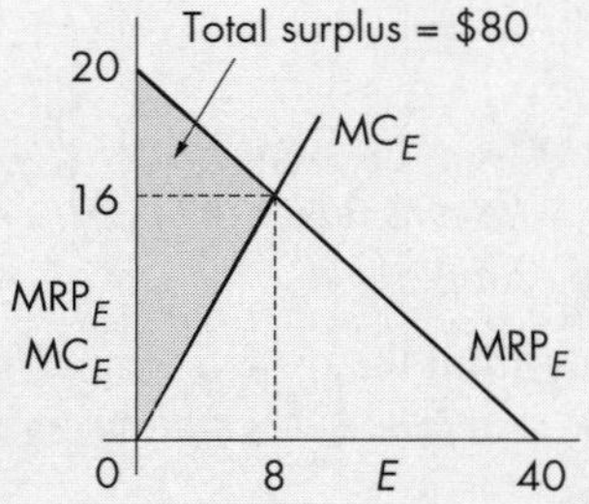

Contingent contract: a commission

Real estate commissions for selling a home have traditionally averaged 6–7 percent of the gross sales price of the property. However, the recent proliferation of discount commissions and flat fees has created a downward pressure on commissions, with the national average being just above 5 percent. Such real estate commissions are a **contingent contract**, where the agent's share of payoff (the real estate commission) depends on the expected total payoff. In cases where the cost of taking precaution by both the agent and the principal are similar, this alternative contract may be more efficient. Thus, a contingent contract is one type of scheme that is popular when the possible losses in profits are only partially affected by the principal's and agent's precaution levels. Their lack of control in reducing the uncertainty on profits results in the sharing of the risk.

A type of contingent contract is where the expected payoff (profit) is shared by the principal and agent. A fraction of the payoff, say 40 percent, is retained by the agent, and the remainder, 60 percent, is transferred to the agent. An example of a contingent contract is an attorney (agent) taking a case with no set fee, but 40 percent of any court settlement after expenses. In terms of employer and employee relations, year-end bonuses based on the firm's annual profits or stock options are types of contingent contracts.

Contingent contract. The agent's share of payoff depends on the expected total payoff. *E.g. a sharecropper receiving a proportion of the harvest, with the remaining crop being transferred to the landlord.*

A contingent contract where the expected payoff is shared by the agent will receive a portion α of the consumer surplus and economic rent. The agent will then attempt to maximize this payoff. Specifically,

$$\max_{E} \alpha\, [pf(E) - \mathrm{TC}_E(E)].$$

The FOC is again

$$\mathrm{MRP}_E = \mathrm{MC}_E.$$

In this case, expected marginal benefit equals marginal cost and both the principal and agent share in the payoff and jointly bear the risk. If either or both are risk-averse, then this results in a second-best Pareto-efficient allocation with neither of them able to fully insure against losses.

The proportion α depends on the relative bargaining powers of the principal and the agent. If the principal has a great deal of power, then the agent's expected payoff will be driven to her reservation payoff, where she is indifferent to participating or not. In agriculture, sharecropping is an example where the landlord can generally extract must of the surplus from the sharecropper. In contrast, attorneys and real estate agents generally have greater bargaining powers and are able to retain more of the surplus (payoff). A used car salesman working on a commission may not be as fortunate.

Example 23.10 Contingent contract

Using the same production function and participation constraint as in Example 23.7, and again letting the output price $p = 1$, the agent's objective is to

$$\max_{E} \alpha \left[20E - \tfrac{1}{4}E^2 - E^2\right],$$

where α is the proportion of profits retained by the agent. The FOC is the same as in Example 23.7, so $E^* = 8$, and the total surplus as calculated in Example 23.9 is \$80. If the principal and agent set $\alpha = 40$ percent, then the agent retains 0.40(80) = \$32 and the principal receives 0.60(80) = \$48.

Application: Sharecropping

Sharecropping as a contingent contract became widely used in the South following the Civil War. Plantations had a large supply of land but limited financial resources for wages or taxes. Most of the labor, mainly from former slaves, was generally unemployed, with limited endowments (limited financial capital and no land). The solution was sharecropping (contingent contract) cotton, which was the only crop that could generate cash for the croppers (agents) and landlords (principals). Thus, sharecropping was a mechanism for differently endowed agents (principals and agents) to pool their resources for joint benefit. This allowed risk management and credit constraint avoidance. However, sharecropping was also a mechanism for former slave owners to take advantage of uneducated freedmen (former slaves). Freedmen had little or no education, allowing landlords to write contacts with upwards of a 70–30 split instead of 50–50 or less.

Generally, sharecroppers were faced with both monopoly power for their inputs and monopsony power for selling their output. In some cases, they purchased inputs and sold their output through their landlord who exercised monopoly price setting power. The sharecropper was sometimes compensated in scrip redeemable only within the plantation.

During and after World War II, labor for industry was in demand and mechanization of agriculture practically ended sharecropping within the United States. This resulted in sharecroppers migrating to the industrialized North.

Source: D. Sen, "A Theory of Sharecropping: The Role of Price Behavior and Imperfect Competition," *Journal of Economic Behavior and Organization* 80 (2011): 181–199.

Bonding: a security deposit

Florida is a popular college student destination over spring break. Every year, we see film footage of wild (drunken?) students having an uncultured time on the beach. Ever consider what happens inside the hotel rooms? Hotel managers have, and they often require students to pay a security deposit when they book a room. This security deposit is a posted bond to cover any room damage when students shirk and do not take the desired effort level to avoid any damage.

The second-best Pareto-efficient mechanisms of residual claimant and contingent contract work well when the agent is generating revenue, so a portion of the revenue can then be transferred to the principal. In many employer–employee relations, the employee is not directly generating revenue that can then be collected by the principal. Instead, the employee is part of an overall production process where the final product is then sold. Examples are a landlord (principal) wanting to provide incentive for the tenant (agent) to take proper care of the apartment, a guard for a precious antique not to shirk, and keeping an accused felon from fleeing. In such cases, the residual claimant and contingent contract mechanisms are not an option. With moral hazard, some other mechanisms are required on the part of the principal to provide incentives for the agent to put forth the optimum effort level E^*.

One mechanism is **bonding**, which requires an agent to post a bond, which is a sum of money either paid to the principal or deposited with some other party such as an insurance company. A landlord requiring a security deposit, a guard required to post a bond against theft, and an accused felon posting a bond before he can be released from jail are all examples of using bonding as a mechanism for providing agents incentives to put forth effort E^*.

Why does an accused felon not flee? The accused must post a bond, which he will forfeit if he flees.

Bonding. A sum of money set aside by agents to insure they will not shirk. *E.g., a $500 deposit required for a jet-ski rental.*

With principals setting the bond, they will require the agent to post a bond of sufficient amount to provide the agent an incentive to put forth effort E^*. As long as the incentive-compatibility constraint

$$w(E^*)E^* - TC_E(E^*) \geq w(E)E - TC_E(E)$$

holds, the agent will not forfeit the bond. However, if the agent shirks (wrecks the apartment or hotel room, allows a theft, or flees) the agent will forfeit the bond. Without a bond, this occurs when the optimal effort level E^* results in an agent being better off shirking:

$$w(E^*)E^* - TC_E(E^*) < w(E)E - TC_E(E).$$

With bonding, the agent will only shirk if the utility from shirking is greater than the bond:

$$[w(E)E - TC_E(E)] - [w(E^*)E^* - TC_E(E^*)] > \text{Fee}.$$

The agent is then willing to forfeit the bond and pay a fee for shirking. The principal will set the bond at a level where shirking does not pay. This occurs where the agent is indifferent between the payoff received from E^* and shirking:

$$[w(E)E - TC_E(E)] - [w(E^*)E^* - TC_E(E^*)] = \text{Fee}.$$

Rearranging terms results in a similar condition as the residual claimant mechanism:

$$w(E^*)E^* - TC_E(E^*) + \text{Fee} = w(E)E - TC_E(E).$$

The only difference is that under the residual claimant mechanism, the agent pays a fee for cooperating with the principal, while with bonding, the agent pays a fee for noncooperation. Thus, the FOC is the same, with

$$\text{MRP}_E = \text{MC}_E,$$

and a risk-averse agent will not be able to fully insure against losses, yielding a second-best Pareto-efficient allocation.

An employer may also post bonds for their new employees. They may hire interns at low or zero wages and not hire those who shirk. The interns who shirk then forfeit the bond (their reservation wage minus any internship wage). *Deferred payments* in the form of higher wages are then paid to the interns who are hired to compensate them for the low or zero wage as interns.

Why are some interns not paid or are paid a low wage? Those interns who shirk are not hired and the others who put forth the desired effort are hired and paid a higher wage that compensates them for their time as interns.

For current employees, an employer may pay an *efficiency wage* where the wage rate is above the market wage. By receiving the efficiency wage, an employee will be less likely to shirk in order to reduce the probability of being fired and having to take a pay cut (the difference in the efficiency and market wage rates). This difference in wages is a bond, where on getting fired the employee forfeits the bond—the wage differential. Reducing the efficiency wage lowers the bond, leading to possibly more employee shirking. An example is the Greek economic crisis that started in 2009. Dimitra Koutsomba, president of the Greek Archaeologists Association, stated, “It is the first time that we have an armed robbery at a museum during operating hours. … It shows that the cuts the Culture Ministry has made since the crisis hit in 2009 make it easier for such incidents to take place." The cuts in museum guards' efficient wages may have resulted in increased shirking, leading to the museums' loss of a Pablo Picasso and other artworks in a number of museum robberies.

Example 23.11 Bonding

Using the same production function and participation constraint as in Example 23.7, and again letting the output price $p = 1$, the agent's objective is to

$$\max_{E}\left[20E - \tfrac{1}{4}E^2 - E^2\right].$$

The FOC is the same as in Example 23.7, so $E^* = 8$. The agent engages in the optimal level of effort, so he does not forfeit the bond. Total surplus as calculated in Example 23.9 is \$80. In contrast to the residual claimant mechanism with the principal capturing all the surplus (Example 23.9), the agent receives economic rent of $16(8)/2 = \$64$ and the principal receives consumer surplus of $(20 - 16)8 = \$16$. When the agent is generating revenue, a residual claimant mechanism allows the principal to capture the entire surplus as opposed to only a portion (consumer surplus) with a bonding mechanism.

Similar to bonding, a principal can fine (penalize) an agent for shirking. This is a post-shirking mechanism as opposed to a pre-shirking mechanism of bonding. Sport players can be fined for not showing up to practice, with possible monetary fines for professional players and nonmonetary fines for collegiate athletes (50 pushups and running around the track). In game theory, this is a form of repeated games, where the principal can reward good behavior and punish bad behavior in an attempt to minimize shirking and obtain a desired level of effort.

> *Two stone cutters were asked what they were doing. The first said, "I am cutting this stone into blocks." The second replied, "I am on a team building a cathedral".*
>
> (Old Adage)

Translation: Proper employee motivation will increase effort and reduce shirking.

Summary

1. Asymmetric information exists when market information is costly and varies between buyers and sellers. This asymmetric information generates two types of outcomes: adverse selection and moral hazard.
2. Adverse selection exists when an informed agent's decision depends on unobservable characteristics that adversely affect uninformed agents.
3. Adverse selection results in an inefficient allocation (called the lemons problem), where only a market for the lowest-quality group of commodities prevails, with missing markets for higher-quality commodities.

4. Pooling all consumers together is one mechanism for addressing the inefficiencies associated with adverse selection in health insurance. Rates are set at the average cost of health care and adverse selection is eliminated by requiring all consumers to participate.
5. A mechanism provided by firms that transfers information from the informed agent to the uninformed agent is called signaling. Firms may employ strong signals such as reputation, guarantees, warranties, and standardized products to create a market for their level of quality products.
6. A mechanism employed for sorting the commodities offered by sellers is called screening. By screening commodities in terms of characteristics, a market for alternative characteristics can develop.
7. Moral hazard may exist when future returns of an agent are dependent on the actions of another agent. An example is an employer unable to observe an employee's work ethic.
8. In the insurance market, the optimal level of precaution for a consumer is to equate the marginal cost with the marginal benefits of precaution. Assuming no moral hazard, an actuarially fair insurance policy will result in this optimal level of precaution.
9. Moral hazard will result in insurance companies being unable to cover all the claims from their premiums unless mechanisms are designed that provide incentives for consumers to take precaution. Coinsurance and deductibles are mechanisms designed by insurance companies to encourage consumers to take some level of precaution.
10. A particular form of moral hazard is called shirking, where an employee engages in leisure while working. An employee's level of effort depends on her participation constraint where the employee will be willing to work if the payoff is at least as great as the next highest payoff.
11. An employer can increase an employee's effort by offering a compensation scheme, called an incentive-compatibility constraint, which gives the employee an incentive to choose the required effort level.
12. Residual claimant, contingent contract, and bonding are mechanism designs that consider employees' incentive-compatibility constraints.

Key concepts

Key equations

$$TC'(P) = -EL'(P)$$

A condition for Pareto efficiency with no moral hazard is equating the marginal cost of precaution to the marginal benefit of reducing expected losses.

$$TC'(P) = -A'(P)$$

A condition for Pareto efficiency with an insurance market and no moral hazard is equating the marginal cost of precaution to the additional savings in premium costs.

$$-0.2EL'(P) = TC'(P)$$

With moral hazard and given a 20 percent coinsurance, the second-best Pareto-efficient equilibrium level of precaution is where 20 percent of the marginal benefit of reducing expected losses is equal to the marginal cost of precaution.

$$\text{MRP}_E = \text{MC}_E$$

Pareto efficiency with no moral hazard results when an employer equates the marginal revenue product of employees' effort to his marginal opportunity cost of effect. With moral hazard, this equality is a second-best Pareto-efficient condition under a residual claimant scheme.

Questions

A mind is like a parachute—it only works when it is opened.

(Matthias Elter)

1. An automobile dealer sells autos to both informed and uninformed buyers. Why would an informed buyer generally pay a lower price for a car than an uninformed buyer would?
2. Assume a new car sells for $20,000 and the same model sells for only $10,000 when it is five years old. Why should the used model sell for half the price of a new one?
3. Why will an economist not stop to pick up a $20 bill on the walkway of a busy airport?
4. Government building codes and inspectors are an example of governmental interference in the efficient free-market allocation of resources. Do you agree or disagree with this statement? Explain.
5. Does requiring firms to be equal-opportunity employers, prohibiting them from screening by race, religion, color, or national origin, result in asymmetric and inefficient labor markets? Explain.

6. A small number of universities do not assign grades to students. This allows students the opportunity to learn without the stress of potentially performing below expectations. What possible problems does this cause and how could they be remedied?
7. Can adverse selection and moral hazard coexist? Explain by providing an example.
8. One section of campaign finance reform is designed to reduce the time politicians spend seeking campaign funds instead of working for their electorate. What is the cause of politicians seeking funds? What other solutions could be employed?
9. In terms of the principal-agent model, why may government-owned firms, such as a municipal water district, have different objectives than a city manager?
10. Will a policy that requires the firm responsible for an oil spill to pay the average cost of a spill result in the Pareto-efficient level of precaution?

Exercises

1. In a large city, the used car market at any one time has 16,000 autos offered for sale. The values of these used autos range from \$2000 to \$18,000, with one car being worth each dollar amount between this range. Used car owners are willing to sell their autos for what they are worth, but used car buyers do not know the value of a particular automobile. Their demand Q^D depends on the average value of autos offered in the market, μ_p, and on the price of the autos, p:

$$Q^D = 3\mu_p - p.$$

   a. Assuming that buyers base their estimate of μ_p on the entire used car market, what is μ_p and what is the equilibrium price of used cars?
   b. Given the equilibrium price in (a), what will be the average value of used cars actually traded?
   c. If buyers revise their estimate of μ_p on the basis of the average value of cars actually traded, what will be the new equilibrium price of used cars and what is the average value of cars traded?
   d. Is there a market equilibrium where the actual value of μ_p is consistent with the equilibrium of supply and demand at a positive price and quantity?

2. Suppose that the cost to a firm for supplying a reliable automobile is \$10,000 and that consumers are willing to pay \$12,000 for a reliable vehicle and \$6000 for a lemon, what is the percentage α of reliable automobiles necessary for reliable vehicles to enter the market?

3. A travel agency is offering a package cruise for \$4000 to a honeymoon couple. There is a 30 percent chance that the agency is selling a low-amenities cruise in place of a first-class cruise. The honeymooners cannot observe the quality before taking the cruise and value a first-class cruise at \$5000 and a low-class one at \$2500.

The cost of production for a first-class cruise is \$2000 and that for a low-class cruise is \$1000.

a. Assuming that the honeymooners are risk-neutral, will they purchase the cruise?
b. If Alice the bride observes that the travel agency is spending \$2500 on advertising, will the honeymooners purchase the cruise? Explain.

4. Sara, whose utility function for wealth is represented in logarithmic form, is a poor student with only \$5000 in wealth and an expensive \$800 bike. At a fair insurance premium of \$50.71, she is indifferent between insuring the bike against a 5 percent probability of loss or not. However, with insurance, she realizes she does not have to be as cautious in protecting her bike against any loss, so her probability of loss increases to 10 percent. What is the actuarially fair insurance premium now?
5. Suppose that 16-year-olds have a 90 percent probability of having an automobile accident that results in damages of \$10,000. However, only a 10 percent probability exists for 20-year-olds having a similar accident resulting in the same level of damages.

a. Assuming that an insurance company believes that 16-year-olds and 20-year-olds are equally represented in the population and are equally likely to purchase insurance, what will be the actuarially fair insurance premium?
b. Assuming a logarithmic utility function in terms of wealth and a current wealth level of \$20,000 for both ages, will 16- and/or 20-year-olds purchase insurance? What is the utility for an individual in each age group?
c. Given the solution to (b), what should the fair premium be? What is the utility for an individual in each age group?
d. If the insurance company can price-discriminate between 16- and 20-year-olds, what are the insurance premiums for each age group and the level of utilities?

6. Consider a game where an employee is first endowed by nature with either a high level of productivity or a low level of productivity. She can take a test that will reveal her productivity to an employer. The employer will offer a higher wage for the higher level of productivity, which results in the following payoff matrix:

		Employee productivity	
		Low	High
Employer	Low wage	(5, 5)	(0, –)
	High wage	(2, 7)	(5, 6)

Note: the payoff (0, –) indicates that a high-productivity worker will not accept a low wage.

a. If no testing is done, determine the Nash equilibrium for this game.
b. With testing, what are the Nash equilibria?

7. Consider the production function

$$f(E) = 20E - E^2,$$

where E is the level of agent's effort, and the agent's opportunity cost is $\mathrm{TC}_E = 4E$. With an output price $p = 1$, determine the level of effort, E, along with profits for the principal and the agent for each of the following situations.

a. Fixed compensation: the agent receives a compensation of \$160.
b. Residual claimant: the agent pays a franchise fee of \$64 to operate the enterprise.
c. Sharecropping: the agent receives a 50 percent share of the output.

8. Donald is a manager who must choose one of two shirking levels. If he chooses to surf the Net, Donald will have a 0.8 probability of earning a return of \$700 and a 0.2 probability of a \$1600 return. If he instead puts out some effort, he has a 0.1 probability of a \$100 return and a 0.9 probability of a \$1000 return. The returns are lower for effort because of the cost of effort.

a. Assuming that Donald is risk-neutral, show that a residual claimant contract would be effective in preventing his shirking?
b. If Donald is instead risk-averse (represented by a logarithmic utility function), will a residual claimant contract still be effective? Explain.

9. Two Cournot firms are producing undifferentiated products at zero cost and both face the market demand

$$p = 30 - (q_1 + q_2).$$

The two firms are identical except that firm 1 is owner-managed—output is determined by the owner, who receives all the profits. In contrast, the owner of firm 2 has hired a manager based on a contract where the manager's salary I_2 is

$$I_2 = \tfrac{1}{4}\pi_2 + 3q_2.$$

The owner of firm 2 receives profits net of the manager's salary. The manager of firm 2 makes all the output decisions and attempts to maximize her salary.

a. Determine the Cournot equilibrium for this market. What is the profit for the owner of firm 1? For firm 2, what are the manager's salary and the net profit for owner?
b. Determine the optimal contract for the owner of firm 2 where the owner is paid a franchise fee and the manager's salary is $I_2 = \pi_2 - \text{Fee}$.

10. A landowner has hired a peasant to tend her land. If the crop fails, the landowner will lose \$10,000; if it is harvested, the landowner will make \$50,000 minus any

compensation to the peasant. The peasant can choose to work the land or totally shirk. If he shirks, the crop will fail; if he works, the crop has a 50–50 chance of failing. The peasant's utility, measured in monetary units, is $5000 lower if he works versus shirking. The landowner must choose between either paying the peasant a fixed annual salary of $10,000 or a profit-sharing plan where the peasant earns nothing if the crop fails and $20,000 if it is harvested. Assuming that both the landowner and the peasant are risk-neutral, draw a game tree that determines the landowner's optimal strategy.

Internet case studies

1. Develop a list of large companies that are owned and operated by employees.
2. Discuss a number of incentive mechanisms that firms use to increase employees' productivity.
3. Provide a brief history of sharecropping and why it developed.

What is important is to keep learning, to enjoy challenge, and to tolerate ambiguity. In the end there are no certain answers.

(Martina Horner)

Appendix A Mathematical review

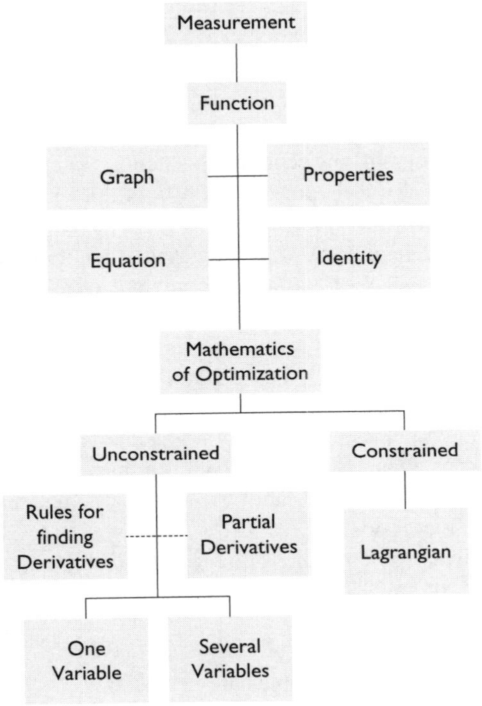

Outline and Conceptual Inquiries

Measurement

Is your class ranking measured differently than your grade-point average?

Functions

Graphs

Is a picture worth a thousand words?

Properties of functions

Equations and identities

Slope and intercept

Linear and nonlinear equations

Absolute values

Exponents

Logarithms

Summation notation, Σ

Mathematics of maximization (optimization)

Maximization of a function with one variable

Are you on a horizontal surface?

Are you in a valley, on top of a mountain, or on a terrace?

Rules for finding derivatives

Functions of several variables

Does only one person move at a time?

Does everyone move at one time?

Maximization of functions with several variables

Is everyone at the bottom of the valley or on top of a mountain?

Constrained maximization

Are you subject to any constraints?

Is this economics or mathematics?

Convexity

Useful quantitative relations

Homogeneous functions

Euler's Theorem

Key concepts

Questions

Exercises

Internet case studies

I cannot understand it. I cannot even understand the people who can understand it.

(Queen Juliana)

Mathematics makes the invisible visible. It provides the window for viewing how a system operates. For example, employing mathematics in the development of economic theory reveals the workings of our economic systems. Specifically, economic theory makes Adam Smith's invisible hand visible, but without mathematics much of the invisible hand would remain invisible.

To understand economic theory, it is important to not only have the ability to do mathematical calculations but also to comprehend why the manipulations of the variables work the way they do. When an equation or identity is presented as a method of solution to an economic problem, it is important to understand the theory on which the equation or identity is based. Understanding the basis of an equation or identity will often allow its modification for a particular case. Thus, this appendix provides a brief review of the mathematical concepts used throughout the chapters. We intend this review as an aid for recalling definitions and concepts, not as a tutorial in mathematics. For additional understanding of the mathematical concepts presented, refer to a mathematical textbook.

In doing mathematical problems, the following algorithm will aid in determining the most efficient method for solving the problem and to reduce error:

1. Read the problem carefully.
2. Determine what theory and principles are involved.
3. Know what the general results are to be produced by the calculations.
4. Think about the possible methods to use in solving the problem.
5. Write the intermediate stages of the calculations clearly. Avoid writing one number on top of another as a method of correction. Make each digit legible.
6. Recognize different forms of the same value. For example, $1/2 = ½ = \frac{1}{2} = 2^{-1} = 0.5 = 50$ percent.
7. Mentally estimate an answer before working the problem.

Measurement

Two is not equal to three, not even for large values of two.

(Grabel's Law)

Any review of mathematical concepts involving the manipulation of numbers will be aided by a discussion of how things are measured in terms of these numbers. In general, the types of mathematical tools that can be used on numbers depend on how these numbers are measured. **Measurement** is the assignment of numbers to observations, where numbers can then be used for analysis. It is the description of something in terms of numerical values. Analysis of the numbers then reveals new information about the objects being measured. For example, the average cost of producing a given output may be determined by dividing the observed total cost for a given output by that output.

Analysis of the numbers assigned to observations is dependent on the method used in mapping numbers to observations. This analysis must be **isomorphic**, meaning that two systems have the same relations and operations they allow. For example, manipulating the assignment of numbers to output levels by adding or subtracting them assumes that the structure of the measurement is isomorphic to arithmetic. That is, we assume that the level of measurement is precise enough to allow such arithmetical analysis.

Levels of measurement may be divided into four scales, with the type of analysis allowed varying for each scale. Measurement at its weakest level is when numbers or other symbols are used simply to classify an object, person, or characteristic. This is called a **nominal scale** (or **classificatory scale**), where numbers or other symbols are used to identify the groups to which various objects belong. This nominal scale partitions the observations into mutually exclusive subclasses. Objects of any one subclass are equivalent in the property being scaled. Examples are automobile license plates, where automobiles can be classified according to which state they are from, and numbers assigned to football players, where 01 to 20 may represent quarterbacks, 90s defensive guards, and 00 water boys.

The next level of measurement is called the **ordinal scale** (or **ranking scale**). For an ordinal level of measurement, the objects in one subclass of a scale are not just different from the objects in another subclass, but they stand in some kind of relation to them. Typical relations among classes are "higher," "preferred," or "more difficult." However, the magnitude of the relation between these different subclasses is not known. One subclass may, for example, be higher than another subclass, but it is not known by how much higher. An example of an ordinal scale introduced in Chapter 2 is the preference relation "is preferred to or indifferent to," written $\succcurlyeq$. This preference relation assumes an ordinal level of measurement. Other examples are 1st, 2nd, and 3rd grade in elementary school and 1st, 2nd, and 3rd place in a race. The grade levels could just as well be assigned names as in high school and college (freshman, sophomore, junior, and senior) or assigned symbols as in Boy Scouts (Tiger Cub, Cub Scout, Webelo, Boy Scout, and Eagle Scout).

> *My dog is worried about the economy because Alpo is up to 99 cents a can. That is almost $7.00 in dog money.*
>
> (Joe Weinstein)

The two highest levels of measurement scales, interval scale and ratio scale, are called **cardinal scale** measurements. At the cardinal measurement level, the magnitude of the relation between different subclasses is known. An **interval scale** has all the characteristics of an ordinal scale plus the known distances or magnitude between any two numbers on the scale. The measurement of temperature is an example of an interval scale, and, as discussed in Chapter 18, the expected utility function is also measured at an interval level.

The distinction between the interval and ratio scales is that for an interval scale, the ratio of any two intervals is independent of the unit of measurement and of the zero point. At an interval level of measurement, the zero point and unit of measurement are arbitrary. For example, temperature is generally measured by three different interval scales, Fahrenheit, °F, Kelvin, K, and Celsius, °C. The unit of measurement and point of zero in measuring temperature are different for each of the scales, but they all convey the same amount of information. This is because they are positively linearly related (by what are called **positive affine transformations**):

$$°C = (5/9)(°F - 32),$$

$$K = °C + 273.$$

The Fahrenheit scale has a zero point set at the lowest temperature attainable from a mixture of table salt and ice, and 100°F was set at the body temperature of a small animal. Absolute zero is 0 K. Water freezes at 0° on the Celsius scale, 273 on the Kelvin scale and 32° on the Fahrenheit scale. Water boils at 100°C, 373 K, and 212°F, and when it is a comfortable 68°F, it is 20°C and 313 K.

The ratio of the difference between temperatures on one scale is the same as the ratio between equivalent differences on the other scale. For example, on the Celsius scale, the ratio of the differences between 100° and 20° and between 20° and 0° is

$$\frac{100-20}{20-0} = 4.$$

This ratio is the same for a comparable reading in Fahrenheit degrees:

$$\frac{212-68}{68-32} = 4$$

A **ratio scale** is an interval scale with a true zero point as its origin. Similar to the interval scale, on a ratio scale, the ratio of any two scale points is independent of the unit of measurement. However, in contrast to the interval scale, the ratio scale is not independent of the true zero point. For example, output is measured on a ratio scale. Output has a true zero point and, whether it is measured in gallons or liters, the ratio of any two points is the same. For example, the ratio of 2 gallons to 1 gallon is the same as the ratio of 7.571 liters to 3.785 liters. What is the level of measurement between dollars and dog money? A ratio scale, given that the cost of the dog food in both scales starts at the same zero point: free food.

Is your class ranking measured differently than your grade-point average? Yes, your class ranking is an ordinal measure and your grade-point average is a ratio scale.

Functions

Arithmetic is being able to count up to twenty without taking off your shoes.

(Mickey Mouse)

A fundamental area of mathematics is arithmetic. **Arithmetic** is the mathematics involving real numbers and their manipulation by the four basic operations (addition, subtraction, multiplication, and division). **Algebra** is a direct outgrowth of arithmetic, where letters or other symbols are used to represent real numbers. Algebra provides rules for determining the order and kind of basic operations necessary to solve a problem. One such rule is a **function**, which describes a relationship among numbers. The general functional expression $y = f(x)$ states "y is a function of x" (and does not represent some number x multiplied by another number f). This function means there is some, perhaps unspecified, relationship between the values of the variables y and x. The variable y is called the **dependent variable** and x the **independent variable**. Specifically, for some values of x, such a relationship specifies corresponding values for y. For example, one functional relationship is summarized in the following table:

x	1	5	6	9	10
y	15	−22	0	9	12

This functional relationship states that when $x = 1$, $y = f(1) = 15$. The function $y = f(x)$ is a symbol that represents such a table of values. The variable x is transformed into the variable y, so functions are also called **transformations**. A function represented as $y = f(x)$ is called an **explicit function**. The variable y is explicitly represented by the function $f(x)$. Alternatively, a function may be represented in implicit form (called an **implicit function**), by an equation, for example $y - f(x) = 0$. In this case, y is implicitly a function of x.

An economic example of a function is the demand function

$$Q^D = f(p).$$

The quantity demanded of some commodity (good or service), Q^D, depends on p, the per-unit price of the commodity. If a second functional relationship is introduced—for example a supply function—it should be distinguished from any previous functional relationship. To make such a distinction, we use other symbols such as F, g, ϕ (the Greek letter phi), or f_1 instead of f. Thus, we could represent a supply function as

$$Q^S = g(p),$$

where Q^S denotes the quantity supplied.

If the quantity of a commodity also depends on the values of variables other than price, then we use a multivariable demand function. For example, if quantity demanded is also a function of income I, then

$$Q^D = f(p, I).$$

This function states that both price p and income I influence the level of demand Q^D. In general, the demand function may be a function of $k + 1$ independent variables:

$$Q^D = f(p_1, p_2, \ldots, p_k, I),$$

which states that the value of Q^D is dependent on the values of k prices and income.

Graphs

> *I must see it to believe it. However, the words Figure and fictitious both derive from the same Latin root fingere, so beware.*
>
> (M.J. Moroney)

Describing something, either in prose or mathematics, is much easier with the aid of a picture. For example, an outstanding novelist may be able to provide an excellent description of an ocean sunset, but only from seeing it for yourself is the true magnificence revealed. Similarly, a graph of a function can reveal much of a function's properties. A **graph** is a pictorial representation of one or more functions. For example, a graph of functions $y = f(x)$ and

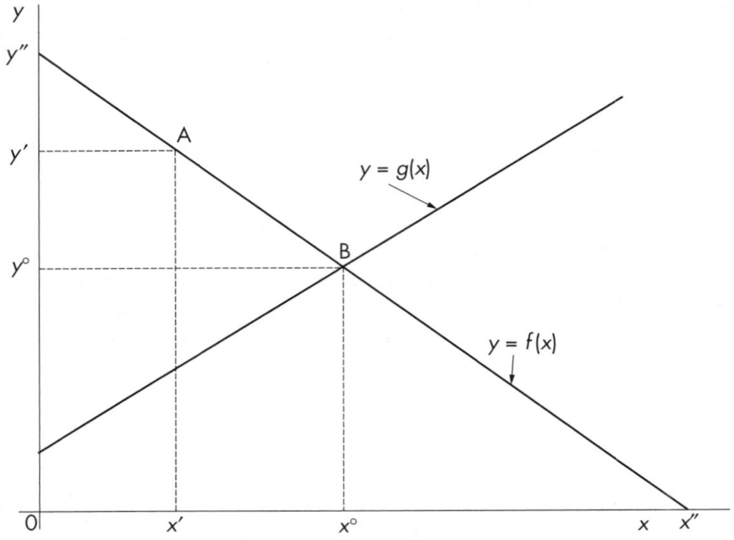

Figure A.1 **Slope of a line.** The two functions $y = f(x)$ and $y = g(x)$ are both represented in the figure. The slope of the line $y = f(x)$ is given by the increase in the vertical coordinates (rise) of points A and B divided by the increase in their horizontal coordinates (run).

$y = g(x)$ is illustrated in Figure A.1. In mathematics, the independent variable is usually depicted on the horizontal (x) axis and the dependent variable on the vertical (y) axis. However, in economics, it is common to graph some functions with the independent variable on the vertical axis and the dependent variable on the horizontal axis. For example, demand functions are usually depicted with the price on the vertical axis and the amount demanded on the horizontal axis (see Chapter 4).

Is a picture worth a thousand words? Yes, a picture can reveal the true image of what is being described.

In Figure A.1, values of x are represented on the horizontal axis starting from zero and going to infinity, so $x \geq 0$. Similarly, values of y are represented on the vertical axis with $y \geq 0$. For some value of x, say x', the associated value of $y = f(x)$ can be determined from the graph by going up from x' to the curve $y = f(x)$ (point A) and then across. For x', this results in y'. We determine the same relation between x and y by inserting the value of x, x', into the function $y = f(x)$ and calculating y, $y' = f(x')$.

A graph can also represent the relation between x and y, given negative values for x. Negative numbers are not natural numbers, so they are not observed in reality. For example, having -2 fish does not make any sense. Thus, most graphs in economic theory are restricted to the positive quadrant, where both y and x are nonnegative.

Properties of functions

A **continuous function** is one that can be drawn without lifting a pencil from the paper. Such a continuous function is illustrated in panel (a) of Figure A.2 for the interval between x^o and x'.

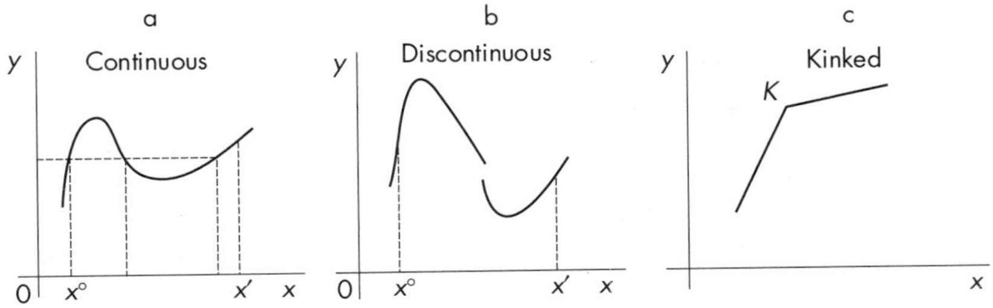

Figure A.2 **Continuous, discontinuous, and kinked functions.** A continuous function is represented by a curve that can be drawn without any breaks. A discontinuous function is associated with breaks in the curve. A function is kinked if the associated curve has sharp corners (not smooth).

In contrast, panel (b) depicts a discontinuous function between x^o and x'. A discontinuous function results in gaps where the relation between the variables makes a discrete jump. A **smooth function** is one that has no kinks (corners). The graph in panel (a) and the two segments in panel (b) represent smooth functions. In contrast, the curve in panel (c) is not smooth, it has a kink at K, where the slope of the function is undefined. An example of a continuous and smooth function is any function that is amenable to taking a derivative, for example, $y = \ln x$. For either functions with kinks or discontinuous functions, a derivative cannot be calculated at the kink or at the discrete jump, and thus the functions are not smooth.

A **monotonic function** is a function that is always increasing or always decreasing. Specifically, a **positive monotonic** function is always increasing and a **negative monotonic** function is always decreasing. For example, a function relating total human population to time is a positive monotonic function and a function relating total elephant population to time is a negative monotonic function. One example of a positive monotonic function is $y = \ln x$, where $dy/dx = 1/x > 0$ for $x > 0$. The slope is always positive, so y is always rising as x increases. An example of a negative monotonic function is $y = -\ln x$, where $dy/dx = -1/x < 0$. The slope is always negative, so y is always declining as x increases. Positive monotonic and negative monotonic functions are illustrated in Figure A.3. Monotonic functions have the **single-value** property, where for any value of x there is only one unique associated value for y. In contrast, a function that is not single-valued is illustrated in panel (a) of Figure A.2. Within the interval (x^o, x'), a number of x values can result in the same value for y.

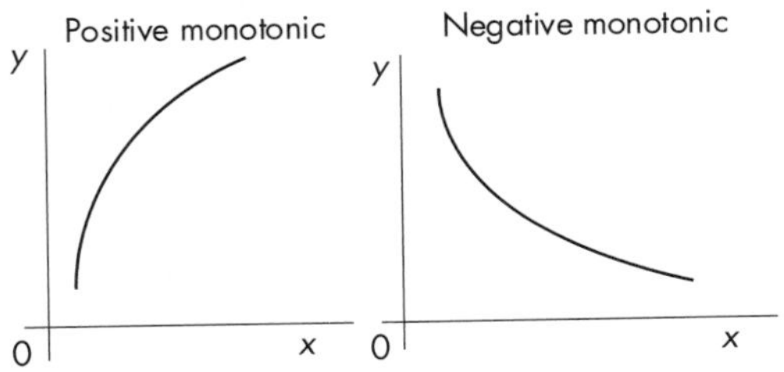

Figure A.3 **Monotonic functions.** Curves associated with monotonic functions are increasing or decreasing throughout the whole range of x.

Equations and identities

The fundamental tool of algebra is the equation. An **equation** indicates when a function is equal to a particular number—for example, $3x = 9$, $x^2 = 4$ and $f(x) = 0$. The solution to an equation is a value of x that satisfies the equation. The first equation has the solution $x = 3$, and the second has the solution $x = 2$ and -2. The third equation is called a **general equation**. A solution of a general equation, typically denoted x^*, requires knowledge of the actual rule associated with f. The solution x^* is the number that satisfies the equation $f(x) = 0$.

An **identity** is a relation among variables that holds for all values of the variables—for example,

$$(x+y)^2 \equiv x^2 + 2xy + y^2.$$

The symbol $\equiv$ means that the left-hand side and the right-hand side are equal for all values of the variables. An equation only holds for some values of the variables, whereas an identity is true for all values of the variables.

Slope and intercept

The **slope** of a line is a measure of its steepness and is determined by how much a curve rises per unit move to the right (rise over run). Specifically, if moving 5 units to the right involves a 3-unit rise in the curve, its slope is 3/5. It rises at an average rate of 3/5 per unit for a 1-unit move to the right. If moving 2 units to the right involves a 4-unit fall in the curve, its slope is -2. The curve falls at an average rate of 2 units for a 1-unit move to the right.

As illustrated in Figure A.1, the slope of a curve is given by the increase in the vertical coordinates (rise) of points A and B divided by the increase in their horizontal coordinates (run):

$$\text{slope} = \frac{y' - y^{\text{o}}}{x' - x^{\text{o}}}.$$

For the line $y = f(x)$ in Figure A.1, the slope is negative (slope < 0). If slope > 0 (positive slope), it represents a line segment of the form $y = g(x)$ in Figure A.1. In panel (c) of Figure A.2, the slope at the kink (point K) is undefined, and in Figure A.3, a positive monotonic function has a positive slope and a negative monotonic function has a negative slope.

The difference between a curve that is straight (linear) and one that is not is that the slope of a straight line never changes. For example, the slope of the line $y = f(x)$ in Figure A.1 is the same for all points on the line. In contrast, the slopes of the lines in Figure A.3 are changing throughout.

The **vertical intercept** of a function is the value of y when $x = 0$, and the **horizontal intercept** is the value of x when $y = 0$. In Figure A.1, for the line $y = f(x)$, the vertical intercept is y'' and the horizontal intercept is x''.

Linear and nonlinear equations

The equation $y = ax + b$, where a and b are any constants (parameters), is called a **linear equation**. A parameter represents any number, for example 5. The constant a is the slope and b is the y-intercept.

The graph of a three-variable relationship such as $y = 3x_1 + 4x_2 - 6$ is the three-dimensional analogue of a straight line (linear curve). This graph is a plane in a three-dimensional diagram whose three axes represent the values of x_1, x_2, and y. Generally, by analogy, the term *linear equation* is applied for any relationship such as

$$y = a_1x_1 + a_2x_2 + \ldots + a_kx_k + b,$$

where $y, x_1, x_2, \ldots, x_k$ are all variables and $a_1, a_2, \ldots, a_k$ and b are all parameters.

A linear function and a number of nonlinear functions are illustrated in Figures A.4 and A.5. For the cubic function, within the interval (x^o, x'), a maximum critical point occurs. Such a maximum within an interval is called a **local maximum**. Similarly, within the interval (x', x''), a **local minimum** exists. In Figure A.5, the quadratic function results in a minimum considering all values of x, called a **global minimum**.

Absolute values

I value your decision regardless of the sign.

(Michael Wetzstein)

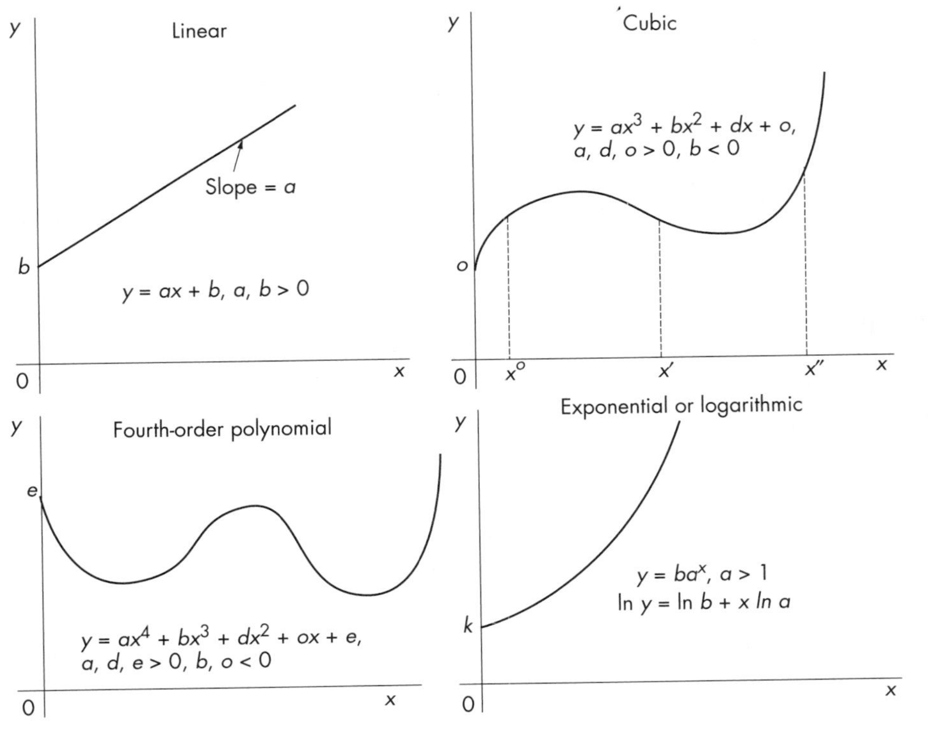

Figure A.4 **Graphs of linear, cubic, fourth-order polynomial and exponential or logarithmic equations.** A linear curve has a constant slope over the whole range of x. For the exponential or logarithmic curve, the slope is increasing as x increases (positive monotonic).

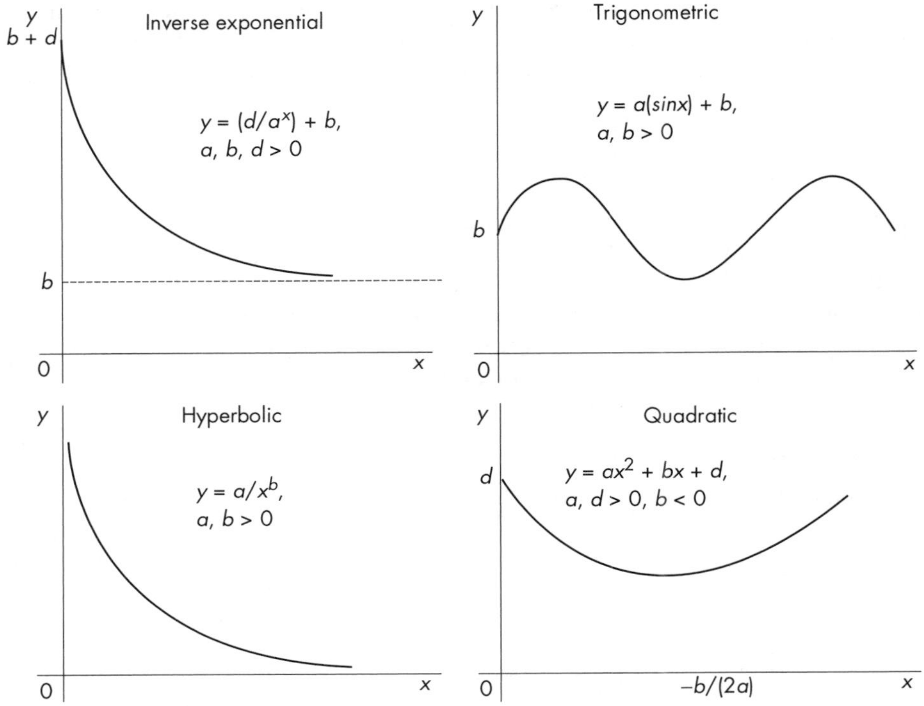

Figure A.5 **Graphs of inverse exponential, trigonometric, hyperbolic, and quadratic equations.** The inverse exponential and hyperbolic functions are monotonic; however, the trigonometric and (in this case) the quadratic functions are not monotonic.

The **absolute value** of a number is a function that states that the solution is determined by dropping any negative sign associated with the number. It is the numerical value of a real number without regard to sign. The absolute-value function is usually written as $y = |x| > 0$, for both $x > 0$ and $x < 0$. For example, $y = |-2| = 2$.

Exponents

The **exponential** relation $x^k = x \bullet x \cdots x$ (k times) states that x is multiplied by itself k times. The following rules apply to exponentials:

1. **Zero exponent.** $x^0 = 1$. For example, $2^0 = 1$.
2. **Reciprocal.** $x^{-a} = \frac{1}{x^a}$. For example, $x^{-2} = \frac{1}{x^2}$.
3. **Multiplication.** $x^a x^b = x^{a+b}$. For example, $x^2 x^3 = x^5$.
4. **Division.** $\frac{x^a}{x^b} = x^{a-b}$. For example, $\frac{x^2}{x^3} = x^{-1}$.
5. **Powers.** $(x^a)^b = x^{ab}$. For example, $(x^6)^{1/2} = x^{6/2} = x^3$.
6. **Roots.** $x^{1/b}$ is the bth root of x. For example, $x^{1/2}$ is the square root of x.

Logarithms

> *Compared to you, my lack of understanding is on a common logarithmic scale. For each thing you misunderstand, I misunderstand ten times that.*
>
> (Michael Wetzstein)

Exponent rules 3 and 5 that state multiplication can be reduced to addition of exponents and a variable can be raised to a higher power by multiplication, provide the basis for logarithmic computation. Logarithms were developed to simplify the mathematical operations of multiplication and division to the level of addition and subtraction. **Logarithmic functions** are the exponent of some number. There are two main systems of logarithms: base 10 and base e. Logarithms to the base 10 are called **common logarithms** (or **Briggs logarithms**), and they are exponents of the number 10. Generally, in economics, a system of logarithms is used in which the base is the number $e = 2.718281828459045\ldots$. Logarithms to the base e are known as **hyperbolic logarithms**, **Naperian logarithms**, or **natural logarithms**. When no base is designated, natural logarithms are usually assumed. Natural logarithms are the inverses of exponential functions (Figure A.6). The inverse of the function f defined by $f(x) = e^x$ is called the logarithm function with base e and is denoted by ln. The logarithmic function associates with each number x the exponent y, where the power e^y is equal to x. We can use ln if we want to know the value of y for which $e^y = x$. The term $\ln x$ can be thought of as an exponent on e. Thus, $e^{\ln x} = x$. Specifically, given any number x, the logarithm of x (to the base e) is defined to be a number that satisfies the relationship $x = e^{\ln x}$. The term $\ln x$ is a number such that, if e is raised to the power of $\ln x$, then the result is equal to x. Note that $1 = \ln e$.

Logarithms can be combined according to the rules for exponents as follows:

7. **Logarithmic multiplication.** Given $y = ab$, then

$$\ln y = \ln a + \ln b.$$

Given $y = a/b$, then

$$\ln y = \ln a - \ln b.$$

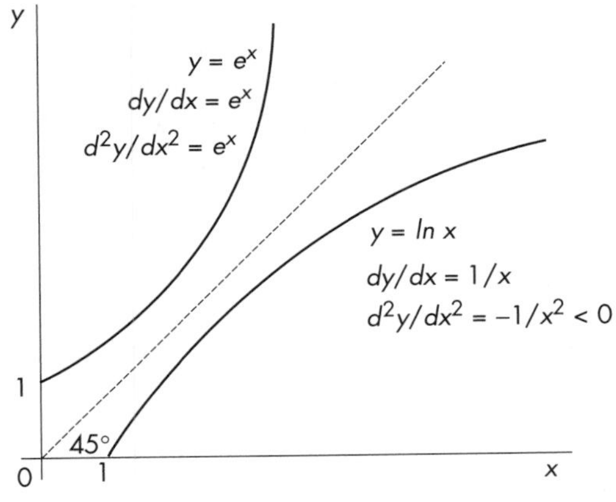

Figure A.6 **Graph of $y = \ln x$ and its inverse $y = e^x$.** Natural logarithms are the inverse of exponential functions.

8. **Logarithmic powers.** Given $y = x^a$, then

$$\ln y = a \ln x.$$

Summation notation, $\sum$

Let $x_1 = 6, x_2 = 0, x_3 = -3$ and $x_4 = 15$. Using the Greek Letter $\sum$ (an upper-case sigma) to indicate a summation, we denote the addition of these four numbers as

$$\sum_{j=1}^{4} x_j$$

In other words, to add the numbers x_j ($j = 1, \ldots, 4$) we successively let j be equal to 1, then to 2, all the way up to $j = 4$:

$$\sum_{j=1}^{4} x_j = x_1 + x_2 + x_3 + x_4 = 6 + 0 + (-3) + 15 = 18.$$

When a large number of terms are involved, this notation saves both time and space.

Mathematics of maximization (optimization)

Central to many economic models is the hypothesis that agents attempt to maximize or minimize certain outcomes (called **optimizing**). For example, firms attempt to maximize profit π for a given technology, which requires minimizing cost for a given level of output. Consumers attempt to maximize utility (satisfaction) for a given level of income, and governments attempt to maximize social welfare for a given resource constraint. This optimization by economic agents generally assumes (an abstraction) rational behavior by firms, consumers, and government.

Economists adopt optimization hypotheses to explain and predict market behavior. Such hypotheses are very useful in explaining all types of economic phenomena, and the method of mathematical optimization is precise, assuming that what is being optimized is consistent with agents' actual behavior. The development of the mathematics of maximization is extensive, and alternatives to optimization hypotheses are very limited in their ability to yield satisfactory explanations of agents' market behavior. For example, if we used the hypothesis that firms or consumers strive toward satisfactory performance, difficulties in determining "satisfactory performance" would limit the usefulness of this hypothesis.

Maximization of a function with one variable

As an example of employing mathematical optimization to an economic problem, assume that a manager of a firm desires to maximize pure profit π, where

$$\pi = f(q)$$

and q is the quantity of the good sold by the firm. A possible relationship between π and q is illustrated in Figure A.7, where π^* is the maximum level of profit considering all values of q.

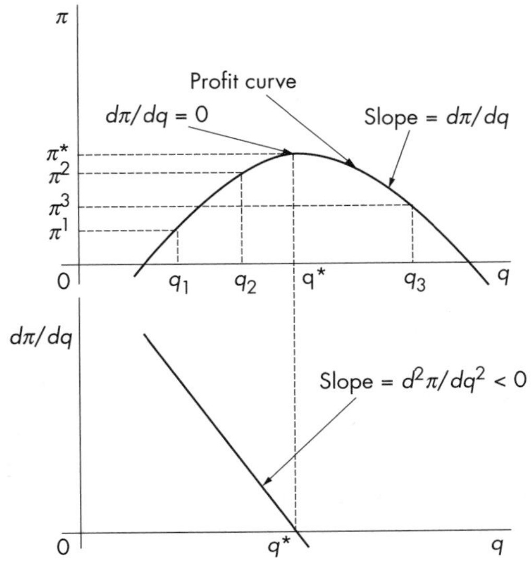

Figure A.7 **Profit curve.** Profit is maximized at output q^*, where $d\pi/dq = 0$ and $d^2\pi/dq^2 < 0$.

This maximum level of profit is called a **global maximum**. The firm should produce q^* units of output to maximize π at π^*. If more or less of this amount were produced, π would not be maximized.

If Figure A.7 were not available, the firm could vary q, assess the associated profit levels, and then select the profit-maximizing output. For example, q_1 yields a profit of π_1 and q_2 a profit of π_2. Increasing q from q_1 to q_2 enhances profit. Specifically

$$\frac{\pi_2 - \pi_1}{q_2 - q_1} = \frac{\Delta\pi}{\Delta q} > 0,$$

where Δ denotes change. As long as $\Delta\pi/\Delta q$ is positive, profit increases by increasing q, so a profit-maximizing firm will continue to increase output. However, increasing q beyond q^* results in $\Delta\pi/\Delta q < 0$, so the firm will move toward q^* by cutting back on q.

In general, assume that the function $\pi = f(q)$ is continuous on some interval. With calculus, we can determine the limit of ratios such as $\Delta\pi/\Delta q$ for very small changes in q. If the independent variable q changes by a small quantity Δq, then the value of the function will change by the quantity $\Delta\pi$. Thus,

$$\pi + \Delta\pi = f(q + \Delta q).$$

Solving for $\Delta\pi$, we express the change in the value of the function as

$$\Delta\pi = f(q + \Delta q) - f(q).$$

Dividing both sides by Δq, we have

$$\frac{\Delta\pi}{\Delta q} = \frac{f(q + \Delta q) - f(q)}{\Delta q}.$$

The average rate of change of π per unit change of q for the interval $(q, q+\Delta q)$ is $\Delta\pi/\Delta q$. The **derivative** of $\pi = f(q)$, denoted by

$$\frac{d\pi}{dq},\ f'(q),\ \pi',\ \text{or}\ \dot{\pi},$$

is defined as the rate of change of $f(q)$ as Δq approaches zero:

$$\frac{d\pi}{dq} = f'(q) = \lim_{\Delta q \to 0}\left[\frac{f(q+\Delta q) - f(q)}{\Delta q}\right],$$

where dq is an increment (small change) in the independent variable and $d\pi$ is the resulting increment in the dependent variable. The derivative is the limit of the rate of change of π with respect to q as the change in q goes to zero, and it provides precise meaning to the rate of change in π with respect to q for small changes in q. In terms of economics, the derivative is the marginal change in π resulting from a small change in q. This is called the **marginal value**. In this case, the value is profit, so it is called **marginal profit**. If $f(q)$ is plotted (Figure A.8), the derivative calculated at the point $q = a$ is the slope of the curve representing $f(q)$ at the point $q = a$.

In Figure A.7 at q^*, the value of $d\pi/dq$ is zero, which corresponds to the maximum profit level. A point such as q^* where $d\pi/dq = 0$ is called a **critical point**. As illustrated in Figure A.7, the value of $d\pi/dq$ is positive for values of q less than q^* and negative for values greater than q^*. The derivative is the slope of the curve in question, in this case the profit curve. Thus, if a firm could estimate the function $f(q)$ from market data, it would be theoretically possible to find the point where $d\pi/dq = 0$.

Generally, firms do not estimate a profit function and then take the derivative with respect to output for determining their profit-maximizing level of output. Rather, through trial and error (called **tâtonnement**), firms adjust output in attempting to maximize profits. In modeling firms' behavior with the calculus of maximization, we assume that firms are successful in reaching this point of maximum output in some tâtonnement process. Thus, a model of firm

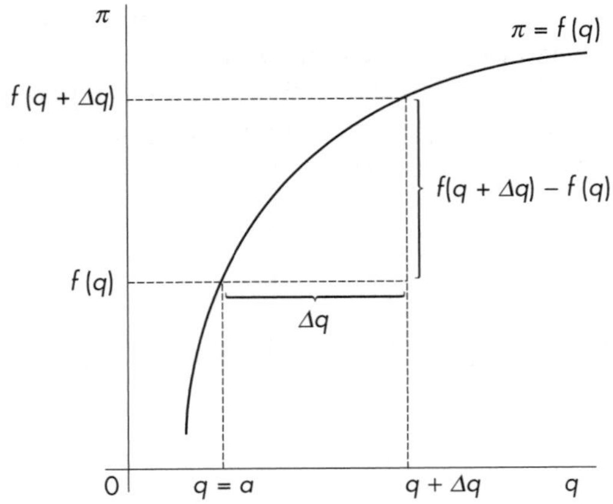

Figure A.8 **Change in q yielding a change in π.** In the limit as Δq approaches zero, the slope of the curve at $q = a$ is the derivative evaluated at a.

behavior with the calculus of maximization is an abstraction from actual firm behavior but leads to the same market behavior in terms of the output a firm will supply. Such an abstraction allows for the development of economic models that simplify market behavior. These models can then be used for explaining, predicting, or controlling economic agents' behavior. This method of abstracting from reality is called the **scientific method**, which is discussed further in Chapter 1.

First-order condition (FOC)

The requirement of $d\pi/dq = 0$ is called the **first-order condition (FOC)** for determining a maximum or minimum of a function. The FOC along with the second-order condition (SOC) are the necessary and sufficient conditions for a maximum or a minimum.

Are you on a horizontal surface? If so, you have satisfied the FOC for being on top of a hill, in the bottom of a valley, or on a terrace.

Second-order condition (SOC)

When attempting to maximize a function by setting $d\pi/dq = 0$ (FOC), the firm could be misled. For example, suppose that the profit function appears as in panel (a) of Figure A.9.

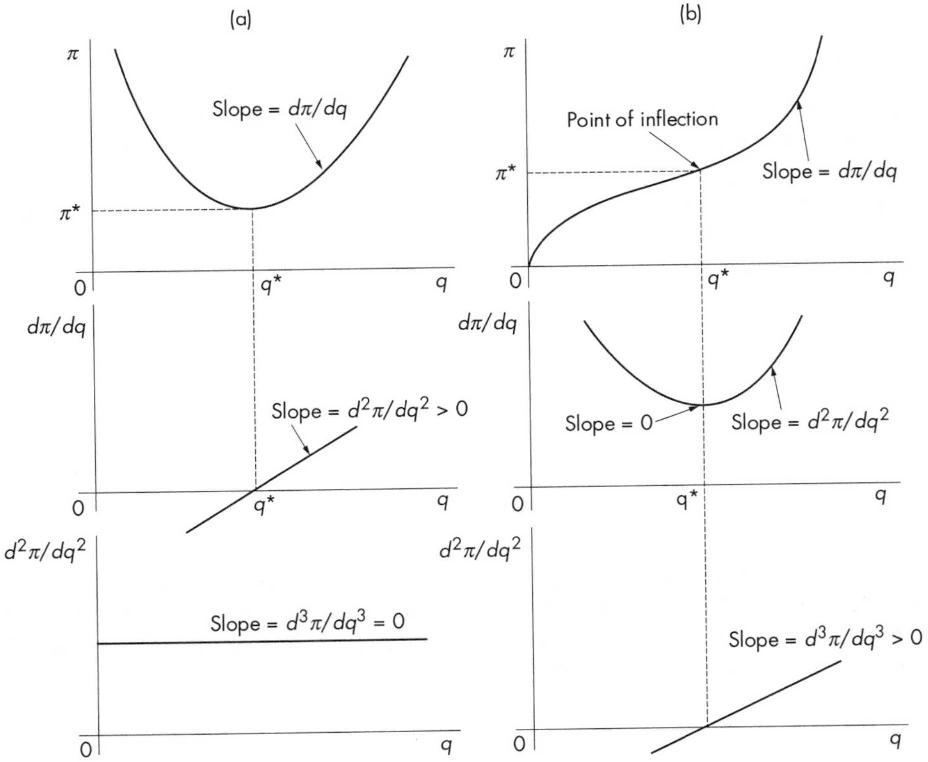

Figure A.9 **Consideration of second-order conditions.** In panel (a), the critical point q^* results in the minimum level of profit, and in panel (b), the critical point is an inflection point.

The firm produces where $d\pi/dq = 0$ and minimizes rather than finding the maximum profits. Thus, the mathematical condition $d\pi/dq = 0$ alone is not a sufficient condition for a maximum. The additional condition required is that the profit available by producing either a bit more or a bit less than q^* must be smaller than the profit available from q^*. If this is not the case, then the firm can do better by changing output from q^*. Mathematically, this means that $d\pi/dq$ must be greater than 0 for $q < q^*$ and less than 0 for $q > q^*$, Figure A.7. Specifically, at q^*, $d\pi/dq$ must be decreasing.

The derivative of what is already a derivative (the derivative of a derivative) is called a **second derivative**. The second derivative of $\pi = f(q)$ is denoted by

$$\frac{d^2\pi}{dq^2}, \; f''(q), \; \pi'', \; \text{or} \; \ddot{\pi},$$

and is defined as

$$\frac{d^2\pi}{dq^2} = \lim_{\Delta q \to 0}\left[\frac{f'(q+\Delta q) - f'(q)}{\Delta q}\right].$$

The second derivative is the rate of change of the first derivative, or the rate at which the slope of the function is changing. Thus, the additional condition for q^* to represent a true maximum is the **second-order condition (SOC)**

$$\frac{d^2\pi}{dq^2} < 0 \;\text{ at }\; q^*.$$

As indicated in Figure A.7, the second derivative measures the curvature of a function. A function with a negative second derivative at some point is concave near that point; its slope is decreasing (Figure A.7). A function with a positive second derivative at some point is convex near that point; its slope is increasing [Figure A.9, panel (a)]. A function with a zero second derivative at a critical point, such as q^* in panel (b) of Figure A.9, has an inflection point at q^*. Specifically, given $d\pi/dq = 0$ at q^*,

$$\frac{d^2\pi}{dq^2} < 0 \;\text{ at }\; q^* \quad \text{results in a maximum,}$$

$$\frac{d^2\pi}{dq^2} > 0 \;\text{ at }\; q^* \quad \text{results in a minimum,}$$

$$\frac{d^2\pi}{dq^2} = 0 \;\text{ at }\; q^* \quad \text{results in an inflection point.}$$

Are you in a valley, on top of a mountain, or on a terrace? Look to the right and left. If the slope is falling in both directions, you are on a mountain; if it is rising in both directions, you are in a valley; and if it is neither falling nor rising in both directions, you are on a terrace.

Example

In Star Trek, would you trust Mr Spock's guess over a mathematical formula?

(Michael Wetzstein)

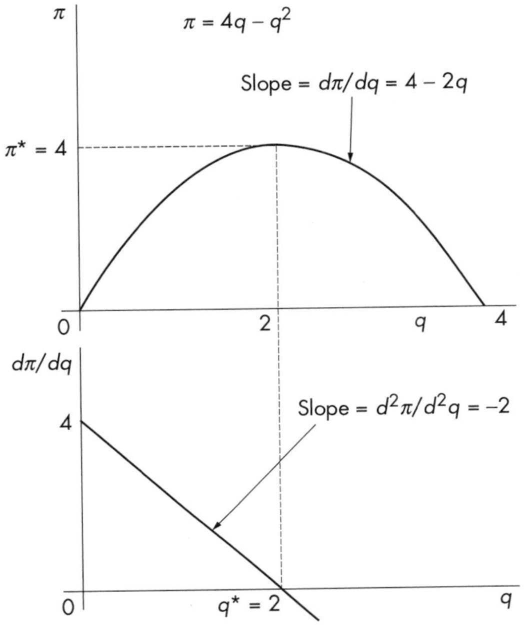

Figure A.10 **Profit maximum.** The critical point of maximum profit is $q^* = 2$ with $\pi^* = 4$.

Suppose that the specific relationship between profit π and output q is

$$\pi = 4q - q^2,$$

with the associated graph shown in Figure A.10. To find the maximum level of profit, we could do any of the following:

(1) trial and error, tâtonnement;
(2) graph the function;
(3) apply mathematics:

$$\frac{d\pi}{dq} = f'(q) = \lim_{\Delta q \to 0} \left[\frac{f(q + \Delta q) - f(q)}{\Delta q} \right].$$

To apply mathematics, we determine the FOC by taking the derivative of profit with respect to output:

$$\begin{aligned} \frac{d\pi}{dq} = f'(q) &= \lim_{\Delta q \to 0} \left[\frac{4(q + \Delta q) - (q + \Delta q)^2 - 4q + q^2}{\Delta q} \right] \\ &= \lim_{\Delta q \to 0} \left(\frac{4q + 4\Delta q - q^2 - 2q\Delta q - \Delta q^2 - 4q + q^2}{\Delta q} \right) \\ &= \lim_{\Delta q \to 0} \left(\frac{4\Delta q - 2q\Delta q - \Delta q^2}{\Delta q} \right) \end{aligned}$$

$$= \lim_{\Delta q \to 0} (4 - 2q - \Delta q)$$
$$= 4 - 2q.$$

Setting this derivative equal to zero and solving for q yields the critical point q^*:

$$4 - 2q^* = 0,$$
$$q^* = 2.$$

We determine the SOC by taking the derivative of the first derivative $d\pi/dq = 4 - 2q$:

$$\frac{d^2\pi}{dq^2} = \lim_{\Delta q \to 0} \left[\frac{4 - 2(q + \Delta q) - 4 + 2q}{\Delta q}\right]$$
$$= \lim_{\Delta q \to 0} \left(\frac{4 - 2q - 2\Delta q - 4 + 2q}{\Delta q}\right)$$
$$= \lim_{\Delta q \to 0} \left(\frac{-2\Delta q}{\Delta q}\right) = -2 < 0.$$

Thus, profit is maximized at $q^* = 2$, resulting in $\pi^* = 4$ (Figure A.10).

Rules for finding derivatives

Like a formal dinner, calculus is ritual.

(Michael Wetzstein)

Rather than having to take the limit every time we want to take a derivative, the following rules offer a number of shortcuts. Considering the function $y = f(x)$.

1. If b is a constant and $y = f(x) = b$, then

$$\frac{dy}{dx} = 0.$$

As an example, if $y = 5$, then $dy/dx = 0$ [Figure A.11, panel (a)].

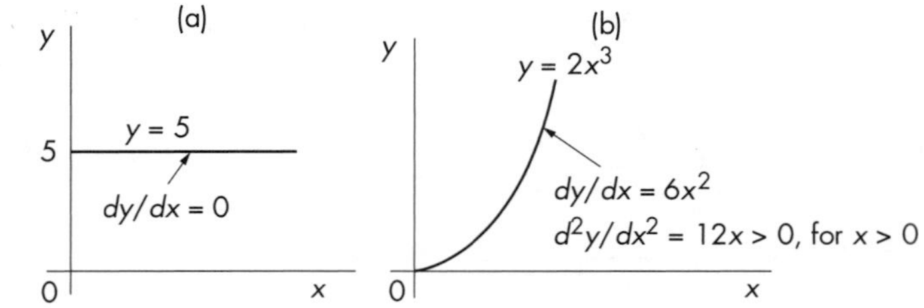

Figure A.11 **Graphs of $y = 5$ and $y = 2x^3$.** In panel (a), the curve is horizontal; in panel (b), it is increasing at an increasing rate.

2. If a and b are constants, $b \neq 0$, and $y = f(x) = ax^b$, then

$$\frac{dy}{dx} = bax^{b-1} = bx^{-1}y.$$

As an example, if $y = 2x^3$, then $dy/dx = 6x^2 = 3x^{-1}y$ [Figure A.11, panel (b)].

3. If $y = f(x) = \ln x$, then

$$\frac{dy}{dx} = \frac{1}{x}.$$

Refer to Figure A.6.

4. If a is a constant and $y = f(x) = a^x$, then

$$\frac{dy}{dx} = a^x \ln a.$$

A particular case of this rule is $de^x/dx = e^x$ (Figure A.6).

Suppose that $g(x)$ and $h(x)$ are two functions of x and that both $g'(x)$ and $h'(x)$ exist.

5. If $y = f(x) = e^{g(x)}$, then

$$\frac{dy}{dx} = g'(x)e^{g(x)}.$$

As an example, if $y = e^{3x}$, then $dy/dx = 3e^{3x}$.

6. **Product rule**. If $y = f(x) = g(x)h(x)$, then

$$\frac{dy}{dx} = g(x)h'(x) + g'(x)h(x).$$

As an example, if $y = (x+1)^2x^3$, then

$$\frac{dy}{dx} = (x+1)^2 3x^2 + 2(x+1)x^3 = x^2(x+1)(5x+3).$$

7. **Quotient rule**. If $y = f(x) = \frac{g(x)}{h(x)}$, then

$$\frac{dy}{dx} = \frac{g'(x)h(x) - g(x)h'(x)}{[h(x)]^2},$$

given $h(x) \neq 0$. As an example, if $y = \frac{(x+1)^2}{(x-1)^2}$, then

$$\frac{dy}{dx} = \frac{2(x+1)(x-1)^2 - (x+1)^2 2(x-1)}{(x-1)^4} = -4(x+1)(x-1)^{-3}.$$

8. **"Function of a function" rule**. If $y = f(x) = g(h(x))$, then

$$\frac{dy}{dx} = g'(h(x))\,h'(x).$$

Note that $g(h(x))$ is called a **composite function**. For a function within a function, calculus always works from the outside in. In this case, the derivative of the outside function $g(h)$ is taken first, followed by the derivative of the inside function $h(x)$. (This is analogous to using tableware at formal dinners: You always use the outside silver first and then work your way in.) As an example of this function of a function rule, if $y = (2x + 1)^3$, then

$$\frac{dy}{dx} = 3(2x+1)^2 2 = 6(2x+1)^2.$$

9. **Chain rule**. If $y = f(x_1)$ and $x_1 = g(x_2)$ and if both $f'(x_1)$ and $g'(x_2)$ exist, then

$$\frac{dy}{dx_2} = \frac{dy}{dx_1}\frac{dx_1}{dx_2} \quad \text{or} \quad \frac{df}{dx_1}\frac{dg}{dx_2}.$$

As an example, if $y = x_1^3$ and $x_1 = x_2^2 + 1$, then

$$\frac{dy}{dx_2} = \left(3x_1^2\right)2x_2 = 6\left(x_2^2+1\right)^2 x_2.$$

10. If $y = f(x)$ is single-valued, continuous, and can be written in inverse form as $x = g(y)$, and is such that $f'(x)$ is continuous and not equal to zero, then

$$f'(x) = \frac{1}{g'(y)} \quad \text{or} \quad \frac{dy}{dx} = \left(\frac{dx}{dy}\right)^{-1} = \frac{1}{dx/dy}.$$

For example, let $y = x^2$; then $x = y^{1/2}$ and

$$\frac{dy}{dx} = 2x = \frac{1}{dx/dy} = \frac{1}{\frac{1}{2}y^{-1/2}} = 2y^{1/2}$$

Functions of several variables

Economic problems seldom involve functions of only a single variable. In many cases, a dependent variable is a function of several variables. For example, a consumer's utility (satisfaction) may be a function of a number of commodities. In general, consider a function with k independent variables:

$$y = f(x_1, x_2, \ldots, x_k).$$

Partial derivative

To determine the critical point where y is a maximum or a minimum, we must determine the effect on y from changing one of the x's while all the other variables are held constant (called a **first-order partial derivative**).

In general, for x_j, where $j = 1, 2, \ldots, k$, the partial derivative of $y = f(x_1, x_2, \ldots, x_k)$ with respect to x_j is denoted by

$$\frac{\partial y}{\partial x_j}, \frac{\partial f}{\partial x_j}, \quad \text{or } f_j.$$

This represents the change in y given a change (in the limit) in x_j, holding all the other x's constant. Formally, partial derivatives are defined as

$$\left.\frac{\partial f}{\partial x_1}\right|_{x_2,\ldots,x_k} = \lim_{\Delta x_1 \to 0}\left[\frac{f(x_1+\Delta x_1,\, x_2,\,\ldots,\, x_k)-f(x_1,\, x_2,\ldots,\, x_k)}{\Delta x_1}\right],$$

$$\left.\frac{\partial f}{\partial x_2}\right|_{x_1,x_3,\ldots,x_k} = \lim_{\Delta x_2 \to 0}\left[\frac{f(x_1,\, x_2+\Delta x_2,\,\ldots,\, x_k)-f(x_1,\, x_2,\ldots,\, x_k)}{\Delta x_2}\right],$$

$$\vdots$$

$$\left.\frac{\partial f}{\partial x_k}\right|_{x_1,\ldots,x_{k-1}} = \lim_{\Delta x_k \to 0}\left[\frac{f(x_1,\, x_2,\,\ldots,\, x_k+\Delta x_k)-f(x_1,\, x_2,\ldots,\, x_k)}{\Delta x_k}\right].$$

In the notation for the partial derivative, the subscripts to the right of the vertical bar indicate variables that are being held constant. Partial derivatives of a function of two or more variables obey the same rules for finding derivatives as a function with one variable. A partial derivative of y with respect to x_j is the marginal contribution to y for a change in x_j, holding all other variables constant. The marginal value of x_j (partial derivative) measures the change in y from a change in x_j, holding all other variables constant.

Does only one person move at a time? In the world of partial derivatives, yes.

Examples

Some examples of calculating first-order partial derivatives are

1. If $y = f(x_1, x_2) = 3x_1^2 + 2x_1x_2 + 5x_2^2$, then

$$\partial f/\partial x_1 = f_1 = 6x_1 + 2x_2,$$
$$\partial f/\partial x_2 = f_2 = 2x_1 + 10x_2.$$

2. If $y = f(x_1, x_2) = \exp(ax_1 + bx_2) = e^{ax_1+bx_2}$, then

$$\partial f/\partial x_1 = f_1 = a\exp(ax_1 + bx_2),$$
$$\partial f/\partial x_2 = f_2 = b\exp(ax_1 + bx_2).$$

3. If $y = f(x_1, x_2) = 2\ln x_1 + 4\ln x_2$, then

$$\partial f/\partial x_1 = f_1 = 2/x_1,$$
$$\partial f/\partial x_2 = f_2 = 4/x_2.$$

Second-order partial derivatives

A **second-order partial derivative** obeys the same rules as a second derivative of a function of one variable and is denoted by

$$\frac{\partial^2 f}{\partial x_j \partial x_i} = f_{ji} = \frac{\partial}{\partial x_i}\left(\frac{\partial f}{\partial x_j}\right), \quad \text{for all} \quad i \text{ and } j = 1, 2, \ldots, k.$$

In the cases where $j=i$, $\partial^2 f/\partial x_j^2$ is the partial derivative of f_j with respect to x_j, also denoted by f_{jj}. When $j \neq i$, the second-order partial derivative $f_{ji} = \partial^2 f/\partial x_j \partial x_i$ is called the **second-cross partial derivative**.

Similar to the calculation of first-order partial derivatives, in calculating second-order partial derivatives, we change only one variable and hold all other variables constant. For the case of $y = f(x_1, x_2)$,

$$\frac{\partial}{\partial x_1}\left(\frac{\partial f}{\partial x_1}\right) = \frac{\partial^2 f}{\partial x_1^2} = f_{11},$$

$$\frac{\partial}{\partial x_2}\left(\frac{\partial f}{\partial x_1}\right) = \frac{\partial^2 f}{\partial x_1 \partial x_2} = f_{12},$$

$$\frac{\partial}{\partial x_1}\left(\frac{\partial f}{\partial x_2}\right) = \frac{\partial^2 f}{\partial x_2 \partial x_1} = f_{21},$$

$$\frac{\partial}{\partial x_2}\left(\frac{\partial f}{\partial x_2}\right) = \frac{\partial^2 f}{\partial x_2^2} = f_{22}.$$

Note that according to **Young's Theorem**, $f_{ji} = f_{ij}$. If the first- and second-cross partial derivatives are continuous, the order in which second-order partial differentiation is taken does not matter.

Examples

Continuing with the same examples employed for the first-order partial derivatives, the second-order partial derivatives are as follows:

1. $\partial f/\partial x_1 = f_1 = 6x_1 + 2x_2$ and $\partial f/\partial x_2 = f_2 = 2x_1 + 10x_2$, so

$$\partial^2 f/\partial x_1^2 = \partial^2 f/\partial x_1 \partial x_1 = f_{11} = 6,$$

$$f_{12} = f_{21} = 2, \quad \text{and} \quad f_{22} = 10.$$

2. $\partial f/\partial x_1 = f_1 = a\exp(ax_1 + bx_2)$ and $\partial f/\partial x_2 = f_2 = b\exp(ax_1 + bx_2)$, so

$$f_{11} = a^2 \exp(ax_1 + bx_2),$$

$$f_{12} = f_{21} = ab\exp(ax_1 + bx_2), \quad \text{and}$$

$$f_{22} = b^2 \exp(ax_1 + bx_2).$$

3. $\partial f/\partial x_1 = f_1 = 2/x_1$ and $\partial f/\partial x_2 = f_2 = 4/x_2$, so

$$f_{11} = -2/x_1^2,$$

$$f_{12} = f_{21} = 0, \quad \text{and}$$

$$f_{22} = -4/x_2^2.$$

Total differential

The **total differential** is a direct extension of the idea of partial differentiation. It determines the total effect of a change in the independent variables $x_1, x_2, \ldots, x_k$ on the dependent variable y. For a function of a single variable, with $dy/dx = f'(x)$, with dx defined as an increment or change in the independent variable, the total differential dy is defined as

$$dy = f'(x)\,dx.$$

This is the differential equation for $f(x)$. The term $f'(x)dx$ represents the influence on y of an incremental change in x. At a given point x^o, the value of the function is $y^o = f(x^o)$, and we can rewrite $dy = f'(x)dx$ in terms of deviations from this point as

$$y - y^o = f'(x^o)(x - x^o),$$

which is the equation of the tangent line to $y = f(x)$ at the point (x^o, y^o). Thus, $dy = f'(x)dx$ is the general form of the equation of the tangent line to the function. For small changes in x, $y - y^o = f'(x^o)(x - x^o)$ gives the approximate value of the corresponding change of $f(x)$.

The total differential of a function with k variables is defined as

$$dy = f_1\,dx_1 + f_2\,dx_2 + \ldots + f_k\,dx_k,$$

which is the general form of the equation for the tangent plane (or hyperplane) to the surface (or hypersurface) defined by

$$y = f(x_1, x_2, \ldots, x_k).$$

For $y = f(x_1, x_2)$, the total differential is

$$dy = f_1\,dx_1 + f_2\,dx_2.$$

The change in x_1, dx_1, times the influence that this change has on y, f_1, plus the change in x_2, dx_2, times its influence on y, f_2, equals the total change in y, dy. Total differentiation provides an approximate value of the change in the function when all variables are permitted to vary, provided the variations in the independent variables are small. This is in contrast to partial differentiation, where only one of the independent variables changes, holding all other variables constant.

Does everyone move at one time? Yes, we live in a total differential world.

Dividing the total differential by $dx_j (j = 1, \ldots, k)$ yields the total derivative of the function with respect to x_j:

$$\frac{dy}{dx_j} = f_1\frac{dx_1}{dx_j} + \ldots + f_j + \ldots + f_k\frac{dx_k}{dx_j},$$

where $dx_j/dx_j = 1$. This total differential measures the rate of change of y with respect to x_j when all other variables are permitted to vary and where all $x_i, j \neq i$, are specified functions of x_j. The effect of x_j on y is composed of two parts: the direct effect f_j and the sum of x_j's indirect effects via all other variables. The partial derivative $f_j = \partial f / \partial x_j$ measures the direct effect that x_j has on y. However, changing x_j also changes all the other independent variables. Thus, in addition to the direct effect, there are the indirect effects on y of the changes in the x_i's due to the change in x_j. The term dx_i/dx_j measures the change in x_i due to a change in x_j, so multiplying this change in x_i by the influence this change has on y, f_i, yields the indirect effect that a change in x_j has on y through the change in x_i. Summing this indirect effect over all x_i, $i \neq j$, yields the indirect effect of x_j on y from the influence x_j has on all the other independent variables.

For the case of $y = f(x_1, x_2)$, the total derivative is

$$\frac{dy}{dx_1} = f_1 + f_2 \frac{dx_2}{dx_1}$$
$$= \text{Direct Effect} + \text{Indirect Effect}.$$

Second-order differential

We obtain the **second-order total differential** of $y = f(x_1, x_2, \ldots, x_k)$ by first taking the total differential of y:

$$dy = f_1\, dx_1 + f_2\, dx_2 + \ldots + f_k\, dx_k.$$

Now, taking the total differential of dy yields the second-order total differential:

$$\begin{aligned} d^2y &= \sum_{j=1}^{k} \sum_{i=1}^{k} f_{ji}\, dx_j\, dx_i \\ &= f_{11}\, dx_1^2 + f_{12}\, dx_1\, dx_2 + \ldots + f_{1k}\, dx_1\, dx_k \\ &\quad + f_{21}\, dx_2\, dx_1 + f_{22}\, dx_2^2 + \ldots + f_{2k}\, dx_2\, dx_k \\ &\quad + \ldots + f_{kk}\, dx_k^2. \end{aligned}$$

The second-order total differential provides an approximate value of the change in the change in the value of the function when all variables are permitted to vary within a small neighborhood. For the case of $y = f(x_1, x_2)$, the second-order total differential is

$$d^2y = f_{11}\, dx_1^2 + 2f_{12}\, dx_1 dx_2 + f_{22}\, dx_2^2.$$

Maximization of functions with several variables

Assuming that the SOC for maximization of one independent variable is satisfied, the FOC for maximization of one variable can be regarded as $dy = 0$ for small changes in x. When $dy = 0$, small changes in x will not increase or decrease y, which indicates the maximum level of y. However, in many cases, a firm or consumer problem involves finding a set of x's, rather than just one x, that will maximize the value of $y = f(x_1, x_2, \ldots, x_k)$.

A firm or consumer might consider changing only one of the x's, say x_1, while holding all others constant. The change in y resulting from this change in x_1 is

$$dy = \frac{\partial f}{\partial x_1} dx_1 = f_1\, dx_1.$$

In other words, the change in y is equal to the change in x_1 times the degree x_1 changes y.

If all x's are varied by a small amount, then the total effect on y will be the total differential of y:

$$dy = \frac{\partial f}{\partial x_1}dx_1 + \frac{\partial f}{\partial x_2}dx_2 + \ldots + \frac{\partial f}{\partial x_k}dx_k$$
$$= f_1\,dx_1 + f_2\,dx_2 + \ldots + f_k\,dx_k.$$

Thus, the total change in y is the sum of changes brought about by varying each of the x's.

Is everyone at the bottom of the valley or on top of a mountain? If it is possible for one individual to change his position and increase or decrease the combined elevation of everyone, then everyone is not at the bottom of the valley or on top of a mountain.

FOCs for a function of several variables

The FOC for a maximum is $dy = 0$ for small changes in the x's. Specifically,

$$f_1 = f_2 = \ldots = f_k = 0$$

is required for $dy = 0$. When all the partial derivatives are zero, dy will be zero and a critical point is reached. The SOC requires that we investigate the second partial derivatives. By design, most functions encountered in this text will obey this SOC, so this condition is not developed here.

Example

As an example of determining the maximum of a function with several variables, consider

$$y = 4x_1 - x_1^2 + 6x_2 - x_2^2 + 5.$$

The FOCs are

$$\partial y/\partial x_1 = 4 - 2x_1^* = 0,$$
$$\partial y/\partial x_2 = 6 - 2x_2^* = 0.$$

Solving these two equations for x_1 and x_2 yields

$$x_1^* = 2 \quad \text{and} \quad x_2^* = 3,$$

where the asterisk * denotes the critical value. Thus, the function has a critical point at $x_1^* = 2$ and $x_2^* = 3$, which results in $y^* = 18$.

Constrained maximization

Lagrangian

The Lagrangian is the missile for hitting economic targets.

(Michael Wetzstein)

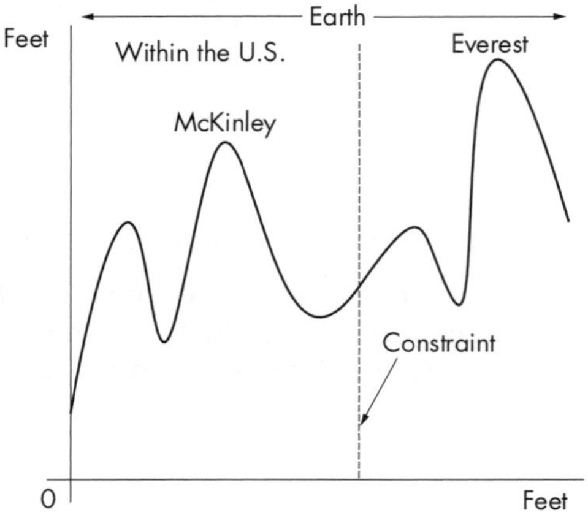

Figure A.12 **Geographic analogy of constrained maxima.** On earth, the tallest mountain above sea level is Mount Everest; however, limiting (constraining) mountains to only within the United States results in Mount McKinley being the tallest.

In the preceding section, our discussion centered on finding the maximum value of a function f without restricting the choices of the x's available. This is termed global maximization. However, many maximization problems involve some restrictions on the choice of variables. For example, as illustrated in Figure A.12, the highest mountain on earth is Mount Everest. If we constrain the search to only the United States, the highest mountain is Mount McKinley.

In economic problems, not all values for the x's are generally permissible. For example, consumers are constrained by their budgets, which limit their consumption of commodities. Such constraints necessarily cannot increase the maximum value for the function to be maximized, and will lower the maximum value if a constraint prevents obtaining the global maximum.

Are you subject to any constraints? Yes, your limited income constrains you from satisfying all your desires.

One method for solving constrained maximization problems is the Lagrange multiplier method. To develop this method, we recall the FOCs for an unconstrained maximum

$$f_1 = f_2 = \ldots = f_k = 0.$$

We solve the k equations and k unknowns for the optimal values of the x's, the critical point. When the x's are constrained, however, there is at least one additional equation—the constraint—but no additional variables. The set of equations is thus over-determined. The Lagrangian technique introduces an additional variable—the Lagrange multiplier—which not only helps in solving the problem but also has a useful economic interpretation. Specifically, for only one constraint, consider

$$\max y = \max f(x_1, x_2, \ldots, x_k)$$

subject to (s.t.)

$$g(x_1, x_2, \ldots, x_k) = 0,$$

where $f(x_1, x_2, \ldots, x_k)$ is called the **objective function** to be maximized and $g(x_1, x_2, \ldots, x_k) = 0$ is called the **constraint**. The first step in the Lagrange multiplier method is setting up the expression

$$\mathcal{L}(x_1, x_2, \ldots, x_k, \lambda) = f(x_1, x_2, \ldots, x_k) + \lambda g(x_1, x_2, \ldots, x_k),$$

which is called the **Lagrangian**. The variable λ is the additional variable called the **Lagrange multiplier**. Note that when the constraint is satisfied $[g(x_1, x_2, \ldots, x_k) = 0]$, $\mathcal{L}$ and f have the same values. Thus, finding the maximum of $\mathcal{L}$ is equivalent to finding the maximum value of f that satisfies the constraint.

The FOCs for finding the maximum value of $\mathcal{L}$ are the unconstrained conditions

$$\begin{aligned}
\partial\mathcal{L}/\partial x_1 &= f_1 + \lambda^* g_1 = 0, \\
\partial\mathcal{L}/\partial x_2 &= f_2 + \lambda^* g_2 = 0, \\
&\vdots \\
\partial\mathcal{L}/\partial x_k &= f_k + \lambda^* g_k = 0, \\
\partial\mathcal{L}/\partial \lambda &= g(x_1, x_2, \ldots, x_k) = 0.
\end{aligned}$$

The last FOC guarantees that the constraint will be satisfied. Solving these $k+1$ equations for the $k+1$ unknowns will yield the optimal values of x_1, …, x_k plus λ, subject to the constraint being satisfied.

Example

As an example, consider maximizing the function

$$y = 4x_1 - x_1^2 + 6x_2 - x_2^2 + 5 \text{ s.t. } 3 - x_1 - x_2 = 0.$$

The Lagrangian is then

$$\mathcal{L}(x_1, x_2, \lambda) = 4x_1 - x_1^2 + 6x_2 - x_2^2 + 5 + \lambda(3 - x_1 - x_2).$$

The FOCs are

$$\begin{aligned}
\partial\mathcal{L}/\partial x_1 &= 4 - 2x_1^* - \lambda^* = 0, \\
\partial\mathcal{L}/\partial x_2 &= 6 - 2x_2^* - \lambda^* = 0, \\
\partial\mathcal{L}/\partial \lambda &= 3 - x_1^* - x_2^* = 0.
\end{aligned}$$

Solving the three equations for the three unknowns, by solving the first two equations for λ and then equating them, yields

$$\begin{aligned}
4 - 2x_1^* = \lambda^* &= 6 - 2x_2^*, \\
x_1^* &= x_2^* - 1.
\end{aligned}$$

Substituting this value for x_1^* into the constraint yields

$$x_2^* = 2, \quad x_1^* = 1, \quad \lambda^* = 2, \quad y^* = 16.$$

Referring to a text on mathematics for economists will provide a discussion on the SOCs.

Multiple constraints

In general, a problem may have more than one constraint, which may affect the optimal solution. In the example involving determination of the highest mountain, an additional constraint could be requiring the top of the mountain to be tree-covered. This would prevent Mount McKinley from being considered as a possible solution. For mathematical problems involving the Lagrangian, each additional constraint requires an additional Lagrange multiplier. If there are m constraints, then a maximization problem would be

$$\begin{aligned}
\max y = \max f(x_1, x_2, \ldots, x_k) \\
\text{s.t.} \\
g^1(x_1, x_2, \ldots, x_k) = 0, \\
g^2(x_1, x_2, \ldots, x_k) = 0, \\
\vdots \\
g^m(x_1, x_2, \ldots, x_k) = 0.
\end{aligned}$$

Given the Lagrange multipliers $\lambda_1, \lambda_2, \ldots, \lambda_m$ associated with these constraints, the Lagrangian is then

$$\begin{aligned}
\mathcal{L}(x_1, x_2, \ldots, x_k, \lambda_1, \lambda_2, \ldots, \lambda_m) = f(x_1, x_2, \ldots, x_k) + \lambda_1 g^1(x_1, x_2, \ldots, x_k) \\
+ \lambda_2 g^2(x_1, x_2, \ldots, x_k) + \ldots + \lambda_m g^m(x_1, x_2, \ldots, x_k).
\end{aligned}$$

The FOCs are

$$\begin{aligned}
\partial\mathcal{L}/\partial x_1 &= f_1 + \lambda_1 g_1^1 + \lambda_2 g_1^2 + \ldots + \lambda_m g_1^m = 0, \\
\partial\mathcal{L}/\partial x_2 &= f_2 + \lambda_1 g_2^1 + \lambda_2 g_2^2 + \ldots + \lambda_m g_2^m = 0, \\
&\vdots \\
\partial\mathcal{L}/\partial x_k &= f_k + \lambda_1 g_k^1 + \lambda_2 g_k^2 + \ldots + \lambda_m g_k^m = 0, \\
\partial\mathcal{L}/\partial \lambda_1 &= g^1(x_1, x_2, \ldots, x_k) = 0, \\
\partial\mathcal{L}/\partial \lambda_2 &= g^2(x_1, x_2, \ldots, x_k) = 0, \\
&\vdots \\
\partial\mathcal{L}/\partial \lambda_m &= g^m(x_1, x_2, \ldots, x_k) = 0,
\end{aligned}$$

where $g_j^i = \partial g^i/\partial x_j$ for all $i = 1, 2, \ldots, m$ and $j = 1, 2, \ldots, k$. Solving these $k + m$ unknowns will yield the optimal values of $x_1, x_2, \ldots, x_k$, subject to the m constraints.

Example

As an example, consider the following maximization problem:

$$\max y = \max (x_1 x_2 x_3) \quad \text{s.t.} \quad x_1^2 + x_2^2 + x_3^2 = 3 \quad \text{and} \quad x_1 x_2 - x_3 = 0.$$

The Lagrangian is then

$$\mathcal{L}(x_1, x_2, x_3, \lambda_1, \lambda_2) = x_1 x_2 x_3 + \lambda_1 \left(3 - x_1^2 - x_2^2 - x_3^2\right) + \lambda_2 (x_1 x_2 - x_3).$$

The FOCs are

$$\begin{aligned}
\partial \mathcal{L}/\partial x_1 &= x_2^* x_3^* - \lambda_1^* 2 x_1^* + \lambda_2^* x_2^* = 0, \\
\partial \mathcal{L}/\partial x_2 &= x_1^* x_3^* - \lambda_1^* 2 x_2^* + \lambda_2^* x_1^* = 0, \\
\partial \mathcal{L}/\partial x_3 &= x_1^* x_2^* - \lambda_1^* 2 x_3^* - \lambda_2^* = 0, \\
\partial \mathcal{L}/\partial \lambda_1 &= 3 - x_1^{*2} - x_2^{*2} - x_3^{*2} = 0, \\
\partial \mathcal{L}/\partial \lambda_2 &= x_1^* x_2^* - x_3^* = 0.
\end{aligned}$$

The five equations and five unknowns may be solved by collecting terms in the first two FOCs:

$$\begin{aligned}
x_2^* \left(x_3^* + \lambda_2^*\right) &= 2\lambda_1^* x_1^*, \\
x_1^* \left(x_3^* + \lambda_2^*\right) &= 2\lambda_1^* x_2^*.
\end{aligned}$$

Taking the ratio of these two equations yields

$$\begin{aligned}
\frac{x_2^* \left(x_3^* + \lambda_2^*\right)}{x_1^* \left(x_3^* + \lambda_2^*\right)} &= \frac{2\lambda_1^* x_1^*}{2\lambda_1^* x_2^*}, \\
x_2^*/x_1^* &= x_1^*/x_2^*, \\
x_1^* &= x_2^*.
\end{aligned}$$

Substituting the condition $x_1^* = x_2^*$ into the fourth FOC results in

$$2x_1^{*2} + x_3^{*2} = 3.$$

Solving for x_1^{*2},

$$x_1^{*2} = \tfrac{1}{2}\left(3 - x_3^{*2}\right).$$

From the last FOC, $x_1^{*2} = x_3^*$, substitution yields

$$x_3^* = \tfrac{1}{2}\left(3 - x_3^{*2}\right).$$

Solving for x_3^* gives $x_3^* = 1, x_1^* = 1$, and $x_2^* = 1$.

Interpretation of the Lagrange multiplier

How does the missile work?

(Michael Wetzstein)

We develop the interpretation of the Lagrange multiplier by rewriting the first k FOCs from the single-constraint case as

$$\frac{f_1}{-g_1} = \frac{f_2}{-g_2} = \ldots = \frac{f_k}{-g_k} = \lambda^*.$$

At the maximum critical point, the ratio of f_j to g_j is the same for every x_j. The function f_j is the marginal value of each x to the function f. This is the marginal value that one more unit of x_j will have for the function to be maximized.

We can interpret the terms $g_j = \partial g/\partial x_j$, for all $j = 1, 2, \ldots, k$, by taking the total differential of the constraint $g(x_1, x_2, \ldots, x_k) = 0$:

$$g_1\, dx_1 + g_2\, dx_2 + \ldots + g_k\, dx_k = 0.$$

Increasing x_1 by 1 unit, $dx_1 = 1$, gives

$$g_1 + g_2\, dx_2 + \ldots + g_k\, dx_k = 0.$$

Then, solving for $-g_1$ yields

$$-g_1 = g_2\, dx_2 + \ldots + g_k\, dx_k.$$

This indicates how the x's other than x_1 must change for the constraint to continue to hold when x_1 is increased by 1 unit. For example, when a consumer facing an income constraint increases her consumption of food, the consumption of some other goods and services must decline. Otherwise, she will exceed her income. Thus, the expression $-g_1$ represents the marginal cost necessary for an increase in x_1. This marginal cost is the loss in the value of the objective function from a reduction in the x's other than x_1 necessary to increase x_1.

The Lagrange multiplier λ at the optimal choices for the x's is then the ratio of the marginal benefit of increasing x_j to the marginal cost of increasing x_j. This is the benefit/cost ratio for x_j:

$$\lambda^* = \frac{f_j}{-g_j} = \frac{\text{marginal benefit of } x_j}{\text{marginal cost of } x_j} \quad \text{for all } j = 1, \ldots, k.$$

At the optimum, this ratio is the same for every x. If it were not the same, then it would be possible to change the values of the x's in such a way to increase the value of the objective function.

If the constraint were relaxed slightly, it would not matter which x is changed. The Lagrange multiplier then provides a measure of how such an overall relaxation of the constraint would affect the value of y. The multiplier λ is the value of the constraint. A high λ indicates that y could be increased substantially by relaxing the constraint, because each x has a high benefit/cost ratio. For example, in the problem with one constraint $\lambda^* = 2$, relaxing the constant by 1 unit from 3 to 4 will increase y by approximately 2, from 16 to 17.5. Specifically, the Lagrange multiplier is the derivative of the objective function with respect to the constraint: $\lambda^* = d(\text{objective function})/d(\text{constraint})$.

Direct substitution with one constraint

We can also solve constrained maximization problems by directly substituting the constraint into the objective function. For example, again consider the problem of maximizing

$$y = 4x_1 - x_1^2 + 6x_2 - x_2^2 + 5 \quad \text{s.t.} \quad 3 - x_1 - x_2 = 0.$$

We can solve the constraint for x_1,

$$x_1 = 3 - x_2,$$

and substitute into the objective function

$$y = 4x_1 - x_1^2 + 6x_2 - x_2^2 + 5.$$

This results in

$$\max_{x_2} y(x_2) = \max_{x_2} \left[4(3 - x_2) - (3 - x_2)^2 + 6x_2 - x_2^2 + 5\right].$$

The objective function is now transformed by the constraint being incorporated into the objective function. The objective function is solely a function of x_2 without any constraints and may be maximized as a single-variable function without a constraint. The FOC is then

$$\frac{dy}{dx_2} = -4 + 2\left(3 - x_2^*\right) + 6 - 2x_2^* = 0.$$

Solving for x_2^* gives $x_2^* = 2$, and $x_1^* = 1$.

The SOC is

$$\frac{d^2y}{dx_2^2} = -2 - 2 = -4 < 0, \quad \text{therefore a maximum.}$$

Fence building example

Suppose that a manager of a public park has 2000 linear feet of fencing material and wishes to use this material to enclose the largest possible rectangular park. The problem is determining how long and wide the park should be. Let x_L represent the length and x_W the width of the park. Thus, the manager wants to determine the length x_L and width x_W that maximize

$$\text{area} = x_L x_W \quad \text{s.t.} \quad 2x_L + 2x_W = 2000.$$

The Lagrangian is

$$\mathcal{L}(x_L, x_W, \lambda) = x_L x_W + \lambda(2000 - 2x_L - 2x_W).$$

The FOCs are then

$$\partial \mathcal{L}/\partial x_L = x_W^* - 2\lambda^* = 0,$$

$$\partial \mathcal{L}/\partial x_W = x_L^* - 2\lambda^* = 0,$$

$$\partial \mathcal{L}/\partial \lambda = 2000 - 2x_L^* - 2x_W^* = 0.$$

We then solve the three FOCs for the three unknowns. One method is to add $2\lambda^*$ to both sides of the first two FOCs and then take the ratio

$$x_W^*/x_L^* = 2\lambda^*/2\lambda^* = 1.$$

This reduces to $x_W^* = x_L^*$. Substituting this result into the third FOC (the constraint) results in

$$4x_L^* = 2000.$$

Solving for x_L^* gives $x_W^* = x_L^* = 500$. We then determine the Lagrange multiplier by substituting the optimal values for x_W or x_L into the first or second FOCs:

$$500 - 2\lambda^* = 0,$$
$$\lambda^* = 250.$$

Figure A.13 shows the effect that increasing fencing material by 1 foot has on the area. The resulting increase in area is

$$4\{(1/8)[500 + (1/8)]\} = 250.0625,$$

which matches the value of the Lagrange multiplier $\lambda^* = d(\text{area})/d(\text{fencing}) = 250$.

Alternatively, we could solve this fencing problem by directly substituting the constraint into the objective function. For example, solving the constraint for x_W yields

$$x_W = \frac{2000 - 2x_L}{2}$$
$$= 1000 - x_L.$$

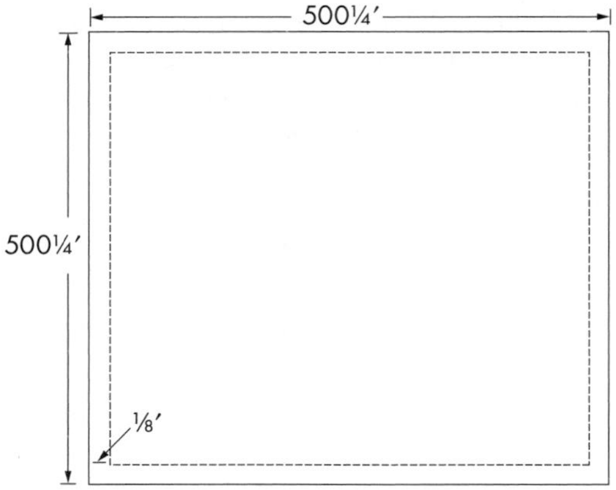

Figure A.13 **Fenced area with a one-foot increase in fencing.** Relaxing the constraint with a one-foot increase in fencing material yields a 250-square-foot increase in area, so $\lambda^* = 250$.

The objective function then becomes

$$\begin{aligned}\text{area} &= x_L(1000 - x_L), \\ &= 1000x_L - x_L^2.\end{aligned}$$

The FOC is

$$\frac{d(\text{area})}{dx_L} = 1000 - 2x_L^* = 0.$$

Solving for x_L^* gives $x_L^* = 500$, so $x_W^* = 500$. This is the same solution that we found using the Lagrangian method.

Economics example

Consider a firm interested in producing 250 units of an output, with labor and capital as inputs. Let L be the number of workers it hires, with a wage rate per worker of \$2, and let K be the quantity of capital, with a per-unit rental rate of \$1. The firm's objective is to minimize cost subject to producing 250 units of output. The cost equation (called an isocost equation) is

$$2L + K = \text{TC},$$

where TC denotes total cost.

The firm will combine labor L with capital K to produce an output q. We represent the technology that the firm can use to produce q with L and K by the function $q = 5LK$ (called a production function). For minimizing cost given 250 units of output, the firm must find the least-cost combination of L and K. To solve this problem, we first put the production function in implicit form:

$$q - 5LK = 0.$$

The Lagrangian is then

$$\mathcal{L}(L, K, \lambda) = 2L + K + \lambda(q - 5LK).$$

If the constraint is always satisfied, then the expression in parentheses ($q - 5LK$) will be equal to zero, so the Lagrangian expression will behave exactly in the same way as does the isocost equation (the objective function).

Is this economics or mathematics? Both: the procedure is mathematics as a tool for finding solutions to economic problems.

The three unknowns in this problem are L, K, and λ. We solve for the three unknowns by partially differentiating with respect to each of them, setting the three resulting equations equal to zero, and then solving these three equations for the three unknown values.

The FOCs are

$$\left.\begin{aligned}\frac{\partial \mathcal{L}}{\partial L} &= 2 - 5\lambda^* K^* = 0,\\ \frac{\partial \mathcal{L}}{\partial K} &= 1 - 5\lambda^* L^* = 0,\end{aligned}\right\} \Rightarrow 2L^* = K^*,$$

$$\frac{\partial \mathcal{L}}{\partial \lambda} = q - 5L^* K^* = 0.$$

Substituting $K^* = 2L^*$ into the third equation gives

$$q - 5L^*(2L^*) = 0,$$

$$L^{*2} = q/10.$$

Recalling that $q = 250$, we have

$$L^* = 5, K^* = 10, \quad \text{and} \quad \lambda^* = 1/25.$$

The minimum cost of producing 250 units of output is then $\text{TC}^* = \$20$. Note that the constraint is automatically guaranteed to be satisfied as the third FOC. The variable λ^* in this case is marginal cost, $\partial\text{TC}/\partial q$. Total cost TC is the level of the objective function and output q is the level of the constraint. Reducing output by 1 unit will lower TC by 1/25. This optimal solution is illustrated in Figure A.14, which is examined in detail in Chapters 9 and 10. The least-cost combination of inputs is $L^* = 5$ and $K^* = 10$, with \$20 as the minimum cost of producing $q = 250$.

Convexity

May the walls of the Grand Canyon be represented as a convex or a concave function?
(Michael Wetzstein)

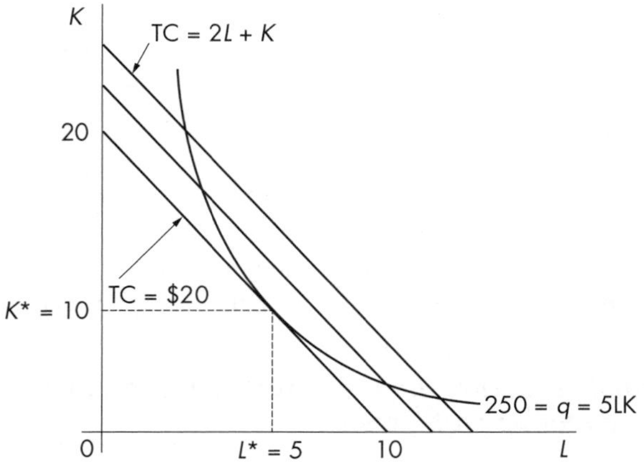

Figure A.14 **Minimizing cost for a given level of output.** The least-cost combination of labor and capital, for a given level of output $q = 250$, is $L^* = 5$ and $K^* = 10$.

A function $f(x)$ is defined as being **convex** over the interval (a, b) if

$$f\left(\alpha x' + (1-\alpha)x''\right) \leq \alpha f\left(x'\right) + (1-\alpha) f\left(x''\right) \text{ for all } a \leq x', x'' \leq b \text{ and all } 0 \leq \alpha \leq 1.$$

It is **strictly convex** over the interval if the strict inequality, $<$, holds for all $0 < \alpha < 1$.

A function is defined as being **concave** over the interval (a, b) if

$$f\left(\alpha x' + (1-\alpha)x''\right) \geq \alpha f\left(x'\right) + (1-\alpha) f\left(x''\right) \text{ for all } 0 \leq \alpha \leq 1,$$

and **strictly concave** if the strict inequality, $>$, holds for all $0 < \alpha < 1$.

Illustrations of concave and convex functions are provided in Figure A.15. A linear function is both convex and concave, but not strictly convex or concave. Figure A.16 illustrates strictly concave and convex functions.

Satisfaction of the FOCs at the critical point on an interval in which a twice-differentiable function is strictly concave (convex) is a necessary and sufficient condition for the existence of a maximum (minimum) at that critical point.

Useful quantitative relations

A number of relations among total, average, and marginal values are often employed in economic theory. As an illustration of these relations, let $f(x)$ be a continuous and differentiable function of the variable x. The marginal value MV(x) is then defined as

$$\mathrm{MV}(x) = \frac{df(x)}{dx}.$$

This marginal value is the change in the total, $f(x)$, given a small change in x, holding all other variables constant.

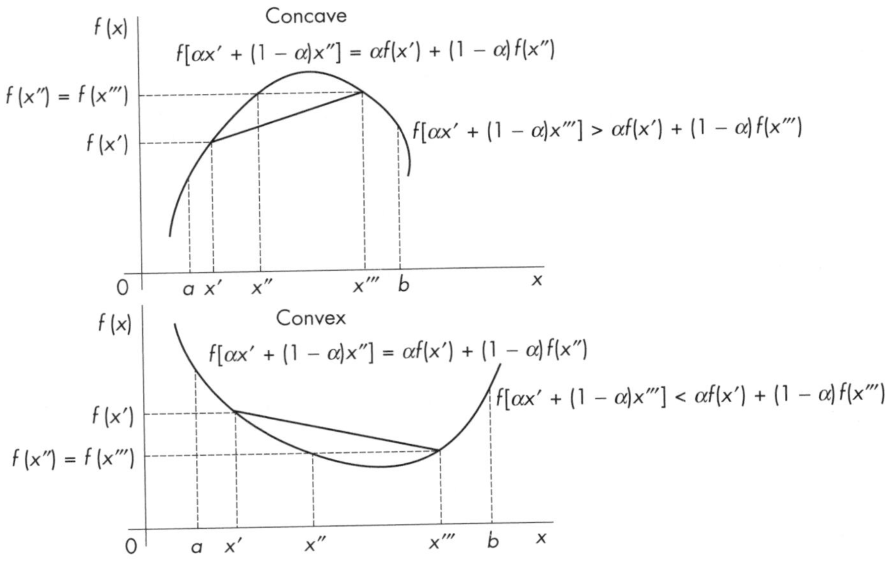

Figure A.15 **Concave and convex functions are functions where linear segments within the interval are possible.** Within the interval between x'' and x', the functions are linear.

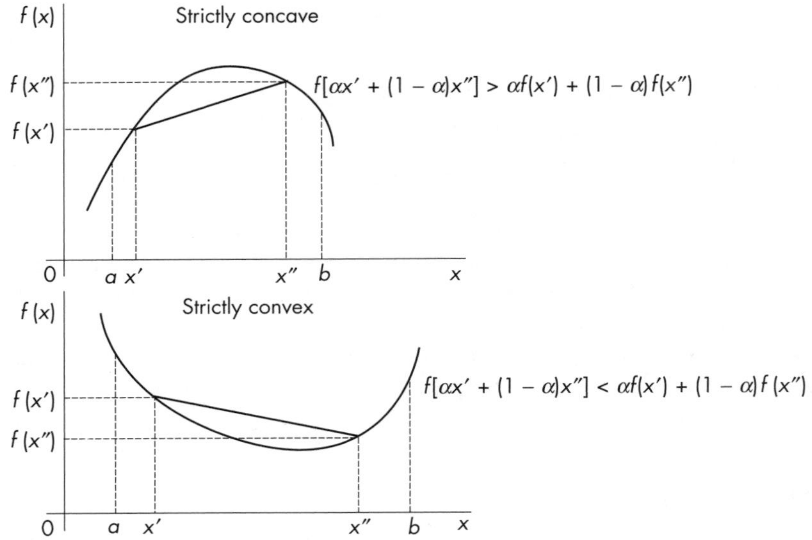

Figure A.16 **Strictly concave and convex functions are functions where no linear segments within the interval exist.** Throughout the interval *a* to *b*, there are no linear segments along the curves.

Relation I

Given that the derivative of a constant is zero, the marginal value is unchanged by adding a constant *a* to the total value:

$$\frac{d[f(x)+a]}{dx} = \frac{df(x)}{dx}.$$

For example, let $f(x) = x^2$; then $df(x)/dx = 2x$. Adding 5 to $f(x)$ does not change the derivative:

$$d(x^2+5)/dx = 2x.$$

We can write the total, $f(x)$, in terms of a variable value and a fixed value:

$$f(x) = g(x) + a,$$

where $g(x)$ is the variable value and a is the fixed value. For example, if the function is short-run total cost, we write it in terms of short-run total variable cost plus total fixed cost. Dividing by x yields

$$\text{AT}(x) = f(x)/x,$$

$$\text{AV}(x) = g(x)/x,$$

$$\text{AF}(x) = a/x,$$

where AT is the average of the total $f(x)$, AV is the average of the variable value, and AF is the average of the fixed value. For example, given $f(x) = x^2 + 5$, then $\mathrm{AT}(x) = x + 5/x$, $\mathrm{AV}(x) = x$ and $\mathrm{AF}(x) = 5/x$.

Relation II

The marginal value intersects the average total value at any critical points of the average.

A critical point for the average total value is where the derivative of this average total value equals zero:

$$\frac{d[f(x)/x]}{dx} = 0.$$

Evaluating this derivative establishes Relation II. Using the product rule of differentiation, we have

$$\frac{1}{x}\frac{df(x)}{dx} - \frac{f(x)}{x^2} = 0.$$

Multiplying through by x gives

$$\frac{df(x)}{dx} - \frac{f(x)}{x} = 0,$$

$$\mathrm{MV}(x) - \mathrm{AT}(x) = 0,$$

$$\mathrm{MV}(x) = \mathrm{AT}(x).$$

Thus, the marginal value equals the average total value at the average total value's critical points. For example, marginal cost equals average total cost at the minimum point of average total cost.

As an example, assume again $f(x) = x^2 + 5$, so $\mathrm{AT}(x) = x + 5/x$ and $\mathrm{MV}(x) = 2x$. Equating $\mathrm{MV}(x)$ to $\mathrm{AT}(x)$ yields

$$2x = x + \frac{5}{x},$$

$$x - \frac{5}{x} = 0,$$

$$1 - \frac{5}{x^2} = 0.$$

This same solution results when taking the derivative of $\mathrm{AT}(x)$ and set it equal to zero:

$$\frac{d\mathrm{AT}(x)}{dx} = 1 - \frac{5}{x^2} = 0.$$

Relation III

If the average (total or variable) value is rising, then the marginal value lies above it; if the average (total or variable) value is falling, then the marginal value lies below it; if the average (total or variable) value is neither rising nor falling, then the marginal value is equal to it.

The average total is increasing if the derivative of the average total value is positive:

$$\frac{d[f(x)/x]}{dx} > 0.$$

Then, according to Relation III,

$$MV(x) > f(x)/x.$$

Again, evaluating the derivative of AT(x),

$$\frac{d[f(x)/x]}{dx} = \frac{1}{x}\frac{df(x)}{dx} - \frac{1}{x^2}f(x) > 0.$$

Multiplying through by x,

$$\frac{df(x)}{dx} - \frac{1}{x}f(x) > 0,$$

$$\text{MV}(x) > f(x)/x.$$

For example, if average total cost is rising, then marginal cost will be above it and if average total cost is falling, then marginal cost will be below it. This general relationship between the average and marginal values is illustrated in Figure A.17. If the marginal value is above the average, then the average is rising. If the marginal value is below the average, then the average is falling. If the marginal value is equal to the average, then the average is neither rising nor falling.

Homogeneous functions

A function $y = f(x_1, x_2)$ is **homogeneous of degree** κ if

$$f(\alpha x_1, \alpha x_2) = \alpha^{\kappa} f(x_1, x_2),$$

where κ is an integer and α is any positive real number. If multiplying the variables of a function by some positive constant α results in the value of the function changing by α^{κ} times the function, then the function is homogeneous of degree κ. For example, the function

$$y = x_1 x_2,$$

is homogeneous of degree $\kappa = 2$:

$$(\alpha x_1)(\alpha x_2) = \alpha^2 x_1 x_2 = \alpha^2 y.$$

If the variables x_1 and x_2 are doubled, $\alpha = 2$, the value of the function will increase by $2^2 = 4$ times.

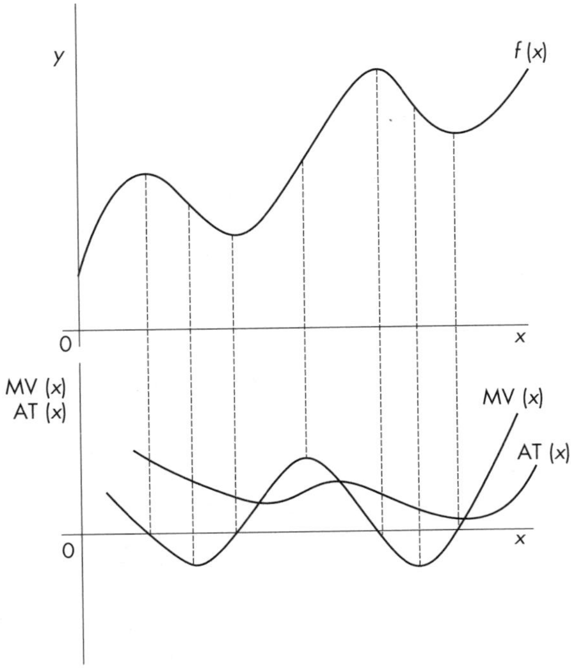

Figure A.17 **Figure A.17 Relationship between the marginal and average values.** If the marginal value is above the average, then the average is rising. If the marginal value is below the average, then the average is falling. If the marginal value is equal to the average, then the average is neither rising nor falling.

Euler's Theorem

Euler's Theorem states that the following condition is satisfied by a homogeneous function $y = f(x_1, x_2)$:

$$x_1 \frac{\partial y}{\partial x_1} + x_2 \frac{\partial y}{\partial x_2} = \kappa f(x_1, x_2),$$

where κ is the degree of homogeneity.

Proof: Given a homogeneous of degree κ function

$$f(\alpha x_1, \alpha x_2) = \alpha^{\kappa} f(x_1, x_2), \alpha > 0,$$

the derivative of this function with respect to α is

$$x_1 f_1(\alpha x_1, \alpha x_2) + x_2 f_2(\alpha x_1, \alpha x_2) = \kappa \alpha^{\kappa-1} f(x_1, x_2),$$

where

$$f_1(\alpha x_1, \alpha x_2) = \frac{\partial f}{\partial(\alpha x_1)},$$

$$f_2(\alpha x_1, \alpha x_2) = \frac{\partial f}{\partial(\alpha x_2)}.$$

Setting $\alpha = 1$, since α can take any positive value, results in

$$x_1 \frac{\partial y}{\partial x_1} + x_2 \frac{\partial y}{\partial x_2} = \kappa f(x_1, x_2).$$

QED (*quod erat demonstrandum*, which was to be demonstrated).

Key concepts

Questions

1. Determine the level of measurement for the following scales:
   a. Consumer price index.
   b. Dow Jones industrial average.
   c. Olympic medals.
   d. Automobile model numbers.
   e. Channels on a cable television system.
   f. Numbers on a telephone.
   g. Numbers on a manual transmission.
   h. Numbers indicating floors in a dormitory.
2. Are the following relationships positive or negative monotonic functions?
   a. Your age and time.
   b. Firm's total cost and output.
   c. A strictly convex function continuously declining toward zero.
3. Interpret in economic terms the Lagrange multiplier that would be associated with the constraint in the following optimization problem:

   A central planner in a developing country wishes to maximize GNP, subject to the constraint that the balance of payments deficit may not exceed a given level.

4. Recalling the interpretation of a Lagrange multiplier, give an economic interpretation of the case $\lambda^* = 0$.
5. Economic theory is based on agents (households and firms) attempting to maximize their satisfaction. What major constraints are they facing?
6. Determine whether each of the following generally are convex, concave, strictly convex, strictly concave, or none of these classifications:
   a. Concrete irrigation ditch.
   b. Roof of a barn.
   c. A balance beam.
   d. A telephone line between two poles.
   e. A river bottom.
   f. A granite hill worn away by erosion.
   g. A hillside with terracing.
7. For each of the items in Question 6, determine whether it is possible to obtain a unique critical point given only the FOCs.
8. How is the partial derivative related to the concept of a marginal unit in economics?
9. Describe, in terms of marginal and average values, how a baseball player's batting average will change if he is in a slump.
10. Do production technologies generally have homogeneous of degree one characteristics? For example, if all inputs are all doubled, will output then also double?

Exercises

Each problem that I solved became a rule which served afterwards to solve other problems.

(Rene Descartes)

1. Given $y = f(x)$, find dy/dx and d^2y/dx^2 for each of the following functions:
   a. $y = 358$;
   b. $y = e^x$;
   c. $y = 9x^3$;
   d. $y = 5e^{6x}$;
   e. $y = 4x^{1/4}$;
   f. $y = x^3 - 2x^2 + x + 5$;
   g. $y = 1/x^3$;
   h. $y = x^3x^2$;
   i. $y = \ln(x^2)$;
   j. $y = e^x(x^3 - 2x + 7)$;
   k. $y = x^3 - (1/x^2)$;
   l. $y = x^a/b$;
   m. $y = e^{-x}$;
   n. $y = x\ln x - x$;
   o. $y = e^{a+bx}$;
   p. $y = \ln(\ln x)$, $x > 1$;
   q. $y = (x^3/3) - (x^2/2) + x - 1$;
   r. $y = e^{5x3}$;
   s. $y = (2x + 5)/(3x - 2)$;
   t. $y = 3\ln x - b$;
   u. $y = x^e$;
   v. $y = a\ln x^e$;
   w. $y = 2^x$.
2. Given $y = f(x)$, find the relative maxima and relative minima, if they exist, for each of the following functions:
   a. $y = 4x^2 - 8x$;
   b. $y = 8x - 2x^2$;
   c. $y = x^3$;
   d. $y = x^2 - 6x + 10$;
   e. $y = -3x^2 + 4x - 2$;
   f. $y = 358$;
   g. $y = 2x - (1/x)$;
   h. $y = 2x^3 - 24x^2 + 10$;
   i. $y = b\ln x$, $b > 0$.
3. Given $y = f(x_1, x_2)$, find f_1, f_2, f_{12}, and f_{21} for each of the following functions. Also, verify that $f_{12} = f_{21}$ for each function.
   a. $y = x_1x_2$;
   b. $y = x_1/x_2$;
   c. $y = \exp(x_1/x_2)$;
   d. $y = x_1^4x_2^3 + \exp\left(x_1^2x_2\right)$;
   e. $y = 2x_1 + 3x_2 + x_1^2 + \ln\left(x_1^2 + x_2^2\right)$;
   f. $y = x_1/\left(x_1^2 + x_2^3\right)$;
   g. $y = x_1^2x_2^2$;
   h. $y = \left(x_1^2 + x_2\right)/(x_1 + x_2)$;
   i. $y = x_1\ln x_2$;
   j. $y = x_1^2e^{x_2}$;
   k. $y = x_1^{x_2}$;
   l. $y = x_1^{1/2}x_2^{1/2}$;
   m. $y = (x_1 + x_2)/(x_1 + x_2)^2$.
4. Find the total differentials of the functions in Exercise 3.
5. Using the method of direct substitution and Lagrange multipliers, find the maximum or minimum values of the following functions $f(x_1, x_2)$ subject to the constraint $g(x_1, x_2) = 0$:

a. $f(x_1, x_2) = x_1 x_2, \quad g(x_1, x_2) = 2 - (x_1 + x_2);$

b. $f(x_1, x_2) = x_1 + x_2, \quad g(x_1, x_2) = 1 - x_1 x_2;$

c. $f(x_1, x_2) = x_1 x_2, \quad g(x_1, x_2) = I - p_1 x_1 - p_2 x_2,$

where p_1, p_2, and I are parameters;

d. $f(x_1, x_2) = wx_1 + vx_2, \quad g(x_1, x_2) = q - x_1 x_2,$

where w, v, and q are parameters.

6. Carly must decide how to allocate her time in answering the questions on a Microeconomics Examination. Let

Q = total number of questions,
T = total number of minutes,
P_q = the maximum number of points a student can earn on the qth question,
f_q = the fraction of P_q a student actually earns on the qth question,
t_q = the amount of time Carly spends on answering the qth question,
A_q = Carly's ability to answer the qth question,

where f_q is a strictly increasing concave function of t_q and a strictly increasing concave function of A_q. Assume that Carly wishes to allocate her time to maximize the total number of points she receives on the examination.

a. State Carly's maximization problem.
b. Derive the FOCs.
c. Can it be optimal for Carly to leave the exam early? Explain.

7. During a day, Miss Sweets enjoys consuming candy C and donuts D, represented by

$$U(C, D) = 20C - 2C^2 + 18D - 3D^2.$$

a. For her to maximize her satisfaction, how much candy and donuts does she consume during a day?
b. Unfortunately, Miss Sweets is now a diabetic and must curtail her consumption of candy and donuts to only three a day. How does this constraint affect her consumption decisions?

8. Nomadic tribes have a serious portability problem, so they are somewhat reluctant to acquire heavy material possessions. Let x_1 and x_2 denote possessions that the nomads transport, with associated per-unit prices p_1 and p_2 and total income I. Each of these goods also has an associated weight per unit, denoted by w_1 and w_2 and a total carrying capacity W. Consider the nomads' income and carrying capacity as multiple constraints with the objective of maximizing their satisfaction represented by the function $U(x_1, x_2)$. Derive and interpret the FOCs for this problem.

9. Determine if the following functions are convex or concave:
   a. $y = 5x + 10$;
   b. $y = 2x^2 - 4x$;
   c. $y = -2x^2 + 12x$;
   d. $y = \ln x$;
   e. $y = e^x$.

10. For the short-run total cost function

$$STC = \tfrac{1}{6}q^3 - q^2 + 4q + 36,$$

show that marginal cost intersects average total cost and average variable cost at their minimum points.

Internet case studies

1. Distinguish among the different measurement scales and state the appropriate test statistics to use for deriving inferences.
2. Discuss the implications of isomorphic representations.
3. Provide a biography of Henry Briggs.

Glossary

Absolute advantage. The input cost for the additional production of a commodity is lower for the firm (country) compared with another firm (country).

Actuarially fair games. The cost of playing the game is equivalent to the game's expected value.

Actuarially favorable. The cost of an asset is less than the asset's expected value.

Adverse selection (hidden information). An informed agent's decision depends on unobservable characteristics that adversely affect uninformed agents.

Affiliation. A bidder's estimated value for a commodity increases as other bidders' estimates increase.

Agent. A household or firm within an economy.

Allocation Condition 1 (opportunity cost condition). No more of one output can be produced without having to cut back on the production of other commodities.

Allocation Condition 2 (marginal product condition). Resources should be allocated to the point where the marginal product of any resource in the production of a particular commodity is the same no matter which firm produces the commodity.

Allocation Condition 3 (comparative advantage condition). If two or more firms produce the same outputs, they must operate at points on their respective production possibility frontiers where their marginal rates of product transformation are equal.

Allocative efficiency. Employing the least-cost combination of inputs for a given level of output.

Analytical solution. Solving a mathematical model with algebra.

Antitrust. Prohibiting the establishment and operation of cartels.

Applied economics. The application of economic theory and statistics, combined with a knowledge of institutions, to explain the behavior of real world phenomena.

Arbitrage. The ability to buy in one market and then sell in another market at a higher price.

Arrow's Impossibility Theorem. A social preference ranking satisfying a set of reasonable axioms is impossible, given an ordinal ranking of individual agent preferences.

Art of economics. Relating the conclusions derived from positive economics to the goals determined in normative economics.

Asset. The title to receive commodities or monetary returns at some period in time.

Assumptions. Statements about the conditions of some system.

Asymmetric information. Market information varies across agents.

Auction. For a thin market commodity, agents state a bid they are willing to pay (sell), and the agent with the highest (lowest) bid purchases (sells) the commodity.

Average fixed cost (AFC). Total fixed cost divided by output.

Average input cost (AIC). The per-unit cost of a given amount of an input.

Average product (AP). Output divided by an input.

Average revenue (AR). Revenue per unit of output.

Backward-bending labor supply curve. A labor supply curve illustrating how at some point further increases in wages will result in a decrease in hours worked.

Backward induction. In a game tree, the equilibrium strategies are determined by working backward toward the root.

Bad (or undesirable) commodity. More of the commodity is not preferred to less.

Bandwagon effect. Individual demand is based on the number of other households consuming a commodity.

Barriers to entry. Obstacles that allow existing firms to earn pure profits without a threat of entry by other firms.

Bayesian game. A game where players have imperfect knowledge about each other's strategies and payoffs.

Behavioral economics. A field of economics that relaxes assumptions on economic behavior by incorporating findings from related disciplines such as psychology and sociology.

Bertrand model. An oligopoly model that assumes firms base their price decisions on zero conjectural variations on prices.

Bidding (pools) rings. Buyers form a group (pool) who do not bid against each other.

Bilateral externality. Two agents with one agent's utility affected by the other agent's actions.

Bilateral monopoly. A monopoly selling its output to a monopsony.

Black market. Selling a commodity in violation of some law.

Budget line or budget constraint. A set of bundles that exhaust a household's income.

Bundling. Requiring consumers to purchase a set of commodities rather than some subset of the commodities.

Cardinal utility. The ability of a household to determine the change in magnitude of satisfaction between bundles.

Cartel. A collusive agreement among agents.

Ceiling price. An established price maximum (ceiling) where the selling price is not allowed to rise above it.

Certainty equivalent (C). The amount of return C a household would receive from a certain outcome so that it is indifferent between a risky outcome and this certain outcome.

Ceteris paribus. With all other factors remaining the same.

Coase Theorem. If a market can be established for an externality, an efficient outcome will result, regardless of how property rights are allocated.

Collusion. A joint strategy among a set of players that improves their payoff.

Commodity. A particular good or service delivered at a specific time and at a specific location.

Commodity bundle. A set of commodities that a household may consume.

Commodity space. The set of all possible commodity bundles.

Commodity tax (τ). A payment increasing what consumers pay for a commodity above the price that firms receive for supplying the commodity.

Common property. A resource owned in common by all the agents in an economy.

Comparative advantage. The sacrifice in terms of other commodities for the additional production of a commodity is lower for the firm (country) compared with another firm (country).

Comparative statics analysis. Investigating a change in one parameter, holding all other parameters constant.

Compensation principle. Compensating agents who are harmed by the selection of a choice, so by this selection no agent is made worse off and at least one agent is made better off.

Complete, perfect, or first-degree price discrimination. Selling each unit of a commodity for the maximum price that a consumer is willing to pay.

Composite commodity (numeraire commodity). A group of commodities represented as one combined commodity.

Conjectural variation. A firm's expectation of how another firm's action (output) will change as a result of its own actions (change in output).

Constant-cost industry. A market with a horizontal long-run supply curve.

Constant returns to scale. A proportional change in inputs results in the same proportional change in output.

Constant returns to scope. No gains from jointly producing products.

Consumer Price Index (CPI). An index that states the amount of income required in the current year to purchase the same consumption bundle in some base year.

Consumer sovereignty. Consumers' preferences are reflected in the market.

Consumer surplus (CS). The net benefit that a consumer receives from a commodity.

Consumers. Households or firms purchasing commodities for direct consumption or as inputs in a production process.

Contestable markets. Markets characterized by little or no firm sunk costs, so firms set price equal to average cost to prevent entrant firms employing hit-and run-tactics.

Contingent commodity. A commodity whose level of consumption depends on which state of nature occurs.

Contract curve. The locus of Pareto-efficient allocations.

Control. Altering a model's exogenous variables to predict a particular outcome.

Cooperative game theory. A game where binding agreements among agents exist.

Core solution. Points where all gains from trade are exhausted.

Corner solution. An optimal solution at one of the axes.

Cournot model. An oligopoly model that assumes firms base their output decisions on zero conjectural variations.

Cross-price elasticity (ε_{ji}). The percentage change in quantity of commodity x_j given a percentage change in the price of commodity x_i.

Data. A collection of values for model variables.

Deadweight loss (excess burden). The decrease in total surplus that is not transferred to some other agent.

Decreasing-cost industry. A market with a downward-sloping long-run supply curve.

Decreasing returns to scale. A proportional change in inputs results in less of a proportional change in output.

Demand. How much of a commodity consumers are willing and able to purchase at a given price.

Direct demand functions. Quantity demanded is a function of price.

Discount rate (*r*). Rate of return used to compare the value of a dollar received sometime in the future with that of a dollar received today.

Diseconomies of scope (decreasing returns to scope). One firm jointly producing a set of products results in a lower level of output than a set of separate firms each uniquely producing one of the products.

Dominant firm. A firm with a greater influence on the market than other firms in the industry.
Dominant strategy. A strategy that is preferred to another strategy no matter what the other players' strategies are.
Duopoly. A market composed of two firms.
Durable inputs (commodities). Commodities that may not be exhausted in the current production process.
Dutch auction. For buyers (sellers) of a commodity, the price decreases (increases) with the first bidder purchasing (selling) the commodity.
Econometrics. Based on economic theory, the application of mathematical statistics to economic data.
Economic efficiency. The three allocation conditions for Pareto efficiency in production are satisfied along with output efficiency.
Economic rate of substitution or marginal rate of transformation. The market rate at which one commodity can be purchased in place of another, holding income constant.
Economic rent. The portion of total payment to a factor that is in excess of what is required to keep the factor in its current occupation.
Economics. A social science concerned with the allocation of scarce resources for satisfying unlimited wants.
Economics of scope (increasing returns to scope). One firm jointly producing a set of products results in a higher level of output than a set of separate firms each uniquely producing one of the products.
Economy. A group of agents interacting to improve their individual and joint satisfaction.
Edgeworth box. A diagram illustrating the feasible allocations of two commodities between two agents.
Elasticity (ε). A standardized (unit-free) measure of responsiveness.
Elasticity of demand. The percentage change in quantity demanded given a percentage change in price.
Elasticity of substitution (ξ). Measures how easy it is to substitute one input (commodity) for another.
Elasticity of supply. The percentage change in quantity supplied given a percentage change in price.
Emissions standard. A quota on the level of emissions.
Employee buyout. Employees purchasing a company from the owners.
Endogenous variables. Variables whose values are determined within a model and depend on the values of the exogenous variables.
Engel's Law. The proportion of total expenditure devoted to food declines as income rises.
English auction. For buyers (sellers) of a commodity, the price increases (decreases) with the highest (lowest) bidder purchasing (selling) the commodity.
Equitable. No household prefers any other household's initial endowment.
Exogenous variables. Variables whose values are predetermined outside a model.
Expected (von Neumann–Morgenstern) utility function. The weighted average of utility obtained from alternative states of nature.
Explanation. Determining relationships among variables.
Explicit (expenditure) costs. Costs of employing inputs not owned by the firm.
Exploiters. Players who invade a cooperative society and attempt to maximize their payoff given the strategies of the other players.
Extensive form. An extended description of a game.

Externality (*z*). An agent's utility includes commodities whose amounts are determined by other agents who pay no particular attention to the effect on the agent's welfare.

Fair allocation. An equitable and Pareto-efficient allocation.

Fallacy of composition. What is true of the parts is not necessarily true of the whole.

Fallacy of division. What is true of the whole is not necessarily true of the parts.

Finitely repeated game. A game that is repeated a fixed number of times.

Firm. An agent using inputs to produce commodities for consumers.

Firm economic efficiency. A condition where a firm is technologically, allocatively, and scale-efficient.

Firm's short-run supply curve. How much a firm is willing and able to supply at a given price.

First-bid auction. The buyer (seller) who submitted the highest (lowest) bid wins the commodity and pays the bid price.

First-degree (perfect) wage discrimination. Employing each worker at his or her reservation wage.

First Fundamental Theorem of Welfare Economics. Every perfectly competitive allocation is Pareto-optimal.

Free markets. Markets not controlled by any governmental constraints.

Free rider. A consumer who cannot be excluded from receiving the benefits of a nonrival commodity and who is unwilling to pay her portion of the cost.

Full capacity. Average cost of production is at a minimum.

Game. A model representing the strategic interdependence of agents.

Game or payoff matrix. Lists the payoffs associated with each strategy for each player.

Game theory. The theory of how agents interact.

Game tree. A figure representing the extensive form of a game.

General-equilibrium analysis. Analysis of the interaction among agents across markets within an economy.

General-equilibrium model. Modeling the interrelationships among a number of markets or the whole economy.

Giffen good. Price and quantity demanded move in the same direction.

Global bliss (or bliss). A state in which there are no resource constraints and all wants are satisfied.

Good (or desirable) commodity. More of the commodity is preferred to less.

Homothetic preferences. Consumer preferences resulting in the proportion of income spent on a commodity remaining the same at all levels of income.

Household. A group of individuals sharing income for purchasing commodities.

Household's demand curve. A curve illustrating how much of a commodity a household is willing and able to purchase at a given price.

Household's labor supply curve. A labor supply curve illustrating how much labor a household is willing and able to supply at a given wage rate.

Human capital. An individual's abilities and knowledge.

Human-capital production function. A function describing how investment in human capital enhances future income.

Hyperbolic discounting. Discounting outcomes in the short run more than outcomes in the long run.

Hypothesis. A logical conclusion based on a theoretical model.

Idle (empty) threat. Threat by an agent who has no commitment to follow through.

Impatient. Consumer preference of preferring current consumption to postponing consumption into the future.

Imperfect competition. Markets between the polar cases of perfect competition and monopoly.

Imperfect substitutes. As the amount of consumption for a commodity decreases, a household would be willing to substitute more of other commodities for an additional unit of the commodity

Implicit (nonexpenditure, imputed, entrepreneurial) costs. Costs charged to inputs owned by the firm.

Income. The monetary return from resources owned by a household at a given time period.

Income effect. The change in purchasing power resulting from a price change.

Income elasticity (η). The percentage change in quantity given a percentage change in income.

Income subsidy. Direct cash payment to a household.

Increasing-cost industry. A market with an upward-sloping long-run supply curve.

Increasing returns to scale. A proportional change in inputs results in more than a proportional change in output.

Independence Axiom. The preference a household has for one state of nature over another state is independent from other states of nature.

Indifference. A household is just as satisfied consuming one commodity bundle as it is consuming some other commodity bundle.

Indifference curve. A locus of points that yield the same level of utility.

Indifference set. The set of all commodity bundles where a household receives the same level of satisfaction for each bundle consumed.

Industry. A group of firms offering the same or like commodities.

Inferior good. The expenditures on a commodity decline as income increases.

Infinitely repeated game. A game that is repeated forever.

Inflation. A general rise in prices.

Inputs. Factors used in the production of outputs.

Interest rate (i). The rate at which agents can borrow and lend money.

Interior optimum. The utility-maximizing solution results in some of all commodities being consumed.

Interloper. A firm who markets the commodity but is not a member of the cartel.

Intertemporal choice. Consumption choices made over time.

Intertemporal price discrimination. Price discrimination based on different points in time.

Inverse demand functions. Price per unit is a function of quantity demanded.

Investment. Purchase of a capital item.

Invisible hand. The ability of markets to allocate resources without planning or programs by governmental agencies.

Isocost curve. A locus of points where the total cost is the same for alternative input combinations.

Isoprofit curve. A curve representing an equal level of profit for alternative levels of a firm's output.

Isoprofit line. A locus of points where the level of pure profit is the same for various levels of a variable input.

Isoquant. A locus of points that yield the same level of output.

Iterated deletion. Reducing the set of choice strategies based on rational behavior.

Labor market supply curve. The horizontal summation of individual workers' labor supply curves.

Labor union. A cartel of workers with the objective of promoting the interest of the union membership.

Law of Demand. As the price of a commodity declines, quantity demanded for the commodity increases.

Law of Diminishing Marginal Returns. As more of a variable input is added to a constant amount of the fixed inputs, the marginal product of the variable input will eventually decline.

Law of One Price. Given a perfectly competitive market, there is only one market price for a commodity.

Lerner Index (L_I). A measure of the degree of monopoly power.

Limit price analysis. The threat of governmental regulation or entry by other firms into the market restricts a firm from increasing price above marginal cost.

Lindahl price. Each agent's per-unit reservation price for a pure public good.

Local bliss. A state where social welfare is maximized for a given resource constraint.

Long-run average cost (LAC). Long-run total cost divided by output.

Long-run marginal cost (LMC). The additional cost associated with an additional unit increase in output when all inputs are variable.

Long-run period. All inputs are variable.

Long-run total cost (LTC). Total cost when all inputs are variable.

Lump-sum tax. A fixed level of tax independent of the output level.

Lump-sum income tax. A tax on income.

Luxury good. The proportion of income spent on a commodity increases as income rises.

Macroeconomics. Investigates the economy as a whole.

Marginal benefit of the externality (MBE). A decrease in the cost of production when employing more of the externality.

Marginal input cost (MIC). The addition to total input cost from employing an additional unit of an input.

Marginal product (MP). The additional output associated with an additional unit of an input, holding all other inputs constant.

Marginal rate of product transformation (MRPT). The rate at which one output can be substituted for another, holding the level of inputs constant.

Marginal rate of substitution x_2 for x_1 [MRS(x_2 for x_1)]. The rate at which a household is willing to substitute commodity x_2 for x_1.

Marginal rate of technical substitution [MRTS(K for L)]. With a given level of technology, the rate at which a firm can substitute capital for labor, holding output constant.

Marginal rate of time preference. The rate at which a consumer is willing to substitute future consumption for current consumption.

Marginal revenue (MR). The change in total revenue from a change in output.

Marginal revenue product (MRP). The change in total revenue resulting from a change in an input.

Marginal social cost (MSC). An increase in a negative externality increases the cost of an agent affected by the externality.

Marginal utility of income (MU_I). The additional satisfaction received from an additional unit of income.

Marginal utility of x_j (MU_j). The extra utility obtained from consuming slightly more of x_j while holding the amounts consumed of all other commodities constant.

Market. A mechanism for consumers (buyers) and producers (sellers) of a good or service to interact in determining the market price.

Market-clearing price. Market quantity demanded equals quantity supplied.

Market (aggregate) demand. The total amount of demand for a commodity by all households.

Market equilibrium. State of balance in the market.

Market failure. An economic failure (that occurs) when the resulting market is not efficient.

Market niche. A segment of the market that demands a commodity that is slightly differentiated from other commodities.

Market period. All inputs in a production process are fixed.

Market (industry) supply curve. The horizontal summation of individual firms' supply curves.

Maximin strategy. The maximum security value.

Mechanism design. A method for eliciting an agent's preferences for collective decisions.

Microeconomics. Investigates the interactions of individual consumers and producers (agents).

Minimum wage. A price floor below which the wage rate cannot fall.

Mixed strategies. For some strategy set, a player randomly chooses strategies.

Models. Simplified representations of reality.

Monopolistic competition. Firms within a market producing heterogeneous products with relatively easy entry into this market.

Monopoly. Only one firm in an industry.

Monopoly power. A firm's ability to set price above marginal cost.

Monopoly rents. The rent that an entrant would be willing to pay for a monopoly.

Monopsony. Only a single buyer for an input.

Monopsony power. A buyer of an input has some control over the price of the input.

Moral hazard (hidden actions). The actions of an agent affecting another agent (the principal) are hidden from the principal.

Multilateral externalities. Externalities affecting numerous agents.

Multiple plants. The ability of a firm to enhance its profits by having more than one physical plant.

Nash equilibrium. Each player's selected strategy is his or her preferred response to the strategies actually played by all the other players.

Natural monopoly. Market forces result in only one firm in an industry.

Necessary good. The proportion of income spent on a commodity decreases as income rises.

Negative externality. Negative external effects.

Negative network externalities. The value that one household places on a commodity declines as other households purchase the item.

Net present value. The present value of discounting the future costs and returns from an investment to the present.

Net present value criterion. A condition for undertaking an investment if the net present value is positive and known with certainty.

No-arbitrage condition. Markets will result in the same equilibrium rate of return for all investments.

Nominal rate of interest (*i*). Observed market interest rate.

Noncooperative game theory. A game where binding agreements among agents are not assumed.

Nondurable inputs (commodities). Commodities that are exhausted in the current production period.

Normal good. An increase in income results in purchasing more of the commodity.

Normal (necessary, ordinary, opportunity-cost) profit. The minimum total return to the inputs necessary to keep a firm in a given production activity.

Normative economics. The study of what ought to be.

Numeraire price. The relative price against which all other prices and income are compared.

Numerical solution. Solving a mathematical model by computation

Oligopolistic market. A market comprised of a relatively small number of interdependent firms.

Oligopsony. A buyer in a market with only a few other buyers.

Opportunity cost. The cost of increasing the consumption of one commodity measured by the resulting decrease in consumption of another commodity.

Opportunity cost of capital. The profit forgone by not investing financial capital in another activity.

Optimal choice. The point where utility is maximized for a given budget constraint.

Option value. The value of waiting before exercising an option.

Ordinal utility. The ability of a household to rank a set of commodity bundles.

Ordinary good. Price and quantity demanded move in opposite directions.

Outcome. A particular result when undertaking some action.

Output effect. The effect on an input from a change in output resulting from an input price change.

Output efficiency. The condition where the MRS for each household equals the MRPT.

Output elasticity (ω_j). The percentage change in output q given a percentage change in input j.

Paradigm. A theory that has been tested a number of times and its explanatory power accepted.

Pareto-efficient allocation. There is no way to make one agent better off without making some other agent worse off.

Pareto improvement. A reallocation of commodity bundles among agents resulting in at least one agent being made better off without any loss incurred by another agent.

Partial-equilibrium analysis. Only one segment of an economy is analyzed, without consideration of possible interactions with other segments.

Partial-equilibrium model. Modeling one market with limited effects from other markets.

Patient. Willing to postpone some current consumption even for less of it in the future.

Payoff. A reward or consequence of playing a game.

Pecuniary externalities. External effects transmitted through changes in prices.

Perfect complements. Commodities consumed in a fixed proportion.

Perfect (complete) information game. A game where players have perfect knowledge about each other's strategies and payoffs.

Perfect substitutes. A household's willingness to exchange one commodity for another is constant and does not depend on the relative quantities of the commodities consumed.

Perfectly competitive market. Agents have no incentive to alter the market price they face for a product.

Perfectly competitive price system. Agents have no control over the market prices, so they take such prices as given.

Perfectly elastic demand ($\varepsilon_{Q,p} = -\infty$). Quantity demanded is infinitely responsive to a percentage change in price.

Perfectly inelastic demand ($\varepsilon_{Q,p} = 0$). Quantity demanded is not at all responsive to a price change.

Permit. Permission to extract a certain quantity of a resource.

Pigouvian tax. A tax on a negative externality.

Player. An agent in a game.

Positive economics. The study of what is, was, or will be.

Positive externality. Positive external effects.

Positive network externalities. The value that one household places on a commodity increases as other households purchase the item.

Prediction. Deriving conclusions before they are observed.

Preemption game. A games where agents moving first have an advantage.

Present value (PV). The current value of an item received in some future time period.

Price efficiency. When a firm is both allocatively and scale-efficient.

Price leadership. When one firm adjusts its price, all other firms follow suit.

Price maker. An agent who sets the market price.

Price system. All commodities are valued in the market by their money equivalence.

Price taker. An agent who considers the prices associated with the commodities as fixed.

Price wars. All firms attempt to undercut their competitors' prices, resulting in a large decline in price.

Principal. An agent who depends on another agent to undertake some actions.

Principal-agent problem. A problem of moral hazard when the principal depends on an agent to undertake some actions.

Principle of sequential rationality. At any point in a game tree, a player's strategy is consistent with future optimal actions.

Prisoners' Dilemma. A game illustrating the difficulties of obtaining a cooperative solution without some binding agreement.

Private good. A rival commodity, where each additional unit consumed by one consumer results in less of the commodity available for other consumers.

Private property rights. Property entitlements vested with individual agents.

Probability (ρ). The likelihood that an outcome will occur.

Producer surplus (PS). Pure profit plus total fixed cost, which is equivalent to total revenue minus total variable cost.

Product differentiation (D). Commodities closely related, but not identical.

Production. The process of transferring a set of elements into a different set of elements.

Production contract curve (efficiency locus). Locus of Pareto-efficient input allocations.

Production function. Restriction on how inputs are transformed into outputs.

Production possibilities frontier. The locus of Pareto-efficient output levels for a given set of inputs and production technology.

Profit tax. A tax on a firm's profit.

Properties. The traits and attributes of a system.

Property rights. A bundle of entitlements.

Public good. A nonrival commodity, where one consumer's consumption of a commodity does not preclude other consumers from consuming it.

Pure (economic) profit (π). Total revenue minus total cost.

Pure-exchange economy. Households trading, given that they are initially endowed with some quantities of commodities and there is no production.
Pure Nash equilibrium. An equilibrium associated with pure strategies.
Pure private good. A rival and exclusive commodity.
Pure public good. A nonrival and nonexclusive commodity.
Pure strategies. For some strategy set, a player has a 100 percent probability of selecting one strategy.
Quid pro quo. Something for something else.
Quota. Restriction on the volume of a commodity imported.
Rate of return (discount rate) or real interest rate (*r*). Nominal interest rate adjusted for the expected inflation rate.
Rationality. Households can maximize satisfaction by ranking a set of commodity bundles.
Rationalizable strategy. One strategy is preferred to another based on the rational behavior of the other players.
Reaction function. How one firm reacts to a change in another firm's action (output).
Rent-seeking behavior. Expense incurred to obtain and maintain monopoly power.
Reservation price. For a seller, the lowest price that he or she is willing to accept, and for a buyer the highest price that he or she is willing to pay.
Reservation wage. The lowest wage that a worker is willing to accept to work in a given occupation.
Residual claimant. The agent who receives the payoff from the output after any fees have been paid to a principal.
Returns to scale. A measurement of how output changes with a proportionate change in inputs.
Revealed preference theory. Determining a household's preference ordering for commodity bundles based on the observed market choices that it makes.
Ricardian rent. Profit accruing to an input.
Risk. Variability in the outcomes associated with a state of nature.
Risk-averse preferences. A household that will not play actuarially fair games.
Risk-neutral preferences. A household that is indifferent between playing an actuarially fair game or not.
Risk premium. The cost of risk for an asset.
Risk-seeking (risk-loving) preferences. A household that will play actuarially fair games.
Rival good. Each additional unit consumed by one consumer results in less of the commodity being available for other consumers.
Root. The initial decision node.
Salvage value (SV). The value of a capital item at the end of the production process.
Scale efficiency. Output price equals marginal cost.
Scientific method. Reducing the complexity of reality to manageable proportions, formulating a hypothesis that explains reality, and then testing the hypothesis.
Screening. An agent employs a mechanism for sorting commodities.
Second-best Pareto-optimal allocations. Allocations based on mechanisms (besides price signals) designed for improving society's allocation of resources.
Second-bid (Vickrey) auction. The buyer (seller) with the highest (lowest) bid wins, but pays (receives) the second highest (lowest) bid.
Second-degree price discrimination (nonlinear pricing). A firm sells different units of output at different per-unit prices, and every consumer who buys the same unit quantity of the commodity pays the same per-unit price.

Second-degree wage discrimination. Employees of the same type receive different wages based on their level of effort.

Second Fundamental Theorem of Welfare Economics. Every Pareto-efficient allocation has an associated perfectly competitive set of prices.

Security value. The minimum payoff for a given strategy.

Selling costs (information differentiation). Marketing expenditures aimed at adopting the buyer to the product.

Separation Theorem. The existence of markets allows agents to separate production decisions from consumption decisions.

Sequential (dynamic) game. In making a choice of strategies, a player already knows the other player's choice.

Shirking. Employees engaging in leisure while working.

Short-run average total cost (SATC). Short-run total cost divided by output.

Short-run average variable cost (SAVC). Short-run total variable cost divided by output.

Short-run marginal cost (SMC). In the short run, the additional cost associated with an additional increase in output.

Short-run period. Some inputs are fixed and some are variable.

Short-run total cost (STC). Short-run total variable cost plus total fixed cost.

Short-run total variable cost (STVC). Total cost associated with the variable inputs.

Signaling. A transfer of information from the informed agent to the uninformed agent.

Slutsky equation. An equation that decomposes the effects of a price change.

Social indifference (isowelfare) curves. A locus of points that yield the same level of social welfare.

Social welfare. Happiness for society as a whole.

Social-welfare function. A function that orders commodity bundles for a society.

Society. The interaction of individuals within an environment.

Spatial differentiation. Products differentiated by location.

Stackelberg model. A duopoly quantity leadership model where one firm (the leader) takes the likely response of the competitor (the follower) into consideration when maximizing profit.

State of nature. A set of probabilities associated with all possible outcomes.

Strategic (normal) form. A condensed form of a game.

Strategic interdependence. Each agent's welfare depends on the actions of other agents.

Strategy. A set of actions that a player may take specifying how he will act in every possible distinguishable circumstance in which he may be placed.

Strategy pair. A combination of strategies for two players.

Subsidy (*S*). A payment reducing what consumers pay for a commodity below the price that firms receive for supplying the commodity.

Substitution effect (Hicksian substitution). The incentive to purchase more of a lower-priced commodity and less of a higher-priced commodity.

Sunk cost. Cost that cannot be recovered once incurred.

Support price. An established price minimum (floor) below which the selling price is not allowed to fall.

System. A group of units interacting to form a whole.

Tacit collusion. Firms behave as a cartel without ever developing an explicit joint-marketing strategy.

Tariff. Tax on imports.

Tâtonnement. French for trial and error.

Technological efficiency. A production process that yields the highest level of output for a given set of inputs.

Theory of the Second Best. A second-best solution stating the satisfaction of Pareto-efficient conditions in at least some but not all markets will improve social welfare.

Thin markets. A commodity market without a recent history of many transactions, so information is lacking on the demand for the commodity.

Third-degree price discrimination. A firm sells its output at different per-unit prices based on different categories of consumers, and all consumers within a category pay the same price.

Third-degree wage discrimination. The wage rate is the same within a particular class of workers, but differs across classes.

Tie-in-sales. A firm requires consumers to purchase two or more commodities that are complementary goods.

Tit-for-tat (trigger). A strategy that immediately rewards good behavior and punishes bad behavior.

Total cost (TC). The sum of explicit and implicit costs; also, the sum of fixed and variable costs.

Total expenditures. Per-unit price of a commodity times the quantity that a household purchases.

Total fixed cost (TFC). The total cost for employing the fixed inputs in production.

Total input cost (TIC). The total cost of employing a given level of an input.

Total product (TP). Output of a particular commodity.

Total revenue (TR). Per-unit price of a commodity times the quantity a firm sells.

Treble damage. Three times the damages from illegal price setting.

Trembling-hand game. A game where players may make mistakes.

Trembling-hand Nash equilibrium. A Nash equilibrium associated with a trembling-hand game.

Two-part tariff. Consumers pay for the ability to purchase a commodity and possibly again for the actual commodity.

Utility. Ability or power of a commodity to satisfy a want.

Utility function (U). A function that orders commodity bundles based on household preferences.

Utility possibilities frontier. The locus of Pareto-efficient utility levels for a given set of outputs.

Value of the marginal product (VMP). Output price times the marginal product.

Variable. A symbol, such as x, that may change within a model.

Walras' Law. The value of aggregate excess demand is zero.

Welfare economics. The study of criteria for a society's selection among feasible allocations of resources.

Well-developed markets. A commodity market with a recent history of many transactions yielding information on the demand for the commodity.

Win-stay/lose-shift. If a player wins, the strategy is retained on the next round; if a player loses, the strategy is changed on the next round.

Winner's curse. A buyer (seller) with the highest error above (below) the true value wins, but actually loses since the bid is greater (less) than the true value.

Notes

1 Introduction

1 J. Keynes, *The Scope and Method of Political Economy,* London: Macmillan (1891).
2 In Chapter 3, we develop this model of consumer behavior and discuss the resulting conclusion.
3 The Pythagorean Theorem states that, given a right triangle, the sum of the squared sides forming the right angle equals the square of the hypotenuse.
4 A. Marshall, *Principles of Economics*, 8th ed., London: Macmillan (1920).
5 L. Walras, *Éléments d'économie politique pure,* Lausanne: L. Corbaz (1874, 1877). Translated by W. Jaffe as *Elements of Pure Economics,* Homewood, IL: Irwin (1954).

Part I Consumers' sovereignty

1 The study of satisfying wants with a given fixed amount of resources is economics.

2 Consumer preferences

1 The Law of Demand holds given that an increase in income results in an increase in the demand for the commodity, called a *normal good*. See Chapter 4.
2 In Chapter 4, we discuss how time, as a limited resource, is allocated between work and leisure in the development of an individual's labor supply curve.
3 The movie *Father of the Bride* provides an excellent illustration of splitting open a package of hotdog buns.
4 J. Bentham, *Introduction to the Principles of Morals and Legislation,* London: Hafner (1848).
5 This ability to distinguish different levels of utility is based on the Weber–Fechner Law of the just-noticeable difference. In 1834, Ernst Weber determined the just-noticeable difference to any stimulus was a constant related to the level of the basic stimulus. Gustav Theodor Fechner, known as the father of psychophysics, conducted experiments measuring by how much any sensation had to be increased before the increase was noticed. G. Fechner, *Elemente der Psychophysik*, Leipzig: von Breitkopf und Härtel (1860). Translated by H. Adler, *Elements of Psychophysics.* New York: Holt, Rinehart and Winston (1966).
6 As discussed in Chapter 18, an exception to the assumption of ordinal utility is the expected utility function, which is measured on a cardinal scale.

3 Utility maximization

1 B. Caldwell, *Beyond Positivism: Economic Methodology i the Twentieth Century*, London: George Allen & Unwin (1982).
2 Universality is one principle that will result in well-defined private-property rights. See Chapter 21.
3 Firms that offer differing per-unit prices depending on the quantity purchased are practicing price discrimination. See Chapter 13.

4 Comparative statics

1 The term $(\partial x_j/\partial I)I/x_j$ measures the percentage change in x_j given a small change in I and is called the income elasticity of demand. See Chapter 5.
2 A positively sloping demand curve is also possible in the case of a Veblen good where quality demanded increases with a rise in price. A higher price for a commodity implies greater status in owning it, and so increases its demand. This is a form of conspicuous consumption and status-seeking. Thorstein Veblen (1857–1929) was an American institutional economist.
3 In the following sections, after the development of the Slutsky equation, we address the reasoning behind this example.
4 J.R. Hicks, *Value and Capital*, Oxford: Oxford University Press (1939).
5 The US Bureau of Labor Statistics collects price data by making personal phone calls to firms. In a month or so, the data is then summarized. To avoid costly personal phone calls and to generate a more rapid analysis, A. Cavallo and R. Rigobon developed the Billion Prices Project (bpp.mit.edu). Software indexes use websites to track prices of over five million goods in 70-plus countries and then generates inflation rates in real time.

5 Market demand

1 See Chapter 22. A private good is a rival commodity, where each additional unit consumed by one consumer results in less of the commodity available for other consumers.
2 Elasticity of demand measures how responsive quantity demanded is to a change in price, so it is the $\partial x_1/\partial p_1$ weighted by p_1/x_1. Note the slope in Figure 5.7 is $\partial p_1/\partial x_1 = -1/2$. The inverse of the slope is 1/slope $= \partial x_1/\partial p_1 = -2$.
3 S. Berry, J. Levinson, and A. Parks, "Automobile Prices in Market Equilibrium," *Econometrica* 63 (1995): 841–890.
4 G.S. Maddala, R.P. Trost, H. Li, and F. Joutz, "Estimation of Short-Run and Long-Run Elasticities of Energy Demand from Panel Data Using Shrinkage Estimators," *Journal of Business and Economic Statistics* 15 (1997): 90–100.
5 See the Chapter 9 application on new technology.
6 See Chapter 23 for solutions to this information asymmetry problem.
7 See Chapter 15 for an investigation on product differentiation.
8 See the appendices to Chapters 18 and 19.

6 Pure exchange

1 Was it a good deal for Peter Minuit? See Chapter 19.
2 The compensation principle, discussed in Chapter 20, is one possible approach for determining the social desirability of a policy.
3 The cumbersome nature of bartering is the result of higher transaction costs. It generally takes longer to find and negotiate (barter) an exchange of commodities without some medium of exchange. However, the Internet has mitigated some of these transaction costs by spawning cooperative consumption, where, through social sharing networks—known as peer-to-peer (P2P) networks—consumers buy, sell, borrow, and rent from one another, thereby avoiding a retailer (firm). The Internet allows any consumer to connect around the utility of mutually beneficial trading of commodities.
4 D. Klein and C. Stern, "Economists' Policy Views and Voting," *Public Choice Journal* 126 (2006): 331–342.

7 Production technology

1 See the Mathematical Review. Since production is measured on a ratio scale, it is invalid to take any transformation of a production function.
2 Note that $AP_L = MP_L$ at point B only for a constant returns to scale production function (defined in the next section).
3 A. Smith, *The Wealth of Nations,* New York: Modern Library (1937).
4 In consumer theory, elasticity of substitution also results between two commodities. In Chapter 5, the Slutsky equation is represented in elasticity form resulting in a substitution elasticity.

8 Theory of cost

1 See Chapter 19. Besides costs being explicit or implicit and fixed or variable, they may also be sunk. Sunk cost or historical cost is a cost that cannot be recovered once incurred, for example, the cost of labor. In contrast, an automobile can be resold, so some of the cost is recoverable. Only the depreciated value of the automobile is a sunk cost.
2 See Chapter 5. Total return to inputs is the total revenue a firm receives from selling its output. It is output price times quantity sold.
3 See Chapters 3 and 4. The expansion path in production is analogous to the income-expansion path in consumer theory.
4 In contrast, neoclassical economic approaches have tended to model an economy based on a Newtonian system, with a unique equilibrium solution determined completely by resource constraints, consumer preferences, and technological possibilities. In this view, perturbations such as the terrorist attack of 2001 are quickly negated by the opposing forces they elicit. Given technological progress, this economic theory will forecast accurately the resulting effect on the economy.

9 Perfect competition

1 M.S. Luchansky and J. Monks, "Supply and Demand Elasticities in the U.S. Ethanol Fuel Market," *Energy Economics* 31 (2009): 403–410.
2 See Chapter 3. The invisible hand is referenced in Adam Smith's *Wealth of Nations*.
3 J. Roosen, "Regulation in Quality Differentiated Markets: Pesticide Cancellations in U.S. Apple Production," *Journal of Agricultural and Applied Economics* 33 (2001): 117–133.

10 Economic efficiency

1 See Chapter 20. Societies have alternative criteria for social welfare. For example, some may have the objective of egalitarianism, others utilitarianism. However, given limited resources, we assume that, regardless of a society's social welfare criteria, it will attempt to improve its welfare in an efficient manner.
2 See Chapter 23. Edison's sleeping on the job is an example of moral hazard, a form of asymmetric information addressed in principal-agent models.
3 A.C. Harberger, "The Measurement of Waste," *American Economic Review* 54 (1964): 58–76.
4 See the Appendix to Chapter 13.
5 In Chapter 20, we investigate alternative mechanisms designed for improving social welfare
6 See Chapter 21 for a discussion on externalities.
7 Alternatively, instead of firms paying the commodity tax, with a resulting supply curve shift, as illustrated in Figure 10.13, consumers could pay the tax, with the demand curve shifting to the left. For a quantity tax, this results in the same equilibrium quantity and prices for the firms and consumers. The welfare effects are the same and the portion of the tax borne by consumers and producers is also the same. However, for a sales tax, the results will differ slightly depending on who pays the tax.
8 This illustration of a perfectly elastic supply curve is similar to the illustration in Chapter 9 of an output tax for a constant-cost industry.
9 See Chapter 14. In a game-theory context, governments may employ protectionist policies as a preemption strategy.
See Chapter 12. Firms may also lobby for trade protection where such activity is a form of rent seeking.

11 General competitive equilibrium

1 See Chapter 6. A production contract curve is analogous to the contract curve in the pure-exchange model.
2 See Chapter 8. Determining that the area under a MP curve represents total output is similar to determining that the area under a SMC curve is STVC.
3 See Chapter 6. The condition for Pareto efficiency in exchange requires equivalence of every household's marginal rate of substitution (MRS) between any two commodities.

4 See Chapter 2. Recall that the four preference axioms are Completeness, Transitivity, Nonsatiation, and Diminishing Marginal Rate of Substitution.
5 See Chapter 2. A commodity is desirable if more of it is preferred to less. See Chapter 6. The condition of no excess demand is a Walrasian equilibrium.
6 O. Lange and F. Taylor, "On the Economic Theory of Socialism," in *Government Control of the Economic Order*, Vol. 2, edited by B.E. Lippincott, Minneapolis: University of Minnesota Press (1938).

12 Monopoly and regulation

1 See Chapter 10. Tariffs and quotas are examples of this type of barriers to entry, where a government deems competition from foreign suppliers as undesirable.
2 A. Lerner, "The Concept of Monopoly and the Measurement of Monopoly Power," *Review of Economic Studies* 1 (1934): 157–175.
3 Auctions are discussed in Chapter 13.
4 See Chapter 13. Bundling forces consumers to purchase a set of commodities rather than being allowed to purchase one subset of the commodities from one firm and another subset from another firm as they choose.
5 See Chapter 20. A first-best solution is where an optimal allocation of resources is only constrained by technology. A second-best solution involves other constraints on resource allocation.
6 See Chapter 13. This is an example of second-degree price discrimination.

13 Price discrimination

1 In 1936, Section 2 of the Clayton Antitrust Act was amended by the Robinson–Patman Act. Robinson–Patman prohibits sellers from price discrimination if it injures or threatens to injure competition. Called the Anti-Chain-Store Act, this act was directed at protecting "mom-and-pop" stores from chain-store competition. The government rarely enforces this act; the majority of suits are brought by private individuals.
2 See Chapter 19. Once an investment is made in the particular test kit or printer, the sunk cost of this investment results in a household being locked in, so switching to another kit or printer is prohibitively costly.
3 In terms of an Edgeworth box, if total output does not increase, the size of the box does not enlarge. However, with price discrimination resulting in prices not being equal, agents' allocations are not on the contract curve. This results in a Pareto-inefficient allocation.
4 See Chapter 23. An example of a welfare gain from third-degree price discrimination allowing for the existence of markets is the lemons problem caused by adverse selection.
5 A model for quality discrimination is developed in Chapter 23 for automobiles.
6 See Chapter 14. A dominant strategy is a strategy that is preferred to another strategy no matter what other agents do.
7 In Chapter 20, we define mechanism design as a set of rules governing a procedure for social choice.
8 P. Milgrom, "Auctions and Bidding: A Primer," *Journal of Economic Perspectives* 3 (1989): 3–22.
9 See Chapter 17. A closer analogy is monopsony power in the input market, where a buyer of an input lowers the price offered for employing an input.

14 Game theory

1 J. Nash, "Non-Cooperative Games," *Annals of Mathematics* 54 (1951): 289–295.
2 R. Axelrod, *The Evolution of Cooperation,* New York: Basic Books (1984).
3 See Chapter 15. This results in a great deal of real or imaginary product differentiation.
4 Chapter 23. Asymmetric information exists when one agent has more knowledge concerning something than another agent.
5 See Chapter 23. A principal/agent model is where one agent depends on another agent to undertake some actions.
6 J. von Neumann and O. Morgenstern, *Theory of Games and Economic Behavior,* Princeton, NJ: Princeton University Press (1944).

7 Note that the Rock, Paper, Scissors game in Table 14.1 is another example of a non-Nash-equilibrium solution. At each strategy pair, at least one of the players has an incentive to change his or her strategy.

15 Industrial organization

1 See Chapter 12. MR $= p(1 + 1/\varepsilon^D)$.
2 Chapter 14. This is an example of an infinitely repeated game where a cooperative strategy may be a Nash equilibrium.
3 See Chapter 17. A labor union is a cartel of workers with the objective of promoting the interest of the union members.
4 Chapter 21. An externality is where an agent's utility includes commodities whose amounts are determined by other agents without particular attention to the effect on the agent's welfare.
5 S. Salant. "Treble Damage Awards in Private Lawsuits for Price Fixing," *Journal of Political Economy* 95 (1987): 1326–1336.
6 P.W. Sweezy. "Demand under Conditions of Oligopoly," *Journal of Political Economy* 47 (1939): 568–573.

16 Competitive input markets

1 In Chapter 17, we relax this assumption.
2 Elizabeth (Lizzie) Magie Phillips invented the board game Monopoly in 1904 to help instill the principles of this single-tax scheme promoted by the economist Henry George. In the first part of her game, each player tries to become a monarch of the world (obtain monopolies). Phillips hoped, in this part, to point out the folly of the current system of property ownership. As the game became popular on college campuses, this monopolizing part of the game flourished, while the second half of the game, which taught the single-tax scheme, was abandoned.
3 D. Ricardo, "Letter to T.R. Malthus, October 9, 1820," in *The Works and Correspondence of David Ricardo,* edited by P. Sraffa, Cambridge: Cambridge University Press for the Royal Economic Society, Volume VIII (1952): 278–279.

17 Monopoly power in input markets

1 An interloper is an example of the free-rider problem discussed in Chapter 22.
2 Such a win/win situation for a union was dramatized in the 1979 movie *Norma Rae*. Sally Field stars as a southern textile mill worker, widowed with two children, in a poverty-stricken mill town in the late 1960s and early 1970s. She becomes involved in organizing a union that at the end of the movie is successful in increasing working conditions, wages, and the number of workers employed. The movie was based on the real-life activities of Crystal Lee Sutton (1940–2009), dramatized as Norma Rae.

Unfortunately, after the victorious election that ends the movie, the real-life scene was that Sutton got fired in 1974 for insubordination. In 1977, she was reinstated by a court order and awarded \$13,436 in back wages. She went back to work for two days just to prove a point.
3 C.A. Carter, D.L. Hueth, J.W. Mamer, and A. Schmitz, "Labor Strikes and the Price of Lettuce," *Western Journal of Agricultural Economics* 6 (1981): 1–14; and "Agricultural Labor Strikes and Farmers' Income," *Economic Inquiry* 25 (1987): 121–134.
4 See Chapter 23. Shirking is where employees engage in leisure while working.
5 In Chapter 23, we discuss the optimal conditions that cause employees to put forth effort that maximizes a firm's profit.
6 In terms of an Edgeworth box, if total employment does not increase, the size of the box does not enlarge. However, with wage discrimination, the firms' allocations are not on the production contract curve. This results in a Pareto-inefficient allocation where Allocation Condition 1 fails.

18 Risky choice and risk aversion

1 See Chapter 23. Asymmetric information exists when one set of agents is more knowledgeable about a commodity than another set.

2 See Chapter 13. Well-developed markets yield a history of many market transactions that provide information on the market price for a commodity.

19 Intertemporal choice and capital decisions

1 In contrast, the discussion focusing on labor supply in Chapter 4 assumed that consumers have no control over their wage rate.
2 The Stafford Loan is a Federal Government-guaranteed simple-interest loan where a student borrows money in his or her own name. Students have the option of postponing repayment until their education has been completed. The Stafford Loan is the most popular education loan, with students borrowing nearly $145 billion annually.
3 This relationship $r = i - \alpha$ is associated with the Fisherian law on the constancy of the real rate of interest. In 1930, Irving Fisher maintained that if inflation increased, then the nominal interest rate would rise at the same rate to keep the real interest rate constant. This law was disputed by Keynes in 1937 and further discredited in 1963 by Mundell. Note that both this law of constancy and the Separation Theorem were advanced by Fisher in his 1930 book *The Theory of Interest*.
4 The prime interest rate is the rate charged by banks to their most creditworthy customers (prominent and stable business customers). As a result of price leadership (Chapter 15), the prime rates are almost the same among banks, and any adjustments occur at the same time.
5 See Chapter 23. Selling costs are a type of transaction cost that can prevent a market yielding a Pareto-optimal allocation.
6 A.K. Dixit and R.S. Pindyck, *Investment Under Uncertainty*, Princeton: Princeton University Press (1994).
7 We have made use of the formula for a geometric series,

$$1 + x + x^2 + x^3 + \ldots = 1/(1 - x),$$

where $x = 1/1.1$.

Part IX Missing markets

1 In Chapters 6 and 11, we established the connection between perfectly competitive markets and Pareto optimality in terms of the two fundamental welfare theorems.

20 Welfare economics

1 See Chapter 6 for a discussion of equitable and fair allocations.
2 Paternalistic government supervises the lives of its citizens. For example, in current welfare reform, there are rules that require adults receiving assistance to work or stay in school. Paternalism is also apparent for the homeless, where shelters increasingly set rules for their residents, in education with tougher standards for children, and in drug programs that test addicts for compliance. With the support of the public, paternalism is a major trend in social policy.
3 In Chapter 22, we discuss the Clarke tax as a mechanism design that provides incentives for agents to reveal their preferences for the joint purchase of a commodity.
4 R.G. Lipsey and K.J. Lancaster, "The General Theory of the Second Best," *Review of Economic Studies* 24 (1956): 11–32.

21 Externalities

1 We discuss a Lindahl tax for addressing inefficiencies associated with allocating resources for public goods in Chapter 22.

22 Public goods

1 See Chapter 12 for a discussion on monopoly power regulation.

23 Asymmetric information

1 After the US 1929 stock market crash, Congress enacted the Securities Act of 1933 and the Securities Exchange Act of 1934 aimed at controlling stock abuses. Section 16(b) of the 1934 Act prohibits short-swing profits (profits realized in any period less than six weeks) by corporate insiders. Under Rule 10b-5 of the Securities and Exchange Commission, it is illegal for stock brokers to use nonpublic information (insider trading).

2 In Chapter 13, we provide a discussion in terms of auctions, where a Pareto-efficient allocation results when the buyer with the highest willingness to pay receives the commodity.

3 Recall from Chapter 16 that perfectly competitive equilibrium in the factor markets is established where the marginal revenue product of the input (labor) is equal to the input price (wage rate). Measuring labor input in terms of effort and setting the wage rate to the marginal-opportunity cost of effect results in identical equilibrium conditions.

4 See Chapter 17. By setting an employee's compensation level to her level of effort, an employee is practicing wage discrimination.

Index

Page numbers in **bold** indicate figures and tables.